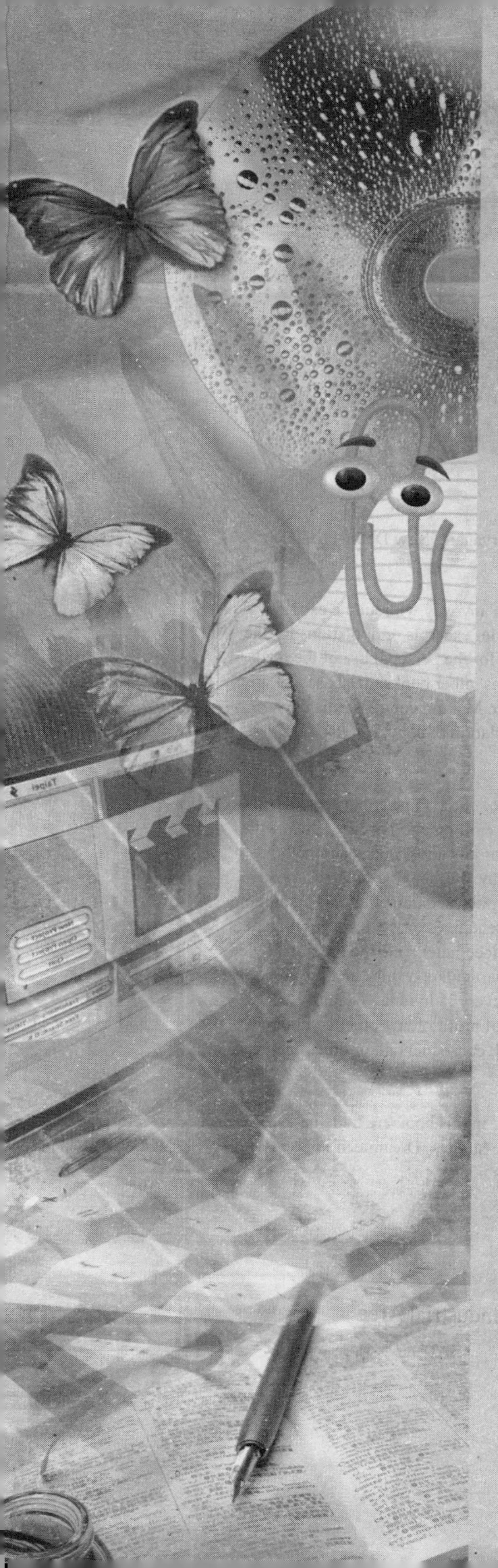

Comdex®

Computer Course Kit

(Covers all versions up to Office 2003)

Revolutionary 3 - Stage Self-learning System (Book + CD)

Vikas Gupta

B.E., D.P.P.S. (London), D.S.M.

dreamtech PRESS

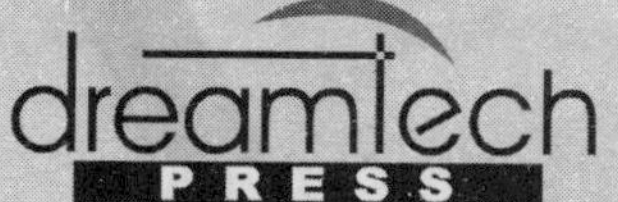

19-A, Ansari Road, Darya Ganj,
New Delhi-110002

Edition : 2008

Printed at: PrintMan (India), 477 Patparganj Industrial Area

PREFACE

If asked to describe the Comdex Computer Course Kit in a single sentence, I would simply say, "It's a kit that makes learning computers easy for anyone." A slogan for the kit describes it even better: **Learn computer at your will.** The first half of the slogan, of course, remains a claim until the reader actually uses the kit and realizes that it is truly oriented towards his needs. Only qualification needed to benefit from this kit is the elementary reading ability which a computer learner like you won't be lacking.

I had originally conceptualized this kit based on my perception of exactly what does a common person need to learn computer. This perception grew out of my personal interaction with thousands of students and computer learners. So, I instinctly followed a practical down-to-earth approach in developing this kit. The slogan reflects this approach as it puts you in command of the learning process.

My first book on computer learning had sold over a million copies in India alone, and the second stage of its evolution—the Book + CD kit—sold over a quarter million. I was moved by the generally applauding feedback. Despite huge sales, I felt that kit was not perfect as reader's needs keep changing. Rather, I would say, their needs keep *evolving*. So must this course kit. Putting myself in the reader's position, I found they had to contend with the mismatch between the colour display on their monitors and the black-and-white pages of the book. They had the basic computer learning tool in hand but they wanted to use it in style—they wanted to see the real computer monitor come alive on the book pages.

The original orientation and fabric of the kit remain unaltered. The book presents the subject in a lucid and easy-to-understand language. The CD contains the following highly useful content:

1. Self-learning tutorial software for learning Windows XP, Word, Excel, Access and Internet.
2. The BUSYLITE financial accounting package. This special version of the best-selling `Busy` financial accounting software allows you to do financial accounting using your computer.
3. The SmartCOP anti-virus software that is designed to save your computer from virus attacks.

The kit follows a three-stage learning process

Stage 1: Explanation Mode (Book)

Learning from the book is the first stage. All the concepts are explained in a clear, simple language along with hundreds of illustrations and graphics. The step-wise description is function-oriented: the steps guide you to performing a certain function and almost each step is accompanied by a screenshot or illustration. The exhilarating screenshots show you exactly what you will see on the screen as you carry out the described steps, one after the other. But is that the end of your computer learning? No, unlike other books, we have provided you a means to practice what you have learnt from the book. This practical means is a teaching software on accompanying CD. To learn through CD, move on to the next mode.

Stage 2: Audio-Video Demo Mode (CD)

Insert the accompanying CD in your computer and the tutorial starts automatically. Click on the topic you want to learn and the software automatically teaches you the desired topic step-by-step through audio-visual, graphic simulations. You don't have to do anything—just sit back and watch. The software demonstrates what you have already read in the book to enhance your understanding.

You get a rich learning experience with this process. But your learning process doesn't end with this stage. The next stage allows you to test your newly-acquired computer skills. So, move on to the next mode—the Practice Mode.

Stage 3: Self-Learning/Practice Mode (CD)

Here you can test the skills you have developed from the previous two modes. In this mode, the practice software instructs you to carry out the steps on a given topic. If you do it right, it allows you to go to the next step. And if you do it wrong, it points out the mistake and helps you correct it. You proceed to the next step only after you have performed the current step correctly.

The book has four types of special instructions sprinkled liberally to strengthen your learning. Each has its own icon. The special instructions appear in following forms:

NOTE gives you additional information that you may require at a certain step.

CAUTION acts like a teacher and imparts you the information that is important to a certain step.

HOT TIP gives you some real hot tips that are indispensable in computer learning.

TEST helps you to test and assess your performance as you complete a section.

My motivation in bringing out the original book was to bring computers closer to the masses. Then it evolved into a Book + CD kit. And, now in your hands is the improved, version of the kit. As it has always remained our motivation, the current kit has been so priced that people from every walk of life, who want to learn computer, can afford to have it.

I request every user of this kit to send feedback on their learning experience with it. Your suggestions and opinions would serve as the most important guideline in making the kit more user-friendly.

I thank Mr. Manish Nath Srivastava for his invaluable contribution to developing the kit through his unwavering hard work. I also thank Mr. M.V. Shastri and Mr. S.P. Chopra for their determined effort that proved of immense help in developing this kit. Mr. Anil Kumar Baranwal has done a great job in developing the software on the CD.

I dedicate this work to my parents and my wife for their unwavering support and encouragement which always inspire me in all my endeavours, and to the kids for imbuing me with confidence.

New Delhi
1st January, 2005

Vikas Gupta
Email: vikas@wileydt.com
vikasgupta@bol.net.in

TABLE OF CONTENTS

Chapter 1 Fundamentals of Computer

Chapter 2 Introducing Windows XP

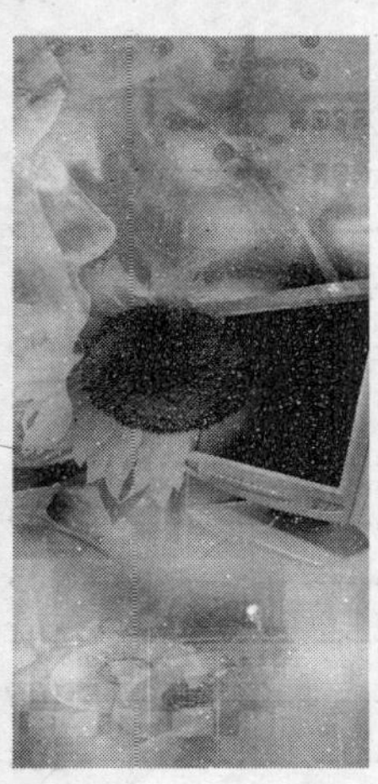

Chapter 3 Starting Windows XP

Chapter 4 Windows Explorer

Chapter 5 Windows Accessories

MICROSOFT WORD

Chapter 1 Introducing Microsoft Word

Chapter 2 Familiarizing with Microsoft Word

Chapter 3 Typing Your First Document

Chapter 4 Editing the Document

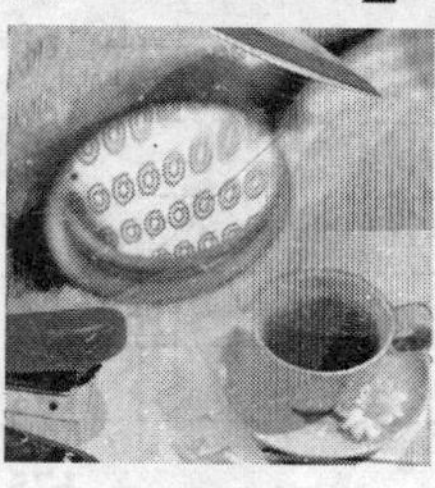

Chapter 5 Designing the Document

Chapter 6 Mail Merge

MICROSOFT EXCEL

Chapter 1 Introduction to Spreadsheets

Chapter 2 Simple Charts

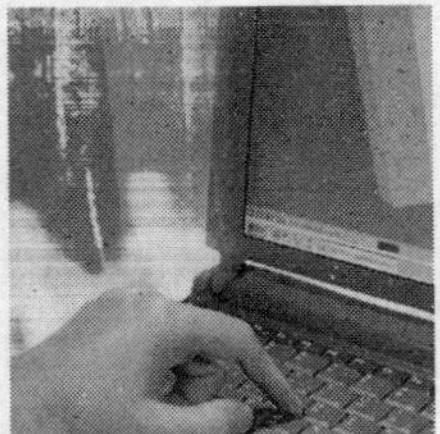

Chapter 3 Manipulating Data

Chapter 4 Changing the Layout

MICROSOFT ACCESS

Chapter 1 Introduction to Databases

Chapter 2 Creating Tables

Chapter 3 Updating Tables

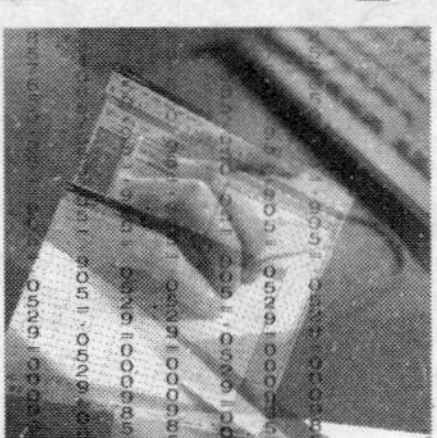

Chapter 4 Working with Forms

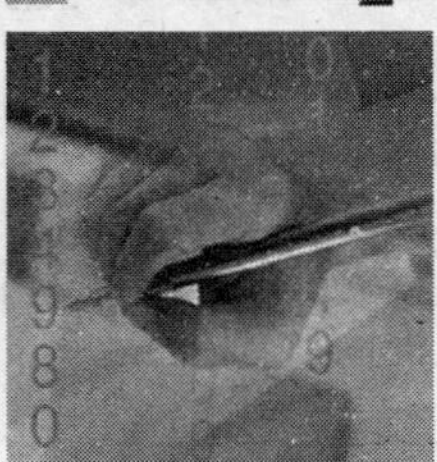

Chapter 5 Handling Queries

Fig. 3 Blaise Pascal

Fig. 4 Pascaline

Charles Babbage

The real beginning of computers as we know them today started with the efforts of English mathematics professor Charles Babbage (Fig. 5). Son of a banker father, Babbage was every intelligent in his childhood itself. He was excellent in mathematics. In 1821, Babbage invented a machine known as the **Difference Engine** (Fig. 6) to perform mathematical calculations. In 1832, he got an idea to develop another machine that could perform not only mathematical tasks but also any type of calculation. Soon, he began work on the new machine, and in 1856 he succeeded in developing it. The new machine was named the **Analytical Engine.** Due to his contribution in the field of computers, Charles Babbage is also known as *father of modern computers.*

Fig. 5 Charles Babbage

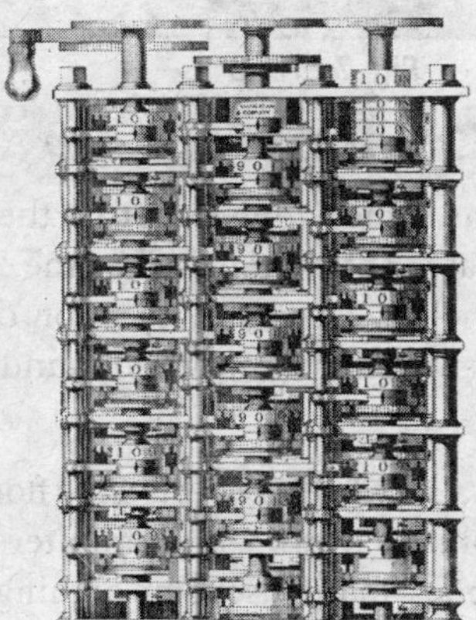

Fig. 6 Difference Engine

So far, we have talked about mechanical computers that used no software. Let us now learn about early electronic computers that actually laid the foundation of today's computer.

ENIAC

ENIAC was the first electronic computer. ENIAC stands for **Electronic Numerical Integrator and Calculator** (Fig. 7). Three American scientists—John von Neumann, Eckert and Mauchly—jointly developed the ENIAC on February 19, 1946. Impressed by their invention, the American Government decided to use it. ENIAC performed mathematical calculations at a very fast speed. It could do 5,000 additions and 360 multiplications in just one second. As compared to today's computer, ENIAC was very big. It was 100 feet long, weighed 80 tons and consumed lot of electricity. It was very expensive and beyond common man's reach.

IBM Personal Computer

In the late 1970s, the computer company IBM decided to provide computers to common people. IBM stands for **International Business Machine.** IBM developed PC or "personal computer" in 1981 (Fig. 8). A personal computer can be used anywhere and by anyone. Plus it fits on your study table. PC is the most popular type of computer these days.

Fig. 7 ENIAC

Fig. 8 IBM Personal Computer of 1981

Modern Computer

Today the man has come a long way from the Neolithic Computer. Now, you would hardly find an area of modern living that is not yet touched by the computer. If it has become indispensable for critical areas of information technology, telecommunication, defence preparedness, medical and space research, it is equally adept at handling with lightning speed mundane tasks like railway booking, electricity billing and online shopping.

In business world also, whether it's the shop floor or the showroom, most of the activities are controlled by the computer. The ability to work with computers is a pre-prequisite for most job profiles. Educationists have also given it due place in their scheme of things. Computer science is now being offered as a core subject in schools and colleges.

What is computer?

The term computer is derived from the word *compute*. In simple words, computer is an electronic device, which takes input from the user in the form of data and instructions. Then it processes the input as per the user's instructions and generates some output that is displayed before the user. Computer processes data with the help of hardware and software. Soon, we will discuss hardware and software in detail.

Let us now understand **data processing**. By data, we mean any text, numbers, audio, video, and images—whether they are useful or not. Such raw data may not make any sense to the user. We need to process this data to convert it into a form that is useful and meaningful for the user. The processed data becomes information. Figure 9 attempts to illustrate the sequence of data processing.

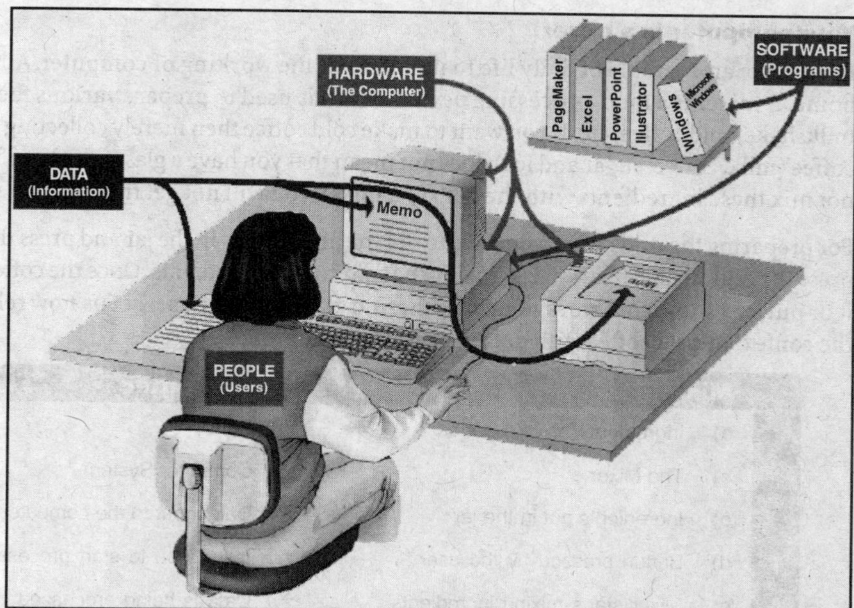

Fig. 9 Data Processing

Basically, a computer performs the following tasks:

- **Input:** Sending the data and command to the computer is known as input.
- **Processing:** Work done by the computer to produce results is known as processing.
- **Output:** The result displayed by the computer is known as output.
- **Storage:** A place to save result inside or outside the computer is known as storage. You may be having a vague idea of various parts of a computer system. To get a clear picture of all these parts, carefully observe Fig. 10.

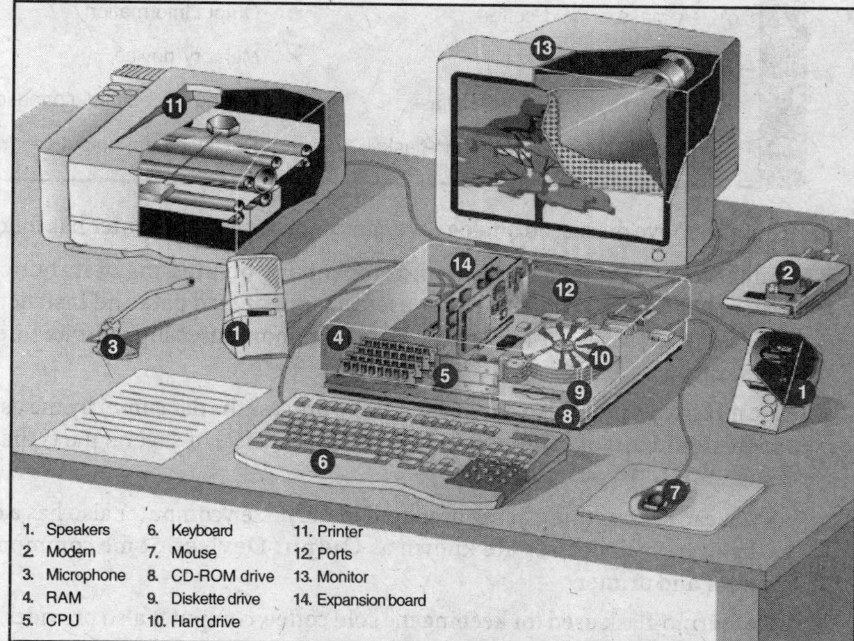

Fig. 10 An overview of a computer system

Your computer is a mixer!

Let us take an example of daily life to understand the working of computer. All of us must have a mixer at home. A mixer is a food-processing device, which is used to prepare various food products and drinks like milkshake, cold coffee, etc. If you want to make cold coffee then merely collecting the ingredients used in cold coffee (milk, coffee, sugar and ice) does not mean that you have a glass of cold coffee. Until and unless you do not mix these ingredients with the help of a mixer, you will not get the cold coffee.

For preparing the cold coffee, you have to put the ingredients in the jar and press the mixer's button. When you press the button, the mixer starts mixing the cold coffee ingredients. Once the coffee is prepared, you can serve it or put it in some cold storage such as thermo-flask for later use. Let us now relate the working of mixer in the context of cold coffee with data processing by computer.

TABLE

Mixer		Computer
a) Ingredients of cold coffee	→	Data
b) The Mixer	→	Computer System
c) Ingredients put in the jar	→	Data input to the computer
d) Button pressed by the user	→	Instruction to start processing the data
e) Mixer starts mixing ingredients	→	Data is being processed
f) Button pressed by the user to stop the mixing	→	Instruction to display result
g) A glass of cold coffee	→	Output/Information
h) Thermo-flask	→	Memory device
i) Putting coffee in thermo-flask	→	Saving the output/information in memory
j) Bring coffee out of thermo-flask	→	Retrieving the output/information from the memory

Thus from the above discussed analogy, we can conclude that computer has following basic operations:

- Similar to a mixer that can start and stop mixing on pressing of its buttons by the user, a computer system has devices, which the user uses to input or feed data and instructions to the computer. Such devices are known as **Input Devices.** Some commonly used input devices are keyboard, mouse, trackball and scanner.
- Like mixer, computer also has machinery to process the data input by the user. Such machinery is called the **System Unit** of computer. A system unit consists of several parts that work together to produce results.
- As you can see anything being prepared in the mixer, computer also has a device to display the output to the user. Such devices are known as **Output Devices.** Some commonly used output devices are monitor and printer
- Like thermo-flask used for keeping the cold coffee, computer also provides some way or devices to save the output for later use. Such devices are known as **Memory** and **Storage Devices.** Commonly used storage devices are floppy, hard disk, CD-ROM and magnetic tape.

Input Devices, System Unit, Output Devices and Memory Devices are collectively known as hardware of computer. Anything that you can see and touch in your computer system is known as hardware.

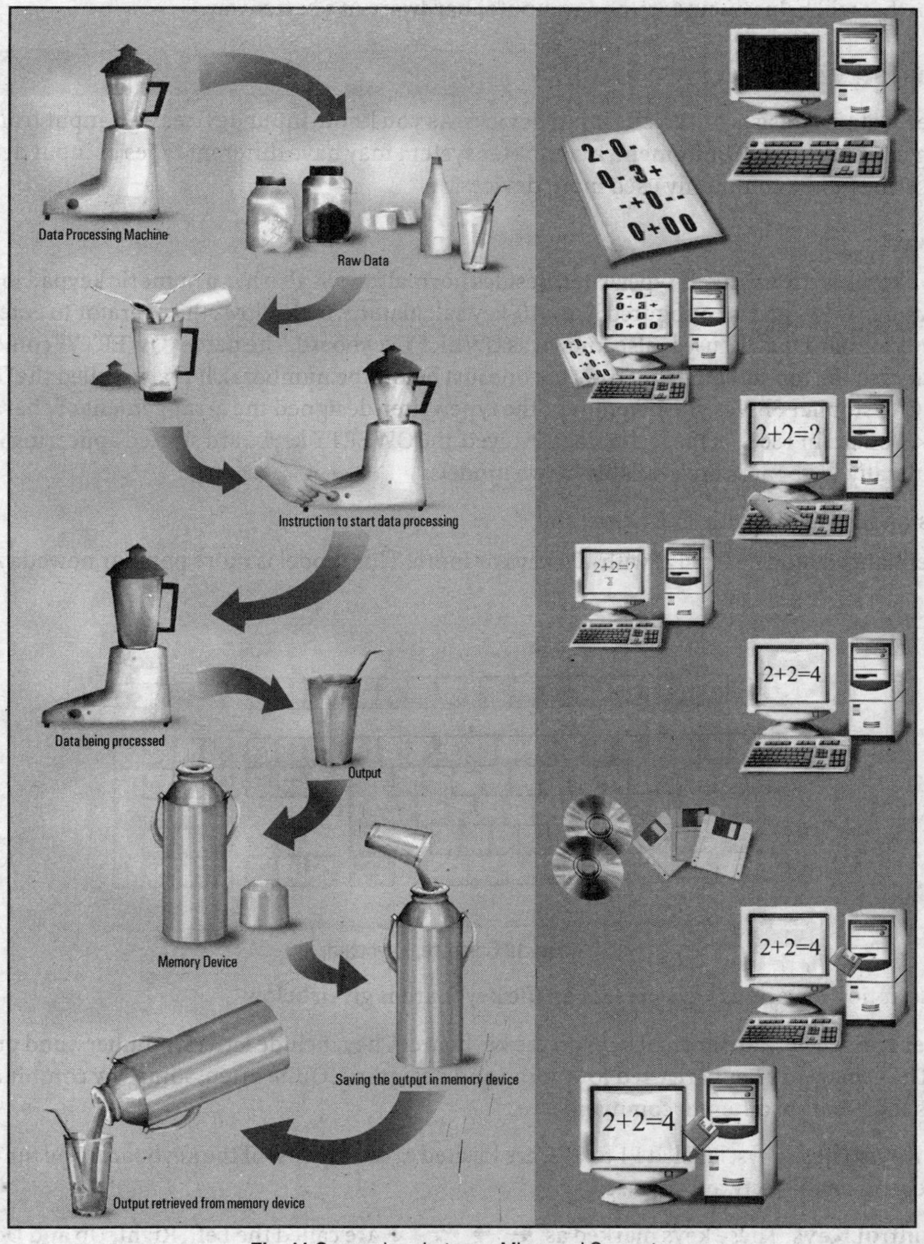

Data Processing Machine

Raw Data

Instruction to start data processing

Data being processed

Output

Memory Device

Saving the output in memory device

Output retrieved from memory device

2-0-
0-3+
-+0--
0+00

2+2=?

2+2=4

Fig. 11 Comparison between Mixer and Computer

Computer Hardware

In the last section, you have gone through a sketchy description of computer hardware. Now, here is a detailed description that will help you understand computer hardware in a better way.

Input Devices

A computer system consists of various input devices. As you know, input devices take input from the user. Depending upon the user requirement, a computer system may have different types of input devices. This section describes some commonly used input devices.

Keyboard

A computer keyboard looks like a typewriter. Besides normal keys, it also has a numeric keypad located to its right. The numeric keypad is configured like a 10-key calculator, which allows the operator to enter numbers rapidly. The keyboard that we use is also known as QWERTY keyboard. The name "QWERTY" comes from the first six letters in the top-left alphabet row (the one just below the numbers). It is also called the "Universal" keyboard. Christopher Sholes, the inventor of the typewriter, designed the arrangement of characters on a QWERTY keyboard in 1868. As the technology evolved, the QWERTY keyboard started appearing in different shapes. Generally, keyboards are available in two models:

- The standard model with 83-84 keys; and
- The enhanced model (Fig. 12) with 104 keys or more. This model is more popular nowadays.

Fig. 12 Computer Keyboard

A brief description of various keys present on the keyboard is given below

Typewriter Keys: These are normal keys on the keyboard. They include letters, numbers, and punctuation symbols. The typewriter keys are used for typing and designing. Quite often, some key combinations also function as short-cuts to different commands.

Function Keys: These keys, labeled F1 to F12, are located at the top row of the keyboard. The functions they perform depend on the software you use.

Cursor Control Keys: These keys marked as ← → ↑ ↓ are called the Left, Right, Up and Down Arrow keys, respectively. These keys enable you to move the cursor to the left, right, up or down the screen—one line or one character at a time.

TABLE

Numeric Keys:	The numeric keys are located just below the function keys. They also have some special characters printed on the topside. The keyboard also contains a numeric key pad located to the right. The numeric key pad has a calculator-like configuration. Some numeric pad keys have double functions. The switch-over between two functions of a numeric key pad is controlled by the key marked NUM LOCK. For example, the key marked 7 also works as a Home key when the NUM LOCK key is OFF. When the NUM LOCK key is ON (indicated by a green light on top of the keyboard), the keys marked 1, 2, 3, 4, 5, 6, 7, 8, 9, 0 function as numeric keys. Then pressing any one displays its respective number.
Page Up and Page Down keys:	The Page Up and Page Down keys are used to move to the preceding and next pages of the document, respectively.
Home and End keys:	The Home and End keys take the cursor to the top and end of the document, line or window, respectively.
Caps Lock key:	Normally, an alphabet is typed in the lower case. If you press the Caps Lock key once (i.e. when the LED status indicator of Caps Lock is lit), any letter you type will appear in the uppercase (capital). This effect can be reversed by simply pressing the Caps Lock once again.
Shift key:	Holding the Shift key down and then pressing a letter key creates an upper case letter. However, if the Caps Lock is ON, then this effect is reversed. Pressing any key with two symbols or characters while holding down the Shift key causes the upper symbol to appear. The upper symbols are ~ ! @ # $ % ^ & * ( ) _ + | : { } " : < > ? etc. Shift key is also used extensively in short-cut commands.
Ctrl and Alt keys:	The Ctrl (Control) and Alt (Alternate) keys are often used in combination with other keys to carry out special actions. For example, in MS-DOS, pressing Ctrl and C simultaneously aborts the current task or command from being executed and the user returns to DOS prompt. By pressing Ctrl, Alt and Del (Delete) keys simultaneously, the machine automatically restarts.
Enter key:	The Enter key is also referred to as the Return key. The Enter key is mainly used for two purposes. First, when you press it, your PC gets the signal that you have finished giving an instruction so that it can execute the instruction. Second, in a Microsoft Word document, pressing the Enter key begins a new paragraph or a new line.
Tab key:	The Tab key moves the cursor along a line to a preset point. It lets you indent paragraphs and line up columns, text or numbers. In some software menus, the Tab key helps you to move from one option to another.
Esc key:	In most applications, you can use the Esc key to cancel or ignore the entry or command that you have just entered. Esc key is also used to exit a program.
Delete and Backspace keys:	Pressing Delete erases a space or character (one space/character at a time) that is placed to the right side of the blinking cursor. On the contrary, the Backspace key erases the character to the left side of the blinking cursor. It moves the cursor back, one character at a time – erasing what you typed last.

Dvorak Keyboard

This is another type of keyboard designed for speed typing. The Dvorak keyboard was designed in the 1930s by August Dvorak, a professor of education, and his brother-in-law, William Dealy. Unlike the traditional QWERTY keyboard, the Dvorak keyboard has in its middle row keys of the most common letters. Besides, common letter combinations are positioned in such a way that they can be typed quickly. Apart from a standard Dvorak keyboard, there are also two additional Dvorak models—left-handed and right-handed keyboards. These keyboards are designed for people who function with only one hand.

Mouse

A mouse is a handheld device, which allows you to control your computer without having to type instructions from the keyboard. It helps you to move around your computer screen, select any object and activate commands. The computer mouse shape resembles an actual mouse. It has a rubber ball embedded at its lower side and buttons on the top. As the user places palm over the top of the mouse and moves it across the mouse-pad, the ball at lower side also moves. The movement of the ball determines the location of the arrow or mouse-pointer on the computer screen. A mouse-pointer is small arrow or other symbol on the computer screen that moves as you move the mouse.

The buttons of the mouse are used to select objects on the screen and execute commands. Typically a mouse has three buttons—Left, Center, and Right button. The Left button is primary button of the mouse as most of time it is used to select objects and execute commands. You can select commands, icons and options by positioning the arrow or pointer over them and clicking the left mouse button. The Right mouse button is considered as secondary button because it is not used very often. The Right mouse button is used for accomplishing special tasks on the screen such as opening shortcut menus for executing a command.

Different shapes of Computer Mouse

Mouse comes in different shapes, sizes and buttons. There are three broad categories of computer mouse:

- **Three-button mouse:** This type of mouse has primary button, secondary button and a middle button between these two (Fig. 13).
- **Scroll mouse:** This type of mouse replaces the middle button of the three-button mouse with a small roller (Fig. 14). When the user moves the roller forward and backward, the screen moves in downward and upward direction, respectively.
- **Cordless mouse:** Cordless mice (Fig. 15) aren't physically connected with the computer. Instead, they rely on infrared or radio waves to communicate with the computer. Cordless mice are more expensive than both three-button and scroll mice, but they do eliminate the cord, which can sometimes get in the way.

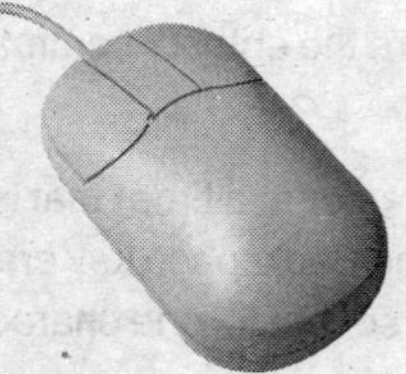

Fig. 13 Three-button Mouse

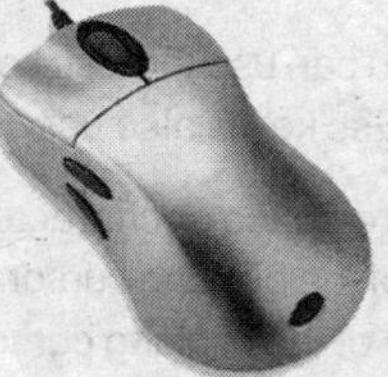

Fig. 14 Scroll Mouse

Fig. 15 Cordless Mouse

Trackball

Trackball (Fig. 16) is an alternative to a mouse. It operates in the same way as a mouse except that the ball is on the top. It is less complicated than a mouse and is designed for the use of children. Turning the ball with your hand moves the pointer on the screen. Trackballs are useful when there is not enough space for a mouse, e.g. in portable computers. Most trackballs have buttons which can be used to select options on the screen.

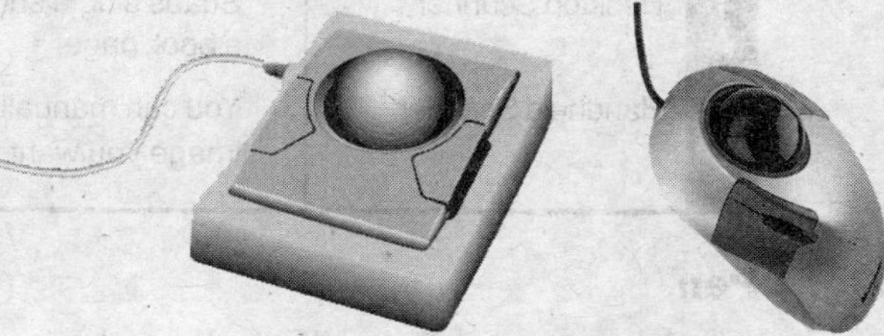

Fig. 16 Trackball

Joystick

While playing a racing video game, the user needs to move the vehicle quickly across the screen. Although this can be done by pressing arrow keys on the keyboard, it is neither convenient nor comfortable for small children to use the keyboard. This type of action can be better done with the help of a joystick (Fig. 17). Joystick is not only easier to use but also provides a better control. As you move the stick around its socket, the movements are translated into binary instructions with the help of electrical contacts in the base of the joystick. Nowadays, Joystick has become a favourite playing tool among kids specially for playing video games. With joystick in hand, kids can perform gaming manouvres like taking aim and firing shots at enemies, driving the car, etc. The trackball also does the same thing but it is small and hence not suitable for playing games. Both these devices allow you to move the objects around the screen easily.

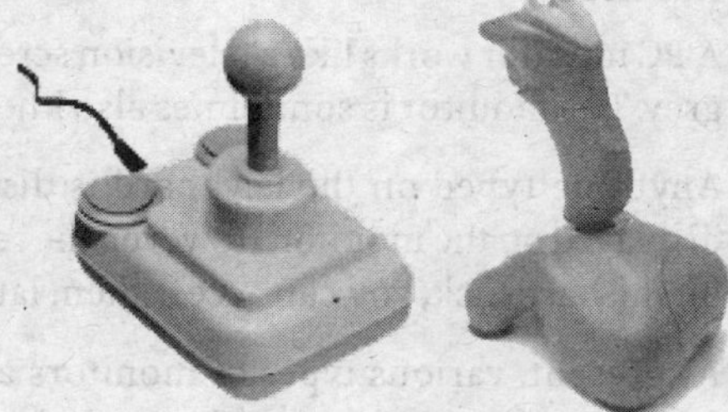

Fig. 17 Joystick

Scanner

Scanner is a device that can transfer typed or handwritten texts, graphs, diagrams and photographs to the computer. Instead of making a duplicate copy on paper of the required data or photograph, scanner copies them to the memory of the computer. Scanners can do a wide variety of jobs. They can be used for storing photographs and important documents in their original forms. They may also be used to take in enormous text material that otherwise would be very tedious to type manually.

Two types of scanners —Desktop (Fig. 18) and Handheld (Fig. 19)—are used. A handheld scanner is used in medical science and departmental stores for reading bar codes pertaining to product information like date of manufacture, expiry date, price etc.

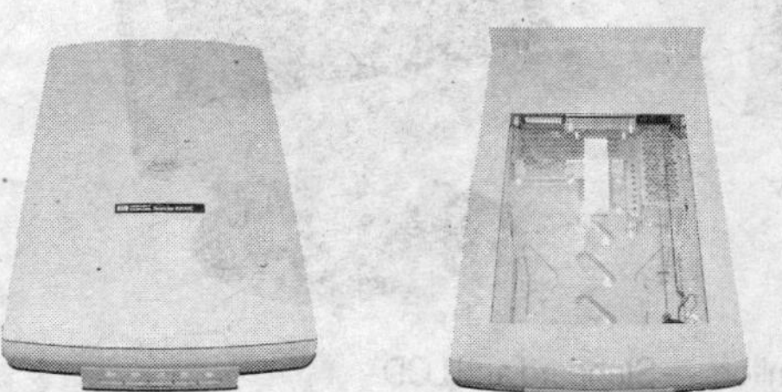

Fig. 18 Desktop Scanner

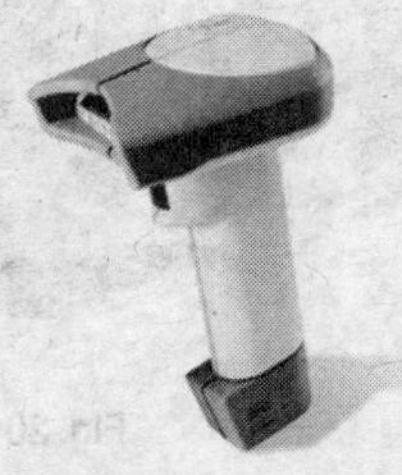

Fig. 19 Handheld Scanner

	Scanner Name	How it Works	Features
TABLE	Desktop Scanner	Scans single sheet of paper or a book page	Expensive and less compact
	Handheld Scanner	You can manually move it over the image you want to scan	Inexpensive and portable

Light Pen

Light pen is an input device that utilizes a light-sensitive detector to select objects on a display screen. Light pen is similar to a mouse, except that you can directly move the pen pointer to the objects on the display screen to select them.

Output Devices

Monitor

A PC monitor works like a television screen. It displays text characters and graphics in colors or in shades of grey. The monitor is sometimes also known as screen, display or a **CRT** (Cathode Ray Tube). See Fig. 20.

Anything typed on the keyboard is displayed on the monitor. When a program is executed, results are displayed on the monitor. However, the results stay on the screen temporarily. Only when you save the results on the hard disk, you can access them later on.

At present, various types of monitors are available in the market – such as monochrome (single color) monitor, color monitor, etc. The monochrome monitor and the color monitor differ in terms of their resolution (i.e. the sharpness of the image on the screen). Higher the resolution, higher the cost. Generally color monitors have a higher resolution. High resolution monitors are used for specialized jobs like creating graphics and images. Monochrome monitors comes in single color and are rarely available.

Fig. 20 Computer Monitors — Standard and LCD

Factors deciding the performance of a monitor

- **Dot Pitch**—The dot pitch is a standard to measure how close together the dots (pixels) should be to create an image on the monitor. More closer the dots, better quality of the image would be.
- **Resolution and Refresh Rate**—Resolution and refresh rate are two factors that depend upon each other. They work hand-in-hand to produce a clean image, and they both depend on the video card and monitor (display screen) installed on your computer. **Refresh rate** is the rate at which each pixel on a screen is re-drawn.

  Resolution means the sharpness and clarity of an image. The sharpness of an image on a computer monitor depends on the size and resolution of the monitor. The term refresh rate means the ability of a computer monitor to redraw the image information from memory. The refresh rate of the computer monitor is measured in **Hertz** (Hz). For example, if a computer has refresh rate of 75 Hz then it means a monitor can redraw the image 75 times per second. Faster the refresh rate, less the monitor flickers.

Printer

A device that prints images (numbers, alphabets, graphs, etc.) on paper is known as **printer**. After creating a document on the computer, you can send it to the printer for printing its **hard-copy** which is generally called a **printout**. The speed of a printer is rated either by pages per minute (ppm) or by characters per second (cps). You can take printout in full colors or in black color only. Printers which can print in full colors are expensive. Different types of printer are as follows:

Dot Matrix printer: This type of printer makes use of pins. The pins strike an ink ribbon. As each pin hits the ink ribbon, a dot appears on the paper, and combinations of dots form characters and illustrations. A dot matrix printer (Fig. 21) can print 1 to 18 pages in one minute. Use of dot-matrix printer is now limited to printing invoices and bills.

Line Printer: This type of printer contains a chain of characters or pins that print an entire line at one time. Line printers (Fig. 22) are very fast, but produce low-quality prints. The line printer is now used for mass printing and publishing.

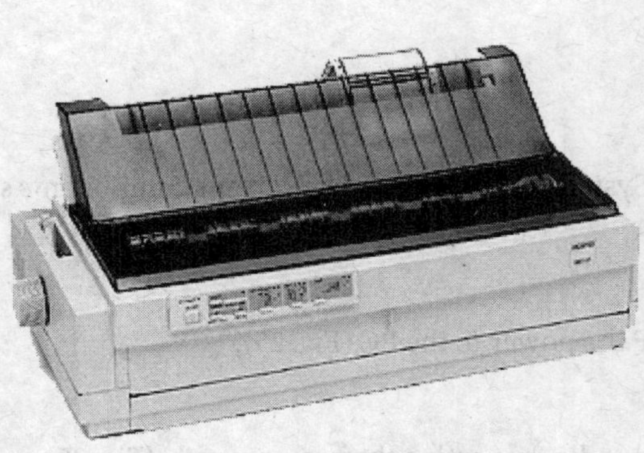

Fig. 21 Dot Matrix Printer

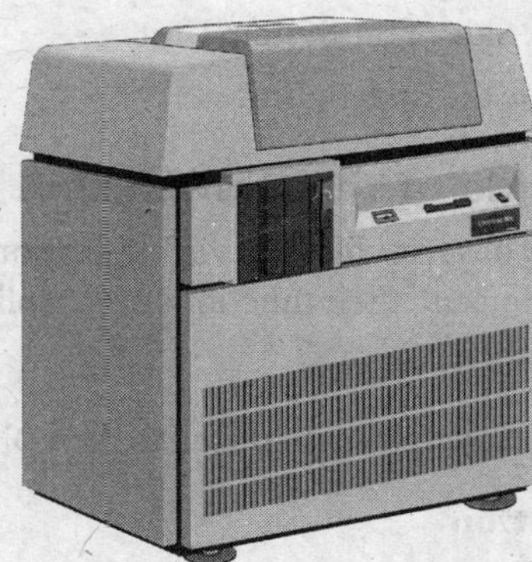

Fig. 22 Line Printer

Inkjet printer: This type of printer sprays ink on a sheet of paper. Ink-jet printers (Fig. 23) produce high-quality text and graphics. An inkjet printer can print 4 to 6 pages in one minute. Due to its low price and affordability, the inkjet printer is popular in homes specially among kids.

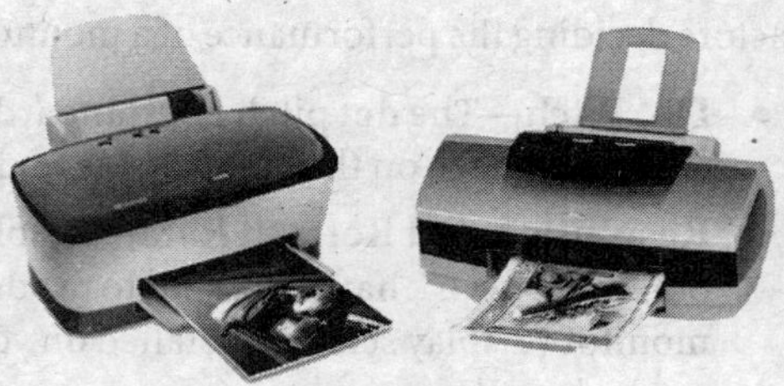

Fig. 23 Inkjet Printer

Laser printer: This type of printer uses fine powder ink called toner. Laser printers (Fig. 24) use the same technology as photocopy machines. They produce high quality text and graphics prints. The laser printer is quite popular in corporate world and printing houses.

Fig. 24 Laser Printer

Some other printers, which are gaining in popularity, are the **LED** (Light Emitting Diode) printer and the **multi-functional** printer. LED printers are similar to laser printers. A multi- functional printer, as the name suggests, can perform more than one task. It can also work as a fax machine, a photocopier and a scanner.

System Unit

The System Unit is the most important part of a PC. It may be called the brain behind every action of a PC since it controls and executes all the operations performed by the PC. It contains everything that is essential for your computer's effective functioning. The System Unit holds the Windows Operating System. The keyboard, monitor, mouse, printer, etc. are all linked to the System Unit through cables which are plugged into its back. The hard disk, the floppy disk drive and the CD-ROM drive are placed inside this unit. You may also find the DVD drive attached to the System Unit.

In this section, we will discuss vital components of the System Unit so as to enable you understand the working of the System. Our discussion focuses on the following three sections of the System Unit:

- Front Side of the System Unit
- Back Side of the System Unit
- Inside the System Unit

Front Side of the System Unit

Let us now observe the front visible portion of the System Unit (Fig. 25). The various components seen in the front portion and their functions are as follows:

Power switch

The power on/off switch is used to turn ON or OFF the power to the PC (Fig. 25).

Reset button

This button helps you restart your computer without disconnecting the power supply (Fig. 25).

Lights

The front portion may display some colored indicator lights (Fig. 25). These lights indicate whether the hard disk, the floppy disk or the CD-ROM is being read or written.

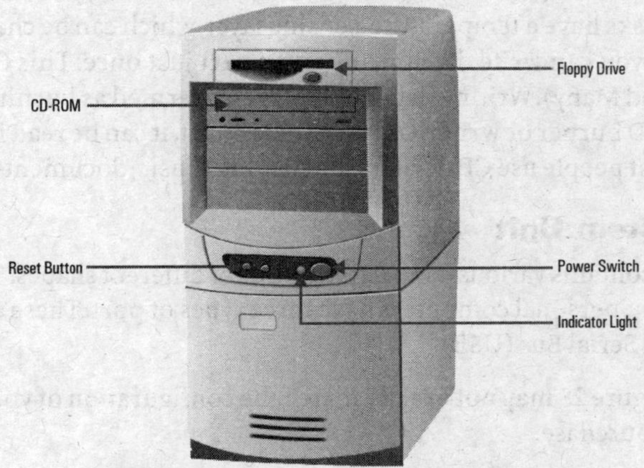

Fig. 25 Front portion of the System Unit

Floppy Disk drive

Fig. 26 Floppy Drive

The floppy disk drive (Fig. 26) is used to read the information stored in floppy disks (also called diskettes). The System Unit contains a slit (drive) in which the floppy disk can be inserted. The floppy disk drive consists of a slot to accept a floppy disk, a motor to spin the disk, and a recording/reading device that moves across the disk to read or write data. A floppy disk, like a hard disk, is used to store information.

CD-ROM Drive

Fig. 27 CD-ROM Drive

CD-ROM drive (Fig. 27) is a device that reads the information stored on CD-ROM disks and displays it on the monitor. CD-ROM stands for 'Compact Disk-Read Only Memory'. The information stored in a CD-ROM can neither be changed nor new information be added to it. That is why, it is called Read Only Memory (ROM). The speed of a CD-ROM drive is indicated by a number followed by the alphabet "X". Greater the number faster the spin of disk. And, faster the spin, faster is the transfer of information from the disk to the computer. The 56X CD-ROM is currently the most popular drive specification. For recording information on a CD, a special CD drive known as 'CD-RW' is used. The CD-ROM disk is flat and circular in shape and can store lot more information as compared to a floppy disk.

CD-Writer

In 1990, the CD-ROM technique was further refined to enable the user write data on CD. To make your own CD-ROMs, you use a drive, which can write on special CD-ROM disks. Now, two types of writable CDs are available. One is the CD-ReWritable (CD-RW) on which you can write data many times by erasing the data written on it earlier. These disks have a temperature-sensing layer, which can be changed by writing. On the second type of writable CD, you can write data on any given part just once. This CDR disk is also called a WORM disk (Write Once Read Many). Writing data on a CD is also termed as burning a CD. The device used for CD writing is known as CD burner or writer. Once a CDR is burnt, it can be read in most newer CD drives for sound, video, or data. Most people use CD-writers for copying music, documents, images and programs.

Back Side of the System Unit

The back of the System Unit contains various connection points of different shapes. These connection points are known as **Ports.** Generally, personal computers have three types of port. These are: the Parallel Port, the Serial Port and the Universal Serial Bus (USB).

The photograph shown in Figure 28 may not exactly match the configuration of your System Unit and may include options you did not purchase.

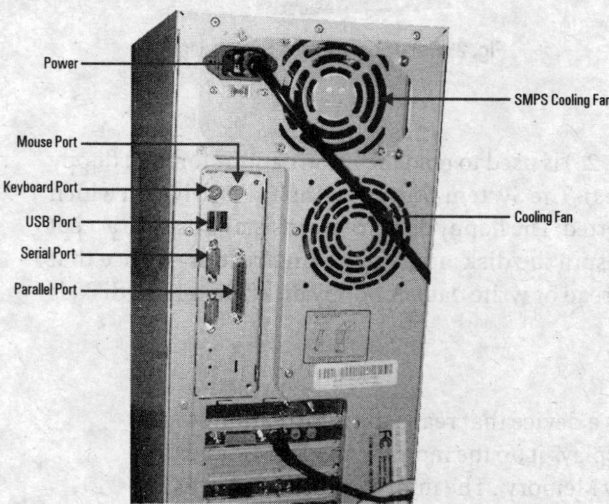

Fig. 28 Back side of System Unit

Let us briefly discuss each type of port.

Serial Port

A serial port is a general-purpose interface that can be used for almost any type of device, including modems, mouse and keyboard. Most PCs are fitted with two serial ports. The connector used for a serial port is shown in Figure 29.

Parallel Port

The parallel port is usually used for connecting the computer to a printer. Very often, it is referred to as the printer port.

The port for connecting the Keyboard is marked by ⌨ . Similarly the port for connecting the Mouse port is marked by ⎕ and the USB port is marked by ⭠ .

USB Port

USB (Universal Serial Bus) is a plug-and-play port on your computer. You can attach to it devices such as audio players, joysticks, keyboards, telephones, scanners, and printers. With USB, a new device can be added to your computer without adding additional hardware or even having to turn the computer off. A single USB port can be used to connect up to 127 peripheral devices. Soon USB ports will replace serial and parallel ports. The connector used for USB port is shown in Fig. 30.

Power socket

Power socket supplies electricity to your computer. A power cable is plugged into the power socket, which carries the power from the electrical outlet to the System Unit, and from the System Unit to your monitor. The connector used for power socket is shown in Fig. 31.

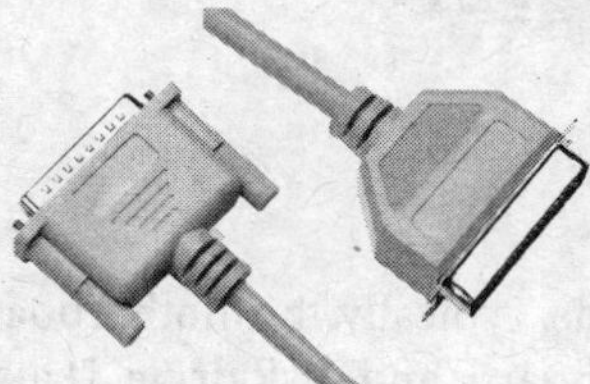

Fig. 29 Serial Port Connector

Fig. 30 USB Port Connector

Fig. 31 Power Connector

Cooling Fan

The back of the System Unit has a fan which works like an exhaust fan. When you are working on computer, its machinery produces lot of heat. If this heat is not moved out from the System Unit, it can cause havoc to the computer machinery. Here, fan is a great help to your computer. No sooner you switch on the computer, its fan starts rotating and throwing out heat from the System Unit. The fan keeps on rotating all the time your computer is on.

Inside the System Unit

The inside of a System Unit consists of several devices and chains of colored electronic wires running from one end to another. If you look inside the System Unit, you will find green boards with mysterious circuit paths and soldering joints. These boards play essential role in running your computer.

Motherboard

A motherboard is the physical arrangement in a computer that contains the computer's basic circuitry and components. On a typical motherboard (Fig. 32), the circuitry is imprinted or affixed to a firm planar surface and usually manufactured in a single step. The motherboard is also called Printed Circuit Board (PCB).

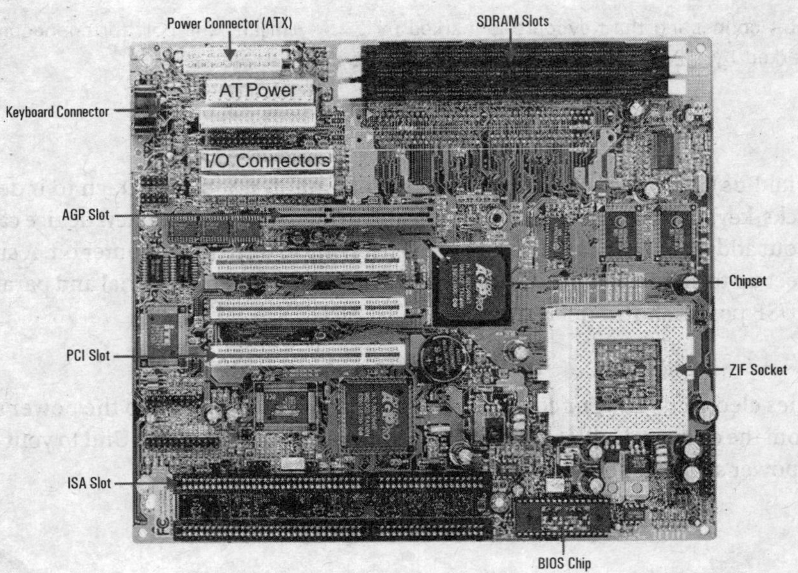

Fig. 32 A typical Motherboard

The motherboard contains connectors for attaching additional boards. Typically, the motherboard contains controllers for all standard devices such as the display screen, keyboard, and disk drive. It also contains controllers for ports and mass storage devices. Collectively, all chips that reside on the motherboard are known as the motherboard's **chipset**.

The most common motherboard design used in desktop computers today is the AT, based on the IBM AT motherboard. A more recent motherboard specification, ATX, improves on the AT design.

Central Processing Unit

Central Processing Unit (CPU) is the most important part of computer where actual processing, i.e. the mathematical and logical processing, takes place. It is the brain behind all PC operations. Within a CPU, instructions are written in the form of computer programs, which are carried out by the CPU sequentially. The power of a CPU lies in the ability of its processor (Fig. 33) to carry out these instructions rapidly and flawlessly. A PC's processing capability is measured in terms of the amount of data processed by the CPU processor in one operation. The processor speed is measured in **MegaHertz (MHz)** and **GigaHertz**. A computer has a central clock that keeps all its components in tune with one another. Quicker the clock ticks, faster the computer runs. Over the years, there has been a gradual improvement in the processor speed. Intel is a major producer of computer processors. Among popular Intel processors is the Pentium IV series, whose speed ranges from 1.3 GigaHertz to 2.6 GigaHertz or more. Apart from Pentium, there are other processors like Intel Celeron, AMD Athlon, AMD Duron etc. **Centrino** is the latest Pentium processor for mobile computers like Laptop and Notebook.

Fig. 33 Processor

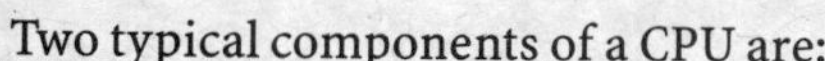

Two typical components of a CPU are:

- The Arithmetic Logic Unit (ALU), which performs arithmetic and logical operations.
- The Control Unit, which extracts instructions from memory and decodes and executes them. It also calls on the ALU when necessary.

Switch Mode Power Supply

In personal computer, the power supply unit is a metal box usually found in a corner of the System Unit (Fig. 34). This box is known as SMPS (Switch Mode Power Supply) box. Visible from the back of the System Unit, the power supply box contains the power-cord receptacle and a cooling fan. Power supply, often referred to as 'switching power supply', uses switcher technology to convert the AC current into DC current. Once the current is converted to DC, the power supply unit sends the required wattage to different components of the computer like monitor, hard disk, CD-ROM, floppy disk drive etc. The measurement unit of voltage is **watts.**

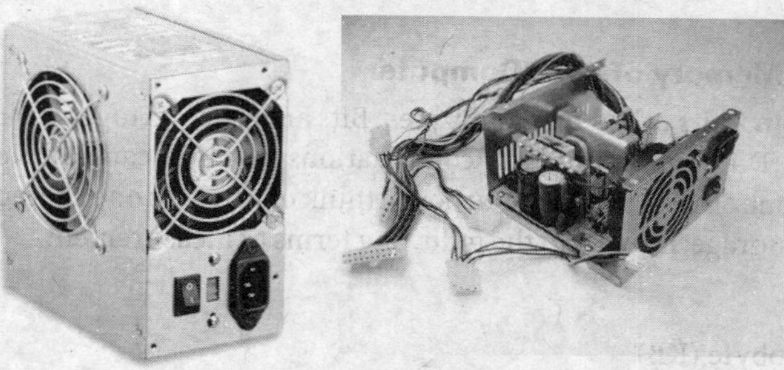

Fig. 34 SMPS Box

The power consumption values (in watts) for common devices in a personal computer are:

TABLE

Accelerated Graphics Port (AGP) card	20 to 30W
Peripheral Component Interconnect (PCI) card	5W
Small computer system interface (SCSI) PCI card	20 to 25W
Floppy Disk Drive	5W
Network interface card	4W
50X CD-ROM drive	10 to 25W
RAM	10W per 128MB
5200 RPM HDD	5 to 11W
7200 RPM IDE hard disk drive	5 to 15W
Motherboard (without CPU or RAM)	20 to 30W
550 MHz Pentium III	30W
733 MHz Pentium III	23.5W
300 MHz Celeron	18W
600 MHz Athlon	45W

Basic Input Output Software

The Basic Input Output Software (BIOS) is a built-in software, which keeps track of all devices attached to the computer and acts as an inter-communication channel between these devices. The devices include keyboard, monitor, disk drives, and other miscellaneous devices. Older computers contained read-only BIOS that could not be altered. This means that new components could not be added to the computer because the BIOS would not know how to communicate with them. This limited the user's ability to upgrade their computers. So Flash BIOS was introduced. Now when a new component is installed in the computer, the Flash BIOS can be electronically upgraded so that it can recognize and communicate with the new devices.

The BIOS is typically placed in a ROM chip that comes with the computer (it is often called a ROM BIOS). This ensures that the BIOS will always be available and will not be damaged by disk failures. It also makes it possible for a computer to boot itself. As RAM is faster than ROM, therefore many computer manufacturers design systems for copying the BIOS from ROM to RAM each time the computer is booted. This is known as **shadowing.**

RAM/ROM—Primary Memory of your Computer

A computer stores data in units called **bits and bytes.** Bits are grouped together in sets of eight. Each set of eight bits is called a byte. Different "on and off" combinations for a byte can be developed to stand for letters, numbers, spaces, and symbols. For practical purposes, think of a byte as one character. When your computer refers to its memory or storage, it refers to the following terms of measurement.

- 8 bits = 1 byte
- 1024 bytes = 1 Kilobyte (KB)
- 1024 Kilobytes = 1 Megabyte (MB)
- 1024 Megabytes = 1 Gigabyte (GB)

The term **memory** stands for data storage that comes in the form of chips, and the term **storage** is used for memory that exists on tapes or disks. Memory is usually used as a short reference for physical memory, related with actual chips. The word 'main' added to the computer's memory distinguishes it from external mass storage devices like floppy disks, CDs and memory sticks.

Besides the main memory, your computer also has a physical temporary internal storage place. That place is known as **RAM** or **Random Access Memory.**

RAM is the place in a computer where the operating system, application programs, and data in current use are kept so that they can be quickly accessed by the computer's processor. RAM is much faster to read from and write to than other kinds of storage in your computer, like hard disk, floppy disk, and CD-ROM. However, data stays in RAM only as long as your computer is running. When you turn the computer off, RAM loses its data. When you turn on your computer again, the operating system and other files are once again loaded into RAM, usually from the hard disk. In order words, we can say that RAM is volatile memory (memory that loses the data when the computer is turned off). Information of any kind can be stored permanently only when it is stored in the hard disk. RAM chips (Fig. 35) come in memory sizes of 64 MB, 128 MB, 256 MB, and so on.

Fig. 35 RAM Chips

There are two types of RAM, **Static RAM (SRAM)** and **Dynamic RAM (DRAM)**. The second type is used more commonly. The two types differ in the technology they use to hold data. Dynamic RAM needs to be refreshed thousands of times per second. Static RAM does not need to be refreshed, which makes it faster; but it is also more expensive than dynamic RAM. Both types of RAM are volatile, meaning that they lose their contents when the power is turned off. Let us discuss them briefly.

- **Dynamic RAM (DRAM):** As you know, it is temporary physical memory of your computer. The term dynamic indicates that the memory must be constantly refreshed (re-energized) or it will lose its contents. Dynamic RAM has more access time and is more volatile than Static RAM (SRAM).
- **Static RAM (SRAM):** SRAM is also a type of temporary memory but more faster and more reliable than DRAM. The term static means that SRAM doesn't need to be refreshed like Dynamic RAM. While DRAM supports access times of about 60 nanoseconds, SRAM can give access times as low as 10 nanoseconds. Besides, its cycle time is much shorter than that of DRAM because it does not need to pause between accesses.
- **Extended Data Out RAM (EDO RAM):** EDO RAM is an improved version of DRAM. EDO RAM can perform more than one task at a time. When some data is sent to the processor, another chunk of data is retrieved from the RAM module. It means while some data processing is on in your computer, EDO RAM is looking for the next piece of data for the processor. This process enables the chip's data to be accessed at very high speed. EDO RAM can be used only in that computer system whose processor and motherboard support its use.

Read Only Memory

Read Only Memory or ROM is a built-in computer memory containing data that normally can only be read, not written to (Fig. 36). ROM contains the programming that allows your computer to "boot up" or regenerate each time you turn it on. Unlike a computer's Random Access Memory (RAM), the data in ROM is not lost when the computer power is turned off. The ROM is sustained by a small long-life battery in your computer. If you configure hardware of your computer, you will be writing to ROM.

Besides computers, ROMs are used extensively in calculators and peripheral devices such as laser printers, whose fonts are often stored in ROMs. A variation of ROM is PROM (programmable read-only memory).

Fig. 36 ROM

- **PROM:** The Programmable Read-Only Memory (PROM) is a memory chip on which data can be written only once. A program written on a PROM remains there forever. Unlike RAM, PROMs retain their contents when the computer is turned off. The difference between PROM and ROM (read-only memory) is that PROM is manufactured as blank memory, whereas ROM is programmed during the manufacturing process. To write data onto a PROM chip, you need a special device called PROM programmer or PROM burner. The process of programming a PROM is sometimes called burning the PROM. A type of PROM is EPROM (erasable programmable read-only memory).
- **EPROM:** This erasable programmable read-only memory can be erased and re-used. Erasure is caused by an intense ultraviolet light through a window that is designed into the EPROM chip. Normal light in a room does not contain enough ultraviolet light to cause EPROM erasure. Only bright sunlight can cause erasure.

Hard Disk Drive

Hard disk is a device which stores all programs and data in the computer. Hence, the hard disk is referred to as the memory bank of a computer. The hard disk memory is permanent. Programs and data stored on it are not lost when the computer is turned off. Earlier, the memory capacity of computers was limited to Mega Bytes (MB). But, today PCs having hard disks of capacities like 10 GB, 20 GB or 30 GB are popular. Larger the hard disk capacity more the amount of software programs and information that can be stored on it. Let us now briefly discuss various components of the Hard Disk Assembly (HDA) (Fig. 37). The Hard Disk Assembly is a sealed metal unit, which contains the following components.

- **Platters:** The platters are the actual disks inside the drive that store the data. Most drives have at least two platters. The larger the storage capacity of the drive more platters it would have. A platter can store data on its both sides, so a drive with 2 platters has 4 sides to store data (Fig.37).
- **Spindle and Spindle Motor:** The platters in a drive are separated by disk spacers and are clamped to a rotating spindle that turns all the platters in unison. The spindle motor is built right into the spindle or mounted directly below it. The motor spins the platters at a constant set rate ranging from 7,200 to 12,000 RPM (rotations per minute) (Fig.37).
- **Read/Write Heads:** The read/write heads read and write data to the platters. There is typically one head per platter side. Each head is attached to a single actuator shaft so that all the heads move in unison. When one head is over a track, i.e. working, all the other heads remain stationary over their respective surfaces. Typically, only one of the heads is active at a time, i.e. reading or writing data. The space between the platter and the head is so minute that even one dust particle or a fingerprint could disable the spin (Fig.37).
- **Head Actuator:** All the heads are attached to a single head actuator, or actuator arm, that moves the heads around the platters (Fig.37).

Fig. 37 Hard Disk Assembly

As you know, the platters, spindle, spindle motor, head actuator and the read/write heads are all contained in the Hard Disk Assembly (HDA). Outside the HDA is the logic board that controls the movements of the internal parts. It also controls the movement of data into and out of the drive.

Cards

Cards are printed circuit boards that you can insert into an expansion slot of your computer to give it added capabilities. Expansion slots are long and narrow connectors. Cards are also called expansion boards, adaptors, add-ins, and add-ons.

- **Disk Drive Control Card:** This card controls the disk drive motors of your PC. It transfers data to the control circuitry and directs the read/write heads to access data on the disk. Earlier computers carried a slot in which the card could be inserted. Nowadays, computers do not contain a separate slot for the disk drive control card. Instead, it is permanently inserted in the motherboard.
- **Display/Video/Graphic Card:** Display card is used to display the data to the user. It is indirectly linked with the computer memory and is inbuilt in the motherboard. Two types of display cards are available. These are the PCI graphics card and the AGP card.
- **Printer Adaptor Card:** To make use of the information stored in the computer memory, you need to either see it on the monitor or print it. The display/printer adaptor card is the link between the PC's memory, the monitor and the printer. It displays the information on the monitor as well as allows it to be printed.
- **Sound Card:** This card allows you to play sound and music. The sound card (Fig. 38) converts the digital information into electrical signals that speakers use. When the speaker is connected to the sound card, the sound can be heard on the speaker.
- **Network Interface Card (NIC):** NIC is another type of expansion board that you can insert into your computer to connect to a network. Most NICs are designed for a particular type of network although some can serve multiple networks.

Fig. 38 Sound Card

Storage Devices

Mass storage devices include all types of disk drives and tape drives. Mass storage is distinct from main memory, which refers to temporary storage areas within the computer. Unlike main memory, mass storage devices retain data even when the computer is turned off. The main types of storage device are:

- **Floppy Disk:** The floppy disk drive continues to be included in new PC systems, even though years ago it was made obsolete by newer storage devices. A floppy disk uses electromagnetism to encode data. The floppy disk (Fig. 39) has come in a variety of sizes during its lifetime, including 8-inch, 5.25-inch, and 3.5-inch disks. The 3.5-inch disk has been the most popular size for about the past 10 years. The floppy disk drive is an internal device mounted into an open drive bay of the system case. Even though it is an internal device, its bezel extends through the drive bay opening and should be visible through a removable bay cover on the case as well. The floppy disk drive comprises a number of components that are very similar in name and function to those of a hard disk drive.

- **Optical disks:** Unlike floppy and hard disks, which use electromagnetism to encode data, optical disk systems use a laser beam to read and write data. Optical disks, also called compact disks (CDs), have very large storage capacity, but they are not as fast as hard disks. Disks (Fig. 40) are random-access media because a disk drive can access any point on the disk at random without passing through intervening points. Both disk drives and disks come in two types—read-only and read/write. Read/write CDs are expensive than read-only CDs.
- **Memory Stick:** In 1998, Sony (a popular electronic goods manufacturing company) started promoting a new storage device called Memory Stick. Within a short span of time, the memory stick became a preferred way of transferring files, songs and data among computers and different compact electronic devices such as digital camera, MP3 player etc. It is extremely compact in comparison to conventional storage devices such as CD or floppy disk. In looks, a memory stick (Fig. 41) is just like a flat AA battery (pencil cell). Memory sticks are available in 32MB, 64MB and 128MB sizes. Despite its compact size, a memory stick can hold photos, movie clips, and hundreds of MP3 files and transfer files easier and much faster. To retrieve data directly from a memory stick, you need a special device known as a memory stick reader. With the help of this device, you can read and transfer data from memory stick to your computer. Although some devices like digital camera employ memory sticks, they have the option of reading and transferring data without the help of memory stick reader.

Mass storage is measured in kilobytes (1,024 bytes), megabytes (1,024 kilobytes), gigabytes (1,024 megabytes) and terabytes (1,024 gigabytes). Mass storage is sometimes called auxiliary storage.

Fig. 39 Floppy Disk

Fig. 40 Compact Disk

Fig. 41 Memory Stick and Reader

So far, we have discussed various peripheral and machinery of computer. Let us know take a brief journey of various types of computers available.

Types of Computer

Computers come in various shapes and sizes. A computer can be as small as your palm, and it can also occupy many rooms of a building. The computer that you use at your home is known as Personal Computer. Besides shape and size, computers also vary in terms of data processing speed. Computers, based upon their sizes, are listed as follows:

Personal Computer

Personal Computer (PC) is a small but powerful computer primarily used in an office or home without the need to connect it to a larger computer. PCs evolved after the development of the Microprocessor popularised the hobby-computer movement in the late 1970s, when some computers were built from components or kits. In the early 1980s, the first low-cost, fully assembled units were mass-marketed. A typical PC configuration consists of a video display, keyboard, mouse, logic unit and memory, storage device. Most current PCs have more computing power, memory, and storage than the large mainframe computers of the 1950s and early 60s. PCs equipped with networking and communications hardware are often used as **computer terminals.**

Today, PCs are generally categorized in a variety of ways. A common categorization is by form rather than function. Most PCs come in one of two shapes: towers and desktops. Desktops (Fig. 42) are perhaps the most familiar. Their system unit is shaped like a tall rectangular box. These personal computers (PCs) are what you see most often on the retail shelves and in homes.

Fig. 42 Personal Computer

Palmtop : Personal Digital Assistant

Personal Digital Assistant (PDA) is a lightweight, hand-held computer designed for use as a personal organizer with communication capabilities (Fig.43). A typical PDA has no keyboard, instead it relies on a pen-like pointing device. The working of this pen is similar to a computer mouse. The user uses the pen to select icons and execute commands. Equipped with applications like word processor, spreadsheet, calendar, and address book, PDAs are used as notepads, appointment schedulers, and wireless communicators for sending and receiving data, faxes, and electronic-mail messages.

Laptop

Laptop computer is also known as notebook. Laptops are portable computers that are integrated with display screen, keyboard, trackball, processor and memory (Fig.44). For power supply, the laptop and all its components depend on rechargeable batteries. You can carry a laptop computer anywhere and also work on it while on the move. Laptops are expensive than personal computers. They are generally used by people who travel frequently.

Fig. 43 Palmtop

Fig. 44 Laptop

Embedded Computers and Special-purpose Computers

There are also special-purpose (dedicated) computers that perform specific tasks, ranging from controlling the temperature and humidity in high-rise buildings to monitoring your heart rate while you work out. Embedded computers enhance the utility of consumer goods like wristwatches, game machines, stereos, video cassette recorders (VCRs), ovens, and even automobiles. Embedded computers are also widely used in industry, defence and science for controlling a variety of hardware devices, including robots.

Main Frame Computers

Mainframe is an industry term for a large computer, typically manufactured by a large company such as IBM for commercial applications and other large-scale computing purposes. In the sixties and seventies, mainframe computers became an important part of many American businesses. These are the large-size computers which occupy a large air-conditioned roomful space and main memory size up to 128 megabytes. Since all peripherals of such a computer are mounted in a large cabinet-type frame, it is also known as Main Frame Computer (Fig. 45). This type of computer system can be used by 128 users simultaneously in time sharing mode and employing mini computers as front end processors. All the first to third generation computers, which work with the speed of 5 to 100 million instructions per second, fall under this group. IBM's 308x-580 series, IBM-3090, 4300, 4381, DEC 1090, 10 20, Cyber's 170, ICL's Series 9, Honeywells DPS 88/860, etc. Burrough 7800, UNIVAC 1100/60, ACOS 100 are the popular main frame computers. Historically, a mainframe is associated with centralized rather than distributed computing. Today, IBM refers to its larger processors as large servers and emphasizes that they can be used to serve distributed users and smaller servers in a computing network.

Super Computers

Super computers are the largest, fastest and most expensive computers made so far. By definition, super computer means a computer having main memory of 256 megabytes working on vector architecture with 64-bit words and performance peak time in the range of 500 M flops. Flops stands for million floating point operations per second. It is a measure of optimum computer efficiency. As compared to an educational computer with only 32 kilobyte memory, a super computer (Fig. 46) has 8000 times more memory. Early computers like ENIAC and Colossus had speeds of 100 flops only as compared to super computer's speed of 500 M flops. Thanks to their fantastic speeds, super computers execute 400,000,000 to 600,000,000 operations per second. The CRay-2, for example, operates at speeds of 1.2 billion flops. It can perform calculations in one minute which a personal computer could perform in three weeks.

Fig. 45 Mainframe Computer

Fig. 46 Super Computer

Mini Computer

The term mini computer originated in the 1960s when it was realized that many computing tasks do not require an expensive mainframe computer but can be done by a small, inexpensive computer. By 1970s, mini computers became powerful machines, which could be used in a variety of applications and could support business applications as well as scientific applications. Soon, with the increase in processor speed, disk memory size and addition of new features, mini computer was found useful in various stand-alone or dedicated applications. Gradually the architectural requirements of mini computers grew and a 32-bit mini computer, which was called supermini, was introduced. It had more peripheral devices, larger memory and could support more users working simultaneously on the computer in comparison to the previous mini computers.

Tablet PC

Tablet PC is a kind of micro-computer (Fig.W-47), which offers a host of new features to today's IT savvy user. It is Microsoft's entry into the world of natural interfaces. Computer manufacturers for years have tried to incorporate new data transfer techniques such as handwriting recognition, voice command and fingerprint authentication. However, now the required processing power and the software base are available that can smoothly absorb written words. With its electromagnetic pen, touch screen and software that recognizes letters written on screen, the Tablet PC hopes to be the Notepad of the 21st century. Ten years of research and analysis of millions of hand writing samples by Microsoft engineers led to the development of the final product. The pen can act like a mouse when moving over a Tablet PC. When the pen touches the screen, it acts like an ink pen, and the user can write directly on the screen.

Fig. 47 Tablet PC

Computer Software

Software of a computer works like its brain. Software can be defined as a set of programs necessary to carry out operations for a specified job. These programs consist of step-by-step instructions telling the computer how to carry out operations for a specific job. Software can be divided into two groups—**System** and **Application software.**

System Software

This consists of all the programs, languages and documentation supplied by the computer manufacturer. This type of software is required to use the computer efficiently and conveniently. System software programs allow the application developers to write and develop their own programs. Examples of system software: Operating Systems (Windows 98, Windows Me, Windows XP), drivers (sound card driver, display driver), and viruses etc.

Application Software

Any software which is designed to accomplish a specific task like accounting, typing, drawing, browsing the Internet, emailing, etc., is known as Application Software. Nowadays, various application softwares are available in the market like Paintbrush, MS Word, MS Excel, Tally, etc.

Word Processing Program

The word processing software enables the PC to function like a sophisticated typewriter. This software allows you to type a letter or report, and change words or move blocks of text around with ease. Further, word processing programs also count your words and even check spellings. **Microsoft Word** (Fig. 48) and **WordPad** of Windows 2000 are the most popular word processing programs.

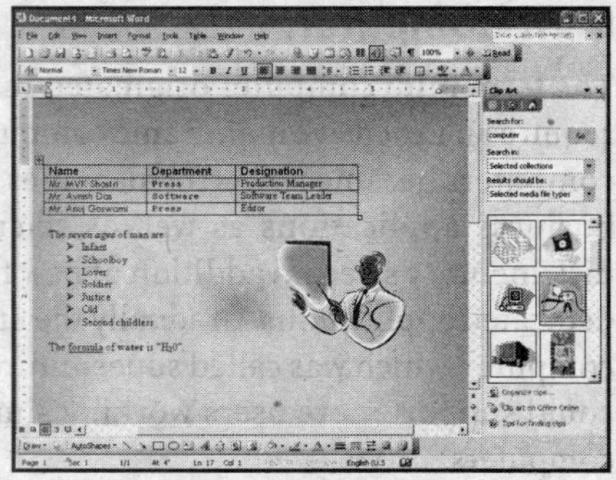

Fig. 48 MS Word

Spreadsheet Program

Spreadsheet program is meant for those who need to do lot of calculation or financial planning. A spreadsheet is made up of cells arranged in a grid. Each cell can contain a number, text or a formula. Sometimes a spreadsheet program may include charting tools that allow you to plot the values stored in rows or columns as a graph or chart. **Microsoft Excel** (Fig. 49) is so far the most popular spreadsheet program.

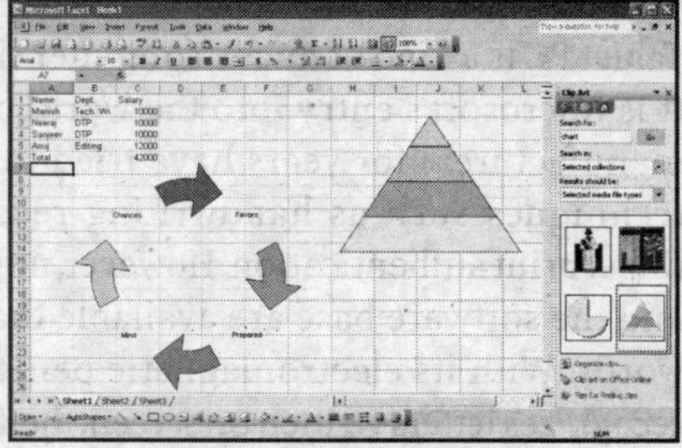

Fig. 49 MS Excel

Database Program

Database programs are useful for storing, sorting and retrieving large amount of data. Invoices or orders, which may be in large numbers, can be managed better by using a database program. Database software allows you to add new information, search through previously stored data, and print records. An organization, for example, might require a database about its various products, suppliers, employees, and customers. Doctors, on the other hand, may need to maintain databases about patients and their individual medical histories. Today, the most widely used database program is **Microsoft Access** (Fig. 50).

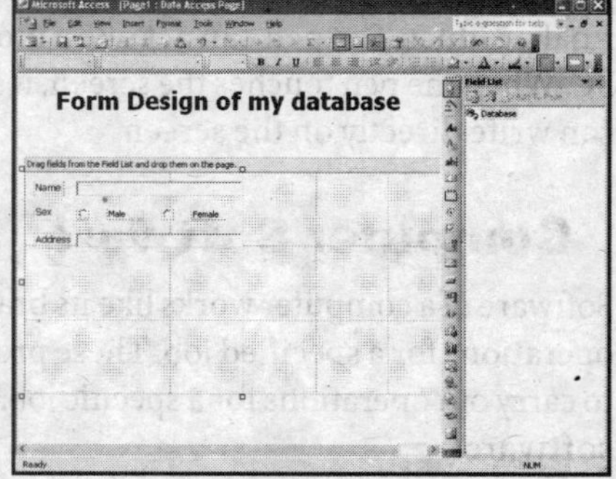

Fig. 50 MS Access

Presentation Program

A Presentation Program enables us to represent information in a number of attractive formats. Such a program is very useful for people who have to prepare reports and proposals. The most commonly used presentation program is **Microsoft PowerPoint** (Fig. 51).

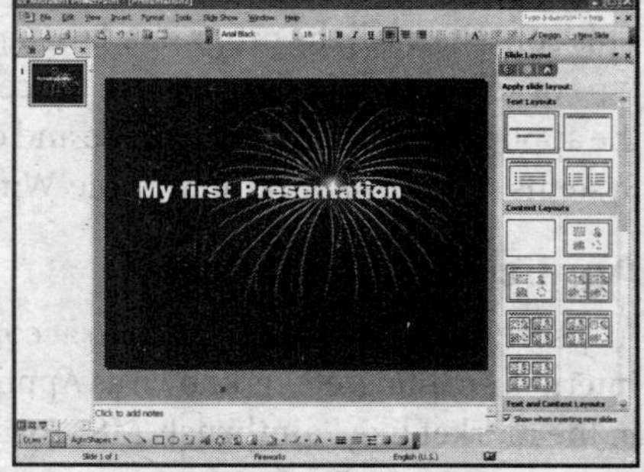

Fig. 51 MS PowerPoint

Painting Program

The purpose of this program is to provide the user with a number of options for drawing and sketching. The pictures we draw on a computer are represented as bit maps. The various paint programs provide tools for drawing and colouring different types of pictures. The most common of these programs is **MS Paint** (Fig. 52) that comes along with the Windows Operating System.

Emailing Software

The term e-mail stands for electronic mail. It is the easiest and the fastest means of sending mails to one's friends and relatives. Whether you send an e-mail to someone next door or a person staying abroad, it will take less than a minute to reach the recipient. **Outlook Express** (Fig. 53) is a popular emailing software.

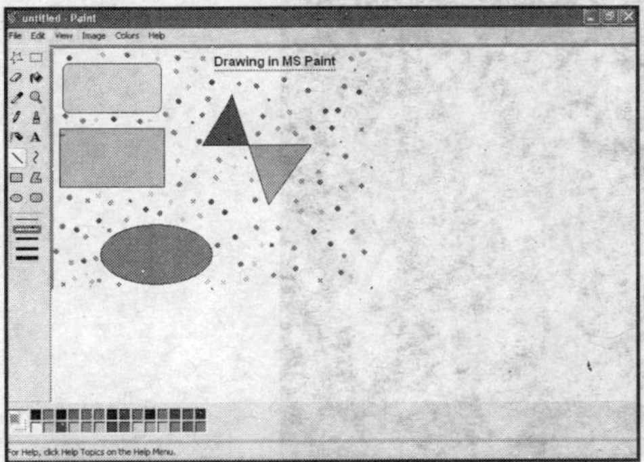

Fig. 52 MS Paint

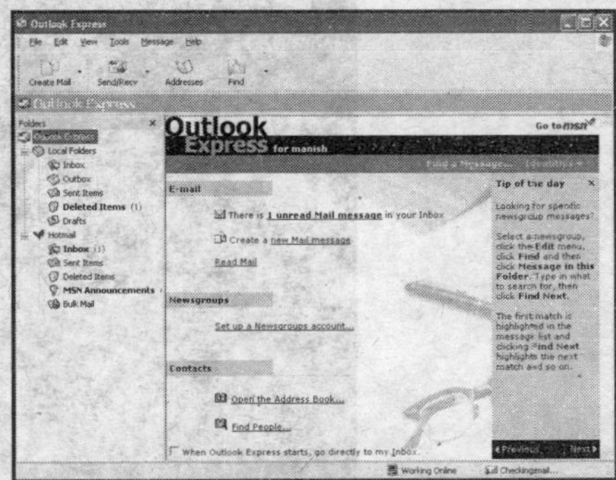

Fig. 53 Outlook Express

Personal Information Manager

Personal Information Manager (PIM) is a type of application software designed to help users organize information. Most PIMs enable you to enter various kinds of textual notes — reminders, lists, and dates — and to link the information together in useful ways. Many PIMs also include calendar, scheduling, and calculator programs. One such PIM is **MS Outlook** (Fig. 54) that comes with the MS Office package. Using **Outlook** one can easily organize one's contacts, phone numbers, set a reminder for a meeting or task etc.

Browser

Browser is a software application used to locate and display web pages. The two most popular browsers are **Netscape Navigator** and **Microsoft Internet Explorer** (Fig. 55). Both are graphical browsers, which means that they can display graphics as well as text. In addition, most modern browsers can present multimedia information, including sound and video, though they require plug-ins for some formats. Another type of browser is Opera.

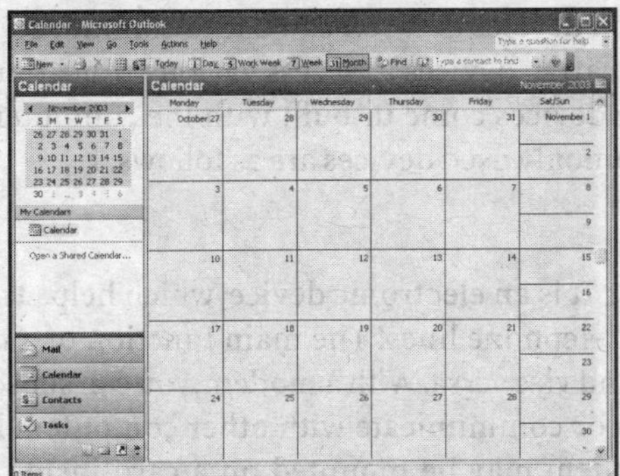

Fig. 54 MS Outlook

Fig. 55 Internet Explorer

Open Source

The software programs that are freely available to everybody on the Internet are known as **Open Source**. This term indicates two things. First, you do not have to pay for installing such a program on your computer, and secondly, the coding of the program is also available to all. One such software is **Linux** (Fig. 56).

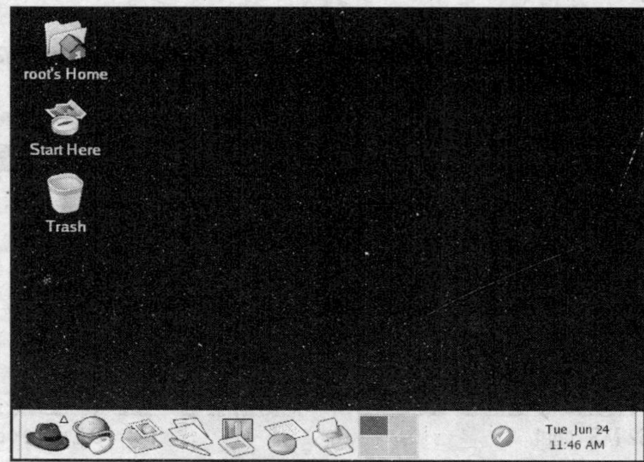

Fig. 56 Linux Desktop

Multimedia Software

Multimedia software packages are the latest craze among the users. Using these programs, one can create 3D objects, move objects on a definite or random path, and can animate objects in a number of ways. Some examples of the multimedia programs are Flash, Director, Maya and Sound Forge.

Computer Aided Design

Computer Aided Design (CAD) is a technique that enables engineers and manufacturers to make the basic design of their product on a computer. CAD packages help engineers to create and analyze the design of a product thoroughly before its actual manufacture. The commonly used CAD softwares are **Max** and **AutoCAD**.

Communication Devices

Your computer system comes with several communication devices that you can use to communicate with your friends over the Internet. You can also use communication devices to access various educational and entertainment resources available on the Internet. Some devices come in-built with the computer, while others can easily be attached to your computer. Some commonly used devices are as follows:

Modem

Modem is technically called the Modulator–Demodulator. It is an electronic device, which helps transmit programs and data locally or around the world through telephone lines. The main function of a modem (Fig. 57) is to transform digital signals into analog signals and vice versa. With a modem, you can subscribe to a growing number of online and bulletin board services or communicate with other computers located elsewhere which have modems attached to them. A modem may be mounted on a card inside the PC (an internal modem), or it may be a separate piece of equipment that connects to the serial port of the PC via a cable (an external modem). Telephone lines then connect the modem to the telephone service. Modems help in carrying out various functions like electronic mail, online banking, travel, reservations etc. Some modems contain software that allow documents (files) created on your computer to be sent to fax machines.

Fig. 57 Modem

Web Camera

Web camera is a video camera, usually attached to a computer, whose current or latest image can be had from a website. A live camera is one that is continually providing new images that are transmitted in rapid succession. Web cameras (Fig. 58) are easy to connect through a USB port (earlier cameras used to be connected through a dedicated card or parallel port). Web camera is also called Webcam. A piece of software connects to the camera and takes an image from it periodically. For example, the software might hold a still image from the camera once every 30 seconds. The software then turns that image into a normal JPG file and uploads it to your Web server. The JPG image can be placed on any web page.

If you don't have a web server, several companies now offer you a free place to upload your images, saving you the trouble of having to set up and maintain a web server or a host website. This is the simplest possible Webcam.

Fig. 58 Web Cameras

Accessories

Speakers, Headphone and Mike

Nowadays, every computer comes with a set of two speakers (Fig. 59). Though speakers could be your personal choice, while buying one, ensure that its has a built-in amplifier and is magnetically-shielded so that it does not interfere with the picture quality of the monitor. Fig. 59 shows a set of latest speakers available in the market.

If you like the computer environment to be quiet, you must purchase a good quality headphone. It also ensures that while doing multimedia tasks on computer, only you hear the resultant sound. Now, mike also comes with headphone (Fig. 60). At home, you can use headphone and mike for voice based chatting and making phone calls over the Internet. With a headphone you can hear the voice and speak to your friend simultaneously.

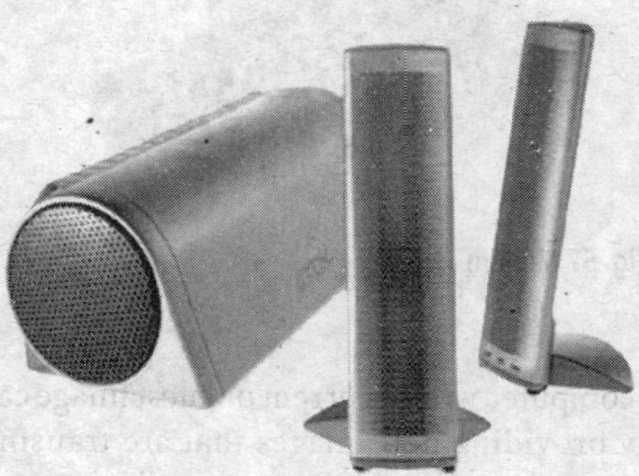

Fig. 59 Speakers

Fig. 60 Headphone with Mike

Digital Camera

In principle, a digital camera (Fig. 61) is similar to a traditional film-based camera. There's a viewfinder to aim it, a lens to focus the image onto a light-sensitive device, some means by which several images can be stored and removed for later use, and the whole lot is fitted into a box. In a conventional camera, light-sensitive film captures images and after development of the film, image prints are taken on photo paper. Digital photography uses a combination of advanced image sensor technology and memory storage, which allows images to be captured in a digital format. The captured images are instantly available to print with no need for a development process.

Fig. 61 Digital Cameras

MP3 Player

Your computer can also work as your music system. For downloadable music, there are many popular formats including MP3, liquid audio, MS audio etc. The MP3 file format is one of the most popular and easy-to-use formats currently available. To listen music on your computer, you will need an MP3 music player and music files.

Fig. 62 Winamp Player

MP3 is a way of storing music in compressed form on your computer so that it takes up relatively little space on your hard disk. An MP3 file works on any MP3 player installed on your computer. For Windows 98/2000/XP, **Winamp** (Fig. 62) is the most popular player for MP3 files and other downloadable music formats. It requires a 486 processor or better and a sound card installed on your computer.

Summary

- Neolithic Computer and Abacus are two ancient computers.
- Calculation done by using the Neolithic Computer is known as Stone-Henge calculation.
- In 1642, French mathematician Blaise Pascal invented a machine for performing basic mathematical calculations. The name of the machine was Pascaline.
- In 1821, English mathematician Charles Babbage (also known as father of modern computers) invented a machine called Difference Engine to perform mathematical calculations. Later in 1856, he invented another machine known as Analytical Engine.
- Three American scientists – John von Neumann, Eckert and Mauchly—jointly developed first electronic computer known as Electronic Numerical Integrator and Calculator (ENIAC).
- International Business Machine (IBM) launched personal computer (PC) in 1981.
- A computer has four basic operations – Input, Processing, Output and Storage.
- The two broad categories of computer hardware are – Input and Output devices. Commonly used input devices are: Keyboard, Mouse, Trackball, Joystick, Scanner and Light pen. Monitor and Printer are examples of Output Devices.

- The System Unit of a computer is also hardware but it is solely used by the computer for processing and generating results for the user. The System Unit is also known as the brain of computer.
  - The front side of the System Unit has Floppy Disk drive and CD-Writer drives.
  - The back side of the System Unit has several connection points of different shapes. These connection points are known as ports.
  - The inside of the System Unit comprises motherboard, Switch Mode Power Supply (SMPS) box, Random Access Memory (RAM), Read Only Memory (ROM), Hard Disk Assembly, and Cards.
- Commonly used storage devices are Floppy Disk, CD and Memory Stick.
- Based upon size and speed, computers come in different shapes and sizes. Some commonly found computers are Personal Computer, Palmtop, Laptop and Tablet PC.
  - Main Frame computers are used for commercial applications and large-scale computing purposes.
  - Super computers are the largest and fastest computers present on earth. Cray-2 and Param are examples of super computer.
- A set of instructions (Program) necessary to carry out a specific job on computer is known as software.
  - Software can be divided into two groups – System and Application software.
  - Windows, Mac, Linux etc. are examples of System Software
  - Tally, MS Paint, Outlook Express, etc. are examples of Application Software.
- Communication devices let you communicate with people over the Internet. Modem and Web Camera are two commonly used communication devices.

CHAPTER 2

Introducing Windows XP

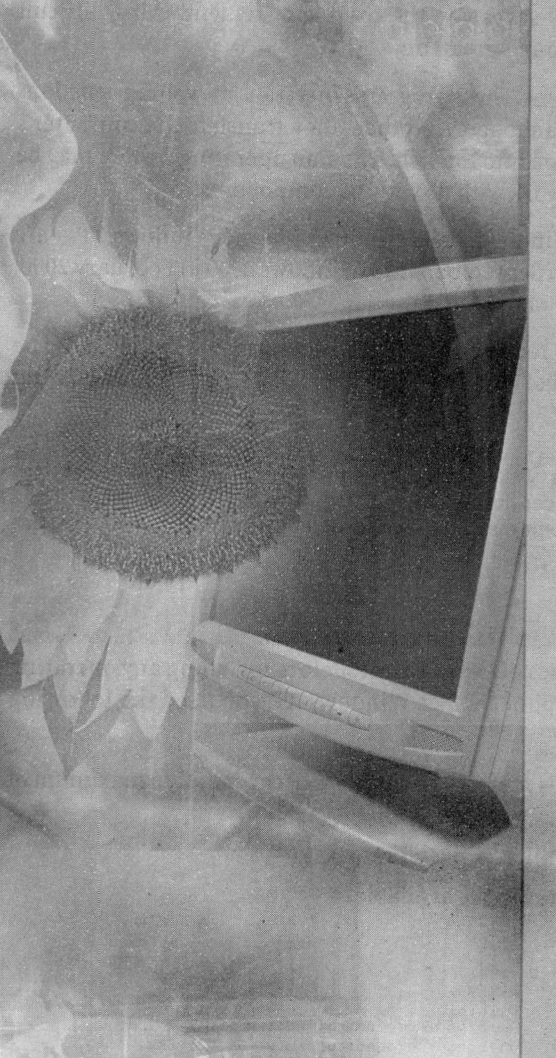

IN THIS CHAPTER

- Windows XP Requirements
- Mouse Basics
- Working in Windows XP
- Learning more about the Mouse
- Components of a Window
- Quitting Windows XP
- Summary
- Exercise

This chapter introduces you to **Windows XP** which is an **operating system** that controls your computer's hardware. Computer hardware is not capable of communicating to you directly. It needs a communication medium to understand your requirements. Such a medium is called the **Operating System**. Similar to a traffic policeman who controls the traffic, the operating system controls the overall working of your computer. It helps you manage files and check the various peripheral devices such as printer, monitor, mouse, etc. DOS is also an operating system, but DOS commands are difficult to understand and even more difficult to remember. Windows XP saves you the trouble of remembering difficult commands. And, the computer learning process becomes great fun.

Basically, an operating system is a collection of programs. These programs first translate your instructions or questions into computer language or machine language. And then, they translate the computer's response to your queries from the computer language into English. Thus, an operating system may be defined as a program that instructs your PC how to work with its various components.

Currently, four operating systems—Windows 98, Windows 2000, Windows Me and Windows XP—are available in the market. Windows 98 was launched in September 1998, Windows 2000 in February 2000, Windows Me in September 2000 and Windows XP in May 2001.

Previous versions of Windows like Windows 3.1/3.11 required MS-DOS to operate. That is, they could be opened only through DOS. However, later versions like Windows 95 and its successors Windows 98 and Windows Me didn't depend too much on DOS.

Windows XP makes it easy for persons having vision, hearing or mobility deficiency to work on computer. For such persons, it offers many accessibility options such as speech recognition. The speech recognition option enables the user to select menu, toolbar, dialog box and task pane by using his voice.

Windows XP Requirements

This chapter concentrates on teaching you the basics of Windows XP. Before installing any operating system, you require some essential hardware components. For Windows XP, you need the following hardware components.

- A minimum of 128 MB of RAM although 256 MB is preferred. Windows XP can handle a maximum of 4GB RAM.
- 533 megahertz (MHz) Pentium III or equivalent microprocessor.
- A 4 GB or larger hard disk with at least 650 MB free space available.
- VGA monitor.
- Keyboard.
- Mouse or compatible pointing device.
- CD-ROM or DVD drive.

If a person has limited mobility and faces difficulty in using a conventional keyboard, he can display a keyboard on his screen. This feature of Windows XP allows a person to use mouse or joystick to do typing on the screen keyboard.

While working in Windows XP, you have to make extensive use of **computer mouse**. Already, we have discussed this device and its features in the last chapter. However here we again describe the mouse briefly to refresh your memory.

Mouse Basics

Mouse is a small object, designed to fit neatly under your palm. It has two main functions: You can use it to move the cursor on the screen in all directions (Left, Right, Up, Down or diagonal), and also select the items displayed on the screen. The most useful feature of the mouse is its buttons which help us in selecting items. Generally a mouse has three buttons. Some mouse models also have a small wheel in the middle (known as roller). Commonly used three-button mouses are shown in Fig. W-2.1(a) and W-2.1(b). The mouse shown in Fig. W-2.1(b) has a small wheel in the middle.

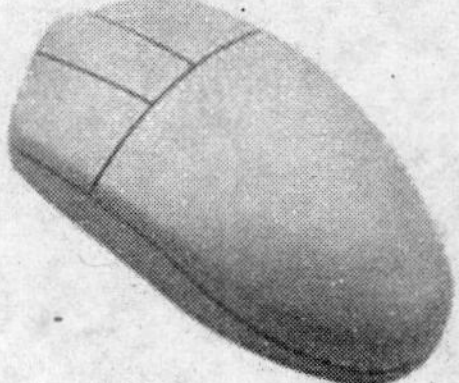

Fig. W-2.1(a)

Fig. W-2.1(b)

Using the Mouse

Before you use a mouse, make sure that it is placed on a flat surface so that you can move it easily. To get a firm grip over the mouse, it is better to keep it on a rectangular pad. This would also ensure its smooth movement. The rectangular pad is called **mouse-pad** (Fig. W-2.2).

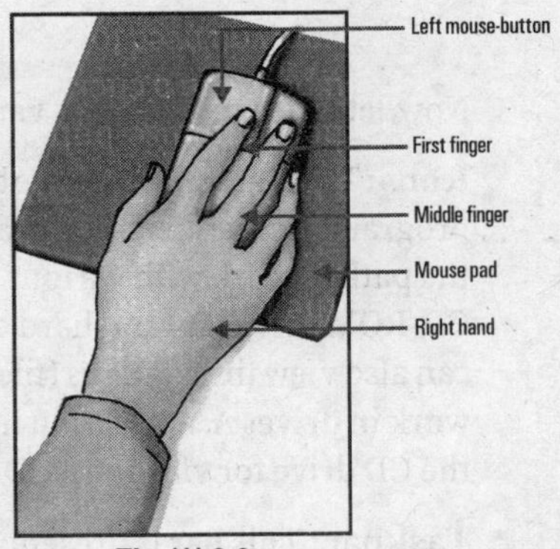

Fig. W-2.2

The left mouse-button is the primary button of the mouse. Its two most common actions are: **Click** (pressing the left mouse-button once) and **Double-click** (pressing the left mouse-button two times). Single click is used to highlight or click on the icons or menu options while double-click is used to open programs or icons. The second mouse-button is the right button that is used to open shortcut menus.

Working in Windows XP

After you switch on the computer or the PC, Windows XP is loaded into the computer's memory. Thereafter, Windows XP tests all the hardware components and loads graphic files, font files, etc. which are needed for displaying the **Desktop**. Finally, after all the checking, Windows XP displays its Desktop (Fig. W-2.3).

Desktop

The Windows XP Desktop (Fig. W-2.3) is a graphical screen containing icons and pictures. The pictures and icons are actually shortcuts to programs. By double-clicking the mouse on these pictures and icons, you can gain access to their respective programs.

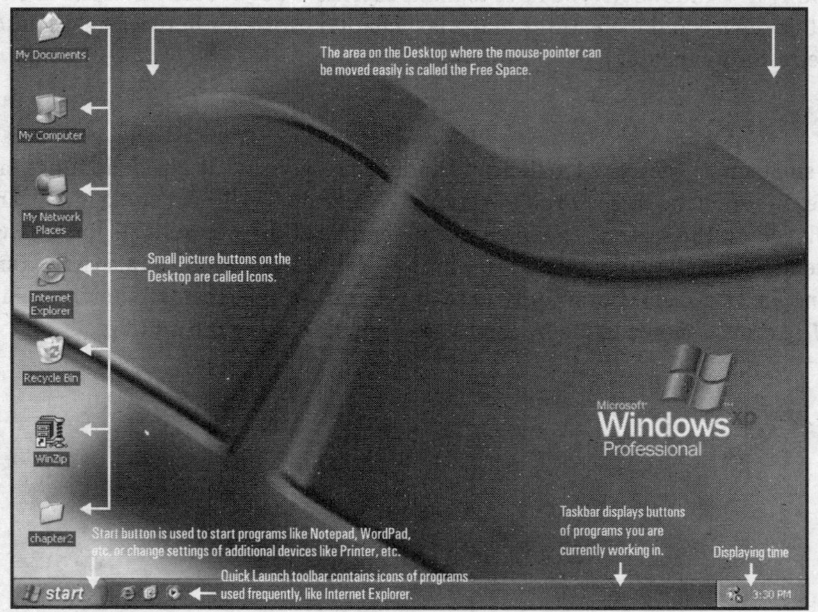

Fig. W-2.3: Windows XP Desktop

Now, let us learn about the various elements of the Windows XP Desktop.

Icons : These are small picture buttons present on the Desktop. The icons represent programs, folders, etc. For example, the **My Computer** icon (Fig. W-2.4) provides the path to work with various computer resources, e.g. the disk drive (A: or B:), CD-ROM drive (D:) and hard disk drive (C:). Through the **My Computer** icon, you can also view the contents (files and folders) present in these drives. However, to work in drives A: and B: you have to insert disks in them. Similarly, you can use the CD drive for viewing a CD-ROM.

Fig. W-2.4

Taskbar : This bar is present at the bottom of the Windows XP Desktop. Apart from displaying the buttons of the currently open programs, the Taskbar also displays information such as time, etc. on the right-hand side. It also shows a **Quick Launch** toolbar containing shortcuts to various useful programs like **Internet Explorer, Windows Media Player** etc.

The **Start** button, present on the left-hand side of the Taskbar, helps you start programs in Windows XP.

Free Space : The free space on the Desktop is used for the free movement of the mouse-pointer(↖) or for file related operations such as copying or moving of files. In this chapter, we will use the free space to work with various examples which will give you a better understanding of mouse functions.

Learning more about the Mouse

You have already gone through a brief description of the mouse, its types, and use of click or double-click on it. Let us now go through a couple of examples for a better understanding of mouse functions.

Working with the Mouse

Mouse is a device attached to your system. With the mouse, you can feel at ease while working on your computer. The mouse has three buttons, viz. the **left button**, the **middle button** and the **right button.** However, Fig. W-2.5 shows a roller instead of middle button. The left and the right buttons are used extensively but the middle button is used rarely while working in Windows XP.

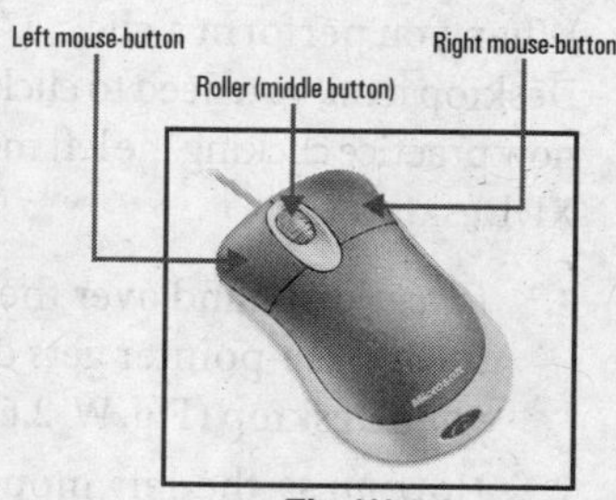

Fig. W-2.5

To make use of the left and right mouse-buttons, the mouse should be held comfortably inside your palm. If you feel comfortable working with your right hand, *place* your right hand on the mouse. Then *place* your first finger on the left mouse-button and the middle finger on the right mouse-button (Fig. W-2.2). Now, *move* the mouse over the mouse-pad in any direction. Notice that as you move the mouse, an arrow( ) also moves in the same direction on your screen. This arrow is called the **mouse-pointer**.

Let us now try working with the mouse by undertaking the following steps:

1. *Raise* the mouse and *place* it beneath your right hand on the mouse-pad.
2. *Hold* the mouse with your first finger on the left mouse-button and middle finger on the right mouse-button.
3. Now *move* the mouse towards the left-hand side on the mouse-pad, keeping it in contact with the mouse-pad all the while. You will observe that the mouse-pointer ( ) shifts to the left on your screen.
4. Similarly, *move* the mouse in other directions by keeping it in contact with the mouse-pad. You will observe that the mouse-pointer ( ) on the screen follows the same direction in which the mouse moves on the pad.

The mouse measures the distance and direction it has moved across the Desktop and delivers that information to the computer. When the mouse-pointer does not move with the mouse, it could be either due to a fault in the mouse, or a problem inside the computer.

If while sliding to the left, mouse goes out of the pad then lift the mouse and put it again on the mouse pad. Thereafter, slide it gradually to the left to move the mouse-pointer to the left of the screen.

Performing Mouse Actions

The four common mouse actions are **Click, Double-click, Drag** and **Select.** Let us understand these actions one-by-one.

Click means moving the mouse-pointer (↖) to the desired option or program on the screen and then pressing the left or the right mouse-button once. Let us now do the click action with each of these buttons.

Clicking with the left mouse-button

To click the left mouse-button, *press* it just once and then *release* it. When you perform a click, a **'tick'** sound is heard. To highlight any Desktop icon, you need to click the left mouse-button just once. Let us now practice clicking the left mouse-button on any icon of the Windows XP Desktop.

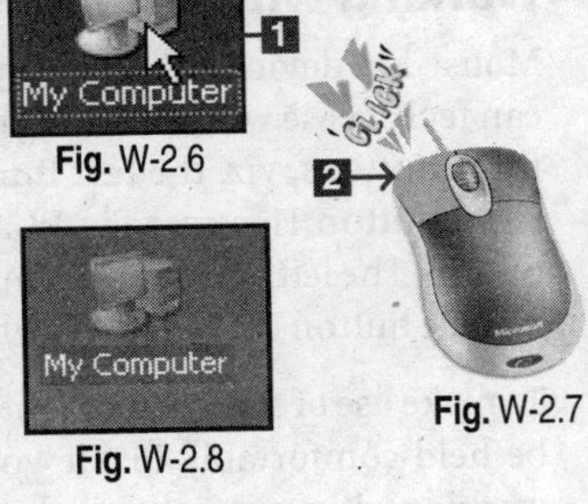

Fig. W-2.6

Fig. W-2.7

Fig. W-2.8

1. *Place* your hand over the mouse and *move* it in such a way that the mouse-pointer gets displayed over the **My Computer** icon on your Desktop (Fig. W-2.6).
2. Now *press* the left mouse-button (depicted in green in Fig. W-2.7) once and then *release* it. You hear a tick sound confirming the click. Now you see that the **My Computer** icon gets highlighted (Fig. W-2.8). This highlight is the result of the click action.
3. To remove the highlight from the **My Computer** icon, *move* the mouse in such a way that the mouse-pointer shifts to the free space of the Windows XP Desktop.
4. Now, *press* the left mouse-button once. This makes the highlight disappear from the **My Computer** icon.

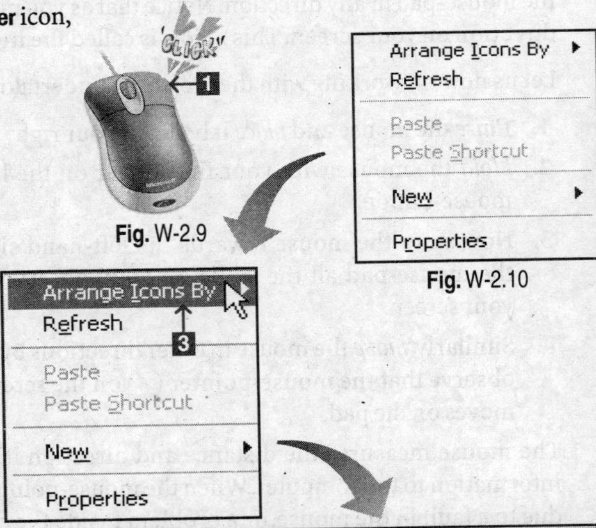

Fig. W-2.9

Fig. W-2.10

Fig. W-2.11

Clicking with the right mouse-button

To perform a right-click, *place* your middle finger over the right mouse-button and *click* it. A click with the right mouse-button is used to bring up pop-up menus of commands and shortcuts. Pop-up menu in also called **shortcut menu.** Let us now use the right click to arrange icons on your Desktop in alphabetical order.

1. *Move* the mouse-pointer over the free space of your Desktop.
2. *Press* the right mouse-button (depicted in green in Fig. W-2.9) just once and *release* it. You hear a tick sound, confirming the click. Instantly, a shortcut menu gets displayed before you (Fig. W-2.10).
3. In the shortcut menu, *place* the mouse-pointer on the **Arrange Icons By** option (Fig. W-2.11). The option gets highlighted.
4. Immediately, a second menu (Fig. W-2.12) appears next to the first one.

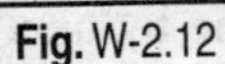
Fig. W-2.12

5. In the second menu, *place* the mouse-pointer on the **Name** option (Fig. W-2.12). The **Name** option also gets highlighted.
6. Now *place* your finger on the left mouse-button.
7. *Press* the left mouse-button just once. A tick sound confirms that the selection is done. You will notice that the shortcut menu as well as the second menu disappear from the screen, and all the icons of the Desktop get arranged automatically in alphabetical order.

Double-Clicking with the left mouse-button

Clicking the left mouse-button two times simultaneously is called a **double-click**. To double-click the mouse-button, *place* your finger on the left mouse-button (Fig. W-2.14) and then quickly *press* and *release* the button two times. On double-clicking, you will hear, a '**tick tick**' sound.

In Windows XP, a double-click can be performed only with the left mouse-button.

The double-clicking operation is used to open an icon. As you know, the icons present on Windows XP Desktop are nothing but programs which are closed. For opening any icon, i.e. program, you have to double-click over its corresponding picture button, i.e. icon.

Let us now perform a double-click operation on any icon. Suppose you want to open the **My Computer** icon present on Windows XP Desktop. To do so, undertake the following steps:

1. *Move* the mouse in such a way that the mouse-pointer gets displayed over the **My Computer** icon (Fig. W-2.13).
2. Now, *press* and *release* the left mouse-button two times as quickly as possible (Fig. W-2.14). Immediately, the **My Computer** icon opens up into a window and displays its contents (Fig. W-2.15).

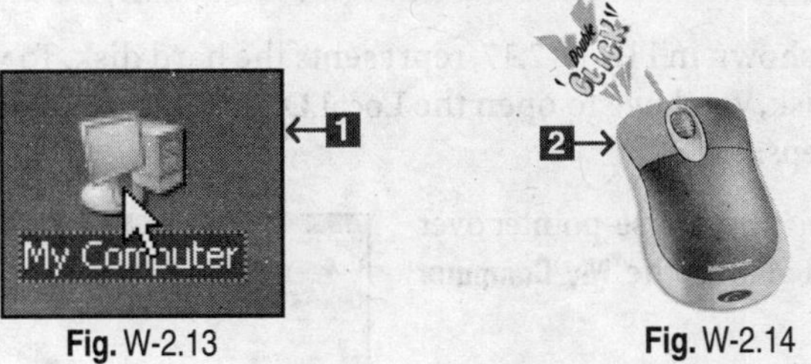

Fig. W-2.13　　**Fig.** W-2.14

In Fig. W-2.15, the **My Computer** window has a toolbar called the **Standard Toolbar** consisting of buttons which are shortcuts to the various commands of Menu bar options.

You may also perform double-clicks with the right mouse-button, but Windows XP ignores them. It considers two right clicks as a single right click. For example, do a right click two times on the My Computer icon. You will observe that the result is same as that of clicking the right mouse-button once.

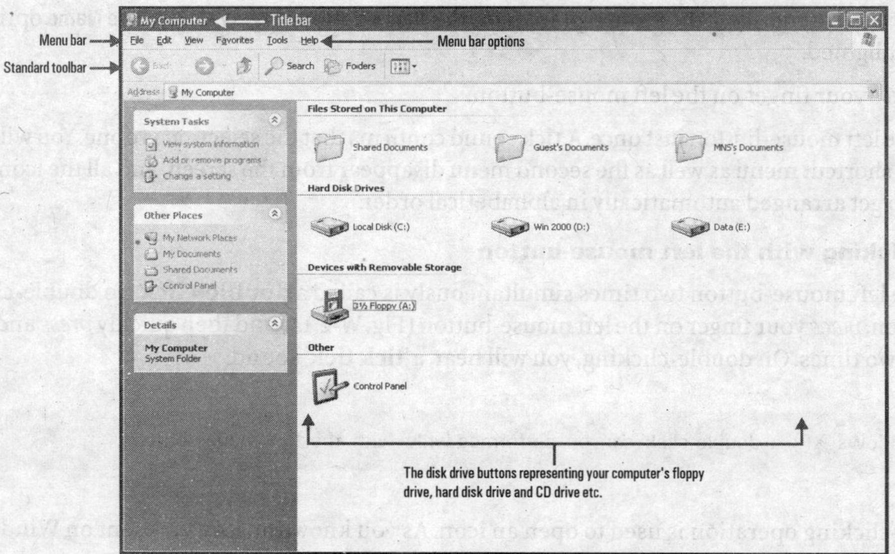

Fig. W-2.15: My Computer Window

Fig. W-2.16

The **My Computer** window has many icons. Each icon represents a particular program. For example, the icon for **3½ Floppy (A:)** shown in Fig. W-2.16 is a program used for showing the contents of a 3½ inch floppy disk. First, you *insert* a floppy disk in A: drive. Then *double-click* the left mouse-button over this icon. Instantly, the contents of the inserted disk get displayed in a window on the screen.

If you have to read a 5½ inch floppy disk then a 5½ inch floppy disk drive is essential for your system. Since our system does not have a 5½ inch floppy disk drive, its icon is not displayed inside the My Computer window.

Fig. W-2.17

The icon for **Local Disk(C:)**, shown in Fig. W-2.17, represents the hard disk. To view the contents of the hard disk, you have to open the **Local Disk(C:)** icon. To do so, undertake the following steps:

1. *Move* the mouse and *place* the mouse-pointer over the **Local Disk (C:)** icon inside the **My Computer** window (Fig. W-2.18).
2. Now *press* the left mouse-button and *release* it two times as quickly as possible. Immediately, the **Local Disk (C:)** icon opens up into a window which contains many more icons. Fig. W-2.19 shows the contents of the **Local Disk (C:)** in Windows XP. The Hard Disk (C:) is called Local Disk (C:) in Windows XP.

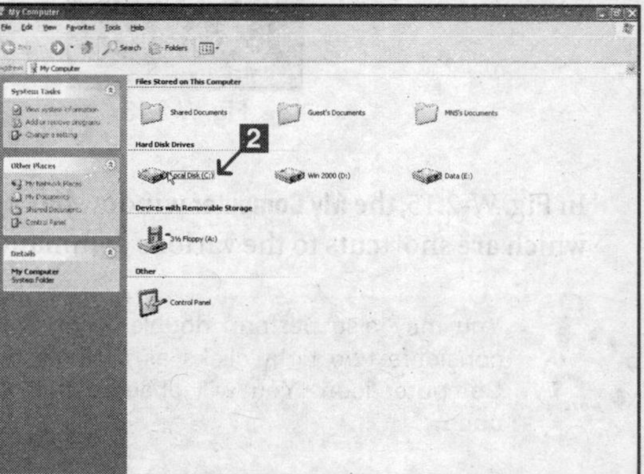

Fig. W-2.18

3. Each icon inside the **Local Disk(C:)** can be opened by double-clicking over it. For example, for opening the **Documents and Settings** icon present inside the **Local Disk (C:)** window (Fig. W-2.19), *double-click* over it. Instantly, this icon opens up to display its contents.

If a CD-ROM is already inserted in your CD drive(D:) then double-clicking its icon in the **My Computer** window will show you the CD-ROM contents as small icons. These icons can also be opened by double-clicking the left mouse-button over them.

The third mouse action is **Dragging.** We will discuss it later on. Now, we will learn more about the various components of a window.

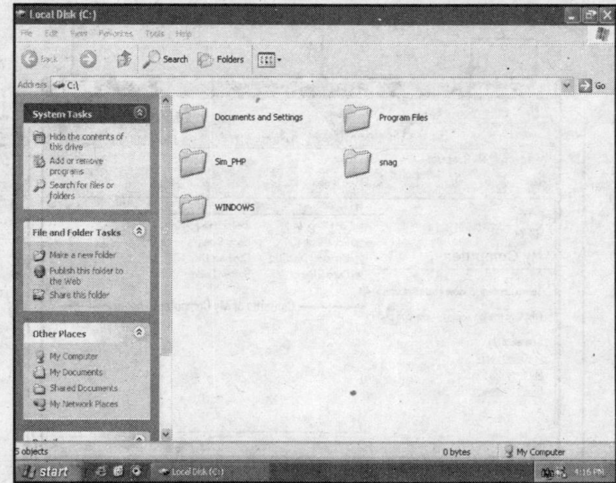

Fig. W-2.19: Local Disk (C:) Window

Components of a Window

Currently your desktop displays two Windows viz. **My computer** and **Local Disk (C:)** or (C:). If you are using Windows XP, these windows will look like Fig. W-2.20. If your version is Windows ME, your screen will display Fig. W-2.21. In both these Figures we have opened the **Local Disk (C:)** by following the steps described above.

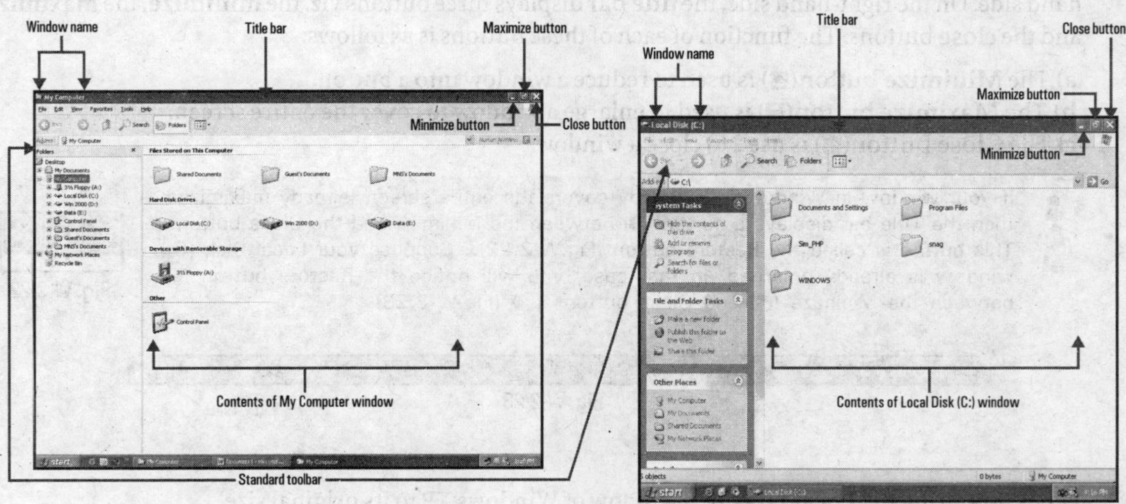

My Computer window of Windows XP

Local Disk [C:] window of Windows XP

Fig. W-2.20

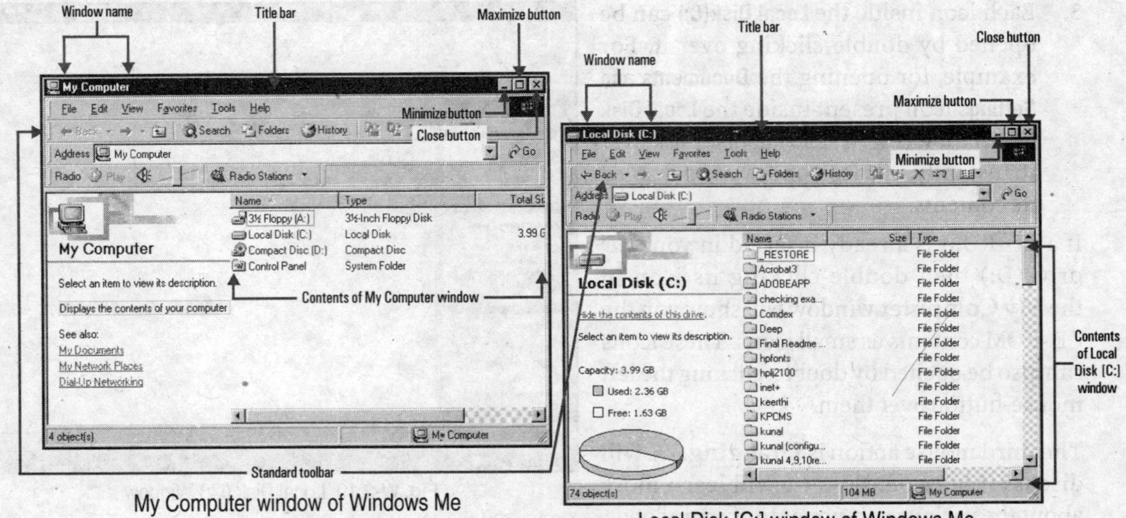

My Computer window of Windows Me

Local Disk [C:] window of Windows Me

Fig. W-2.21

Box displaying contents: In all the windows displayed in the last section, you must have observed a bigger box displaying smaller icons. These icons represent the contents of that particular window.

Title bar: The topmost portion of any window in Windows XP is called the **Title bar.** This bar displays the name of the window on the left-hand side. For example, Fig. W-2.20 displays the names of the **Local Disk (C:)** and **My Computer** windows on the left-hand side. Fig. W-2.21 also displays these names on the left-hand side. On the right-hand side, the **title bar** displays three buttons viz. the **minimize,** the **maximize** and the **close** buttons. The function of each of these buttons is as follows:

a) The **Minimize button**(▬) is used to reduce a window into a button.
b) The **Maximize button**(▭) is used to enlarge a window to cover the entire screen.
c) The **Close button**(☒) is used to close a window.

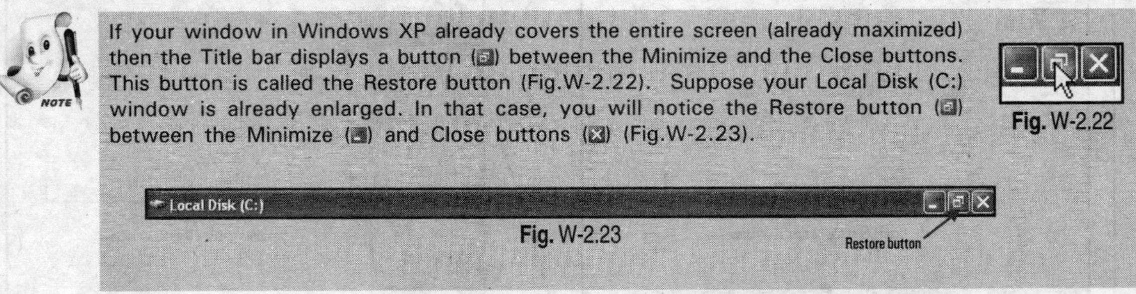

NOTE

If your window in Windows XP already covers the entire screen (already maximized) then the Title bar displays a button (▭) between the Minimize and the Close buttons. This button is called the Restore button (Fig.W-2.22). Suppose your Local Disk (C:) window is already enlarged. In that case, you will notice the Restore button (▭) between the Minimize (▬) and Close buttons (☒) (Fig.W-2.23).

Fig. W-2.22

Fig. W-2.23

Let us now bring the **Local Disk (C:)** window of Windows XP to its original size.

1. *Move* the mouse and *place* the mouse-pointer over the **Restore** button (▭) present on the right-hand side of the **title bar** of the **Local Disk (C:)** window (Fig. W-2.22).

2. Now, *press* the left mouse-button just once. Instantly, the **Local Disk (C:)** window returns to its original size.

You can open any number of windows in Windows XP, but only the window opened last would be currently active. The **Title bar** of the currently active window appears highlighted. So, a currently active window is the one which is opened last.

Now, to have a better understanding of the concept of an active window, let us undertake the following exercise. At present no window is open your desktop.

1. *Double-click* on the **My Computer** icon on the **Desktop** to open it (Fig. W-2.13). In the **My Computer** contents box, *double-click* the **Local Disk (C:)** icon to open it (Fig. W-2.18).
2. *Click* on the **Restore** (▣) button of the **Title bar** of the **Local Disk (C:)** window to reduce it into a small window on the desktop.
3. *Now, click* the left mouse-button on the **Title bar** (not on its buttons) of the **My Computer** window. Instantly, the **My Computer** window gets displayed over the **Local Disk (C:)** window (Fig. W-2.24).
4. To see the **Local Disk (C:)** window **Title bar** clearly, *move* the mouse-pointer over the **title bar** of the **My Computer** window.
5. *Press* the left mouse-button.
6. Keeping the left mouse-button *pressed*, *drag* the mouse a little downwards and *release* the left button.

You can now clearly see the **Title bar** of the **Local Disk (C:)** window. The **My Computer** window is the currently active window because its **Title bar** appears more highlighted than that of the **Local Disk (C:)** window. Fig. W-2.24 shows the **Local Disk (C:)** window and the **My Computer** window of Windows XP.

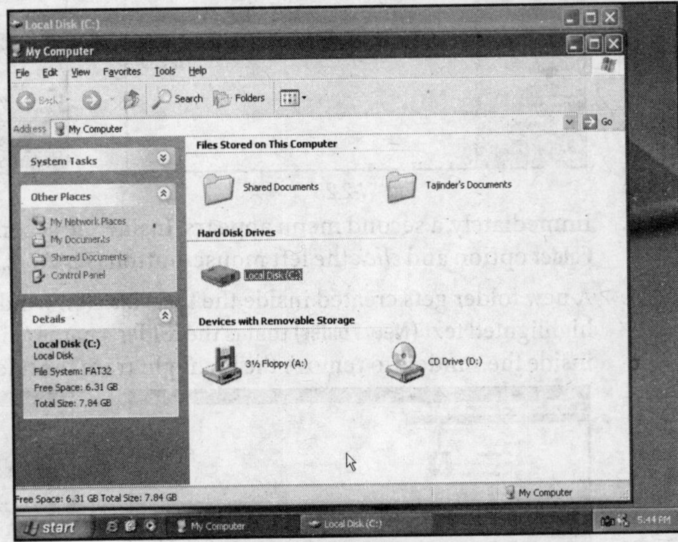

Fig. W 2.24

Menu bar

Every window displays the **Menu bar** just below the **Title bar.** In any open window of Windows XP, the **menu bar** looks like Fig. W-2.25. It contains certain options such as **File, Edit, View, Favorites, Tools** and **Help.**

Fig. W-2.25

These options are used to perform specific operations. For example, the **File** option is used for carrying out file-related operations, the **Edit** option is used for editing purpose, the **View** option is used for changing the appearance of a window, and the **Help** option provides help in case of problems. Let us now learn how to work with these options.

Menu Bar Options

First, we will work with the **File** option of the **Menu bar.** The File option has many sub-options like **Open, Explore, Search, Format, New,** etc. These options appear in the pull-down menu of the **File** option. However, the File pull-down menu differs from window to window. Now we will work with the **New** sub-option to create a new folder in the **Local Disk (C:).** We assume that the My Computer and the Local Disk (C:) windows are open on your Desktop and the Local Disk (C:) window is currently active. Now, undertake the following steps to create a new folder in the Local Disk (C:).

1. *Click* on the **File** option on the **Local Disk (C:)** Menu bar (Fig. W-2.26). Instantly, a pull-down menu gets displayed on the screen (Fig. W-2.27).
2. Inside the pull-down menu, *move* the mouse-pointer over the **New** option (Fig. W-2.27).

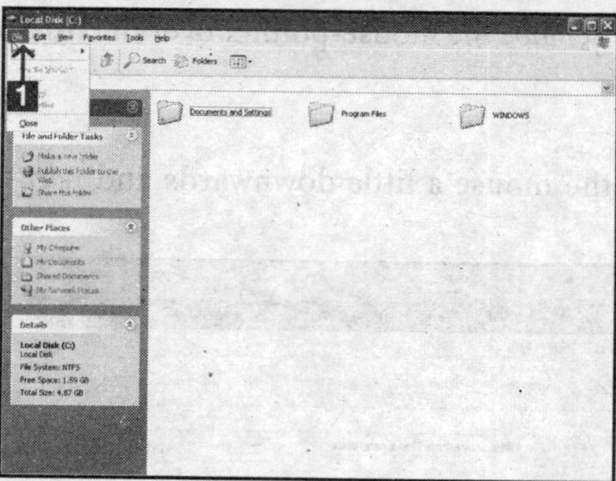

Fig. W-2.26

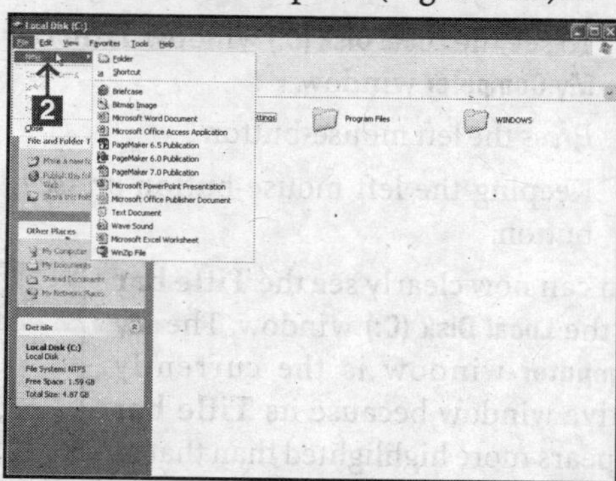

Fig. W-2.27

3. Immediately, a second menu appears. Inside the second menu, *move* the mouse-pointer over the **Folder** option and *click* the left mouse-button (Fig. W-2.28).
4. A new folder gets created inside the **Local Disk (C:)** window with a box beside it. The box has some highlighted text (**New Folder**) that is the folder's name (Fig. W-2.29). *Click* anywhere in the empty area inside the window to remove the highlight from the folder name.

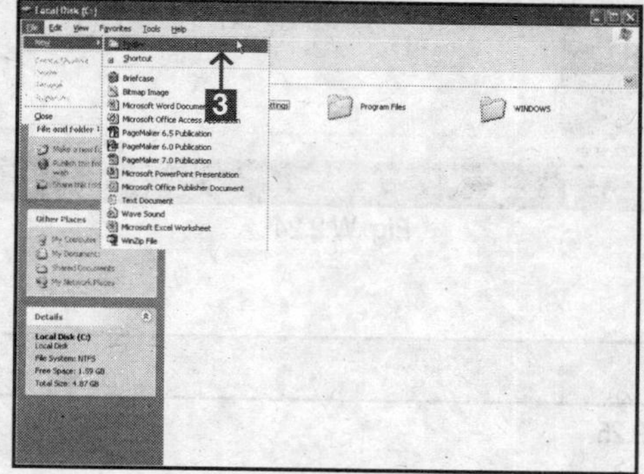

Fig. W-2.28

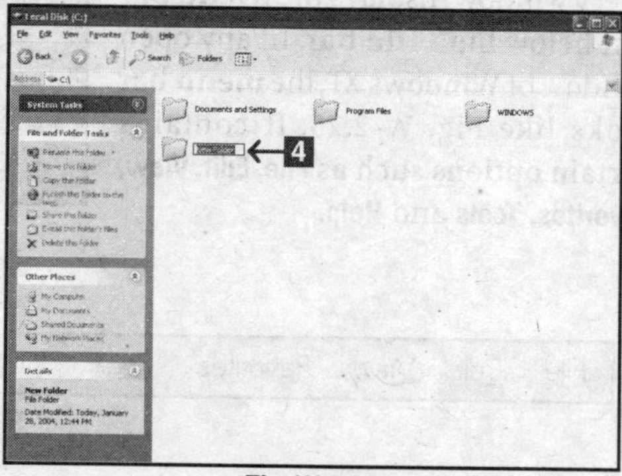

Fig. W-2.29

The **Edit** menu bar option helps you to copy/move the folder or files and paste them at any desired location. Let us now copy the **New Folder**, just created in the **Local Disk (C:)**, to the **My Pictures** folder.

1. Start with your monitor displaying the **My Computer** window. Now, *move* the mouse pointer on the **Local Disk (C:)** icon and *double-click* the left mouse-button (Fig. W-2.18).
2. The **Local Disk (C:)** folder opens, displaying its contents on the screen (Fig. W-2.19). In the contents, *move* the mouse-pointer over the **New Folder** and *click* the left mouse-button once to highlight it.
3. Once the folder is highlighted, *click* on the **Edit** option in the **Menu bar** of **Local Disk (C:)**. The **Edit** pull-down menu gets displayed (Fig. W-2.30).
4. Inside the pull-down menu, *click* on the **Copy To Folder** option (Fig. W-2.30). Instantly the **Copy Items** box appears on the screen (Fig. W-2.31).
5. In the **Copy Items** box, *click* on the **plus sign** (⊞) beside the **My Documents** icon (Fig. W-2.31). The contents of the **My Documents** folder get displayed in the contents box (Fig. W-2.32).
6. *Click* on the **My Pictures** folder (Fig. W-2.32).
7. Finally, *click* on the **Copy** button (Fig. W-2.32). The **New Folder** gets copied to the **My Pictures** folder and we return to the **Local Disk (C:)** window.
8. Now, to view the copied folder, *double-click* on the **My Documents** folder inside the **Local Disk (C:)** window. Do another *double-click* on the **My Pictures** folder in the **My Documents** folder. You will see a copy of the **New Folder** in the **My Pictures** folder (Fig. W-2.33).

The **View** option in the Windows XP **Menu bar** contains

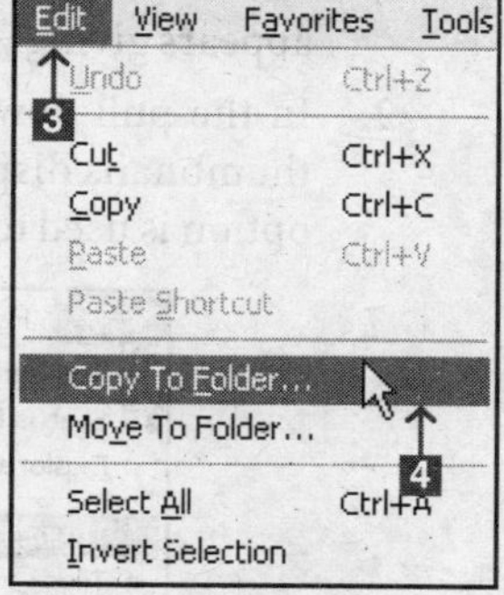

Fig. W-2.30

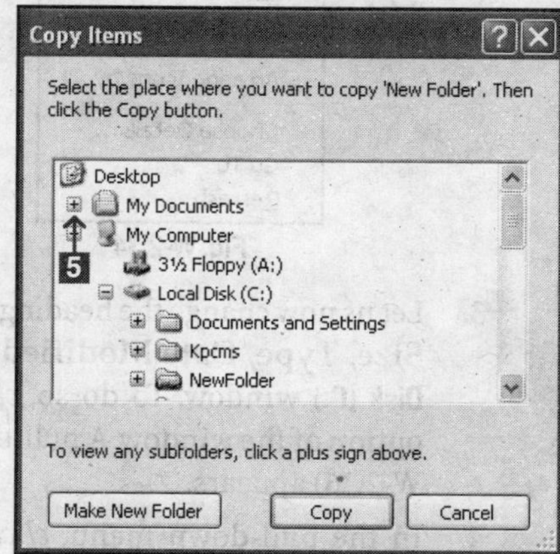

Fig. W-2.31

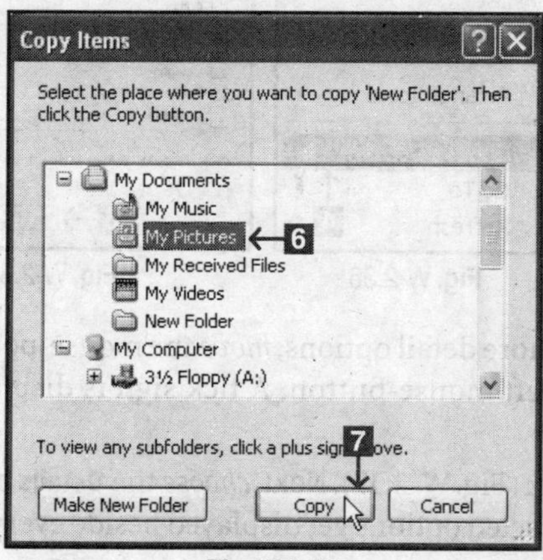

Fig. W-2.32

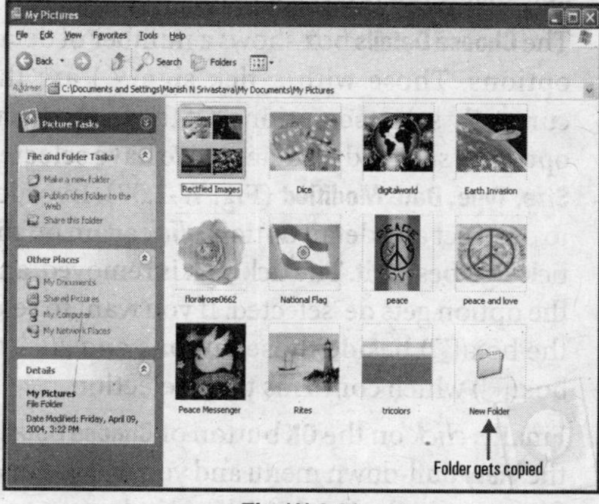

Fig. W-2.33

additional view features to enhance your display. Let us now work with the **View** option in the **Local Disk(C:)** window:

1. *Click* on the **View** option in the **Menu bar** of the **Local Disk (C:)** window. Instantly, a pull-down menu appears giving you various options to change the display (Fig. W-2.34).
2. In the pull-down menu, *click* on the **Thumbnails** option (Fig. W-2.34). Immediately, you get the thumbnails display of files and folders in the **Local Disk (C:) window** (Fig. W-2.35). The **Thumbnails** option is used to display folders in form of miniatures along with content present inside folders.

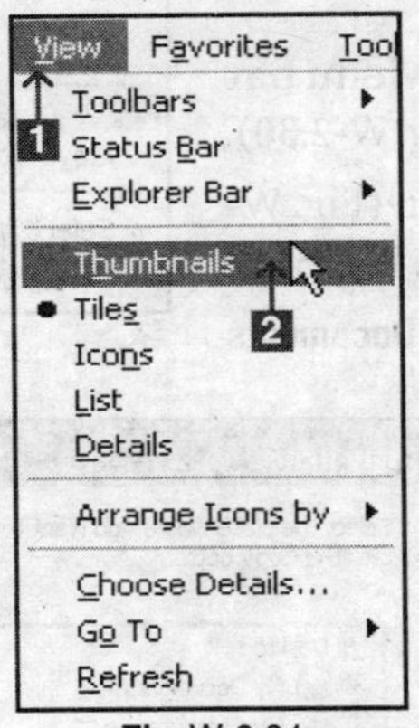

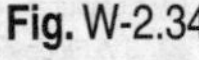
Fig. W-2.34

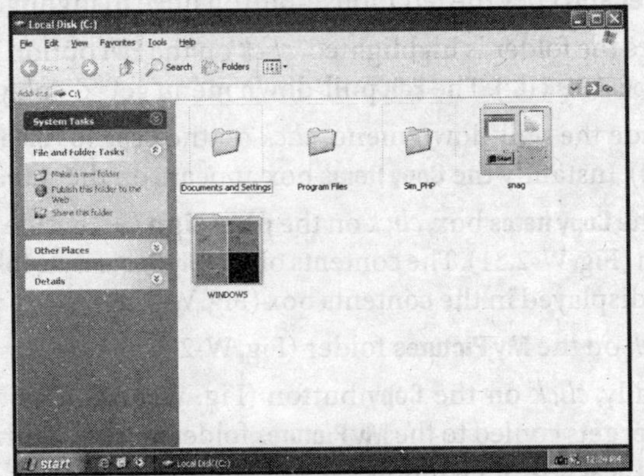

Fig. W-2.35

3. Let us now change the headings such as **Name, Size, Type, Date Modified**, etc of the **Local Disk (C:)** window. To do so, *click* on the **View** option of the window. A pull-down menu (Fig. W-2.36) appears.
4. In the pull-down menu, *click* on the **Choose Details** option (Fig. W-2.36). A **Choose Details** box gets displayed (Fig. W-2.37).
5. The **Choose Details** box shows a number of detail options. Those with a tick sign(✓) are the currently selected options. Of these, the **Name** option is selected by default. We have selected **Size, Type, Date Modified** (Fig. W-2.37). In order to deselect any detail option, *click* again on the tick sign beside it. The tick sign is removed, and the option gets de-selected. If you want to select more detail options, *move* the mouse-pointer inside the box(☐) beside those options and *click* the left mouse-button. A tick sign is displayed in the box(☑) which confirms their selection.

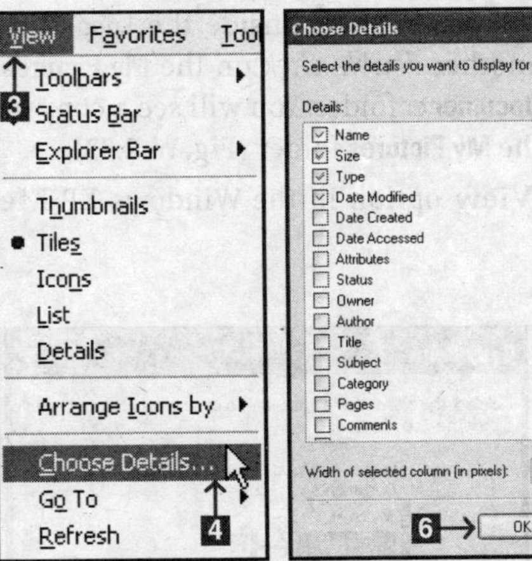

Fig. W-2.36

Fig. W-2.37

6. Finally, *click* on the **OK** button of **Choose Details** box (Fig. W-2.37). Next, *choose* the **Details** option from the **View** pull-down menu and you will see that selected options get displayed beside every folder and file name in the **Local Disk (C:)** window.

Status bar : The Status bar of any window in Windows XP displays information such as the total number of items present inside the window, the total memory space occupied by the items and the name of window which in our case is **My Computer** (Fig. W-2.38).

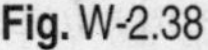

Fig. W-2.38

Sometimes the Status bar is not displayed in a window of Windows XP. To display the Status bar, undertake the following steps :

1. Move the mouse-pointer over the View menu in the Menu bar and click the left mouse-button.
2. In the pull-down menu that appears, move the mouse-pointer over the Status Bar option (Fig.W-2.39), and click the left mouse-button. Immediately, a click mark appears beside the Status Bar option and the Status bar gets displayed at the bottom of the window.

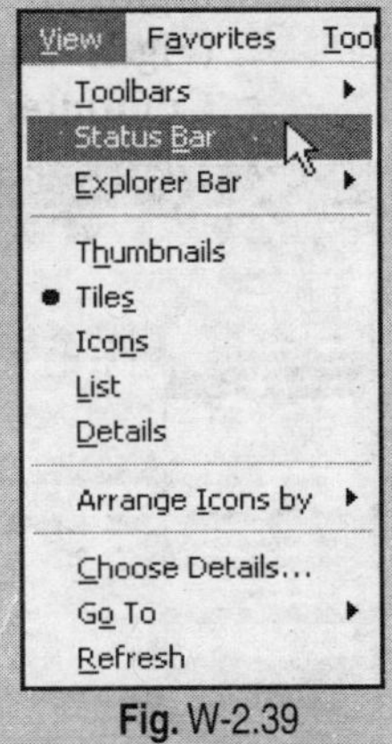

Fig. W-2.39

As you have become familiar with the components of a window, now let us try to understand the third common mouse action, i.e. **dragging.**

Dragging with Mouse

Moving the mouse on your mouse-pad in any direction while keeping the left mouse-button pressed is called **dragging.** While dragging, make sure that the mouse remains in contact with the mouse-pad all the time. The **dragging** action is used to move icons, windows, etc.

Let us now learn how to drag any window. We assume your Windows XP Desktop is currently displaying two windows, viz. the **My Computer** window and the **Local Disk (C:)** window. We will drag the **My Computer** window from one position to another on the Desktop.

Dragging the My Computer window in Windows XP : To drag the **My Computer** window across the Desktop, undertake the following steps :

1. *Move* the mouse and *place* the mouse-pointer over the **Title bar** of the **My Computer** window (Fig. W-2.40).

Fig. W-2.40

2. *Press* the left mouse-button. Keeping the left mouse-button *pressed*, *move* the mouse to your right on the mouse-pad.
3. You will notice that the **My Computer** window now shifts to the position where you dragged the mouse (Fig. W-2.41).

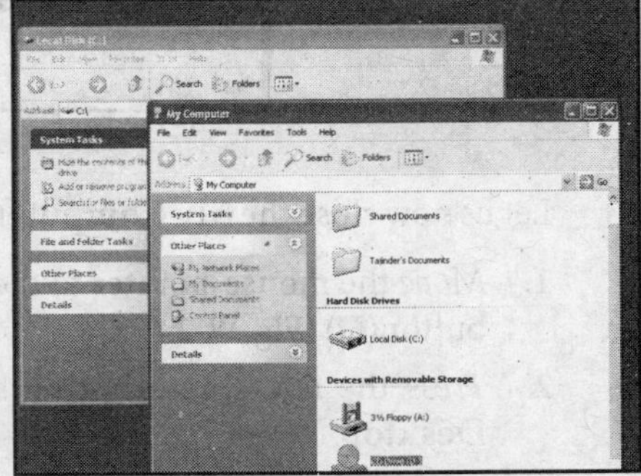

Fig. W-2.41

Let us now try dragging the **Local Disk (C:)** window present on your **Desktop.** But before doing so, the **Local Disk (C:)** window needs to be made an active window.

Making the Local Disk (C:) window active: As you notice, the **Title bar** of the **Local Disk (C:)** window (Fig. W-2.40) is not highlighted. To highlight it, i.e. to make the **Local Disk(C:)** window active, undertake the following steps:

1. *Move* the mouse-pointer over the **Title bar** of the **Local Disk (C:)** window (Fig. W-2.42).
2. *Press* the left mouse-button just once and *release* it. The **Title bar** of the **Local Disk (C:)** window gets highlighted and the **Local Disk (C)**: window gets displayed over the **My Computer** window (Fig. W-2.43). Now you can drag this window by following Steps 1 to 3 of topic '**Dragging the My Computer window.**'

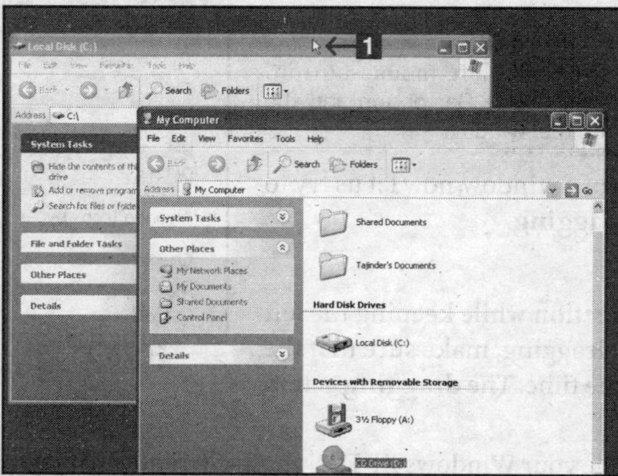

Fig. W-2.42

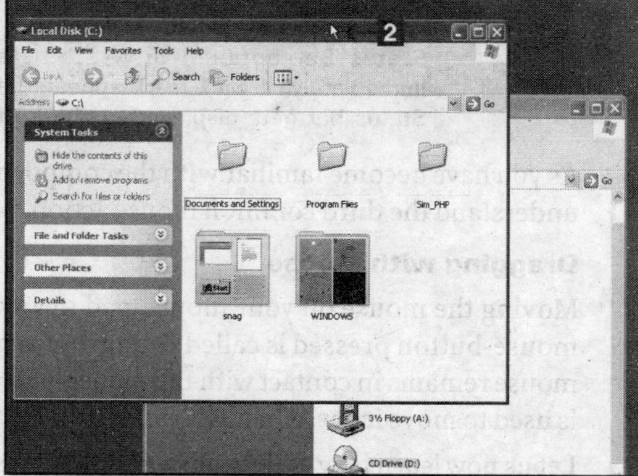

Fig. W-2.43

Apart from dragging windows, we can also drag icons. Dragging an icon on the Desktop is quite easy. Your Desktop at the moment is covered by two windows: the **Local Disk (C:)** and **My Computer.** Therefore, before doing the dragging operation on icons, we need to close these windows one by one. To close the **Local Disk (C:)** window, undertake the following steps :

1. *Move* the mouse-pointer to the **Title bar** of the **Local Disk (C:)** window and place it over the **Close** button (☒) (Fig. W-2.44).
2. *Press* the left mouse-button once. The **Local Disk (C:)** window closes, making the **My Computer** window active.

Fig. W-2.44

Let us now close the **My Computer** window through the following steps:

1. *Move* the mouse-pointer to the **Title bar** of the **My Computer** window and place it over the **Close** button(☒) (Fig. W-2.45).
2. *Press* the left mouse-button once. Instantly, the **My Computer** window disappears from your **Desktop.**

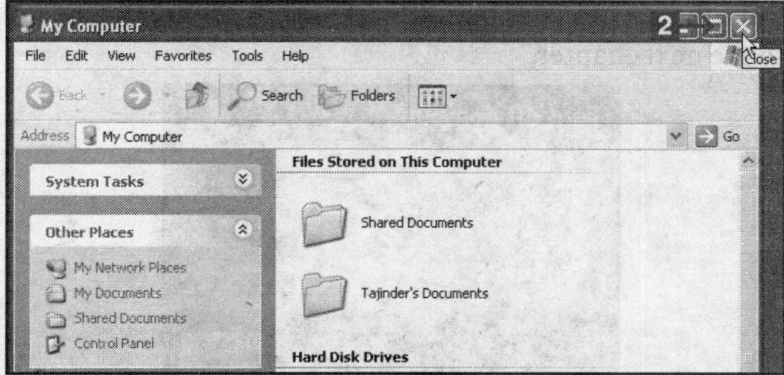

Fig. W-2.45

Dragging an Icon on the Desktop : Now that the Desktop area of Windows XP is vacant, you can drag any of its icons. Let us try dragging the **New Folder** icon.

To do so, undertake the following steps:

1. *Move* the mouse and place the mouse-pointer over the **New Folder** icon.
2. *Press* the left mouse-button and keeping it *pressed*, *move* the mouse towards your right side on the mouse-pad. You see a greyish shadow of the icon moving on the screen along with the pointer (Fig. W-2.46).
3. *Release* the left mouse-button. As soon as you release it, the **New Folder** icon occupies its new location on the **Desktop.**

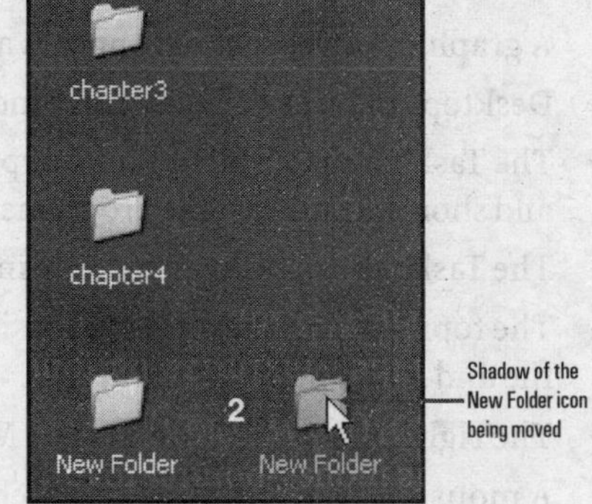

Fig. W-2.46

You can also repeat Steps 1 to 3 to drag **My Computer, My Documents, Internet Explorer,** etc. icons on the desktop.

Quitting Windows XP

By now you must have become quite familiar with Windows XP. In the next chapter, we will discuss some new features of this operating system. Let us now learn the steps for quitting Windows XP:

1. *Place* the mouse-pointer on the **Start** button (start) of the **Taskbar,** and then *press* the left mouse-button. Immediately, a push-up menu appears (Fig. W-2.47).
2. Inside the push-up menu, *move* the mouse-pointer over the **Turn Off Computer** option (Fig. W-2.47).
3. Now, *press* the left mouse-button. Immediately, a **Turn Off Computer** box gets displayed (Fig. W-2.48).
4. Inside the **Turn Off Computer** box, *click* on the **Turn Off** option (Fig. W-2.48).

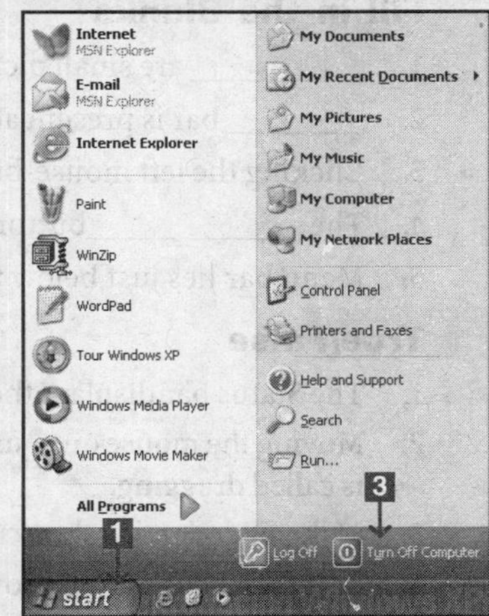

Fig. W-2.47

5. After a few seconds, the screen goes blank. Now, switch off the power supply and refresh yourself before heading to the next chapter.

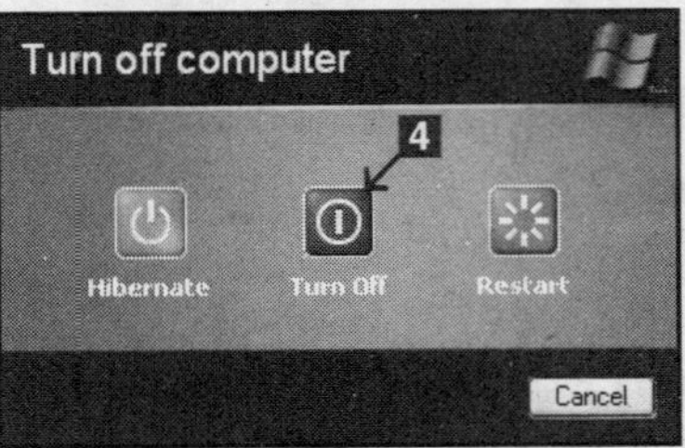

Fig. W-2.48

Summary

- A graphical screen which appears after starting the computer is known as Desktop.
- Desktop contains various icons and a bar at its bottom. This bar is known as Taskbar.
- The Taskbar displays the name of program, window or file which is currently open on the computer and shortcuts for various programs.
- The Taskbar can be used for viewing date and time.
- The topmost bar of every window is known as Title bar. This bar displays the name of the program, file and icon on the left hand side.
- The right side of the Title bar has Minimize, Maximize and Close buttons.
- A mouse is a pointing device which you use to select icons, drag icons and execute commands.
- The left mouse-button is always considered as primary button of the mouse whereas the right mouse-button is treated as secondary mouse-button.

Exercise

Fill in the Blanks

1. __________ are small picture buttons present on the Desktop.
2. __________ bar is present at the bottom of the Windows XP Desktop.
3. Clicking the left mouse-button twice simultaneously is called __________.
4. The __________ button is used to reduce the window into a button.
5. Menu bar lies just below the __________.

True/False

1. The Status bar displays the title of the window.
2. Moving the mouse on your mouse pad in any direction while keeping the left mouse-button pressed is called dragging.
3. Menu bar contains shortcut icons for performing various tasks.
4. Edit menu bar option provides the facility for creating a new file.
5. A click with the right mouse-button is used to bring up pop-up menus of commands and shortcuts.

CHAPTER 3

Starting Windows XP

IN THIS CHAPTER

- Getting familiar with the Desktop
- Moving from One Window to Another
- Enlarging a Window to Screen Size
- Reverting a Window to its Previous Size
- Reducing a Window to a Taskbar Button
- Opening a Taskbar Button into a Window
- Adjusting the Window Size Freely
- Closing a Window
- Creating Shortcut for a Program
- Deleting the Shortcut Icon
- Deleting the Contents of the Recycle Bin
- Quitting Windows XP
- Summary
- Exercise

The Desktop of Windows XP displays many icons. Each icon represents a program. These icons can be opened by double-clicking over them. On double-clicking an icon, a window appears which displays the contents of the program represented by that icon. Further, the program contents are also displayed as icons which can also open up into their respective windows. This arrangement helps you open and view the desired programs without any hassles. For example, when you double-click on the My Computer icon, it opens up into a window displaying its contents in the form of icons. Double-clicking on any content icon further opens into its respective window.

As you know, several small windows can be opened simultaneously on your Desktop. And, you can move the open windows to rearrange their position on the Desktop. To view all the icons in a window, you can enlarge the window to cover the whole screen. And, to create space on your Desktop, you can reduce an open window into a button on the Taskbar. Apart from these, you can also adjust a window size by stretching it from its edges.

Let us proceed to work with these useful features of Windows XP.

Getting Familiar with the Desktop

When you switch on your computer, Windows XP Desktop gets displayed before you in a short while.

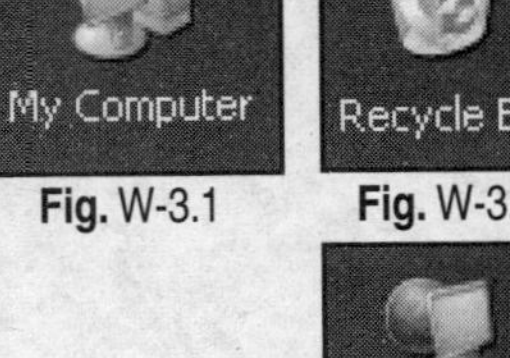

Fig. W-3.1 **Fig.** W-3.2

Let us now get familiar with the icons on the Desktop.

- The **My Computer** icon (Fig.W-3.1) lets you view the files, folders, drives and other tools in your system.
- The **Recycle Bin** icon (Fig.W-3.2) lets you store deleted files and recover them later, if required.
- The **My Network Places** icon (Fig.W-3.3) helps you view all the shared files and folders of different users in a local network.

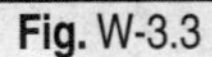

My Network Places

Fig. W-3.3

- The **Taskbar** (Fig.W-3.4) displays a button for each open window. These buttons can be used to move from one window to the other.

Buttons on the Taskbar

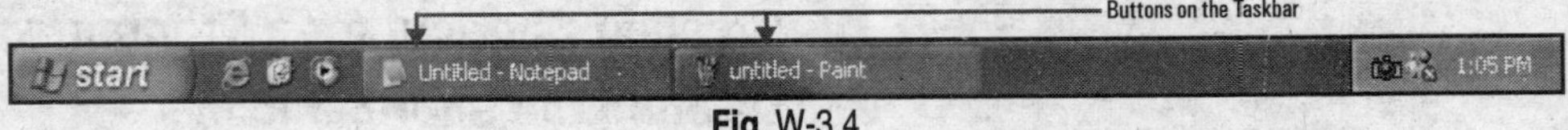

Fig. W-3.4

The Taskbar makes it easier for you to keep track of open programs and applications. The Taskbar displays the time on the right-hand side. Other icons may also appear next to time depending upon what your computer is doing. For example, if you were printing a document, a printer icon shows up on the Taskbar. As you go through this chapter, you will know about more uses of the Taskbar.

- The **Start** button (Fig.W-3.5) gives you a quicker access to the programs of Windows XP. It is present on the extreme left side of the Taskbar.

Fig. W-3.5

Opening an Icon from the Desktop

Let us now refresh the steps we had followed in the last chapter to open a Desktop icon. Here, we will try opening the **My Computer** icon from the **Desktop**. To do so, perform the steps given on the next page.

1. *Move* the mouse on the mouse-pad so that the mouse-pointer gets positioned over the **My Computer** icon (Fig. W-3.6).
2. After positioning the mouse-pointer over the **My Computer** icon, *double-click* the left mouse-button (shown in green in Fig.W-3.7). Instantly, the **My Computer** icon opens into a window (Fig.W-3.8). This window displays several icons which represent the disk drives and other important tools.

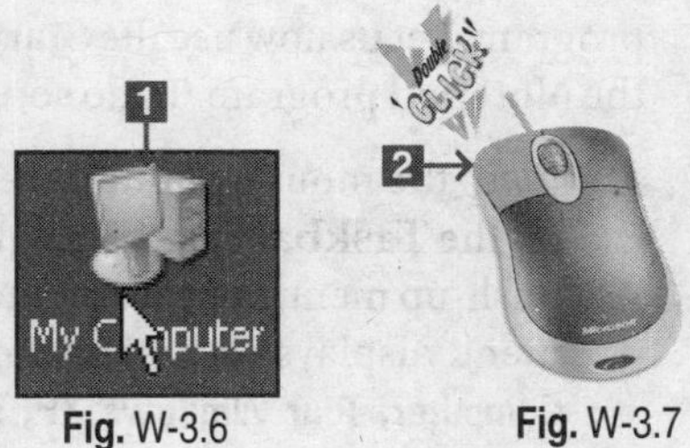

Fig. W-3.6 **Fig.** W-3.7

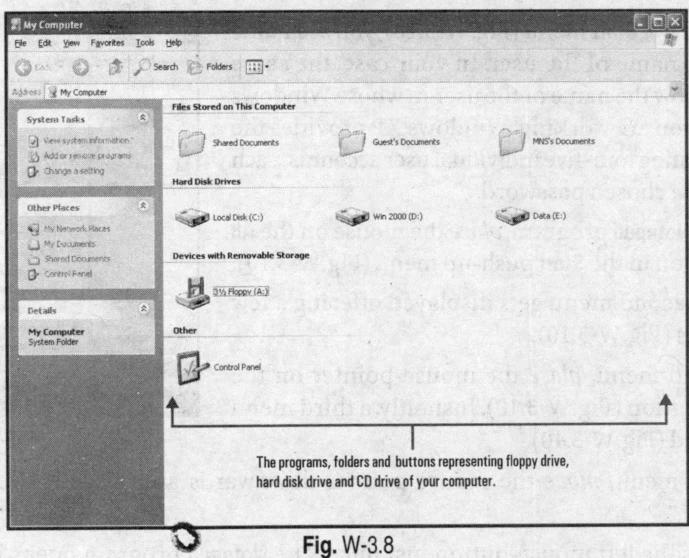

Fig. W-3.8

While going through this book, you will come across the terms Windows and windows. Windows (with capital W) denotes Windows XP, which is an operating system. Windows (with small w) refers to all open window screens in which you work while using Windows XP. In this book, in all the headlines, window is written with a capital W, irrespective of whether it represents Windows XP or a small window screen.

Leaving the **My Computer** window open on the **Desktop**, let us now work with the **Start** button present on the extreme left of the **Taskbar**.

Starting a Program through Start button

You can start any program by using the **Start** button (start). When you click on the **Start** button, a push-up menu appears, providing a list of programs and functions you can use. Apart from opening various programs, you can also use the **Start** menu to find documents, to get help or to shut down your computer.

An additional advantage of the **Start** button is that you can use it while working in another program. It allows you to quickly start a new program without having to close or minimize the currently open program. Let us now use the **Start** button to open any program, say the **Notepad** program. To do so, undertake the following steps:

Fig. W-3.9

1. *Place* the mouse-pointer over the **Start** button (start) present on the **Taskbar** (Fig.W-3.9) and *click* the left mouse-button. A push-up menu appears on the screen (Fig.W-3.10). This menu displays several options, such as **Log Off, Turn Off Computer, Tour Windows XP, Windows Media Player, My Documents, My Pictures, My Music, Control Panel, Search** and **Run** etc.

   On the top of the **Start** menu (Fig. W-3.10), you see name **MNS.** It's the name of the user. In your case, the same figure will show the name of the user in whose Windows XP account you are working. Windows XP provides the facility of creating four-five individual user accounts, each protected by a chosen password.

2. To open the **Notepad** program, *place* the mouse on the **All Programs** option in the **Start** push-up menu (Fig.W-3.10).

   Instantly, a second menu gets displayed offering a few more options (Fig.W-3.10).

3. In the second menu, *place* the mouse-pointer on the **Accessories** option (Fig.W-3.10). Instantly, a third menu gets displayed (Fig.W-3.10).

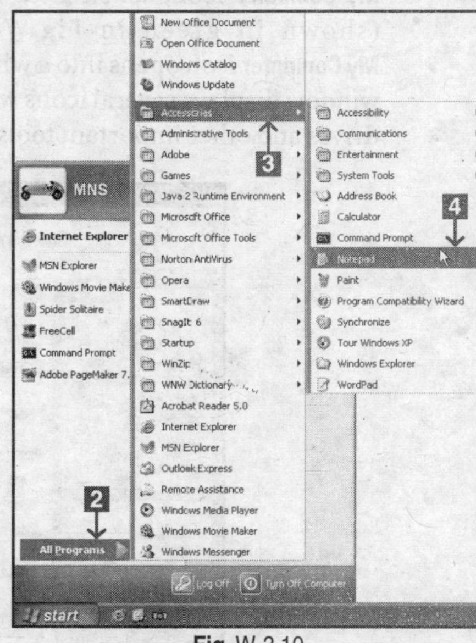

Fig. W-3.10

4. In the third menu, *move* the mouse-pointer downwards and place it over the **Notepad** option (Fig.W-3.10).

5. Finally, *press* the left mouse-button just once. The **Notepad** program opens into a window on the screen and gets displayed over the **My Computer** window (Fig.W-3.11).

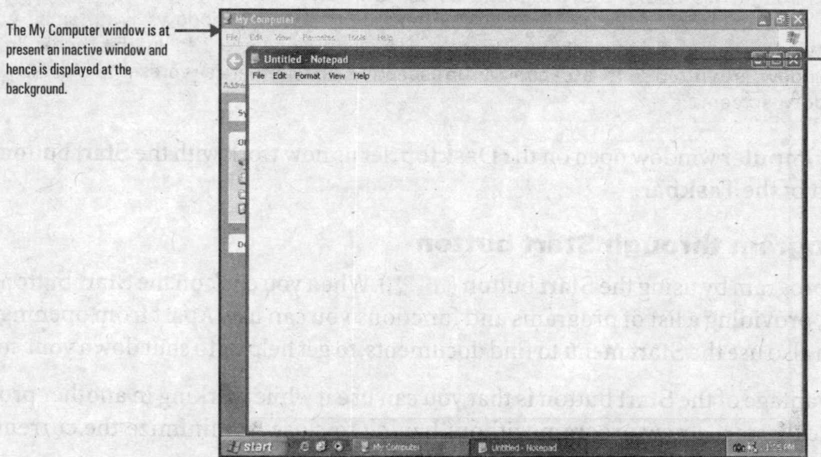

Fig. W-3.11

Moving from One Window to Another

As mentioned earlier, you can have a number of windows simultaneously open on your screen, and you can easily move from one window to another. In other words, all open windows are accessible to you. However, you can work in only one window at a time. The window in which you work is called the **active window.** The **Title bar** of an active window is always highlighted while those of the other open windows are disabled. The **Taskbar** displays buttons for all open windows.

In Fig.W-3.11, the **Taskbar** shows buttons for both the **My Computer** and **Notepad** windows. However, the button of the **My Computer** window appears less bright as compared to the **Notepad** button. This is because the **Notepad** window is currently active. Let us now make the **My Computer** window the active window.

Making the My Computer Window Active

1. *Move* the mouse-pointer over the **My Computer** button (My Computer) present on the **Taskbar** (Fig.W-3.12).

Fig. W-3.12

2. *Press* the left mouse-button just once. Immediately, the **My Computer** window becomes active with its **Title bar** shown highlighted (Fig. W-3.13). It completely covers the **Notepad** window.

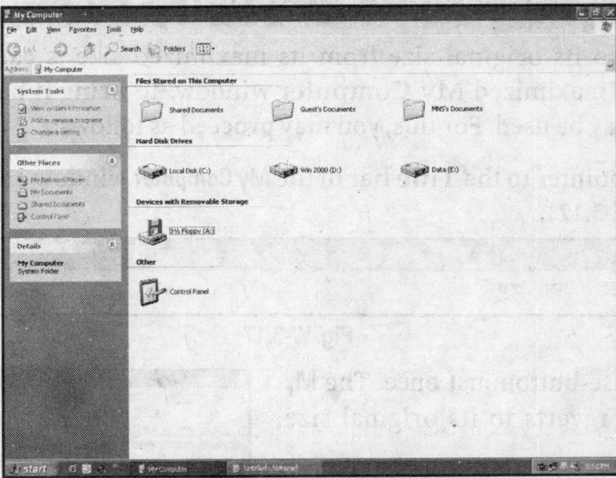

Fig. W-3.13

Making the Notepad Window Active

1. *Move* the mouse-pointer over the **Notepad** button (Untitled - Notepad) present on the **Taskbar** (Fig.W-3.14) and *click* the left mouse-button.

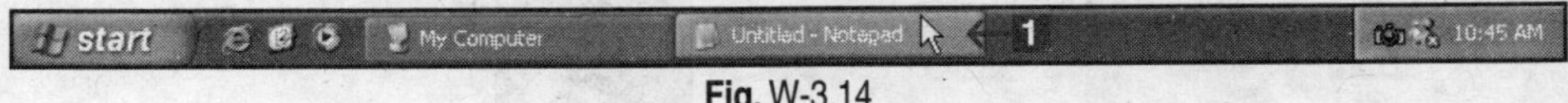

Fig. W-3.14

2. Instantly, the **Notepad** window appears over the **My Computer** window (Fig.W-3.11).

Enlarging a Window to Screen Size

You may want to enlarge a window on your screen so that you can see more of its contents. For this, you have to maximize it. For example, the **Notepad** window, displayed on the **Desktop** of Windows XP (Fig. W-3.11), does not fit the entire screen. You can enlarge this window by using the following steps:

1. *Move* the mouse-pointer to the **Title bar** of the **Notepad** window and *position* it on the **Maximize** button(▭) (Fig.W-3.15).
2. *Click* on the **Maximize** button(▭). Instantly, the **Notepad** window grows in size to fill the whole screen (Fig.W-3.16).

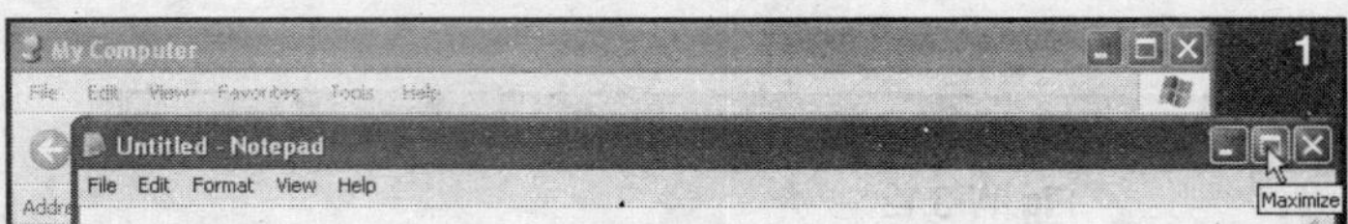

Fig. W-3.15

Fig. W-3.16

Reverting a Window to its Previous Size

Reverting a window to its original size from its maximized size is called **Restoring** a window. Fig. W-3.13 shows the maximized **My Computer** window. To bring it back to its original size, the **Restore** button (⧉) may be used. For this, you may proceed as follows:

1. *Move* the mouse-pointer to the **Title bar** of the **My Computer** window and place it over the **Restore** button (⧉) (Fig.W-3.17).

Fig. W-3.17

2. *Press* the left mouse-button just once. The **My Computer** window reverts to its original size (Fig.W-3.18).

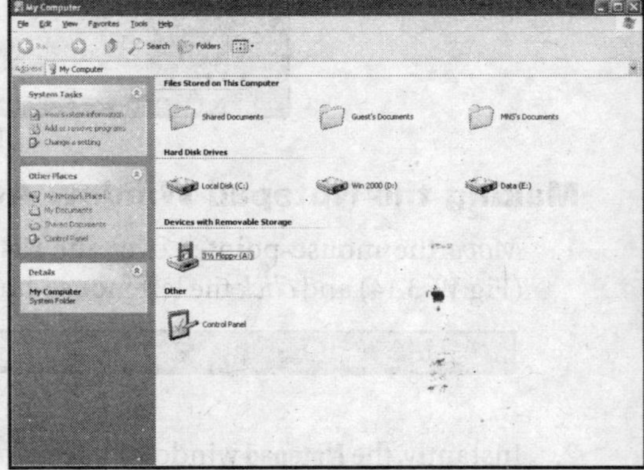

Fig. W-3.18

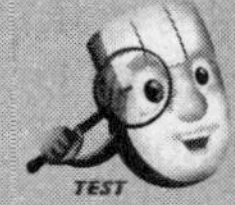

How to restore the maximized Notepad window to its original size?

- Move the mouse-pointer over the Restore button (🗗) of the Notepad window.
- Press the left mouse-button once.

Reducing a Window to a Taskbar Button

When you are not using a window, you can minimize it and remove it temporarily from the screen. On minimizing a window, it appears as a button on the **Taskbar.**

Your **Desktop** now displays two windows – the **Notepad** window and the **My Computer** window. Let us now make one of these, say the **Notepad** window, appear as a small button on the **taskbar** to get a clear view of the other window. To do so, undertake the following steps :

1. *Move* the mouse-pointer to the **Title bar** of the **Notepad** window and place it over the **Minimize** button (▬) (Fig.W-3.19).

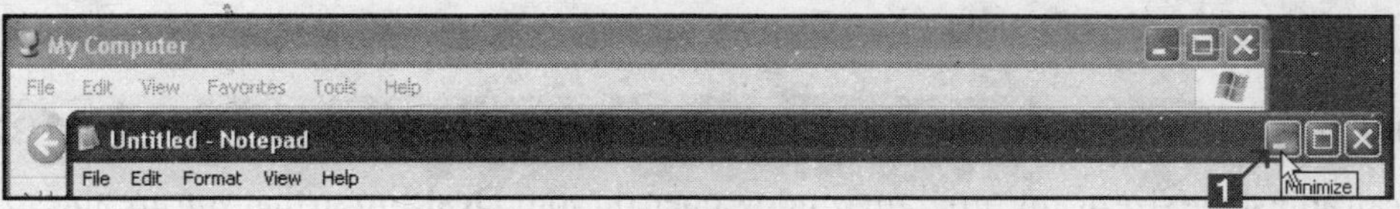

Fig. W-3.19

2. Now *press* the left mouse-button just once. The **Notepad** window disappears and gets reduced to a button on the **Taskbar** (Fig.W-3.20).

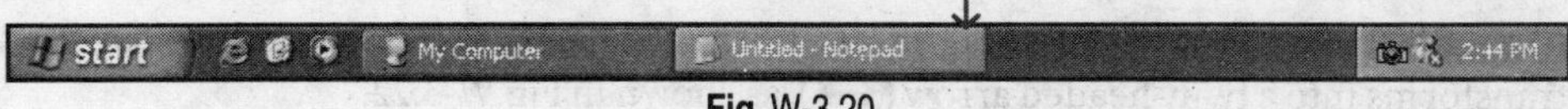

Fig. W-3.20

As soon as you minimize the **Notepad** window, the **My Computer** window becomes the active window.

Remember that minimizing a window into a Taskbar button does not close that window. It just transforms the window into a button.

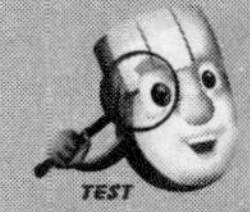

How to minimize the My Computer window which is open on your Desktop?

- Move the mouse-pointer over the Minimize button (▬) of the My Computer window.
- Click the left mouse-button once.

Opening a Taskbar Button into a Window

As you know, on minimizing a window, it gets reduced to a button on the **taskbar.** To display that window once again on the screen, *click* on its button on the **taskbar.** The window reappears on the screen in the same size as it was before its transformation into a button.

On your screen, the **taskbar** shows two buttons, (Untitled - Notepad) and (My Computer). This indicates that two programs namely **Notepad** and **My Computer** are currently running in Windows XP. Let us now display the **Notepad** program window on the screen by performing the steps given below:

1. *Move* the mouse-pointer to the **Taskbar** and place it on the minimized **Notepad** button (Untitled - Notepad) (Fig.W-3.21).

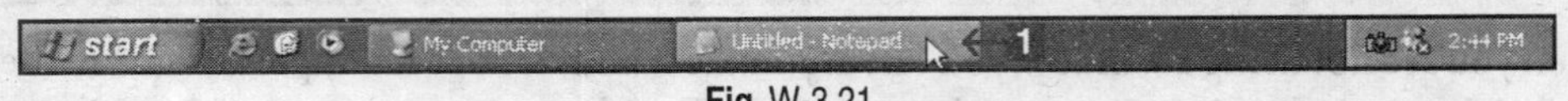

Fig. W-3.21

2. *Press* the left mouse-button once and *release* it. Instantly, the minimized **Notepad** window opens up on your **Desktop** (Fig. W-3.16).

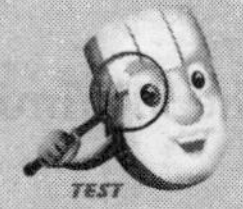

How to display the My Computer window through its taskbar button?

- Move the mouse-pointer to the Taskbar and place it on the My Computer button (My Computer).
- Click the left mouse-button once.

Adjusting the Window Size Freely

You can adjust the size of any program window open on your **Desktop** so that you are able to work more easily with its contents. At present, the **My computer** window is active on your **Desktop** and completely covers the **Notepad** window. Now suppose you want to adjust the size of this window from the right side. For this, you have to undertake the following steps:

1. *Move* the mouse-pointer to the right-side border of the **My Computer** window. The mouse-pointer transforms into a twin-headed arrow (↔), as shown in Fig. W-3.22.
2. *Press* the left mouse-button.
3. Keeping the left mouse-button *pressed*, *drag* the mouse to the left-side.
4. Keep *dragging* the mouse until the window is reduced to the size of your choice.
5. After reaching the desired size, *release* the left mouse-button. The window gets displayed in its new changed size (Fig. W-3.23).

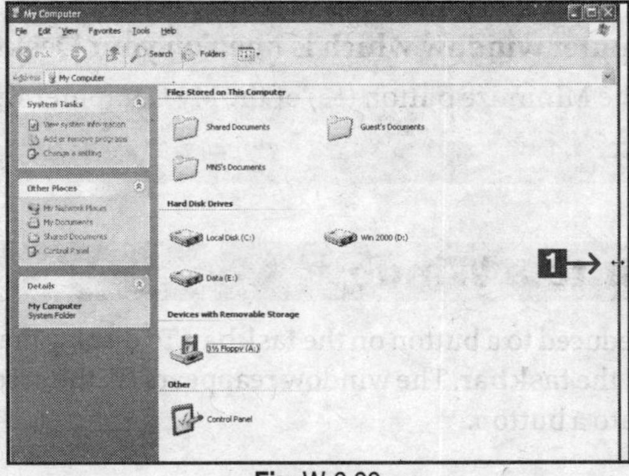

Fig. W-3.22

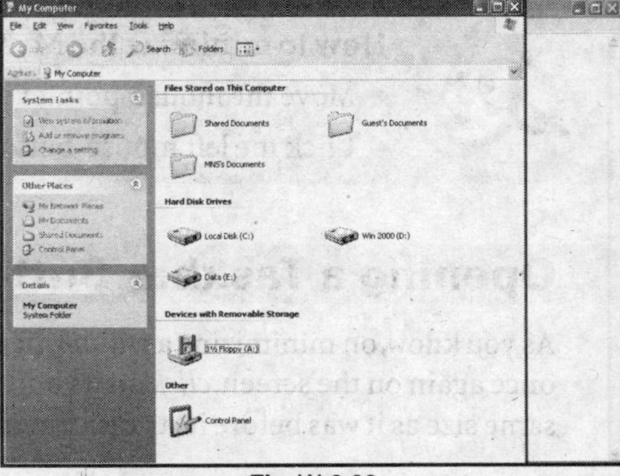

Fig. W-3.23

How to stretch the top outline of the inactive Notepad window?

- Click on the Notepad button present on the Taskbar.
- When the Notepad window becomes active, move the mouse-pointer over its top outline.
- When the mouse-pointer changes to a twin-headed arrow(↕), press the left mouse-button.
- Keeping the left mouse-button pressed, drag the mouse upwards.
- When the desired size is reached, release the left mouse-button.

Closing a Window

Let us now learn how to close the **My Computer** and the **Notepad** windows. To do so, we will proceed as follows:

1. Start with Fig. 3.23 displayed on your Desktop.
2. *Move* the mouse-pointer over the **Close** button(☒) on the **Title bar** of the **My Computer** window (Fig. W-3.24).
3. *Press* the left mouse-button. Instantly, the **My Computer** window closes and the **Notepad** window becomes visible on the screen (Fig. W-3.25). In the **Notepad** window, repeat Steps 2 and 3 to close it.

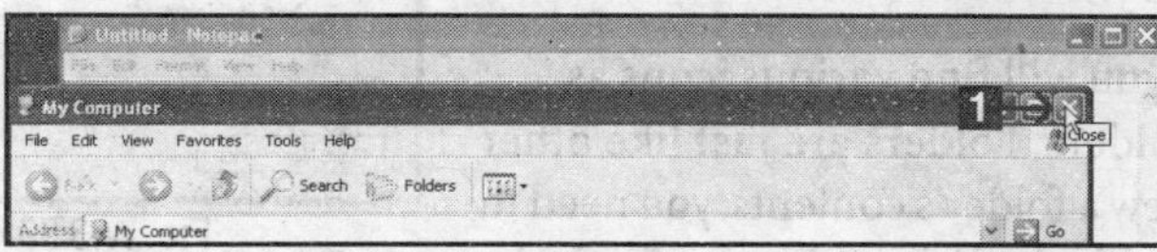

Fig. W-3.24

Fig. W-3.25

Creating Shortcut for a Program

In the topic **Opening an Icon from the Desktop**, you could easily open the **My Computer** icon because it was visible on your Desktop.

However, in case of the **Notepad** window, you had to first click on the **Start** button and then locate the **Notepad** program in the **All Programs** menu option. This process took some time. To save time, you can have a **Notepad** icon on your **Desktop** so that you can quickly open the **Notepad** program. This can be done by creating a **shortcut** icon for this program.

A **shortcut** is basically a quick link to a program, a file or a folder that is located at a different place. You can create a **shortcut** icon on your **Desktop**. Let us now create a shortcut for the **Notepad** program through the following steps:

1. *Place* the mouse-pointer anywhere in the free space of the **Desktop** of Windows XP and *click* the right mouse-button (Fig. W-3.26). This instantly displays a shortcut menu (Fig. W-3.27).

Fig. W-3.26

2. Now *move* the mouse-pointer over the **New** option inside this menu. The **New** option gets highlighted, and a second menu appears on the screen (Fig.W-3.27).
3. In the second menu, *move* the mouse-pointer over the **Shortcut** option (Fig.W-3.27) and *press* the left mouse-button. The **Create Shortcut** box opens up on the screen (Fig.W 3.28).
4. *Move* the mouse-pointer over the **Browse** button in this box (Fig.W-3.28), and *click* the left mouse-button. The **Browse For Folder** box opens up on your **Desktop** (Fig.W-3.29).

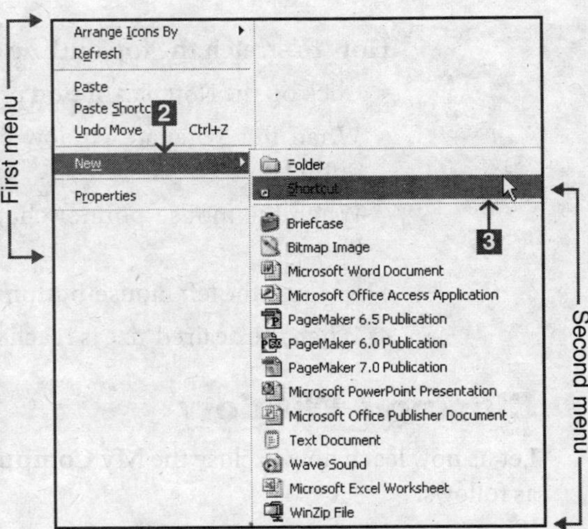

Fig. W-3.27

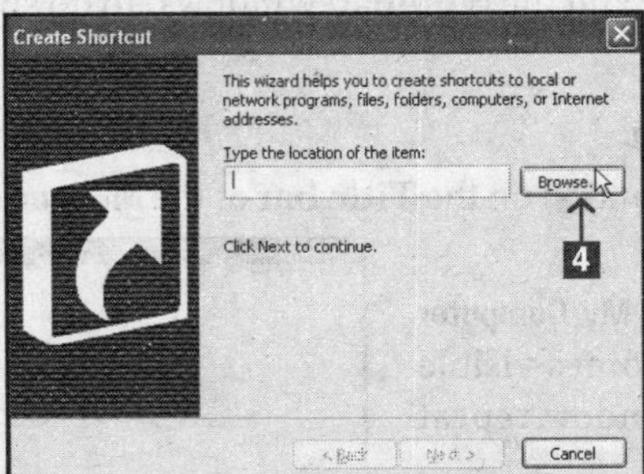

Fig. W-3.28

Fig. W-3.29

Inside the **Browse For Folder** box, you will find various icons as . These icons are termed as folders. Folders are just like other icons which can be opened. To view a folder's contents, you need to *double-click* over its icon. Now, with the help of **Browse For Folder** box, first we will search the **Notepad** program that resides in the **Windows** folder of the Local Disk (C:) folder in My Computer contents.

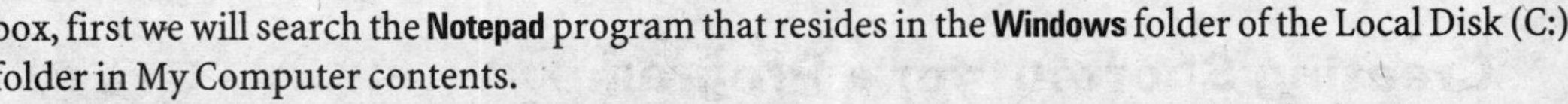

5. In the **Browse For Folder** box, *move* the mouse-pointer over the plus sign (⊞) beside the **My Computer** icon and *click* the left mouse-button (Fig.W-3.30). Now, the **Browse For Folder** box changes to Fig. W-3.31 that displays the contents of the **My Computer** folder.

Fig. W-3.30

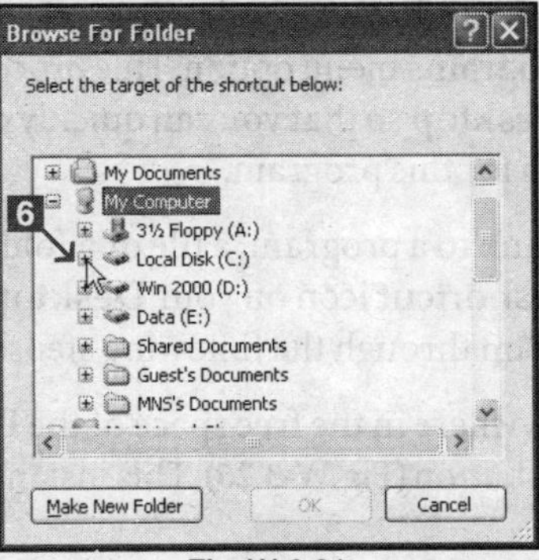

Fig. W-3.31

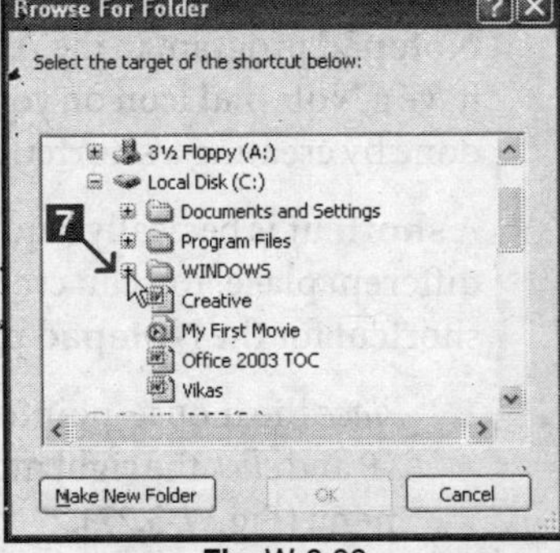

Fig. W-3.32

6. In the contents of the **My Computer** folder, *move* the mouse-pointer over the plus sign (⊞) beside the **Local Disk (C:)** icon and *click* the left mouse-button (Fig.W-3.31). The **Browse For Folder** box changes to Fig W-3.32 that displays the contents of the **Local Disk (C:)**.

7. In the **Local Disk (C):** contents, *move* the mouse-pointer over the plus-sign (⊞) beside the **WINDOWS** folder and *click* the left mouse-button (Fig.W-3.32).

   If the **WINDOWS** folder is not visible to you in the box, then *click* on the down-arrow scroll button (⌄) of the **Browse For Folder** box. This will enable you to view all the contents of the **Local Disk (C:)**.

8. *Move* the mouse-pointer over the file name **notepad** and *click* the left mouse button. The file is selected (Fig.W-3.33).

Fig. W-3.33

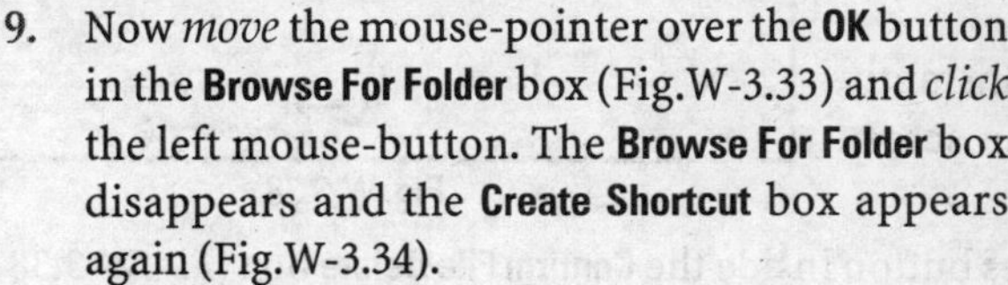

If the NOTEPAD.EXE option is not visible to you in the big box then click on the down-arrow scroll button (⌄) of the Browse For Folder box (Fig. W-3.33). When you move downward, you see the notepad icon in the Windows contents.

9. Now *move* the mouse-pointer over the **OK** button in the **Browse For Folder** box (Fig.W-3.33) and *click* the left mouse-button. The **Browse For Folder** box disappears and the **Create Shortcut** box appears again (Fig.W-3.34).

10. *Move* the mouse-pointer over the **Next** button of the **Create Shortcut** box and *press* the left mouse-button once (Fig.W-3.34).

11. Instantly, a box titled **Select a Title for the Program** opens up on the screen (Fig.W-3.34).

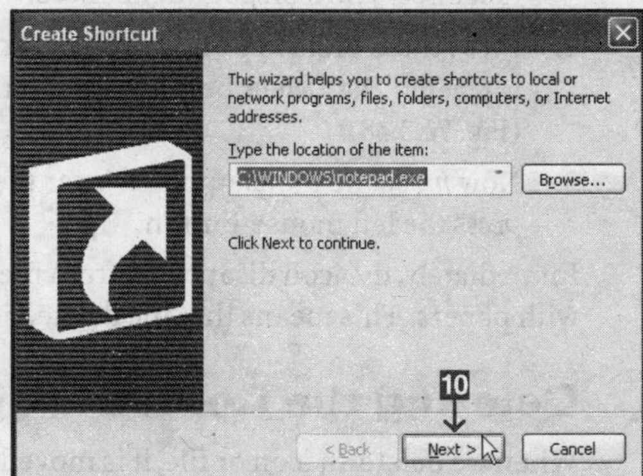

Fig. W-3.34

12. The **Select a Title for the Program** box displays a default name for the shortcut under the **Type a name for this shortcut** option. To create a shortcut with the default name, *click* on the **Finish** button.

    To change the default name, you can type the new name in the box displaying the default name.

13. Finally, *move* the mouse-pointer over the **Finish** button (Fig.W-3.35), and *click* the left mouse-button.

The **Select a Title for the Program** box disappears and a shortcut to the **Notepad** program appears on the **Desktop** with a small arrow sign below it (⬈) (Fig.W-3.36).

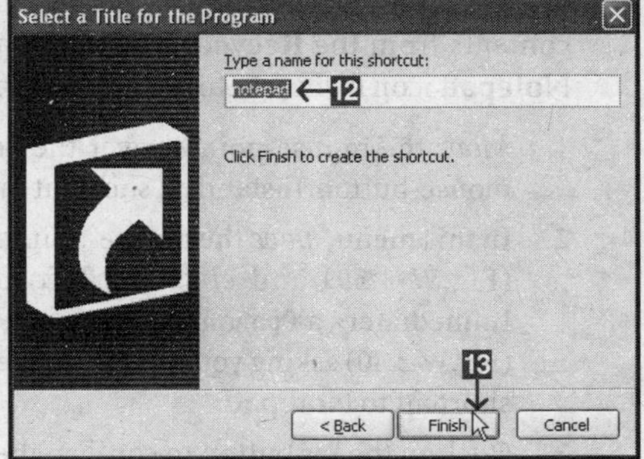

Fig. W-3.35

You can create shortcut for any programs in Windows XP by undertaking the steps listed above.

Fig. W-3.36

To open the **Notepad** program through its just created icon on the **Desktop**, undertake the following steps:

1. *Place* the mouse-pointer over the **Notepad** icon present on the **Desktop**.
2. *Double-click* the left mouse-button. The Notepad window instantly opens up on your screen.

Deleting the Shortcut Icon

If you start creating short-cut icons for a number of programs, your **Desktop** will soon get cluttered with icons. To make your Windows XP Desktop less crowded, you should delete the icons of those programs in which you do not work regularly. And, be sure that deleting an icon won't affect its program that would stay in your system intact.

Fig. W-3.37

Let us learn how to delete a shortcut icon. We will delete the **Notepad** program icon from the **Desktop** through the following steps:

1. *Move* the mouse-pointer over the shortcut **notepad** icon (Fig.W-3.37) and *click* the left mouse-button just once. The icon gets highlighted.
2. *Press* the **Delete** key on your keyboard. Instantly, a **Confirm File Delete** box appears on the screen (Fig. W-3.38).

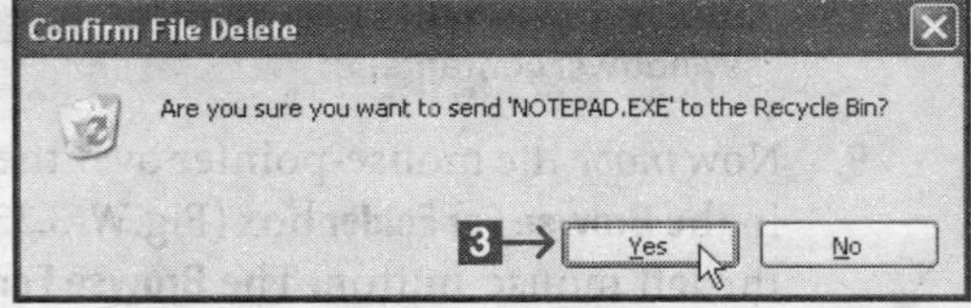

Fig. W-3.38

3. Now *move* the mouse-pointer over the **Yes** button inside the **Confirm File Delete** box (Fig. W-3.38) and *press* the left mouse-button.

Immediately, the icon disappears from the **Desktop**, and the **Recycle Bin** icon changes into a bin filled with papers. This means that the deleted icon is stored in the **Recycle Bin** and could be recovered.

Deleting the Contents of the Recycle Bin

When we delete an icon or file, it is moved to the **Recycle bin**. We can easily recover the deleted file as it still resides in the hard disk. However, you can delete this file permanently by deleting it from the **Recycle bin**. To delete the contents from the **Recycle Bin**, you have to empty it. Now to delete the **Notepad** icon from the **Recycle Bin**, perform the following steps :

Fig. W-3.39

1. *Move* the mouse-pointer over the **Recycle Bin** icon and *click* the right mouse-button. Instantly, a shortcut menu gets displayed (Fig. W-3.39).
2. In this menu, *move* the mouse-pointer over the **Empty Recycle Bin** option (Fig. W-3.39) and *click* the left mouse-button. Immediately, a **Confirm File Delete** box gets displayed (Fig. W-3.40) asking you to confirm the deletion of the shortcut to **Notepad**.
3. *Click* on the **Yes** button to confirm the file delete.

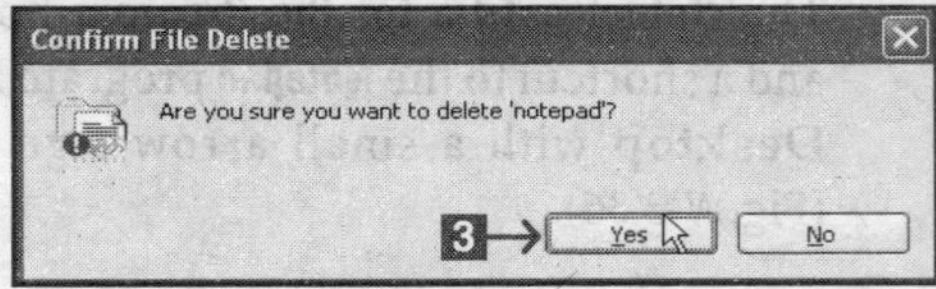

Fig. W-3.40

If you have accidentally deleted an icon or a file and it gets transferred to the Recycle Bin, you can retrieve it easily through the following steps:

1. Double-click on the Recycle Bin. Instantly, the Recycle Bin opens up into a window.
2. Now right click on the icon or file which you wish to retrieve.
3. When a shortcut menu gets displayed, click the left mouse-button on the Restore option. Immediately, the selected file gets restored to its original position.

Quitting Windows XP

To quit Windows XP, you may proceed as follows:

1. *Move* the mouse-pointer to the **Taskbar**.
2. *Click* on the **Start** button (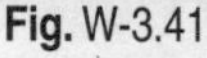). A push-up menu appears (Fig.W-3.41).
3. In the push-up menu, move the mouse-pointer over the **Turn Off Computer** option and *click* the left mouse-button (Fig.W-3.41). Instantly, the **Turn Off Computer** box appears on the screen (Fig.W-3.42).
4. In the **Turn Off Computer** box, *move* the mouse-pointer over the **Turn Off** button (Fig.W-3.42) and *click* the left mouse-button.
5. After a few seconds, the screen goes blank. Now, switch off the power supply and refresh yourself before heading to the next chapter.

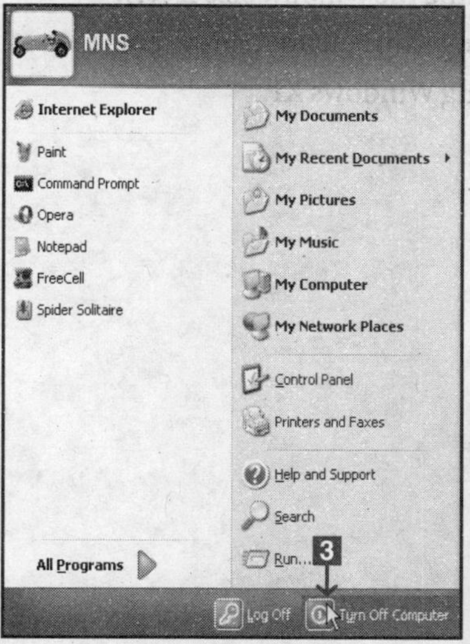

Fig. W-3.41

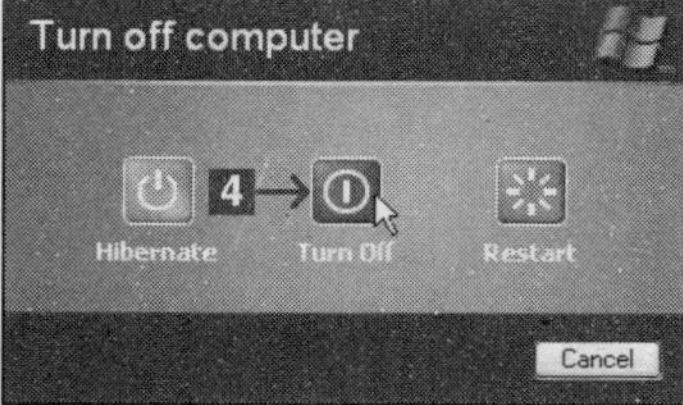

Fig. W-3.42

Summary

- The Recycle Bin icon lets you store deleted files and recover them if required.
- The My Network Places icon helps you view all computers connected to a network and their shared files and folders.
- The Start button of Taskbar gives you a quicker access to launch programs installed on your computer.
- The size of a window can be changed by clicking over Minimize, Maximize and Restore buttons.
- A window can be sized freely by placing the mouse at the edge of a window and dragging the mouse-pointer.

Exercise

Fill in the Blanks

1. For enlarging a window you can also double-click on its __________ bar.
2. ____________ is basically a quick link to a program, a file or a folder.
3. Reverting a window to its original size from its maximized size is called ______________ a window.
4. The icon that helps you view all the files and folders of different users in a local network is known as ________________________.

Short Questions

1. Write the steps for adjusting the window size freely.
2. Write the steps for creating short cut for a program.
3. Write the steps for quitting Windows XP.

CHAPTER 4

Windows Explorer

IN THIS CHAPTER

- Opening a Program
- Working in a File
- Saving a File
- Printing a File
- Installing the Printer
- Quitting the WordPad Program
- Files and Folders in Windows
- Opening the Explorer Program
- Parts of the Explorer Window
- Working in Explorer
- Opening the Local Disk (C:) through Explorer
- Opening and Closing a Folder and File in Explorer
- Creating a New Folder through Explorer
- Copying and Renaming a File
- Copying and Renaming a Folder
- Moving a File and Folder
- Deleting a File and Folder
- Emptying the Recycle Bin
- Closing Explorer and Quitting Windows
- Summary
- Exercise

After mastering the basic operations in Windows, you are no more stranger to Windows XP. Now, to further enhance your capability to use the computer, we introduce you to a powerful feature of Windows XP called **Windows Explorer.** The Windows Explorer is a program which enables you to systematically arrange and access various files, folders and disk drives on your computer.

What is the role of files and folders in a computer and how are they arranged? To understand this, let us take the example of a filing cabinet in which files are stored. A filing cabinet has folders pertaining to various subjects. Your filing cabinet may have folders of your clients, projects, etc. that may or may not be logically arranged. Each folder may have articles, letters, diagrams, reports – anything that you want to keep. Similar to a filing cabinet, Windows XP provides the Windows Explorer program to logically store all the files and folders in your hard disk. Using Explorer, you can also perform various operations on files, such as cutting, copying, pasting, etc.

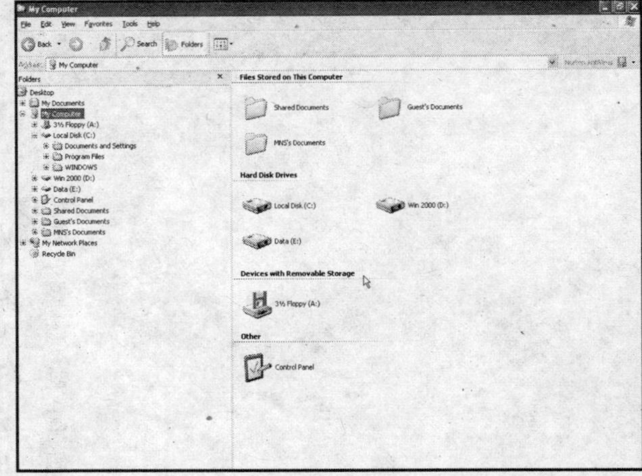

Fig. W-4.1

Any folder window can be transformed into the Explorer window. Later in this chapter, you will learn how to do this. For now, observe the Explorer window of the My Computer folder, shown in Fig. W-4.1. This window is divided into two portions. The left hand side portion displays the folders. The right hand side portion displays the contents of the folder that has been selected.

Before working with the Explorer program, let us learn to create and save a file. You will need this file to understand the functioning of the Explorer program. If you want to work in Explorer directly then simply move to the topic, "Opening the Explorer", of this chapter.

Opening a Program

In the previous chapter, you have learnt how to open the Notepad program. Let us now open another program called **WordPad** in Windows XP and work in it. Let us open the WordPad program by undertaking the following steps:

1. *Move* the mouse and *place* the mouse-pointer over the **Start** button (start) on the **Taskbar.** *Click* the left-mouse button on it (Fig. W-4.2).
2. Immediately, a push-up menu appears on the screen (Fig. W-4.2).
3. Inside the push-up menu, *place* the mouse pointer on the **All Programs** option. A second menu appears immediately (Fig. W-4.2).
4. Inside the second menu, *move* the mouse-pointer over the **Accessories** option. A third menu appears next to the second menu (Fig. W-4.2).
5. In the third menu, *place* the mouse-pointer over the **WordPad** option (Fig. W-4.2) and *click* the left mouse-button. The **WordPad** window opens up on your screen (Fig. W-4.3).

Let us refresh our familiarity with some common window components shown in Fig. 4.3.

Title bar : The top-most bar present in any window.

Menu bar : The bar just below the Title bar with some menus.

Menus : A set of major menus such as **File, Edit, View, Insert, Format** and **Help**. Each menu has its own commands which you can use to save a file, print a file, open a file, etc.

Pull-down menu : When you click on any menu in the Menu bar, it generates a list of commands. This list is called pull-down menu.

Standard Toolbar : It lies below the Menu bar and contains buttons for performing operations like printing, saving a file, copy, cut, paste etc.

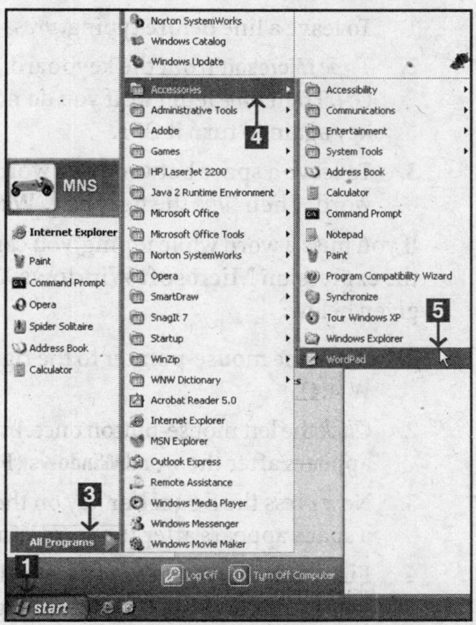

Fig. W-4.2

Working in a File

WordPad is a word processing program. As you know, a word processing program is useful for jobs such as drafting letters, printing mailing lists, producing reports, etc. As soon as the WordPad window opens up, you will notice a blinking line on the top left hand corner of the empty space in the window (Fig. W-4.3). This blinking line is known as **cursor** and its appearance indicates that the WordPad program is ready to accept any text you type.

Let us now create a simple file in WordPad and then store it in the hard disk. First, let us type the text given below in the open WordPad screen. If you face any difficulty while typing this text, follow the tips given after this text.

Microsoft Windows XP Edition gives the best in digital media, improved user experience and rich internet experience. It supports new and cutting edge technology. This edition starts faster and as you use your PC, the new smart menu simplifies your desktop to show only the items you wish to use the most.

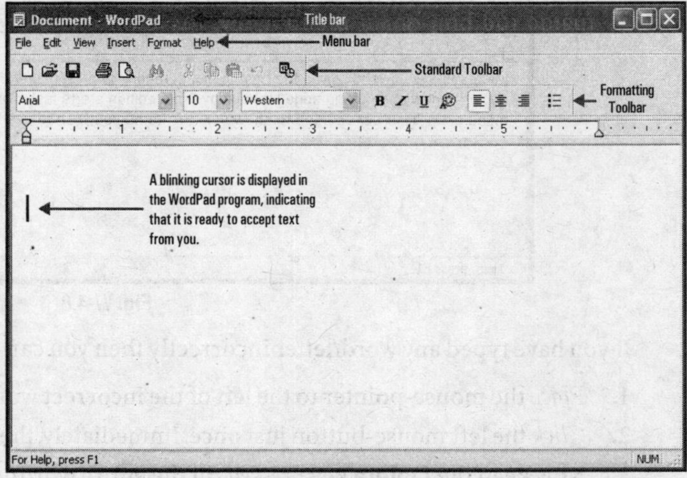

Fig. W-4.3

1. To leave a line before typing, *press* the **Enter** key on the keyboard.
2. *Type* **Microsoft** from the keyboard. To type a capital letter, say **M**, *press* the **Caps Lock** key to turn it ON. Then *type* letter **M**. If you do not want to display the capital letters further, *press* the **Caps Lock** key again to turn it OFF.
3. To leave a space between two words, *press* the **Spacebar** key on the keyboard after typing the first word. Then *type* the next text, **Windows XP Edition.**

If you miss a word while typing, you can insert it easily. Suppose in the first line, you forgot to type **XP** in the expression **Microsoft Windows XP Edition.** You can insert the missing text by following the steps given below:

1. *Move* the mouse-pointer to the right of the word **Windows** (Fig. W-4.4).
2. *Click* the left mouse-button once. Immediately, a blinking cursor appears after the word **Windows** (Fig. W-4.5).
3. Now *press* the **Spacebar** key on the keyboard. You will see that a space appears after the word **Windows** (Fig. W-4.6).
4. Finally *type* **XP** from the keyboard. The text **XP** gets displayed where the cursor was blinking (Fig. W-4.7).
5. *Type* rest of the text as shown in Fig. W-4.8.

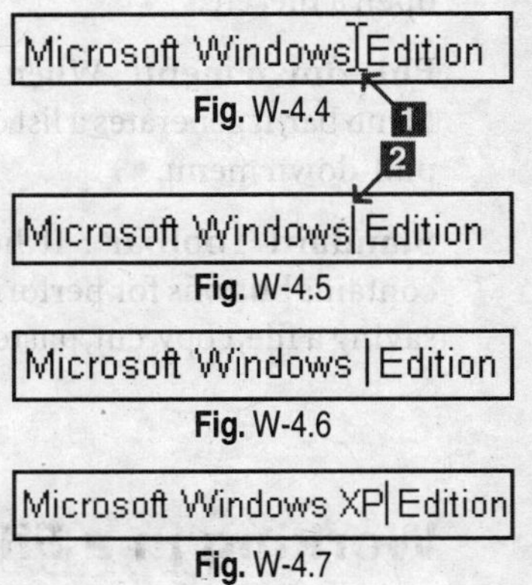

Fig. W-4.4
Fig. W-4.5
Fig. W-4.6
Fig. W-4.7

Fig. W-4.8 shows the **WordPad** screen with the typed text in Windows XP.

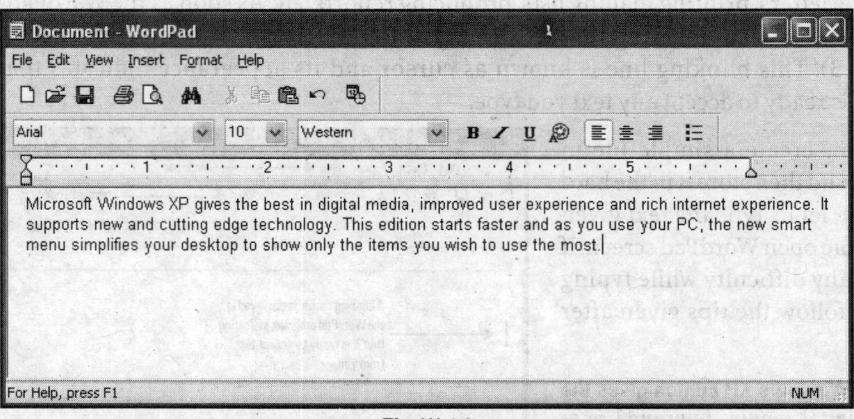

Fig. W-4.8

If you have typed any word/letter incorrectly then you can correct it in the following way:

1. *Place* the mouse-pointer to the left of the incorrect word/letter.
2. *Click* the left mouse-button just once. Immediately, the blinking cursor appears at that point.
3. Now keep the **Delete** key *pressed* till the entire word/letter gets deleted. After the word or letter is erased, *type* in the correct word.

Saving a File

As you type some text in your file, it gets stored temporarily in the computer memory. The contents in the memory, if not saved, will be lost when your computer is switched off, or if there is a power failure. Chances are that you may lose valuable data.

To avoid loss of data, you should save the text you have typed. Saving means storing the text safely as a file in the hard disk. You can save the typed text as a file using the following steps.

1. Start with the window of Fig. W-4.8. *Move* the mouse-pointer over the **File** menu in the Menu bar. *Click* the left mouse-button.
2. Immediately, a pull-down menu appears on the screen (Fig. W-4.9).

Every menu present on the Menu bar can be click-opened to display a pull-down menu. The following list shows various options under the File menu in a WordPad window:

New	:	Creates a new file	Save As	:	Saves file with another name
Close	:	Closes a file	Save	:	Saves a file
Open	:	Opens an existing file	Print	:	Prints the existing file

3. Now *move* the mouse-pointer over the **Save** option and *click* the left mouse-button (Fig. W-4.9). Instantly, a **Save As** box gets displayed on the screen (Fig. W-4.10).

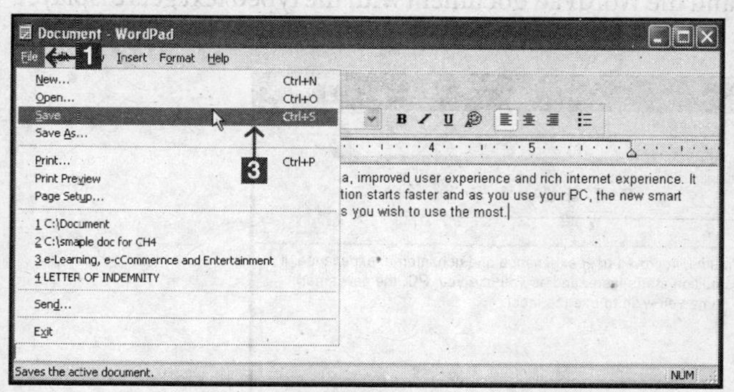

Fig. W-4.9

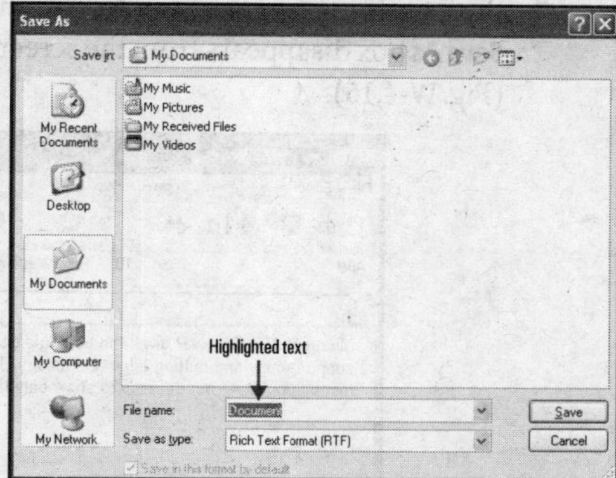

Fig. W-4.10

4. In the **Save As** box, you will find some highlighted text inside the rectangular box beside the **File name** option (Fig. W-4.10). In the rectangular box, *type* a file name for the typed text, say **Vikas.** This name replaces the default highlighted text beside the **File name** option (Fig. W-4.11).

File name: Vikas ← 4

Fig. W-4.11

5. Now you must choose a folder where you wish to store the **Vikas** file, otherwise it will be stored in the folder that is opened in the **Save As** box by default. Let us save this file in the **Local Disk (C:)**. To do so, *move* the mouse-pointer over the down-arrow button (⌄) in the box beside the **Save in** option. Then *click* the left mouse-button on it (Fig. W-4.12).

Save in: My Documents 5 →

Fig. W-4.12

6. Immediately, a pull-down menu appears (Fig. W-4.13).

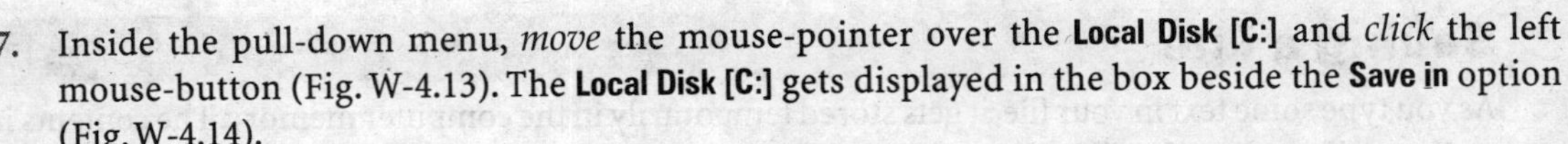

7. Inside the pull-down menu, *move* the mouse-pointer over the **Local Disk [C:]** and *click* the left mouse-button (Fig. W-4.13). The **Local Disk [C:]** gets displayed in the box beside the **Save in** option (Fig. W-4.14).

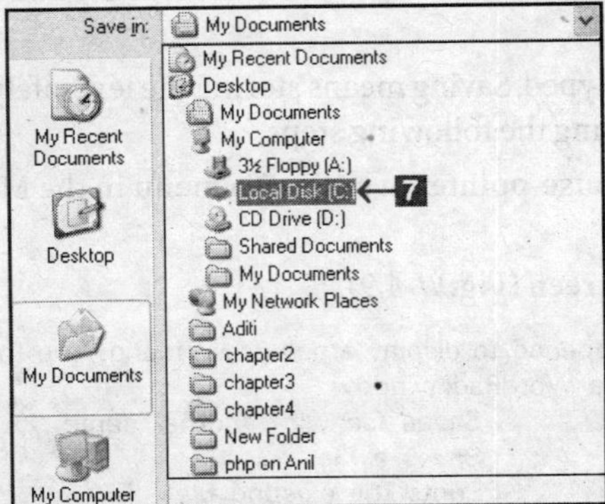

Fig. W-4.13

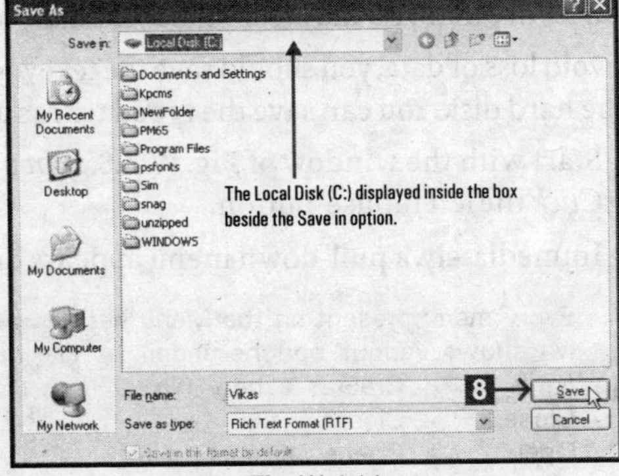

Fig. W-4.14

8. Now, you are one click away from saving your first file, i.e. **Vikas.** *Move* the mouse-pointer over the **Save** button of the **Save As** box and *click* the left mouse-button (Fig. W-4.14). Immediately, the **Save As** box disappears from the screen and the WordPad document with the typed text gets displayed (Fig. W-4.15).

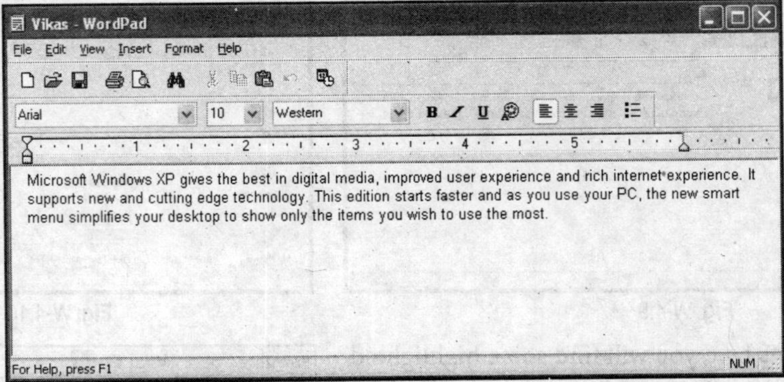

Fig. W-4.15

This Wordpad document is actually the **Vikas** file you have just saved. Its **Title bar** shows the name **Vikas.** Remember, the Title bar of any saved file displays the name given to it. Once you save a file in your computer, you can edit, modify and change it whenever required.

When you save your file for the first time, you will see the Save As box (Fig. W-4.10). Thereafter, whenever you save the same file, the Save As box will not appear. Instead, the WordPad program will automatically save the new changes when you will press the Ctrl and S keys simultaneously.

If you wish to give a different name to the Vikas file then click the Save As option inside the File pull-down menu. This will display the Save As box, in which you can specify another name and location for the Vikas file.

Printing a File

Sometimes you need a hard copy or printout of your file for your record. Now, let us take a printout of our file **Vikas** through the following steps.

1. Make sure that your printer is **ON** and connected to your computer.
2. Start with the window of Fig. W-4.15. *Move* the mouse-pointer over the **File** menu in the **Menu bar**.
3. *Click* the left mouse-button. Immediately, a pull-down menu appears on the screen (Fig. W-4.16).
4. In the pull-down menu, *move* the mouse-pointer on the **Print** option (Fig. W-4.16) and *click* the left mouse-button. Immediately, a **Print** dialog box opens up on the screen (Fig. W-4.17).
5. Finally *click* over the **Print** button (Fig. W-4.17). The **Print** dialog box disappears and the **Vikas** file gets printed.

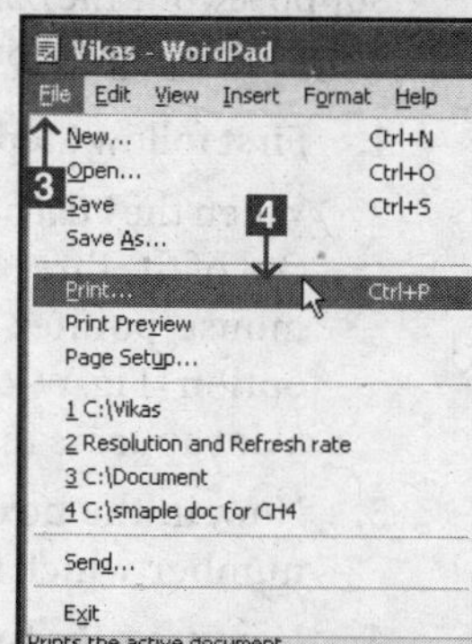

Fig. W-4.16

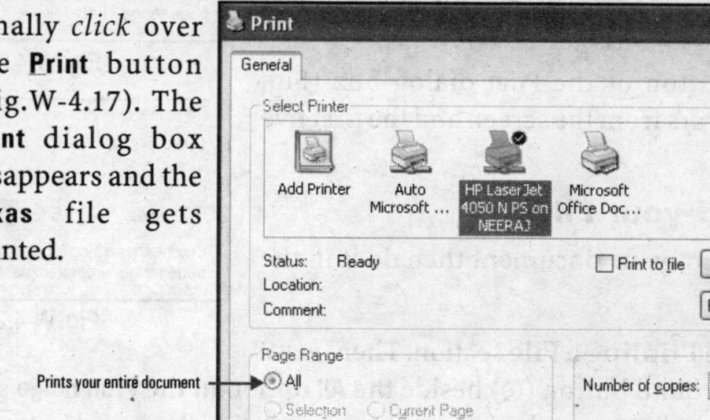

Fig. W-4.17

You have just learned about printing a single-page file. This process is different from the one employed for printing multi-page files. To know more about other printing methods, move onto the next page.

Sometimes when you click on the File menu and then on the Print option, a message box gets displayed as shown in Fig. W-4.18.

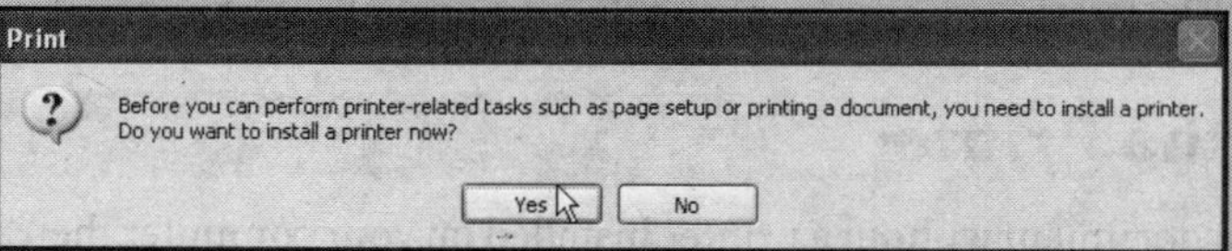

Fig. W-4.18

This message box tells you that the printer is not installed in your system and asks you to install it by following certain steps. Installation of the printer in Windows XP may be done as described in the topic 'Installing the Printer' later in this chapter. After installing the printer, return to the topic 'Printing Selected Pages of Your File'.

Printing Selected Pages of Your File

Suppose your file contains 20 pages and you wish to take print-outs of only first 5 pages. You can do so by performing the following steps.

1. First follow Steps 1 to 4 of the previous section, **Printing a File.**
2. When the **Print** box gets displayed, *locate* the **Print range** section in it. Out of the three sub-options inside the **Print range** section, *move* the mouse-pointer over the round button (◯) beside the **Pages** sub-option (Fig. W-4.19) and *click* the left mouse-button. Immediately, a dot appears inside the round button (Fig. W-4.20).
3. Now, in the box beside the **Pages** option, *type* the starting page number, which in our case is **1** (Fig. W-4.20).
4. Now *press* the **hyphen**(-) from the keyboard and then *type* the last page number, which in our case is **5** (Fig. W-4.21).
5. Finally, *click* on the **Print** button of the **Print** dialog box (Fig. W-4.17). The **Print** box disappears from the screen and the first five pages of your file get printed.

Page Range
All
Selection Current Page
Pages: 1-65535
2
Enter either a single page number or a single page range. For example, 5-12

Fig. W-4.19

Page Range
All
Selection Current Page
Pages: 1
3
Enter either a single page number or a single page range. For example, 5-12

Fig. W-4.20

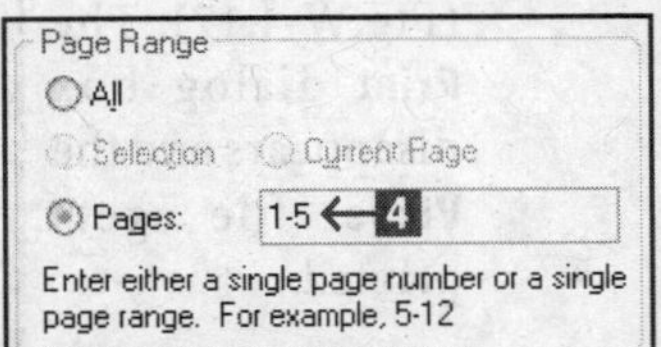

Fig. W-4.21

Printing All the Pages of your File

If you want to print all the pages of your document then do it in the following manner:

1. First, follow Steps 1 to 4 of the **Printing a File** section. Then, *move* the mouse-pointer over the round button (◯) beside the **All** option in the **Print range** section (Fig. W-4.22) and *click* the left mouse-button. A dot instantly appears inside the round button indicating its selection (Fig. W-4.23).

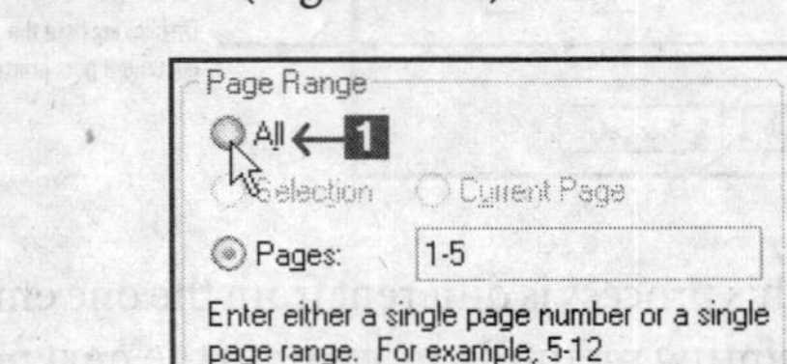

Fig. W-4.22

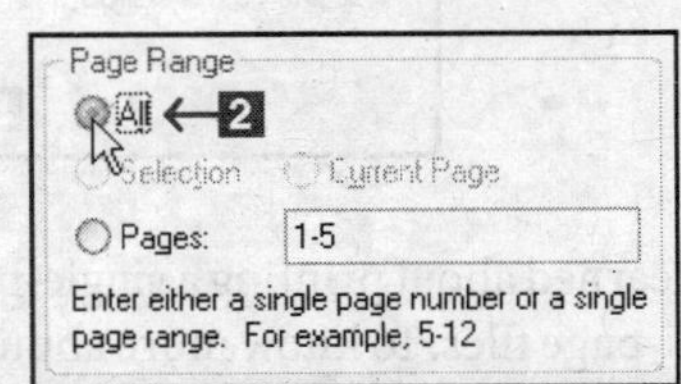

Fig. W-4.23

2. Now, *move* the mouse-pointer over the **Print** button in the **Print** box and *click* the left mouse-button (Fig. W-4.17). The **Print** box disappears from the screen, and all the pages of your file get printed.

Installing the Printer

If you try to print a document without a printer installed on your computer then a message box as shown in Fig. W-4.18 appears. For installing a printer on your computer, carry out the following steps:

1. When a message box as shown in Fig. W-4.18 gets displayed, *click* on the **OK** button in it.
2. Now *click* on the **Start** button (start) of the **Taskbar.** A push-up menu gets displayed (Fig. W-4.24).

3. Inside the push-up menu, *click* the **Printer and Faxes** option (Fig. W-4.24). The **Printer and Faxes** window appears (Fig. W-4.25).
4. In the **Printer and faxes** window, *move* the mouse-pointer over the **Add a Printer** option under the **Printer Tasks** category and *click* the left mouse-button (Fig. W-4.25). Instantly, an **Add Printer Wizard** (Fig. W-4.26) appears on the screen which starts the printer installation process.
5. To move ahead, *click* on the **Next** button (Fig. W-4.26). The next screen of the **Add Printer Wizard** appears (Fig. W-4.27).

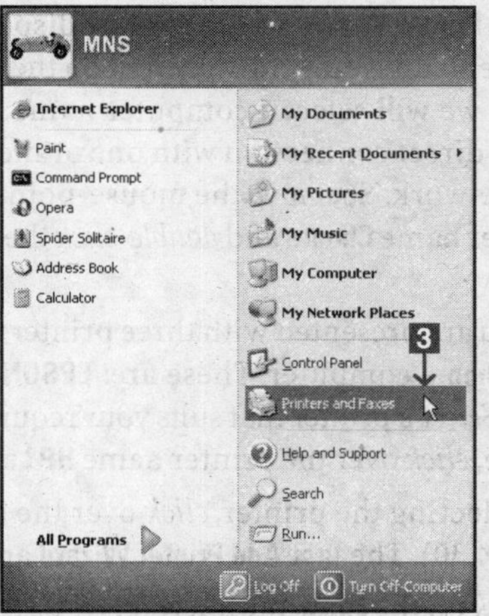

Fig. W-4.24

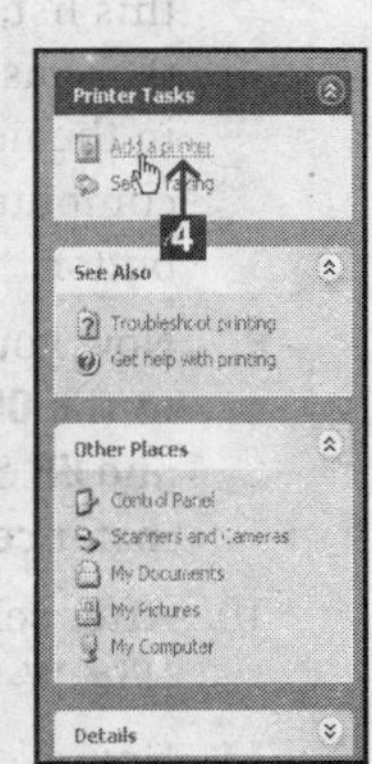

Fig. W-4.25

Fig. W-4.26

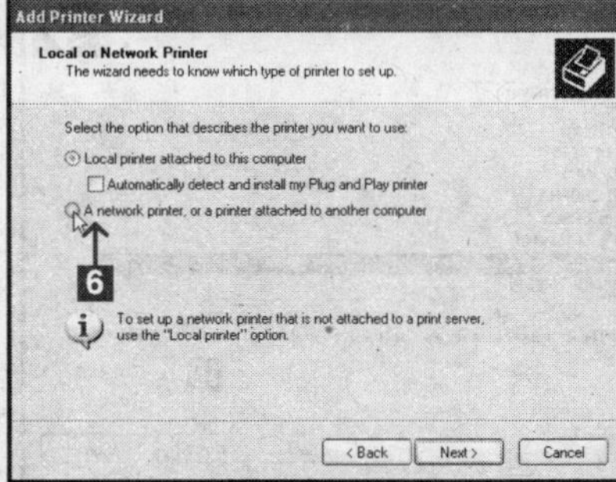

Fig. W-4.27

6. The **Add Printer Wizard** window has two options—**Local printer attached to this computer,** and **A network printer, or a printer attached to another computer.** You can select the first option if your printer is attached directly to the system. However, we will work with the second option since our printer is attached to the network. So, *click* on the round button beside **A network printer, or a printer attached to another computer** option (Fig. W-4.27) and *click* on the **Next** button. The next screen of the **Add Printer Wizard** appears (Fig. W-4.28).
7. In the new screen, **Browse for a printer** is selected by default. So, *click* on the **Next** button to move on to the next **Add Printer Wizard** screen (Fig. W-4.29).

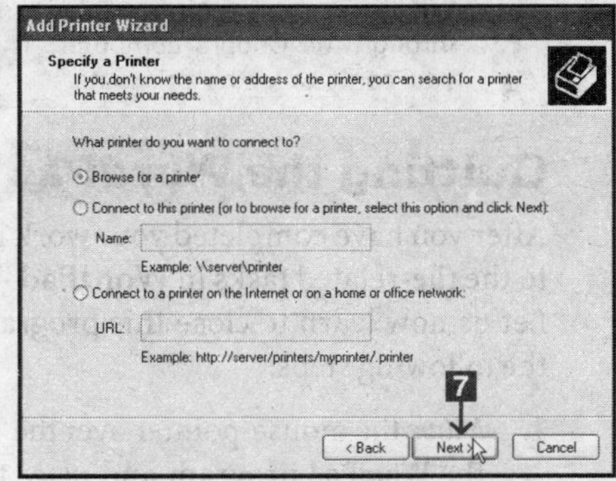

Fig. W-4.28

If you are not connected to a network then to install a printer on your computer, insert the printer CD in the CD Drive of your computer and follow the instructions of the Printer Wizard.

8. The **Add Printer Wizard** of Fig. W-4.29 displays a list of computer names currently present on the network. In this list, we will select a computer name, say **Chopra**, that has direct connection with one or more printers in the network. So, *move* the mouse-pointer over the computer name **Chopra** and *double-click* the left mouse-button.
9. Now, you are presented with three printers connected to the **Chopra** computer. These are: **EPSON, EPSON 440** and **HP**. *Select* a printer that suits your requirement. For instance, *click* over the printer name **HP Laser 4050.**

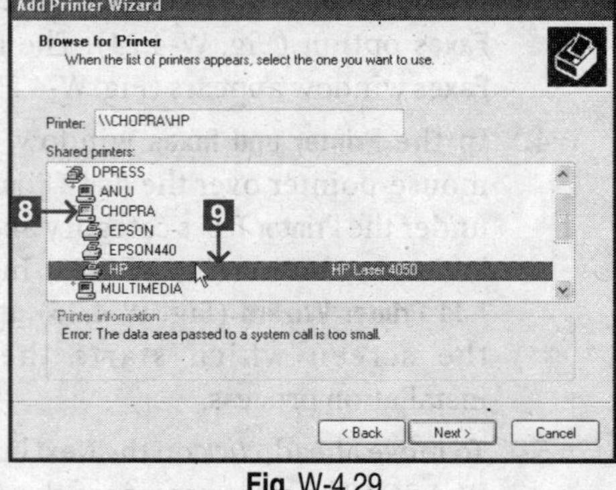

Fig. W-4.29

10. After selecting the printer, *click* over the **Next** button (Fig. W-4.30). The last **Add Printer Wizard** appears (Fig. W-4.31).
11. Now *click* on the **Finish** button (Fig. W-4.31). This ends the printer installation process.

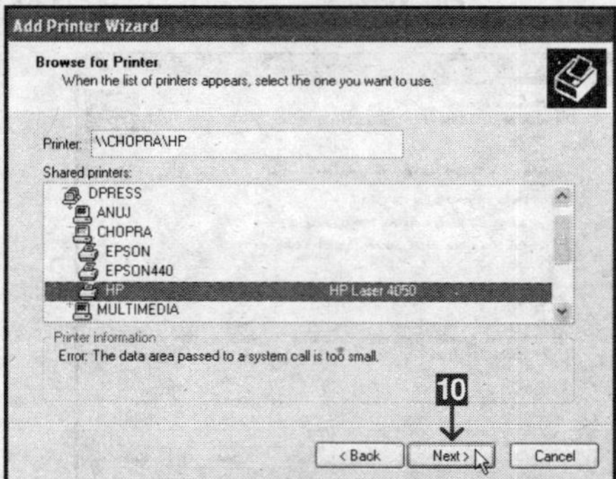

Fig. W-4.30

Fig. W-4.31

Whenever next time you give a print command to print a file, the command will reach the printer through the Chopra computer. Thus, in case, Chopra computer is off or not present on the network, you can't take the printouts.

Quitting the WordPad Program

After you have completed your work in a program, don't forget to close it. You have already given a try to the file-related tasks in **WordPad** – creating a file, saving it under a name and printing its contents. Let us now learn to close this program through the following steps:

1. *Move* the mouse-pointer over the **Title bar** of the **WordPad** program and *place* the mouse-pointer on the **Close** button (☒) (Fig. W-4.32).
2. Now, *click* the left mouse-button once (Fig. W-4.32). The **WordPad** window closes instantly and we return to the **Desktop**.

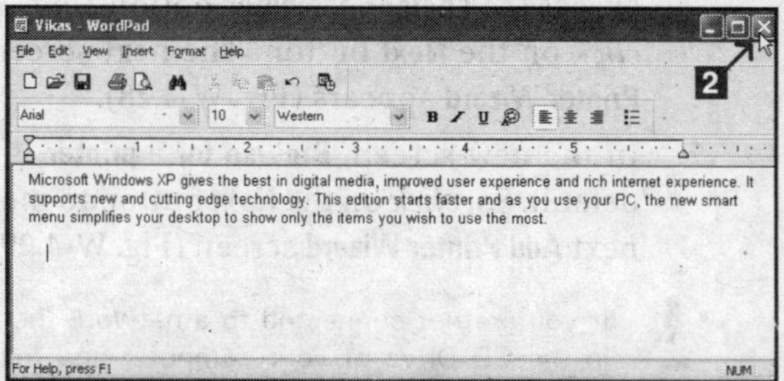

Fig. W-4.32

If you have made some changes to the Vikas file and before saving it you clicked on the Close button(☒) then a message box (Fig. W-4.33) appears on your screen.

If you do not wish to save changes made to this file, move the mouse-pointer over the No button and click the left mouse-button. Otherwise, click on the Yes button. This instantly closes the WordPad and the Desktop gets displayed before you.

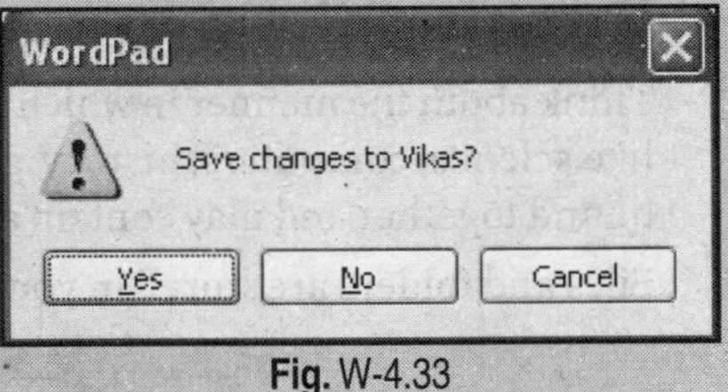

Fig. W-4.33

Let us now perform the following workout.

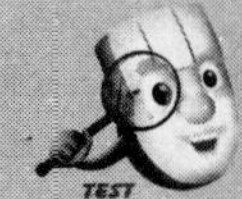

How to print an open file in WordPad and close WordPad?

- Move the mouse-pointer our the Menu bar and click on the File menu.
- In the pull-down menu, click on the Print option. The Print box appears.
- Click on the OK button. Your file gets printed.
- Now click on the Close button (☒) located on the Title bar of the open file window. The WordPad window immediately closes.

Let us now learn about files and folders. No operating system can function without files and folders. And, you must also have a fair understanding of them to work efficiently on your computer. The following text will certainly enable you to feel at ease while working with files and folders in your system.

Files and Folders in Windows

When not working on computer, you use paper sheets to write important information. You would obviously like to keep safely organized the paper sheets containing important information. And, to be doubly sure about the safety of your sheets, you may prefer to bind them together in a book form.

In computer terminology, 'file' is like a paper sheet and a 'folder' is akin to a book. Just as a book contains pages, a computer folder consists of files. Fig. W-4.34 illustrates the relationship between files and folders.

Fig. W-4.34

We can therefore say that in Windows, a **Book** is referred to as **Folder** and a **Paper Sheet** as **File**.

Opening the Explorer Program

Think about the manner in which books are arranged on a bookshelf. Books may be on various subjects like science, computers, history, geography, etc. Within each book (folder), sheets of paper (files) are bound together and may contain articles, diagrams, reports, etc. (Fig. W-4.35).

Files and folders are stored in your system in the same way as illustrated in Fig. W-4.35.

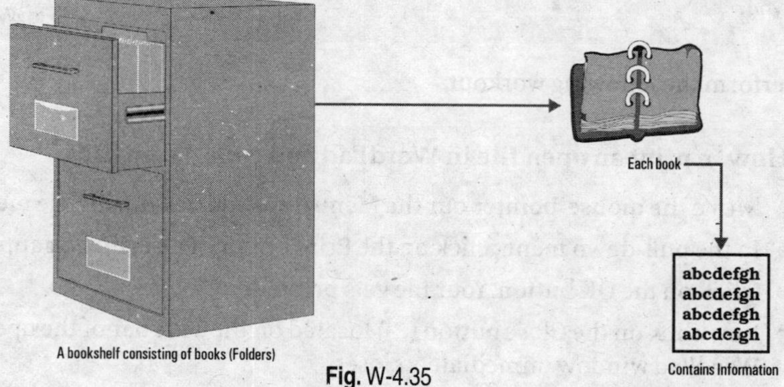

Fig. W-4.35

To work with files and folders in your computer, you must learn the use of the **Windows Explorer** program of Windows XP. With the help of Windows Explorer program, let us now understand the arrangement of files and folders in a computer. We will also use this program to copy, paste, rename and search files and folders. But first, it is necessary to open the Windows Explorer program. You can do so through the following steps:

1. Make sure that the **Desktop** of Windows XP is displayed before you. *Move* the mouse-pointer over the **My Computer** icon (Fig. W-4.36).
2. *Press* the right mouse-button once. (The right mouse-button is shown in green in Fig. W-4.37). A shortcut menu appears (Fig. W-4.38).
3. Now *move* the mouse-pointer over the **Explore** option of the shortcut menu and *press* the left mouse-button. This opens up the Explorer window of **My Computer** on your screen (Fig. W-4.39).

My Computer
1

Fig. W-4.36

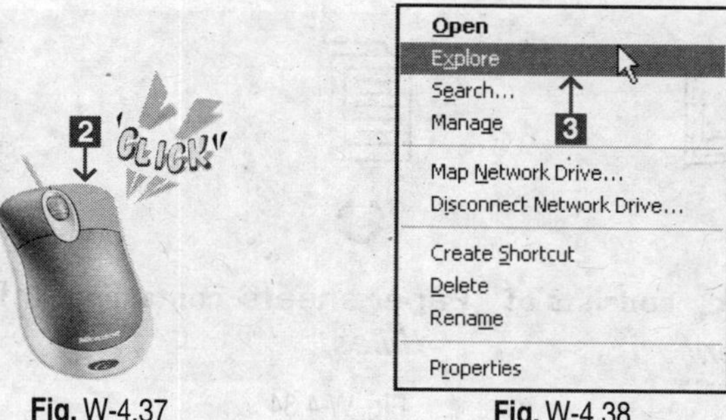

Fig. W-4.37 **Fig.** W-4.38

By following Steps 1 to 3, you can transform a folder or drive window into the Explorer window.

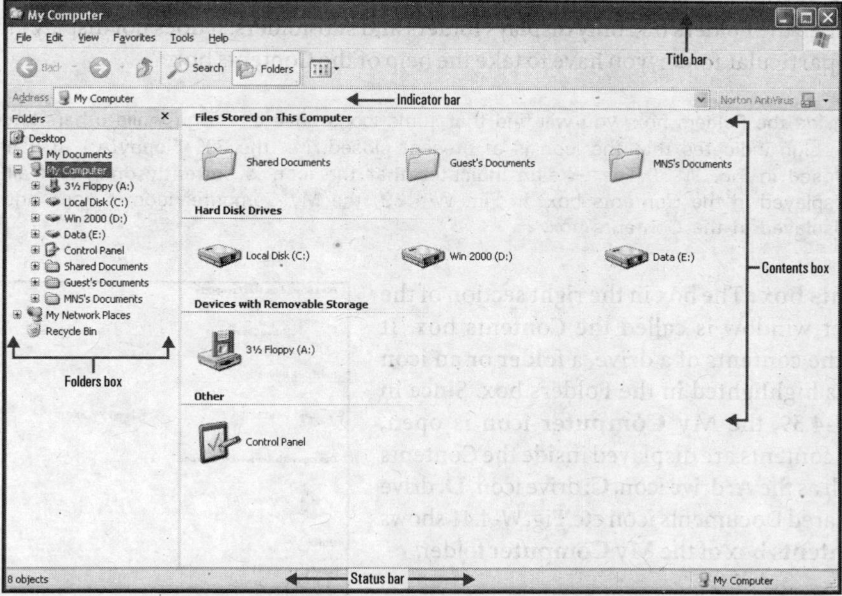

Fig. W-4.39: Explorer window of the My Computer folder

Parts of the Explorer Window

The various parts of the Explorer window are as follows:

Title bar : The Title bar is situated at the top of the Explorer window. It displays the name of the icon, My computer, from where you had started the Explorer program. You can also start the Explorer program from the **Start** button of the Taskbar or the **Network Neighbourhood** icon or the **Recycle Bin**, etc.

Menu bar : The Menu bar consists of various options such as **File, Edit, View, Tools** and **Help**. These options are called **menus**.

Indicator bar : The Explorer window is divided into two parts. The box on the left hand side is termed as the **Folders box**, and the one on the right hand side is called the **Contents box.** At the top of the Contents box, the name of the currently open folder, **My Computer** in Fig.W-4.39, is displayed in a bar which is called the **indicator bar.**

Status bar : The Status bar, by default, indicates the number of items in the Contents box. In Fig. W-4.39 it shows eight objects.

Folders box : As you know, the box on the left side of the Explorer window is called the Folders box. This box, as shown in Fig.W-4.40, displays the icons for various folders and drives present on a computer. All folders and drives are displayed in the form of a folder tree. In other words, the folder tree is a hierarchical representation of the folders, files, disk drives, and other resources connected to a computer or

Folders
Desktop
My Documents
My Computer
3½ Floppy (A:)
Local Disk (C:)
Win 2000 (D:)
Data (E:)
Control Panel
Shared Documents
Guest's Documents
MNS's Documents
My Network Places

Fig. W-4.40

network. If you click on any icon in the folder tree, its contents get displayed inside the Contents box. Remember, the Folders box only displays folders and sub-folders. It does not display any file. To view any file of a particular folder, you have to take the help of the Contents box.

Inside the Folders box, you will find that some icons have a + sign while others have a − sign. The + sign indicates that the icon is at present closed, i.e. the 3½ Floppy(A:), (C:) and (D:) icons are closed in Fig. W-39.The − sign indicates that the icon is currently open and all its contents are displayed in the Contents box. In Fig. W-4.39, the My Computer icon is open and its contents are displayed in the Contents box.

Contents box : The box in the right section of the Explorer window is called the Contents box. It shows the contents of a drive, a folder or an icon which is highlighted in the Folders box. Since in Fig. W-4.39, the **My Computer** icon is open, only its contents are displayed inside the Contents box such as the **A:** drive icon, **C:** drive icon, **D:** drive icon, Shared Documents icon etc. Fig. W-4.41 shows the **Contents** box of the **My Computer** folder.

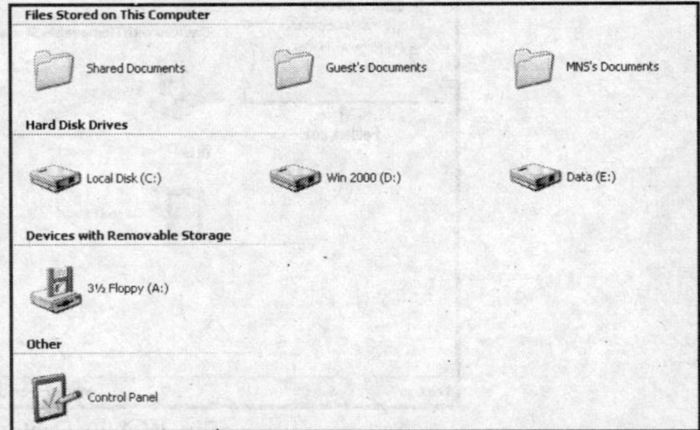

Fig. W-4.41

Get familiar with the following terms which you will frequently encounter:

Folders : Folders are containers that may have many files or sub-folders under them. Folders form the first level of contents in Local Disk (C:). Folders can never be copied or moved into a file.

Local Disk (C:) : It is the head of all folders in your hard disk. It can be renamed, but it cannot be copied or moved into a file or sub-folder or a sub-sub-folder, etc. The following diagram shows the way in which folders are arranged in the hard disk:

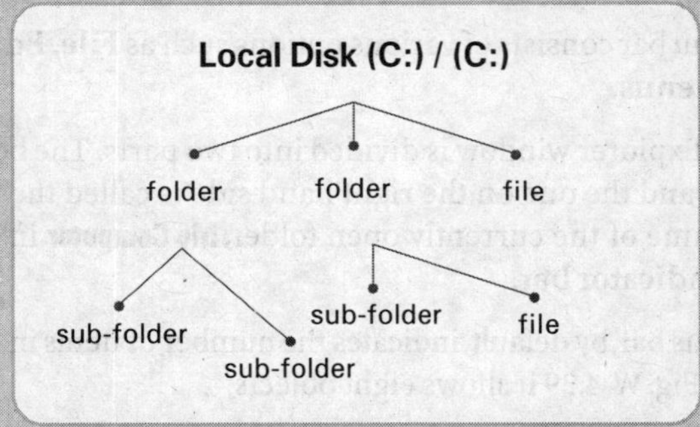

Sub-folders : All the folders just below main folders of the Local Disk (C:) are called sub-folders. These can be renamed, copied or moved into another sub-folder or sub-sub-folder. However, they cannot be copied into files.

Sub-sub-folders : All the folders existing inside any sub-folder are termed as sub-sub-folders. These can be renamed, copied or moved to a sub-folder or a sub-sub-folder or the Local Disk (C:). However, these cannot be copied into files.

Working in Explorer

You can term the explorer as a mini library. As you know, a library is a place where books are stored. Each book consists of a number of paper sheets and each paper sheet contains information. Similarly, in your computer, Explorer is used to store folders. Each folder consists of a number of files, and each file contains certain information.

Opening an Icon from the Explorer Window

Let us now learn to open a folder or disk drive icon from an Explorer window and display its contents in the Contents box. Suppose, you wish to open the **Desktop** icon. For this, you have to undertake the following steps.

1. We assume that the Explorer window of **My Computer** (Fig. W-4.42) is open on your computer.
2. *Place* the mouse-pointer over the **Desktop** icon in the **Folders** box (Fig. W-4.43), and *click* the left mouse-button. Immediately, the My Computer Explorer window changes into the Desktop window. The **Desktop** icon opens up and displays its contents in the **Contents** box (Fig. W-4.43). Both the Indicator bar and the Title bar display the name **Desktop.**

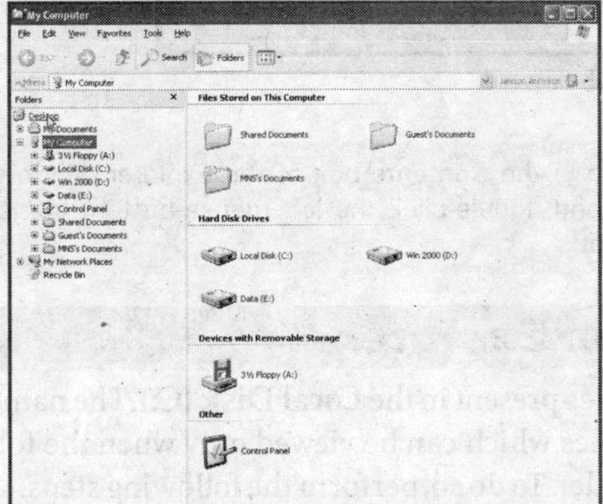

Fig. W-4.42

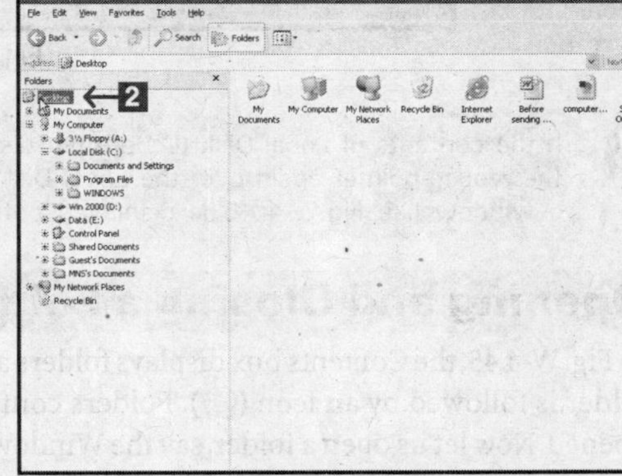

Fig. W-4.43

Opening the Local Disk (C:) through Explorer

Let us now locate the **Local Disk (C:)** and open it. For this, we proceed as follows:

1. The Local Disk (C:) resides inside the My Computer icon. So, start with the Explorer window of the **My Computer** folder (Fig. W-4.42).
2. Now *move* the mouse-pointer over the **Local Disk (C:)** in the **Folders** box (Fig. W-4.44) and *click* the left mouse-button. The Explorer window changes into the **Local Disk (C:)** window, whose contents get displayed in the **Contents** box (Fig. W-4.45).

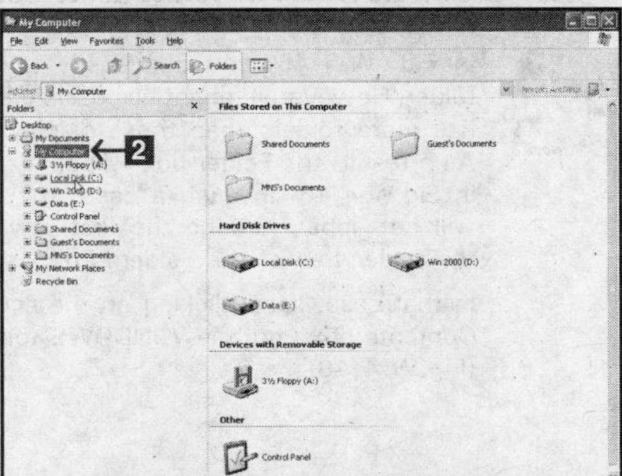

Fig. W-4.44

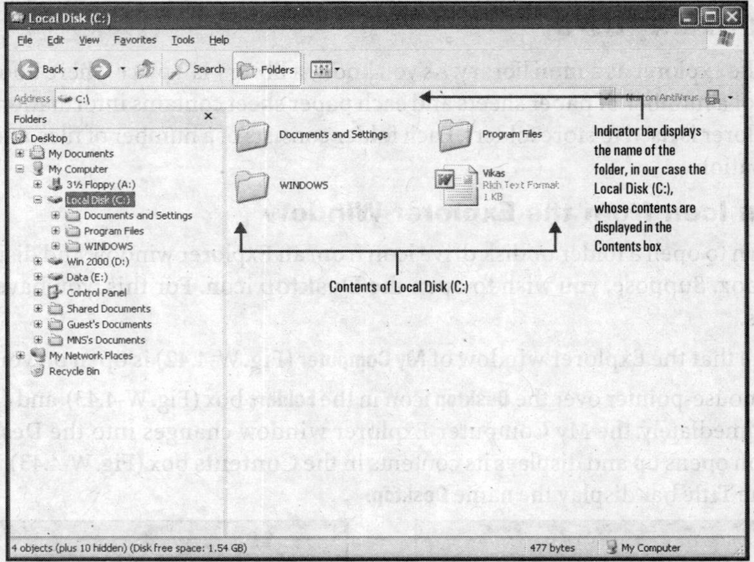

Fig. W-4.45

If the contents of Local Disk (C:) are not displayed in the Contents box of the Explorer window, move the mouse-pointer again over the Local Disk (C:) and double-click the left mouse-button. Immediately, a window like Fig.W-4.45 is displayed before you.

Opening and Closing a Folder in Explorer

In Fig. W-4.45, the Contents box displays folders and files present in the **Local Disk (C:)**. The name of each folder is followed by an icon (📁). Folders contain files which can be viewed only when the folders are opened. Now let us open a folder, say the Windows folder. To do so, perform the following steps.

1. First, make sure the **Local Disk (C:)** drive window is open as shown in Fig. W-4.45. Then, *move* the mouse-pointer over the **Contents** box.
2. *Locate* the **WINDOWS** folder in the **Contents** box.

In Fig. W-4.45, you can easily find the WINDOWS folder. However, it might be possible that your computer has more folders than those displayed in Fig.W-4.45. As a result, the Folder box will appear longer as shown in Fig.W-4.46. In such a case, the WINDOWS folder will not appear among the first few folders displayed the folder tree of the Folders box.

In that case, keep clicking on the scroll buttons of the Contents box until the WINDOWS folder gets displayed (Fig.W-4.46).

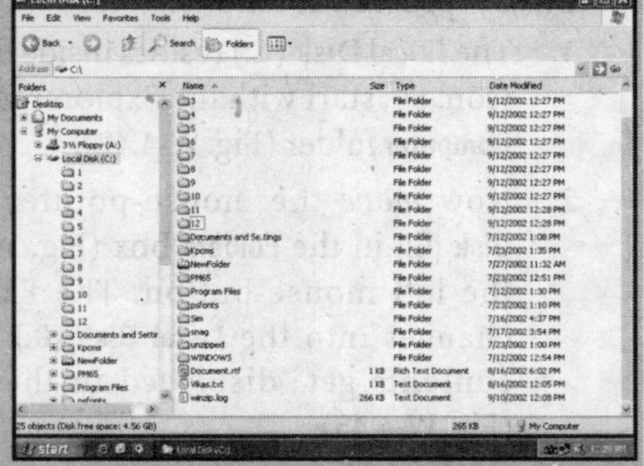

Fig. W-4.46

3. After locating the **WINDOWS** folder, *move* the mouse-pointer over it (Fig. W-4.47) and *double-click* the left mouse-button. Instantly, the Local Disk (C:) window changes into **WINDOWS** folder window. The **WINDOWS** folder also opens up displaying its contents in the **Contents** box (Fig. W-4.48).

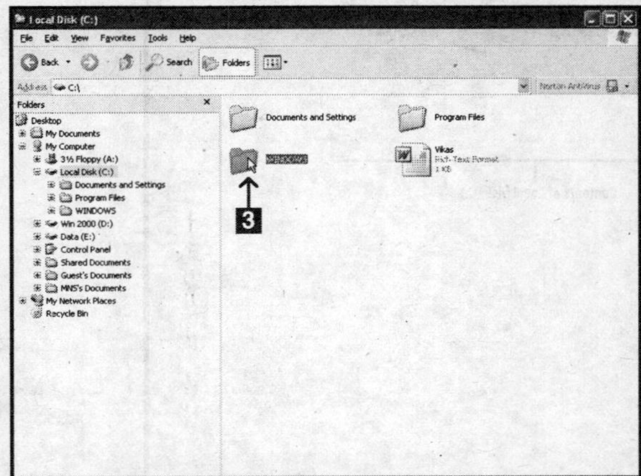

Fig. W-4.47

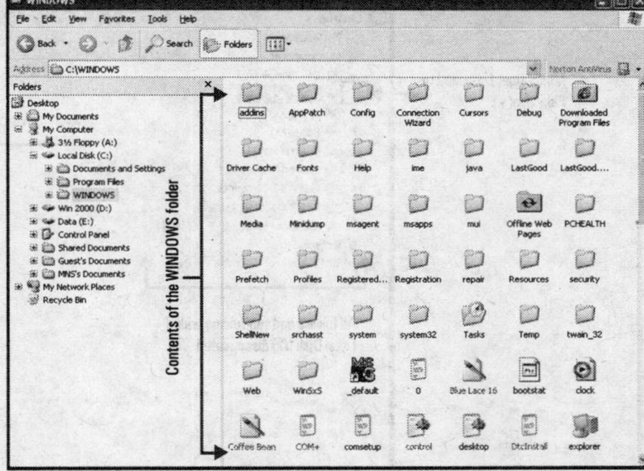

Fig. W-4.48

The **Indicator bar** over the **Contents** box displays the address as **C:\WINDOWS**. It means the **WINDOWS** folder that resides in **Local Disk (C:)** is now open. This address may also be termed as the path of the **WINDOWS** folder.

Closing a folder in Explorer

Let us now close the **Local Disk (C:)**. For this, you may undertake the following steps:

1. In the window shown in Fig. W-4.48, *move* the mouse-pointer over the minus sign (⊟) beside the **Local Disk (C:)** (Fig. W-4.49) and *click* the left mouse-button. Now you will notice three changes:

   (i) The ⊟ sign beside the **Local Disk (C:)** changes to a ⊞ sign (Fig. W-4.50) indicating that the folder is closed.

   (ii) The **WINDOWS** folder window changes into the **Local Disk (C:)** window. The contents of the **WINDOWS** folder disappear and those of **Local Disk (C:)** get displayed in the **Contents** box (Fig. W-4.50).

   (iii) All the sub-folders under **Local Disk (C:)** disappear from the **Folders** box (Fig. W-4.50).

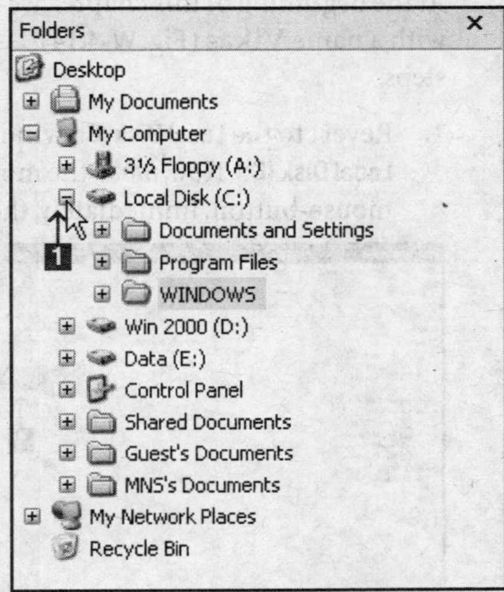

Fig. W-4.49

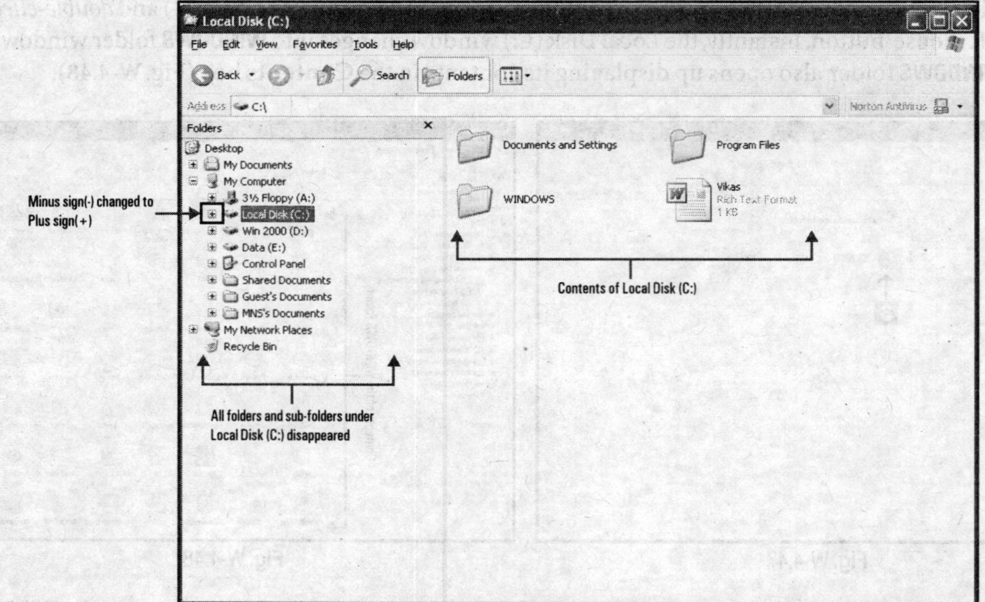

Fig. W-4.50

Opening and Closing a File in Explorer

The **Local Disk (C:)** or **(C:)** displays the files of a folder in the **Contents** box. The files are represented by symbols such as , , , , , , , , , etc.

At the beginning of this chapter, we had created a file in WordPad and saved it under the Local Disk (C:) with a name **Vikas** (Fig. W-4.14). Let us open this file using Explorer. To do so, undertake the following steps:

1. Revert to the **Local Disk (C:)** window of Fig. W-4.45. The **Vikas** file is displayed in the **Contents** box of **Local Disk (C:)**. Now, *move* the mouse-pointer over the **Vikas** file (Fig. W-4.51) and *double-click* the left mouse-button. Immediately, the file opens up in **WordPad** program (Fig. W-4.52).

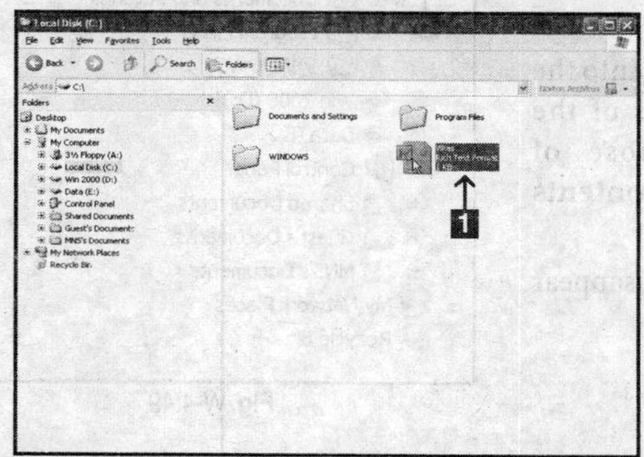

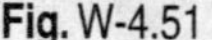

Fig. W-4.51

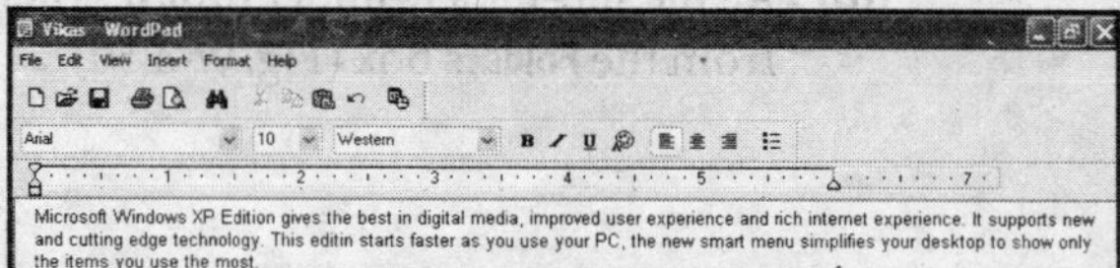

Fig. W-4.52

If Microsoft Word is installed in your system then the 'Vikas' file will open in Microsoft Word. If it is not installed, like in our case, the file will open in the WordPad program only.

2. Let us now close the **WordPad** program along with the **Vikas** file, and return to the Explorer window. For this, *move* the mouse-pointer over the **Close** button (☒) present on the **Title bar** of the **Vikas** file (Fig. W-4.53) and *click* the left mouse-button.

Fig. W-4.53

The **Vikas** file closes immediately and the Explorer window of the Local Disk (C:) is displayed before you.

Suppose you have made some changes to the Vikas file. If you click on the Close button(☒) to close this file, a dialog box (Fig.W-4.54) appears, asking you whether you want to save the changes to the file or not. To save the changes, move the mouse-pointer over the Yes button (Fig. W-4.54) and click the left mouse-button. The changes get saved and the WordPad screen closes.

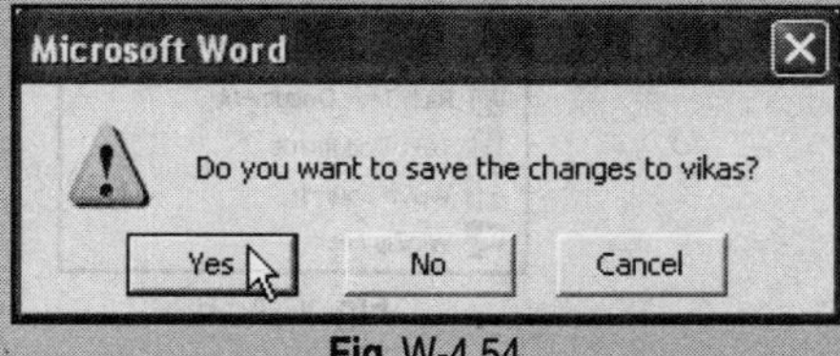

Fig. W-4.54

Creating a New Folder through Explorer

So, you have learnt how to locate files and folders through the Explorer program. Now, we will learn how to create new folders or sub-folders in Explorer. Let us create a new folder inside the **Local Disk (C:)**. To do so, undertake the following steps:

1. Make sure the Explorer window of **Local Disk (C:)** as shown in Fig. W-4.45, is open on your computer. *Move* the mouse-pointer to an empty area inside the **Contents** box of this window.
2. *Click* the right mouse-button. Immediately, a shortcut menu appears on the screen (Fig. W-4.55).
3. In the shortcut menu, *move* the mouse-pointer over the **New** option (Fig. W-4.55). This displays a sub-menu beside the **New** option (Fig. W-4.56).

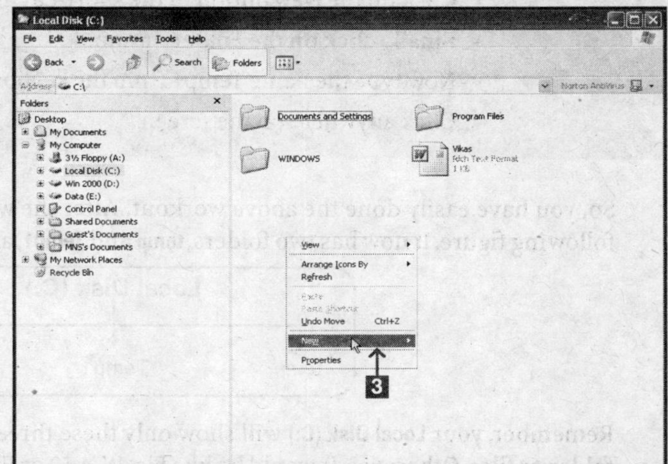

Fig. W-4.55

4. In the sub-menu, *move* the mouse-pointer over the **Folder** option (Fig. W-4.56) and *click* the left mouse-button. Instantly, a new folder with some highlighted text gets displayed in the **Contents** box of the **Local Disk (C:)** window (Fig. W-4.57).

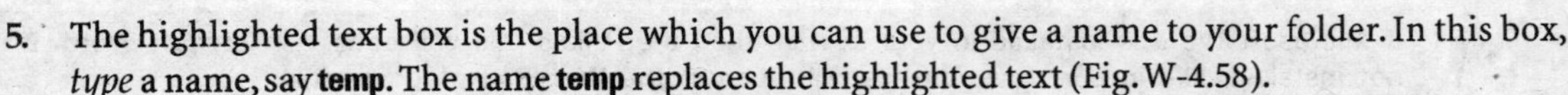

5. The highlighted text box is the place which you can use to give a name to your folder. In this box, *type* a name, say **temp**. The name **temp** replaces the highlighted text (Fig. W-4.58).
6. To confirm the name given to the new folder, *move* the mouse-pointer anywhere on the screen, and *click* the left mouse-button. The new folder **temp** is now created in **Local Disk (C:)** (Fig. W-4.59).

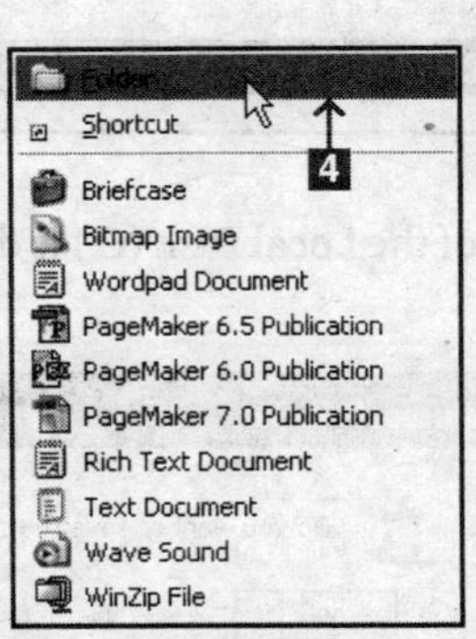

Fig. W-4.56

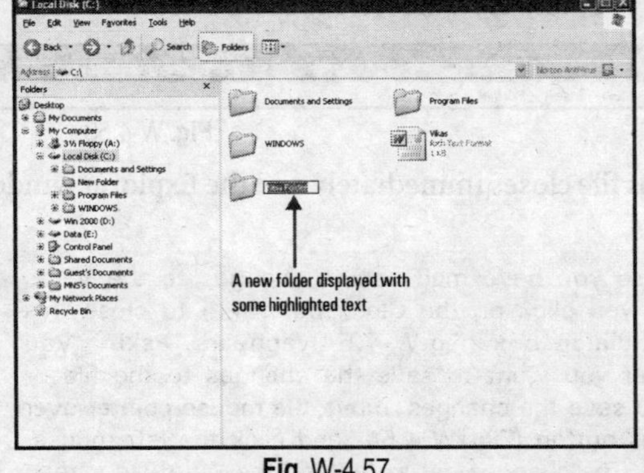

Fig. W-4.57

Fig. W-4.58

temp

Fig. W-4.59

Now to refresh your learning, do the following workout to create another folder.

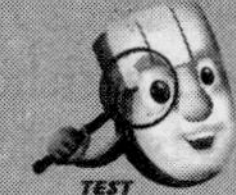

Create a folder, Temp1, under the Local Disk (C:).

- Begin with the Explorer window of the Local Disk (C:).
- Click the right mouse-button at an empty space in the Local Disk (C:) Contents box.
- Click on the New option in the short-cut menu.
- Finally click on the Folder option.
- Now type the name Temp1 from the keyboard.
- Click anywhere on the screen.

So, you have easily done the above workout. After the workout, your **Local Disk (C:)** will resemble the following figure. It now has two folders, **temp** and **Temp1**, and a file, **Vikas**.

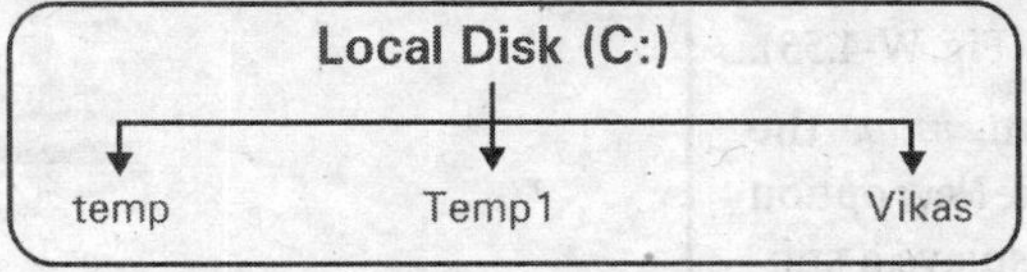

Remember, your **Local Disk (C:)** will show only these three contents if doesn't have any other program folder or files. Otherwise, it would be like Fig. W-4.50 or Fig. W-4.57.

Copying a File

You never forget to keep duplicate copies of your important documents. These copies save you from trouble when the original documents are lost or get damaged. Similarly, a computer file may also get corrupted. This corruption will make you lose important information stored in it. The best solution then is to have more than one copy of your important files in computer.

You can have a duplicate copy of your file in a different folder under the same name or a different name. You can also make its duplicate copy in its original folder but with a different name.

Let us now make a duplicate copy of the **Vikas** file, present under the **Local Disk (C:)**. We will also store it inside a folder, say, **temp**. To do the desired task, we proceed in the following way:

1. Start with the Explorer window of **My Computer** (Fig. W-4.44). In the **Folders** box of this window, *move* the mouse-pointer over the **Local Disk (C:)** and *click* the left mouse-button.

2. When the contents of the **Local Disk (C:)** get displayed in the **Contents** box, *move* the mouse-pointer over the **Vikas** file and *click* the left mouse-button once to highlight it (Fig. W-4.60).

3. Now, *move* the mouse-pointer over the **Edit** option on the Menu bar, and *click* the left mouse-button. Immediately, a pull-down menu appears (Fig. W-4.60).

4. Inside the pull-down menu, *move* the mouse-pointer over the **Copy** option (Fig. W-4.60) and *click* the left mouse-button. Now, your computer has made a copy of the **Vikas** file, and it awaits your instruction to paste it at a location of your choice.

5. To copy the **Vikas** file to the **temp** folder, you have to locate the folder in the **Contents** box.

6. After locating the **temp** folder, *move* the mouse-pointer over it and *double-click* the left mouse-button. Immediately, the empty **temp** folder opens on the screen (Fig. W-4.61). The **temp** folder is empty because we have not stored any files in it.

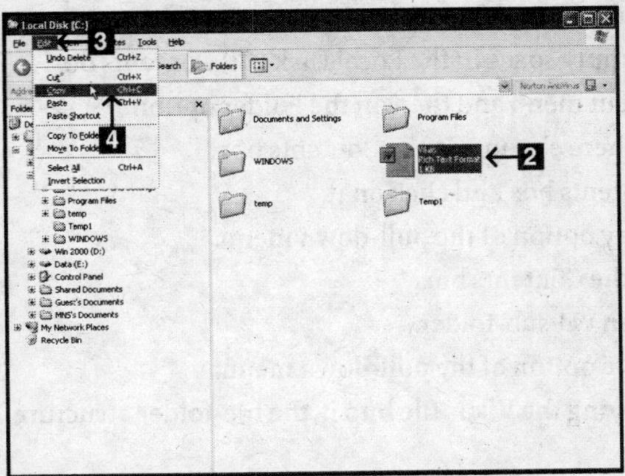

Fig. W-4.60

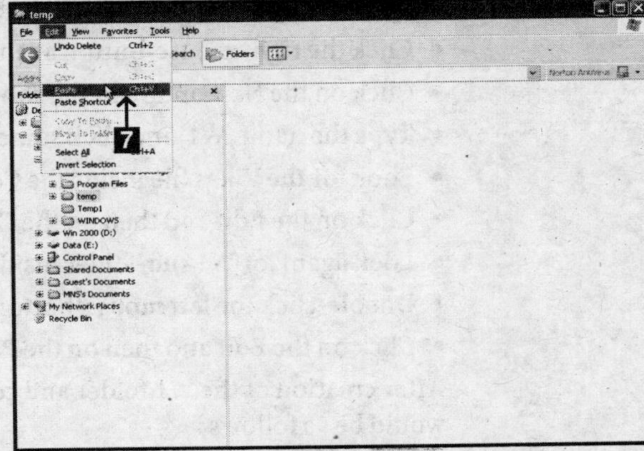

Fig. W-4.61

7. Now *click* the left mouse-button on the **Edit** option of the Menu bar of the **temp** window. In the pull-down menu that appears, *move* the mouse pointer to the **Paste** option and *click* the left mouse-button (Fig. W-4.61). Instantly, the **Vikas** file gets copied inside the **temp** folder. Now the **temp** folder's **Contents** box displays the **Vikas** file (Fig. W-4.62).

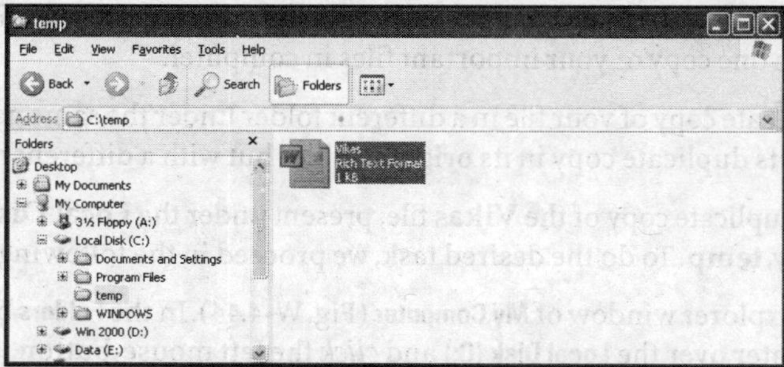

Fig. W-4.62

After making a duplicate copy of the **Vikas** file and storing it in the **temp** folder, your file-folder structure will be as follows:

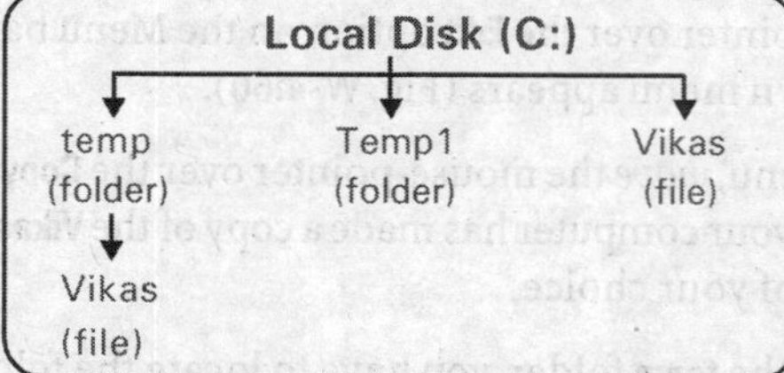

Now to refresh your learning, do the following workout to create another folder and copy a file into it.

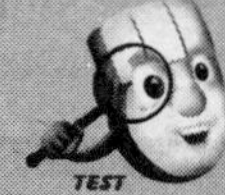

Create a new folder W1 under the Local Disk (C:) and copy a file, say Vikas, into it. Also draw the file-folder structure.

- Begin with the Explorer window of Local Disk (C:).
- Click the right mouse-button at an empty space in the Local Disk (C:) Contents box.
- Click on the New option in the shortcut menu and then on the Folder option.
- Type the name, W1, and click somewhere else inside the Contents box.
- Look for the Vikas file inside the Contents box and click on it.
- Click on the Edit and then on the Copy option of the pull-down menu.
- Look again for W1 sub-folder inside the Contents box.
- Double-click the left mouse-button on W1 sub-folder.
- Click on the Edit and then on the Paste option of the pull-down menu.

After creation of the W1 folder and copying the Vikas file into it, the file-folder structure would be as follows :

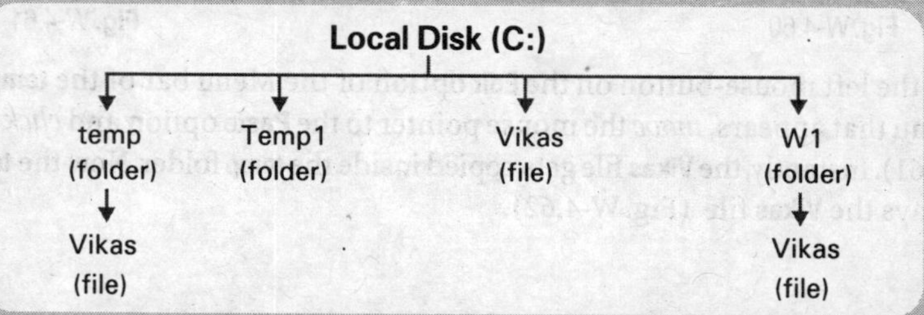

Renaming a File

You can change the name of a file to a more suitable one, which gives you precise indication about its contents. Such a name makes it easy for you to search the file later on. In Windows 98/2000/Me/XP, you can use up to 255 characters to name a file. Some of the characters which cannot be used in a file name are \/:*? | "<or>. If you use a dot (.) in the file name, the letters after the dot would be considered as the file extension. For example, files made in the Word program have a **.doc** extension.

Fig. W-4.62 shows the **Vikas** file copied into the **temp** folder. Let us now rename it as **Sachin** through the following steps:

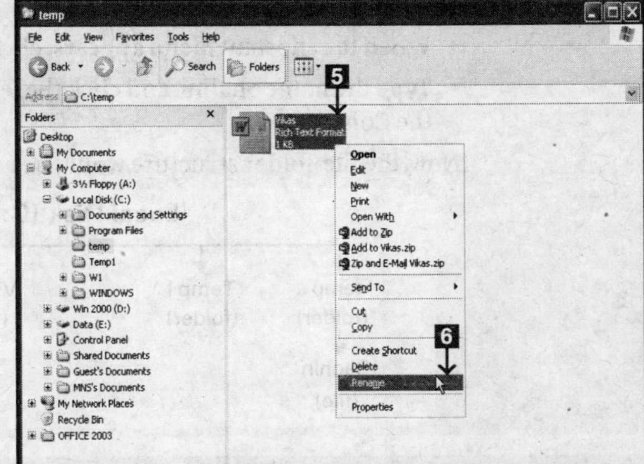

Fig. W-4.63

1. Start with the Explorer window of **My Computer**. First, to search the **temp** folder, *locate* the **Local Disk (C:)** in the **My Computer Folders** box.
2. *Move* the mouse-pointer on the plus sign(⊞) beside the **Local Disk C**: and *click* the left mouse-button. Instantly, the **Local Disk C**: contents get displayed in the **Contents** box.
3. If the **temp** folder is not visible, use the down-arrow scroll button (⌄) of the **Contents** box to locate it.
4. On locating the **temp** folder, *double-click* the left mouse-button on it. Instantly, the **temp** folder opens up displaying its contents, i.e. the **Vikas** file, inside the **Contents** box (Fig. W-4.63).
5. Now, *move* the mouse-pointer over the **Vikas** file (Fig. W-4.63), and *click* the right mouse-button just once. Immediately, a shortcut menu appears (Fig. W-4.63).
6. In the shortcut menu, *move* the mouse-pointer over the **Rename** option (Fig. W-4.63) and *click* the left mouse-button just once.
7. The file name **Vikas** gets highlighted (Fig. W-4.64). Now, *type* the new name **Sachin.** The new name overwrites the old one (Fig. W-4.65).
8. *Click* the left mouse-button anywhere in the **Contents** box to save this file with the new name **Sachin.** Now, your file-folder structure will be:

Vikas

Fig. W-4.64

7

Sachin

Fig. W-4.65

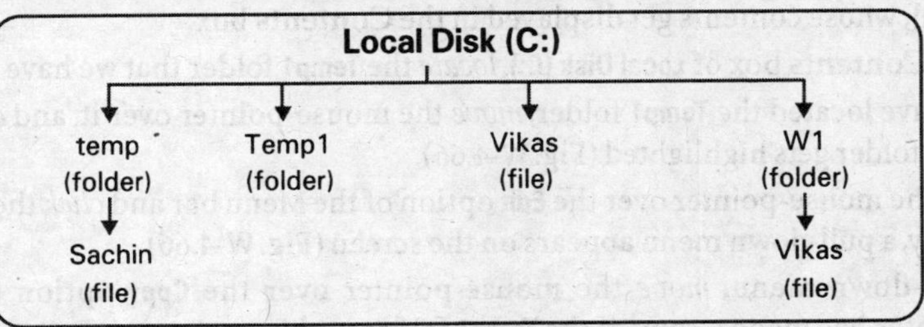

Now, to refresh our understanding of the renaming procedure, let us do the following workout.

Inside the W1 folder, rename file Vikas to Shalini. Also draw the file-folder structure.

- Begin with the Explorer window of the Local Disk (C:).
- In the Contents box of the Local Disk (C:), locate the W1 folder.
- Double-click the left mouse-button on the W1 folder.
- Move the mouse-pointer over the Vikas file in the Contents box.
- Click the right mouse-button on it.
- When the shortcut menu appears, click on the Rename option.
- Type the name Shalini, and click the left mouse-button anywhere inside the Contents box.

Now, the file-folder structure would be as follows:

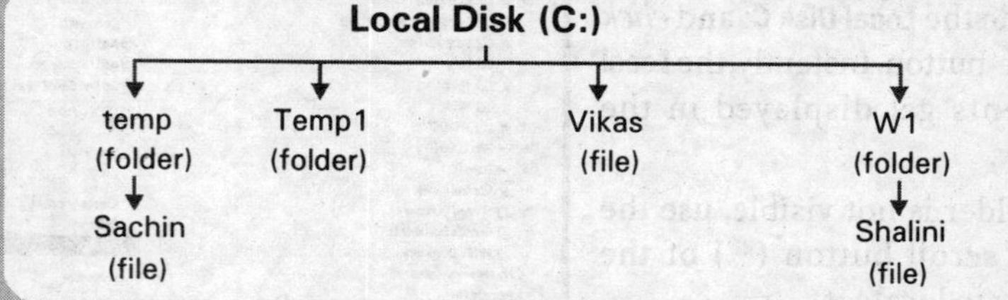

Copying a folder

When you copy a folder or sub-folder or sub-sub-folder to a new location, all its contents also get copied with it. Let us copy the **Temp1** folder to the **temp** folder. In our case, both these folders reside in the **Local Disk** (C:). To do the folder copying, we proceed in the following way. For our current task and other tasks in this chapter, we will mostly work in the Explorer window of the Local Disk (C:). You have to master the steps needed to open this important window. So, read carefully and practice the method of opening the Explorer window of the Local Disk (C:) described below.

1. We assume that you have gone through the last workout.
2. Start with the Explorer window of **My Computer.** In the **Folders** box of this window, locate the **Local Disk (C:)** and *move* the mouse-pointer over its plus sign (⊞). Then *click* the left mouse button. The plus sign (⊞) changes to the minus (⊟) sign. The **My Computer** window changes to the Explorer window of the **Local Disk (C:)**, whose contents get displayed in the **Contents** box.
3. Now in the **Contents** box of **Local Disk** (C:), *locate* the **Temp1** folder that we have to copy.
4. Once you have located the **Temp1** folder, *move* the mouse-pointer over it, and *click* the left mouse-button. The folder gets highlighted (Fig. W-4.66).
5. Now, *move* the mouse-pointer over the **Edit** option of the Menu bar and *click* the left mouse-button. Immediately, a pull-down menu appears on the screen (Fig. W-4.66).
6. In the pull-down menu, *move* the mouse-pointer over the **Copy** option (Fig. W-4.66). Now your computer has made a copy of the **Temp1** folder, and it awaits your instruction to paste it at a location of your choice.

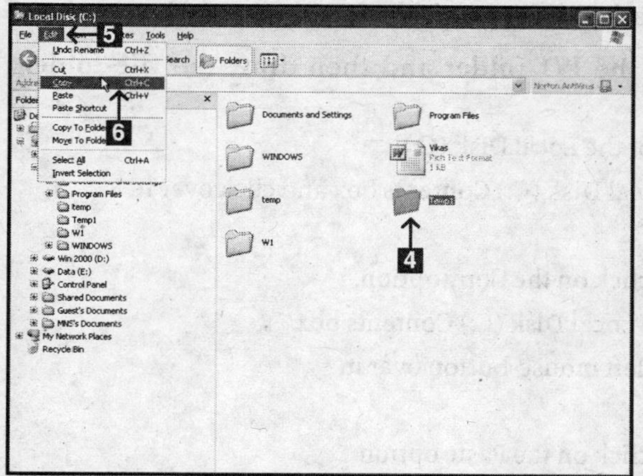

Fig. W-4.66

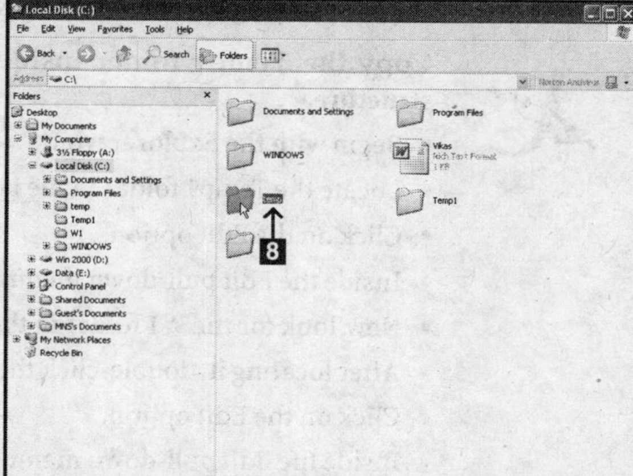

Fig. W-4.67

7. Now in the **Contents** box, *locate* the **temp** folder where you have to paste **Temp1** .
8. After finding the **temp** folder, *move* the mouse-pointer over it and *double-click* the left mouse-button (Fig.W-4.67). Immediately the contents of the **temp** folder, i.e. the **Sachin** file, get displayed in the **Contents** box.
9. You are now ready to paste the copied folder, i.e. **Temp1**. So *click* on the **Edit** Menu bar option. A pull-down menu gets displayed on the screen.
10. Inside the pull-down menu, *move* the mouse-pointer over the **Paste** option, and *click* the left mouse-button. Instantly, the **Temp1** folder gets copied into the **temp** folder (Fig. W-4.68).

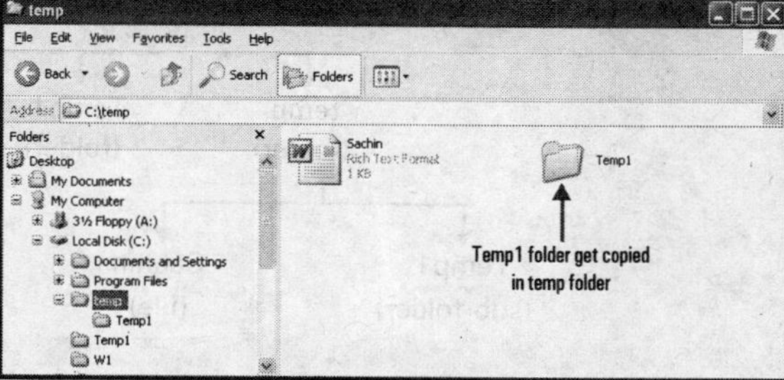

Fig. W-4.68

Now, your file-folder structure would be as follows:

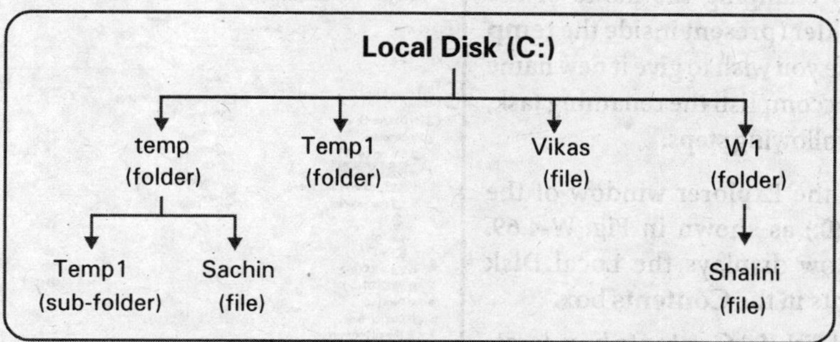

Similarly, you can copy a sub-sub-folder or a sub-sub-sub-folder and so on.

Now to refresh your learning, do the following workout to copy a folder into another folder.

Copy the Temp1 folder inside the W1 folder and then draw the file-folder structure.

- Begin with the Explorer window of the Local Disk (C:)
- Locate the Temp1 folder in the Local Disk (C:) Contents box and click over it.
- Click on the Edit option.
- Inside the Edit pull-down menu, click on the Copy option.
- Now, look for the W1 folder in the Local Disk (C:) Contents box.
- After locating it, double-click the left mouse-button over it.
- Click on the Edit option.
- Inside the Edit pull-down menu, click on the Paste option.

The file-folder structure would be as follows:

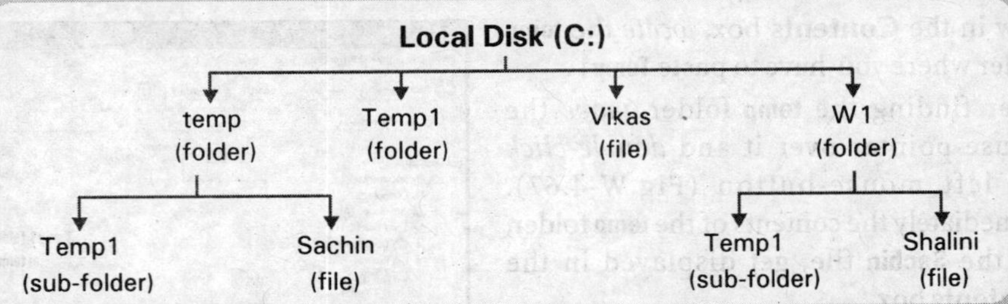

Renaming a Folder (or a sub-folder)

Suppose, you wish to delete the contents of a sub-folder and store new files into it. In such a case, the name of that sub-folder also needs to be changed so as to enable you easily identify its changed contents by its new name. Just as you renamed a file, you can also rename a sub-folder.

Let us now try changing the name of the **Temp1** sub-folder (present inside the **temp** folder). Suppose you wish to give it new name **Accounts.** To accomplish the renaming task, undertake the following steps:

1. Start with the Explorer window of the **Local Disk (C:)** as shown in Fig. W-4.69. This window displays the Local Disk (C:) contents in the **Contents** box.
2. In the **Local Disk (C:) Contents** box, *locate* the **temp** folder.

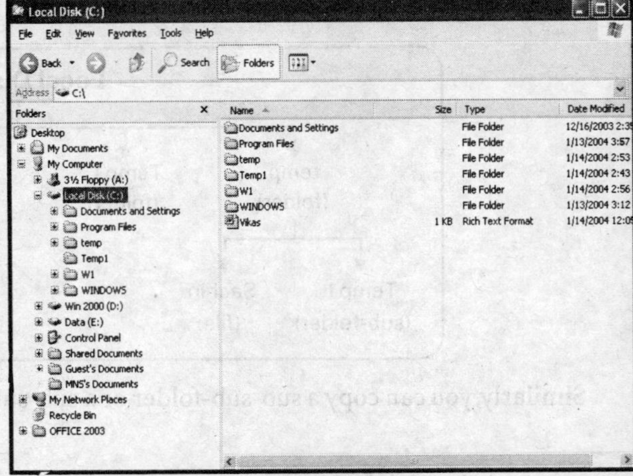

Fig. W-4.69

3. Now, *move* the mouse-pointer over the **temp** folder and *double-click* the left mouse-button. The **Local Disk (C:)** window changes into the **temp** folder window. The **temp** folder contents, i.e. the **Sachin** file and the **Temp1** sub-folder, get displayed inside its **contents** box (Fig. W-4.70).

4. In the **Contents** box of **temp** folder window, *move* the mouse-pointer to the **Temp1** sub-folder, and *click* the right mouse-button once. A shortcut menu appears (Fig. W-4.70).

5. Inside the shortcut menu, *move* the mouse-pointer over the **Rename** option (Fig. W-4.70) and *click* the left mouse-button. The **Temp1** sub-folder gets highlighted instantly (Fig. W-4.70).

6. Now *type* the new name **Accounts** from the keyboard and *click* the left mouse-button anywhere inside the **Contents** box (Fig. W-4.71).

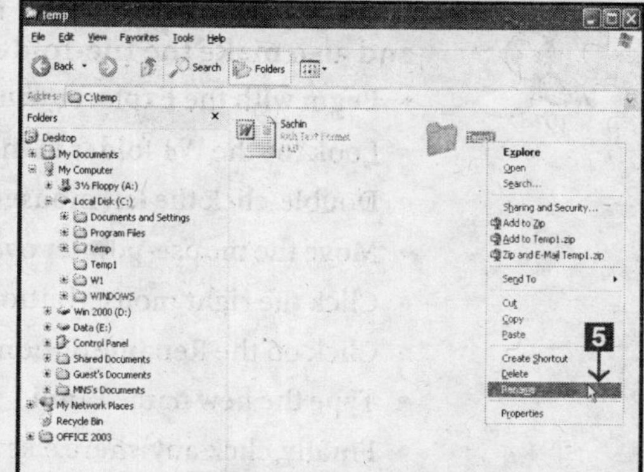

Fig. W-4.70

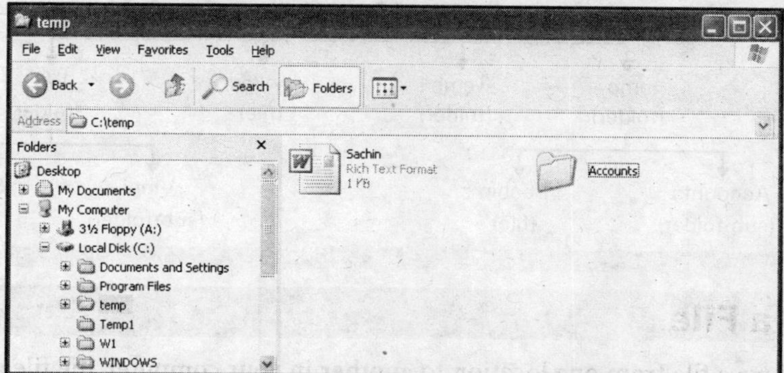

Fig. W-4.71

Now, the file-folder structure would be as follows:

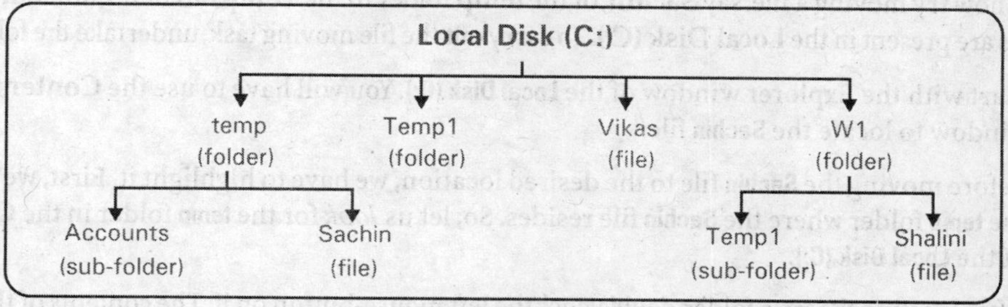

Do not try to rename the Local Disk (C:) as such an attempt can cause harm to the working of your computer.

Now to refresh your learning, do the following workout to rename a sub-folder.

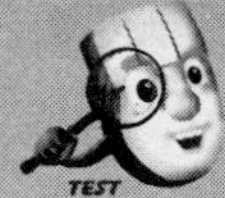

Change the name of the Temp1 sub-folder (inside the W1 folder) to Vinni and also make the file-folder structure?

- Begin with the Explorer window of the Local Disk (C:).
- Look for the W1 folder in the Local Disk (C:) Contents box.
- Double-click the left mouse-button over the W1 folder.
- Move the mouse-pointer over the Temp1 sub-folder.
- Click the right mouse-button.
- Click on the Rename option.
- Type the new name Vinni.
- Finally, click anywhere else inside the Contents box.

The file-folder structure will now be as follows:

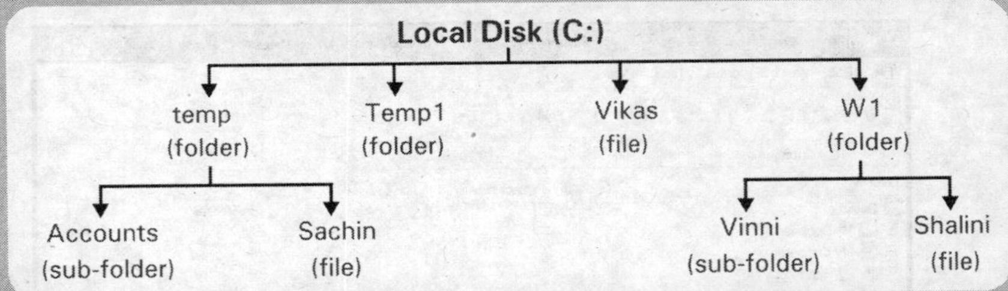

Moving a File

When you move a file from one location to another in your computer, the file gets deleted from its original place and moves to its new location. In other words, when you move a file, no duplicate copy of it is made.

Let us now try moving a file, say **Sachin**, of the **temp** folder to the **Temp1** folder. Both **temp** and **temp1** folders are present in the **Local Disk (C:)**. To carry out the file moving task, undertake the following steps:

1. Start with the Explorer window of the **Local Disk (C:)**. You will have to use the **Contents** box of this window to locate the **Sachin** file.
2. Before moving the **Sachin** file to the desired location, we have to highlight it. First, we should open the **temp** folder where the **Sachin** file resides. So, let us *look* for the **temp** folder in the **Contents** box of the **Local Disk (C:)**.
3. After locating the **temp** folder, *double-click* the left mouse-button on it. The contents of the **temp** folder get displayed in its **Contents** box (Fig. W-4.72). In this box you can see the **Sachin** file.
4. The next task is to *locate* the **Temp1** folder in the **Folders** box of the **Local Disk (C:)**.

5. After locating the **Temp1** folder, *move* the mouse-pointer over the **Sachin** file, and *click* the left mouse-button. The file gets highlighted (Fig. W-4.73).

6. Keeping the left mouse-button *pressed* on the **Sachin** file, *drag* the file towards the **Folders** box. As you drag the file, you will see that a shadow of the file also moves along, into the **Folders** box (Fig. W-4.73).

7. The **Sachin** file, which in being dragged, has to be shifted to the **Temp1** folder. So, keeping the left mouse-button *pressed*, *place* the file over the **Temp1** folder in the **Folders** box (Fig. W-4.74).

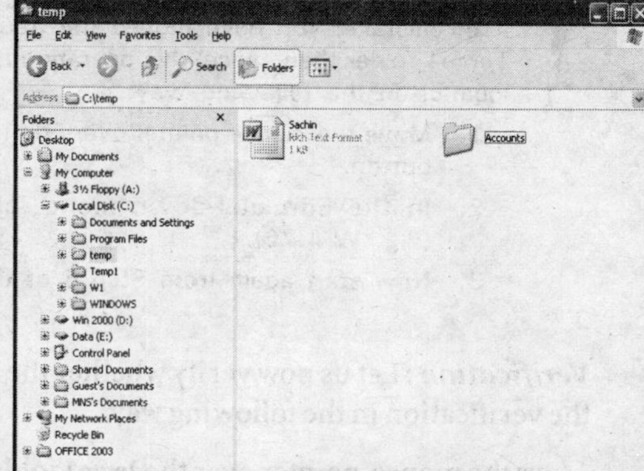

Fig. W-4.72

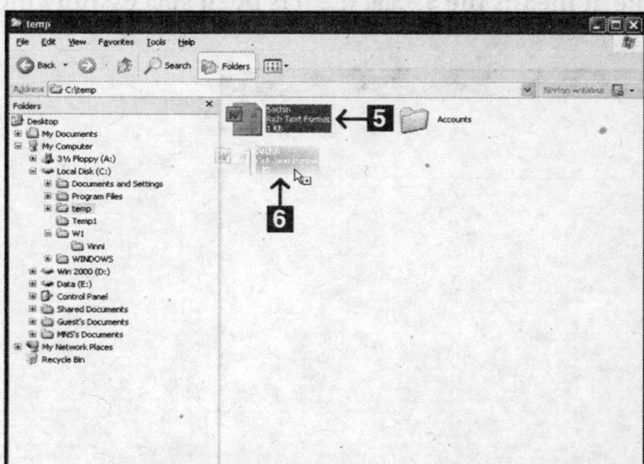

Fig. W-4.73

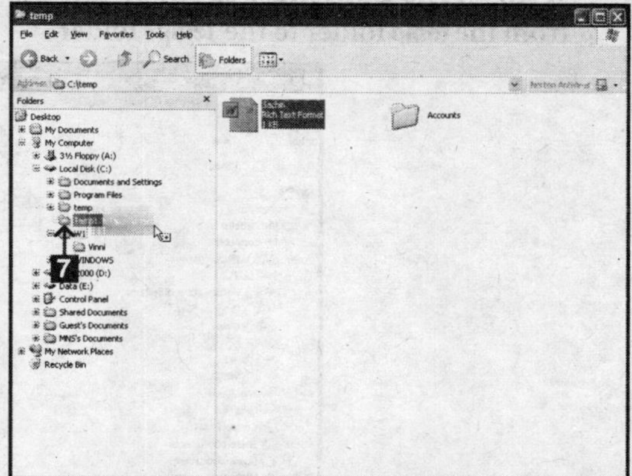

Fig. W-4.74

8. When the **Temp1** folder gets highlighted, *release* the left mouse-button. Now, the **Sachin** file disappears from the **Contents** box of the **temp** folder (Fig. W-4.75).

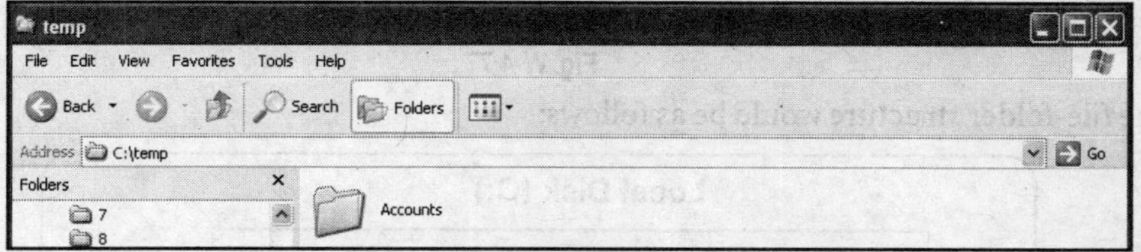

Fig. W-4.75

While dragging a file to the Temp1 sub-folder of the Folders box, sometimes you miss the target folder. It goes either up or down due to the shaky mouse movement. In that case, without releasing the left mouse-button, bring the file back into the Contents box. Then release the left mouse-button and again perform Steps 5 to 9 given under the heading 'Moving a File.'

If by mistake, you have moved the Sachin file into a folder other than the Temp1 folder then cancel this operation and move the file back to its previous location in the following way:

1. Move the mouse-pointer over Edit menu option and click the left mouse-button.
2. In the Edit pull-down menu, click over the Undo Move option (Fig. W-4.76).
3. Now start again from Step 5 of the topic 'Moving a file.'

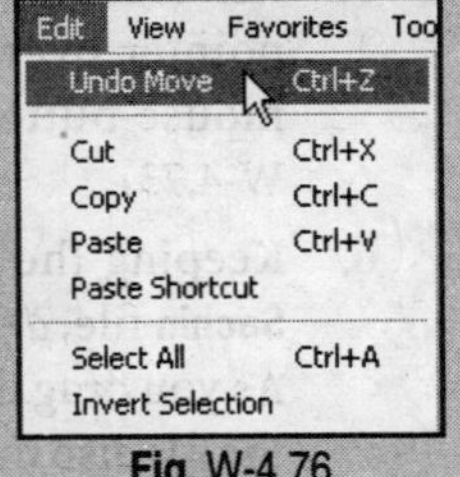

Fig. W-4.76

Verification : Let us now verify whether the **Sachin** file has really moved into the **Temp1** folder. We will do the verification in the following way:

Move the mouse-pointer over the **Temp1** folder in the **Folders** box (Fig. W-4.74). Then *click* the left mouse-button on it. Immediately, the **Temp1** folder opens up to display its contents in the **Contents** box (Fig. W-4.77). The **Contents** box shows the **Sachin** file. It means the **Sachin** file has been successfully moved from the **temp** folder to the **Temp1** folder.

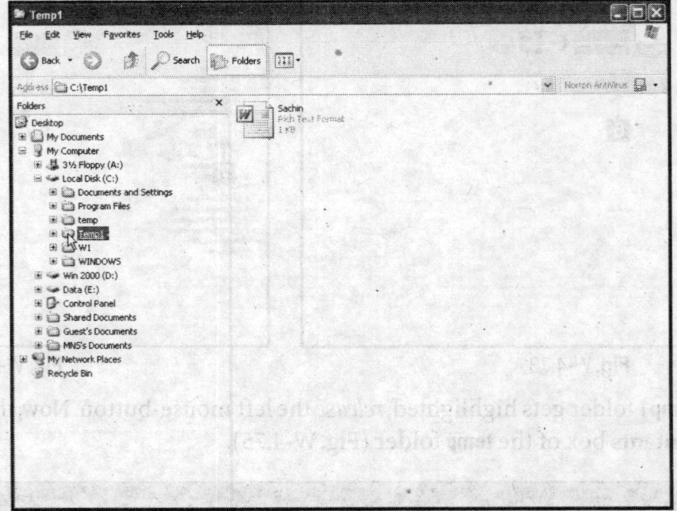

Fig. W-4.77

Now the file-folder structure would be as follows:

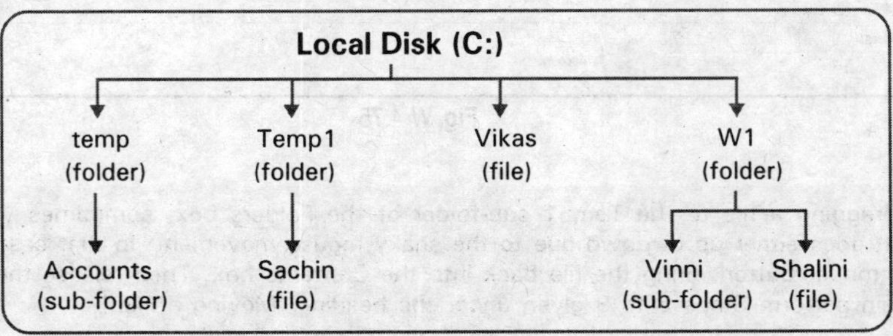

Now to refresh your learning, do the following workout to move a file into a sub-folder.

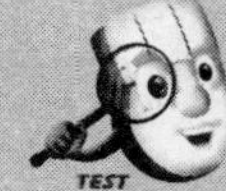

Move the Shalini file to the Vinni sub-folder. The Shalini file and Vinni sub-folder are present in the W1 folder. Also make the file-folder structure at the end of this workout.

- Begin with the Explorer window of the Local Disk (C:).
- Locate the W1 folder in the Contents box of Local Disk (C:).
- Double-click the left mouse-button on the W1 folder.
- Move the mouse-pointer over the Shalini file.
- Click the left mouse-button on the file to highlight it.
- Keeping the left mouse-button pressed, drag the Shalini file into the Vinni sub-folder, which is also present inside the Contents box.
- When the Vinni sub-folder gets highlighted, release the left mouse-button.

The file-folder structure would be as follows:

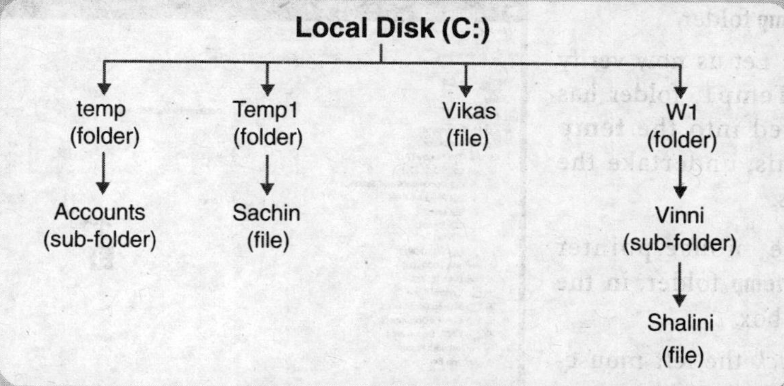

- To verify whether the Shalini file has really moved into the Vinni sub-folder, move the mouse-pointer over the Vinni sub-folder and double-click the left mouse-button.

Moving a Folder

A folder or sub-folder can be moved into another folder or sub-folder or to any level below it. When you move a folder or sub-folder to a new location, all its contents also move to that location.

Do not attempt to move the Local Disk (C:) as it cannot be moved into any folder or sub-folder.

Let us now move the **Temp1** folder into the **temp** folder. Both these folders are present in the **Local Disk** (C:). Let us undertake the desired moving operation through the following steps:

1. Start with the Explorer window of the **Local Disk (C:)**. In the **Contents** box of this window, you will see the **temp** and **Temp1** folders (Fig. W-4.78).

2. Now, *click* the left mouse button on the **Temp1** folder to highlight it (Fig. W-4.78).

3. Now *press* the left mouse-button, and *keeping it pressed, drag* the **Temp1** folder over the **temp** folder (also present in **Contents** box) (Fig. W-4.79). As you move the **Temp1** sub-folder, its shadow moves along with the mouse-pointer.

4. When the **temp** folder gets highlighted, *release* the mouse-button. Immediately, the **Temp1** sub-folder disappears from the **Contents** box as it has moved into the **temp** folder.

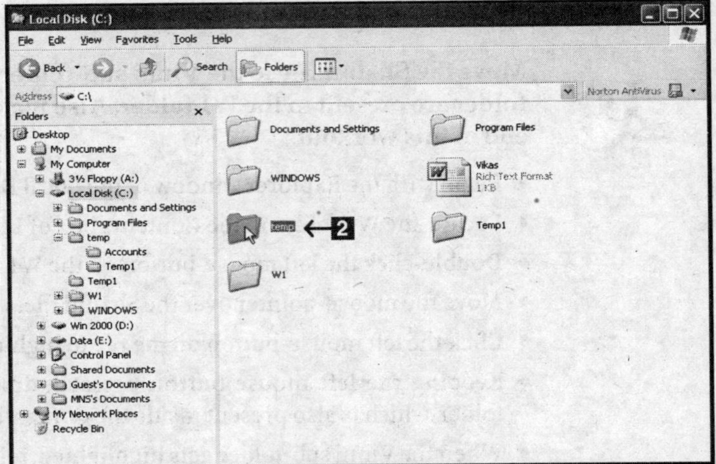

Fig. W-4.78

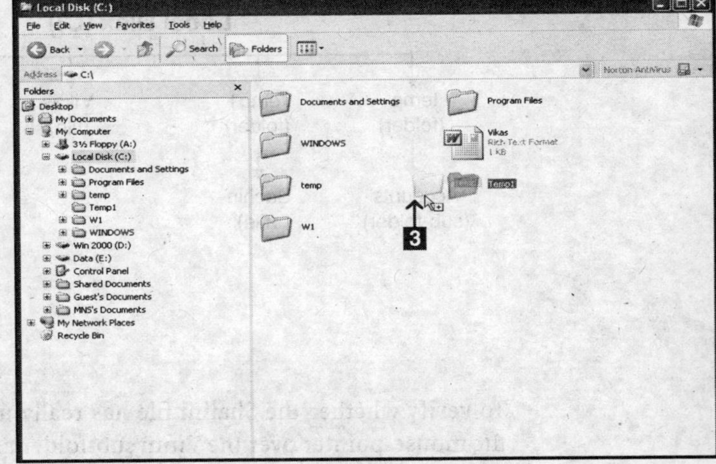

Fig. W-4.79

Verification : Let us now verify whether the **Temp1** folder has actually moved into the **temp** folder. For this, undertake the following steps:

1. *Move* the mouse-pointer over the **temp** folder, in the **Contents** box.

2. *Double-click* the left mouse-button. The **temp** folder opens up displaying its contents in the **Contents** box (Fig. W-4.80).

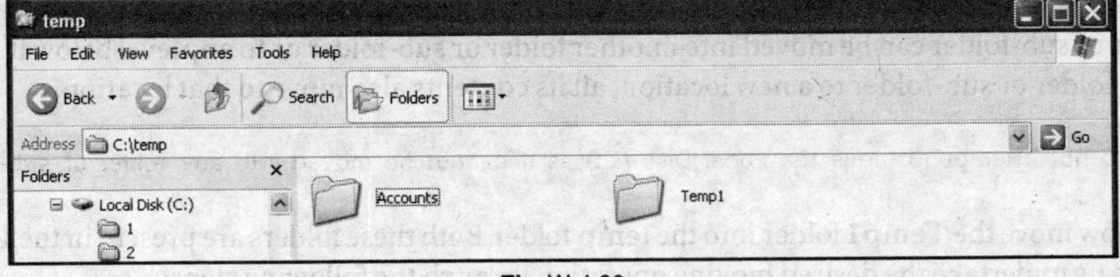

Fig. W-4.80

Inside the **Contents** box, you will notice the **Temp1** folder. This means that the **Temp1** folder has been successfully moved to the **temp** folder.

3. The file-folder structure in the previous workout showed that the **Temp1** folder contained the **Sachin** file. Now to see whether this file has also moved to the new location, *move* the mouse-pointer over the **Temp1** sub-folder displayed inside the **Contents** box (Fig. W-4.80) and *double-click* the left mouse-button. You will notice that the **Sachin** file is displayed inside the **Temp1** sub-folder.

   The file-folder structure would now be as follows :

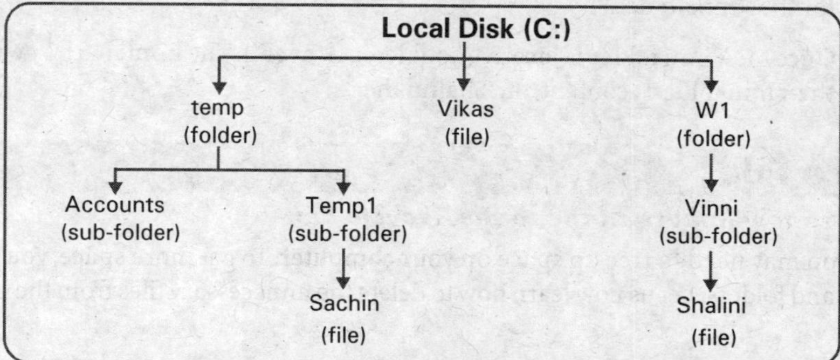

Now, to refresh your learning, do the following work out to convert a sub-folder into a folder.

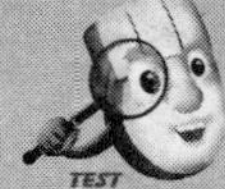

Make the Vinni sub-folder a main folder in the Local Disk (C:). Also make the file-folder structure.

- Begin with the Explorer window of the Local Disk C:.
- Look for the W1 folder in the Contents box of the Local Disk (C:).
- After locating it, double-click the left mouse-button on it.
- Move the mouse-pointer over the Vinni sub-folder in the W1 folder Contents box.
- Click the left mouse-button on the Vinni sub-folder to highlight it.
- Keeping the left mouse-button pressed, drag the Vinni sub-folder into the Folders box.
- Then move it over the Local Disk (C:).
- When the Local Disk (C:) gets highlighted, release the left mouse-button. The Vinni sub-folder now becomes the Vinni folder.

Now, the file-folder structure would be as shown below:

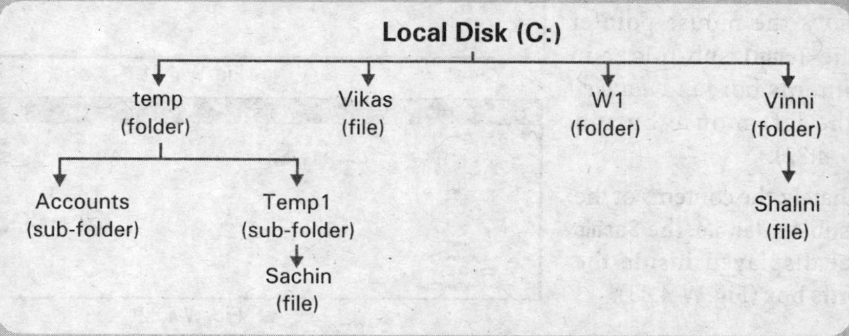

- To verify the new location of the Vinni folder, move the mouse-pointer over the plus sign (+) beside the Local Disk (C:) in the Folders box and click the left mouse-button over it.
- Use the down-arrow scroll button (⌄) of the Contents box of the Local Disk (C:) to look for the Vinni folder.
- Once the Vinni folder is located, double-click over it. The Contents box will then display the Vinni folder's content, the Shalini file.

Deleting a File

(How to Move an unimportant file to the Recycle Bin)

Many a time, you may need to free up space on your computer. To get more space, you need to remove unwanted files and folders. Let us now learn how to delete the unnecessary files from the hard disk of your computer.

Let us remove the **Sachin** file present inside the **Temp1** sub-folder. To do so, undertake the following steps:

1. As you know, the **Temp1** sub-folder is present in the **temp** folder of the **Local Disk (C:)**, we start with the Explorer window of the **Local Disk (C:)**. The **Contents** box of this window displays the contents of the **Local Disk (C:)** as shown in Fig. W-4.81.
2. Now *look* for the **temp** folder in the **contents** box and *move* the mouse-pointer over it (Fig. W-4.81).
3. Then *double-click* the left mouse-button. Immediately, the **temp** folder's contents get displayed in its **Contents** box (Fig. W-4.82).
4. Now *move* the mouse-pointer over the **Temp1** sub-folder in the **Contents** box, and *double-click* the left mouse-button (Fig. W-4.82).
5. Immediately, the contents of the **Temp1** sub-folder, i.e. the **Sachin** file, get displayed inside the **Contents** box (Fig. W-4.83).

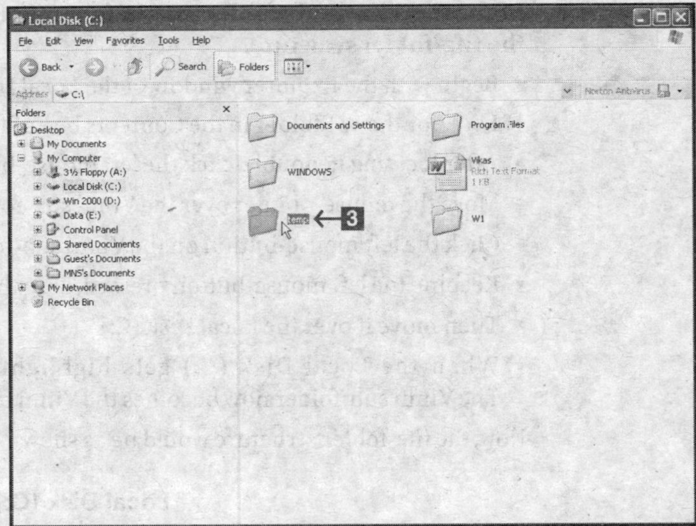

Fig. W-4.81

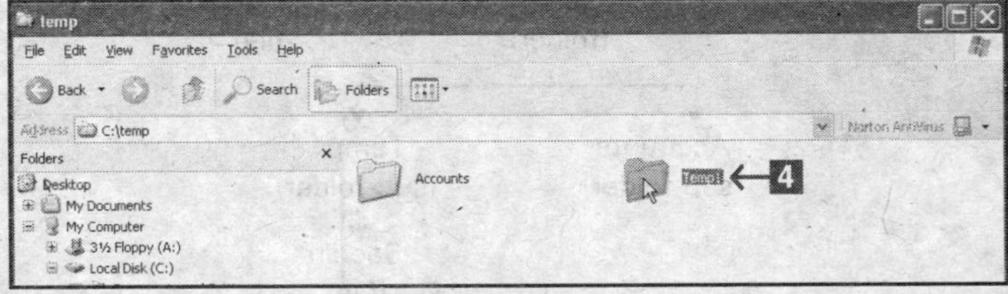

Fig. W-4.82

6. Now, *move* the mouse-pointer over the **Sachin** file and *click* the left mouse-button just once to highlight it (Fig. W-4.83).
7. Next, *click* the left mouse-button on the **File** option of the Menu bar. Instantly, a pull-down menu appears (Fig. W-4.84).
8. Inside the **File** pull-down menu, *move* the mouse-pointer over the **Delete** option (Fig. W-4.84) and *click* the left mouse-button. Immediately, a **Confirm File Delete** dialog box (Fig. W-4.85) appears on the screen.

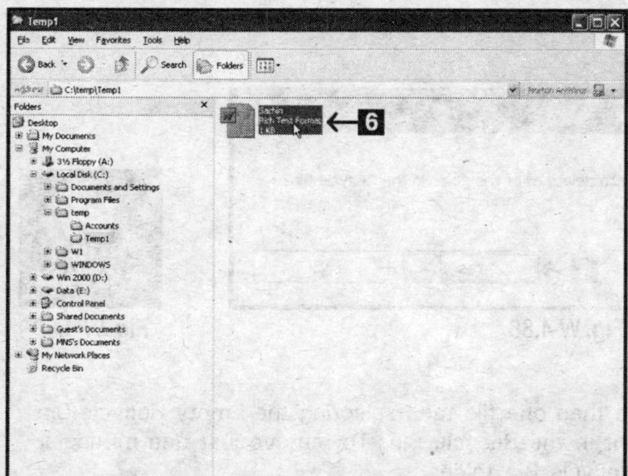

Fig. W-4.83

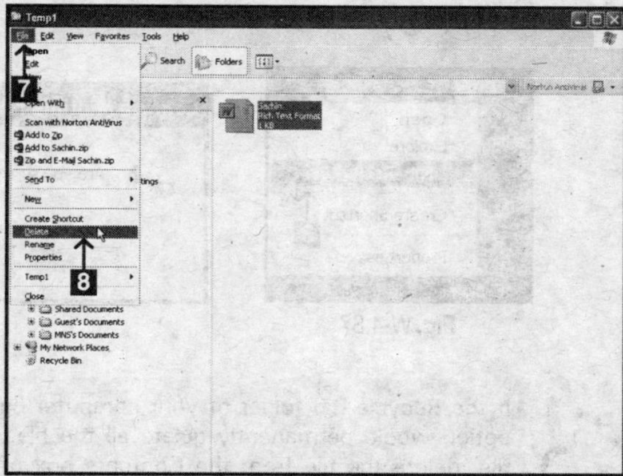

Fig. W-4.84

9. Finally, *click* on the **Yes** button in the **Confirm File Delete** box (Fig. W-4.85). The **Sachin** file now disappears from the **Temp 1 Contents** box which means it has been successfully removed to the **Recycle Bin**. Similarly, you can delete any folder and send it in the recycle bin. However, for deleting a folder, you may not need to follow steps 1 to 9 listed above. You can simply select a folder by clicking over it and then press the delete key from the keyboard. A message box similar to Fig. W-4.85 appears on the screen. Click over the yes button to proceed ahead and delete the folder.

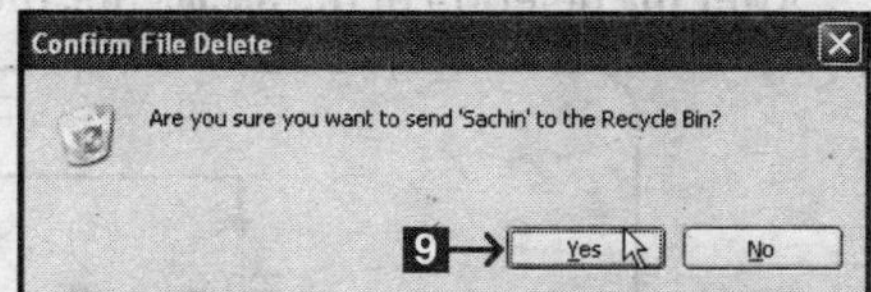

Fig. W-4.85

To prevent accidental removal of any important file, Windows provides the Recycle Bin. Any file, when deleted, gets automatically shifted to the Recycle Bin. It means the deleted file has not been removed permanently from the computer's memory. The main advantage of Recycle Bin is that you can retrieve a deleted file from it, if you require it again.

Emptying the Recycle Bin

To remove a deleted file permanently from your computer, you have to remove it from the **Recycle Bin**. Let us now remove the **Sachin** file from the **Recycle Bin**. To do so, undertake the following steps:

Fig. W-4.86

1. *Move* the mouse-pointer over the **Recycle Bin** icon on the **Desktop** (Fig. W-4.86).

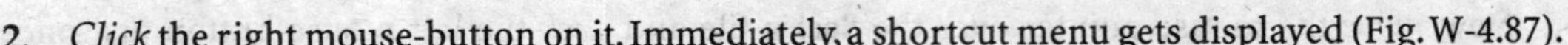

2. *Click* the right mouse-button on it. Immediately, a shortcut menu gets displayed (Fig. W-4.87).
3. Inside the shortcut menu, *move* the mouse-pointer over the **Empty Recycle Bin** option (Fig. W-4.87), and *click* the left mouse-button.

   Immediately, the **Confirm File Delete** dialog box appears on the screen (Fig. W-4.88), asking you to confirm whether the items, including the **Sachin** file, have to be erased.
4. Inside the **Confirm File Delete** box, *move* the mouse-pointer over the **Yes** button (Fig. W-4.88) and *click* the left mouse-button. Instantly, the **Sachin** file is removed from the **Recycle Bin**, which becomes empty (Fig. W-4.89).

Fig. W-4.87

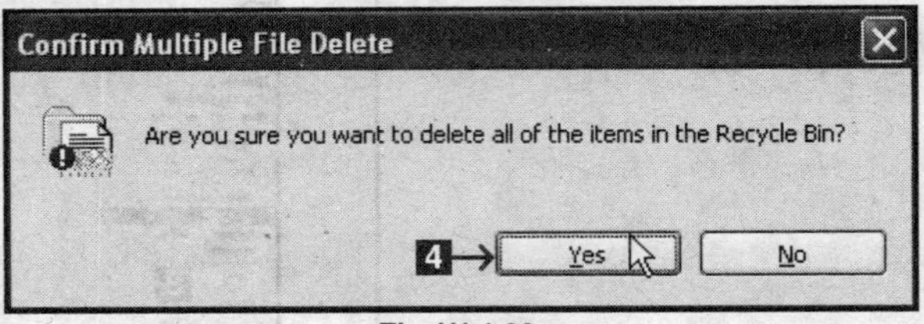

Fig. W-4.88

Fig. W-4.89

NOTE: If the Recycle Bin folder of your computer has more than one file then selecting the Empty Recycle Bin option would permanently delete all the files present in the Recycle Bin. To remove just one particular file, delete the file from the Contents box of the Recycle Bin folder.

After the deletion of the **Sachin** file, the file-folder structure would be as follows:

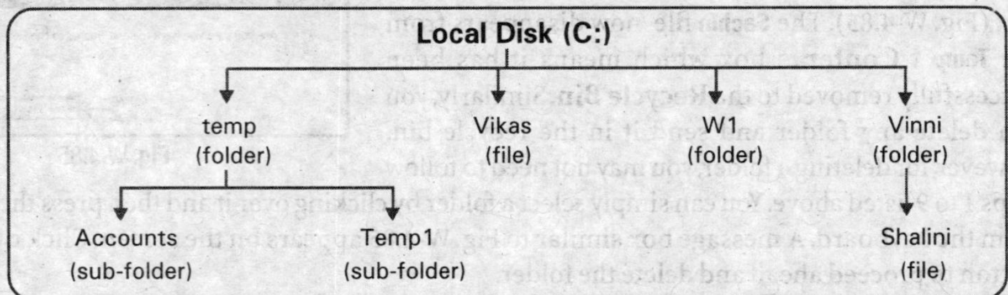

Closing Explorer and Quitting Windows

So, after reading this chapter, now you understand the importance of the Explorer program in Windows XP. Let us now quit this program and turn off the computer through the following steps.

1. *Move* the mouse-pointer over the **Close** button (☒) on the **Title bar** of the **Local Disk C**: Explorer window (Fig. W-4.90), and *click* the left mouse-button. Immediately, the Explorer program closes and the **Desktop** is displayed on the screen.

Fig. W-4.90

2. *Press* the left mouse-button once on the **Start** button (start) present on the **Taskbar**. Immediately, a push-up menu appears (Fig. W-4.91).
3. Inside the push-up menu, *click* over the **Turn Off Computer** option (Fig. W-4.91). Immediately, a **Turn Off Computer** dialog box gets displayed (Fig. W-4.92).
4. Inside the box, *click* the left mouse-button on the **Turn Off** option (Fig. W-4.92). Soon, your monitor screen goes blank. Then turn off the UPS supply to your computer and take a break.

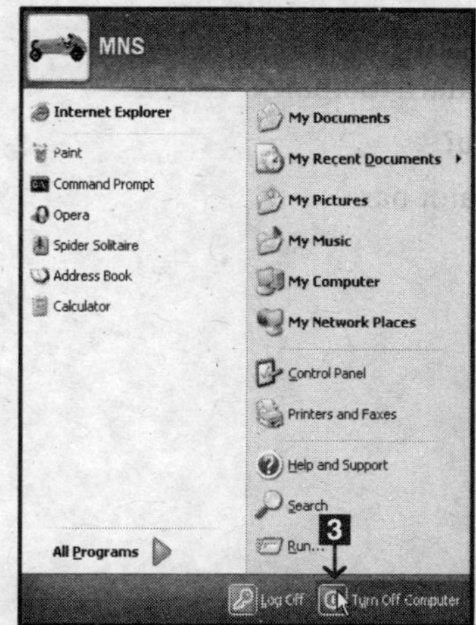

Fig. W-4.91

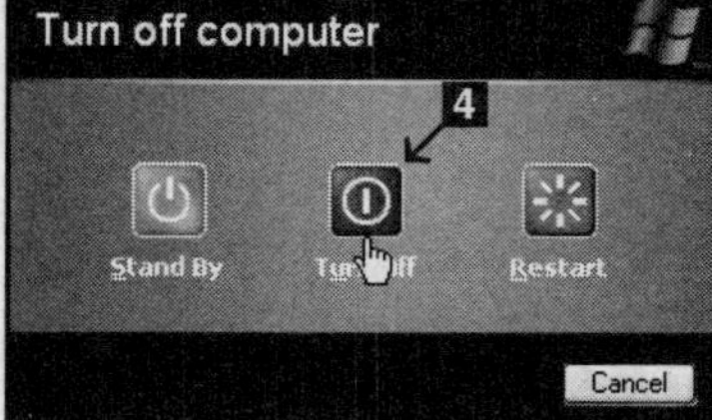

Fig. W-4.92

Summary

- The Windows Explorer is a program which enables you to systematically arrange and access various files, folders and disk drives on your computer.
- The Explorer window is divided into two parts – The left part of the Explorer window is known as Folders box whereas the right part of the Explorer window is known as Contents box.
- The Folder box displays the icons for various folders and drives present on a computer. All folders and drives are displayed in the form of a folder tree. If you click on any icon in the folder tree, its contents get displayed inside the Contents box.
- The Folders box only displays folders and sub-folders. It does not display any file. To view any file of a particular folder, you have to take the help of the Contents box.
- The box in the right section of the Explorer window is called the Contents box. It shows the contents of a drive, a folder or an icon which is highlighted in the Folders box.

Exercise

Fill in the Blanks

1. When you save your file for the first time, you will see the ____________ box.
2. ____________ option is used for printing the pages.
3. The Copy option is present inside the __________ menu bar option.
4. _________ option creates a new file.
5. To type a capital letter, press _______________ key once to turn it ON.

Short Questions

1. Write a short note on Standard toolbar.
2. What is a pull-down menu?
3. Briefly describe the Indicator bar.
4. What is the Contents box?
5. What are sub-folders?

CHAPTER 5

Windows Accessories

IN THIS CHAPTER

- Opening the WordPad Program
- Entering and Editing Text in WordPad
- Saving and Closing a Document
- Quitting WordPad
- Printing a Document and Quitting Windows
- Opening the Paint program
- Selecting Tools and Colours
- Saving and Printing a Paint File
- Quitting the Paint Program
- Calculator and Closing Calculator
- Windows Media Player
- Opening the Windows Media Player
- Playing VCDs & DVDs
- Play Back Control Area
- Playing Movie in Full Screen Mode
- Changing the Appearance
- Closing the Windows Media Player
- Windows Movie Maker
- Opening Windows Movie Maker
- Importing Video in Windows Movie Maker
- Adding Clips to the Storyboard
- Adding Video and Transition Effects
- Playing Storyboard Clips
- Introduction to Digital Photography
- How to Select the Right Digital Camera
- Making Necessary Arrangements
- Working with Images
- Copying Photograph from the Digital Camera
- Copying Photograph to the Digital Camera
- Rename and Email a Photograph
- Deleting Picture from Digital Camera

Let us now explore the most exciting feature of Windows XP, i.e. the **Accessories** program. It consists of some very handy tools which are useful for everyone – from novices to professionals. The Accessories tools like **WordPad, Paintbrush, Calculator, Windows Media Player** and **Windows Movie Maker** will help you easily manage your common tasks as well as entertain you.

WordPad is a simple word processor program that is used to create documents such as letters and memos. It offers basic features for formatting the documents, such as boldfacing, italicizing and underlining the text. Further, it offers the opportunity to add new text to a document and remove the unwanted text. It also enables the user to move lines of text from one location to another inside the document. However, in comparison to WordPad, Microsoft Word is a better word processor with additional features. Microsoft Word is the most commonly used word processor.

Paintbrush may be used to draw pictures on your computer. You can draw and modify the pictures using the various tools provided in Paintbrush. The **Calculator** program of Windows performs various mathematical and scientific calculations easily. Two calculators are built into this program—Standard Calculator and Scientific Calculator.

The **Accessories** program also contains a **Notepad**. This is a text editor program, which is used for writing short letters, memos and create text file. However, while working in **Notepad**, formatting is difficult as it is a simple program for entering text. The Accessories program also contains the **Windows Media Player** program which is quite useful for playing music and watching movies. A new addition to the Accessories program is **Windows Movie Maker** that you can use to edit your videos and still pictures and convert them into a movie.

Opening the WordPad Program

As you know, **WordPad** is a simple word processor program incorporated in Windows XP, which can be used to create any number of simple documents. Some commands and procedures, used in the powerful word processor Microsoft Word, are also included in WordPad. One such feature is that we do not need to press the Enter key at the end of each line. The text you enter fits automatically into lines of equal length.

Before we start working with WordPad, let us learn to open it. Undertake the following steps to open the WordPad program.

1. *Switch on* your computer system.
2. After a few seconds, the logo of Windows XP appears on the screen and thereafter Windows XP **Desktop** is displayed on the screen.
3. *Click* on the **Start** button (start) on the **Taskbar**. Immediately, a push-up menu appears on the screen (Fig. W-5.1).
4. In this push-up menu, *move* the mouse-pointer over the **All Programs** option. Instantly, a sub-menu appears (Fig. W-5.1).

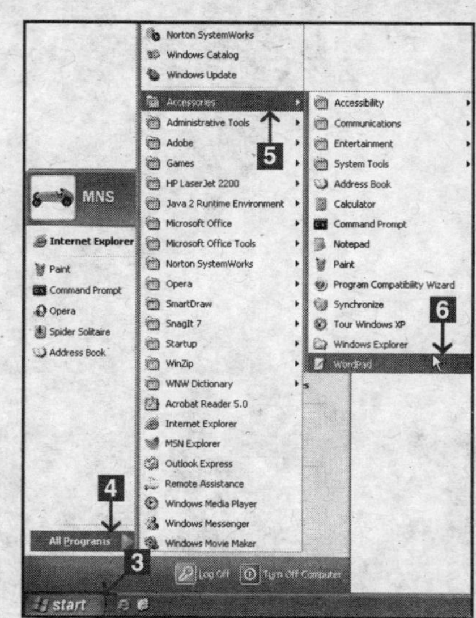

Fig. W-5.1

5. In the sub-menu, *move* the mouse-pointer over the **Accessories** option. Another sub-menu appears beside the **Accessories** option (Fig. W-5.1).
6. In the second sub-menu, *place* the mouse-pointer over the **WordPad** option, and *click* the left mouse-button. Instantly, the **WordPad** window (Fig. W-5.2) opens up on the screen.

Entering Text in WordPad

The newly opened WordPad window (Fig. 5.2) has a blinking cursor. In Fig. W-5.2, you also see important parts of the WordPad window like Menu bar, Standard toolbar, Title bar, Formatting toolbar, etc. The blinking cursor indicates that the WordPad is ready to accept text.

Now, type the text shown below:

MICROSOFT WINDOWS Me

MICROSOFT WINDOWS 2000

MICROSOFT WINDOWS XP

While typing the text, you must follow the steps given below:

- To type the text in capitals, *press* the **Caps Lock** key once. To type small letters, again *press* the **Caps Lock** key to turn it off.
- *Type* the first line of your text, **MICROSOFT WINDOWS Me.**
- To leave a space between two words, *press* the **Spacebar** key from the keyboard every time you finish typing a word. For example,

MICROSOFT WINDOWS Me.

- Before typing the next line, *press* the **Enter** key once. When the cursor jumps to the next line, start *typing* **MICROSOFT WINDOWS 2000.**
- Similarly, *press* the **Enter** key once again before typing the last line of the text, **MICROSOFT WINDOWS XP.**

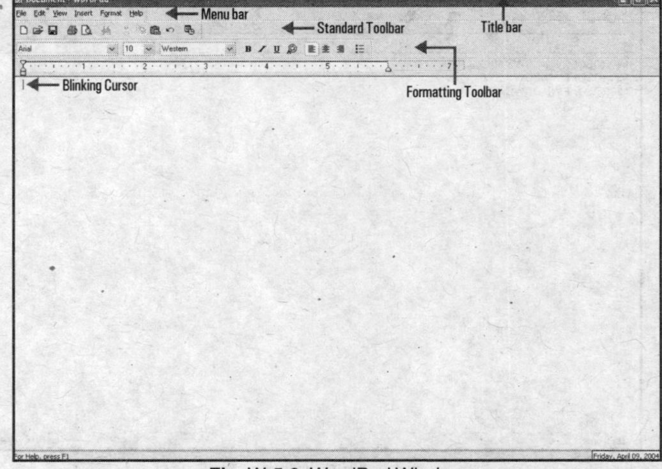

Fig. W-5.2: WordPad Window

- As you type, you may miss some text. Suppose, you have skipped the word **WINDOWS** from the third line which appears as **MICROSOFT XP**. You can insert this word by undertaking the following steps :

MICROSOFT 1 WINDOWS Me
MICROSOFT WINDOWS 2000
MICROSOFT XP

Fig. W-5.3

1. *Move* the mouse-pointer after the word **MICROSOFT** (Fig. W-5.3).
2. *Press* the left mouse-button once and release it. Immediately, you see a blinking cursor at that position (Fig. W-5.3).

MICROSOFT 3 WINDOWS Me
MICROSOFT WINDOWS 2000
MICROSOFT XP

Fig. W-5.4

3. Now *press* the **Spacebar** key once. You will see that a space gets inserted between the words **MICROSOFT** and **XP** (Fig. W-5.4).

MICROSOFT WINDOWS 4 Me
MICROSOFT WINDOWS 2000
MICROSOFT WINDOWS XP

Fig. W-5.5

4. Finally, *type* **WINDOWS** from the keyboard. As you see in Fig. W-5.5, the text **WINDOWS** gets displayed at the desired location.

MICROSOFT 1 WINDOWS Me
MICROSEFT WINDOWS 2000
MICROSOFT WINDOWS XP

Fig. W-5.6

- It may also happen that you incorrectly type one or more letters in a word. Suppose you have typed the word **MICROSOFT** as **MICROSEFT** in the second line. To correct the spelling error, undertake the following steps:

MICROSOFT 2 WINDOWS Me
MICROSEFT WINDOWS 2000
MICROSOFT WINDOWS XP

Fig. W-5.7

1. *Place* the mouse-pointer just before the letter **E** of the word **MICROSEFT** (Fig. W-5.6).
2. *Click* the left mouse-button just once. Immediately, a blinking cursor appears at that point (Fig. W-5.7).

MICROSOFT 3 WINDOWS Me
MICROSO T WINDOWS 2000
MICROSOFT WINDOWS XP

Fig. W-5.8

3. Now *press* the **Delete** key just once. The letter **E** gets deleted. After erasing the letter **E**, *type* the letter **O** (Fig. W-5.8).

After entering the desired text, the WordPad document in Windows XP looks like Fig. W-5.9.

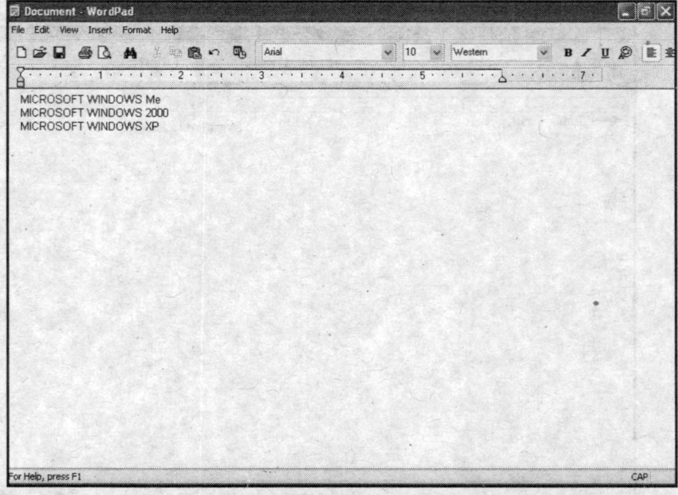

Fig. W-5.9

Editing Text in WordPad

When you write notes on paper, you sometimes perform some editing operations like underlining important text or boldfacing important lines to make them stand out in the text.

WordPad also enables you to perform various editing operations. You can centralize, underline, boldface and italicize important portions of text. However, before actually changing the appearance of the text, you need to select the text whose appearance you wish to change. Let us now perform some editing operations on the three-line text of our WordPad document as shown in Fig. W-5.9.

Selecting the Text

Highlighting a particular text is termed as **selection.** You may select an alphabet/number or a word/line/paragraph or the entire text of your document. Let us now go through the basic steps involved in the selection procedure. Right now, do not perform any of these steps on your computer. We will do it later on. Just read on.

1. *Move* the mouse-pointer to the left of the alphabet, word, line or the entire paragraph that you wish to select.
2. *Click* the left mouse-button. Instantly, a blinking cursor appears beside the mouse-pointer.
3. *Place* the mouse-pointer on the blinking cursor. Keeping the left mouse-button *pressed*, *drag* the mouse to the right on the mouse pad such that the desired alphabet, word, line or the entire paragraph gets selected.
4. Now *release* the left mouse-button.
5. To remove the highlight from the selected alphabet, word, line or paragraph, *click* the left mouse-button anywhere else in the document.

Let us now practice the selection operation on an alphabet, a word, a line and a paragraph – one by one. We will perform this operation on the typed text of Fig. W-5.9. To select the desired text, you may follow any of the methods described below:

Selecting an Alphabet or a Number

To select an alphabet or a number – in our case first letter **W** of the first line, undertake the following steps:

1. *Move* the mouse-pointer to the left of alphabet **W** of the word **WINDOWS** in the line **MICROSOFT WINDOWS Me** (Fig. W-5.10).
2. *Click* the left mouse-button. A blinking cursor appears beside the mouse-pointer (Fig. W-5.11).
3. *Place* the mouse-pointer at the position of the blinking cursor. Keeping the left mouse-button *pressed*, *move* the mouse such that alphabet **W** gets highlighted (Fig. W-5.12).
4. Once **W** is highlighted, *release* the left mouse-button.

MICROSOFT WINDOWS Me
MICROSOFT WINDOWS 2000
MICROSOFT WINDOWS XP

Fig. W-5.10

MICROSOFT WINDOWS Me
MICROSOFT WINDOWS 2000
MICROSOFT WINDOWS XP

Fig. W-5.11

MICROSOFT WINDOWS Me
MICROSOFT WINDOWS 2000
MICROSOFT WINDOWS XP

Fig. W-5.12

If you have accidentally released the mouse-button before highlighting the desired letter then start from the beginning, i.e. from Step 1 of the topic 'Selecting an Alphabet or a Number'.

5. To remove the highlight from letter **W**, just *move* the mouse-pointer anywhere inside the WordPad document and *click* the left mouse-button.

Selecting a Word

Suppose you wish to highlight word **WINDOWS** in the second line. For this, undertake the following steps:

1. *Move* the mouse-pointer to the left of word **WINDOWS** in the second line (Fig. W-5.13).
2. *Click* the left mouse-button. A blinking cursor instantly appears at that point (Fig. W-5.14).
3. *Place* the mouse-pointer at the blinking cursor position. Then keeping the left mouse-button *pressed*, *move* the mouse to the right such that word **WINDOWS** gets highlighted (Fig. W-5.15).
4. Now *release* the left mouse-button.

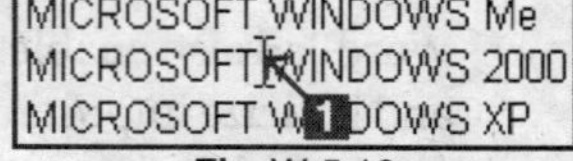

Fig. W-5.13

MICROSOFT WINDOWS Me
MICROSOFT WINDOWS 2000
MICROSOFT WINDOWS XP

Fig. W-5.14

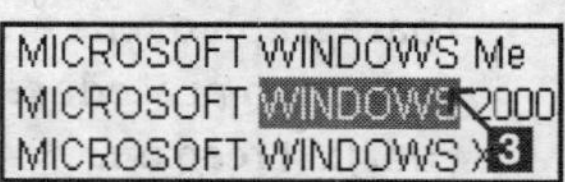

Fig. W-5.15

If you released the mouse-button accidentally before highlighting the whole word, start from the beginning, i.e. from Step 1 of the topic 'Selecting a Word'.

5. To remove the highlight from word **WINDOWS**, *move* the mouse-pointer anywhere inside the WordPad document, and *click* the left mouse-button.

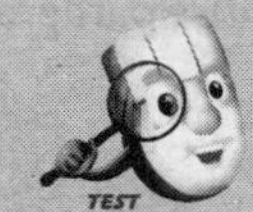

Now that you are familiar with the selection procedure, try doing the following workout.

Select the line MICROSOFT WINDOWS Me in Fig. W-5.10.

- Click the left mouse-button at the left of the line MICROSOFT WINDOWS Me.
- Keeping the left mouse-button pressed, drag the mouse to the right on the mouse-pad.
- Once the line MICROSOFT WINDOWS ME gets highlighted, release the left mouse-button.
- To remove highlight from the line, click anywhere in your document.

Selecting a Paragraph

Let us consider the three lines in the document (Fig. W-5.9) as a paragraph and try selecting all of them. To do so, undertake the following steps:

1. *Move* the mouse-pointer to the left of the first line **MICROSOFT WINDOWS Me** (Fig. W-5.16).
2. *Click* the left mouse-button. A blinking cursor instantly appears beside the mouse-pointer (Fig. W-5.17).
3. *Place* the mouse-pointer on the blinking cursor position. Then keeping the left mouse-button *pressed*, *move* the mouse downwards and highlight all the three lines (Fig. W-5.18).
4. Once the entire paragraph gets highlighted, *release* the left mouse-button.

MICROSOFT WINDOWS Me
MICROSOFT WINDOWS 2000
MICROSOFT WINDOWS XP

Fig. W-5.16

MICROSOFT WINDOWS Me
MICROSOFT WINDOWS 2000
MICROSOFT WINDOWS XP

Fig. W-5.17

MICROSOFT WINDOWS Me
MICROSOFT WINDOWS 2000
MICROSOFT WINDOWS XP

Fig. W-5.18

If you have accidentally released the mouse-button before the entire paragraph is highlighted, start from Step 1 of the topic 'Selecting a Paragraph'.

5. To remove the highlight from the paragraph, **MICROSOFT...WINDOWS XP**, *move* the mouse-pointer anywhere inside the WordPad document, and *click* the left mouse-button.

Remember, for performing any editing or formatting operation on a text, it is essential to select it. In a document, do not select that portion of the text on which you don't want to perform any operation. Let us now practice one by one various formatting operations on the desired text like centering, boldfacing, underlining, italicizing, etc. For various formatting tasks, you will find the **Formatting Toolbar** (Fig. 5.19) quite handy.

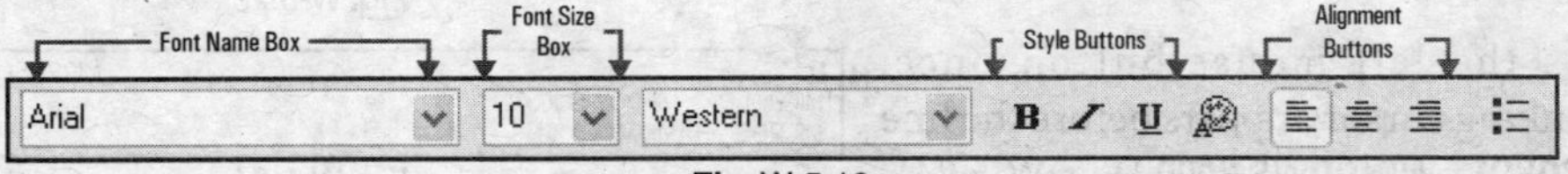

Fig. W-5.19

Centering the Text

Normally in a document, headings are positioned at the center of a page. So, the centering feature is basically used for headings. Before performing the centering operation on a text, you must select/highlight that text. Let us practice centering the line MICROSOFT WINDOWS Me in our document by undertaking the following steps :

1. Start with the window of Fig.W-5.9. *Bring* the mouse-pointer to the left of the line **MICROSOFT WINDOWS Me** (Fig. W-5.16).
2. *Press* the left mouse-button once. Instantly, a blinking cursor appears before the line **MICROSOFT WINDOWS Me.**
3. Now *place* the mouse-pointer over the blinking cursor. Keeping the left mouse-button *pressed*, *drag* the mouse-pointer across the text **MICROSOFT WINDOWS Me** and highlight it (Fig. W-5.20).

Fig. W-5.20

4. When the desired text gets highlighted, *release* the left mouse-button.

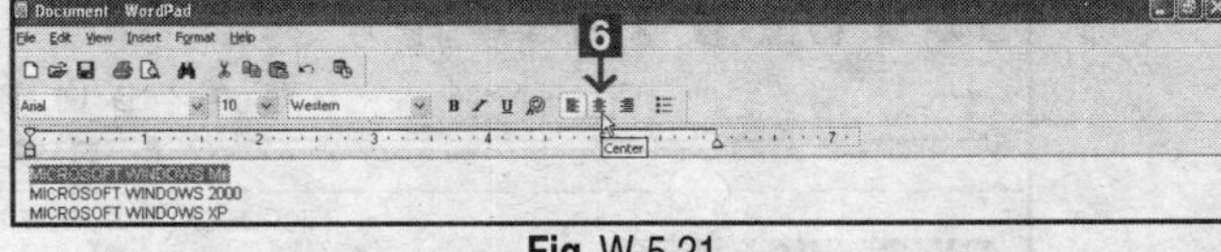

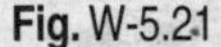

Fig. W-5.21

5. Now *move* the mouse-pointer to the **Formatting Toolbar** and *position* it on the **Center** button (≡) (Fig. W-5.21).

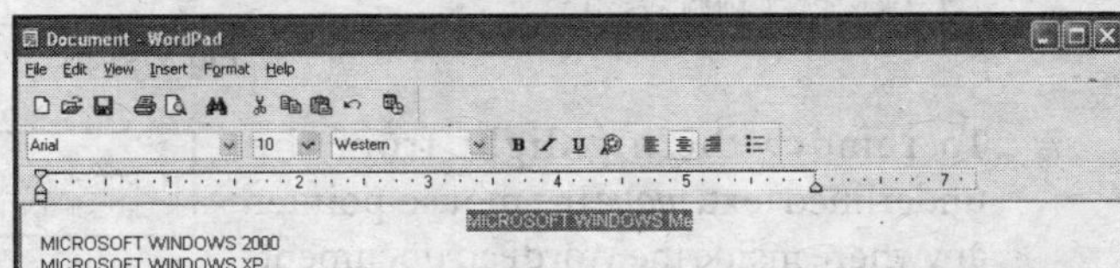

Fig. W-5.22

6. Finally, *click* the left mouse-button on the **Center** button (≡). Thereafter, the highlighted text, i.e **MICROSOFT WINDOWS Me** gets centered (Fig. W-5.22).
7. In Fig. W-5.22, you will notice that the text **MICROSOFT WINDOWS Me** remains highlighted even after getting centralized. To remove the highlight, *move* the mouse-pointer anywhere inside the WordPad document and *click* the left mouse-button.

Do not press the Enter key or any other key while the text is highlighted; else the text will be deleted.

Underlining the Text

We generally underline important points in a document. Suppose, we want to underline the text **MICROSOFT WINDOWS 2000**. This can be done through the following steps :

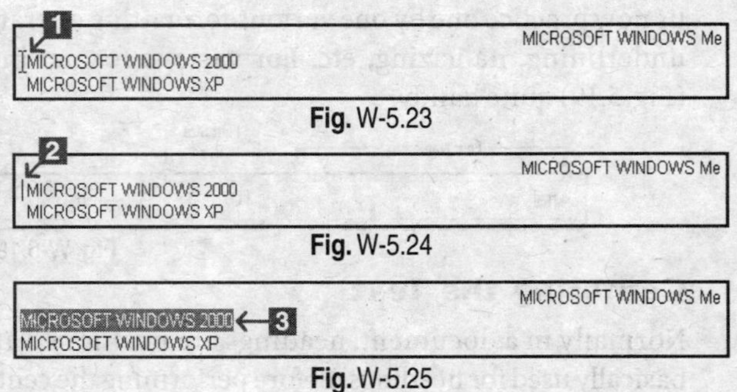

Fig. W-5.23

Fig. W-5.24

Fig. W-5.25

1. Start with the window shown in Fig. 5.22. *Move* the mouse- pointer to the left of the line **MICROSOFT WINDOWS 2000** (Fig. W-5.23).
2. *Press* the left mouse-button once. A blinking cursor appears before the line **MICROSOFT WINDOWS 2000** (Fig. W-5.24).
3. Now *place* the mouse-pointer over the blinking cursor. Then keeping the left mouse-button *pressed*, *drag* the mouse across the entire line. The text **MICROSOFT WINDOWS 2000** gets highlighted (Fig. W-5.25).
4. *Release* the left mouse-button.
5. Now, *move* the mouse-pointer to the **Underline** button (U) on the **Formatting Toolbar** (Fig. W-5.26).
6. Now *click* the left mouse-button on the **Underline** button (U). Immediately, the selected text gets underlined and remains highlighted (Fig. W-5.26).

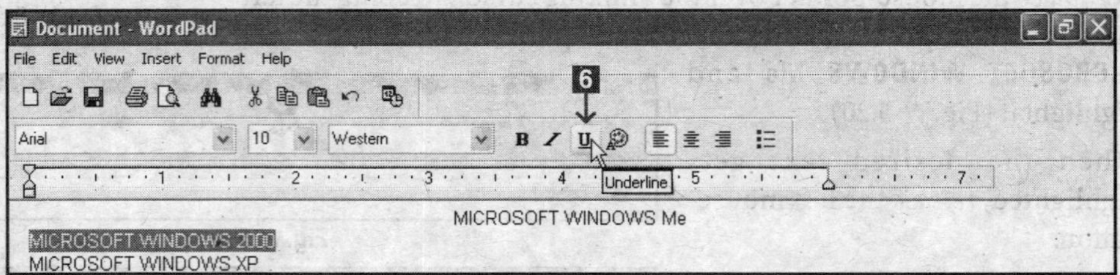

Fig. W-5.26

7. To remove the highlight from the underlined text, *move* the mouse-pointer anywhere inside the WordPad document, and *click* the left mouse-button. The highlight is removed from the text (Fig. W-5.27).

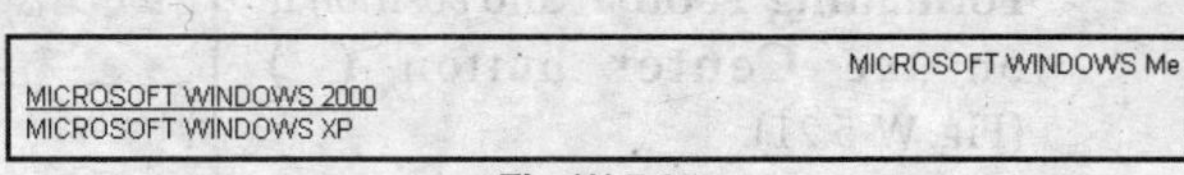

Fig. W-5.27

HOT TIP!

As soon as you place the mouse-pointer at any button on the Formatting Toolbar, a label describing the formatting function of that button appears automatically. Fig. W-5.26 displays the text Underline below the Underline button. Such a label is known as Tooltip.
Similarly, if you place the mouse-pointer over the Center button or the Italic button, their respective Tooltips would automatically get displayed below them.

Making Entries in Bold

Let us assume that you need to talk on your project report before a group of people. Instead of searching the entire document for important points, you can quickly get an idea of the key points if you type them in a different format. One suitable format for this is the bold format. If you make the important points bold, they can be easily identified.

Let us now try to make the line **MICROSOFT WINDOWS XP** appear in bold through the following steps:

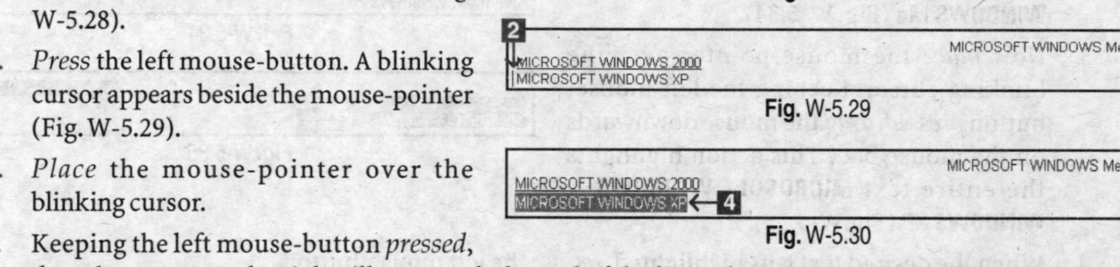

Fig. W-5.28

Fig. W-5.29

Fig. W-5.30

1. Start with the window of Fig. W-5.27. *Bring* the mouse-pointer to the left of the line **MICROSOFT WINDOWS XP** (Fig. W-5.28).
2. *Press* the left mouse-button. A blinking cursor appears beside the mouse-pointer (Fig. W-5.29).
3. *Place* the mouse-pointer over the blinking cursor.
4. Keeping the left mouse-button *pressed*, *drag* the mouse to the right till you reach the end of the line. The text **MICROSOFT WINDOWS XP** gets highlighted (Fig. W-5.30).
5. Now, *move* the mouse-pointer over the **Bold** button (**B**) on the **formatting Toolbar** (Fig. W-5.31), and *click* the left mouse-button. **MICROSOFT WINDOWS XP** appears in bold format and remains highlighted (Fig. W-5.31).

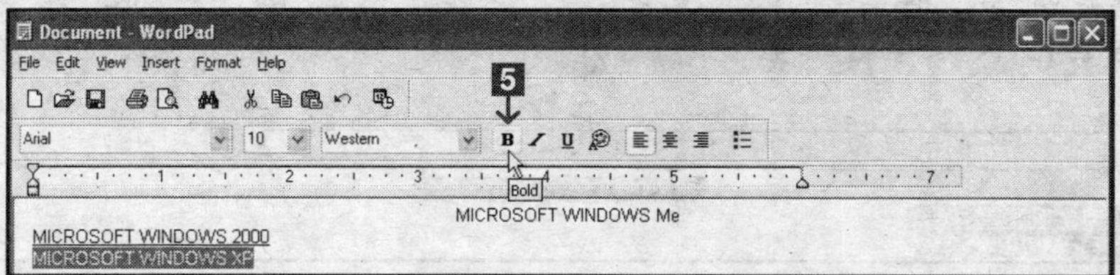

Fig. W-5.31

6. *Click* anywhere in your document to remove the highlight (Fig. W-5.32).

Fig. W-5.32

For doing a formatting operation on any text, it first needs to be highlighted. However after the completion of the formatting operation, the text still remains highlighted (Fig.W-5.31). For removing the highlight, click anywhere else in the document.

Making Entries in Italics

Italicizing is yet another formatting operation, which would help you to go through important points of your project report quickly. The text on which you perform this operation appears a little tilted. Let us now learn how to italicize the entire text of your document, i.e. from **MICROSOFT WINDOWS Me** to **WINDOWS XP.** To do so, undertake the following steps:

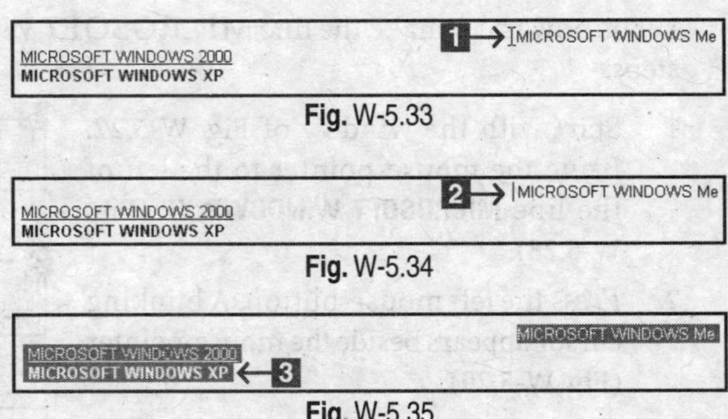

Fig. W-5.33

Fig. W-5.34

Fig. W-5.35

1. Start with the window of Fig.W-5.32. *Bring* the mouse-pointer to the left of the line **MICROSOFT WINDOWS Me** (Fig. W-5.33).
2. *Press* the left mouse-button once. A blinking cursor appears before the line **MICROSOFT WINDOWS Me** (Fig. W-5.34).
3. Now *place* the mouse-pointer over the blinking cursor. Keeping the left mouse-button *pressed*, *drag* the mouse downwards on the mouse pad. This action highlights the entire text **MICROSOFT WINDOWS... WINDOWS XP** (Fig.W-5.35).
4. When the desired text gets highlighted, *release* the left mouse-button.
5. Next, *move* the mouse-pointer over the **Italic** button ( ) present on the **Formatting Toolbar** (Fig. W-5.36).
6. Now *click* the left mouse-button on the **Italic** button ( ). The text gets italicized.

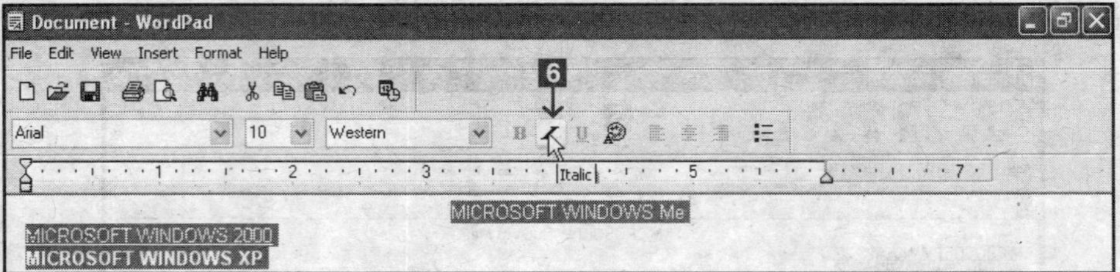

Fig. W-5.36

7. To see the actual italicized text, *click* anywhere inside the document. Instantly, the entire text appears in italics (Fig. W-5.37).

Fig. W-5.37

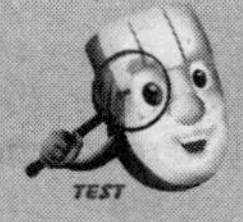

Practice centering, underlining, boldfacing and italicizing by writing and formatting the text exactly as shown below on the Wordpad document.

HIMANI

TECHNICAL EDITOR

DREAMTECH PRESS

Saving a WordPad Document

After you have created a document, you may want to keep it for future use. For this, you have to save your document on the disk. Let us now learn how to save the currently open document (Fig.W-5.37). Follow the steps given below:

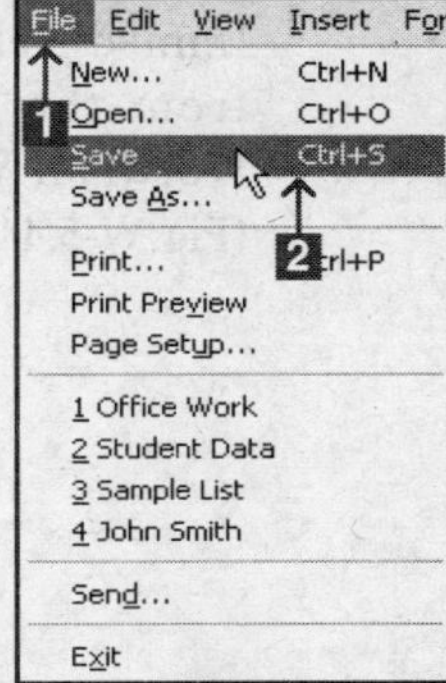

Fig. W-5.38

1. On the Menu bar of the currently open document, *move* the mouse-pointer over the **File** option and *click* the left mouse-button. Instantly, a pull-down menu appears on the screen (Fig. W-5.38).
2. Inside the pull- down menu, *move* the mouse-pointer over the **Save** option and *click* the left mouse-button once (Fig W-5.38).
3. Instantly, a **Save As** dialog box appears on the screen (Fig. W-5.39). In this dialog box, we can specify the name of the file and the location where we want to save it.

Giving a unique name to a document is essential to distinguish it from other documents. Also while naming a document, take care to give it such a name that will help you in quickly recalling its contents.

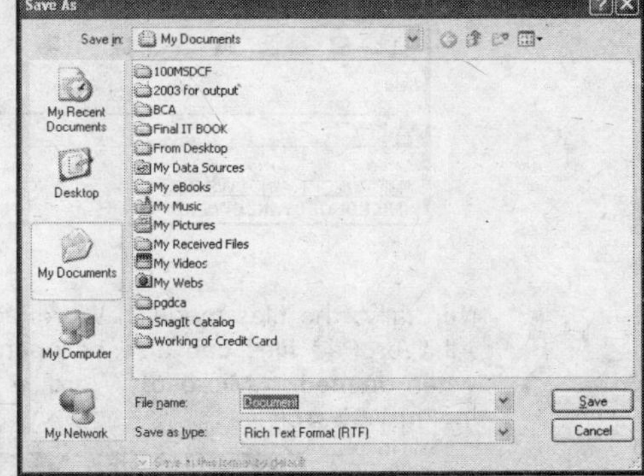

Fig. W-5.39

4. Let us name our document as **Creative** and save it on the **Desktop**. So, *type* **Creative** in the box beside the **File name** option in the **Save As** box (Fig. W-5.40).

Beside the File name option in the Save As box some text, i.e. document.rtf in Fig. 5.39, is highlighted by default. So, whatever name we give to our document, it immediately replaces the highlighted text.

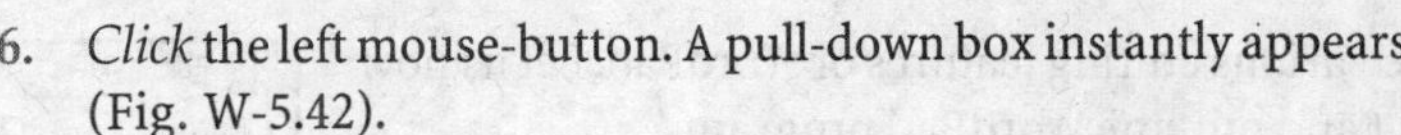

5. Now, you have to select a folder, say **Desktop**, in which you would save your document. Here comes the use of **Save in** option. To reach the **Desktop** folder, *move* the mouse-pointer over the down-arrow button (⌄) beside the **Save in** option (Fig. W-5.41).

Fig. W-5.40

Fig. W-5.41

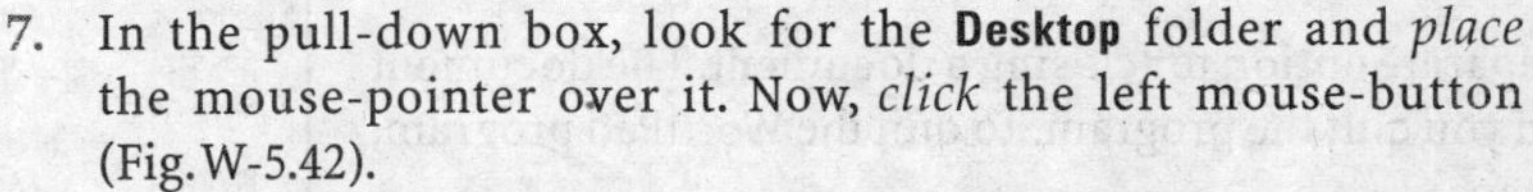

6. *Click* the left mouse-button. A pull-down box instantly appears (Fig. W-5.42).
7. In the pull-down box, look for the **Desktop** folder and *place* the mouse-pointer over it. Now, *click* the left mouse-button (Fig. W-5.42).
8. The action taken in Step 7 brings two changes in the **Save As** box (Fig. W-5.43). First, **Desktop** folder name appears in the box beside the **Save in** option. It indicates that the **Desktop** folder has been chosen to save the desired file. Second, the contents of the **Desktop** folder are displayed in the rectangular box below the **Save in** option.

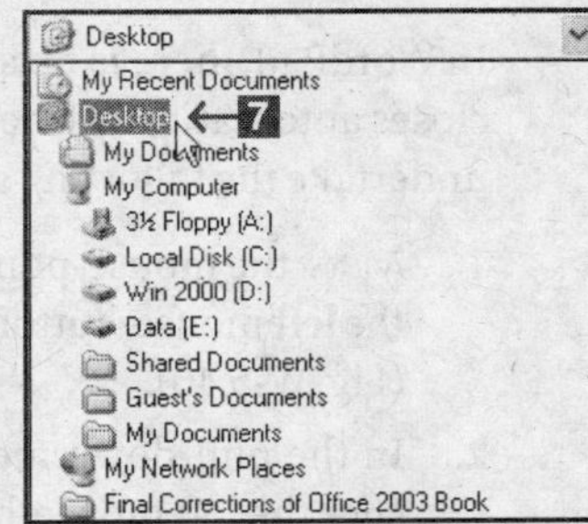

Fig. W-5.42

9. Finally, *move* the mouse-pointer over the **Save** button (Fig. W-5.43) and *click* the left mouse-button. Immediately, the **Save As** dialog box disappears from the screen and the **Title Bar** of the WordPad window displays the name **Creative** (Fig. W-5.44).

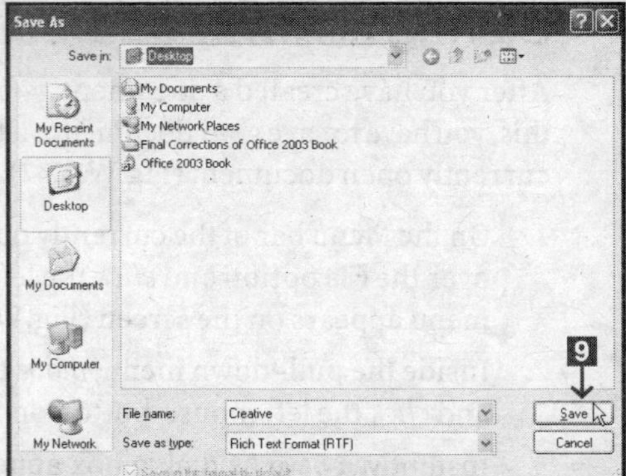

Fig. W-5.43

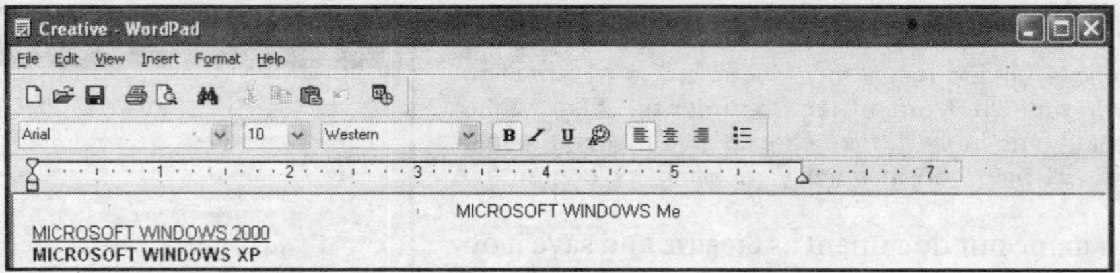

Fig. W-5.44

Normally, the files made in WordPad have the .rtf extension and open in the WordPad program itself. All WordPad files can also be opened in the Microsoft Word if it is installed in your computer. But, when opened in Microsoft Word, a WordPad file, like Creative, won't display any extension as shown in Fig.W-5.45

Fig. W-5.45

A file originally made in Microsoft Word (explained later) with a .doc extension cannot be opened in the WordPad program.

Closing a Document and Quitting WordPad

So, now you know how to use the various editing features of WordPad. Let us now learn how to close the document and quit the WordPad program.

In WordPad, there is no separate option for closing a document. The document closes automatically when you quit the program. To quit the WordPad program, undertake the following steps :

1. *Move* the mouse-pointer over the **File** in the Menu bar of **Creative** file and *click* the left mouse-button. Immediately, a pull-down menu appears on the screen (Fig. W-5.46).
2. In the pull-down menu, *move* the mouse-pointer over the **Exit** option and *click* the left mouse-button (Fig. W-5.46).

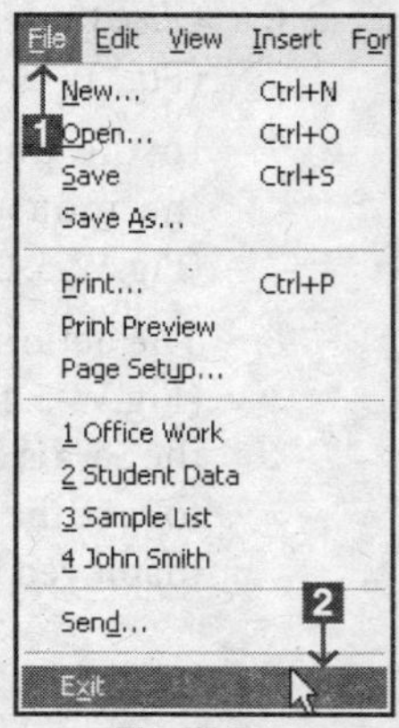

Fig. W-5.46

3. Immediately, WordPad program closes along with your document **Creative**.

Suppose you have made some changes to your document. If you choose the Exit option without saving those changes then a message box would get displayed. This box asks whether you wish to save the changes to your document. If you do not want to save the changes, click on the No button; otherwise, click on the Yes button.

Printing a Document and Quitting Windows

As you have saved your document **Creative** in the **Desktop** folder, its icon gets displayed along with other icons on the Desktop (Fig. W-5.47). An advantage of saving a file or document on your **Desktop** is that you can print it without opening it.

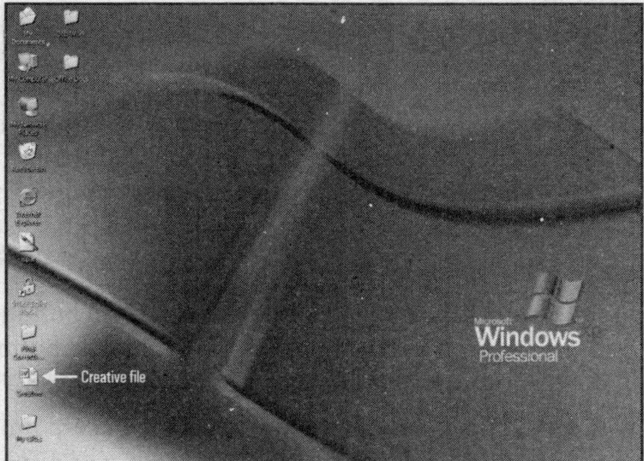

Fig. W-5.47

Let us now try printing the document **Creative** from the Desktop itself. Here, we assume that a printer is connected to your computer. Now, undertake the following steps:

1. *Move* the mouse-pointer over the icon named **Creative** on your **Desktop** (Fig. W-5.48).
2. Then *click* the right mouse-button just once. A shortcut menu appears on the screen (Fig. W-5.48).
3. Inside the shortcut menu, *move* the mouse-pointer over the **Print** option (Fig. W-5.48) and *click* the left mouse-button. This instantly opens up the WordPad window and displays your document, **Creative.**

   A message box appears with a message that the document is currently getting printed. Within a few seconds, your document gets printed and the message box disappears. The WordPad program also closes and you return to your **Desktop** again.

Fig. W-5.48

In case you have not installed any printer, a message box, as shown in Fig.W-5.49, gets displayed on your screen.
Click on the OK button of the message box. The message box disappears. If you wish to install a network printer on your computer then follow the steps listed under the topic 'Installing the Printer' of Chapter 4—"Windows Explorer". If you are not connected to a network then insert the printer CD in the CD Drive of your computer and follow the instructions of the Printer Wizard to set up the printer.

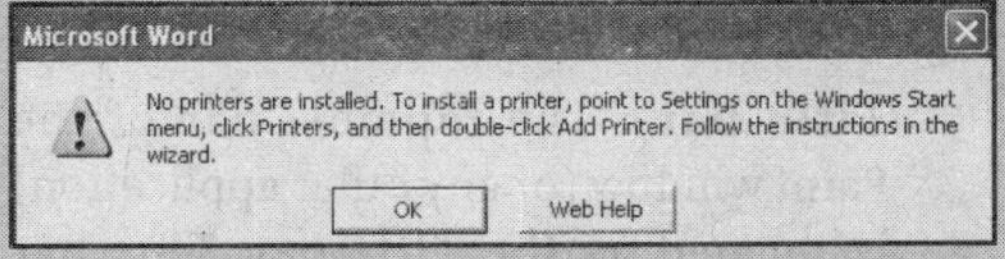

Fig. W-5.49

Let us take a break now. After the break, we will work on another program of **Accessories**, called **Paint**. If you wish to quit Windows XP now, undertake the following steps:

1. *Click* on the **Start** button (start).
2. Inside the **Start** push-up menu, *click* on the **Turn Off Computer** option.
3. Immediately a **Turn Off Computer** box gets displayed. Inside the box, *click* the left mouse-button on the **Turn Off** option. Soon, your monitor screen goes blank. Then turn off the UPS supply to your computer and take a break.

Opening the Paint Program

Hope after the break you are refreshed and ready to work in a new Accessories program called **Paint**. It is a drawing and painting program. The various tools and colours available in Paint help you create useful and informative graphics to make your reports and letters impressive. Let us open the Paint program by following the steps given below:

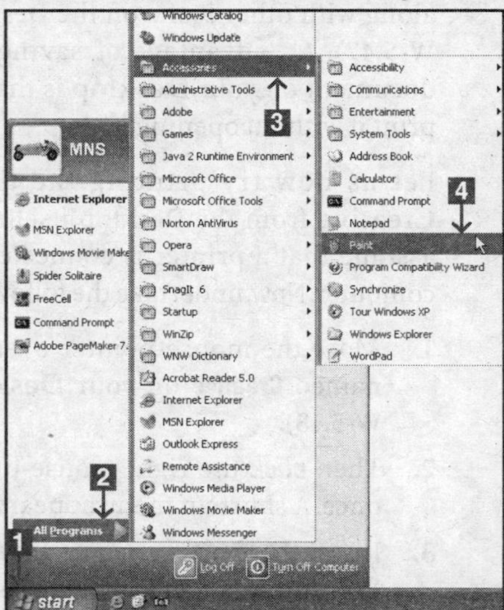

Fig. W-5.50

1. *Move* the mouse-pointer over the **Start** button (start) on the **Taskbar** and *click* the left mouse-button on it. A push-up menu appears on the screen (Fig. W-5.50).
2. In the push-up menu, *place* the mouse-pointer on the **All Programs** option. A second menu gets displayed (Fig. W-5.50).
3. *Move* the mouse-pointer over the second menu and *place it* on the **Accessories** option. Immediately, a third menu gets displayed (Fig. W-5.50).
4. Inside the third menu, *move* the mouse-pointer over the **Paint** option (Fig. W-5.50), and *click* the left mouse-button. Instantly, the **Paint** window opens up on your screen (Fig. W-5.51).

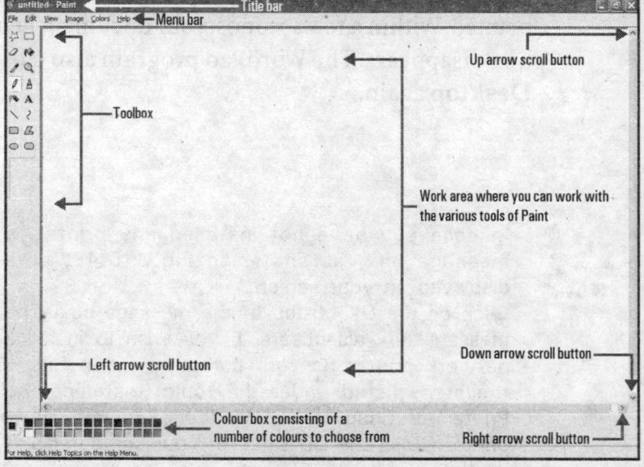

Fig. W-5.51

Parts of Paint Window

The Paint window (Fig. W-5.51) is made up of several parts. Following is a brief description of these parts.

Title bar : The topmost bar of the Paint window (or any other application) is termed as the Title bar. This bar usually displays the program name and the name of the file you are currently working in.

Menu bar : The Menu bar displays a number of options, like **File, Edit, View,...Help.** You can select any option by moving the mouse-pointer over it and then clicking the left mouse-button.

Workarea : The Workarea is empty space and covers a major part of the **Paint** window. The scroll buttons – the left arrow scroll button, the right arrow scroll button, the down arrow scroll button and the up arrow scroll button – are displayed on two sides of the Workarea. The entire Workarea space is not displayed on the screen. You can see the entire Workarea by scrolling through the screen using the scroll buttons.

Colour box : The Colour box is present at the bottom of the **Paint** window. From this box you can select the colour of your choice and then apply this colour using different tools of the Toolbox. For example, to write some text in red colour, you first need to select the red colour from the Colour box and then click over the Text tool in the Toolbox. After this, whatever you type in the Workarea would appear in red colour. But remember, the Colour box does not work with the Eraser tool.

Toolbox : On the left side of the Workarea, you see the Toolbox that consists of various tools. These tools help you create drawings and fill them with colours in the Workarea. As you move the mouse-pointer over a tool, a tool tip appears along with the mouse-pointer. This tool tip mentions the name of the tool. On clicking over a tool, the mouse-pointer acquires the shape of the selected tool. For example, if you click on Airbrush ( ) tool, the mouse-pointer changes to a spray bottle. On selection of the Filler tool ( ), the cursor acquires the shape of a tilted bucket. But on selecting certain tools, like Rectangle, Ellipse, Line, Text, Round Rectangle, the mouse-pointer changes to a cross (+). Let us take a quick look at the functions of various tools.

Eraser tool ( ): It is used to erase colours, text or even image.

Fill tool ( ): It is used to fill objects and Workarea with desired colour.

Pencil tool ( ): It is used to draw free-hand lines.

Brush tool ( ): It is used to paint the images with chosen colour.

Airbrush tool ( ): It gives the spraying effect to the selected images with chosen colour. Whenever you use this tool on a desired image, a spray of dots appears over the image.

Text tool(A): It is used to type text in Paint window in different types of font.

Line tool (\\): It is used to draw horizontal and vertical lines.

Ellipse tool ( ): It is used to draw circular shapes.

Selecting Tools

To work efficiently in the **Paint** program, carefully follow the description given below about the procedures that are employed to work with tools of the Toolbox. Let us first start with the **Text tool.**

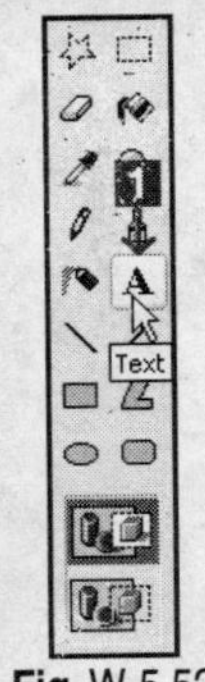

Fig. W-5.52

Text tool

The **Text tool (A)** allows you to write any text on the screen. Let us test this tool by writing some text, say **Happy New Year.** To do so, follow the steps given below:

1. Start with the Paint window of Fig.W-5.51. *Move* the mouse-pointer over the **Text** tool (**A**) in the Toolbox, and *click* the left mouse-button. Instantly, the tool gets highlighted indicating that it has been selected (Fig. W-5.52).

2. Now *move* the mouse-pointer to the Workarea of the **Paint** window. In the Workarea, the mouse-pointer changes into a cross (+) (Fig. W-5.52).
3. Let us now type the text **Happy New Year** in the Workarea. First, you have to select the specific area where you wish to type the text. For this, *move* the mouse-pointer to the top left corner of the **Paint** window (Fig. W-5.53).
4. Keeping the left mouse-button *pressed*, *drag* the mouse-pointer to the right to such a length that a dotted box is formed to accommodate the text **Happy New Year** (Fig. W-5.54).
5. A dotted box appears in the area where you dragged the mouse (Fig. W-5.54). *Release* the mouse-button.
6. When you *release* the left mouse-button, a **Fonts** dialog box (Fig. W-5.55) also gets displayed on the screen. Fig W-5.56 shows the bigger image of the **Fonts** dialog box..

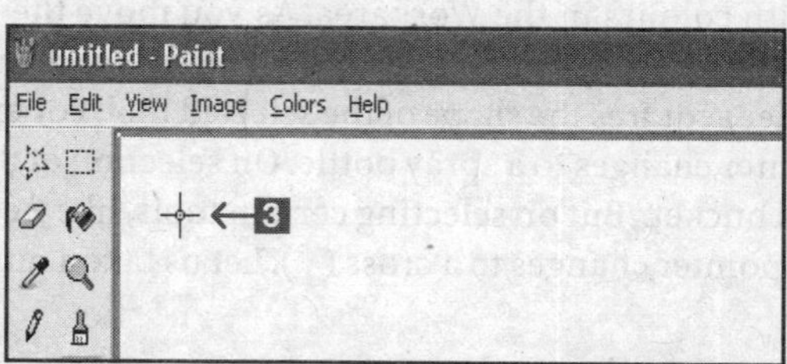

Fig. W-5.53

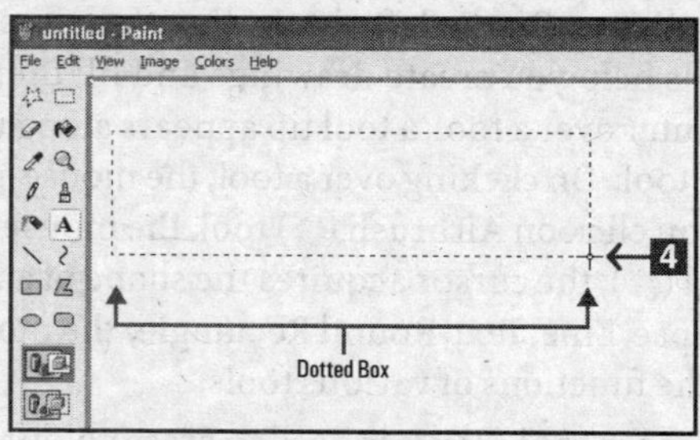

Fig. W-5.54

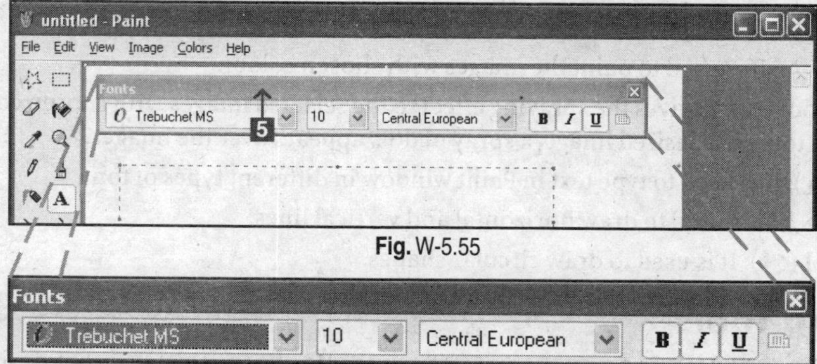

Fig. W-5.55

Fig. W-5.56

If the Fonts box is not displayed automatically then perform the following steps to bring it on the screen:

1. Move the mouse-pointer over View menu in the Menu bar and click the left mouse-button. A pull-down menu appears.
2. In this pull-down menu, move the mouse-pointer over the Text Toolbar option (Fig. W-5.57), and click the left-mouse button. Immediately the Fonts box appears on the screen.

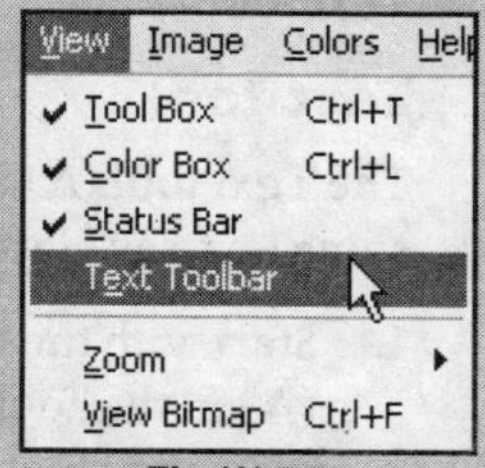

Fig. W-5.57

Choosing a Font

After drawing the dotted box, you have to choose a font for the text to be typed. For this selection, undertake the following steps.

1. *Move* the mouse-pointer over the down-arrow button ( ) in the first rectangular box (Fig. W-5.58) of the **Fonts** dialog box, which displays the font name. *Click* the left mouse-button. Instantly, a pull-down menu appears (Fig. W-5.59).

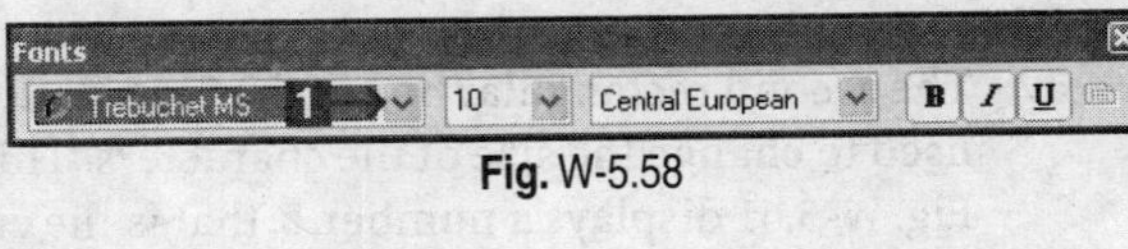

Fig. W-5.58

2. Suppose you want to select the **Times New Roman** font. However, in Fig. W-5.59, the pull-down menu does not display the **Times New Roman** font. To locate it, *move* the mouse-pointer over one of the scroll buttons, in our case the up-arrow scroll button ( ), as shown in Fig. W-5.59.
3. *Click* the left mouse-button. Keep *clicking* the button until you see the **Times New Roman** font.
4. After locating the **Times New Roman** font, *move* the mouse-pointer over it and *click* the left mouse-button (Fig. W-5.60).

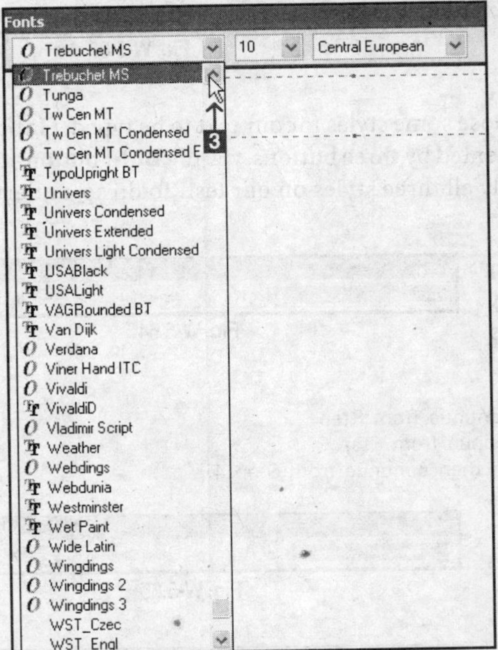

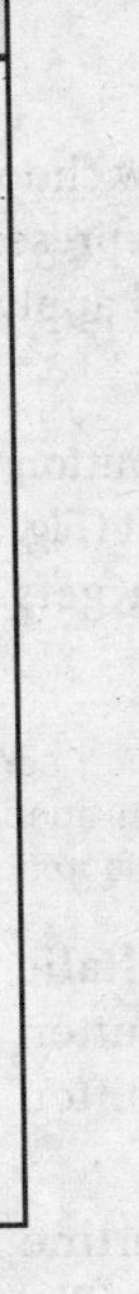

Fig. W-5.59

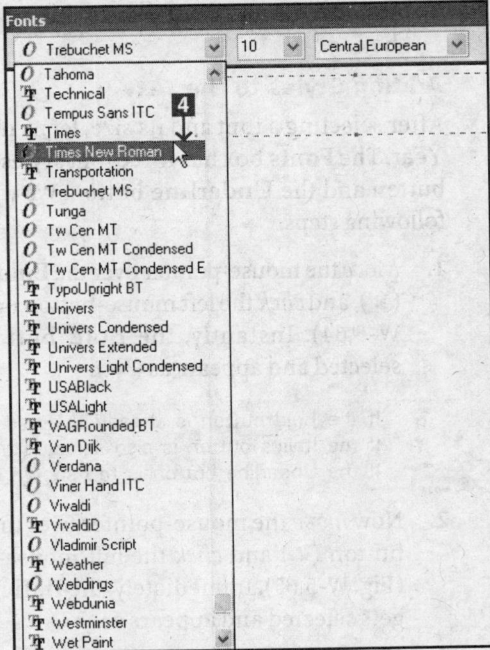

Fig. W-5.60

5. Instantly, the pull-down menu disappears, and the selected font name, i.e. **Times New Roman**, gets displayed inside the first rectangular box of the **Fonts** box (Fig. W-5.61).

Selected font displayed here

Fig. W-5.61

Choosing a Font Size

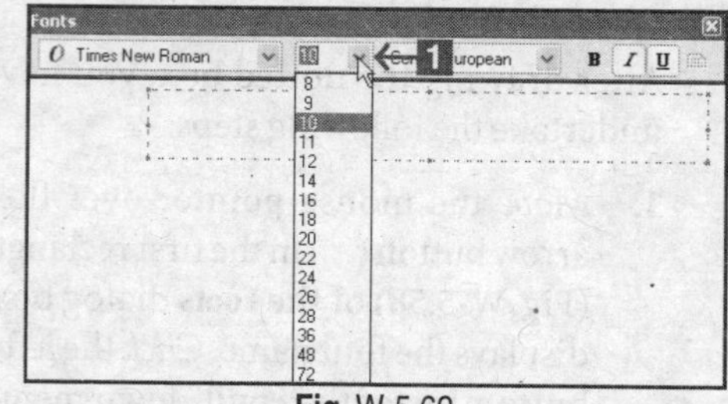

Fig. W-5.62

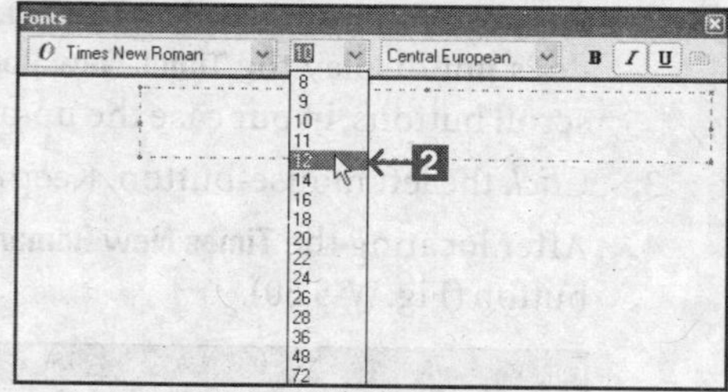

Fig. W-5.63

Now, you have to select the font size, i.e. the size of characters for the text to be typed. Do this selection in the following way.

1. The second rectangular box in the **Fonts** dialog box is used to change the size of the characters. This box in Fig. W-5.61 displays a number, **8**, that is the currently set size of the characters to be typed. Let us change this size to **12.** To do so, *move* the mouse-pointer over the down-arrow button (⌄) in the **Font size** box and *click* the left mouse-button (Fig. W-5.61). Immediately, a pull-down menu appears (Fig. W-5.62).
2. In the pull-down menu, *move* the mouse-pointer over size **12** and *click* the left mouse-button (Fig. W-5.63). Immediately, the pull-down menu disappears, and the number **12** gets displayed in the second rectangular box.

Adding Styles to the Text

After selecting a font and its size, let us now choose some styles for our text to be typed, **Happy New Year.** The **Fonts** box has three font styles represented by three buttons, viz. the **Bold** button, the **Italic** button and the **Underline** button. We will apply all three styles on our test. To do so, undertake the following steps.

1. *Move* the mouse-pointer over the **Bold** button (**B**), and *click* the left mouse-button on it (Fig. W-5.64). Instantly, the **Bold** button gets selected and appears as (**B**).

Fig. W-5.64

If the Bold button is already selected then continue from Step 2.
If the Italics button is also selected then continue from Step 3
If the Underline button is too shown selected then continue from Step 4.

2. Now *move* the mouse-pointer over the **Italic** button (*I*) and *click* the left mouse-button (Fig. W-5.65). Immediately, the **Italic** button gets selected and appears as *I*.

Fig. W-5.65

3. *Move* the mouse-pointer over the **Underline** button(U) and *click* the left mouse-button (Fig. W-5.66). The **Underline** button gets selected and appears as (U).

Fig. W-5.66

4. Having selected all the style options, let us now type the text **Happy New Year.** To do so, *move* the mouse-pointer inside the dotted box of Fig. W-5.67, and *click* the left mouse-button. Immediately, a blinking cursor appears inside the dotted box (Fig. W-5.67).

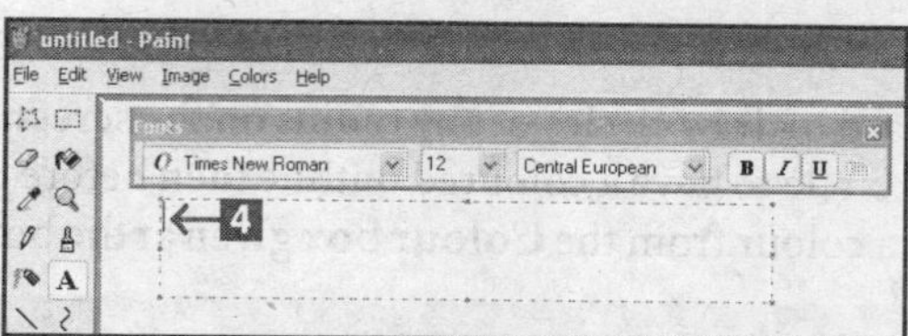

Fig. W-5.67

For typing capital letters H, N and Y of the text Happy New Year, type these letters while keeping the Shift key pressed.

Fig. W-5.68

5. Now *type* the text **Happy New Year.** This text appears inside the dotted box (Fig. W-5.68). All the selected formats (i.e. **Times New Roman** font, size **12**, **bold**, **underlined** and **italicized**) have been applied on the typed text.

Fig. W-5.69

Now let us work with another tool in the Toolbox, namely the **Rectangle** tool. But before that, it is better if we remove the **Fonts** dialog box from the screen. To close the **Fonts** box, proceed as follows:

1. *Move* the mouse-pointer over the **Close** button (☒) present on the **title bar** of the **Fonts** dialog box (Fig. W-5.69).
2. *Click* the left mouse-button. Immediately, the **Fonts** box disappears and your screen looks like Fig. W-5.70.

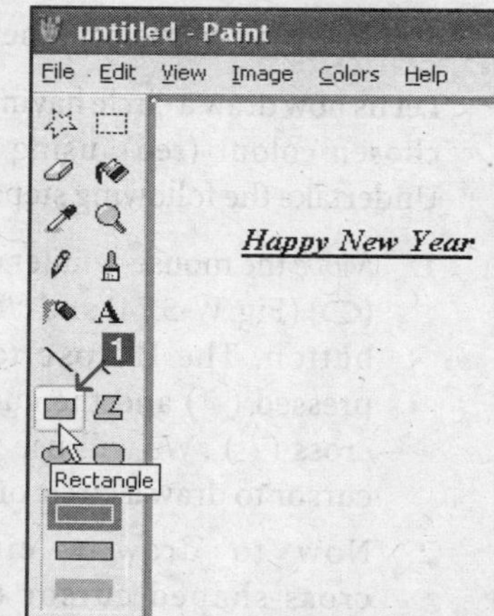

Fig. W-5.70

Rectangle Tool

The **Rectangle** tool (▭) helps you draw a box, either square or rectangle, of any size. To learn how to work with this tool, undertake the following steps.

1. Start with Fig. W-5.70 open on your screen. *Move* the mouse-pointer over the **Rectangle** tool (▭) of the Toolbox (Fig. W-5.70) and *click* the left mouse-button.
2. Now, *move* the mouse-pointer over the Workarea of the **Paint** window and *press* the left mouse-button. The cursor instantly changes into a cross shape (+).
3. Keeping the left mouse-button *pressed*, *drag* the mouse so that a rectangular box is displayed in the Workarea (Fig. W-5.71).
4. When the box of the desired size is created, *release* the left mouse-button. Fig. W-5.71 shows the newly-formed rectangular box in the Workarea.

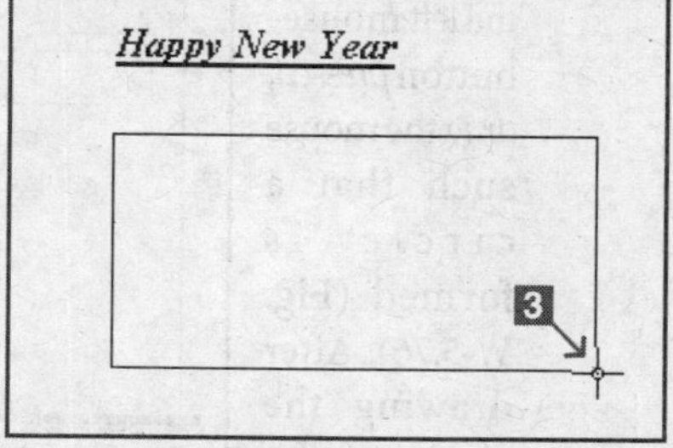

Fig. W-5.71

Ellipse Tool

The **Ellipse** tool (⬭) is used to draw circles of any radius on the screen. We will draw a circle using this tool. But, if you wish your circle to have a coloured outline then before drawing a circle, select a colour. Let us learn how to select a colour from the **Colour box** given at the bottom of the Paint window.

Selecting Colours

The **Colour box** (Fig. W-5.72) helps you draw or fill your drawing with the colour of your choice. It contains a variety of colours. To select a colour from the Colour Box, undertake the following steps:

1. *Move* the mouse-pointer over the colour of your choice, say **Red** colour present in the second row of the third column of the **Colour box** (Fig. W-5.72).
2. *Click* the left mouse-button (Fig. W-5.72).
3. The colour you have chosen gets selected and is displayed in the **Colour Selection** box (Fig. W-5.73).

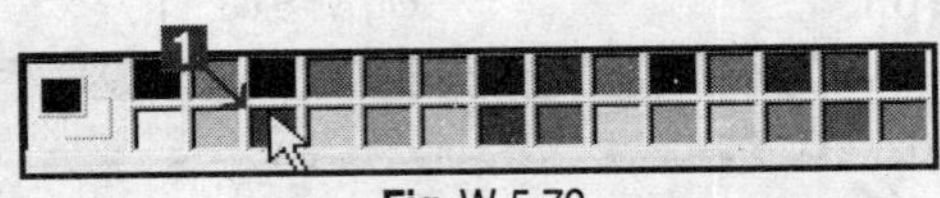

Fig. W-5.72

The selected colour appears in the Colour Selection Box

2

Fig. W-5.73

Similarly, you can select other colours.

Let us now draw a circle having an outline of our chosen colour (red), using the **Ellipse** tool. Undertake the following steps:

1. *Move* the mouse-pointer on the **Ellipse** tool (⬭) (Fig. W-5.74) and *click* the left mouse-button. The **Ellipse** tool now appears pressed (⊜) and the cursor changes to a cross (+). We will use this cross-shaped cursor to draw a circle of desired radius.
2. Now to draw a circle, *move* the cross-shaped cursor to the Workarea of the **Paint** window (Fig. W-5.75)

Fig. W-5.74 **Fig.** W-5.75

3. Then keeping the left mouse-button *pressed*, *drag* the mouse such that a circle is formed (Fig. W-5.76). After drawing the circle of the desired radius, *release* the left mouse-button (Fig. W-5.77).

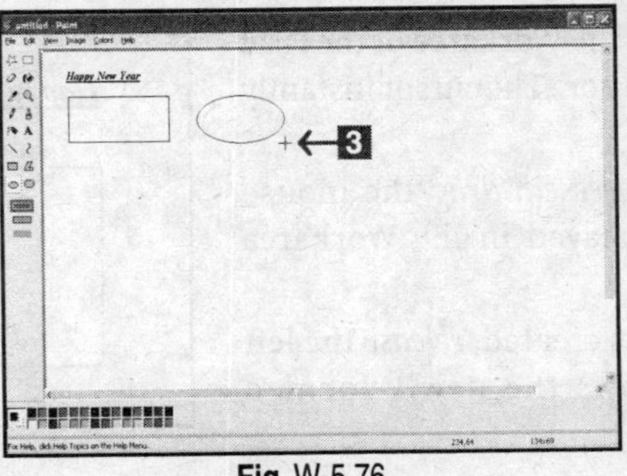

Fig. W-5.76

Fig. W-5.77

Let us now learn how to draw lines in Paint program using the **Line** tool.

Line Tool

With the **Line** tool you can not only draw lines in a Paint document but also change the thickness of a line, using options provided in its Width box. To make use of the Line tool, proceed as follows:

1. *Move* the mouse-pointer over the **Line** tool (\) and *click* the left mouse-button (Fig. W-5.78). The **Line** tool gets highlighted and a **Width** box (Fig. W-5.79) also appears at the bottom of the Toolbox. You can choose the width for your line to be drawn from different line widths displayed in the **Width** box.
2. If you wish to draw a thin line then *move* the mouse-pointer over the first line width in the **Width** box (Fig. W-5.79) and *click* the left mouse-button over it.
3. Next, *move* the mouse-pointer inside the Workarea and *press* the left mouse-button.
4. Now, keeping the left mouse-button *pressed*, *drag* the mouse on the mouse-pad. A line of your chosen width gets drawn on the screen (Fig. W-5.80). Now *release* the left mouse-button.

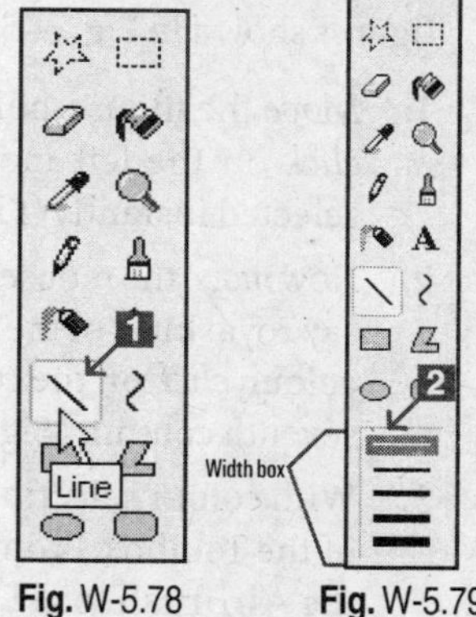

Fig. W-5.78 **Fig.** W-5.79

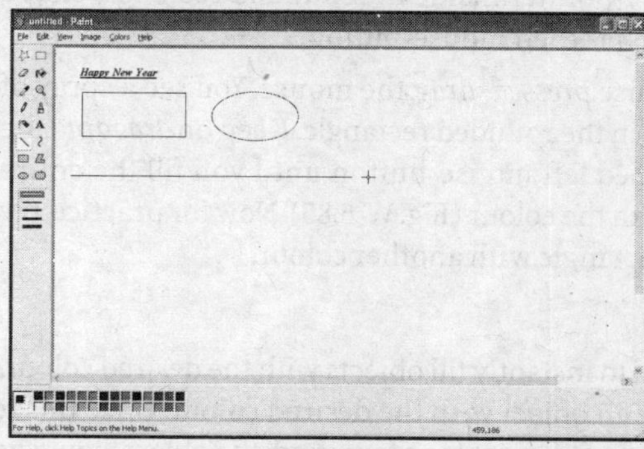

Fig. W-5.80

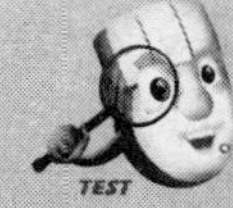

So, you have learnt how to draw different types of figure in the Paint window. Let us now perform a workout.

Draw a black Rounded Rectangle inside the Paint window.

- Click on Rounded Rectangle tool (⬭).
- Move the mouse-pointer to the workarea.
- Keeping the left mouse-button pressed, drag the mouse down-wards and towards the right to draw a rounded rectangle.
- Release the left mouse-button after you have drawn the rounded rectangle.
- Your screen now displays a rectangle, a circle, a line and a rounded rectangle (Fig. W-5.81).

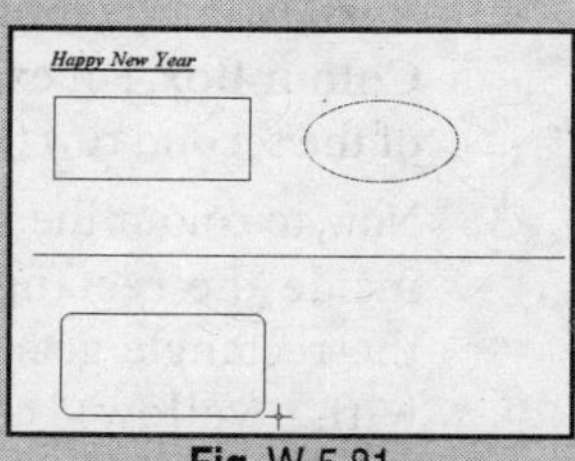

Fig. W-5.81

Airbrush Tool

Let us now work with another tool of the Paint window, which will help you in filling a chosen colour in the figures you have drawn. This tool is called the **Airbrush** (🖌) tool. It fills the desired figure with a circular spray of dots of a chosen colour. You can also increase or decrease the circular spray of dots using the Width box of the Toolbar. Undertake the following steps to use the **Airbrush** tool to fill colour in figures shown in Fig. W-5.81.

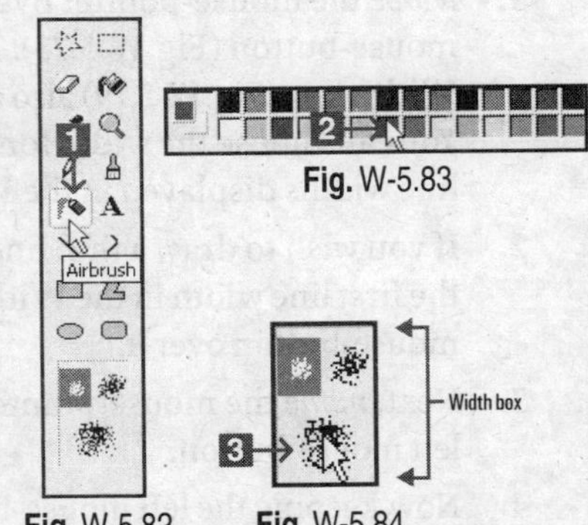

Fig. W-5.82 Fig. W-5.83 Fig. W-5.84

1. *Move* the mouse-pointer over the **Airbrush** (🖌) tool and *click* on the left mouse-button. The **Airbrush** tool gets selected instantly (Fig. W-5.82).
2. Now *move* the mouse-pointer over the colour of your choice, say royal blue, in the **Colour box**. To select the **Royal blue** colour, *click* on the colour present in the second row of the seventh column (Fig. W-5.83).
3. With colour selection, a **Width box** appears at the bottom of the Toolbox. From this box, you can select any width for the **Airbrush** tool. Let us *click* over the third width to select it (Fig. W-5.84).
4. Next, *move* the mouse-pointer inside the rounded rectangle shape drawn earlier and *press* the left mouse-button.
5. Now keeping the mouse *pressed, drag* the mouse. You see a spray of colour gets displayed in the rounded rectangle. Keep on *dragging* the mouse with the pressed left mouse-button until you fill the entire rounded rectangle with the colour (Fig. W-5.85). Now for practice, try filling the rounded rectangle with another colour.

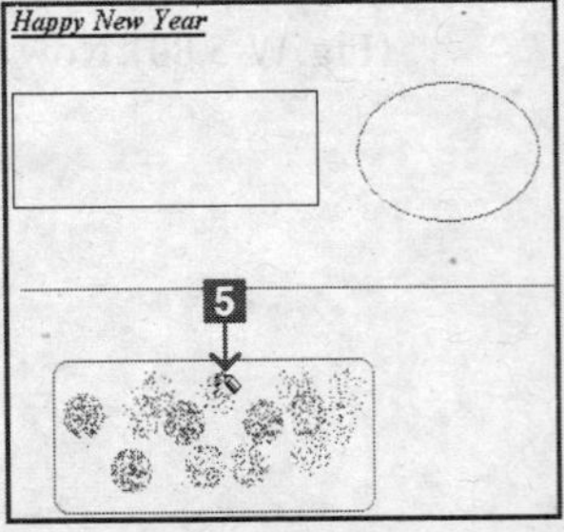

Fig. W-5.85

Filler Tool

The **Filler** (🪣) tool is used to instantly fill objects with the desired colour. While using this tool, you need not drag the mouse to fill an object with the desired colour. Once this tool is selected, you just have to click it inside the object that you want to colour. And, the object would get filled with the chosen colour. To work with the **Filler** tool, undertake the following steps:

1. *Move* the mouse-pointer over the **Filler** (🪣) tool, and *click* the left mouse-button (Fig. W-5.86).
2. Next, *move* the mouse-pointer over the colour of your choice on the **Colour Box**. For example, *click* on the colour present at fourth column of the second row (Fig. W-5.87). You will get **Yellow** colour.
3. Now, to colour the rectangle already drawn by you, *move* the mouse-pointer inside the rectangle. *Click* the left mouse-button once. Immediately, the rectangle gets filled with yellow colour (Fig. W-5.88).

Happy new Year

Fill With Color

Fig. W-5.86

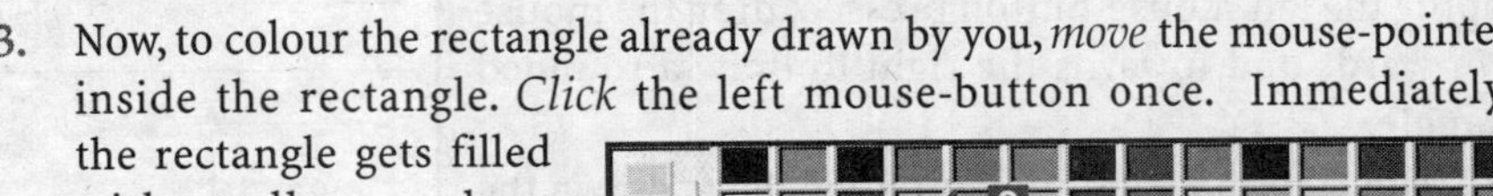

Fig. W-5.87

Happy New Year

Fig. W-5.88

Let us now undertake the following workout:

Use the Filler tool to fill the circle with cyan colour.

- Click on the Filler tool (🖌).
- Click on the Cyan colour in the Colour Box.
- Move the mouse-pointer inside the circle and click the left mouse button.
- Immediately, the circle gets filled with cyan colour.

After this workout, the Paint window looks like Fig. W-5.89.

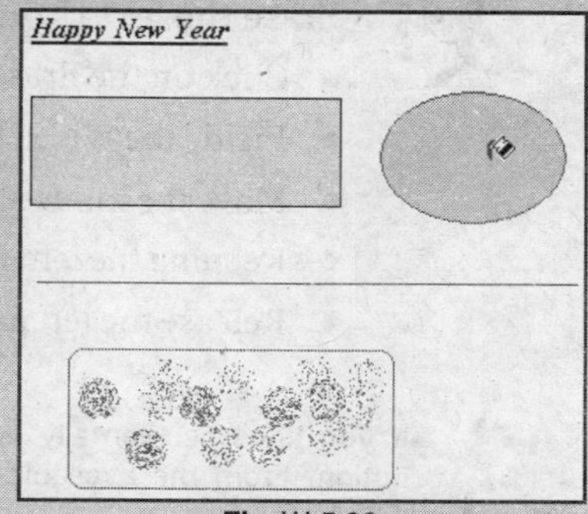

Fig. W-5.89

Eraser Tool

Normally, while making a drawing on paper, you use a rubber to remove unwanted pencil marks. In the Paint program, the **Eraser** tool performs the same function, i.e. rubs off unwanted marks or lines. An added advantage of the Eraser tool over ordinary eraser is that its size can be changed according to your requirement. Now let us understand the working of the Eraser tool by undertaking the following steps:

1. *Move* the mouse-pointer over the **Eraser** tool (⌫) in the Toolbox and *click* the left mouse button. Immediately, the tool gets highlighted (Fig. W-5.90). A **Width box** also appears at the bottom of the Toolbox, containing different sizes of eraser (Fig. W-5.91). You can select a desired size of the eraser just by clicking over it. For example, we will select the third size.

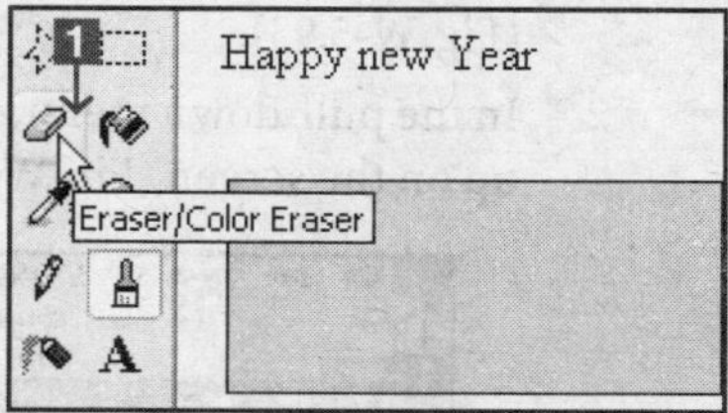

Fig. W-5.90

2. To select the third size, *move* the mouse-pointer over it and *click* the left mouse-button. Immediately, the third size gets highlighted (Fig. W-5.91).
3. Let us now delete the circle from Fig. W-5.89. To do so, *move* the mouse-pointer over the circle in the Workarea of the **Paint** window. You will observe that the mouse-pointer gets changed into a small white square.
4. Now keeping the left mouse-button *pressed*, *drag* the mouse on the mouse pad. The mouse-pointer starts working as eraser. It deletes the circle as it moves on it (Fig. W-5.92). Keep *moving* the mouse with the left mouse-button *pressed* until the whole circle gets deleted.

Fig. W-5.91

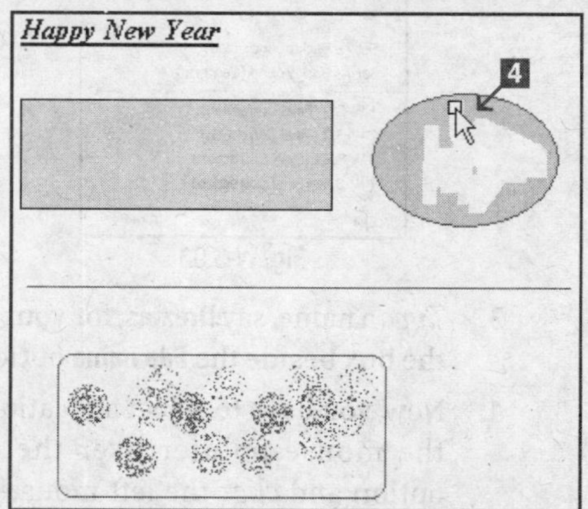

Fig. W-5.92

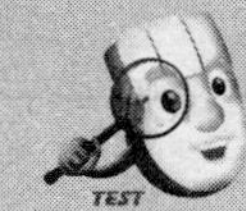

Let us now do a workout to practise the erasing operation.

Erase the text Happy New Year from Fig. W-5.92.

- Click on the Eraser tool ( ).
- Inside the Width box, click on the fourth width, i.e. the maximum eraser size.
- Move the mouse-pointer over the text Happy New Year.
- Keeping the left mouse-button pressed, drag the mouse-pointer over the text.
- Release the left mouse-button when the text has been completely erased.

If you have accidentally erased some part of a figure then to restore it, click on the Edit menu bar option. From the available options of the pull-down menu, choose the Undo option.

Saving a Paint File

Once you have given final touches to your drawing, you can save it as a your file for later use. To distinguish one file from another, each file must possess a unique name. To save your file, as it appears in Fig W-5.92, undertake the following steps:

1. *Move* the mouse-pointer over the Menu bar and *click* on the **File** option. A pull-down menu appears (Fig. W-5.93).
2. In the pull-down menu, *choose* the **Save** option by *clicking* over it (Fig. W-5.93). A **Save As** box opens up on the screen (Fig. W-5.94) with a highlight beside the **File name** option.

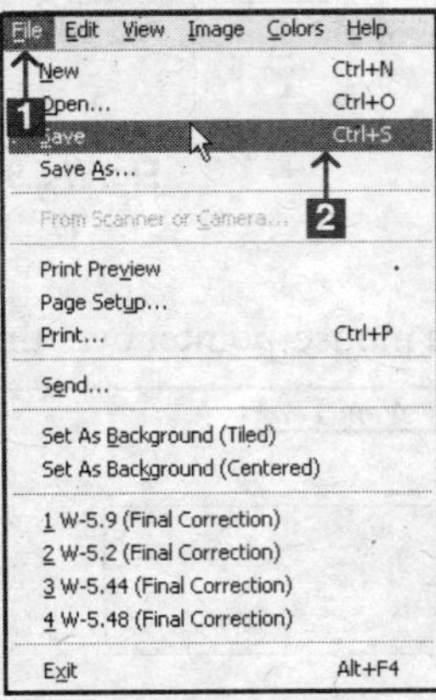

Fig. W-5.93

Fig. W-5.94

3. *Type* a name, say **Dreams**, for your drawing. As you type the name, it automatically gets written inside the box beside the **File name** option (Fig. W-5.95).
4. Now, you have to select a location through the **Save in** option to save your drawing. For this, *move* the mouse-pointer over the down-arrow button ( ) inside the box beside the **Save in** option and *click* the left mouse-button. Immediately, a pull-down menu appears on the screen (Fig. W-5.96).

5. Inside the pull-down menu, *move* the mouse-pointer over the **Local Disk (C:)** and *click* the left mouse-button (Fig. W-5.96). The **Local Disk (C:)** gets displayed in the box beside the **Save in** option (Fig. W-5.97).

6. Finally, *click* on the **Save** button. The **Save As** box disappears from the screen and you return to the **Paint** window. Your file gets saved with the name **Dreams** under the **Local Disk (C:)**. You will notice the filename **Dreams** displayed on the **title bar** (Fig. W-5.98).

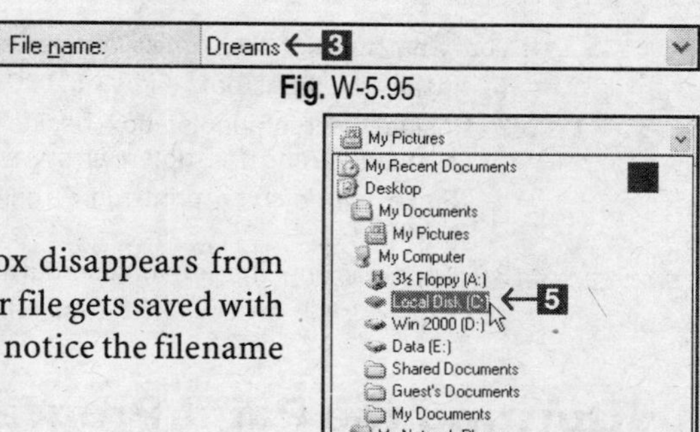

Fig. W-5.95

Fig. W-5.96

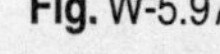

Fig. W-5.97

Fig. W-5.98

Printing a Paint File

You have just created a file, **Dreams**, through the Paint program. Let us now print this file through the following steps.

1. *Click* the left mouse-button over the **File** menu bar option. Instantly, a pull-down menu appears on the screen (Fig. W-5.99).

2. Inside the pull-down menu, *click* the **Print** option (Fig. W-5.99). Instantly, a **Print** box appears on your screen (Fig. W-5.100). As the box beside the **Number of copies** option displays **1**, only one copy of your file will be printed.

3. Inside the **Print** box, *move* the mouse-pointer over the **Print** button and *click* the left mouse-button (Fig. W-5.100). This confirms the printing procedure, and your file starts printing.

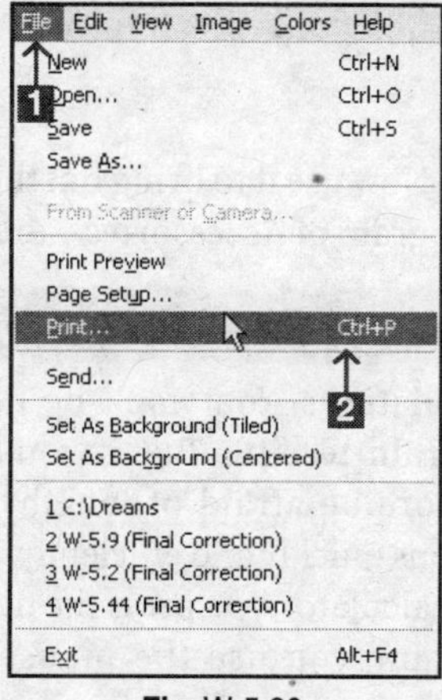

Fig. W-5.99

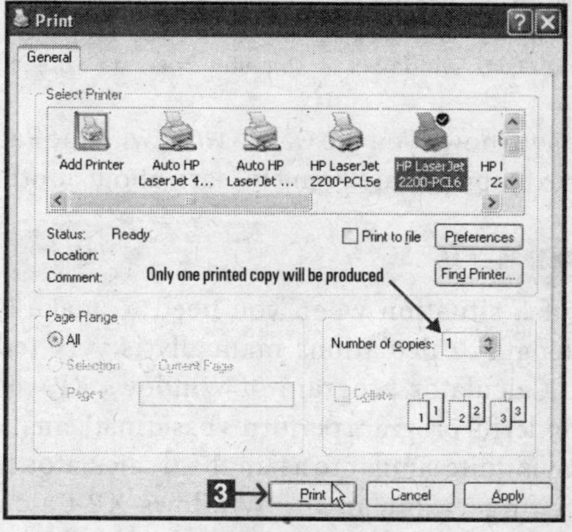

Fig. W-5.100

If you want to print five copies of the Dreams file, undertake the following steps :

1. Inside the Print box (Fig.W-5.100), look for the Number of copies option.
2. Inside the rectangular box beside this option, you will see two buttons – the up arrow scroll button (⌃) and the down arrow scroll button (⌄).
   Since you wish to print more than one copy, move the mouse-pointer over the up arrow scroll button (⌃).
3. Keep clicking the left mouse-button over it till the number 5 gets displayed.
4. Finally, click on the OK button of the Print box to start printing the file.

Quitting the Paint Program

Hope now you would feel comfortable while in the **Paint** program. Let us proceed to quit the **Paint** program. To do so, undertake the following steps.

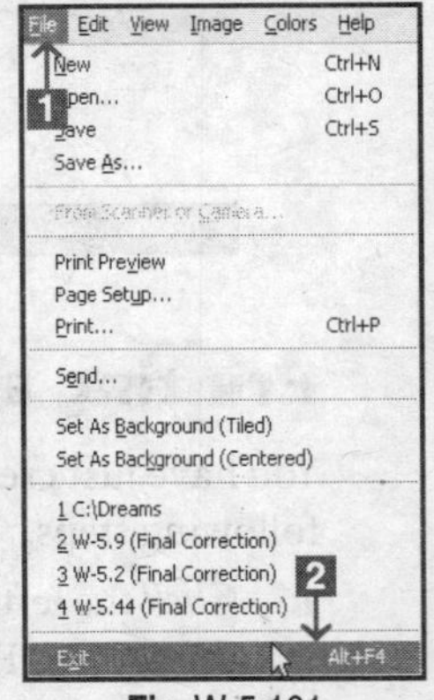

Fig. W-5.101

1. *Move* the mouse-pointer over the **File** Menu bar option of the **Dreams** window and *click* the left mouse-button. Instantly, a pull-down menu gets displayed (Fig. W-5.101).
2. Inside the pull-down menu, *click* the left mouse-button over the **Exit** option (Fig. W-5.101). Immediately, the **Paint** window closes along with the file **Dreams**, and you return to the **Desktop** of Windows XP.

Suppose you have made some changes to the file earlier but forgot to save those changes while quitting the Paint program. In such a case, a message box appears (Fig.W-5.102), asking you whether you wish to save the changes effected in your file.

If you like to save the changes, click on the Yes button.

If you do not want to save the changes to the file, click on the No button. If you click on the Cancel button, the message box closes but the Paint window still remains open on your screen.

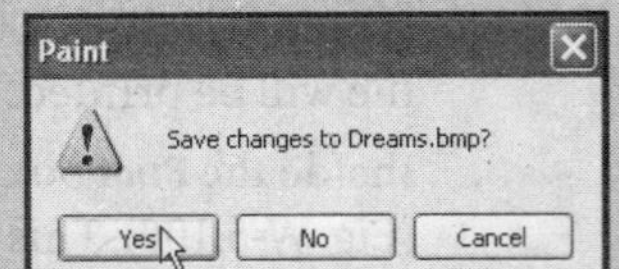

Fig. W-5.102

So, we have shown you the way to work with the Paint program. Now use it to bring out the artist in you. In the next topic, we are going to learn about another useful program of Accessories – the **Calculator**.

Calculator

Think of a situation when you need to make lengthy calculations. You won't be happy because doing lengthy calculations manually is very tedious and brain-teasing. But if you know how to use the Calculator program of Windows XP, you will no more be afraid of lengthy calculations. This wonderful program performs basic mathematical calculations quickly and efficiently. The Calculator program is quite similar to a handheld calculator. In handheld calculator, you press the number buttons by your fingers, but in the Windows XP Calculator program, you use the mouse to press the number buttons.

To work in the **Calculator** program, you first need to open it. This program resides in the Accessories. To open it, undertake the following steps.

1. *Move* the mouse-pointer over the **Start** button (start) and *click* the left mouse-button on it. Instantly, a push-up menu appears on the screen (Fig. W-5.103).
2. Inside the push-up menu, *move* the mouse-pointer over the **All Programs** option. Instantly, a second menu pops up on the screen (Fig. W-5.103).
3. Inside the second menu, *move* the mouse-pointer over the **Accessories** option. A third menu gets instantly displayed (Fig. W-5.103).
4. Inside the third menu, *move* the mouse-pointer over the **Calculator** option, and *click* the left mouse-button (Fig. W-5.103). Immediately, a **Calculator** window opens up on your screen (Fig. W-5.104).

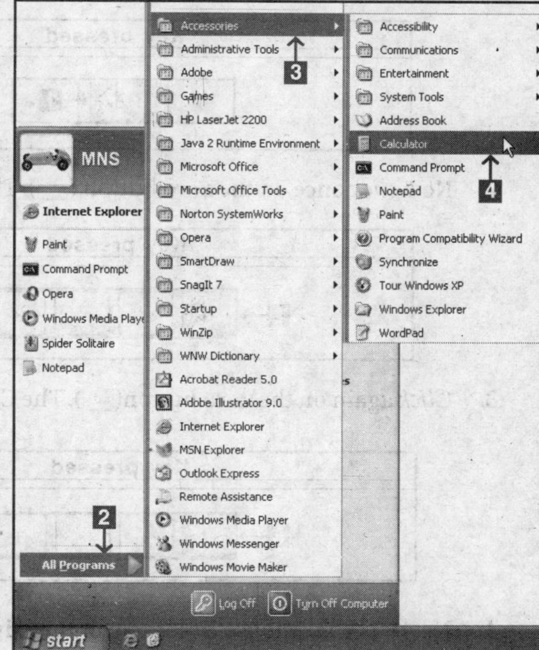

Fig. W-5.103

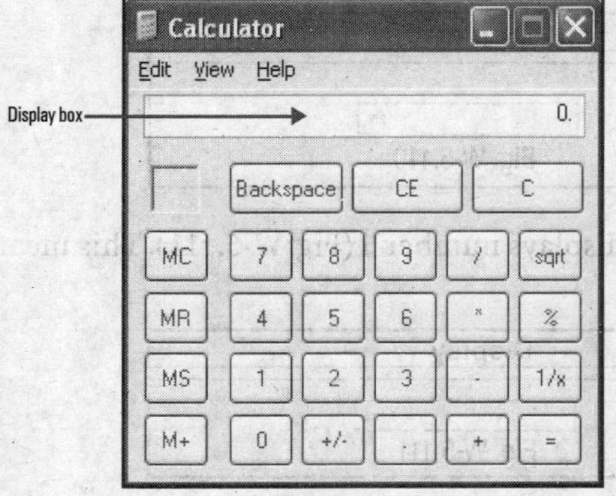

Fig. W-5.104

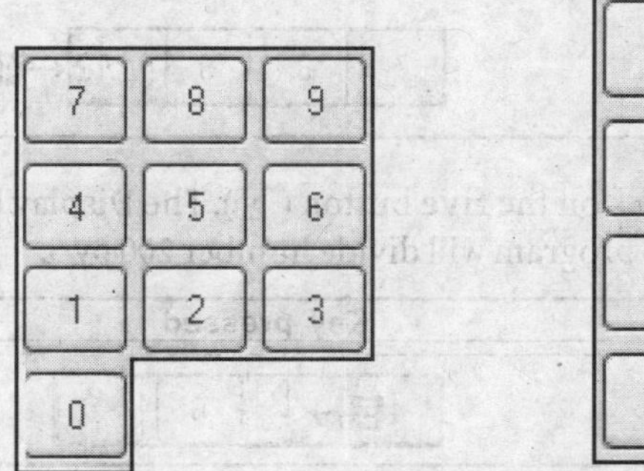

Fig. W-5.105: Numeric buttons

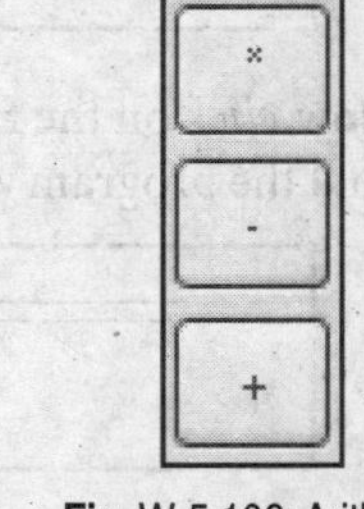

Fig. W-5.106: Arithmetic Operator buttons

Inside the Calculator window, you will see various buttons. The **Numeric** buttons (0 – 9) are shown in Fig. W-5.105, while Fig. W-5.106 shows various other buttons such as the **Arithmetic Operator** buttons (/, *, - and +), **Equal to** button(=), etc.

Let us perform a simple calculation to learn how to use the calculator buttons in Windows XP. Suppose, you wish to divide 200 by 5. To do this calculation with the **Calculator** program, undertake the steps described in the next page.

1. *Move* the mouse-pointer on the **two** button (2), and *click* the left mouse-button. Number **2** appears in the Display box of calculator (Fig. W-5.107).

Key pressed	Display
1 · 2 ← **1**	2

Fig. W-5.107

2. Now *click* once on the **zero** button (0). The Calculator Display box shows **20** (Fig. W-5.108).

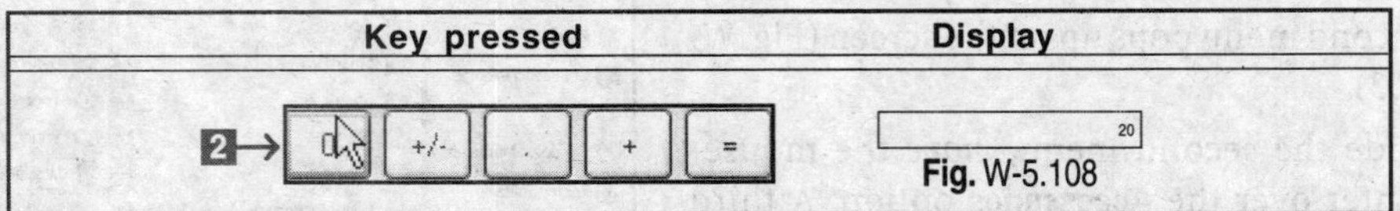

Fig. W-5.108

3. *Click* again on the **zero** button(0). The Calculator Display box shows number **200** (Fig. W-5.109).

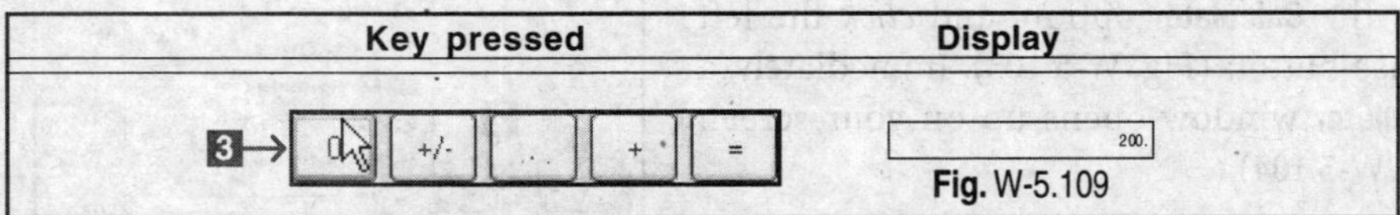

Fig. W-5.109

4. Now *move* the mouse-pointer over the **Division** button (/), and *click* the left mouse-button (Fig. W-5.110). As you *click*, the program is instantly informed that it has to divide the selected number.

Key pressed	Display
7 · 8 · 9 · / ← **4**	200.

Fig. W-5.110

5. Now, *click* on the **five** button (5). The Display box displays number **5** (Fig. W-5.111). This means that the program will divide number 200 by 5.

Key pressed	Display
4 · **5** → 5 · 6 · *	5

Fig. W-5.111

6. Finally, *move* the mouse-pointer on the **equal to** button (=), as seen in Fig. W-5.112, and *click* the left mouse-button. Immediately, the answer **40** gets displayed in the Display box (Fig. W-5.112).

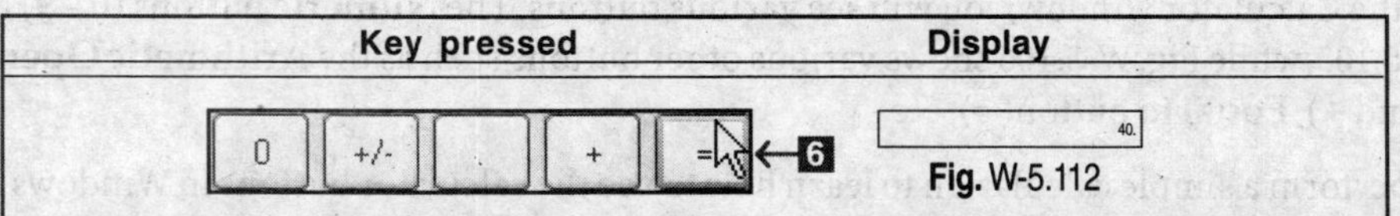

Fig. W-5.112

Closing Calculator

Let us now exit the Calculator program through the following steps.

1. *Move* the mouse-pointer over the **Close** button (☒) on the **title bar** of the **Calculator** window (Fig.W-5.113).
2. *Click* the left mouse-button on it. Immediately, the **Calculator** window disappears and the **Desktop** gets displayed on the screen.

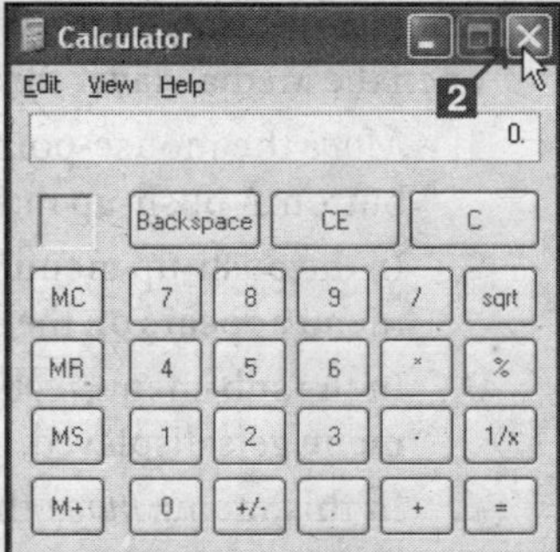

Fig. W-5.113

Windows Media Player

People generally play **VCD** (Visual Compact Disk) and **DVD** (Digital Video Disk) on computer. These CDs give better picture, good resolution and better performance. The storing capacity of a CD is approximately 650 MB. On one CD, you can store a full three-hour movie.

Do you know how to play a CD on computer? If not, don't worry. You can quickly learn playing CDs on your computer with the help of **Windows Media Player** program. This program comes with Windows XP. When you instal Windows XP, the Windows Media Player program by default gets loaded in your computer's memory. It finds place among **Entertainment** tools and is listed under the **Accessories** option.

Once you learn the use of Windows Media Player, you can use your computer as an all-in-one entertaining medium. You can play music on it, watch movies, hear radio station, play and copy your own CD, store movies and look for movies that are available on the Internet.

Windows Media Player provides several skins which are nothing but display themes. Whenever you select a skin, the appearance of the Windows Media Player changes. You can choose a skin from the list of skins that comes in-built with the Windows Media Player. You can also download skins from the web. The Windows Media Player can serve as all the devices listed below:

- CD player
- Audio and video Player
- Media Juke Box
- Media Guide
- Internet Radio Tuner
- Portable Device to Transfer Music Files
- Audio CD Burner

If the Windows Media Player is not installed in your computer then insert the Windows Operating System CD and install the Windows Media Player or call your vendor.

Opening the Windows Media Player

After learning about the Windows Media Player's entertaining features, you may be eager to use it. Let us open the Media Player through following steps:

1. *Move* the mouse-pointer on the **Start** button (start) over the **Taskbar** and *click* the left mouse-button. A push-up menu appears (Fig. W-5.114).
2. In the push-up menu, *position* the mouse-pointer over the **All Programs** option (Fig. W-5.114). A sub-menu appears on the screen.
3. In the sub-menu, *move* the mouse-pointer over the **Accessories** option (Fig. W-5.114). Another sub-menu gets displayed.
4. In this menu, *move* the mouse-pointer over the **Entertainment** option (Fig. W-5.114). Another sub-menu appears on the screen.
5. In the new sub-menu, *click* the left-mouse button on the **Windows Media Player** option (Fig. W-5.114). The **Windows Media Player** opens up on the screen (Fig. W-5.115).

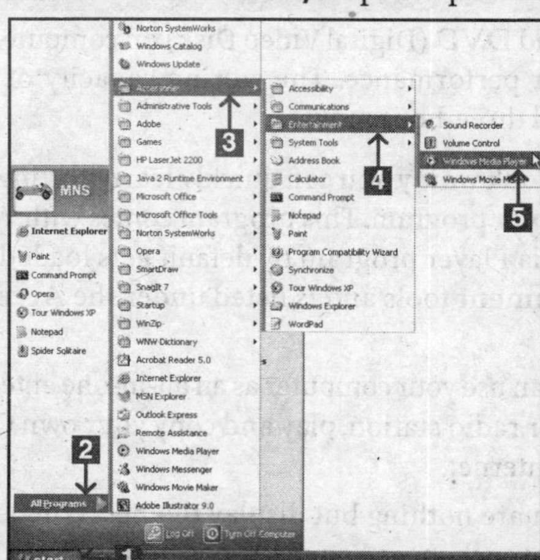
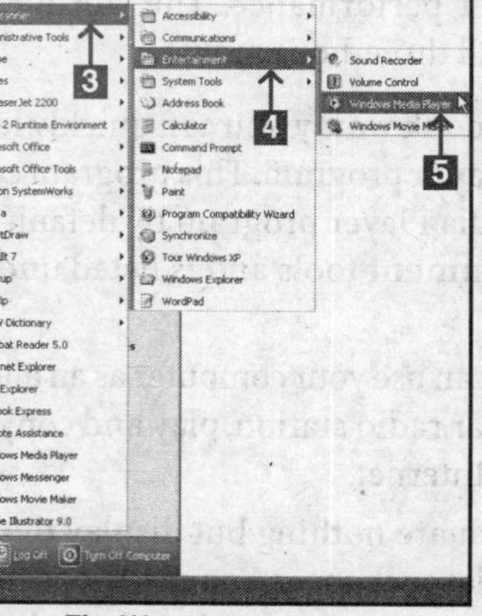

Fig. W-5.114

Fig. W-5.115

Playing VCDs and DVDs

Let us now play a VCD or a DVD on your computer. To do so, undertake the following steps:

1. If the **Windows Media Player** is not displayed on your screen, open it through Steps 1 to 6 described in the heading **opening Windows Media Player.**
2. *Insert* the **VCD** you want to watch into the **CD** drive.
3. *Click* on the **File** Menu bar option of the **Windows Media Player** window. A pull-down menu appears on the screen (Fig. W-5.116).
4. In the pull-down menu, *click* over the **Open** option (Fig. W-5.116). The **Open** dialog box appears (Fig. W-5.117).

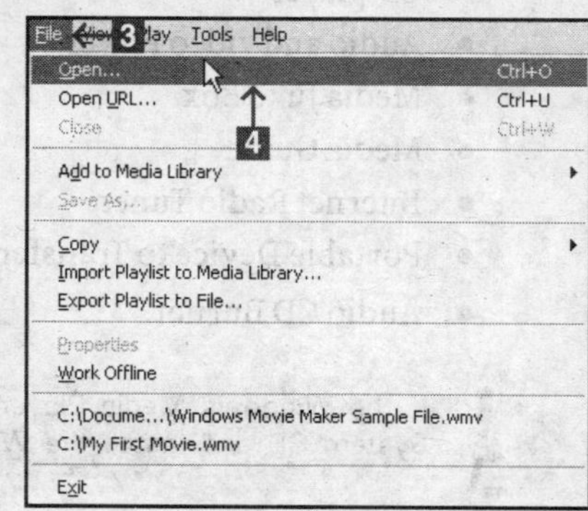

Fig. W-5.116

5. Whatever you want to open in the Media Player must be mentioned in the **Look in** option of the **Open** dialog box. Currently, **My Videos** folder appears in the **Look in** option and the contents of this folder are displayed in the **Open** dialog box.
6. Now, to display the contents of your VCD, first locate the CD drive, in our case **E:**, in which you have inserted the VCD. For this, *click* on the down-arrow button (▾) in the box beside the **Look in** option (Fig. W-5.117). A list displaying the names of various drives and folders in your computer appears.
7. *Click* on the CD drive name, i.e. **E:** (Fig. W-5.118). The contents of the inserted VCD are displayed in the dialog box window (Fig. W-5.119).

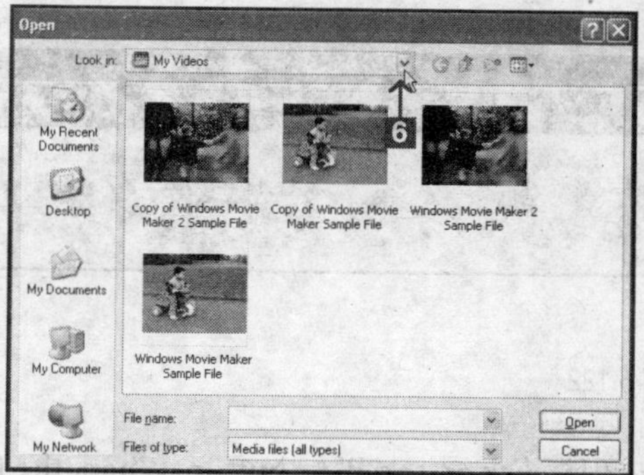

Fig. W-5.117

Fig. W-5.118

8. In the displayed VCD contents, you have to look for the **MPEGAV** folder because this folder contains the file that can be played the Media Player. So, locate the **MPEGAV** folder and *double-click* on it.
9. The **MPEGAV** folder opens up. It has only one file, **MUSIC01**. To open this file, *click* on the **Open** button in the **Open** dialog box (Fig. W-5.120). After a few seconds, **Windows Media Player** will start playing the movie on the screen of your computer (Fig. W-5.121).

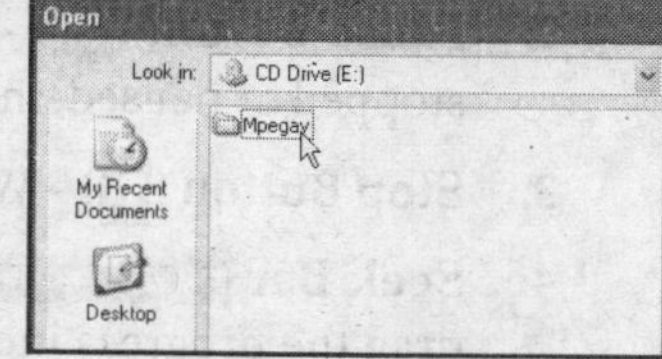

Fig. W-5.119

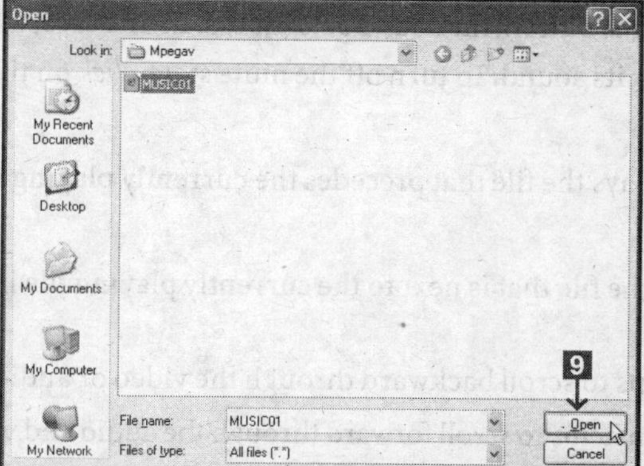

Fig. W-5.120

Fig. W-5.121

Similarly, you can play the song files and DVDs (if your computer is DVD compatible) in the **Windows Media Player.**

Play Back Control Area

The **Play Back Control Area** (Fig. W-5.122) is displayed at the bottom of the **Media Player.** You can use these controls to adjust the volume level and to do basic playback tasks such as playing, pausing, stopping, rewinding and fast-forwarding audio and video files. Following is a brief description of each control .

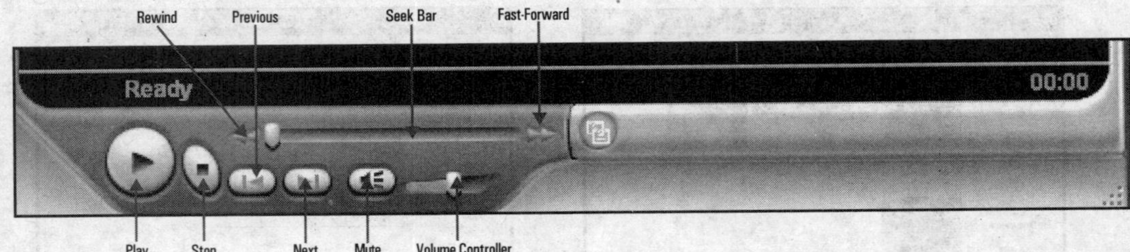

Fig. W-5.122

1. **Play Button** ( ) – To play a movie or a song file, *click* on the **Play** button. When the file starts playing, the **Play** button changes to the **Pause** button.
2. **Pause Button** ( ) – When you want to pause a file, *click* on the **Pause** button. When a file is stopped or paused, the **Pause** button changes to the **Play** button.
3. **Stop Button** ( ) – When you want to stop playing the selected file, *click* on the **Stop** button.
4. **Seek Bar** ( ) – The **Seek Bar** indicates the play progress of a selected item. You can drag the progress indicator anywhere in the selected file to play the desired portion of the song or movie.
5. **Volume Controller** ( ) – This button controls the **Volume** level of the file you are playing.
6. **Mute Button** ( ) – When we *click* on this button, the sound gets muted. In this case, the song or movie is still running, but we cannot hear its sound. To turn off the mute state, *click* on this button again
7. **Previous Button** ( ) – This button plays the file that precedes the currently playing file in the play list.
8. **Next Button** ( ) – This button plays the file that is next to the currently playing file in the play list.
9. **Rewind Button** ( ) – This button helps to scroll backward through the video or audio files.
10. **Fast-Forward Button** ( ) – This button helps to scroll forward through the audio and video files.

Playing Movie in Full Screen Mode

In default settings of the Media Player, a movie appears in the Movie Play Area only and other components of the Windows Media Player also appear on the screen. But, you can display the movie on your entire Desktop. This is called the **full screen mode.** To go into this mode, carry out the following steps:

1. Perform Steps **1** through **9** given under the heading **Playing VCDs and DVDs.**
2. When your movie gets started in the **Movie Play Area,** *click* on the **View** Menu bar option of the Media Player. A drop-down menu appears on the screen (Fig. W-5.123).
3. In the drop-down menu, *click* on the **Full Screen** option (Fig. W-5.123). The movie now plays in full screen (Fig. W-5.124).

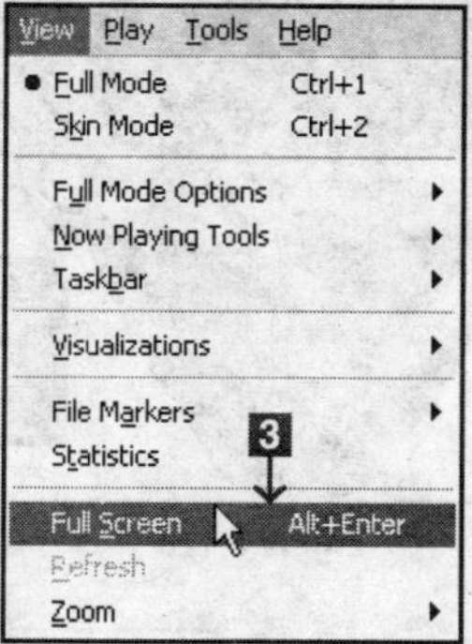

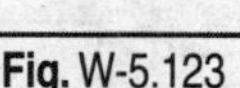
Fig. W-5.123

Fig. W-5.124

To revert to the normal appearance from the Full Screen Mode, press the escape key of your keyboard.

Changing the Appearance

You can change the default appearance, i.e. **Full Mode** view, of the Windows Media Player by applying a skin to it. Windows XP provides your various skins. When a skin is applied to the Media Player, it is said to be in the **Skin Mode.** To change the skin of the Media Player, follow the steps given below.

1. *Click* on the **View** Menu bar option of the Media Player. Immediately, a drop-down menu appears (Fig. W-5.125).
2. In the drop-down menu, position the mouse-pointer on the **Taskbar** option. A sub-menu appears on the screen (Fig. W-5.125).

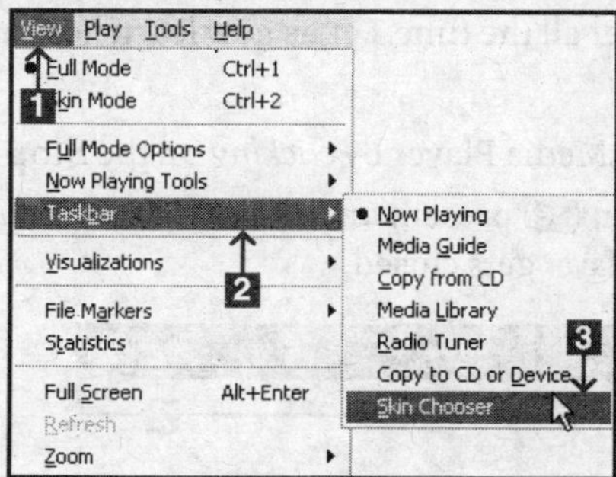

Fig. W-5.125

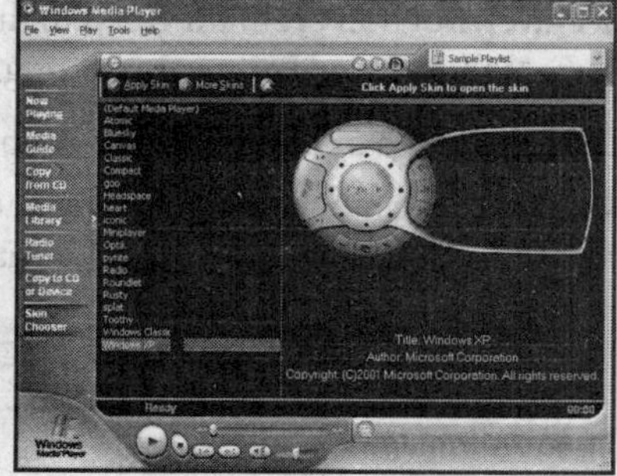

Fig. W-5.126

3. *Click* on the **Skin Chooser** option of this sub-menu (Fig. W-5.125). The **Windows Media Player** dialog box appears on the screen displaying a list of different types of skin (Fig. W-5.126).
4. *Click* on one of the skins, say, **Headspace** (Fig. W-5.127).
5. *Click* on the **Apply Skin** button. The selected skin is applied to the Windows Media Player (Fig. W-5.128).

Fig. W-5.127

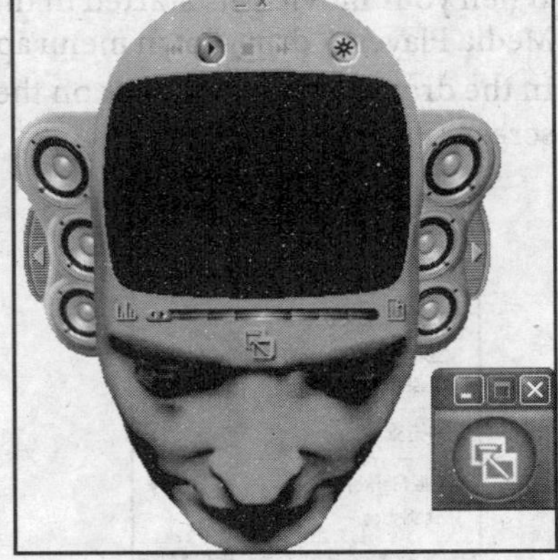
Fig. W-5,128

You can easily return from the Skin Mode to the Full Mode i.e. default appearance of the Media Player, in the following way:

1. Click the right mouse button, a menu appears on the screen (Fig. W-5.129).
2. In this menu, click over the Switch to Full Mode option (Fig. W-5.129). The default appearance of the Media Player is restored.

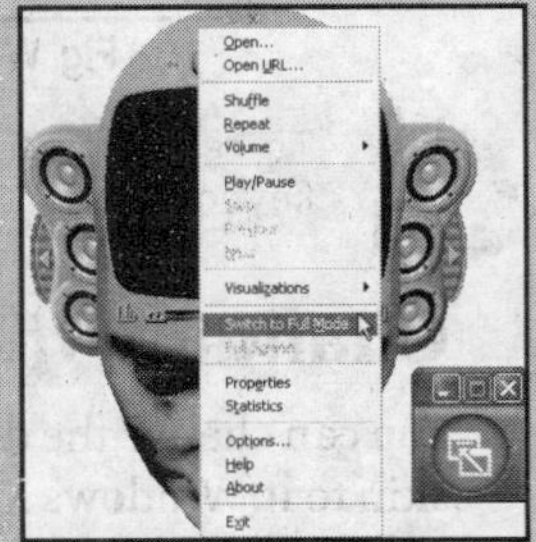

Fig. W-5.129

Closing the Windows Media Player

So, you have learnt how to turn your computer into an entertainment medium through the Windows Media Player. But don't remain glued to the Media Player all the time. Let us now learn how to close the Windows Media Player. Follow the steps given below.

1. *Close* the video or audio file you are playing on the Media Player by *clicking* on the **Stop** button.
2. Now, *move* the mouse-pointer over the **Close** button (☒) present on the **Title Bar** and *click* the left mouse-button (Fig. W-5.130). The **Windows Media Player** gets closed.

Fig. W-5.130

Windows Movie Maker

Movies are always a great attraction for people. While watching movies, many of us often dream of making movies ourselves. But, before taking a big leap towards the silver screen, it's better to try making movies sitting at home. Yes, it's possible thanks to Windows Movie Maker program that comes in-built with Windows XP. Widows Movie Maker is a video editing tool and the first step of Microsoft in digital video editing. It is designed to help you edit both your home videos and pictures. While editing the audio and video content in Windows Movie Maker, you can include titles, video transitions or effects. When your movie is ready, don't forget to share it with your friends and family members. Windows Movie Maker helps you send the movie to anyone through Internet.

You can use Windows Movie Maker to capture audio and video to your computer through a video camera, Web camera, or other video source, and then use the captured content in your movies. You can also import existing audio, video, or still pictures for use in your movies. Windows Movie Maker is fully compatible with Windows Media Player in-built into Windows Operating System such as Windows 98, Windows Me and Windows 2000.

In this section we will learn to do the following movie-related tasks in Windows Movie Maker.

- Opening Windows Movie Maker
- Importing video into Windows Movie Maker from a digital camera and creating clips
- Adding video and transition effects to the imported video
- Deleting effects
- Saving the video file or your movie on the computer and then viewing it in Windows Media Player

But before going through above listed steps, make sure that camera is properly connected to you computer. In case, the camera is not connected to your computer then go through the following steps:

1. *Insert* the smaller terminal of the USB cable into the camera's USB port (Fig.W-5.131).
2. *Plug* the other end of the USB cable into the USB port of your computer (Fig.W-5.131).

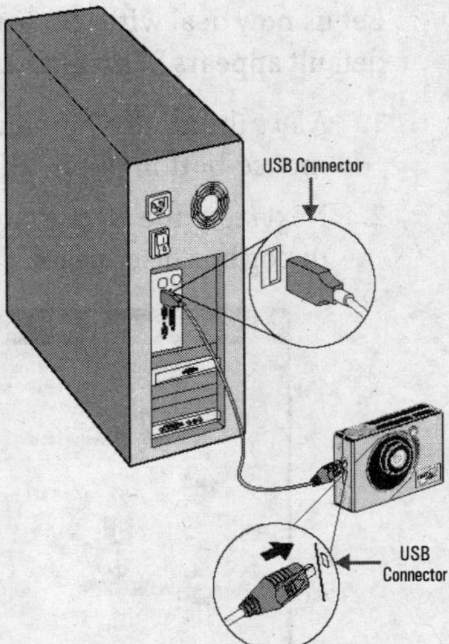

Fig. W-5.131: Connecting Camera

After ensuring the right connection, switch the camera on. Instantly, a dialog box, **Sony MemoryStick (F:)** (Fig. W-5.132), appears. This box prompts you to take some action to view the pictures/video stored in the camera. Before taking any action, carefully observe the name **Sony MemoryStick (F:)** of the dialog box. This drive name represents the camera that is connected to your computer. It contains the name of the camera's manufacturer (**Sony**, in our case) and name of the storing device installed inside the camera (**MemoryStick**, in our case). **F:** represents temporary drive which gets created automatically each time you connect the camera to the computer. The temporary drive appears in the **My Computer** window under the **Devices with Removable**

Storage category (Fig.W-5.133). No sooner, you remove the camera from the computer, the temporary drive disappears automatically from the **My Computer** window. The drive letter, which in our case is **F:** could vary from computer to computer as it is automatically generated by the Windows.

The names of files and folders present under the temporary drive are automatically generated and their naming depends on the name, model and manufacturer of camera. In our case, the video folder is named as **MSSONY**. In this chapter, while working with Windows Movie Maker, we will import a video file from **MSSONY**.

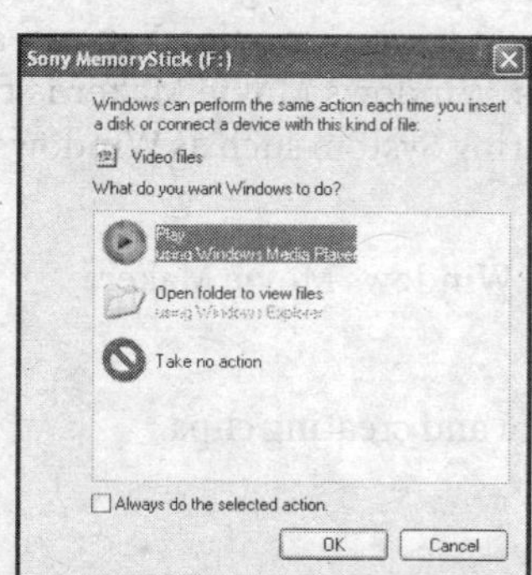

Fig. W-5.132

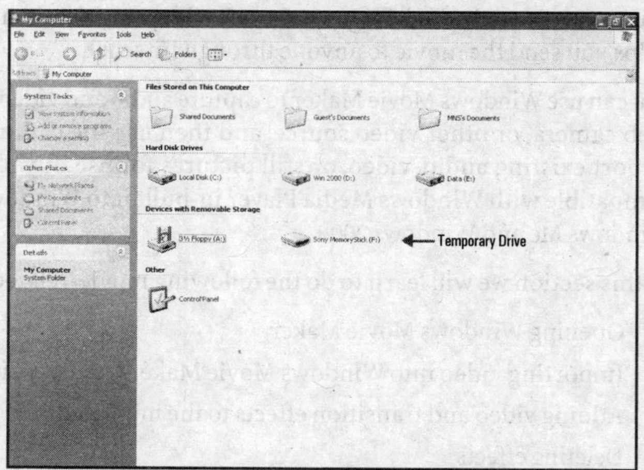

Fig. W-5.133: My Computer Window after connecting the camera

Let us now deal with the **Sony MemoryStick (F:)** dialog box (Fig. W-5.132). In this box, the **Play** option by default appears highlighted. For the time being, we will close this box through the following steps:

1. *Move* the mouse-pointer over the **Take no action** option present inside the dialog box and *click* the left mouse-button (Fig.W-5.134).
2. Next *move* the mouse-pointer over the **OK** button and *click* the left mouse-button (Fig. W-5.135). The dialog box disappears.

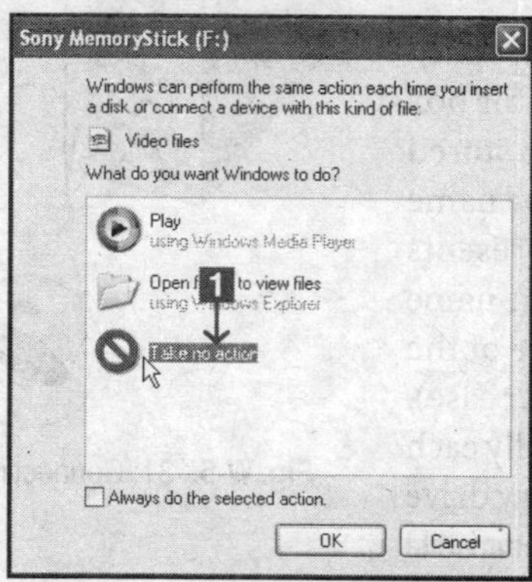

Fig. W-5.134

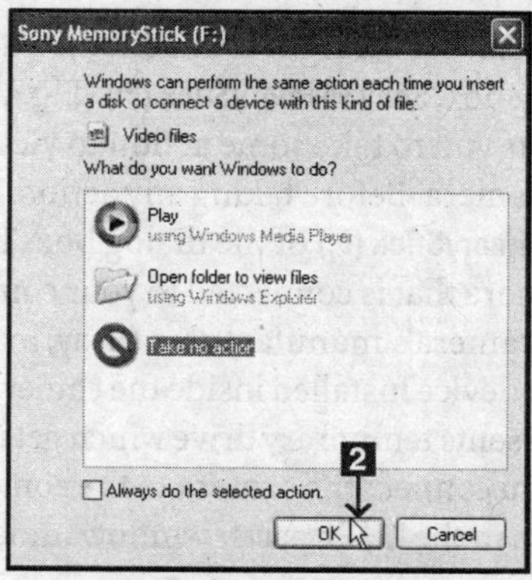

Fig. W-5.135

Opening Windows Movie Maker

Now, we will work with Windows Movie Maker. First, undertake the following steps to open Windows Movie Maker:

1. *Place* the mouse-pointer over the **Start** button (start) and *click* the left mouse-button. A push-up menu appears (Fig.W-5.136).
2. In the push-up menu, *place* the mouse-pointer over the **All Programs.** A second menu appears (Fig. W-5.136).
3. In the second menu, *move* the mouse-pointer over the **Windows Movie Maker** and *click* the left mouse-button (Fig.W-5.136).
4. The window of **Windows Movie Maker** appears on the screen (Fig.W-5.137).

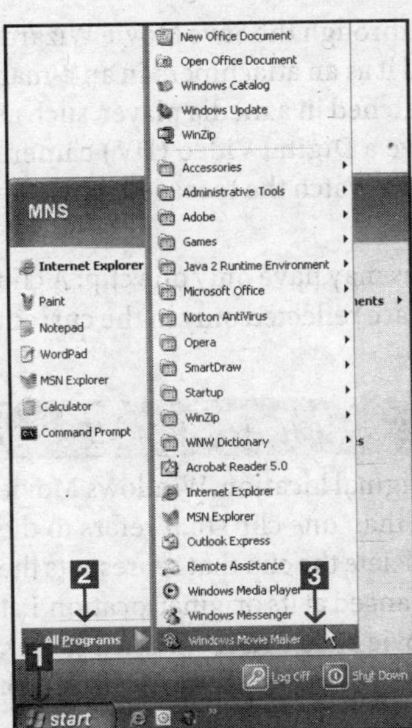

Fig. W-5.136

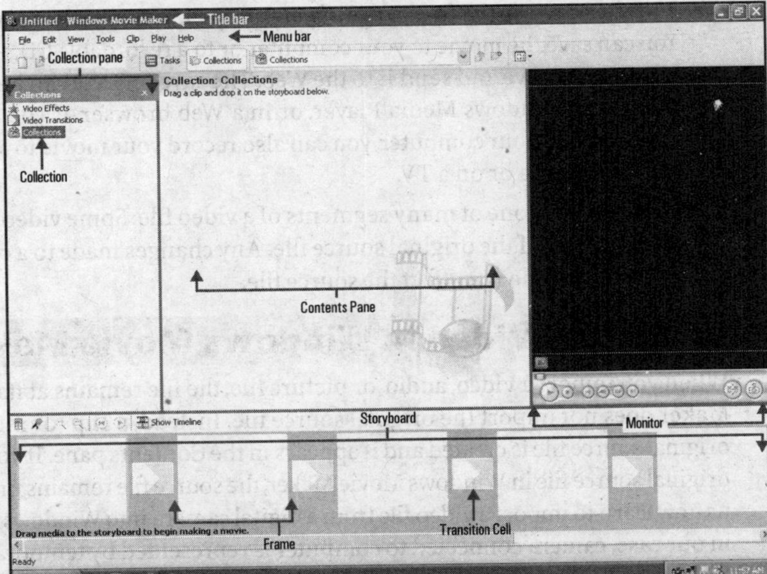

Fig. W-5.137

Let us now understand various terms and parts associated with the Movie Maker Window.

1. **Collection:** A collection contains audio clips, video clips, or pictures that you have imported or captured in Windows Movie Maker. In other words, a collection acts as a container for your clips, which are smaller segments of audio and video. It helps you organize the imported or captured content. Your collections appear in the Collections Pane on the left side of the Movie Maker Window (Fig.W-5.137).
2. **Collections Pane:** The Collections Pane displays your collections. The collections get listed by name in the Collections Pane when the Collections folder is double-clicked. You can display the clips of a particular collection in the Contents Pane on the right by double clicking it. The Collection Pane also contains options for adding **Video Effects** and **Video Transitions** (Fig.W-5.137).

3. **Contents Pane:** The Contents Pane displays the clips of collections. You can drag clips from the Contents Pane to the Storyboard. You can also drag clips to the monitor to play them.
4. **Monitor:** The black screen on the right of the Movie Maker Window is called monitor. It is meant to view video clips or entire movie. On monitor, you can preview your project before saving it as a movie. You can use the playback controls to navigate through an individual clip or an entire project (Fig.W-5.137).
5. **Storyboard:** The Storyboard consists of frames (a location on storyboard where you actually place the clips) and is positioned at the bottom in default view of the Movie Maker. You can use the Storyboard to look at the sequence of clips in your project and easily rearrange them, if necessary. This view also lets you see any video effects or video transitions that have been added (Fig.W-5.137).
6. **Transition Cells:** The empty spaces between various Storyboard frames are known as Transition Cells. You can use the Transition Cell to add Transition Effect between two clips (Fig.W-5.137).
7. **Movie:** Movie is the final stage of your project. You save the movie through the Save Movie Wizard. You can save the movie to your computer or to a recordable CD, send it as an attachment in an e-mail message, or save and send it to the Web. The saved movie can be watched in a media player, such as Microsoft Windows Media Player, or in a Web browser. If you have a Digital Video (DV) camera connected to your computer, you can also record your movie to a tape. Watch the recorded movie on the DV camera or on a TV.
8. **Clip:** A clip is one of many segments of a video file. Some video files may have only one clip. A clip is just a copy of the original source file. Any changes made to a clip are reflected only in the current project. They do not affect the source file.

Importing Video in Windows Movie Maker

When you import a video, audio, or picture file, the file remains at its original location. Windows Movie Maker does not import the original source file. Instead, a clip (or more than one clip) that refers to the original source file is created and it appears in the Contents pane. If you delete the clip that represents the original source file in Windows Movie Maker, the source file remains unchanged at its original location. Let us now learn to import a video file from a digital camera into Windows Movie Maker. As mentioned earlier, in our case, camera connected to computer is represented by temporary drive **Sony MemoryStick (F:)**. First, we will locate this drive in our system and then open it to access our video folder **MSSONY**. This folder has a sub-folder **MOML0001** that contains a video file, **Mov0062**. We will import this video file to our computer through the following steps.

1. Start with the Movie Maker window, i.e. Fig. W-5.137. *Move* the mouse-pointer over the **File** Menu bar option of the and *click* the left mouse-button. Instantly a pull-down menu appears (Fig.W-5.138).
2. In the pull-down menu, *move* the mouse-pointer over the **Import Collections** option and *click* the left mouse-button (Fig.W-5.139).

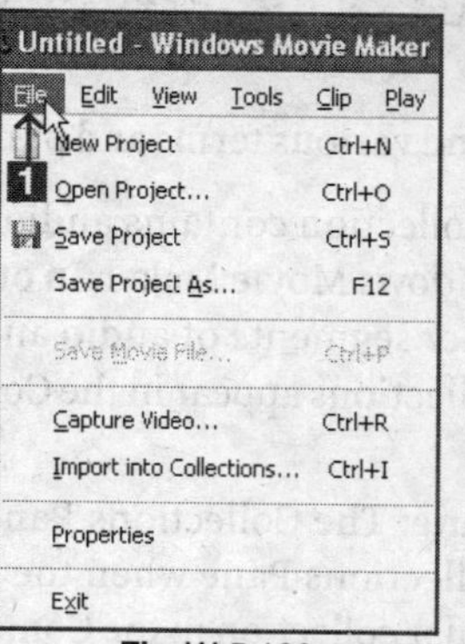

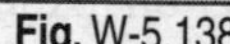
Fig. W-5.138

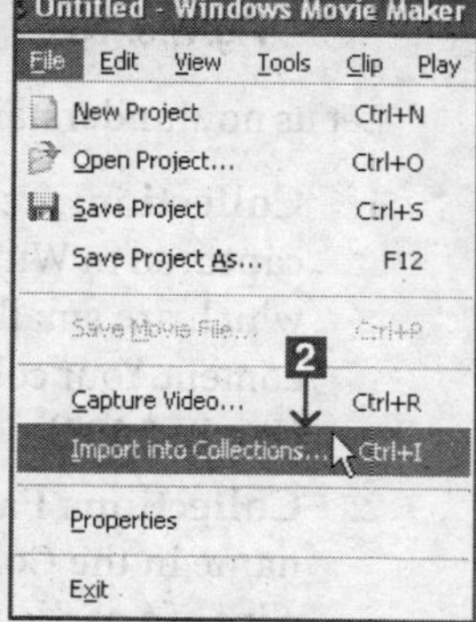

Fig. W-5.139

3. The **Import File** box, as shown in Fig.W-5.140, appears on the screen.
4. Now, we will search the temporary drive **Sony MemorySTick (F:)** through the **Import File** box. So, in this box *place* the mouse-pointer over the down-arrow button (⌄) beside the **Look in** option and *click* the left mouse-button. Instantly, a pull-down menu appears (Fig.W-5.141).

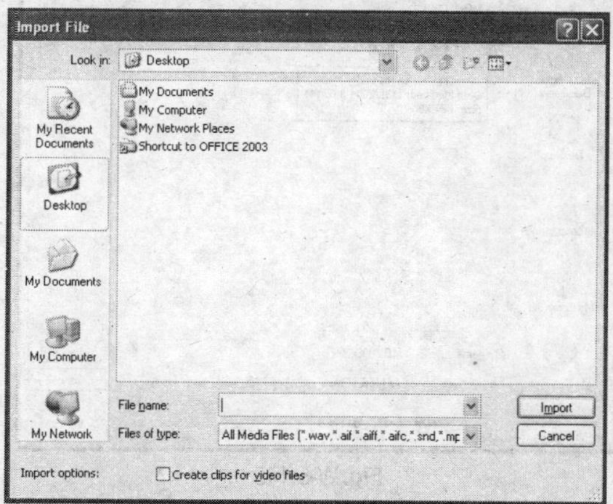

Fig. W-5.140

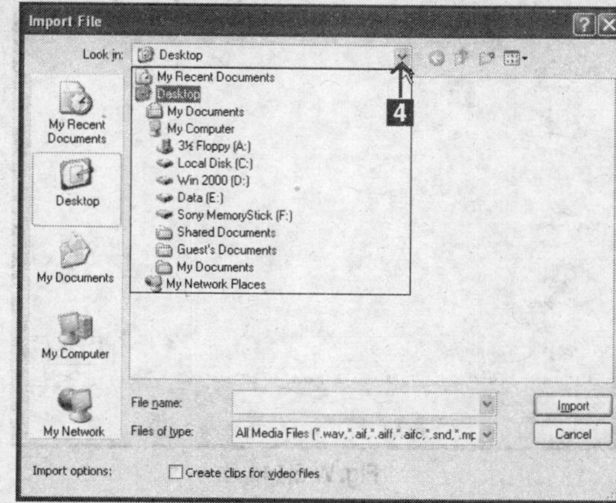

Fig. W-5.141

5. In the pull-down menu, *move* the mouse-pointer over the **Sony MemoryStick (F:)** and *click* the left mouse-button (Fig.W-5.142).
6. The **Sony MemoryStick (F:)** appears inside the rectangular box beside the **Look in** option and its contents appear in the bigger rectangular box. Now, *move* the mouse-pointer over the **MSSONY** folder and *double-click* the left mouse-button (Fig. W-5.143). The **MSSONY** folder appears beside the **Look in** option. This folder has a sub-folder, **MOML0001** that appears in the bigger rectangular box (Fig. W-5.144).

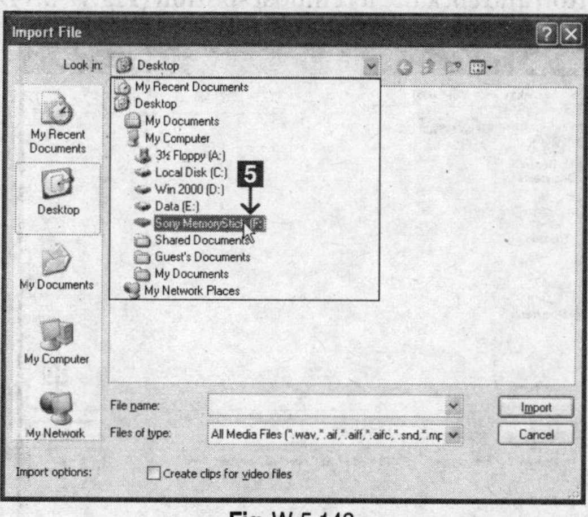

Fig. W-5.142

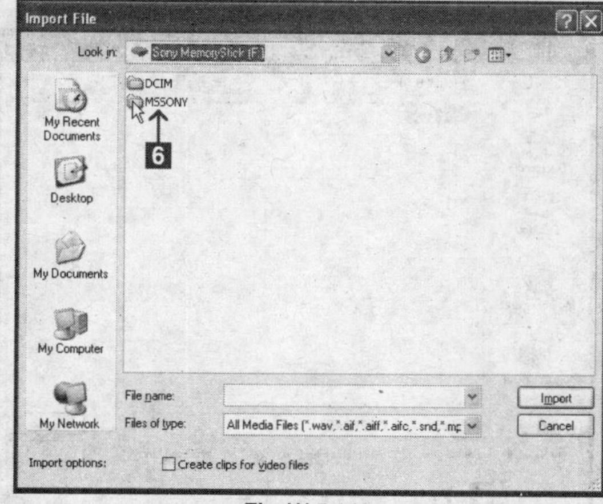

Fig. W-5.143

7. Now, to open the **MOML0001** sub-folder, *move* the mouse-pointer over it and *double-click* the left mouse-button (Fig.W-5.144).

8. The sub-folder opens up to display a video file, **MOV00662** (Fig. W-5.145). Now to create, clips for the video file, *move* the mouse-pointer over it and *click* the left mouse-button once to highlight it (Fig. W-5.145).

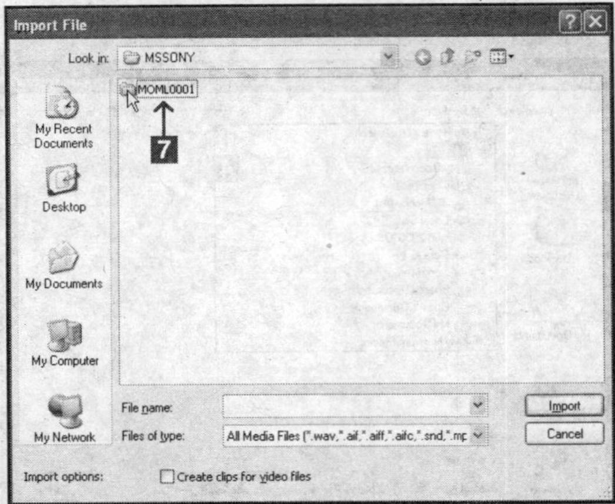

Fig. W-5.144

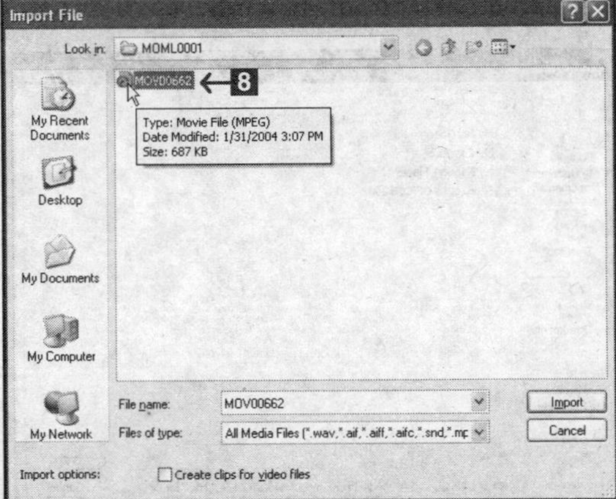

Fig. W-5.145

9. Now, *move* the mouse-pointer over the square box (☐) beside the **Create clips for video files** option at the bottom of the **Import File** window and *click* the left mouse-button (Fig. W-5.146). A check sign (☑) appears inside the box indicating that the option has been selected.

If you select the 'Create clips for video files' option in the Import File box, Windows Movie Maker automatically divides the video file into a number of clips each having its own duration (in minutes). The number of clips depends on the total duration of the video file. Larger the duration of the video file, more will be the number of clips to be created by Windows Movie Maker.

10. Next, *move* the mouse-pointer over the **Import** button and *click* the left mouse-button (Fig. W-5.147).

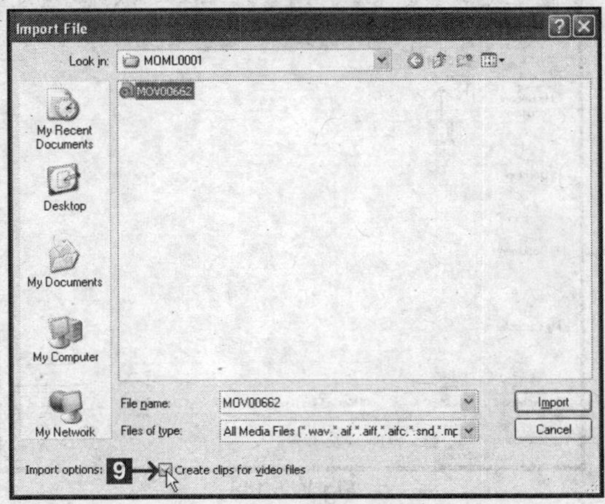

Fig. W-5.146

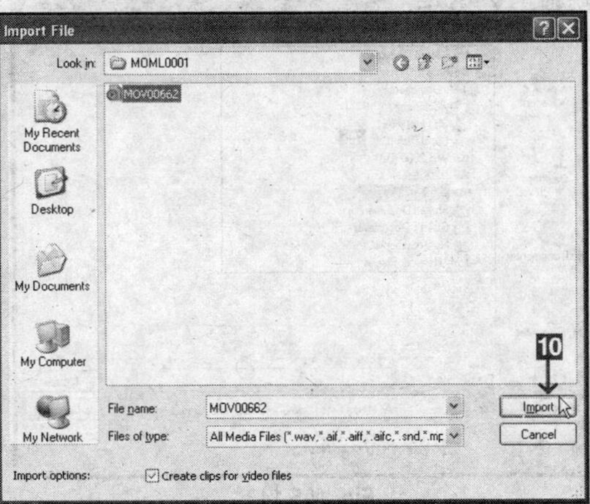

Fig. W-5.147

11. The **Import** box appears with progress bars (Fig.W-5.148). The progress bars indicates how much of the video file **MOV00662** has been imported from the video camera connected to your computer.

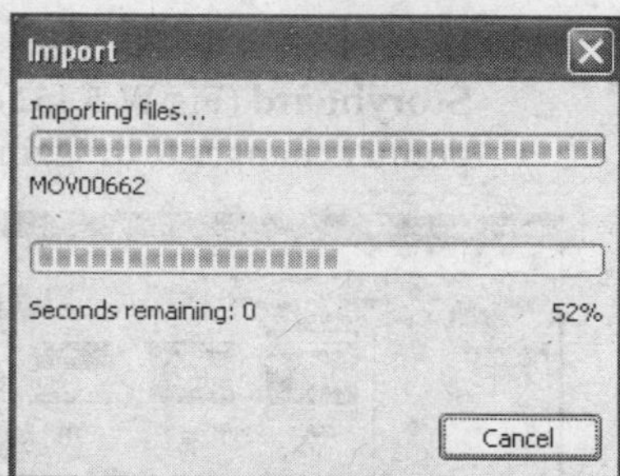

Fig. W-5.148

While importing a video file from the camera, never click over the Cancel button.

12. Once the video is imported, the Movie Maker window looks like Fig.W-5.149. This window shows three clips— **MOV00662**, **MOV00662 002**, and **MOV00662 003**. It means our video file **MOV00662** has been divided into three clips.

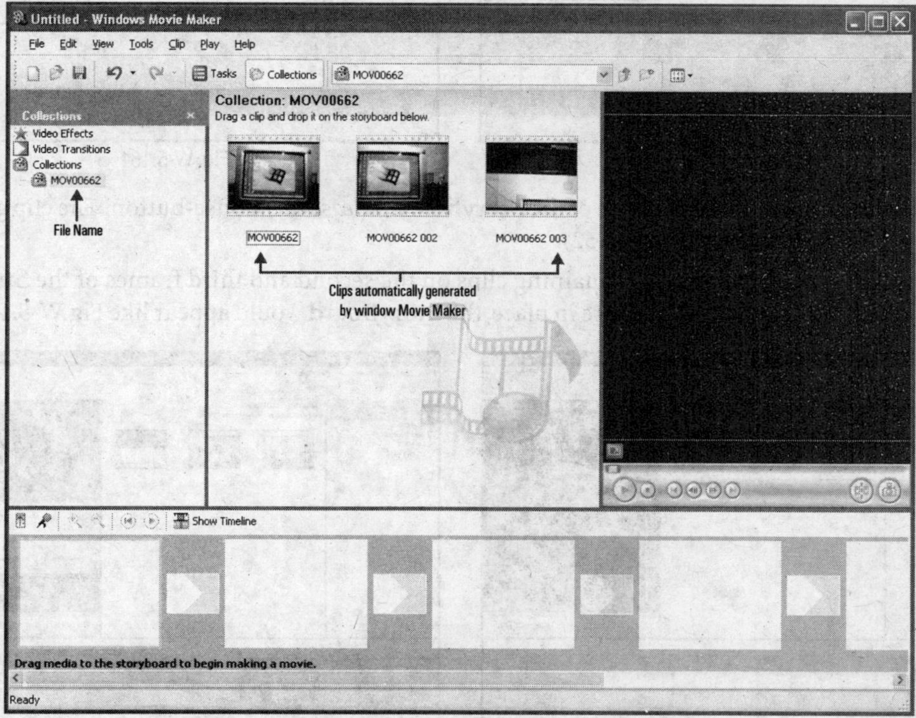

Fig. W-5.149

Adding Clips to the Storyboard

So, you have learnt to make clips of a video file while importing it your computer. Now, let us learn how to add the clips of the imported video file to the Storyboard so that a movie could be created with video and transition effects. Undertake the following steps to add clips to the Storyboard.

1. Proceed with Fig. W-5.149 open on your screen. *Move* the mouse-pointer over the first clip and *click* the left mouse-button (Fig.W-5.150).

2. Now, keeping the left mouse-button *pressed*, *drag* the mouse-pointer towards the first frame of the **Storyboard** (Fig.W-5.151). As you drag the clip, a shadow follows the clip and the default mouse-pointer changes to dragging-pointer (⦸).

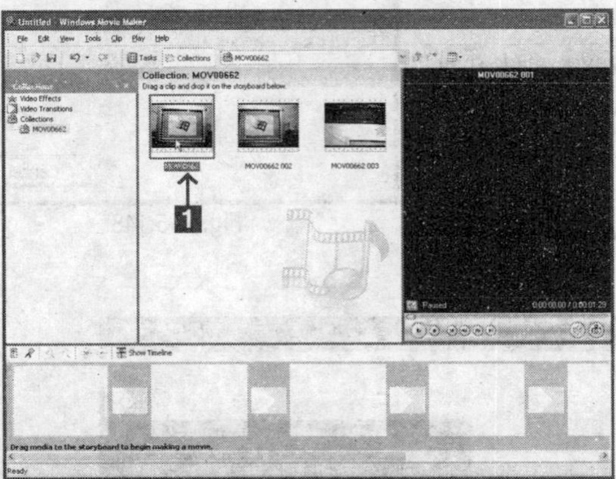

Fig. W-5.150

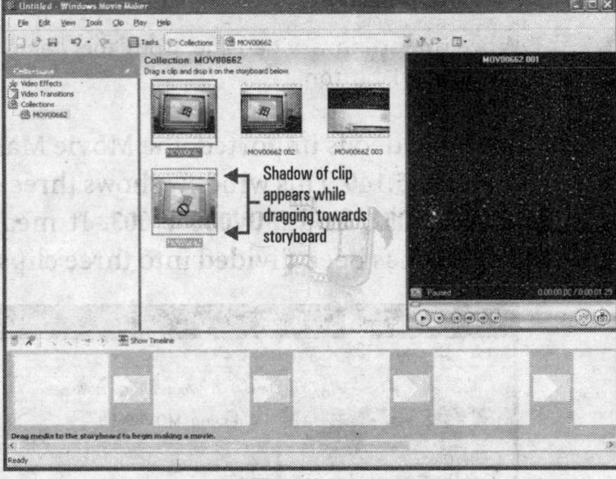

Fig. W-5.151

3. On reaching over the first frame of the **Storyboard**, *release* the mouse-button. The clip gets placed over the **Storyboard** (Fig. W-5.152).
4. Similarly, *drag* and *place* the remaining clips on the second and third frames of the **Storyboard.** Once all clips of our video file are in place, the **Storyboard** would appear like Fig.W-5.153.

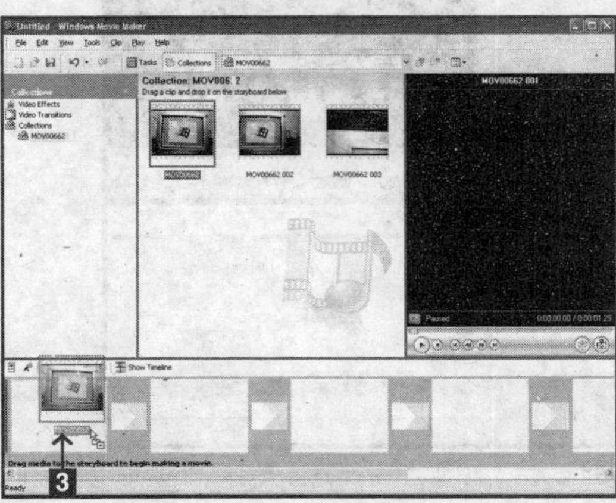

Fig. W-5.152

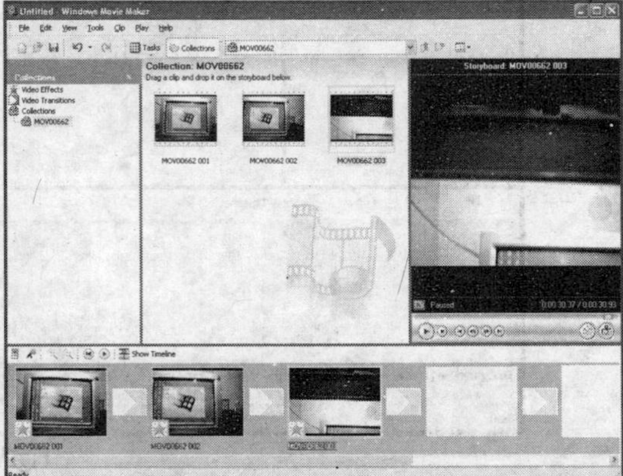

Fig. W-5.153

Adding Video and Transition Effects

While placing clips over the Storyboard, you must have noticed an empty space ( ) between two consecutive frames of the Storyboard. This space is known as **Transition Cell** and it is used to add **Video Transition** between two clips. The **Video Transition** controls the way your video moves from one clip to the other. In other words, it is meant to fill the time gap between the playing of two video clips. It plays after one clip ends and the other clip has yet to start. You can add similar or dissimilar Video Transitions for different pairs of clips. You can also make your clips impressive using video effects. These are special effects that determine how a video clip or picture would play in your final movie. A video effect is applied on the clip for its entire play duration.

You can apply video effects on one or all clips. It's up to you whether you choose a similar video effect for all clips or go for different video effects for each clip present on your Storyboard.

Adding a Video effect

Let us now learn to apply Video and Video Transition effects to the clips present on our Storyboard.

1. Start with Fig. W-5.153 displayed on your monitor. *Move* the mouse-pointer over the **Video Effects** option present in the **Collections** pane and *click* the left mouse-button. Various video effects provided by the Windows Movie Maker get displayed in the **Video Effects** pane beside the **Collections** pane (Fig.W-5.154).
2. Now *move* the mouse-pointer over the desired video effect, say **Fade In, From Black**, and *click* the left mouse-button over it to select it (Fig.W-5.155).

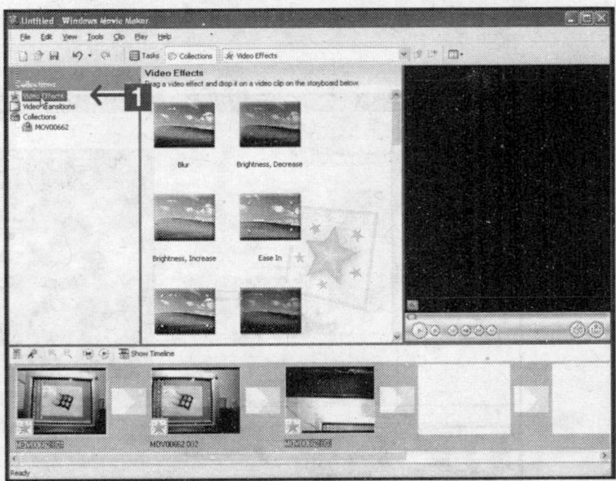

Fig. W-5.154

Fig. W-5.155

3. Next, keeping the left-mouse-button *pressed*, *drag* the mouse-pointer towards the video clip in the first frame of the **Storyboard**. As you *move* the mouse, a shadow follows the video effect (Fig. W-5.156).
4. On reaching the desired clip, *release* the mouse-button. The **Disabled Video Effect** symbol (⊠) turns into **Enabled Video** symbol (⊠) indicating that a video effect has been added to the clip in the first frame (Fig. W-5.157).

Fig. W-5.156

Similarly, you can add video effects to other clips on the Storyboard. Let us now learn how to add Video Transition between two clips.

Fig. W-5.157

Adding Video Transition

Just like video effect, Video Transition can also be added between any two clips present on the Storyboard. Let us add a Video Transition between first and second clips of the Storyboard. To do so, undertake the following steps:

1. Start with the window of Fig. W-5.156 displayed on your computer. *Move* the mouse-pointer over the **Video Transition** option in the **Collections** pane and *click* the left mouse-button (Fig. W-5.158). Immediately, various transition effects offered by the Windows Movie Maker appear in the **Video Transitions** pane beside the **Collections** pane (Fig. W-5.159).
2. Now, *move* the mouse-pointer over the desired Video Transition, say **Checkboard, Across**, and *click* the left mouse-button (Fig. W-5.159).

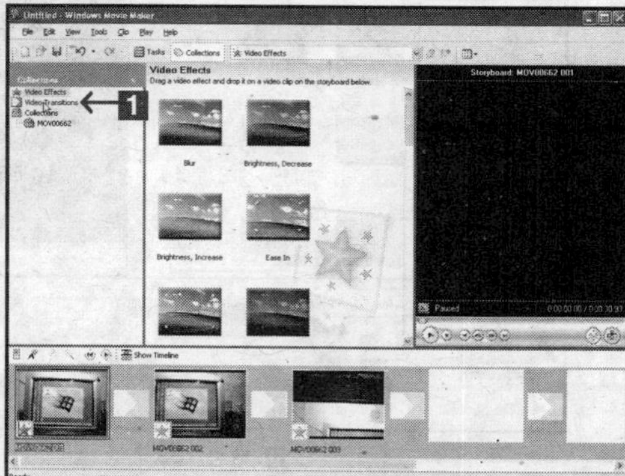

Fig. W-5.158

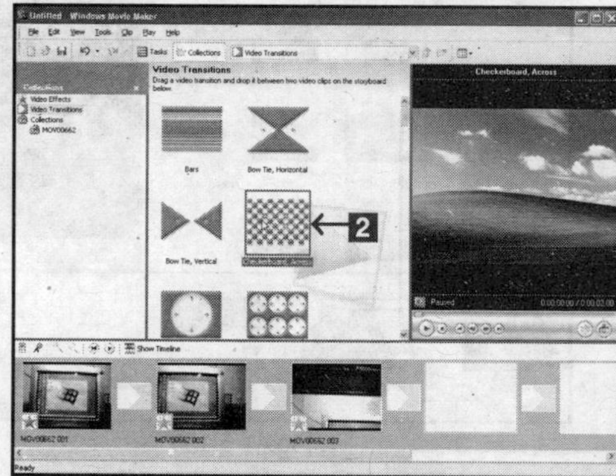

Fig. W-5.159

3. Keeping the left mouse-button *pressed*, *drag* the mouse-pointer towards the **Transition Cell** ( ) between the first and second frames of the **Storyboard.** As you *move* the mouse, a shadow follows the Video Transition (Fig. W-5.160).
4. On reaching over the desired **Transition Cell**, *release* the mouse-pointer. The **Empty Transition Cell** ( ) turns into a **Filled Transition Cell** ( ) (Fig. W-5.161).

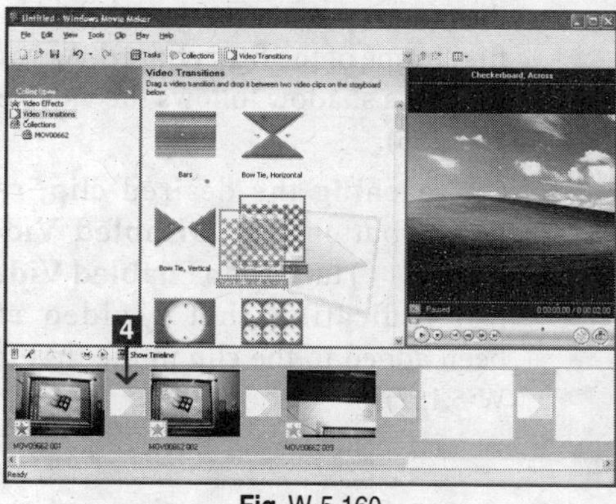

Fig. W-5.160

Similarly, you can add Video Transition to other clips on the Storyboard. After adding effects to all clips, the Storyboard appears like Fig. W-5.162. Now, you may be

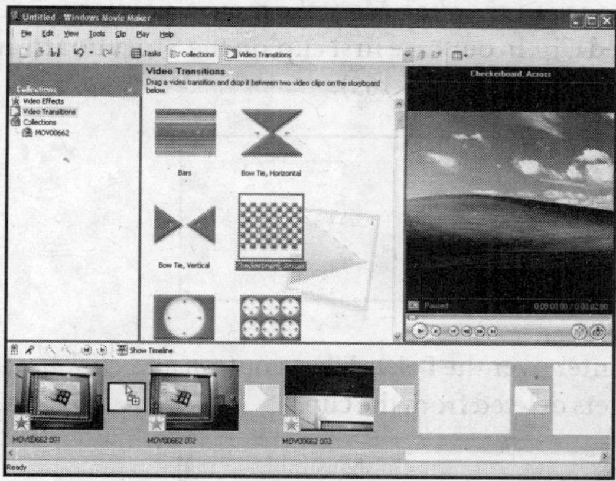

Fig. W-5.161

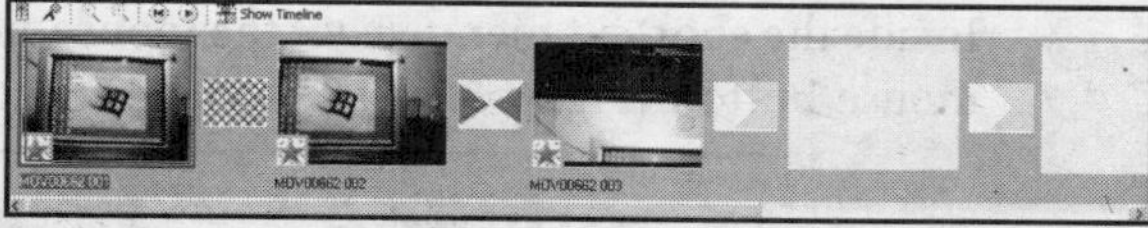

Fig. W-5.162

curious to see the result of these effects when the Storyboard clips are played. So, read on to learn how to play the Storyboard clips.

Playing Storyboard Clips

To play the Storyboard clips, go through the steps listed below:

1. *Move* the mouse-pointer over the **Play** (⊙) button present under the **Monitor** and *click* the left mouse-button (Fig.W-5.163).
2. The **Windows Movie Maker** starts playing the **Storyboard** clips with added effects (Fig.W-5.164).

Fig. W-5.163

Fig. W-5.164

Deleting a Video Effect

After viewing the clips on the monitor, you may not like the video or audio transition effects. Don't worry, you can delete the existing effects and add the new ones. Let us learn how to do that. To delete a video effect from a clip, undertake the following steps.

1. Start with the window of Fig.W-5.164 displayed on your monitor. *Move* the mouse-pointer over the **Enabled Video Effect** ( ) symbol of the desired clip, in our case first clip, on the **Storyboard** and *click* the right-mouse-button. A shortcut menu appears (Fig.W-5.165).

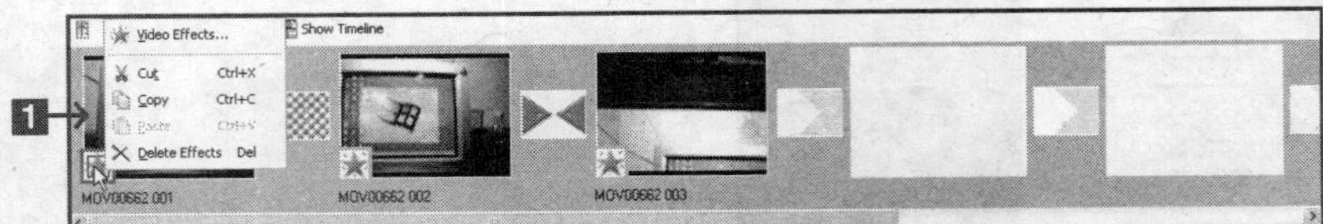

Fig. W-5.165

2. Inside the shortcut menu, *move* the mouse-pointer over the **Delete Effects** option and *click* the left mouse-button (Fig.W-5.166). The video effect gets deleted from the clip.

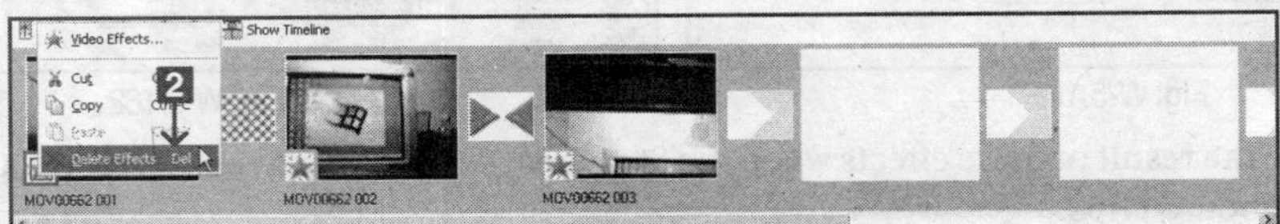

Fig. W-5.166

Deleting a Video Transition

To delete a transition effect between two clips, undertake the following steps.

1. *Move* the mouse-pointer over the **Filled Transition Cell** ( ) between two clips, in our case first and second, and *click* the right mouse-button. A shortcut menu appears (Fig.W-5.167).

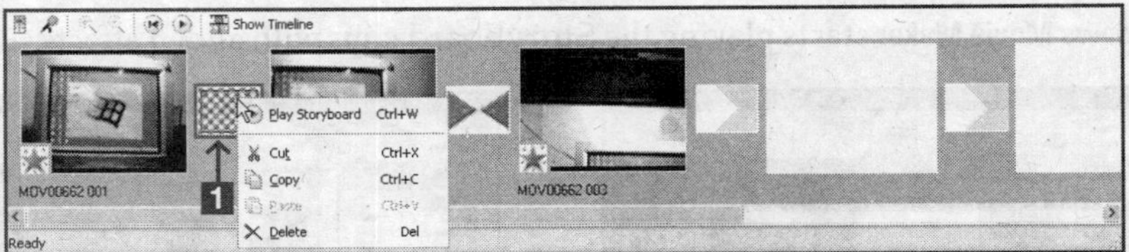

Fig. W-5.167

2. In the shortcut menu, *move* the mouse-pointer over the **Delete** option and *click* the left mouse-button (Fig.W-5.168). The video transition effect gets deleted from the selected **Transition Cell.**

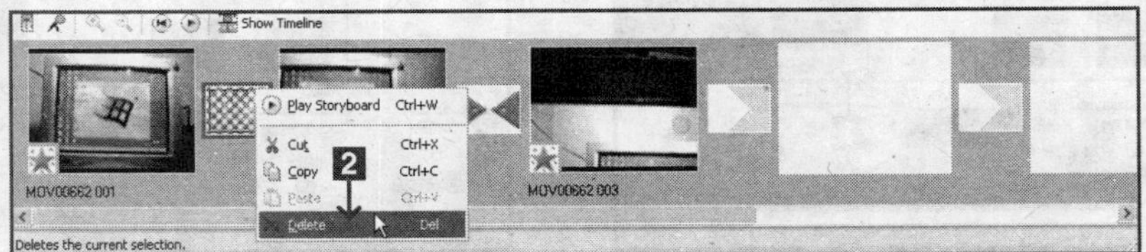

Fig. W-5.168

Saving the Movie

After editing, playing and making necessary changes to your movie, it's time to save it. Let us save our movie file in the **Local Disk (C:)** In Movie Maker, a movie is saved through the **Save Movie Wizard.** You can save your movie quickly through the steps listed on the next page.

1. *Move* the mouse-pointer over the **File** menu bar option and *click* the left mouse-button. Instantly, a pull-down menu appears (Fig.W-5.169).
2. In the pull-down menu, *move* the mouse-pointer over the **Save Movie File** option and *click* the left mouse-button (Fig.W-5.170).

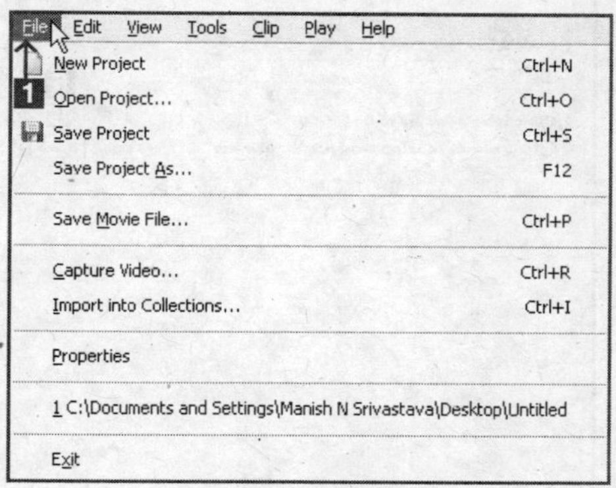

Fig. W-5.169

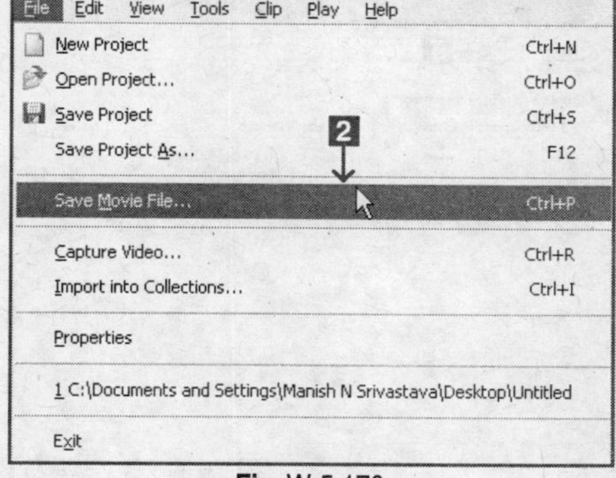

Fig. W-5.170

3. The **Save Movie Wizard** appears on the screen. Using the **Movie Location** box of this wizard, you can specify the location for your movie. In the **Movie Location** box, the **My Computer** option appears highlighted by default. Let us go by the default save location, **My Computer**, for saving our movie. So, *click* over the **Next** button and *move* ahead (Fig.W-5.171).
4. The **Saved Movie File** box of the **Save Movie Wizard** appears on the screen (Fig. W-5.172). In this box, you need to specify the name for the movie and the location where you want to save it. First, we will assign a name to the movie. You see a highlighted default text in the box under the **Enter a file name for your saved movie** option (Fig.W-5.172). We will replace the default text by the name that we want to give to our movie.

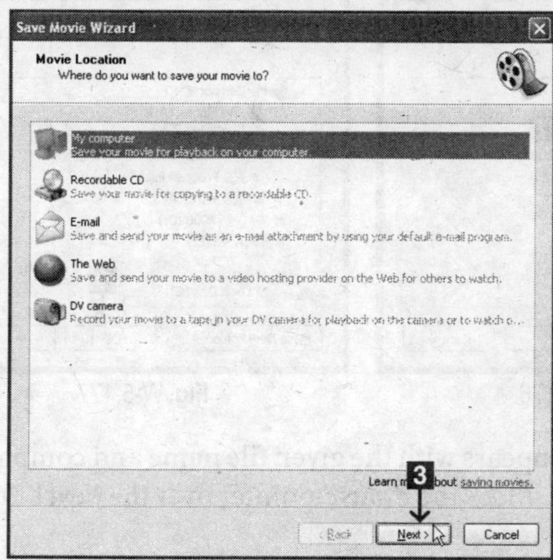

Fig. W-5.171

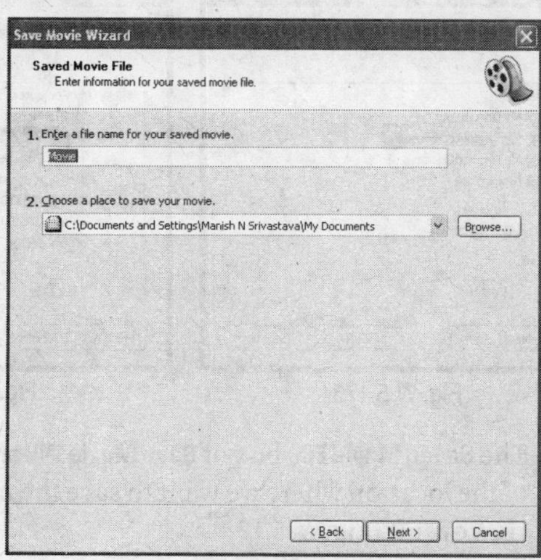

Fig. W-5.172

5. *Type* **My First Movie** as the name of the movie (Fig.W-5.173).
6. Now, *move* the mouse-pointer over the **Browse** button and *click* the left mouse-button (Fig.W-5.174).

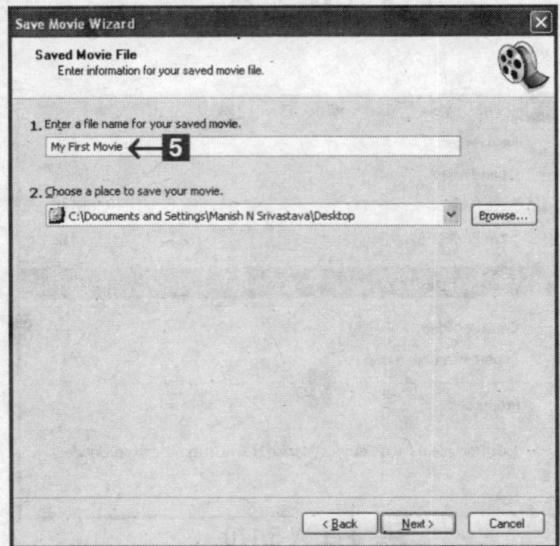

Fig. W-5.173

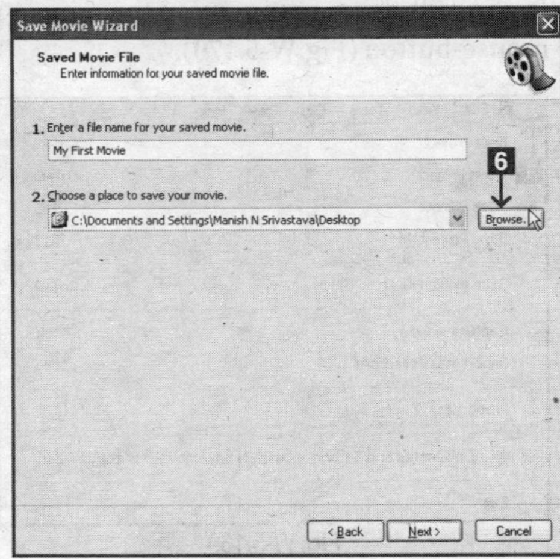

Fig. W-5.174

7. The **Browse for Folder** box appears (Fig. W-5.175). This box displays a small folder tree of your computer. In the folder tree, *move* the mouse-pointer over the **My Computer** and *click* the left mouse-button (Fig.W-5.175).
8. The folder tree expands, showing the contents of **My Computer** folder. Now *move* the mouse-pointer over the **Local Disk (C:)** and *click* the left mouse-button (Fig.W-5.176).
9. Finally, *move* the mouse-pointer over the **OK** button and *click* the left mouse-button (Fig.W-5.177). The **Browse for Folder** box disappears.

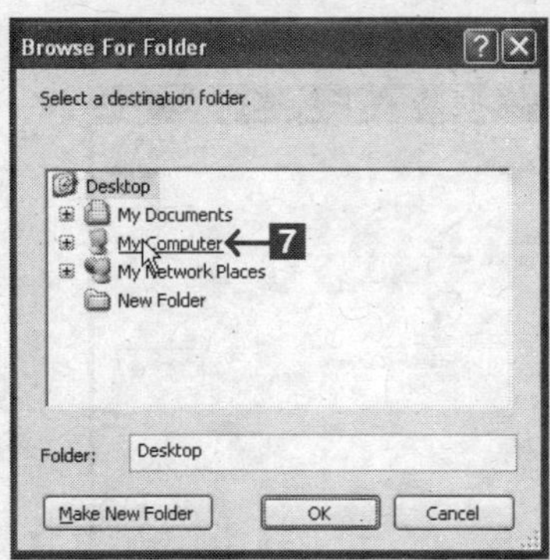

Fig. W-5.175

Fig. W-5.176

Fig. W-5.177

10. The **Saved Movie File** box of **Save Movie Wizard** reappears with the given file name and complete path of the location where we want to save the movie. *Move* the mouse-pointer over the **Next** button and *click* over it (Fig.W-5.178).

11. The **Movie Setting** box of the **Save Movie Wizard** appears (Fig. W-5.179). In this box, the **Best Quality for playback on my computer (recommended)** option is selected by default. If it's not selected then *move* the mouse-pointer over the round button (◯) beside this option and *click* over it. The round button changes to (◉) indicating that the option has been selected. Now, *click* over the **Next** button in the **Movie Setting** box (Fig. W-5.179).

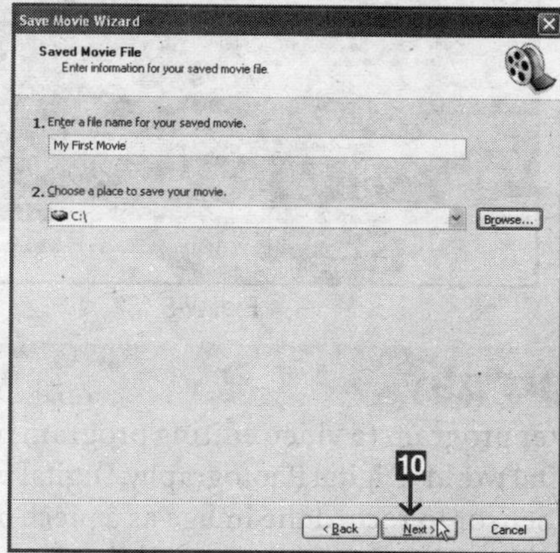

Fig. W-5.178

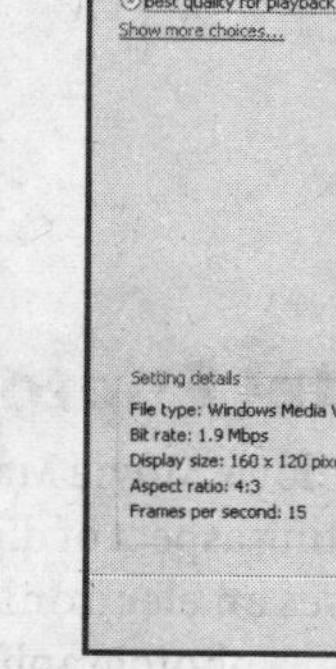

Fig. W-5.179

12. The **Saving Movie** box of **Save Movie Wizard** appears with a progress bar (Fig. W-5.180). Wait for a few moments as you are one step away from saving and viewing your movie file.

13. The **Completing the Save Movie Wizard** box of the **Save Movie Wizard** appears. In this box, make sure that a tick mark appears inside the square box beside the **Play movie when I click Finish** option. This option lets you view the saved file instantly. Finally, *click* over the **Finish** button (Fig. W-5.181).

NOTE

In case the 'Play movie when I click Finish' option is not selected then move the mouse-pointer over the square box (☐) beside this option and click the left mouse-button. A tick mark (☑) appears inside the box indicating that the option has been selected.

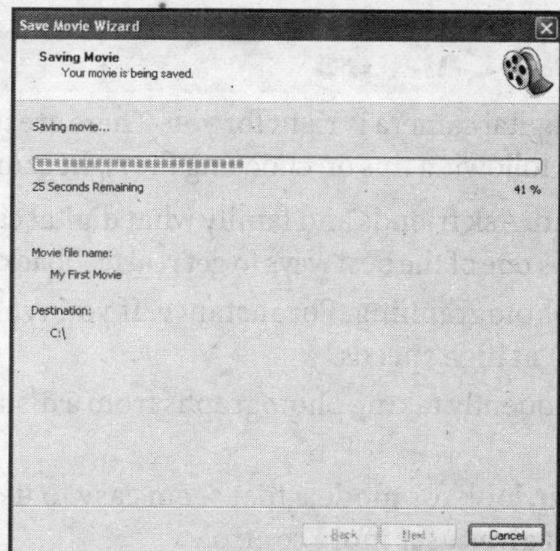

Fig. W-5.180

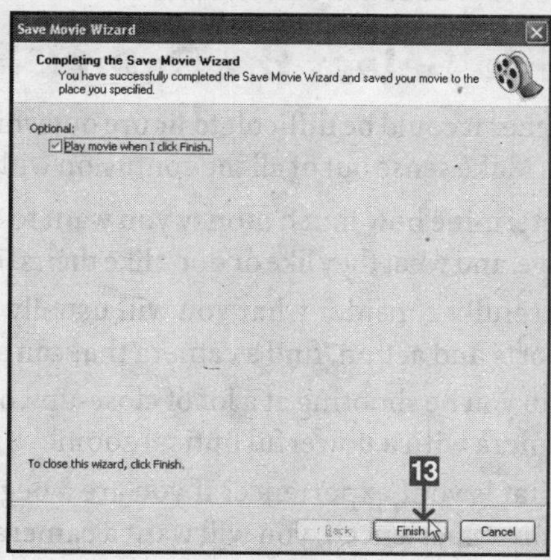

Fig. W-5.181

14. The Save Movie Wizard function is completed and your movie is saved at the desired location. Instantly, the saved movie starts playing in the Windows Media Player as shown in Fig.W-5.182

    Your first movie is permanently saved on your computer. Anytime, you can open the Windows Movie Maker and watch the movie. You can also send movie to your friends through email and copy it on the CD.

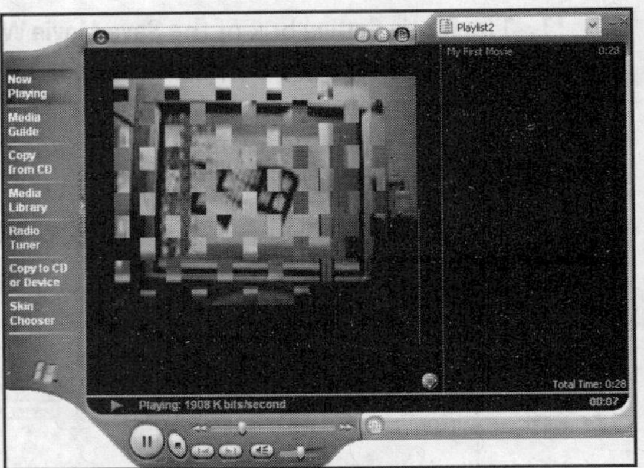

Fig. W-5.182

Introduction to Digital Photography

In the previous section we discuss Windows Movie Maker program (a video editing program) of Windows XP. Let us now look into another interesting aspect of digital world- Digital Photography. Digital photography is photography using a camera that uses an electronic sensor to record the image as a piece of electronic data rather than as chemical changes on a photographic film. Digital Cameras records images using pixels. Depending upon your camera, each photograph you shoot contains 1 to 5 thousand pixels (tiny dots that make up the representation of a picture on computer monitor. Usually, the dots are so small and numerous that, when printed on a paper or displayed on computer monitor, they appear to merge into a smooth image) or millions of pixels. For storing images, Digital Camera uses a compact memory device known as Memory Stick. Once saved, images can easily be transferred on the computer. Digital cameras can be smaller and lighter than film cameras of equivalent quality. The advantages of digital photography over the conventional one include:

- Instant review of pictures, i.e. no wait for the film to be developed
- One only pays for any images one wants to print and one can delete the images one doesn't want to keep
- Color reproduction and range is not dependent on film quality

How to Select the Right Digital Camera

Sometimes it could be difficult to figure out which digital camera is right for you. There are just so many factors. Make sense out of all the confusion with the following tips on choosing the right camera for you.

- Determine how much money you want to spend. Ask friends and family what digital cameras they have, and what they like or don't like theirs. This is one of the best ways to get real feedback on a model.
- Carefully consider what you will usually be photographing. For instance, if you typically shoot sports and action, find a camera that can shoot at high speeds.
- Will you be shooting at a lot of close-ups, or frequently taking photographs from a distance? Find a camera with a powerful optical zoom.
- What is your experience? If you are a beginner, look for models that seem easy to use. If you are more experienced, you will want a camera that gives user more control.
- Be sure to select a model with a good LCD screen, even if you don't think you need one at all.

Making Necessary Arrangements

When you connect a digital camera to a computer running windows XP, Windows immediately attempts to recognize the device by displaying a dialog box (see Fig.W-5.131 and associated text on page number 151). By default, Windows XP contains all necessary files and programs for various hardware devices, including digital camera thus you rarely need to install driver files. Incase, after connecting the digital camera, Windows prompts for the driver files then undertake the following steps.

1. *Move* the mouse-pointer over the **Start** button (start) present on the **Taskbar** and *click* the left mouse-button. Instantly, a push-up menu appears (Fig.W-5.183).
2. Inside the push-up menu, *move* the mouse-pointer over the **Control Panel** option and *click* the left mouse-button (Fig.W-5.184).

If you find difficult to locate options in the Control Panel window of Fig.W-5.185 then click over the Switch to Classic View option.

3. The **Control Panel** window appears. *Move* the mouse-pointer over the **Printers and Other Hardware** option and *click* the left mouse-button (Fig.W-5.185).

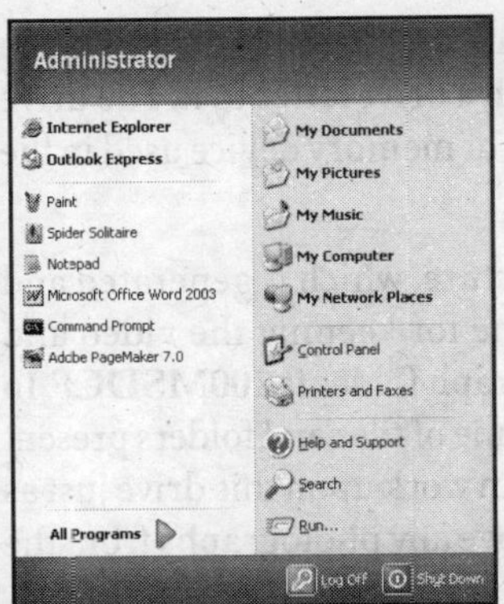

Fig. W-5.183

Fig. W-5.184

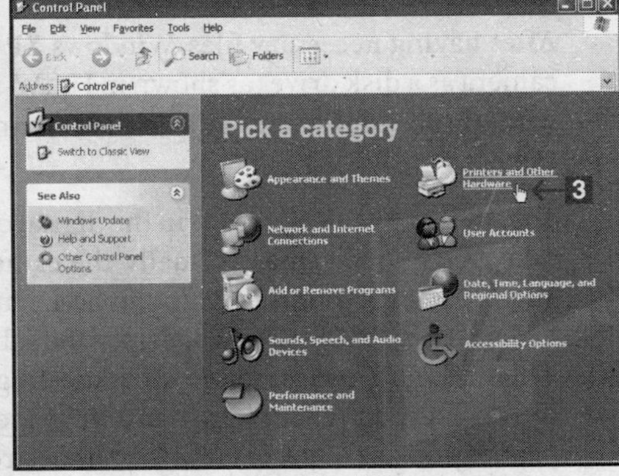

Fig. W-5.185

4. The **Printers and Other Hardware** window appears. *Move* the mouse-pointer over the **Scanners and Cameras** option and *click* the left mouse-button (Fig.W-5.186).
5. Next, the **Scanners and Cameras** window appears. On the left side of the window you will see the **Imaging Tasks** Task Pane. In this Task pane, *move* the mouse-pointer over the **Add an Imaging Device** option and *click* the left mouse-button (Fig.W-5.187).

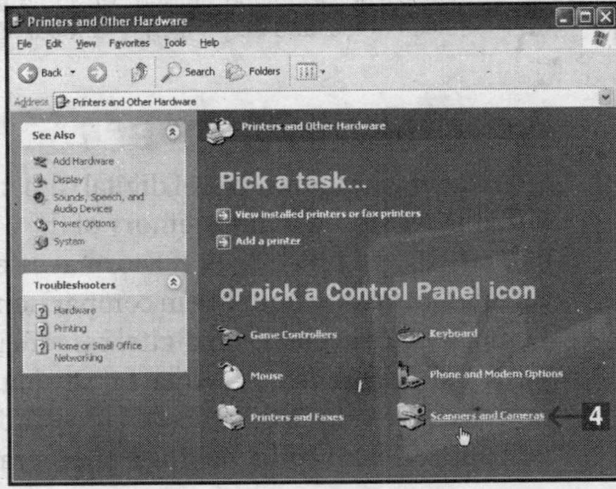

Fig. W-5.186

6. Instantly, the first window of **Scanner and Camera Installation Wizard** appears. In this window, *click* over the **Next** button and follow the instructions of the wizard to install necessary files required for the digital camera connected to your computer (Fig.W-5.188). Once all files are copied, the computer will be able to interact with the digital camera.

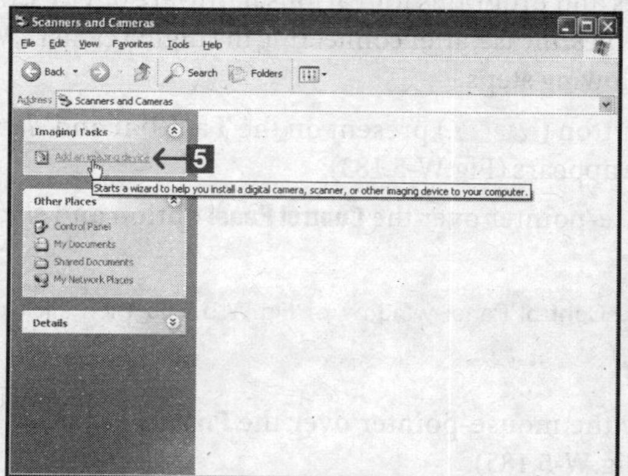

Fig. W-5.187

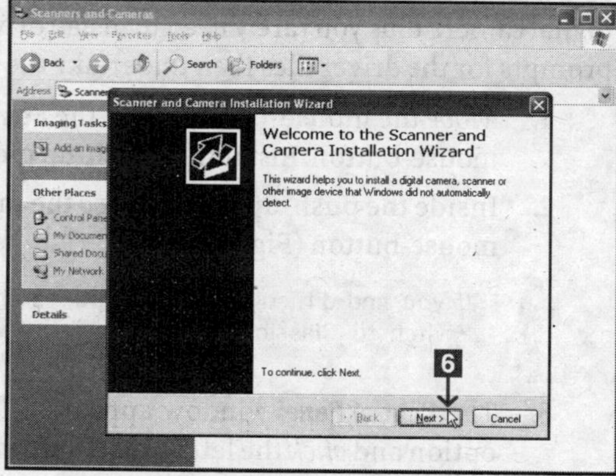

Fig. W-5.188

After having necessary files, Windows XP recognizes the camera. It treats the memory device of the camera as a disk drive (as shown in Fig. W-5.133) and automatically assign a drive letter to it. The drive name displays the name of the camera's manufacturer along with the name of memory device used in the camera.

The memory device present in the digital camera has its own folder structure, which is generated and managed by the camera. Usually, the camera generates two folders – one for keeping the video and another one keeping the photographs. In our case, the name of the photograph folder is **100MSDCF**. In folder tree, the 100MSDCF appears as the subfolder of **DCIM** folder. The name of files and folders present in the memory device is also automatically generated by the camera. You can work upon this drive just as you do with computer's hard disk, which means you can view, copy, and move any photographs from the memory device of the camera to your desired location on the computer.

Incase you are using camera of some other company (other than Sony) then names of drive, memory device, files and folders may appear different as illustrated in this book.

Working with Images

After having the knowledge of digital camera and bridging up the gap with the computer, let us now work with images stored in the memory of the camera. A digital camera store photographs in two formats – TIFF or TIF and JPEG. The TIFF format offers highest picture quality while JPEG format is space-saving but offer low picture quality in comparison to TIFF format. In comparison to computer's hard disk, the memory space available in digital camera is less and that is why most manufacturers of digital camera prefer JPEG as the default format for storing the images. The photographs used or illustrated in upcoming sections have JPEG format. Let us now undergo the upcoming sections and learn to perform tasks like copying a photograph, emailing a photograph, setting up photograph as desktop's background etc.

Copying Photograph from the Digital Camera

You can copy photograph from digital camera on your computer just as you copy any other file or folder from one location in the computer to another one. Once transferred on the computer, you can use photograph as desktop's background and can even email photographs to your love ones. Let us now undertake the following steps to copy a photograph from the digital camera.

1. *Move* the mouse-pointer over the **My Computer** icon present on the **Desktop** and *click* the right mouse-button. Instantly, a shortcut menu appears (Fig.W-5.189).
2. Inside the shortcut menu, *move* the mouse-pointer over the **Explore** option and *click* the left mouse-button (Fig.W-5.190).
3. The Explorer window of **My Computer** appears on the screen (Fig.W-5.191). As you can see, the Explorer window is divided into two boxes. The left box – **Folders** – displays the name of disk drives, important folders and locations of your computer. The left box – **Contents** – displays the content of a folder selected in the Folders box.

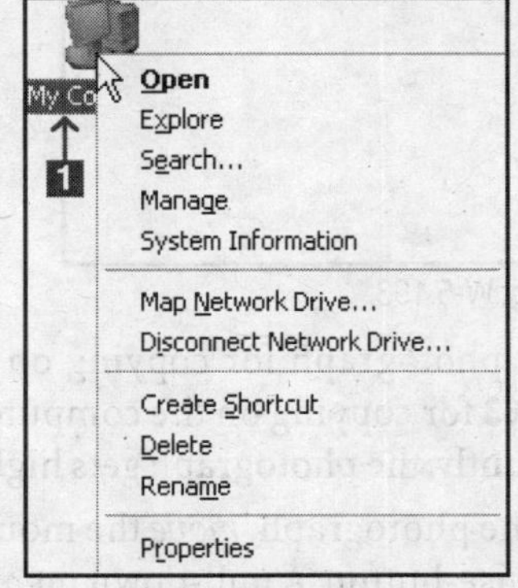

Fig. W-5.189

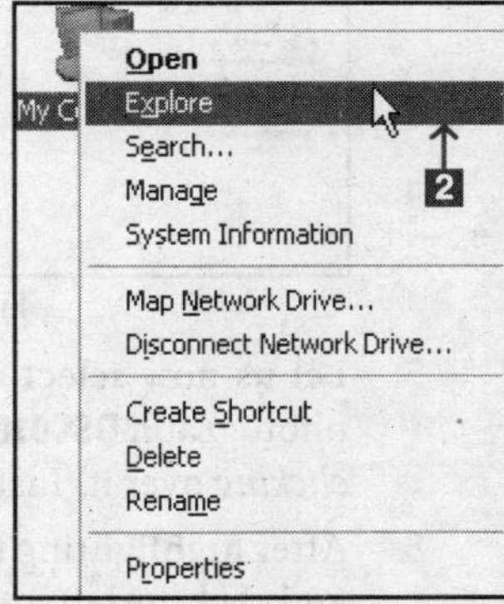

Fig. W-5.190

4. In the **Folders** box of the Explorer widow, *move* the mouse-pointer over the **Sony MemoryStick (G:)** drive name and *click* the left mouse-button. The folders present under the selected drive appear in the **Contents** box. Also, the folders tree in the **Folders** box expands (Fig.W-5.192).

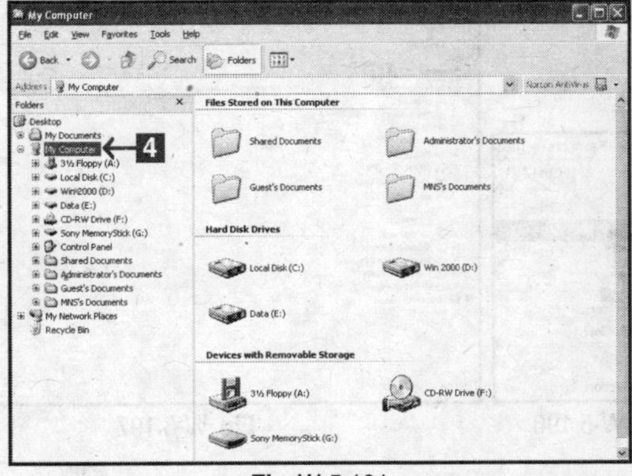

Fig. W-5.191

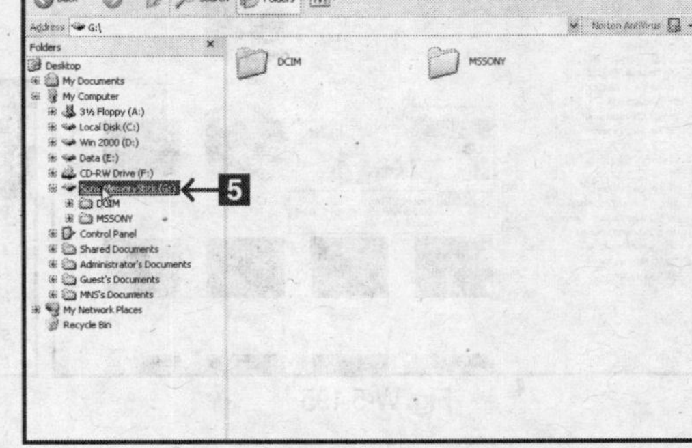

Fig. W-5.192

5. Next, *move* the mouse-pointer over the **DCIM** subfolder present under the **Folders** box and *click* the left mouse-button (Fig.W-5.193).
6. Once again, *move* the mouse-pointer over the **100MSDCF** subfolder present under the **Folders** box and *click* the left mouse-button. All photographs shoot through the digital camera appears on the right side of the Explorer window. Among the displayed photographs, you can select one or more than one photograph for copying on your computer (Fig.W-5.194).

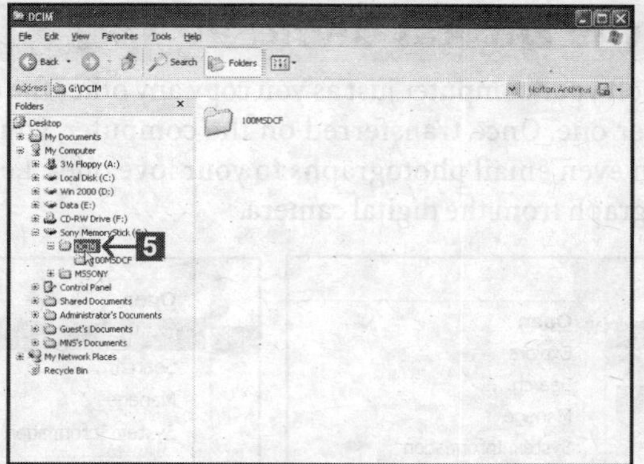

Fig. W-5.193

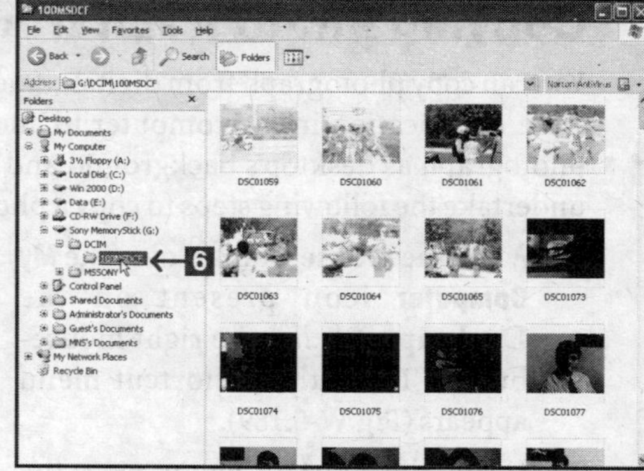

Fig. W-5.194

7. Let us now select a photograph for copying on the computer. For instance, let us choose the photograph **DSC01063** for copying on the computer. To do so, first of all select the photograph by *clicking* over it. Instantly, the photograph gets highlighted (Fig.W-5.195).
8. After highlighting the photograph, *move* the mouse-pointer over the **Edit** option of the Menu bar and *click* the left mouse-button. A pull-down menu appears (Fig.W-5.196).
9. Inside the pull-down menu, *move* the mouse-pointer over the **Copy** option and *click* the left mouse-button (Fig.W-5.196).
10. After copying the photograph, it is time to decide the location on the computer where you want to transfer or place the photograph. Let us transfer the photograph on the Desktop. In the **Folders** box, *move* the mouse-pointer over the **Desktop** folder and *click* the left mouse-button (Fig.W-5.197).

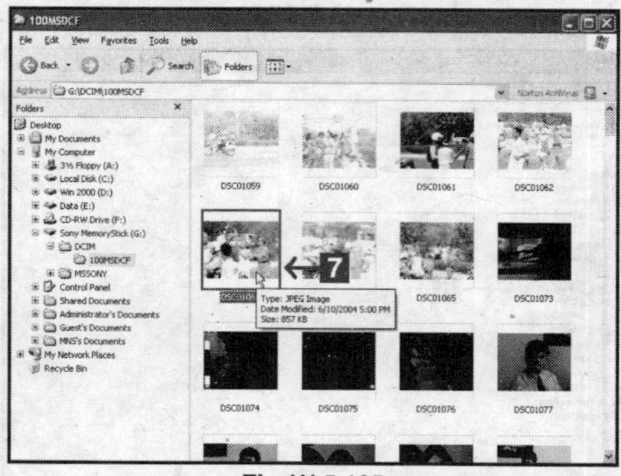

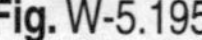

Fig. W-5.195

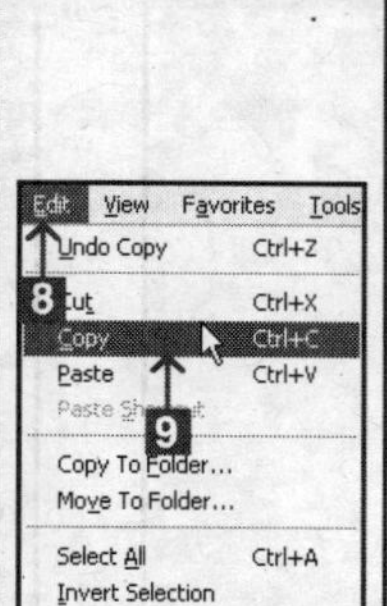

Fig. W-5.196

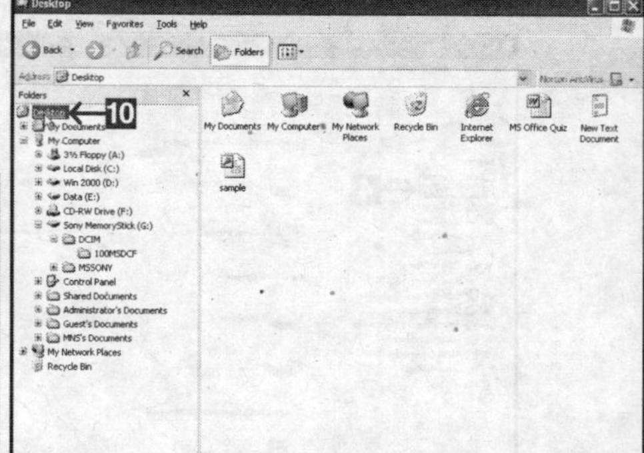

Fig. W-5.197

11. Once again, *move* the mouse-pointer over the **Edit** option of the Menu bar and *click* the left mouse-button. A pull-down menu appears (Fig.W-5.198).
12. Inside the pull-down menu, *move* the mouse-pointer over the **Paste** option and *click* the left mouse-button (Fig.W-5.198).

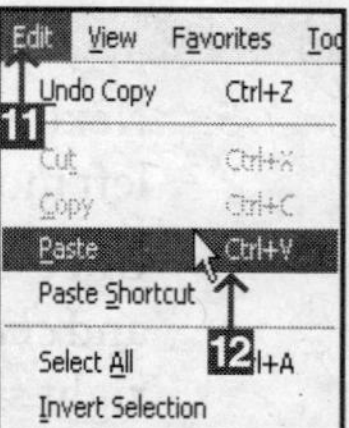

Fig. W-5.198

13. The selected photograph (DCS01063, in our case) gets transferred from Digital camera to the Desktop of the computer (Fig.W-5.199).

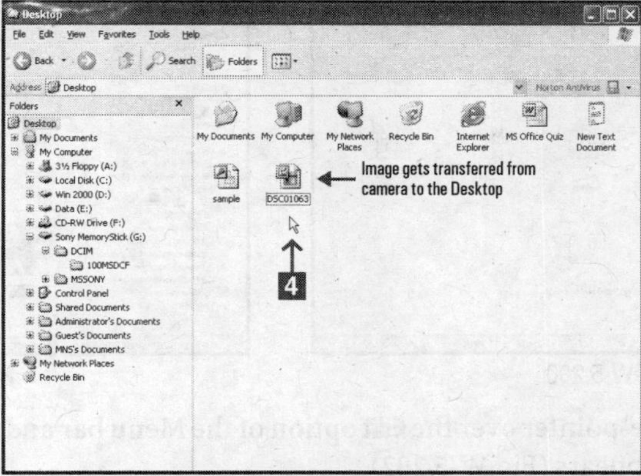

Fig. W-5.199

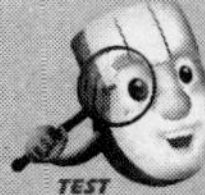

How to select multiple photographs at a time, copy them and transfer on the computer's Desktop?

- Open the Explorer window and locate the folder, in the Digital camera's drive, containing photographs.
- Once photographs appear in the Contents box, keep the Ctrl key pressed, move the mouse-pointer over the desired photographs and click the left mouse button. The desired photographs get highlighted.
- Click over the Edit option of the Menu bar. A pull-down menu appears.
- Inside the pull-down menu, click over the Copy option.
- In the Folders box of the Explorer window, click over Desktop.
- Click over the Edit option of the Menu bar. A pull-down menu appears.
- Inside pull-down menu, click over the Paste option.

Copying Photograph to the Digital Camera

In this section we will look into the procedure of copying picture to the camera from a location on the computer. The picture we will going to copy resides in the **My Documents** folder of the computer and name of the picture is **IMG1**. Let us now undertake the following steps and copy IMG1 to the camera.

1. Start from Fig.W-5.199. In the **Folders** box of the Explorer window, *move* the mouse-pointer over the **My Documents** folder and *click* the left mouse-button. The contents of My Documents folder appear on the right side (In Contents box) of the Explorer window (Fig.W-5.200).
2. Among the displayed contents, *move* the mouse-pointer over picture **IMG1** and *click* the left mouse-button to highlight it (Fig.W-5.201).

Fig. W-5.200

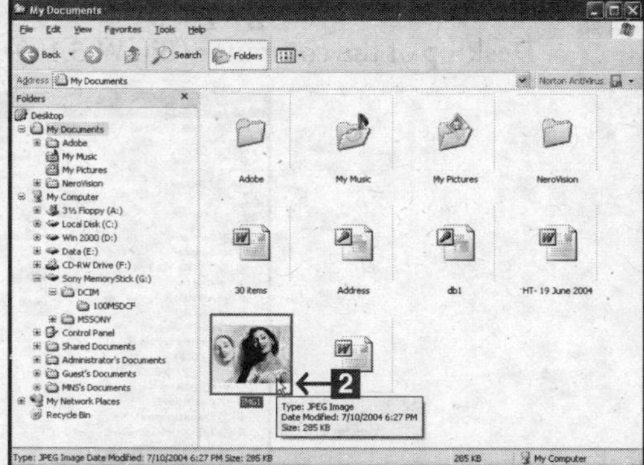

Fig. W-5.201

3. Next, *move* the mouse-pointer over the **Edit** option of the Menu bar and *click* the left mouse-button. A pull-down menu appears (Fig.W-5.202).
4. Inside the pull-down menu, *move* the mouse-pointer over the **Copy** option and *click* the left mouse-button (Fig.W-5.202).
5. After copying the picture, it is time to transfer it into the picture folder of the camera. For doing so, *move* the mouse-pointer over the subfolder **100MSDCF**, present in the **Folders** box, and *click* the left mouse-button. Various pictures present in the subfolder appear in the **Contents** box (Fig.W-5.203).

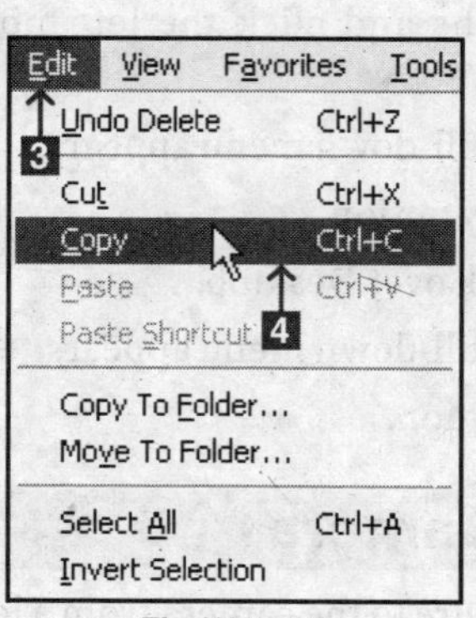

Fig. W-5.202

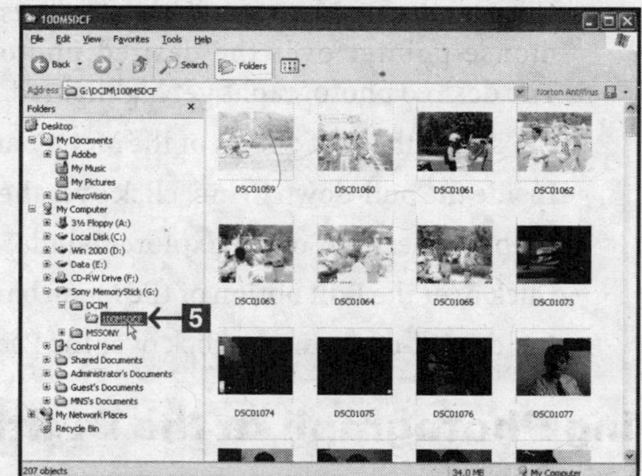

Fig. W-5.203

6. Lastly, *move* the mouse-pointer over the **Edit** option of the Menu bar and *click* the left mouse-button. A pull-down menu appears (Fig.W-5.204).
7. Inside the pull-down menu, *move* the mouse-pointer over the **Paste** option and *click* the left mouse-button (Fig.W-5.204).
8. Picture **IMG1** appears gets copied to the camera and appear along with other images present in **100MSDCF** subfolder (Fig.W-5.205).

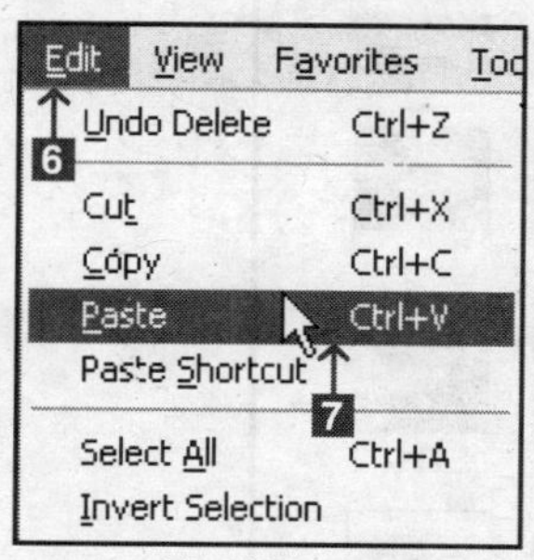

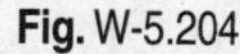
Fig. W-5.204

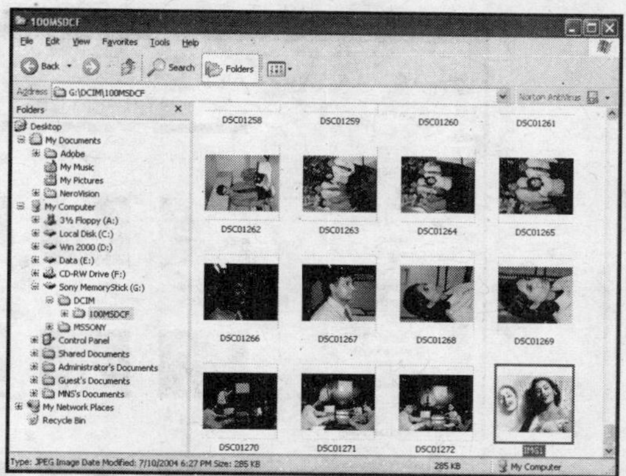

Fig. W-5.205

Rename a Photograph

As we know, now, that picture names are automatically assigned by the camera. The names assigned to pictures are usually in form of alpha-numerical characters like MD10DCR03, which sometimes cause difficulty in remembering the names. However, you can avoid this situation by renaming your favorite pictures according to your needs. In the last section we upload the **IMG1** picture to the camera. Let us now learn to rename it as **Madhubala** by undertaking the following steps.

1. Start from Fig. W-5.205. Incase the picture is not highlighted then *move* the mouse-pointer over it and *click* the left mouse-button. Next, *move* the mouse-pointer over the **File** option of the Menu bar and *click* the left mouse-button. A pull-down menu appears (Fig. W-5.206).

2. Inside the pull-down menu, *move* the mouse-pointer over the **Rename** option and *click* the left mouse-button (Fig. W-5.206).

3. Now, *type* **Madhubala** as the new name for the picture (Fig. W-5.207).

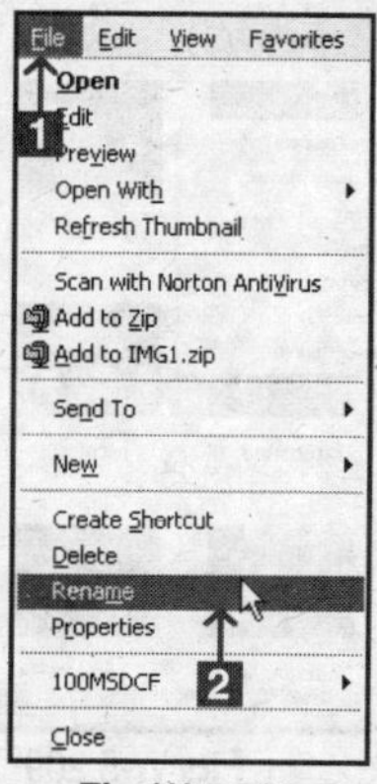

Fig. W-5.206

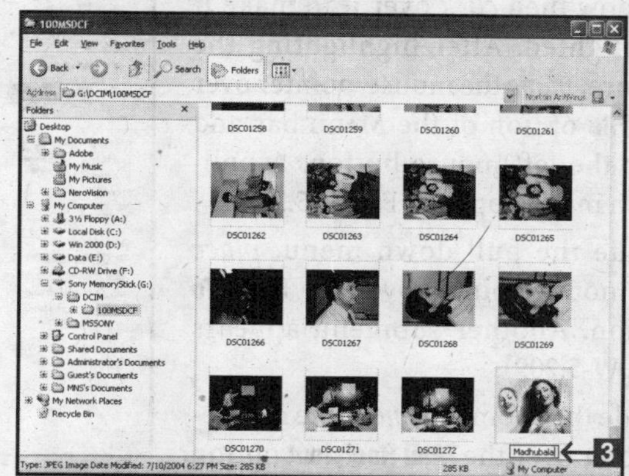

Fig. W-5.207

4. After typing the name, *click* anywhere in the Contents box. Figure W-5.208 shows the picture with the new name.

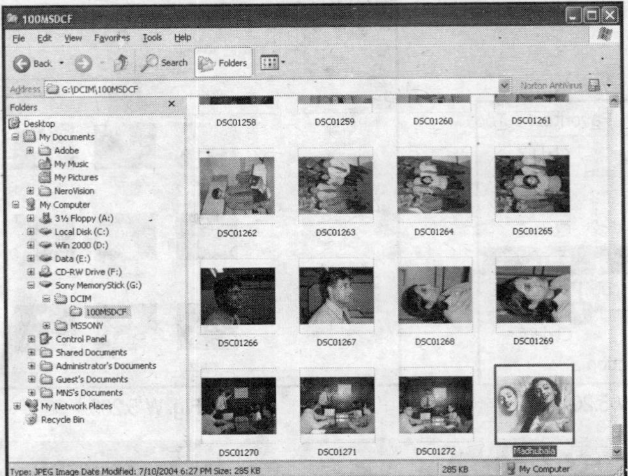

Fig. W-5.208

Email a Photograph

You can share favorite photographs between distant friends and family members by emailing them. For emailing the photograph, the Outlook Express software installed on your computer must be properly configured to the Internet settings of your computer However, due to some reasons you do not use Outlook Express then do not feel disappointed. You can still email photographs to your friends and family by referring the section 'Sending Email with Attachment' of Internet. Lets us now undertake the following steps and learn to email the picture that you have just copied in the camera.

1. Start with Fig.W-5.208. Incase the picture **Madhubala** is not highlighted in the **Contents** box of the Explorer window then *click* over it to make it highlighted. After highlighting the picture, *move* the mouse-pointer over the **File** option of the Menu bar and *click* the left mouse-button. A pull-down menu appears (Fig.W-5.209).
2. Inside the pull-down menu, *place* the mouse-pointer over the **Send To** option. Another submenu appears (Fig.W-5.209).
3. Inside the submenu, *move* the mouse-pointer over the **Mail Recipient** option and *click* the left mouse-button (Fig. W-5.210).

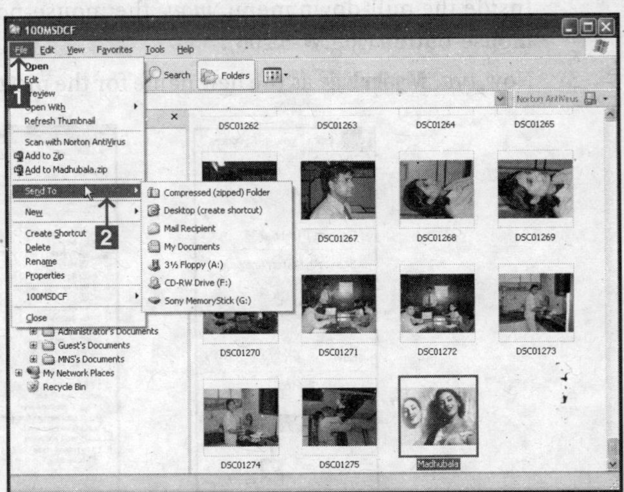

Fig. W-5.209

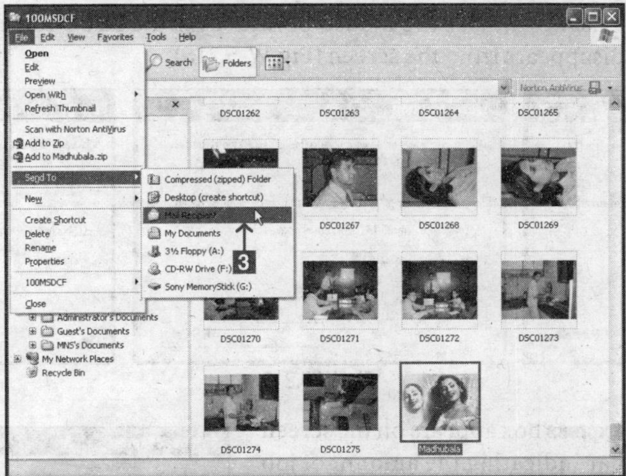

Fig. W-5.210

4. An emailing window, similar to Fig.W-5.211 appears with a blinking cursor beside the **To** option.
5. Type the email address of the person whom you want to send the photograph. For example, *type* **johnsmith@yahoo.com** as the email address (Fig.W-5.212).
6. Lastly, *move* the mouse-pointer over the **Send** button and *click* the left mouse-button (Fig.W-5.213).

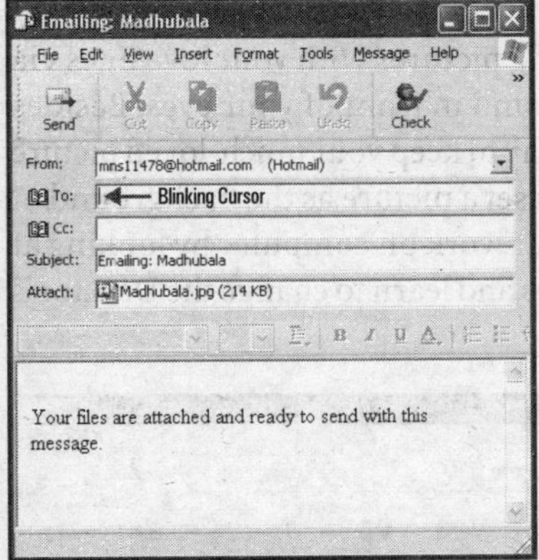

Fig. W-5.211

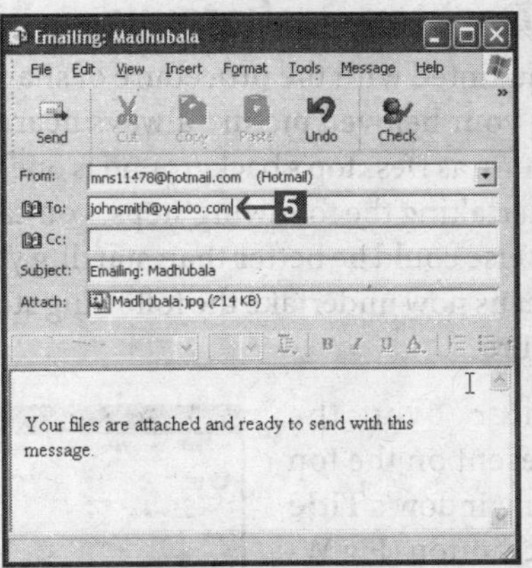

Fig. W-5.212

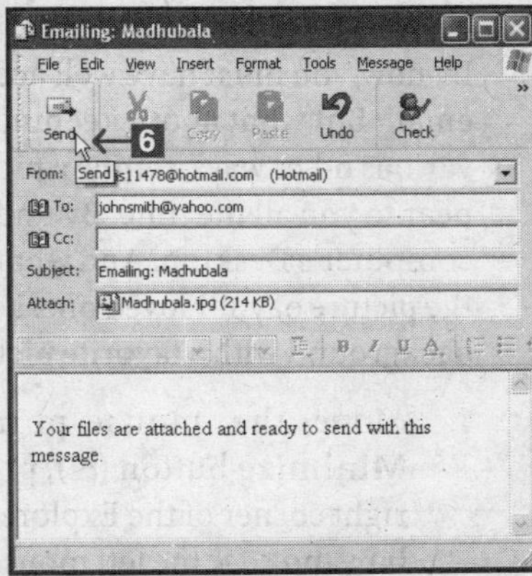

Fig. W-5.213

The Title bar of the emailing window displays the same text that appears beside the Subject option. If you change the text beside the Subject option then text on the Title bar changes correspondingly.

7. Immediately, the **Login – Hotmail** box appears on the screen (Fig.W-5.214).
8. You will notice the blinking cursor inside the text box beside the **Password** option. *Type* the password of your Hotmail email account. Due to security reasons, the password's characters appear in asterisk symbols (Fig.W-5.215).

9. After typing the password, *move* the mouse-pointer over the **OK** button and *click* the left mouse-button. The box disappears from the screen (Fig.W-5.216).

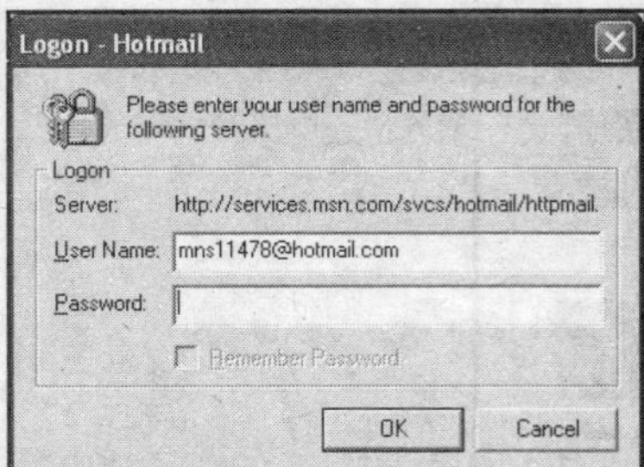

Fig. W-5.214

Fig. W-5.215

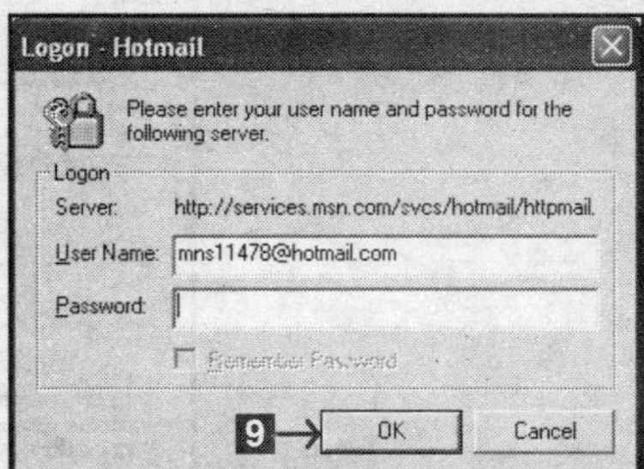

Fig. W-5.216

10. Next, the **Outlook Express** box appears on the screen with a progress bar indicating the amount of job done (Fig.W-5.217). Once the job of emailing the picture is done, the box disappears and once again screen of Internet Explorer similar to Fig.W-5.208 appears. Within few minutes picture reaches in the recipient's mail box.

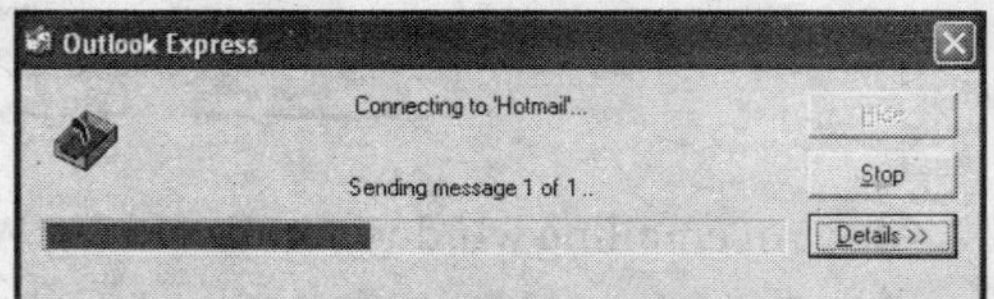

Fig. W-5.217

Using the Photograph Desktop Background

By now, you must have well acquainted with the procedure of sharing pictures with your love ones via email. But what about keeping your beloved picture always nearer and in front of your eyes. Besides various other ways, setting a picture as Desktop's background is one way to keep your much-loved picture near to you all the time. By undertaking the following steps, you can set a picture as the background of computer's Desktop. And what else could be better than starting your work on computer by looking at the picture of your loved one. Let us now undertake the following steps and learn to change the Desktop's background with a favorite picture.

1. *Move* the mouse-pointer over the **Minimize** button (▬), present on the top right corner of the Explorer window's **Title bar**, and *click* the left mouse-button (Fig.W-5.218). Instantly, the Explorer window reduces into a button on the **Taskbar**. Repeat this step to minimize other windows, if they are open on your computer's screen.

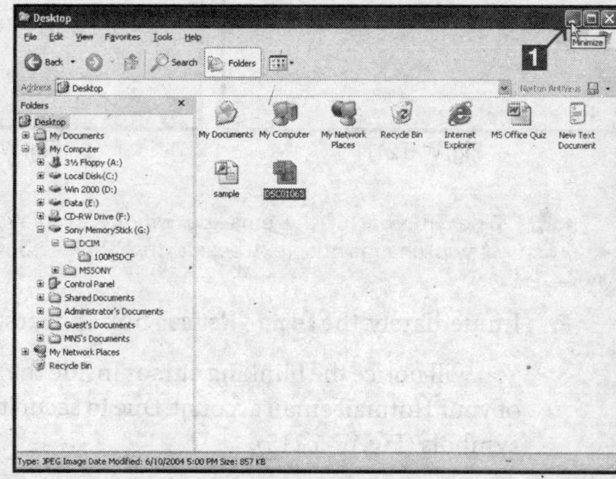

Fig. W-5.218

2. Once the **Desktop** appears, *click* the right mouse-button anywhere in the empty region of the Desktop. A shortcut menu appears (Fig.W-5.219).
3. Inside the shortcut menu, *move* the mouse-pointer over the **Properties** option and *click* the left mouse-button (Fig.W-5.220).
4. The **Display Properties** box with several tabs appears on the screen (Fig.W-5.221).

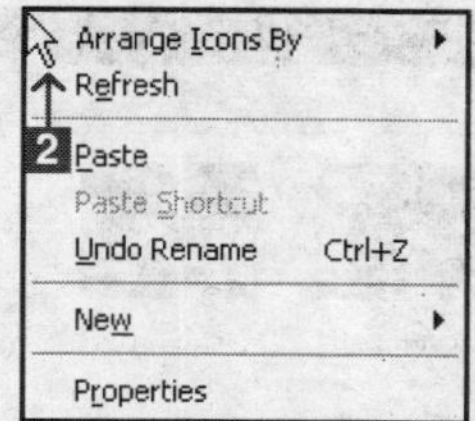

Fig. W-5.219

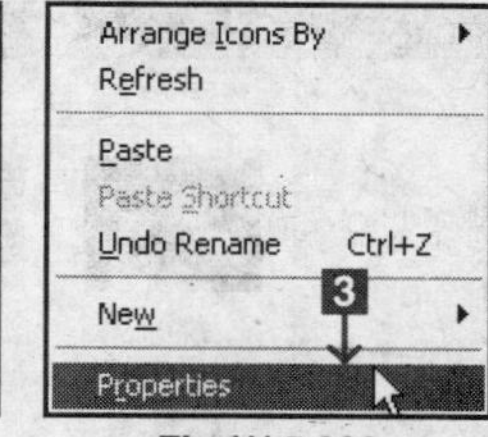

Fig. W-5.220

5. *Move* the mouse-pointer over the **Desktop** tab and *click* the left mouse-button. Various options present under this tab appear (Fig.W-5.222).
6. Next, *move* the mouse-pointer over the **Browse** button and *click* the left mouse-button (Fig.W-5.223).

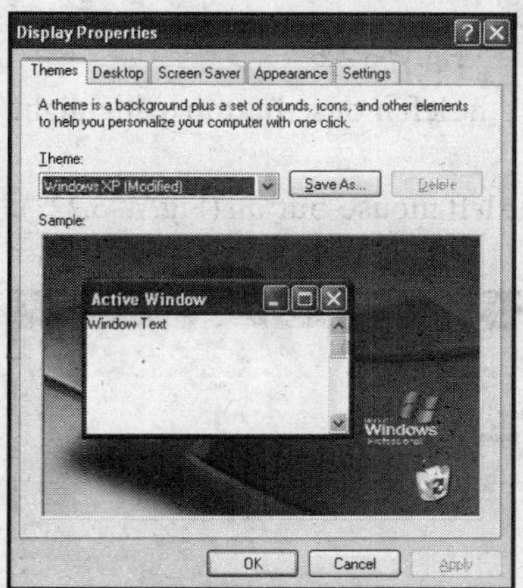

Fig. W-5.221

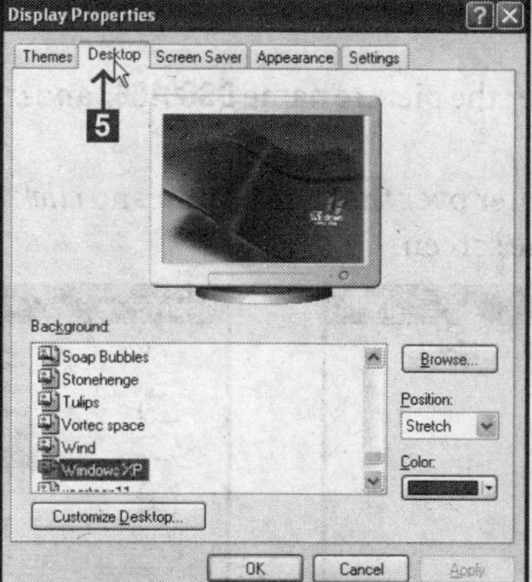

Fig. W-5.222

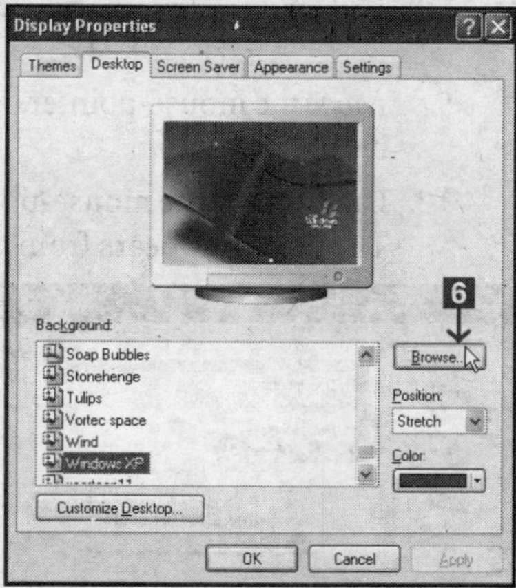

Fig. W-5.223

7. The **Browse** box appears (Fig.W-5.224). Using this box, you can navigate all locations and folders on your computer to look for a picture and later set the chosen picture as Desktop's background. For quick and easy navigation, some icons with captions are provided on the left side of the Browse box. Actually, these icons are buttons. If you click over any button, the Browse box takes you to the specific computer location. By default, the Browse box displays contents of My Pictures, subfolder, which is present under the My Documents folder.
8. *Move* the mouse-pointer over the **Desktop** button and *click* the left mouse-button. The contents present on your computer's desktop appear in the box (Fig.W-5.225).

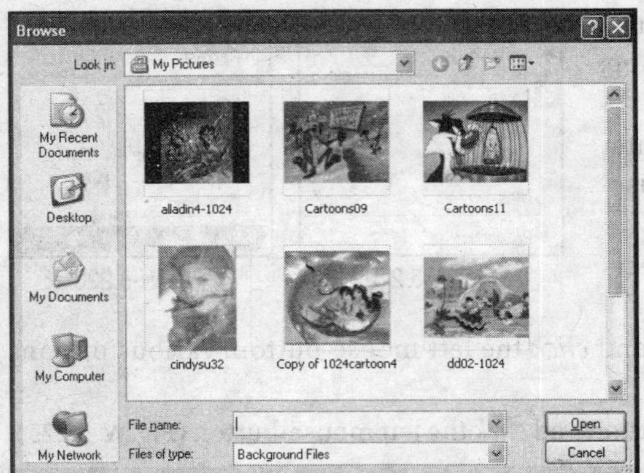

Fig. W-5.224

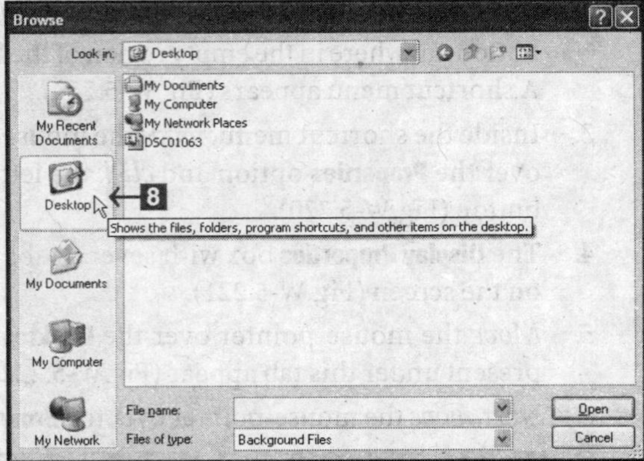

Fig. W-5.225

9. *Move* the mouse-pointer over the picture name **DSC01063** and *click* the left mouse-button to highlight it (Fig.W-5.226).
10. Lastly, *move* the mouse-pointer over the **Open** button and *click* the left mouse-button (Fig.W-5.227). The box disappears from the screen.

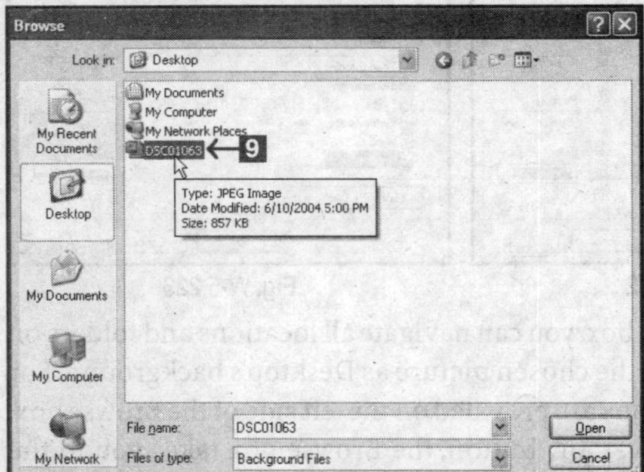

Fig. W-5.226

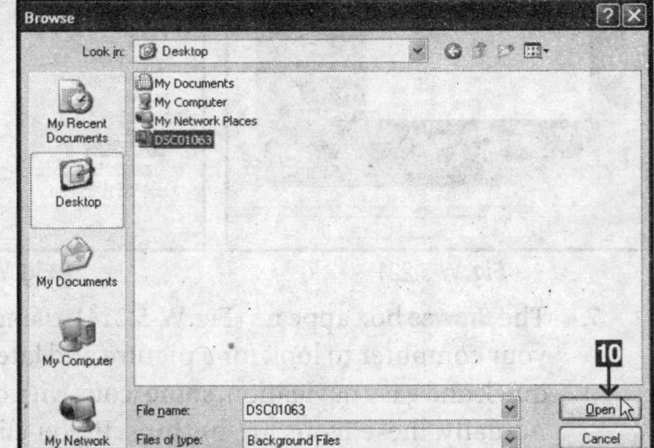

Fig. W-5.227

11. The **Display Properties** box reappears. *Move* the mouse-pointer over the **Apply** button and *click* the left mouse-button (Fig.W-5.228).
12. Once again inside the **Display Properties** box, *move* the mouse-pointer over the **OK** button and *click* the left mouse-button (Fig. W-5.229).

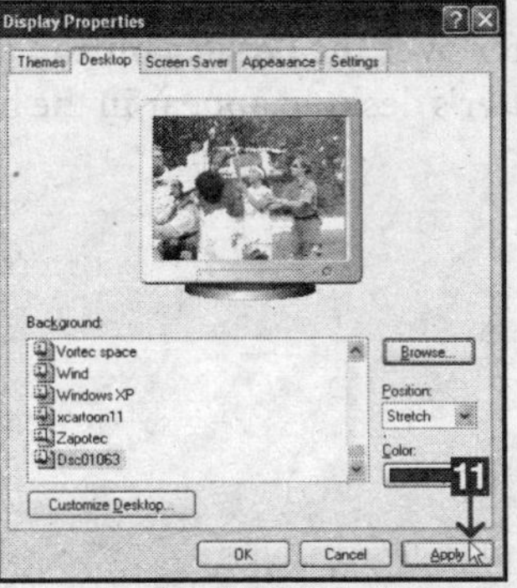

Fig. W-5.228

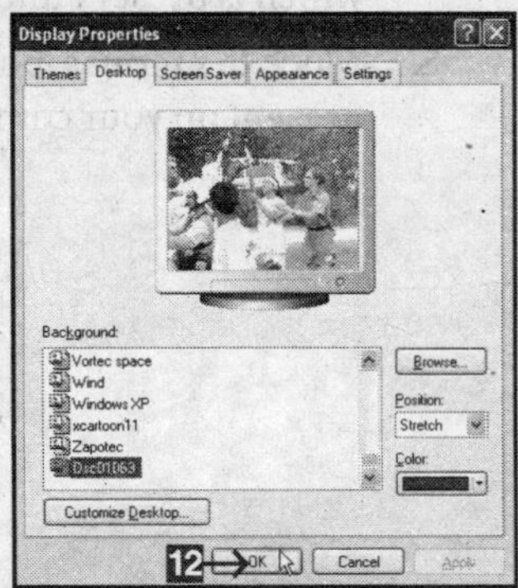

Fig. W-5.229

The dialog box disappears and your selected photograph appears as the background of computer's Desktop, as shown in Fig.W-5.228.

Fig. W-5.230

Deleting Picture from Digital Camera

Just as you delete any file or folder from your computer, you can remove unnecessary photographs from digital camera. But while removing photographs think twice as once deleted from the camera, the photograph will be permanently gone. There is no provision of restoring it back from the Recycle Bin. So pay extreme attention. Let us now undertake the following steps to remove an unwanted photograph **DSC01061** from the digital camera.

1. *Move* the mouse-pointer over the photograph name **DSC01061** and *click* the left mouse-button. The photograph gets highlighted (Fig.W-5.331).
2. Next, *move* the mouse-pointer over **File** option of the Menu bar and *click* the left mouse-button. A pull-down menu appears (Fig.W-5.232).
3. Inside the pull-down menu, *move* the mouse-pointer over the **Delete** option and *click* the left mouse-button (Fig.W-5.232).

Fig. W-5.231

4. The **Confirm File Delete** box appears. *Move* the mouse-pointer over **Yes** button and *click* the left mouse-button. The selected photograph gets deleted permanently from the camera (Fig.W-5.233).

It's time you took a break. When you return refreshed, we will learn how to use the Microsoft Word application to make impressive and attractive letters and documents on your computer.

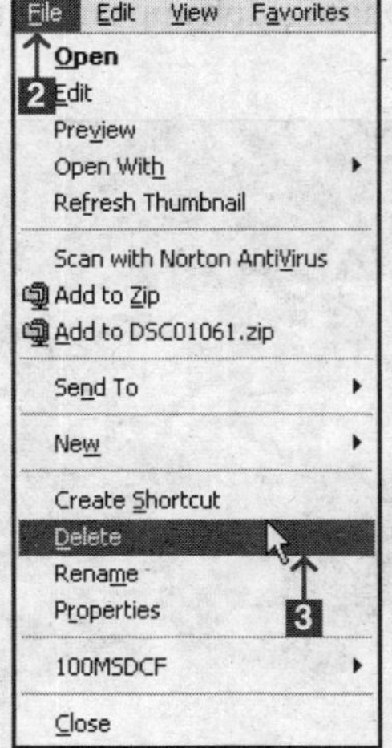

Fig. W-5.232

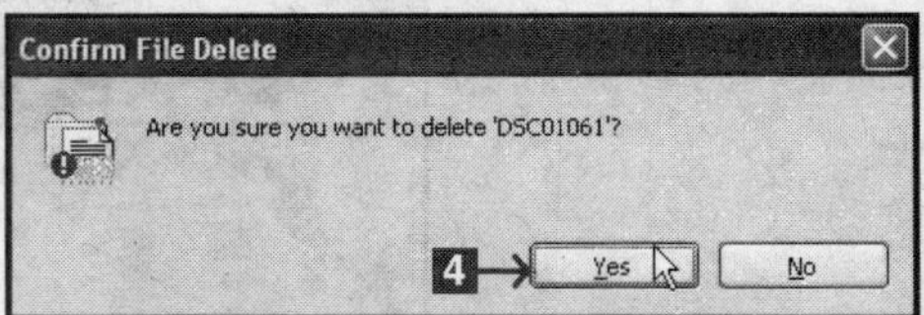

Fig. W-5.233

Summary

- The chapter starts with the basic word processing application—**WordPad** which you can use to create and edit simple text documents and apply basic formatting features on them. You can save your WordPad file as a text file or rich text file.
- Another Accessories feature explained in this chapter is **MS Paint**. It helps you create simple or elaborate drawings that can be saved as bitmap files. You can print your drawing, use it for your desktop background, or paste it in another document.
- If you work with numbers then Accessories application—**Calculator**—saves you from getting lost in the numbers world. With Calculator you can easily perform basic arithmetic tasks such as addition and subtraction, as well as scientific calculations like logarithms and factorials.
- Then there is **Microsoft Media Player** that soothes your overworked brain with music or movies. It is like having a radio, video player, CD player, and information database all-in-one. You can use Windows Media Player to listen to radio stations from all over the world, play and copy your CDs, look for videos on the Internet, and create customized lists of all the digital media files on your computer.
- Another Accessories application—**Windows Movie Maker**—can transform you into a filmmaker. With the Movie Maker you can capture audio and video to your computer from a video camera, Web camera, or other video source, and then use the captured content in your movies. You can also edit, the audio and video content by adding titles, video transitions, or effects and then save your final movie and share it with friends and family through email. You can save your movies to your computer or to a recordable or rewriteable CD.

Microsoft Word

IN THIS SECTION

- Introducing Microsoft Word
- Familiarizing with Microsoft Word
- Typing Your First Document
- Editing the Document
- Designing the Document
- Mail Merge

Introducing Microsoft Word 1

IN THIS CHAPTER

- Word Processor Basics
- Document View
- Exercise

Microsoft Word XP is a word processor program that helps you create neat and attractive documents easily and quickly. You will find its multi-faceted capability quite handy in drafting letters (casual and official), preparing mailing lists and reports. As compared to a typewriter, a word processor produces better looking documents which can be stored in your computer and reused easily whenever needed. Features like spell and grammar check, easy insertion of new sentences and paragraphs in the already entered text, page numbering, etc., make the functioning of a word processor easier, faster and more accurate than a typewriter. Unlike a typewriter, a word processor enables you store important documents in its hard disk, and reuse them.

Microsoft Word also allows you to change the appearance of text and organize the information in your document in a systematic manner. The appearance of the text can be changed by changing the font sizes, styles and colours. A document looks more organized if you add page numbers, page borders, headers and footers at the top and bottom of a page to display useful information.

Word also allows you to present the information in your document in a tabular form, i.e. within tables. After finishing the formatting of your document, you can take its printout. Word also enables you to preview the document before printing.

Word Processor Basics

Here, we briefly introduce you to some useful word processor features. In the following chapters, you will learn how to use these features in professional or personal work.

Word Wrapping (Word Adjusting)

In Word XP, margins of a new document or file are set by default. However, you can also set the width of the text line you want to type. Whether you go by the default margin setting or choose a new setting, in both cases you need not press the Enter key after the end of each line. The word processor automatically takes you to the next line when the current line attains the set width, and rearranges the text accordingly. This is called word wrapping.

Adding or Deleting Text

When you type a document on a typewriter, you generally commit mistakes like sentences being missed out, or an extra word being typed. This calls for retyping the whole document. By using a word processor, you can easily correct all such mistakes on the screen itself without retyping the whole document. New text can also be inserted easily into the document. The words, sentences or paragraphs between which you add the new text will themselves shift to make room for the new addition. Similarly, when you delete or remove text, the words surrounding it will occupy the additional space created after the deletion and adjust accordingly. The adjacent figures show the new text insertion and automatic adjustment of the existing text.

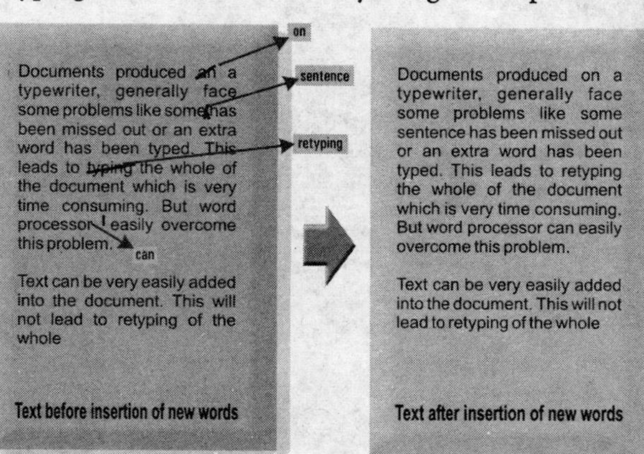

Text before insertion of new words

Text after insertion of new words

Selecting Blocks of Text

A word processor also allows you to copy or move text from one place to another. But before doing any operation on the desired text, you have to select it. The selected text is generally called **block text**. Word XP recognizes the selected text as a block of text which is to be copied or moved. Given below is a portion of the selected text:

Copying Text

The text from one part of a document can be very easily copied to another part with the help of a word processor. The original text remains in its place.

Moving Text

Moving a text basically means copying it to another place by removing it from its original place. So **move** performs two functions – copying the text to a new place and also removing it from the original place.

Search and Replace

This facility of the Word XP helps you correct a particular word misspelt at many places in your document in one go. Suppose you have misspelt Delhi as Dellhi in your document. Here, you can use the word processor to search through your entire document and simultaneously replace the incorrect word with the correct one at all the places where it appears.

Editing a Document

Checking and improving the text of your document is a very strong feature of the word processor. It checks your document in following three ways to make it grammatically correct and free from spelling mistakes.

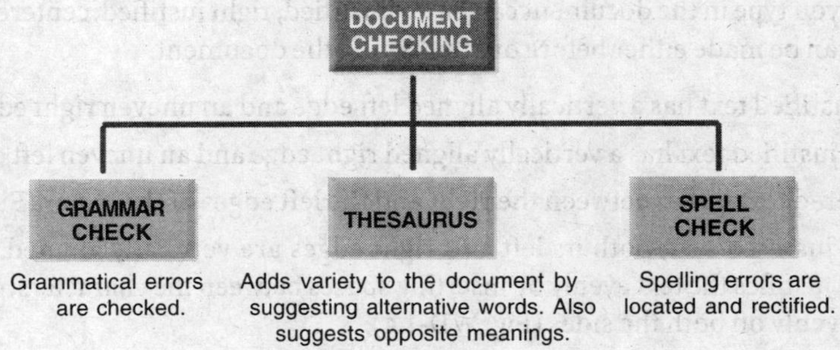

Character Formatting and Style

The design, style or size of the letters can also be changed through a word processor. By using different fonts, you can make the text distinct and attractive. With formatting and style feature, you can even turn your simple letter into an attractive and easy-to-read document. Some samples of the letter size and font are given here.

STYLE	SIZE
BOLD	5 times
Italic	10 times
Bold Italic	20 times
Underline	50 times
Subscript	H_2O
Supersubscript	$(A+B)^2$

Page Formatting – Headers, Footers and Page Numbers

Headers (printed at the top of each page) and footers (printed at the bottom of each page) can be written in your document using the word processor. You can also use the word processor to automatically give number to the pages in your document.

Margin Settings and Columns

Margin is the distance between the text and the edges of the paper. You can yourself set the margin for your document or go by the default margin of the word processor.

Some word processing programs can even split the text, i.e. set it into two or more columns.

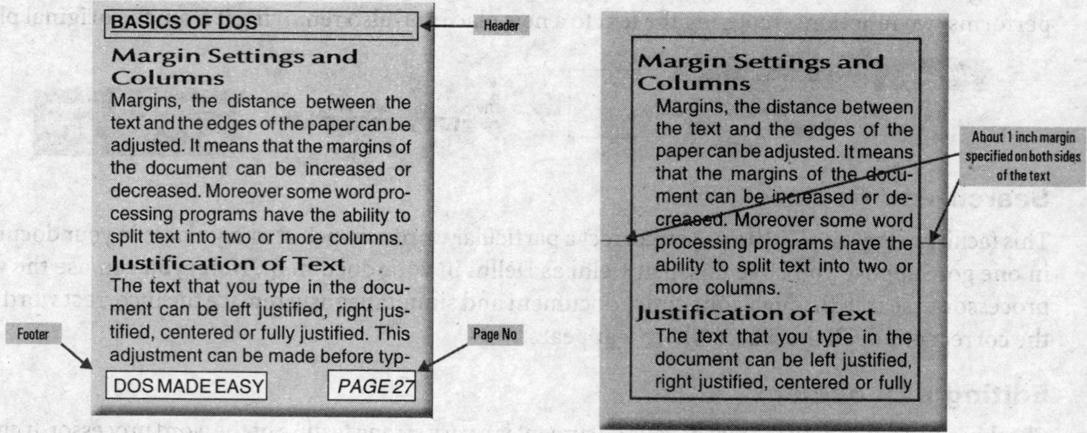

Justification of Text

The text that you type in the document can be left justified, right justified, centered or fully justified. This adjustment can be made either before or after typing the document.

- The left justified text has a vertically aligned left edge and an uneven right edge (Fig. WD-1.1).
- The right justified text has a vertically aligned right edge and an uneven left edge (Fig. WD-1.2).
- The centered text lies in between the right and the left edges of the paper (Fig. WD-1.3).
- In a fully justified text, both its left and right edges are vertically aligned. In this case, the word processor justifies the text evenly by inserting spaces between the characters, on its own, until the text lines up evenly on both the sides (Fig. WD-1.4).

The text that you type in the document can be left justified, right justified, centered or fully justified. This adjustment can be made before typing the document or after typing.

Fig. WD-1.1

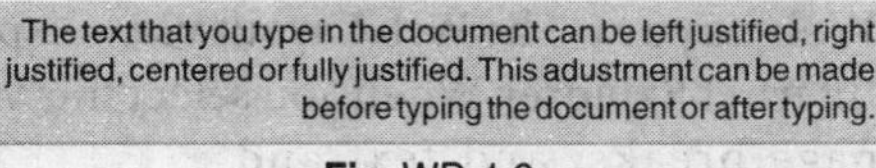

The text that you type in the document can be left justified, right justified, centered or fully justified. This adjustment can be made before typing the document or after typing.

Fig. WD-1.2

The text that you type in the document can be left justified, right justified, centered or fully justified. This adjustment can be made before typing the document or after typing.

Fig. WD-1.3

The text that you type in the document can be left justified, right justified, centered or fully justified. This adjustment can be made before typing the document or after typing.

Fig. WD-1.4

Line Spacing

The word processor allows you to adjust the number of blank lines in between the text, which is known as **line spacing.** This is generally done to make the document appear neat and clean. Line spacing can be done either before or after typing the document.

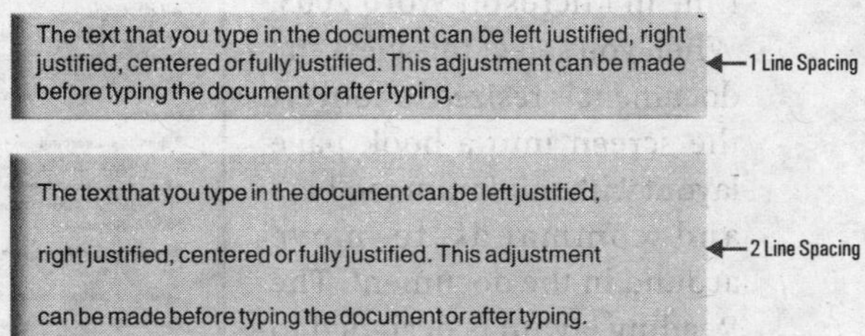

The text that you type in the document can be left justified, right justified, centered or fully justified. This adjustment can be made before typing the document or after typing. ← 1 Line Spacing

The text that you type in the document can be left justified,

right justified, centered or fully justified. This adjustment ← 2 Line Spacing

can be made before typing the document or after typing.

Setting Tabs

Setting tabs in a word processor is similar to that in a typewriter. It helps you arrange the text in columns and add, delete or move tab, as you desire.

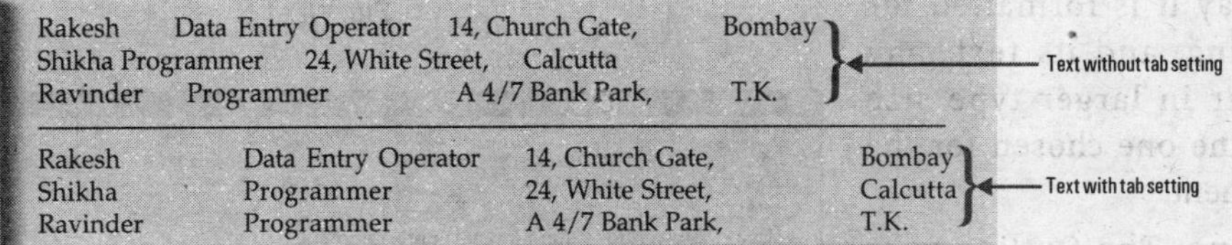

Rakesh Data Entry Operator 14, Church Gate, Bombay
Shikha Programmer 24, White Street, Calcutta
Ravinder Programmer A 4/7 Bank Park, T.K.

← Text without tab setting

Rakesh	Data Entry Operator	14, Church Gate,	Bombay
Shikha	Programmer	24, White Street,	Calcutta
Ravinder	Programmer	A 4/7 Bank Park,	T.K.

← Text with tab setting

Automating Tasks

Word XP has a very useful feature of keeping a record of the words, which you may find difficult to memorize. For typing such a word, you just need to type a part of it, and Word XP completes it for you. This feature is termed as the AutoCorrect facility.

Creating Letters in Readymade Formats

You can easily create letters through readymade formats which are provided in the word processor. These readymade formats are called **Templates** or **Wizards.**

Document View

Microsoft Word XP offers you different ways to view the document you work upon. These ways are known as Views. You have seven view options under the View menu of Word XP. Let us briefly discuss each view option.

- **Normal:** The Normal view shows the document in a simple page layout that you can type and edit quickly. The Normal view is convenient for most editing and formatting tasks.
- **Print Layout:** The Print view shows the view of a document as it will appear when you print it.

- **Web Layout**: The Web Layout view displays the document as it will appear in a Web browser, like Internet Explorer. When you select this view, your document appears as one long page without any page breaks, and text and images wrap to fit into the window.

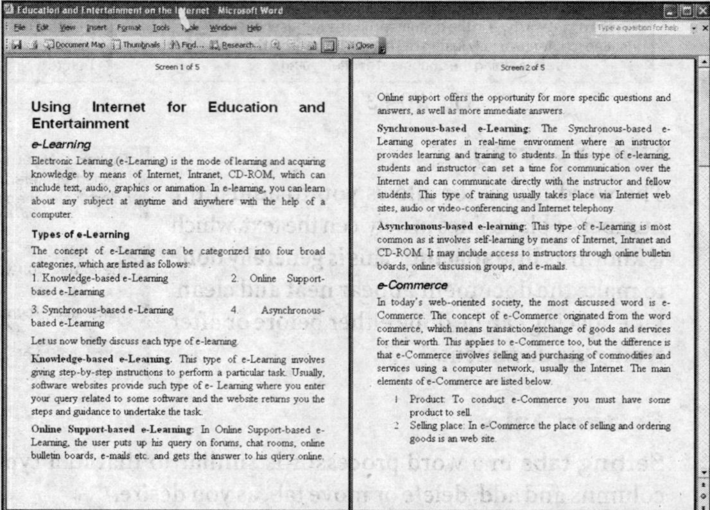

Fig. WD-1.5

- **Reading Layout**: This type of view was included for the first time in Microsoft Word 2003. When you select this view, the document is resized to convert the screen into a book page layout with minimum toolbars and commands to move around in the document. The Reading layout is designed to make reading of documents on screen more comfortable. This view, as shown in Fig. WD-1.5, does not display the document the way it is formatted for printing, and its text may appear in larger type size than the one chosen for the document.

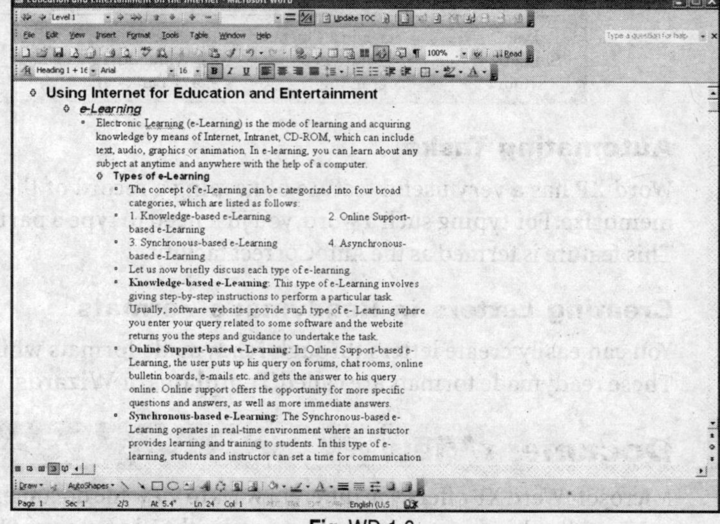

Fig. WD-1.6

- **Outline**: The Outline view shows the headings and their levels in the document (Fig. WD-1.6). In this view, you can minimize the layout of the document to view only headings and also expand it to see headings with the body text.
- **Document Map**: The Document Map view enables you to have a quick look at different heading levels on all pages of your document. And, through any heading you can also quickly access its page and view the contents below the heading. Whenever you select this view, a pane appears on the left side of the document window as shown in Fig. WD-1.7. This pane displays an outline of the various headings present in the document. Whenever you click over a heading in the pane, the selected heading appears on top in the adjacent window that also displays the contents below the heading.

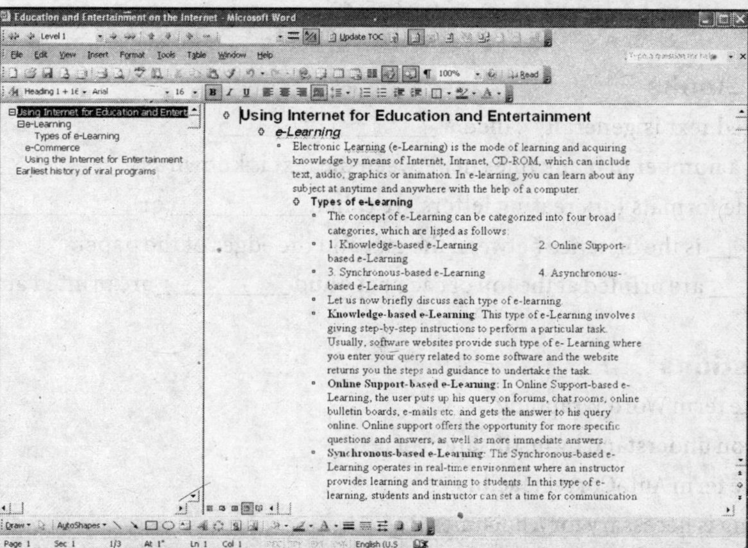

Fig. WD-1.7

- **Thumbnails**: The Thumbnails view provides a small visual impression of each page present in the document (Fig.WD-1.8). It helps you to quickly access a page and have a look at its contents.

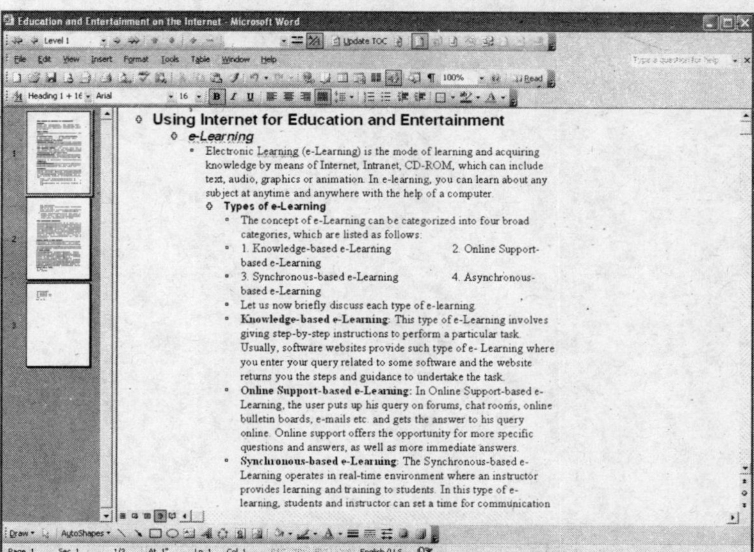

Fig. WD-1.8

Whenever you select this view, a pane appears on the left side of the document window with thumbnail of each page in the document. To access a particular page, you have to click on its thumbnail in the pane. Immediately, the page contents appear in the adjacent window.

Exercise

Fill in the Blanks

1. The selected text is generally called a _______________.
2. Adjusting a number of blank lines in between the text is known as _______________.
3. Readymade formats for creating letters are called __________ or ___________.
4. ___________ is the distance between the text and the edges of the paper.
5. ___________ are printed at the top of each page and __________ are printed at the bottom of each page.

Short Questions

1. Explain the term Word Wrapping.
2. What do you understand by justification of text?
3. Explain the term AutoCorrect facility.
4. Why editing is necessary for a document?

Familiarizing with Microsoft Word 2

IN THIS CHAPTER

- Menus
- Creating a New Blank Document
- Toolbars
- Changing the Size of a Document
- Closing the Document and Quitting Word
- Exercise

As you know, Microsoft Word is a word processing package. It is used to create professional documents such as letters, reports, etc. Microsoft Word is part of MS Office suite. You can have your own copy of Microsoft Word by purchasing a genuine copy of Microsoft Office from your authorized software vendor. While running the setup of MS Office, choose the Microsoft Word for installation on your computer.

Here we are assuming that you already have the Microsoft Word program installed on your computer with Windows XP as the Operating System.

For working in Microsoft Word, first we have to open it. To do so, follow the steps given below:

1. *Move* the mouse-pointer over the **Start** button (start) present on the **Taskbar** (Fig. WD-2.1).

Fig. WD-2.1

2. *Click* the left mouse-button on it. Immediately, a push-up menu gets displayed. (Fig. WD-2.2).
3. Inside the push-up menu, *move* the mouse-pointer over the **All Programs** option. A second menu appears.
4. Inside the second menu, *place* the mouse-pointer over the **Microsoft Office** option (Fig. WD-2.3).
5. Immediately, a third menu appears. In the third menu, *move* the mouse-pointer over the **Microsoft Word 2003** option and *click* the left mouse button. Immediately, the **Microsoft Word** window opens up on your screen (Fig. WD-2.3). Carefully observe the Word window shown in Fig. WD-2.3. It is actually a blank Word document, named as **Document 1**. Normally, a Microsoft Word document window contains all the parts described in Fig. WD-2.3.

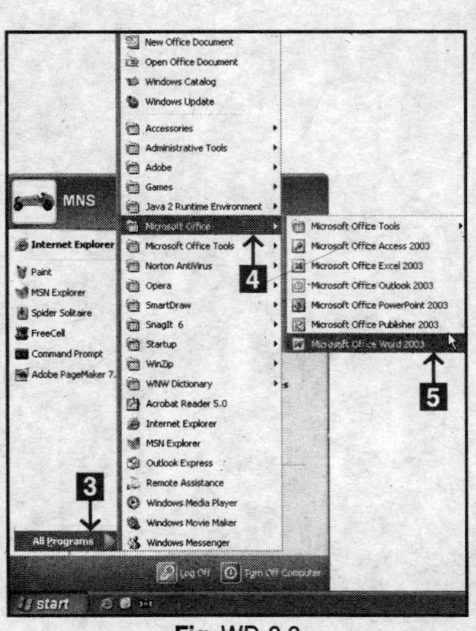

Fig. WD-2.2

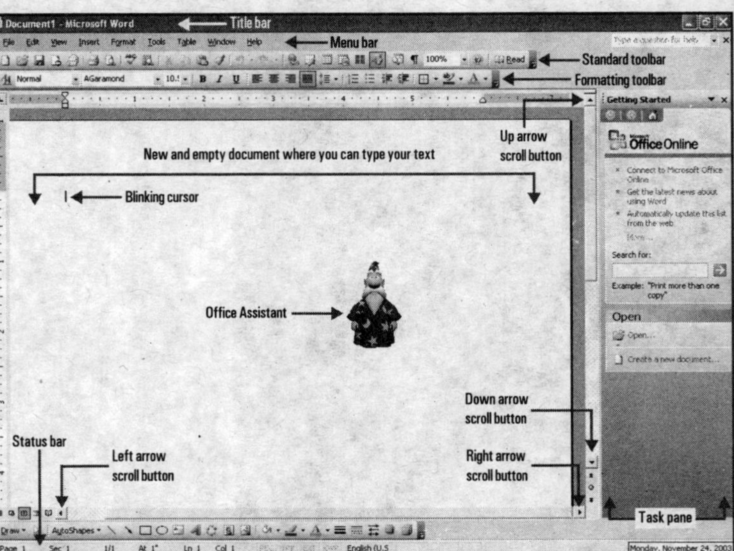

Fig. WD-2.3

Let us now get familiar with some of the Word window parts indicated in Fig. WD-2.3.

Title bar : The topmost portion of any window.

Menu bar : The bar just below the Title bar.

Menu bar options : These are command categories on the Menu bar. For example, Microsoft Word has Menu bar options like **File**, **Edit**, **View**, etc.

Pull-down menu : Clicking on each Menu bar option generates a list of commands called the pull-down menu.

Toolbar : A horizontal bar lying below the Menu bar containing pictorial buttons of commands is called the Toolbar. Two important toolbars which you use frequently are the Standard Toolbar and the Formatting Toolbar.

Menus

As you know, computer programs work only when you give them commands. To work efficiently in the Word program, you must have a fair knowledge of all the commands used in this program.

In Microsoft Word, commands are arranged in a systematic manner, i.e. in the form of menus. This arrangement makes it easy for the user to give appropriate commands when needed without having to remember all of them. The menus in a Word document are displayed in the form of horizontal bars (Fig. WD-2.3). These bars are generally grouped in two categories—**Menu bar** and **Toolbar**. Let us learn about each category.

Menu bar

The **Menu bar** appears just below the **Title bar** of the Microsoft Word window. It consists of nine options (Fig. WD-2.4).

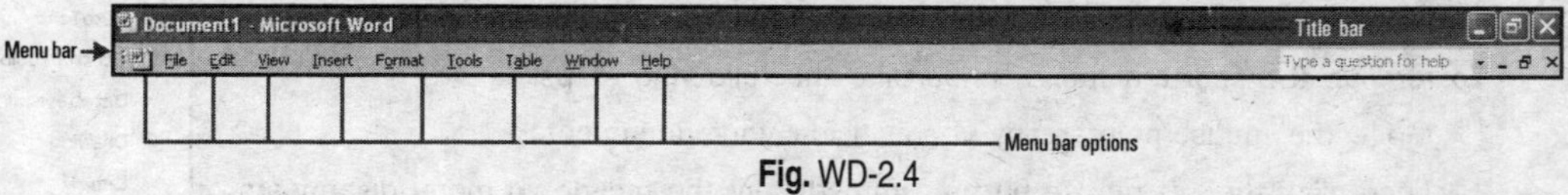

Fig. WD-2.4

Each Menu bar option represents a category of commands. When you click on any Menu bar option, its pull-down menu gets displayed with a list of commands. For example, when the **File** Menu bar option is clicked, its pull-down menu lists all the commands to carry out various file-related operations like creating a new file, opening an existing file, printing a file, saving a file, etc. Similarly, when the **Edit** menu bar option is clicked, its pull-down menu lists all the commands related to editing operations done within a file, such as copying, moving, deleting, etc.

Selecting the required Menu bar option

Selecting a Menu bar option becomes very simple when you use the mouse. Let us now learn how to select a Menu bar option. Suppose, you wish to select the **File** option of the Menu bar. This you can do through the following steps.

1. Start with the Word document as shown in Fig. WD-2.3. *Place* the mouse-pointer over the **File** option of the Menu bar (Fig. WD-2.5). *Click* the left mouse-button once.
2. Immediately, a pull-down menu appears (Fig. WD-2.5). Similarly, you can open the pull down menu of any Menu bar option.

For a better understanding of the pull-down menu, read on.

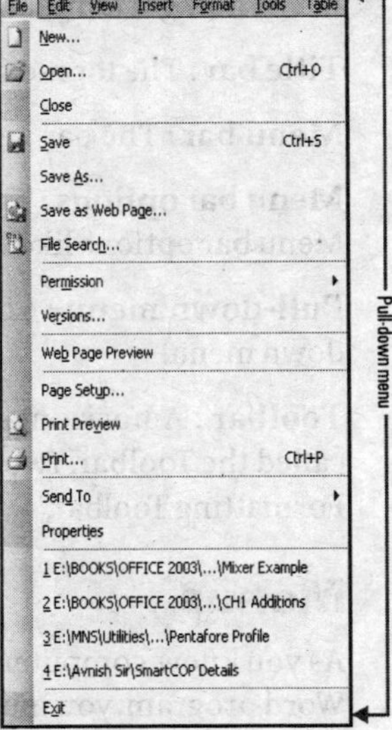

Fig. WD-2.5

Pull-down menu

As you know, the pull-down menu is a vertical box of commands that appears when a Menu bar option is clicked. Remember, a pull-down menu is not permanently visible on the screen. It appears only when you click on its corresponding menu bar option. For example, in Fig.WD-2.5, the pull-down menu of the **File** option appears only when the **File** option is clicked. The important commands of the File pull-down menu are explained in the following Table.

TABLE

New	:	Create a new file
Open	:	Open an existing file
Close	:	Close an open file
Print	:	Print a file
Save	:	Store a file in memory with a name
Save As	:	Store a file in memory with a different name
Exit	:	Exit from the program

After opening the Microsoft Word document, suppose you have accidentally clicked the right mouse-button on a Menu bar option or on any button of the Toolbar. This results in appearance of a shortcut menu (Fig.WD-2.6).

To remove the shortcut menu, undertake the following steps:

1. Move the mouse-pointer anywhere inside your document.
2. Then click the left mouse button. Immediately the pull-down menu disappears from the screen, and you can now carry on with your work.

Similarly, when you click the left mouse-button on any Menu bar option, a pull-down menu gets displayed with a set of commands related to that option.

To remove such a pull-down menu from the screen, just click the left mouse-button anywhere inside the document.

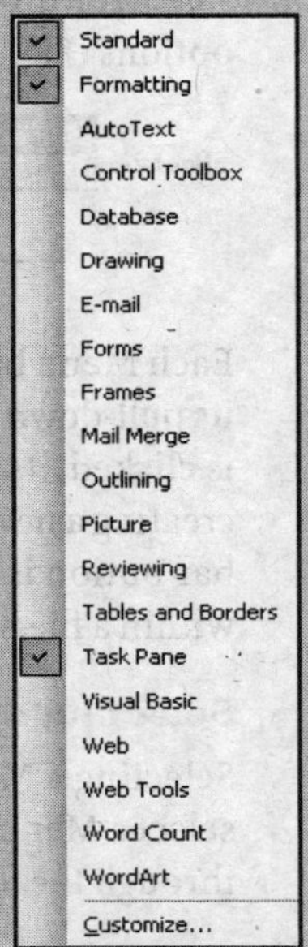

Fig. WD-2.6

Let us now practice selecting a command or option from the pull-down menu of the **File** Menu bar option.

Selecting the Close option for Closing a Document

The **File** pull-down menu has the **Close** option to close an open file or document. To use the **Close** option, undertake the following steps:

1. We assume that a Microsoft Word document is open on your **Desktop**. *Move* the mouse-pointer over the **File** Menu bar option (Fig. WD-2.7).
2. *Click* the left mouse-button on it. Immediately, a pull-down menu appears on your screen (Fig. WD-2.7).
3. Now *place* the mouse-pointer over the **Close** option (Fig. WD-2.7). Next, *press* the left mouse-button once.
4. Immediately, the currently open document closes and the Microsoft Word window appears on your monitor (Fig. WD-2.8).

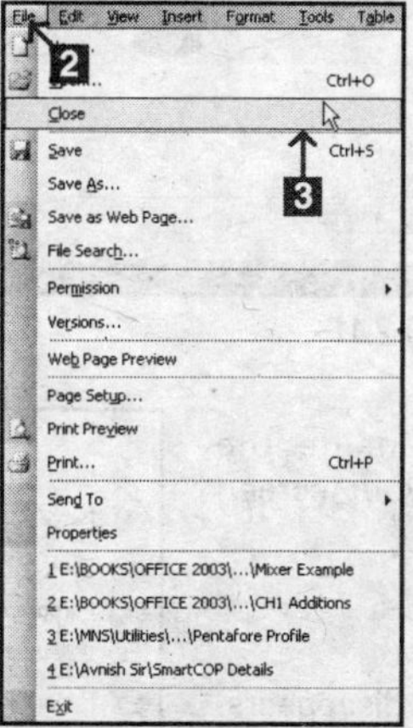

Fig. WD-2.7

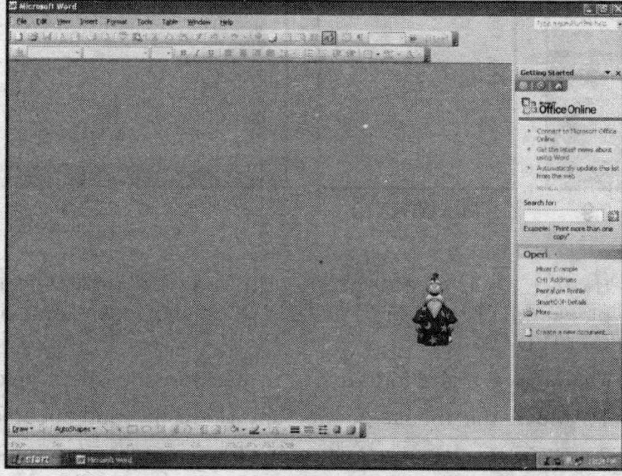

Fig. WD-2.8

The pull-down menus cover up a certain portion of the screen. Therefore, the document text gets partially hidden behind them.

Creating a New Blank Document

Let us now use Task Pane to perform an operation, say, creating a new document. **Task pane** is a vertical narrow window within an MS Office application that provides commonly used commands, such as opening an existing file, creating a new file, search for topics, etc. Its location and narrow width allow you to use these commands while still working in your document. When you open the Microsoft Word, the Getting Started Task pane appears on the right side of blank document window. Let us now learn to use the Getting Started Task pane for creating a blank document. To do so, go through the following steps:

1. Begin with the window of Fig. WD-2.8 *move* the mouse-pointer over the **Create a new document** option in the **Getting Started** Task pane and *click* the left mouse-button (Fig. WD-2.9). The **Getting Started** Task pane changes to **New Document** Task pane of Fig. WD-2.10.

2. In the **New Document** Task pane of Fig. WD-2.10, *click* over **Blank document** option. A blank document opens up on your screen (Fig. WD-2.11). It looks like a blank piece of paper where you can type text appears.

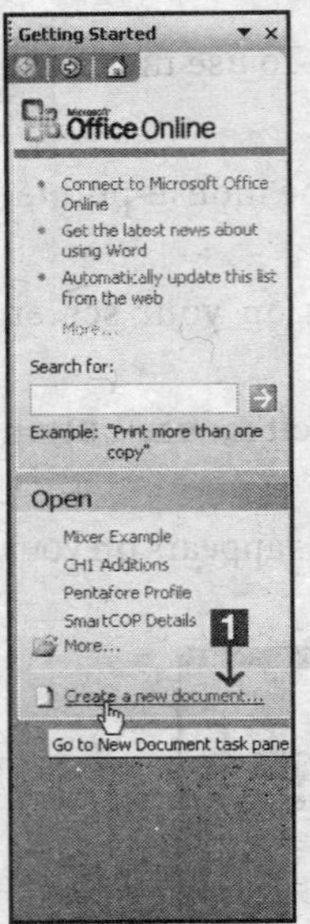

Fig. WD-2.9

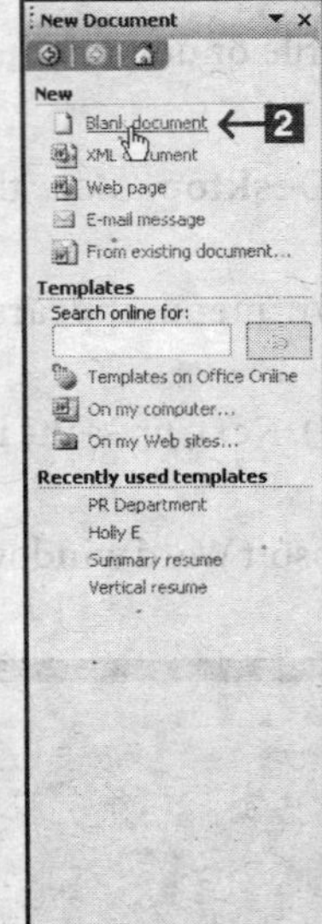

Fig. WD-2.10

Fig. WD-2.11

If you have accidentally clicked the right mouse-button inside the blank document (Fig. WD-2.11), a shortcut menu appears on your screen (Fig.WD-2.12).

To remove this shortcut menu, perform the steps given below:

1. Move the mouse-pointer anywhere in your document.
2. Click the left mouse-button. Immediately, the pull-down menu disappears.

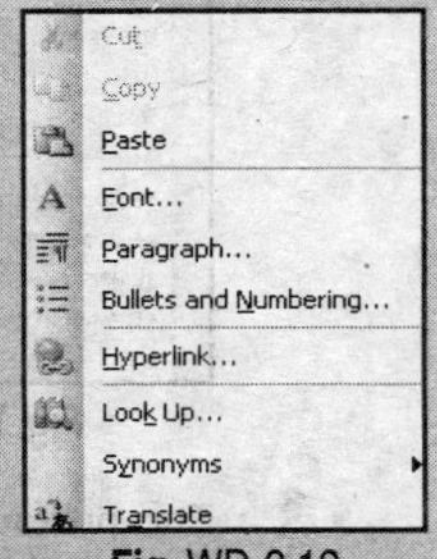

Fig. WD-2.12

How to start when you don't see the Getting Started Task pane?

If you don't see the Getting Started Task pane, it means the option responsible to display it every time MS Word starts is currently switched off. To turn this option on, undertake the following steps:

1. Start with the MS Word window. *Click* on the **Tools** Menu bar option. In the pull-down menu, *click* over the **Options** option (Fig. WD-2.13)
2. The **Options** box (Fig. WD-2.14) appears. In this box, under the **View** tab locate the **Startup Task Pane** option and *click* over the square box beside it. A check sign appears in the box, indicating that the option has been turned on (Fig. WD-2.14).
3. Next, *click* over the **OK** button (Fig. WD-2.15). The **Options** box disappears. Now when you start the MS Word program, the **Getting Started** Task pane will appear along with the default document.

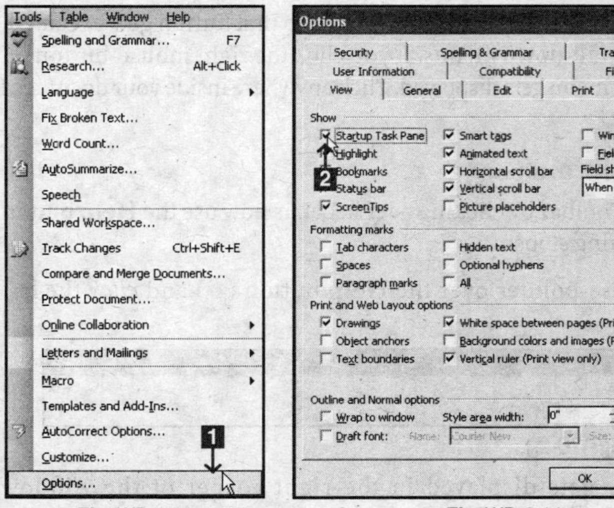

Fig. WD-2.13 **Fig.** WD-2.14

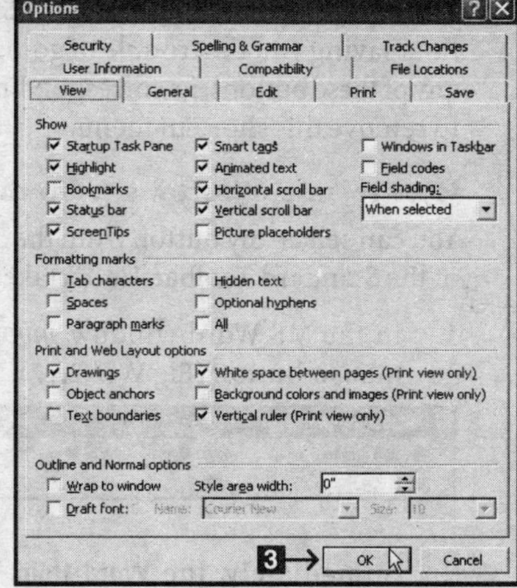

Fig. WD-2.15

Toolbars

Toolbar is a set of buttons located below the Menu bar in the Microsoft Word and various Microsoft Office programs, like Microsoft Excel, Microsoft Access, Microsoft PowerPoint and Microsoft Outlook. The toolbar buttons are equivalents of various pull-down menu commands of Menu bar options. As compared to commands, it is easier to remember toolbar buttons since they display the pictures of the tasks they accomplish. Toolbar buttons are also easier to use as they get activated with only one click.

In Microsoft Word, there are many toolbars, viz. the Standard Toolbar, the Formatting Toolbar, the Drawing Toolbar, Forms Toolbar, Tables and Borders Toolbar, etc. Among these, the **Standard** and the **Formatting Toolbars** are quite important. So, our current discussion will concentrate on these two toolbars.

Standard Toolbar

The **Standard Toolbar** in a Word document window looks like Fig. WD-2.16. And, you know, it is present just below the Menu bar. The picture buttons of the Standard Toolbar are shortcuts to frequently used pull-down commands of various menu bar options. Carefully observe Fig. WD-2.16 and memorise the tasks related to various buttons.

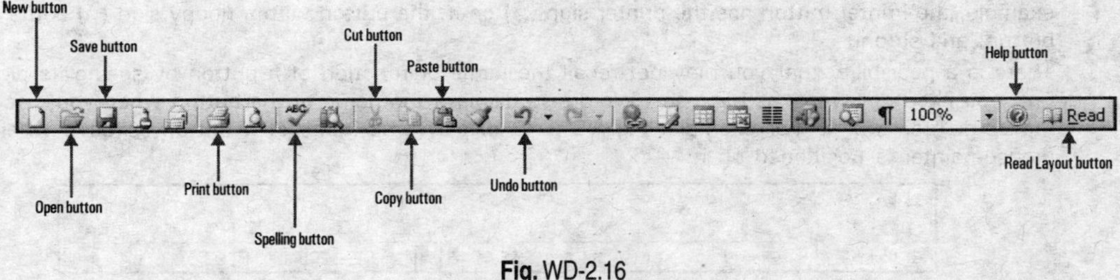

Fig. WD-2.16

When you click on a button of the Standard Toolbar, the command related to that button gets executed, thus saving you the trouble of going through pull-down menus. If you click the right mouse-button on any of these buttons, its corresponding shortcut menu gets displayed. Click anywhere inside your document to remove this shortcut menu.

How to select buttons from the Standard Toolbar?

You can select any button from the Standard Toolbar by clicking over it. Let us now use the **Help** button of the Standard Toolbar. Undertake the following steps:

1. In the MS Word window, *move* the mouse-pointer over the **Help** button (◉) and *click* the left mouse-button (Fig.WD-2.17).

Fig. WD-2.17

2. Immediately, the **Word Help** Task pane gets displayed in the right corner of the window (Fig. WD-2.18). From the **Word Help** Task pane, you can seek assistance for a topic related to the MS Word (as discussed later in the chapter).

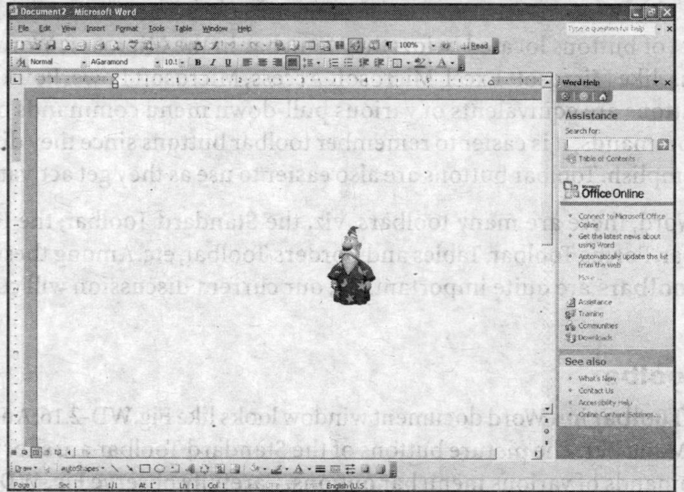

Fig. WD-2.18

Every button on the Standard Toolbar has a picture so that you can easily recall its function. For example, the Printer button has the printer sign (🖨) on it, the button with a floppy sign (💾) is the Save button, and so on.

There is a possibility that you may not recall the name or function of a button by seeing its picture. But, you need not worry as Microsoft Word also displays the name of the button when you place the mouse-pointer over it. For example, Fig.WD-2.19 displays the name of a button as Save when the mouse-pointer is positioned on it.

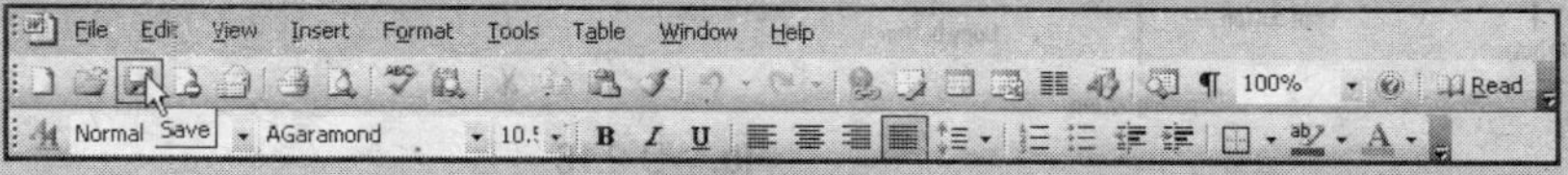

Fig. WD-2.19

Let us now know more about other picture buttons of the Standard Toolbar which we will use frequently. Please do not try to perform the following steps practically on your computer now. You can do that later on. But, you can perform the steps given under the topics 'Office Assistant' and 'Formatting Toolbar' while reading the text.

New button ( ) : This button is used for creating a blank new file to work in. To create a new file, follow the steps given below:

1. *Move* the mouse-pointer over the **New** button.
2. Then *click* the left mouse-button on it. Immediately, a blank file opens up on your screen.

Copy button ( ) : The **Copy** button is used to make a duplicate copy of any block of text. Any text can be copied from one location in your document to another through the copy operation. Copying can be done not only within a document, but also from one document to another.

Cut button ( ) : The **Cut** button is used to move any block of text from one location in your document to another. During the Cut operation, no duplicate copy of the text is made. Instead, when the text is moved to the new location, it gets deleted from its previous location. With the **Cut** button, text can be moved not only within a document but also from one document to another.

If you are not sure about the actual operation of a particular button, just bring the mouse-pointer over it, and the name of the button will appear below as shown in Fig.WD-2.16.

If you click the right mouse-button on any of these buttons, its corresponding shortcut menu gets displayed. Click anywhere inside your document to remove this shortcut menu.

Paste button ( ) : The process of displaying data at a certain location, after a copy or cut operation, is called **Pasting** of data. It can be quickly done with the help of the **Paste** button. Any copy or cut operation is usually followed by the use of the **Paste** button. This button becomes enabled only when you move or copy text. Any text can be copied or moved from one document and pasted in the same or different document.

Spelling and Grammar button ( ): As the name suggests, this button is used to check spelling and grammatical errors in your document. Generally, the **Spelling and Grammar** button is used after the whole text has been typed.

Save button ( ) : With the help of the **Save** button, you can save your file quickly and easily. To save the document in which you are currently working, click on the **Save** button. While doing your work, keep clicking on the **Save** button at regular intervals to protect your work from being lost in case your computer is turned off accidentally.

Undo button ( ) : Suppose, you have created a document and typed some text into it. While reading through the text, you perform certain modifications. After doing all the changes, you realize that you have performed them at wrong places. But, you need not worry because you can restore the text to its original form by removing all the changes using the **Undo** button. To remove the changes, keep clicking on the **Undo** button till you reach the original form of your document.

Office Assistant

It is an animation character that appears on screen when the MS Word window is opened. It gives answers to the queries typed by you. Microsoft Office offers various types of Office Assistants, shown in Fig. WD-2.20 to WD-2.24. Depending upon your requirement and preference, you can select any assistant.

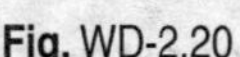

Fig. WD-2.20

Fig. WD-2.21

Fig. WD-2.22

Fig. WD-2.23

Fig. WD-2.24

If you are unable to see the Office Assistant icon on the screen then move the mouse-pointer over the Help Menu bar option and click the left mouse button. A pull-down menu appears. Move the mouse-pointer over the Show Office Assistant option and click the left mouse button (Fig. WD-2.25).

Immediately, the Office Assistant icon gets displayed on your screen asking you to type the name of the topic on which you need help.

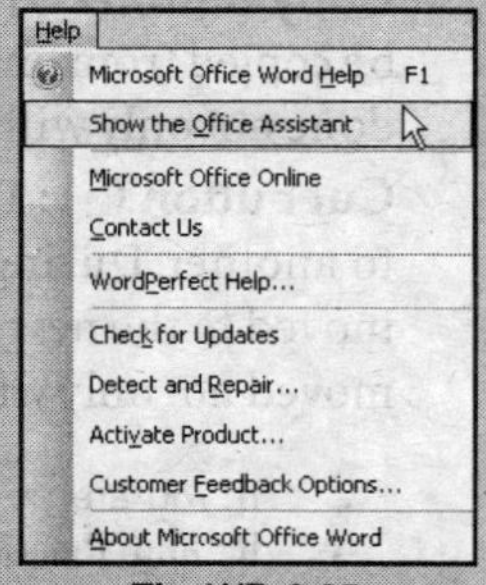

Fig. WD-2.25

Choosing an Office Assistant

Just now you have seen various animation characters that you can use as an Office Assistant in MS Office applications. Depending upon your liking and requirement, you can select any character as your Office Assistant. Let us now learn to select an Office Assistant by undertaking the following steps:

1. Start with a MS Word window showing an Office Assistant. *Move* the mouse-pointer over the displayed Office Assistant and *click* the left mouse-button. Instantly, a **What would you like to do?** box appears above the Office Assistant (Fig.WD-2.26).
2. *Move* the mouse-pointer over the **Options** button and *click* the left mouse-button (Fig.WD-2.27).

Fig. WD-2.26

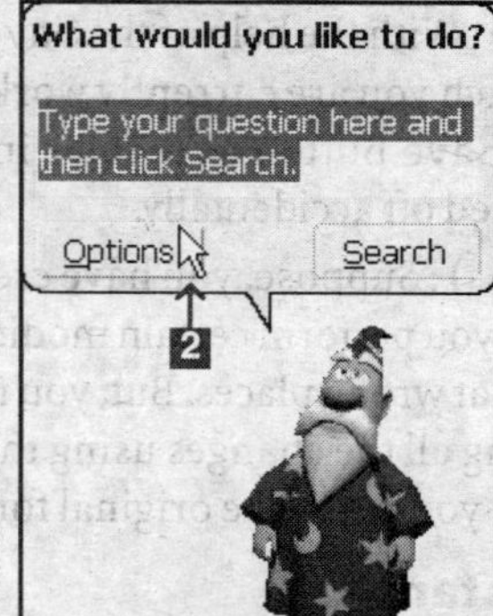

Fig. WD-2.27

3. An **Office Assistant** box with two tabs – **Gallery** and **Options**, appears (Fig.WD-2.28).
4. In the **Office Assistant** box, *move* the mouse-pointer over the **Gallery** tab and *click* the left mouse-button (Fig.WD-2.29).

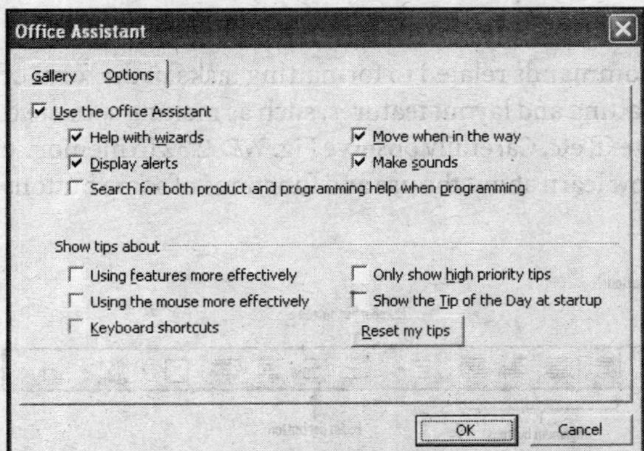

Fig. WD-2.28

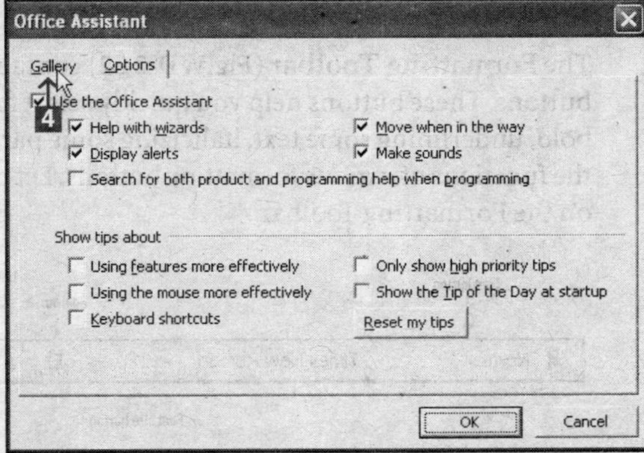

Fig. WD-2.29

5. A preview of various Office Assistants is shown under the **Gallery** tab. To view all the characters, *click* over **Back** or **Next** buttons. In our case, *click* over the **Back** button two times. As you *click* the **Back** button, the preview of Office Assistant appears (**Genie,** in our case) with a callout and the name of the Office Assistant (Fig.WD-2.30).

6. After selecting an Office Assistant of your choice, *move* the mouse-pointer over the **OK** button of **Office Assistant** box and *click* the left mouse-button (Fig.WD-2.31). The selected character, in our case Genie, will serve as our Office Assistant.

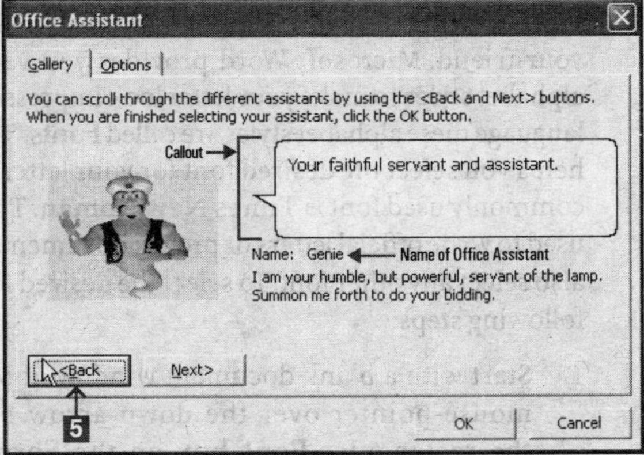

Fig. WD-2.30

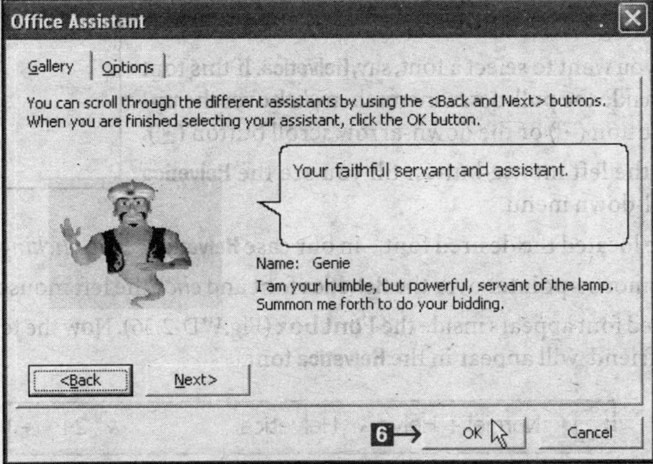

Fig. WD-2.31

Formatting Toolbar

The **Formatting Toolbar** (Fig.WD-2.32) contains commands related to formatting tasks in the form of buttons. These buttons help you quickly select formatting and layout features, such as making some text bold, underlining some text, italicizing some part of text, etc. Carefully observe Fig. WD-2.32 to memorise the functions of various formatting buttons. Let us now learn about the use and functions of some buttons on the Formatting Toolbar.

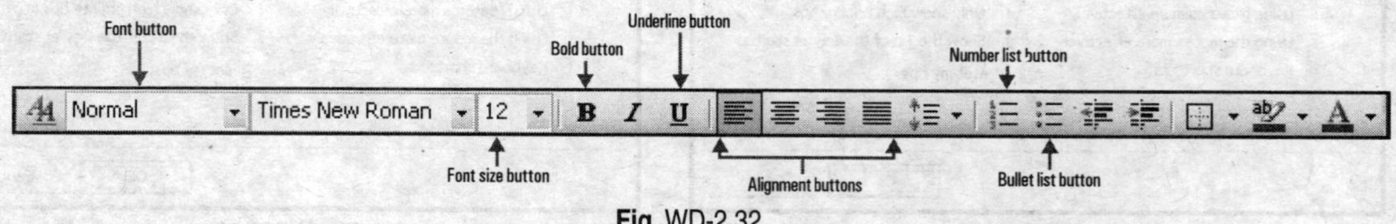

Fig. WD-2.32

Font button (Minion Web): Suppose you wish to write a letter to your friend. Microsoft Word provides you various types of alphabet styles to make your letter look impressive. In printing language these alphabet styles are called **Fonts.** The Font button helps you select the desired font for your letter text.The most commonly used font is **Times New Roman.** This font is generally used to write official letters or project documents. However, you can also select any other font. To select the desired font, go through the following steps:

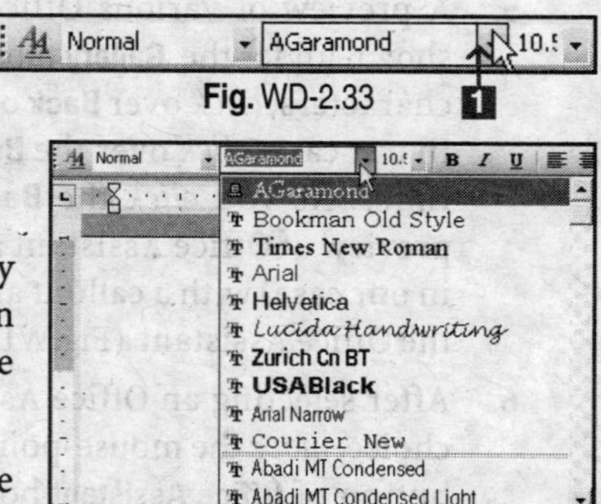

Fig. WD-2.33

Fig. WD-2.34

1. Start with a blank document window of MS Word. *Place* the mouse-pointer over the down-arrow button (▾) inside the rectangular **Font box** on the **Formatting Toolbar** (Fig.WD-2.33). *Press* the left mouse-button just once.
2. Immediately, a small pull-down menu appears displaying the available fonts (Fig.WD-2.34).
3. Now suppose you want to select a font, say, **Helvetica.** If this font is not visible inside the pull-down menu then *click* over the up-arrow scroll button (▴) or the down-arrow scroll button (▾).
4. Keep *clicking* the left mouse-button till you see the **Helvetica** font in the pull-down menu.

Fig. WD-2.35

5. Once you have located the desired font – in our case **Helvetica**– stop *clicking* the left mouse-button.
6. Now *move* the mouse-pointer over the **Helvetica** font and *click* the left mouse-button (Fig.WD-2.35).
7. Now the selected font appears inside the **Font box** (Fig.WD-2.36). Now the text you would type in the letter to your friend, will appear in the **Helvetica** font.

Fig. WD-2.36

Font Size button (10 ▾) : The **Font Size** button is used to set the size of the alphabets. To select a size for the text you are going to type, follow these steps :

1. *Move* the mouse-pointer over the down-arrow button (▾) of the **Font Size** box (Fig. WD-2.37).
2. *Click* the left mouse-button. Immediately, a pull-down menu appears displaying the available sizes (Fig. WD-2.38).
3. Suppose, you wish to select the size **24**. For this, *move* the mouse-pointer over the number **24** (Fig. WD-2.38).
4. Then *click* the left mouse-button. Immediately, the selected size gets displayed in the **Font Size** box.

Fig. WD-2.37

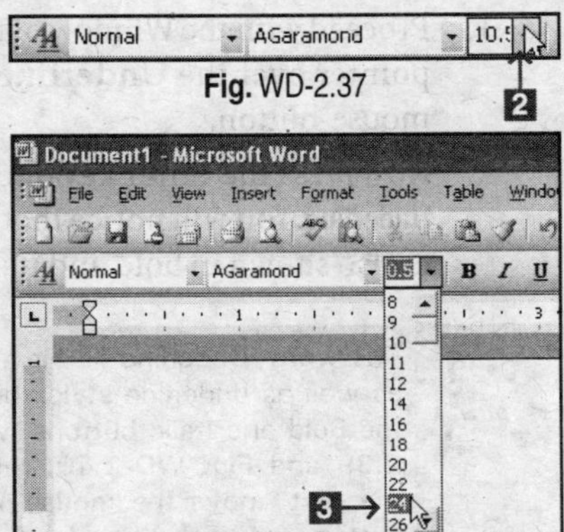

Fig. WD-2.38

If you click on a higher number, the size of the alphabets of your text will become larger. Similarly, selecting a smaller number will make the size of the alphabets smaller.

Apart from selecting the size and appearance of your text, you can also add styles to some important portion of your text to make it look different from the rest. This is done with the help of the **Bold** button, *Italic* button and the Underline button, present on the Formatting Toolbar.

Bold button (**B**) : If you want to make some text look bold than the rest, follow the steps given below:

1. Proceed with the window of Fig. WD-2.38. *Position* the mouse-pointer over the **Bold** button (**B**).
2. *Click* the left mouse-button.
3. Now *type* any word, say **Bold**. This word gets displayed in a bold format in size 24 (Fig. WD-2.39).

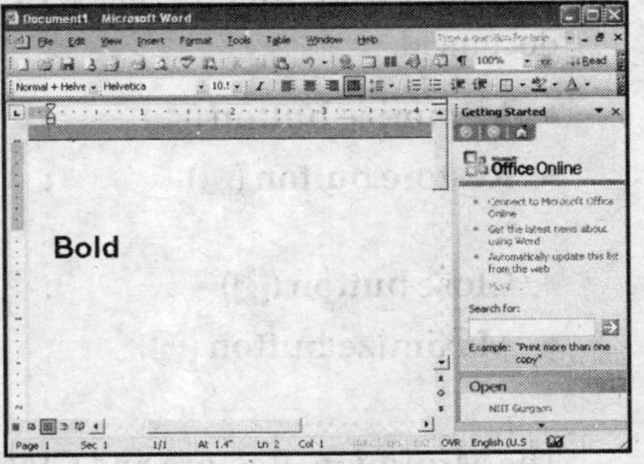

Fig. WD-2.39

To stop boldfacing the characters of your text, move the mouse-pointer again over the Bold button and click the left mouse-button.

Italic button (*I*) : If you want to make the text appear slanted or tilted, follow the steps given below:

1. Proceed with the window of Fig. WD-2.39. *Position* the mouse-pointer over the **Italic** button (*I*).
2. *Click* the left mouse-button.
3. Now *press* the **Enter** key once and then *type* any word, say **Italics.** This word gets displayed in bold and italics format in size 24 (Fig. WD-2.40).

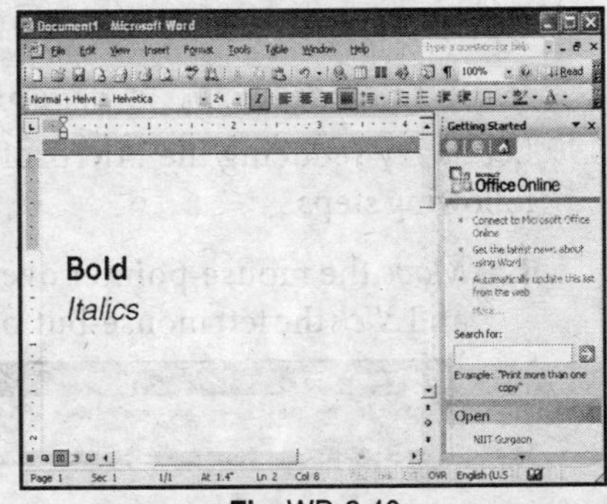

Fig. WD-2.40

To stop italicizing characters of your text, move the mouse-pointer again over the Italics button and click the left mouse-button. The word 'Italics' in Fig WD-2.40 appears bold as well as italicized because we have not de-selected the Bold button that was selected in Fig. WD-2.39.

Underline button (U) : If you wish to underline some text then undertake the following steps.

1. Proceed with the Window of Fig. WD-2.40. *Move* the mouse-pointer over the **Underline** button (U) and *click* the left mouse-button.
2. Now *press* the **Enter** key once and then *type* any word, say **Underline.** You will notice that the word gets underlined and is also shown in bold and italic styles. (Fig. WD-2.41).

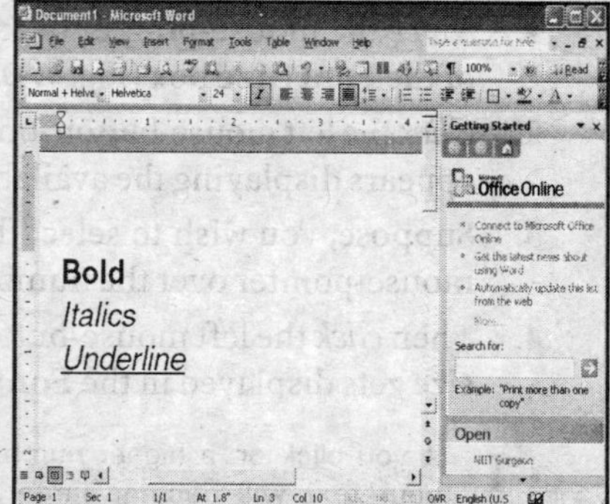

Fig. WD-2.41

The word 'Underline' in Fig WD-2.41 is shown in bold, italics as well as underline styles because we have not de-selected the Bold and Italic buttons, which were selected in Fig. WD-2.39 and Fig. WD-2.40, respectively. To stop underlining the text, move the mouse-pointer again over the Underline button and click the left mouse-button.

Changing the Size of a Document

Let us now try adjusting the size of a Word window. Before doing so, it is better that you get familiar with Microsoft Word window (Fig. WD-3.40). You have to make use of these buttons to adjust the size of your document.

- **Minimize button** ( ) : Used for changing a window into a button.
- **Restore button** ( ) : Used for adjusting the size of a window according to the user's requirement.
- **Close button** ( ) : Used for closing a window.
- **Maximize button** ( ) : Used for enlarging a window after it has been minimized or restored.

The **Minimize, Restore** and **Close** buttons present on the **Title bar** of a every document opened in Microsoft Word will show these buttons. Let us now use these buttons.

Reducing the Microsoft Word Window

(How to Reduce the Microsoft Word window into a Taskbar button)

Let us try reducing the Microsoft Word window into a Taskbar button. For this task, undertake the following steps.

1. *Move* the mouse-pointer over the **Minimize** button ( ) present on the **Title bar** (Fig. WD-2.42) and *click* the left mouse-button.

Fig. WD-2.42

2. Immediately, **Microsoft Word** window reduces into a **Taskbar** button (Fig. WD-2.43).

Fig. WD-2.43

Maximizing a Taskbar button into a Window

(How to Enlarge the Microsoft Word Taskbar button into a window)

To enlarge a Taskbar button of Microsoft Word into a window, undertake the following steps :

1. *Move* the mouse-pointer over **Microsoft Word** button present on the **Taskbar** (Fig. WD-2.44).

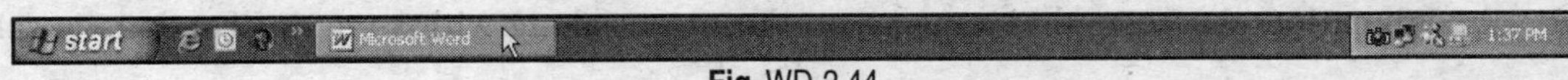

Fig. WD-2.44

2. *Click* the left mouse-button. Immediately, **Microsoft Word** window opens up on your screen.

Closing the Document and Quitting Word

Now, let us proceed to close the file that is open on your screen (Fig. WD-2.41) and then quit Microsoft Word. Undertake the following steps to do so:

1. *Move* the mouse-pointer over **File** Menu bar option of the open file and *click* the left mouse-button. Instantly, a pull-down menu gets displayed (Fig. WD-2.45).
2. Inside the pull-down menu, *move* the mouse-pointer over the **Close** option and *click* the left mouse-button (Fig. WD-2.45). Immediately, a message box is displayed asking whether you need to save the changes to the document (Fig. WD-2.46).
3. If you do not wish to save your document, *click* the left mouse-button over the **No** button (Fig. WD-2.46). Immediately, the message box disappears and the document also closes, and you return to the Microsoft Word window.

   Here we have closed the document without saving it. Every document created in your computer can be saved into the computer's memory. When you save a document, you always give a name to it. We will deal with the saving procedure in the next chapter.

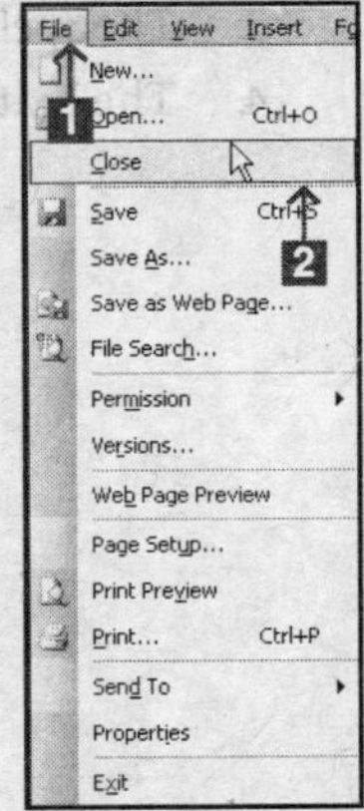

Fig. WD-2.45

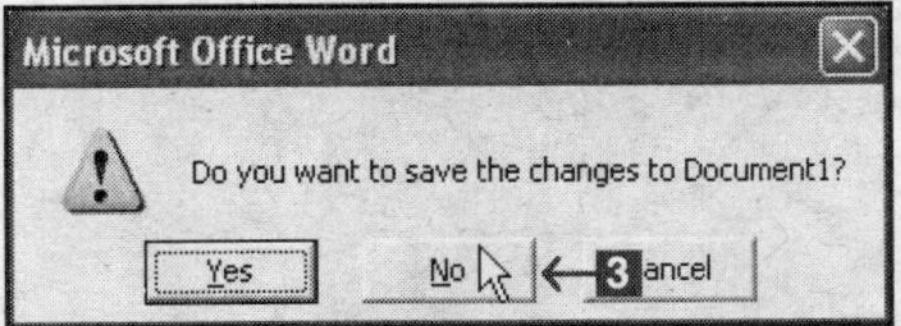

Fig. WD-2.46

4. Now, let us proceed to quit Microsoft Word. To do so, *move* the mouse-pointer over the **Close** button (☒) on the **title bar** of the **Microsoft Word** window (Fig. WD-2.47).
5. *Click* the left mouse-button. Immediately, Microsoft Word closes and you return to your **Desktop**.

Fig. WD-2.47

Exercise

Fill in the Blanks

1. A __________ consists of various buttons, which are shortcuts to the commands available on the Menu bar.
2. An animation character that appears on the screen along with some instructions is called ________________.
3. The _____________ button is used for making some text look bolder than the rest of the text.
4. The ________________ button is used to set the size of the alphabets.

True/False

1. New button is used for opening an existing file to work in.
2. During the cut operation, a duplicate copy of the text is made.
3. The Spelling and Grammar button is used to check spelling and grammatical errors in your document.
4. The Exit button is used to close an open file.

Typing Your First Document 3

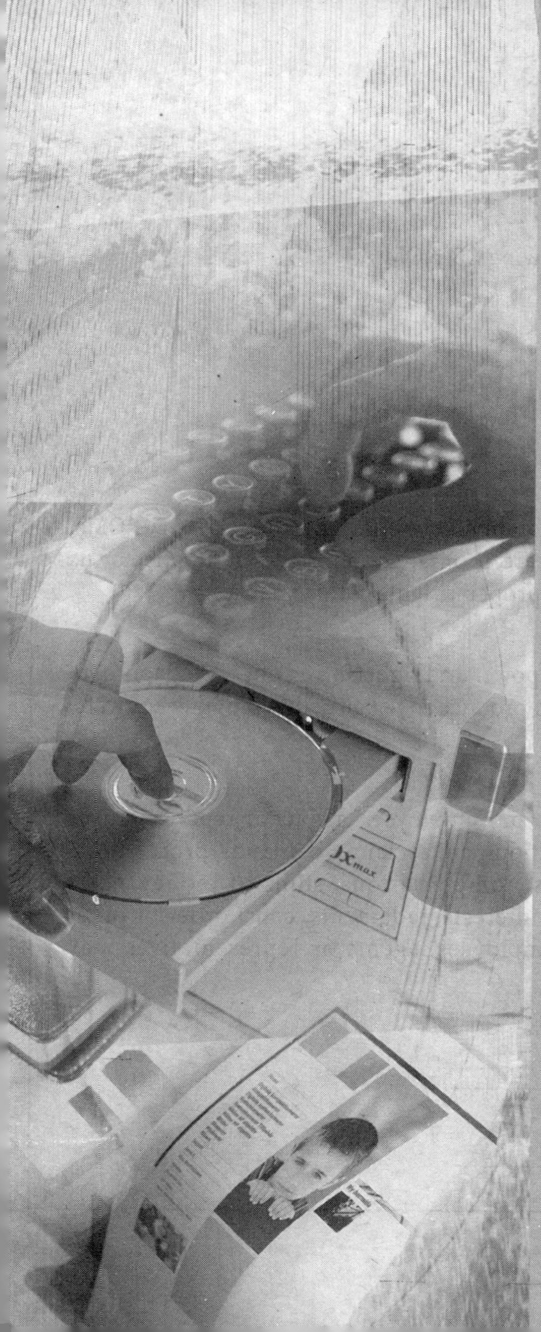

IN THIS CHAPTER

- Starting Microsoft Word
- Saving the Document
- Previewing the Document
- Printing the Document
- Closing the Word Document
- Exercise

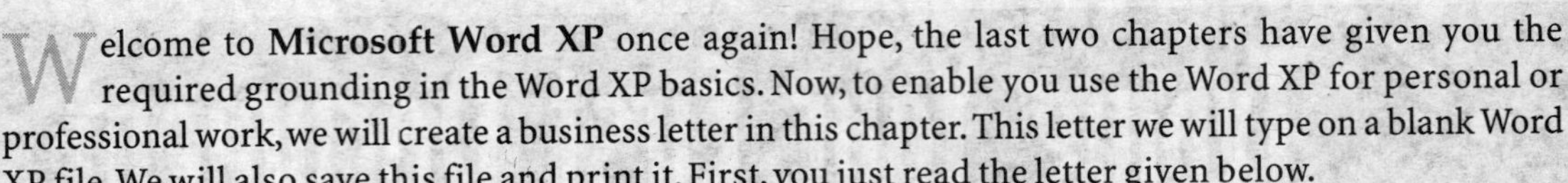

Welcome to **Microsoft Word XP** once again! Hope, the last two chapters have given you the required grounding in the Word XP basics. Now, to enable you use the Word XP for personal or professional work, we will create a business letter in this chapter. This letter we will type on a blank Word XP file. We will also save this file and print it. First, you just read the letter given below.

Dated: 5th January 2004

M/s Concord Computers Pvt. Ltd.
Singapore

Dear Sir,

RE: LETTER OF INDEMNITY

In respect of our request to you to replicate the following CD-ROM.

Name the of CD-ROM	Quantity
1. Word XP for Dummies	3000
2. Teach Yourself CorelDraw	3000
3. Teach Yourself MS-Office XP	2000

We hereby warrant that :

1. The use, testing, replicating and mass production of any or all of the aforesaid CD-ROMs, CD-ROM software and any other computer software, program or information supplied by us will not result in the infringement of intellectual property rights of third parties.

2. We are permitted by law which authorises us full power and right (in and out of Singapore) to instruct or advise you to use, test, replicate or mass-produce any or all of the computer software, software program or information.

3. We will indemnify and agree to keep you and your employees, agents or representatives fully and effectively indemnified against any actions, suits, claims, demands, proceedings, governmental prosecutions, losses, damages, compensations, sums of money, costs (including solicitor and client costs), charges, interests, judgments, court order or other liabilities whatsoever which you and your employees, agents or representatives may incur.

Signed by :__________________ Dated :__________________

NRIC NO :__________________ Company Stamp : __________

Starting Microsoft Word

Now, open the Word XP program on your computer through the following steps:

1. *Click* the left mouse-button over the **Start** button ( ). Immediately, a push-up menu gets displayed.
2. Inside the push-up menu, *place* the mouse-pointer over the **All Programs** option. Instantly, a second menu gets displayed.
3. Inside the second menu, *move* the mouse-pointer over the **Microsoft Office** option. A third menu appears
4. In the third menu, *move* the mouse-pointer over the **Microsoft Office Word 2003** option and *click* the left mouse-button. Immediately, Microsoft Word window opens up with a blank Word document in which we will type the letter given on the preceding page.

Guidelines for Typing

1. Before typing the first line, *press* the **Enter** key two times. This is done to leave a line blank before you begin the letter text. Wherever you need to leave a line blank after a text portion, just press the **Enter** key twice.
2. After typing the text, **Dated: 5th January 2004,** *press* the **Enter** key two times. After the text **M/s Concord Computers Pvt. Ltd.**, you need to press the Enter key just once. However, the Enter key would be pressed twice after the lines **Singapore, Dear Sir, RE: LETTER OF INDEMNITY, In respect... following CD-ROM, Name of the CD-ROM.** Also *press* the **Enter** key twice after each paragraph and at the end of the third paragraph and after the text **Dated:**__________.
3. When the text in your current line ends before attaining the set line width, and you have to start a new line, then just *press* the **Enter** key once and start typing text in a new line. For example:
   - (i) *Type* **M/s Concord Computers Pvt. Ltd.** (Fig.WD-3.1).
   - (ii) Then *press* the **Enter** key. The blinking cursor now shifts to the next line (Fig.WD-3.2).
   - (iii) Now *type* **Singapore**, which gets displayed in the next line (Fig.WD-3.3).

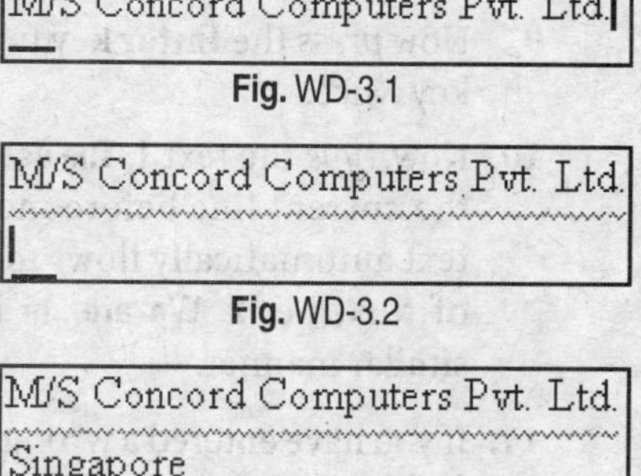

Fig. WD-3.1

Fig. WD-3.2

Fig. WD-3.3

4. After you type **Dear Sir** in your document, a box gets displayed before you with a message, **Dear Sir** *or* **Madam.** Ignore it by *pressing* **Esc** key. Now, *press* the **Enter** key twice for leaving one line blank.
5. For typing the subject of the letter, i.e. **RE: LETTER OF INDEMNITY** in capitals, undertake the following steps.
   - (i) *Press* the **Caps Lock** key of your keyboard once. This sets the **Caps Lock** ON.
   - (ii) Now *type* the text **RE: LETTER OF INDEMNITY.**
   - (iii) Next, again *press* the **Caps Lock** key once for turning the capital mode off. Thereafter, *press* the **Enter** key two times before typing the next line. **In respect....CD-ROM.** After this line, again *press* the **Enter** key twice.

6. *Press* the **Spacebar** key of your keyboard once to create a space between two words such as **LETTER** and **OF** or between a serial number and the text following it, such as **1. The use...third parties.**

7. Sometimes you may need to type a word in the same line, after leaving some spaces. For example, the word **Quantity** has to be displayed some spaces after the text **Name of CD-ROM**. To undertake this task, carry out the following steps:

   (i) *Type* the text **Name of CD-ROM** (Fig.WD-3.4).

   Name of CD-ROM

   Fig. WD-3.4

   (ii) Now *press* the **Tab key 5 times** from the keyboard. This action takes the blinking cursor five spaces away from its position (Fig.WD-3.5).

   (iii) Then *type* the word **Quantity.** It gets displayed at the desired place (Fig.WD-3.6).

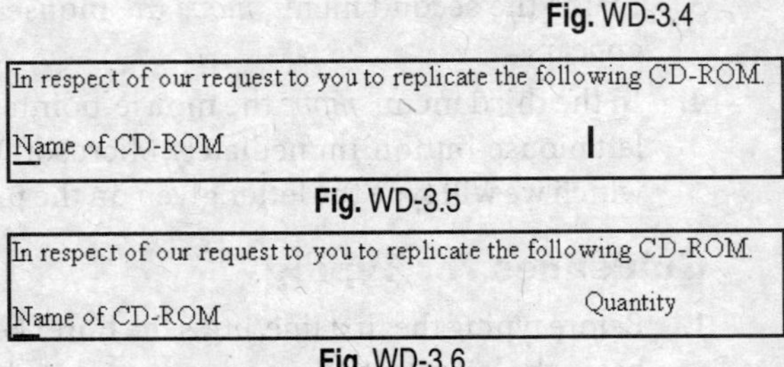

Fig. WD-3.5

Fig. WD-3.6

8. Now follow the steps given below for typing the line **1. Word XP for Dummies.**

   (i) *Press* the **Enter** key two times after the word Quantity.

   (ii) *Type* the text **1. Word XP for Dummies.**

   (iii) Then *press* the **Tab** key **five times.**

   (iv) *Type* **3000.**

   (v) *Press* the **Enter** key only once.

   (vi) *Type* the other two lines, i.e. **2. Teach Yourself CorelDraw...**(press Tab key five times) **3000** and **3. Teach Yourself MS-Office XP...**(press Tab key five times) **2000** in the same manner.

9. Now *press* the **Enter** key twice and type the next line **We hereby warrant that:.** Again press the **Enter** key twice.

10. Now, *type* the text **1. The use...third parties** without worrying whether you have to stop at the end of the current line before moving onto the next line. As soon as your current line gets filled, the text automatically flows to the next line. Now *press* the **Enter** key two times and enter other lines of text, i.e. **2. We are...or information** and **3. We will...agents or representatives may incur** in the similar manner.

11. If you have entered a wrong letter, or pressed the **Enter** key by mistake then *press* the **Backspace** key from the keyboard to delete the incorrect letter, the extra space or the line.

    After you have typed **Signed by:**, *press* the **Dash** key (-) ten to twelve times. You will see that a line gets displayed on the screen.

12. *Press* the **Tab** key just once, then *type* the text to be displayed in the same line, in our case **Dated.** Similarly, draw a line after the text. Write the rest of the text in the same manner.

    Hope, after going through the typing tips described in the above steps, you will type the letter quickly. So, don't wait, just type the letter.

Saving the Document

The letter which you have just typed is written in the computer's memory only temporarily. It would be lost as soon as the computer is switched off, or if there is a power failure.

To avoid the loss, save your document as a named file in the computer's memory. To do so, undertake the following steps :

1. We assume that your monitor displays the letter you have just typed. *Move* the mouse-pointer over the **File** Menu bar option of the window displaying the letter. *Click* the left mouse-button. Immediately, a pull-down menu (Fig.WD-3.7) appears.

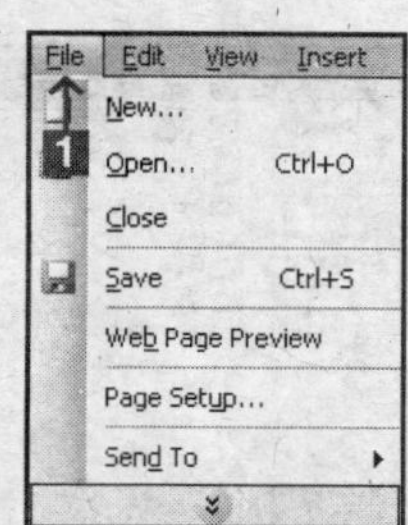

Fig. WD-3.7

2. Now *move* the mouse-pointer over the **Save** option inside the pull-down menu, and *click* on it (Fig.WD-3.8). Immediately, a **Save As** box appears (Fig.WD-3.9).

   In the previous chapters, you had used the **Save As** box. So, you know it has two options—**File name** and **Save in**—that we use to save our documents. A box beside the **File name** option (Fig. WD-3.9 & 3.10) has some highlighted text. This box is meant for entering a name for your document.

3. Now *type* the document name as **Letter.** This name automatically gets written inside the box beside the **File name** option (Fig.WD-3.11).

4. Now, we come to the **Save in** option. A box beside it displays the folder name **My Documents.** Actually this box is meant to mention the location where we would save our letter. Let us save our letter in **Local Disk (C:).** Now, *click* on the down-arrow button (▾) of the box beside the **Save in** option (Fig. WD-3.12).

5. A pull-down menu appears below the **Save in** option. In this menu, locate the **Local Disk (C:)** and *click* over it (Fig. WD-3.13).

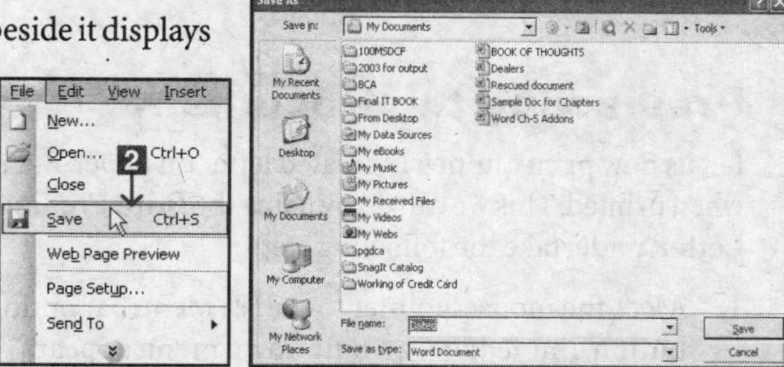

Fig. WD-3.8

Fig. WD-3.9

Fig. WD-3.10

Fig. WD-3.11

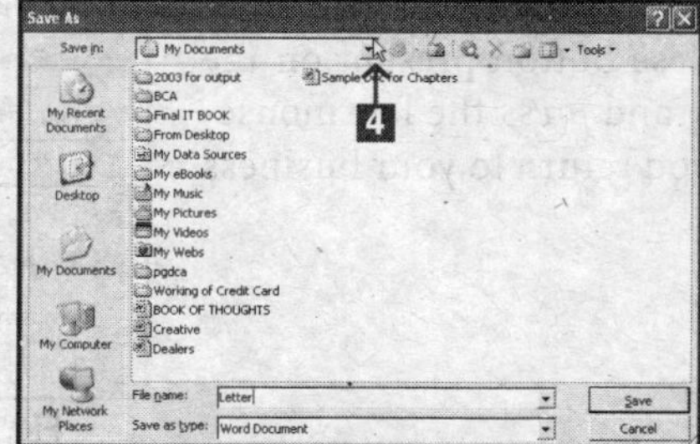

Fig. WD-3.12

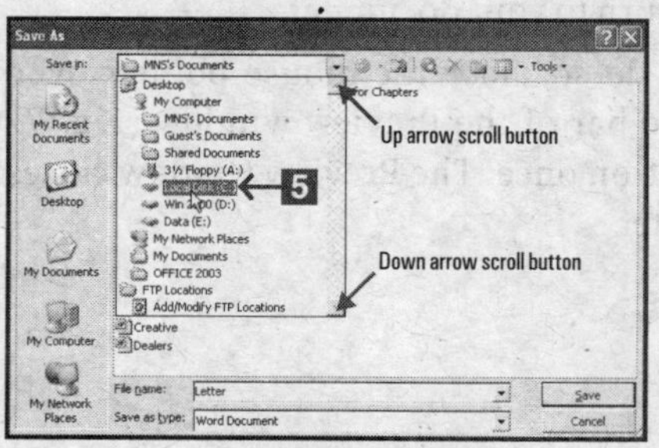

Fig. WD-3.13

6. The **Local Disk (C:)** option gets highlighted and appears inside the box beside the **Save in** option. The contents of the **Local Disk (C:)** gets displayed in the **Save As** box (Fig. WD-3.14).

7. Now *move* the mouse-pointer over the **Save** button in the **Save As** box (Fig.WD-3.15) and *click* the left mouse-button. Immediately, the **Save As** box disappears and you return to your business letter.

   The **Title bar** now displays the name **Letter.** We have saved our business letter as **Letter** and **.doc** is the extension which is given automatically to every Word document.

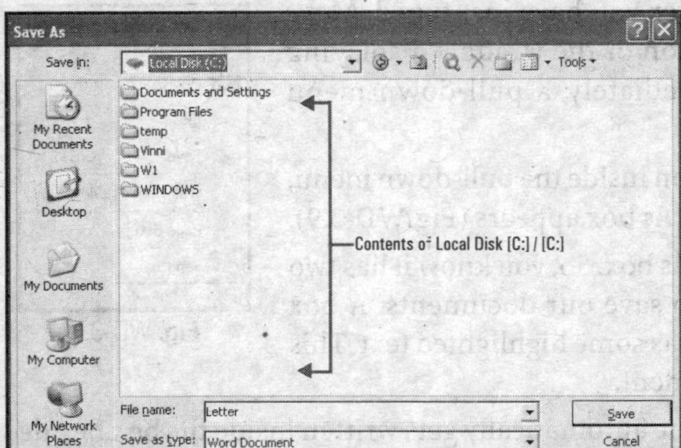

Fig. WD-3.14

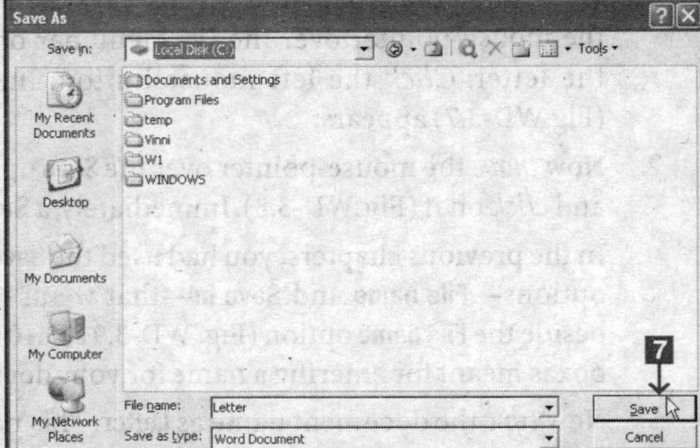

Fig. WD-3.15

Previewing the Document

Let us now print our newly created letter on paper. But before this, let us see on the screen how it will look when printed. This we can do by using the **Print Preview** feature of Microsoft Word. To preview document **Letter**, undertake the following steps:

1. *Move* the mouse-pointer to the **File** Menu bar option and *click* the left mouse-button. Immediately, a pull-down menu appears (Fig.WD-3.16).

2. Inside the pull-down menu, *move* the mouse-pointer over the **Print Preview** option and *click* the left mouse-button (Fig.WD-3.16).

3. Instantly, Microsoft Word shows you the print preview of your letter (Fig.WD-3.17).

4. After seeing the print preview of your document, you need to close it and return to your document.

   To do so, *move* the mouse-pointer over the **Close** button present on the Toolbar of the Preview window (Fig.WD-3.18) and *press* the left mouse-button once. The Preview window closes and you return to your business letter.

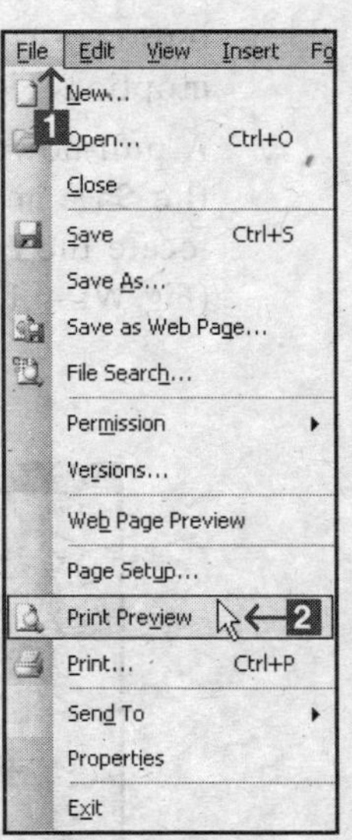

Fig. WD-3.16

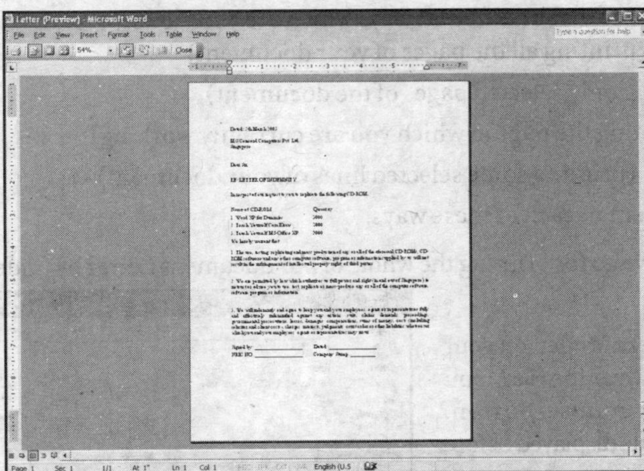

Fig. WD-3.17

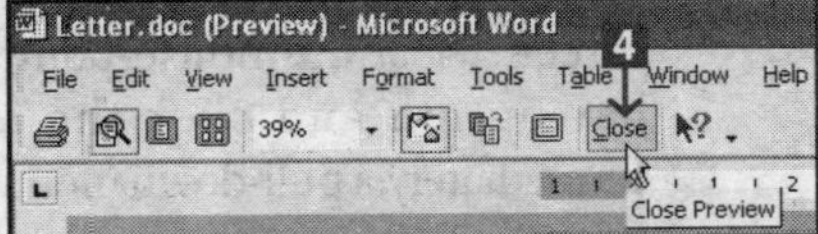

Fig. WD-3.18

To quickly preview any Word document click on the Print Preview button (🔍) present on the Standard Toolbar. This shortcut method saves you the trouble of going through Steps 1 to 3 of the topic Previewing the Document.

Printing the Document

Let us now print the **Letter** document. If printer is not installed on your computer then read the topic Installing the Printer in Chapter 4 - Windows Explorer to install a printer on your computer.

1. *Move* the mouse-pointer over the **File** Menu bar option, and *click* on it. Immediately, a pull-down menu gets displayed (Fig.WD-3.19).
2. Inside the pull-down menu, *move* the mouse-pointer over the **Print** option (Fig.WD-3.19) and *click* the left mouse-button. Immediately, the **Print** box appears on your screen (Fig.WD-3.20).

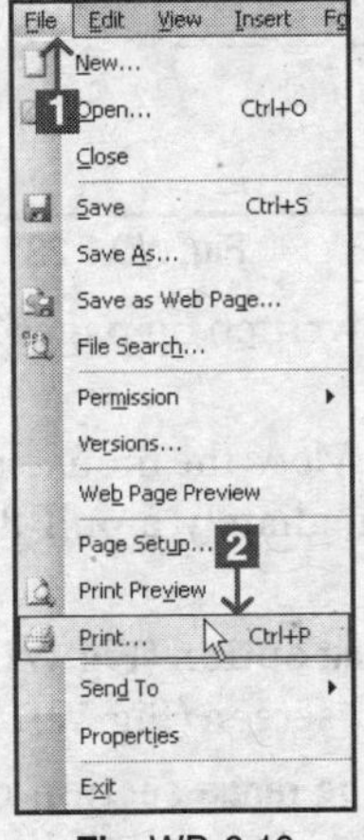

Fig. WD-3.19

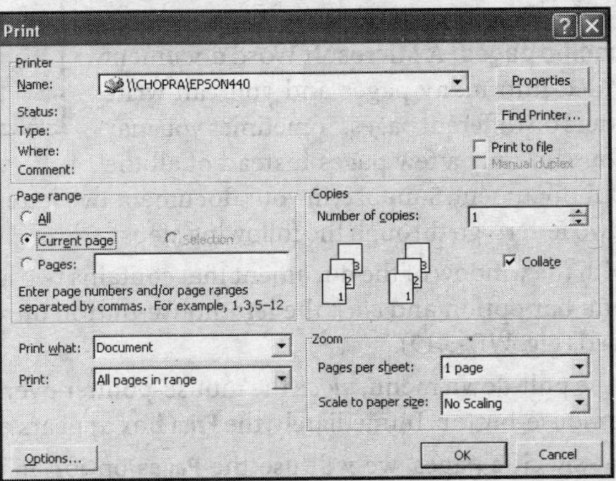

Fig. WD-3.20

In Microsoft Word, printing can be done in four different ways which are as follows:

- **Printing the whole document** (printing all the pages of your document)
- **Printing specific pages** (printing only selected pages of the document)
- **Printing the current page** (printing the page in which you are currently working)
- **Printing a small section of text** (printing some selected lines of your document)

Let us learn how to print our document in each of these ways:

Printing the whole document: First, we go for printing the whole of our document **Letter** by undertaking the following steps:

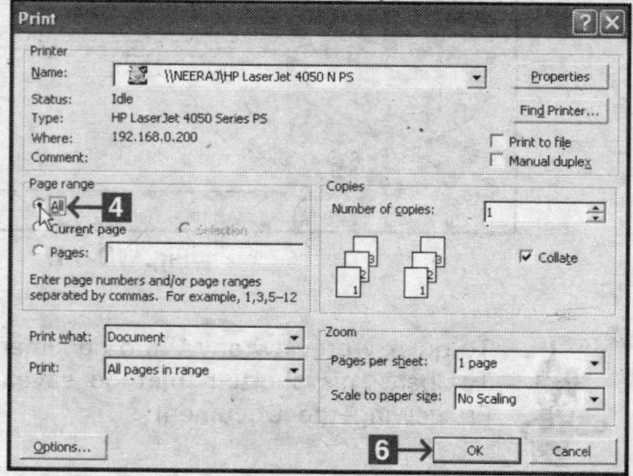

Fig. WD-3.21

1. We assume that the **Letter** document is open on your screen. *Move* the mouse-pointer over the **File** Menu bar option and *click* the left mouse-button. Immediately, a pull-down menu gets displayed before you (Fig.WD-3.19).
2. Inside the pull-down menu, *move* the mouse-pointer over the **Print** option (Fig.WD-3.19) and *click* the mouse-button.
3. Immediately, the **Print** box appears on your screen (Fig.WD-3.21).
4. Inside the **Print** box, *locate* the **Page range** section. To print the whole document, you have to select the **All** option in the **Page range** section. So, *move* the mouse-pointer over the round button beside the **All** option and *click* the left mouse-button once (Fig.WD-3.21).
5. A dot appears inside the round button, indicating the selection of the **All** option.
6. Finally, *click* on the **OK** button to start printing (Fig.WD-3.21).

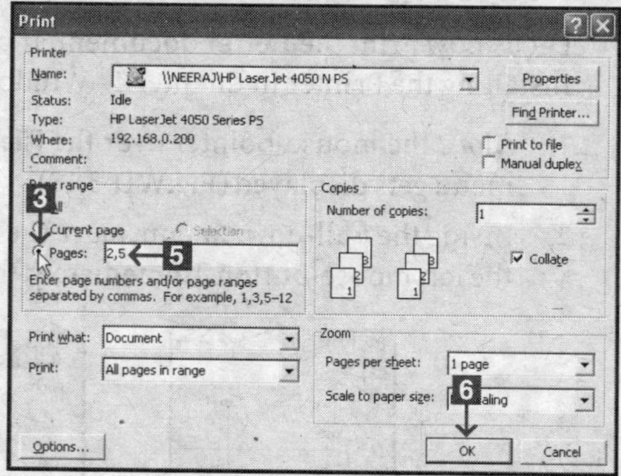

Fig. WD-3.22

Printing specific pages: A Microsoft Word document can be divided into many pages and you can write different letters on different pages. Sometimes you may need printouts of only a few pages instead of all the pages of your document. Suppose, in your document two letters are written on pages 2 and 5. To print only these two letters, go through the following steps:

1. Start with the window of the document that contains two letters. *Move* the mouse-pointer over the **File** Menu bar option and *click* the left mouse-button once. Immediately, a pull-down menu gets displayed (Fig. WD-3.19).
2. Inside the pull-down menu, *move* the mouse-pointer over the **Print** option (Fig.WD-3.19) and *click* the left mouse-button. Immediately, the **Print** box appears on your screen (Fig. WD-3.22).
3. To print specific pages, we will use the **Pages** option in the **Page range** section of the **Print** box. So, *move* the mouse-pointer over the round button beside the **Pages** option and *click* the left mouse-button over it (Fig. WD-3.22).

4. Instantly, a blinking cursor appears inside the rectangular box beside the **Pages** option.
5. Now *type* **2, 5** (Fig.WD-3.22). This indicates that pages **2** and **5** have to be printed.
6. Finally, *click* on the **OK** button to print pages **2** and **5** (Fig.WD-3.22).

To print continuous pages, e.g. from page three through page nine, just type 3-9 in step 5 above, and click on the OK button.

Printing the Current Page: Suppose you wish to print that page of your document in which you are currently working, but you do not have any idea about its page number. In such a case, undertake the following steps :

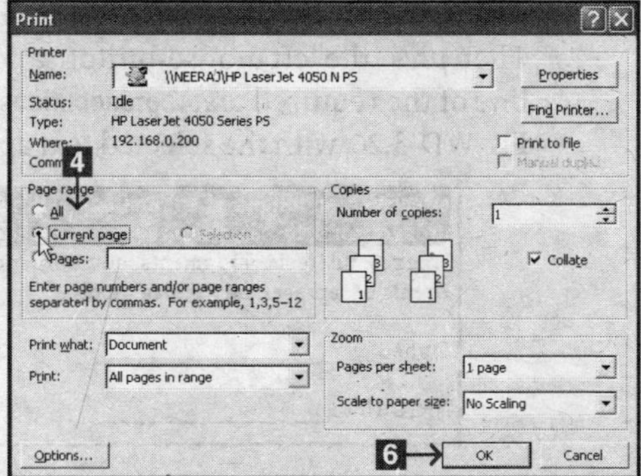

Fig. WD-3.23

1. We assume that the **Letter** document is open on your screen. *Move* the mouse-pointer over the **File** Menu bar option and *click* the left mouse-button. Immediately, a pull-down menu gets displayed before you (Fig. WD-3.19).
2. Inside the pull-down menu, *move* the mouse-pointer over the **Print** option (Fig.WD-3.19). and *click* the left mouse-button over it.
3. Immediately, the **Print** box appears on your screen (Fig.WD-3.23).
4. To print the page in which we are currently working, we will use the **Current page** option in the **Page range** section of the **Print** box. So *move* the mouse-pointer over the round button beside the **Current page** option (Fig.WD-3.23).
5. *Click* the left mouse-button. A dot appears in the round button indicating the selection of the **Current page** option (Fig.WD-3.23).
6. Finally, *click* on the **OK** button to start printing (Fig.WD-3.23).

Printing a Small Section of Text : You can also print a portion of the text instead of the entire page. To do so, first you have to select that portion of the text which you wish to print and then give the print command.

Suppose, you wish to print the following lines from the third paragraph of the **Letter** document.

3. We will indemnify and agree to keep you and your employees, agents or representatives fully and effectively indemnified against any actions, suits, claims, demands, proceedings, governmental prosecutions, losses, damages, compensations,...

To print the above text, undertake the following steps:

1. We assume that the **Letter** document is open on your screen. *Move* the mouse-pointer to the left of line **3. We will indemnify...** (Fig.WD-3.24).

1 → 3. We will indemnify and agree to keep you and your employees, agents or representatives fully and effectively indemnified against any actions, suits, claims, demands, proceedings, governmental prosecutions, losses, damages, compensations, sums of money, costs (including solicitor and client costs), charges, interests, judgments, court order or other liabilities whatsoever which you and your employees, agents or representatives may incur.

Fig. WD-3.24

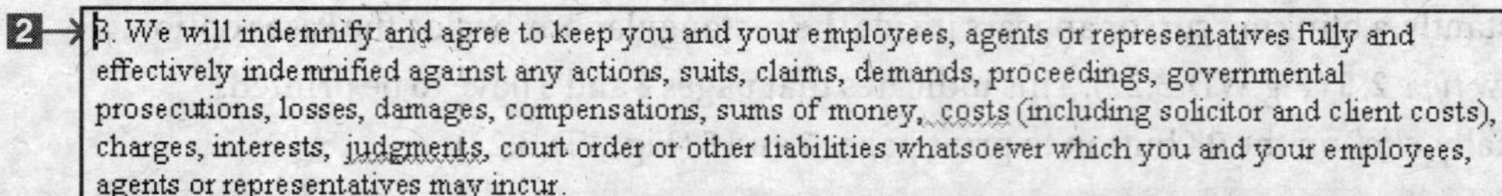

2 → 3. We will indemnify and agree to keep you and your employees, agents or representatives fully and effectively indemnified against any actions, suits, claims, demands, proceedings, governmental prosecutions, losses, damages, compensations, sums of money, costs (including solicitor and client costs), charges, interests, judgments, court order or other liabilities whatsoever which you and your employees, agents or representatives may incur.

Fig. WD-3.25

2. And *press* the left mouse-button once. A blinking cursor appears at that point (Fig.W D-3.25).
3. Now *move* the mouse-pointer to the place where the cursor is currently blinking.
4. Then *press* the left mouse-button, and keeping it *pressed*, *drag* the mouse vertically down to the last line of the required text **...prosecutions, losses, damages, compensations.** Now, your screen will look like Fig.WD-3.26, with the selected text appearing highlighted.

effectively indemnified against any actions, suits, claims, demands, proceedings, governmental prosecutions, losses, damages, compensations, sums of money, costs (including solicitor and client costs), charges, interests, judgments, court order or other liabilities whatsoever which you and your employees, agents or representatives may incur.

Signed by : ______________ Dated : ______________

NRIC NO : ______________ Company Stamp : ______________

Fig. WD-3.26

5. After the text portion to be printed gets highlighted, *stop pressing* the left mouse-button.
6. Now, *move* the mouse-pointer over the **File** menu bar option and *click* the left mouse-button. Immediately, a pull-down menu gets displayed (Fig.WD-3.19).
7. Inside the pull-down menu, *move* the mouse-pointer over the **Print** option (Fig.WD-3.19).
8. *Click* the left mouse-button over it. Immediately, the **Print** box appears on your screen (Fig.WD-3.27).
9. Now, to print the selected text, we will use the **Selection** option in the **Print range** section of the **Print** box. So, *move* the mouse-pointer over the round button beside the **Selection** option and *click* the left mouse-button over it. A dot appears in the round button, indicating the selection of the **Selection** option .
10. Finally, *click* on the **OK** button to start printing the selected portion (Fig.WD-3.27).

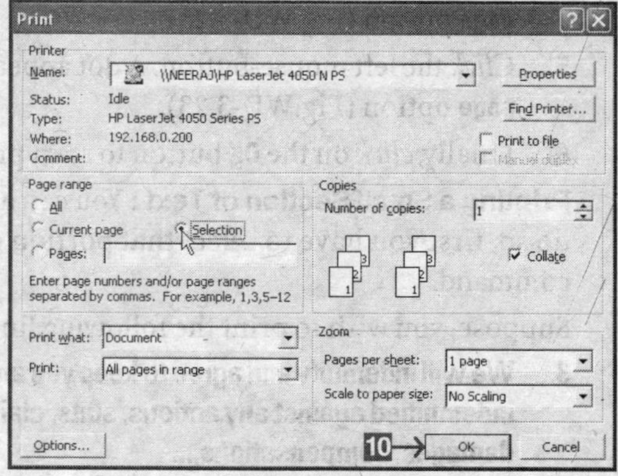

Fig. WD-3.27

Closing the Word Document

Let us now learn how to close the document Letter.doc and Microsoft Word program. To do so, undertake the following steps:

1. We assume that the **Letter** document is open on your screen. *move* the mouse-pointer over the **File** Menu bar option and *click* the left mouse-button. Instantly, a pull-down menu appears (Fig.WD-3.28).

2. Inside the pull-down menu, *move* the mouse-pointer on the **Close** option (Fig.WD-3.28) and *click* the left mouse-button.

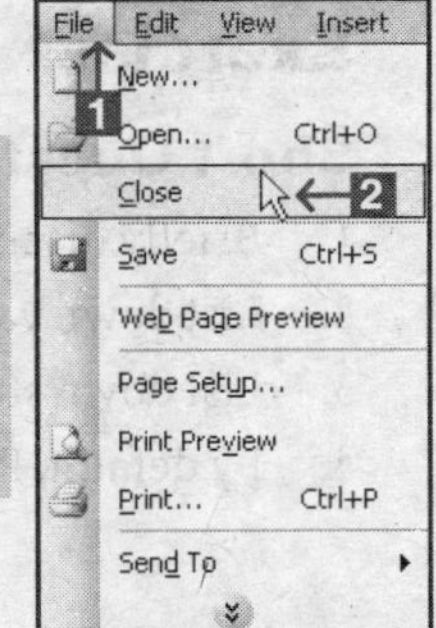

Fig. WD-3.28

If you have made some changes to your document, Letter.doc, then a message box (Fig. WD-3.29) gets displayed. It asks whether you wish to save the changes to your document. To save the changes click on Yes button or else click on No button.

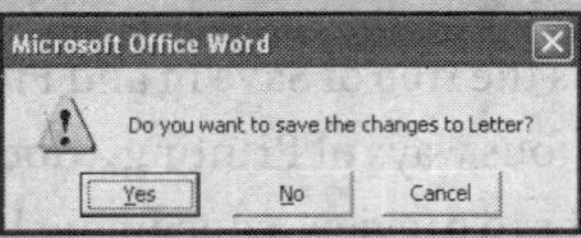

Fig. WD-3.29

Instantly, the document closes. The Microsoft Word window has no open document now.

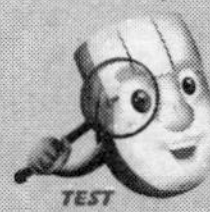

Type the following text in a new MS Office document. After typing the text, save the document as 'Early History of Computer Virus' in 'Local Disk (C:)'.

Earliest history of virus programs

Virus programs have a long, and sometimes honourable, history. In the earliest computers it was vital that you knew the initial state of the computer. It was also important that no remnants of other programs remain. An instruction was often implemented that had only one function: it would copy itself to the next memory location and then proceed on to that location. Thus, by starting this instruction at the beginning of memory, the entire memory space could be "filled" with a known value. This single instruction could be seen as the 1st viral type application.

In the early 1980s, Fred Cohen did extensive theoretical research, as well as setting up and performing numerous practical experiments, regarding viral type applications. His dissertation was presented in 1986 as part of the requirements for a doctorate in electrical engineering from the University of Southern California. This work is foundational, and any serious student of viral applications disregards it at his own risk.

Dr. Cohen's definition of a computer virus as "a program that can 'infect' other applications by modifying them to include a ... version of itself" is generally accepted as a standard. On occasion it presents problems with the acceptance of, say, boot sector viral programs and entities such as the Internet/UNIX/Morris worm. However, his work did experimentally demonstrate and theoretically prove many vital issues. Some popular computer viruses are a follows:

Fred Cohen
Pranks and Trojans
Apple Virus 1, 2 and 3
The Jerusalem virus
The Jerusalem virus - part II
The Jerusalem virus - part III
Brain
Brain - part II
Brain - part III

Exercise

Short Questions

1. Briefly discuss the role of Save in and File name options of Save As dialog box.
2. List down various ways of Printing a document in Microsoft Word.
3. List down steps to preview a document before printing.
4. By default, Print dialog box displays how much number of copies to print a document?

MICROSOFT WORD

Editing the Document 4

IN THIS CHAPTER

- Starting Microsoft Word
- Opening an Existing Word Document
- Moving the Cursor
- Making Changes in Your Document (Editing)
- Selecting the Text
- Operations Done with Selection
- Undoing any Operation
- Checking Spellings in the Document
- Automatic Correction of Errors
- Printing the File
- Find and Replace
- Replacing Text
- Saving and Closing the Document
- Quitting Microsoft Word
- Exercise

In the previous chapter, you created two Microsoft Word documents—**Letter** and **History of Computer Virus**—and also printed them. After seeing the printout of the **History of Computer Virus** document, you may have noticed some errors in the text. But, don't worry about errors. You need not retype the entire text of this document because Microsoft Word provides you various editing features to correct errors in a document.

To render the **History of Computer Virus** document error-free, you may need to insert or delete text (letters/words/sentences) or blank lines. You can do all this easily in Microsoft Word. Creating space for new text in your document is no problem. Nor does filling up the space left by the deleted text pose any difficulty. Microsoft Word automatically adjusts the gap left in the document by the deleted text.

There is also the useful **Undo** feature that helps you restore the changes made or text deleted accidentally from a Word document. Among other useful editing features of Microsoft Word are the **Spell and Grammar checking, Find and Replace, Automatic correction**, etc.

Starting Microsoft Word

Let us now open the **History of Computer Virus** document, saved in **Local Disk (C:)**, to correct its errors. First, we open the Microsoft Word program through the following steps.

1. *Click* the left mouse-button over the **Start** button. Immediately, a push-up menu gets displayed.
2. Inside the push-up menu, *place* the mouse-pointer over the **All Programs** option. Instantly, a second menu gets displayed.
3. Inside the second menu, *move* the mouse-pointer over the **Microsoft Office** option. A third menu appears. In this menu, *place* the mouse-pointer over the **Microsoft Word 2003** option and *click* the left mouse-button. Immediately, **Microsoft Word** window opens up with a blank document (Fig. WD-4.1).

Opening an Existing Word Document

Let us now learn how to open a saved or existing document in Microsoft Word. As we wish to make changes in the **History of Computer Virus** document, we will open it through the following steps.

1. *Move* the mouse-pointer over the **More...** option present in the **Getting Started** Task pane of **Microsoft Word** window and *click* the left mouse-button (Fig. WD-4.1).
2. Instantly, the **Open** box appears on the screen (Fig. WD-4.2).
3. In the **Open** box, *move* the mouse-pointer over the down-arrow button (▾) of the box beside the **Look in** option and *click* the left mouse-button. Immediately, a pull-down menu gets displayed (Fig. WD-4.3).

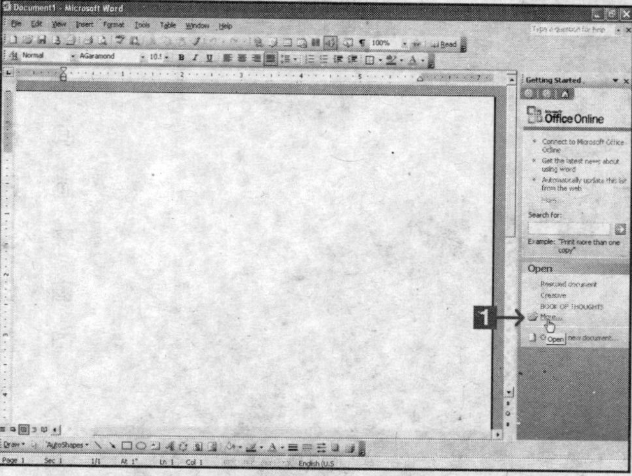

Fig. WD-4.1

4. Inside the pull-down menu, *move* the mouse-pointer over the **Local Disk (C:)** and *click* the left mouse-button (Fig. WD-4.3).
5. Immediately, the **Local Disk (C:)** gets displayed inside the box beside the **Look in** option. Also, the contents of **Local Disk (C:)** get displayed in the **Open** box below the **Look in** option (Fig. WD-4.4).

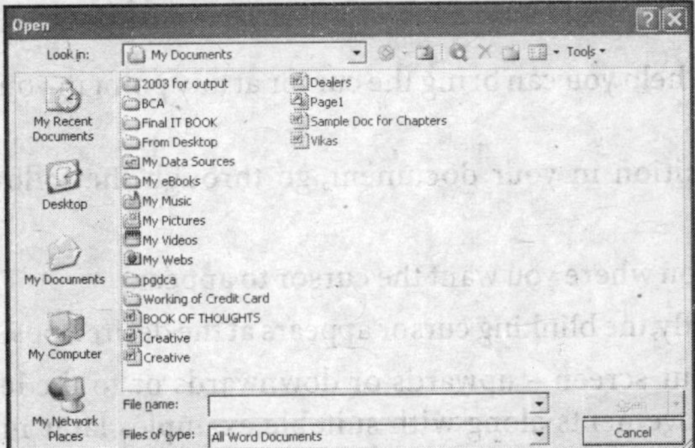

Fig. WD-4.2

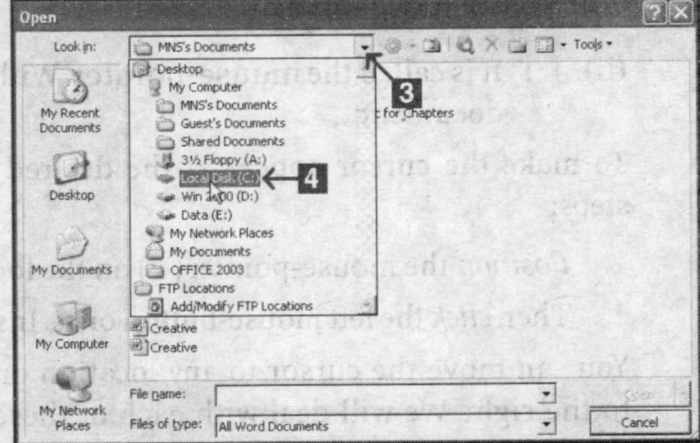

Fig. WD-4.3

5. In the **Local Disk (C:)** contents, the **History of Computer Virus** document is displayed. To open this document, first *click* the left mouse-button on it. The document name gets highlighted (Fig. WD-4.4).
6. Finally, *move* the mouse-pointer over the **Open** button (Fig.WD-4.4) and *click* the left mouse-button. The **History of Computer Virus** document opens on the screen (Fig.WD-4.5).

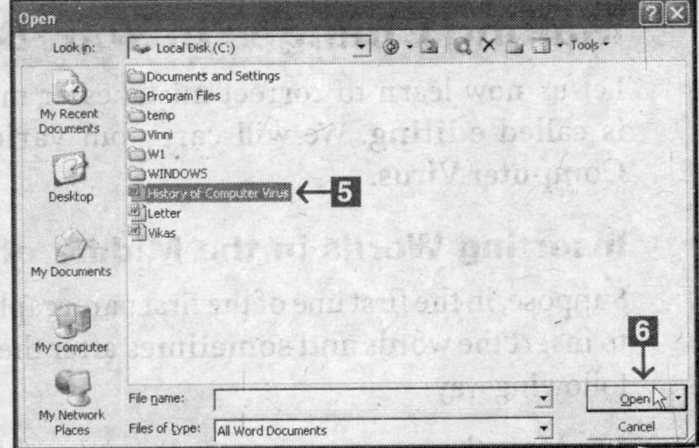

Fig. WD-4.4

The **Status bar** of the Microsoft Word window of Fig. WD-4.5 displays information regarding the open document. Some of the important details are as follows:

Page 1 : Displays the page number of the currently open page of the History of Computer Virus document.

1/1 : Displays the total number of pages present in the document and the page number currently displayed on the screen, which is 1/1.

Sec 1 : Displays the line number where the cursor is blinking. Fig.WD-4.5 shows the cursor blinking at the first or the starting line.

Col 1 : Displays the column number where the cursor is blinking (Fig.WD-4.5).

OVR : Indicates whether the **Insert** key is currently active (ON) or not (OFF). Fig. WD-4.5 shows the OVR button as de-highlighted which indicates that the insert mode is currently active (ON).

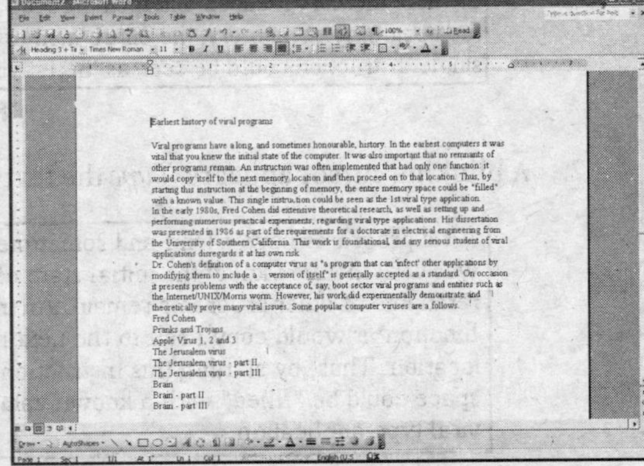

Fig. WD-4.5

Moving the Cursor

On your screen, you see the cursor and the mouse pointer explained below.

(i) **|** : It is called the **blinking cursor.** It displays the position where the characters typed from your keyboard are placed.

(ii) I : It is called the **mouse-pointer.** With its help you can bring the cursor at any point in your document.

To make the cursor appear at the desired position in your document, go through the following steps:

1. *Position* the mouse-pointer(I) on the location where you want the cursor to appear.
2. Then *click* the left mouse-button once. Instantly, the blinking cursor appears at the desired position.

You can move the cursor to any location on your screen – upwards or downwards or to the left or to the right. We will deal with each of these movements along with suitable examples later in this chapter.

Making Changes in Your Document (Editing)

Let us now learn to correct mistakes or make changes in a Word document. Correcting mistakes is called **editing.** We will carry out various editing tasks in the open document, **History of Computer Virus.**

Inserting Words in the Middle of a Line

Suppose, in the first line of the first paragraph of the **History of Computer Virus** document, you want to insert the words **and sometimes** after the word **long.** You can easily insert the desired words in the following way:

1. *Move* the mouse-pointer to the right of the word **long** and *click* the left mouse button (Fig.WD-4.6).

Viral programs have a long 1 [illegible]rable, history. In the earliest computers it was vital that you knew the initial state of the computer. It was also important that no remnants of other programs remain. An instruction was often implemented that had only one function: it would copy itself to the next memory location and then proceed on to that location. Thus, by starting this instruction at the beginning of memory, the entire memory space could be "filled" with a known value. This single instruction could be seen as the 1st viral type application.

Fig. WD-4.6

2. A blinking cursor appears. *Type* the text **and sometimes** (Fig.WD-4.7).

Viral programs have a long and sometimes 2 [illegible]urable, history. In the earliest computers it was vital that you knew the initial state of the computer. It was also important that no remnants of other programs remain. An instruction was often implemented that had only one function: it would copy itself to the next memory location and then proceed on to that location. Thus, by starting this instruction at the beginning of memory, the entire memory space could be "filled" with a known value. This single instruction could be seen as the 1st viral type application.

Fig. WD-4.7

Inserting a Blank line

You can easily insert blank lines in your document using the mouse and the keyboard. Let us now insert a blank line after the first paragraph in the **History of computer virus** document through the following steps:

1. *Move* the mouse-pointer to the end of the last line of the first paragraph (Fig.WD-4.8).

> Viral programs have a long and sometimes honourable, history. In the earliest computers it was vital that you knew the initial state of the computer. It was also important that no remnants of other programs remain. An instruction was often implemented that had only one function: it would copy itself to the next memory location and then proceed on to that location. Thus, by starting this instruction at the beginning of memory, the entire memory space could be "filled" with a known value. This single instruction could be seen as the 1st viral type application. ← 1

Fig. WD-4.8

2. *Click* the left mouse-button. Immediately, a blinking cursor appears at that point (Fig.WD-4.9).

> Viral programs have a long and sometimes honourable, history. In the earliest computers it was vital that you knew the initial state of the computer. It was also important that no remnants of other programs remain. An instruction was often implemented that had only one function: it would copy itself to the next memory location and then proceed on to that location. Thus, by starting this instruction at the beginning of memory, the entire memory space could be "filled" with a known value. This single instruction could be seen as the 1st viral type application. ← 2

Fig. WD-4.9

3. Finally, *press* the **Enter** key once from the keyboard. Immediately, a blank line gets inserted (Fig.WD-4.10).

> Viral programs have a long and sometimes honourable, history. In the earliest computers it was vital that you knew the initial state of the computer. It was also important that no remnants of other programs remain. An instruction was often implemented that had only one function: it would copy itself to the next memory location and then proceed on to that location. Thus, by starting this instruction at the beginning of memory, the entire memory space could be "filled" with a known value. This single instruction could be seen as the 1st viral type application.
>
> ← Blank line gets inserted in the document

Fig. WD-4.10

You need not check the location of the cursor on the screen before performing any cursor-related function. The cursor will always shift to the position where you place the mouse-pointer and click the left mouse-button.

Selecting the Text

Selecting any text refers to **highlighting** that text. You can select, i.e. highlight, the text in the form of a single letter, a word, a line or a paragraph.

You have to always select, i.e. highlight, that text on which you need to perform some editing or formatting operation, like making it bold or italic, underlining it and so on.

Let us understand some basic steps required for highlighting the desired text. Just read through the basic steps described below without performing them on your document.

1. *Move* the mouse-pointer to the beginning of the text to be selected (letter, word, line or paragraph) of your document.

2. *Click* the left mouse-button. A blinking cursor gets displayed at that point.
3. *Place* the mouse-pointer over the cursor and then *press* the left mouse-button.
4. Keeping the left mouse-button *pressed*, *drag* the mouse-pointer over the relevant text (letter, word, line or paragraph). This highlights the relevant text.
5. When the required text gets highlighted, *release* the left mouse-button.
6. To remove the highlight from the text, *click* anywhere else in your document.

If you have accidentally released the left mouse-button before completely highlighting the desired text then move the mouse-pointer somewhere else on the screen, and click the left mouse-button once. The highlight will immediately disappear from the text. Now restart the procedure to highlight the required text.

Selecting a Letter (Alphabet) or any Number

We assume that the **History of Computer Virus** document is open on your Desktop. Suppose you wish to highlight the letter V of the word **Viral** present at the beginning of your document. You can do so through the following steps.

1. *Move* the mouse-pointer to the left of the letter **V** (Fig. WD-4.11).

1 → Viral programs have a long and sometimes honourable, history. In the earliest computers it was vital that you knew the initial state of the computer. It was also important that no remnants of other programs remain. An instruction was often implemented that had only one function: it would copy itself to the next memory location and then proceed on to that location. Thus, by starting this instruction at the beginning of memory, the entire memory space could be "filled" with a known value. This single instruction could be seen as the 1st viral type application.

Fig. WD-4.11

2. Then *click* the left mouse-button. Instantly, a blinking cursor appears at that point (Fig. WD-4.12).
3. *Place* the mouse-pointer over the cursor and then *press* the left mouse-button .

2 → Viral programs have a long and sometimes honourable, history. In the earliest computers it was vital that you knew the initial state of the computer. It was also important that no remnants of other programs remain. An instruction was often implemented that had only one function: it would copy itself to the next memory location and then proceed on to that location. Thus, by starting this instruction at the beginning of memory, the entire memory space could be "filled" with a known value. This single instruction could be seen as the 1st viral type application.

Fig. WD-4.12

4. Keeping the left mouse-button *pressed*, *drag* the mouse-pointer over the letter **V**.
5. When the letter **V** gets highlighted, *release* the left mouse-button (Fig. WD-4.13).

Viral programs have a long and sometimes honourable, history. In the earliest computers it was vital that you knew the initial state of the computer. It was also important that no remnants of other programs remain. An instruction was often implemented that had only one function: it would copy itself to the next memory location and then proceed on to that location. Thus, by starting this instruction at the beginning of memory, the entire memory space could be "filled" with a known value. This single instruction could be seen as the 1st viral type application.

Fig. WD-4.13

6. To remove the highlight from letter **V**, *move* the mouse-pointer somewhere else in your document and *click* the left mouse-button once.

Selecting a Word

Suppose you wish to highlight the word **vital** present in the second line of the first paragraph in your document, **History of Computer Virus.** To do so, undertake the following steps.

1. *Move* the mouse-pointer to the left of the word **vital** (Fig.WD-4.14).

> **1** → Viral programs have a long and sometimes honourable, history. In the earliest computers it was vital that you knew the initial state of the computer. It was also important that no remnants of other programs remain. An instruction was often implemented that had only one function: it would copy itself to the next memory location and then proceed on to that location. Thus, by starting this instruction at the beginning of memory, the entire memory space could be "filled" with a known value. This single instruction could be seen as the 1st viral type application.

Fig. WD-4.14

2. Then *click* the left mouse-button. Immediately, a blinking cursor appears at that point (Fig.WD-4.15).

> **2** → Viral programs have a long and sometimes honourable, history. In the earliest computers it was vital that you knew the initial state of the computer. It was also important that no remnants of other programs remain. An instruction was often implemented that had only one function: it would copy itself to the next memory location and then proceed on to that location. Thus, by starting this instruction at the beginning of memory, the entire memory space could be "filled" with a known value. This single instruction could be seen as the 1st viral type application.

Fig. W-4.15

3. *Place* the mouse-pointer over the blinking cursor and then *press* the left mouse-button.
4. Keeping the left mouse-button *pressed*, *drag* the mouse-pointer over the word **vital** (Fig. WD-4.16).
5. When the word **vital** gets highlighted (Fig.WD-4.16), *release* the left mouse-button.

> Viral programs have a long and sometimes honourable, history. In the earliest computers it was vital that you knew the initial state of the computer. It was also important that no remnants of other programs remain. An instruction was often implemented that had only one function: it would copy itself to the next memory location and then proceed on to that location. Thus, by starting this instruction at the beginning of memory, the entire memory space could be "filled" with a known value. This single instruction could be seen as the 1st viral type application.

Fig. WD-4.16

> Suppose, you have accidentally released the left mouse-button when only half of the word 'vital' was highlighted. In such a case, click at any place inside your document to remove the incomplete highlight. Again go through Steps 1 to 5 of the topic 'Selecting a Word' to correctly highlight the word 'vital'.

6. To remove the highlight from the word **vital**, *click* anywhere in the document.

Selecting a Line

Suppose you wish to highlight the last line **This single instruction could be seen as the 1st viral type application** in the first paragraph of the **History of Computer Virus** document. You can do so in the following way:

1. *Move* the mouse-pointer to the left of the line **This single instruction could be......** and *click* the left mouse-button. A blinking cursor appears before the word **This** (Fig.WD-4.17).

Viral programs have a long and sometimes honourable, history. In the earliest computers it was vital that you knew the initial state of the computer. It was also important that no remnants of other programs remain. An instruction was often implemented that had only one function: it would copy itself to the next memory location and then proceed on to that location. Thus, by starting this instruction at the beginning of memory, the entire memory space could be "filled" with a known value. This single instruction could be seen as the 1st viral type application.

1

Fig. WD-4.17

2. Keeping the left mouse button *pressed*, *drag* the mouse over the mouse-pad such that the line **This single instruction could be......** gets highlighted (Fig. WD-4.18).

Viral programs have a long and sometimes honourable, history. In the earliest computers it was vital that you knew the initial state of the computer. It was also important that no remnants of other programs remain. An instruction was often implemented that had only one function: it would copy itself to the next memory location and then proceed on to that location. Thus, by starting this instruction at the beginning of memory, the entire memory space could be "filled" with a known value. This single instruction could be seen as the 1st viral type application. 2

Fig. WD-4.18

3. Once the entire line is highlighted, *release* the left mouse-button.
4. To *remove* the highlight from the line, *click* anywhere in your document.

Selecting a Paragraph

Suppose, you wish to highlight a group of lines, i.e. the first paragraph, of the **History of Computer Virus** document, **Viral programs have a long................ as the 1st viral type application.** You can do the desired job easily through the following steps.

1. *Move* the mouse-pointer to the left of the first word of the first paragraph, i.e. **Viral** (Fig.WD-4.19).

1 → Viral programs have a long and sometimes honourable, history. In the earliest computers it was vital that you knew the initial state of the computer. It was also important that no remnants of other programs remain. An instruction was often implemented that had only one function: it would copy itself to the next memory location and then proceed on to that location. Thus, by starting this instruction at the beginning of memory, the entire memory space could be "filled" with a known value. This single instruction could be seen as the 1st viral type application.

Fig. WD-4.19

2. *Click* the left mouse-button. A blinking cursor appears before the word **Viral** (Fig. WD-4.20).

2 → Viral programs have a long and sometimes honourable, history. In the earliest computers it was vital that you knew the initial state of the computer. It was also important that no remnants of other programs remain. An instruction was often implemented that had only one function: it would copy itself to the next memory location and then proceed on to that location. Thus, by starting this instruction at the beginning of memory, the entire memory space could be "filled" with a known value. This single instruction could be seen as the 1st viral type application.

Fig. WD-4.20

3. *Place* the mouse-pointer over the cursor and then *press* the left mouse-button.
4. Keeping the left mouse button *pressed*, *drag* the mouse over the mouse-pad such that the complete paragraph gets highlighted (Fig.WD-4.21).

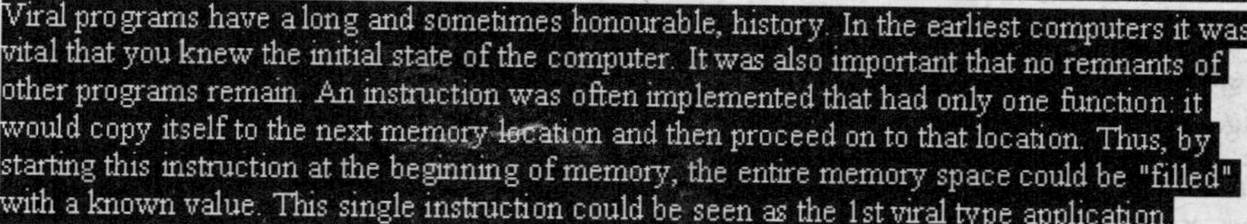
Viral programs have a long and sometimes honourable, history. In the earliest computers it was vital that you knew the initial state of the computer. It was also important that no remnants of other programs remain. An instruction was often implemented that had only one function: it would copy itself to the next memory location and then proceed on to that location. Thus, by starting this instruction at the beginning of memory, the entire memory space could be "filled" with a known value. This single instruction could be seen as the 1st viral type application.

Fig. WD-4.21

5. When the entire paragraph is highlighted, *release* the left mouse-button.

Suppose, you have accidentally released the left mouse-button when only half of the first paragraph of your document was highlighted. In such a case, click at any place inside your document to remove the incomplete highlight from the paragraph. Repeat Steps 1 to 4 to highlight the entire paragraph.

6. To remove the highlight from the paragraph, *click* anywhere inside your document.

Operations Done with Selection

(How to Substitute or Replace a Text with new Text)

For substituting some text with new text in your document, you always have to go through basic steps briefly described below:

1. *Move* the mouse-pointer to the left of the text you wish to substitute.
2. *Click* the left mouse-button so that a blinking cursor appears.
3. *Place* the mouse-pointer over the cursor, and then *press* the left mouse-button.
4. Keeping it *pressed*, *drag* the mouse over the mouse-pad such that a highlight appears over the desired letter/word/line/paragraph to be substituted.
5. Now *release* the left mouse-button.
6. *Type* the new text (letter or word or line or paragraph) from the keyboard. The new text replaces the highlighted text. The highlight disappears automatically when you substitute the old text with the new text.

Let us now do text substitution in the **History of Computer Virus** document.

Substituting a Word

Let us now replace the word **extensive** with the word **widespread** in the first line of second paragraph through the following steps:

1. *Move* the mouse-pointer to the left of the word **extensive** and *click* the left mouse-button. A blinking cursor appears (Fig. WD-4.22).

1

In the early 1980s, Fred Cohen did extensive theoretical research, as well as setting up and performing numerous practical experiments, regarding viral type applications. His dissertation was presented in 1986 as part of the requirements for a doctorate in electrical engineering from the University of Southern California. This work is foundational, and any serious student of viral applications disregards it at his own risk.

Fig. WD-4.22

2. *Place* the mouse-pointer over the blinking cursor and *press* the left mouse-button.
3. Keeping it *pressed*, *drag* the mouse over the mouse-pad such that the word **extensive** gets highlighted (Fig. WD-4.23).

3

In the early 1980s, Fred Cohen did extensive theoretical research, as well as setting up and performing numerous practical experiments, regarding viral type applications. His dissertation was presented in 1986 as part of the requirements for a doctorate in electrical engineering from the University of Southern California. This work is foundational, and any serious student of viral applications disregards it at his own risk.

Fig. WD-4.23

4. After highlighting the word **extensive,** *release* the left mouse-button.
5. Now *type* the word **widespread** from the keyboard. This word replaces the word **extensive** on the screen (Fig. WD-4.24).

In the early 1980s, Fred Cohen did widespread theoretical research, as well as setting up and performing numerous practical experiments, regarding viral type applications. His dissertation was presented in 1986 as part of the requirements for a doctorate in electrical engineering from the University of Southern California. This work is foundational, and any serious student of viral applications disregards it at his own risk.

Fig. W-4.24

Substituting a Line

Suppose, in the third paragraph of your document, you want to replace the expression **'s definition of** with the word **defines.** To do so, perform the following steps.

1. *Move* the mouse-pointer to the left of the text **'s definition of** and *click* the left mouse-button. Instantly, a blinking cursor appears (Fig. WD-4.25).

1

Dr. Cohen's definition of a computer virus as "a program that can 'infect' other applications by modifying them to include a ... version of itself" is generally accepted as a standard. On occasion it presents problems with the acceptance of, say, boot sector viral programs and entities such as the Internet/UNIX/Morris worm. However, his work did experimentally demonstrate and theoretically prove many vital issues. Some popular computer viruses are a follows:

Fig. WD-4.25

2. Now *place* the mouse-pointer over the blinking cursor and *press* the left mouse-button.
3. Keeping the left mouse-button *pressed*, *drag* the mouse over the mouse-pad such that the text **'s definition of** gets highlighted (Fig. WD-4.26).

Dr. Cohen's definition of a computer virus as "a program that can 'infect' other applications by modifying them to include a ... version of itself" is generally accepted as a standard. On occasion it presents problems with the acceptance of, say, boot sector viral programs and entities such as the Internet/UNIX/Morris worm. However, his work did experimentally demonstrate and theoretically prove many vital issues. Some popular computer viruses are a follows:

Fig: WD-4.26

4. *Release* the left mouse-button when the required expression gets highlighted.
5. Now, type the word **defines.** This word replaces the highlighted expression **'s definition of** (Fig. WD-4.27).

Dr. Cohen defines computer virus as "a program that can 'infect' other applications by modifying them to include a ... version of itself" is generally accepted as a standard. On occasion it presents problems with the acceptance of, say, boot sector viral programs and entities such as the Internet/UNIX/Morris worm. However, his work did experimentally demonstrate and theoretically prove many vital issues. Some popular computer viruses are a follows:

Fig. WD-4.27

Copying a Section of Text

Copying text means creating a copy of the text and placing it in some new location in the document. Whenever you copy the text, it does not move from its original location. Let us now learn the steps for copying a section of text.

Suppose you wish to copy the entire paragraph, i.e. **Viral programs have a long....... application** after the text at the end of your document, i.e. **Brain-part III.** To do the desired copying, perform the following steps:

1. *Position* the mouse-pointer at the beginning of the text, i.e. to the left of the line **Viral programs have a long........** and *click* the left mouse-button. Immediately, a blinking cursor appears at that point (Fig.WD-4.28).

1→ Viral programs have a long and sometimes honourable, history. In the earliest computers it was vital that you knew the initial state of the computer. It was also important that no remnants of other programs remain. An instruction was often implemented that had only one function: it would copy itself to the next memory location and then proceed on to that location. Thus, by starting this instruction at the beginning of memory, the entire memory space could be "filled" with a known value. This single instruction could be seen as the 1st viral type application.

Fig. WD-4.28

2. Now *place* the mouse-pointer over the blinking cursor and *press* the left mouse-button.
3. Keeping the left mouse-button *pressed*, *drag* the mouse-pointer over the entire paragraph that gets highlighted (Fig.WD-4.29).

Viral programs have a long and sometimes honourable, history. In the earliest computers it was vital that you knew the initial state of the computer. It was also important that no remnants of other programs remain. An instruction was often implemented that had only one function: it would copy itself to the next memory location and then proceed on to that location. Thus, by starting this instruction at the beginning of memory, the entire memory space could be "filled" with a known value. This single instruction could be seen as the 1st viral type application.

Fig. WD-4.29

4. After highlighting the paragraph, *release* the left mouse-button.

Do not press the Enter key once the text has been highlighted, or else the text will be deleted.

5. Now *click* on the **Edit** option of the Menu bar. A pull-down menu appears (Fig.WD-4.30).

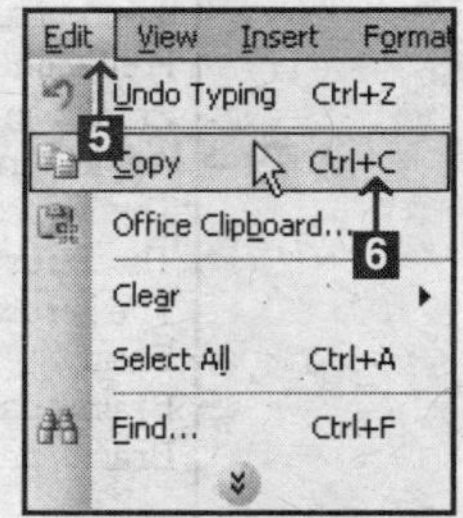

Fig. WD-4.30

6. Inside the pull-down menu, *move* the mouse-pointer on the **Copy** option (Fig.WD-4.30), and *click* the left mouse-button. Now the selected text gets stored temporarily in the memory of your computer.

7. *Click* anywhere else in your document to remove the highlight from the paragraph.
8. Now *move* the mouse-pointer at the end of the last line of your document, i.e. after the text **Brain-part III** and *click* the left mouse-button. Immediately, a blinking cursor appears at that point (Fig. WD-4.31). *Press* the **Enter** key two times.

In the early 1980s, Fred Cohen did widespread theoretical research, as well as setting up and performing numerous practical experiments, regarding viral type applications. His dissertation was presented in 1986 as part of the requirements for a doctorate in electrical engineering from the University of Southern California. This work is foundational, and any serious student of viral applications disregards it at his own risk.
Dr. Cohen defines computer virus as "a program that can 'infect' other applications by modifying them to include a ... version of itself" is generally accepted as a standard. On occasion it presents problems with the acceptance of, say, boot sector viral programs and entities such as the Internet/UNIX/Morris worm. However, his work did experimentally demonstrate and theoretically prove many vital issues. Some popular computer viruses are a follows:
Fred Cohen
Pranks and Trojans
Apple Virus 1, 2 and 3
The Jerusalem virus
The Jerusalem virus - part II
The Jerusalem virus - part III
Brain
Brain - part II
Brain - part III ← 8

Fig. WD-4.31

9. Again *click* on the **Edit** option of the Menu bar (Fig.WD-4.32). Instantly, a pull-down menu gets displayed.

Fig. WD-4.32

10. Inside the pull-down menu, *move* the mouse-pointer over the **Paste** option (Fig.WD-4.32) and *click* the left mouse-button.

The execution of the **Paste** command leads to copying of the first paragraph at the end of document. The first paragraph also stays at its original position.

For copying any highlighted text, press the Ctrl key and C key together. For pasting the copied text to a new location, click at the new location and press Ctrl and V keys together.

Moving a Section of Text

Unlike copying, moving a section of text means removing it from its original location and shifting it to a new place in the document.

Let us now move the text **apple Virus 1, 2, and 3** after the paragraph that you have just pasted at the end of the document. To do so, undertake the following steps.

1. *Click* the left mouse-button at the beginning of the text **Apple Virus 1, 2 and 3.** Instantly, a blinking cursor gets displayed before it (Fig.WD-4.33).

Dr. Cohen defines computer virus as "a program that can 'infect' other applications by modifying them to include a ... version of itself" is generally accepted as a standard. On occasion it presents problems with the acceptance of, say, boot sector viral programs and entities such as the Internet/UNIX/Morris worm. However, his work did experimentally demonstrate and theoretically prove many vital issues. Some popular computer viruses are a follows:
Fred Cohen
Pranks and Trojans
1 → Apple Virus 1, 2 and 3
The Jerusalem virus
The Jerusalem virus - part II
The Jerusalem virus - part III
Brain
Brain - part II
Brain - part III

Fig. WD-4.33

2. Next, keeping the left mouse-button *pressed*, *drag* the mouse-pointer over the required text to highlight it (Fig.WD-4.34).

Dr. Cohen defines computer virus as "a program that can 'infect' other applications by modifying them to include a ... version of itself" is generally accepted as a standard. On occasion it presents problems with the acceptance of, say, boot sector viral programs and entities such as the Internet/UNIX/Morris worm. However, his work did experimentally demonstrate and theoretically prove many vital issues. Some popular computer viruses are a follows:
Fred Cohen
Pranks and Trojans
Apple Virus 1, 2 and 3 ←2
The Jerusalem virus
The Jerusalem virus - part II
The Jerusalem virus - part III
Brain
Brain - part II
Brain - part III

Fig. WD-4.34

3. Next, *move* the mouse-pointer to the Menu bar and *click* on the **Edit** option. Immediately, a pull-down menu gets displayed (Fig.WD-4.35).
4. Inside the pull-down menu, *click* on the **Cut** option (Fig.WD-4.35).
5. The highlighted text disappears leaving a blinking cursor in its place (Fig. WD-4.36).
6. Now *move* the mouse-pointer to the end of the last paragraph and *click* the left mouse-button. Instantly, a blinking cursor appears at that point (Fig.WD-4.37).
7. *Press* the **Enter** key two times.
8. Again, *click* on the **Edit** option of the Menu bar. Immediately, a pull-down menu gets displayed (Fig.WD-4.38).

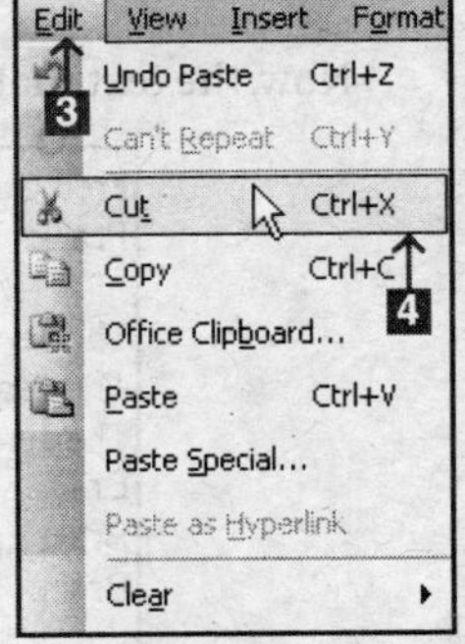

Fig. WD-4.35

9. Inside the pull-down menu, *move* the mouse-pointer over the **Paste** option (Fig.WD-4.38) and *click* the left mouse-button.

Dr. Cohen's defines computer virus as "a program that can 'infect' other applications by modifying them to include a ... version of itself" is generally accepted as a standard. On occasion it presents problems with the acceptance of, say, boot sector viral programs and entities such as the Internet/UNIX/Morris worm. However, his work did experimentally demonstrate and theoretically prove many vital issues. Some popular computer viruses are a follows:
Fred Cohen
Pranks and Trojans
|←5
The Jerusalem virus
The Jerusalem virus - part II
The Jerusalem virus - part III
Brain
Brain - part II
Brain - part III

Fig. WD-4.36

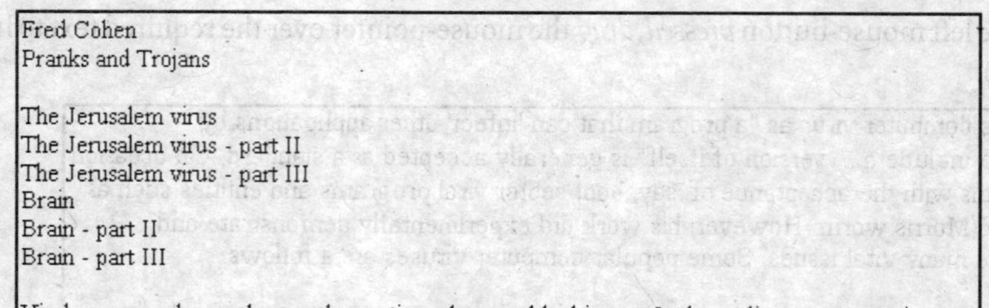

Fred Cohen
Pranks and Trojans

The Jerusalem virus
The Jerusalem virus - part II
The Jerusalem virus - part III
Brain
Brain - part II
Brain - part III

Viral programs have a long and sometimes honourable, history. In the earliest computers it was vital that you knew the initial state of the computer. It was also important that no remnants of other programs remain. An instruction was often implemented that had only one function: it would copy itself to the next memory location and then proceed on to that location. Thus, by starting this instruction at the beginning of memory, the entire memory space could be "filled" with a known value. This single instruction could be seen as the 1st viral type application. ← 6

Fig. WD-4.37

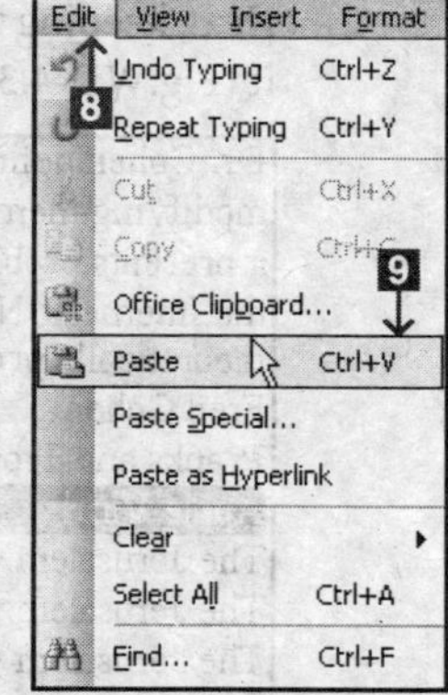

Fig. WD-4.38

You can cut any highlighted text by pressing Ctrl and X keys together. Thereafter, to move this text to a new location, i.e. paste it, press Ctrl and V keys together.

Now, the text that was cut in Step 4 gets pasted or shifted the new position (Fig. WD-4.39).

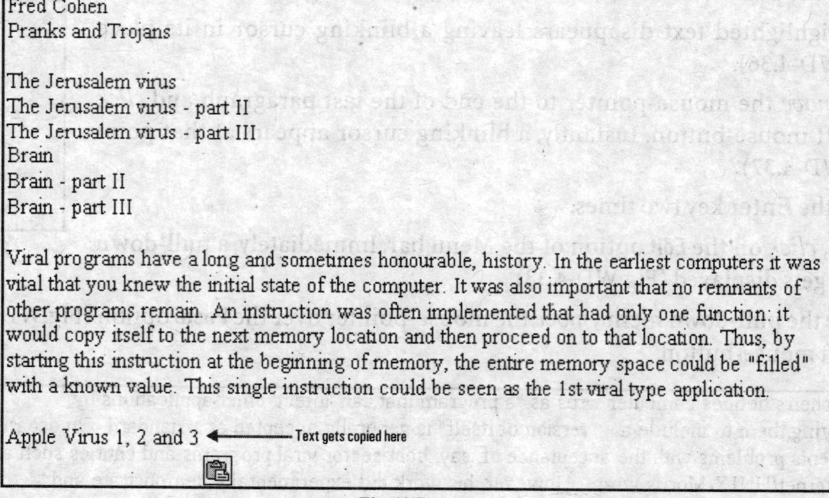

Fred Cohen
Pranks and Trojans

The Jerusalem virus
The Jerusalem virus - part II
The Jerusalem virus - part III
Brain
Brain - part II
Brain - part III

Viral programs have a long and sometimes honourable, history. In the earliest computers it was vital that you knew the initial state of the computer. It was also important that no remnants of other programs remain. An instruction was often implemented that had only one function: it would copy itself to the next memory location and then proceed on to that location. Thus, by starting this instruction at the beginning of memory, the entire memory space could be "filled" with a known value. This single instruction could be seen as the 1st viral type application.

Apple Virus 1, 2 and 3 ← Text gets copied here

Fig. WD-4.39

Removing Text after Selecting it

Many a time, it may happen that while typing you enter some wrong text. To remove or delete the wrong text from your document, you have to always go through three basic steps, described here briefly. For the moment, just read them without working on your document.

1. *Move* the mouse-pointer to the left of the required text (letter, word, line or paragraph) to be removed or deleted.
2. *Click* the left mouse-button. A blinking cursor appears.

3. a) To delete a letter, just *press* the **Delete** key from the keyboard.

   b) To delete a word, line or paragraph, *move* the mouse-pointer over the blinking cursor and *press* the left mouse-button. Keeping the left mouse-button *pressed*, *drag* the mouse on the mouse-pad such that the required word or line or paragraph gets highlighted. Then *press* the **Delete** key from the keyboard.

Let us now learn to delete a word. Suppose you want to delete the word **theoretical** from the first line of the second paragraph in the **History of Computer Virus** document. To do so, undertake the following steps:

1. *Move* the mouse-pointer to the left of the word **theoretical** in the second paragraph.
2. Then *click* the left mouse-button. Immediately, a blinking cursor appears at that point (Fig.WD-4.40).

> In the early 1980s, Fred Cohen did extensive theoretical research, as well as setting up and performing numerous practical experiments, regarding viral type applications. His dissertation was presented in 1986 as part of the requirements for a doctorate in electrical engineering from the University of Southern California. This work is foundational, and any serious student of viral applications disregards it at his own risk.

Fig. WD-4.40

3. Now keeping the left mouse-button *pressed*, *drag* the mouse over the mouse-pad such that the word **theoretical** gets highlighted (Fig.WD-4.41).

> In the early 1980s, Fred Cohen did extensive theoretical research, as well as setting up and performing numerous practical experiments, regarding viral type applications. His dissertation was presented in 1986 as part of the requirements for a doctorate in electrical engineering from the University of Southern California. This work is foundational, and any serious student of viral applications disregards it at his own risk.

Fig. WD-4.41

4. *Press* the **Delete** key from the keyboard. Immediately, the highlighted word **theoretical** gets deleted.

Similarly, you can highlight any line or paragraph you wish to delete and then *press* the **Delete** key to remove it.

Undoing any Operation

Let us now learn about another very useful feature of Microsoft Word – the **Undo** feature. Using this feature, you can reverse any operation, such as deletion, insertion or modification, performed on your text. Suppose you have unknowingly deleted some important paragraph, word or alphabet in the document. And later on, realizing the importance of the deleted content, you wish to retrieve it. Here, the **Undo** feature comes to your help. Using this feature, you can display the deleted text at its original location.

Let us now delete the third paragraph from the **History of Computer Virus** document, and then reverse this operation through the **Undo** feature. To do so undertake the following steps:

Deleting a Paragraph

1. Repeat Steps 1 to 4 of the **Selecting a Paragraph** section to highlight the third paragraph in the document (Fig.WD-4.42).

> In the early 1980s, Fred Cohen did widespread theoretical research, as well as setting up and performing numerous practical experiments, regarding viral type applications. His dissertation was presented in 1986 as part of the requirements for a doctorate in electrical engineering from the University of Southern California. This work is foundational, and any serious student of viral applications disregards it at his own risk.
> Dr. Cohen defines computer virus as "a program that can 'infect' other applications by modifying them to include a ... version of itself" is generally accepted as a standard. On occasion it presents problems with the acceptance of, say, boot sector viral programs and entities such as the Internet/UNIX/Morris worm. However, his work did experimentally demonstrate and theoretically prove many vital issues. Some popular computer viruses are a follows:

Fig. WD-4.42

2. Now *press* the **Delete** key from the keyboard. The selected paragraph gets deleted.

Undoing the Deletion Operation

Now let us reverse the deletion operation to restore the deleted third paragraph to its original position. To reverse the deletion operation, perform the following steps:

1. *Move* the mouse-pointer over the **Undo** button ( ) present on the **Standard Toolbar** of the document window and *click* the left mouse-button (Fig.WD-4.43).

Fig. WD-4.43

2. On *pressing* the **Undo** button, the deleted paragraph reappears. If you go on pressing the **Undo** button, you would see the sequential reversal of operations which you had done earlier on your document.

HOT TIP!

For undoing any operation, press control and Z keys together.

Checking Spellings in the Document

The **Spelling and Grammar Check** feature of the Microsoft Word helps you search spelling errors in your document and then correct them. To spell-check the **History of Computer Virus** document undertake the following steps:

1. We assume that the **History of Computer Virus** document is open on your screen. *Move* the mouse-pointer over the **Spelling and Grammar** button ( ) present on the **Standard Toolbar** (Fig.WD-4.44) and *click* the left mouse-button.

Fig. WD-4.44

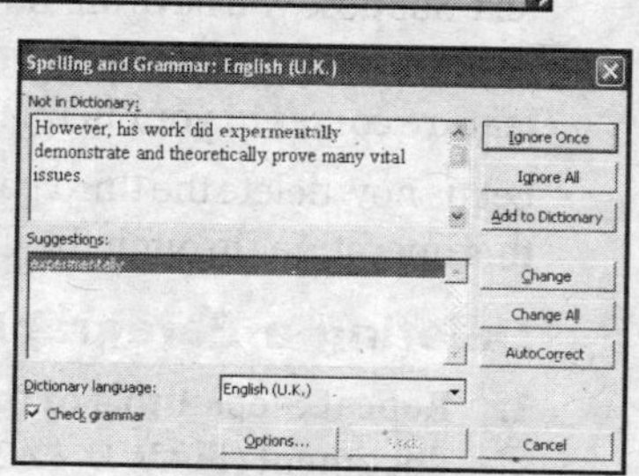

Fig. WD-4.45

Instantly, the **Spelling and Grammar** box appears on your screen (Fig.WD-4.45). This box has two options with boxes below them. The options are: **Not in Dictionary:** and **Suggestions:**. Under the **Suggestions:** option are displayed the words that could replace the incorrect word or line. In our case, the word **expermentally** is shown as misspelt word in the box below the **Not in Dictionary:** option. The suggested substitute for the word **expermentally** is also given in the **Suggestions** box.

Press F7 key to start spelling and grammar checking in the document.

Replacing an Incorrect Word with a Correct Word

Let us now learn to substitute the incorrect word with a correct word given in the **Suggestions**: option. To replace the incorrect word **expermentally** with the correct word **experimentally**, given in the box below the **Suggestions**: option, undertake the following steps:

1. *Move* the mouse-pointer over the correct word **experimentally** inside the box below the **Suggestions**: option and *click* the left mouse-button (Fig.WD-4.46).
2. The word **experimentally** gets highlighted.
3. Now *move* the mouse-pointer over the **Change** button (Fig.WD-4.47) and *click* the left mouse-button. This action replaces the word **expermentally** with **experimentally** in your document. After this change, Word continues checking your document, and moves on to the next incorrect word.

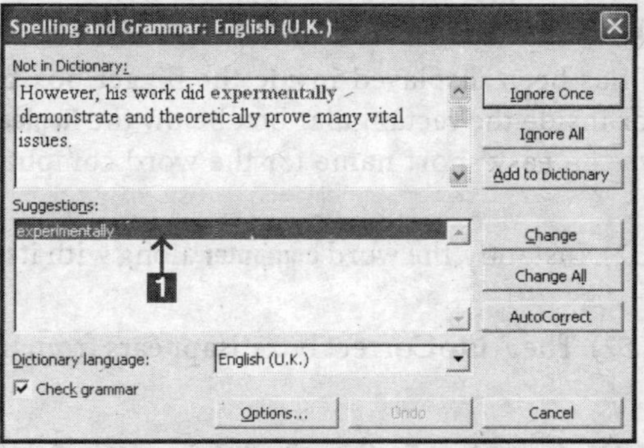

Fig. WD-4.46

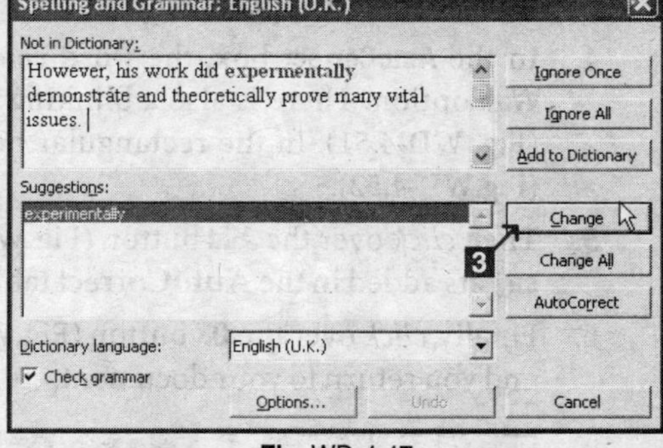

Fig. WD-4.47

Completing the Spell-check

1. Until the entire document is spell-checked, go on repeating the steps given under the topic **Replacing an Incorrect Word with a Correct Word**.
2. When the whole document is checked, a message box (Fig.WD-4.48) appears informing you that the spelling check is complete. *Click* on the **OK** button.

Fig. WD-4.48

If you want to stop the spell and grammar-check procedure before the complete checking of your document, click over the Cancel button of the Spelling and Grammar box, Immediately, you will return to your document.

Automatic Correction of Errors

The **AutoCorrect** facility is a unique feature of Microsoft Word. It helps you write correctly the words whose spellings are often difficult to remember. You just have to type short forms of difficult words which you frequently forget and the Microsoft Word would automatically expand them.

Suppose, you find it difficult to memorize the spelling of the word **computer**. As a result, there is always a spelling mistake when you type this word. To overcome this problem, undertake the following steps.

1. We assume that the **History of Computer Virus** document is open on your screen. *Locate* the word **computer** in the document and highlight it as shown in Fig. WD-4.49.

> Viral programs have a long and sometimes honourable, history. In the earliest computers it was vital that you knew the initial state of the computer. It was also important that no remnants of other programs remain. An instruction was often implemented that had only one function: it would copy itself to the next memory location and then proceed on to that location. Thus, by starting this instruction at the beginning of memory, the entire memory space could be "filled" with a known value. This single instruction could be seen as the 1st viral type application.

Fig. WD-4.49

2. Now *click* on the **Tools** option of the Menu bar. Immediately, a pull-down menu gets displayed before you (Fig.WD-4.50).
3. Inside the pull-down menu, *click* on the **AutoCorrect Options...** option (Fig.WD-4.50). Immediately, an **AutoCorrect** box appears on your screen (Fig.WD-4.51).
4. In the **AutoCorrect** box, the word **computer** has been displayed inside the bigger box below the **With** option. There is also a blinking cursor inside the rectangular box below the **Replace** option (Fig. WD-4.51). In the rectangular box, *type* an easy short name for the word computer, say **co** (Fig.WD-4.52).
5. Then *click* over the **Add** button (Fig.WD-4.52). Instantly, the word **computer** along with its shortcut **co** gets added in the **AutoCorrect** table.
6. Finally, *click* over the **OK** button (Fig.WD-4.52). The **AutoCorrect** box disappears from the screen and you return to your document.

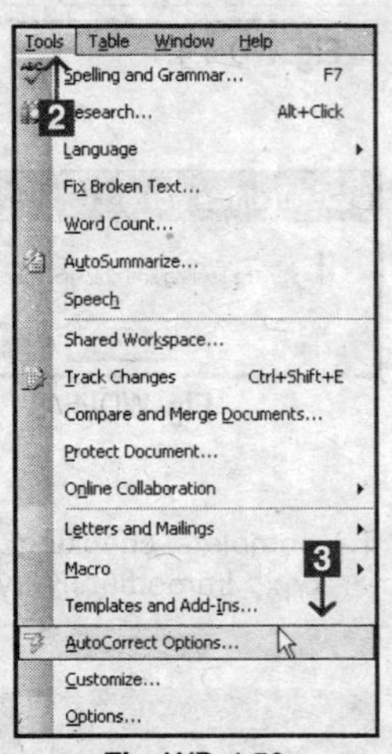

Fig. WD-4.50

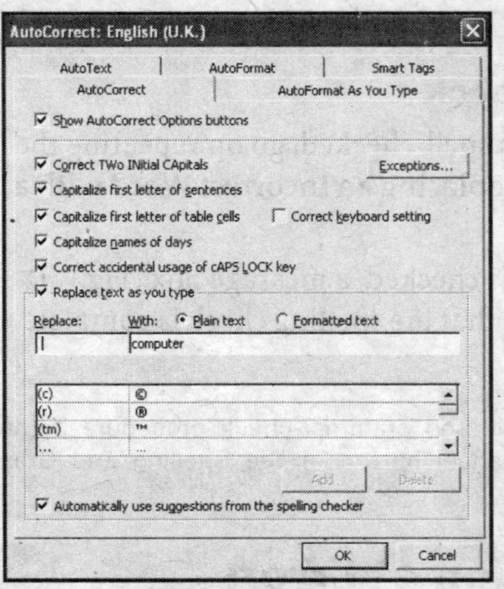

Fig. WD-4.51

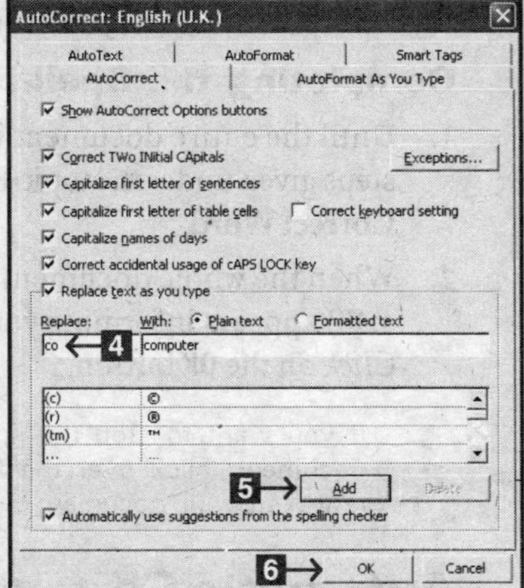

Fig. WD-4.52

7. To test whether the short form of word **computer** will work, *type* **co** anywhere in your document.

8. Then *press* the **Spacebar** key from the keyboard. Immediately, the short form gets expanded and becomes **computer.**

You can now practise creating shortcut spellings for other difficult words and add them to the AutoCorrect table.

Deleting a Shortcut from AutoCorrect

Suppose you have created shortcuts for so many words that now you find it difficult to remember them all. So, the best way to overcome this confusion is to remove some shortcut spellings from AutoCorrect. Let us now remove the shortcut for the word **computer** through the following steps:

1. We assume that the **History of Computer Virus** document is open on your screen. *Click* on **Tools** Menu bar option. A pull-down menu appears (Fig. WD-4.50).
2. Inside the pull-down menu, *click* on the **AutoCorrect Options.....** option (Fig. WD-4.50). The **AutoCorrect** box comes up on your screen (Fig. WD-4.51).
3. In the **AutoCorrect** box, you will find a box under the **Replace** option. In this box, *type* **co** (Fig. WD-4.53). Instantly, the shortcut as well as its expanded form appears as highlighted in the **AutoCorrect** box (Fig.WD-4.54)
4. Now *move* the mouse-pointer over the **Delete** button (Fig.WD-4.54) and *click* the left mouse-button. After this action, the shortcut and its expansion **computer** get deleted from the **AutoCorrect** table.
5. Finally, *click* on the **OK** button of the **AutoCorrect** box (Fig.WD-4.54).

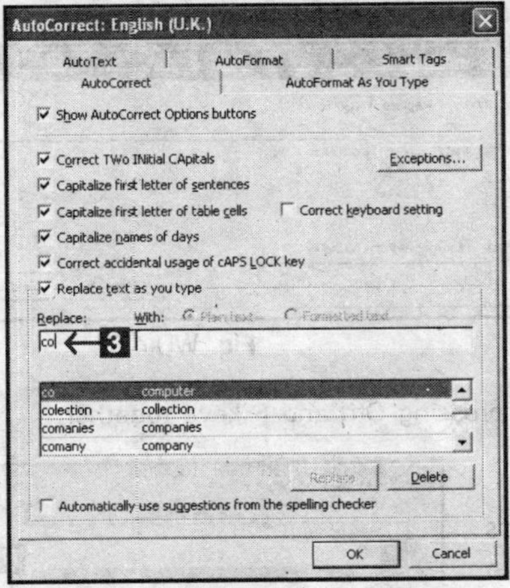

Fig. WD-4.53

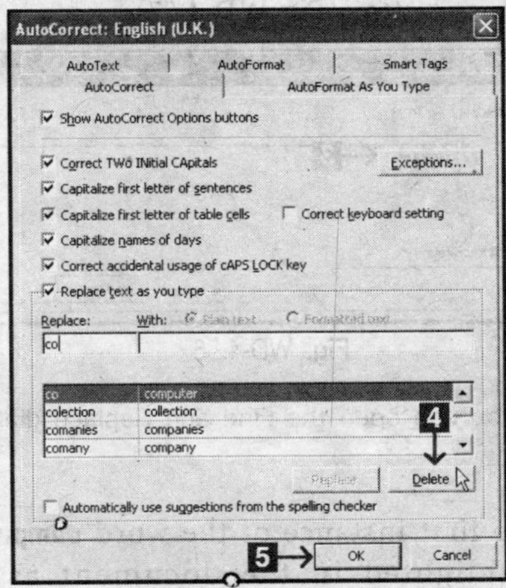

Fig. WD-4.54

Printing the File

Now that you have done lot of modifications on your document, **History of Computer Virus**, by editing it, let us try printing it. To do so, undertake the following steps:

1. Make sure that printer is connected to your computer and is ON.
2. *Move* the mouse-pointer over the **Print** ( ) button present on the **Standard Toolbar** and *click* the left mouse-button. Your document gets printed.

Find and Replace

The **Find and Replace** feature of the Word XP helps the user to quickly search the document for some word, phrase or text and replace it with the desired text. This feature has two parts—**Find and Replace.** Through **Find**, we search the document for specific word or phrase. Then using **Replace**, we can substitute the searched word or phrase with the desired text. You can use the Find and Replace option for the entire document as well as for a selected section of document.

Let us now learn to use the **Find and Replace** feature.

Suppose, you want to find the word **computer** in the **History of Computer Virus** document. To do so, undertake the following steps:

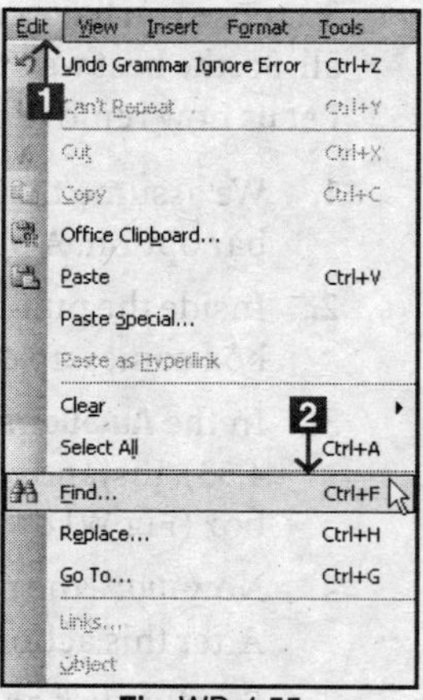

Fig. WD-4.55

1. We assume that the **History of Computer Virus** document is open on your screen. *Click* over the **Edit** option of the Menu bar (Fig. WD-4.55).
2. Instantly, a pull-down menu appears. In the pull-down menu, *click* over the **Find** option (Fig. WD-4.55).
3. Instantly, the **Find and Replace** dialog box appears over the document (Fig. WD-4.56). This box has three tabs—**Find, Replace** and **GoTo.** Currently, the **Find** tab is active. Now, to do your search, *type* the word **computer** in the box beside the **Find what** option (Fig. WD-4.56).
4. Next, *move* the mouse-pointer over the **Find Next** button and *click* the left mouse-button (Fig. WD-4.57).

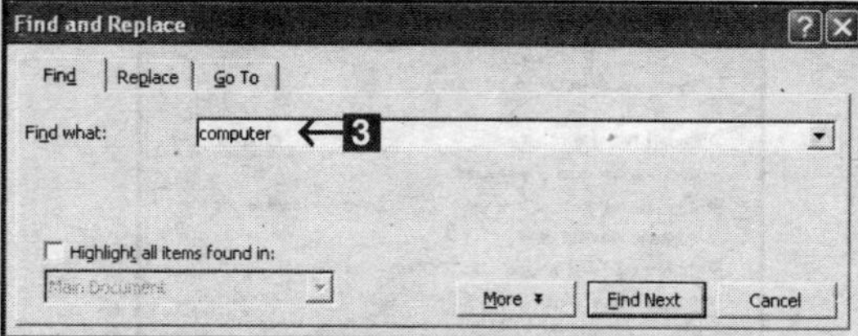

Fig. WD-4.56

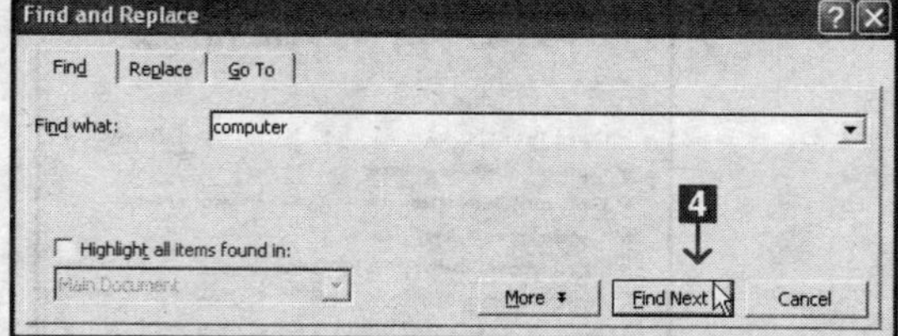

Fig. WD-4.57

HOT TIP!

You can open the Find and Replace dialog box by pressing Ctrl and F keys together.

5. The first instance of the word **computer** appears highlighted in the document as shown in Fig. WD-4.58. If you want to search more instances of the word **computer** then again *click* the **Find Next** button. In this way, you can have a look at all the places in the document where the word **computer** has been used.

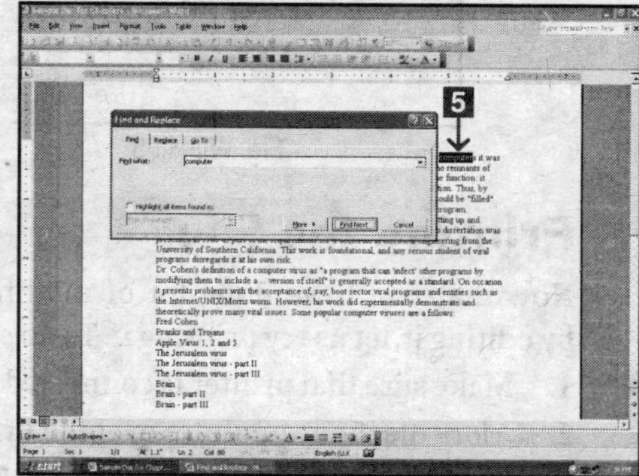

Fig. WD-4.58

Using the Find option for Selected Text

The **Find** option can also be used for a selected portion of text in your document. For this, you first need to select the desired portion of text in your document in which you want to search a particular word or phrase. Then, you can use the **Find** option on the selected text. Let us now use the **Find** option for finding the word **program** in the selected text in the first paragraph of the **History of Computer Virus** document.

1. We assume that the **History of Computer Virus** document is open on your screen. *Highlight* some text in the document, as shown in Fig. WD-4.59. After highlighting the text, *click* over the **Edit** option of the Menu bar (Fig. WD-4.55). In the **Edit** pull-down menu, *click* over the **Find** option (Fig. WD-4.55).
2. The **Find and Replace** box appears. *Type* the word **program** in the box beside the **Find what** option (Fig. WD-4.60).
3. Next, *click* over the **Find Next** button (Fig. WD-4.60). The **Find** option will start searching the word **program** in the selected text.
4. The **program** word, when found in the selected text, will be highlighted as shown in Fig. WD-4.61. Go on clicking till the entire highlighted text is searched for the word **program**.

Earliest history of viral programs

Viral programs have a long, and sometimes honourable, history. In the earliest computers it was vital that you knew the initial state of the computer. It was also important that no remnants of other programs remain. An instruction was often implemented that had only one function: it would copy itself to the next memory location and then proceed on to that location. Thus, by starting this instruction at the beginning of memory, the entire memory space could be "filled" with a known value. This single instruction could be seen as the 1st viral type program.

In the early 1980s, Fred Cohen did extensive theoretical research, as well as setting up and performing numerous practical experiments, regarding viral type programs. His dissertation was presented in 1986 as part of the requirements for a doctorate in electrical engineering from the University of Southern California. This work is foundational, and any serious student of viral programs disregards it at his own risk.

Dr. Cohen's definition of a computer virus as "a program that can 'infect' other programs by modifying them to include a ... version of itself" is generally accepted as a standard. On occasion it presents problems with the acceptance of, say, boot sector viral programs and entities such as the Internet/UNIX/Morris worm. However, his work did experimentally demonstrate and theoretically prove many vital issues. Some popular computer viruses are a follows:

Fig. WD-4.59

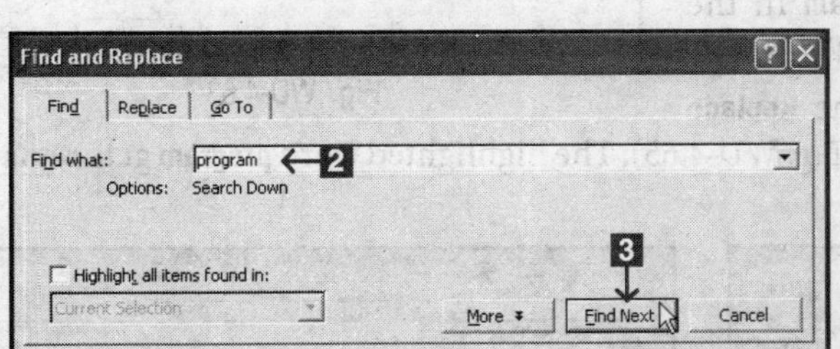

Fig. WD-4.60

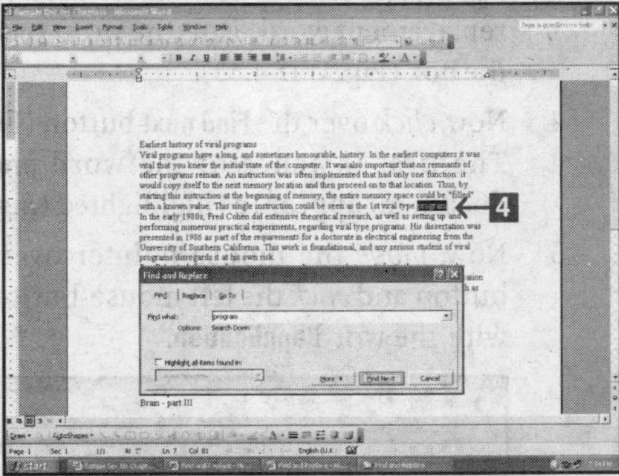

Fig. WD-4.61

Replacing Text

Now, we will learn to use the **Replace** option of the Microsoft Word. Using the **Replace** option, you can find the desired word or phrase as well as substitute it with an alternative word or phrase. For example, suppose you want to change all occurrences of the expression "mouse-arrow" with the term "mouse-pointer" in selected text or the entire document. You can do this change easily through the **Replace** option.

There are two ways to replace words and phrases in the document.

Replace with confirmation: In this replacement method, the word to be replaced is first highlighted. Thereafter, the user has to click on the **Replace** button in the **Find and Replace** dialog box to replace the highlighted word.

Replace without confirmation: In this replacement method, the word to be replaced is not highlighted before being substituted. The Find and Replace option searches the document or selected text and makes replacements on its own.

Replace with confirmation

Let us now understand to use the **Replace** option for searching and replacing the desired text in entire document.

Suppose you want to replace the word **program** with **application** in entire document. To do so, undertake the following steps:

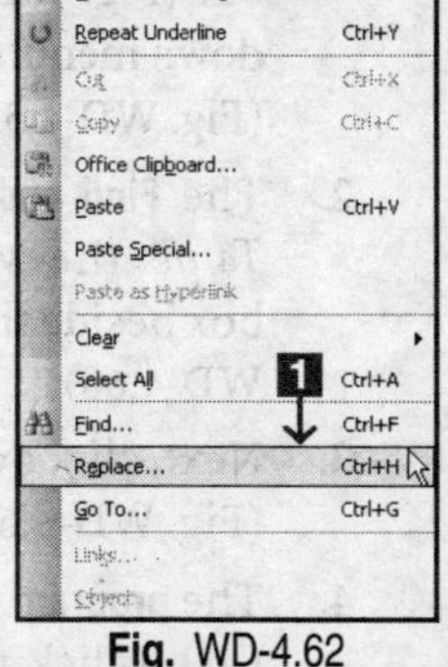

Fig. WD-4.62

1. Start with the **History of Computer Virus** document open on your screen. *Click* over the **Edit** option of the Menu bar. In the pull-down menu, *click* over the **Replace** option (Fig. WD-4.62).
2. The **Find and Replace** dialog box appears. In this box, the **Replace** tab is currently active. *Type* the word **program** inside box beside the **Find what** option (Fig. WD-4.63). As you know, the **Find what** option is used to specify the word you want to search in the document.

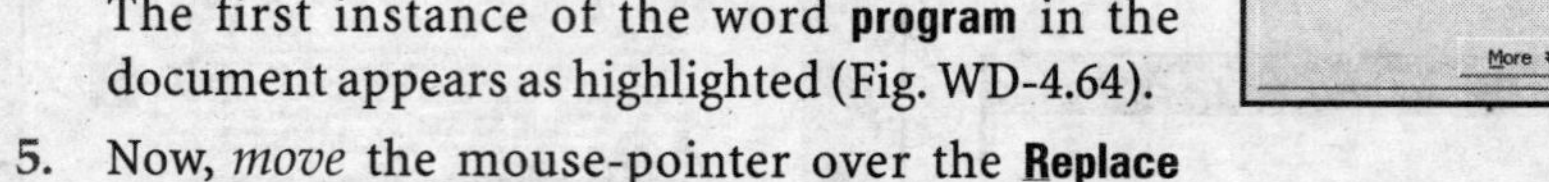

3. Next, *press* the **Tab** key in the keyboard. The cursor jumps to the box beside the **Replace with** option that is used to specify the replacement word. *Type* the word **application** inside the box (Fig. WD-4.63).

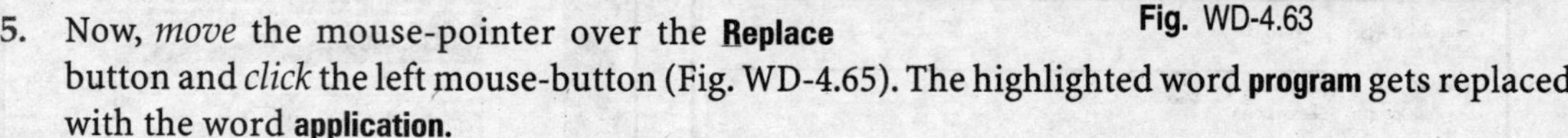

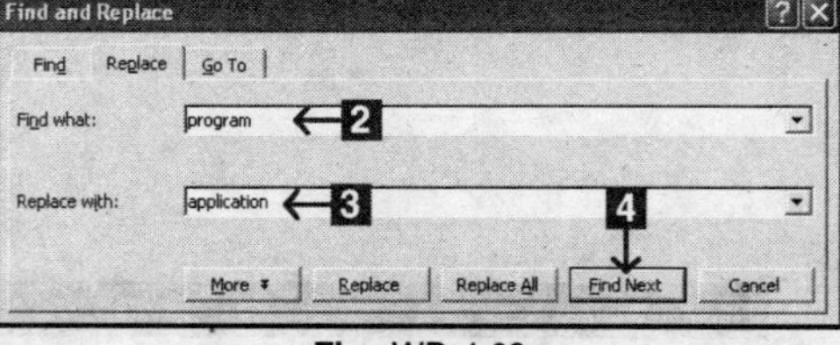

Fig. WD-4.63

4. Now, *click* over the **Find next** button (Fig. WD-4.63). The first instance of the word **program** in the document appears as highlighted (Fig. WD-4.64).
5. Now, *move* the mouse-pointer over the **Replace** button and *click* the left mouse-button (Fig. WD-4.65). The highlighted word **program** gets replaced with the word **application**.

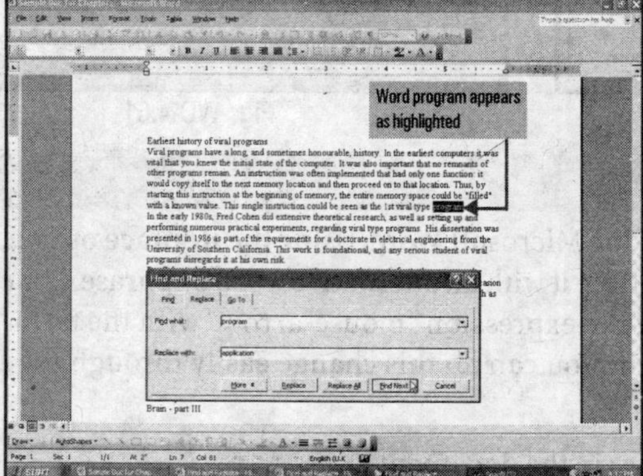

Fig. WD-4.64

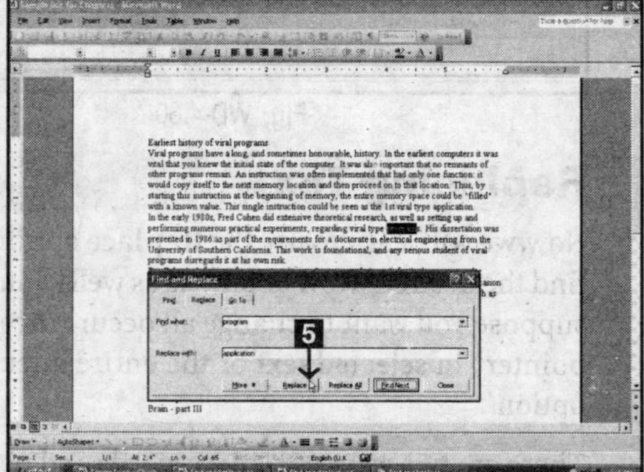

Fig. WD-4.65

Replace Without Confirmation

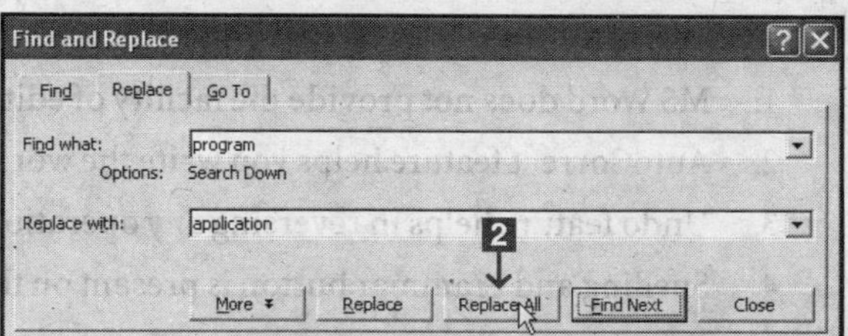

Fig. WD-4.66

If you are sure that you want to replace all instances of the word **program** with **application** in entire document with a single step then **Replace All** button in the **Find and Replace** dialog box can help you. All you have to do is:

1. Repeat Steps 1 to 4 of the topic **Replace with confirmation.**
2. Next, *click* over the **Replace All** button as shown in Fig. WD-4.66.

Saving and Closing the Document

You have done various editing modifications on the text of your document, **History of Computer Virus,** as per your requirement. You have also printed the document. Let us now proceed to close this document. For this, undertake the following steps.

1. *Click* on the **File** option of the Menu bar. Immediately, a pull-down menu appears.
2. Inside the pull-down menu, *click* on the **Close** option.
3. As you have not saved the document since you last edited it, a dialog box appears asking you whether the changes made to the document need to be saved or not. For saving the changes to the document, *click* on the **Yes** button. Immediately, the dialog box disappears and changes made to the **History of Computer Virus** document are saved, and the document closes.

Quitting Microsoft Word

Let us now quit Microsoft Word by undertaking the following steps:

1. *Move* the mouse-pointer over the **Close** button (☒) present on the **Title bar.**
2. Now, *click* the left mouse-button. Immediately, Microsoft Word window closes and you return to your Desktop.

Exercise

Fill in the Blanks

1. Correcting the mistakes in a document is called ____________.
2. ____________ Mode inserts the characters typed from the keyboard at the current cursor position on the screen.
3. OVR button stands for ____________ button.
4. For copying the highlighted text press _______ key and ______ key together.
5. To cut any highlighted text press _______ key and ________ key together.

True/False

1. MS Word does not provide the facility of editing any Word document.
2. AutoCorrect feature helps you write the words whose spellings are difficult to remember.
3. Undo feature helps in reversing any operation performed on the text.
4. Spelling and grammar button is present on the formatting toolbar.

MICROSOFT WORD

Designing the Document 5

IN THIS CHAPTER

- Opening Windows and Microsoft Word
- Creating a Well Formatted Document
- Setting Left, Right, Top and Bottom Margins
- Previewing the Document before Printing
- Setting Page Numbers on Your Document
- Specifying Text at the Top and the Bottom of Each Page
- Creating Tables
- Selecting Text in a Table
- Inserting Rows in an Existing Table
- Inserting Columns
- Deleting a Row and a Column
- Formatting the Document
- Creating Bulleted and Numbered List
- Exercise

When it comes to giving a nice, distinct look to your document, you will find various formatting features of Microsoft Word quite useful. Using these features, you can make the headlines stand out from general text, highlight certain important points of the text, set up margins, or change the writing style and size of some characters, and display some details neatly in rows and columns. Let us now learn to work with all these formatting features of the Microsoft Word.

Opening Windows and Microsoft Word

1. *Switch on* your computer.
2. When the **Desktop** appears, *move* the mouse-pointer over the **Start** button on the **Taskbar**, and then *click* the left mouse-button. Immediately, a push-up menu appears on the screen (Fig. WD-5.1).
3. *Place* the mouse-pointer over the **All Programs** option. A second menu appears next to the push-up menu (Fig.WD-5.1).
4. In the second menu, *move* the mouse-pointer over the **Microsoft Office** option (Fig. WD-5.1).
5. A third menu appears. *Move* the mouse-pointer over the **Microsoft Office Word 2003** and *click* the left mouse-button (Fig. WD-5.1). Immediately, the **Microsoft Word** window appears with a blank document (Fig. WD-5.2).

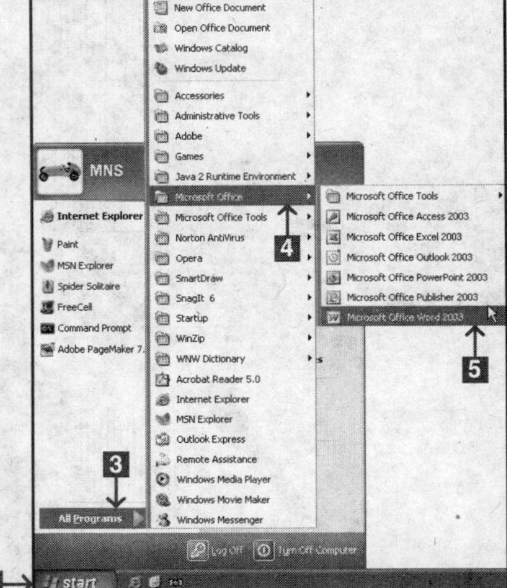

Fig. WD-5.1

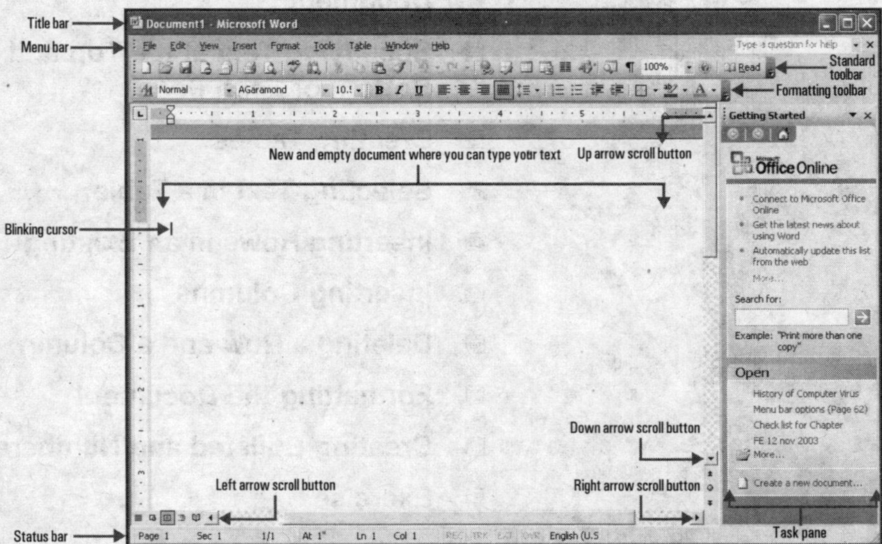

Fig. WD-5.2

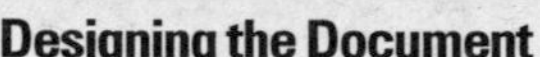

If Microsoft Word window is already open on your screen, you can straightaway start from the topic 'Creating a Well Formatted Document'.

Creating a Well Formatted Document

Now, we will learn how to create a well-formatted document. We will apply various formatting features to our existing Word document, **History of Computer Virus**. To open this document, undertake the following steps:

1. We assume that the Microsoft Word is open on your screen. *Move* the mouse-pointer over the **More...** option of the **Getting Started** Task pane, and *click* the left mouse-button once (Fig. WD-5.3). Immediately, an **Open** box appears before you (Fig. WD-5.4).
2. Remember that you had saved the **History of Computer Virus** document in the **Local Disk (C:)**. So, to reach the **Local Disk (C:)**, *click* over the down-arrow button (▾) of the box beside the **Look in** option (Fig. WD-5.5). A pull-down menu instantly appears (Fig. WD-5.5).

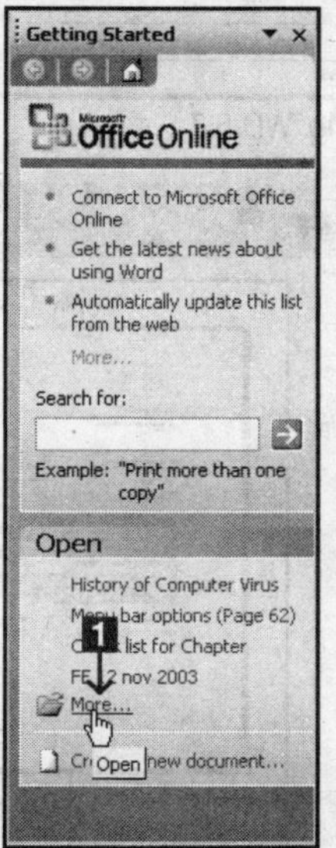

Fig. WD-5.3

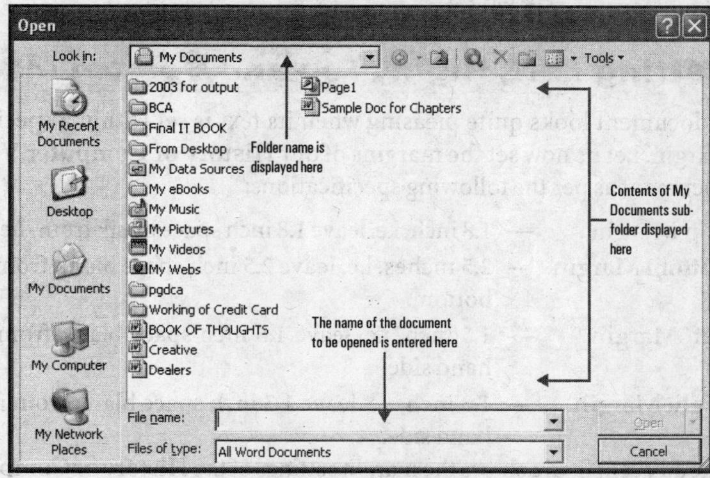

Fig. WD-5.4

3. Inside the pull-down menu, *move* the mouse-pointer over the **Local Disk (C:)**, and *click* the left mouse-button on it (Fig. WD-5.6). Instantly, the **Local Disk (C:)** gets displayed inside the box beside the **Look in** option and its contents appear in the bigger box below the **Look in** option (Fig. WD-5.7).
4. Now, in the **Local Disk (C:)** contents, *move* the mouse-pointer over the **History of Computer Virus** (Fig. WD-5.7) and *click* the left mouse-button once.

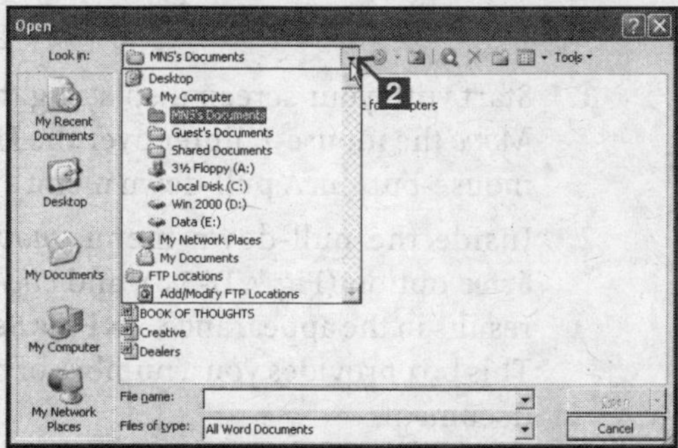

Fig. WD-5.5

5. Finally, *move* the mouse-pointer over the **Open** button and *click* the left mouse-button (Fig. WD-5.7). The **Open** box disappears and the **History of Computer Virus** document gets displayed on the screen.

NOTE: All the folders shown in the pull-down menu in Fig.WD-5.6 may not be present in your computer. Your computer may show different folders names.

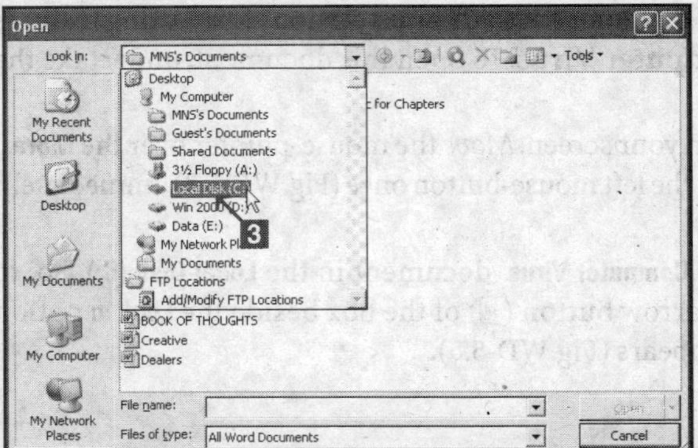

Fig. WD-5.6

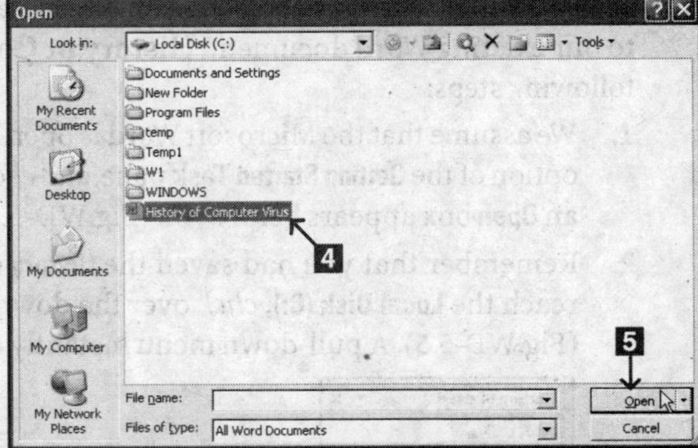

Fig. WD-5.7

Setting Left, Right, Top and Bottom Margins

A document looks quite pleasing when its text is set within a specified margin. Let us now set the margins of our **History of Computer Virus** document as per the following specifications:

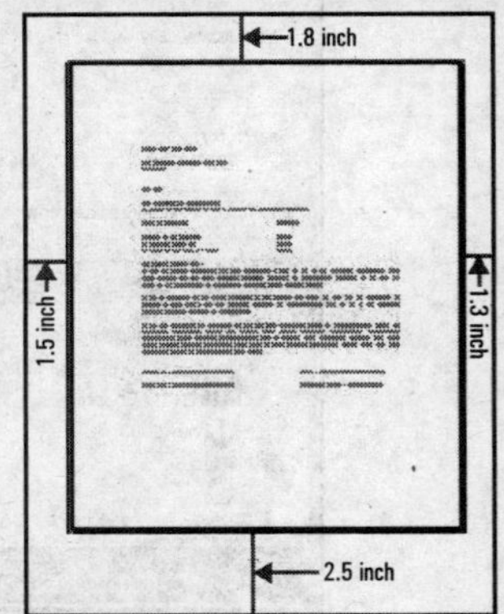

Top Margin — 1.8 inch, i.e. leave 1.8 inch space blank from the top.

Bottom Margin — 2.5 inches, i.e. leave 2.5 inch space blank from the bottom.

Left Margin — 1.5 inch, i.e. leave 1.5 inch space blank from left hand side.

Right Margin — 1.3 inch, i.e. leave 1.3 inch space blank from right hand side.

The adjacent figure shows the margin settings of the **History of Computer Virus** document as per our specifications. For setting the required margins of the document, undertake the following steps:

1. Start with your screen displaying the **History of Computer Virus** document. *Move* the mouse-pointer over the **File** Menu bar option and *click* the left mouse-button. A pull-down menu appears (Fig. WD-5.8).

2. Inside the pull-down menu, *move* the mouse-pointer on the **Page Setup** option (Fig.WD-5.8), and *click* the left mouse-button. This action results in the appearance of a **Page Setup** box on your screen (Fig.WD-5.9). This box provides you a number of options to change the settings of your document.

Fig. WD-5.8

3. In the **Page Setup** box (Fig. WD-5.9), you see the **Margins** tab with four sub-options—**Top**, **Bottom**, **Left** and **Right.** Each sub-option has a rectangular box showing the margin measurement in inches. Each rectangular box also contains scroll buttons (⬍). The symbol ▲ represents the up-arrow scroll button. If you click over the up-arrow scroll button, the number inside the box increases. The symbol ▼ represents the down-arrow scroll button. If you click over the down-arrow scroll button, the number inside the box decreases.

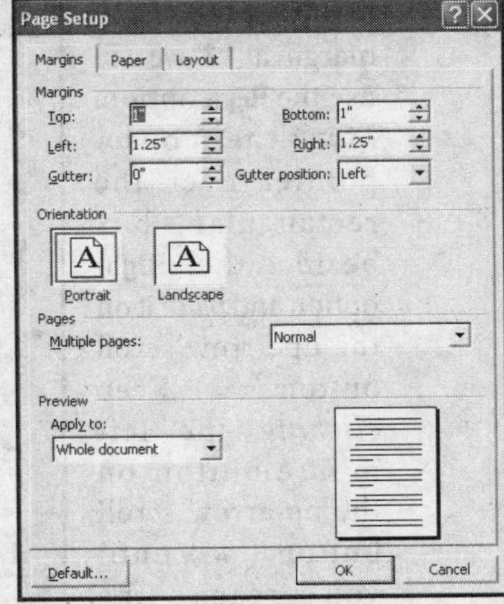

Fig. WD-5.9

Let us now give the desired settings to the **History of Computer Virus** document. To set the desired top margin of **1.8"**, we will use the **Top** option. *Move* the mouse-pointer over the up-arrow scroll button (▲) of the rectangular box beside the **Top** option and *click* the left mouse-button. With this action, the number inside the box increases.

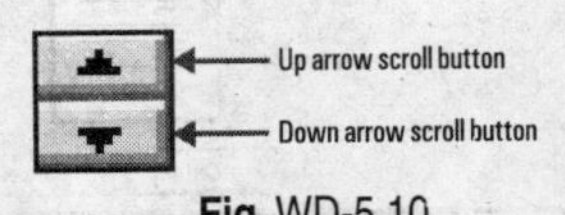

Fig. WD-5.10

4. Keep *clicking* the up-arrow scroll button (▲) until you reach the required number **1.8"** (Fig. WD-5.11).

Sometimes, due to excessive clicking, you may set the top margin measure more than the desired one in the box. In such a case, use the down arrow scroll button (▼) to come back to 1.8".

5. Similarly, for setting the bottom margin at **2.5"**, we will use the **Bottom** option. Now *move* the mouse-pointer over the up-arrow scroll button (▲) of the box beside the **Bottom** option and *click* the left mouse-button. Keep *clicking* the left mouse-button until you reach the number **2.5"** (Fig. WD-5.12).

6. Now, to set the left margin at **1.5"**, we will use the **Left** option. *Place* the mouse-pointer over the up-arrow scroll button (▲) of the box beside the **Left** option and *click* the left mouse-button. Keep *clicking* the left mouse-button until you reach the number **1.5"** (Fig. WD-5.13).

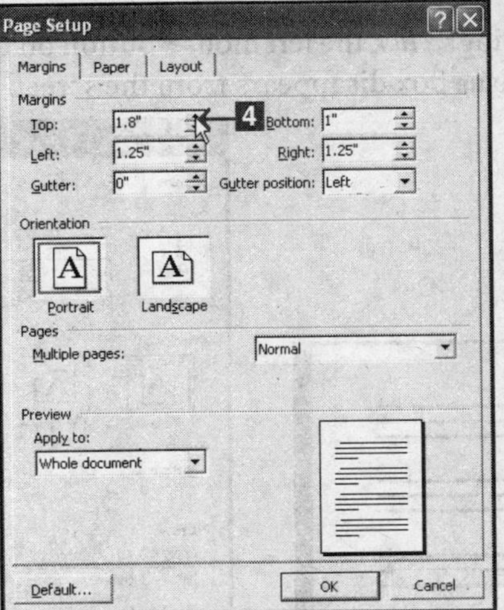

Fig. WD-5.11

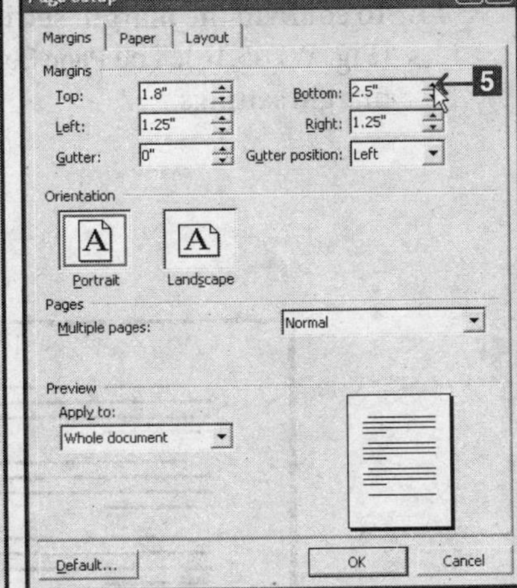

Fig. WD-5.12

7. Now to set the right margin at **1.3"** we will use the **Right** option. *Move* the mouse-pointer over the rectangular box beside the **Right** option and *place* it on the up-arrow scroll button (▲). Keep *clicking* the left mouse-button on the up-arrow scroll button (▲) until you reach the number **1.3"** (Fig. WD-5.14).

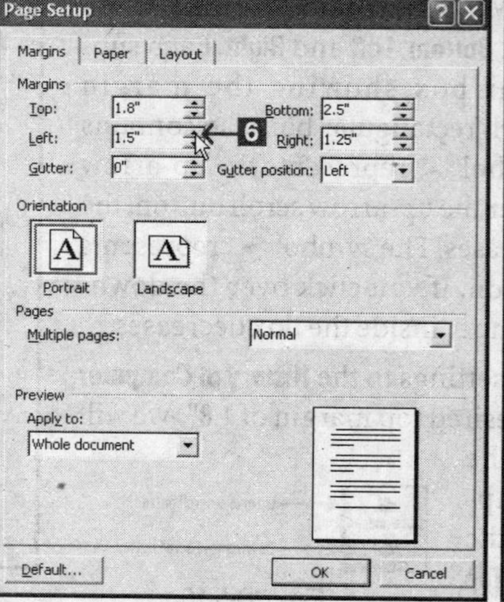

Fig. WD-5.13

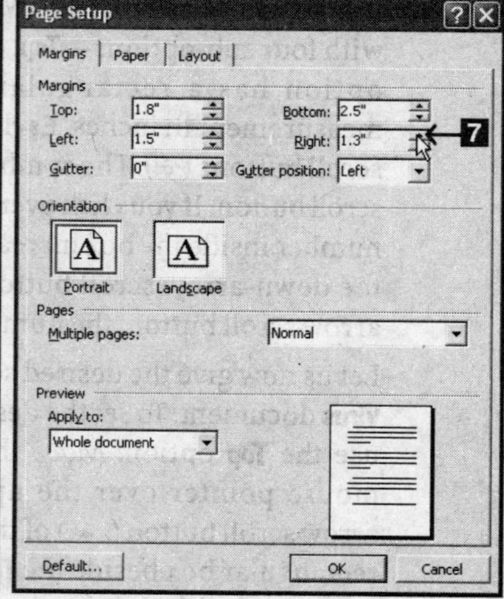

Fig. WD-5.14

If by mistake you click more, i.e. if you get the right margin more than the desired one, then use the down-arrow scroll button (▼) to come back to 1.3".

So, you have successfully given the new margin settings to all the four sides of the **History of Computer Virus** document. Before confirming these settings, you would like to see a preview of your document set within new margins. This can be seen under the **Preview** option in the **Page Setup** box (Fig. WD-5.14). The enlarged preview of the **History of Computer Virus** document is shown in Fig.WD-5.15.

11. To confirm the margin settings, *click* the left mouse-button on the **OK** button of the **Page Setup** box (Fig. WD-5.16). The **Page Setup** box disappears from the screen and your document gets the new margin settings.

Fig. WD-5.15

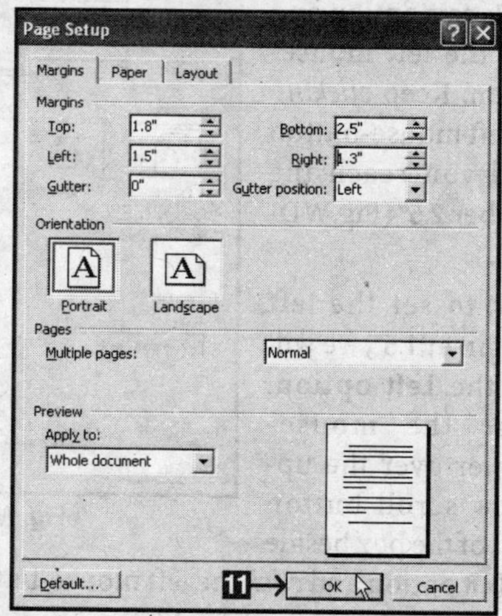

Fig. WD-5.16

Previewing the Document before Printing

You can now print your document with its new margin settings. But before taking a printout, it is better to once again verify the margin settings of your document through the **Print Preview** option. This option helps you visualize how your document will look like after printing. To use the **Print Preview** option, undertake the following steps:

1. *Move* the mouse-pointer over the **Print Preview** button (🔍) on the **Standard Toolbar** (Fig.WD-5.17) and *click* the left mouse-button.

Fig. WD-5.17

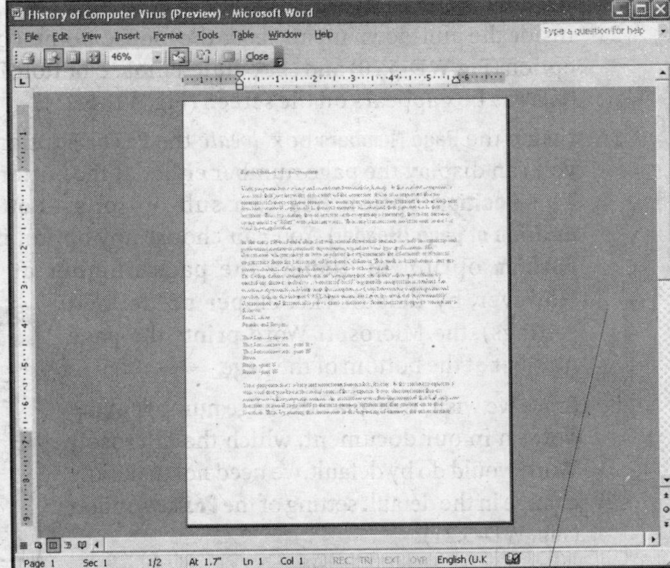

Fig. WD-5.18

Immediately, the screen displays the print preview of the **History of Computer Virus** document (Fig. WD-5.18). The print preview screen is a non-readable outline of the text in your document. If you want to make this text readable then follow the Hot Tip given at the bottom.

2. Suppose you are not satisfied with the document layout and you wish to make certain changes to it. This cannot be done in the print preview screen. For making changes, you have to return to the original document.
3. To return to the original document, *move* the mouse-pointer over the **Close** button present on the **Toolbar** of the print preview window (Fig.WD-5.19) and *click* the left mouse-button.

Fig. WD-5.19

4. Immediately, you return to the original document, **History of Computer Virus.**

To make the text of the Print Preview screen readable, undertake the following steps.

1. Move the mouse-pointer over the document in the Print Preview screen. Instantly the cursor changes into a magnifier symbol (🔍).
2. Now click the left mouse-button. The document becomes clearly readable.

Setting Page Numbers on Your Document

When a document is printed, Microsoft Word does not display a page number automatically at the end of every page. However, it has a feature through which you can get the page numbers displayed automatically either at the bottom or top of the page. Now let us learn to display the page number at the bottom in the **History of Computer Virus** document through the following steps:

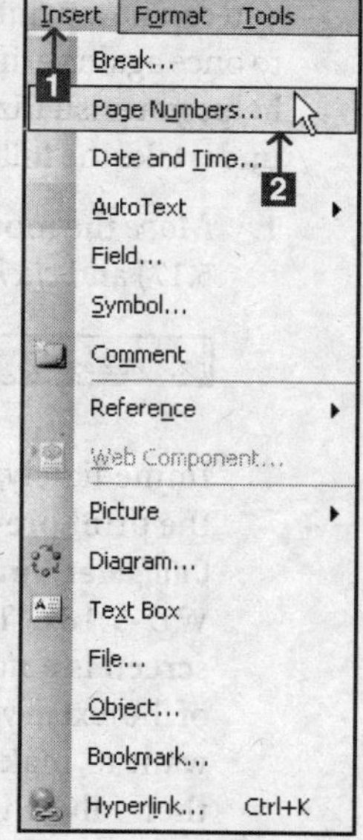

Fig. WD-5.20

1. We assume that the **History of Computer Virus** document is open on your screen. *Move* the mouse-pointer over the **Insert** option of the Menu bar, and *click* the left mouse-button. Immediately, a pull-down menu appears (Fig.WD-5.20).
2. Inside the pull-down menu, *move* the mouse-pointer over the **Page Numbers** option (Fig.WD-5.20) and *click* the left mouse-button. Immediately, the **Page Numbers** box appears on the screen (Fig.WD-5.21).
3. Inside the **Page Numbers** box, *locate* the **Position** option. Using this option, you can display the page number either at the bottom or top of the page. The **Position** option has two sub-options—**Bottom of page (Footer)** and **Top of page (Header)**. You can choose any option in the box below the **Position** option to display the page number at the desired place. However, by default (i.e. as per predefined settings), the Microsoft Word prints the page number at the bottom of the page.

   Since we wish to display the page number at the bottom in our document, which the Microsoft Word would do by default, we need not make any change in the default setting of the **Position** option (Fig. WD-5.21).

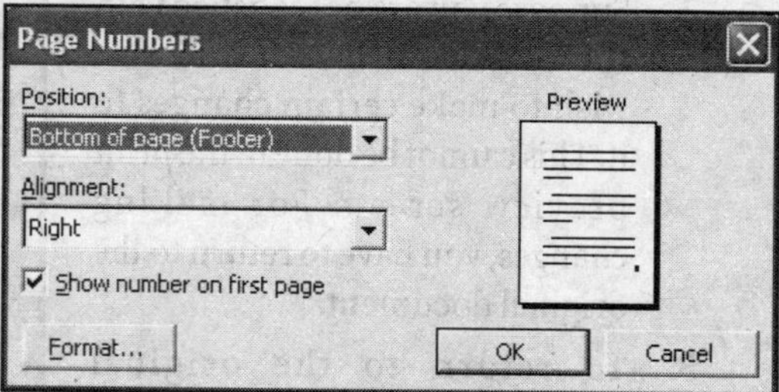

Fig. WD-5.21

If you wish to display the page number at the top of the page, undertake the following steps:

1. In the Page Numbers box, move the mouse-pointer over the down-arrow button (▾) of the box below the Position option, and click the left mouse-button. Immediately, a pull-down menu gets displayed on the screen (Fig.W-5.22).
2. In the pull-down menu, move the mouse-pointer over the Top of Page (Header) option and click the left mouse-button (Fig.WD-5.22).
3. Lastly, move the mouse-pointer over the OK button and click the left mouse-button. The Page Numbers box disappears and the page number appears on top of the page.

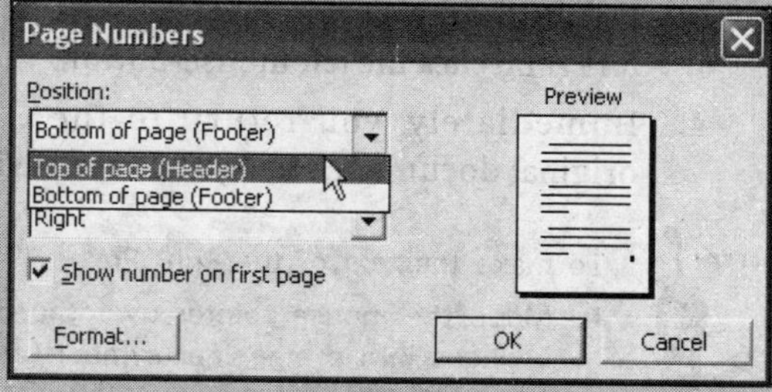

Fig. WD-5.22

4. Now, we will use another option, i.e. the **Alignment** option, in the **Page Numbers** box, to display the page number at a specific location on the page, i.e. to the left hand side or the right hand side or at the center. In the **Page Numbers** box, the **Alignment** option appears just below the **Position** option.

   Let us place the page number at the center. To do so, *move* the mouse-pointer over the down-arrow button (▾) of the box below the **Alignment** option and *click* the left mouse-button over it. A pull-down menu appears (Fig.WD-5.23).

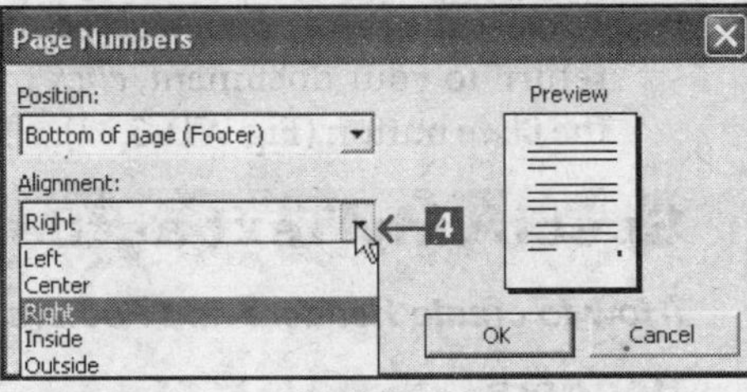

Fig. WD-5.23

5. Inside the pull-down menu, *move* the mouse-pointer over the **Center** option and *click* the left mouse-button (Fig.WD-5.24). The **Center** option gets displayed in the box just below the **Alignment** option (Fig.WD-5.25).

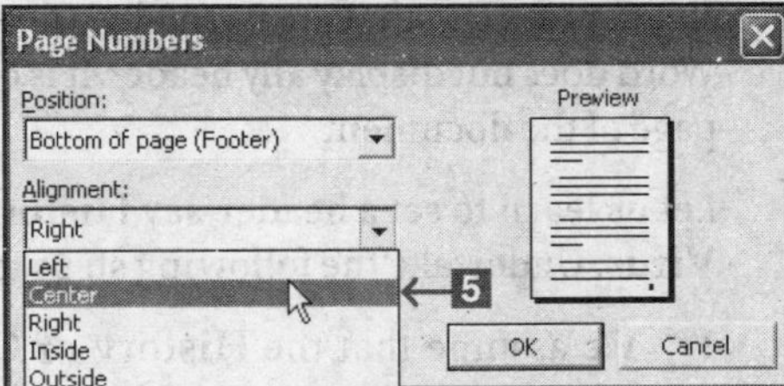

Fig. WD-5.24

6. Through the preview screen present just below the **Preview** option in the **Page Numbers** box you can have a glimpse of your chosen page number placement in the document. On the Preview screen, you will not be able to see the number clearly. Only a dot at the center of page indicates the page number.

In the Page Numbers box, you see a square box beside the Show number on first page option. If you leave this box blank, the page number would appear only from the second page of your document. If you want to have a page number on your first page also then move the mouse-pointer over the square box and click the left mouse-button. A tick mark appears in the box, indicating the selection of the option, Show number on first page.

7. Now *click* on the **OK** button of the **Page Numbers** box (Fig.WD-5.25). Instantly, the box disappears from the screen.

8. To verify whether the page numbers have been positioned at the desired place in your document, preview your document by *clicking* on the **Print Preview** button (🔍) (Fig.WD-5.17).

   Immediately, the print preview screen (Fig.WD-5.26) gets displayed before you. In this screen, the page number is indicated by a dot at the bottom of the page.

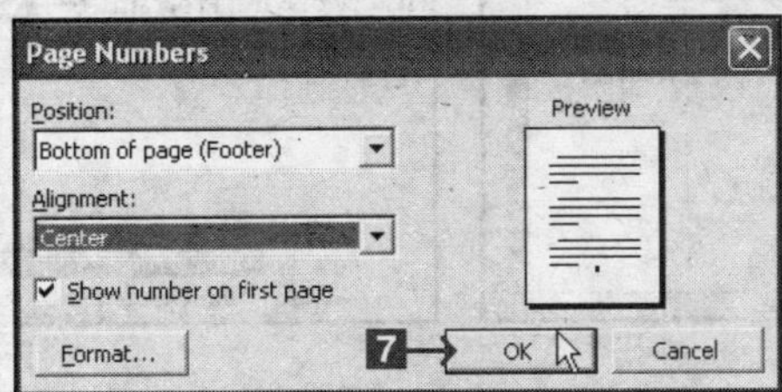

Fig. WD-5.25

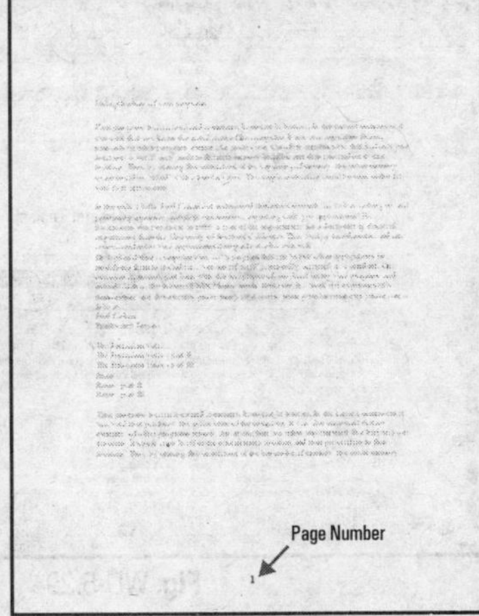

Fig. WD-5.26

After looking at the Print Preview of your document, if you are dissatisfied with the position of the page number, you can again start from step 1 of the topic 'Setting the Page Numbers on Your Document' to do the desired changes.

9. To close the print preview screen and return to your document, *click* over the **Close** button (Fig.WD-5.27).

Fig. WD-5.27

Specifying Text at the Top and the Bottom of Each Page

(How to create Headers and Footers for your Document)

Headers

Headers are text that are normally printed at the top of each page of your document. By default, Microsoft Word does not display any header. It is only when you specify some text as header that it appears on every page of the document.

Let us learn to set a header, say **History of Viral Programs**, in our document, **History of Computer Virus.** Undertake the following steps to set the desired header.

1. We assume that the **History of Computer Virus** document is open on your screen. *Move* the mouse-pointer over the **View** option on the Menu bar, and *click* the left mouse-button. Immediately, a pull-down menu gets displayed on the screen (Fig.WD-5.28).
2. Inside the pull-down menu, *move* the mouse-pointer over the **Header and Footer** option (Fig.WD-5.28) and *click* the left mouse-button. Immediately the **Header and Footer** box along with a dotted line box comes up on the screen (Fig.WD-5.29). Inside the dotted line box – where the cursor is blinking – you have to enter the header text.
3. Now, *type* the header text, **History of Viral Programs** (Fig.WD-5.30). Now we proceed to set a footer for our document.

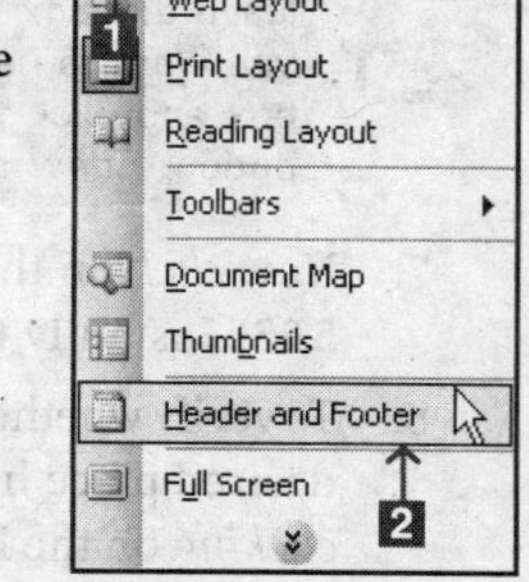

Fig. WD-5.28

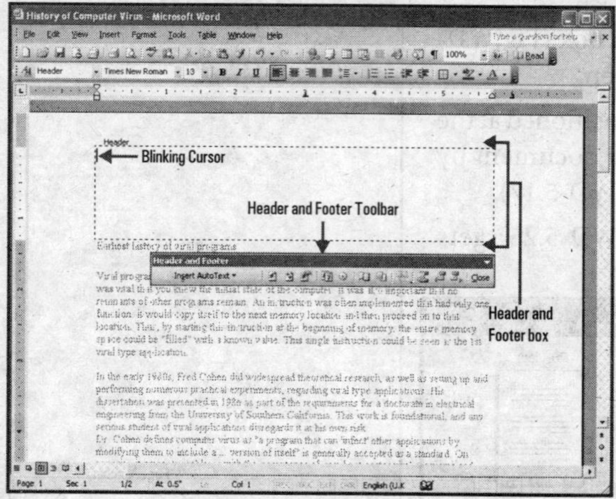

Fig. WD-5.29

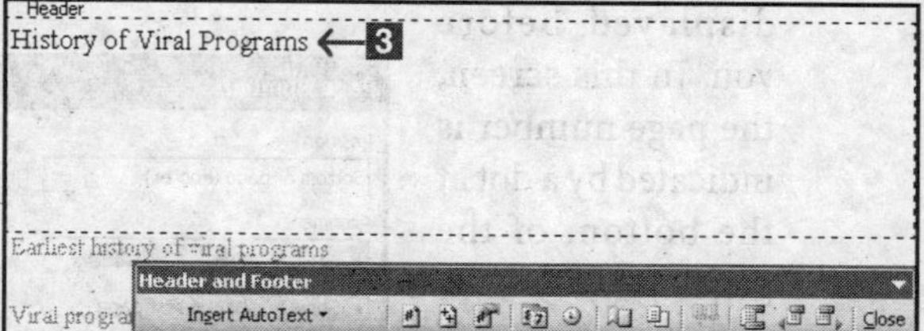

Fig. WD-5.30

Footers

Footer is the text that appears at the bottom of every page in a document. We will set a dotted line as the footer of our document, **History of Computer Virus.** To set the desired footer, go through the following procedure:

1. Start with Fig. WD-5.30. *Move* the mouse-pointer over the **switch between header and footer button** (▣) in the **Header and Footer** Toolbar (Fig. WD-5.31) and *click* the left mouse-button. Instantly, another dotted box with a blinking cursor and the page number appears at the bottom of your document (Fig.WD-5.32).

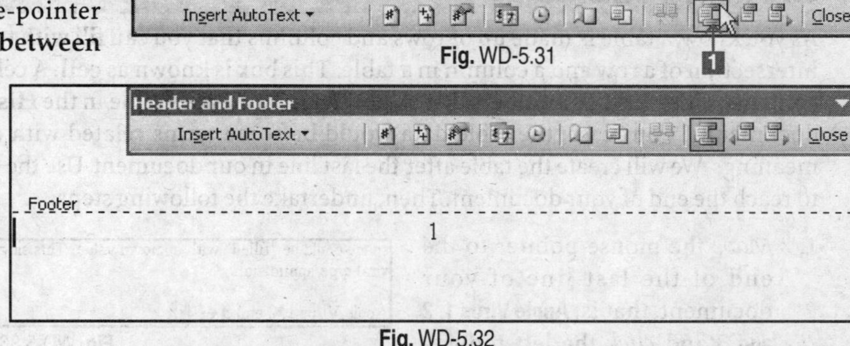

Fig. WD-5.31

Fig. WD-5.32

2. As we want a dotted line as footer, *keep pressing* the **hyphen** (–) key from the keyboard such that a line gets drawn (Fig.WD-5.33).

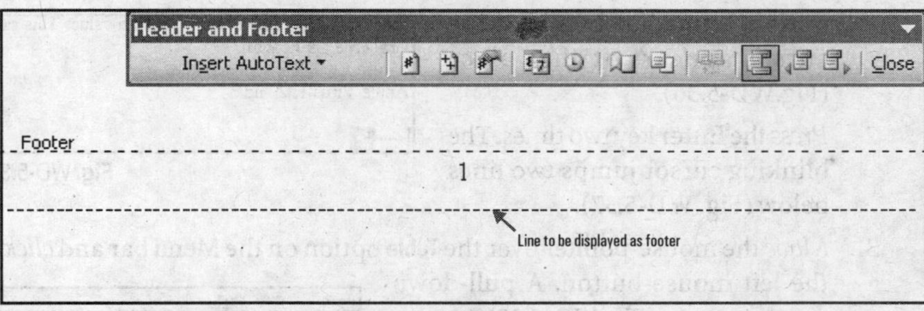

Fig. WD-5.33

3. Once the line attains the desired length, stop *pressing* the **hyphen** (–) key.

If you keep pressing the hyphen key even after the dotted line attains the document width, a second line starts getting displayed automatically. To remove the second dotted line, keep pressing the Backspace key from the keyboard until the second dotted line gets deleted.

4. Now *move* the mouse-pointer over the **Close** button present on the **Header and Footer** box (Fig.WD-5.34) and *click* the left mouse-button. Immediately, the **Header and Footer** box disappears and your document gets displayed.

Fig. WD-5.34

5. Now, to verify whether the header and footer are displayed at the proper place, take the help of the print preview feature. *Move* the mouse-pointer over the **Print Preview** button (▣) present on the **Standard Toolbar** (Fig.WD-5.17) and *click* the left mouse-button.
6. Instantly, the print preview of your document gets displayed (Fig. WD-5.35). As you know, the print preview screen displays the layout in which your document would be printed.
7. After seeing the print preview, return to your document by clicking on the **Close** button. Immediately, the print preview screen disappears and you return to the **History of Computer Virus** document.

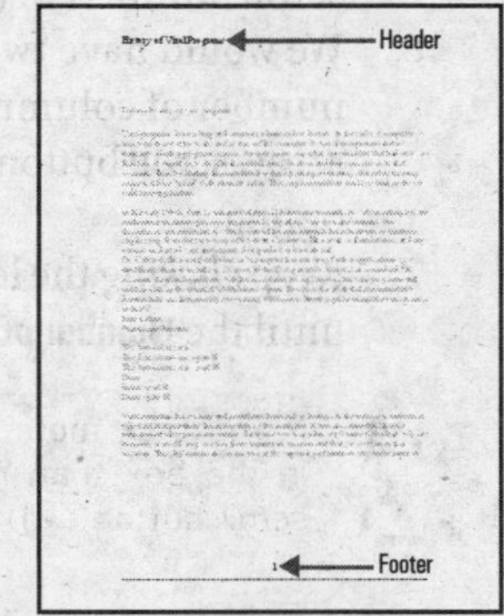

Fig. WD-5.35

Creating Tables

As you know, a table is made up of rows and columns that you can fill with text. A box is formed by the intersection of a row and a column in a table. This box is known as **cell.** A cell is meant for typing table contents, either text or numbers. Let us now learn to create a table in the **History of Computer Virus** document. In our case, the table data would be some terms related with computer virus and their meanings. We will create the table after the last line in our document. Use the down-arrow-scroll button to reach the end of your document. Then, undertake the following steps:

1. *Move* the mouse-pointer to the end of the last line of your document, that is, **Apple Virus 1, 2 and 3** and *click* the left mouse-button. Immediately, a blinking cursor appears at that place (Fig.WD-5.36).

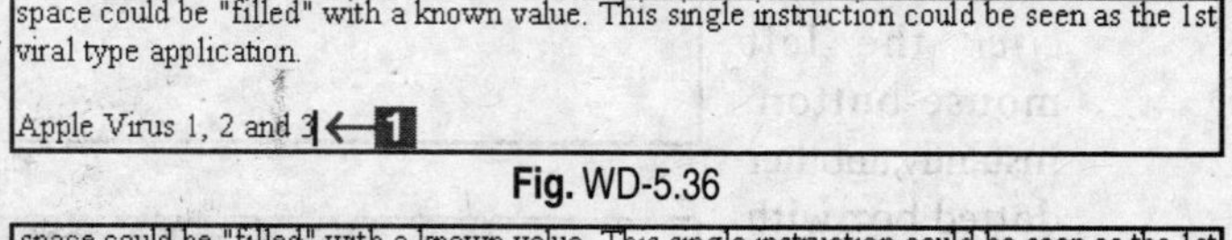

Fig. WD-5.36

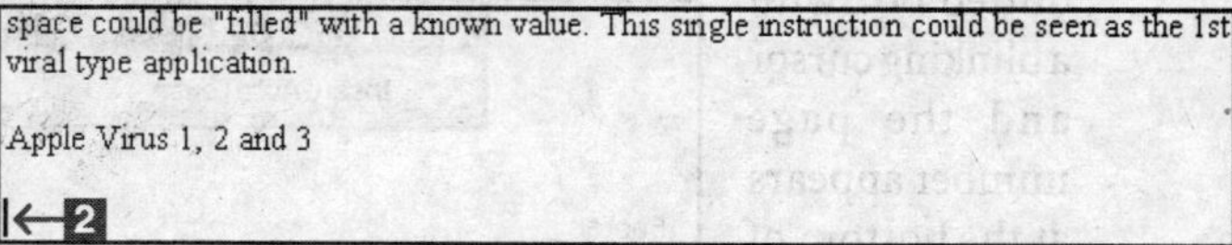

Fig. WD-5.37

2. *Press* the **Enter** key two times. The blinking cursor jumps two lines below (Fig. WD-5.37).
3. *Move* the mouse-pointer over the **Table** option on the Menu bar and *click* the left mouse-button. A pull-down menu appears (Fig. WD-5.38).
4. Inside the pull-down menu, *click* over the **Insert** option. A sub-menu appears (Fig. WD-5.38).
5. In the sub-menu, *click* the left mouse-button on the **Table** option (Fig.WD-5.38). Immediately, an **Insert Table** box appears on the screen (Fig.WD-5.39). The **Insert Table** box has a number of options. Using these options, you can specify the number of columns and rows and other details for your table. Beside each option, there is a rectangular box with two scroll buttons (⬍) (Fig.WD-5.40).

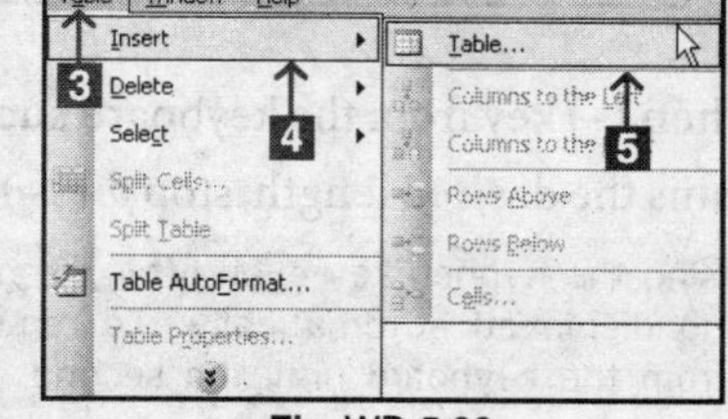

Fig. WD-5.38

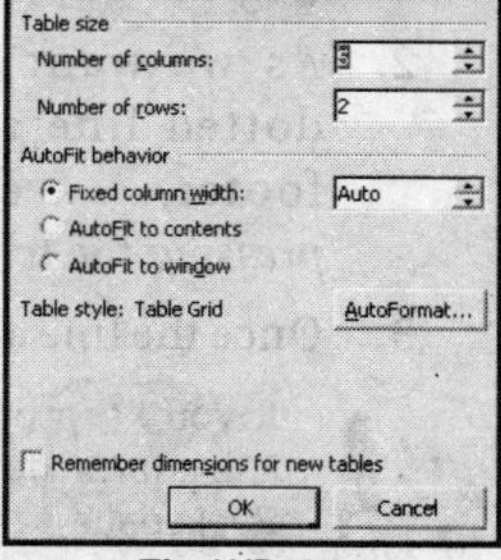

Fig. WD-5.39

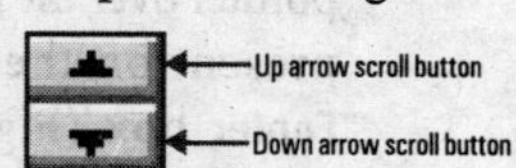

Fig. WD-5.40

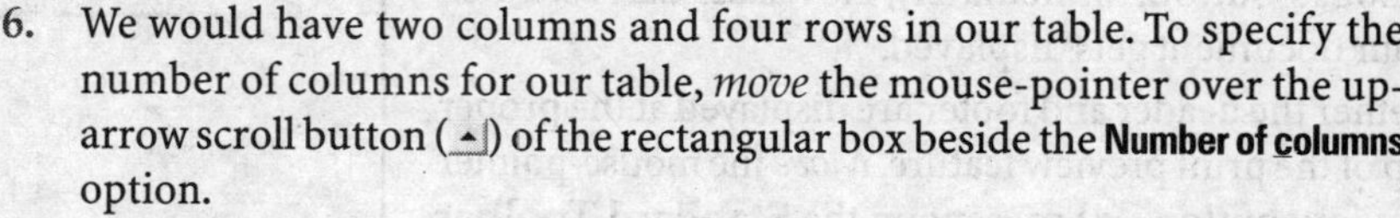

6. We would have two columns and four rows in our table. To specify the number of columns for our table, *move* the mouse-pointer over the up-arrow scroll button (▲) of the rectangular box beside the **Number of columns** option.
7. Keep *clicking* the left mouse-button over the up-arrow scroll button (▲) until the **Number of columns** option displays **2** (Fig.WD-5.41).

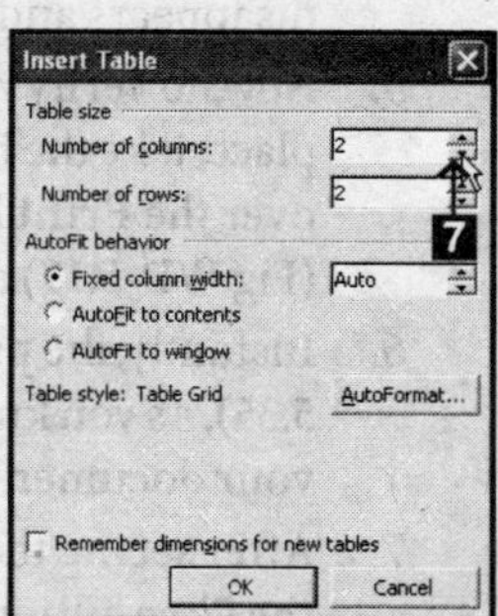

Fig. WD-5.41

If you click more by mistake then you would get more number of columns in the box than required. In that case, start clicking on the down-arrow scroll button (▼) to return to number 3.

8. Now, to specify the number of rows needed for our table, we will use the **Number of rows** option of the **Insert Table** box.
9. *Move* the mouse-pointer over the up-arrow scroll button (▲) of the box beside the **Number of rows** option. Keep *clicking* the left mouse-button on it until the number increases to **4** (Fig.W-5.42).

> If you click more by mistake then you would get more number of rows than required. In that case, start clicking on the down arrow-scroll button (▼) to come back to number 4.

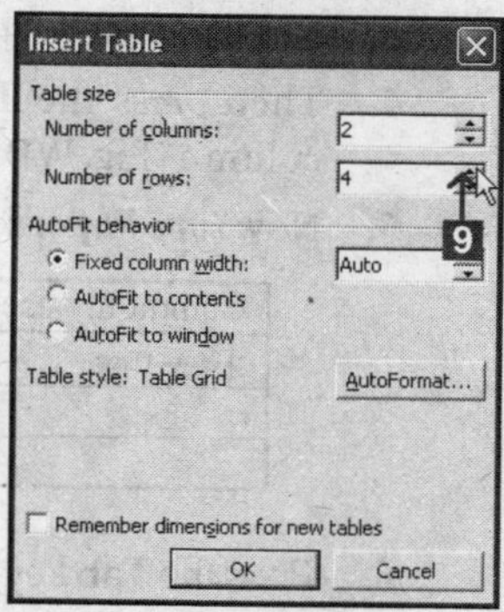

Fig. WD-5.42

10. Having specified the number of columns and rows for your table, *move* the mouse-pointer over the **OK** button in the **Insert Table** box and *click* the left mouse-button (Fig.WD-5.43).

    Immediately, the **Insert Table** box disappears from the screen, and a table is inserted at the end of the **History of Computer Virus** document (Fig.WD-5.44). This table has three columns and four rows. The cursor is blinking in the first row of the first column of the table.

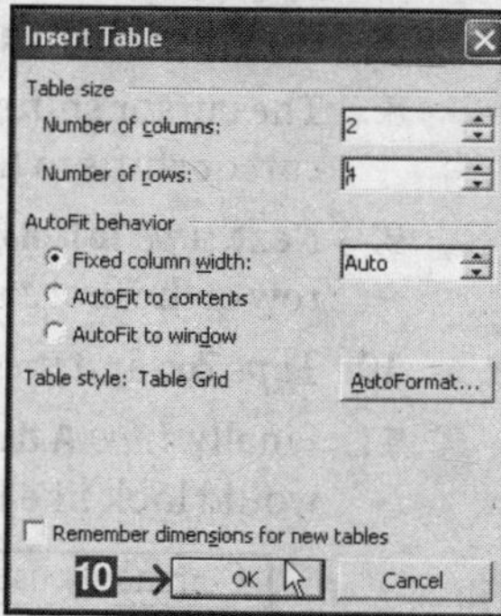

Fig. WD-5.43

Fig. WD-5.44

Entering Text into Table

Let us now fill the table with the following text related with computer virus.

Commonly used Terms	Meaning
Payload	The malicious activity that a virus performs.
Quarantine	To isolate files suspected to contain a virus.
Zoo	A threat that exists only in antivirus labs.

Now, to enter the above details in the table, undertake the following steps:

1. As the cursor is blinking in the first row of the first column of table (Fig.WD-5.44), the first text entry will be made at this position. *Type* **Commonly used Terms** from the keyboard (Fig.WD-5.45). This text gets displayed in the first row of the first column of your table.
2. After writing the text in the first column, *press* the **Tab** key from the keyboard. This makes the cursor jump to the second column (Fig.WD-5.45).

Fig. WD-5.45

3. Now *type* the second column heading, i.e. **Meaning** (Fig. WD-5.46).
4. Then *press* the **Tab** key again. The cursor now starts blinking in the second row of the first column (Fig. WD-5.46).
5. Now *type* **Payload** at the place where the cursor is blinking.

Commonly used Terms	Meaning ← 3
← Cursor	

Fig. WD-5.46

6. *Press* the **Tab** key from the keyboard. The cursor jumps from the second row first column to the second row second column.
7. Now, *type* **The malicious activity that virus performs** and *press* the **Tab** key.
8. The cursor shifts to the third row first column. Now, *type* **Quarantine** and then *press* the **Tab** key. The cursor shifts to the third row second column.
9. Next, *type* **To isolate file suspected to contain virus** and *press* the **Tab** key. The cursor shifts to the fourth row of the first column.
10. *Type* **Zoo** and *press* the **Tab** key once. The cursor shifts to the fourth row of the second column.
11. Finally, *type* **A threat that exists only in antivirus labs.** Once you have entered the all details, the table would look like Fig.WD-5.47.

Commonly used Terms	Meaning
Payload	The malicious activity that a virus performs.
Quarantine	To isolate files suspected to contain a virus.
Zoo	A threat that exists only in antivirus labs.

Fig. WD-5.47

Sometimes you need to expand your existing table for accommodating more details. For that, you have to insert new rows and columns in the table. But, before learning how to insert columns and rows into an existing table, let us refresh the procedure of selecting the text (a word, a sentence or a paragraph).

Selecting Text in a Table

How to Select a Word

Suppose you want to select the word **Payload** in the table. For this, you may proceed as follows:

1. *Move* the mouse-pointer(I) to the left of the word **Payload** (Fig.WD-5.48) and *press* the left mouse-button. A blinking cursor appears at that position.

Commonly used Terms	Meaning
1 → Payload	The malicious activity that a virus performs.
Quarantine	To isolate files suspected to contain a virus.
Zoo	A threat that exists only in antivirus labs.

Fig. WD-5.48

2. Now *move* the mouse-pointer over the blinking cursor and *press* the left mouse-button.

3. Keeping the left mouse button *pressed*, *drag* the mouse on the mouse pad till the word **Payload** gets highlighted (Fig.WD-5.49).

Commonly used Terms	Meaning
Payload ← (3)	The malicious activity that a virus performs.
Quarantine	To isolate files suspected to contain a virus.
Zoo	A threat that exists only in antivirus labs.

Fig. WD-5.49

4. After highlighting the desired word, *release* the left mouse-button.
5. To remove the highlight from the word **Payload**, *click* the left mouse-button anywhere else in your document.

To quickly highlight a word in a table or document, move the mouse-pointer anywhere over the word and double-click the left mouse-button.

How to Select a Sentence

Suppose, you want to select the text, **Quarantine To isolate files suspected to contain a virus**, in the third row of your table. You can do so by undertaking the following steps.

1. *Move* the mouse-pointer to the left of the text **Quarantine** and *click* the left mouse-button (Fig.WD-5.50). A blinking cursor appears at that place.

Commonly used Terms	Meaning
Payload	The malicious activity that a virus performs.
(1) → Quarantine	To isolate files suspected to contain a virus.
Zoo	A threat that exists only in antivirus labs.

Fig. WD-5.50

2. Now *place* the mouse-pointer over the blinking cursor.
3. Keeping the left mouse-button *pressed*, *drag* the mouse-pointer over the line, i.e. whole of the third row of your table, to highlight it (Fig.WD-5.51).

Commonly used Terms	Meaning
Payload	The malicious activity that a virus performs.
(3) → Quarantine	To isolate files suspected to contain a virus.
Zoo	A threat that exists only in antivirus labs.

Fig. WD-5.51

4. When the required line gets highlighted, *release* the left mouse-button.
5. For removing the highlight from the line, *move* the mouse-pointer anywhere else in the document and *click* the left mouse-button.

For quickly selecting a sentence in your document, first press the Ctrl key. Keeping it pressed, click the left mouse button once on the sentence. The required sentence gets selected.

Inserting Rows in an Existing Table

How to Insert a Row between two Existing Rows in Table

Sometimes you may need to add some new information in your table. You can include new information in your table by inserting rows and columns. You can insert a new row before or after an existing row or at the end of table. Let us now undertake the following steps to insert a new row after the third row of our table.

1. *Move* the mouse-pointer in the third row of the first column, and *place* it to the right of the text **Quarantine.** Then *click* the left mouse-button. Immediately, a blinking cursor appears (Fig. WD-5.52).

Commonly used Terms	Meaning
Payload	The malicious activity that a virus performs.
Quarantine ← 1	To isolate files suspected to contain a virus.
Zoo	A threat that exists only in antivirus labs.

Fig. WD-5.52

2. Now *move* the mouse-pointer over the **Table** option of the Menu bar, and *click* the left mouse-button. Immediately, a pull-down menu gets displayed (Fig. WD-5.53).
3. Inside the pull-down menu, *move* the mouse-pointer over the **Insert** option (Fig. WD-5.53). A sub-menu appears next to the pull-down menu.
4. In the sub-menu, *move* the mouse pointer over the **Rows Below** option and *click* the left mouse button (Fig. WD-5.53).
5. A new row gets inserted after the third row in your table (Fig. WD-5.54). The table now has five rows and two columns.

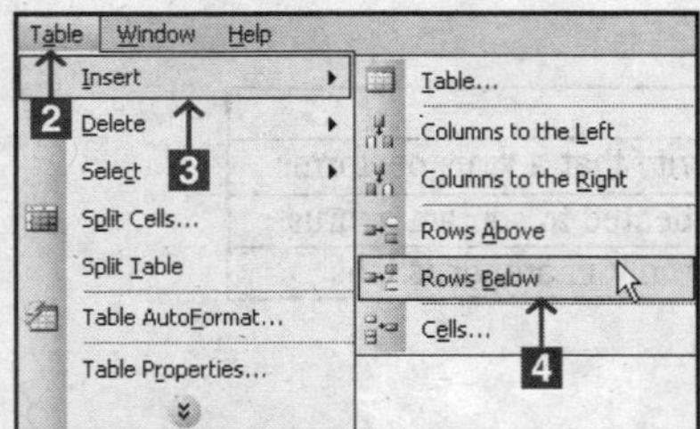

Fig. WD-5.53

Commonly used Terms	Meaning
Payload	The malicious activity that a virus performs.
Quarantine	To isolate files suspected to contain a virus.
← New row	
Zoo	A threat that exists only in antivirus labs.

Fig. WD-5.54

You can also insert rows at the end of the table. The following topic tells you how to go about doing this.

How to Insert Rows at the End of Table

Undertake the following steps to insert a row at the end of table.

Commonly used Terms	Meaning
Payload	The malicious activity that a virus performs.
Quarantine	To isolate files suspected to contain a virus.
Zoo	A threat that exists only in antivirus labs. ← 1

Fig. WD-5.55

1. Start with your screen displaying Fig. WD-5.54. *Move* the mouse-pointer at the end of the text **A threat that exists only in antivirus labs** present in the fifth row of the second column and *click* the left mouse-button. Immediately, a blinking cursor appears at that place (Fig. WD-5.55).
2. *Click* over the **Table** option of the Menu bar. Immediately, a pull-down menu appears (Fig. WD-5.56).
3. Inside the pull-down menu, *move* the mouse-pointer over the **Insert** option (Fig. WD-5.56). A sub-menu appears beside the pull-down menu.

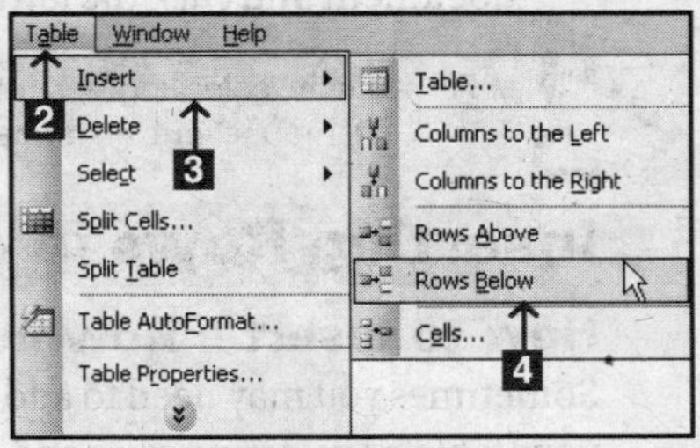

Fig. WD-5.56

4. In the sub-menu, *move* the mouse-pointer over the **Rows Below** option and *click* the left mouse button (Fig.WD-5.56).
5. Immediately a new row appears at the end of the table.

Now your table has six rows and two columns (Fig.WD-5.57).

Commonly used Terms	Meaning
Payload	The malicious activity that a virus performs.
Quarantine	To isolate files suspected to contain a virus.
Zoo	A threat that exists only in antivirus labs.

Fig. WD-5.57

Whenever you insert a new row, it appears highlighted in the table. To remove highlight from the newly inserted row, click anywhere in your document.

Inserting Columns

How to Insert a Column in the Table

You can also add new columns in a table. The new column would be placed to the left or right side of an existing column or after the last column in the table. Let us now learn to add a new column between two existing columns in our table.

1. Start with your screen displaying Fig. WD-5.57. *Move* the mouse-pointer to the right of the text **Commonly used terms** and *click* the left mouse-button. A blinking cursor appears at that place (Fig.WD-5.58).

Commonly used Terms ← 1	Meaning
Payload	The malicious activity that a virus performs.
Quarantine	To isolate files suspected to contain a virus.
Zoo	A threat that exists only in antivirus labs.

Fig. WD-5.58

2. Now *click* over the **Table** option of the Menu bar. Immediately, a pull-down menu gets displayed (Fig.WD-5.59).
3. Inside the pull-down menu, *move* the mouse-pointer over the **Insert** option (Fig.WD-5.59).
4. A sub-menu appears next to the pull-down menu. In the sub-menu, *move* the mouse-pointer over the **Columns to the Right** option and *click* the left mouse-button (Fig.WD-5.59).
5. In your table, a new column gets inserted between the existing columns **Commonly used Terms** and **Meaning**. Your table now has three columns and six rows (Fig.WD-5.60).

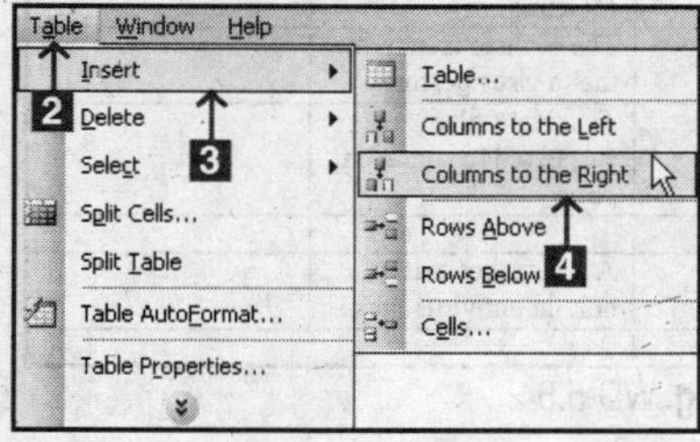

Fig. WD-5.59

New Column

Commonly used Terms		Meaning
Payload		The malicious activity that a virus performs.
Quarantine		To isolate files suspected to contain a virus.
Zoo		A threat that exists only in antivirus labs.

Fig. WD-5.60

How to Insert a Column after the Last Column

If you wish to insert a new column after the last column of your table, undertake the following steps:

1. Start with your screen displaying Fig. WD-5.60. *Move* the mouse-pointer to the end of the first row in third column and *click* the left mouse-button. Immediately, a blinking cursor appears at that point (Fig.WD-5.61).

Commonly used Terms		Meaning ← 1
Payload		The malicious activity that a virus performs.
Quarantine		To isolate files suspected to contain a virus.
Zoo		A threat that exists only in antivirus labs.

Fig. WD-5.61

2. Now *click* over the **Table** option of the Menu bar. Immediately, a pull-down menu appears on the screen (Fig.WD-5.62).
3. Inside the pull-down menu, *move* the mouse-pointer over the **Insert** option (Fig.WD-5.62).
4. A sub-menu appears next to the pull-down menu. In the sub-menu, *move* the mouse-pointer over the **Columns to the Right** option and *click* the left mouse-button (Fig. WD-5.62).
5. A new column gets inserted after the existing last column in your table. Now your table, as shown in Fig. WD-5.63, has six rows and four columns.

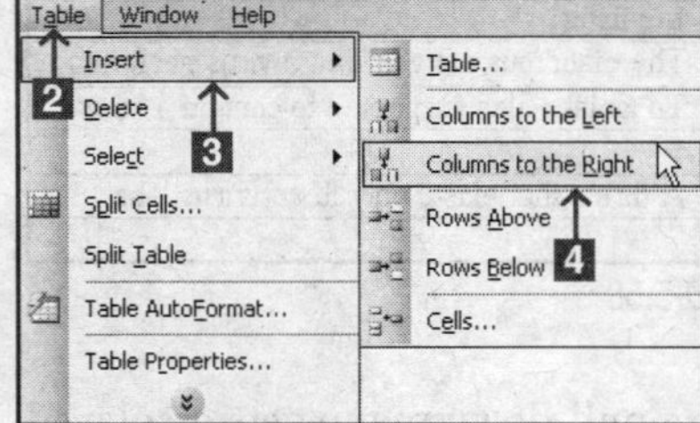

Fig. WD-5.62

Commonly used Terms		Meaning	New Column
Payload		The malicious activity that a virus performs.	
Quarantine		To isolate files suspected to contain a virus.	
Zoo		A threat that exists only in antivirus labs.	

Fig. WD-5.63

Deleting a Row

Sometimes, you may need to delete one or more rows from your table. Let us now learn how to delete an existing row from our table. Suppose, you wish to delete the fourth row from your table. To do so, undertake the following steps:

1. Start with your screen displaying Fig. WD-5.63. *Move* the mouse-pointer to the fourth row of the first column of your table, and *click* the left mouse-button. Immediately, a blinking cursor appears (Fig. W-5.64).

Commonly used Terms		Meaning	
Payload		The malicious activity that a virus performs.	
Quarantine		To isolate files suspected to contain a virus.	
← 1			
Zoo		A threat that exists only in antivirus labs.	

Fig. WD-5.64

2. Now *click* on the **Table** option of Menu bar. A pull-down menu appears (Fig.WD-5.65).

3. Inside the pull-down menu, *move* the mouse-pointer over the **Delete** option (Fig.WD-5.65).
4. A sub-menu appears next to the pull-down menu. In the sub-menu, *move* the mouse-pointer over the **Rows** option and *click* the left mouse-button (Fig.WD-5.65). The fourth row disappears from the table (Fig.WD-5.66). Now, your table is left with five rows and four columns.

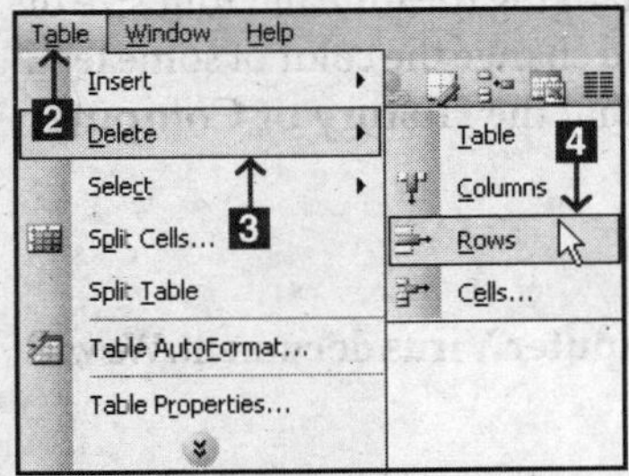

Fig. WD-5.65

Commonly used Terms		Meaning	
Payload		The malicious activity that a virus performs.	
Quarantine		To isolate files suspected to contain a virus.	
Zoo		A threat that exists only in antivirus labs.	

Fig. WD-5.66

Deleting a Column

Suppose, you want to delete the column which you had earlier inserted between **Commonly used Terms** and **Meaning** columns. It is the second column of your table. To delete the second column, undertake the following steps:

1. *Move* the mouse-pointer to the first row of the second column of your table, and *click* the left mouse-button. Immediately, a blinking cursor appears at that position (Fig.WD-5.67).

Commonly used Terms		Meaning	
Payload		The malicious activity that a virus performs.	
Quarantine		To isolate files suspected to contain a virus.	
Zoo		A threat that exists only in antivirus labs.	

Fig. WD-5.67

2. Now *move* the mouse-pointer over the **Table** option of the Menu bar, and *click* the left mouse-button. Immediately, a pull-down menu gets displayed (Fig. WD-5.68).
3. Inside the pull-down menu, *move* the mouse-pointer over the **Delete** option (Fig.WD-5.68).
4. A sub-menu appears beside the pull-down menu. In the sub-menu, *move* the mouse pointer over the **Columns** option and *click* the left mouse-button (Fig.WD-5.68). Immediately, the desired column, i.e. column number two, gets deleted and the third column takes its place. Thus, the third column becomes the second column, and so on. Our table is now left with three columns and five rows as shown in Fig.WD-5.69.

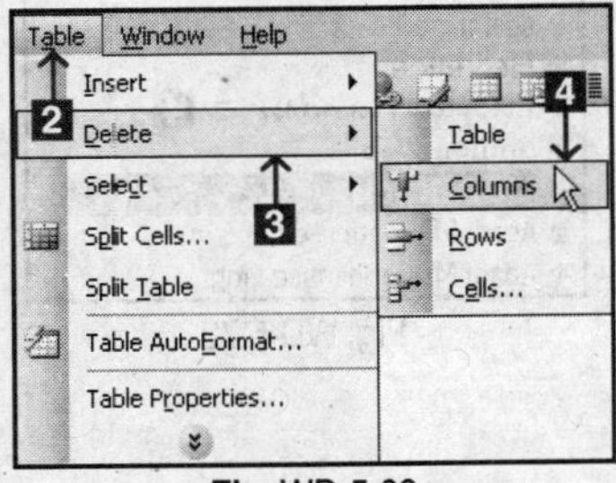

Fig. WD-5.68

Commonly used Terms	Meaning	
Quarantine	To isolate files suspected to contain a virus.	
Zoo	A threat that exists only in antivirus labs.	

Fig. WD-5.69

Formatting the Document

You can use Microsoft Word to impose spectacular formatting on any documents. With few mouse clicks, you can create a document that looks like a graphic designer's spread for the world's most popular magazine. In this section, we discuss various formatting options like changing the font and font size of some text, italicizing and underlining some text, highlighting the text and change the color of some text. While learning the steps of applying formatting features, we assume that the **History of Computer Virus** document is open on the monitor of your computer.

Changing the Font

Let us change the font and font size of the first line of the **History of Computer Virus** document. We will set this line as a heading of the document.

1. *Move* the mouse-pointer to the left of the text **Earliest history of....** and *click* the left mouse button. Instantly a blinking cursor appears at that place (Fig. WD-5.70).

1 → Earliest history of viral programs

Viral programs have a long, and sometimes honourable, history. In the earliest computers it was vital that you knew the initial state of the computer. It was also important that no remnants of other programs remain. An instruction was often implemented that had only one function: it would copy itself to the next memory location and then proceed on to that location. Thus, by starting this instruction at the beginning of memory, the entire memory space could be "filled" with a known value. This single instruction could be seen as the 1st viral type application.

Fig. WD-5.70

2. Keeping the left mouse-button *pressed*, *drag* the mouse in such a way that the first line gets highlighted (Fig. WD-5.71).

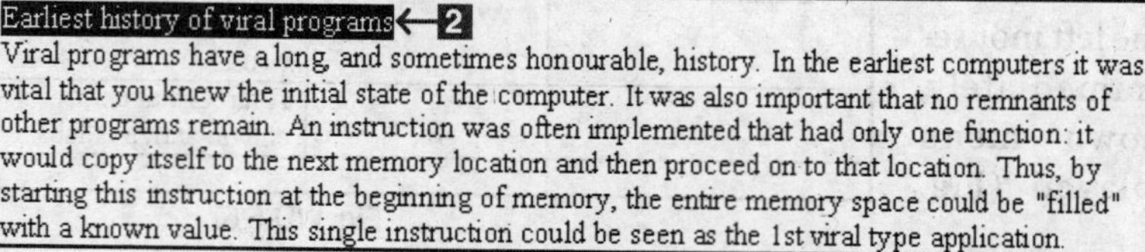

Earliest history of viral programs ← 2

Viral programs have a long, and sometimes honourable, history. In the earliest computers it was vital that you knew the initial state of the computer. It was also important that no remnants of other programs remain. An instruction was often implemented that had only one function: it would copy itself to the next memory location and then proceed on to that location. Thus, by starting this instruction at the beginning of memory, the entire memory space could be "filled" with a known value. This single instruction could be seen as the 1st viral type application.

Fig. WD-5.71

3. Take care that the first line remains highlighted. Next, *move* the mouse-pointer over the down-arrow button (⌄) beside the **Font** box, present on the **Formatting Toolbar**. Instantly, a pull-down menu with names of several fonts with their font face appears (Fig. WD-5.72).

4. Among the displayed fonts, *move* the mouse-pointer over the font name **USA Black** and *click* the left mouse-button (Fig. WD-5.73).

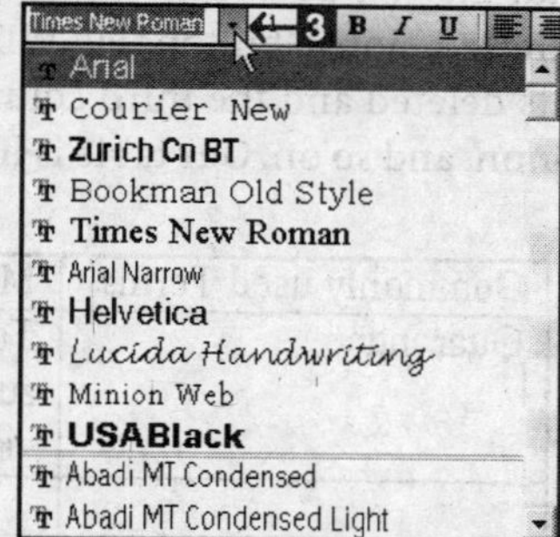

Fig. WD-5.72

Fig. WD-5.73

5. The pull-down menu disappears and the font of the selected text, i.e. first line, changes. *Click* anywhere in the document to remove the highlight. After removing the highlight the first line appears like Fig.WD-5.74.

Earliest history of viral programs
Viral programs have a long, and sometimes honourable, history. In the earliest computers it was vital that you knew the initial state of the computer. It was also important that no remnants of other programs remain. An instruction was often implemented that had only one function: it would copy itself to the next memory location and then proceed on to that location. Thus, by starting this instruction at the beginning of memory, the entire memory space could be "filled" with a known value. This single instruction could be seen as the 1st viral type application.

Fig. WD-5.74

Changing the Font Size

Sometimes you may need to set certain text in bigger size to make it stand out in your document. This you can do by increasing the font size of the desired text. Suppose you wish to increase the size of the first line in your document to make it distinct from the rest of the text. To do so, undertake the following steps:

1. Repeat Steps 1 and 2 of the section **Changing the Font** to select the first line in your document. The selected first line appears as shown in Fig. WD-5.75.

Earliest history of viral programs ← 1
Viral programs have a long, and sometimes honourable, history. In the earliest computers it was vital that you knew the initial state of the computer. It was also important that no remnants of other programs remain. An instruction was often implemented that had only one function: it would copy itself to the next memory location and then proceed on to that location. Thus, by starting this instruction at the beginning of memory, the entire memory space could be "filled" with a known value. This single instruction could be seen as the 1st viral type application.

Fig. WD-5.75

2. Now *move* the mouse-pointer over the down-arrow button (▾) of the **Font size** box and *click* the left mouse-button. A thin pull-down menu appears (Fig. WD-5.76.)
3. In the pull-down menu, *move* the mouse-pointer over a bigger font size, say **14**, and *click* the left mouse-button (Fig. WD-5.77.)
4. The pull-down menu disappears and the size of the selected text changes. *Click* anywhere in the document to remove the highlight from the text. The changed text appears like Fig.WD-5.78.

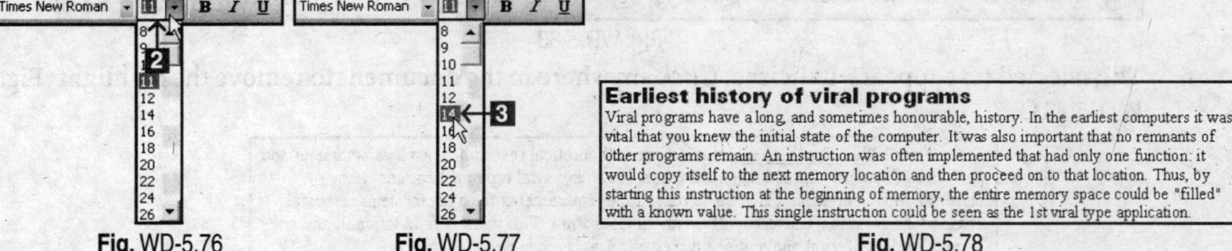

Earliest history of viral programs
Viral programs have a long, and sometimes honourable, history. In the earliest computers it was vital that you knew the initial state of the computer. It was also important that no remnants of other programs remain. An instruction was often implemented that had only one function: it would copy itself to the next memory location and then proceed on to that location. Thus, by starting this instruction at the beginning of memory, the entire memory space could be "filled" with a known value. This single instruction could be seen as the 1st viral type application.

Fig. WD-5.76 **Fig.** WD-5.77 **Fig.** WD-5.78

Underlining and Italicizing the Text

Underlining and Italicizing the text is just another way to make your document impressive. You can use these options to highlight some important text or points in your document. The underline option helps you place a line below the desired text. Using Italics option, you can make the desired text appear slightly tilted. Let us now learn the steps to use these two formatting options.

1. Start with your screen showing Fig. WD-5.78. *Move* the mouse-pointer to the left of the text **Fred Cohen** and *click* the left mouse-button. Immediately, a blinking cursor appears. Keeping the left mouse button *pressed*, *drag* the mouse-pointer in such a way that text **Fred Cohen** gets selected (Fig. WD-5.79).

> In the early 1980s, Fred Cohen did widespread theoretical research, as well as setting up and performing numerous practical experiments, regarding viral type applications. His dissertation was presented in 1986 as part of the requirements for a doctorate in electrical engineering from the University of Southern California. This work is foundational, and any serious student of viral applications disregards it at his own risk.

Fig. WD-5.79

2. *Move* the mouse-pointer over the **Underline** button (U) present on the **Formatting Toolbar** and *click* the left mouse-button (Fig.WD-5.80).

Fig. WD-5.80

3. A line appears under the selected text. *Click* anywhere in the document to remove the highlight from the text (Fig.WD-5.81).

> In the early 1980s, <u>Fred Cohen</u> did widespread theoretical research, as well as setting up and performing numerous practical experiments, regarding viral type applications. His dissertation was presented in 1986 as part of the requirements for a doctorate in electrical engineering from the University of Southern California. This work is foundational, and any serious student of viral applications disregards it at his own risk.

Fig. WD-5.81

4. Let us now italicize some text. Suppose you want to italicize first two lines of the third paragraph. To do so, *move* the mouse-pointer before the text **Dr. Cohen defines computer virus...** in the first line of the third paragraph and *click* the left mouse button. A blinking cursor appears. Keeping the left mouse-button *pressed*, *drag* the mouse-pointer in such a way that the text till **accepted as a standard** in the second line gets selected (Fig.WD-5.82).

> In the early 1980s, <u>Fred Cohen</u> did widespread theoretical research, as well as setting up and performing numerous practical experiments, regarding viral type applications. His dissertation was presented in 1986 as part of the requirements for a doctorate in electrical engineering from the University of Southern California. This work is foundational, and any serious student of viral applications disregards it at his own risk.
> Dr. Cohen defines computer virus as "a program that can 'infect' other applications by modifying them to include a ... version of itself" is generally accepted as a standard. On occasion it presents problems with the acceptance of, say, boot sector viral programs and entities such as the Internet/UNIX/Morris worm. However, his work did experimentally demonstrate and theoretically prove many vital issues. Some popular computer viruses are a follows:

Fig. WD-5.82

5. *Move* the mouse-pointer over the **Italic** button (I) present on the **Standard Toolbar** and *click* the left mouse-button (Fig. WD-5.83).

Fig. WD-5.83

6. The selected text appears italicized. *Click* anywhere in the document to remove the highlight (Fig. WD-5.84).

> In the early 1980s, <u>Fred Cohen</u> did widespread theoretical research, as well as setting up and performing numerous practical experiments, regarding viral type applications. His dissertation was presented in 1986 as part of the requirements for a doctorate in electrical engineering from the University of Southern California. This work is foundational, and any serious student of viral applications disregards it at his own risk.
> *Dr. Cohen defines computer virus as "a program that can 'infect' other applications by modifying them to include a ... version of itself" is generally accepted as a standard.* On occasion it presents problems with the acceptance of, say, boot sector viral programs and entities such as the Internet/UNIX/Morris worm. However, his work did experimentally demonstrate and theoretically prove many vital issues. Some popular computer viruses are a follows:

Fig. WD-5.84

Working with Colors

We all are fascinated by colors. You can also use colours in your document text to enhance its appeal. MS Word allows you to add colors to the selected text in two ways – by highlighting it with a desired color or by changing the color of its font. Let us learn both these ways.

Highlighting the text

Highlighting the text means adding color to the background of the text without changing the original color of the text font. Usually, we use the marker to highlight some important text in the textbook to make it stand out from rest of the text. The marker only changes the colour of the background of the text without changing the original colour of the font. Now, let us highlight words **Earliest History** in the first line of the document. To do so, undertake the following steps:

1. Start with your screen displaying Fig. WD-5.84. *Move* the mouse-pointer to the beginning of the first line in the document and *click* the left mouse-button. Keeping the left mouse-button *pressed*, *drag* the mouse in such a way that text **Earliest history** gets highlighted (Fig. WD-5.85).

Earliest history of viral programs
Viral programs have a long, and sometimes honourable, history. In the earliest computers it was vital that you knew the initial state of the computer. It was also important that no remnants of other programs remain. An instruction was often implemented that had only one function: it would copy itself to the next memory location and then proceed on to that location. Thus, by starting this instruction at the beginning of memory, the entire memory space could be "filled" with a known value. This single instruction could be seen as the 1st viral type application.
In the early 1980s, Fred Cohen did extensive theoretical research, as well as setting up and performing numerous practical experiments, regarding viral type applications. His dissertation was presented in 1986 as part of the requirements for a doctorate in electrical engineering from the University of Southern California. This work is foundational, and any serious student of viral applications disregards it at his own risk.

Fig. WD-5.85

2. After highlighting the text, *move* the mouse-pointer over the down-arrow button beside the **Highlight** button ( ) of **Formatting Toolbar** (Fig. WD-5.86).
3. A small color palette appears (Fig. WD-5.86). *Click* over the desired color as shown in Fig. WD-5.87.
4. The colour palette disappears and the selected text appears highlighted in the chosen color (Fig. WD-5.88). *Click* anywhere in the document to remove the highlight. You can repeat Steps 1 to 4 to highlight any word, phrase, sentence or paragraph in a desired color in your document.

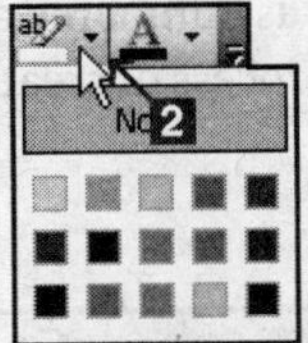

Fig. WD-5.86

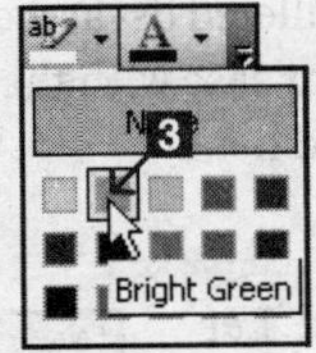

Fig. WD-5.87

Earliest history of viral programs
Viral programs have a long, and sometimes honourable, history. In the earliest computers it was vital that you knew the initial state of the computer. It was also important that no remnants of other programs remain. An instruction was often implemented that had only one function: it would copy itself to the next memory location and then proceed on to that location. Thus, by starting this instruction at the beginning of memory, the entire memory space could be "filled" with a known value. This single instruction could be seen as the 1st viral type application.

Fig. WD-5.88

Changing Font Color

Changing the font color is another way to make the document impressive. A change in the font color changes the color of the text without altering the background. Let us now learn the steps to change the colour of the font. Suppose you want to change the font color of words **viral programs** in the first line of the document. To do so, undertake the following steps:

1. Start with your screen displaying Fig. WD-5.88. *Move* the mouse-pointer to the left of the word **viral** in the first line and *click* the left mouse-button. Keeping the left mouse-button *pressed*, *drag* the mouse in such a way that words **viral programs** get highlighted (Fig. WD-5.89).

Viral programs have a long, and sometimes honourable, history. In the earliest computers it was vital that you knew the initial state of the computer. It was also important that no remnants of other programs remain. An instruction was often implemented that had only one function: it would copy itself to the next memory location and then proceed on to that location. Thus, by starting this instruction at the beginning of memory, the entire memory space could be "filled" with a known value. This single instruction could be seen as the 1st viral type application.

Fig. WD-5.89

2. Next, *click* over the down-arrow button beside the **Font Color** button (A·) of the **Formatting Toolbar** (Fig. WD-5.90).
3. A small color palette appears. *Click* over the desired color as shown in Fig.WD-5.91.
4. The color palette disappears and the font color of the selected words changes. *Click* anywhere in the document to remove the highlight from words **viral programs** that appear in the chosen colour (Fig. WD-5.92).

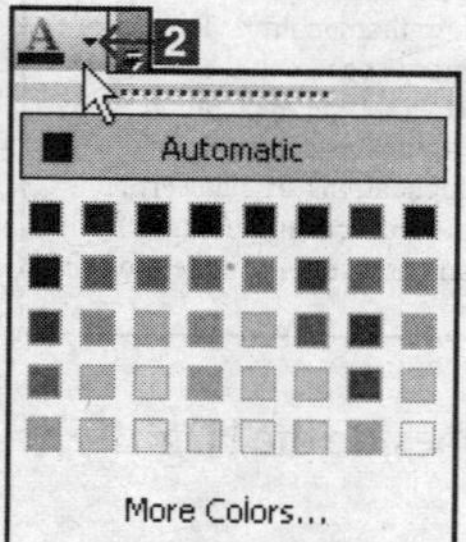

Fig. WD-5.90

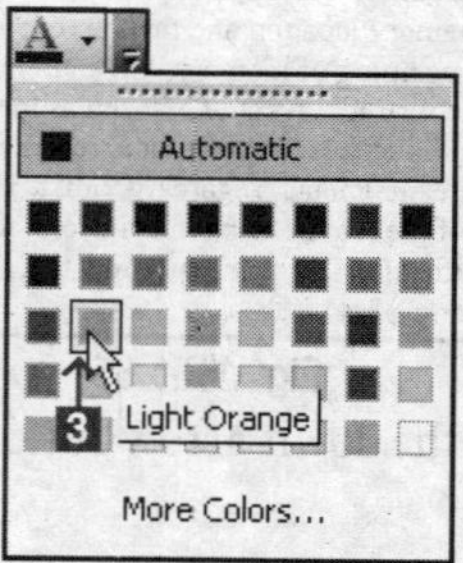

Fig. WD-5.91

Earliest history of viral programs

Viral programs have a long, and sometimes honourable, history. In the earliest computers it was vital that you knew the initial state of the computer. It was also important that no remnants of other programs remain. An instruction was often implemented that had only one function: it would copy itself to the next memory location and then proceed on to that location. Thus, by starting this instruction at the beginning of memory, the entire memory space could be "filled" with a known value. This single instruction could be seen as the 1st viral type application.
In the early 1980s, Fred Cohen did extensive theoretical research, as well as setting up and performing numerous practical experiments, regarding viral type applications. His dissertation was presented in 1986 as part of the requirements for a doctorate in electrical engineering from the University of Southern California. This work is foundational, and any serious student of viral applications disregards it at his own risk.

Fig. WD-5.92

Creating Bulleted and Numbered List

A dot or any other symbol that is placed before the text, particularly in an items list, to add emphasis is known as **bullet.** MS Word provides you with the options to create a bulleted list as well as numbered and outline list. Once you have learnt to create a bulleted list, you will feel at ease with the process of creating a numbered list. Let us now proceed with steps for creating a bulleted list.

Creating a Bulleted List

The **History of Computer Virus** document has a virus list at the end. Let us add bullets to this list through the following steps:

1. *Move* the mouse-pointer to the beginning of the virus list and *click* the left mouse-button on the left of the text **Fred Cohen.** Keeping the left mouse-button *pressed*, *drag* the mouse-pointer in such a way that the entire list gets selected (Fig. WD-5.93).
2. Now, *move* the mouse-pointer over the **Format** option of the Menu bar and *click* the left mouse-button. A pull-down menu appears (Fig. WD-5.94).

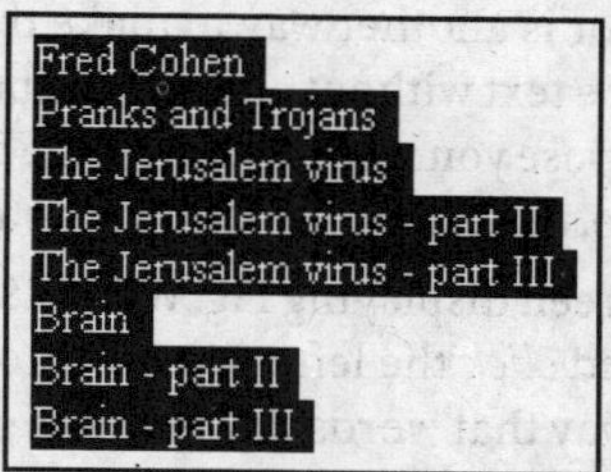

Fig. WD-5.93

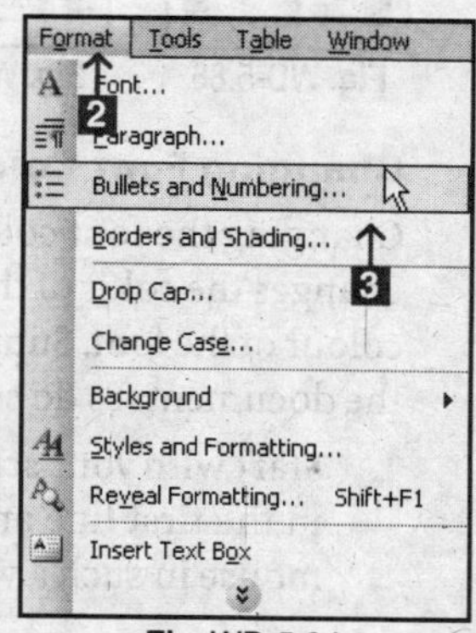

Fig. WD-5.94

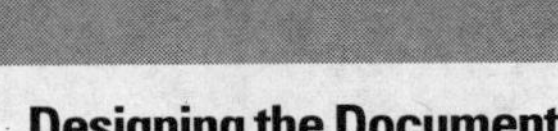

3. In the pull-down menu, *click* over the **Bullets and Numbering** option (Fig. WD-5.94).

4. The **Bullets and Numbering** box appears with the **Bulleted** tab being currently active (Fig. WD-95). Among the displayed bullet lists, *click* over any desired bullet list as shown in Fig. WD-5.95.

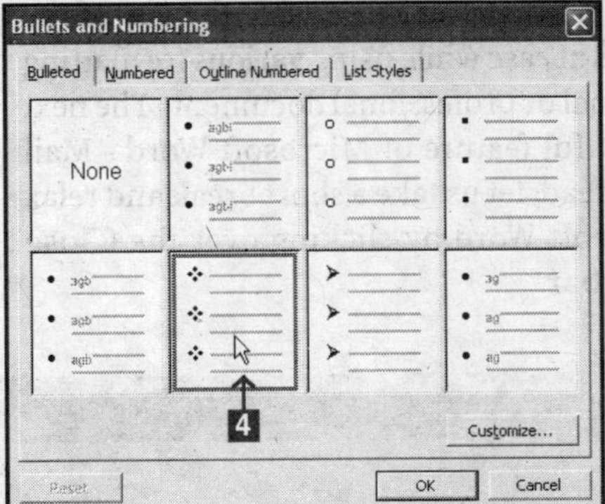

Fig. WD-5.95

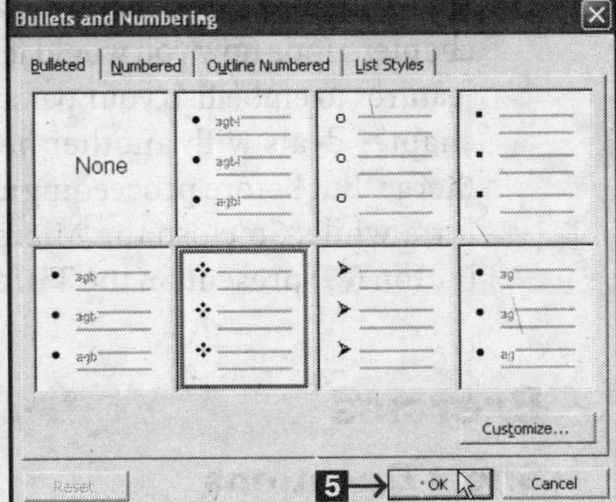

Fig. WD-5.96

5. Next, *click* over the **OK** button of the **Bullets and Numbering** box (Fig.WD-5.96).

6. The virus list appears with the selected bullets as shown in Fig. WD-5.97.

- Fred Cohen
- Pranks and Trojans
- Apple Virus 1, 2 and 3
- The Jerusalem virus
- The Jerusalem virus - part II
- The Jerusalem virus - part III
- Brain
- Brain - part II
- Brain - part III

Fig. WD-5.97

Numbered List

A numbered list is another way to add emphasis to an items list. In a numbered list, numbers are used to give serial nos. to items. We have just created a bulleted list, shown in Fig. WD-5.97. Now, to learn the use of number list, we will convert this bulleted list into a numbered list.

1. Repeat Steps 1 to 3 of the topic **Creating a Bulleted List.**
2. The **Bullets and Numbering** box appears. *Click* over the **Numbered** tab. Various types of numbered list including numbered, alphabetical and roman appear (Fig. WD-5.98).
3. *Move* the mouse-pointer over the desired numbered list as shown in Fig. W-5.99 and *click* the left mouse-button.
4. *Move* the mouse-pointer over the **OK** button and *click* the left mouse-button (Fig. WD-5.100).

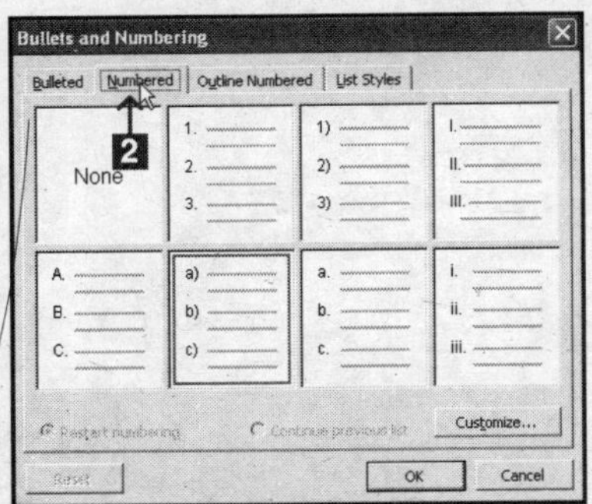

Fig. WD-5.98

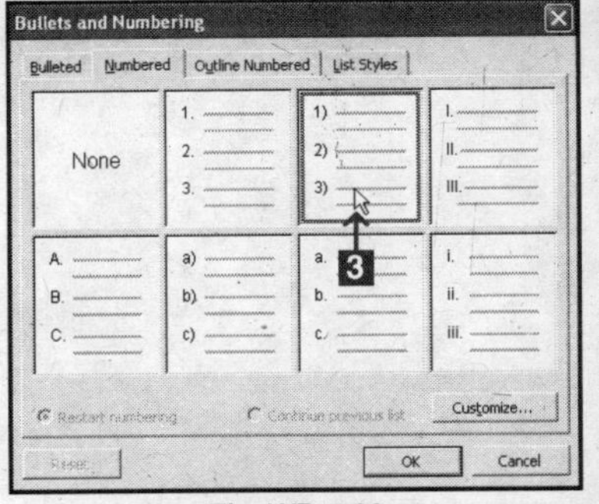

Fig. WD-5.99

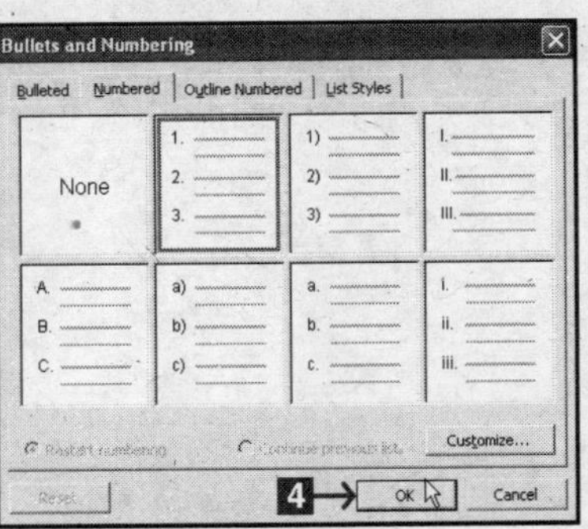

Fig. WD-5.100

5. The bulleted virus list gets converted into a numbered list as shown in Fig. W-5.101.

With the final step of creating a number list we come to the end of the chapter. Hope now you would feel at ease while using various formatting features to embellish your personal or professional document. The next chapter deals with another helpful feature of Microsoft Word - Mail Merge. But before proceeding ahead, let us take a short break and relax for a while. So close the Microsoft Word by clicking over the **Close** button (☒) present on the **Title bar**.

1) Fred Cohen
2) Pranks and Trojans
3) Apple Virus 1, 2 and 3
4) The Jerusalem virus
5) The Jerusalem virus - part II
6) The Jerusalem virus - part III
7) Brain
8) Brain - part II
9) Brain - part III

Fig. WD-5.101

Exercise

Short Questions

1. What do you understand by the term Formatting Text?
2. What does the Position option in the Page Numbers dialog box indicate?
3. What will you do to display the page number at the top of the page?
4. What is a table?

True/False

1. Rows can be inserted only at the end of the table.
2. You can delete only one row at a time.
3. Microsoft Word displays a page number automatically at the end of every page.
4. In the Page Setup dialog box we can set the margins for the document.

Mail Merge 6

IN THIS CHAPTER

- Creating a Mail Merge Project
- Creating Data Source
- Creating the Main Document
- Merging the Main Document with Data Source
- Sending the Merged Document to the printer
- Saving the Main Document
- Modifying Records in the Data Source
- Printing the New Dealer's Letter
- Changing an Existing Record
- Deleting an Existing Record
- Closing the Main Document
- Quitting Microsoft Word
- Exercise
- Summary

Suppose your company has a number of book dealers to whom you often send business letters. However, typing the same letter for different dealers becomes a very tedious job. But, do not worry. Your computer has a solution to save you from this tedious job. The solution lies in a unique and extremely useful feature of Microsoft Word called **Mail Merge**. Using this feature, you can quickly create personalized letters for every dealer in your mailing list. Let us now learn how the Mail Merge is created and executed. To use Mail Merge, you need two documents—Main Document and Data Source.

Main Document: It is a text and format file that contains any common text, like a business letter you want to send to all book dealers on your mailing list. It also contains Merge Fields to bring in information from your Data Source at appropriate positions in the document. A Merge Field is meant for inserting specific information into the Main Document from the Data Source. For example, you may have a Merge Field for city to insert a city name into the Main Document from the Data Source during Mail Merge.

Data Source: The Data Source can be any database of information, like names, addresses and other details of persons on your mailing list. It contains the information that will vary with each letter that will result from the Mail Merge procedure.

Creating a Mail Merge Project

To create a Mail Merge project, you need to undertake the following three basic tasks—

1. Create a Data Source
2. Create a Main Document
3. Merge the Main Document with the Data Source

First, you have to decide on the type of the Main Document you would like to have, such as a letter, a label or a catalogue, etc. Next, you have to collect data for the Data Source. In our case, an invitation letter addressed to all dealers will serve as the Main Document. And, the document or file containing names and addresses of all dealers will become the Data Source. Let us now go through the actual procedure for creating a Mail Merge project.

Suppose you wish to write invitation letters to all your dealers in the format shown on the next page. This letter should have the following Merge Fields—Dealer's First Name, Last Name, Company Name, Address, City, State and Reference. The information in these fields will vary from dealer to dealer.

First name	Last Name	Company Name	Address Line 1	City	State	Zip Code	Ref.
Anuj	Mathur	Anuma Books	MPR-325, Sarojani Nagar	New Delhi	Delhi	110023	12-12-2003
Neeraj	Khanna	Khanna Book Mart	20-E, Pitampura	New Delhi	Delhi	110082	12-12-2003
MVK	Shastri	Dreamtech Press	4435/7, Ansari Road	New Delhi	Delhi	110002	14-12-2003
Chandani	Gupta	Best Book Store	49, Roop Nagar	New Delhi	Delhi	110007	15-12-2003

To
Dealer's First Name Last Name
Company Name,
Address,
City,
State,
Pin Code

Sub: With Reference to your letter dated Reference

Dear Dealer's First Name

This is to inform you that our company is holding the annual meeting of all dealers at **Hotel Taj Conference Room**, Sardar Patel Marg, **New Delhi** on **7th March 2004**. You are requested to attend the meeting at **6 PM** sharp. Dinner will be served at 9 PM.

Sincerely,

V. Gupta
Managing Director
InfoBook Publishing House

For working in Mail Merge, you have to open Microsoft Word. Undertake the following steps to open the Microsoft Word.

1. *Click* on the **Start** button (start) of the **Taskbar** (Fig. WD-6.1). A push-up menu appears.
2. Inside the push up menu, *place* the mouse-pointer over the **All Programs** option. Instantly, a second menu gets displayed on the screen (Fig. WD-6.1).
3. In the second menu, *place* the mouse-pointer over the **Microsoft Office** option. A third menu gets displayed.
4. In the third menu, *move* the mouse-pointer over the **Microsoft Office Word 2003** option and *click* the left mouse-button (Fig.WD-6.1). Immediately, a blank document opens up on the screen (Fig. WD-6.2).

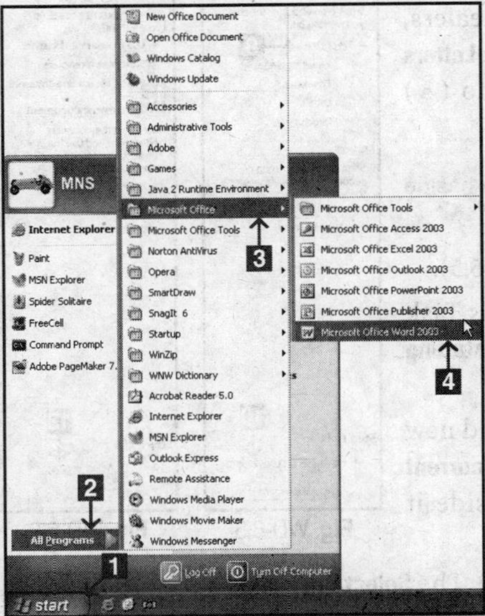

Fig. WD-6.1

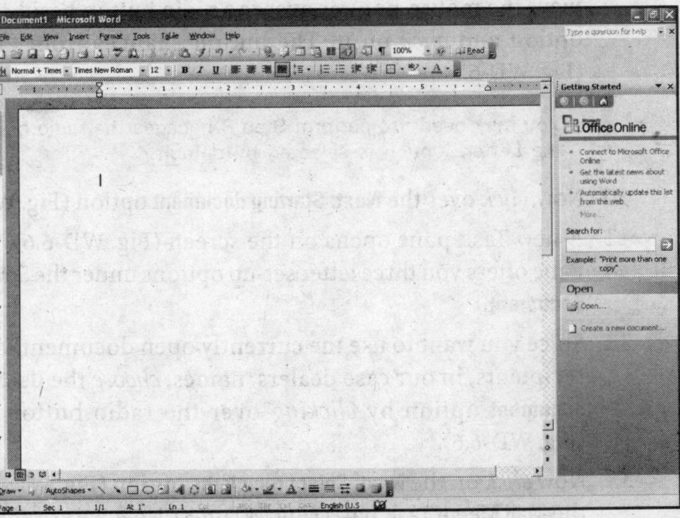
Fig. WD-6.2

5. Now, we proceed to access and use the Mail Merge option of the MS Word. *Click* on the **Tools** option of the Menu bar. Instantly, a pull-down menu gets displayed on the screen (Fig. WD-6.3).
6. Inside the pull-down menu, *move* the mouse-pointer over the **Letters and Mailings** option. A sub-menu appears on the screen (Fig. WD-6.3).
7. In the sub-menu, *move* the mouse-pointer over the **Mail Merge** option and *click* over it (Fig. WD-6.3). Immediately, **Mail Merge** Task pane gets displayed on the screen (Fig. WD-6.4).

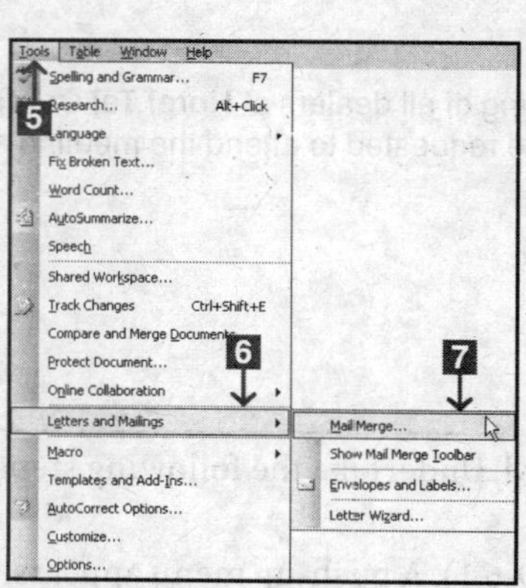

Fig. WD-6.3

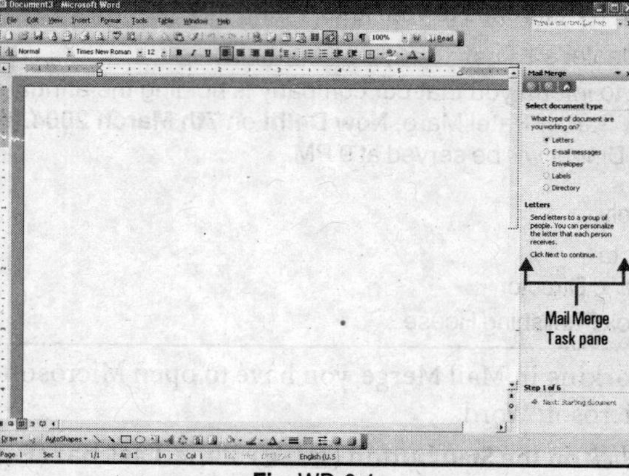

Fig. WD-6.4

HOT TIP!

Word takes the advantage of the Task pane to deliver a new and easy way to connect to your data source and create form letters, mailing labels, envelopes and directories.

8. This Task pane has a **Select document type** option that asks you about the type of document you are working on (Fig. WD-6.4).
9. Since you wish to send invitation letters to all your dealers, *move* the mouse-pointer over the radio button beside the **Letters** option and *click* on it. The button changes from (◉) to (◉) (Fig. WD-6.5).

NOTE

You may need not perform Step 8 because the radio button beside the Letters option is selected by default.

10. Now, *click* over the **Next: Starting document** option (Fig. WD-6.5).
11. A new Task pane opens on the screen (Fig. WD-6.6). This Task Pane offers you three letter set-up options under the **Select starting document.**
12. Since you want to use the currently-open document to add new recipients, in our case dealers' names, *choose* the **Use the current document** option by *clicking* over the radio button beside it (Fig. WD-6.6).

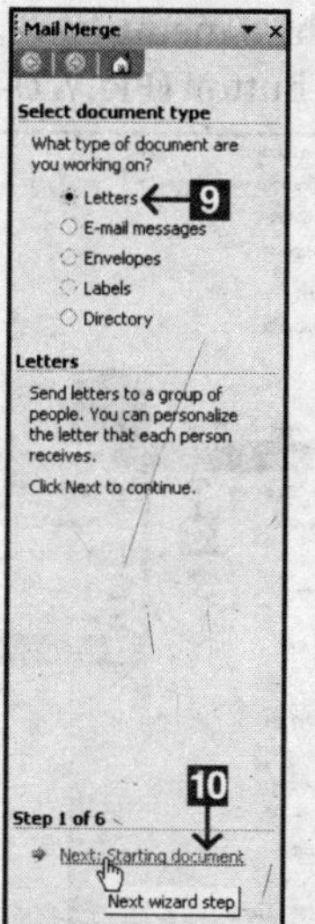

Fig. WD-6.5

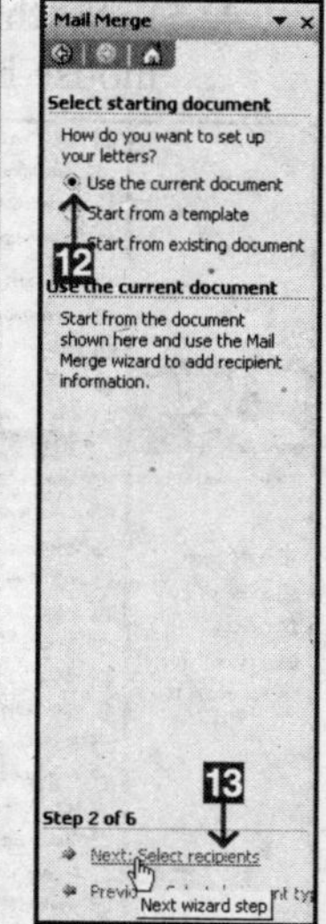

Fig. WD-6.6

13. Now *click* on the **Next: Select recipients** option (Fig. WD-6.6). The **Select Recipients** option appears on the **Mail Merge** Task pane (Fig. WD-6.8). Now, we are at the first step of creating our Data source.

You can set up your letters by three ways. The three options, shown in Fig. WD-6.7, have been discussed below briefly.

(i) Use the current document—By choosing this option you can start from the document shown here and use the Mail Merge to add recipient information.

(ii) Start from a template—In this option you can set up your letter by starting from a ready-to-use Mail Merge template that can be customized to suit your needs.

(iii) Start from existing document—By choosing this option you can start from an existing Mail Merge document and make changes to the contents or recipients.

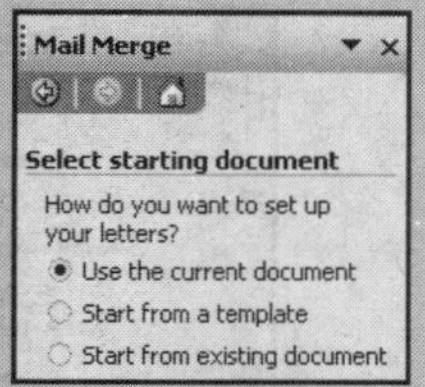

Fig. WD-6.7

Creating Data Source

As you know, a list containing addresses of our dealers will form our Data Source. While creating our Data Source, we will add or delete certain fields so that the Data Source has all the Merge Fields of our Main Document. Just to remind you, the format of the invitation letter that forms our Main Document has the following Merge Fields—Dealer's First Name Last Name, Company Name, Address, City, State, Zipcode. After inserting the required fields in the Data Source we will add the following names and addresses of our dealers in the Data Source. Data relating to a particular dealer is also known as record. Undertake the following steps to create the Data Source.

1. Start with the **Mail Merge** Task pane of (Fig. WD-6.8).
2. As you want to make a new list, *move* the mouse-pointer over the radio button beside the **Type a new list** option and *click* the left mouse-button (Fig.WD-6.9).
3. Next, *move* the mouse-pointer over the **Create** option and *click* the left mouse-button (Fig. WD-6.10). A **New Address List** dialog box gets displayed on the screen (Fig. WD-6.11).
4. In the **New Address List** dialog box, you see a number of fields with their corresponding boxes under the **Enter Address Information** option. By default, the cursor appears in the box beside the first field, **Title** (Fig. WD-6.11). Since the format of our letter that forms the Main Document does not have any field for Title, it is better to remove it. So *click* over the **Customize** button (Fig. WD-6.11). Immediately, a **Customize Address List** dialog box appears on the screen (Fig. WD-6.12).

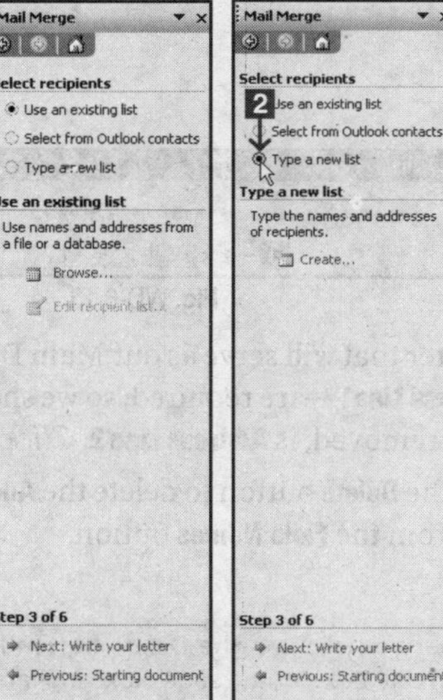

Fig. WD-6.8

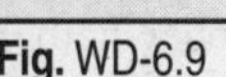

Fig. WD-6.9

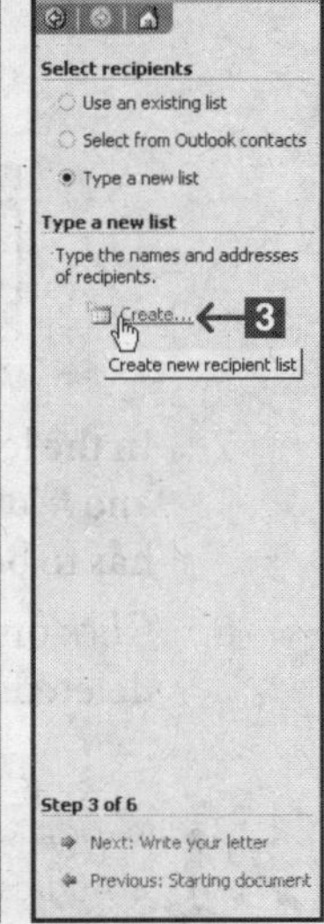

Fig. WD-6.10

5. In the **Customize Address List** dialog box, all the fields are displayed below the **Field Names** option. The field **Title** is already highlighted (Fig. WD-6.12). Now, to remove the **Title** field from our list, *move* the mouse-pointer over the **Delete** button and *click* on it (Fig. WD-6.12). Immediately, a message box (Fig. WD-6.13) appears asking us whether we want to delete the field.

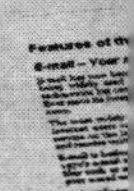

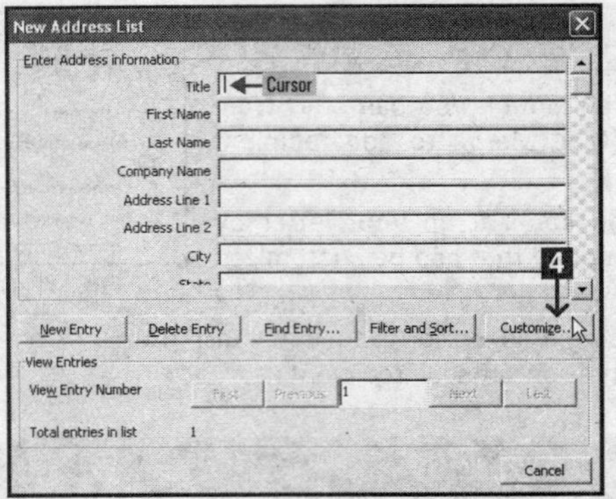

Fig. WD-6.11

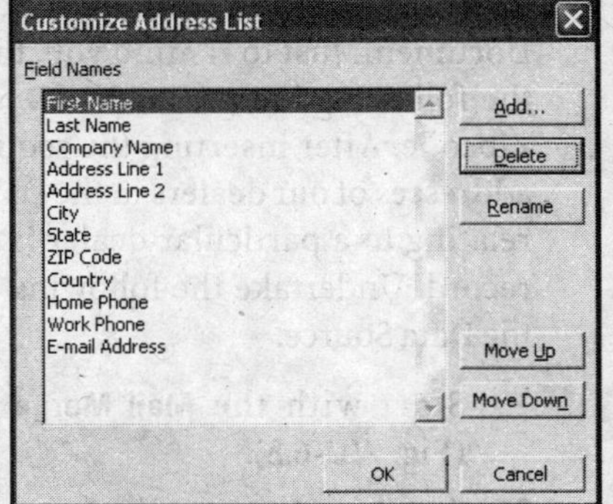

Fig. WD-6.12

6. *Click* on the **Yes** button of this dialog box (Fig. WD-6.13). The Title field gets deleted from the list and next field **First Name** gets highlighted (Fig. WD-6.14).

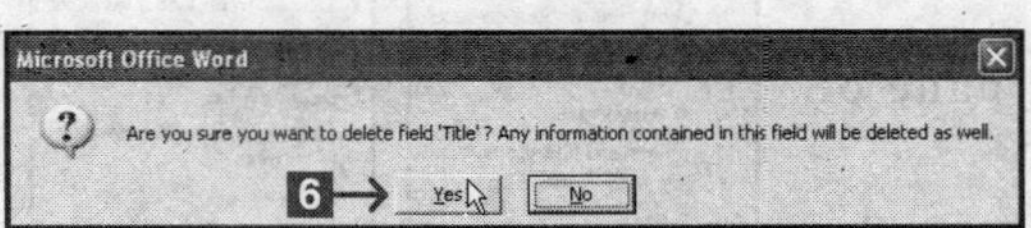

Fig. WD-6.13

Customize Address List

Field Names

First Name
Last Name
Company Name
Address Line 1
Address Line 2
City
State
ZIP Code
Country
Home Phone
Work Phone
E-mail Address

Add...
Delete
Rename
Move Up
Move Down
OK
Cancel

Fig. WD-6.14

7. In the letter that will serve as our Main Document, the fields—**First Name, Last Name, Company Name** and **Address Line1**—are required, so we should not remove them from the list. The next field, which has to be removed, is **Address Line 2**. *Click* on the **Address Line2** field to highlight it (Fig. WD-6.15).
8. *Click* on the **Delete** button to delete the **Address Line2** field (Fig. WD-6.15). The **Address Line2** field gets deleted from the **Field Names** option.

Whenever you click on the Delete button in the Customize Address List box, a message box appears on the screen, asking you whether you want to delete the highlighted field. Clicking on the Yes button of this message box will delete the highlighted field from the list.

The fields **City, State** and **Zip Code** are required by in our letter whereas the fields **Country, Home Phone, Work Phone** and **E-mail Address** can be deleted. So remove them in the same manner as explained above.

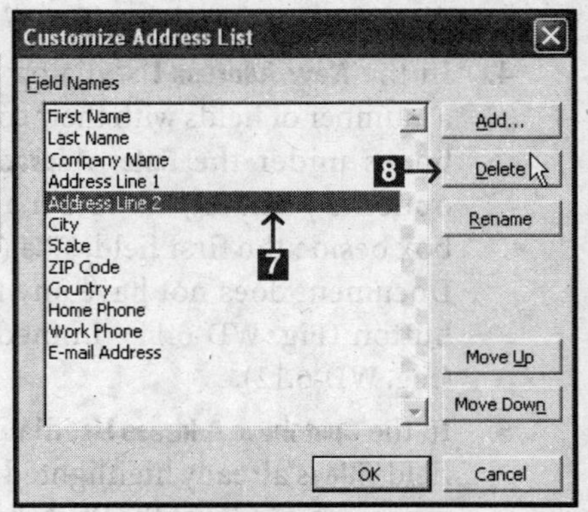

Fig. WD-6.15

After deleting the extra fields, we are left with the seven fields shown in Fig. WD-6.16. However, these seven fields do not have field, **Reference**, that is required in our letter format. So, to add the **Reference** field, undertake the following steps:

9. Start with Fig. WD-6.16. *Move* the mouse-pointer over the **Add** button of the **Customize Address List** box and *click* the left mouse-button (Fig. WD-6.17). An **Add Field** dialog box appears (Fig. WD-6.18).
10. *Type* the field **Reference** in the box below the **Type a name for your field** option (Fig. WD-6.19).
11. *Click* on the **OK** button of this dialog box (Fig. WD-6.19). The field **Reference** gets added to your list of fields under the **Field Names** option (Fig. WD-6.20).

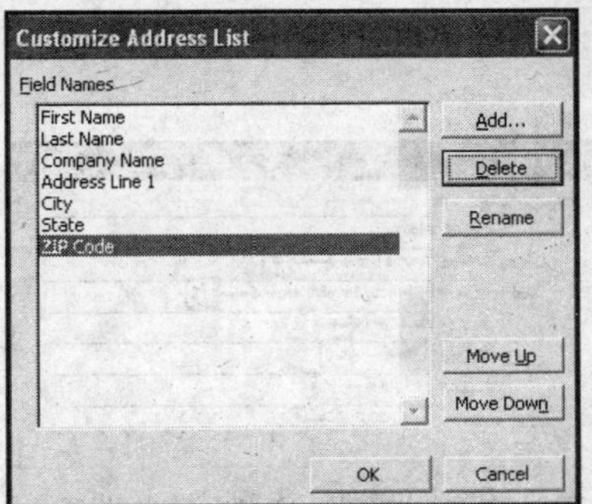

Fig. WD-6.16

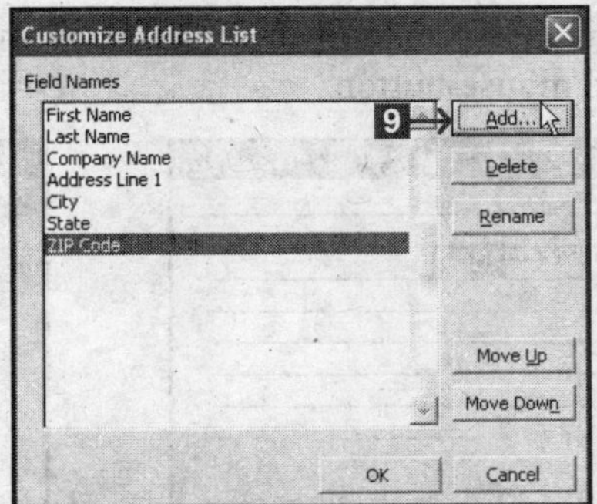

Fig. WD-6.17

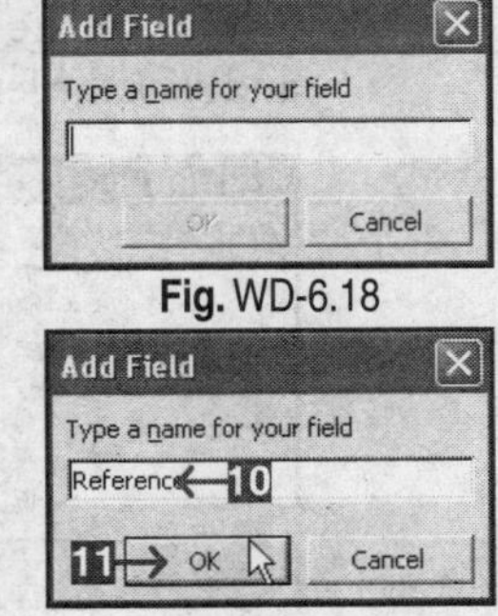

Fig. WD-6.18

Fig. WD-6.19

12. Finally *click* on the **OK** button of the **Customize Address List** dialog box. The box disappears and you return to the **New Address List** box. The changes that you have made through the **Customize Address List** dialog box reflect in the fields shown in the **New Address List** dialog box (Fig. WD-6.21).
13. Now, we will use the **New Address List** dialog box to enter the names and addresses of our dealers to create the required Data Source for our Mail Merge project. *Click* inside the box beside the **First Name** field. A blinking cursor gets displayed in that box (Fig. WD-6.21).
14. Let us now enter details of the first dealer. *Type* **Anuj** as first name (Fig. WD-6.22).
15. *Press* the **Tab** key from the keyboard. On *pressing* the **Tab** key, the blinking cursor gets displayed inside the box beside the next field name, i.e. **Last Name** (Fig. WD-6.22).

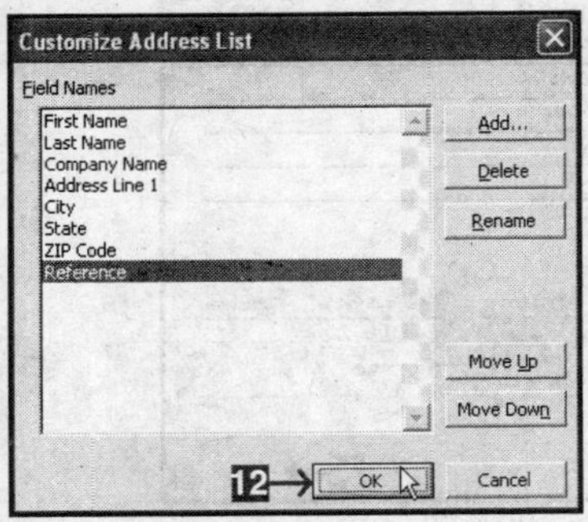

Fig. WD-6.20

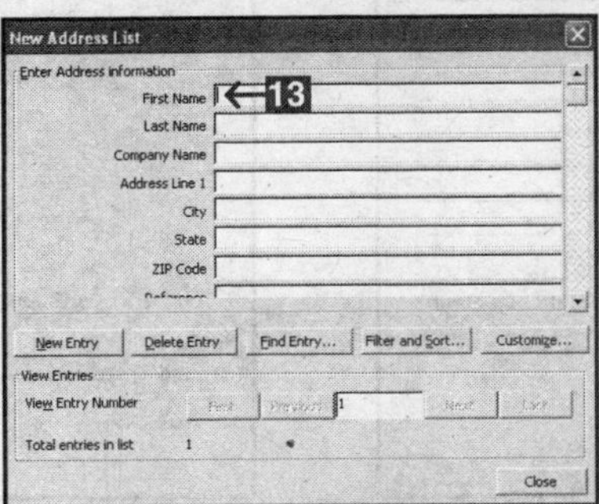

Fig. WD-6.21

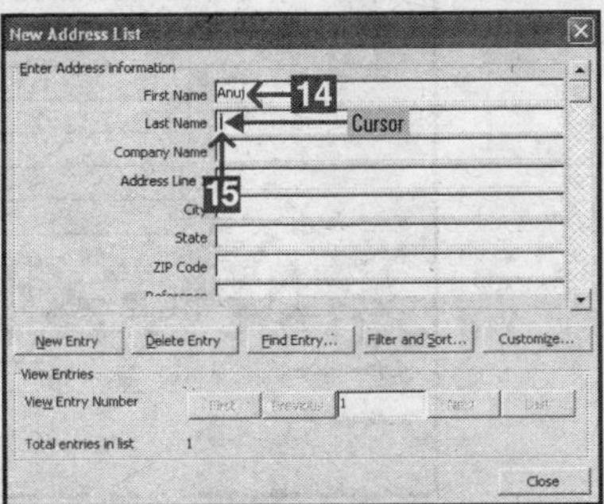

Fig. WD-6.22

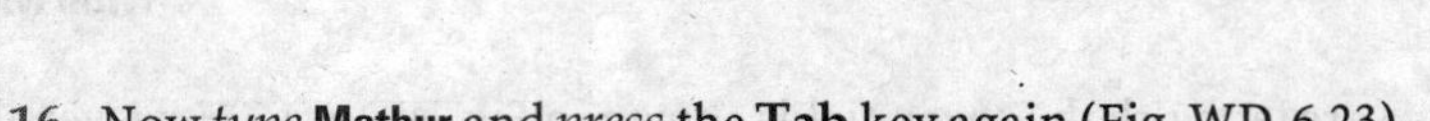

16. Now *type* **Mathur** and *press* the **Tab** key again (Fig. WD-6.23).
17. *Type* the **Company Name** as **Anuma Books** and *press* the **Tab** key (Fig. WD-6.24).
18. Now *type* **MPR - 325, Sarojani Nagar** as **Address Line1** and *press* the **Tab** key again (Fig. WD-6.24).
19. *Type* the **City** as **New Delhi** and again *press* the **Tab** key (Fig. WD-6.24).
20. Then *type* **Delhi** as the **State** name and *press* the **Tab** key again (Fig. WD-6.24).
21. *Type* the **Zip Code** as **110023** and *press* the **Tab** key (Fig. WD-6.24).
22. Finally, *type* the **Reference** as **12-12-2003** (Fig. WD-6.24). So, you have completed entering the details of the first dealer.
23. Now, *move* the mouse-pointer over the **New Entry** button of the **New Address List** box (Fig. WD-6.24) and *click* the left mouse-button.

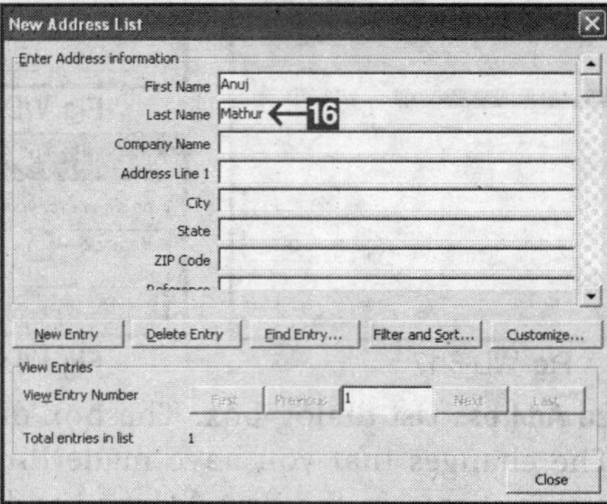

Fig. WD-6.23

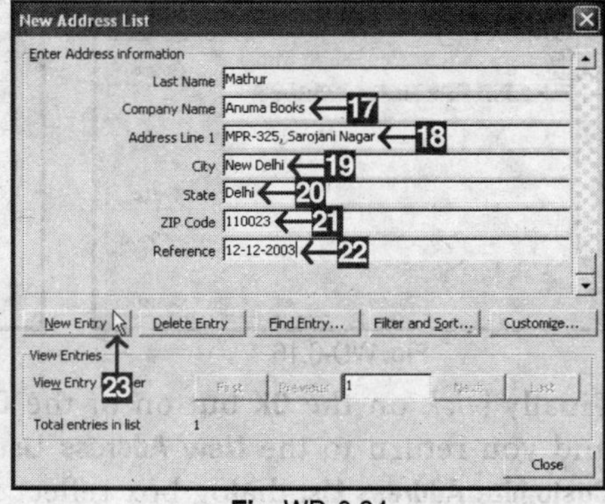

Fig. WD-6.24

Another blank form gets displayed (Fig. WD-6.25). In this form, enter the next record, i.e. details of next dealer **Neeraj Khanna**. Similarly, you can enter information about rest of the dealers in the **New Address List** box.

24. After adding all the details, *click* on the **Close** button of the **New Address List** box (Fig. WD-6.26). Immediately, the **Save Address List** dialog box appears on the screen (Fig. WD-6.27).

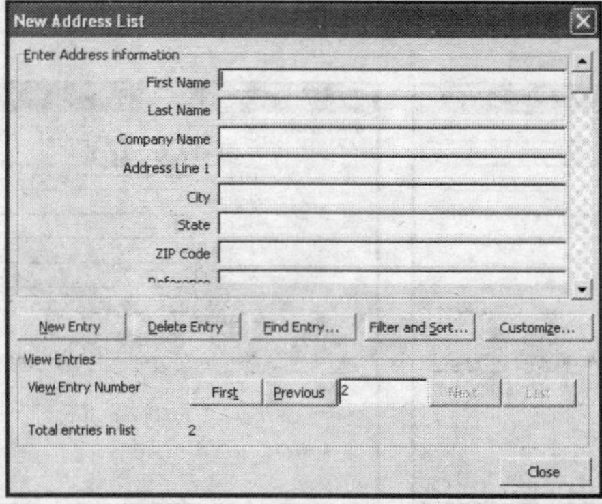

Fig. WD-6.25

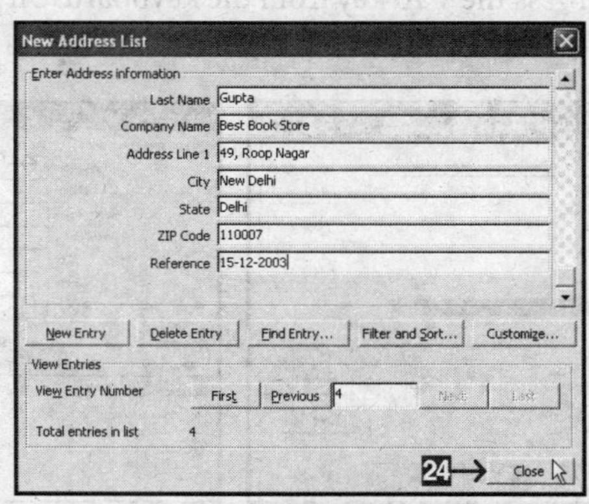

Fig. WD-6.26

25. *Type* a name for the data source, say, **My Books Dealer** in the box beside the **File name** option (Fig. WD-6.27). You can save this document in any folder. Let us save it in the **My Documents** folder.
26. *Move* the mouse-pointer over the down-arrow button of the rectangular box beside the **Save in** option and *click* the left mouse-button. Immediately, a pull-down menu gets displayed (Fig. WD-6.28).
27. Inside the pull-down menu, *move* the mouse-pointer over the **My Documents** folder and *click* the left mouse-button (Fig. WD-6.28). The folder gets selected and appears in the rectangular box beside the **Save in** option (Fig. WD-6.29).

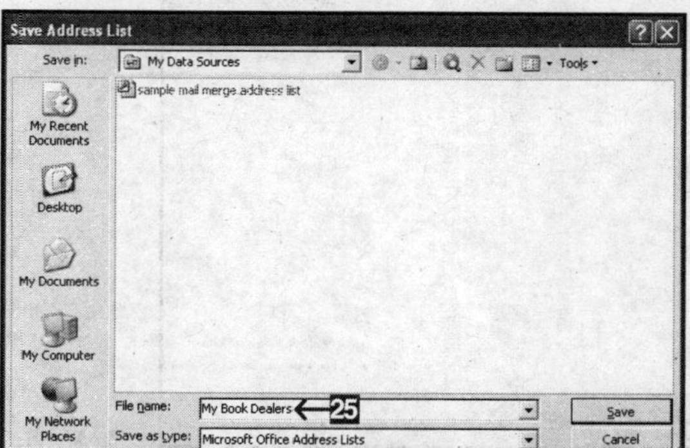

Fig. WD-6.27

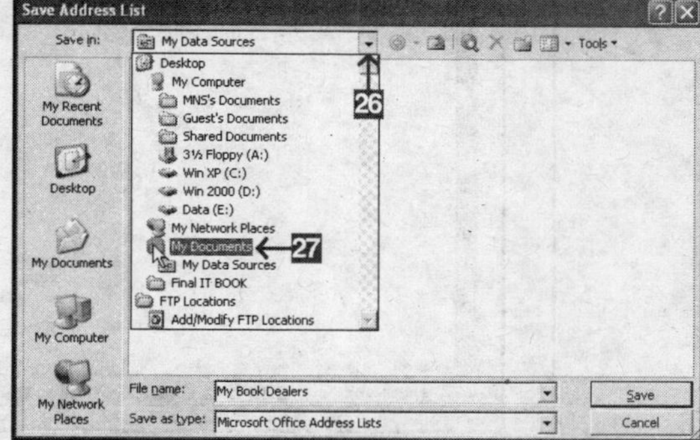

Fig. WD-6.28

28. Finally, *click* on the **Save** button of the **Save Address List** box (Fig. WD-6.29).
29. Immediately, **Mail Merge Recipients** dialog box appears on the screen, containing all the information about the dealers in rows and columns. Now, *move* the mouse-pointer over the **OK** button and *click* the left mouse-button (Fig. WD-6.30).

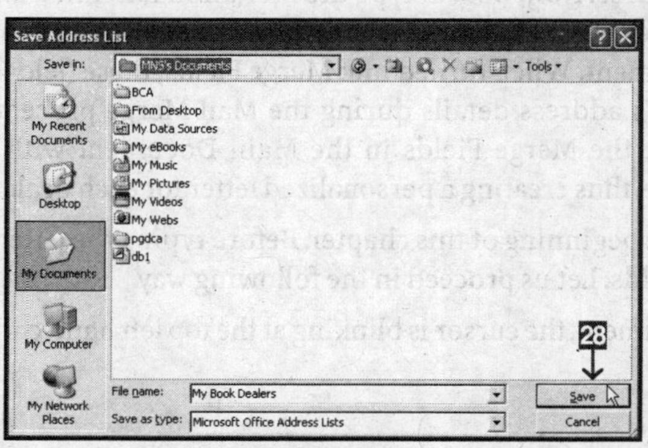

Fig. WD-6.29

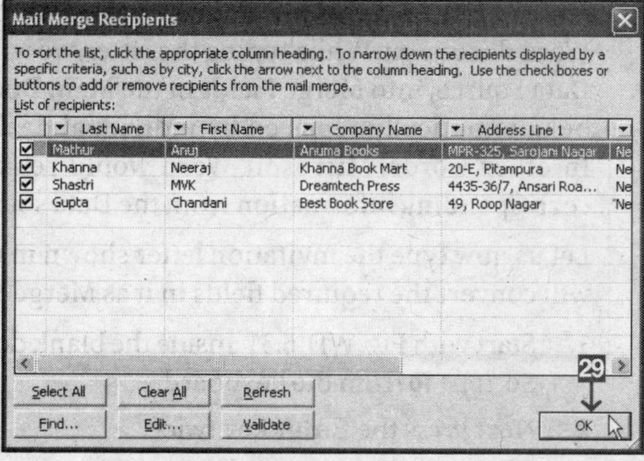

Fig. WD-6.30

30. Instantly, the dialog box gets closed followed by the display of a blank document. A new toolbar, called the **Mail Merge Toolbar,** is displayed along with the **Standard Toolbar** and **Formatting Toolbar** in the blank document (Fig. WD-6.31).

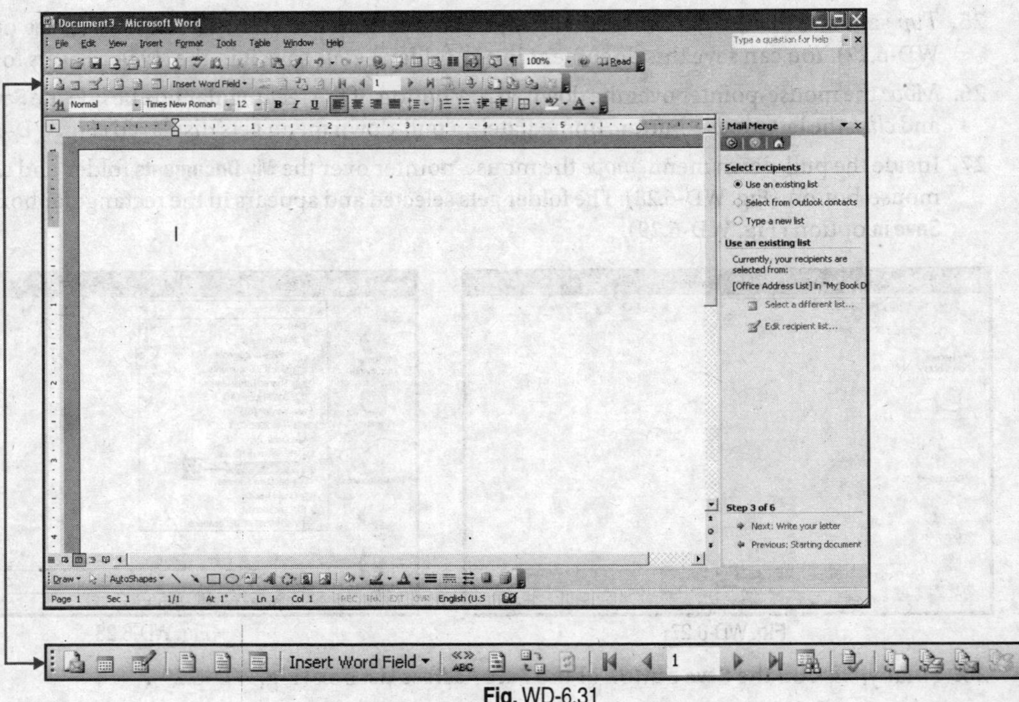

Fig. WD-6.31

Creating the Main Document

As you know, our Main Document is an invitation letter that has to be sent to all the dealers listed in the mailing list. And, this mailing list is our Data Source. Now, we will type the invitation letter in a blank Word document. While typing the letter, we will take the required steps to turn the fields selected in the Data Source, into Merge Fields of the Main Document. When turned into Merge Fields, these fields will be automatically replaced by individual dealer's address details during the Mail Merge procedure. In other words, Microsoft Word would replace the Merge Fields in the Main Document with the corresponding information from the Data source, thus creating a personalized letter for each dealer.

Let us now type the invitation letter shown in the beginning of this chapter. Before typing the letter, we will convert the required fields in it as Merge Fields. Let us proceed in the following way.

1. Start with Fig. WD-6.31. Inside the blank document, the cursor is blinking at the top left hand corner. So, *type* **To** from the keyboard.
2. Next *press* the **Enter** key twice.
3. Now, let us make First Name a Merge field. *Move* the mouse-pointer over the **Mail Merge Toolbar**, and *click* over the **Insert Merge Fields** (▤) button (Fig. WD-6.32). Immediately, the **Insert Merge Field** dialog box gets displayed (Fig. WD-6.33).

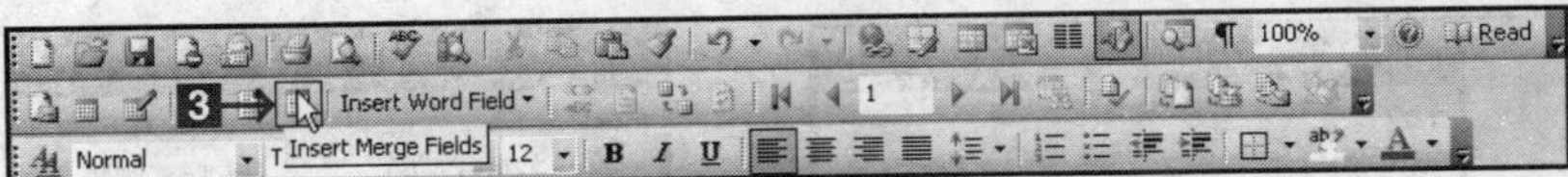

Fig. WD-6.32

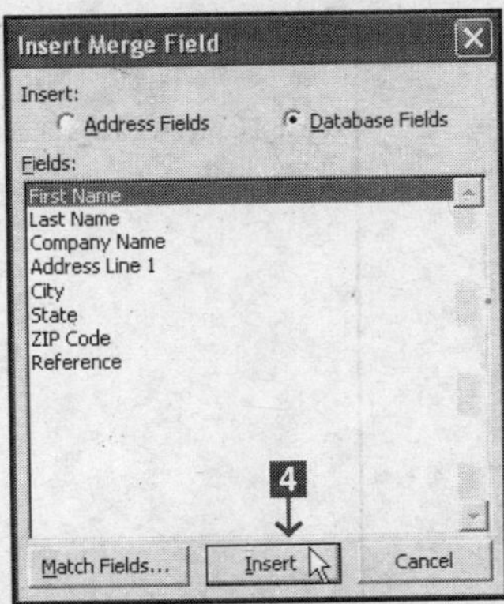

Fig. WD-6.33

4. The **First Name** field is already highlighted in the **Insert Merge Field** dialog box. To turn the highlighted field into a Merge Field, *move* the mouse-pointer over the **Insert** button and *click* the left mouse-button (Fig. WD-6.33). The dealer's first name gets inserted as a Merge Field in your Main Document (Fig. WD-6.34).
5. Now, before adding another Merge Field in your document, you need to close the **Insert Merge Field** dialog box. So, *move* the mouse-pointer over the **Close** button and *click* the left mouse-button (Fig. WD-6.34). The dialog box gets closed and the Merge Field **First Name** appears in your document as shown in Fig. WD-6.36.

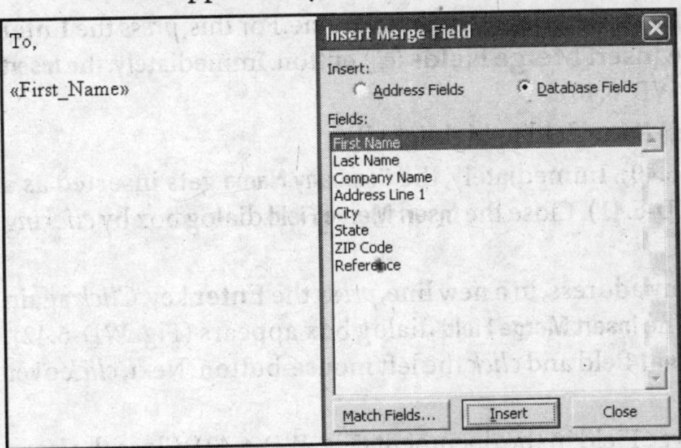

Fig. WD-6.34

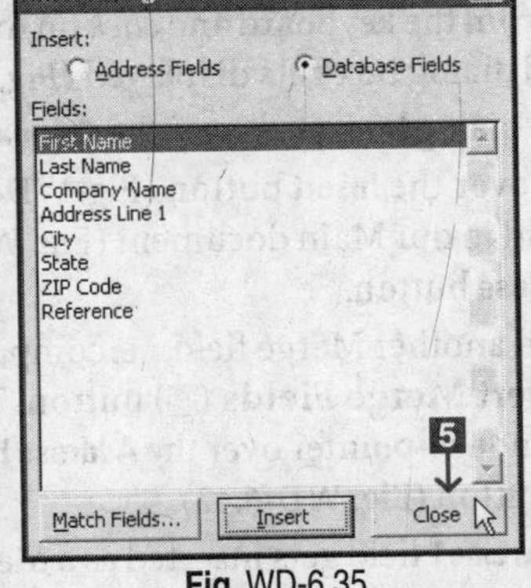

Fig. WD-6.35

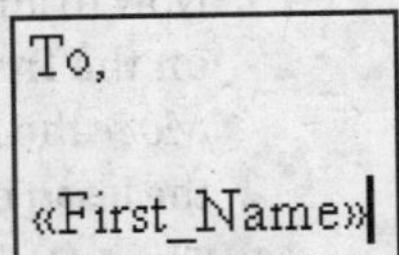

Fig. WD-6.36

6. Now, we will insert the dealer's Last Name as a Merge Field in our Main Document. The fields First Name and the Last Name should be displayed together in the invitation letter. So *press* the **Spacebar** from the keyboard. The cursor shifts to the right side of the First Name field, leaving some blank space (Fig. WD-6.37). Now, *click* on the **Insert Merge Fields** (▤) button of the **Mail Merge Toolbar**. Immediately, the **Insert Merge Field** dialog box gets displayed (Fig. WD-6.38).
7. Inside the **Insert Merge Field** box, *click* over the **Last Name** field to highlight it (Fig. WD-6.38).
8. Now, *move* the mouse-pointer over the **Insert** button and *click* on it. Immediately, the dealer's Last Name gets inserted as a Merge Field in our main document (Fig. WD-6.39).
9. Now close the **Insert Merge Field** dialog box by *clicking* on the **Close** button (Fig. WD-6.39).

To,

«First_Name»

Fig. WD-6.37

Fig. WD-6.38

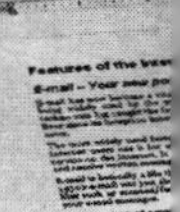

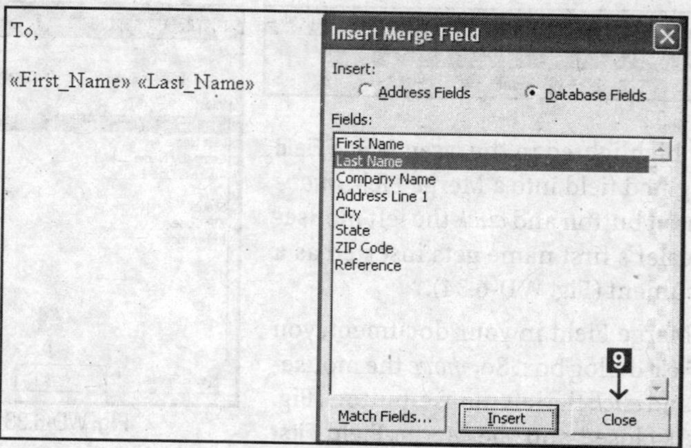

Fig. WD-6.39

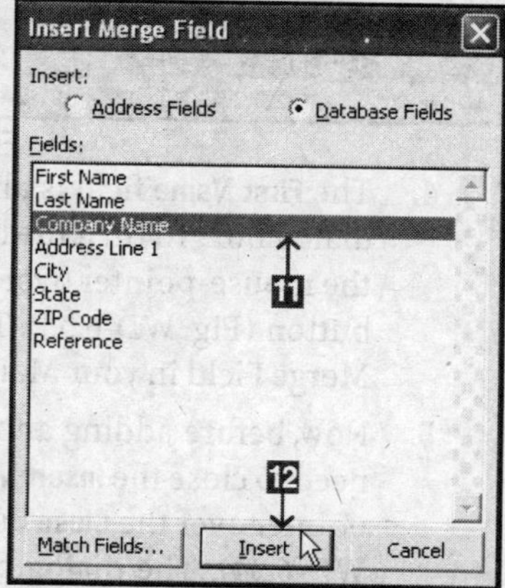

Fig. WD-6.40

10. Now you have to insert the company's name as a Merge Field in the next line. For this, *press* the **Enter** key once from the keyboard and *click* on the **Insert Merge Fields** (▤) button. Immediately, the **Insert Merge Field** dialog box gets displayed (Fig. WD-6.40).
11. Inside the dialog box, *click* over the **Company Name** field to highlight it.
12. Now *click* over the **Insert** button (Fig. WD-6.40). Immediately, the **Company Name** gets inserted as a Merge Field in our Main document (Fig. WD-6.41). Close the **Insert Merge Field** dialog box by *clicking* over the **Close** button.
13. Now to add another Merge field, i.e. company address, in a new line, *press* the **Enter** key. *Click* again on the **Insert Merge Fields** (▤) button. The **Insert Merge Field** dialog box appears (Fig. WD-6.42). *Move* the mouse-pointer over the **Address Line1** field and *click* the left mouse-button. Next, *click* over the **Insert** button (Fig. WD-6.42).
14. The **Address Line1** field gets inserted as a Merge Field in the document (Fig. WD-6.42). Close the **Insert Merge Field** dialog box *clicking* over the **Close** button (Fig. WD-6.42).

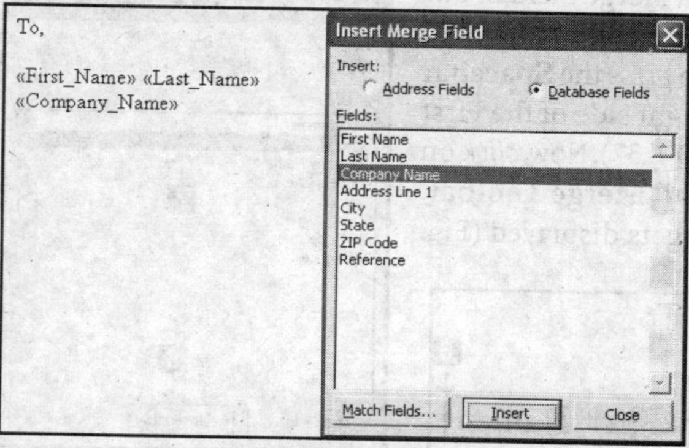

Fig. WD-6.41

Fig. WD-6.42

15. Now, we will insert another Merge Field, i.e. **City**, in a new line. First, *press* the **Enter** key. Then *click* over the **Insert Merge Fields** (▤) button. The **Insert Merge Field** dialog box appears In the dialog box, *click* on the **City** field to highlight it (Fig. WD-6.43).

16. *Click* over the **Insert** button (Fig. WD-6.43). The **City** field gets inserted in the Main Document (Fig. WD-6.44). Again close the Insert Merge Field dialog box.

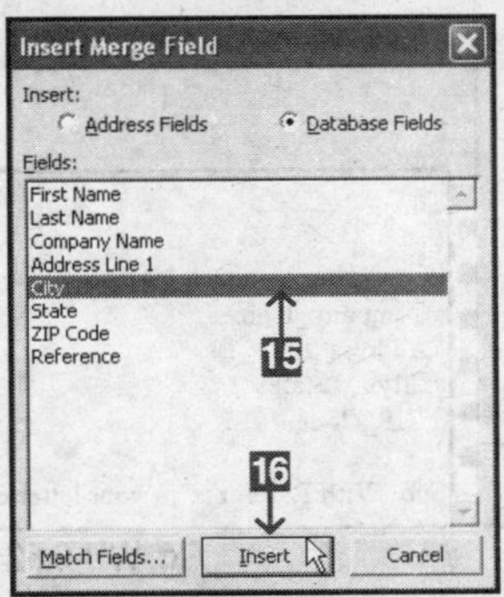

Fig. WD-6.43

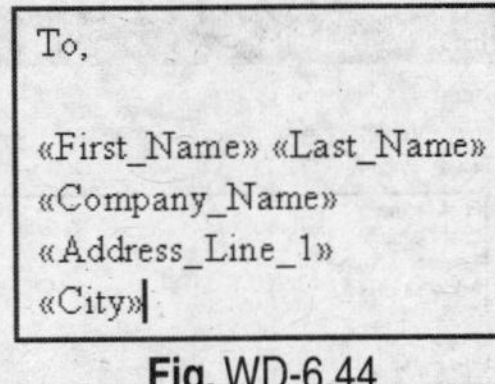

Fig. WD-6.44

17. Now, the **State** field has to be displayed. Both the **City** and **State** fields will appear in the same line. So, press the **comma** (,) key from the keyboard. Then *press* the **Spacebar** once from the keyboard (Fig. WD-6.45). Next, *click* over the **Insert Merge Fields** (▤) button. The **Insert Merge Field** dialog box gets displayed (Fig. WD-6.46).

Fig. WD-6.45

18. Inside the **Insert Merge Field** dialog box, *click* over the **State** field to highlight it (Fig. WD-6.46).

19. Now *click* over the **Insert** button (Fig. WD-6.46). The **State** field gets inserted in the document (Fig. WD-6.47). Now close the dialog box.

20. Now, to insert the **Zip Code** field in a new line, *press* the **Enter** key once. The cursor moves to next line (Fig.WD-6.47). *Click* on the **Insert Merge Fields** (▤) button. Immediately, the **Insert Merge Field** dialog box gets displayed.

21. Inside the dialog box, *move* the mouse-pointer over the **Zip Code** field to highlight it (Fig. WD-6.48).

22. Then *click* over the **Insert** button (Fig. WD-6.48). The **Zip Code** gets inserted in your document (Fig. WD-6.49). Again close the dialog box.

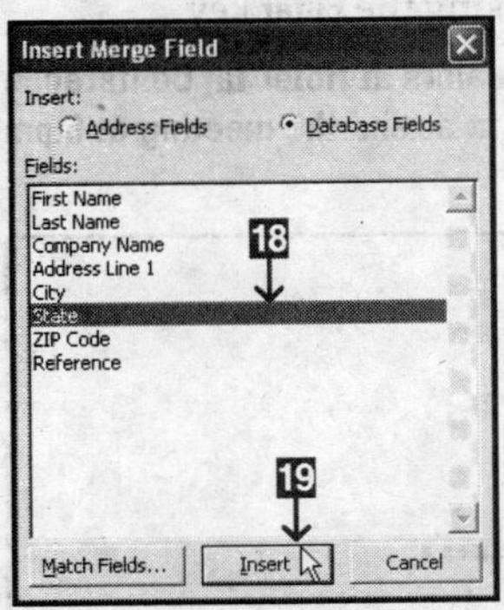

Fig. WD-6.46

Fig. WD-6.47

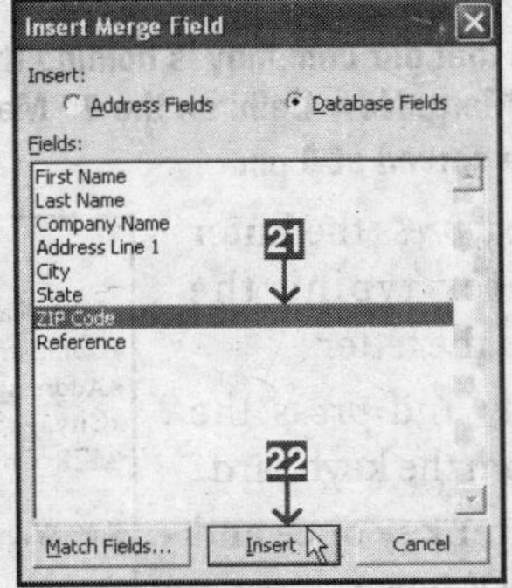

Fig. WD-6.48

Fig. WD-6.49

23. Now, only one field, i.e. **Reference**, has been left. To insert it in your document, *press* the **Enter** key twice and *type* **Sub: With reference to your letter dated** (Fig. WD-6.50).

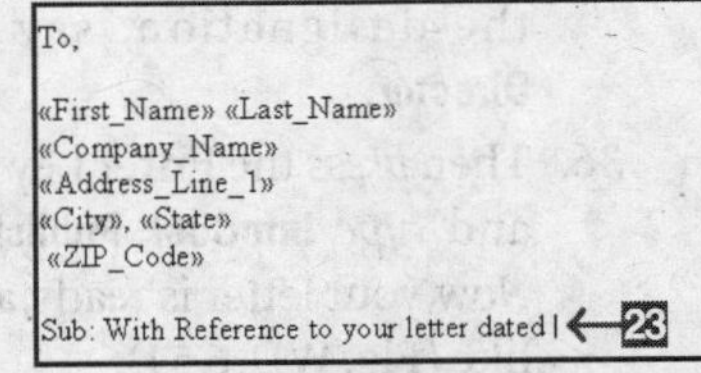

Fig. WD-6.50

24. Now, *press* the **Spacebar** key once from the keyboard for inserting a space before the **Reference** field that we are going to insert.

25. Then *click* over the **Insert Merge Fields** (▤) button. Immediately, the **Insert Merge Field** dialog box gets displayed (Fig. WD-6.51).

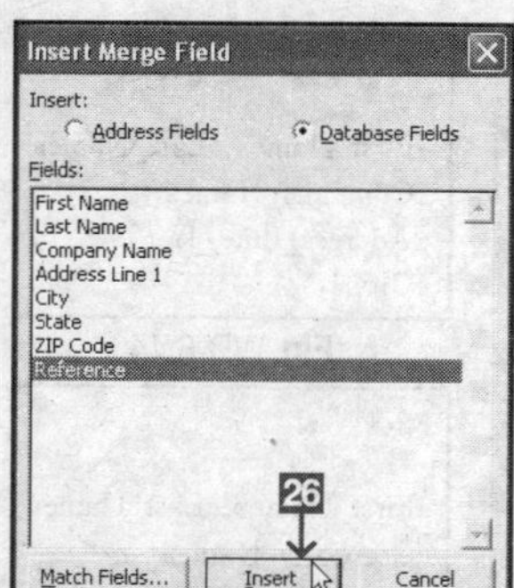

Fig. WD-6.51

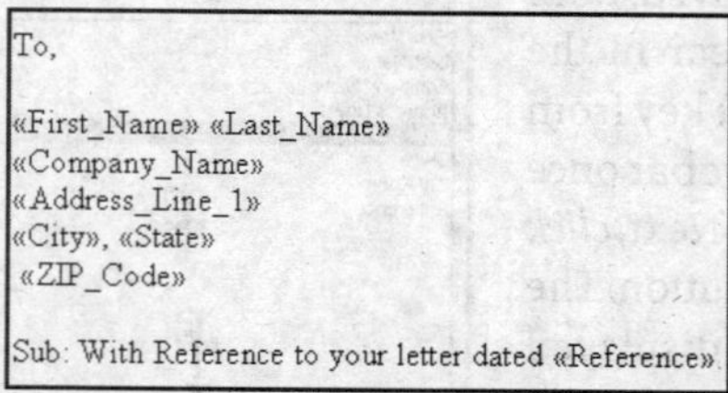

Fig. WD-6.52

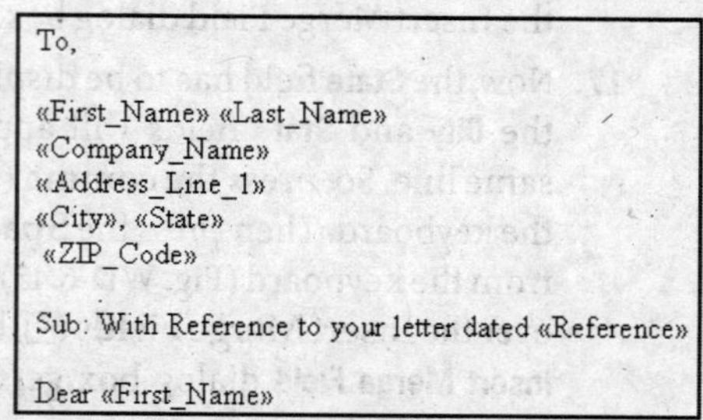

Fig. WD-6.53

26. Inside the dialog box, *select* the **Reference** field. And *click* over the **Insert** button by *moving* the mouse-pointer over it (Fig. WD-6.51). The **Reference** field gets inserted in the document (Fig. WD-6.52).
27. *Press* the **Enter** key twice and then *type* the salutation text, **Dear**.
28. Along with the salutation text, we also need to insert the dealer's First Name. For this, *press* the **Spacebar** key once from the keyboard to insert a space after the salutation text.
29. Then *click* over the **Insert Merge Fields** (▤) button. Inside the **Insert Merge Field** dialog box, *select* the **First Name** field and *click* over the **Insert** button. Immediately, the dealer's First Name field gets inserted after the salutation text (Fig. WD-6.53). Close the dialog box.
30. *Press* the **Comma** key (,) once to insert a comma after the First Name field in your document. Then *press* the **Enter** key.
31. Now *type* the following text of the letter in your document without pressing the **Enter** key.

    This is to inform you that our company is holding the annual meeting of all the dealers at Hotel Taj Conference Room, Sardar Patel Marg, New Delhi on the 7th March 2004. You are requested to attend the meeting at 6 pm sharp. Dinner will be served at 9 pm.

32. After typing the text, *press* the **Enter** key four times for typing the concluding lines of the letter.
33. Now *type* **Sincerely** and *press* the **Comma** key (,) from the keyboard.
34. Next, *press* the **Enter** key once and *type* any name, say **V. Gupta.**
35. *Press* the **Enter** key once and *type* the designation, say **Marketing Director.**
36. Then *press* the **Enter** key once again and *type* **InfoBook Publishing House.** Now, your letter is ready, and it looks like (Fig. WD-6.54).

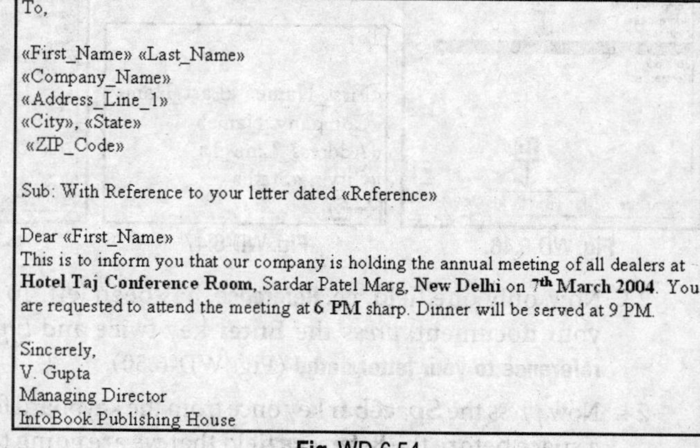
To,

«First_Name» «Last_Name»
«Company_Name»
«Address_Line_1»
«City», «State»
«ZIP_Code»

Sub: With Reference to your letter dated «Reference»

Dear «First_Name»
This is to inform you that our company is holding the annual meeting of all dealers at **Hotel Taj Conference Room**, Sardar Patel Marg, **New Delhi** on **7th March 2004**. You are requested to attend the meeting at **6 PM** sharp. Dinner will be served at 9 PM.

Sincerely,
V. Gupta
Managing Director
InfoBook Publishing House

Fig. WD-6.54

Merging the Main Document with Data Source

After creating the Main Document, you are now ready to combine the Main Document and the Data Source to create a personalized letter for each dealer on your mailing list. To merge the Main Document and the Data Source, undertake the following steps:

1. *Move* the mouse-pointer over the **View Merged Data** ( ) button of the **Mail Merge Toolbar** (Fig. WD-6.55) and *click* the left mouse-button. After this action, all the Merge fields in your main document get replaced with the corresponding information of all dealers from the Data Source. However, your screen shows the merged data for the first dealer i.e. Anuj Mathur (Fig. WD-6.56).

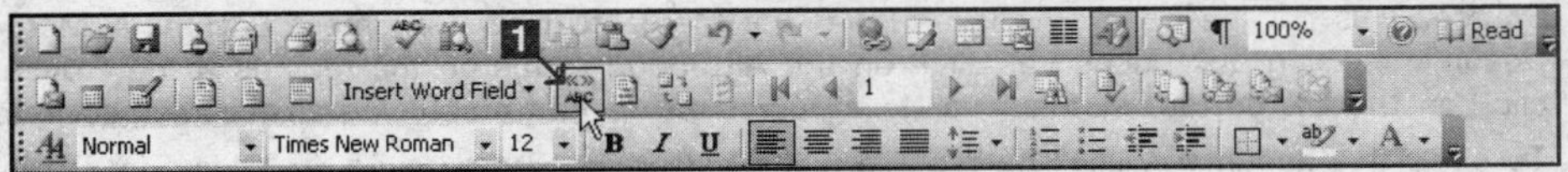

Fig. WD-6.55

2. Now to insert the details of the second dealer's record, *click* over the **Next Record** ( ) button of the **Mail Merge Toolbar** (Fig. WD-6.57). Immediately, the details of the second record get inserted at their respective places in your document.
3. Similarly, keep *clicking* on the **Next Record** ( ) button for inserting details of all from your Data source to your Main Document.

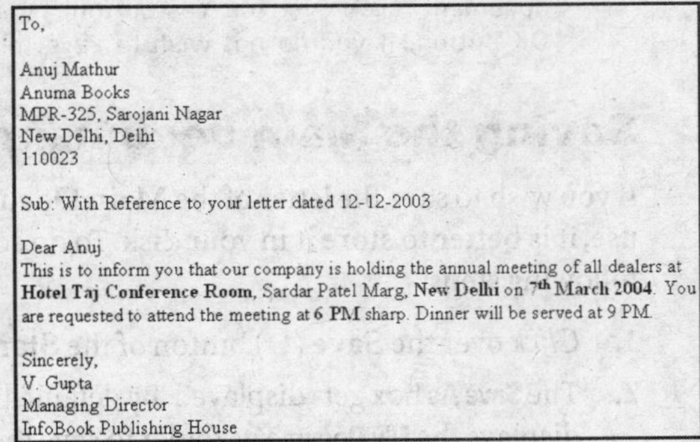

To,

Anuj Mathur
Anuma Books
MPR-325, Sarojani Nagar
New Delhi, Delhi
110023

Sub: With Reference to your letter dated 12-12-2003

Dear Anuj
This is to inform you that our company is holding the annual meeting of all dealers at **Hotel Taj Conference Room**, Sardar Patel Marg, **New Delhi** on **7th March 2004**. You are requested to attend the meeting at **6 PM** sharp. Dinner will be served at 9 PM.

Sincerely,
V. Gupta
Managing Director
InfoBook Publishing House

Fig. WD-6.56

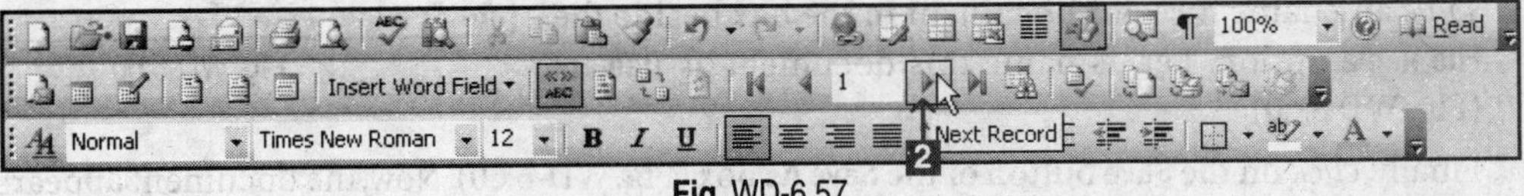

Fig. WD-6.57

Sending the Merged Document to the Printer

Let us now print the letters of all the dealers through the following steps:

1. *Move* the mouse-pointer over the **Merge to Printer** ( ) button of the **Mail Merge Toolbar** and *click* the left mouse-button (Fig. WD-6.58).
2. A **Merge to Printer** dialog box gets displayed (Fig. WD-6.59). *Select* the **All** option to print letters for all your dealers.
3. Finally, *click* over the **OK** button (Fig 6.59).

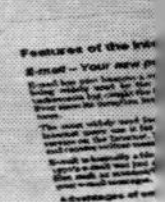

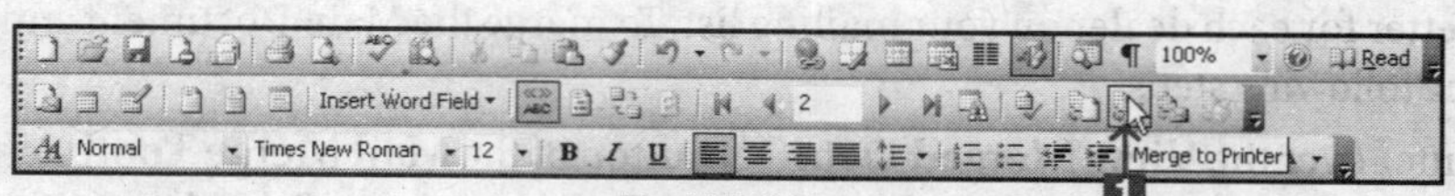

Fig. WD-6.58

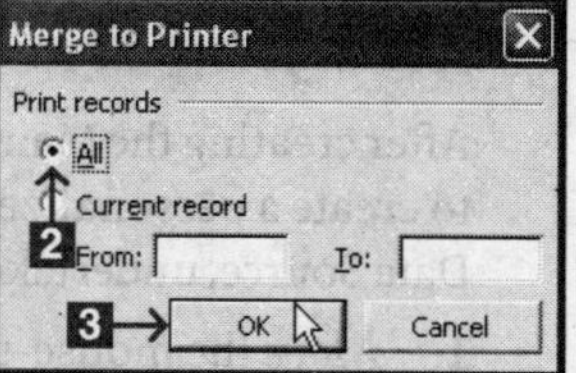

Fig. WD-6.59

You can merge the data into a New Document also. It means you can make a new document containing all the four dealer letters that you get after merging the mail document with the Data Source. This can be done by clicking over the Merge to New Document button. A Merge to New Document dialog box opens up. Click on the All option to merge the records to new document and click on the OK button. Instantly, a New Document opens up showing all the merged letters.

To close this document, click on the File menu bar option and then on the Close option. Instantly, a Message Box appears asking whether you wish to save the document. If you wish to save the document, click over the Yes button, type a suitable name for the new document and then click the OK button. If you do not wish to save this document, click on the No button of the Message Box.

Saving the Main document

If you wish to save the letter of the **Main Document** for future use, it is better to store it in your disk. To do so, undertake the following steps:

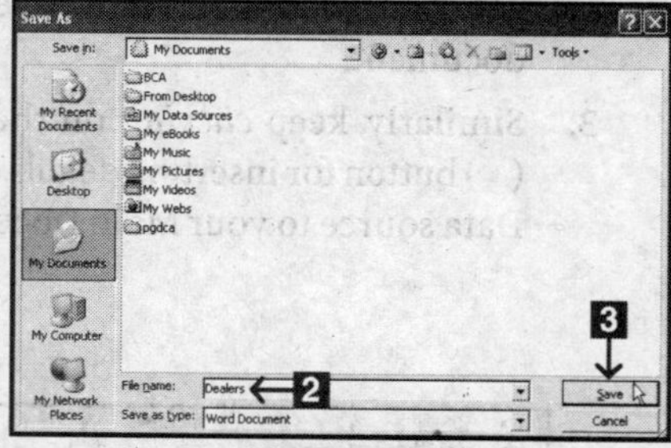

Fig. WD-6.60

1. *Click* over the **Save** (💾) button of the **Standard Toolbar.**
2. The **Save As** box gets displayed. By default, the **Save in** option displays the **My Documents** folder to save the document. Let us choose this default folder to save our main document. *Type* any name for your document in the box beside the **File name** option. Let us name this document as **Dealers** (Fig. WD 6.60).
3. Finally, *click* on the **Save** button of the **Save As** box (Fig. WD-6.60). Now, the document appears on the screen with its name displayed on the **Title bar.**

Modifying Records in the Data Source

You can easily add, delete or change the dealer information, i.e. record, in your Data Source. Let us now learn to do all these functions one by one.

Adding a New Record

Suppose, a new dealer has recently joined in your business and you want to insert his details into your Data Source. The details of the new dealer are as follows:

Fields	First name	Last name	Company	Address line 1	City	State	Zip code	Reference
Entry to be made	Mohit	Bhasin	Bhasin Bros	20, Prashant Vihar	New Delhi	Delhi	110035	23-04-02

Let us now enter these details into the Data Source through the following steps:

1. *Move* the mouse-pointer over the **Mail Merge Recipients** ( ) button of the **Mail Merge Toolbar** (Fig. WD-6.61) and *click* the left mouse-button. Immediately, the **Mail Merge Recipients** box appears on your screen (Fig. WD-6.62).

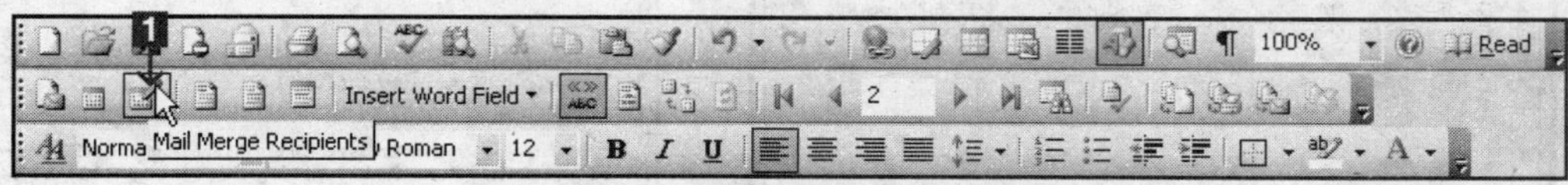

Fig. WD-6.61

2. Now *click* on the **Edit** button of the **Mail Merge Recipients** dialog box (Fig. WD-6.62). Immediately the **New Address List** box appears on the screen (Fig. WD-6.63). The **Title Bar** of this box doesn't have the name, **New Address List.** Instead, it depicts the path where you have saved your Data Source file. In the dialog box of Fig. W-5.63, details of a dealer, **Neeraj Khanna**, are already shown.
3. To add details of a new dealer, *move* the mouse-pointer over the **New Entry** button and *click* once (Fig. WD-6.63). The fields showing a dealer's details get emptied. Now, to fill the empty fields with new details, *type* the new dealer's first name as **Mohit** in the box beside the **First Name** field.

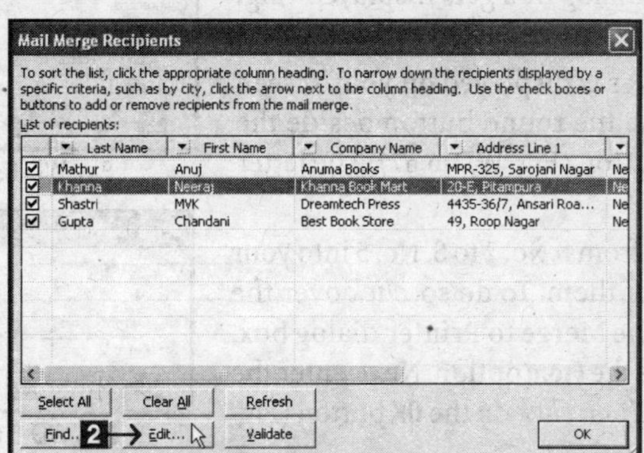

Fig. WD-6.62

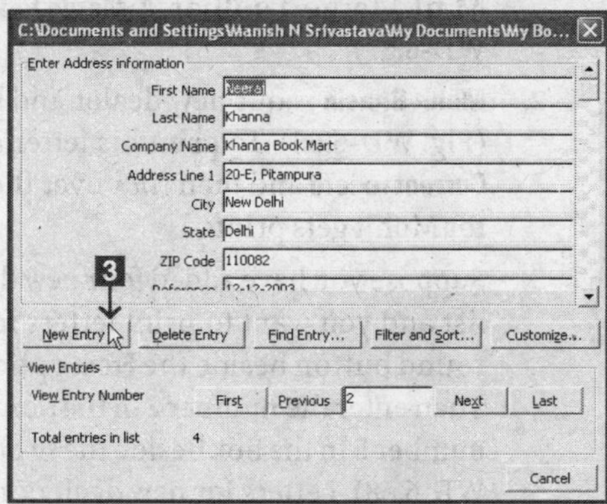

Fig. WD-6.63

4. Then *press* the **Tab** key to move to the next field, i.e. **Last Name**, and *type* **Bhasin**.
5. Similarly, *type* rest of the details of the new dealer.
6. After filling up all the fields, *move* the mouse-pointer over the **Close** button and *click* on it (Fig. WD-6.64). The **New Address List** box disappears. And the new entry can be seen in the **Mail Merge Recipients** dialog box (Fig. WD-6.65).
7. To close the **Mail Merge Recipients** dialog box, *click* on the **OK** button. The dialog box gets closed and the letter for new dealer **Mohit** gets displayed (Fig. WD-6.66).

Fig. WD-6.64

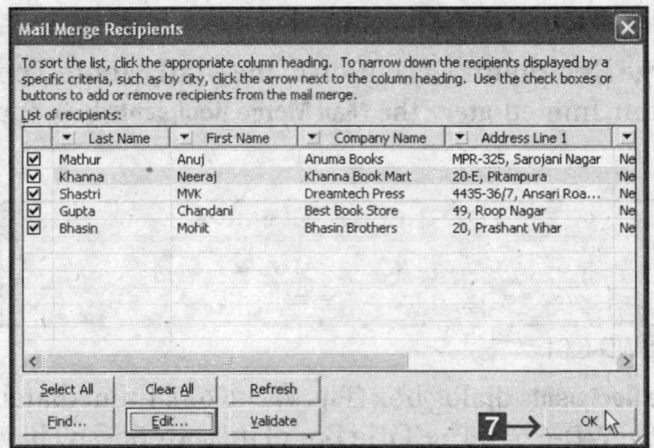

Fig. WD-6.65

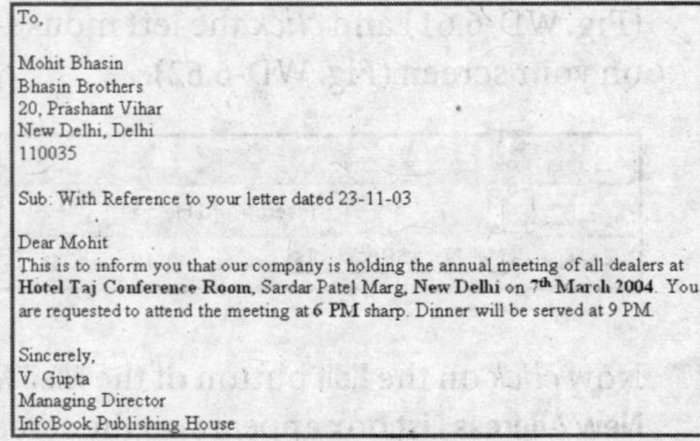

To,

Mohit Bhasin
Bhasin Brothers
20, Prashant Vihar
New Delhi, Delhi
110035

Sub: With Reference to your letter dated 23-11-03

Dear Mohit
This is to inform you that our company is holding the annual meeting of all dealers at **Hotel Taj Conference Room**, Sardar Patel Marg, **New Delhi** on **7th March 2004**. You are requested to attend the meeting at **6 PM** sharp. Dinner will be served at 9 PM.

Sincerely,
V. Gupta
Managing Director
InfoBook Publishing House

Fig. WD-6.66

Printing the New Dealer's Letter

Let us now print only the new dealer's letter by undertaking the following steps.

1. *Move* the mouse-pointer over the **Merge to Printer** (button icon) button of the **Mail Merge Toolbar.** A **Merge to Printer** dialog box gets displayed (Fig. WD-6.67).

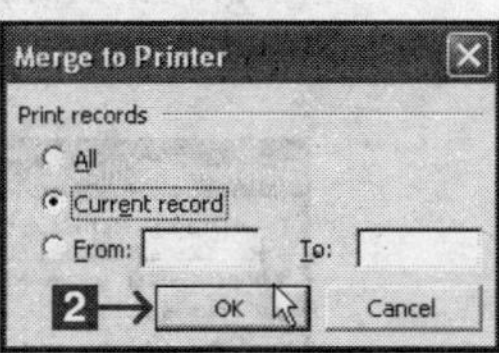

Fig. WD-6.67

2. **Mohit Bhasin** is our new dealer and his letter is displayed on your screen (Fig. WD-6.66). To print his letter *click* on the round button beside the **Current record** and then *click* over the **OK** button (Fig. WD-6.67). The letter for Mohit gets printed.

3. Suppose you have added four new dealers from S.No. 2 to S. No. 5 into your list and you want to print letters for all of them. To do so, *click* over the round button beside the **From** option in the Merge to Printer dialog box. Then enter the number **2** in the box beside the **From** option. Next, enter the number **5** in the box beside the **To** option. Then *click* on the **OK** button (Fig. WD-6.68). Letters for new dealers get printed.

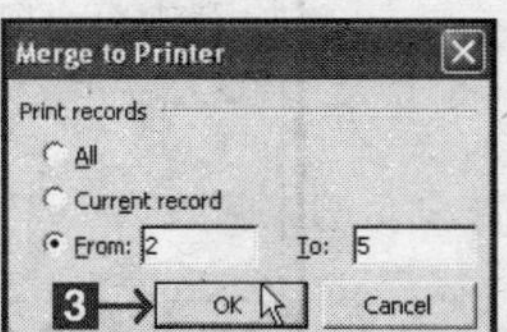

Fig. WD-6.68

Changing an Existing Record

If the address of a particular dealer has been changed, you also need to make corresponding changes in his record in your Data Source. Suppose, you wish to change the details of the **Address Line1** field of the second record, i.e. of dealer **Neeraj**, to **45/C, Prasad Vihar.** To do so, undertake the following steps:

1. *Move* the mouse-pointer over the **Mail Merge Recipients** (button icon) button of the **Mail Merge Toolbar,** and *click* the left mouse-button. Immediately, the **Mail Merge Recipients** dialog box appears on the screen (Fig. WD-6.65).
2. This box displays records of all dealers. Since you want to change the address of the second record, i.e. **Neeraj Khanna,** *move* the mouse-pointer over the dealer name. The details of **Neeraj Khanna** get highlighted (Fig. WD-6.69).
3. Now *move* the mouse-pointer over the **Edit** button and *click* the left mouse-button (Fig. WD-6.70).
4. The details of **Neeraj Khanna** appear in the **New Address List** box (Fig. WD-6.71).

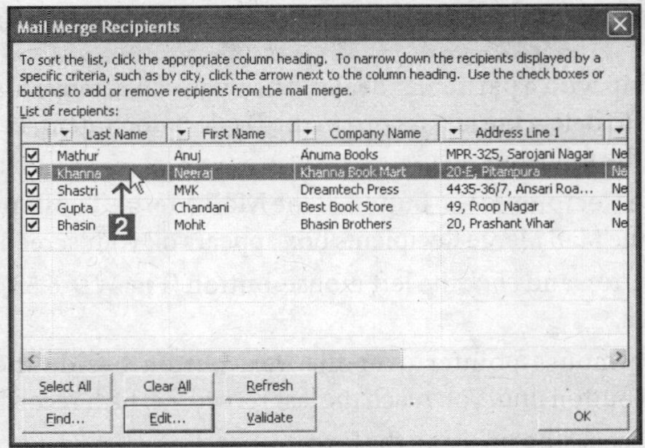

Fig. WD-6.69

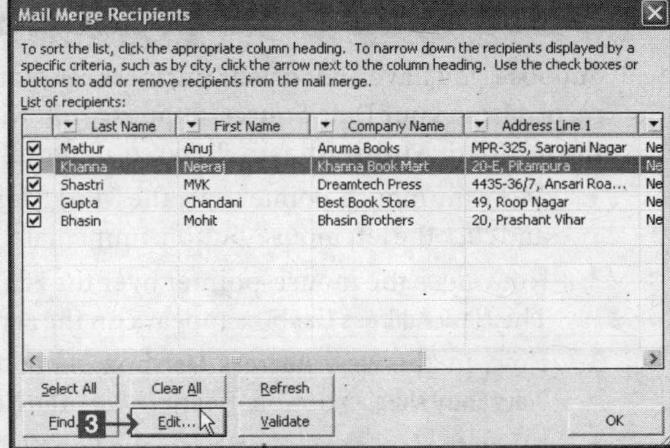

Fig. WD-6.70

5. Now *double-click* inside the box beside the **Address Line1** field to highlight it (Fig. WD-6.71).
6. *Press* the **Backspace** key to erase the contents of the **Address Line1** field.
7. Then *type* the new address **45/C Prasad Vihar** (Fig. WD-6.72).

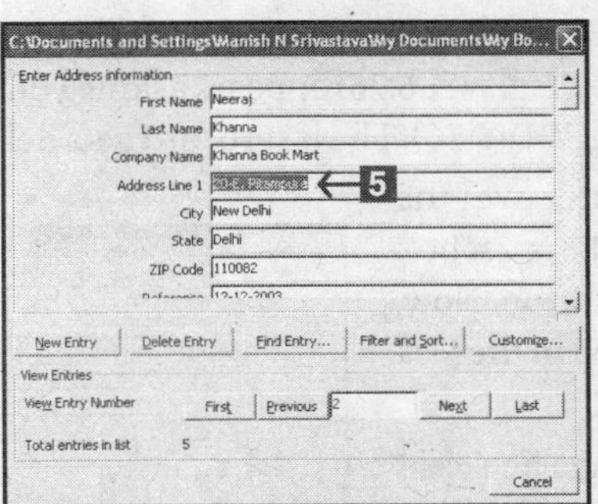

Fig. WD-6.71

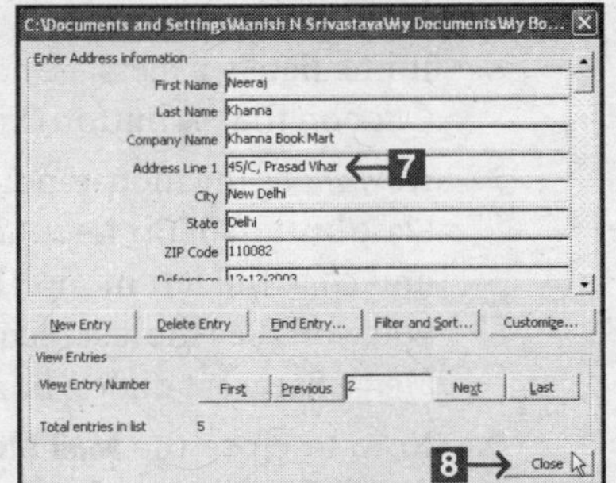

Fig. WD-6.72

8. After making the change, *click* on the **Close** button (Fig. WD-6.72). The **New Address List** dialog box disappears and **Mail Merge Recipients** dialog box appears on the screen. You can see the changes you had made to the second record in this dialog box. *Click* on the **OK** button (Fig. WD-6.73).
9. You can also see the changes made to the address of second record in the **Main Document** (Fig. WD-6.74).

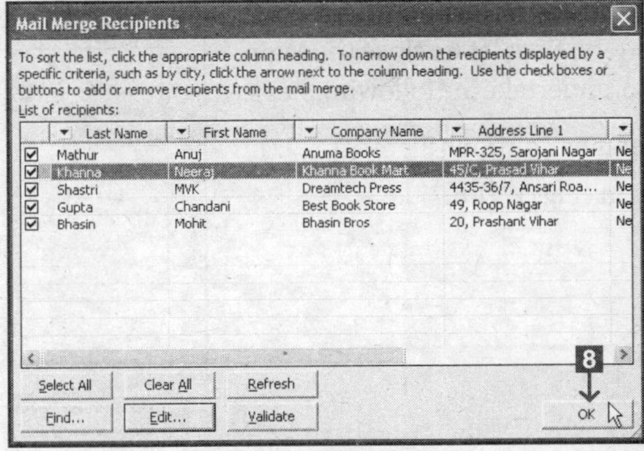

Fig. WD-6.73

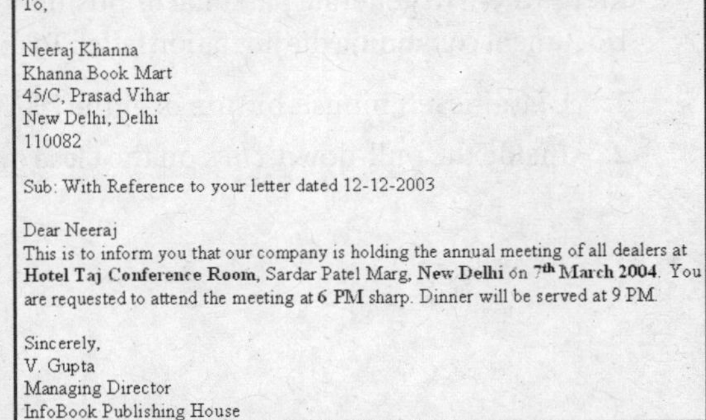
To,

Neeraj Khanna
Khanna Book Mart
45/C, Prasad Vihar
New Delhi, Delhi
110082

Sub: With Reference to your letter dated 12-12-2003

Dear Neeraj
This is to inform you that our company is holding the annual meeting of all dealers at **Hotel Taj Conference Room**, Sardar Patel Marg, **New Delhi** on **7th March 2004**. You are requested to attend the meeting at **6 PM** sharp. Dinner will be served at 9 PM.

Sincerely,
V. Gupta
Managing Director
InfoBook Publishing House

Fig. WD-6.74

Deleting an Existing Record

Suppose, you have ended your business relationship with a particular dealer. Then you can remove his record from your Data Source. Suppose, you wish to delete the last record in the Dealers document, i.e. the record of **Mohit Bhasin.** To do so, undertake the following steps.

1. *Move* the mouse-pointer over the **Mail Merge Recipients** ( ) button of the **Mail Merge Toolbar,** and *click* the left mouse-button. Immediately, the Mail Merge Recipients box appears on your screen.
2. Now, *move* the mouse-pointer over the **Edit** button and *click* the left mouse-button (Fig. WD-6.53). The **New Address List** box appears on the screen.
3. Now, in the **New Address List** box, *move* the mouse-pointer over the **Next** button beside the **View Entry Number** option. Keep *clicking* the **Next** button until you reach the last record, i.e. fifth record.
4. When the last record gets displayed on the screen, stop pressing the **Next** button.
5. Now *move* the mouse-pointer over the **Delete Entry** button and *click* the left mouse-button (Fig. WD-6.75).
6. Immediately, a message box (Fig. WD-6.76) appears asking you, whether you want to delete this entry. *Click* on the **Yes** button (Fig. WD-6.76). The last record gets deleted.
7. Now, *move* the mouse-pointer over the **Close** button of the **New Address List** box and *click* the left mouse-button. Now, you won't see the last record in the **Mail Merge Recipient** dialog box.
8. Now, to close the **Mail Merge Recipient** dialog box, *move* the mouse-pointer over the **OK** button and *click* on it. The **Mail Merge Recipient** dialog box gets closed.

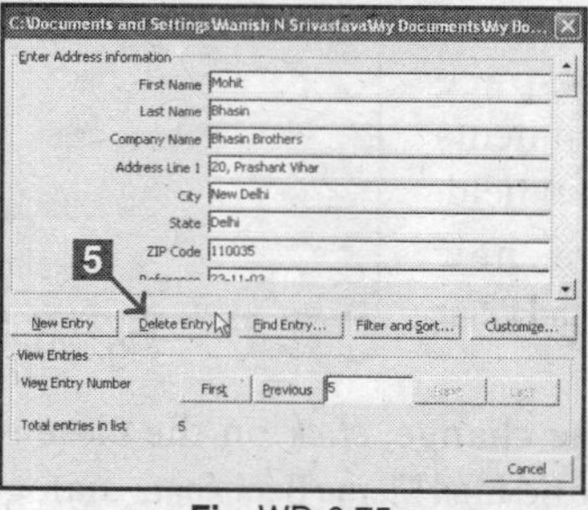

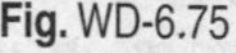

Fig. WD-6.75

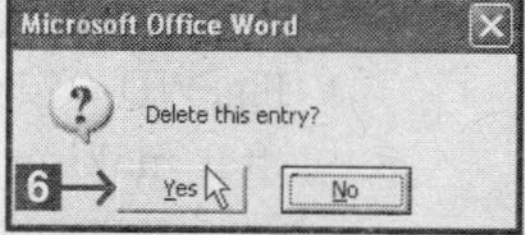

Fig. WD-6.76

Closing the Main Document

So, you have become familiar with the Mail Merge feature of the Microsoft Word. Hope, you would be able to create a Data Source and Main Document, and then merge them to generate personal or business letters. Now, let us close the Main Document containing the invitation letter. To do so, undertake the following steps:

1. *Click* the left mouse-button over the **File** Menu bar option (Fig. WD-6.77).
2. Inside the pull-down, *click* on the **Close** option (Fig. WD-6.77).

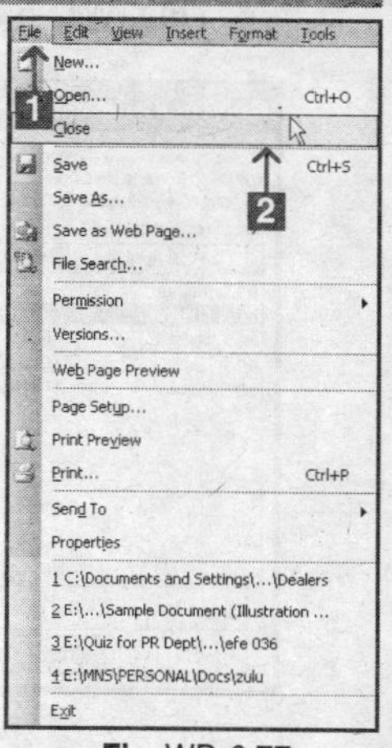

Fig. WD-6.77

3. If you have made some changes to the **Main Document** then on clicking the **Close** option, a message box gets displayed (Fig.WD-6.78). This message box asks whether you wish to save the changes made in your document. For saving the changes *click* on the **Yes** button, otherwise, *click* on the **No** button.

Fig. WD-6.78

Quitting Microsoft Word

Let us now quit the **Microsoft Word** program by going through the following steps:

1. *Move* the mouse-pointer over the **Close** button (☒) present on the **Title bar.**
2. *Click* the left mouse-button. Immediately, the **Microsoft Word** closes and the Windows XP **desktop** gets displayed on the screen.

Exercise

Short Questions

1. Briefly discuss the relevance of Mail Merge option?
2. What is Main document?
3. Write down the three basic steps required to create a Mail Merge Project.
4. Give one line definition of Data Source.
5. Write the steps for creating a new address list.
6. Write the steps for merging the Main Document with the Data Source.
7. Explain the various options for selecting the starting document.

True/False

1. The Letters and Mailing option is present inside the Tools menu.
2. The Mail Merge Recipients button is present on the Mail Merge toolbar.
3. Can you merge the data into a new document also.

Summary

This exhaustive section discusses a vital application of MS Office suite – Microsoft Word. Microsoft Word has something for everyone—whether it be a student preparing his resume or office secretary writing business letters or DTP operator using his computer skills to earn a livelihood. By using Microsoft Word, you can easily create, design and print documents on your computer.

The first chapter of this section introduces you to the features and environment of Microsoft Word and Office Assistant – your friend to advice you how to do things in Microsoft Word. After becoming familiar with these features, you learn to type and print your first document in Microsoft Word. Later, you learn about various document editing techniques like finding and replacing some word in the document, grammar and spelling check to make an error-free document. Besides editing techniques, various designing techniques to produce an attractive document are also discussed in a chapter.

The concluding chapter of the section discusses an important feature of Microsoft Word – Mail Merge. With the help of Mail Merge, any business concern, big or small, can automate the tedious and time-consuming task of creating and printing business letters. Once you have created a data source for the Mail Merge application, you can produce all sorts of mass mailings (both printed and electronic) or print any other information that you maintain in the data source.

Microsoft Excel

IN THIS SECTION

- Introduction to Spreadsheets
- Simple Charts
- Manipulating Data
- Changing the Layout

MICROSOFT EXCEL

Introduction to Spreadsheets 1

IN THIS CHAPTER

- Spreadsheet
- Starting Microsoft Excel
- Spreadsheet Basics
- Excel Work Environment
- Excel Toolbars
- Office Assistant
- Working in Excel Workbook
- Moving inside a Workbook with Cell Pointer
- Entering Data in a Cell Address
- Changing the Cell Content
- Closing Excel Workbook Without Saving
- Quitting Microsoft Excel
- Exercise

Now, we introduce you to the **Microsoft Excel**, a program specifically designed to organize data in tables easily and analyse the tabulated data. **Microsoft Excel** is one of the most versatile and popular spreadsheet programs. It serves as an electronic pad for accountants. It can easily perform simple as well as complex mathematical operations. Excel also provides the facility to convert the spreadsheet data into various charts like Bar, Pie, 2D & 3D. When converted into charts, the spreadsheet data can be easily understood. Before working in Excel, you must understand what a spreadsheet is all about.

Spreadsheet

Spreadsheet is a simple worksheet consisting of rows and columns in which any data can be entered. Spreadsheets are used for performing calculations, recalculating results (if any data stored in them is changed), creating financial reports, comparing reports etc. A very useful feature of the spreadsheet is its ability to create groups. It helps you establish relationship between two or more sets of data and easily understand the trend of data changes.

The report card of a student or the ledger that we create for maintaining bank accounts can be termed as a spreadsheet. Report cards of students are manual spreadsheets. An electronic spreadsheet is similar to a paper spreadsheet. However, an electronic spreadsheet is created on the computer screen while the manual spreadsheet is made on paper. As compared to manual spreadsheets, electronic spreadsheets take less time in getting prepared and it is also quite easy to update them. Let us now consider the following manual spreadsheet prepared by a teacher based on a class report of the students' marks in various subjects.

CLASS REPORT

		RAHUL	ASHA	ANUJ	APARNA
SUBJECT	**MAX MARKS**				
ENGLISH	100	70	80	72	67
HINDI	100	$65^{1}/2$	$76^{1}/2$	67	80
MATHS	100	57	90	80	82
SCIENCE	100	79	79	85	92
SST	100	60	72	60	87
DRAWING	100	67	80	70	80
G.K. GR.	A+	B	A+	B+	A+
TOTAL	600	$398^{1}/2$	$477^{1}/2$	434	488
%(AGE)		66.3%	79.5%	72.33%	81.33%

Fig. EX-1.1

Suppose, in the class report spreadsheet (Fig. EX-1.1), a change is required in the English marks of Aparna. Here, resetting Aparna's marks would be quite tedious and time-consuming as her total marks and the percentage would also need to be changed manually. However, in the case of an electronic spreadsheet, if we change Aparna's English marks, her total marks and percentage get recalculated automatically. We will learn more about various useful features of electronic spreadsheets when we will work in Excel. First, we will learn to open the Excel program.

Starting Microsoft Excel

Let us now start Microsoft Excel through the following steps:

1. *Move* the mouse-pointer over the **Start** button present on the **taskbar** (Fig. EX-1.2) and then *click* the left mouse-button. Instantly, a push-up menu appears (Fig. EX-1.2).
2. Inside the push-up menu, *place* the mouse-pointer over the **All Programs** option. Immediately, a second menu gets displayed (Fig.EX-1.2).
3. In the second menu, *place* the mouse-pointer over the **Microsoft Office** option (Fig.EX-1.2). A third menu appears.
4. In the third menu, *place* the mouse-pointer over the **Microsoft Office Excel 2003**. Finally, *click* the left mouse-button.
5. Instantly, the **Microsoft Excel** window opens up on your screen with a blank document (Fig. EX-1.3). This blank document consisting of rows and columns is called **worksheet.** In a worksheet, you can enter data, perform calculations on the entered data, and so on.

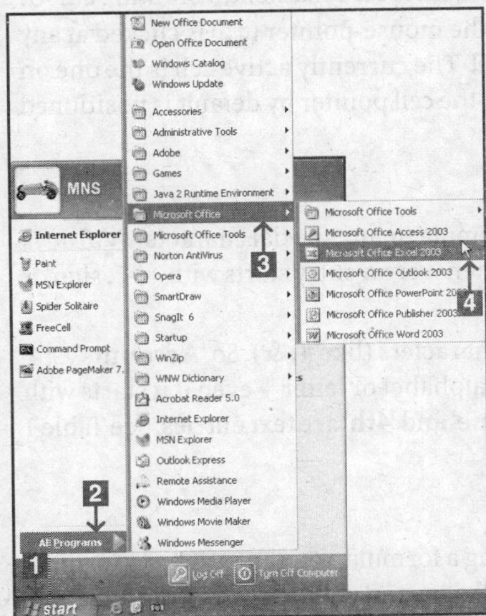

Fig. EX-1.2

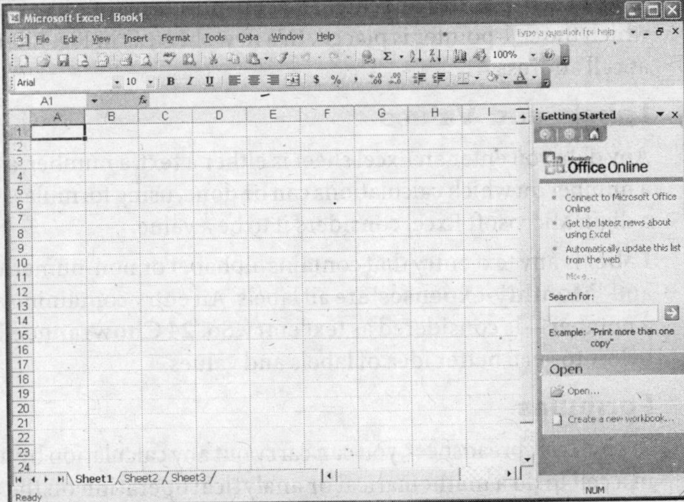

Fig. EX-1.3

Spreadsheet Basics

Let us now understand some essential elements of an electronic spreadsheet like the one shown in Fig. EX-1.3. Their understanding is necessary to work in the Excel program.

Cell and Cell Address

A spreadsheet consists of **rows and columns.** Each row and column intersection creates a **cell,** into which you may enter data. In Fig.EX-1.4, column **A** has **13** cells, column **B** has **13** cells and so on. The cell address identifies the location of each cell. A particular cell is addressed by combining the column letter and the row number. For example, in Fig.EX-1.4, **A1** is the address of the cell that is formed at the intersection of column **A** and row **1.** Cell addresses starting with row numbers, like 3B or 10A, are invalid cell addresses.

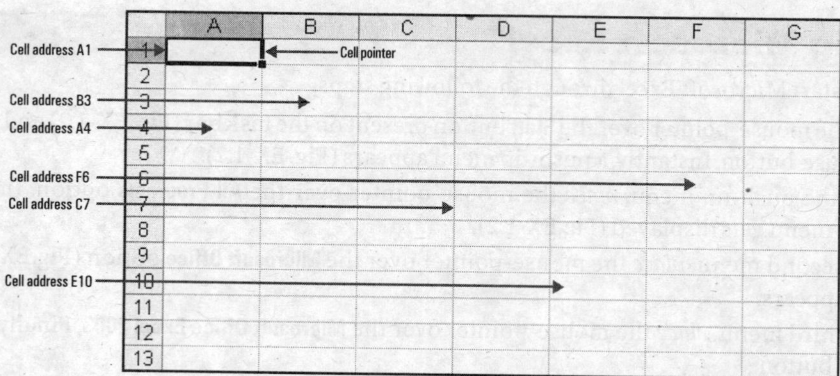

Fig. EX-1.4

Cell Pointer

As we know, in Microsoft Word, when the mouse-pointer is clicked inside a document, a blinking cursor gets displayed. However, in Microsoft Excel spreadsheet, when the mouse-pointer (✥) is clicked at any place, a **cell-pointer** appears. The **cell-pointer** looks like ▭. The currently active cell is the one on which the cell-pointer is placed. In a new sheet, as in Fig. EX-1.4, the cell pointer by default is positioned at cell address **A1**.

Labels and Values

Any data you enter an Excel sheet is either a text, a number, a formula or any special character. **Value** is a number on which calculations can be done, using formulas. Whenever an entry starts with +, -, . sign or a digit, Microsoft Excel considers it to be a value.

Label is any text entry that contains alphabet or non-numeric characters (like #, &). So '**Accounts**', '**#4**' and '**Monthly-expenses**' are all labels. An entry containing an alphabet or letter—even if it starts with a number—is considered as text entry. So, '**24 Chowrangee Lane**' and '**4th**' are text entries. See Table 1 below to get a better idea of labels and values.

Formulas

In an Excel spreadsheet, you can carry out any calculation by using a formula. You can insert any formula in a cell to do a mathematical or analytical operation on the cell data and get the desired output.

For example, in Table 1, cell **C4** contains the formula that calculates the interest. Cell **C1** contains principal (P), **C2** contains time (T) and **C3** contains rate (R). So, according to the formula of **C4**, the interest calculated is **60**.

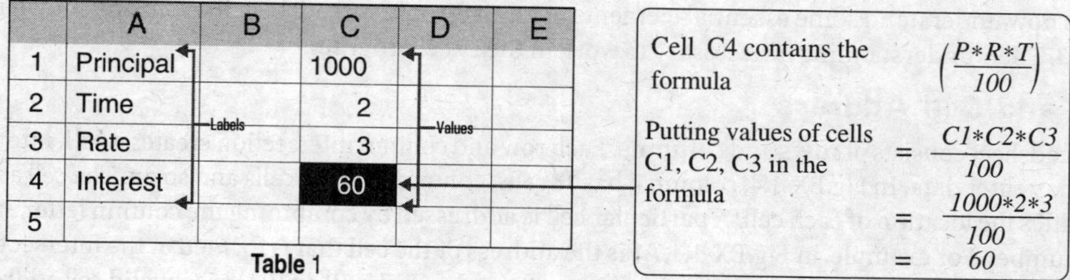

	A	B	C	D	E
1	Principal		1000		
2	Time		2		
3	Rate		3		
4	Interest		60		
5					

Table 1

Cell C4 contains the formula $\left(\frac{P*R*T}{100}\right)$

Putting values of cells C1, C2, C3 in the formula $= \frac{C1*C2*C3}{100}$

$= \frac{1000*2*3}{100}$

$= 60$

Function

Formulas that are inbuilt into a spreadsheet are called functions. In Table 2, formulas in cells B6, C6, D6 calculate the sum, the average and the maximum number of marks awarded to the students in different subjects, respectively. These formulas are built into the spreadsheet that represents Table 2.

	A	B	C	D	E
1		Marks			
2	Chemistry	70	70	70	
3	Biology	73	73	73	
4	Physics	80	80	80	
5	Maths	85	85	85	
6		308	77	85	
7					

This cell contains the sum function, i.e. =Sum (B2..B5) = B2 + B3 + B4 + B5 = 70 + 73 + 80 + 85 = 308

This cell contains the avg. function, i.e. = Average (B2..B5) = (B2 + B3 + B4 + B5)/4 = (70 + 73 + 80 + 85)/4 = 77

This cell contains the max function i.e.= Max (B2..B5) = Max (B2, B3, B4, B5) = Max (70, 73, 80, 85) = 85

Table 2

What-if Analysis

What-if Analysis is a very useful feature of spreadsheets. Using this feature, you can see how would change in values or data of one or more cells affect the outcome of formulas in the worksheet. For example, if Rahul's marks in Science are 90 instead of 79 (Fig. EX-1.1) then using the What-if Analysis you can quickly find out what would be his total marks and how much would be the increase in his percentage.

Automatic Recalculation

A major drawback of the manual spreadsheet is that if any data in it changes, you have to redo all calculations that are affected by the data change. But, an electronic spreadsheet automatically performs all such calculations for you. All you have to do is just change the data and the rest is taken care of by the spreadsheet. The Automatic Recalculation feature proves very useful in the What-if Analysis.

To understand how does Excel carry out the automatic recalculation, let us consider Table 3. Suppose Column **B** of Table 3 contains **Salary** of a person as well as **Expenses** incurred by him on goods, rent and travel. The **Total** displays the sum of expenses on **Goods, Rent** and **Travel.** The **Savings** in Table 3 is calculated as the difference between the **Salary** and the **Total,** i.e. 2800 and 2050 respectively.

If we change the amount spent on **Goods** from **800** to **1000** the **Total** as well as the **Savings** are changed as shown in Table 4. Here it should be noted that the formula applied in both the tables is same. In Table 4, Excel replaces the old value of **Goods** with a new value and recalculates the **Total** and **Savings.** Hence, the **Total** changes from **2050** to **2250** and the **Savings** changes from **750** to **550.**

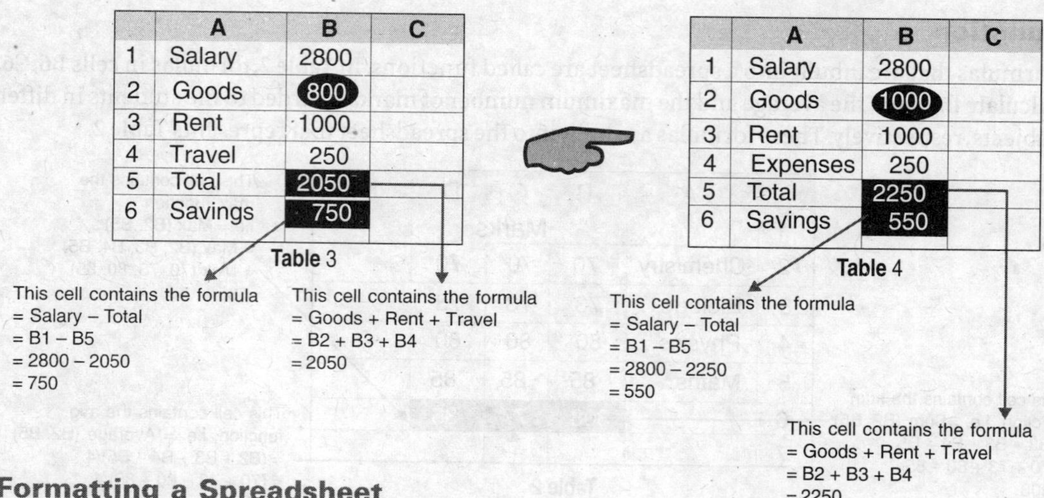

	A	B	C
1	Salary	2800	
2	Goods	800	
3	Rent	1000	
4	Travel	250	
5	Total	2050	
6	Savings	750	

Table 3

	A	B	C
1	Salary	2800	
2	Goods	1000	
3	Rent	1000	
4	Expenses	250	
5	Total	2250	
6	Savings	550	

Table 4

Formatting a Spreadsheet

A spreadsheet can be designed in a number of formats. Basically, number formatting is concerned with how does the data (numeric) in a spreadsheet look on the screen. Table 5 displays frequently used number formats in Microsoft Excel.

Format	Example
Comma	1,750
Percent	63.25%
Currency	Rs. 78,00,000
Scientific	4.00 E + 09

Table 5

The data in a cell may also be right-aligned, left-aligned or centered as shown below.

Example	Alignment
References	Left-aligned
References	Right-aligned
References	Centered

Table 6

Excel Work Environment

Let us now revert to the Excel worksheet (Fig. EX-1.3) open on your computer. The Title bar of this figure is named as Book1. Each file in Excel is termed as **Workbook**. Each workbook consists of worksheets. By default an Excel workbook has three worksheets — Sheet1/Sheet2/Sheet3.

Worksheet

An Excel worksheet, as you know, consists of cells formed by the intersection of rows and columns. Excel worksheet is a large area consisting of 65,536 rows and 256 columns. Only a small portion of the worksheet can be seen on the screen at a time. The worksheet columns are labelled as A-Z, then AA-AZ, then BA-BZ and so on. The rows are labelled from 1 to 65,536.

Task pane

Each time you start the Excel, the **Getting Started** Task pane appears. It is located on the right side of the worksheet as a panel containing various options. The Task pane contains links which can be used to perform common tasks, such as opening or creating a workbook. Let us now briefly discuss the Task pane options.

Office Online — You can use its sub-options to visit the official website of Microsoft which is dedicated to Microsoft Office applications.

Search — This option lets you search help on any topic of your interest.

Open — It displays the name of last four workbooks on which the user has worked. These can be accessed easily

Create a new workbook — This option allows the user to create a new Excel file.

If the Task pane is not visible on the Excel worksheet then undertake the following steps to display it.

1. Move the mouse-pointer over the View Menu bar option of the Excel window and click the left mouse button. A pull-down menu appears.
2. In the pull-down menu, click the Task pane option. Instantly, the Task pane appears.

Excel Toolbars

The Microsoft Excel window comprises a **Menu Bar**, two **Toolbars** and a **Formula Bar**. The Menu bar contains commands for performing tasks. There are two toolbars in the Excel window, one is the **Standard Toolbar** and the other **Formatting Toolbar**. The **Formula Bar** consists of a rectangular box for entering and editing information as well as getting help from Excel in writing formulas. Let us now know more about Excel toolbars.

Title bar

The **Title bar** is present at the top of an Excel window. The Title bar shown in Fig. EX-1.5 displays the name of the program, **Microsoft Excel**, and the name of the currently open workbook, **Book 1**. The three buttons present on the extreme right of the Title bar (Fig. EX-1.5) are used to change the size of the window and close the window.

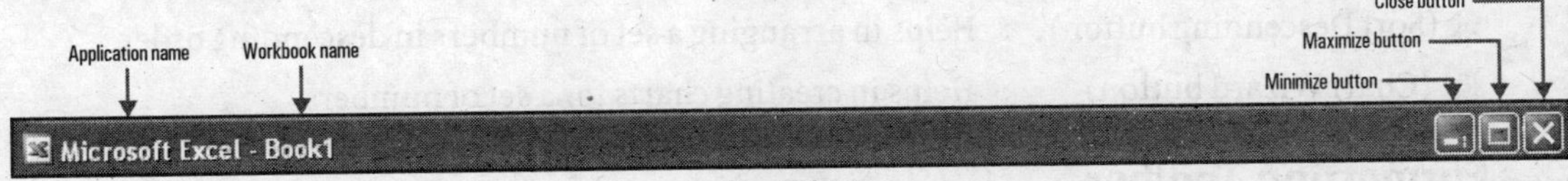

Fig. EX-1.5

Menu Bar

A menu is a list of related options that help you perform operations on the data in your workbook. These options are arranged in a bar. This bar is called **Menu bar** (Fig.EX-1.6) and is placed below the Title bar. Through the Menu bar options, you can perform operations like changing the width of a column, formatting the numbers, erasing a list of cells, copying and retrieving files, and so on.

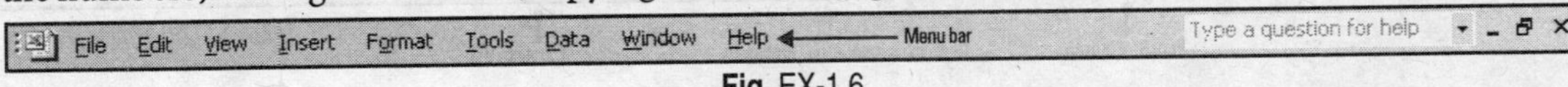

Fig. EX-1.6

A brief description of tasks that can be accomplished with some menu bar options is given as follows:

File : Helps in creating a new file; opening an existing file; setting up margins of the worksheet; saving, printing or closing a particular file after the work has been done; and quitting Microsoft Excel.

Edit : Helps in cutting/copying/deleting a range of text; pasting the text which has been cut or copied from a different location; erasing an entire sheet and quickly moving any sheet.

Insert : Helps in inserting rows or columns in the sheet.

Format : Helps in changing the font style or size of a selected range of text; changing the width of a particular row or a particular column.

Tools : Helps in checking any spelling errors in your current sheet; automatically saves your file on a regular basis; protects your sheet; customizes your sheet according to your specifications, etc.

Data : Helps you in sorting data in an ascending or a descending order, filtering data, adding validations, summarizing data etc.

Standard Toolbar

The **Standard Toolbar**, shown in Fig. EX-1.7, is located just below the Menu bar. It consists of various buttons that provide shortcuts for various editing tasks related to an Excel worksheet.

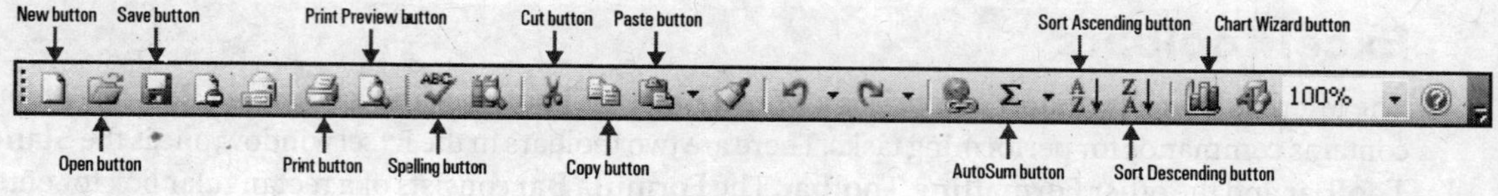

Fig. EX-1.7

In chapters of Microsoft Word, you have worked with the buttons displayed in the left portion of the Standard Toolbar. In Excel also, these buttons work in the same way as in Microsoft Word. Now, read on to understand the functions of some new buttons added to the Standard toolbar to help you in calculations.

Σ (AutoSum button)	:	Helps in calculating the sum of a range of numbers. Also performs various other mathematical operations on them.
(Sort Ascending button)	:	Helps in arranging a set of numbers in ascending order.
(Sort Descending button)	:	Helps in arranging a set of numbers in descending order.
(Chart Wizard button)	:	Helps in creating charts for a set of numbers.

Formatting Toolbar

Just below the Standard Toolbar is the **Formatting Toolbar** as shown in Fig.EX-1.8. It consists of buttons for boldfacing, italicizing, underlining, centering text, and so on.

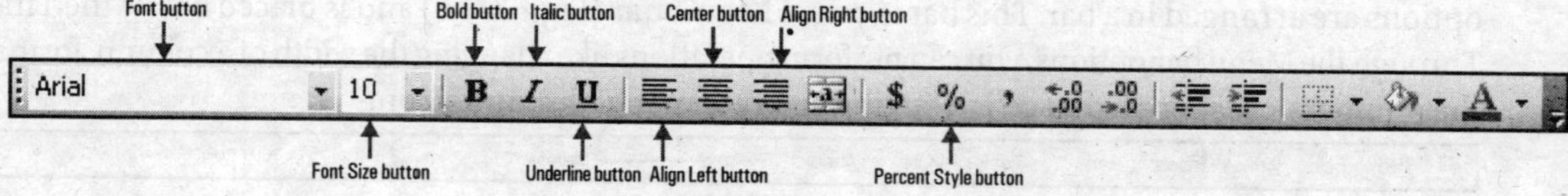

Fig. EX-1.8

Formula Bar

The **Formula Bar** is located just below the Formatting toolbar (Fig.EX-1.9). It has two blank boxes. The box on the left shows the address of the active cell (i.e. name of the cell where the cell pointer is located). The box on the right shows the contents of the active cell. In Fig.EX-1.9, the cell pointer is currently at cell address **A1**. So, the Formula bar indicates the active cell as **A1** and also displays its contents **abc**.

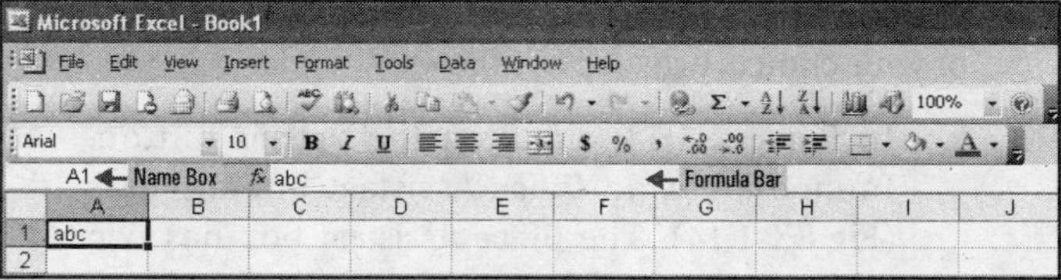

Fig. EX-1.9

Status Bar

The Status Bar is located at the bottom of Microsoft Excel window (Fig.EX-1.10). It displays **Ready** on the left hand side and **NUM** on the right hand side.

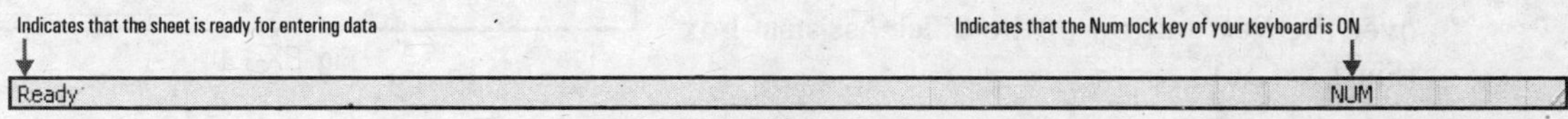

Fig. EX-1.10

The text **Ready** indicates that the workbook is ready to accept data from you. The **NUM** Indicator light of the keyboard can be turned on and off by pressing the **Num** Lock key. When it is ON, the arrow/number keys, lying below the **Lock** key of the keyboard, function as numbers. Press the **Num** Lock key again from the keyboard to turn the Indicator light OFF. When it is OFF, the arrow/number keys function as arrow keys. These can be used to move the cell pointer.

Office Assistant

As soon as you open Microsoft Excel, an animated icon appears on the screen. This icon is called **Office Assistant** (Fig.EX-1.11). It is basically Excel's quick help feature that makes it easy for you to find help on a particular topic to accomplish your tasks. If the Office Assistant is not visible on your screen, undertake the following steps to display it.

Fig. EX-1.11

1. In the Excel window, *move* the mouse-pointer to the **Help** option of the Menu bar and *click* the left mouse-button. A pull-down menu appears (Fig. EX-1.12).
2. In the pull-down menu, *move* the mouse-pointer over the **Show the Office Assistant** option and *click* the left mouse-button (Fig. EX-1.12).
3. Immediately, the **Office Assistant** appears on the screen with some instructions (Fig.EX-1.13) asking you **What would you like to do?** This box has two options: **Options** and **Search.**

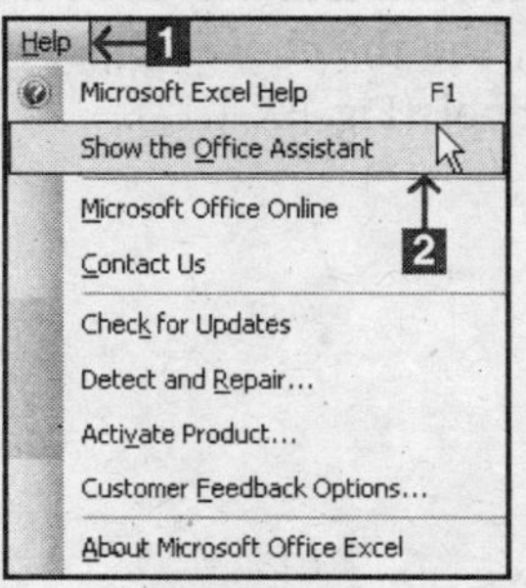

Fig. EX-1.12

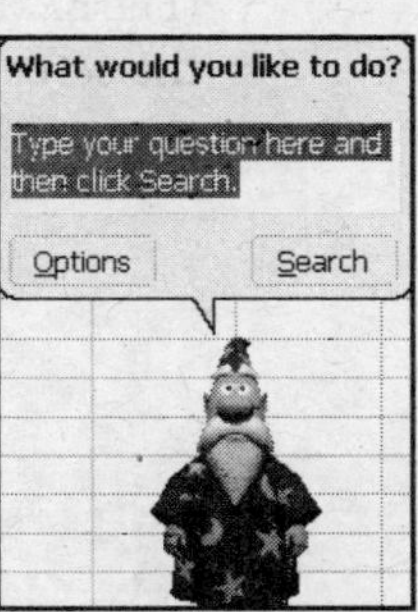

Fig. EX-1.13

Choosing desired Office Assistant

Excel provides eight animated characters to use as Office Assistant icon. To select the Office Assistant of your choice, proceed as follows:

1. In Fig. EX-1.13, *click* on the **Options** button. Immediately, an **Office Assistant** box appears (Fig.EX-1.14). The **Office Assistant** box has two tabs — **Gallery** and **Options**. By default, the **Options** tab appears active.

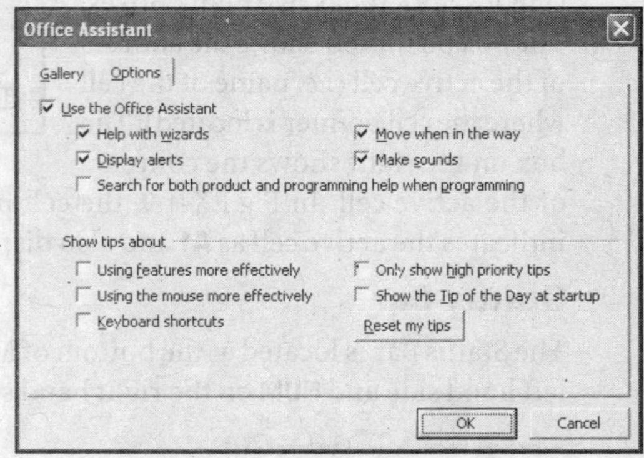

Fig. EX-1.14

2. *Click* on the **Gallery** tab (Fig. EX-1.15). Immediately an animated character appears in the Office Assistant box. This is the default animated character representing the Office Assistant.

3. To view other animated characters, keep *clicking* over the **Next** button of the **Office Assistant** box (Fig. EX-1.16).

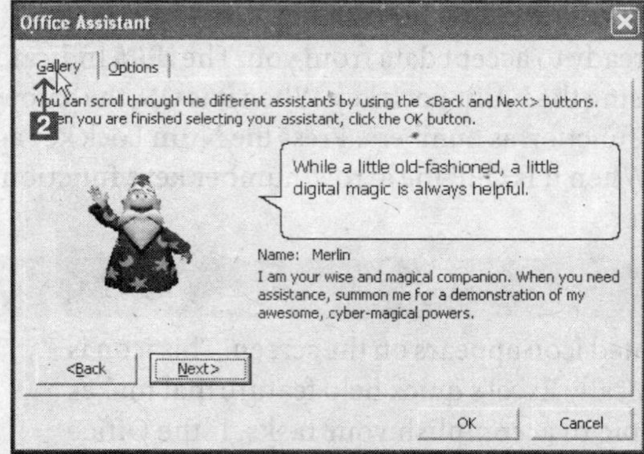

Fig. EX-1.15

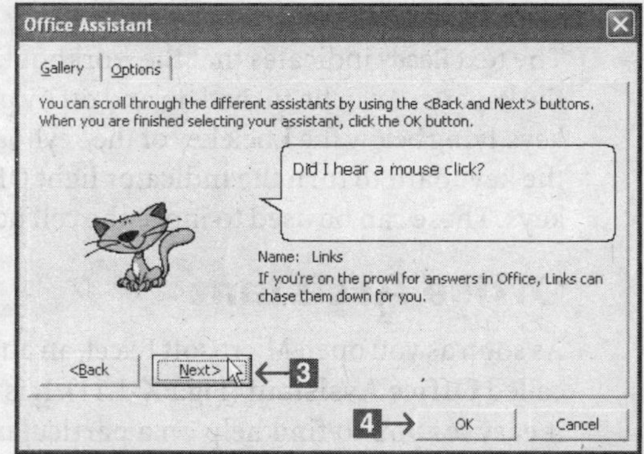

Fig. EX-1.16

4. After choosing an animated character, *stop clicking* over the **Next** button. Thereafter, *click* on the **OK** button of the **Office Assistant** box (Fig. EX-1.16). Immediately, the **Office Assistant** box disappears from the screen, and the chosen **Office Assistant** icon gets displayed on your workbook (Fig. EX-1.17).

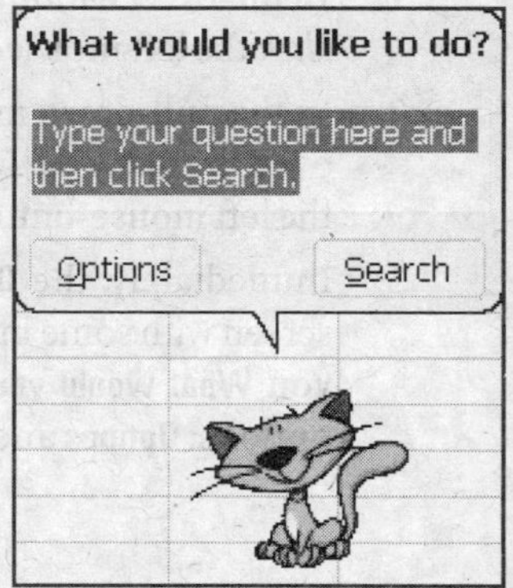

Fig. EX-1.17

Working in Excel Workbook

Now, we will work in the Excel workbook. But, first carefully observe the workbook, i.e. **Book1**, open on your computer. For your convenience we have reproduced Book1 in Fig. EX-1.18 below. We have also explained its essential features.

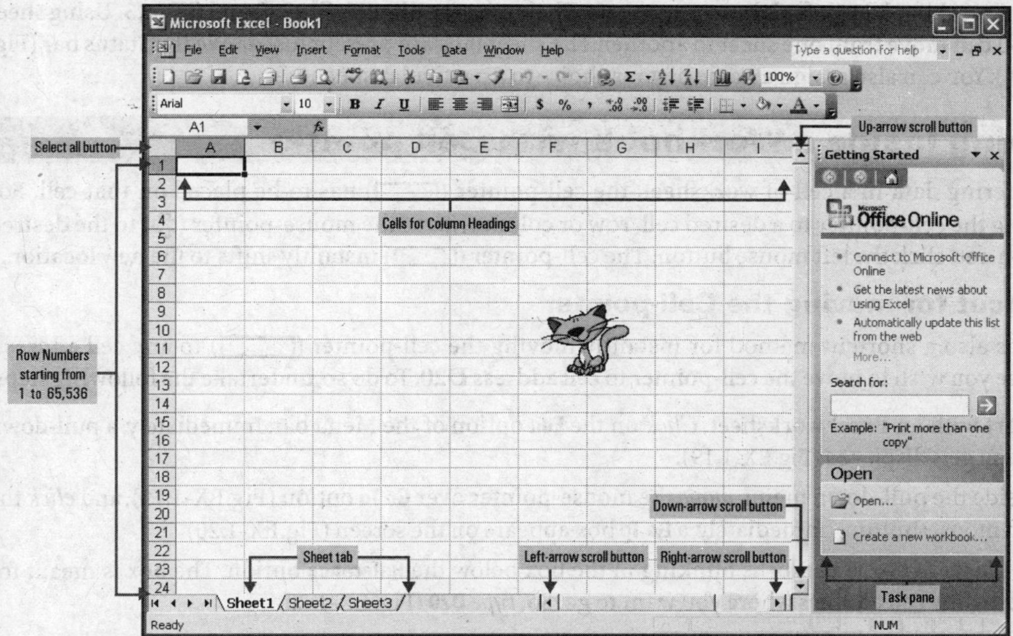

Fig. EX-1.18

Row Numbers

Each row in the Excel worksheet is assigned a number. The row numbers appear on the left side of the worksheet. They start from number **1** and go till number **65,536**, i.e. the last row (Fig.EX-1.18).

Column Headings

The name given to each column is termed as column heading. An Excel worksheet contains **256** columns. The columns are named from **A** through **Z** and they continue from **AA** to **AZ**, **BA** to **BZ** and so on. The column headings appear just below the Formula bar (Fig.EX-1.18).

Vertical Scroll Bar

The vertical scroll bar consists of two buttons—**up-arrow scroll** button (▲) and the **down-arrow scroll** button (▼) (Fig.EX-1.18). Clicking on any scroll button allows you to access the rows not visible on the screen.

Horizontal Scroll Bar

The horizontal scroll bar consists of two buttons—**right-arrow scroll** button and the **left-arrow scroll** button (Fig.EX-1.18). Clicking on any horizontal scroll bar button allows you to see those columns which are not visible on the screen.

Select All button

The Select All button is the first point where the row numbers and column headings meet (Fig.EX-1.18). On clicking this button, all the cells of a worksheet get highlighted.

Sheet Tabs

An Excel workbook by default has three sheets. Their tabs are **Sheet1, Sheet2** and **Sheet3.** Using sheet tabs you can move from one sheet to another. The sheet tabs are present just above the Status bar (Fig. EX-1.18). You can also assign a name of your choice to a particular sheet.

Moving Inside a Workbook with Cell pointer

For entering data in a cell of worksheet, the cell-pointer (▭) has to be placed on that cell. For bringing the cell-pointer to a desired cell, row or column, *move* the mouse-pointer (✚) to the desired location and click the left mouse button. The cell-pointer (▭) instantly shifts to the new location.

Shortcut for moving the Cell-pointer

There is also a shortcut method for instantly moving the cell-pointer (▭) to any cell address. Suppose you wish to move the cell-pointer to cell address D20. To do so, undertake the following steps:

1. Start with an Excel worksheet. *Click* on the **Edit** option of the Menu bar. Immediately, a pull-down menu gets displayed (Fig.EX-1.19).
2. Inside the pull-down menu, *move* the mouse-pointer over **Go To** option (Fig.EX-1.19), and *click* the left mouse-button. Immediately, a **Go To** box appears on the screen (Fig.EX-1.20).
3. In the **Go To** box, a cursor is blinking in the box below the **Reference** option. The box is meant for typing the cell address where you want to go. So, *type* **D20** (Fig. EX-1.20).
4. Finally, *click* on the **OK** button (Fig.EX-1.20). Immediately, the **Go To** box disappears from the screen and the cell-pointer gets displayed at cell address **D20** (Fig.EX-1.21).

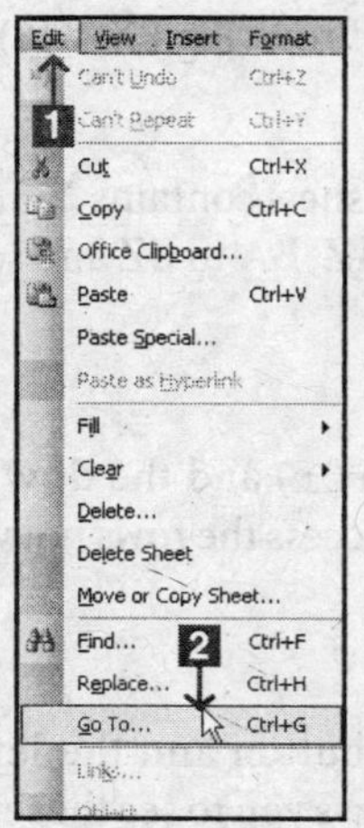

Fig. EX-1.19

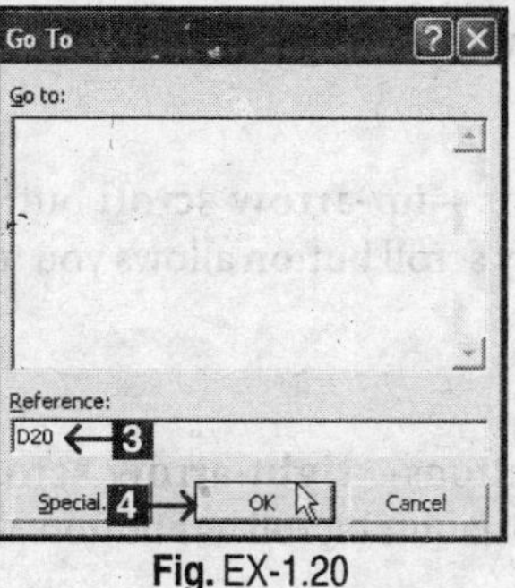

Fig. EX-1.20

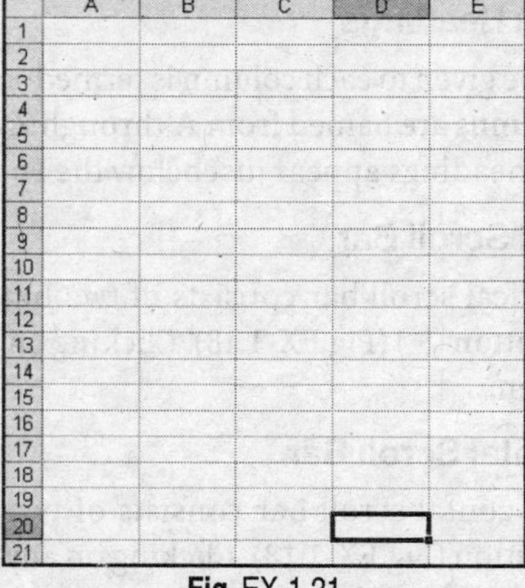

Fig. EX-1.21

Moving Cell pointer Quickly through keys

Some keys, described below, are also used for quick movement of the cell-pointer.

Key	Function
Home	Always moves the cell-pointer back to column A of the row where you are currently positioned.
Tab	Cell-pointer jumps one column to the right of the same row every time this key is pressed.
Shift+Tab	Cell-pointer jumps one column to the left of the same row every time these keys are pressed.
PgDn	Takes you one screen down.
PgUp	Takes you one screen up.

Entering Data in a Cell Address

To enter any data in an Excel worksheet, all you have to do is to *move* the cell-pointer to the cell address where you wish to enter the data and then type the data.

Entering a Label/Text

Text entries are normally used as row and column headings, for entering phone numbers, addresses, and so on. All texts are left aligned. And a formula cannot be applied over text entries. To enter a text, say, **Item** in cell address A2, undertake the following steps:

1. Begin with **Book 1** open on your screen. *Move* the mouse-pointer (✚) to cell address **A2** and *click* the left mouse-button. Instantly, the cell-pointer( ) appears at cell address **A2**.
2. Now *type* **Item** (Fig.EX-1.22).
3. Then *click* the mouse-pointer anywhere in your worksheet. Your worksheet will look like Fig.EX-1.22.

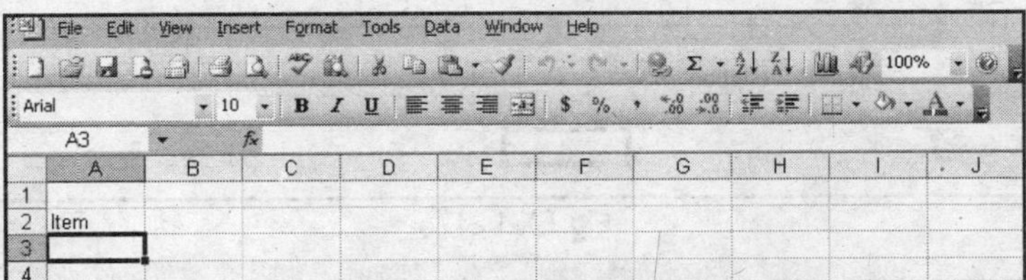

Fig. EX-1.22

Each cell has a default width of 9-10 characters, i.e. each cell can hold up to 9-10 characters. If, the entry of a cell address is more than its default width, its display gets extended to the next cell. This does not mean that it has occupied the space of the next cell.

For instance, when we enter the text Item Description at cell address C1, it gets extended to the next cell D1 (Fig.EX-1.23).

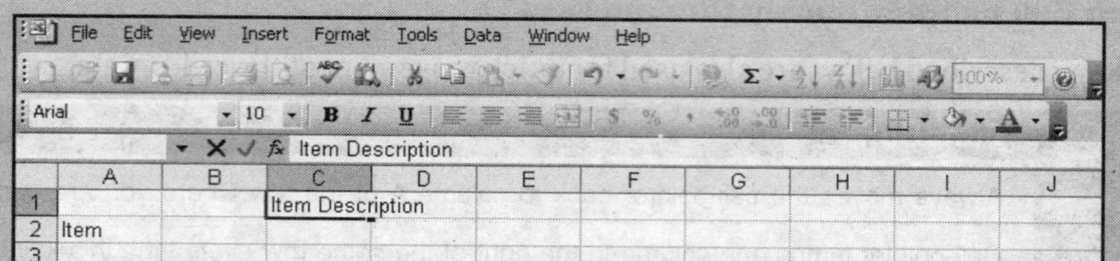

Fig. EX-1.23

Although the text Item Description appears occupying two cell addresses (C1 and D1), it is actually in cell address C1. To find out in which cell the text is actually displayed, undertake the following steps.

Click the left mouse-button over cell address D1. The Formula bar does not display the text entry. Now click the left mouse-button over cell address C1. The Formula bar displays the text Item Description. It means the text has been entered into cell C1.

Entering a Value/Number

Just like a text entry, you can enter a value or number in any cell. Suppose you wish to enter a number, say **400**, at cell address **A3**. To do so, undertake the following steps:

1. Begin with Fig. EX-1.23. *Move* the mouse-pointer (✣) to cell address **A3** and *click* the left mouse-button.
2. Now *type* **400** and then *click* the mouse-pointer (✣) anywhere in the worksheet. The worksheet will now look like Fig.EX-1.24. You will observe that **400**, a number, unlike the text entry, is always aligned to the right of the cell.

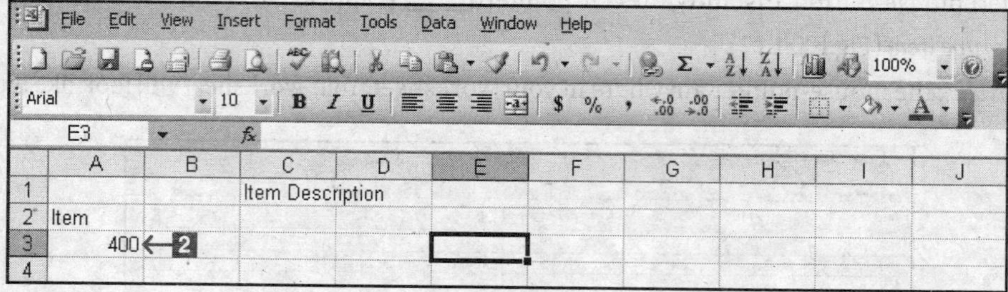

Fig. EX-1.24

You can also display any number as a text. Suppose you wish to type the number 500 as text entry at cell address A4. To do so, first type an apostrophe(') then type 500. On clicking the mouse-pointer anywhere in your sheet, the typed number gets displayed on the left-hand side of the cell (Fig.EX-1.25).

Fig. EX-1.25

> If you type a number without first typing an apostrophe, Microsoft Excel interprets your entry as a value or number and displays it on the right-hand side of the cell.
> Also note that :
> - If you type any number as 7-7-01, Microsoft Excel treats it as date and automatically displays it as 7/7/2001.
> - In the earlier versions of Excel, if you had entered 1000-200 and then pressed the Enter key, you would get the mathematical answer 800. But in XP version, Microsoft Excel treats the minus sign as a hyphen and considers the number 1000-200 as text. Thus, to get the mathematical answer, first you have to type an equal to (=) sign and then type the number 1000-200. Now Microsoft Excel will display the answer 800.
> - If you type a minus sign (-) or a plus sign (+) before a number, Microsoft Excel considers your entry as a negative or a positive number respectively.

Aligning Label/Text in a Cell

Inside a cell, a label or text can be aligned in three ways :

- Left aligned
- Center aligned
- Right aligned

Using different buttons on the Formatting Toolbar, you can center a text or align it on the left or the right side of any cell. Let us now enter a text, say **Rate**, at cell address **B2** and then position it at the center of the cell. Undertake the following steps:

1. Begin with Fig. EX-1.25. *Move* the mouse-pointer over cell address **B2** and then *click* the left mouse-button. Immediately, the cell-pointer shifts to cell **B2** (Fig.EX-1.26).

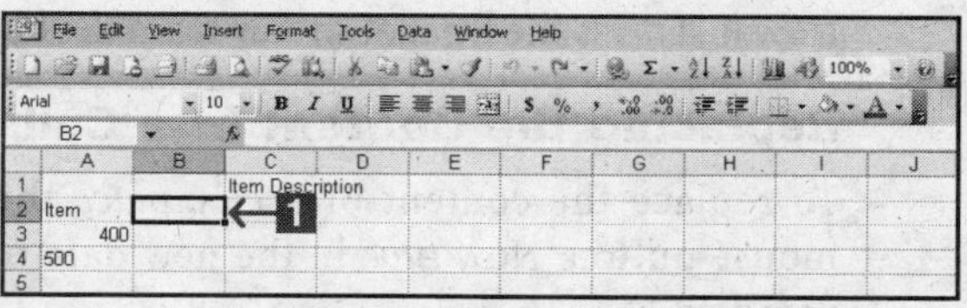

Fig. EX-1.26

2. Now, *type* **Rate**. You will see a blinking cursor inside the cell (Fig. EX-1.27). When a blinking cursor is displayed inside a cell, its text cannot be positioned at the center or aligned to the left or the right side of the cell.

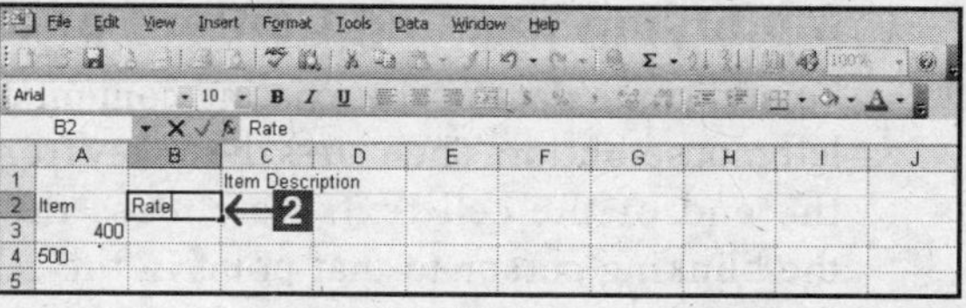

Fig. EX-1.27

3. So *press* the **Enter** key from the keyboard to remove the blinking cursor and *move* the cell-pointer to another cell **B3** (Fig.EX-1.28).

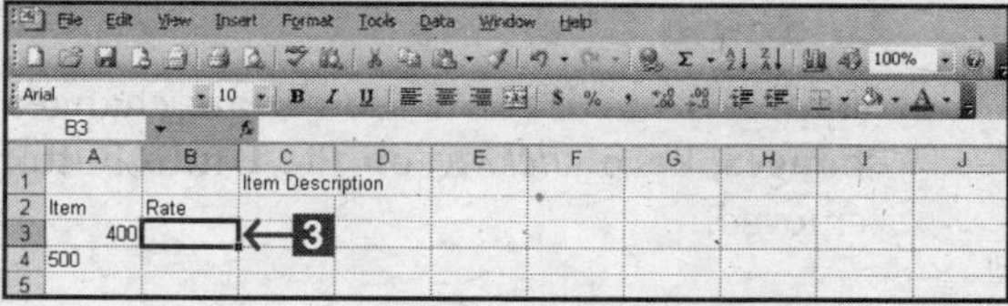

Fig. EX-1.28

4. To position the text **Rate** at the center of the cell, *click* again on cell address **B2**. Then *move* the mouse-pointer to the **Formatting Toolbar**, and *place it* over the **Center** button (≡) (Fig.EX-1.29).
5. Now, *click* the left mouse-button just once. Immediately, the text gets positioned at the center of the cell (Fig.EX-1.30).

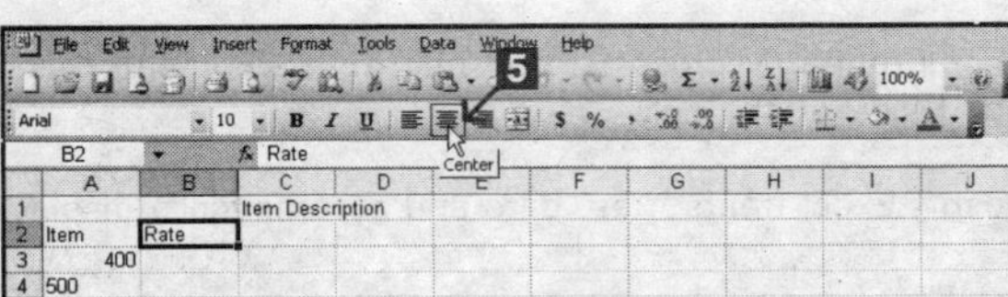

Fig. EX-1.29

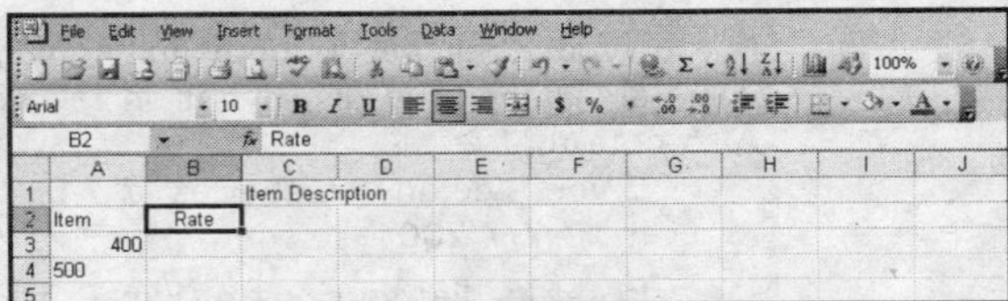

Fig. EX-1.30

If you want to align any text – in our case, Rate—to the right side of the cell, move the mouse-pointer over the Right button (≡) and click the left mouse-button. Immediately, the text gets right-aligned (Fig.EX-1.31).

Similarly, if you wish to align the text to the left side of the cell, click on the Left button (≡).

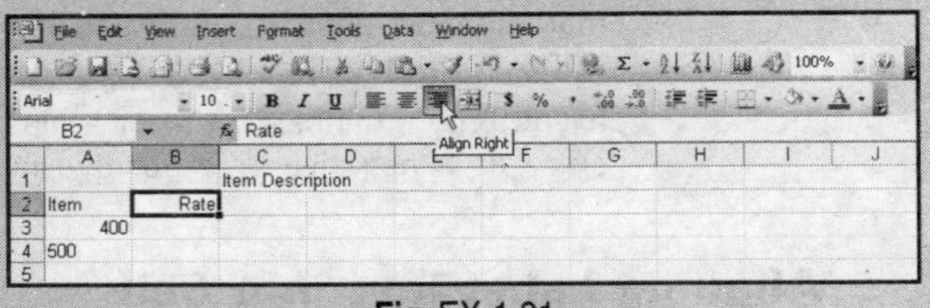

Fig. EX-1.31

Changing the Cell Content

In Microsoft Excel, you can easily delete or modify the contents of a cell. Let us learn to change the cell content.

Deleting the Content of a Cell

To delete the content of a cell, *move* the mouse-pointer (✥) to that cell and *click* the left mouse-button. Now just *press* the **Spacebar** key from the keyboard, and the cell content gets deleted.

Replacing the Content of a Cell

To replace the content of a cell, *place* the mouse-pointer (✥) over that cell and *click* the left mouse-button. Now *type* in the new data from the keyboard. The old content gets replaced by the new data.

Modifying Existing Content of a Cell

To add some data in the existing content of a cell, *move* the cell-pointer to that cell and *click* the left mouse-button. Then *press* the **F2** key from the keyboard. Immediately, a blinking cursor appears at the end of the cell text. Now *press* the right or left arrow keys of the keyboard to move the blinking cursor to that point in the cell where you wish to make the change. Finally, *type* the desired data.

Undoing Changes

Suppose you wish to undo certain changes that you made last time in your sheet. To cancel those changes, keep *clicking* on the **Undo** button (↶) of the **Standard toolbar** till all the changes are removed.

Closing Excel Workbook Without Saving

So, you have become familiar with various features of the Excel program. Let us now close the currently open workbook through the following steps.

1. *Move* the mouse-pointer over the **File** option of the Menu bar and *click* the left mouse-button. Immediately, a pull-down menu gets displayed (Fig.EX-1.32).
2. Inside the pull-down menu, *move* the mouse-pointer over the **Close** option (Fig.EX-1.32) and *click* the left mouse-button. Immediately, a message box (Fig. EX-1.33) appears on your screen, asking whether you need to save **Book 1**.
3. Just *move* the mouse-pointer over the **No** button and *click* the left mouse-button. Immediately, the message box disappears and the workbook gets closed.

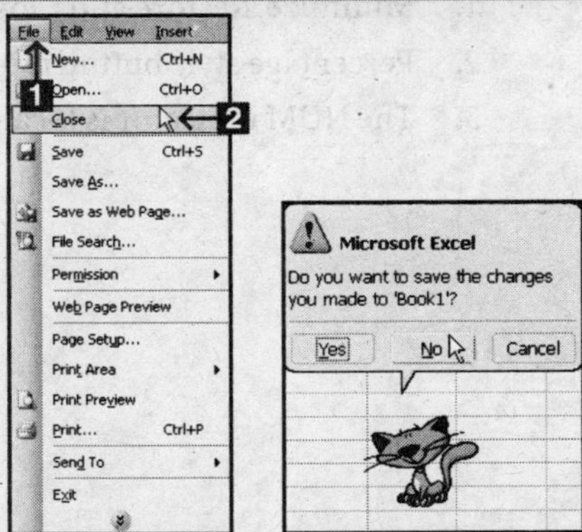

Fig. EX-1.32 **Fig.** EX-1.33

Quitting Microsoft Excel

Let us now close Microsoft Excel program through the following steps.

1. *Move* the mouse-pointer over the **Close** button (☒) (Fig.EX-1.34). *Click* the left mouse-button over it.

Fig. EX-1.34

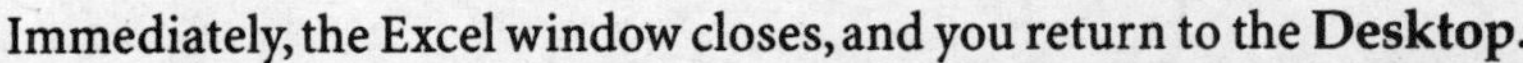

Immediately, the Excel window closes, and you return to the **Desktop**.

Exercise

Short Questions

1. What is cell?
2. What do you understand by the terms Label and Value?
3. Define Office Assistant.
4. In how may ways can you align the text or label in a worksheet?

Fill in the Blanks

1. A highlighted rectangle on an Excel worksheet that indicates the currently activate cell where the data you type will be entered is known as ____________.
2. _______ button allows the user to highlight entire rows and columns in the currently open worksheet.
3. ________ bar displays the address as well as contents of the active cell.
4. A worksheet consists ________ rows and _______ columns.
5. The value in Excel worksheet is always ________ aligned.

True/False

1. Minimize, Restore and Close buttons are present only in the Title bar.
2. Percentage style button is present on the Standard toolbar.
3. The NUM indicator is located on the left side of the Status bar.

MICROSOFT EXCEL

Simple Charts 2

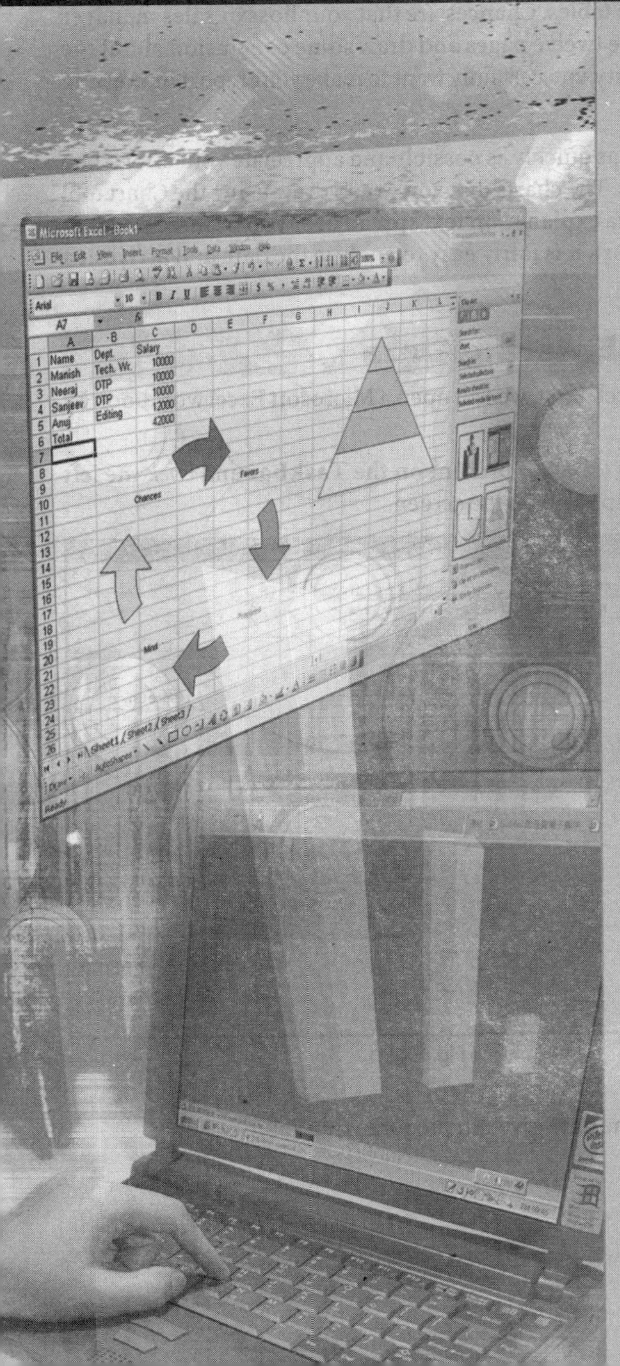

IN THIS CHAPTER

- Opening Microsoft Excel and Entering Data
- Drawing a Chart
- Positioning the Chart
- Changing the Size of a Chart
- Saving the Workbook
- Printing the Chart and Closing the Workbook
- Exercise

Charts also called graphs help us interpret the meaning of data in just one glance without going through a lengthy text. In Microsoft Excel too, you can use graphs to facilitate easy understanding of the data in your sheets. You can draw different types of graphs, such as Bar graph, Pie graph, Area graph, etc.

Suppose, you want to make a sales report for your company, which extends up to twelve pages. The report would also contain lot of data presented in various tables. Chances are that your boss or sales manager may find it quite cumbersome to go through all the twelve pages and draw some conclusion about the company's sales performance. To avoid this possibility, you certainly want to make your report interesting and easy-to-understand.

If you want your boss to go through the sales report as quickly as possible and appreciate your effort then simply replace the data explanation text with charts. The charts that you would draw using the Chart tool of Microsoft Excel will help you summarize the data explanation text spread over two or three pages to just a single page. While going through such a report, it is fairly easy to analyze the data and arrive at a conclusion.

Opening Microsoft Excel and Entering Data

Let us now practice making a chart in Microsoft Excel. First, we will open a Microsoft Excel workbook by undertaking the following steps.

1. *Move* the mouse-pointer over the **Start** button (start) present on the **Taskbar** and *click* the left mouse-button. Immediately, a push-up menu appears on the screen.
2. Next, *place* the mouse-pointer over the **All Programs** option. Instantly, a second menu appears.
3. In the second menu, *place* the mouse-pointer over the **Microsoft Office** option. Instantly, a third menu-appears.
4. In the third menu, *move* the mouse-pointer over the **Microsoft Excel 2003** option and *click* the left mouse-button. Immediately, the **Microsoft Excel** window appears on the screen (Fig. EX-2.1). The window displays blank **Sheet1** of workbook **Book 1**.

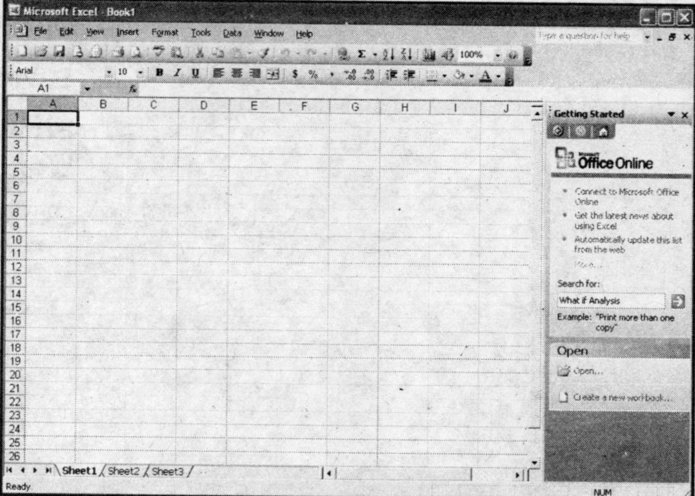

Fig. EX-2.1

Let us now make a sales graph in Sheet1 based on the data given in the following Table.

TABLE	Jan	Feb	Mar	Apr
Total Sales	12000	14000	16000	25000
Sales Goal	15000	20000	20000	25000

To add data of the above table in the currently open Sheet1, we will proceed as follows:

1. *Click* at cell address **B2** and *type* **Quarterly Sales.**
2. Now *move* the mouse-pointer over cell address **B5** and *type* **Total Sales.**
3. Next, *click* at cell address **B6** and type **Sales Goal.**
4. *Move* the mouse-pointer over cell address **C4** and *type* **Jan.** Similarly, *type* rest of the details. After entering all details, Sheet1 looks like Fig. EX-2-2.

	A	B	C	D	E	F	G
1							
2		**Quarterly Sales**					
3							
4			Jan	Feb	Mar	Apr	
5		Total Sales	12000	14000	16000	25000	
6		Sales Goal	15000	20000	20000	25000	
7							

Fig. EX-2.2

Drawing a Chart

A chart or graph has two axes - X axis and Y axis. Let us understand the basic steps of the chart-drawing making procedure. Right now, do not perform these steps on your computer. Just read carefully to have a better understanding of the chart-drawing procedure.

1. *Highlight* the data of which a graph has to be made.
2. *Click* on the **Chart Wizard** button ( ) present on the **Standard Toolbar.**
3. When the **Chart Wizard** box appears on the screen, choose the desired type of graph and enter the data in various dialog boxes of the Chart Wizard to display the chart in a worksheet.
4. To place the graph at the desired location on the sheet, first *position* the mouse-pointer over the white space in the graph, and then *press* the left mouse-button.
5. Then, keeping the left mouse-button *pressed*, *drag* the mouse on the mouse-pad such that the graph is placed at the desired location.
6. *Release* the mouse-button after the graph is placed at the desired location.

Let us now draw a chart, say a column chart on our sheet, through the following steps:

1. Start with Fig. EX-2.2. *Move* the mouse-pointer over cell address **B2** and *press* the left mouse-button (Fig. EX-2.3).

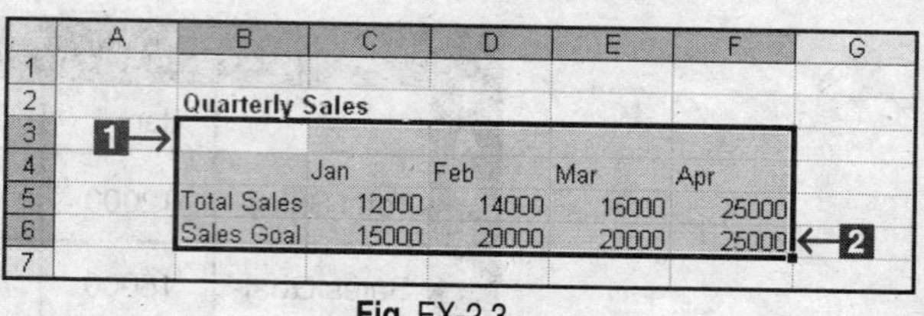

Fig. EX-2.3

2. Keeping the left mouse-button *pressed*, *drag* the mouse-pointer to the last cell address, in our case, cell address **F6** (Fig. EX-2.3).
3. When all five columns containing the data for the proposed chart get highlighted (Fig.EX-2.3), *release* the left mouse-button.
4. Now, *move* the mouse-pointer over the **Chart Wizard** button ( ) on the **Standard Toolbar** and *click* the left mouse-button (Fig. EX-2.4).

Fig. EX-2.4

5. Immediately, a **Chart Wizard - Step 1 of 4 - Chart Type** box appears on the screen (Fig. EX-2.5). In this box, the **Standard Types** tab appears active. Various types of charts present in Microsoft Excel are listed under the **Chart type** option. By default, the **Column** option for **Chart type** appears highlighted (Fig. EX-2.5). Let us use this default option for our chart.
6. Under the **Chart sub-type** option are displayed different types of columnar chart. *Move* the mouse-pointer over the desired columnar chart and *click* the left mouse-button (Fig. EX-2.6).

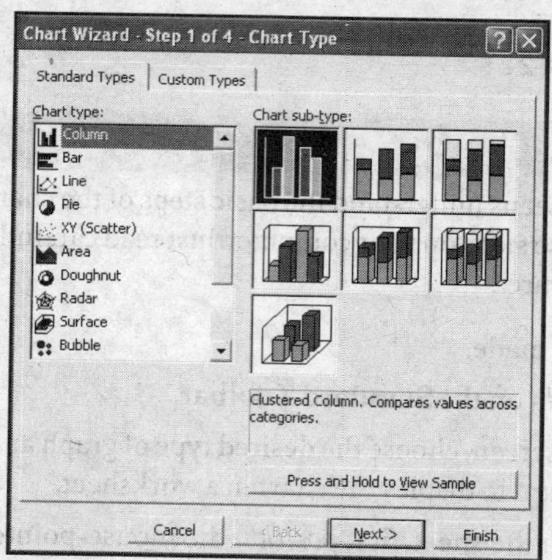

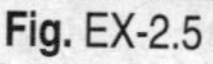

Fig. EX-2.5

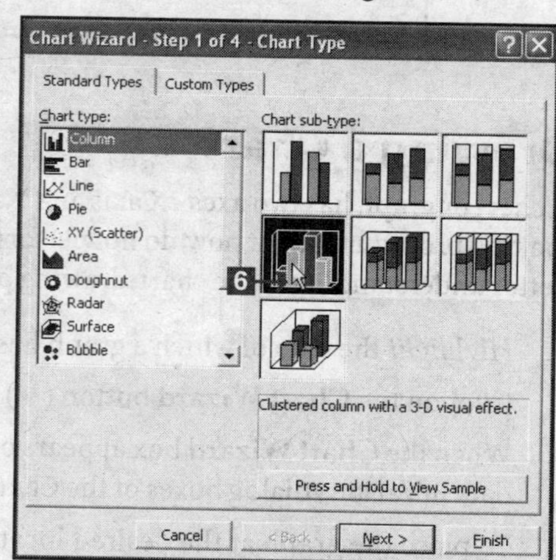

Fig. EX-2.6

7. After selecting the chart type, *move* the mouse-pointer over **Next** button and *click* left mouse-button (Fig. EX-2.7).
8. Immediately, a **Chart Wizard - Step 2 of 4 - Chart Source Data** box (Fig. EX-2.8) opens up showing the preview of the selected chart as well as the range of cell addresses selected by you. If the preview is not to your liking *click* on the **Back** button inside the **Chart Wizard - Step 2 of 4 - Chart Source Data** box to do the desired changes. In our case, we are satisfied with the preview so we *click* the left mouse-button on the **Next** button in Fig. EX-2.8.

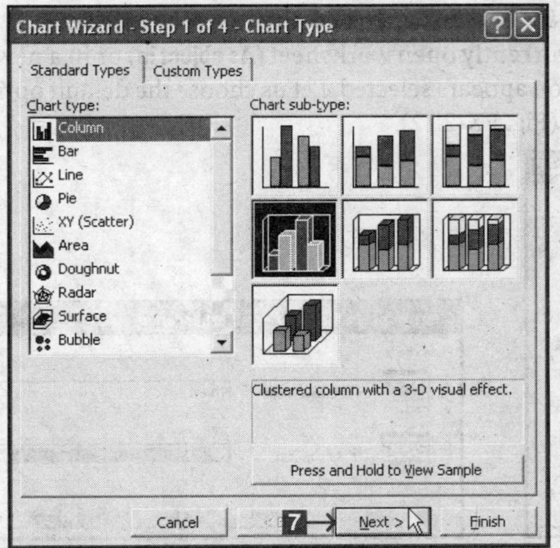

Fig. EX-2.7

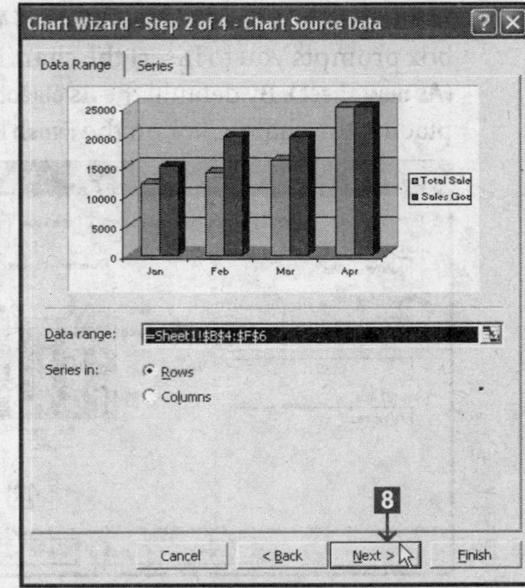

Fig. EX-2.8

9. Immediately, a **Chart Wizard - Step 3 of 4-Chart Options** box gets displayed on the screen (Fig. EX-2.9). In this box, the **Chart title** option is used to give a name to the chart.

10. *Click* inside the box below the **Chart title** option, and *type* **Quarterly Sales** as the name for your chart (Fig. EX-2.10).

11. You also need to give names to X and Z axes of your chart. In the **Chart Wizard** box of Fig. EX-2.9, there is provision to name three axes. But, the second axis option is disabled. So, we will use X and Z axes options for our chart. Now, to give a name, say **Month**, to the X-axis, *click* inside the box below **Category (X) axis** option and then *type* **Month** (Fig. EX-2.10).

12. To give name to the second axis, *type* **In Rupees** inside the box below **Value (Z) axis** option (Fig. EX-2.10).

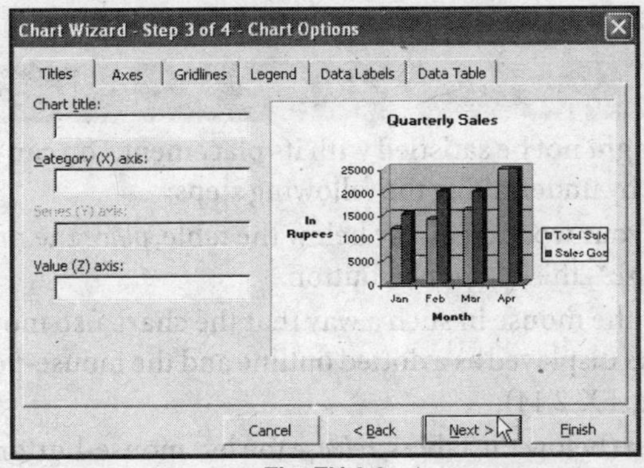

Fig. EX-2.9

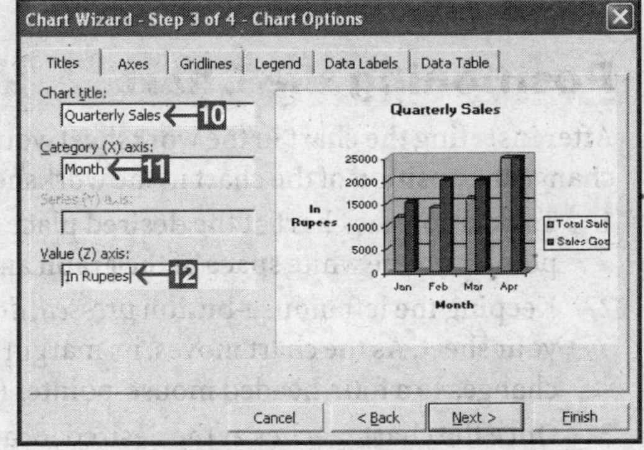

Fig. EX-2.10

13. *Click* on the **Next** button of the **Chart Wizard - Step 3 of 4 - Chart options** (Fig.EX-2.11).

14. Immediately, a **Chart Wizard - Step 4 of 4 - Chart Location** box opens up on the screen (Fig. EX-2.12). This box prompts you to insert the chart in the currently open worksheet (**As object in**) or in a new sheet (**As new sheet**). By default, the **As object in** option appears selected. Let us choose the default option for placing the chart. *Click* on the **Finish** button (Fig. EX-2.12).

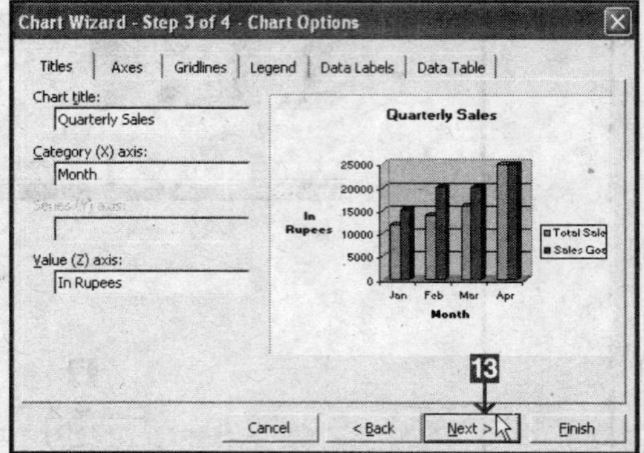

Fig. EX-2.11

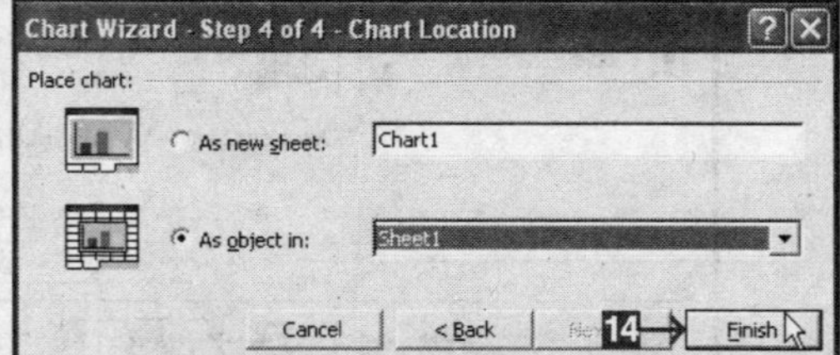

Fig. EX-2.12

15. Immediately, the **Chart Wizard - Step 4 of 4 - Chart Location** box closes, and the chart appears near the data table in your worksheet (Fig. EX-2.13).

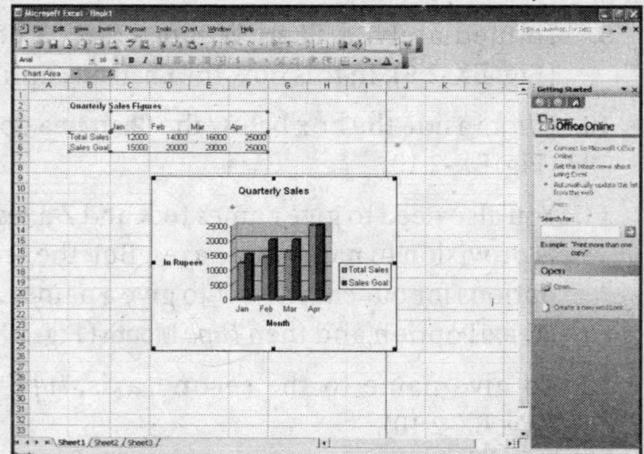

Fig. EX-2.13

Positioning the Chart

After inserting the chart in the worksheet, you might not be satisfied with its placement. You can easily change the position of the chart in the worksheet by undertaking the following steps:

1. To position the chart at the desired place in your worksheet, say below the table, *place* the mouse-pointer on the white space of the graph and *press* the left mouse-button.
2. Keeping the left mouse-button *pressed*, *drag* the mouse in such a way that the chart also moves in your sheet. As the chart moves, its margin gets displayed as a dotted outline and the mouse-pointer changes to a four-headed mouse-pointer (Fig. EX-2.14).
3. Once the chart reaches at the desired location (below the table), *release* the left mouse-button. The chart now gets displayed without the dotted margin (Fig. EX-2.15). You will observe eight dots at the border of the graph. These help in increasing or decreasing the size of the graph.

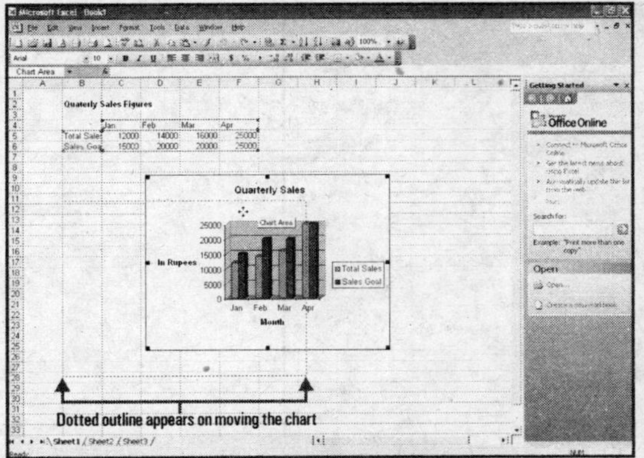

Fig. EX-2.14

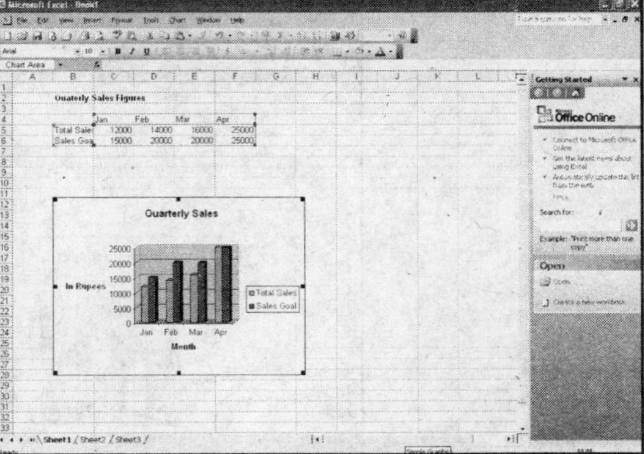

Fig. EX-2.15

Changing the Size of a Chart

You can easily resize the chart in a worksheet. For resizing a chart, eight dots are given on the border of the chart. Figure EX-2.15 displays these dots around the chart. If these dots are not visible on your screen then simply click over the chart. The dots will become visible. You can click over dot and drag the chart either to increase or decrease its size. However, if you click and drag any dot situated on the corners of the chart, the size of the chart increases or decreases in a fixed proportion. Let us now increase the size of the chart through the following steps:

1. Start with Fig. EX-2.15. To increase the size of our graph up to row number 31, *move* the mouse-pointer over any dot present at the bottom border of the graph, say the dot on the extreme right side, and *press* the left mouse-button. The mouse-pointer instantly changes into a diagonal twin-headed arrow (↖↘) (Fig. EX-2.16).
2. Now, keeping the left mouse-button *pressed*, you can *drag* and adjust the chart anywhere on the sheet. As you drag the chart, a dotted outline border around it moves with the mouse-pointer (Fig. EX-2.17).

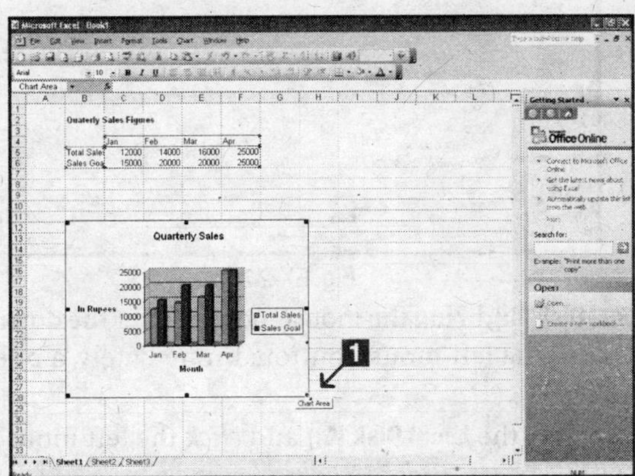

Fig. EX-2.16

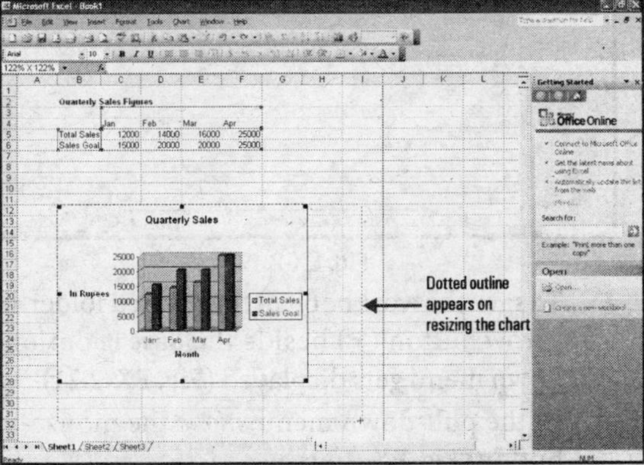

Fig. EX-2.17

3. After resizing the chart, *release* the left mouse-button. The resized chart appears as in Fig. EX-2.18.

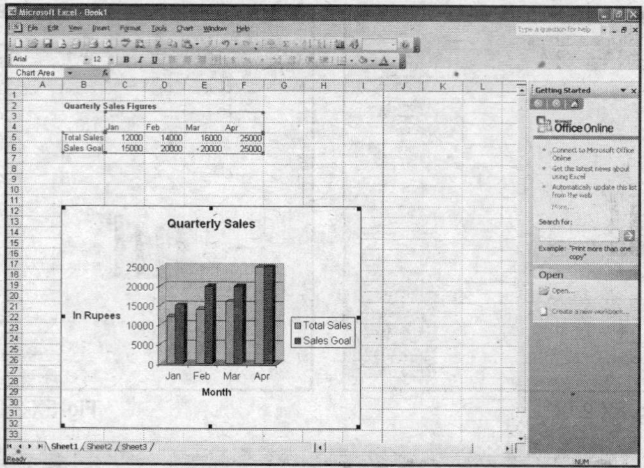

Fig. EX-2.18

Saving the Workbook

Let us now save the chart we have just created. For this, we will have to save the workbook in which we have made the chart. We will save the workbook in the **Local Disk (C:)**. To do so, undertake the following steps:

1. Start with Fig. EX-2.18. *Click* on the **Save** button (💾) present on the **Standard Toolbar**. Immediately, a **Save As** box gets displayed on the screen (Fig. EX-2.19).
2. Now, type any name for your workbook, say **Sales**, in the box beside the **File name** option. (Fig. EX-2.20).

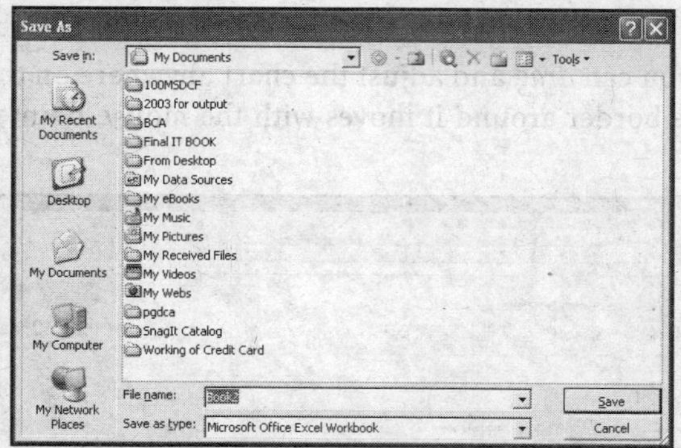

Fig. EX-2.19

Fig. EX-2.20

3. To save the workbook in the desired folder, i.e. **Local Disk (C:)**, bring the mouse-pointer over the down-arrow button (▾) beside the **Save in** option and *click* the left mouse-button. Immediately, a pull-down menu gets displayed (Fig. EX-2.21).
4. In the pull-down menu, *move* the mouse-pointer over the **Local Disk (C:)** and *click* the left mouse-button (Fig. EX-2.22).
5. Finally, *move* the mouse-pointer over the **Save** button, and *click* the left mouse-button (Fig. EX-2.22). The chart now gets saved in **Local Disk (C:)**.

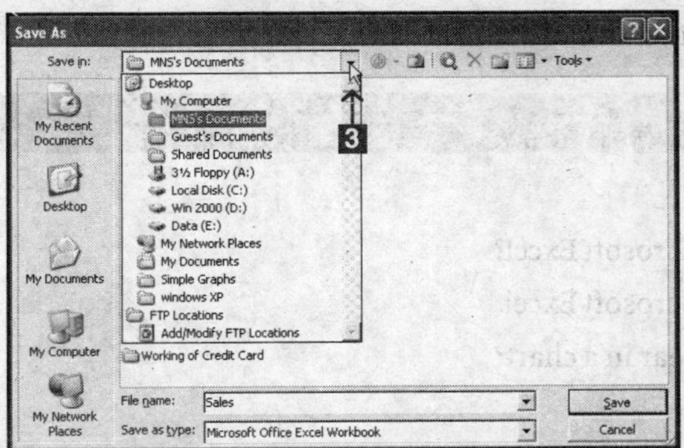

Fig. EX-2.21

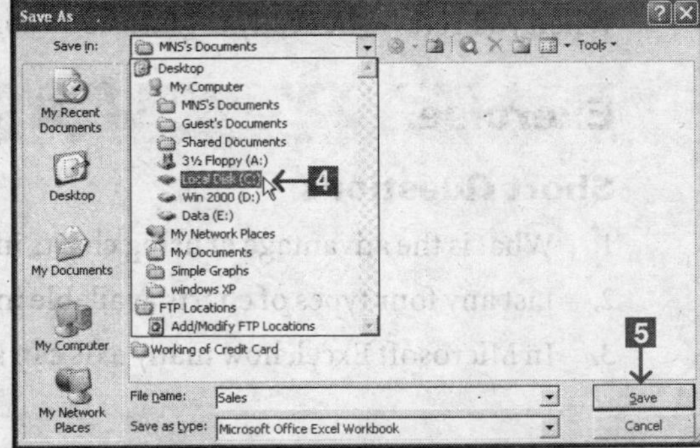

Fig. EX-2.22

Printing the Chart and Closing the Workbook

You may need to print the chart you have just made. For printing the chart, undertake the following steps:

1. Make sure that your printer is **ON** and is connected to your computer. *Move* the mouse-pointer over the **File** Menu bar option, and *click* the left mouse-button. Immediately, a pull-down menu gets displayed on the screen (Fig. EX-2.23).
2. Inside the pull-down menu, *move* the mouse-pointer over the **Print** option (Fig. EX-2.23), and *click* the left mouse-button.
3. Immediately, a **Print** box gets displayed on the screen (Fig. EX-2.24). *Click* on the **OK** button in **Print** box (Fig. EX-2.24). Instantly, the chart gets printed.

After printing the chart, it is time to take a small break before heading to the next chapter. Let us now close the workbook and quit the Excel.

1. To close the workbook, first *click* on the **File** Menu bar option (Fig. EX-2.25).
2. Inside the pull-down menu which appears, *click* on the **Close** option. Your workbook gets closed.
3. After closing the workbook *move* the mouse-pointer over the **Close** button (☒) present on the **Title bar** and *click* the left mouse-button. The **Desktop** appears on your screen.

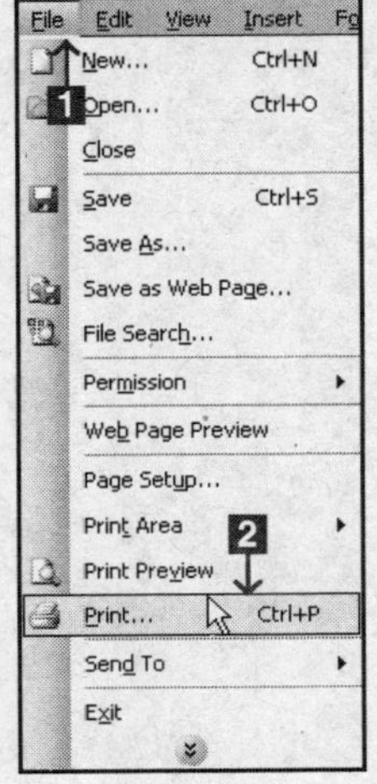

Fig. EX-2.23

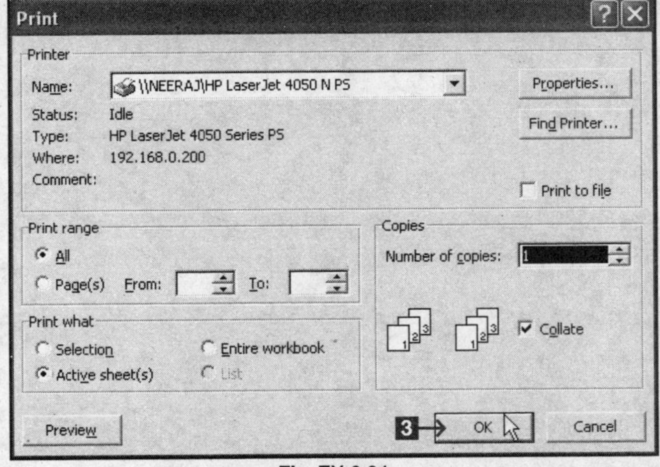

Fig. EX-2.24

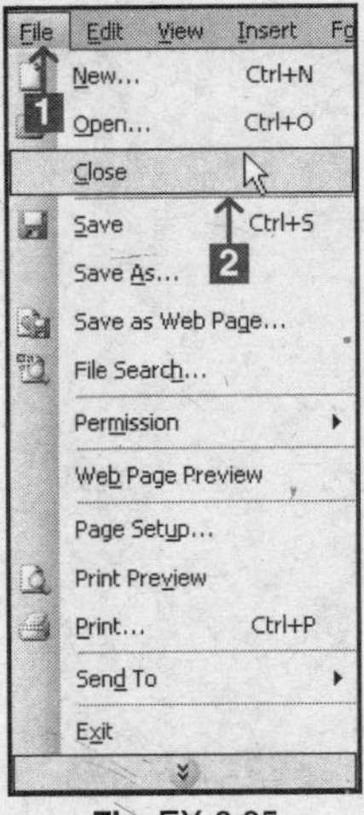

Fig. EX-2.25

When you return, be ready to learn common functions of MS Excel.

Exercise

Short Questions

1. What is the advantage of using charts in Microsoft Excel?
2. List any four types of charts available in Microsoft Excel.
3. In Microsoft Excel, how many axis can appear in a chart?

MICROSOFT EXCEL

Manipulating Data 3

IN THIS CHAPTER

Microsoft Excel works like your calculator. This spreadsheet program helps you perform calculations on numerical data. Whether you need to find simple sum of lengthy data or calculate through a complex set of formulas, Microsoft Excel can quickly provide the answer. Thus by using this program, you can efficiently keep track of your business deals or personal finances.

Formulas and Functions

Formulas and functions are the backbone of the Excel program. They help the Excel users save their brain from the mathematical teasing inflicted by lengthy and complex calculations. Formulas and functions can perform desired calculations on a given data in a jiffy. They can also quickly recalculate the new values whenever data in one or more cells of a table is changed. **Formula**, as you know, is a mathematical expression that produces a new value from the values or numbers on which it is applied. To calculate average marks of ten students, we use a simple formula. In this formula, marks of ten students are first added and then the total is divided by the number of students, i.e. 10, to get the average marks.

Function is a shortcut representation of a formula. It is easier to write a function in comparison to a formula. In Excel, all formulas using numbers start with an equal to (=) sign or a plus (+) sign. If you do not put an equal to (=) or plus (+) sign before a formula, Excel treats the formula as simple text. Let us see how does a function represent a formula. To find sum of numbers in cell addresses C1 to C10 the required formula would be

= C1+C2+C3+C4+C5+C6+C7+C8+C9+C10

The function for the above lengthy formula will be

=Sum (C1:C10)

Colon (:) between two cell addresses (C1:C10) indicates that the function would be applied to all cells from C1 to C10. In other words, to represent a group of cells in a function, we place the colon between the first and the last cell address. As seen in the above example, a formula can also contain cell addresses instead of values or numbers. In that case, the formula is applied on the contents of cell addresses included in it. In a formula, the cell addresses can be used along with numbers, mathematical operators and functions. For example, if the contents of cell address A20 have to be added to that of cell address C13 then the required formula would be:

=A20+C13

Excel Calculation Mode

We often use calculator. As you know, a calculator performs calculation operations like multiplication, addition or division on a given data in any order the user wants it to do. But, this is not the case with the Excel program. Let us understand the difference. In Excel, a formula may use one or all of these operators—plus (+), minus (-), division (/), multiplication (*) and exponential (^). While performing calculation, Excel gives precedence to certain operators contained in the formula.

It performs multiplication before division followed by addition and subtraction. For example, in the formula 2*3+4, Excel will multiply 2 and 3 first. And then, 4 will be added to their product. So the result will be 10 and not 14. However, you may use parenthesis to change this order. For example, if you want to multiply 2 with the sum of 3+4, then write the formula as 2*(3+4). Some formulas valid for Excel are as follows:

+(C2+D3+E4)/3

=D7+D7+62

The default order for calculation is () [parenthesis], * [multiplication], / [division], +[plus] and – [minus]. Between + and –, whichever comes first in the formula is done first.

Opening Microsoft Excel and Entering Data

Let us now start working with Formulas and Functions in an Excel workbook. First, we will open Microsoft Excel program through the following steps.

1. *Click* on the **Start** button (start). Immediately, a push-up menu gets displayed on the screen (Fig. EX-3.1).
2. Inside the push-up menu, *move* the mouse-pointer over **All Programs** option. Instantly, a second menu gets displayed (Fig. EX-3.1).
3. Inside the second menu, *move* the mouse-pointer over the **Microsoft Office** option. Immediately, a third menu appears (Fig. EX-3.1).
4. Inside the third menu, *move* the mouse-pointer over the **Microsoft Office Excel 2003** option and *click* the left mouse-button (Fig. EX-3.1).
5. Immediately, a blank Excel workbook, **Book1**, opens up on your screen (Fig.EX-3.2).

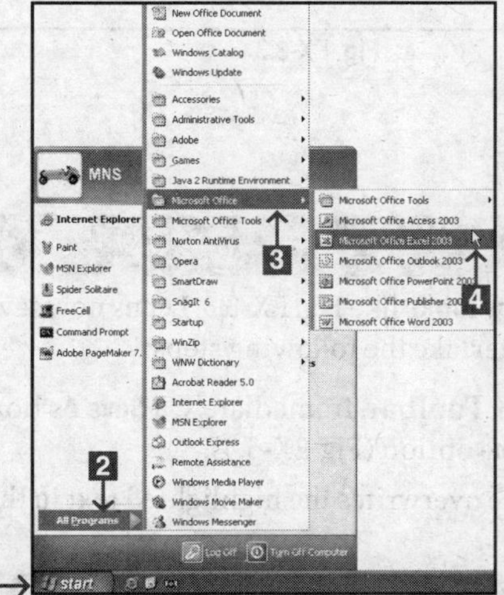

Fig. EX-3.1

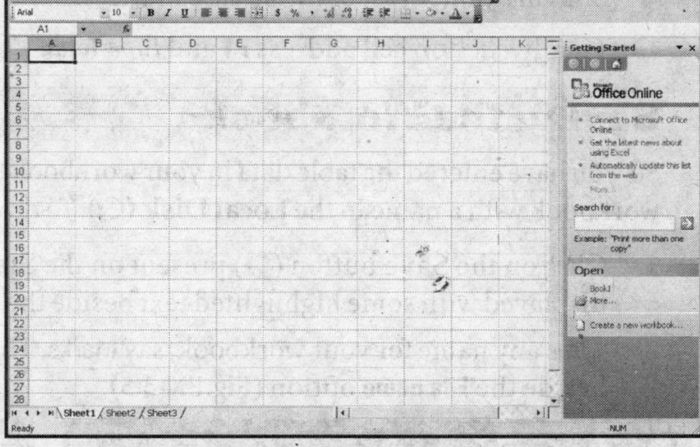

Fig. EX-3.2

Let us now add the following data in the workbook.

TABLE

Name	Roll No.	English	Maths	Science	Total
Sachin	101	80	75	88	
Ajay	102	78	70	75	
Anil	103	70	50	60	
Robin	104	89	65	72	
Dravid	105	65	74	74	
Saurabh	106	90	98	98	

1. First *click* on cell address **A1**.
2. *Type* **Name**. Then *press* the **Enter** key. The cell-pointer (✜) *moves* to cell address **A2**.
3. In cell address **A2**, *type* **Sachin**. *Press* the **Enter** key. The cell pointer moves to cell address **A3**. **Type Ajay** in cell address **A3**. Similarly, enter in the workbook all the names of the table's first column.
4. Now, *click* on cell address **B1** for typing the next column heading **Roll No.**
5. *Type* **Roll No.** and *press* the **Enter** key. The cell pointer moves to cell **B2**.
6. *Type* **101** in cell **B2** and *press* the **Enter** key. Similarly enter all the roll numbers in the workbook.
7. Now, *click* on cell address **C1** and *type* **English** and *press* the **Enter** key. The cell pointer moves to cell **C2**.
8. *Type* **80** in cell **C2** and *press* the **Enter** key. Similarly, enter all the **English** marks.
9. Next, *click* on cell address **D1** and *type* **Maths** and *press* the **Enter** key.
10. Now *type* **75** and *press* the **Enter** key. Similarly, *type* all the marks of **Maths**.
11. *Click* on cell address **E1** and *type* **Science**. *Press* the **Enter** key.
12. *Type* **88** and then *press* the **Enter** key. Similarly, enter rest of the **Science** marks.
13. Finally, *click* on cell address **F1** and *type* **Total**.

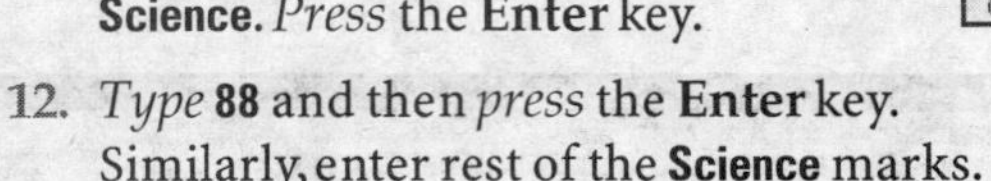

	A	B	C	D	E	F	G
1	Name	Roll No	English	Maths	Science	Total	
2	Sachin	101	80	75	88		
3	Ajay	102	78	70	75		
4	Anil	103	70	50	60		
5	Robin	104	89	65	72		
6	Dravid	105	65	74	74		
7	Saurabh	106	90	98	98		
8							

Fig. EX-3.3

Saving the Workbook

So, you have entered the table data in your workbook that now looks like Fig. EX-3.3. Let us now save this workbook with a name in the **Local Disk (C:)**. To do so, undertake the following steps:

1. *Click* on the **Save** button (💾) present on the **Standard Toolbar**. Immediately, a **Save As** box gets displayed with some highlighted text beside the **File name** option (Fig.EX-3.4).
2. *Type* any name for your workbook, say **Marks**. This name overwrites the highlighted text in the box beside the **File name** option (Fig.EX-3.5).

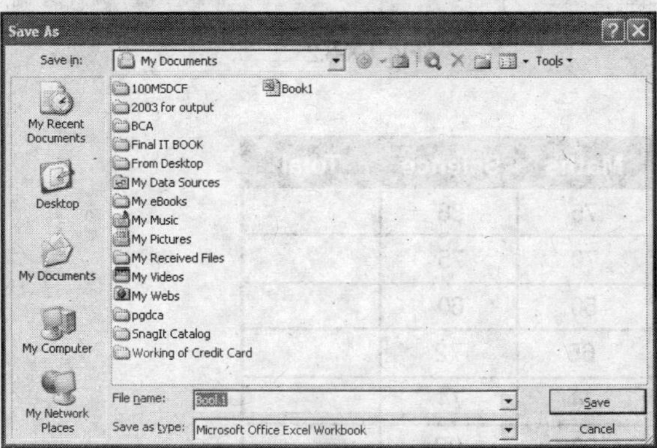

Fig. EX-3.4

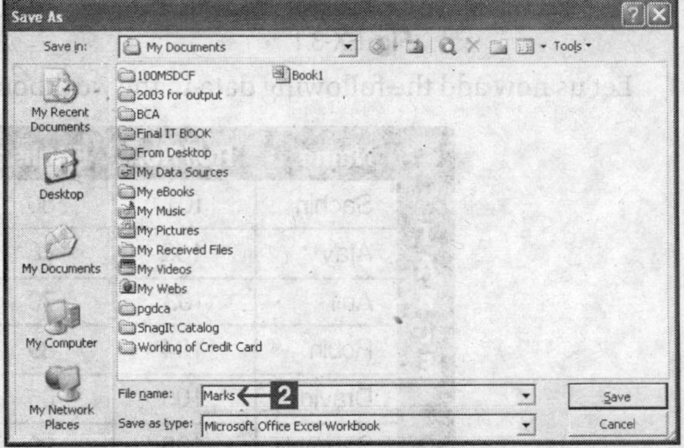

Fig. EX-3.5

3. Now, we will select the location, i.e. **Local Disk (C)**, where we wish to save our workbook. To do so, *move* the mouse-pointer over the down-arrow button of the box (▾) beside the **Save in** option and *click* the left mouse-button. A pull-down menu appears (Fig. EX-3.6).
4. In the pull-down menu, *move* the mouse-pointer over the **Local Disk (C:)** and *click* the left mouse-button (Fig. EX-3.7).

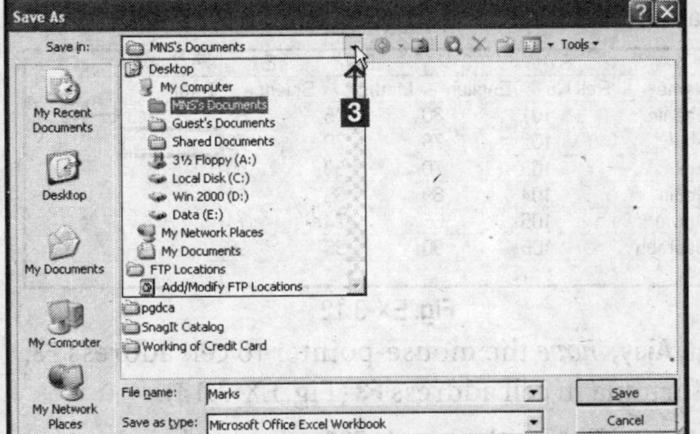

Fig. EX-3.6

Fig. EX-3.7

5. The **Local Disk (C:)** appears inside the box beside the **Save in** option. Finally, *move* the mouse-pointer over the **Save** button and *click* over it (Fig. EX-3.8).
6. The **Save As** box disappears from the screen which now displays your workbook. The **Title bar** displays the name that we have just assigned to the workbook i.e. **Marks** (Fig. EX-3.9).

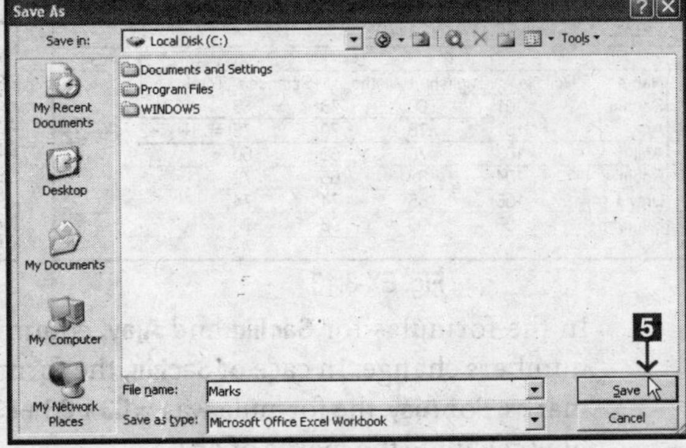

Fig. EX-3.8

Fig. EX-3.9

Using Formula to Calculate the Workbook Data

Let us now calculate and display the total marks of all the students in our workbook. For this, we will use a formula. We start with Sachin. To calculate the total marks of **Sachin**, undertake the following steps :

	A	B	C	D	E	F	G
1	Name	Roll No	English	Maths	Science	Total	
2	Sachin	101	80	75	88		
3	Ajay	102	78	70	75		
4	Anil	103	70	50	60		
5	Robin	104	89	65	72		
6	Dravid	105	65	74	74		
7	Saurabh	106	90	98	98		
8							

Fig. EX-3.10

1. Begin with the **Marks** workbook open on your screen. *Move* the mouse-pointer (✥) over the cell where the total marks have to be displayed – in our case, cell address **F2** and then *click* the left mouse-button. Immediately, the cell-pointer gets displayed at cell address **F2**, making it the active cell (Fig.EX-3.10).

2. Now a formula has to be typed in cell address **F2** for adding **Sachin**'s marks in **English, Maths** and **Science.** The formula is = **C2+D2+E2**. *Type* this formula in cell address **F2**. The formula entered in cell **F2** also gets displayed in the **Formula Bar** (Fig. EX-3.11). We have explained the Formula Bar in the previous chapter.
3. Now *press* the **Enter** key from your keyboard. Immediately, the formula adds the contents of the cells **C2**, **D2** and **E2**, and the result **243** gets displayed in cell address **F2** (Fig. EX-3.12).

DOLLAR ▾ X ✓ fx =C2+D2+E2

	A	B	C	D	E	F	G
1	Name	Roll No	English	Maths	Science	Total	
2	Sachin	101	80	75	88	=C2+D2+E2 ← 2	
3	Ajay	102	78	70	75		
4	Anil	103	70	50	60		
5	Robin	104	89	65	72		
6	Dravid	105	65	74	74		
7	Saurabh	106	90	98	98		
8							

Fig. EX-3.11

	A	B	C	D	E	F	G
1	Name	Roll No	English	Maths	Science	Total	
2	Sachin	101	80	75	88	243 ← 3	
3	Ajay	102	78	70	75		
4	Anil	103	70	50	60		
5	Robin	104	89	65	72		
6	Dravid	105	65	74	74		
7	Saurabh	106	90	98	98		
8							

Fig. EX-3.12

4. Now, to calculate the marks of the next student, **Ajay**, *move* the mouse-pointer to cell address **F3**. For **Ajay**, the formula is = **C3+D3+E3**. *Type* this formula in cell address **F3** (Fig. EX-3.13).
5. Then *press* the **Enter** key from the keyboard. Immediately, the result **223** gets displayed in cell address **F3** (Fig. EX-3.14).

DOLLAR ▾ X ✓ fx =C3+D3+E3

	A	B	C	D	E	F	G
1	Name	Roll No	English	Maths	Science	Total	
2	Sachin	101	80	75	88	243	
3	Ajay	102	78	70	75	=C3+D3+E3 ← 4	
4	Anil	103	70	50	60		
5	Robin	104	89	65	72		
6	Dravid	105	65	74	74		
7	Saurabh	106	90	98	98		
8							

Fig. EX-3.13

	A	B	C	D	E	F	G
1	Name	Roll No	English	Maths	Science	Total	
2	Sachin	101	80	75	88	243	
3	Ajay	102	78	70	75	223 ← 5	
4	Anil	103	70	50	60		
5	Robin	104	89	65	72		
6	Dravid	105	65	74	74		
7	Saurabh	106	90	98	98		
8							

Fig. EX-3.14

In the formulas for **Sachin** and **Ajay**, column names (**C**, **D** and **E**) remain the same, but the row numbers change. In case of **Sachin**, the formula was =**C2+D2+E2** because row 2 contains **Sachin's** marks. For **Ajay**, the formula was =**C3+D3+E3** because the marks of **Ajay** are placed in row 3. Let us now calculate the marks of **Anil**.

6. The total marks of **Anil** would be displayed in cell **F4**. For him, type the formula =**C4+D4+E4**. *Press* the **Enter** key. Anil's marks get displayed in cell **F4**. Similarly calculate total marks of other students. After marks of all the students are placed in column **F** of Sheet1, the Marks workbook looks like Fig.EX-3.15.

	A	B	C	D	E	F	G
1	Name	Roll No	English	Maths	Science	Total	
2	Sachin	101	80	75	88	243	
3	Ajay	102	78	70	75	223	
4	Anil	103	70	50	60	180	
5	Robin	104	89	65	72	226	
6	Dravid	105	65	74	74	213	
7	Saurabh	106	90	98	98	286	
8							

Fig. EX-3.15

Functions

In the preceding topic, you learnt to write a simple formula that calculated total of marks of only three subjects. But imagine calculating total of marks of 50 subjects. In that case, you would have to type a formula with 50 cell addresses to get the answer. Such lengthy calculations can be made simpler with the help of **Functions.** Functions are certain formulas built into the Excel program. Excel offers over 200 functions to help you perform various calculations on your data. A function begins with the = or + sign. For carrying out calculations through functions, you have to make use of a range. So, it's important to understand what exactly a range is.

Range

Range is a sequence of cell addresses. It is written in the following format:

first cell address:last cell address

It can also be written as – **first cell address..last cell address.** However, here we will work with the format – **first cell address:last cell address.** Even a single cell address can be a range, like cell address F1. Given below are a few examples of ranges.

- Range **A1:C1** includes cell addresses **A1, B1** and **C1.**
- Range **B3:E4** includes cell addresses **B3, B4, C3, C4, D3, D4, E3** and **E4.**
- Range **G1:G4** includes cell addresses **G1, G2, G3** and **G4.**

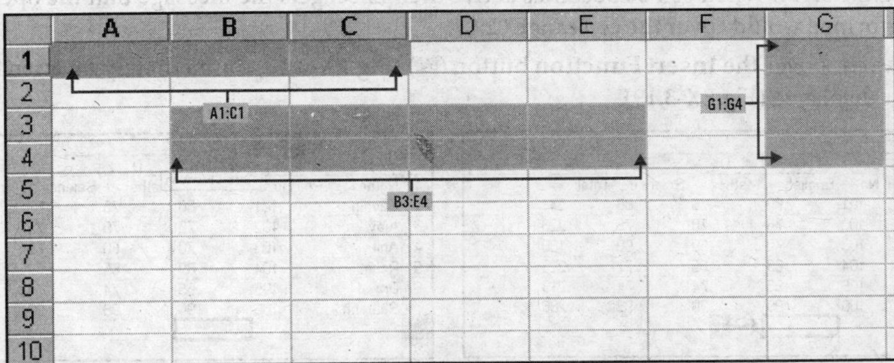

Fig. EX-3.16

Writing a Function

A function is written in the following format :

= Function name(range of cell addresses)

Let us write any function – say the SUM function. The sum of a range, say **B3:E4**, can be calculated with the formula **=SUM(B3:E4).**

You may also enter more than one range of cell addresses in a function. For example, through the SUM function, you can calculate the sum of all the four ranges mentioned above. In that case, the SUM function would be as follows:

=SUM(A1:C1, C8, B3:E4, G1:G4)

Common Excel Functions

Let us now learn how to use some of the common Microsoft Excel functions.

AVERAGE Function

The **AVERAGE** function enables you to find out the average of values in a given range of cell addresses. Let us use this function to calculate the average marks of the English subject in our workbook (Fig. EX-3.15). To display the average marks of the **English** subject at cell address **C8**, the following formula needs to be typed:

=(C2+C3+C4+C5+C6+C7)/6

But this is a very lengthy method as you have to *type* a separate formula at desired cells for calculating average marks of each subject. We will not use this method. Instead, we will use the built-in Average function of the Excel program to quickly find out the average English marks. To learn this method, undertake the following steps:

1. Start with Fig.EX-3.15. First *move* the mouse-pointer (✥) over cell **C8** where you wish to display the average and then *click* the left mouse-button. Cell **C8** now becomes the active cell address (Fig.EX-3.17). When cell **C8** becomes active then Excel gets the message that the operation to be performed would cover the cell range **C2:C7**.
2. Now, *click* over the **Insert Function** button (fx) (Fig.EX-3.18). Immediately, an **Insert Function** box gets displayed (Fig.EX-3.19).

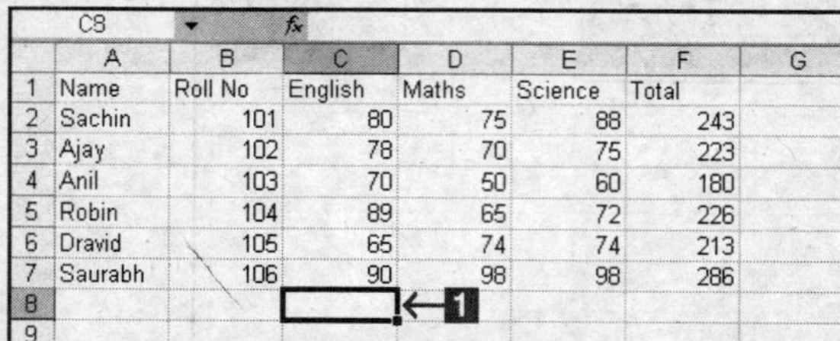

	A	B	C	D	E	F	G
1	Name	Roll No	English	Maths	Science	Total	
2	Sachin	101	80	75	88	243	
3	Ajay	102	78	70	75	223	
4	Anil	103	70	50	60	180	
5	Robin	104	89	65	72	226	
6	Dravid	105	65	74	74	213	
7	Saurabh	106	90	98	98	286	
8							
9							

Fig. EX-3.17

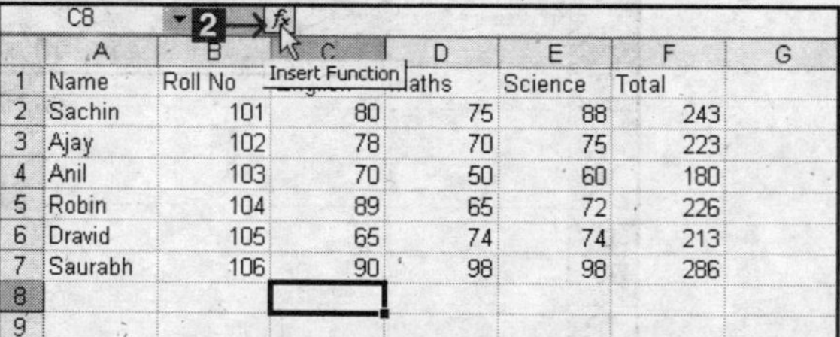

	A	B	C	D	E	F	G
1	Name	Roll No	English	Maths	Science	Total	
2	Sachin	101	80	75	88	243	
3	Ajay	102	78	70	75	223	
4	Anil	103	70	50	60	180	
5	Robin	104	89	65	72	226	
6	Dravid	105	65	74	74	213	
7	Saurabh	106	90	98	98	286	
8							
9							

Fig. EX-3.18

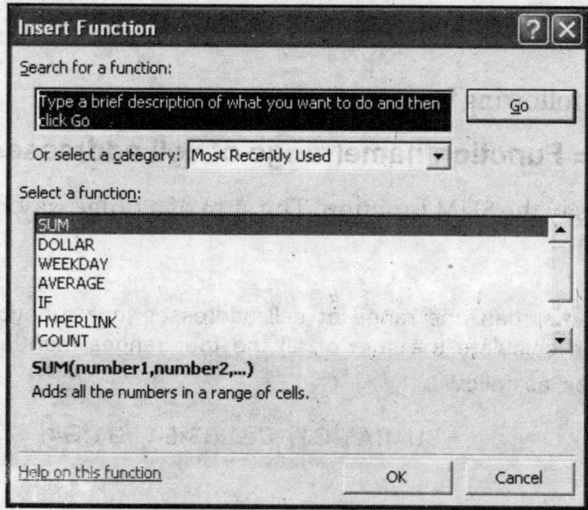

Fig. EX-3.19

3. In the **Insert Function** box, *click* on the **AVERAGE** function in the box below the **Select a function** option (Fig.EX-3.20).
4. *Click* on the **OK** button (Fig.EX-3.21).

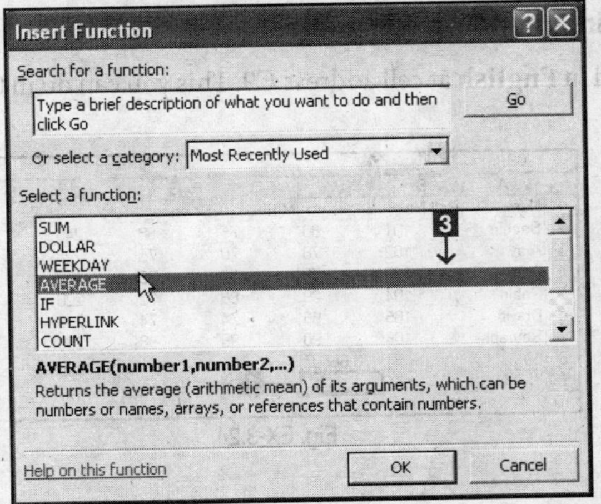

Fig. EX-3.20

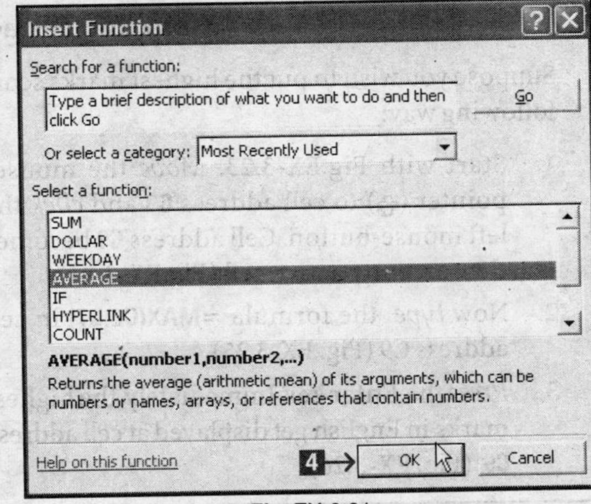

Fig. EX-3.21

5. Instantly, a **Function Arguments** box gets displayed on your screen (Fig.EX-3.22). In this box, under the **AVERAGE** option, the rectangular box beside the **Number1** option shows the **C2:C7** range as highlighted. Also the English marks of all the students are displayed beside the **Number1** option. These placements have occurred due to actions taken in Steps 1 to 4. If the box beside the **Number1** option doesn't show the required cell range, i.e. **C2:C7** then type this range in the box. Now, with just one *click*, you can place the average English marks in cell **C8**.

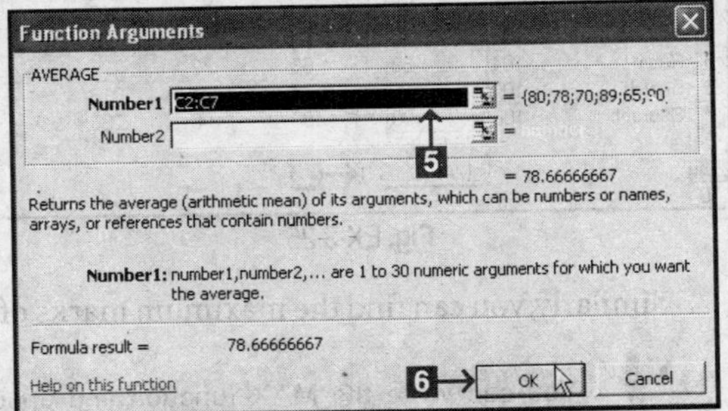

Fig. EX-3.22

6. So, *click* on the **OK** button of the **Function Arguments** box (Fig.EX-3.22).
7. Immediately, the average **English** marks get displayed at cell address **C8** (Fig.EX-3.23), and the function **=AVERAGE(C2:C7)** gets displayed in the **Formula** bar.

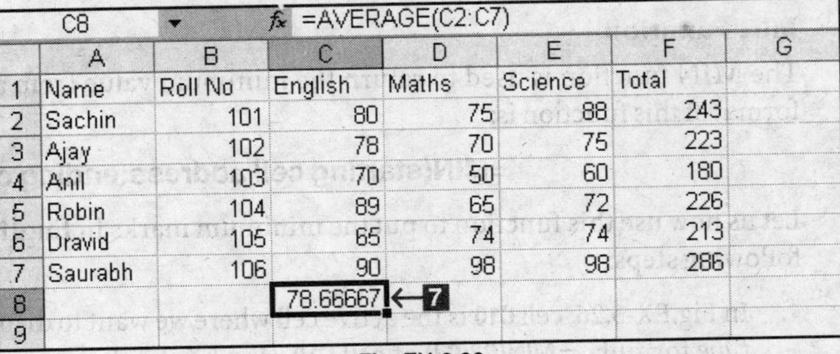

	A	B	C	D	E	F	G
1	Name	Roll No	English	Maths	Science	Total	
2	Sachin	101	80	75	88	243	
3	Ajay	102	78	70	75	223	
4	Anil	103	70	50	60	180	
5	Robin	104	89	65	72	226	
6	Dravid	105	65	74	74	213	
7	Saurabh	106	90	98	98	286	
8			78.66667				
9							

Fig. EX-3.23

MAX Function

Excel has another useful mathematical function i.e. **MAX** Function. It displays the largest value of a cell range in the active cell. Its general format is:

=MAX(starting cell address:ending cell address)

Suppose you wish to put the highest marks scored in **English** at cell address **C9**. This you can do in the following way:

1. Start with Fig.EX-3.23. *Move* the mouse-pointer (✥) to cell address **C9** and *click* the left mouse-button. Cell address **C9** becomes the currently active cell (Fig.EX-3.24).
2. Now *type* the formula **=MAX(C2:C7)** in cell address C9 (Fig. EX-3.25).
3. *Press* the **Enter** key. Immediately, the highest marks in English get displayed at cell address **C9** (Fig. EX-3.26).

C9

	A	B	C	D	E	F	G
1	Name	Roll No	English	Maths	Science	Total	
2	Sachin	101	80	75	88	243	
3	Ajay	102	78	70	75	223	
4	Anil	103	70	50	60	180	
5	Robin	104	89	65	72	226	
6	Dravid	105	65	74	74	213	
7	Saurabh	106	90	98	98	286	
8			78.66667				
9			✥ ← 1				
10							

Fig. EX-3.24

AVERAGE ▾ ✕ ✓ fx =MAX(C2:C7)

	A	B	C	D	E	F	G
1	Name	Roll No	English	Maths	Science	Total	
2	Sachin	101	80	75	88	243	
3	Ajay	102	78	70	75	223	
4	Anil	103	70	50	60	180	
5	Robin	104	89	65	72	226	
6	Dravid	105	65	74	74	213	
7	Saurabh	106	90	98	98	286	
8			78.66667				
9			=MAX(C2:C7) ← 2				
10							

Fig. EX-3.25

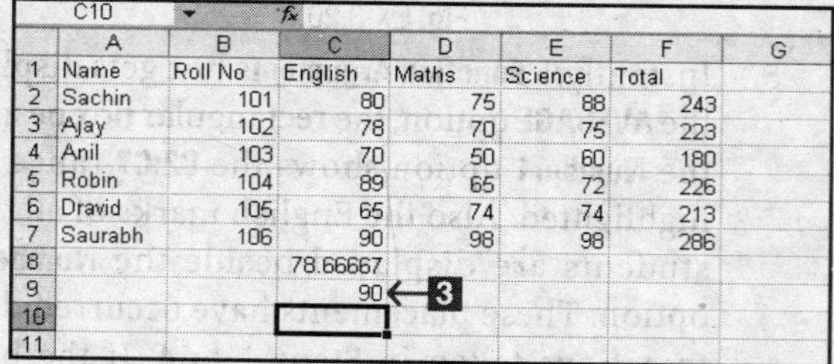

C10

	A	B	C	D	E	F	G
1	Name	Roll No	English	Maths	Science	Total	
2	Sachin	101	80	75	88	243	
3	Ajay	102	78	70	75	223	
4	Anil	103	70	50	60	180	
5	Robin	104	89	65	72	226	
6	Dravid	105	65	74	74	213	
7	Saurabh	106	90	98	98	286	
8			78.66667				
9			90 ← 3				
10							
11							

Fig. EX-3.26

Similarly, you can find the maximum marks of other subjects with the **MAX** function.

You can write the MAX function and upcoming functions through Insert Function dialog box.

MIN Function

The **MIN** function is used to return the minimum value from a range of cell addresses. The general format of this function is:

=MIN(starting cell address:ending cell address)

Let us now use this function to put the minimum marks in **English** at cell address **C10**. Undertake the following steps:

1. In Fig.EX-3.26, cell **C10** is the active cell where we want to display the minimum marks in **English.** So, *type* formula **=MIN(C2:C7)** at cell **C10** (Fig.EX-3.27).
2. Then *press* the **Enter** key. Immediately, the minimum marks in English, **65**, get displayed at cell address **C10** (Fig.EX-3.28).

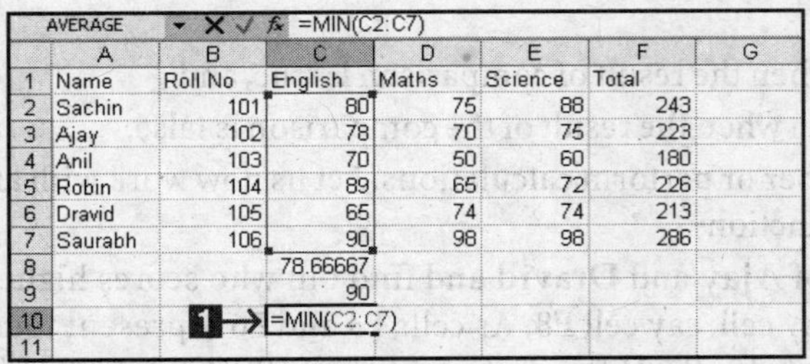

AVERAGE ▾ × ✓ fx =MIN(C2:C7)

	A	B	C	D	E	F	G
1	Name	Roll No	English	Maths	Science	Total	
2	Sachin	101	80	75	88	243	
3	Ajay	102	78	70	75	223	
4	Anil	103	70	50	60	180	
5	Robin	104	89	65	72	226	
6	Dravid	105	65	74	74	213	
7	Saurabh	106	90	98	98	286	
8			78.66667				
9			90				
10		1 →	=MIN(C2:C7)				
11							

Fig. EX-3.27

	A	B	C	D	E	F	G
1	Name	Roll No	English	Maths	Science	Total	
2	Sachin	101	80	75	88	243	
3	Ajay	102	78	70	75	223	
4	Anil	103	70	50	60	180	
5	Robin	104	89	65	72	226	
6	Dravid	105	65	74	74	213	
7	Saurabh	106	90	98	98	286	
8			78.66667				
9			90				
10			65 ← 2				
11							
12							

Fig. EX-3.28

COUNT Function

This function is used to count the number of cell addresses containing the data. The general format of this function is :

=COUNT(starting cell address:ending cell address)

Let us now count the cells containing roll numbers of the students, i.e. entries made in **Column B**, and display the answer at another cell address, say **B8**. To do so, undertake the following steps:

1. Start with Fig. 3.28. *Click* at cell address **B8** to make it the currently active cell (Fig.EX-3.29).
2. Now *type* the function **=COUNT(B2:B7)** in cell address **B8** (Fig.EX-3.30).

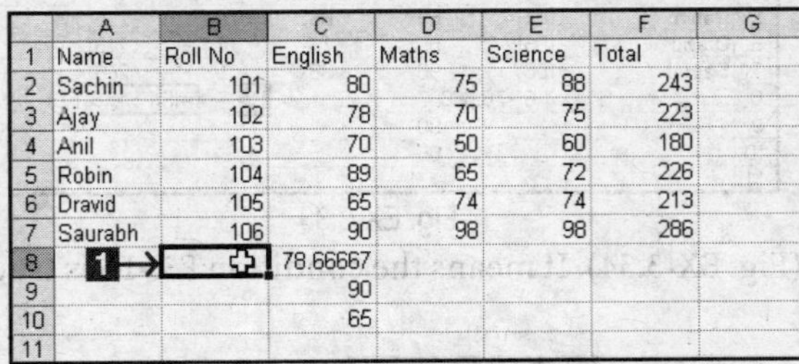

	A	B	C	D	E	F	G
1	Name	Roll No	English	Maths	Science	Total	
2	Sachin	101	80	75	88	243	
3	Ajay	102	78	70	75	223	
4	Anil	103	70	50	60	180	
5	Robin	104	89	65	72	226	
6	Dravid	105	65	74	74	213	
7	Saurabh	106	90	98	98	286	
8	1 →		78.66667				
9			90				
10			65				
11							

Fig. EX-3.29

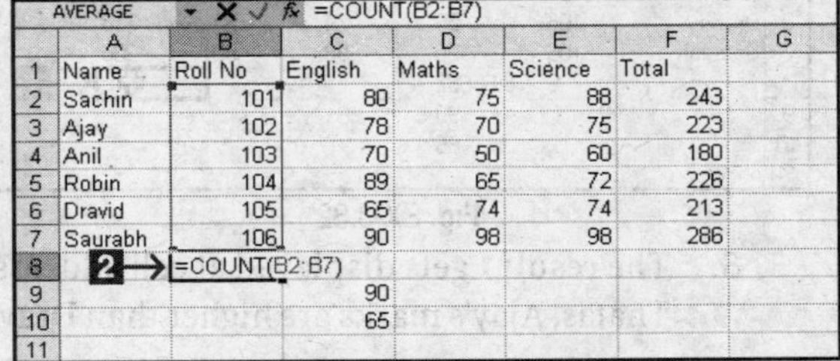

AVERAGE ▾ × ✓ fx =COUNT(B2:B7)

	A	B	C	D	E	F	G
1	Name	Roll No	English	Maths	Science	Total	
2	Sachin	101	80	75	88	243	
3	Ajay	102	78	70	75	223	
4	Anil	103	70	50	60	180	
5	Robin	104	89	65	72	226	
6	Dravid	105	65	74	74	213	
7	Saurabh	106	90	98	98	286	
8	2 →	=COUNT(B2:B7)					
9			90				
10			65				
11							

Fig. EX-3.30

3. After typing the **Count** function, *press* the **Enter** key. Immediately, result **6** gets displayed at cell address **B8** (Fig.EX-3.31).

B9 ▾ fx

	A	B	C	D	E	F	G
1	Name	Roll No	English	Maths	Science	Total	
2	Sachin	101	80	75	88	243	
3	Ajay	102	78	70	75	223	
4	Anil	103	70	50	60	180	
5	Robin	104	89	65	72	226	
6	Dravid	105	65	74	74	213	
7	Saurabh	106	90	98	98	286	
8		3 → 6	78.66667				
9			90				
10			65				
11							

Fig. EX-3.31

IF Function

The **IF** function is a logical function that lets you test the content of a cell—a value or label—on a given condition. If the specified condition is met, Microsoft Excel will perform one action; otherwise, it performs another. The **IF** function is written in the following format:

=IF (comparison, action if match, action if no match)

where, **comparison** tests the condition,

action if match refers to the action to be taken when the result of comparison is true, and

action if no match refers to the action to be taken when the result of the comparison is false.

The action could be to display some text or number or perform calculations. Let us now work with an example to get a better understanding of the **IF** function

Suppose you wish to compare the total marks of **Ajay** and **Dravid** and find out who scores higher marks. Also you want to display the result in any cell, say cell **F8**. As cells F3 and F6 represent total marks of Ajay and Dravid, respectively, the formula for the **If** function would be =IF(F3>F6, 1, 0). This formula will test the condition F3>F6. If Ajay's marks (F3) are greater than Dravid's marks (F6) then the formula is true. In that case, the result 1 would be placed at cell F8. Otherwise, the result 0 would be placed at cell F8. Let us see what is the result.

1. Start with Fig. EX-3.31. *Click* at cell address **F8** where you wish to display the result. This is the place where we will also *type* the **IF** function (Fig.EX-3.32).
2. Now, *type* the formula **=IF(F3>F6,1,0)** and *press* the **Enter** key.

	A	B	C	D	E	F	G
1	Name	Roll No	English	Maths	Science	Total	
2	Sachin	101	80	75	88	243	
3	Ajay	102	78	70	75	223	
4	Anil	103	70	50	60	180	
5	Robin	104	89	65	72	226	
6	Dravid	105	65	74	74	213	
7	Saurabh	106	90	98	98	286	
8		6	78.66667			← 1	
9			90				
10			65				
11							

Fig. EX-3.32

AVERAGE ▾ X ✓ fx =IF(F3>F6,1,0)

	A	B	C	D	E	F	G
1	Name	Roll No	English	Maths	Science	Total	
2	Sachin	101	80	75	88	243	
3	Ajay	102	78	70	75	223	
4	Anil	103	70	50	60	180	
5	Robin	104	89	65	72	226	
6	Dravid	105	65	74	74	213	
7	Saurabh	106	90	98	98	286	
8		6	78.66667		2 →	=IF(F3>F6,1,0)	
9			90				
10			65				
11							

Fig. EX-3.33

3. The result **1** gets displayed at cell address **F8** (Fig. EX-3.34). It means the condition F3>F6 is true. That is, Ajay's marks are higher than Dravid's.

	A	B	C	D	E	F	G
1	Name	Roll No	English	Maths	Science	Total	
2	Sachin	101	80	75	88	243	
3	Ajay	102	78	70	75	223	
4	Anil	103	70	50	60	180	
5	Robin	104	89	65	72	226	
6	Dravid	105	65	74	74	213	
7	Saurabh	106	90	98	98	286	
8		6	78.66667			1	← 3
9			90				
10			65				
11							

Fig. EX-3.34

Editing Data in Excel Workbook

You can reorganize and rearrange data in your Excel workbook by copying and moving data from one location to another or deleting data which you no longer require. This can be made possible by using the **Copy, Cut** or **Delete** editing features provided by Microsoft Excel. You can copy or move data to as many cells as you like. When you move data, it is removed from its original cell and placed at a different cell on the sheet. Copying of data also works in the similar manner except that the data which has been copied to a different cell address also remains at the original cell address.

Moving Data

While working in Excel, you may sometimes by mistake enter data in a wrong cell address. In such a case, you need not delete the data entered at a wrong place and retype it at the correct location. Instead, you can simply move the data to the correct location.

Generally, when a data is moved, it instantly disappears from its original location and gets pasted at a different location. In Excel, when you cut the data for moving, a dotted blinking margin appears around the data indicating that the data is ready to be moved. When the cut data is pasted at the desired location, the dotted blinking margin disappears.

There are several methods to cut the data, but here, you will be using the two easiest methods. In the first method, the **Cut** button (✂) is used. The second method involves dragging the contents of a selected cell address with the mouse. Let us now learn how to move the contents of a cell address within a sheet.

Moving Data in a Sheet

Let us now try moving data from one column to the other, say from Column **A** to Column **G**, in the currently open worksheet of **Marks** workbook. To do so, undertake the following steps:

1. Start with Fig. EX-3.34. *Move* the mouse-pointer (✚) over cell address **A1** and then *press* the left mouse-button. Immediately, the cell-pointer (▭) appears at cell address **A1** making it the active cell (Fig. EX-3.35).
2. Then keeping the left mouse-button *pressed*, *drag* the mouse downwards on your mouse-pad till cell addresses **A1** to **A7** get highlighted (Fig. EX-3.36). After highlighting the cells, *release* the left mouse-button (Fig. EX-3.36).

A1 | fx Name

	A	B	C	D	E	F	G
1	Name	Roll No	English	Maths	Science	Total	
2	Sachin	101	80	75	88	243	
3	Ajay	102	78	70	75	223	
4	Anil	103	70	50	60	180	
5	Robin	104	89	65	72	226	
6	Dravid	105	65	74	74	213	
7	Saurabh	106	90	98	98	286	
8		6	78.66667			1	
9			90				
10			65				
11							

Fig. EX-3.35

7R x 1C | fx Name

	A	B	C	D	E	F	G
1	Name	Roll No	English	Maths	Science	Total	
2	Sachin	101	80	75	88	243	
3	Ajay	102	78	70	75	223	
4	Anil	103	70	50	60	180	
5	Robin	104	89	65	72	226	
6	Dravid	105	65	74	74	213	
7	Saurabh	106	90	98	98	286	
8		6	78.66667			1	
9			90				
10			65				
11							

Fig. EX-3.36

3. Now, *move* the mouse-pointer to the **Standard Toolbar**, and *click* on the **Cut** button (✂). Immediately, a dotted blinking margin appears around the highlighted cells indicating that these cells are going to be moved (Fig. EX-3.37).
4. Now to paste the contents of column **A** at column **G**, i.e. in cell addresses **G1** to **G7**, *click* over the starting cell address **G1** to select it. There is no need to select all the cell addresses where data has to be pasted. Only the starting cell address has to be selected (Fig. EX-3.38).

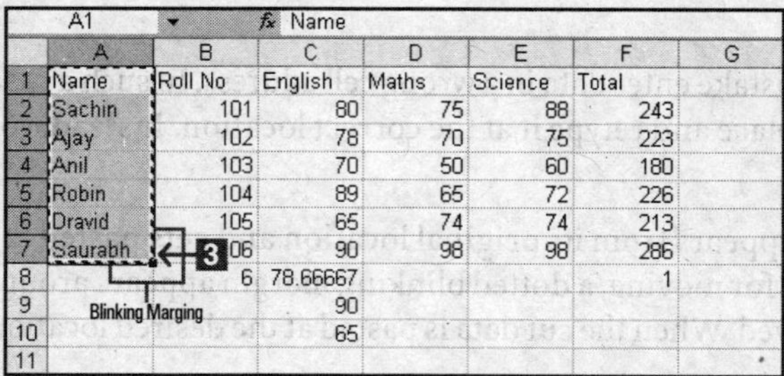

A1 | Name

	A	B	C	D	E	F	G
1	Name	Roll No	English	Maths	Science	Total	
2	Sachin	101	80	75	88	243	
3	Ajay	102	78	70	75	223	
4	Anil	103	70	50	60	180	
5	Robin	104	89	65	72	226	
6	Dravid	105	65	74	74	213	
7	Saurabh	106	90	98	98	286	
8		6	78.66667			1	
9			90				
10			65				
11							

Fig. EX-3.37

G1

	A	B	C	D	E	F	G	H
1	Name	Roll No	English	Maths	Science	Total		
2	Sachin	101	80	75	88	243		
3	Ajay	102	78	70	75	223		
4	Anil	103	70	50	60	180		
5	Robin	104	89	65	72	226		
6	Dravid	105	65	74	74	213		
7	Saurabh	106	90	98	98	286		
8		6	78.66667			1		
9			90					
10			65					
11								

4

Fig. EX-3.38

5. Next, *move* the mouse-pointer over the **Paste** button ( ) present on the **Standard Toolbar**, and *click* the left mouse-button just once. Immediately, the contents of column **A** get shifted to column **G** (Fig. EX-3.39). The new cell entries of column **G** are shown highlighted (Fig.EX-3.39). Just *click* anywhere else on the sheet to remove the highlight from column **G**.

6. Let us now restore the moved data to its original position as later in the chapter we will be requiring it. To do so, *click* on the **Undo** button ( ) on the **Standard Toolbar** to return the moved data from column **G** to column **A** (Fig.EX-3.40).

G1 | Name

	A	B	C	D	E	F	G	H
1		Roll No	English	Maths	Science	Total	Name	
2		101	80	75	88	243	Sachin	
3		102	78	70	75	223	Ajay	
4		103	70	50	60	180	Anil	
5		104	89	65	72	226	Robin	
6		105	65	74	74	213	Dravid	
7		106	90	98	98	286	Saurabh	
8		6	78.66667			1		
9			90					
10			65					
11								

5

Fig. EX-3.39

G1

	A	B	C	D	E	F	G	H
1	Name	Roll No	English	Maths	Science	Total		
2	Sachin	101	80	75	88	243		
3	Ajay	102	78	70	75	223		
4	Anil	103	70	50	60	180		
5	Robin	104	89	65	72	226		
6	Dravid	105	65	74	74	213		
7	Saurabh	106	90	98	98	286		
8		6	78.66667			1		
9			90					
10			65					
11								

Fig. EX-3.40

Copying Data

As you know, the process of copying data is quite similar to moving it, but with one difference. When you copy the content of selected cell addresses, Microsoft Excel makes a duplicate copy of the contents and places it at a new location. For copying the contents of a particular sequence of cell addresses, first these are highlighted and then the **Copy** button ( ) is clicked.

Just like the moving procedure, when you select the desired cells and click on the copy button, a dotted blinking margin appears around the selected cells. This margin is an indication that the data within selected cells is yet to be copied. The dotted blinking margin stays on the selected data until it is pasted at a desired location in your sheet. The copying feature is mostly used to copy formulas so that calculations can be done easily.

Copying Data in a Sheet

Suppose, in the worksheet of Fig.EX-3.40, you wish to copy the contents of cell addresses **B1** to **B7** to empty cell addresses **H1** to **H7**. Undertake the following steps to do so:

1. First, to highlight cell addresses **B1** to **B7** *click* at cell address **B1** and *place* the mouse-pointer (✥) over the cell-pointer (▭) (Fig. W-3.41).
2. Keeping the left mouse-button *pressed*, *drag* the mouse downwards on the mouse-pad. Immediately, cell addresses **B1** to **B7** get highlighted (Fig. W-3.42).

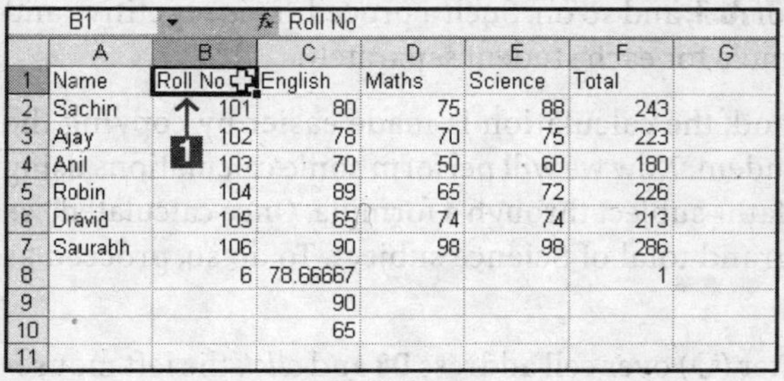

B1 | fx Roll No

	A	B	C	D	E	F	G
1	Name	Roll No	English	Maths	Science	Total	
2	Sachin	101	80	75	88	243	
3	Ajay	102	78	70	75	223	
4	Anil	103	70	50	60	180	
5	Robin	104	89	65	72	226	
6	Dravid	105	65	74	74	213	
7	Saurabh	106	90	98	98	286	
8		6	78.66667			1	
9			90				
10			65				
11							

1

Fig. EX-3.41

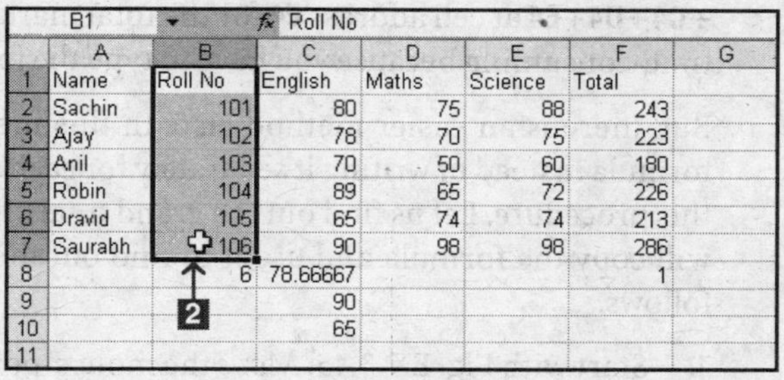

B1 | fx Roll No

	A	B	C	D	E	F	G
1	Name	Roll No	English	Maths	Science	Total	
2	Sachin	101	80	75	88	243	
3	Ajay	102	78	70	75	223	
4	Anil	103	70	50	60	180	
5	Robin	104	89	65	72	226	
6	Dravid	105	65	74	74	213	
7	Saurabh	106	90	98	98	286	
8		6	78.66667			1	
9			90				
10			65				
11							

2

Fig. EX-3.42

3. Next, *click* on the **Copy** button (📋) present on the **Standard Toolbar**. Immediately, a dotted blinking margin gets displayed over cell addresses **B1** to **B7** indicating that the contents of these cell addresses have to be copied (Fig. EX-3.43).
4. Now *bring* the mouse-pointer (✥) to cell address **H1** where you wish to place the selected data and then *press* the left mouse-button. The cell-pointer appears (▭) at cell address **H1** making it the active cell (Fig. EX-3.44).

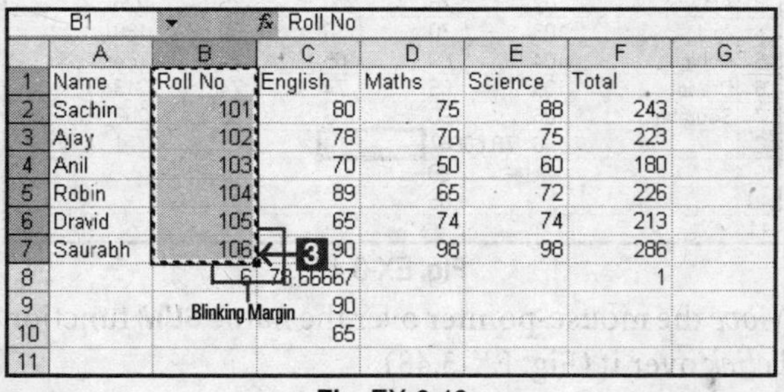

B1 | fx Roll No

	A	B	C	D	E	F	G
1	Name	Roll No	English	Maths	Science	Total	
2	Sachin	101	80	75	88	243	
3	Ajay	102	78	70	75	223	
4	Anil	103	70	50	60	180	
5	Robin	104	89	65	72	226	
6	Dravid	105	65	74	74	213	
7	Saurabh	106	90	98	98	286	
8		6	78.66667			1	
9			90				
10			65				
11							

3 Blinking Margin

Fig. EX-3.43

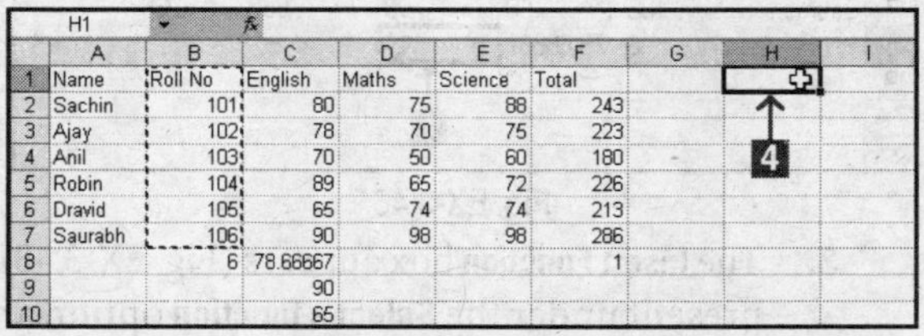

H1 | fx

	A	B	C	D	E	F	G	H	I
1	Name	Roll No	English	Maths	Science	Total			
2	Sachin	101	80	75	88	243			
3	Ajay	102	78	70	75	223			
4	Anil	103	70	50	60	180			
5	Robin	104	89	65	72	226			
6	Dravid	105	65	74	74	213			
7	Saurabh	106	90	98	98	286			
8		6	78.66667			1			
9			90						
10			65						

4

Fig. EX-3.44

5. Finally, *click* on the **Paste** button (📋) present on the **Standard Toolbar**. The copied data gets pasted at cell addresses **H1** to **H7** (Fig. EX-3.45).

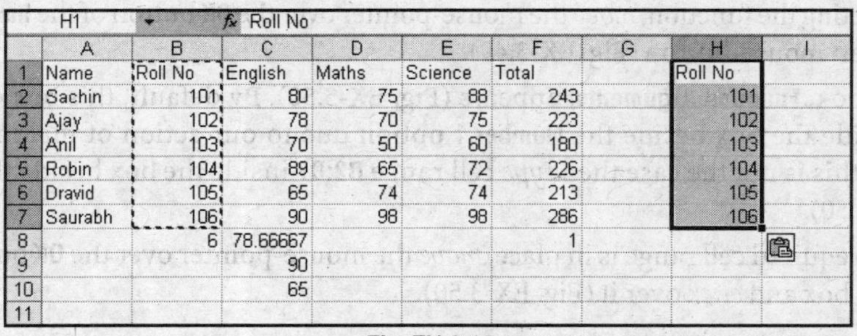

H1 | fx Roll No

	A	B	C	D	E	F	G	H	I
1	Name	Roll No	English	Maths	Science	Total		Roll No	
2	Sachin	101	80	75	88	243		101	
3	Ajay	102	78	70	75	223		102	
4	Anil	103	70	50	60	180		103	
5	Robin	104	89	65	72	226		104	
6	Dravid	105	65	74	74	213		105	
7	Saurabh	106	90	98	98	286		106	
8		6	78.66667			1			
9			90						
10			65						
11									

Fig. EX-3.45

Copying a Formula in a Sheet

Earlier in the chapter, you calculated total marks of seven students in column **F** (Fig. EX-3.15). Remember, the total marks of **Sachin** were calculated by typing the formula **+C2+D2+E2** at cell address **F2**. Then you typed the formula **+C3+D3+E3** at cell address **F3** for calculating the total marks of **Ajay**, and **+C4+D4+E4** at cell address **F4** for the total marks of **Anil**, and so on. Such a procedure is repetitive and time-consuming because you have to type the formula for each student separately.

But, there is an easier method also. In this method, the calculation is made easier by copying the formula instead of writing it separately for each student. Now we will perform some calculations using this procedure. Let us find out the grand total of Maths subject through a formula. Once calculated, we will copy the formula and use it to find out the grand total of Science subject. To do so, proceed as follows.

1. Start with Fig. EX-3.45. *Move* the mouse-pointer (✥) over cell address **D8** and *click* the left mouse-button. Immediately, the cell-pointer appears (▭) at cell address **D8** making it the active cell (Fig. EX-3.46).
2. *Move* the mouse-pointer over the **Insert Function** (fx) button present in the **Formula bar** and *click* the left mouse-button. The mouse-pointer (✥) of worksheet changes to ↖ (Fig. EX-3.47).

	A	B	C	D	E	F	G
1	Name	Roll No	English	Maths	Science	Total	
2	Sachin	101	80	75	88	243	
3	Ajay	102	78	70	75	223	
4	Anil	103	70	50	60	180	
5	Robin	104	89	65	72	226	
6	Dravid	105	65	74	74	213	
7	Saurabh	106	90	98	98	286	
8		6	78.66667			1	
9			90				
10			65				
11							

Fig. EX-3.46

D8 — 2 → fx — Insert Function

	A	B	C	D	E	F	G
1	Name	Roll No	English	Maths	Science	Total	
2	Sachin	101	80	75	88	243	
3	Ajay	102	78	70	75	223	
4	Anil	103	70	50	60	180	
5	Robin	104	89	65	72	226	
6	Dravid	105	65	74	74	213	
7	Saurabh	106	90	98	98	286	
8		6	78.66667			1	
9			90				
10			65				
11							

Fig. EX-3.47

3. The **Insert Function** box appears (Fig. EX-3.48). *Move* the mouse-pointer over the name **SUM** function present under the **Select a function** option and *click* over it (Fig. EX-3.48).

If the SUM function appears highlighted by default in the Insert Function box then skip Step 3 and start from Step 4.

4. After selecting the function, *move* the mouse-pointer over the **OK** button of the **Insert Function** box and *click* the left mouse-button (Fig. EX-3.49).
5. Another box, **Function Arguments**, appears (Fig. EX-3.50). By default, this box displays cell range **D2:D7** inside the box beside the **Number 1** option due to our action of making cell **D8** active in Step 1. If this is not the case then *type* cell range **D2:D7** inside the box beside the **Number 1** option (Fig. EX-3.50).
6. Once the required cell range is in place, *move* the mouse-pointer over the **OK** button of the **Function Arguments** box and *click* over it (Fig. EX-3.50).

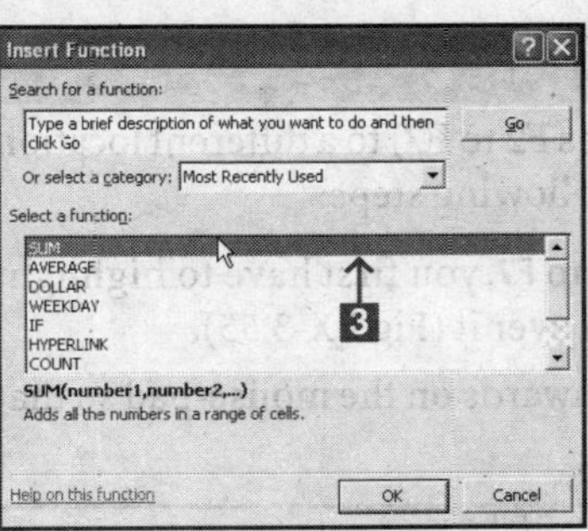

Fig. EX-3.48

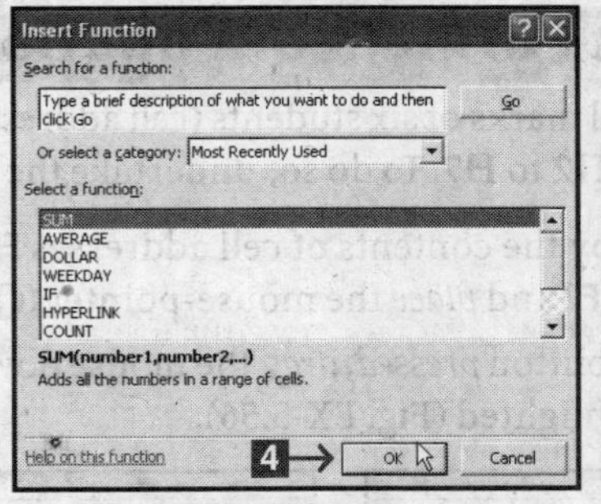

Fig. EX-3.49

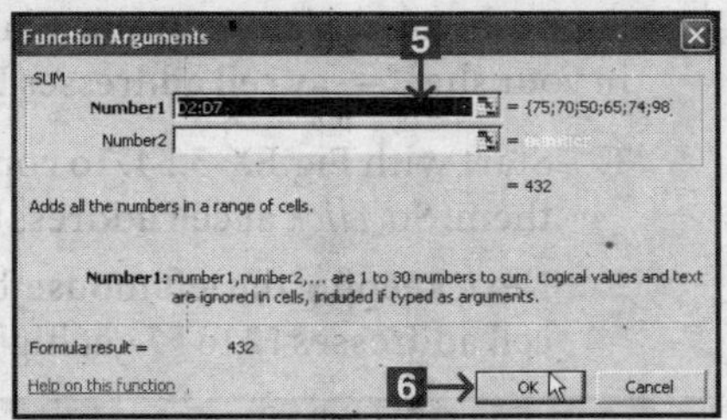

Fig. EX-3.50

7. Instantly, the grand total of **Maths** subject appears at cell address **D8** as shown in Fig. EX-3.51.
8. Without deactivating cell address **D8**, *move* the mouse-pointer over the **Copy** button (), present on the **Standard Toolbar**, and *click* the left mouse-button. Immediately, a blinking margin surrounds cell address **D8** indicating that its formula has been copied (Fig. W-3.52).

D8 =SUM(D2:D7)

	A	B	C	D	E	F	G
1	Name	Roll No	English	Maths	Science	Total	
2	Sachin	101	80	75	88	243	
3	Ajay	102	78	70	75	223	
4	Anil	103	70	50	60	180	
5	Robin	104	89	65	72	226	
6	Dravid	105	65	74	74	213	
7	Saurabh	106	90	98	98	286	
8		6	78.66667	432	← 7	1	
9			90				
10			65				
11							

Fig. EX-3.51

D8 =SUM(D2:D7)

	A	B	C	D	E	F	G
1	Name	Roll No	English	Maths	Science	Total	
2	Sachin	101	80	75	88	243	
3	Ajay	102	78	70	75	223	
4	Anil	103	70	50	60	180	
5	Robin	104	89	65	72	226	
6	Dravid	105	65	74	74	213	
7	Saurabh	106	90	98	98	286	
8		6	78.66667	432			1
9			90	↑ Blinking Margin			
10			65	8			
11							

Fig. EX-3.52

9. Now, *move* the mouse-pointer () over cell address **E8** and *click* the left mouse-button. Instantly, the cell-pointer () appears at cell address **E8** making it the active cell (Fig. EX-3.53).
10. Next, *move* the mouse-pointer over the **Paste** button () of the **Standard Toolbar** and *click* over it. Instantly, the grand total of **Science** subject appears at cell address **E8** (Fig. EX-3.54). So, copying the formula has saved you from typing another formula to calculate the grand total of Science marks.

E8

	A	B	C	D	E	F	G
1	Name	Roll No	English	Maths	Science	Total	
2	Sachin	101	80	75	88	243	
3	Ajay	102	78	70	75	223	
4	Anil	103	70	50	60	180	
5	Robin	104	89	65	72	226	
6	Dravid	105	65	74	74	213	
7	Saurabh	106	90	98	98	286	
8		6	78.66667	432		1	
9			90		↑		
10			65		9		
11							

Fig. EX-3.53

E8 =SUM(E2:E7)

	A	B	C	D	E	F	G
1	Name	Roll No	English	Maths	Science	Total	
2	Sachin	101	80	75	88	243	
3	Ajay	102	78	70	75	223	
4	Anil	103	70	50	60	180	
5	Robin	104	89	65	72	226	
6	Dravid	105	65	74	74	213	
7	Saurabh	106	90	98	98	286	
8		6	78.66667	432	467	1	
9			90		↑		
10			65		10		
11							

Fig. EX-3.54

You can repeat Steps 1 to 10 to insert, copy and paste formulas or functions of any type in your worksheet.

Copying Values, not Formula or Function

Suppose, you wish to copy the total marks of six students (cell addresses **F2** to **F7**) to a different location in your sheet – say cell addresses **H2** to **H7**. To do so, undertake the following steps:

1. Start with Fig.EX-3.54. To copy the contents of cell addresses **F2** to **F7**, you first have to highlight them. So, *click* at cell address **F2** and *place* the mouse-pointer (✥) over it (Fig.EX-3.55).
2. Next, keeping the left mouse-button *pressed*, *drag* the mouse downwards on the mouse-pad so that cell addresses **F2** to **F7** get highlighted (Fig. EX-3.56).

	A	B	C	D	E	F	G	H
1	Name	Roll No	English	Maths	Science	Total		
2	Sachin	101	80	75	88	243 ← 1		
3	Ajay	102	78	70	75	223		
4	Anil	103	70	50	60	180		
5	Robin	104	89	65	72	226		
6	Dravid	105	65	74	74	213		
7	Saurabh	106	90	98	98	286		
8		6	78.66667	432	467	1		
9			90					
10			65					
11								

Fig. EX-3.55

F2 =SUM(C2:E2)

	A	B	C	D	E	F	G	H
1	Name	Roll No	English	Maths	Science	Total		
2	Sachin	101	80	75	88	243		
3	Ajay	102	78	70	75	223		
4	Anil	103	70	50	60	180		
5	Robin	104	89	65	72	226		
6	Dravid	105	65	74	74	213		
7	Saurabh	106	90	98	98	286		
8		6	78.66667	432	467	1		
9			90					
10			65			2		
11								

Fig. EX-3.56

3. Then *click* the **Copy** button (📋) present on the **Standard Toolbar.** Immediately, a blinking margin surrounds cells **F2** to **F7** (Fig. EX-3.57).
4. Now to copy the highlighted contents to cell addresses **H2** to **H7** *click* at cell address **H2** (Fig. W-3.58).

F2 =SUM(C2:E2)

	A	B	C	D	E	F	G	H
1	Name	Roll No	English	Maths	Science	Total		
2	Sachin	101	80	75	88	243		
3	Ajay	102	78	70	75	223		
4	Anil	103	70	50	60	180		
5	Robin	104	89	65	72	226 ← 3		
6	Dravid	105	65	74	74	213	Blinking Margin	
7	Saurabh	106	90	98	98	286		
8		6	78.66667	432	467	1		
9			90					
10			65					
11								

Fig. EX-3.57

H2

	A	B	C	D	E	F	G	H	I
1	Name	Roll No	English	Maths	Science	Total			
2	Sachin	101	80	75	88	243		✥	
3	Ajay	102	78	70	75	223		↑	
4	Anil	103	70	50	60	180			
5	Robin	104	89	65	72	226		4	
6	Dravid	105	65	74	74	213			
7	Saurabh	106	90	98	98	286			
8		6	78.66667	432	467	1			
9			90						
10			65						
11									

Fig. EX-3.58

5. Then *click* on the **Paste** button (📋). As you see in Fig. EX-5.59, instead of total marks some other values get pasted at cell addresses **H2** to **H9**.

	A	B	C	D	E	F	G	H	I
1	Name	Roll No	English	Maths	Science	Total			
2	Sachin	101	80	75	88	243		331	
3	Ajay	102	78	70	75	223		298	
4	Anil	103	70	50	60	180		240	
5	Robin	104	89	65	72	226		298	← 5
6	Dravid	105	65	74	74	213		287	
7	Saurabh	106	90	98	98	286		384	
8		6	78.66667	432	467	1			
9			90						
10			65						
11									

Fig. EX-3.59

This has happened because you had copied a formula from column **F** instead of values of its cells. To understand this occurrence, just go back to an earlier topic of this chapter, **Using Formula to Calculate the Workbook Data.** In this topic, you had placed total marks of all students in column **F** (Fig. EX-3.15) using the formula +Cn+Dn+En where n represented the row number in which the student was placed.

In the present case, the same formula calculated for each student the sum of values in columns **E, F** and **G**. For example, value **331** of cell **H2** is the sum of values in cell addresses **E2, F2** and **G2**. Similar is the case with all cell addresses **H3** to **H9**.

This problem can be solved if you copy values instead of formulas. To do so, proceed as follows:

6. *Press* the **Delete** key to remove the displayed contents of cell addresses **H2** to **H7**.
7. Now repeat Steps 1 to 3 stated earlier in the topic.
8. Then *click* on the **Edit** Menu bar option (Fig. EX-3.60). A pull-down menu appears.
9. Inside the pull-down menu, *click* on the **Paste Special** option (Fig. EX-3.60). Immediately, a **Paste Special** box gets displayed (Fig.EX-3.61).
10. Now, *locate* the **Paste** option in the **Paste Special** box of Fig.EX-3.61
11. Then *move* the mouse-pointer over the round button beside the **Values** option and *click* the left mouse-button (Fig. EX-3.61).
12. Finally, *click* on the **OK** button (Fig. EX-3.62).

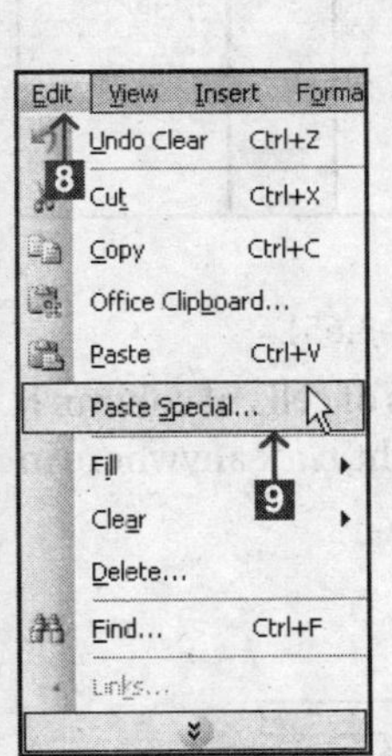

Fig. EX-3.60

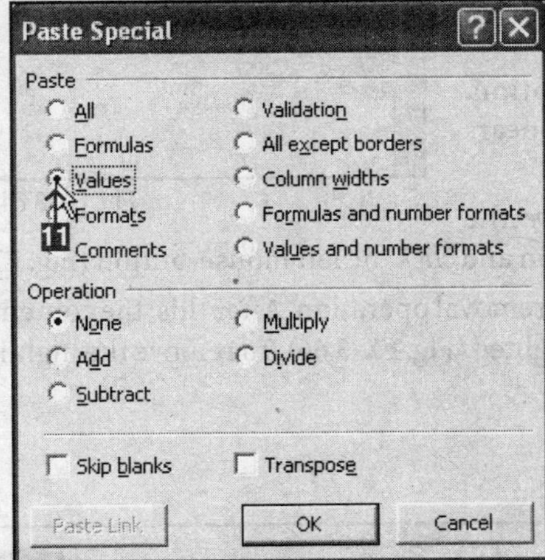

Fig. EX-3.61

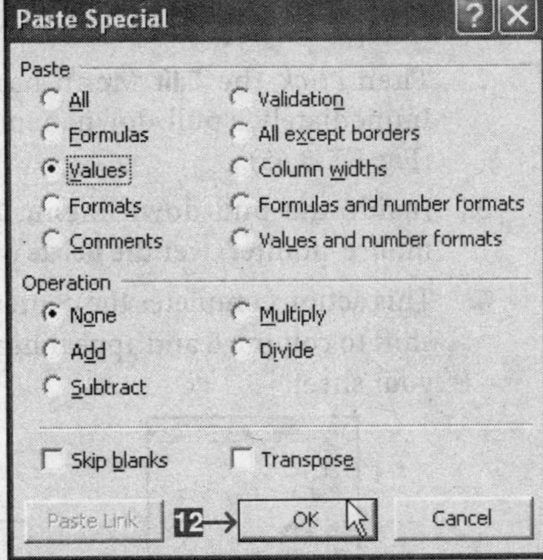

Fig. EX-3.62

13. Immediately, the values of cell addresses **F2** to **F7** get copied to cell addresses **H2** to **H7** (Fig. EX-3.63).

H2 | *fx* 243

	A	B	C	D	E	F	G	H	I
1	Name	Roll No	English	Maths	Science	Total			
2	Sachin	101	80	75	88	243		243	
3	Ajay	102	78	70	75	223		223	
4	Anil	103	70	50	60	180		180	← 13
5	Robin	104	89	65	72	226		226	
6	Dravid	105	65	74	74	213		213	
7	Saurabh	106	90	98	98	286		286	
8		6	78.66667	432	467	1			
9			90						
10			65						
11									

Fig. EX-3.63

Deleting Rows and Columns

Suppose, you no longer require contents of cells of a row or column. Then you can easily delete those contents. However, deletion of contents doesn't delete the row or column. For example, if we delete contents of row 6 then row 6 will remain on our sheet and it will contain contents of row 7. Similar is the case with columns.

When you delete the contents of a particular cell, Microsoft Excel keeps its formatting intact so that you can enter new data in the same format in that cell. Let us now delete the contents of cells in Column G of our sheet. Though these cells are empty, applying the content removal operation on them will bring some changes in our worksheet. Let us observe these changes.

1. Begin with Fig. EX-3.63. *Place* the mouse-pointer (✥) over column **G** and *click* the left mouse-button. The mouse-pointer changes to ↓ (Fig. EX-3.64).
2. Then *click* the **Edit** Menu bar option. Immediately, a pull-down menu appears (Fig. EX-3.65).
3. Inside the pull-down menu, *move* the mouse-pointer over the **Delete** option and *click* the left mouse-button (Fig. EX-3.65).
4. This action completes the contents removal operation. After this, the contents of cells of column **H** shift to column **G** and appear highlighted (Fig. EX-3.66). To remove the highlight, *click* anywhere in your sheet.

G1

	A	B	C	D	E	F	G	H	I
1	Name	Roll No	English	Maths	Science	Total			
2	Sachin	101	80	75	88	243		243	
3	Ajay	102	78	70	75	223		223	
4	Anil	103	70	50	60	180		180	
5	Robin	104	89	65	72	226		226	
6	Dravid	105	65	74	74	213		213	
7	Saurabh	106	90	98	98	286		286	
8		6	78.66667	432	467	1			
9			90						
10			65						
11									

Fig. EX-3.64

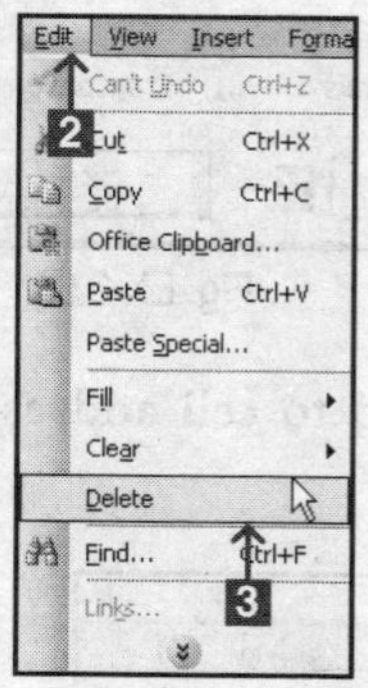

Fig. EX-3.65

G1

	A	B	C	D	E	F	G	H
1	Name	Roll No	English	Maths	Science	Total		
2	Sachin	101	80	75	88	243	243	
3	Ajay	102	78	70	75	223	223	
4	Anil	103	70	50	60	180	180	
5	Robin	104	89	65	72	226	226	
6	Dravid	105	65	74	74	213	213	
7	Saurabh	106	90	98	98	286	286	
8		6	78.66667	432	467	1		
9			90					
10			65					
11								

Fig. EX-3.66

Deleting the Contents of a Row

Let us now learn to delete a row of data. Suppose, you wish to delete the data of the row containing the marks of **Robin**, i.e. the 5th row, in the worksheet. To do so, undertake the following steps:

1. Start with Fig.EX-3.66. First, *move* the mouse-pointer to row **5** and *click* the left mouse-button to highlight this row. Immediately, the entire row gets highlighted (Fig. EX-3.67).
2. Next, *click* the **Edit** option of the Menu bar and *click* the left mouse-button. A pull-down menu appears (Fig. EX-3.68).

3. Inside the pull-down menu, *move* the mouse-pointer over the **Delete** option and *click* the left mouse-button (Fig. EX-3.68).

A5	Robin						
	A	B	C	D	E	F	G
1	Name	Roll No	English	Maths	Science	Total	
2	Sachin	101	80	75	88	243	243
3	Ajay	102	78	70	75	223	223
4	Anil	103	70	50	60	180	180
5	Robin	104	89	65	72	226	226
6	Dravid	105	65	74	74	213	213
7	Saurabh	106	90	98	98	286	286
8		6	78.66667	432	467	1	
9			90				
10			65				

Fig. EX-3.67

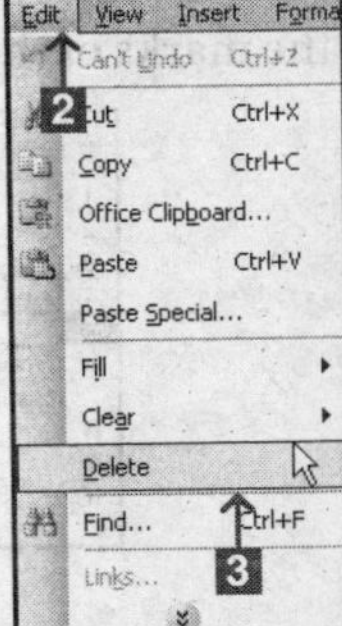

Fig. EX-3.68

4. Robin's marks get deleted from your worksheet. Now, row 6 containing Dravid's marks becomes row 5, which appears highlighted. To remove the highlight *click* the left mouse-button anywhere in your sheet. The contents of row 7 also shift to row 6 (Fig. EX-3.69).

A5	Dravid						
	A	B	C	D	E	F	G
1	Name	Roll No	English	Maths	Science	Total	
2	Sachin	101	80	75	88	243	243
3	Ajay	102	78	70	75	223	223
4	Anil	103	70	50	60	180	180
5	Dravid	105	65	74	74	213	213
6	Saurabh	106	90	98	98	286	286
7		5	76.6	367	395	1	
8			90				
9			65				

Fig. EX-3.69

Inserting Rows

You can add one or more rows anywhere in your sheet by shifting up or down the existing rows. Let us learn how to do this.

Suppose, in your worksheet, you wish to add marks of a new student after the fourth row, i.e. after **Anil**. For this, an empty row has to be inserted after row number **4**. You can do this through the following steps:

1. Begin with Fig.EX-3.69. *Move* the mouse-pointer over row number **5** and then *click* the left mouse-button just once. Immediately, the row gets highlighted (Fig. EX-3.70).
2. Now *click* over the **Insert** option of the Menu bar. A pull-down menu appears (Fig. EX-3.71).
3. Inside the pull-down menu, *click* on the **Rows** option (Fig. EX- 3.71).

	A	B	C	D	E	F	G
1	Name	Roll No	English	Maths	Science	Total	
2	Sachin	101	80	75	88	243	243
3	Ajay	102	78	70	75	223	223
4	Anil	103	70	50	60	180	180
5	Dravid	105	65	74	74	213	213
6	Saurabh	106	90	98	98	286	286
7		5	76.6	367	395	1	
8			90				
9			65				
10							

Fig. EX-3.70

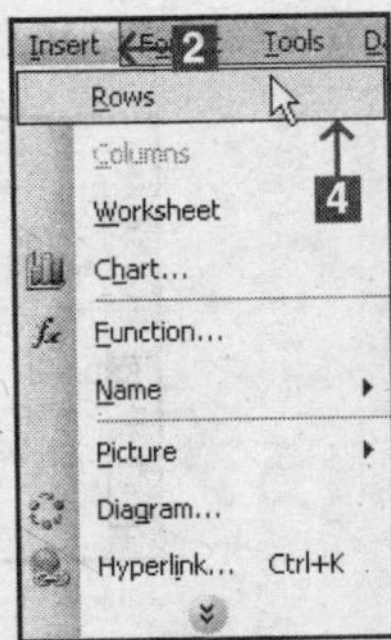

Fig. EX-3.71

4. Immediately, an empty row gets inserted after the fourth row and appears highlighted (Fig. EX-3.72). Now, to remove the highlight *click* the left mouse-button anywhere in your sheet. You can now enter the marks of the new student in the new row.

A5

	A	B	C	D	E	F	G	H
1	Name	Roll No	English	Maths	Science	Total		
2	Sachin	101	80	75	88	243	243	
3	Ajay	102	78	70	75	223	223	
4	Anil	103	70	50	60	180	180	
5			← Empty Row →					
6	Dravid	105	65	74	74	213	213	
7	Saurabh	106	90	98	98	286	286	
8		5	76.6	367	395	1		
9			90					
10			65					
11								

Fig. EX-3.72

Inserting Columns

You can also insert one or more columns between existing columns in your sheet. Let us insert a column in the sheet, say between columns **F** and **H**. To do so, undertake the following steps:

1. Start with Fig.EX-3.72. *Place* the mouse-pointer over column **G** and *click* the left mouse-button. Immediately, column **G** appears highlighted (Fig. EX-3.73).
2. Next, *click* over the **Insert** option of the Menu bar. A pull-down menu appears (Fig. EX-3.74).
3. Inside the pull-down menu, *click* over the **Columns** option (Fig. EX-3.74).

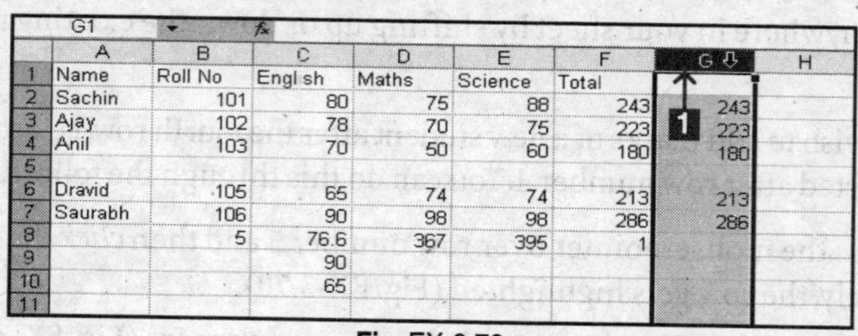

G1

	A	B	C	D	E	F	G	H
1	Name	Roll No	English	Maths	Science	Total		
2	Sachin	101	80	75	88	243	243	
3	Ajay	102	78	70	75	223	223	
4	Anil	103	70	50	60	180	180	
5								
6	Dravid	105	65	74	74	213	213	
7	Saurabh	106	90	98	98	286	286	
8		5	76.6	367	395	1		
9			90					
10			65					
11								

Fig. EX-3.73

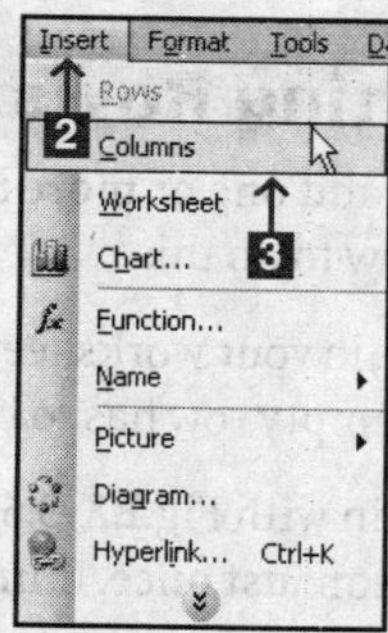

Fig. EX-3.74

4. Immediately, a new column gets displayed between columns **F** and **H** of your sheet. The new column is represented by empty column G whose data has shifted to column **H**. (Fig.EX-3.75).

G1

	A	B	C	D	E	F	G	H	I
1	Name	Roll No	English	Maths	Science	Total			
2	Sachin	101	80	75	88	243		243	
3	Ajay	102	78	70	75	223		223	
4	Anil	103	70	50	60	180		180	
5									
6	Dravid	105	65	74	74	213		213	
7	Saurabh	106	90	98	98	286		286	
8		5	76.6	367	395	1			
9			90						
10			65						
11									

Fig. EX-3.75

Automatic Filling of Entries

Many a time, you are required to fill a range of cells with similar or repeating values or a sequence of values. You can do it very easily in Excel which has provision for automatic filling of repeating values or a sequence of values in a range of cells. Let us learn more about this feature through an example.

Suppose students of your class have been assigned examination roll numbers starting from 1000. One way of writing these roll numbers in a table is that you write each student's roll number in its designated cell. It's a time-consuming method. So, why not use the automatic filling facility of Excel. Suppose you wish to write the students' roll numbers in column I of your worksheet. To do so, undertake the following steps.

1. Start with Fig.EX-3.75. To display a series of examination roll numbers starting from **1000** at column **I**, *click* at the cell address **I2** and then *type* **1000** (Fig. EX-3.76).
2. Now, *highlight* cell addresses **I2** to **I7** (Fig. EX-3.77).

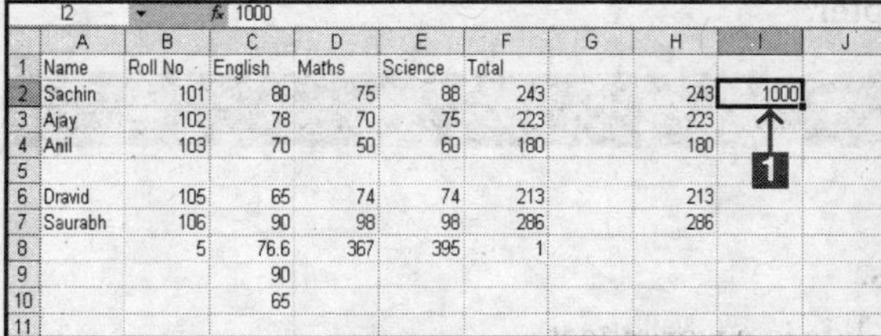

I2 fx 1000

	A	B	C	D	E	F	G	H	I	J
1	Name	Roll No	English	Maths	Science	Total				
2	Sachin	101	80	75	88	243		243	1000	
3	Ajay	102	78	70	75	223		223		
4	Anil	103	70	50	60	180		180		
5										
6	Dravid	105	65	74	74	213		213		
7	Saurabh	106	90	98	98	286		286		
8		5	76.6	367	395	1				
9			90							
10			65							
11										

Fig. EX-3.76

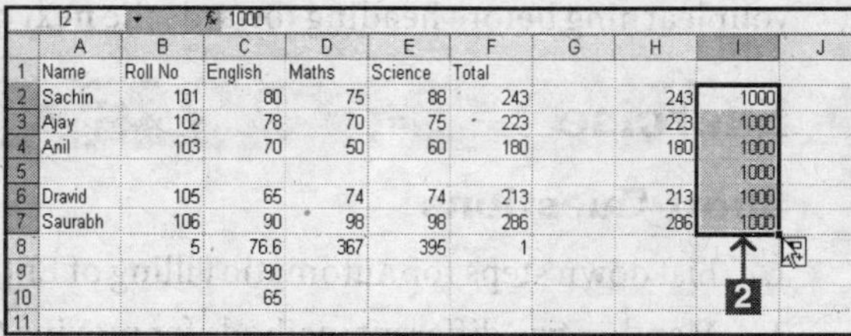

I2 fx 1000

	A	B	C	D	E	F	G	H	I	J
1	Name	Roll No	English	Maths	Science	Total				
2	Sachin	101	80	75	88	243		243	1000	
3	Ajay	102	78	70	75	223		223	1000	
4	Anil	103	70	50	60	180		180	1000	
5									1000	
6	Dravid	105	65	74	74	213		213	1000	
7	Saurabh	106	90	98	98	286		286	1000	
8		5	76.6	367	395	1				
9			90							
10			65							
11										

Fig. EX-3.77

3. Then *move* the mouse-pointer to the Menu bar and *click* on the **Edit** option (Fig.EX-3.78).
4. Inside the pull-down menu, *place* the mouse-pointer over the **Fill** option. Instantly, a second menu appears (Fig.EX-3.78).
5. Inside the second menu, *click* on the **Series** option (Fig.EX-3.78). Immediately, a **Series** box appears (Fig.EX-3.79).
6. Inside this box, the **Step value** option is already set to **1**. Now, to get the final result, *click* on the **OK** button (Fig.EX-3.79).

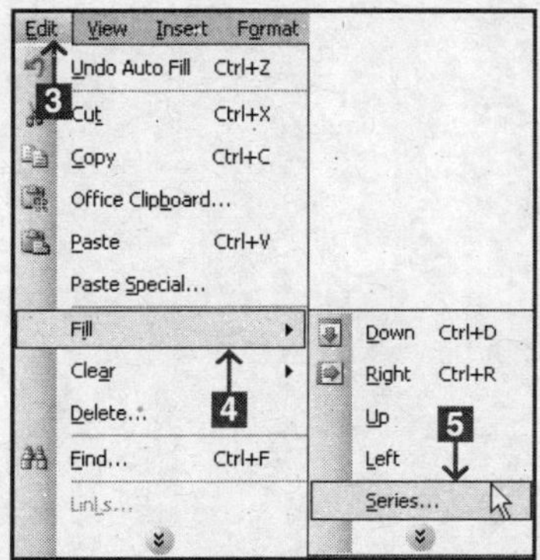

Fig. EX-3.78

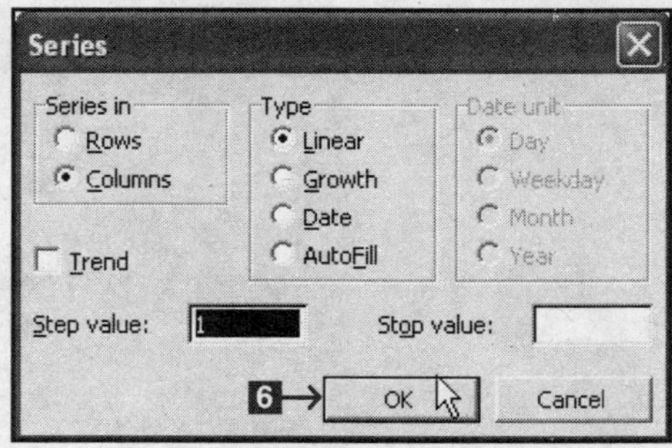

Fig. EX-3.79

7. The final result looks like Fig.EX-3.80 in which the students' roll numbers are automatically numbered serially without your having to type each roll number separately. Now, *click* anywhere else on your screen to remove the highlight from cell addresses **I2** to **I7**.

I2 ▾ fx 1000

	A	B	C	D	E	F	G	H	I	J
1	Name	Roll No	English	Maths	Science	Total				
2	Sachin	101	80	75	88	243		243	1000	
3	Ajay	102	78	70	75	223		223	1001	
4	Anil	103	70	50	60	180		180	1002	
5									1003	
6	Dravid	105	65	74	74	213		213	1004	
7	Saurabh	106	90	98	98	286		286	1005	
8		5	76.6	367	395	1				
9			90							
10			65							
11										

Fig. EX-3.80

With this step, we come to an end of the chapter. Let us go through the exercise given below and refresh your learning before heading towards the next chapter.

Exercise

Short Questions

1. List down steps for Automatic Filling of Entries.
2. Mention two different methods for moving the data in a worksheet.
3. Define formula and function.
4. List down names of any seven functions available in Microsoft Excel.

MICROSOFT EXCEL

Changing the Layout 4

IN THIS CHAPTER

- Aligning Data
- Increasing or Decreasing the Column Width
- Increasing or Decreasing the Height of Rows
- Calculating Net Payable Amount
- Changing the Background of a Worksheet
- Saving the Workbook and Quitting Microsoft Excel
- Exercise
- Summary

Microsoft Excel gives you freedom to design your worksheets by incorporating various styles. A range of design and style options available in Excel play an important role in enhancing the readability of a document or report. Using these options you can make your worksheets attractive. Sometimes, these designs also help in fulfilling your specific requirements.

In Excel, you have choice to change the appearance of text and numbers on the screen. When the data at a particular cell address is formatted, its value remains unaffected, only its appearance is changed. This formatting can be carried out on any number of cell addresses.

Excel also allows you to format a single row or a group of rows. You can change the height of one or more rows and hide or display rows. You can also change the width of one or more columns and hide or display columns.

There is another useful feature called the **Autofit row** feature which automatically fits the cells in a row. The Autofit feature can also be used to fit the cells in a column. Excel also has provision for alignment of data in cells. You can change the position of any data in the cell or selected cells. Alignment changes do not change the data type.

Now, we will work with various design or formatting features of Excel. First, open the Excel program on your computer. To open Excel, *click* on the **Start** button. When the push-up menu appears, *move* the mouse over the **All Programs** option. A second menu appears. Inside the second menu, *click* on the **Microsoft Excel** option. After a few seconds, a blank Excel sheet gets displayed on the screen with the **title bar** displaying **Book 1**.

Let us now start entering the data shown in **Table 1** into the sheet. We can start entering the data from the cell address **A1** (Fig.EX-4.1).

A4 ▾ fx Bhuvan

	A	B	C	D
1	Neeraj			
2	Pooja			
3	Susmita			
4	Bhuvan			
5				

Fig. EX-4.1

TABLE

Neeraj
Pooja
Susmita
Bhuvan

Aligning Data

Data at a particular cell address can be positioned at center, or aligned to the left or the right side. As you know, any text containing alphabets is called a **Label entry**. Microsoft Excel by default aligns all text or label entries to the left. The entries made in **column A** of Fig.EX-4.1 have also been left aligned.

However, Microsoft Excel has some buttons (Fig.EX.4.2) on the Formatting toolbar, such as the **align Left** button, the **Center** button and the **align Right** button. Using these buttons, you can change the alignment of any text or number. Let us now work with these buttons.

Fig. EX-4.2

Changing Alignment of Selected Cells

You have just entered some data in column A of the worksheet open on your screen. By default, this data is aligned to the left hand side in cells. Let us now align this data to the right-hand side of the cells. To do so, undertake the following steps:

1. *Move* the mouse-pointer (✥) over cell address **A1** and *click* the left mouse-button. Instantly, cell address **A1** becomes the active cell (Fig. EX-4.3).

2. Now, keeping the left mouse-button *pressed*, *drag* the mouse downwards on the mouse-pad so that cell addresses **A1** to **A4** get highlighted (Fig. EX-4.4).

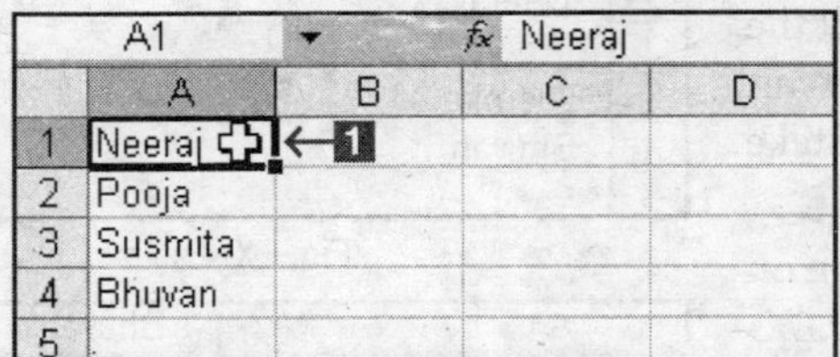

Fig. EX-4.3

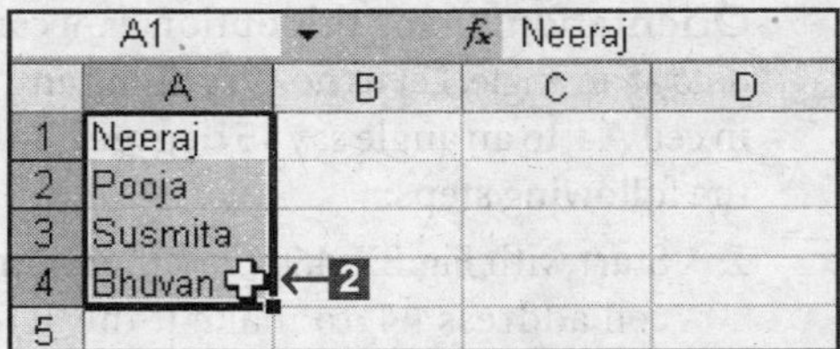

Fig. EX-4.4

3. Now, *move* the mouse-pointer to the **Formatting Toolbar,** and *click* on the **Right** align button (Fig. EX-6.5).

Fig. EX-4.5

4. Immediately, the text gets aligned to the right hand side and appears highlighted. To remove the highlight from the text, *click* anywhere else on the sheet. Now, the worksheet looks like Fig.EX-4.6.

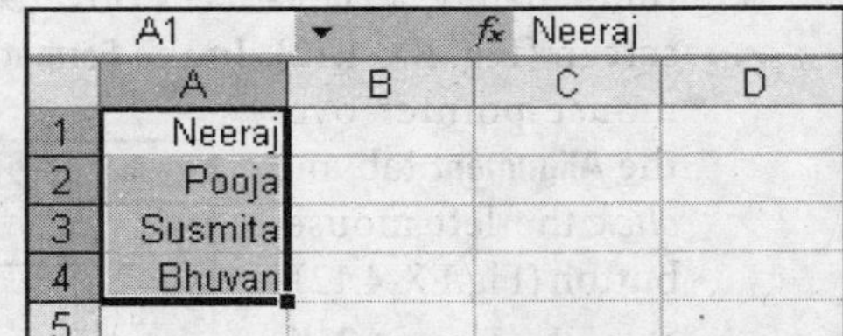

Fig. EX-4.6

Simultaneous Aligning of Data in All Cells

Suppose you have prepared an Excel worksheet. In this worksheet, you wish to position all the entries at the center. One way to do so is by clicking on the **Center** button separately for each row. However, this procedure is time consuming. Let us learn a shortcut method to do this. Undertake the following steps:

1. Begin with Fig.EX-4.6. *Move* the mouse-pointer (✥) over the **Select All** button present at the top-left corner of the worksheet (Fig. EX-4.7) and *click* the left mouse-button. Immediately, the entire sheet gets highlighted.

2. Next, *click* on **Center** align button (≣) present on the **Formatting Toolbar** (Fig.EX-4.8).

3. Now, the right alignment of data in your worksheet has been changed to center alignment. Any entry made at any cell address will now be positioned at the center. Remove the highlight from the text by *clicking* the left mouse-button anywhere inside the sheet (Fig.EX-4.9).

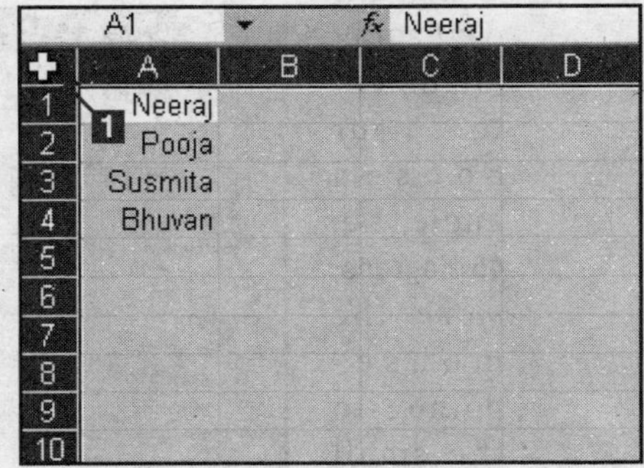

Fig. EX-4.7

Fig. EX-4.8

Aligning Data at an Angle

Microsoft Excel has another very useful option called the **Orientation**. Using this option, you can align or tilt the data at an angle. Let us now try tilting any text, say **Bhuvan** in cell **A4**, to an angle say **45 degrees**. To do so, undertake the following steps:

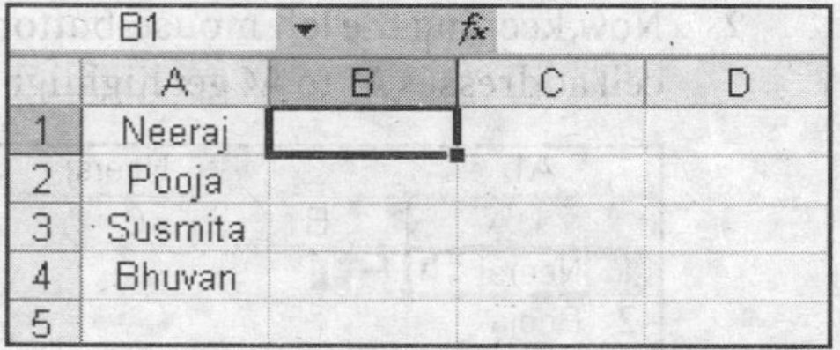

Fig. EX-4.9

1. Start with Fig.EX-4.9. *Click* the left mouse-button on cell address **A4** to make it the active cell (Fig.EX-4.10).

Fig. EX-4.10

2. Now, *click* on the **Format** option in the Menu bar of the Excel workbook. Immediately, a pull-down menu gets displayed (Fig.EX-4.11).
3. Inside the pull-down menu, *click* on the **Cells** option (Fig.EX-4.11).
4. Immediately, a **Format Cells** box gets displayed on the screen (Fig. EX-4.12). In the **Format Cells** box, *move* the mouse-pointer over the **Alignment** tab and *click* the left mouse-button (Fig.EX-4.12).
5. Now, the **Format Cells** box presents various options related to the **Alignment** tab. Microsoft Excel by default aligns all text to zero degree. To change this default alignment to our chosen angle, i.e. **45 degrees**, *move* the mouse-pointer to the small box next to the **Degrees** option and *double-click* the left mouse-button (Fig. EX-4.13).

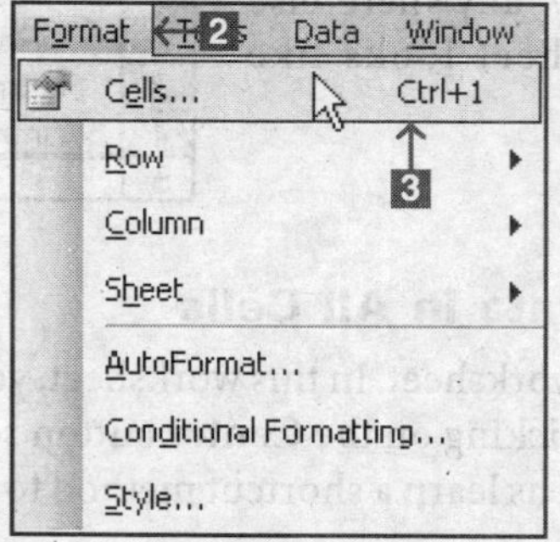

Fig. EX-4.11

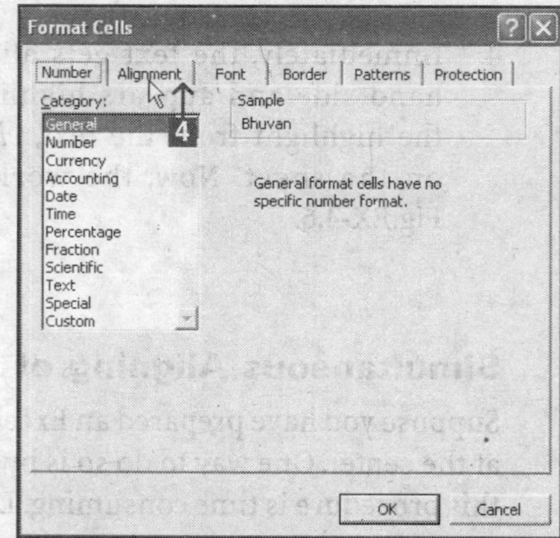

Fig. EX-4.12

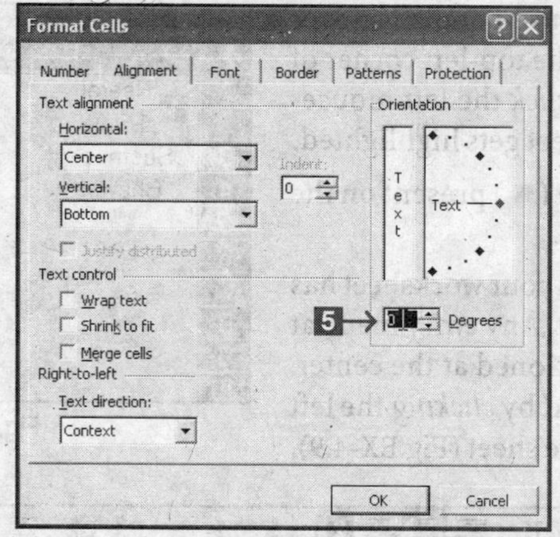

Fig. EX-4.13

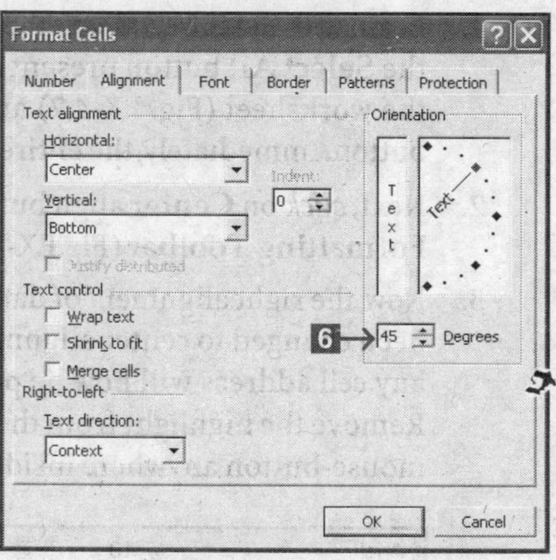

Fig. EX-4.14

6. *Type* **45** in order to tilt text **Bhuvan** to 45 degrees (Fig. EX-4.14).
7. Finally, *click* on the **OK** button (Fig. EX-4.15). Immediately, the **Format Cells** box disappears.
8. The text **Bhuvan** appears tilted to a 45 degree angle at cell address **A4** (Fig. EX-4.16).

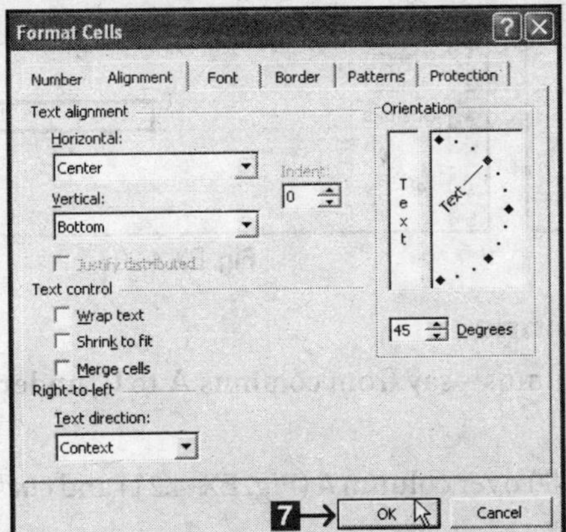

Fig. EX-4.15

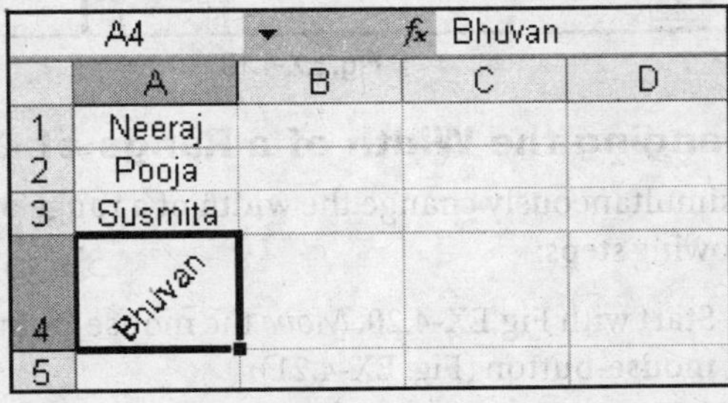

Fig. EX-4.16

Increasing or Decreasing the Column Width

All the cells in a sheet have the default column width of 9 characters, i.e. each cell can fit 9 characters by default. However, Excel allows you to change the width of each column in your sheet. Different columns in a sheet can have different widths. However, all cells in a particular column must have the same width.

Changing the Width of a Column

If you want to change the width of a column, say column D, then proceed as follows:

1. Start with Fig.EX-4.16. *Move* the mouse-pointer over column **D** and *click* the left mouse-button. Immediately, the entire column **D** gets highlighted (Fig.EX-4.17).
2. After highlighting the column, *place* the mouse-pointer over the boundary of the column. The shape of the mouse-pointer changes to (✛) (Fig. EX-4.18).

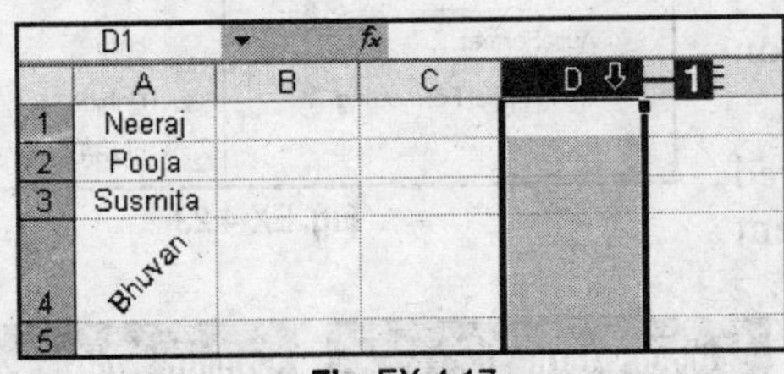

Fig. EX-4.17

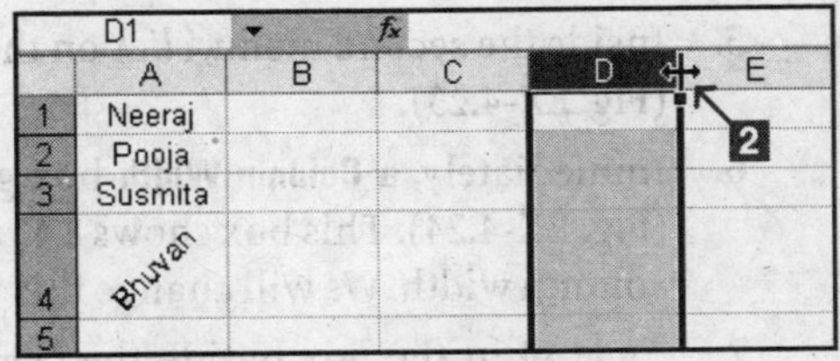

Fig. EX-4.18

3. Now keeping the left mouse-button *pressed*, *drag* the boundary of the highlighted column **D** to the right side. As you drag the boundary, a tooltip appears above column **D**. This tooltip gives you feedback about the current width of the column (Fig. EX-4.19).

4. On attaining the desired column width, *release* the mouse-button. Your worksheet with changed width of column **D** looks like Fig. EX-4.20. *Click* anywhere in the worksheet to remove the highlight from column **D**.

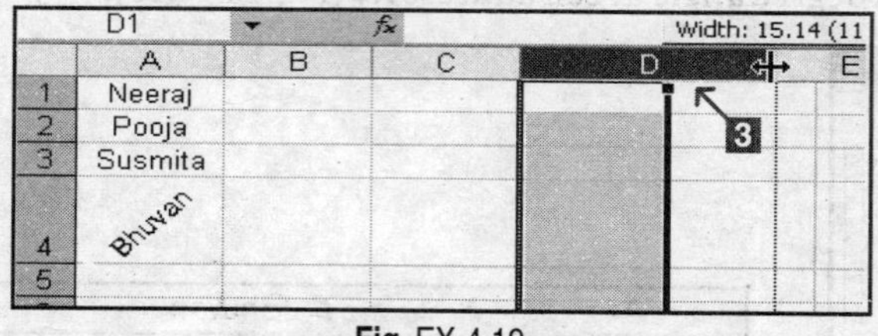

Fig. EX-4.19

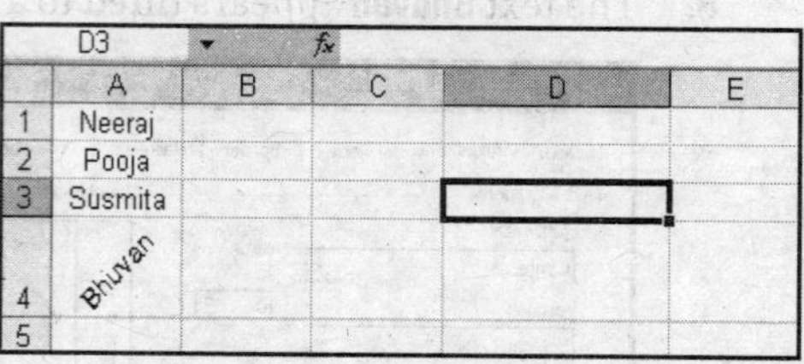

Fig. EX-4.20

Changing the Width of a Range of Columns

To simultaneously change the width of a range of columns – say from columns A to C, undertake the following steps:

1. Start with Fig.EX-4.20. *Move* the mouse-pointer (✥) over column **A** (Fig. EX-4.21) and *click* the left mouse-button (Fig. EX-4.21).
2. Now, keeping the left mouse-button *pressed*, *drag* the mouse-pointer till column **C**. All the cells of columns **A** to **C** get highlighted (Fig. EX-4.22).

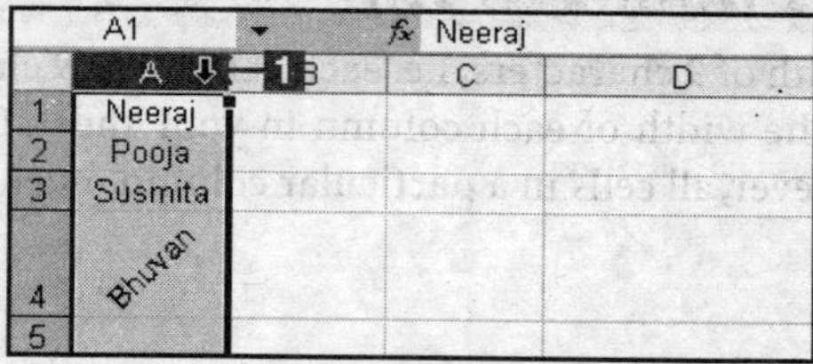

Fig. EX-4.21

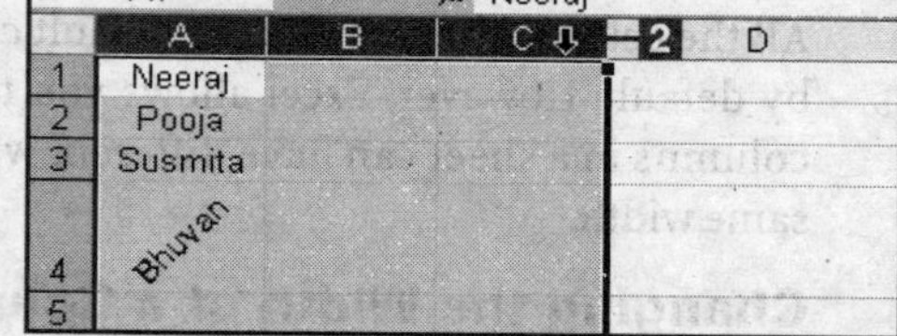

Fig. EX-4.22

3. Next, *choose* the **Format** option from the Menu bar (Fig. EX-4.23).
4. Inside the pull-down menu, *move* the mouse-pointer over the **Column** option. A second menu appears (Fig. EX-4.23).
5. Inside the second menu, *click* on the **Width** option (Fig. EX-4.23).
6. Immediately, a **Column Width** box gets displayed (Fig. EX-4.24). This box shows **8.43** as the present column width. We will change this width to **10**.
7. *Type* **10** in the box beside the **Column width** option (Fig. EX-4.25).
8. Finally, *click* on the **OK** button (Fig. EX-4.26). Now width of all the cells within columns changes to **10**.

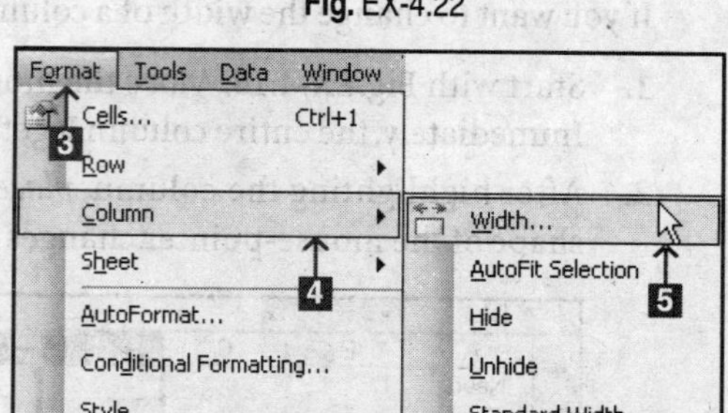

Fig. EX-4.23

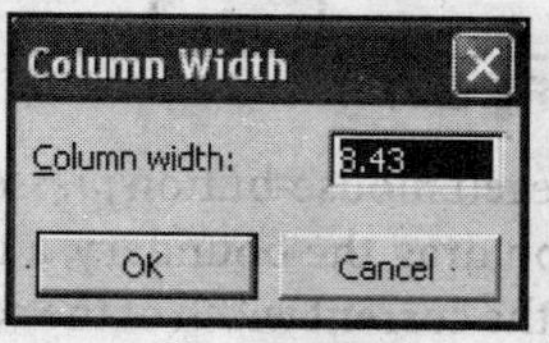

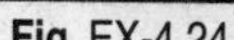

Fig. EX-4.24

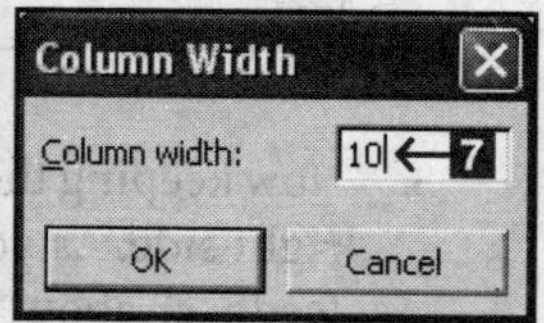

Fig. EX-4.25

9. After removal of the highlight from columns A to C, your worksheet looks like Fig. EX-4.27.

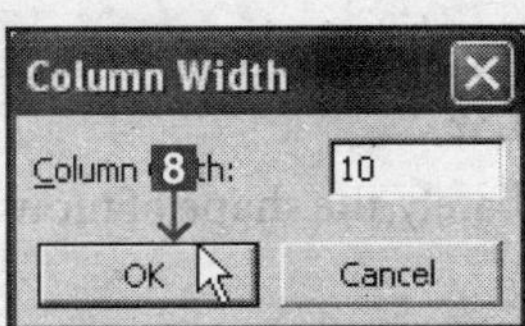

Fig. EX-4.26

Fig. EX-4.27

Changing the Width of all Columns

Suppose, you wish to change the width of all the columns. To do so, undertake the following steps:

1. Begin with Fig.EX-4.27. Since we have to change the width of all the columns, all of them have to be highlighted first. To do so, *move* the mouse-pointer over the **Select All** button (Fig. EX-4.28), and *click* the left mouse-button. Immediately, the whole sheet gets highlighted (Fig.EX-4.29).
2. *Place* the mouse-pointer over the boundary of any column, say column **B**. The shape of mouse-pointer changes to (✛) (Fig. EX-4.29)

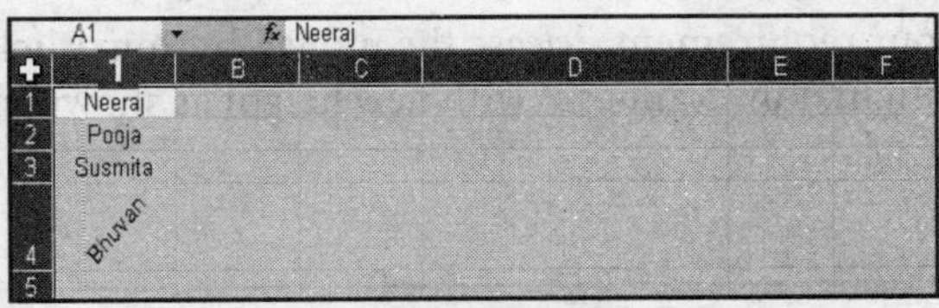

Fig. EX-4.28

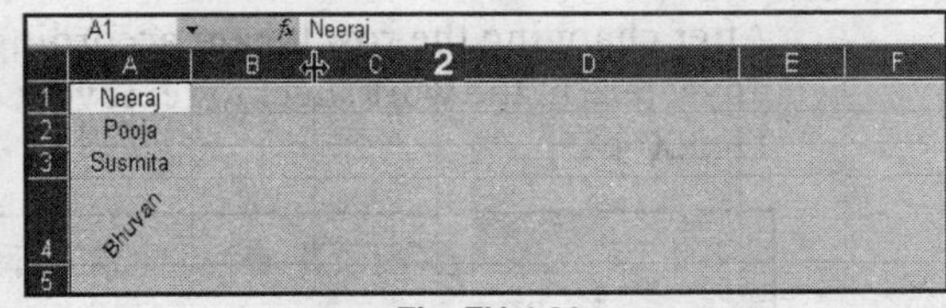

Fig. EX-4.29

3. Now, keeping the left mouse-button *pressed*, *drag* the column boundary towards the right side. As you drag the column boundary, a tool tip appears above the column names giving you the current width of columns (Fig. EX-4.30).
4. Once the column width increases as per your requirement, *release* the left mouse-button. Thereafter, remove the highlight by clicking anywhere in the sheet. Now, the sheet looks like (Fig. EX-4.31).

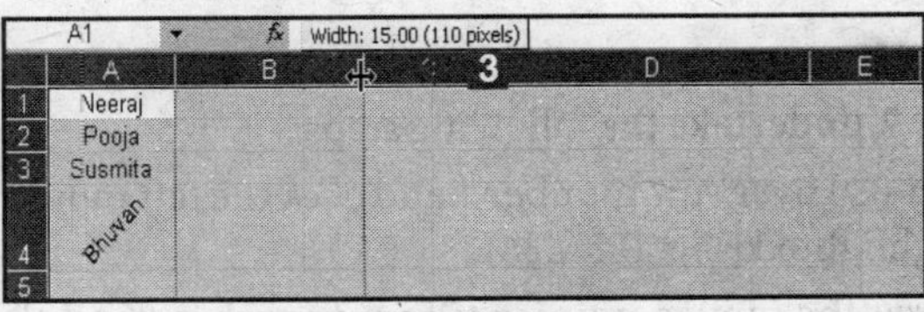

Fig. EX-4.30

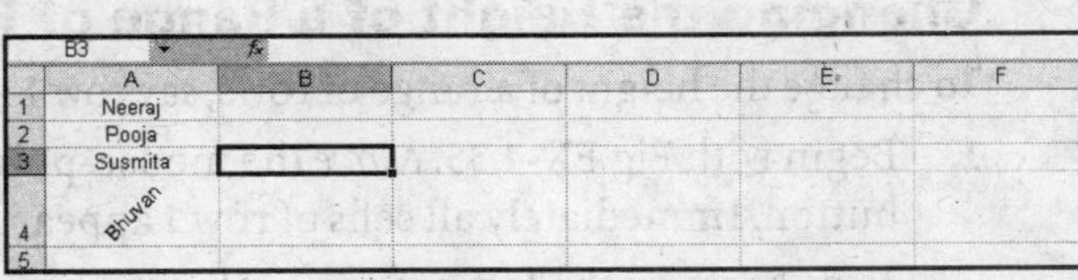

Fig. EX-4.31

Increasing or Decreasing the Height of Rows

All the rows in a sheet have the default height of **12.75**. Excel allows you to change the height of each row in your sheet. Different rows in a sheet can have different heights but all cells in a particular row must have the same height.

Changing the Height of a Row

If you want to change the height of a row, say row number **5**, then proceed as follows:

1. Begin with Fig.EX-4.31. *Move* the mouse-pointer (✥) over row number **5** and *click* the left mouse-button. Immediately, the entire row **5** gets highlighted (Fig. EX-4.32).
2. Next, *place* the mouse-pointer over the boundary of row 5. Immediately, the shape of mouse-pointer changes to ✛ (Fig. EX-4.33).

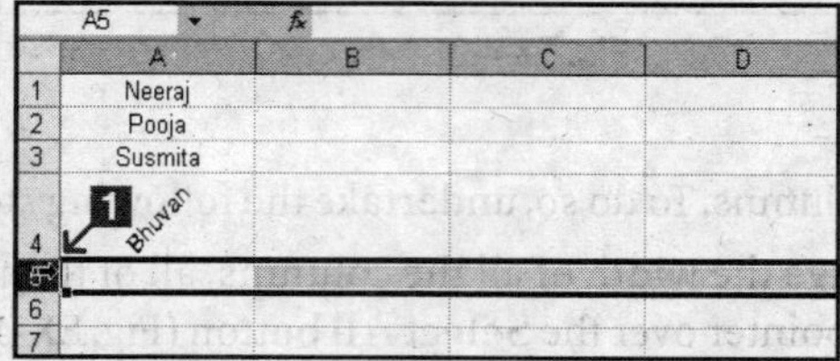

Fig. EX-4.32

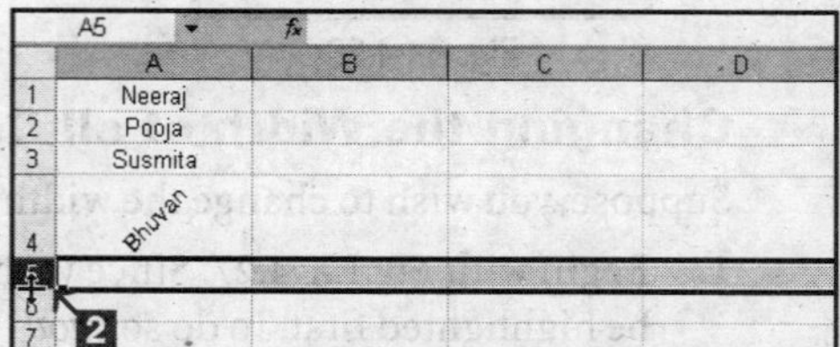

Fig. EX-4.33

3. Now, keeping the left mouse-button *pressed*, *drag* the boundary of the row downwards. As you drag the boundary, a Tool tip appears. This Tool tip mentions the current height of the row (Fig. EX-4.34).
4. After changing the row height according to your requirement, *release* the mouse-button. Click anywhere in the worksheet to remove the highlight. Row 5 appears with new height as shown in Fig.EX-4.35.

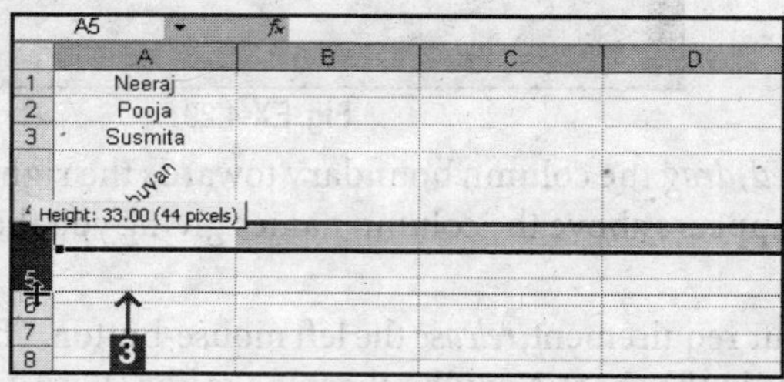

Fig. EX-4.34

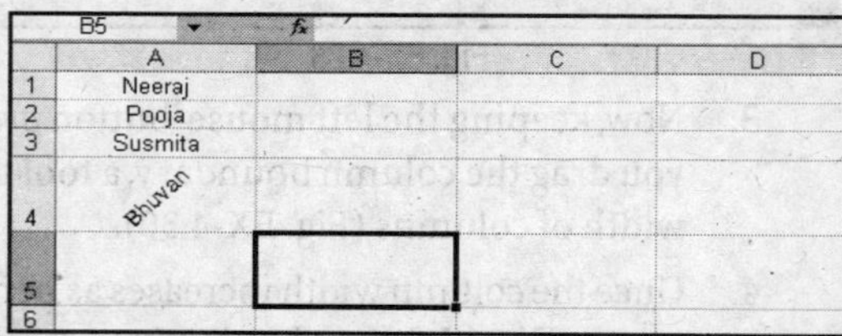

Fig. EX-4.35

Changing the Height of a Range of Rows

To change the height of a range of rows, say row 1 and 2, undertake the following steps:

1. Begin with Fig.EX-4.35. *Move* the mouse-pointer (✥) over row number **1** and *click* the left mouse-button. Immediately all cells of row **1** appear highlighted (Fig. EX-4.36).
2. Now, keeping the left mouse-button *pressed*, *drag* the mouse-pointer till row number **2**. All the cells of rows 1 and 2 get highlighted (Fig.EX-4.37).

Fig. EX-4.36

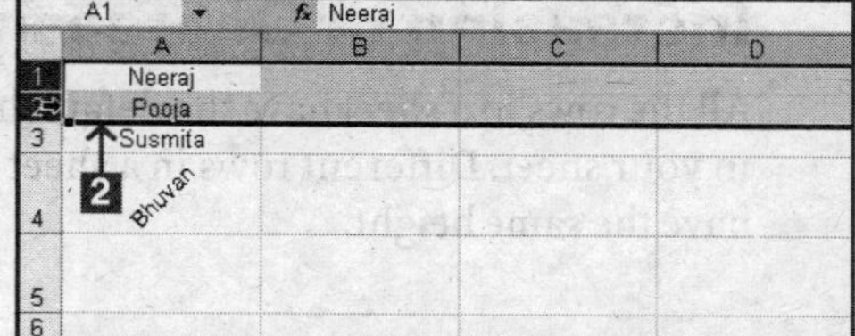

Fig. EX-4.37

3. Then *move* the mouse-pointer over **Format** option in the Menu bar and *click* the left mouse-button (Fig.EX-4.38).
4. Inside the pull-down menu, *move* the mouse-pointer over the **Row** option (Fig.EX-4.38).
5. When a second menu appears, *click* on the **Height** option (Fig. EX-4.38).

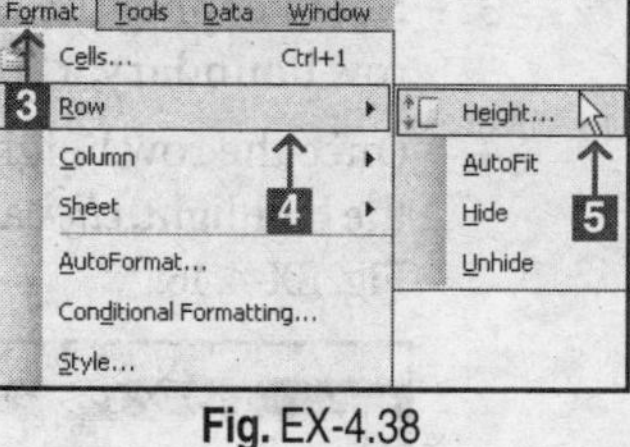

Fig. EX-4.38

6. Immediately, a **Row Height** box appears on the screen (Fig. EX-4.39). In this box, the present row height is shown as **12.75.** Now, we will change this height to 20.

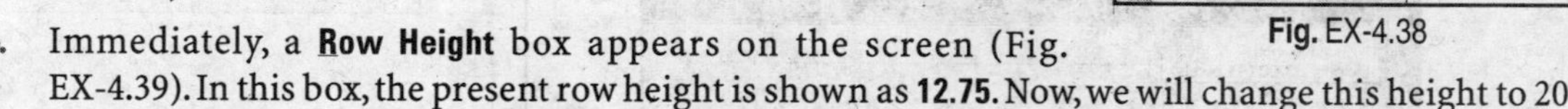

7. *Type* **20** in the box beside the **Row Height** option (Fig.EX-4.40).
8. Finally, *click* on the **OK** button (Fig. EX-4.41). Now, the height of all the cell addresses within rows **1** and **2** changes to **20.**

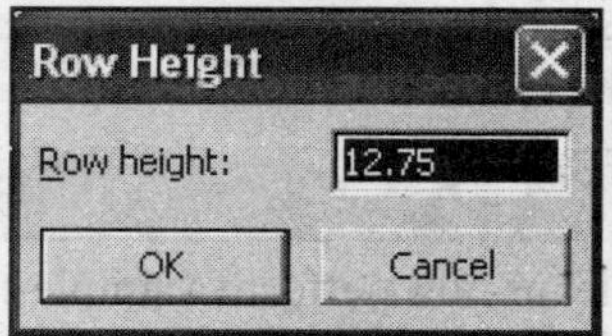

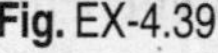
Fig. EX-4.39

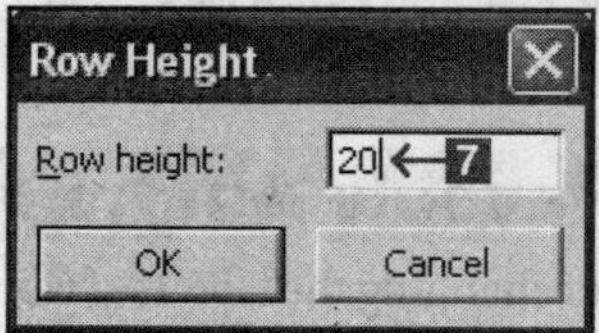

Fig. EX-4.40

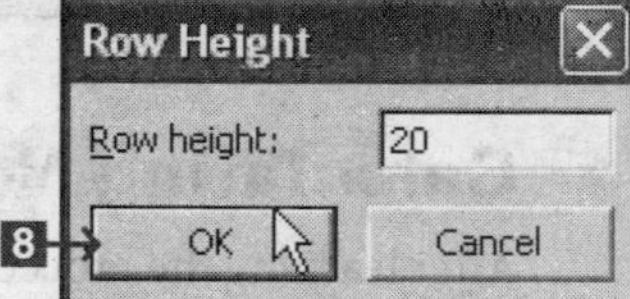

Fig. EX-4.41

9. *Click* anywhere else in your sheet to remove the highlight from rows 1 and 2. Once the highlight is removed, the worksheet looks like Fig. EX-4.42.

Fig. EX-4.42

Changing the Height of all Rows

If you wish to change the height of all the rows of your sheet then undertake the following steps.

1. First, you need to highlight all the rows in your worksheet. To do so, *move* the mouse-pointer (✣) over the **Select** All button (Fig.EX-4.43), and *click* the left mouse-button. Immediately, the whole sheet gets highlighted.
2. *Place* the mouse-pointer over the boundary of any row, say row **2.** The shape of mouse-pointer changes to (✣) (Fig. EX-4.44).

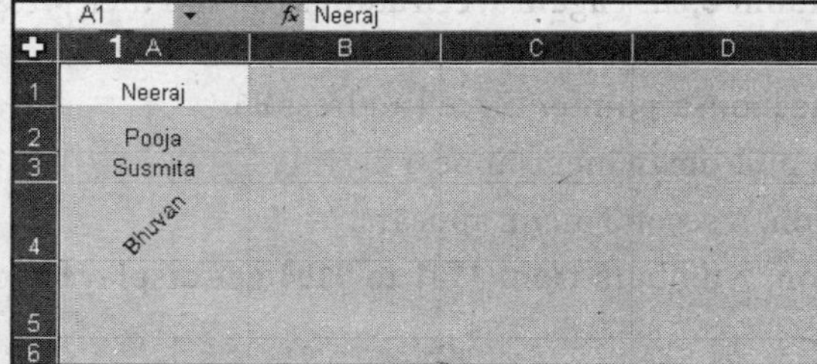

Fig. EX-4.43

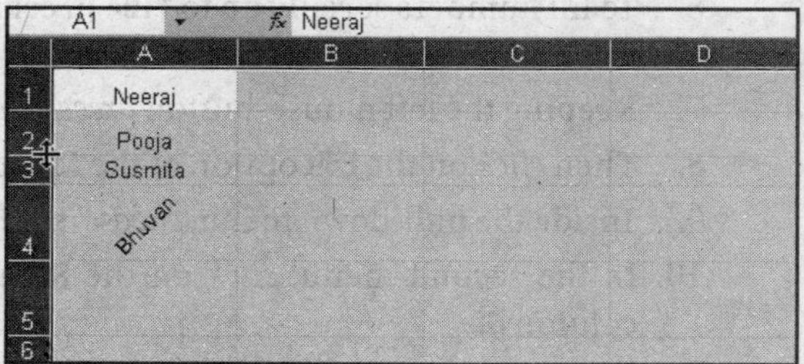

Fig. EX-4.44

3. Now, keeping the left mouse-button *pressed*, *drag* the row boundary downwards. As you drag the row boundary, a Tooltip appears giving you the current height of row 2 (Fig. EX-4.45).
4. Once the row height increases as per your requirement, release the left mouse-button. To remove the highlight, *click* anywhere in the document. Once the highlight is removed, the worksheet looks like Fig. EX-4.46.

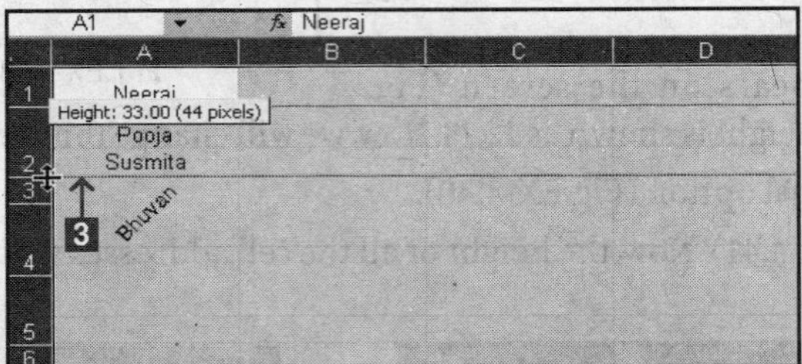

Fig. EX-4.45

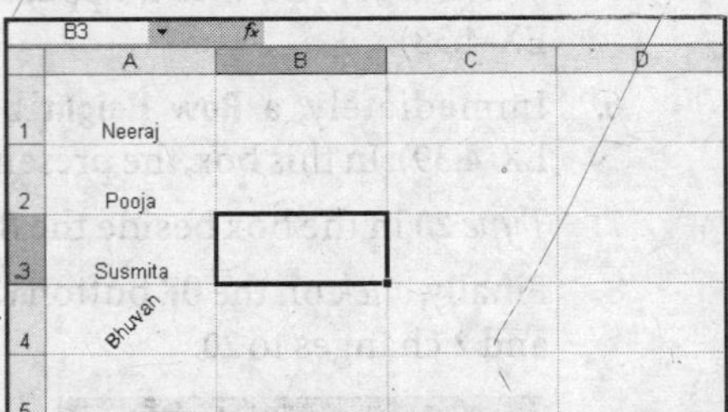

Fig. EX-4.46

Calculating Net Payable Amount

After learning the procedure of changing the layout of worksheet, let us now perform a simple calculation to calculate the net payable amount after the discount. But first of all enter the data given in the underlying table.

TABLE

Sr. No	Name	Rate	Discount	Payable Amount
1101	T-Shirts	400	0.2	
1102	Casual Trousers	750	0.15	
1103	Shirts	500	0.1	
1104	Shoes	1200	0.2	

1. Start with Fig.EX-4.46.
2. *Click* at cell address **B1** and *type* **Sr.No.**
3. Next, *click* at cell address **C1** and *type* **Name.**
4. Similarly at cell address **D1** *type* **Rate,** at **E1** *type* **Discount,** at **F1** *type* **Payable Amount**
5. After typing the heading for each column, *click* at cell address **B2.** *Type* **1101** and *press* the **Enter** key. Now, cell address **B3** becomes the active cell.
6. To fill numbers serially up to **1104** in cells of column **B,** *click* again at cell address **B2** and then *press* the left mouse-button.
7. Keeping the left mouse-button *pressed*, *drag* the mouse-pointer till cell address **B5.**
8. Then *click* on the **Edit** option of the Menu bar. A pull-down menu appears.
9. Inside the pull-down menu, *choose* the **Fill** option. A second menu appears.
10. In the second menu, *click* on the **Series** option. Numbers from **1101** to **1104** get displayed in column **B.**

11. Now, *click* at cell address **C2** and *type* **T-Shirts.** Then *press* the **Enter** key. The mouse-pointer shifts to cell address **C3.**
12. At cell address **C3,** *type* **Casual Trousers** and *press* the **Enter** key. Cell address **C4** becomes active.
13. *Type* **Shirts** at cell address **C4** and *press* the **Enter** key. Similarly, *type* **Shoes** at cell address **C5**
14. Next, *click* at cell address **D2** and *type* **400.** Then *press* the **Enter** key.
15. At cell address **D3,** *type* **750** and *press* the **Enter** key.
16. Similarly, *type* **500** at cell address **D4** and press the **Enter** key.
17. Next, *click* at cell address **D5** and *type* **1200.**
18. Now move the mouse-pointer over cell address **E2** and click the left mouse-button. *Type* **0.2** and press the **Enter** key.
19. The cell-pointer shifts to cell address **E3.** *Type* **0.15** and *press* the **Enter** key. The cell-pointer is now at cell address **E4.** *Type* **0.1** and *press* the **Enter** key.
20. The cell-pointer now shifts to cell address **E5.** At this cell address *type* **0.2.**
21. After typing the entire data of the table, the worksheet appears like Fig.EX-4.47.

E5 | 0.2

	B	C	D	E	F	G
1	Sr. No	Name	Rate	Discount	Payable Amount	
2	1101	T-Shirts	400	0.2		
3	1102	Casual Trouser	750	0.15		
4	1103	Shirts	550	0.1		
5	1104	Shoes	1200	0.2		
6						

Fig. EX-4.47

Making Headings Bold

Let us now undertake the following steps to make column headings – **Sr.No, Name, Rate, Discount** and **Payable Amount** as bold so that they stand out in our worksheet.

1. First, we need to highlight all the column headings. To do so, *move* the mouse-pointer (✥) to cell address **B1** and *click* the left mouse-button. Cell address **B1** becomes active.
2. Next, *press* the left mouse-button at cell address **B1.**
3. Then, keeping the left mouse-button *pressed, drag* the mouse-pointer (✥) till cell address **F1.** When all the cell addresses containing column headings get highlighted, our worksheet looks like Fig. EX-4.48. Now, *release* the left mouse-button.
4. Next, *move* the mouse-pointer over the **Bold** button (B) present on the **Standard Toolbar** and *click* the left mouse-button. The text in selected cells (**B2** to **F2**) appears bold and highlighted. *Click* anywhere in the worksheet to remove the highlight from the cells. After removing the highlight, the worksheet looks like Fig. EX-4.49.

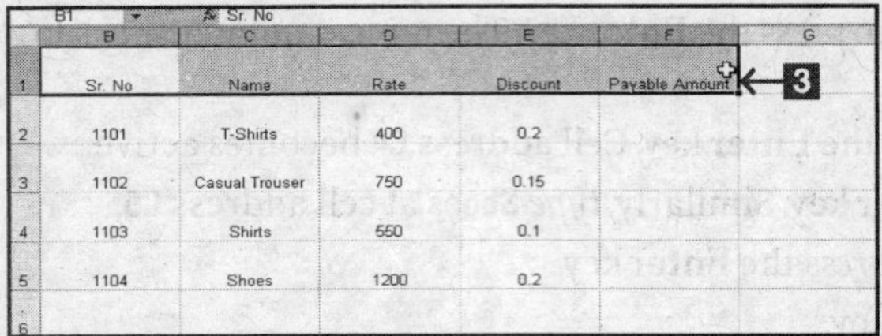

	B	C	D	E	F
1	Sr. No	Name	Rate	Discount	Payable Amount
2	1101	T-Shirts	400	0.2	
3	1102	Casual Trouser	750	0.15	
4	1103	Shirts	550	0.1	
5	1104	Shoes	1200	0.2	

Fig. EX-4.48

	B	C	D	E	F
1	Sr. No	Name	Rate	Discount	Payable Amount
2	1101	T-Shirts	400	0.2	
3	1102	Casual Trouser	750	0.15	
4	1103	Shirts	550	0.1	
5	1104	Shoes	1200	0.2	

Fig. EX-4.49

Displaying the Percentage Sign

To display all the numbers in column E with percentage signs, undertake the following steps.

1. First, we have to highlight cell addresses **E2** to **E5**. So, *place* the mouse-pointer over cell address **E2** (Fig. EX-4.50).
2. Now, keeping the left mouse-button *pressed*, *drag* the mouse downwards on the mouse-pad such that cell addresses **E2** to **E5** get highlighted (Fig. EX-4.51). Then release the mouse-button.

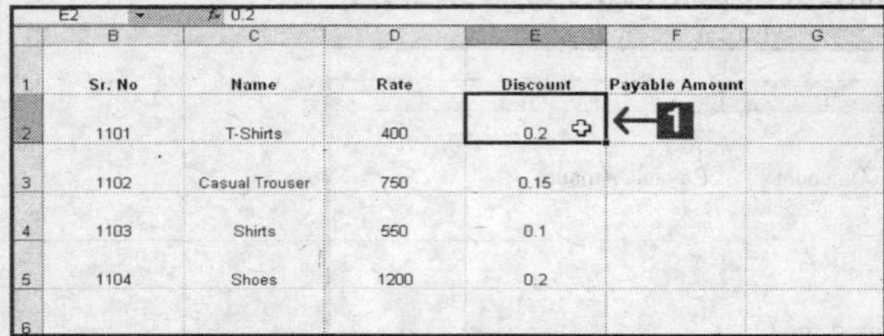

	B	C	D	E	F
1	Sr. No	Name	Rate	Discount	Payable Amount
2	1101	T-Shirts	400	0.2	
3	1102	Casual Trouser	750	0.15	
4	1103	Shirts	550	0.1	
5	1104	Shoes	1200	0.2	

Fig. EX-4.50

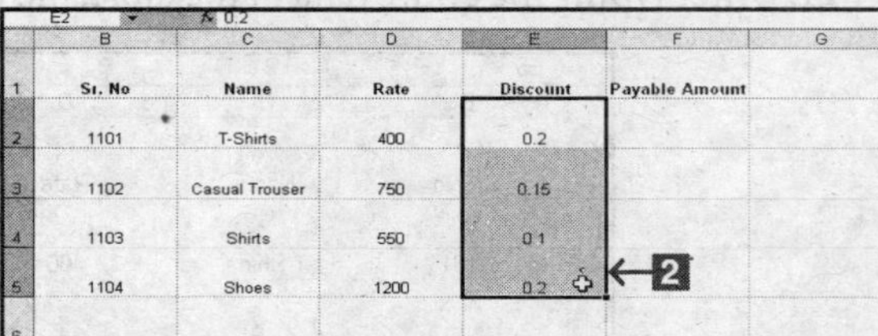

	B	C	D	E	F
1	Sr. No	Name	Rate	Discount	Payable Amount
2	1101	T-Shirts	400	0.2	
3	1102	Casual Trouser	750	0.15	
4	1103	Shirts	550	0.1	
5	1104	Shoes	1200	0.2	

Fig. EX-4.51

3. Next, *move* the mouse-pointer over the **Percent Style** button (%), present on the **Standard Toolbar** (Fig.EX-4.52) and *click* the left mouse-button.

Fig. EX-4.52

4. Immediately, all the highlighted numbers of column **E** change to the percentage style. After removal of the highlight from column **E**, your worksheet looks like Fig.EX-4.53.

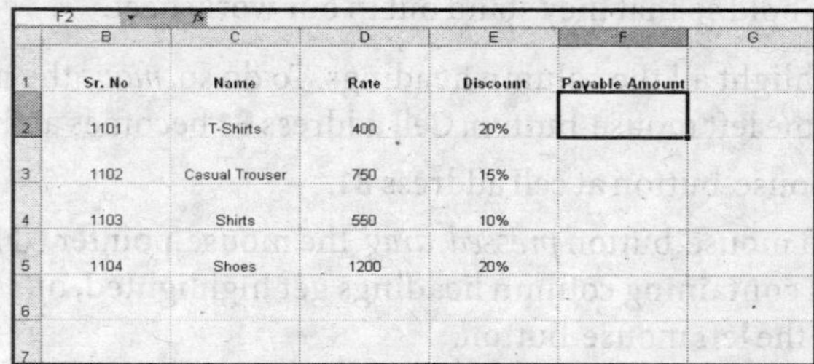

	B	C	D	E	F
1	Sr. No	Name	Rate	Discount	Payable Amount
2	1101	T-Shirts	400	20%	
3	1102	Casual Trouser	750	15%	
4	1103	Shirts	550	10%	
5	1104	Shoes	1200	20%	

Fig. EX-4.53

Calculating the Payable Amount

Let us now calculate the Payable Amount in our worksheet. The net payable amount after adjusting the discount is calculated by the formula

Rate – (Rate*Discount)

Thus if you want to calculate the Payable Amount for T-Shirts then formula will be

400 – (400*20%) = 320

OR

400 – (400*20/100) = 320

We will write this formula only for one item. To calculate Payable Amount for remaining items, we will copy the formula and paste it at the appropriate cells.

1. Start with Fig. EX-4.53. For calculating the Payable Amount for T-Shirts, we will use cell address **F2.** Type formula (**= D2-D2*E2)** in cell **F2**, as shown in Fig. EX-4.54.
2. After typing the formula, *press* the **Enter** key. Immediately, the result **320** i.e. Payable Amount for T-shirts, appears at cell address **F2** (Fig. EX-4.55).

PERCENTILE ▾ X ✓ fx =D2-D2*E2

	B	C	D	E	F	G
1	Sr. No	Name	Rate	Discount	Payable Amount	
2	1101	T-Shirts	400	20%	=D2-D2*E2 ← 1	
3	1102	Casual Trouser	750	15%		
4	1103	Shirts	550	10%		
5	1104	Shoes	1200	20%		
6						

Fig. EX-4.54

3. Again *place* the mouse-pointer over cell **F2** and *click* the left mouse-button. Cell **F2** becomes active. Now, *move* the mouse-pointer over the **Copy** button (), present on the **Standard Toolbar**, and *click* the left mouse-button. Immediately, a box of blinking lines surrounds cell **F2** (Fig. EX-4.56). Appearance of this box indicates that the formula of cell **F2** has been copied.

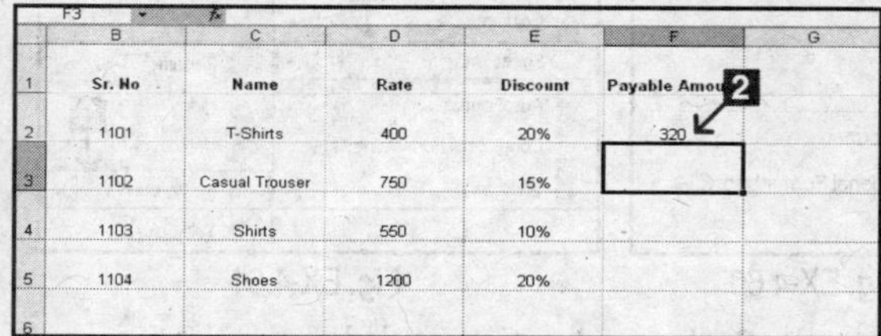

F3 ▾ fx

	B	C	D	E	F	G
1	Sr. No	Name	Rate	Discount	Payable Amou 2	
2	1101	T-Shirts	400	20%	320	
3	1102	Casual Trouser	750	15%		
4	1103	Shirts	550	10%		
5	1104	Shoes	1200	20%		
6						

Fig. EX-4.55

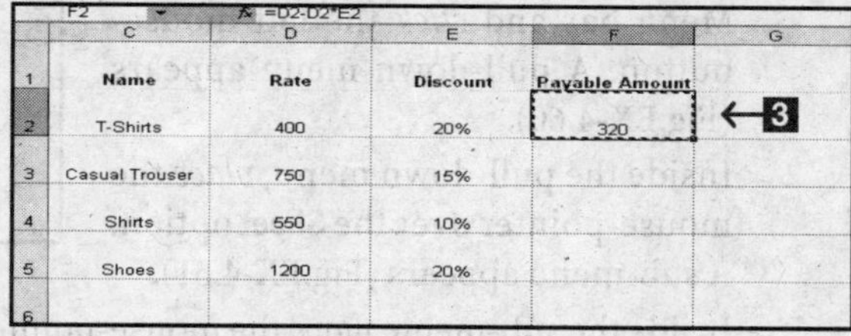

F2 ▾ fx =D2-D2*E2

	C	D	E	F	G
1	Name	Rate	Discount	Payable Amount	
2	T-Shirts	400	20%	320 ← 3	
3	Casual Trouser	750	15%		
4	Shirts	550	10%		
5	Shoes	1200	20%		
6					

Fig. EX-4.56

4. After copying the formula, *place* the mouse-pointer over cell address **F3** and *click* the left mouse-button. Then, keeping the left mouse-button *pressed*, *drag* the mouse-pointer till cell address **F5.** The selected cells appear highlighted (Fig. EX-4.57).
5. Next, *move* the mouse-pointer over the **Paste** button () present on the **Standard Toolbar** and *click* the left mouse-button. Immediately, the Payable Amount for each item appears at its respective cell (Fig. EX-4.58).

F3 ▾ fx

	C	D	E	F	G
1	Name	Rate	Discount	Payable Amount	
2	T-Shirts	400	20%	320	
3	Casual Trouser	750	15%		
4	Shirts	550	10%		
5	Shoes	1200	20%	← 4	
6					

Fig. EX-4.57

F3 ▾ fx =D3-D3*E3

	C	D	E	F	G
1	Name	Rate	Discount	Payable Amount	
2	T-Shirts	400	20%	320	
3	Casual Trouser	750	15%	637.5	
4	Shirts	550	10%	495	
5	Shoes	1200	20%	960	
6					

Fig. EX-4.58

	C	D	E	F	G
1	Name	Rate	Discount	Payable Amount	
2	T-Shirts	400	20%	320	
3	Casual Trouser	750	15%	637.5	
4	Shirts	550	10%	495	
5	Shoes	1200	20%	960	
6					
7					

Fig. EX-4.59

Changing the Background of a Worksheet

In previous sections of the chapter we work upon a worksheet and learn to change the height and width of rows and columns. Let us now learn about another interesting feature to make the worksheet more impressive - Adding a Picture in the Background of a Worksheet. You add any picture from any location of your computer and set is as the background of the worksheet. However, all Microsoft Office applications use My Pictures sub-folder of My Documents folder as the default folder for importing and saving pictures. Let us use the default folder to import a picture in the worksheet and change its background by undertaking the following steps:

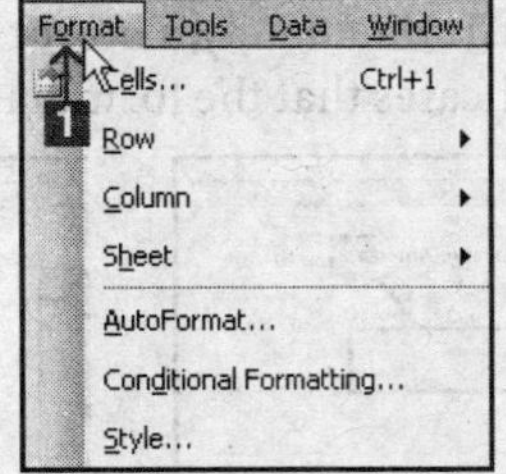

Fig. EX-4.60

Fig. EX-4.61

1. Start with Fig.EX-4.59. *Place* the mouse-pointer over the **Format** option of the Menu bar and *click* the left mouse-button. A pull-down menu appears (Fig.EX-4.60).
2. Inside the pull-down menu, *place* the mouse-pointer over the **Sheet** option. A sub-menu appears (Fig.EX-4.61).
3. Inside the sub-menu, *move* the mouse-pointer over the **Background** option and *click* the left mouse-button (Fig.EX-4.61). Instantly, the **Sheet Background** box appears (Fig.EX-4.62).
4. Among the displayed pictures, *move* the mouse-pointer over the desired picture and *click* over it. The image gets selected and blue lines surround it. For example, *move* the mouse-pointer over the picture name **Rites** and *click* over it (Fig.EX-4.63).

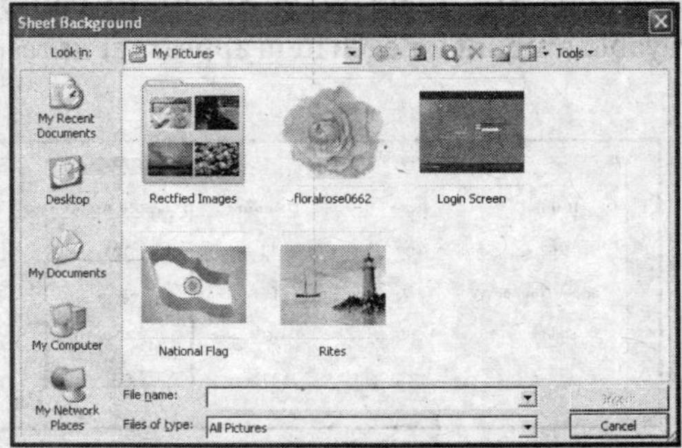

Fig. EX-4.62

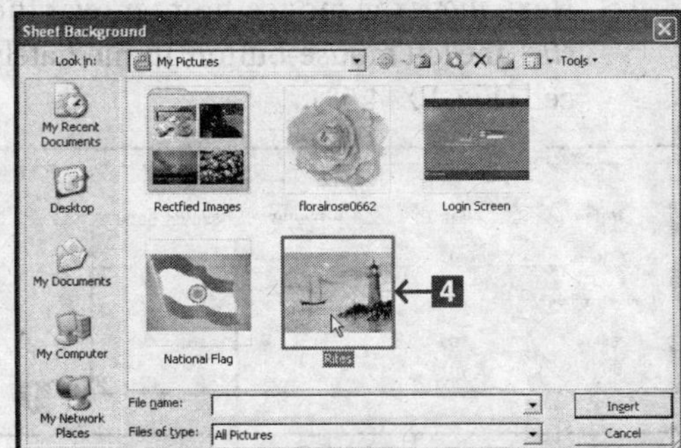

Fig. EX-4.63

5. After selecting the picture for the background, *move* the mouse-pointer over the **Insert** button and *click* the left mouse-button (Fig.EX-4.64).
6. The selected picture appears in the background of the worksheet as shown in Fig.EX-4.65. You can repeat Steps 1 to 6 to insert any image in the background of a worksheet.

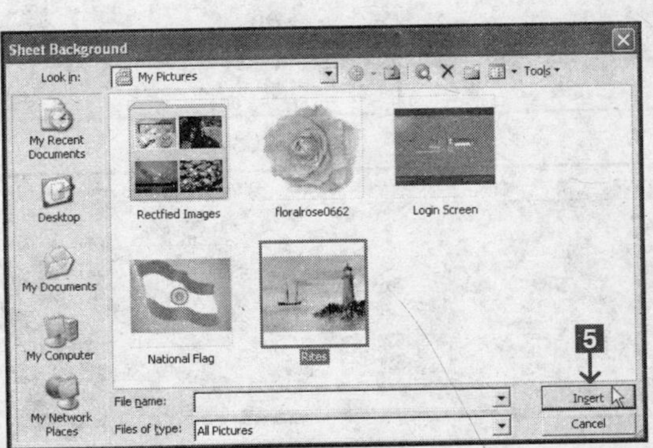

Fig. EX-4.64

Fig. EX-4.65

To remove the picture from the background of the worksheet:

1. Click over the Format option of the Menu bar. Inside the pull-down menu, place the mouse-pointer over the Sheet option.
2. A sub-menu appears. Inside the sub-menu, move the mouse-pointer over Delete Background option and click the left mouse-button.

Renaming a Worksheet and Copying Data between Worksheets

In Microsoft Excel, you can change the name of any worksheet according to your requirement. Also, you can move data between worksheets present in the workbook. Let us now, undertake the following steps to rename a worksheet and move data between worksheets.

1. Start with Fig.EX-4.65. *Move* the mouse-pointer over the sheet tab and *place* it over the **Sheet 1**. Next, *double-click* the left mouse-button. The sheet name gets highlighted (Fig.EX-4.66).
2. Now, type name for the worksheet. For example, *type* **Rites** and press the **Enter** key. The new name of the worksheet appears on the sheet tab (Fig.EX-4.67).

Fig. EX-4.66

Fig. EX-4.67

3. After renaming the worksheet, let us now learn to copy the data between worksheets of a workbook. To do so, *move* the mouse-pointer over the cell address **A1** and *click* the left mouse-button (Fig.EX-4.68).

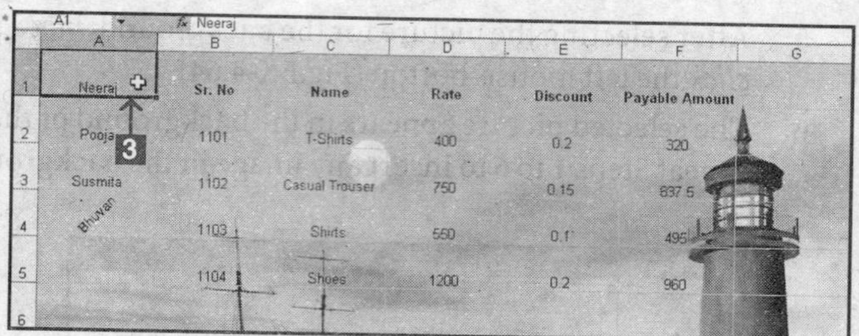

Fig. EX-4.68

4. Keeping the left mouse-button *pressed*, *drag* the mouse-pointer in such a way that data till upto cell address **F5** gets highlighted (Fig.EX-5.69). Once the required data is highlighted, *release* the left mouse-button.

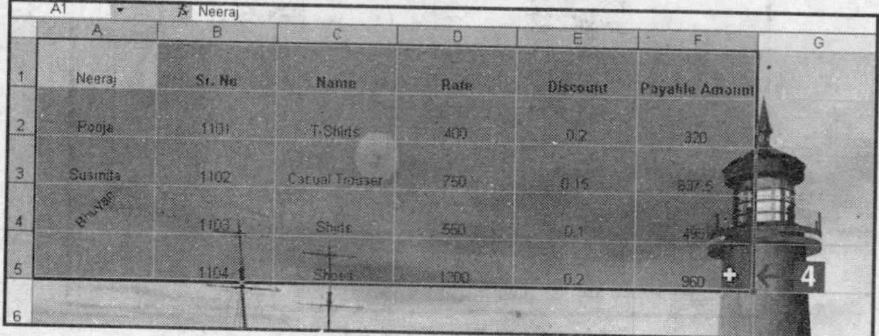

Fig. EX-4.69

5. Without deselecting the data, *move* the mouse-pointer over the **Edit** option of the Menu bar and *click* the left mouse-button (Fig.EX-4.70).
6. A pull-down menu appears. In the pull-down menu, *move* the mouse-pointer over the **Copy** option and *click* the left mouse-button (Fig.EX-4.70).
7. *Move* the mouse-pointer over the **Sheet 2** present in the sheet tab and *click* the left mouse-button (Fig.EX-4.71).
8. Row and columns of **Sheet 2** appears. *Move* the mouse-pointer over the **Edit** option of the Menu bar and *click* the left mouse-button. A pull-down menu appears (Fig.EX-4.72.
9. In the pull-down menu, *move* the mouse-pointer over the **Paste** option and *click* the left mouse-button (Fig.EX-4.72).

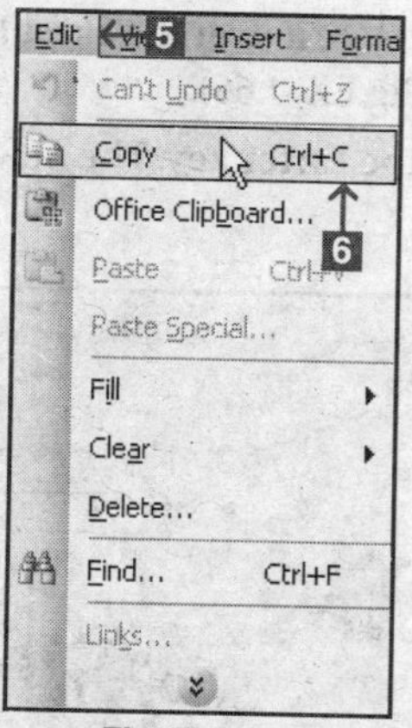

Fig. EX-4.70

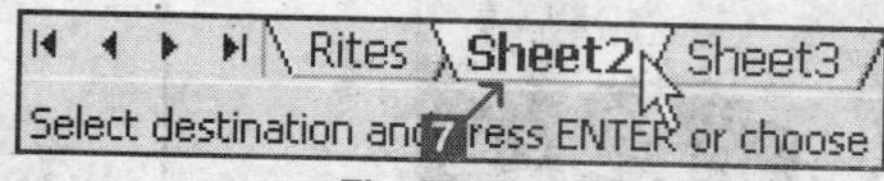

Fig. EX-4.71

Fig. EX-4.72

10. The data of **Rites** worksheet gets appears in **Sheet 2**. *Click* anywhere in the worksheet to remove the highlight from the data. After removing the highlight the worksheet appears like Fig.EX-4.73.

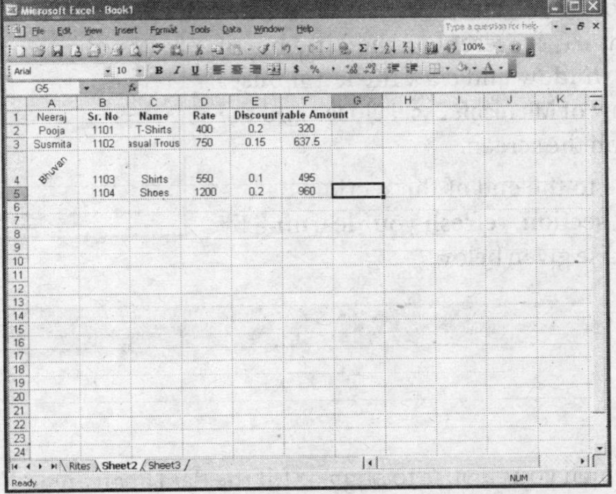

Fig. EX-4.73

Saving the Workbook and Quitting Microsoft Excel

After making required changes in the layout of the worksheet, let us now save the workbook in the Local Disk (C:) by undertaking the following steps:

1. *Move* the mouse-pointer over the **File** option of the Menu bar and *click* the left mouse-button. A pull-down menu appears (Fig.EX-4.74).
2. In the pull-down menu, *move* the mouse-pointer over the **Save** option and *click* the left mouse-button (Fig.EX-4.74).
3. Instantly, the **Save As** dialog box appears. *Type* **Changing the Layout** as the name of the workbook (Fig.EX-4.75).
4. Next, *move* the mouse-pointer over the down-arrow button (▾) beside the **Save in** option and *click* the left mouse-button. Instantly, a pull-down box appears (Fig.EX-4.75).
5. In the pull-down box, *move* the mouse-pointer over the **Local Disk (C:)** option and *click* the left mouse-button (Fig.EX-4.76).

Fig. EX-4.74

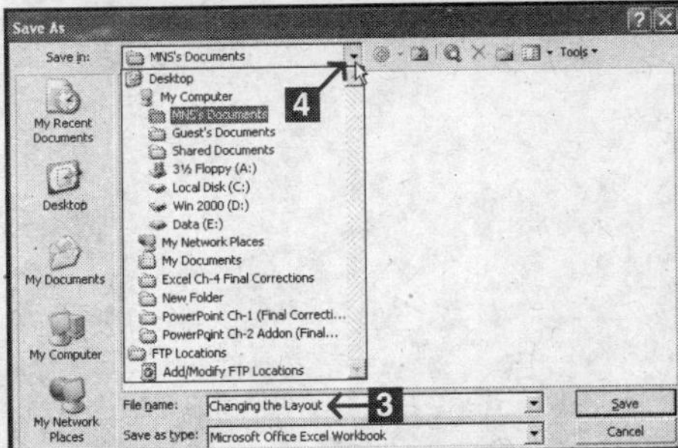

Fig. EX-4.75

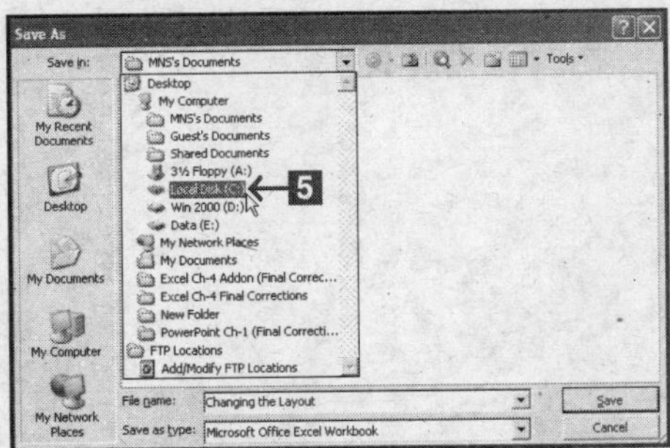

Fig. EX-4.76

6. Lastly, *move* the mouse-pointer over the **Save** option and *click* the left mouse-button (Fig.EX-4.77).
7. After saving the workbook, *move* the mouse-pointer over the **Close** button (☒) present on the **Title bar** of the **Microsoft Excel** window and *click* the left mouse-button. The window of **Microsoft Excel** closes and the **Desktop** appears on the screen.

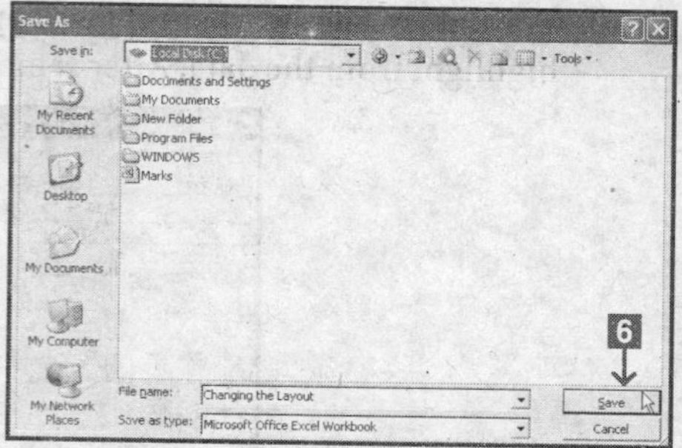

Fig. EX-4.77

With this step, we come to the end of the section. Before proceeding to the next section, refresh your learning by going through the exercise given below.

Exercise

Short Questions

1. What is level entry?
2. Name the option which you can use to align or tilt the data at an angle.
3. By default, how many worksheets appear in a workbook.

Summary

This section introduces you to another very useful application of Microsoft Office suite - Excel. This application is used for sorting and manipulating numbers and data in a spreadsheet. The section starts with a description of the Excel environment, and explains basic Excel terms and techniques for entering and formatting data. Next, we look into an important feature of Excel - Charts, a means to display worksheet data in the form of graphs, pie diagram etc. Charts are free flowing objects appearing anywhere in the worksheet, not confined to any particular cell.

After charts, another important feature of Excel—Functions and Formulas—is explained in detail. The in-built functions of Excel rescue you from typing long equations used to compute the data. Using in-built functions you can perform complex mathematical calculations by typing minimum text. At the end, the section describes techniques for formatting a worksheet, like adding and deleting rows and columns, changing the height and width of rows and columns respectively and changing the background and name of worksheet.

Microsoft Access

IN THIS SECTION

- Introducing to Databases
- Creating Tables
- Updating Tables
- Working with Forms
- Handling Queries
- Generating Reports

MICROSOFT ACCESS

Introduction to Databases 1

IN THIS CHAPTER

- Defining a Database
- Understanding RDBMS
- Objects of a Relational Database
- Functions of a Database Management System (DBMS)
- Starting Microsoft Access
- Closing the Database Window and Quitting Access
- Exercise

To move with the times, you need to keep track of information. The success of a business enterprise today depends much on how quickly it can retrieve the desired information needed for decision-making and routine operations.

Databases are store-houses of information. For retrieving any information, we fall back on databases. Herein comes the role of database management system which helps in systematic organization of information. Amongst the many database management systems available in the market, Access is quite useful and popular because of its unique features.

A database has many advantages. Many of the useful databases are those which can provide latest information. The information in a database should be organized in such a way that it is easy to update. And only then, it can quickly provide the information.

Any stored information or a database, whether electronic or manual, helps you by keeping track of your inventories, payroll, invoicing or anything else that you consider important.

Defining a Database

A database is an organized collection of related information about a particular subject or purpose; for example, information regarding the price of a book or the profile of an individual in any organization. Consider for instance, the example of a box full of index cards carrying the names and prices of the books of a particular author. Every time you juggle through the index cards to set them in an alphabetical order or to look up the price of a particular book, you end up managing the cards.

In computers, a database is like a box containing index cards. The only difference is that instead of index cards, a computer database is filled with **records.** While each index card in the box contains information written in many lines, a record in a database contains all the information related to an item in just one line. Information in a database is stored in **rows** (records) and **columns** (fields), as shown below:

	Column 1	Column 2	Column 3	Column 4	
Row 1	Field 1 **BOOK NAME**	Field 2 **BOOK CODE**	Field 3 **AUTHOR**	Field 4 **PRICE**	
Row 2	Windows 3.1	1002	SANJEEV	500	First Record
Row 3	Windows 95	1001	ASIM	550	Second Record

Table 1

The names given to each column, i.e. BOOK NAME, BOOK CODE, AUTHOR and PRICE are called **field names.** In the given database, the first record (i.e. the second row) contains information about the book Windows 3.1. The second record (i.e. the third row) contains information about the book Windows 95. In the above example (Table 1), we have shown only two records. But in computers, a database can contain large amount of information. Such type of database is called an **electronic database.**

Thus, an electronic database is a collection of logically related information that you store in your computer. It also acts like an assistant to you who is always ready to store, organize and extract information.

Understanding RDBMS

Suppose you have two databases – a database containing book details and the other containing details of the company. Now you wish to display on the screen the information about a book, named A, and the details of the company which published it. What will you do to display the information? You will display the information about that book from the database containing book details. Then you will display the name of the company which has published the book A. To display the information related to book A, we made use of two databases. Both these databases were related. Such a system is called a **RDBMS** (Relational Database Management System).

A Relational Database Management System is defined as a method of viewing information from several, separate databases that relate to one another through keywords or values. The main advantage of a relational database management system is that you can simultaneously use more than one database to see information stored in them.

To have a better understanding of RDBMS, let us take an example of customers ordering products from a dealer. In this case, two databases have to be maintained. The **Customer database** used for storing details of various customers. The **Product Order database** for storing the items ordered by each customer.

Every customer has an identification number which is stored under a fieldname, say Cust-id. This field is present in Customer database as well as the Product Order database. And it is through this field that both these databases are going to be related. Because of this link, it is easy to find out which customer has ordered which item.

If you wish to go through the details about a particular customer stored in the Customer database then just enter the customer identification number and all the information about that customer will be displayed on the screen. Similarly, if you wish to register an order from a particular customer, just enter his customer identification number. When the desired customer's order details are displayed, you can enter his/her new order.

Another advantage of a relational database design is that you can extract fields from different databases and see them on the screen at one time thus reducing the complexity.

Objects of a Relational Database

Microsoft Access is based on RDBMS. Therefore, to have a better understanding of working in Access, you should be familiar with four basic objects of RDBMS as described below:

Tables

A **Table** is a collection of information on a specific topic. In a table, the information is stored in rows and columns. You can store different types of data in different tables.

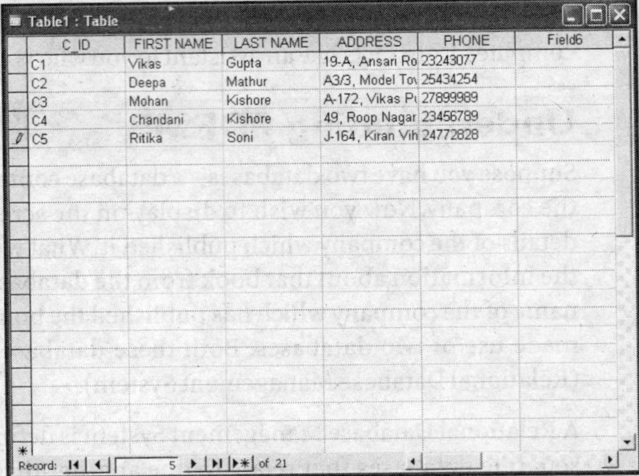

Table1 : Table

C_ID	FIRST NAME	LAST NAME	ADDRESS	PHONE	Field6
C1	Vikas	Gupta	19-A, Ansari Ro	23243077	
C2	Deepa	Mathur	A3/3, Model To	25434254	
C3	Mohan	Kishore	A-172, Vikas Pu	27899989	
C4	Chandani	Kishore	49, Roop Nagar	23456789	
C5	Ritika	Soni	J-164, Kiran Vih	24772828	

Fig. AC-1.1

For example, a table of customers contains all the details regarding the dealings with various customers, whereas a table of suppliers contains the data about various suppliers. When this data is inserted into a table, it will look like Fig.AC-1.1.

Let us now get to know more about the components that make up a table.

Columns

Each column represents a **field.** A field stores only a specific category of information. For example, the field Category Name only stores the name of the food categories.

Rows

Each row in a table is called a record and it consists of a number of related fields. Each field contains some bits of data about the record.

For instance, in the table of Fig. AC-1.1, the listed fields give information about customers such as customer's first and last names, address, and phone nos. When they all are put together, a record is formed.

Domain

The maximum and the minimum values a field can have is called its domain. For example, if you have decided that the field **Book Code** will not contain any three digit number or zero, then its domain will be between 1 to 99. Similarly, if you specify that the field for **Book Name** will not contain any number, its domain will be between **A** to **Z**.

Primary Key

A **Primary key** refers to one or more fields in a table that uniquely identify each record in the table, i.e. it gives a distinct identity to a record. For example, in the table of Fig.AC-1.1 Category ID is the Primary key because it is never repeated. In other words, two different records do not have the same identification number.

Relationships: The tables in a relational database application are tied together by the relationships that bind the records together. Access establishes relationships between tables too, because of which certain fields can be extracted from several tables and displayed on the screen.

Queries

Queries are a systematic way of retrieving information from a database. For example, from Fig.AC-1.1, if you wish to display only those customers whose First Name starts with the alphabet V, then searching through your database and locating such records would be time-consuming. But, you need not worry. You can save your time by using the **Query feature.** Access's Query feature can look for the information that meets the criterion or condition you specify and displays the information on the screen. This information will be displayed in a simple format. But if you wish to present this information to your boss, it is better if you use the **Report feature.**

Forms

Forms present the information stored in a database in an easy to use format. Through Forms, you can view, enter or update information in a database. If you wish to view records in your database, Forms present one record at a time on the screen. But if you wish to enter or update information in your database, Forms become a well-designed data entry form. Fig.AC-1.2 shows a well designed form.

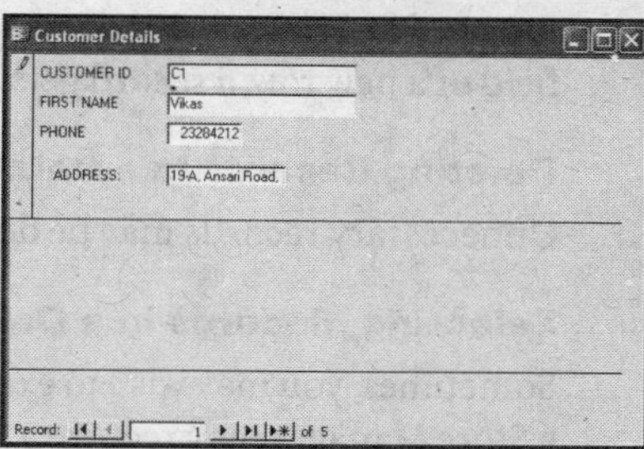

Fig. AC-1.2

Reports

Let us assume that you are in charge of maintaining the list of food items in your company and your boss has asked you to produce a report of the items which have a demand in the market. In such a case, you can use the **Reports feature** to design the required report in such a way that it becomes easy for your boss to quickly understand all its details.

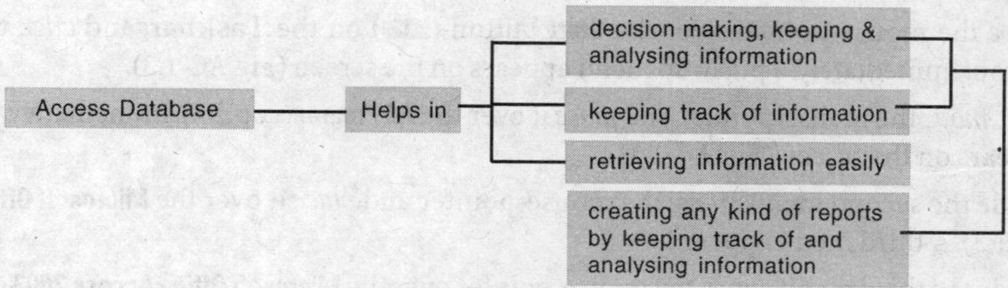

Functions of a Database Management System (DBMS)

A database management system is a tool for managing information, stored in the database. Managing a database includes the following functions:

Database Creation

Creating a database means defining the data to be maintained, and organizing the database to accommodate the data-keeping requirements expected of the system.

Designing a database file means arranging the records, number-wise, type-wise, width-wise and content-wise of each record field. The term **file structure** refers to the manner in which a file is designed. Once a file is designed, data can simply be added to it.

Modifying a Database

Modifying a database means changing its structure. You may wish to add, delete fields or change the width of one or more fields.

Adding Records in a Database

A record or a row of your database is made up of several fields. When new bits of data are entered in every field of a new row, a record gets added.

Deleting Records in a Database

Unnecessary records may be deleted or removed from the datafile.

Selecting Records in a Database

Sometimes, you may wish to examine certain records in a file similar in some characteristic. For example, a Store Manager may require a list of all the items whose quantity on-hand is below the re-order level, or a Sales Manager would require a list of all the sales persons who have achieved their target. All this can be done through a database. The ability to select just those records which meet certain criteria is a very useful feature of DBMS.

Starting Microsoft Access

Let us now start Microsoft Access program through the following steps:

1. *Switch* on your computer. Within a few seconds, Windows XP **Desktop** gets displayed.
2. *Move* the mouse-pointer over the **Start** button (start) on the **Taskbar**, and *click* the left mouse-button. Immediately, a push-up menu appears on the screen (Fig.AC-1.3).
3. Next, *move* the mouse-pointer and *place* it over the **All Programs** option. Immediately, a second menu appears on the screen (Fig.AC-1.3).
4. Inside the second menu, *move* the mouse-pointer and *place* it over the **Microsoft Office** option (Fig. AC-1.3). A third menu appears.
5. Inside the third menu, *move* the mouse-pointer over the **Microsoft Office Access 2003** option and *click* the left mouse-button (Fig.AC-1.3).
6. Immediately, a **Microsoft Access** window appears. On the right side of the window you can see the **Getting Started** Task pane containing various options (Fig.AC-1.4).
7. *Move* the mouse-pointer over the **Create a new file** option and *click* the left mouse-button (Fig.AC-1.4).

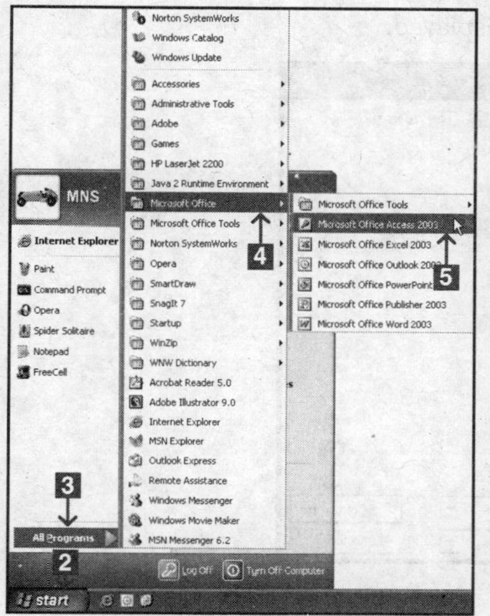

Fig. AC-1.3

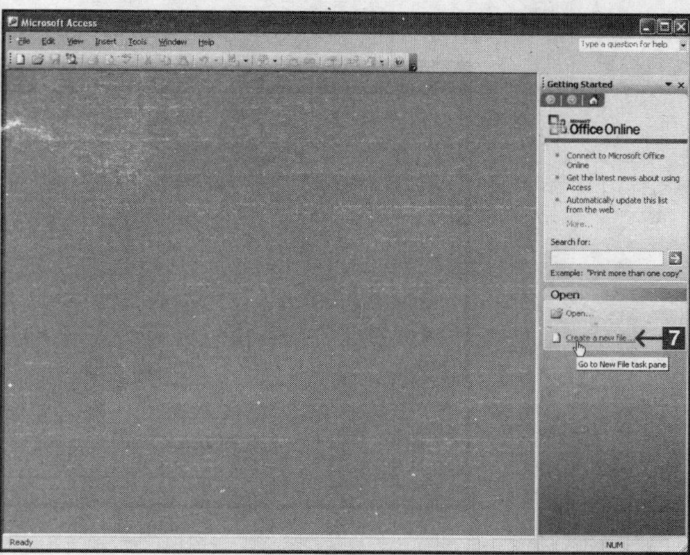

Fig. AC-1.4

8. Instantly, the **New file** Task pane appears. In the Taskpane, *move* the mouse-pointer over the **Blank database** option and *click* the left mouse-button (Fig.AC-1.5).

Fig. AC-1.5

If the New Task pane is not visible undertake the following steps to make it visible.

1. Move the mouse-pointer over the file menu bar option and click the left mouse button. A drop-down appears (Fig.AC-1.6).
2. From this drop-down menu click over the Task pane option (Fig.AC-1.7). Instantly the Getting Started Task pane appears.

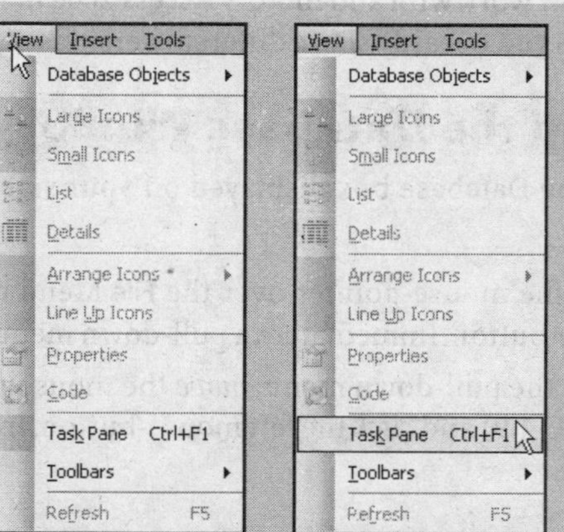

Fig. AC-1.6 Fig. AC-1.7

9. A **File New Database** box gets displayed on the screen (Fig.AC-1.8). Note that the name written against the **File Name** field is **db1** which is the default name that Access assigns to a new database. In this box, *click* on the **Create** button.

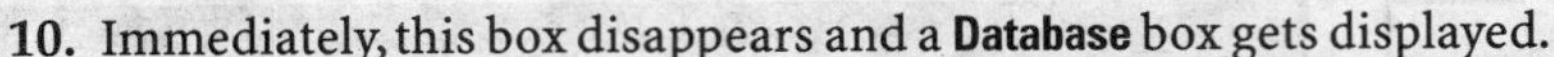

10. Immediately, this box disappears and a **Database** box gets displayed.

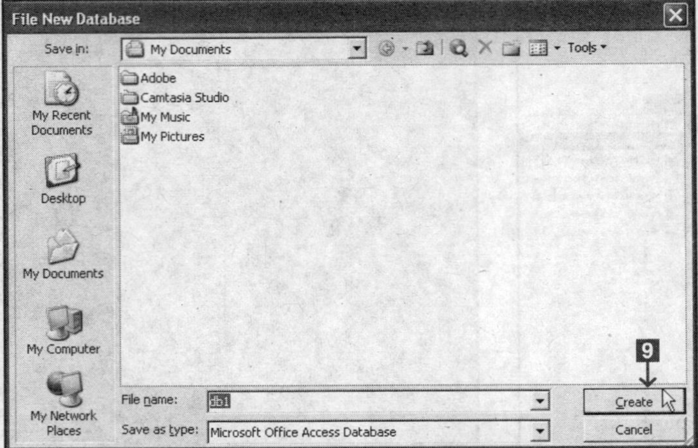

Fig. AC-1.8

A Database box appears whenever you wish to create a database or open an existing one. It always displays on its **Title bar** the name of the open database. In our case, the database was created with a name **db1**. So the **Title bar** displays the name **db1**.

This box is the control center of your database. You can use the **Database** box to open the objects contained within a database, i.e. Tables, Queries, Forms, Reports, Macros and Modules.

Right now we will not work in Access. This program has been opened to help you learn how to open Access. We will work in Access in subsequent chapters. Let us now quit Microsoft Access.

You can now work with and modify Access 2000 files in Access 2003 without converting the file format. This allows you to easily share different versions of database files with other Access users.

Closing the Database Window and Quitting Access

To close the Database box displayed on your screen, undertake the following steps:

1. *Move* the mouse-pointer over the **File** Menu bar option, and *click* the left mouse-button. Immediately, a pull-down menu gets displayed (Fig.AC-9).
2. Inside the pull-down menu, *move* the mouse-pointer over the **Close** option (Fig.AC-1.9) and *click* the left mouse-button. Immediately, the Database box closes.

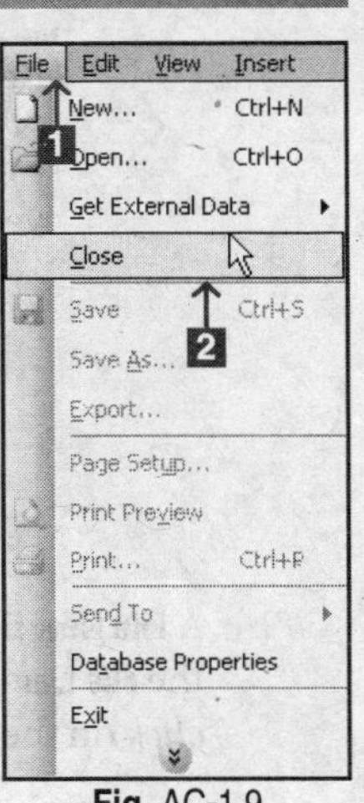

Fig. AC-1.9

3. Now let us close Microsoft Access window. To do so, *move* the mouse-pointer over the **Close** button (☒) present on the **Title bar** of the Microsoft Access window (Fig.AC-1.10), and *click* the left mouse-button. This will close the Microsoft Access window.

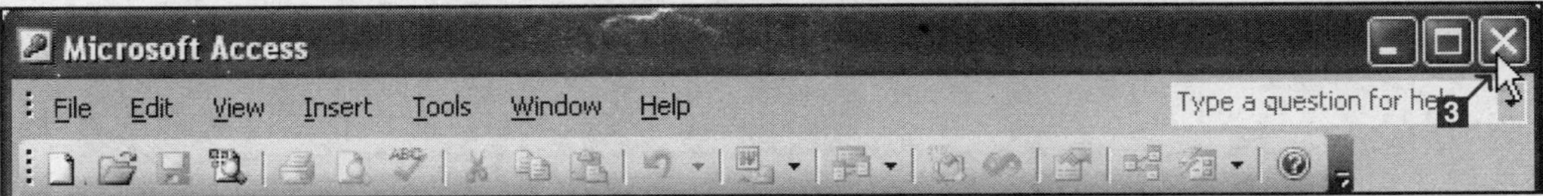

Fig. AC-1.10

Exercise

Fill in the Blanks

1. __________ are the storehouses of information.
2. A computer database is filled with __________.
3. Information in a database is stored in __________ and __________.
4. Access is based on __________.

__________ present the information stored in a database in an easy to use format.

True/False

1. Macros are simple repetitive tasks, which are carried out by Access automatically when you want them to be done.
2. Queries are a non-systematic way of retrieving information from a database.
3. Modifying a database means changing its structure.
4. The term file structure refers to the manner in which a file is designed.
5. Records once entered cannot be deleted or removed from the data file.

MICROSOFT ACCESS

Creating Tables 2

IN THIS CHAPTER

- Understanding Database
- Creating a Database
- Creating a Table
- Working on Table
- Saving the Table
- Defining the Primary Key
- Closing the Table
- Adding Validations to the Table
- Closing the Database and Quitting Access

Microsoft Access is a Window based program created by Microsoft. It helps you store and manage a large collection of information. A systematically arranged database helps you manage the stored information in an efficient way so that it can be accessed quickly whenever needed. You can easily create such a database using Access.

Before creating a database make sure that you design it properly. A good database design ensures that you will be able to perform various tasks on it efficiently and accurately and without any hindrance. Your telephone directory is a good example of a database. It contains the names and addresses of people along with their telephone numbers in alphabetical order. You can also maintain your own telephone book in a computer database.

As you already know, a database consists of four important parts, namely Tables, Forms, Queries and Reports. This means, you have to first create a Database in order to further create Tables, Forms, Queries and Reports. This chapter focuses on Tables.

Understanding Database

Let us learn how to create a database in Microsoft Access. For a better design of your database, keep the following points in mind:

First, *determine the purpose of your database.* In other words, analyze what the database has to do. **Secondly,** *gather all the required information* that you need to store in your database. In a database, information is stored in the form of a table. You can create more than one table. **Thirdly,** *determine the number of fields and field names* required by your table. **Fourthly,** *determine its Primary Key.* And **finally,** if you wish to design more than one table, *determine the relationships between them.* As you know, tables produced in a database system like Access are tied together by the relationship that binds their records together. A relationship in a database brings together the related information stored in different tables.

Let us now create a database and name it as **Address.** This database will contain information about customers such as their identification numbers, names, addresses and phone numbers. You must now determine the number of fields and fieldnames for your proposed table. In our case, the **Address Details** table will contain four fields named as C_ID, First Name, Last Name, Address and Phone as shown in Address Details table.

To give distinction between individual records in the table, each record should have a **Primary Key** attached to it. In our table, the field C_ID contains the identification numbers of all customers. Since no two customers can have the same identification number, **C_ID** becomes the **Primary Key.**

TABLE	Address Details
T	C_ID
A	First Name
B	Last Name
L	Address
E	Phone

TABLE	Order Details
T	P_ID
A	C_ID
B	Product Name
L	Price
E	Quantity

A database can also have more than one table. Let us make another table and name it as **Order Details.** Suppose the second table has five fieldnames P_ID, C_ID, Product Name, Price and Quantity (Order Details table). Here **P_ID** is the field name which uniquely identifies each record. Since the Primary Key can be used to link the two tables, the fieldname C_ID is also inserted into the second table.

A **Primary Key** is a field in the table that uniquely identifies every record in it. The basic purpose of defining a Primary Key is to *avoid duplication of records*. The values in the Primary Key field cannot be repeated. The Primary Key ensures that one and only one record exists of a particular entity. In our case, using Primary key, i.e. C_ID we can find the details of a customer who has ordered a specified quantity of a product.

Creating a Database

Let us now learn how to create the **Address** database, which will maintain address details of the customers. To do so, you may undertake the following steps:

1. *Switch* on your computer. Within a few seconds, Windows XP **Desktop** gets displayed.
2. *Move* the mouse-pointer over the **Start** button (start) on the **Taskbar**, and *click* the left mouse-button. Immediately, a push-up menu appears on the screen (Fig.AC-2.1).
3. Next, *move* the mouse-pointer and *place* it over the **All Programs** option. Immediately, a second menu appears on the screen (Fig.AC-2.1).
4. Inside the second menu, *move* the mouse-pointer and *place* it over the **Microsoft Office** option (Fig.AC-2.1). A third menu appears.
5. Inside the third menu, *move* the mouse-pointer over the **Microsoft Office Access 2003** option and *click* the left mouse-button (Fig.AC-2.1).

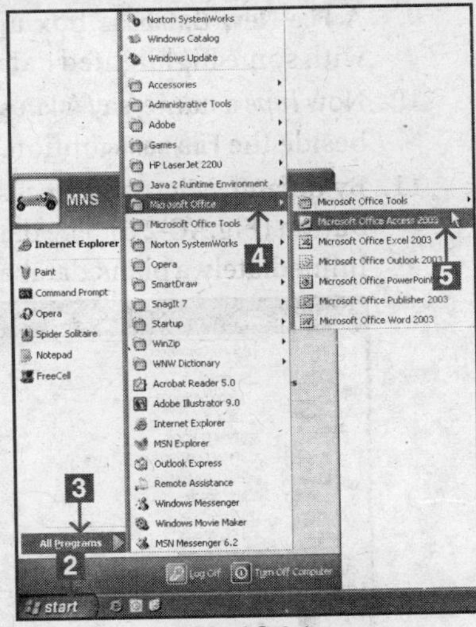

Fig. AC-2.1

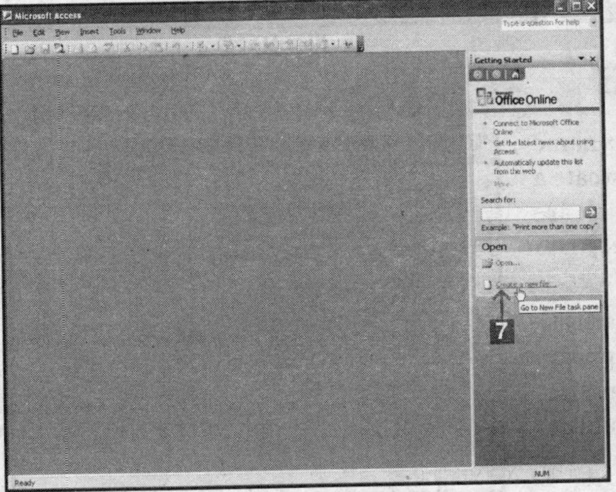

Fig. AC-2.2

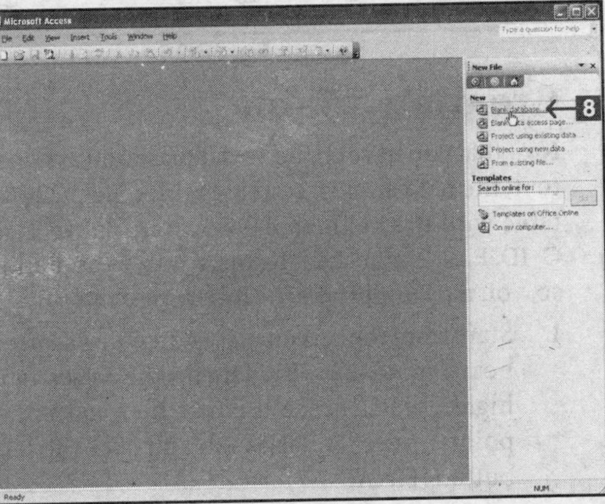

Fig. AC-2.3

6. Immediately, a **Microsoft Access** window appears. On the right side of the window you can see the **Getting Started** Task pane containing various options (Fig.AC-2.2).
7. *Move* the mouse-pointer over the **Create a new file** option and *click* the left mouse-button (Fig.AC-2.2).
8. Immediately, the **New File** Task pane appears. *Move* the mouse-pointer over the **Blank Database** option and *click* the left mouse-button (Fig. AC-2.3).

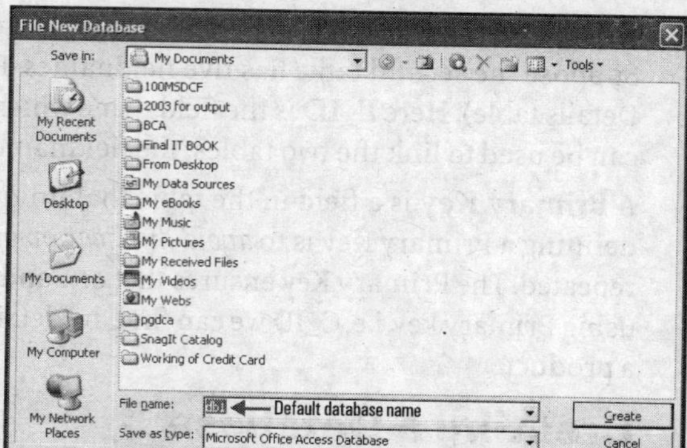

Fig. AC-2.4

9. A **File New Database** box appears on screen with some highlighted database name beside **File name** option (Fig.AC-2.4).
10. Now *type* a name, say **Address**, for the database (Fig.AC-2.5). This name gets displayed inside the box beside the **File name** option.
11. By default, Microsoft Access saves all the databases in **My Documents** folder. So *click* on the **Create** button (Fig.AC-2.6). The database gets saved in My Documents folder. Immediately, a blank database named **Address : Database** gets displayed on the screen (Fig. AC-2.6).

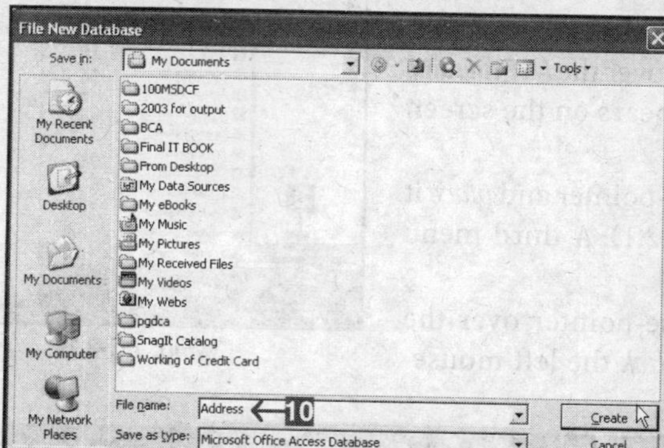

Fig. AC-2.5

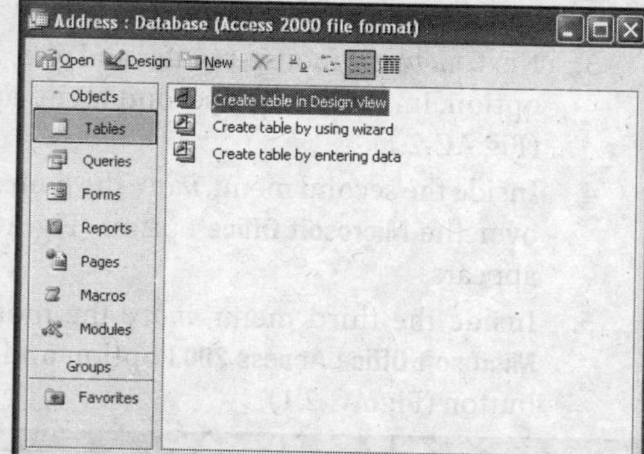

Fig. AC-2.6

Creating a Table

Now that you have created a database and assigned a name to it, the next step is to create tables. Let us now create a table with the fieldnames shown in **Table 1**, which are C_ID, First Name, Last Name, Address and Phone. To do so, you may undertake the following steps:

1. Start from the screen displaying the **Address : Database** box (Fig.AC-2.6). By default, the **Tables** tab appears highlighted. Incase it is not then *move* the mouse-pointer over the **Tables** tab and *click* the left mouse-button (Fig.AC-2.7).

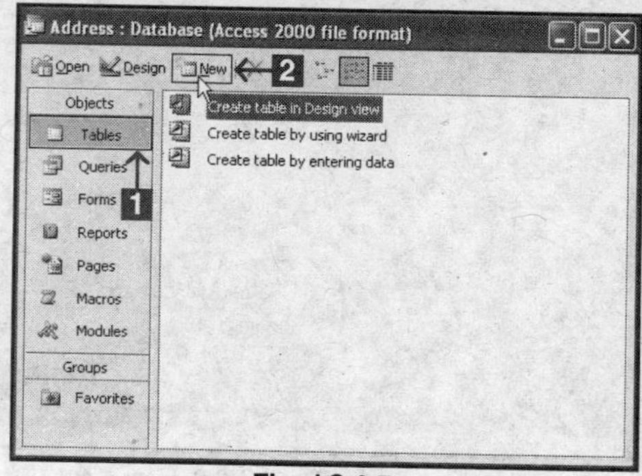

Fig. AC-2.7

2. Then *move* the mouse-pointer over the **New** button (Fig.AC-2.7), and *click* the left mouse-button. Immediately, a **New Table** box appears on the screen (Fig.AC-2.8).
3. In the **New Table** box, the **Datasheet View** option is highlighted by default. In case it is not highlighted then *move* the mouse-pointer and *click* the left mouse-button. Immediately, the option gets highlighted (Fig.AC-2.8).
4. Finally, *click* on the **OK** button (Fig.AC-2.8). Instantly, a blank table appears on the screen (Fig.AC-2.8). You will notice that the Access table of Fig.AC-2.9 is divided into rows and columns. Each column is a **Field** and each row is a **Record**.

Fig. AC-2.8

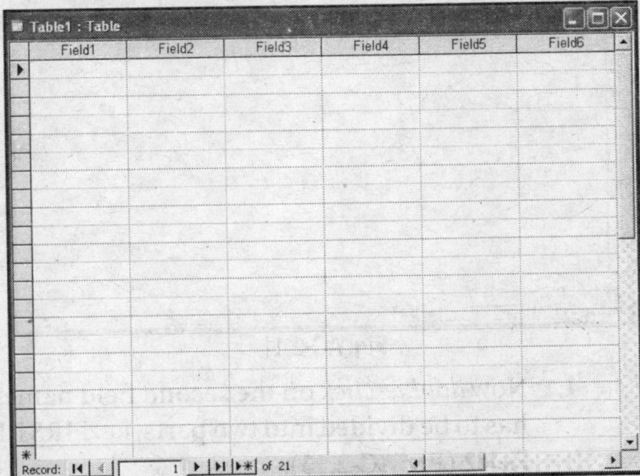

Fig. AC-2.9

Field: A field is a specific category of information. Every field has a unique field name. For example, the column names in a table such as Name of the customer, Address of the customer and Amount in Profit, represent individual fields.

Record: When a collection of information from every field is put together, it forms a record, i.e. a row.

Working on Table

Naming Fields

You will notice that the fields of the table shown in Fig.AC-2.9, are named as **Field1, Field2,** and so on. Microsoft Access allows you to change the names of these fields. So, let us proceed to change these field names to the ones required for our Table.

1. *Move* the mouse-pointer to the field name **Field1** (Fig.AC-2.10). As soon as the mouse-pointer moves on the column name, it changes into an arrow shape (↓).

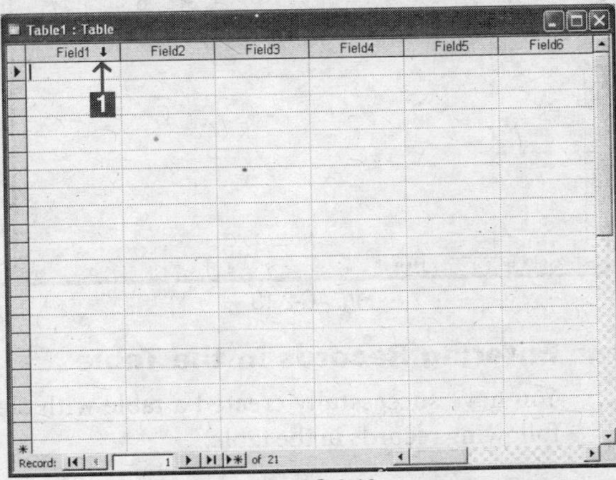

Fig. AC-2.10

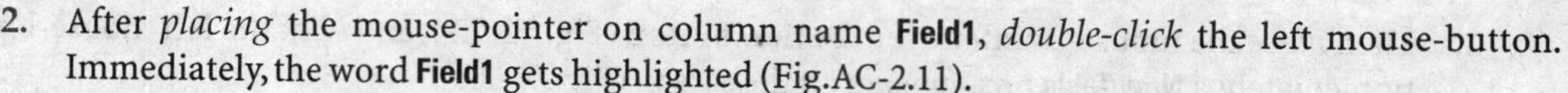

2. After *placing* the mouse-pointer on column name **Field1**, *double-click* the left mouse-button. Immediately, the word **Field1** gets highlighted (Fig.AC-2.11).
3. Next, *type* the new field name of your choice, in our case **C_ID**, from the keyboard. Immediately, the highlighted text gets replaced with the new field name (Fig.AC-2.12).

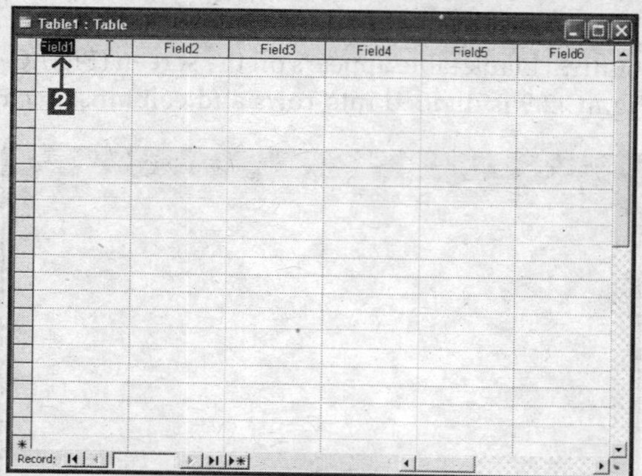

Fig. AC-2.11

Fig. AC-2.12

4. Now *double-click* on the second field name **Field2**. Here you have to type the customer name which has to be divided into two parts, i.e. FIRST NAME and LAST NAME. So, *type* **FIRST NAME** in place of **Field2** (Fig.AC-2.13).
5. Similarly, *type* the second part of the customer name **LAST NAME** to replace **Field3**, **ADDRESS** to replace **Field 3**, and **PHONE** to replace **Field5**. The entire table will now be displayed with the changed field names (Fig.AC-2.14).

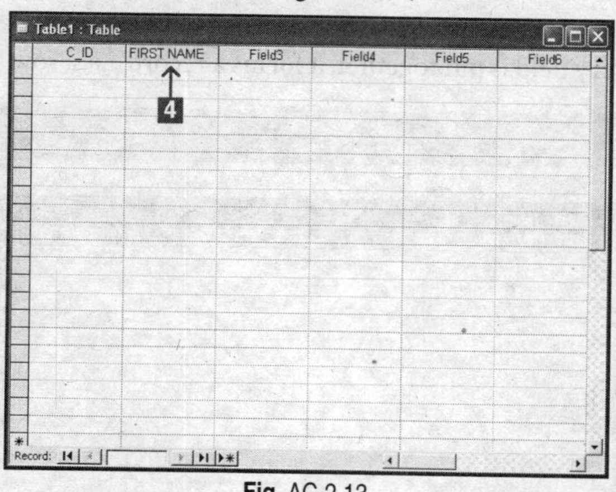

Fig. AC-2.13

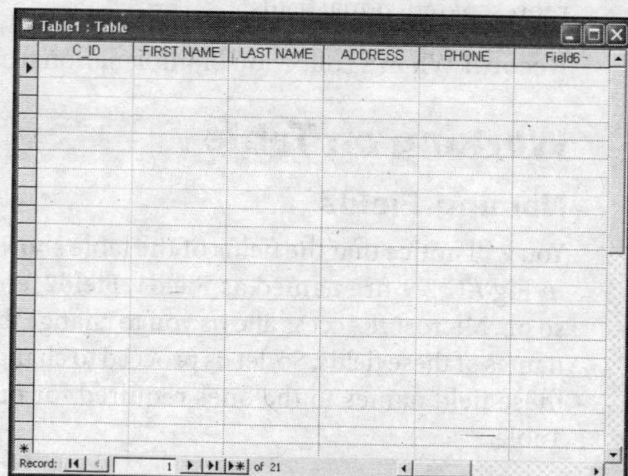

Fig. AC-2.14

Entering Records in the Table

You have successfully created a table with clearly defined fields. Now, the next step is to enter the following records in the table.

TABLE

C_ID	FIRST NAME	LAST NAME	ADDRESS	PHONE
C1	Vikas	Gupta	19-A, Ansari Road Daryaganj, New Delhi-2	23284212
C2	Deepa	Mathur	A3/3 Model Town New Delhi-37	25434254
C3	Mohan	Kishore	A-172, Vikas Puri New Delhi-56	27899989
C4	Chandini	Kishore	49, Roop Nagar Rohtak, Haryana	23456789
C5	Ritika	Soni	J-164 Kiran Vihar New Delhi-43	24772828

To enter the above data in the **Address Details** Table, you may undertake the following steps:

1. For entering the first record, *move* the mouse-pointer to the first cell of the first row (Fig.AC-2.15) and *click* the left mouse-button. Immediately, a blinking cursor appears inside the first cell (Fig.AC-2.16).
2. Now *type* **C1**. It gets displayed below the field name **C_ID** (Fig.AC-2.17).
3. *Press* the **Tab** key on the keyboard to move to the next field. Immediately, a blinking cursor gets displayed in the second cell of the first row. Then *type* **Vikas** (Fig. AC-2.18).
4. Again, *press* the **Tab** key from your keyboard and *type* **Gupta** (Fig.AC-2.19).

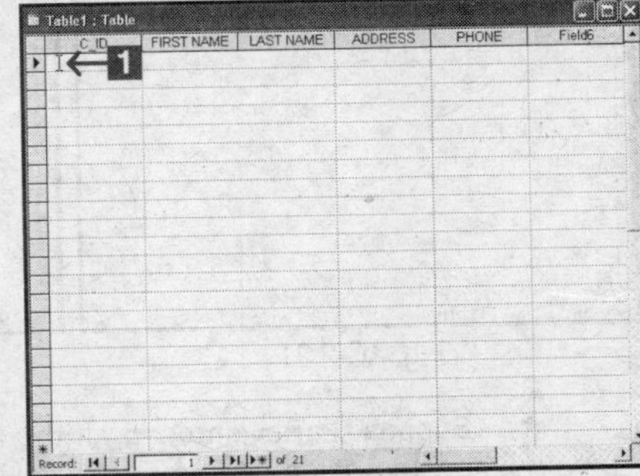

Fig. AC-2.15

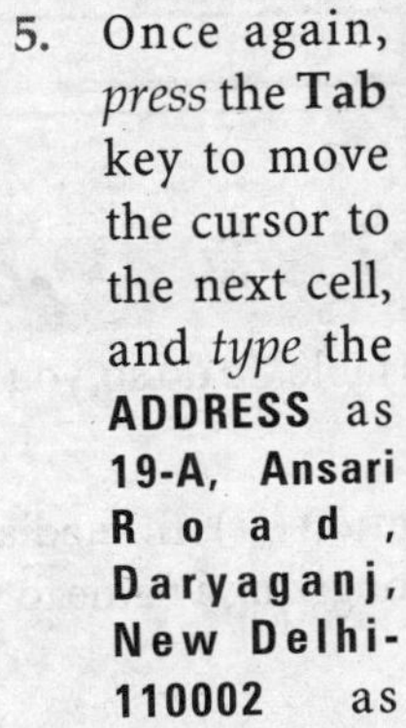

5. Once again, *press* the **Tab** key to move the cursor to the next cell, and *type* the **ADDRESS** as **19-A, Ansari Road, Daryaganj, New Delhi-110002** as shown in Fig. AC-2.20.

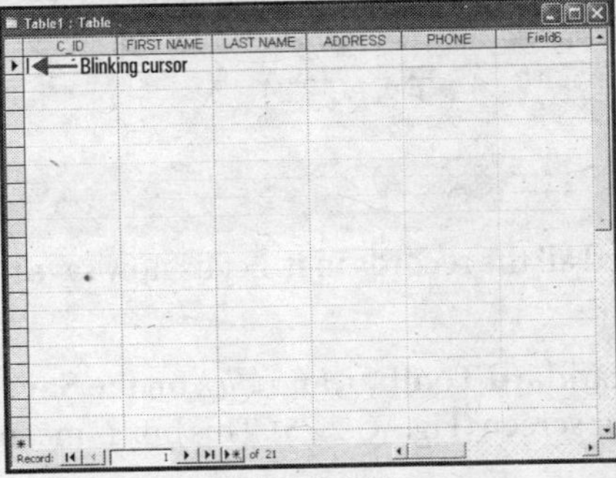

Fig. AC-2.16

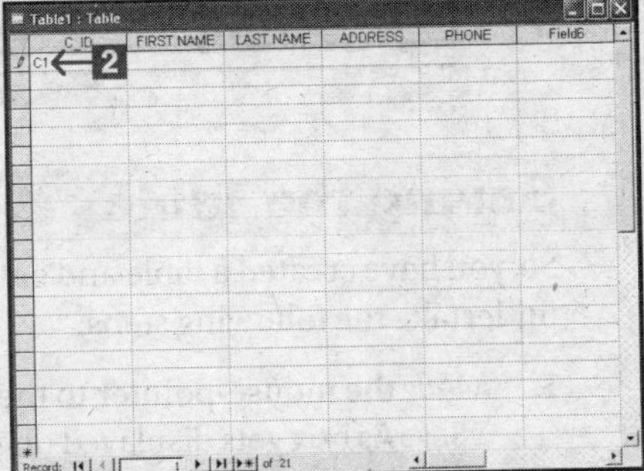

Fig. AC-2.17

6. Finally, *press* the **Tab** key of your keyboard once again to enter the **PHONE** as **23243077** (Fig.AC-2.21).

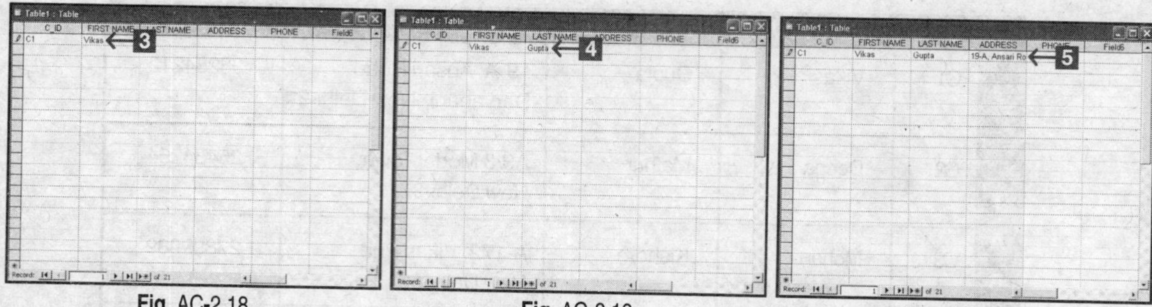

Fig. AC-2.18 Fig. AC-2.19 Fig. AC-2.20

7. So, you have completed the entry of first record. Let us now try to enter the second record. To do so, *move* the mouse-pointer over the second row of **C_ID** field, and *click* the left mouse-button. Immediately, a blinking cursor gets displayed at that point (Fig.AC-2.22).
8. Enter the details of second and other rows as explained above. After entering all the records, the table will look like Fig.AC-2.23.

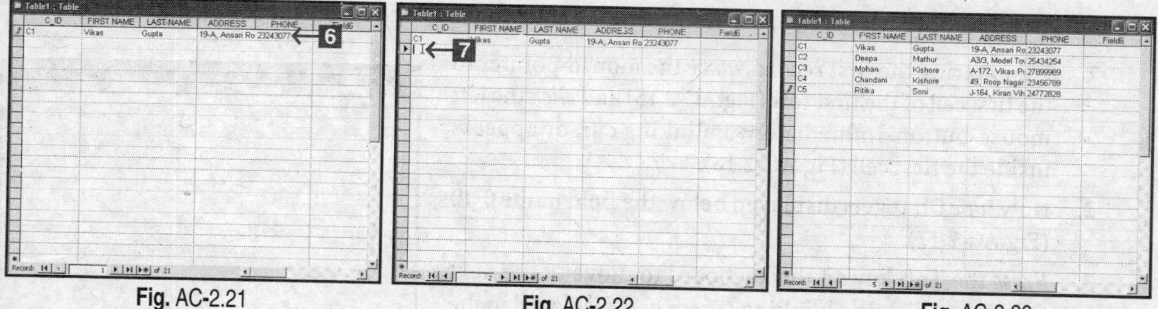

Fig. AC-2.21 Fig. AC-2.22 Fig. AC-2.23

NOTE

Suppose, after entering all the fields of a record, you are unable to see the first field or the last field on the screen for entering fresh data. To overcome such a problem use the left arrow scroll button (◄) or the right arrow scroll button (►) displayed at the bottom of the table (Fig.AC-2.24).

Fig. AC-2.24

Saving the Table

So, you have created a table and entered all the records in it. Let us now save this table. To do so, you may undertake the following steps:

1. *Move* the mouse-pointer to the **Standard Toolbar**, and *click* on the **Save** button (💾). Immediately, a **Save As** box gets displayed on your screen (Fig.AC-2.25). This box is meant for giving a name to your table.

2. Now *type* a name, say **Address Details**, from the keyboard. Instantly, the typed name gets displayed inside the box below **Table Name** option (Fig.AC-2.26).
3. Finally, *click* on the **OK** button. Immediately, a message box appears on your screen asking whether you wish to define the primary key or not (Fig.AC-2.27).
4. Though it is not always essential to define a Primary Key of a table, let us try creating one for the table Address Details. To proceed ahead, *click* on the **Yes** button.

Fig. AC-2.25

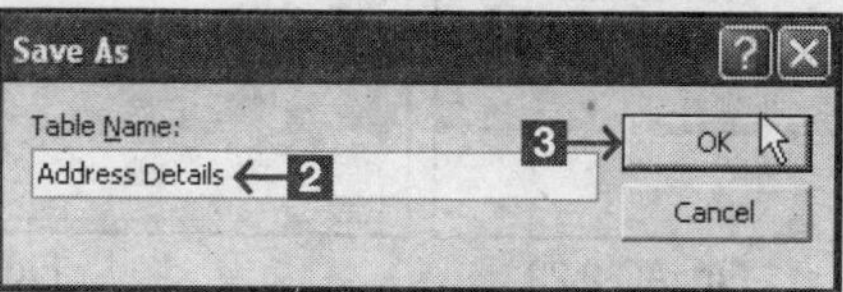

Fig. AC-2.26

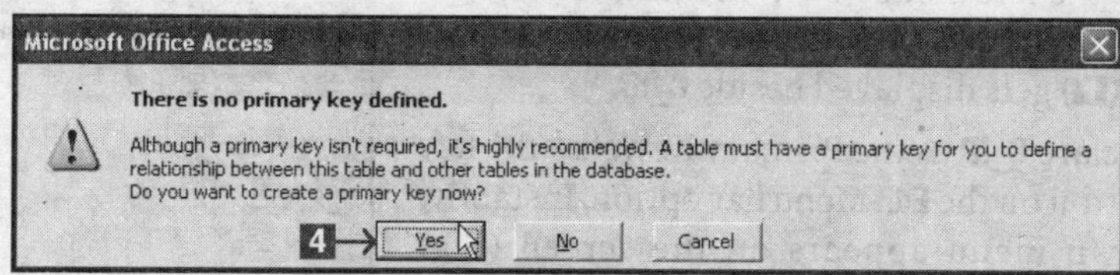

Fig. AC-2.27

Defining the Primary Key

A **Primary Key** is essential for establishing a relationship between two tables of your database. You will create the second table later on in this chapter. Let us first define the Primary key for the first table. For this, you may proceed as follows:

1. After clicking on the **Yes** button (of Fig.AC-2.27), your table will look like Fig.AC-2.28. Notice that Access has added an **ID** field to the table. This field will automatically give a number to each record entered in the table. This field is called **Auto Number.**
2. As you have seen, Access has already created an **ID** field, and automatically made it the Primary key of your table. But, you can also choose any other field to serve as the Primary Key of your table.

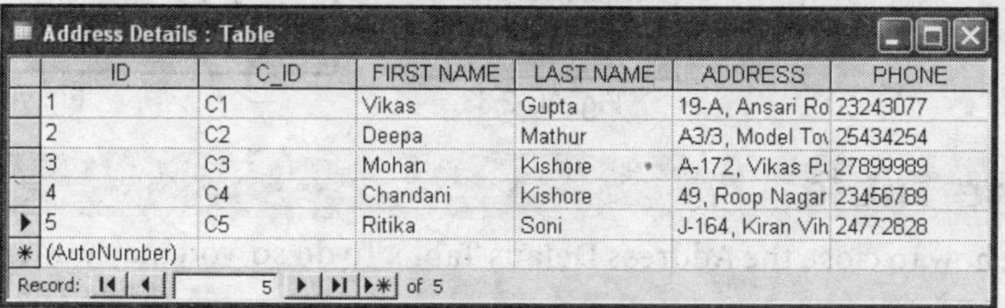

Address Details : Table

ID	C_ID	FIRST NAME	LAST NAME	ADDRESS	PHONE
1	C1	Vikas	Gupta	19-A, Ansari Ro	23243077
2	C2	Deepa	Mathur	A3/3, Model To\	25434254
3	C3	Mohan	Kishore	A-172, Vikas Pu	27899989
4	C4	Chandani	Kishore	49, Roop Nagar	23456789
5	C5	Ritika	Soni	J-164, Kiran Vih	24772828
(AutoNumber)					

Record: 5 of 5

Fig. AC-2.28

3. Now to define the Primary Key for table Address Details, first you have to open the Design View. So, *click* over the **View** Menu bar option. Immediately, a pull-down menu gets displayed on the screen (Fig.AC-2.29). In the pull-down menu *click* on the **Design View** option (Fig.AC-2.29).
4. The table opens in **Design View** (Fig.AC-2.30). Let us define the field **C_ID** as the primary key. To do so, *place* the mouse-pointer to the left of the field name **C_ID** (Fig.AC-2.31). The mouse-pointer now changes to an arrow shape(➡).

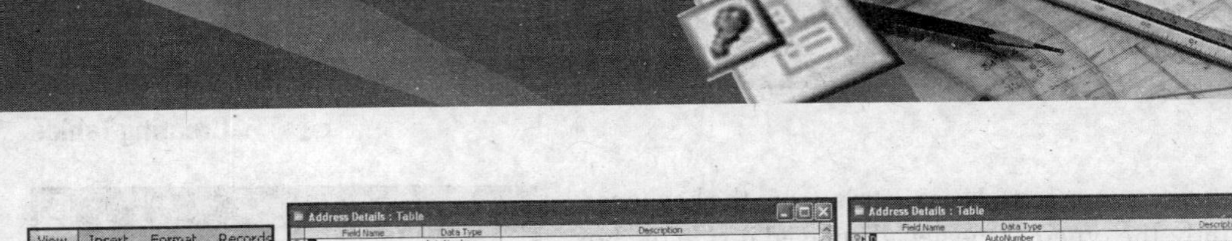

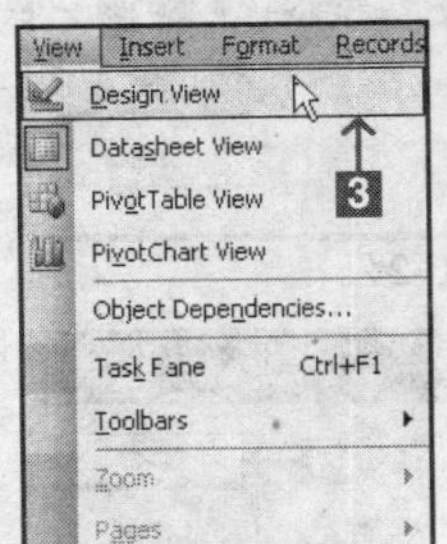

Fig. AC-2.29

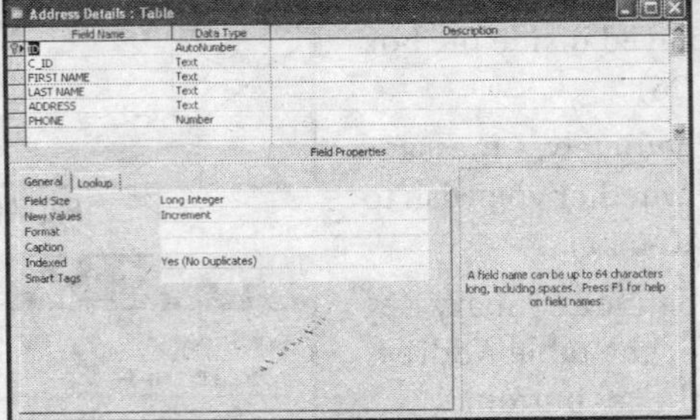

Fig. AC-2.30

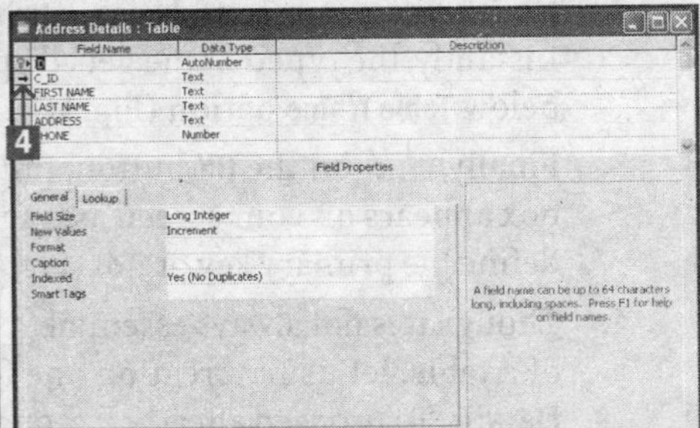

Fig. AC-2.31

5. Then *click* the left mouse-button. Immediately, the entire field name gets highlighted (Fig.AC-2.32), and a triangle (▶) gets displayed beside **C_ID**.
6. Now to declare **C_ID** as the Primary Key, *click* the left mouse-button on the **Edit** Menu bar option. Instantly, a pull-down menu appears on the screen (Fig. AC-2.33).
7. Inside the pull-down menu, *click* over the **Primary Key** option (Fig.AC-2.33). Immediately, a small key (🔑) gets displayed next to the field name **C_ID** (Fig.AC-2.34). This indicates that the field has been selected as the primary key.

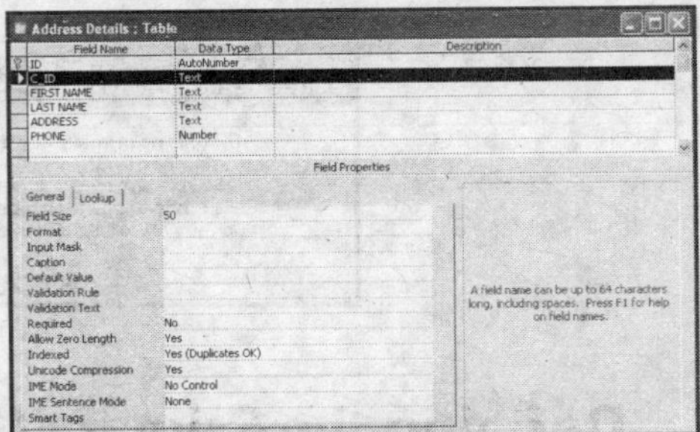

Fig. AC-2.32

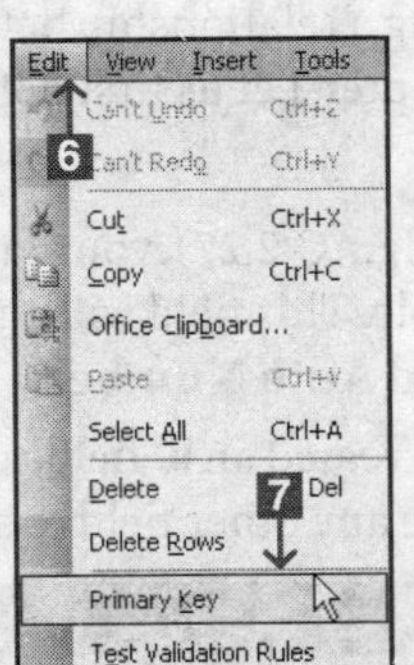

Fig. AC-2.33

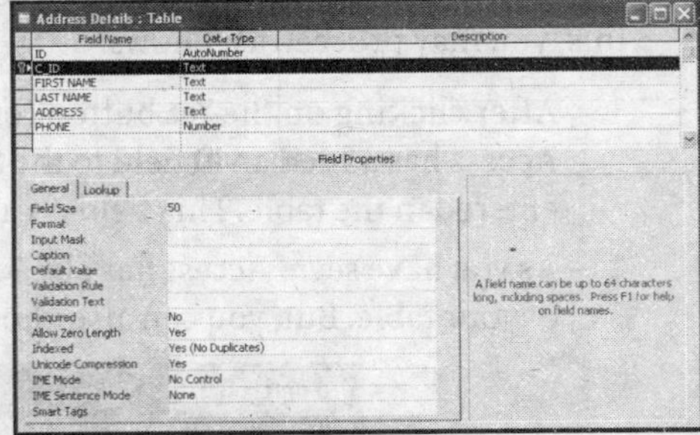

Fig. AC-2.34

Closing the Table

Now let us learn how to close the Address Details Table. To do so, you may undertake the following steps:

1. *Click* on the **File** Menu bar option. Immediately, a pull-down menu gets displayed (Fig.AC-2.35).
2. Inside the pull-down menu, *move* the mouse-pointer over the **Close** option (Fig.AC-2.35) and *click* the left mouse-button. Immediately, a message box (Fig. AC-2.36) appears on your screen asking whether you wish to save the changes made to the table.

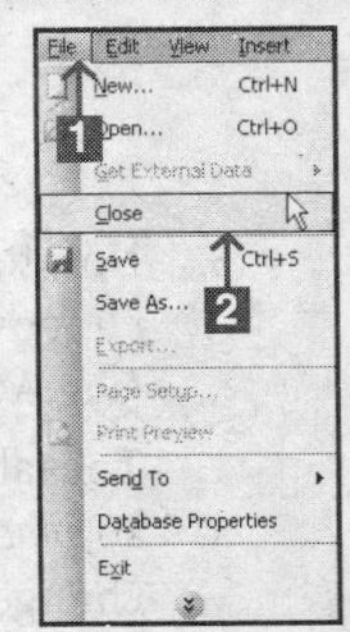

Fig. AC-2.35

3. Since you had performed certain steps to make the field name C_ID as the Primary Key, it is better to save these changes. So *click* on the **Yes** button (Fig.AC-2.36).

Instantly, the Address Details Table gets closed and **Address : Database** box gets displayed on the screen displaying the name of the table (Fig.AC-2.37).

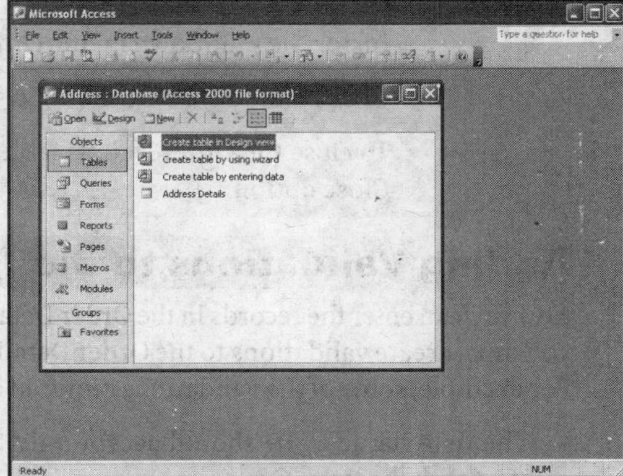

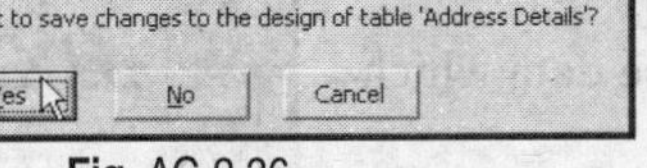

Fig. AC-2.36

Fig. AC-2.37

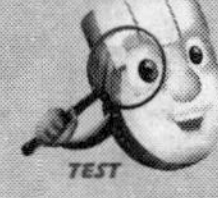

A database can have more than one table. So create another table and save it with the name Order Details. The fields of this table are:

P_ID, C_ID, PRODUCT NAME, PRICE, QUANTITY

- Currently the screen displays Fig.AC-2.37. So, *click* on the New button of the Address : Database box.
- Inside the New Table box, *click* on the OK button (Fig.AC-2.8).
- When the new blank table gets displayed, *double-click* on Field1 and type P_ID.
- Then *double-click* on Field2 and *type* C_ID.
- Next, *double-click* on Field3 and *type* PRODUCT NAME.
- Again *double-click* on Field4 and *type* PRICE.
- Finally, *type* QUANTITY after *double-clicking* on Field5.
- To save the table, *click* on the **Save** button ( ).
- *Type* the Table name as Order Details.
- Then *click* on the OK button. Immediately, a message box gets displayed.
- *Click* on the Yes button to define a Primary Key.
- Now *click* on the View menu bar option.
- Inside the pull-down menu, *click* on the Design View option.

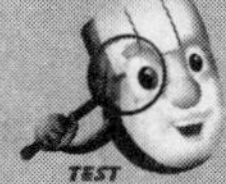

- Since both the tables, i.e. Address Details and Order Details are going to be related through the common field C_ID, it would be better to make C_ID the Primary Key. So, *click* to the left of the fieldname C_ID.
- Now *click* on the Edit menu bar option.
- Inside the pull-down menu, *click* on the Primary Key option.
- *Click* on the Save button ( ) to save the changes.
- To close the Order Details table, *click* on the File menu bar option and then *select* the Close option.

Adding Validations to the Table

Now you can enter the records in the Order Details table. However, before you start entering the records, you must create validations to the Order Details table to ensure that no invalid record is entered in it. For example, some of the validations required are:

- The field name C_ID should accept only those data which start with the letter C.
- If you enter a wrong customer identification number then an error message Please enter Customer ID correctly should be displayed.
- The PRICE entered should not be less than zero.
- If you enter an invalid PRICE, then an error message Price should be greater than zero should be displayed.

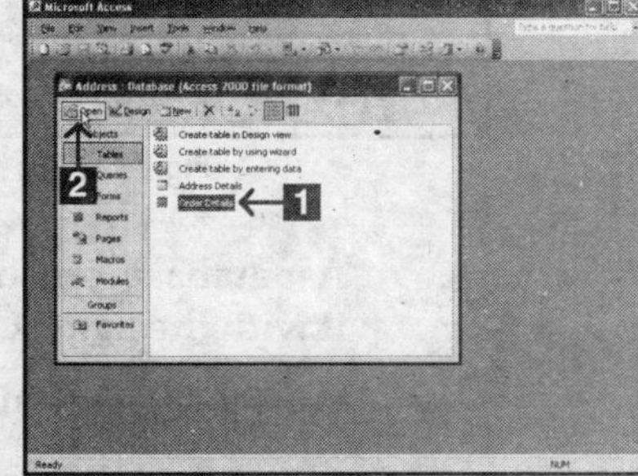

Fig. AC-2.38

Adding Validation to the Fieldname C_ID

To incorporate validations into the **Order Details** table, first *open it* on your screen then proceed further. To do so, you may undertake the following steps:

1. *Start* from the screen displaying the **Address : Database** box (Fig.AC-2.38). Inside the bigger rectangular box, *click* on the **Order Details** table to highlight it.
2. Then *click* on the **Open** button (Fig.AC-2.38). Immediately, the **Order Details : Table** window appears on your screen (Fig.AC-2.39).
3. Now you have to bring the **Design View** on the screen so that the validations can be incorporated. To do so, *move* the mouse-pointer on the **View** button ( ) of the **Standard Toolbar** (Fig.AC-2.40), and *click* the left mouse-button. Immediately, the **Design View** screen gets displayed on the screen (Fig. AC-2.41). Now let us insert a validation rule on the first field – in our case **C_ID**.

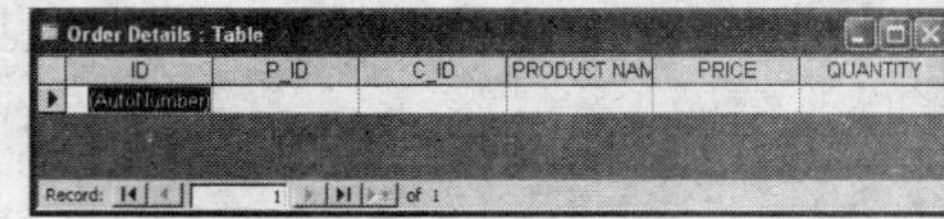

Fig. AC-2.39

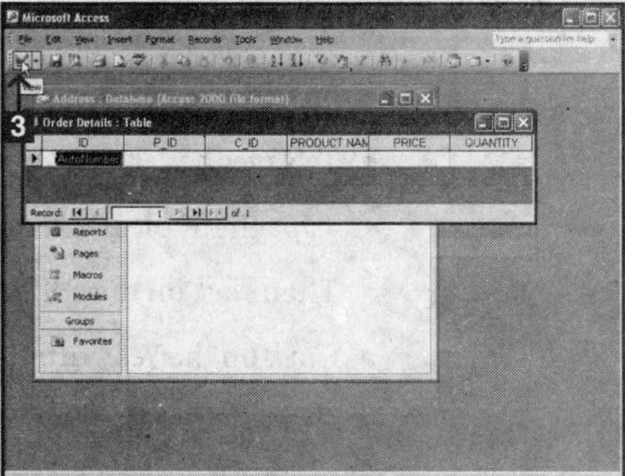

Fig. AC-2.40

4. To do so, *place* the mouse-pointer to the left of the field name **C_ID** (Fig.AC-2.42).
5. Then *click* the left mouse-button. Immediately, the field gets highlighted (Fig.AC-2.43).
6. Below the options inside the **Field Properties** *locate* the **Validation Rule** option. Once you have located it, *move* the mouse-pointer over it and *click* the left mouse-button. Immediately, a blinking cursor appears inside the box beside this option (Fig.AC-2.44).
7. Now *type* the **Validation Rule** as **C*** (Fig. AC-2.45). This will prevent the entry of Customer IDs which do not begin with alphabet C.
8. The next step is to create an error message which has to appear when incorrect Customer ID is entered. To do so, *click* on the **Validation Text** option. Immediately, a blinking cursor appears inside the box beside this option (Fig.AC-2.46).
9. Then *type* the error message as **Please enter Customer ID correctly.** Immediately, the error message gets displayed inside the box beside **Validation Text** option (Fig.AC-2.46).

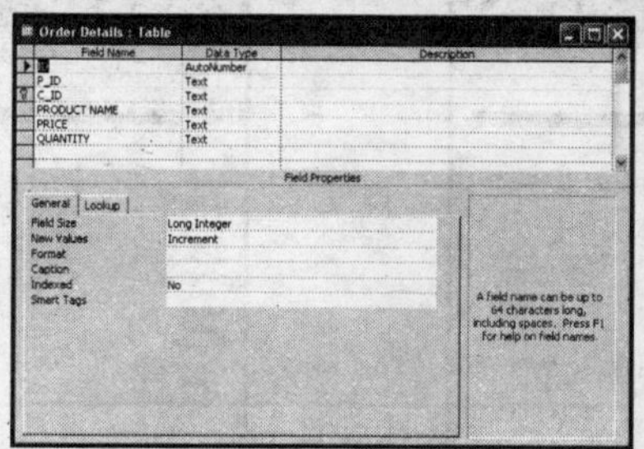

Fig. AC-2.41

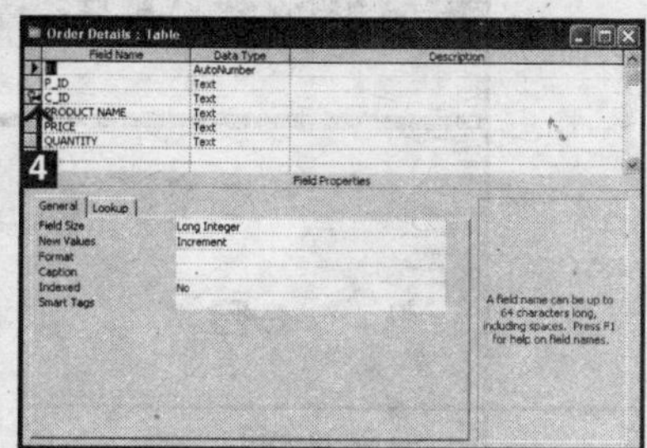

Fig. AC-2.42

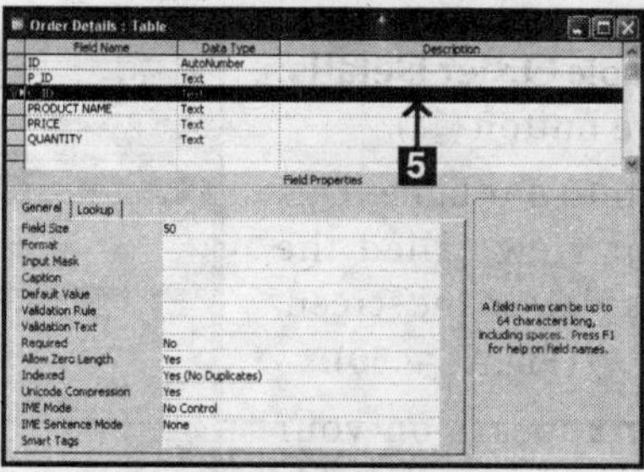

Fig. AC-2.43

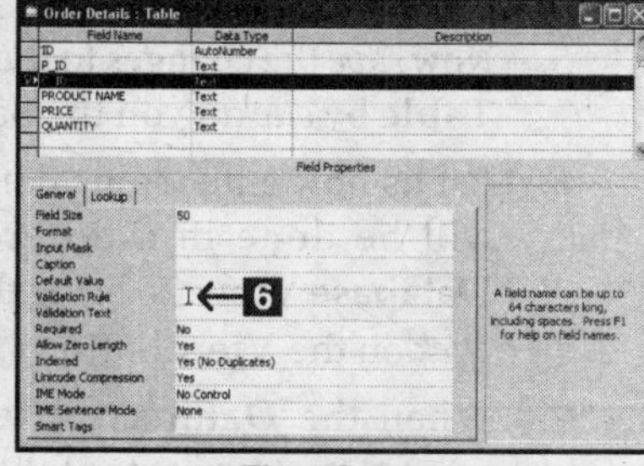

Fig. AC-2.44

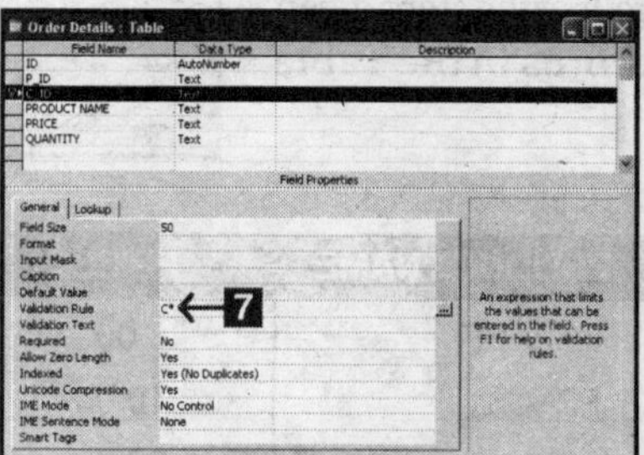

Fig. AC-2.45

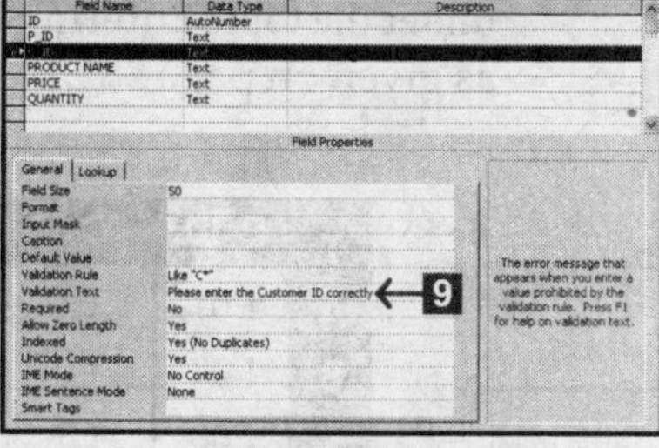

Fig. AC-2.46

Adding Validation to the Fieldname PRICE

Now, to add validations for the field name **PRICE**, undertake the following steps:

1. *Click* on the field name **PRICE** to add a validation rule for this option. Immediately, the field name gets highlighted (Fig. AC-2.47).
2. Next, *locate* the **Validation Rule** option and *click* on it (Fig.AC-2.47).

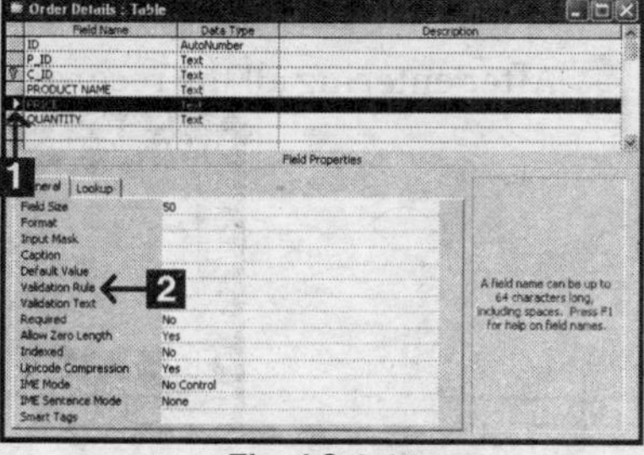

Fig. AC-2.47

3. *Type* **> 0**. This will prevent any value which is less than 0 to be entered in the PRICE field. The **Validation Rule** now gets displayed as in Fig.AC-2.48.

4. Now *click* inside the box beside **Validation Text** option. A blinking cursor gets displayed inside the box beside this option. Here you have to type an error message. So *type* **Price should be greater than zero** (Fig. AC-2.49).

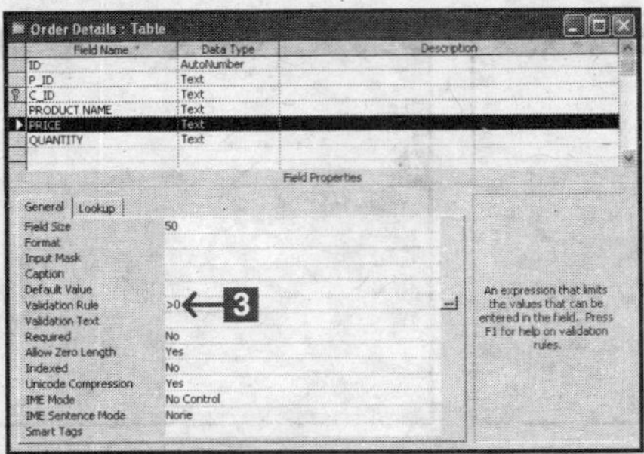

Fig. AC-2.48

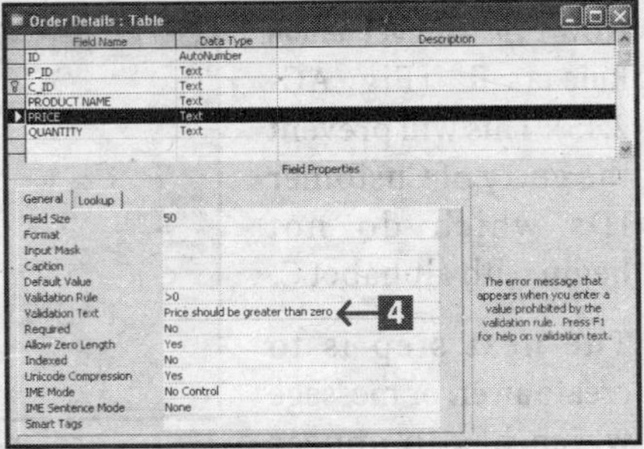

Fig. AC-2.49

5. Now *save* the changes to the table **Order Details: Table** by *clicking* on the **Save** button ( ).

6. Let us now enter some data into our table. This will be done in a different view called the **Database View**. To bring this view on the screen, *click* on the **View** button ( ) (Fig.AC-2.50).

7. When the **Database View** appears on your screen, start *typing* the following data in the table Order Details Table. To do so, follow the steps given under the topic **Entering Records in the Table** as given on page 382.

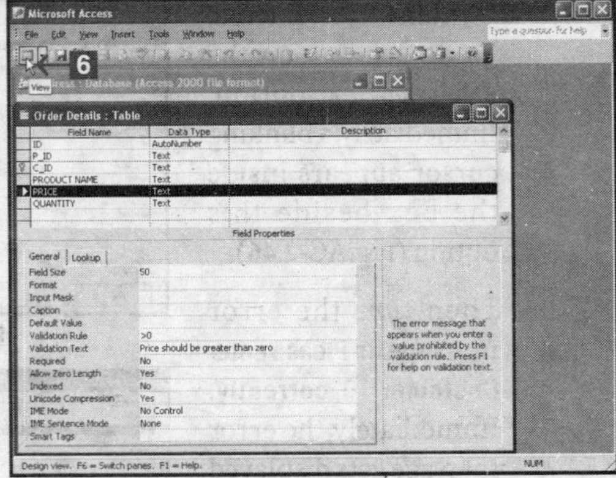

Fig. AC-2.50

TABLE	P_ID	C_ID	PRODUCT NAME	PRICE	QUANTITY
	P01	C1	ERASER	8.00	50
	P02	C2	PENCIL	10.00	40
	P03	C3	PEN	25.00	100
	P04	C4	PENCIL BOX	45.00	25

After entering all the records, the table will look like Fig.AC-2.51.

Order Details : Table

ID	P_ID	C_ID	PRODUCT NAM	PRICE	QUANTITY
22	P01	C1	ERASER	8.00	50
23	P02	C2	PENCIL	10.00	40
24	P03	C3	PEN	25.00	100
25	P04	C4	PENCIL BOX	45.00	25
(AutoNumber)					

Record: 5 of 5

Fig. AC-2.51

If any character other than numeric is entered in a numeric field, then an error message gets displayed (Fig.AC-2.52).

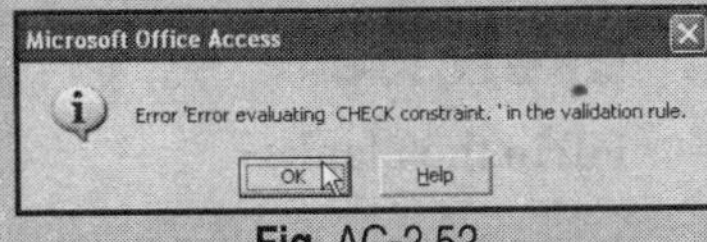

Fig. AC-2.52

If you don't enter any value in the field which is taken as the primary key, then an error message (Fig.AC-2.53) gets displayed.

Fig. AC-2.53

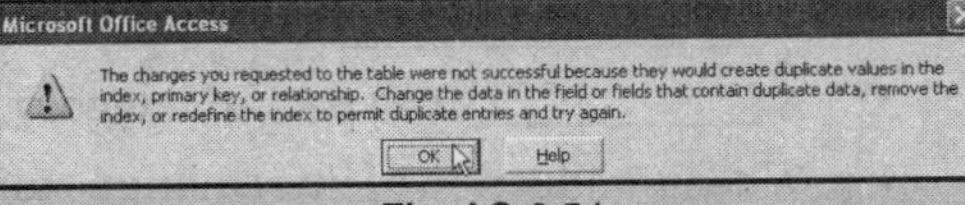

Fig. AC-2.54

If you enter duplicate values in the field which is taken as the primary key, then an error message (Fig.AC-2.52) gets displayed.

8. *Click* on the **Save** button( ) to save the data entered into the table Order Details : Table.
9. So, you have done a lot of modifications in the table Order Details. Now, let us close it. To do so, *click* on **File** Menu bar option (Fig.AC-2.55).
10. Inside the pull-down menu, *click* on the **Close** option (Fig.AC-2.55).

Fig. AC-2.55

Closing the Database and Quitting Access

Let us close the **Address : Database** box. For this, you may undertake the following steps.

1. *Move* the mouse-pointer to the **File** Menu bar option and *click* the left mouse-button. Instantly, a pull-down menu gets displayed (Fig.AC-2.56).
2. Inside the pull-down menu, *move* the mouse-pointer over the **Close** option (Fig.AC-2.55), and then *click* the left mouse-button. Immediately the Address : Database box closes.
3. To quit Microsoft Access, *move* the mouse-pointer to the **Close** button ( ) (Fig.AC-2.57) present on the **Title bar** and *click* the left mouse-button. Immediately, Microsoft Access closes and Windows XP **Desktop** gets displayed on the screen.

Fig. AC-2.56

Fig. AC-2.57

Exercise

Fill in the Blanks

1. A telephone directory is a good example of a ______________.
2. A ________________ is a key in a table that uniquely identifies every record in it.
3. A ___________ is a specific category of information.
4. When a collection of information from every field is put together, it forms a __________.
5. A primary key is essential for establishing a _____________ between two tables of your database.

True/False

1. The basic purpose of defining a primary key is avoiding duplication of records.
2. Blank database option is used to create a new database.
3. The values in a primary key field can be repeated.
4. Every field has a unique field name.
5. Validations can be performed only in the Design view.

MICROSOFT ACCESS

Updating Tables 3

IN THIS CHAPTER

- Opening a Table in Microsoft Access
- Modifying a Table
- Selecting a Field
- Selecting Multiple Fields
- Editing Records in a Table
- Viewing the Table Before Printing
- Printing the Table
- Saving and Closing the Table
- Creating Relationship Between Tables
- Closing the Database and Quitting Access

By now you must have been quite familiar with working in tables. In this chapter, you will learn about another aspect of making tables in Microsoft Access, i.e. updating the tables.

You have already worked with some of the Microsoft Access tools that help you create databases for storing and managing large amount of information. The basic storage element of an Access database is the table. In the previous chapters, you had created two tables, entered records in them and then named them as **Address Details** and **Order Details.** This chapter will teach you in detail how to make changes in the existing records of a table and then print it. Let us begin by making changes in a table, say, **Address Details.** First we need to open the Microsoft Access and then the table in which we want to make the changes.

Opening a Table in Microsoft Access

To open Microsoft Access, you may undertake the following steps:

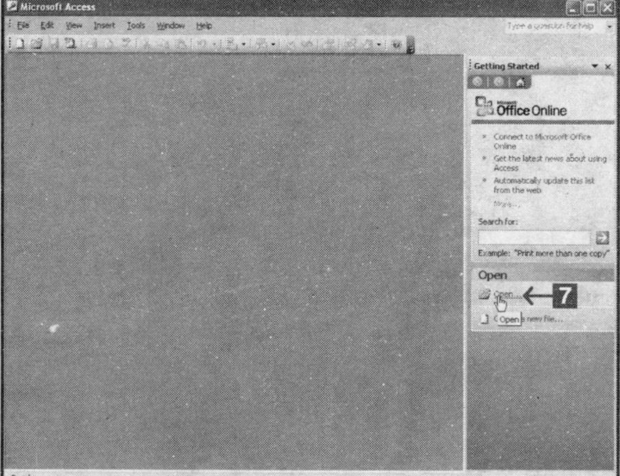

Fig. AC-3.1

1. *Switch* on your computer. Within a few seconds, Windows XP **Desktop** gets displayed.
2. *Move* the mouse-pointer over the **Start** button (start) on the **Taskbar**, and *click* the left mouse-button. Immediately, a push-up menu appears on the screen.
3. Next, *move* the mouse-pointer and *place* it over the **All Programs** option. Immediately, a second menu appears on the screen.
4. Inside the second menu, *move* the mouse-pointer and *place* it over the **Microsoft Office** option. A third menu appears.
5. Inside the third menu, *move* the mouse-pointer over the **Microsoft Office Access 2003** option and *click* the left mouse-button.
6. Immediately, a **Microsoft Access** window appears on the right side of the window you can see the **Getting Started** Task pane containing various options (Fig.AC-3.1).
7. Inside the **Getting Started** Task pane, *move* the mouse-pointer over the **Open** option and *click* the left mouse-button (Fig.AC-3.1).
8. Instantly, the **Open** dialog box appears on the screen displaying the contents of **My Documents** folder, which is also the same folder where Address database was saved earlier (Fig.AC-3.2).

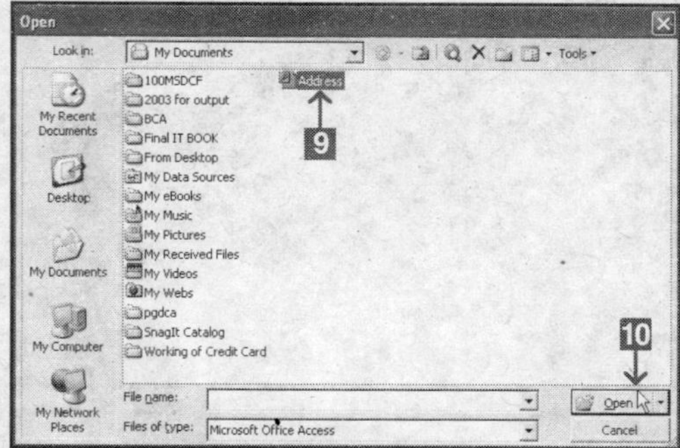

Fig. AC-3.2

9. *Move* the mouse-pointer over the **Address** database and *click* the left mouse-button just once. The database name gets highlighted (Fig.AC-3.2).
10. *Click* over the **Open** button (Fig.AC-3.2). The **Address:Database (Access 2000 file format)** box appears on the screen (Fig.AC-3.3). By default, the **Tables** tab should appear highlighted. Incase it is not then *move* the mouse-pointer over it and *click* the left mouse-button.

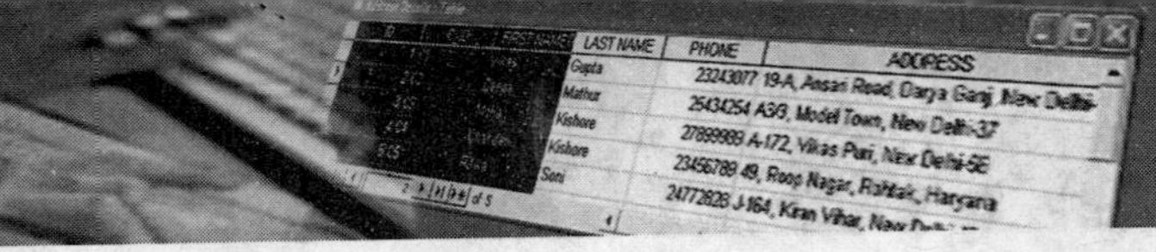

11. Next, *move* the mouse-pointer over the **Address Details** table and *click* the left mouse-button (Fig.AC-3.3).

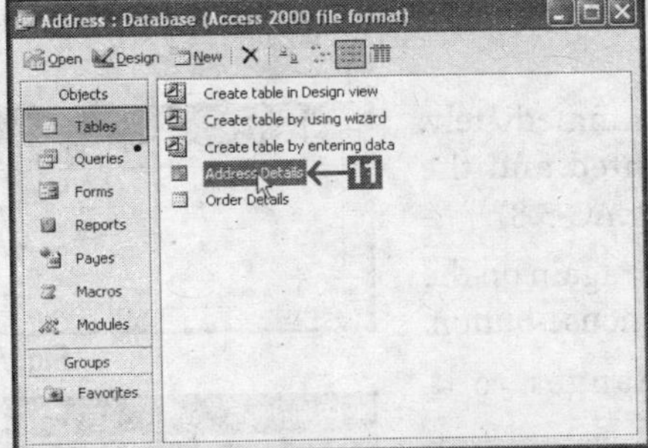

Fig. AC-3.3

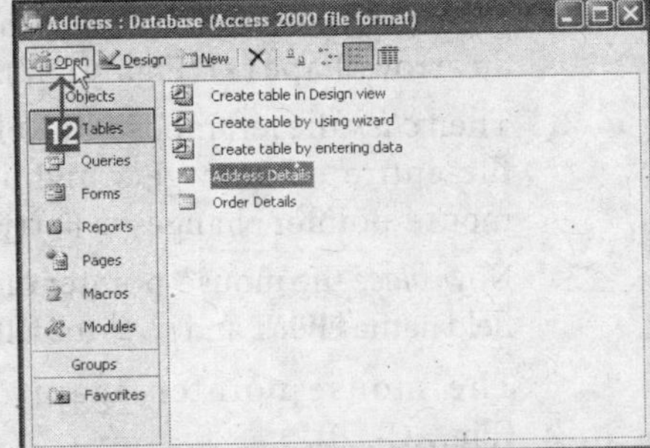

Fig. AC-3.4

12. Lastly, *move* the mouse-pointer over the **Open** button and click the left mouse-button (Fig.AC-3.4).
13. The Address Details table opens upon screen, as shown in Fig.AC-3.5.

Address Details : Table

	ID	C_ID	FIRST NAME	LAST NAME	ADDRESS	PHONE
▶	1	C1	Vikas	Gupta	19-A, Ansari Ro	23243077
	2	C2	Deepa	Mathur	A3/3, Model Tov	25434254
	3	C3	Mohan	Kishore	A-172, Vikas Pu	27899989
	4	C4	Chandani	Kishore	49, Roop Nagar	23456789
	5	C5	Ritika	Soni	J-164, Kiran Vih	24772828
*	(AutoNumber)					

Record: 1 of 5

Fig. AC-3.5

If your file does not appear in the list then move the mouse pointer over the more fields option an click the left mouse button. Immediately Open dialog box gets displayed (Fig.AC-3.6). Now move the mouse pointer over the desired file in our case "Address". The file will get highlighted. Then click in the Open button. The address database box gets displayed on the screen.

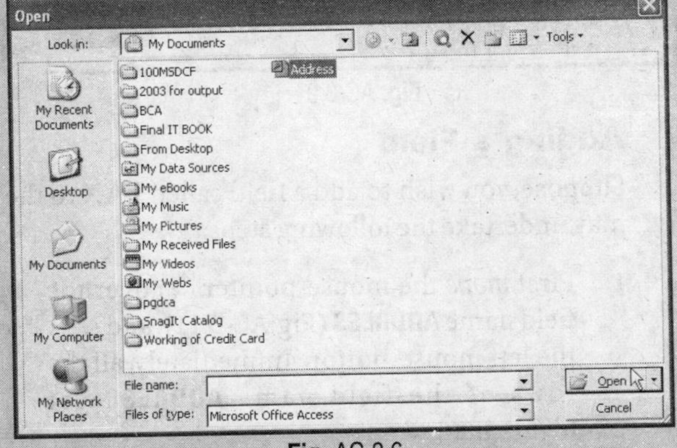

Fig. AC-3.6

Modifying a Table

So, you have successfully opened the Address Detail Table. Let us proceed to modify it. Read on to become well-versed with various modification tasks like editing field names, adding and deleting a field and changing the row height and column width.

Rearranging Fields

You can rearrange fields in a table to suit your needs. Suppose, in the Address Details: Table, you want the field name **PHONE** to be displayed after the field name **LAST NAME**. To do so, you may undertake the following steps:

1. *Place* the mouse-pointer over the field name **PHONE**. Immediately, the mouse-pointer changes into an arrow shape (⬇) (Fig.AC-3.7).
2. Then *click* the left mouse-button. Immediately, the entire column gets highlighted and the mouse-pointer changes to (↖) (Fig.AC-3.8).
3. Now, *place* the mouse-pointer once again on the field name **PHONE** and *press* the left mouse-button. The mouse-pointer again changes to ↖ (Fig. AC-3.9).
4. Then, keeping the left mouse-button *pressed*, *drag* the mouse-pointer on the field name **ADDRESS**. Instantly, a highlighted thick line appears between the field names **LASTNAME** and **ADDRESS** (Fig.AC-3.9).

Fig. AC-3.7

Fig. AC-3.8

5. Finally, *release* the left mouse-button. The field name **PHONE** now appears between the field names **LASTNAME** and **ADDRESS** (Fig.AC-3.10).

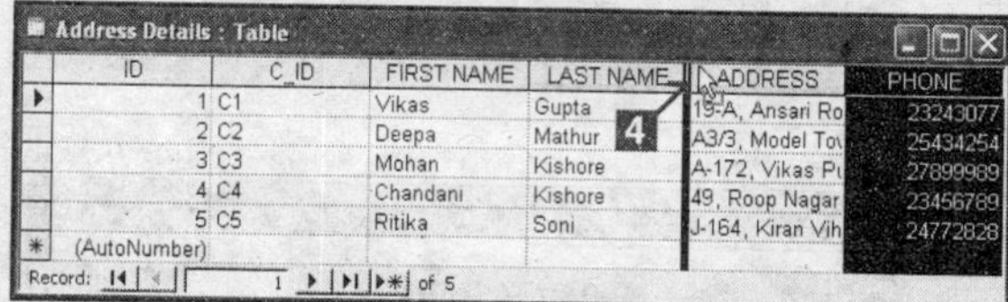

Fig. AC-3.9

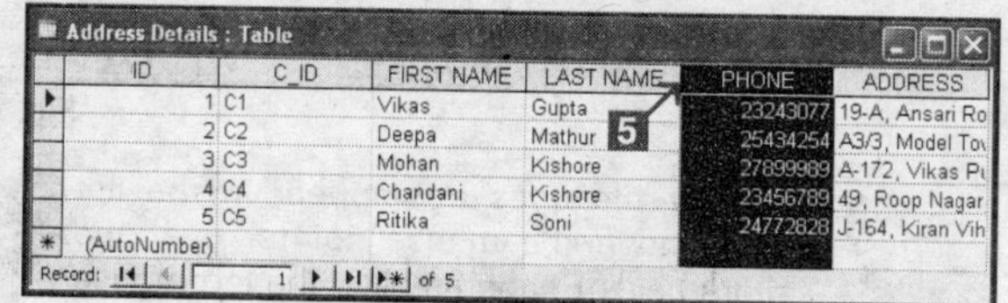

Fig. AC-3.10

Adding a Field

Suppose, you wish to add a field called **FAX** to the right hand side of the field **PHONE**. To do so, you may undertake the following steps:

1. First *move* the mouse-pointer (↖) over the field name **ADDRESS** (Fig.AC-3.11), and *click* the left mouse-button. Immediately, all the rows of the field name **ADDRESS** get highlighted.

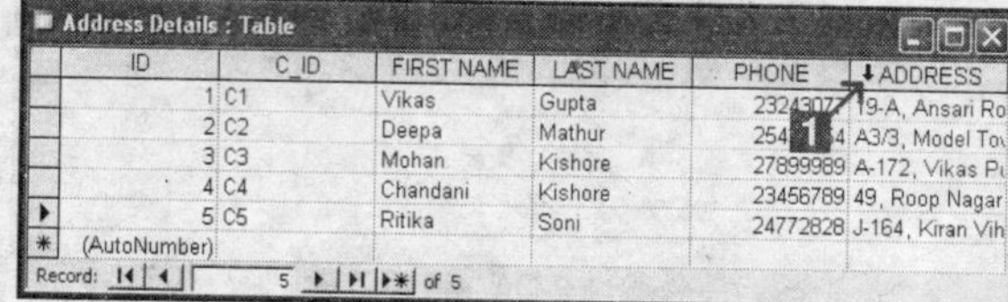

Fig. AC-3.11

2. Now, *move* the mouse-pointer over the **Insert** option on the Menu bar, and *click* on it. Immediately, a pull-down menu appears on the screen (Fig.AC-3.12).
3. Inside the pull-down menu, *click* on the **Column** option (Fig. AC-3.12). You will notice that a new field, **Field1** appears between the **PHONE** and **ADDRESS** fields (Fig.AC-3.13).
4. To give a name to the new field, *move* the mouse-pointer over **Field1** and *double-click* the left mouse-button. Immediately, the new field **Field1** gets highlighted (Fig.AC-3.14).

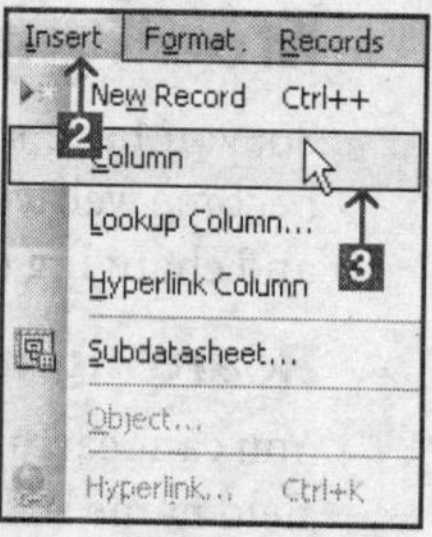

Fig. AC-3.12

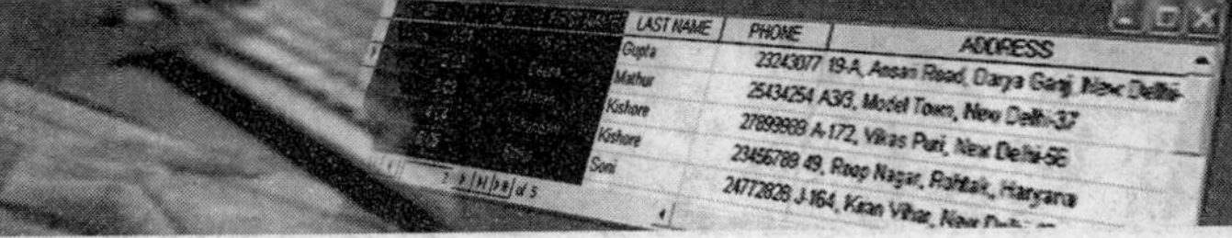

ID	C_ID	FIRST NAME	LAST NAME	PHONE	Field1	ADDRESS
1	C1	Vikas	Gupta	23243077		19-A, Ansari R
2	C2	Deepa	Mathur	25434254		A3/3, Model To
3	C3	Mohan	Kishore	27899989		A-172, Vikas P
4	C4	Chandani	Kishore	23456789		49, Roop Nagai
5	C5	Ritika	Soni	24772828		J-164, Kiran Vil
(AutoNumber)						

Fig. AC-3.13

ID	C_ID	FIRST NAME	LAST NAME	PHONE	Field1	ADDRESS
1	C1	Vikas	Gupta	23243077		19-A, Ansari R
2	C2	Deepa	Mathur	25434254		A3/3, Model To
3	C3	Mohan	Kishore	27899989		A-172, Vikas P
4	C4	Chandani	Kishore	23456789		49, Roop Nagai
5	C5	Ritika	Soni	24772828		J-164, Kiran Vil
(AutoNumber)						

Fig. AC-3.14

5. Now, *type* **FAX** and *press* the **Enter** key (Fig.AC-3.15). After the insertion of the **FAX** field (Fig.AC-3.12) the number of fields in the **Address Details** table has risen to seven (including the **ID** field).

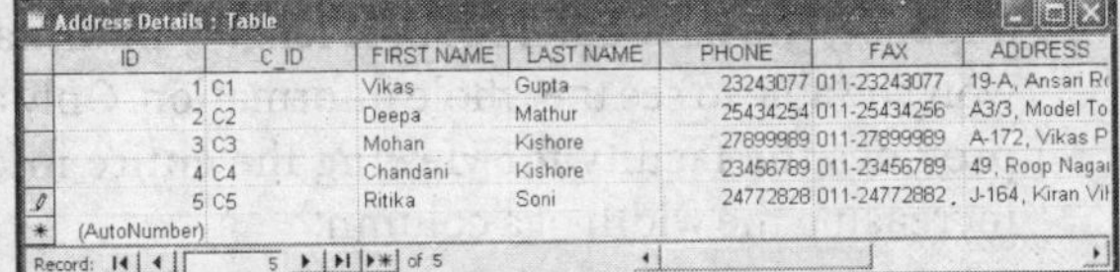

ID	C_ID	FIRST NAME	LAST NAME	PHONE	FAX	ADDRESS
1	C1	Vikas	Gupta	23243077		19-A, Ansari R
2	C2	Deepa	Mathur	25434254		A3/3, Model To
3	C3	Mohan	Kishore	27899989		A-172, Vikas P
4	C4	Chandani	Kishore	23456789		49, Roop Nagai
5	C5	Ritika	Soni	24772828		J-164, Kiran Vil
(AutoNumber)						

Fig. AC-3.15

6. Let us now enter the following fax numbers under the new field **FAX**.

   011-23243077 **011-25434256** **011-27899989** **011-23456789** **011-24772882**

   To do so, *click* the mouse-pointer on the first row of the field **FAX** and *type* **011-23243077**. Then *click* on the second row under the field **FAX** and *type* **011-25434256**.

7. Similarly, *type* the rest of the numbers in the **FAX** field. After entering all the fax numbers, the **Address Details** table will look like Fig.AC-3.16.

ID	C_ID	FIRST NAME	LAST NAME	PHONE	FAX	ADDRESS
1	C1	Vikas	Gupta	23243077	011-23243077	19-A, Ansari R
2	C2	Deepa	Mathur	25434254	011-25434256	A3/3, Model To
3	C3	Mohan	Kishore	27899989	011-27899989	A-172, Vikas P
4	C4	Chandani	Kishore	23456789	011-23456789	49, Roop Nagai
5	C5	Ritika	Soni	24772828	011-24772882	J-164, Kiran Vil
(AutoNumber)						

Fig. AC-3.16

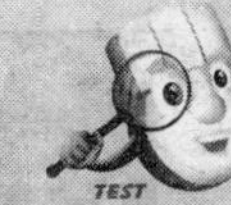

How to insert another field between the field names LAST NAME and PHONE?

- *Place* the mouse-pointer on the field name PHONE and *click* the left mouse-button.
- Then *click* on Insert menu bar option.
- Inside the pull-down menu, *click* on the Column option.

Deleting a Field

A field, no more required, can be deleted from a table. Let us delete the field which we had created in the last workout between field names PHONE and ADDRESS, i.e. FAX. For this, you may undertake the following steps:

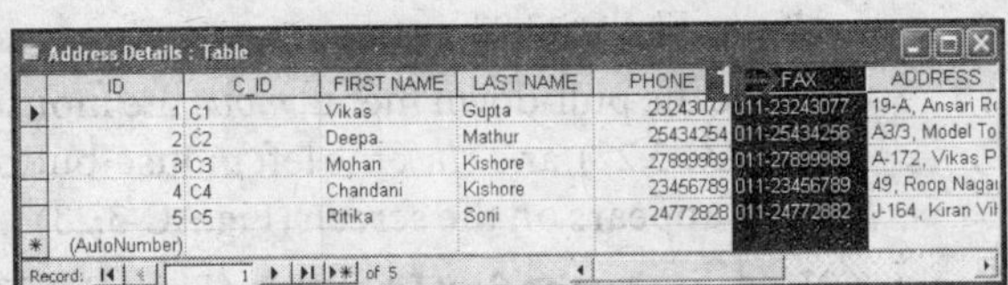

ID	C_ID	FIRST NAME	LAST NAME	PHONE	FAX	ADDRESS
1	C1	Vikas	Gupta	23243077	011-23243077	19-A, Ansari R
2	C2	Deepa	Mathur	25434254	011-25434256	A3/3, Model To
3	C3	Mohan	Kishore	27899989	011-27899989	A-172, Vikas P
4	C4	Chandani	Kishore	23456789	011-23456789	49, Roop Nagai
5	C5	Ritika	Soni	24772828	011-24772882	J-164, Kiran Vil
(AutoNumber)						

Fig. AC-3.17

1. *Move* the mouse-pointer on the field name **FAX** and *click* the left mouse-button. Instantly, the entire column gets highlighted (Fig.AC-3.17).
2. Now *click* on the **Edit** Menu bar option. Immediately, a pull-down menu gets displayed (Fig.AC-3.18).
3. Inside the pull-down menu, *move* the mouse-pointer on **Delete Column** option (Fig.AC-3.18), and *click* the left mouse-button. Immediately, a message box gets displayed (Fig.AC-3.19), asking whether you wish to permanently delete the field or not.

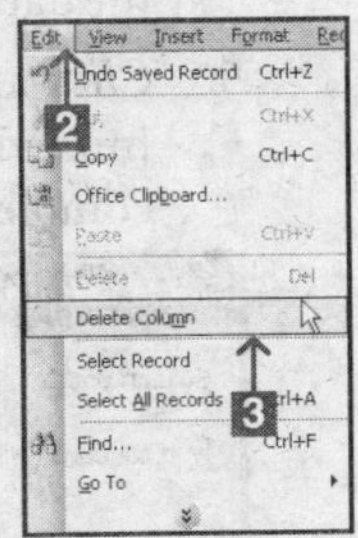

Fig. AC-3.18

4. Since you wish to permanently delete **FAX**, *move* the mouse-pointer over the **Yes** button (Fig.AC-3.19), and *click* the left mouse-button. Instantly, the field gets deleted and the table looks like Fig.AC-3.20.

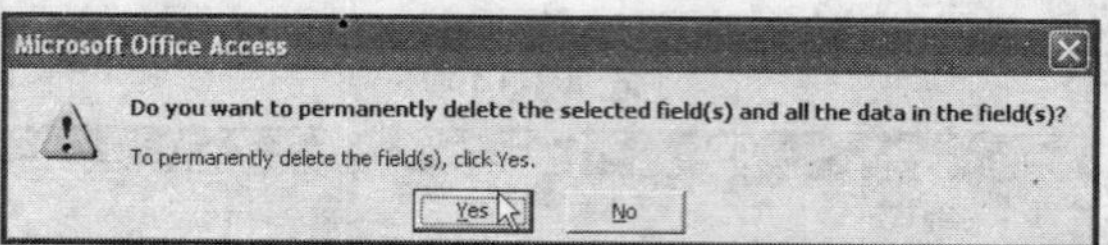

Fig. AC-3.19

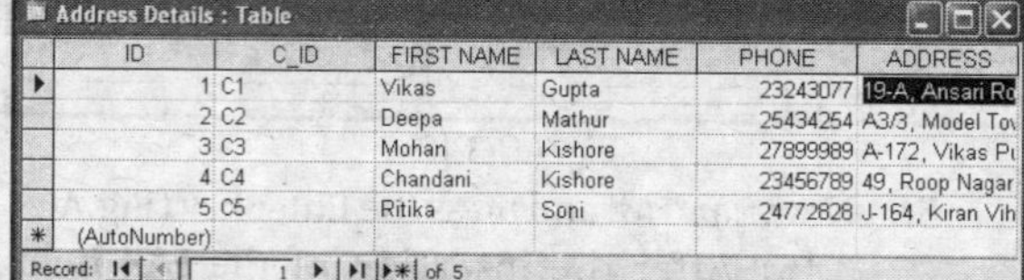

ID	C_ID	FIRST NAME	LAST NAME	PHONE	ADDRESS
1	C1	Vikas	Gupta	23243077	19-A, Ansari Ro
2	C2	Deepa	Mathur	25434254	A3/3, Model To
3	C3	Mohan	Kishore	27899989	A-172, Vikas Pu
4	C4	Chandani	Kishore	23456789	49, Roop Nagar
5	C5	Ritika	Soni	24772828	J-164, Kiran Vih
(AutoNumber)					

Fig. AC-3.20

Click on the Undo button (↶) present on the Standard Toolbar. The recently deleted field-fax, will re-appear in the table.

Changing Column Width

Suppose, you have entered some lengthy information in one of the fields of your table. In such a case, you won't be able to see the whole information. Only a part of it is visible in the column. But Microsoft Access provides the facility for viewing the entire information in a column in one glance. This is done by increasing the width of a column.

For example, in the table Address Details, the field name **ADDRESS** displays only a part of the address entries. And rest of the address remains hidden. To see the entire address at a glance, undertake the following steps:

1. *Move* the mouse-pointer over the field name **ADDRESS** and *click* the left mouse-button. Immediately, all the rows of this field get highlighted (Fig.AC-3.21).

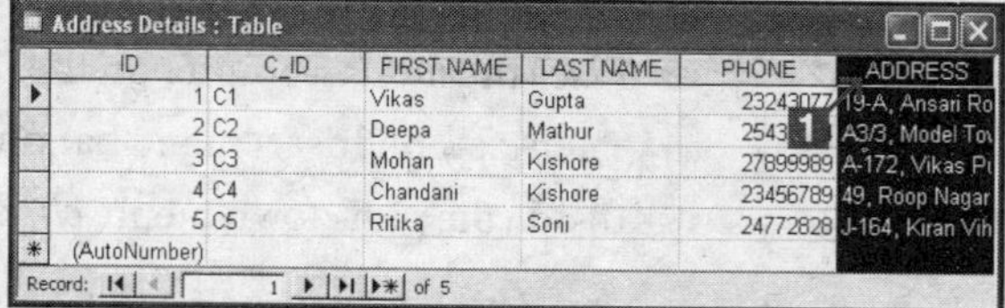

ID	C_ID	FIRST NAME	LAST NAME	PHONE	ADDRESS
1	C1	Vikas	Gupta	23243077	19-A, Ansari Ro
2	C2	Deepa	Mathur	2543	A3/3, Model To
3	C3	Mohan	Kishore	27899989	A-172, Vikas Pu
4	C4	Chandani	Kishore	23456789	49, Roop Nagar
5	C5	Ritika	Soni	24772828	J-164, Kiran Vih
(AutoNumber)					

Fig. AC-3.21

2. Then *click* on the **Format** option on the Menu bar. A pull-down menu appears on the screen, Fig.AC-3.22.
3. Inside the pull-down menu, *move* the mouse-pointer on the **Column Width** option (Fig.AC-3.22), and *click* the left mouse-button. Immediately, a box named **Column Width** appears on the screen (Fig.AC-3.23).
4. Now *click* on the **Best Fit** button (Fig.AC-3.23). This option manages and adjusts the data in a column with maximum efficiency.
5. *Click* anywhere else in the table to remove the highlight from **ADDRESS** field. Immediately, the contents of address entries in the field **ADDRESS** become completely visible on the screen (Fig.AC-3.24).

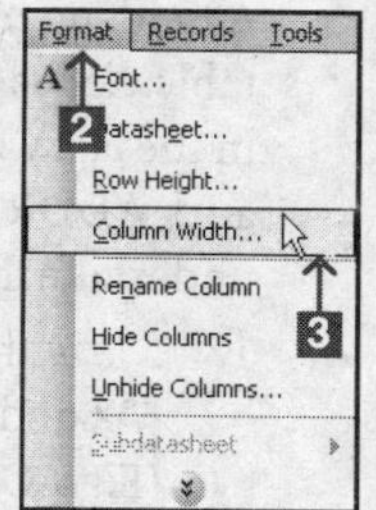

Fig. AC-3.22

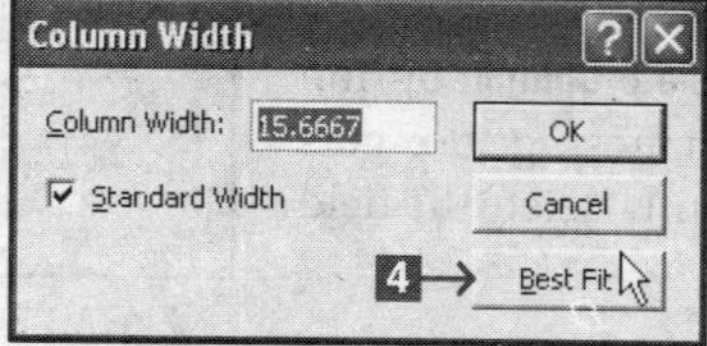

Fig. AC-3.23

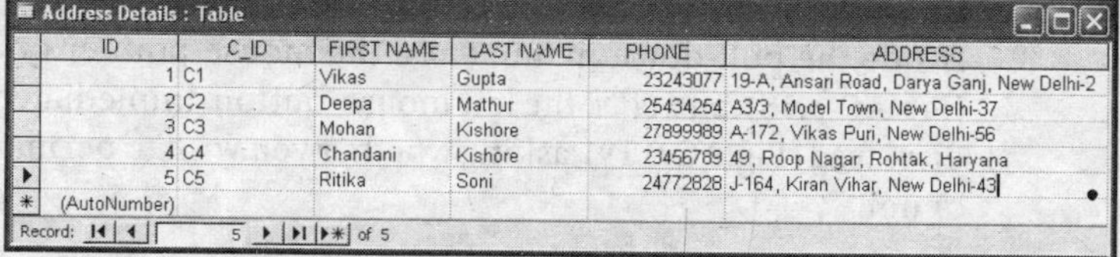

ID	C_ID	FIRST NAME	LAST NAME	PHONE	ADDRESS
1	C1	Vikas	Gupta	23243077	19-A, Ansari Road, Darya Ganj, New Delhi-2
2	C2	Deepa	Mathur	25434254	A3/3, Model Town, New Delhi-37
3	C3	Mohan	Kishore	27899989	A-172, Vikas Puri, New Delhi-56
4	C4	Chandani	Kishore	23456789	49, Roop Nagar, Rohtak, Haryana
5	C5	Ritika	Soni	24772828	J-164, Kiran Vihar, New Delhi-43
(AutoNumber)					

Fig. AC-3.24

Changing the Height of Rows

The standard height of all the rows in Microsoft Access tables is **12.75**. But, you can also change the height of these rows as per your requirement.

Let us now try to increase the height of the rows to **15** in the table Address Details. To do so, undertake the steps listed hereunder.

1. *Move* the mouse-pointer over the **Select All** button and *click* the left mouse-button. Instantly, entire records gets highlighted (Fig.AC-3.25).

Address Details : Table

ID	C_ID	FIRST NAME	LAST NAME	PHONE	ADDRESS
1	C1	Vikas	Gupta	23243077	19-A, Ansari Road, Darya Ganj, New Delhi-2
2	C2	Deepa	Mathur	25434254	A3/3, Model Town, New Delhi-37
3	C3	Mohan	Kishore	27899989	A-172, Vikas Puri, New Delhi-56
4	C4	Chandani	Kishore	23456789	49, Roop Nagar, Rohtak, Haryana
5	C5	Ritika	Soni	24772828	J-164, Kiran Vihar, New Delhi-43
(AutoNumber)					

Record: 1 of 5

Fig. AC-3.25

2. *Click* on the **Format** Menu bar option. Immediately, a pull down menu gets displayed (Fig.AC-3.26).
3. Inside the pull-down menu, *move* the mouse-pointer on the **Row Height** option (Fig.AC-3.26), and *click* the left mouse-button. Instantly, box named **Row Height** appears on the screen (Fig.AC-3.27).
4. Now, *type* **15** in the box beside the **Row Height** option (Fig.AC-3.28).
5. Finally, *click* on the **OK** button, (Fig.AC-3.28). The height of all rows in the **Address Details** table changes, as shown in Fig.AC-3.29.

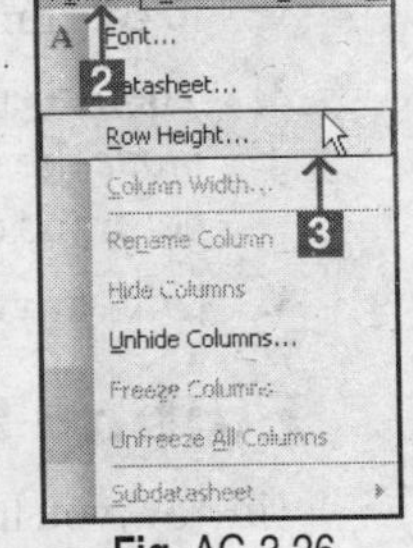

Fig. AC-3.26

Fig. AC-3.27

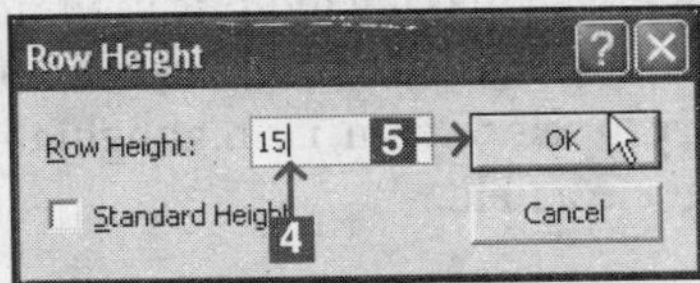

Fig. AC-3.28

Address Details : Table

ID	C_ID	FIRST NAME	LAST NAME	PHONE	ADDRESS
1	C1	Vikas	Gupta	23243077	19-A, Ansari Road, Darya Ganj, New Delhi-
2	C2	Deepa	Mathur	25434254	A3/3, Model Town, New Delhi-37
3	C3	Mohan	Kishore	27899989	A-172, Vikas Puri, New Delhi-56
4	C4	Chandani	Kishore	23456789	49, Roop Nagar, Rohtak, Haryana
5	C5	Ritika	Soni	24772828	J-164, Kiran Vihar, New Delhi-43

Record: 5 of 5

Fig. AC-3.29

Selecting a Field

Any column or field of your table which has been selected appears highlighted on the screen. To understand the selection procedure, let us now select a field, say **ID**, in our table Address Details through the following steps:

1. *Place* the mouse-pointer over the **ID** field in the table (Fig.AC-3.30). The mouse-pointer changes into an arrow shape (↓).
2. Then *click* the left mouse-button to select the **ID** column. Now the entire column **ID** appear highlighted (Fig.AC-3.31). This means that you have selected the column **ID**.
3. *Click* anywhere inside the table to remove the highlight from the **ID** column.

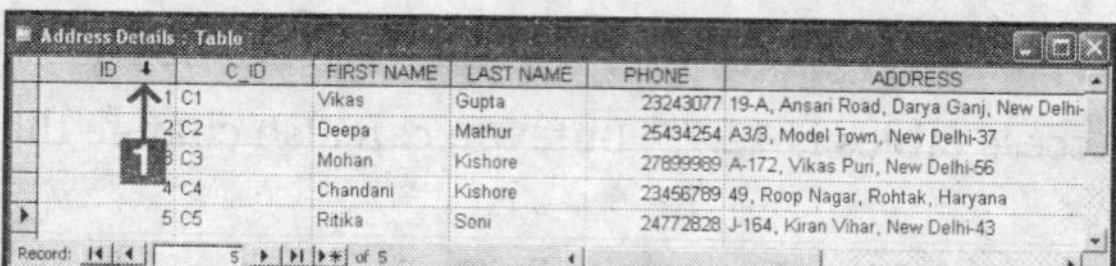

Fig. AC-3.30

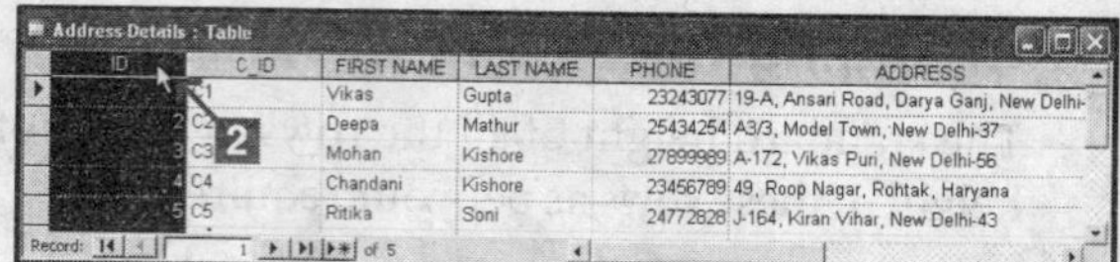

Fig. AC-3.31

Selecting Multiple Fields

You can also select more than one field at a time. Now, let us select any number of fields in sequence, say fields **ID, C_ID** and **FIRST NAME,** from Address Details table. To do so, undertake the following steps:

1. First, *place* the mouse-pointer over the **ID** field name (Fig.AC-3.32), and *press* the left mouse-button. Immediately, all the rows of **ID** column get highlighted.

Fig. AC-3.32

2. Then keeping the left mouse-button *pressed*, *move* the mouse-pointer till the **FIRST NAME** field (Fig.AC-3.32). Instantly, all rows of the first three columns of our table get highlighted.
3. *Click* anywhere inside the table to remove the highlight from the selected fields.

Editing Records in a Table

Till now, you have been making modifications to the fields of a table. Microsoft Access also allows you to make changes on the entered data. However, before making any changes to the desired data entries, it is always necessary to select them, i.e. highlight them. Let us now go through various ways of highlighting the required data in a field.

Selecting a Record

All the records of your table are rows. Selecting a record means highlighting a row of your table. Let us now select a record, say first record, of the table Address Details. To do so, undertake the following steps:

1. *Place* the mouse-pointer over the area to the left of the record you want to select, in our case the first record (Fig.AC-3.33). You will notice that the mouse-pointer changes into an arrow shape (➡).
2. Now, *click* the left mouse-button. The first record gets highlighted (Fig.AC-3.34).
3. *Click* anywhere inside the table to remove the highlight.

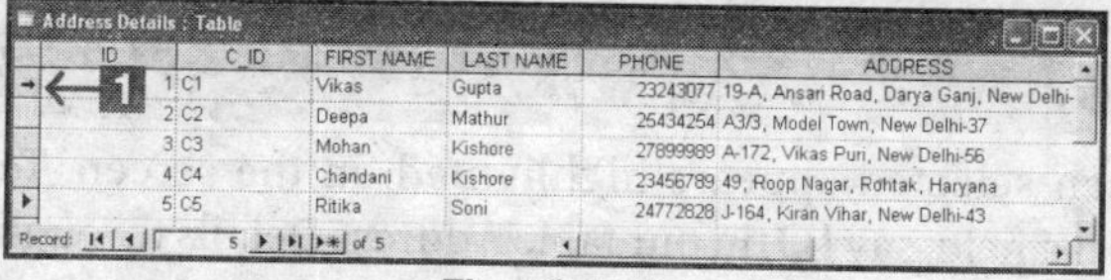

Fig. AC-3.33

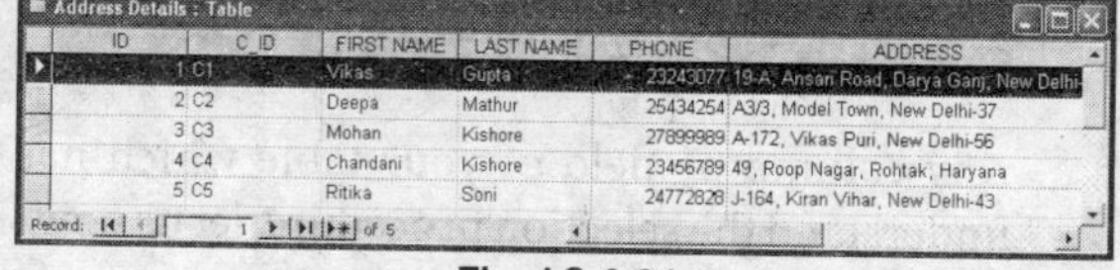

Fig. AC-3.34

Selecting Multiple Records

You can also select more than one record at a time. For example, let us select the first three records of the table Address Details. To do so, undertake the following steps:

1. *Place* the mouse-pointer over the area to the left of the first record. Immediately, the mouse-pointer changes its shape to an arrow (Fig.AC-3.35).

2. Then *press* the left mouse-button, and keeping it *pressed move* the mouse-pointer downwards till you reach the third record. Instantly, all the three records get highlighted (Fig.AC-3.35).
3. Finally *release* the left mouse-button.
4. For removing the highlight from selected records, *click* anywhere else in the table.

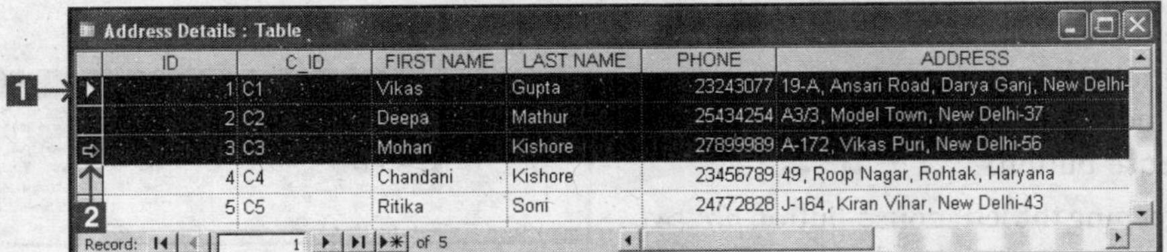

ID	C_ID	FIRST NAME	LAST NAME	PHONE	ADDRESS
1	C1	Vikas	Gupta	23243077	19-A, Ansari Road, Darya Ganj, New Delhi-
2	C2	Deepa	Mathur	25434254	A3/3, Model Town, New Delhi-37
3	C3	Mohan	Kishore	27899989	A-172, Vikas Puri, New Delhi-56
4	C4	Chandani	Kishore	23456789	49, Roop Nagar, Rohtak, Haryana
5	C5	Ritika	Soni	24772828	J-164, Kiran Vihar, New Delhi-43

Fig. AC-3.35

Selecting all the Records in a Table

If you wish to select all the rows of the Address Details table then undertake the following steps:

1. *Move* the mouse-pointer to the top left cell, where rows and columns meet (Fig.AC-3.36).
2. Then *click* the left mouse-button. Immediately, all the records of the table get selected (Fig.AC-3.37).
3. *Click* anywhere in the table to remove the highlight from the selected records.

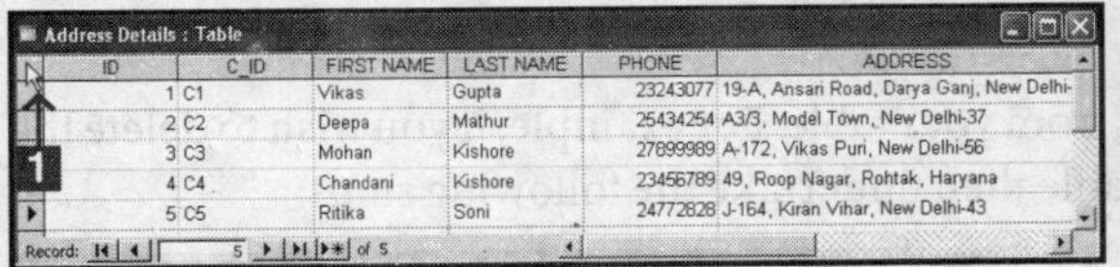

Fig. AC-3.36

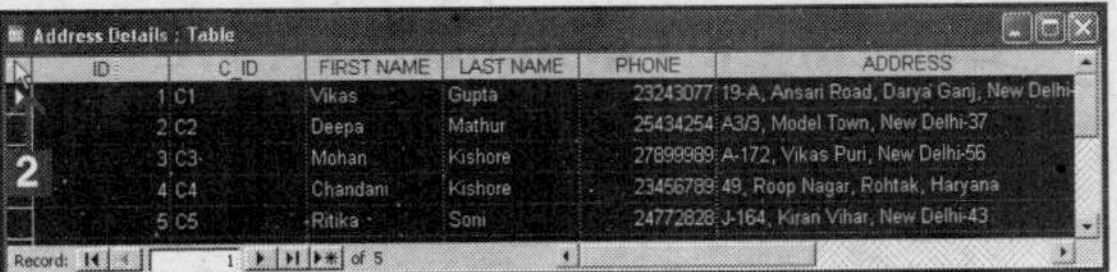

Fig. AC-3.37

Selecting Text in a Cell

Let us now learn how to select text in a particular cell. Suppose, you want to select the data, say name **Vikas**, in the **FIRST NAME** field of Address Details table. To do so, undertake the following steps:

1. *Place* the mouse-pointer (I) to the left of the text you wish to select, i.e. to the left of the name **Vikas** (Fig.AC-3.38).
2. Then *click* the left mouse-button. Immediately, a blinking cursor gets displayed to the left of the name **Vikas** (Fig.AC-3.39).
3. Now, *place* the mouse-pointer over the blinking cursor, and *press* the left mouse-button. Keeping the left mouse-button *pressed*, *drag* the mouse-pointer over the name **Vikas**. Instantly, the name gets highlighted (Fig.AC-3.40).
4. When the entire text of the required cell gets highlighted, *release* the left mouse-button.

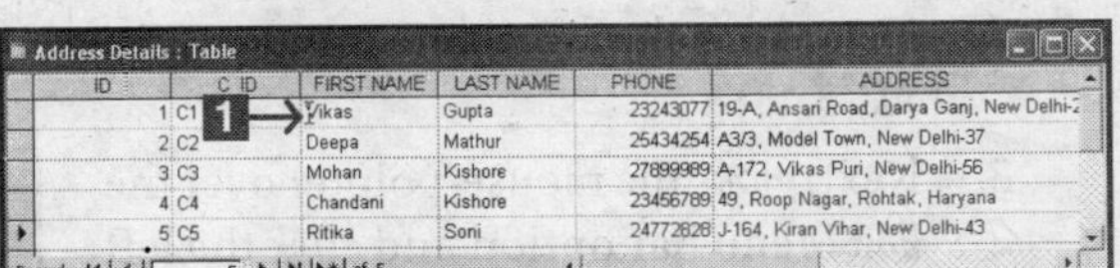

Fig. AC-3.38

Fig. AC-3.39

Fig. AC-3.40

5. *Click* anywhere in the table to remove the highlight from the selected text.

Selecting Text in Multiple Cells

You can also select text simultaneously in more than one cell in a sequence. For example, if you wish to select the text of first four entries under the field **FIRST NAME** of the Address Details table then undertake the following steps:

1. *Place* the mouse-pointer (✥) to the left of the name **Vikas** (Fig.AC-3.41), and *press* the left mouse-button.
2. Now, keeping the left mouse-button *pressed*, *move* the mouse-pointer downwards to the cell containing the name **Chandni**. Immediately, all the four names of the **FIRST NAME** field get highlighted (Fig.AC-3.42).
3. Then *release* the left mouse button.
4. *Click* anywhere in your table to remove the highlight from the cells of the selected names.

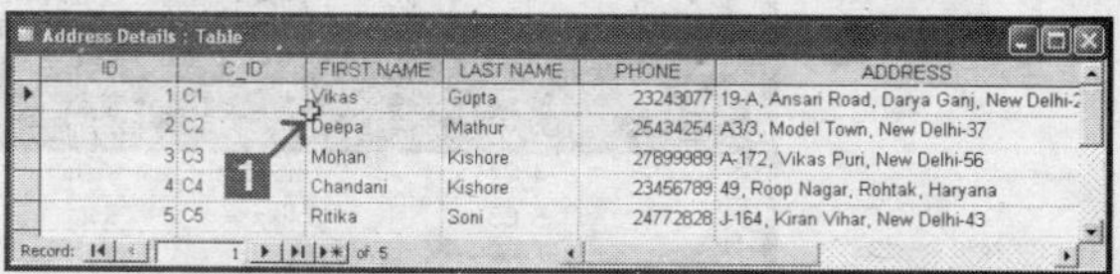

Fig. AC-3.41

Fig. AC-3.42

Deleting a Particular Record

A record which you no longer need can be deleted from your table. For example, if you wish to delete the record of **Ritika Soni** from the Address Details table then undertake the following steps:

1. First, you have to highlight the record to be deleted. So, *place* the mouse-pointer to the left of the record of **Ritika Soni** in **Address Details** table. As usual, the cursor changes to an arrow shape (➡) (Fig.AC-3.43).

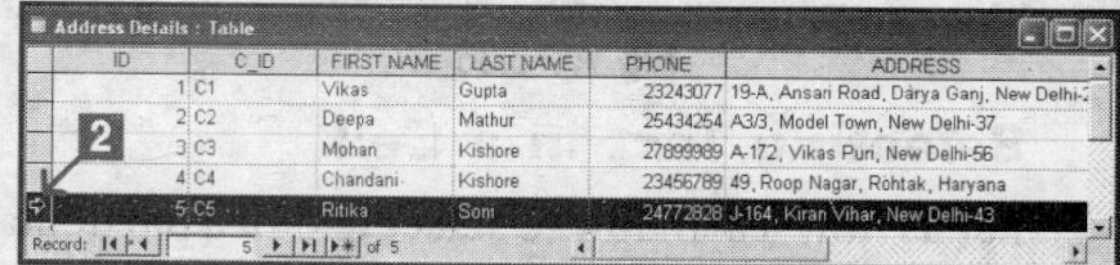

Fig. AC-3.43

2. Now, *click* the left mouse-button. Immediately, the record of **Ritika Soni** gets highlighted (Fig. AC-3.43).
3. Next, *move* the mouse-pointer over the **Edit** Menu bar option and *click* the left mouse-button (Fig.AC-3.44). A pull-down menu appears.
4. In the pull-down menu, *move* the mouse-pointer over the **Delete Record** option and *click* the left mouse-button (Fig.AC-3.44). Immediately, a message box appears (Fig.AC-3.45) to confirm the deletion operation.

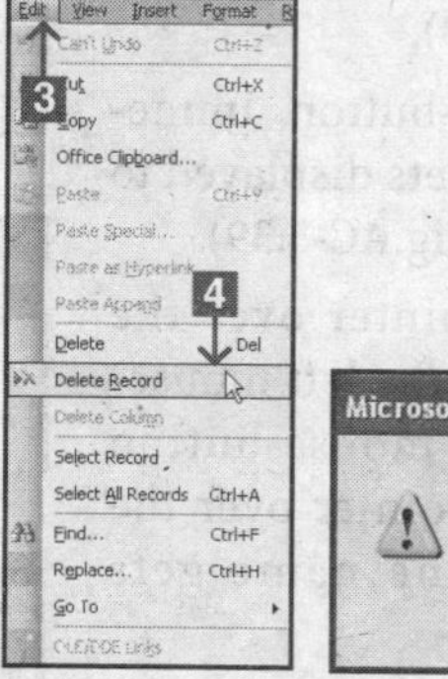

Fig. AC-3.44

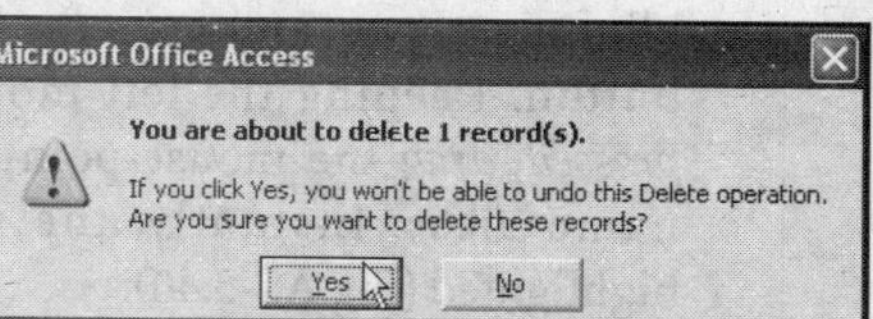

Fig. AC-3.45

5. In this box, simply *click* on the **Yes** button (Fig.AC-3.45). This results in the deletion of the record of **Ritika Soni** from the **Address Details** table, as shown in Fig.AC-3.46.

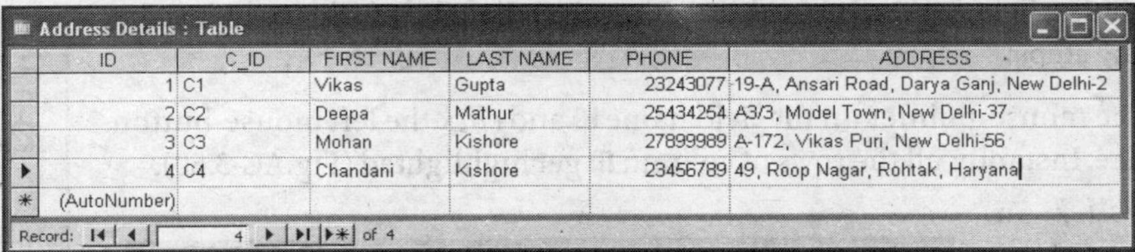

Address Details : Table

ID	C_ID	FIRST NAME	LAST NAME	PHONE	ADDRESS
1	C1	Vikas	Gupta	23243077	19-A, Ansari Road, Darya Ganj, New Delhi-2
2	C2	Deepa	Mathur	25434254	A3/3, Model Town, New Delhi-37
3	C3	Mohan	Kishore	27899989	A-172, Vikas Puri, New Delhi-56
4	C4	Chandani	Kishore	23456789	49, Roop Nagar, Rohtak, Haryana
(AutoNumber)					

Record: 4 of 4

Fig. AC-3.46

If you wish to delete more than one record, say sequential records 4, 5 and 6 then follow steps 1 and 2 of the topic 'Deleting a Particular Record'. Thereafter, press the left mouse-button, and keeping it pressed, drag the mouse-pointer till the last record, i.e the sixth record. Finally, follow steps 3 and 4 of the same topic to complete the deletion process.

Adding a New Record

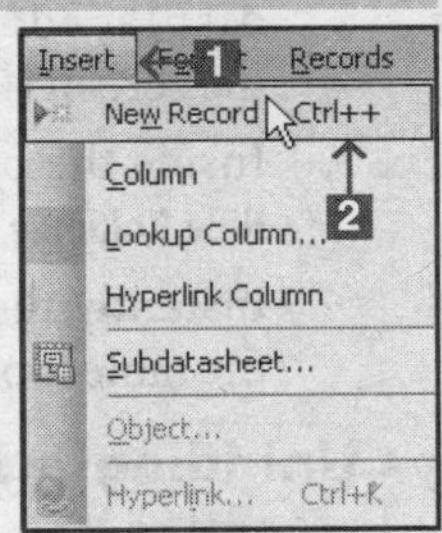

Fig. AC-3.47

New records can be added to an existing table. To add new records in the Address Details table, undertake the following steps.

1. *Move* the mouse-pointer over the **Insert** Menu bar option and *click* the left mouse-button. Instantly, a pull-down menu appears (Fig.AC-3.47).
2. Inside the pull-down menu, *move* the mouse-pointer over the **New Record** option and *click* the left mouse-button (Fig.AC-3.47). A blank row gets inserted in the table. In this blank row, add the following details.

T A B L E

C_ID	FIRST NAME	LAST NAME	PHONE	ADDRESS
C5	ISHAN	MOHAN	26565465	12/60, South Exn. Part-2, New Delhi

You will notice that the AutoNumber displays number 6 instead of 5. As the fifth record of Ritika Soni has already been deleted from Address Details table, Microsoft Access assigns a new number to the new record.

3. *Press* **Tab** key and *type* **C5**.
4. Again *press* the **Tab** key, and *type* the **FIRST NAME** as **Ishan.**
5. For entering the **LAST NAME** *press* the **Tab** key from the keyboard and *type* **Mohan** as **LAST NAME.**
6. Follow the same procedure for entering rest of the details of **Ishan.** Your table will then look like Fig.AC-3.49.
7. Similarly, you can add other records into the **Address Details** table.

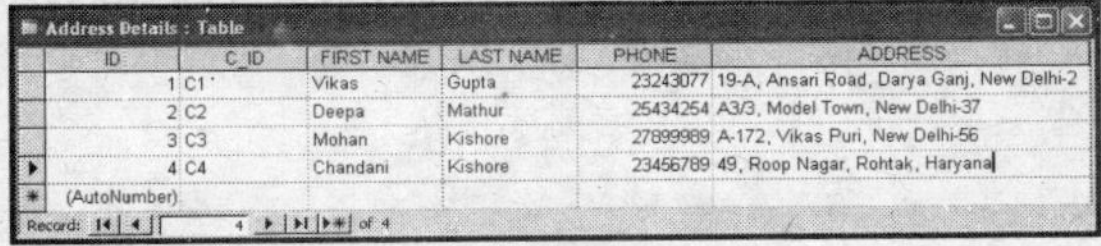

Address Details : Table

ID	C_ID	FIRST NAME	LAST NAME	PHONE	ADDRESS
1	C1	Vikas	Gupta	23243077	19-A, Ansari Road, Darya Ganj, New Delhi-2
2	C2	Deepa	Mathur	25434254	A3/3, Model Town, New Delhi-37
3	C3	Mohan	Kishore	27899989	A-172, Vikas Puri, New Delhi-56
4	C4	Chandani	Kishore	23456789	49, Roop Nagar, Rohtak, Haryana
(AutoNumber)					

Record: 4 of 4

Fig. AC-3.48

Address Details : Table

ID	C_ID	FIRST NAME	LAST NAME	PHONE	ADDRESS
1	C1	Vikas	Gupta	23243077	19-A, Ansari Road, Darya Ganj, New Delhi-
2	C2	Deepa	Mathur	25434254	A3/3, Model Town, New Delhi-37
3	C3	Mohan	Kishore	27899989	A-172, Vikas Puri, New Delhi-56
4	C4	Chandani	Kishore	23456789	49, Roop Nagar, Rohtak, Haryana
6	C5	ISHAN	MOHAN	26565465	12/60, South Ext., Part-2, New Delhi

Record: 5 of 5

Fig. AC-3.49

Hiding a Field

Suppose, your table is so long that you are unable to see all the fields on the screen at once. For viewing all the fields you have to repeatedly use the scroll button which is quite time consuming. To solve this problem, Microsoft Access provides the facility of hiding fields. Using this facility, you can temporarily hide one or more fields of your table and then redisplay them when required. This way you can view only those fields which you urgently require. This feature also helps you to take print-outs of only certain fields.

Let us also hide a field, say the **ID** field, in Address Details table. To do so, undertake the following steps:

1. *Place* the mouse-pointer on the field name **ID** and *click* the left mouse-button just once. Instantly, all the rows of column **ID** get highlighted (Fig.AC-3.50).
2. Then *click* on the **Format** Menu bar option. Immediately, a pull-down menu gets displayed on the screen (Fig.AC-3.51).

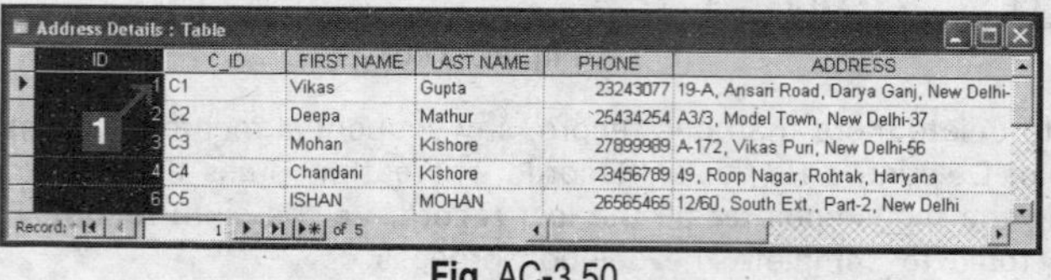

Address Details : Table

ID	C_ID	FIRST NAME	LAST NAME	PHONE	ADDRESS
1	C1	Vikas	Gupta	23243077	19-A, Ansari Road, Darya Ganj, New Delhi-
2	C2	Deepa	Mathur	25434254	A3/3, Model Town, New Delhi-37
3	C3	Mohan	Kishore	27899989	A-172, Vikas Puri, New Delhi-56
4	C4	Chandani	Kishore	23456789	49, Roop Nagar, Rohtak, Haryana
6	C5	ISHAN	MOHAN	26565465	12/60, South Ext., Part-2, New Delhi

Fig. AC-3.50

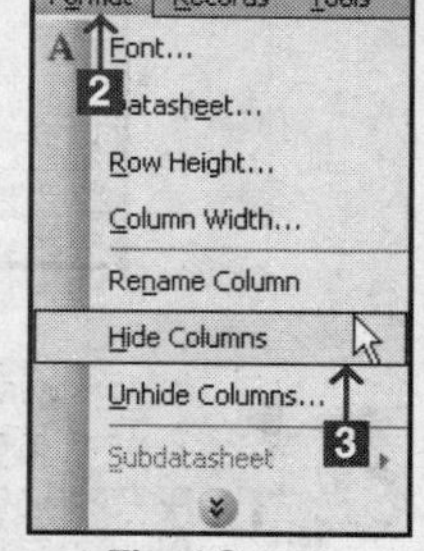

Fig. AC-3.51

3. Inside the pull-down menu, *click* on **Hide Columns** option (Fig.AC-3.51).

   Instantly, the field **ID** gets hidden and the table look like Fig.AC-3.52.

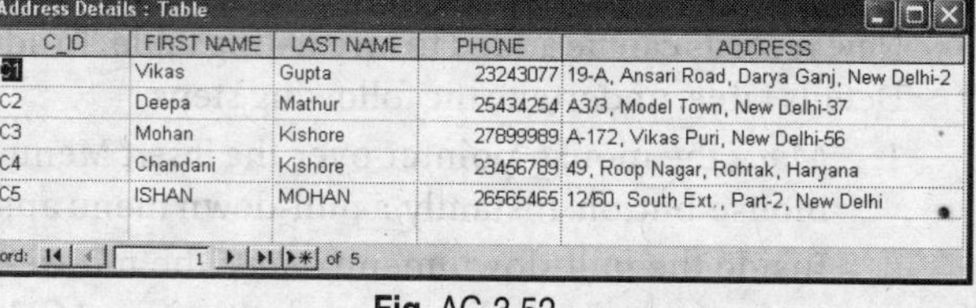

Address Details : Table

C_ID	FIRST NAME	LAST NAME	PHONE	ADDRESS
C1	Vikas	Gupta	23243077	19-A, Ansari Road, Darya Ganj, New Delhi-2
C2	Deepa	Mathur	25434254	A3/3, Model Town, New Delhi-37
C3	Mohan	Kishore	27899989	A-172, Vikas Puri, New Delhi-56
C4	Chandani	Kishore	23456789	49, Roop Nagar, Rohtak, Haryana
C5	ISHAN	MOHAN	26565465	12/60, South Ext., Part-2, New Delhi

Fig. AC-3.52

Unhiding a Field

You can also unhide the field which you had hidden earlier. To unhide a field, in our case ID, in the Address Details table, undertake the following steps:

1. *Click* on the **Format** Menu bar option. Immediately, a pull-down menu gets displayed on the screen (Fig.AC-3.53).
2. Inside the pull-down menu, *move* the mouse-pointer on **Unhide Columns** option (Fig.AC-3.53), and *click* the left mouse-button. Immediately, an **Unhide Columns** box appears on the screen containing a list of fields (Fig.AC-3.54).

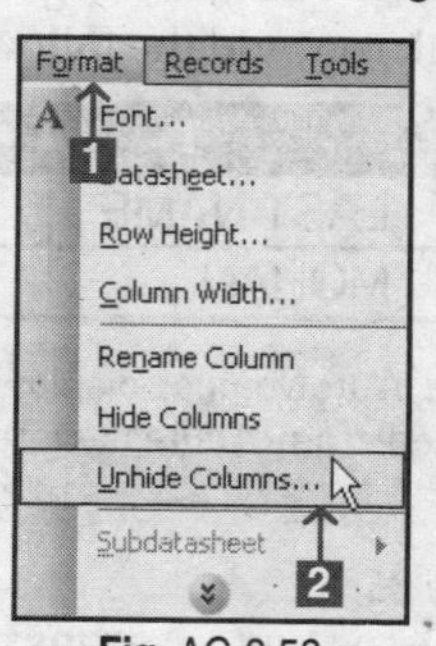

Fig. AC-3.53

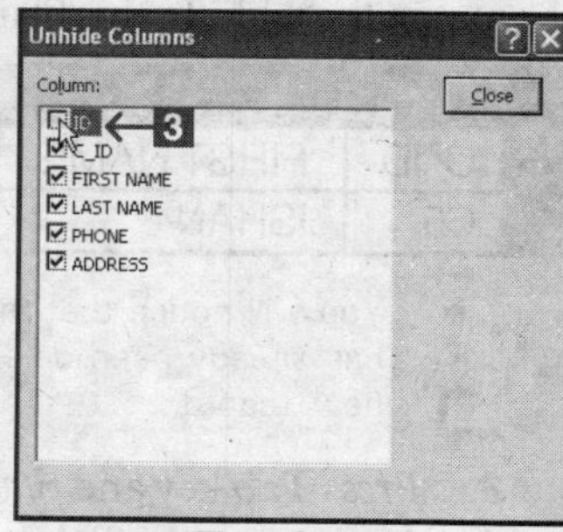

Fig. AC-3.54

3. You will notice that a tick mark (✔) beside all the field names confirming their appearances in the **Address Details** table (except the **ID** field), as shown in Fig.AC-3.54. So, *move* the mouse-pointer over the blank box beside **ID** field, and *click* the left mouse-button. Immediately, a tick mark(✔) appears inside the blank box (Fig.AC-3.55).
4. Finally, *click* on the **Close** button (Fig.AC-3.55). Instantly, the hidden field name **ID** re-appears in the table (Fig.AC-3.56).

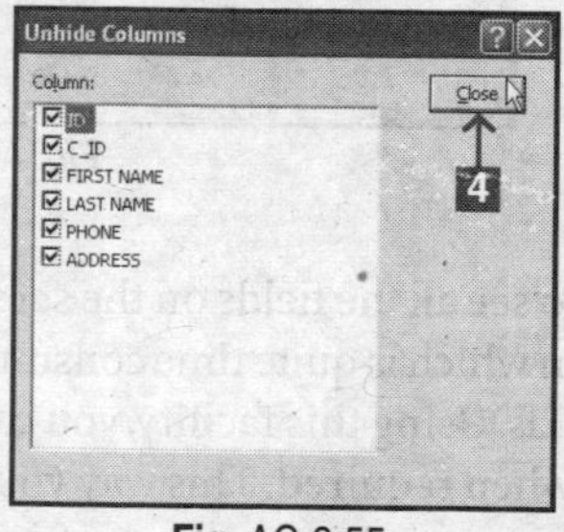

Fig. AC-3.55

Address Details : Table

ID	C_ID	FIRST NAME	LAST NAME	PHONE	ADDRESS
1	C1	Vikas	Gupta	23243077	19-A, Ansari Road, Darya Ga
2	C2	Deepa	Mathur	25434254	A3/3, Model Town, New Delhi
3	C3	Mohan	Kishore	27899989	A-172, Vikas Puri, New Delhi-
4	C4	Chandani	Kishore	23456789	49, Roop Nagar, Rohtak, Har
6	C5	ISHAN	MOHAN	26565465	12/60, South Ext., Part-2, Ne
(AutoNumber)					

Fig. AC-3.56

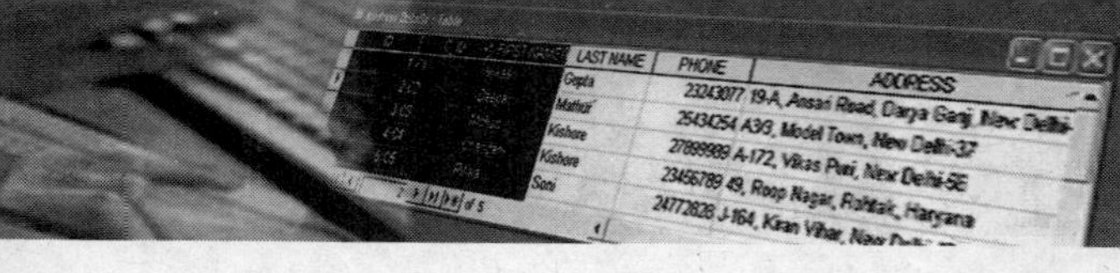

To hide more than one field, say fields PHONE and FAX, first click on the field name PHONE. Then keeping the left mouse-button pressed, drag the mouse-pointer to the field name FAX. Now follow steps 2 and 3 of the topic 'Hiding a Field'.

To unhide the hidden fields, follow steps 1 and 2 of the topic 'Unhiding a Field'. Then select the fields displayed below Columns option, in the Unhide Columns box. Finally, click on the Close button.

Freezing a Field

Suppose, you have a table containing customer salary details in twenty fields. When you move to the last field using scroll buttons, some field names present at the beginning of the table disappear from the screen. Now to see these hidden fields, you again have to use the scroll buttons to move to the beginning of the table.

But, you may not like to use scroll buttons every time you need to see the desired fields which remain hidden. In that case, the freezing feature of Microsoft Access comes to your help. Using this feature, you can freeze a field so that it always remains displayed on your screen while you move on to other fields in the large table.

Now, in our Address Details table, let us freeze a field, say **FIRST NAME**. In order to do so, undertake the following steps:

1. *Move* the mouse-pointer over the field **FIRST NAME** and *click* the left mouse-button. Immediately, all the rows of this field get highlighted (Fig.AC-3.57).
2. Now, *click* over the **Format** Menu bar option. Immediately, a pull-down menu appears on the screen (Fig.AC-3.58).
3. Inside the pull-down menu, *move* the mouse-pointer on **Freeze Columns** option (Fig.AC-3.58), and *click* the left mouse-button. This action freezes the field **FIRST NAME**. In other words, when you *click* on the scroll bar to view other fields, the **FIRST NAME** column remains static, i.e. it does not disappear from the screen.
4. Now, *click* anywhere in your table to remove the highlight from the freezed field. In the table (Fig.AC-3.59), the **FIRST NAME** column is shown as the first column which is not its original place.

Address Details : Table

ID	C_ID	FIRST NAME	LAST NAME	PHONE	ADDRESS
1	C1	Vikas	Gupta	23243077	19-A, Ansari Road, Darya Ga
2	C2	Deepa	Mathur	25434254	A3/3, Model Town, New Delhi
3	C3	Mohan	Kishore	27899989	A-172, Vikas Puri, New Delhi
4	C4	Chandani	Kishore	23456789	49, Roop Nagar, Rohtak, Har
6	C5	ISHAN	MOHAN	26565465	12/60, South Ext., Part-2, Ne
(AutoNumber)					

Record: 1 of 5

Fig. AC-3.57

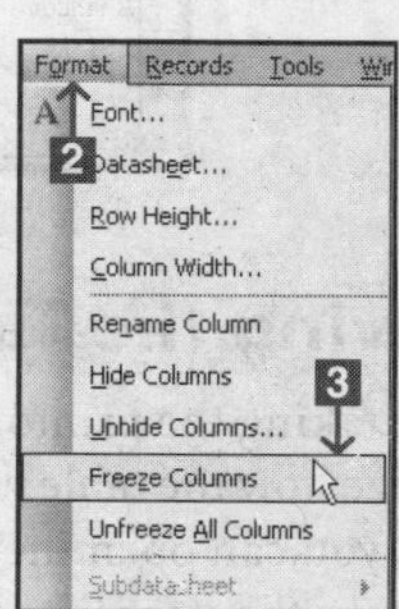

Fig. AC-3.58

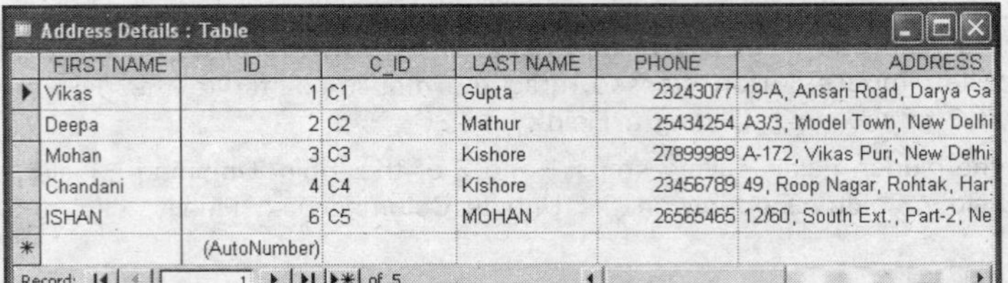

Address Details : Table

	FIRST NAME	ID	C_ID	LAST NAME	PHONE	ADDRESS
▶	Vikas	1	C1	Gupta	23243077	19-A, Ansari Road, Darya Ga
	Deepa	2	C2	Mathur	25434254	A3/3, Model Town, New Delhi
	Mohan	3	C3	Kishore	27899989	A-172, Vikas Puri, New Delhi
	Chandani	4	C4	Kishore	23456789	49, Roop Nagar, Rohtak, Har
	ISHAN	6	C5	MOHAN	26565465	12/60, South Ext., Part-2, Ne
*		(AutoNumber)				

Record: 1 of 5

Fig. AC-3.59

You can also freeze more than one field of the Address Details table. To do so, first highlight the number of columns which you need to freeze. Then click on Format option, and choose Freeze Columns from the pull-down menu.

Unfreezing a Field

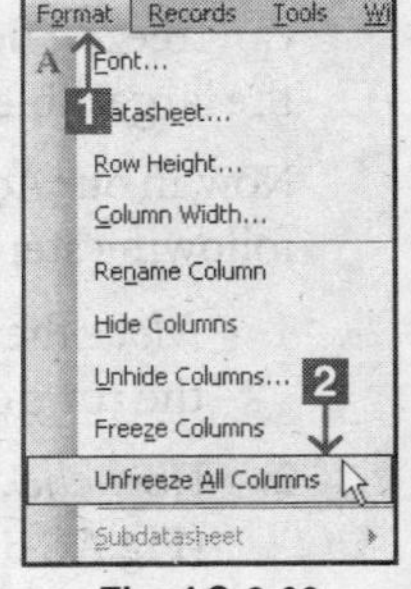

Fig. AC-3.60

If you no more require the continuous appearance of a field on the screen, you can unfreeze it. Let us now unfreeze the field **FIRST NAME** in the Address Details table. To do so, undertake the following steps:

1. *Move* the mouse-pointer over the **Format** menu bar option, and *click* the left mouse-button. Immediately, a pull-down menu appears on the screen (Fig. AC-3.60).
2. Inside the pull-down menu, *click* over **Unfreeze All Columns** option (Fig.AC-3.60), and *click* the left mouse-button. Now, the field **FIRST NAME** no more remains static on the screen but starts moving along with other fields. Also notice that now the field **FIRST NAME** is not at its original place but at the beginning of the **Address Details** table (Fig.AC-3.61).

Address Details : Table

	FIRST NAME	ID	C_ID	LAST NAME	PHONE	ADDRESS
▶	Vikas	1	C1	Gupta	23243077	19-A, Ansari Road, Darya Ga
	Deepa	2	C2	Mathur	25434254	A3/3, Model Town, New Delhi
	Mohan	3	C3	Kishore	27899989	A-172, Vikas Puri, New Delhi
	Chandani	4	C4	Kishore	23456789	49, Roop Nagar, Rohtak, Har
	ISHAN	6	C5	MOHAN	26565465	12/60, South Ext., Part-2, Ne
*		(AutoNumber)				

Record: 1 of 5

Fig. AC-3.61

Viewing the Table Before Printing

Before taking the printout of your table, it is better to have a look at its print preview. It will help you visualize how the table when printed on paper would look. If you don't find the print preview to your liking, you can open the table and modify it. Now, to look at the preview of our table **Address Details**, undertake the steps listed here under.

1. *Move* the mouse-pointer over the **Print Preview** button (🔍) present on the **Standard Toolbar** (Fig.AC-3.62), and *click* the left mouse-button.

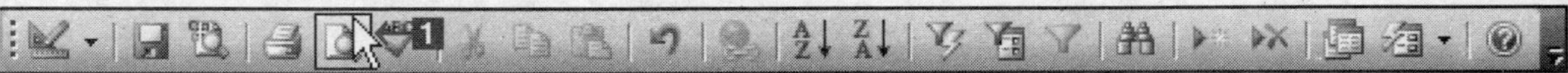

Fig. AC-3.62

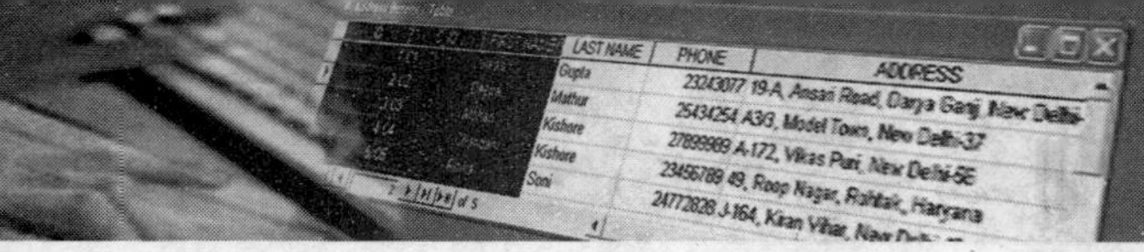

Instantly, a window opens up showing the preview of the table (Fig.AC-3.63).

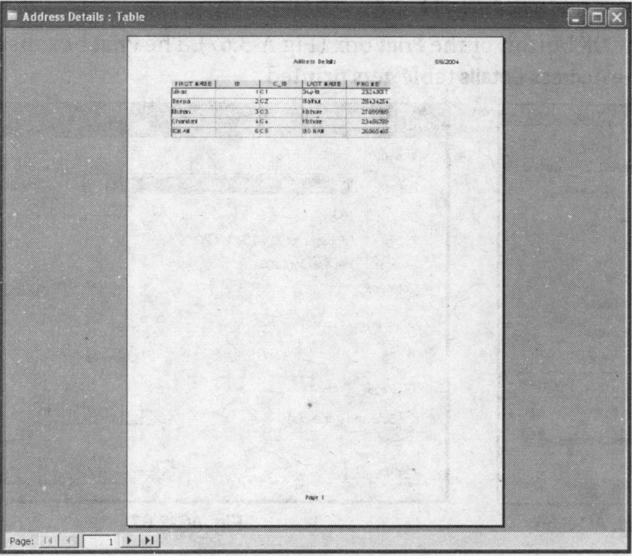

Fig. AC-3.63

When you *move* the mouse-pointer over the sheet containing the table, it automatically changes into a magnifying symbol (🔍).

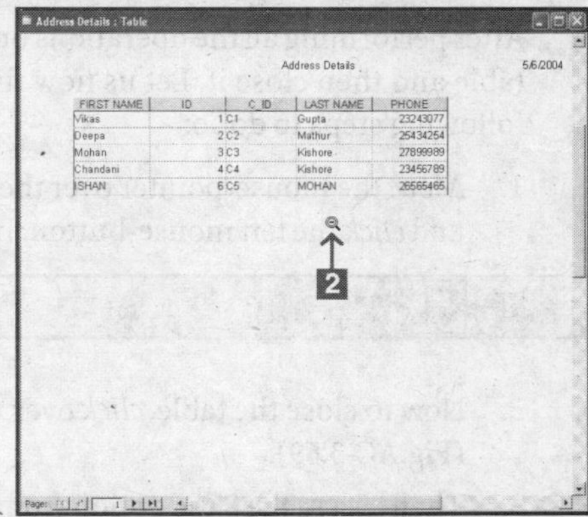

Fig. AC-3.64

2. Now, if you wish to have a look at the enlarged view of the table, *move* the mouse-pointer (🔍) over the text, and *click* the left mouse-button. Immediately, the text gets enlarged on the screen (Fig.AC-3.64).

   You will also notice that the appearance of the mouse-pointer changes to 🔍. Remember, you will not be able to perform any modifications on this text.

3. To close the print preview and return to the table, *click* on the **Close** button of the **Print Preview** screen as shown in Fig.AC-3.65.

Fig. AC-3.65

Printing the Table

Now to take a printout of Address Details table, undertake the following steps:

1. *Move* the mouse-pointer over **File** Menu bar option and *click* the left mouse-button. Immediately, a pull-down menu gets displayed on the screen (Fig.AC-3.66).

2. Inside the pull-down menu, *move* the mouse-pointer on the **Print** option (Fig.AC-3.66). Immediately, a **Print** box appears on the screen (Fig.AC-3.67).
3. Now, *click* on the **OK** button of the **Print** box (Fig A-3.67). The **Print** box disappears from the screen instantly and the **Address Details** table gets printed.

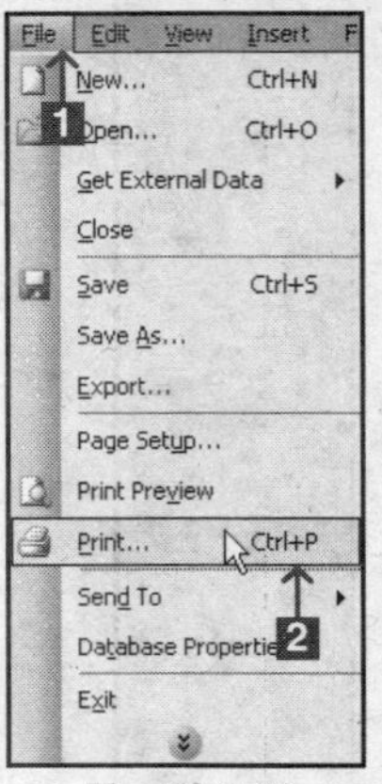

Fig. AC-3.66

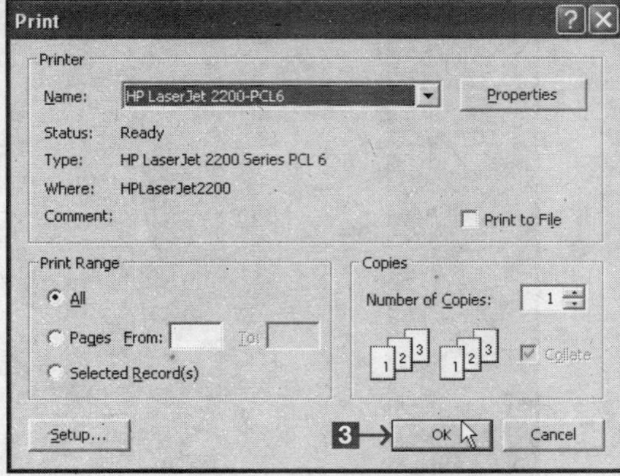

Fig. AC-3.67

Saving and Closing the Table

After performing all the operations on the **Address Details** table, it is better to save the changes made to the table and then close it. Let us now first save the **Address Details** table and then close it. Undertake the following steps to do so:

1. *Move* the mouse-pointer over the **Save** button (🖫) present on the **Standard Toolbar** (Fig.AC-3.68), and *click* the left mouse-button. Instantly the changes made get saved.

Fig. AC-3.68

2. Now to close the table, *click* over the **File** Menu bar option. Immediately, a pull-down menu appears (Fig.AC-3.69).
3. Then *choose* the **Close** option from the pull-down menu, (Fig.AC-3.69). The **Address Details** table closes instantly and the **Address Database** gets displayed on the screen (Fig.AC-3.70). You need not close the **Address Database** right now because it is required in the next topic Creating Relationship Between Tables.

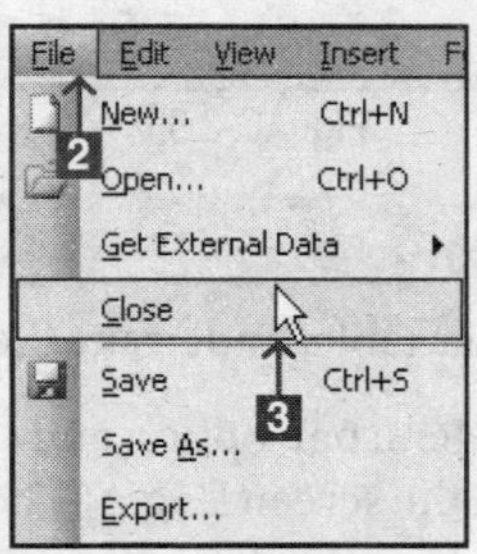

Fig. AC-3.69

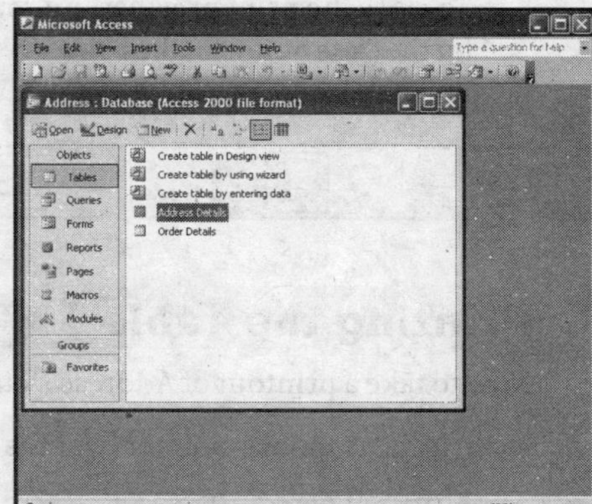

Fig. AC-3.70

Creating Relationship Between Tables

Sometimes the information stored in a database may be repetitive in nature. Let us take an example of a table containing details of publishers (A, B, C & D) who publish books on various subjects, say **Maths, Science, History,** etc.

TABLE

Subjects	Publishers
Maths	A B D
Science	A B C D
History	A B C

Now arrange the book details in one column. The second column will have the names of publishers of these books. In this arrangement, you will find that the name of the publishers get repeated because the books on a particular subject may be printed by more than one publisher.

But this is not the correct way of arranging information. To arrange the books-related repetitive data in a better and simple way, Microsoft Access provides the facility of separating repetitive information into various tables and then relating them. In the above example (Table 1), three separate tables would be created for storing information on books of three subjects. And then, a relationship would be developed among them.

When we say that a number of tables, say three tables, are related to one another, it means all the three tables have at least one common field.

Let us now create a relation between our two tables, **Address Details** and **Order Details.** To do so, undertake the steps described on the following steps:

1. *Revert* to the **Address Database** box displayed on the screen (Fig.AC-3.70). *Click* on the **Tables** tab.
2. Then *move* the mouse-pointer over the **Relationships** button ( ), present on the **Standard toolbar** (Fig.AC-3.71), and *click* the left mouse-button.

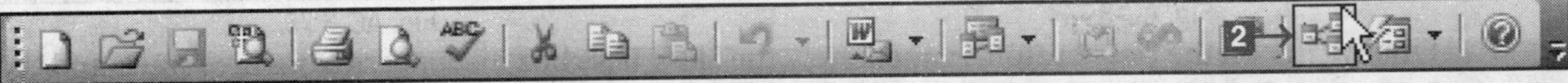

Fig. AC-3.71

Immediately, a **Show Table** box (Fig.AC-3.72) gets displayed in the front, and a **Relationships** window gets displayed in the background (Fig.AC-3.73).

The **Show Table** box is used to choose the tables while the **Relationships** window is used to establish relationships between the fields.

3. Inside the **Show Table** box, the table **Address Details** is already highlighted (Fig.AC-3.73).
4. Now, *click* on the **Add** button of **Show Table** box. Immediately, a small box containing the field names of the **Address Details** table gets displayed inside the **Relationships** window (Fig.AC-3.73).

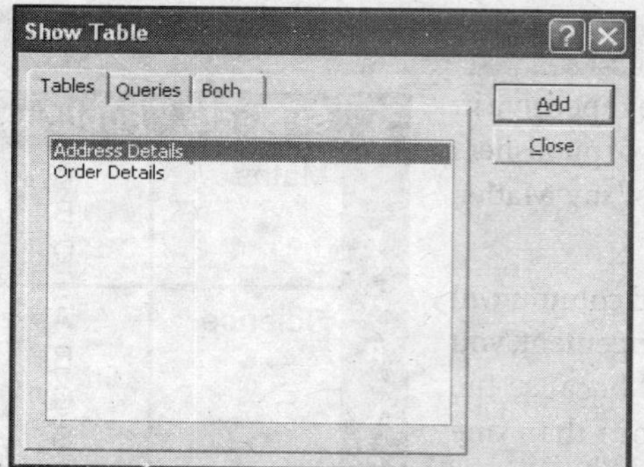

Fig. AC-3.72

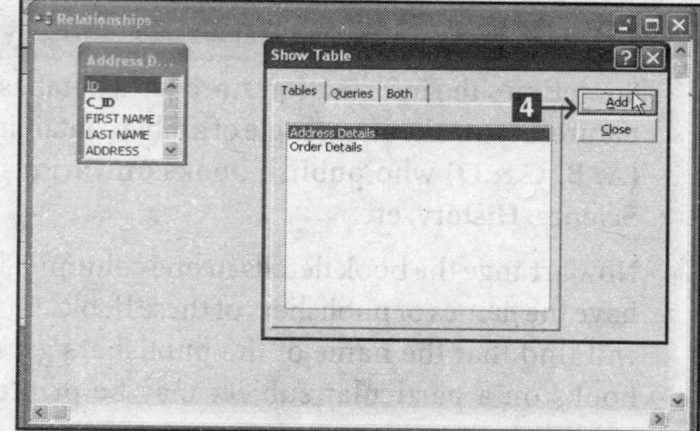

Fig. AC-3.73

5. Now, *click* on **Order Details** inside the **Show Table** box. Immediately, the table name gets highlighted (Fig.AC-3.74).
6. Then *click* on the **Add** button (Fig.AC-3.75) of the **Show Table** box. Instantly, a small box containing the field names of the **Order Details** table gets displayed inside the **Relationships** window (Fig.AC-3.76)

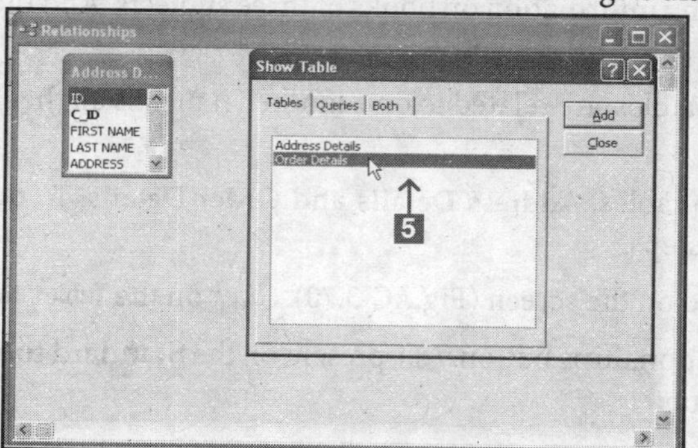

Fig. AC-3.74

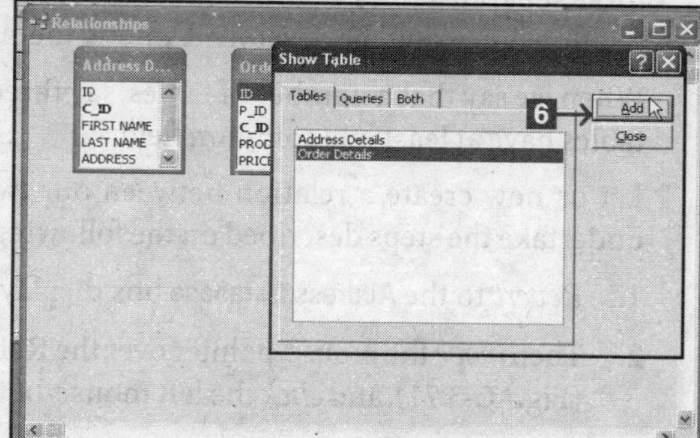

Fig. AC-3.75

7. Finally, *click* on the **Close** button. Immediately, the **Show Table** box disappears from the screen and the **Relationships** window comes to the front (Fig.AC-3.77).
8. Since the field name **C_ID** is the common field in both the tables (**Address Details** and **Order Details**), it gets displayed in both the small boxes in bold format (Fig.AC-3.77). This means that the two tables can be related through the **C_ID** field.

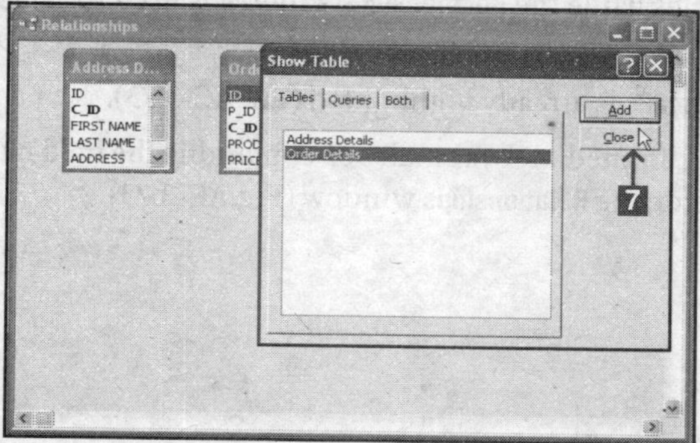

Fig. AC-3.76

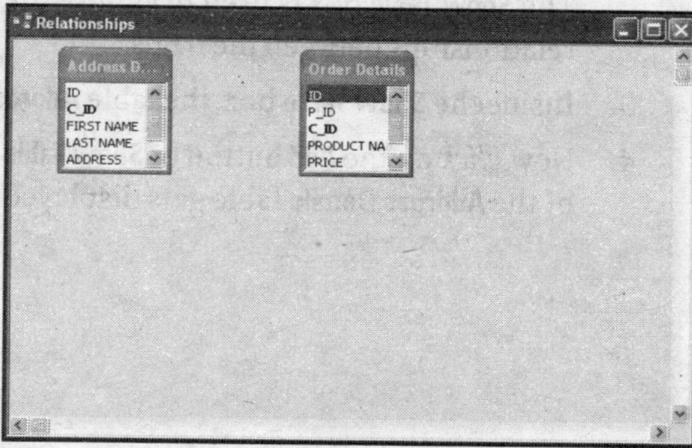

Fig. AC-3.77

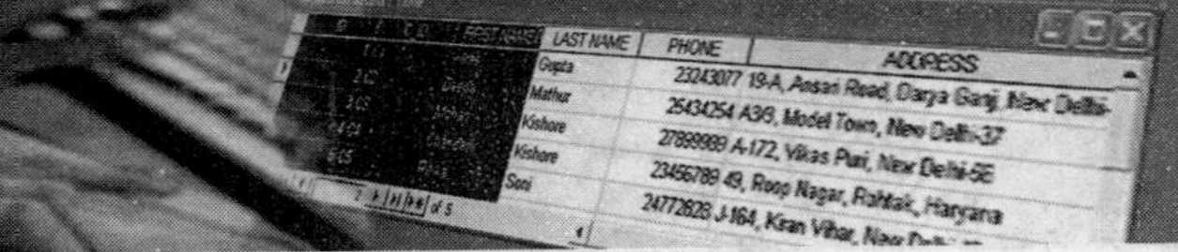

9. Now, let us proceed to establish a relationship between the selected tables through the field name **C_ID**. First, *move* the mouse-pointer over the field name **C_ID** in the **Address Details** box, and *press* the left mouse-button (Fig.AC-3.78).

10. Keeping the left mouse-button *pressed*, *drag* it inside the **Order Details** box (Fig.AC-3.79), and then *release* the mouse-button. Immediately, the **Edit Relationships** box opens up on your screen (Fig.AC-3.80).

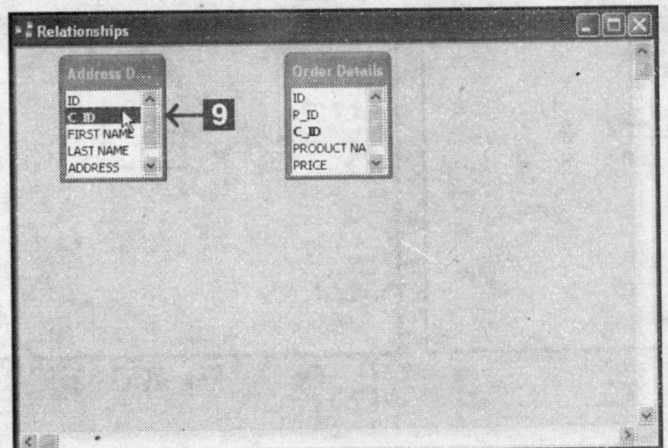

Fig. AC-3.78

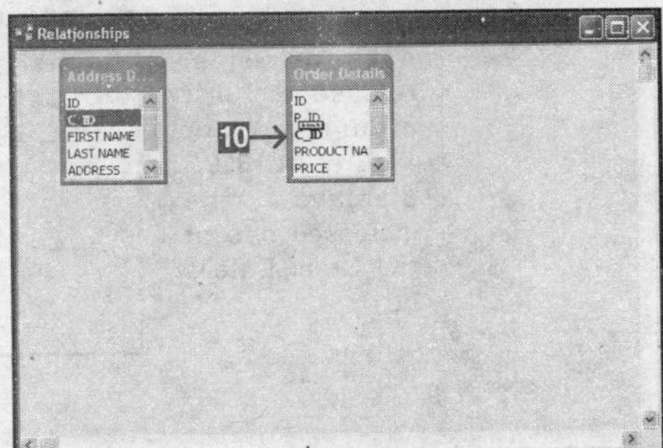

Fig. AC-3.79

11. Now, *click* on **Create** button of the **Edit Relationships** box (Fig.AC-3.80).

Immediately, the box disappears from the screen and the **Relationships** window gets displayed. Inside this window, a thin join line appears between the two boxes containing the field names of **Address Details** and **Order Details** tables (Fig.AC-3.81).

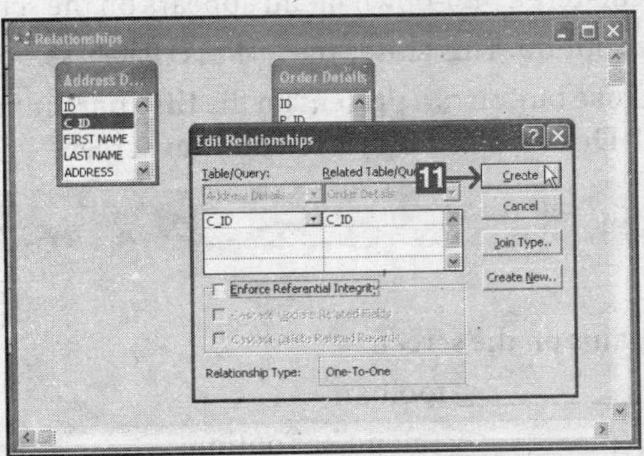

Fig. AC-3.80

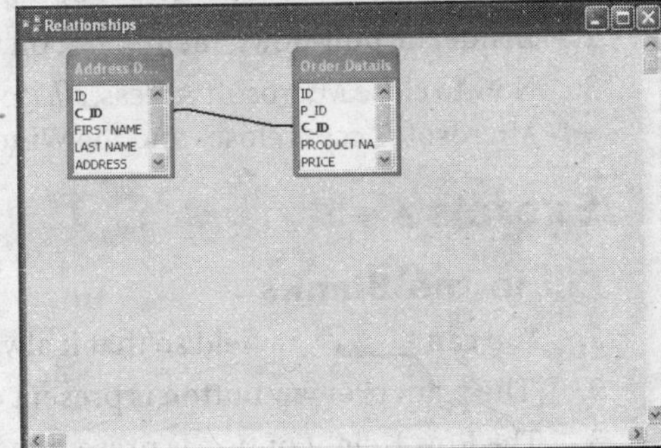

Fig. AC-3.81

12. Next, *move* the mouse-pointer on the **Save** button ( ) present on the **Standard Toolbar** and *click* on the left mouse-button. The relationship that you have created between your two tables now gets saved.

If you are unable to see all the fields in the boxes inside Relationships window then you can increase the size of the boxes. For example, if you wish to increase the size of Order Details box then undertake the following steps:

1. Move the mouse-pointer to the bottom border of the Order Details box (Fig.AC-3.82). Immediately, the mouse-pointer changes into a twin-headed arrow(↕).
2. Now keeping the left mouse-button pressed, drag the mouse downwards on the mouse-pad. A grey outline indicates the increase in the size of the window.
3. On reaching the desired size, release the left mouse-button. Figure AC-3.83 displays the increased size of the Order Details box.

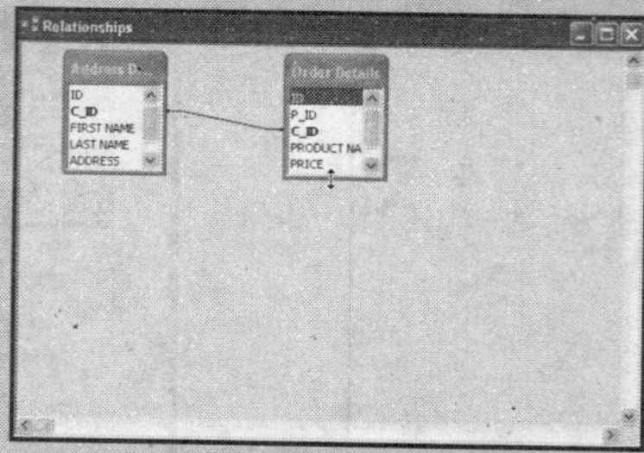

Fig. AC-3.82

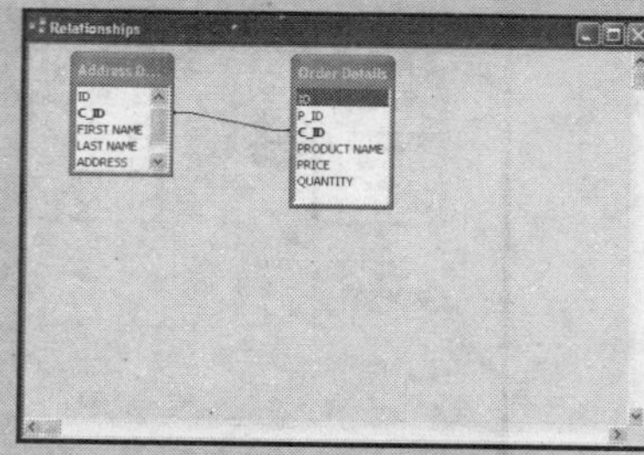

Fig. AC-3.83

13. For closing the **Relationships** window, *move* the mouse-pointer over the **Close** button (☒) present on the **Title bar** of the **Relationships** window and *click* the left mouse-button.

Closing the Database and Quitting Access

Now that you have become familiar with various features of Access, let us quit Microsoft Access. But first let us close any open database box, in our case Address : Database box. To do so, undertake the following steps:

1. First *click* on the **File** menu bar option. Immediately a pull-down menu appears on the screen.
2. Inside the pull-down menu, *click* on the **Close** option. This closes the **Address : Database** box.
3. Now to close Microsoft Access, *click* on the **Close** button (☒) present on the **title bar**. Immediately, Microsoft Access closes and the Windows XP **Desktop** gets displayed on your screen.

Exercise

Fill in the Blanks

1. You can ________ a field so that it always remains on the screen.
2. The print preview button is present on the ____________ toolbar.
3. The Row Height option is present inside the ____________ menu bar option.
4. A new record can be added to an existing table by clicking on the ________________ button.
5. To close the print preview click on the ________ button of the print preview screen.

Short Questions

1. What do you understand by freezing a field?
2. Write the steps for changing the width of a column.
3. Write the steps for hiding a field.
4. How can you create relationships between tables?
5. Write the steps for deleting a particular record.

MICROSOFT ACCESS

Working with Forms 4

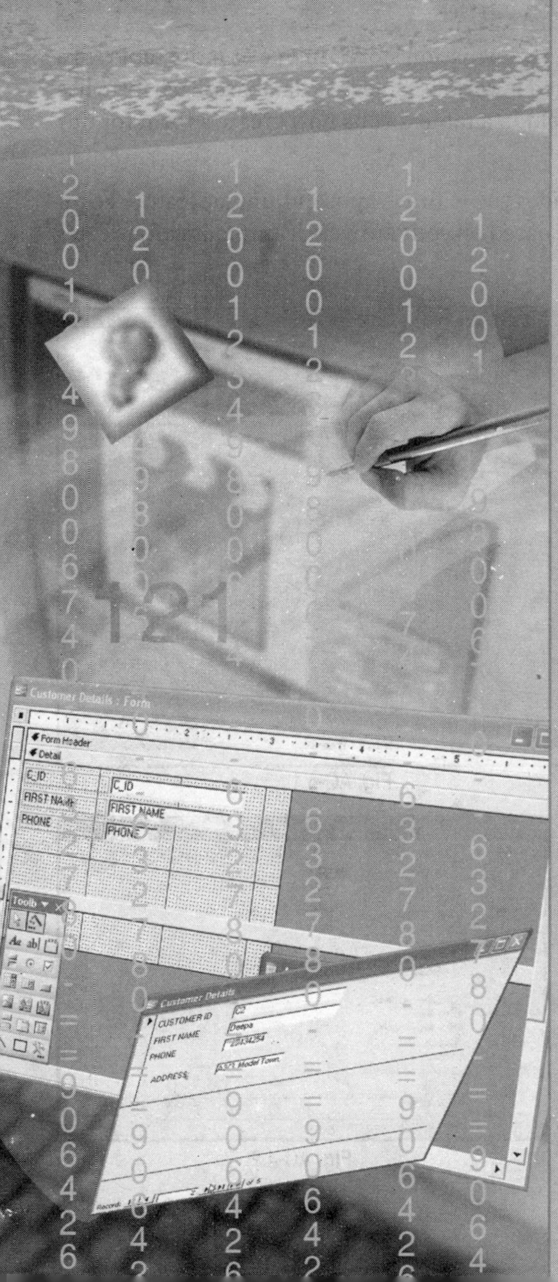

IN THIS CHAPTER

- Opening Database in Microsoft Access
- Creating a Form using the Form Wizard
- Changing the Size of a Form
- Changing the View of a Form
- Moving Through the Records
- Adding a New Field
- Changing the Name of a Field
- Editing the Field Data in the Form
- Deleting a Record from the Form
- Closing the Form
- Renaming the Form and Quitting Microsoft Access

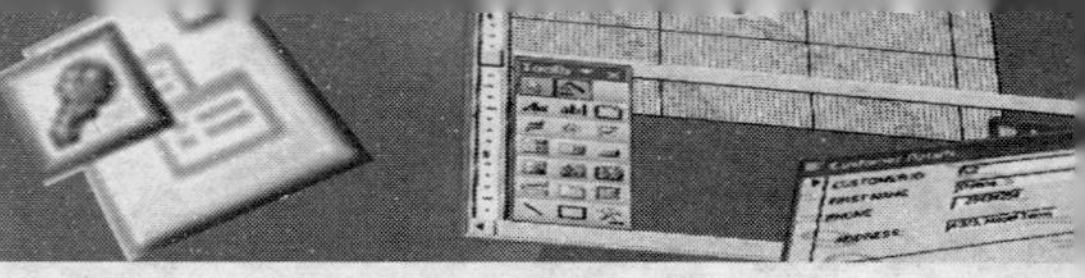

In this chapter, you will learn about **Forms**. Forms provide the most flexible way of viewing and entering data. Even though Forms do not store information, they provide a convenient way to access the information stored in one or more tables. Forms only allow you to view very few records at a time but display all the fields of those records. Tables also let you view records but they are not as flexible as Forms. In Tables, you can see only a limited number of fields at a time. To see the rest of the fields, you need to use the scroll buttons.

Opening Database in Microsoft Access

By using the Form tool, you can view, enter or modify the information stored in one or more tables in a database. It is a convenient way to access information stored in various tables of a database. Each form has a number of controls, and each control accesses one field in a table. Let us now create a form for our **Address Details** table present in **Address Database.**

To create forms easily and quickly, Microsoft Access provides you with a very useful, unique feature **Form Wizards.** This feature asks you a series of questions and based on your answers it automatically creates a Form as per your requirement.

Now, let us first open Microsoft Access, and then proceed to create a form in the following way.

1. *Switch* on your computer. Within a few seconds, Windows XP **Desktop** gets displayed.
2. *Move* the mouse-pointer over the **Start** button (start) on the **Taskbar**, and *click* the left mouse-button. Immediately, a push-up menu appears on the screen.
3. Next, *move* the mouse-pointer and *place* it over the **All Programs** option. Immediately, a second menu appears on the screen.
4. Inside the second menu, *move* the mouse-pointer and *place* it over the **Microsoft Office** option. A third menu appears.
5. Inside the third menu, *move* the mouse-pointer over the **Microsoft Office Access 2003** option and *click* the left mouse-button.
6. Immediately, a **Microsoft Access** window appears on the right side of the window you can see the **Getting Started** Task pane containing various options (Fig.AC-4.1).
7. Inside the **Getting Started** Task pane, *move* the mouse-pointer over the **Open** option and *click* the left mouse-button (Fig.AC-4.1).

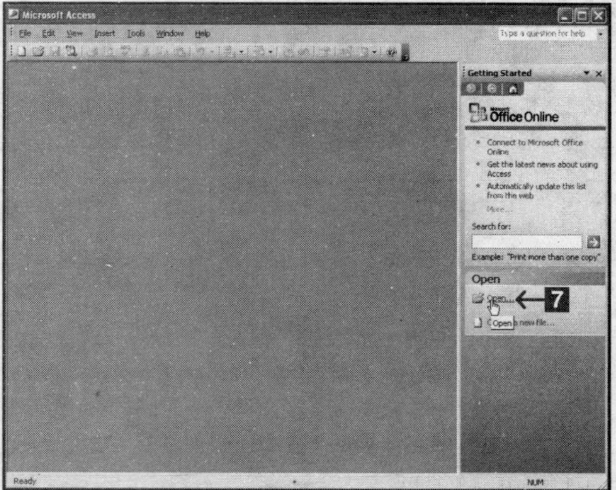

Fig. AC-4.1

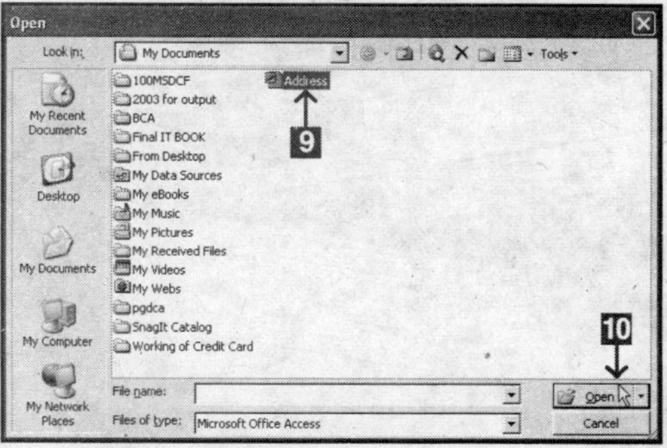

Fig. AC-4.2

8. Instantly, the **Open** dialog box appears on the screen displaying the contents of **My Documents** folder, which is also the same folder where **Address** database was saved earlier (Fig.AC-4.2).
9. *Move* the mouse-pointer over the **Address** database and *click* the left mouse-button just once. The database name gets highlighted (Fig.AC-4.2).
10. *Click* over the **Open** button. The **Address:Database (Access 2000 file format)** box appears on the screen (Fig.AC-4.2).

Creating a Form using the Form Wizard

Once the database opens up, it is time to *decide* on the number of fields to be included in the form which you are going to create. For our Form, let us choose three fields from the **Address Details** table which are **C_ID, FIRST NAME** and **PHONE.** After making decision over the number of fields, proceed as follows.

1. *Move* the mouse-pointer inside the **Address : Database** box, and *click* on the **Forms** tab (Fig. AC-4.3).
2. Next, *move* the mouse-pointer over the **New** button of **Address : Database** box, and *click* the left mouse-button (Fig.AC-4.4). Immediately, a **New Form** box gets displayed on the screen (Fig.AC-4.5).

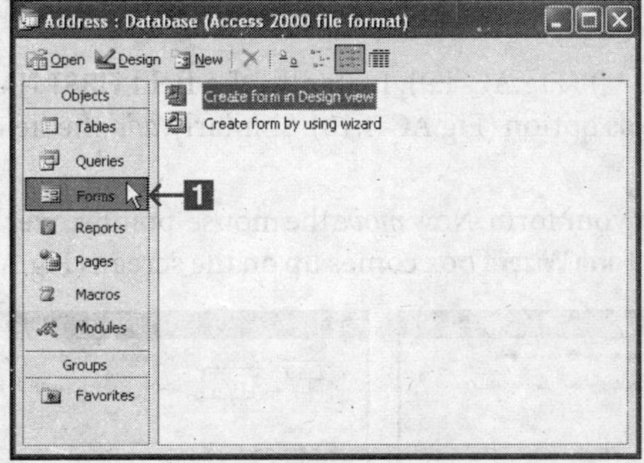

Fig. AC-4.3

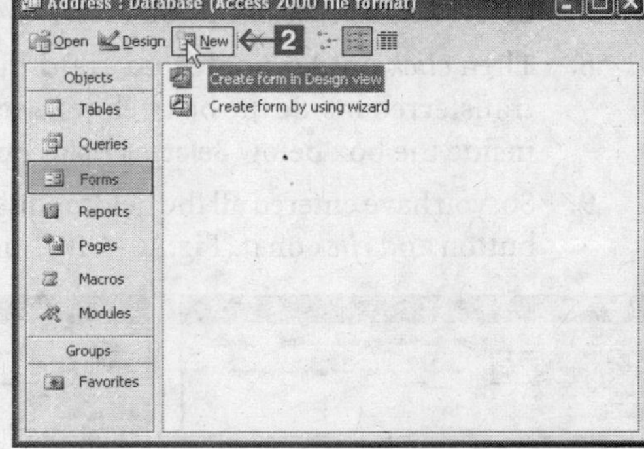

Fig. AC-4.4

3. Inside the **New Form** box, you will see a rectangular box containing some options for creating form. Among these options for creating forms *click* on the **Form Wizard** option. This option gets highlighted (Fig.AC-4.5).
4. Next, *click* on the **OK** button (Fig.AC-4.5). Immediately, a **Form Wizard** box comes up on the screen (Fig.AC-4.6).
5. Inside the **Form Wizard** box below the **Available Fields** option, you have to choose those fields which you want to display in the form. In our case, these fields are **C_ID, FIRST NAME** and **PHONE.** So *move* the mouse-pointer inside the box below the **Available Fields** option and *click* on the **C_ID** field to highlight it (Fig.AC-4.6).
6. The next step is to add the highlighted field into the form. Before doing so, it's better to get familiarized with some buttons inside the box given in Fig.AC-4.6.

   Inside the **Form Wizard** box (Fig. AC-4.6), you will see four buttons. Each of these buttons performs a certain action, as described on the next page.

>	Adds selected field to the Form	>>	Adds all fields to the Form
<	Removes selected field in the Form	<<	Removes all fields in the Form

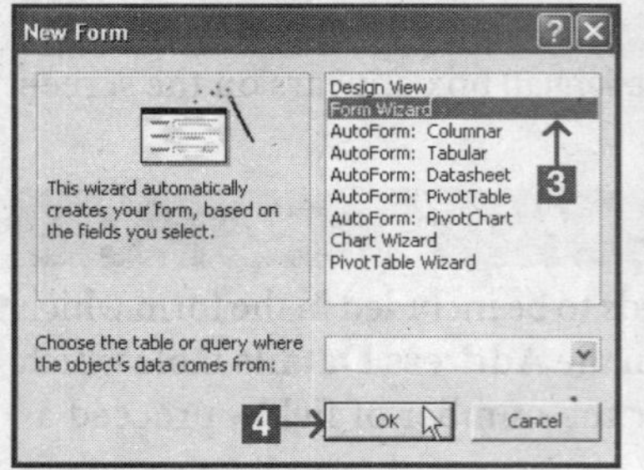

Fig. AC-4.5

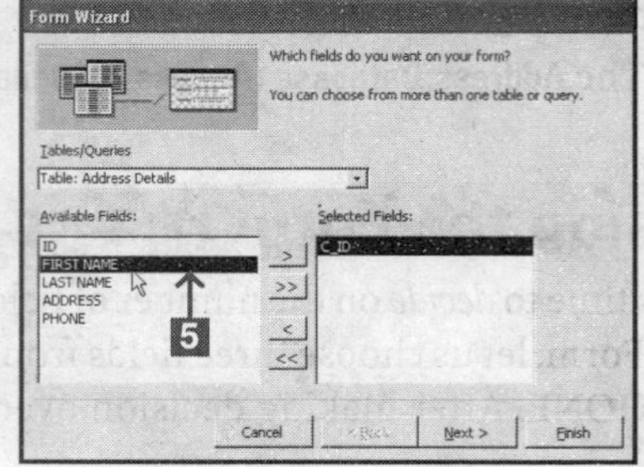

Fig. AC-4.6

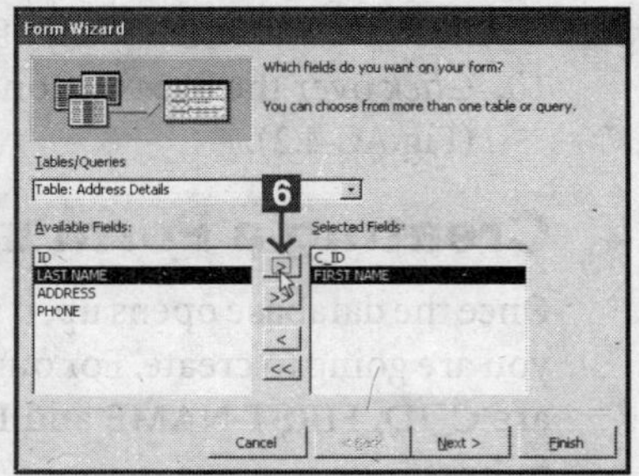

Fig. AC-4.7

Let us now enter the selected field (i.e. the **C_ID** field highlighted in step 6) into the form. To do so, *move* the mouse-pointer over the **Add selected field** button (>) (Fig.AC-4.7) and *click* the left mouse-button on it. Immediately, the field **C_ID** moves inside the box below **Selected Fields** option (Fig.AC-4.8).

7. The next field needed in our form is **FIRST NAME.** So *click* over this field name present inside the box below **Available Fields** option (Fig. AC-4.8).
8. Then *click* on **Add selected field** button (>) (Fig.AC-4.9). Instantly, the field **FIRST NAME** gets transferred inside the box below **Selected Fields** option (Fig.AC-4.10). Similarly, *add* the field **PHONE** inside the box below **Selected Fields** option.
9. So, you have entered all the fields required for your form. Now *move* the mouse-pointer over the **Next** button and *click* on it (Fig.AC-4.10). Another **Form Wizard** box comes up on the screen (Fig.AC-4.11).

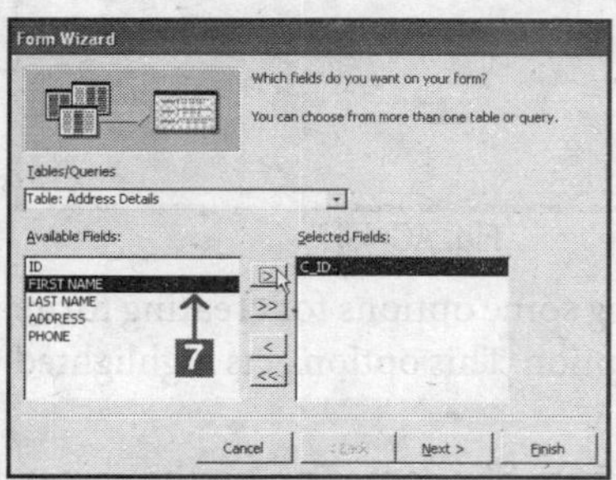

Fig. AC-4.8

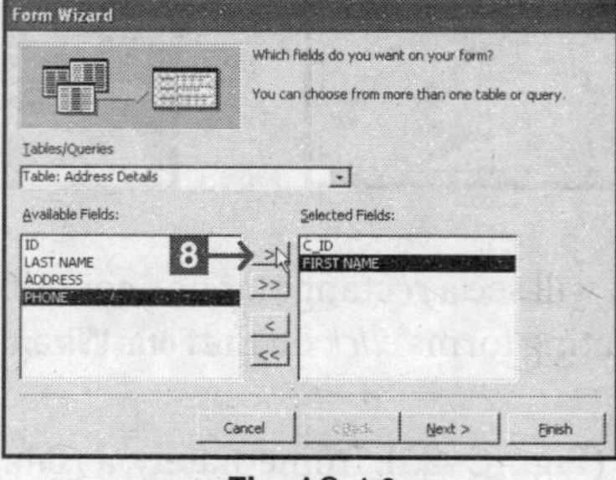

Fig. AC-4.9

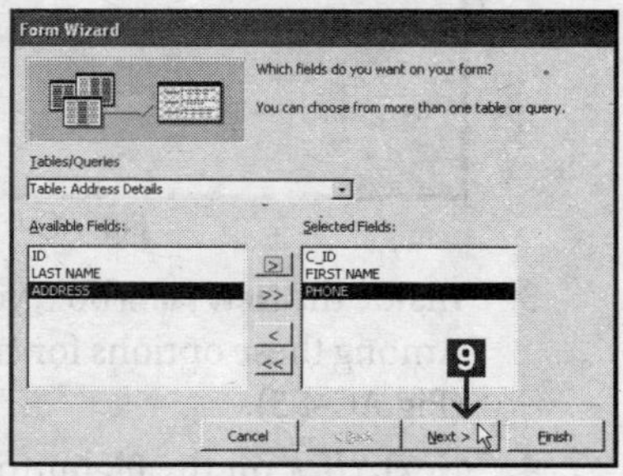

Fig. AC-4.10

10. In this box, you have to choose a **layout** for your document from the available 6 types of layouts. Let us select **Columnar** layout option. The column layout is selected by default. As a dot appears inside the round button beside this option, indicating that the option is selected.

    Now *click* on the **Next** button (Fig. AC-4.11). Immediately, another box gets displayed (Fig.AC-4.12).
11. This **Form Wizard** box asks you to choose a **background** style for your form. The available background styles are given inside a rectangular box. Let us opt for the **Standard** background style. The **Standard** style background is highlighted by default (Fig.AC-4.12). Now *click* on the **Next** button (Fig. AC-4.12).

12. Instantly, another **Form Wizard** window comes up on the screen (Fig.AC-4.13). This window asks you to enter a **title** for the form you are creating. You will notice that the words **Address Details** appear highlighted in Fig.AC-4.13.

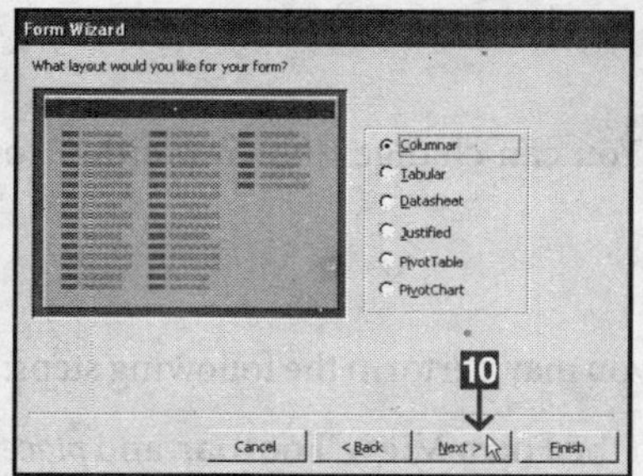

Fig. AC-4.11

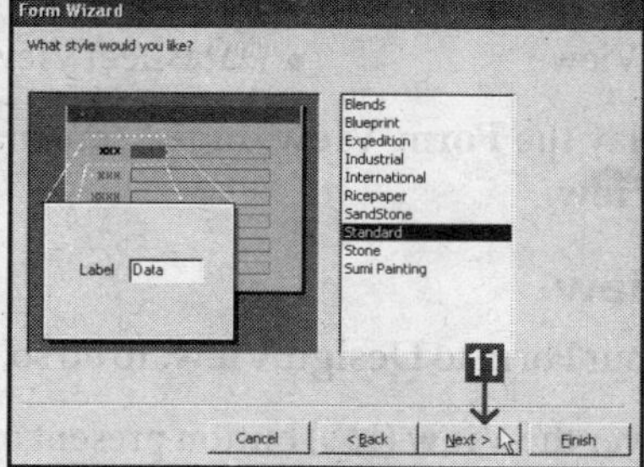

Fig. AC-4.12

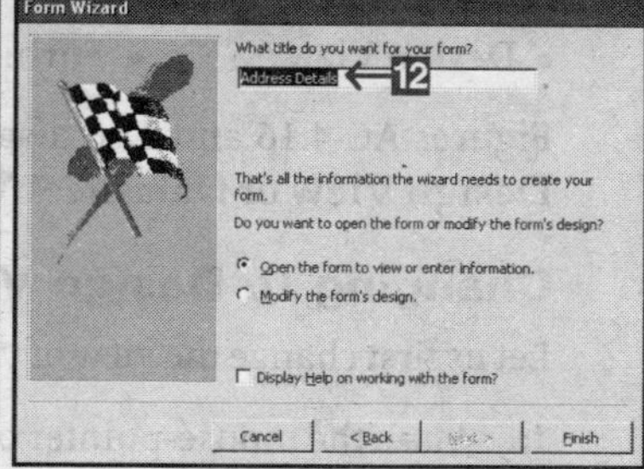

Fig. AC-4.13

13. *Type* in any name, say **Customer Details** (Fig.AC-4.14) for your form.
14. Finally, *click* on the **Finish** button (Fig.AC-4.15). Immediately, your form gets created (Fig.AC-4.16) with its **Title bar** displaying the name you have given to it.

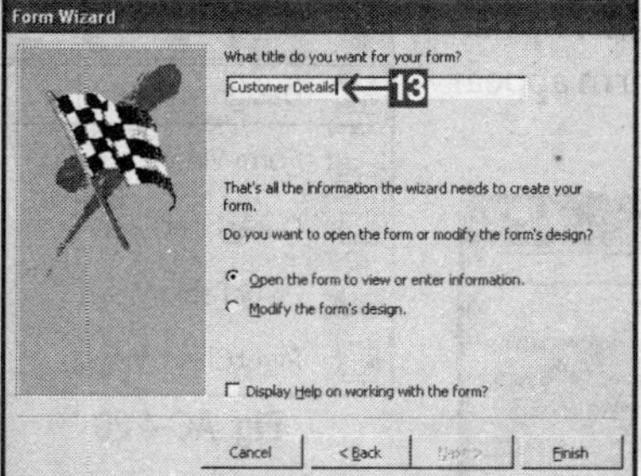

Fig. AC-4.14

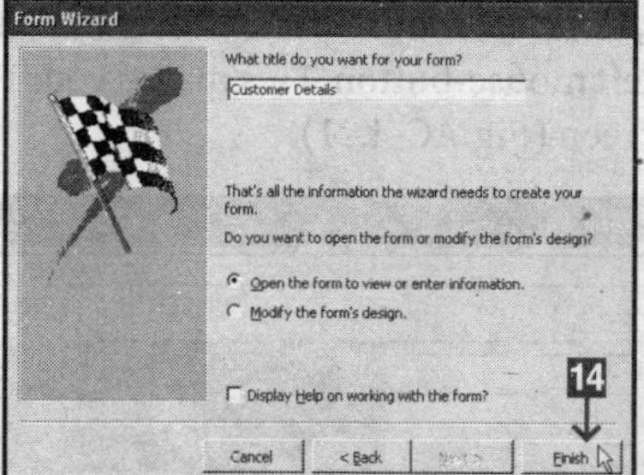

Fig. AC-4.15

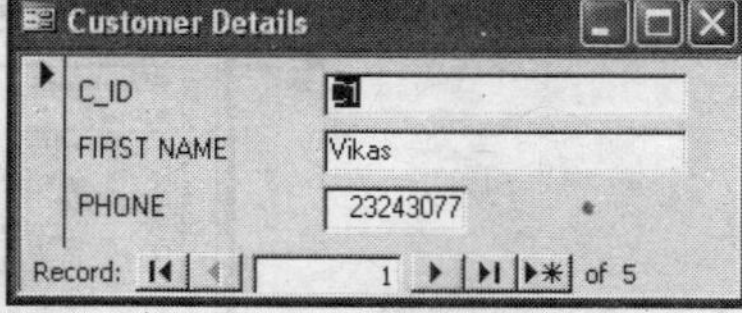

Fig. AC-4.16

Changing the Size of a Form

Microsoft Access offers you the facility to increase or decrease the size of your form as per your requirement. Using this facility, let us now increase the size of the form displayed in Fig.AC-4.16. To do so, you may undertake the following steps:

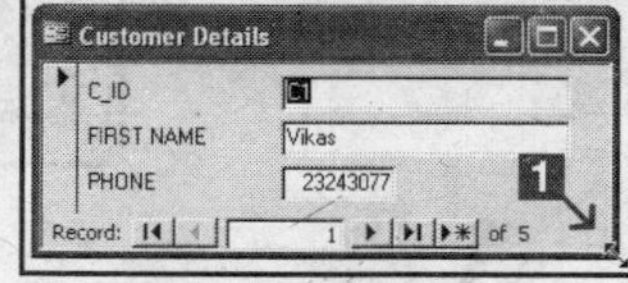

Fig. AC-4.17

1. *Move* the mouse-pointer to the right edge at the bottom of the newly created Form (Fig.AC-4.17). The mouse-pointer then changes to a diagonal two-headed arrow(↘).
2. Now *press* the left mouse-button and keeping it *pressed*, *drag* the mouse downwards.
3. *Release* the left mouse-button when the desired size is achieved. The resized form appears like Fig.AC-4.18.

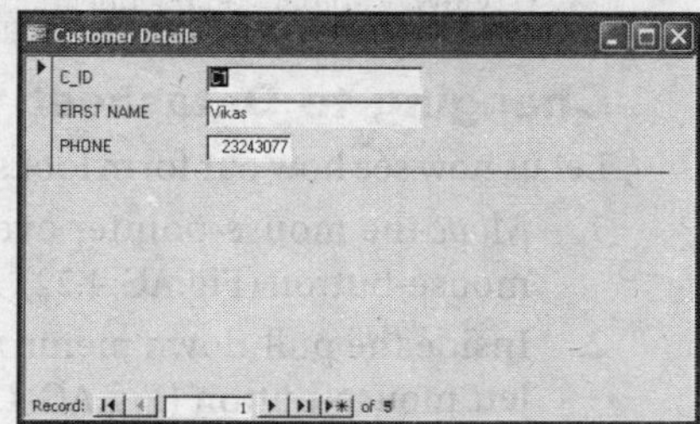

Fig. AC-4.18

Changing the View of a Form

You can also very easily change the view of your forms. For this purpose, Microsoft Access offers three view options. These are:

- Design View
- Form View
- Datasheet View

Figures AC-4.16 and 4.18 display the **Form View** on the screen. You can change this view either to **Design View** or **Datasheet View.**

Changing to Design View

Let us first change the view of your Form to **Design View.** To do so, you may perform the following steps:

1. *Move* the mouse-pointer over the **View** ( ) button present on the **Form View Toolbar,** and *place it* over its down-arrow button (▾) and *click* the left mouse-button. Immediately, a pull-down menu gets displayed (Fig.AC-4.19).

Fig. AC-4.19

2. Inside the pull-down menu, *move* the mouse-pointer over **Design View** option (Fig.AC-4.20), and *click* the left mouse-button. This makes your Form appear in **Design View** on the screen (Fig.AC-4.21).

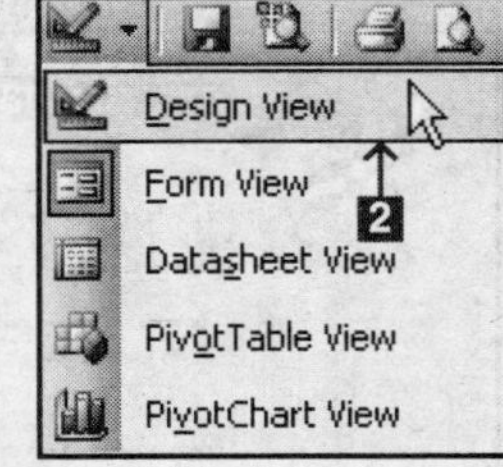

Fig. AC-4.20

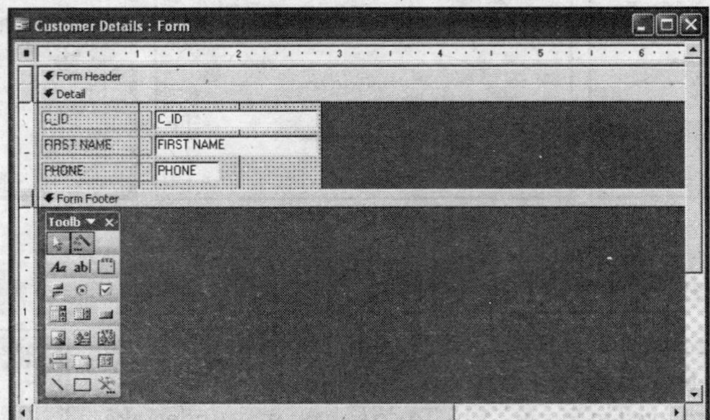

Fig. AC-4.21

Depending upon the form view you are working upon, the appearance of the View button of Form View Toolbar keeps on changing.

Changing to Datasheet View

Let us now see how our form looks in **Datasheet View.** To do so, you may undertake the following steps:

1. *Move* the mouse-pointer over the down arrow button (▾) of **View** button ( ) and *click* the left mouse-button (Fig.AC-4.22). Immediately, a pull-down menu appears.
2. Inside the pull-down menu, *move* the mouse-pointer over the **Datasheet View** option and *click* the left mouse-button (Fig.AC-4.22). Your Form now appears in the **Datasheet View** on the screen (Fig.AC-4.23).

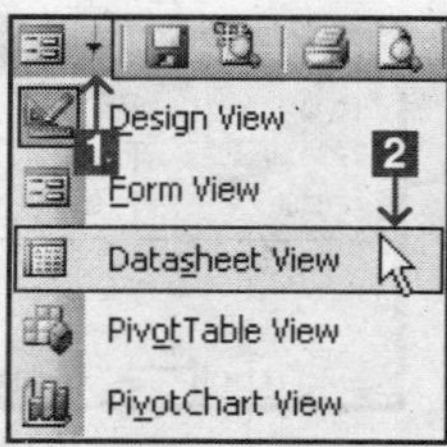

Fig. AC-4.22

Fig. AC-4.23

Changing to Form View

Let us now get back to the original view, i.e. the screen Fig. AC-4.18. To do so, you may undertake the following steps:

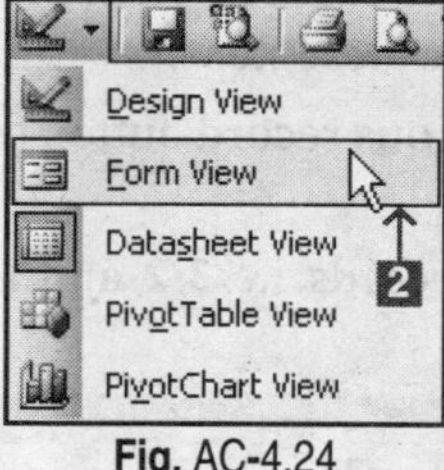

Fig. AC-4.24

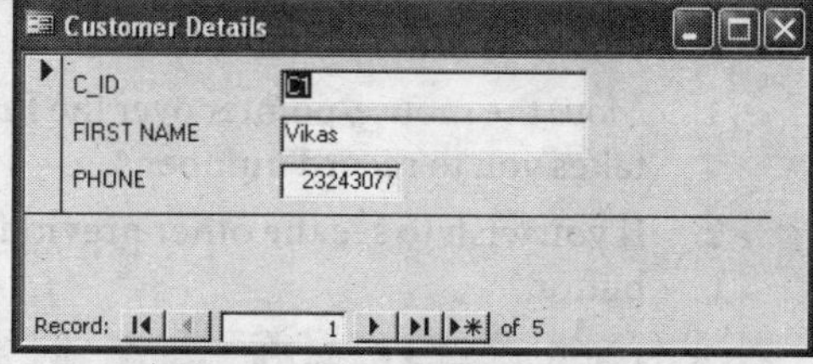

Fig. AC-4.25

1. *Perform* step 1 of the topic **Changing to Datasheet View.**
2. Inside the pull-down menu, *click* on the **Form View** option (Fig.AC-4.24). This will make the **Form View** appear on the screen (Fig.AC-4.25).

Moving Through the Records

You must have noticed that the form you have created displays only one record at a time, i.e. initially the first record is displayed. To view rest of the records, you will have to scroll through them. Another easy method of viewing a desired record in a Form is through the navigation buttons. These are five buttons you will find at the bottom of your **Form View**. By clicking on these buttons you can move to the desired record. The buttons along with their functions are shown in Fig.AC-4.26.

Fig. AC-4.26

Displaying the Next Record

At present, i.e. in Fig.AC-4.25, your form is displaying the first record. To display the next record, i.e. the second record, you may undertake the following steps:

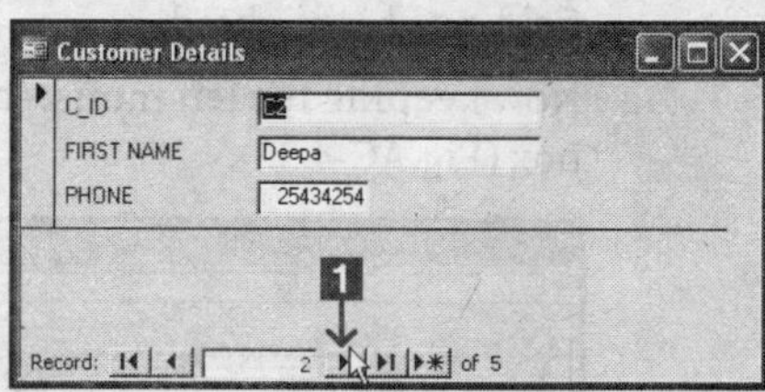

Fig. AC-4.27

1. *Move* the mouse-pointer over the **Next record** button (▶) and *click* the left mouse-button on it. This brings the second record on the screen (Fig.AC-4.27).
2. Now to see other records, *keep clicking* on the **Next record** button. This would bring on the screen all the records one by one.

Moving to the First Record

If you are present in the last record and wish to display the first record directly then

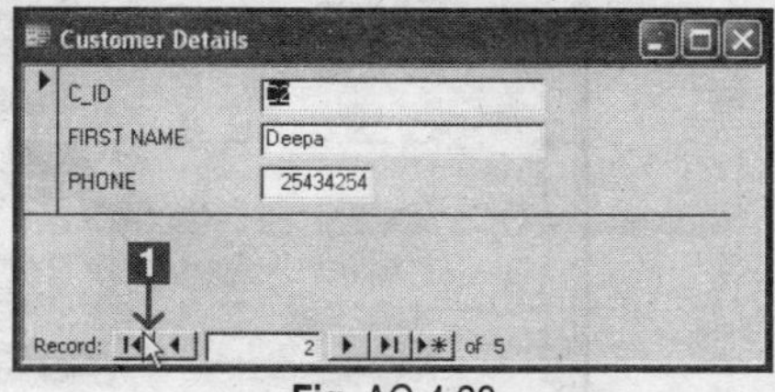

Fig. AC-4.28

1. *Move* the mouse-pointer over the **First record** button (|◀) and *click* the left mouse-button on it. This action will display the first record (Fig.AC-4.28).

Moving to the Last Record

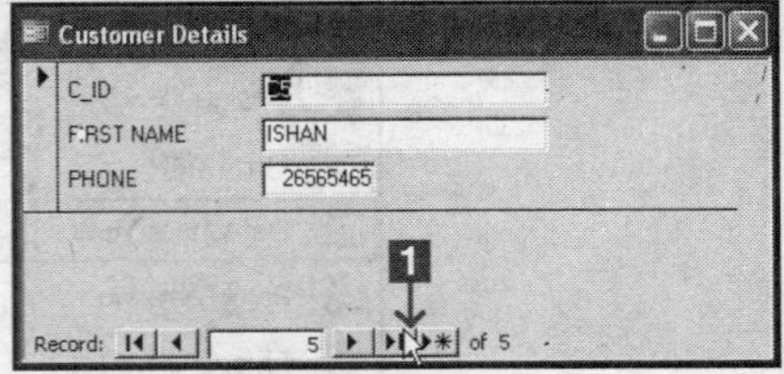

Fig. AC-4.29

If you are at present on the first record (Fig. AC-4.28), then to move to the **Last record** directly.

1. *Move* the mouse-pointer over the **Last record** button (▶|) and *click* the left mouse-button. Instantly, the last record appears on the screen (Fig.AC-4.29).

Moving to the Previous Record

Figure AC-4.29 displays the last record, in our case record number 5. If you wish to display the previous record, i.e. record number 4, then undertake these steps.

1. *Move* the mouse-pointer over the **Previous record** button (◀) and *click* the left mouse-button. This takes you to record number **4.**
2. If you wish to see the other previous records, i.e. **3, 2,** and **1**, keep *clicking* on the **Previous record** button.

Adding a New Field

Suppose you wish to add a new field in your form, say the field Address. To do so, first, you have to bring the **Design View** on the screen and then proceed in the following way.

1. Repeat steps 1 to 2 of section **Changing to Design View.**
2. By default, a small box displaying all fields of Address Details table should appear inside the form's Design View window. In case it does not appear then *move* the mouse-pointer over the **Field list** button (▤) and *click* the left mouse-button (Fig.AC-4.30). Immediately, a box with a list of fields of **Address Details** table appears on the screen (Fig.AC-4.31).

Fig. AC-4.30

3. *Move* the mouse-pointer over the **ADDRESS** field (Fig.AC-4.31) and *press* the left mouse-button. The field gets highlighted.
4. Now keeping the left mouse-button *pressed*, *drag* the **ADDRESS** field inside the **Customer Details : Form** box (Fig.AC-4.32).

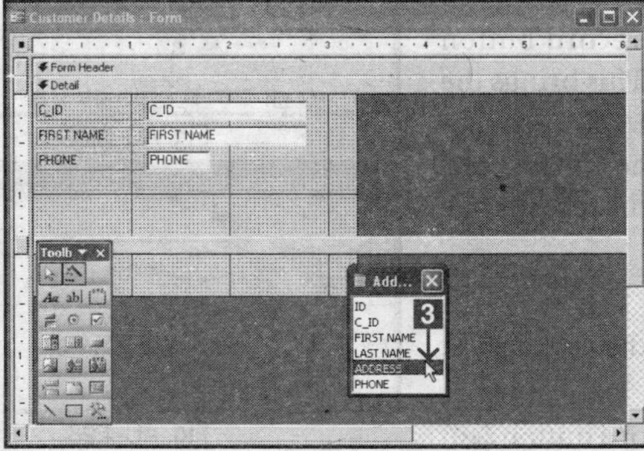

Fig. AC-4.31

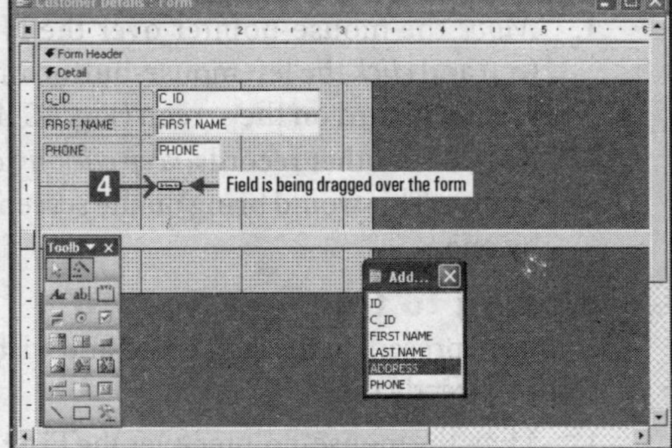

Fig. AC-4.32

5. When you reach the desired place in the **Customer Details : Form**, *release* the mouse-button (Fig. AC-4.33). Then *click* the left mouse-button anywhere in the form to remove the highlight from the field.
6. Finally, *close* the box containing the fields of **Address Details** table by *clicking* on the **Close** button (☒) of its **Title bar** (Fig.AC-4.33).

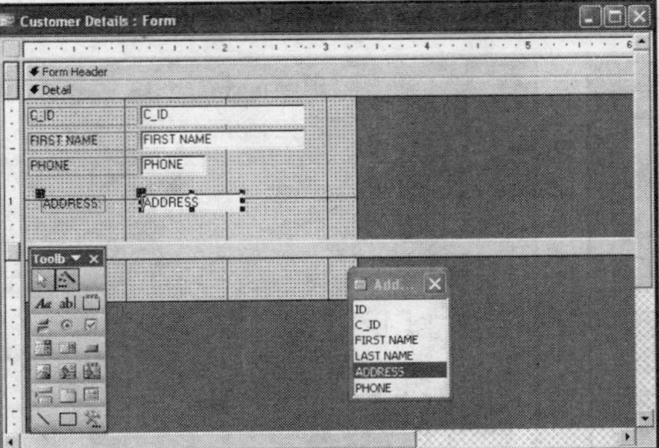

Fig. AC-4.33

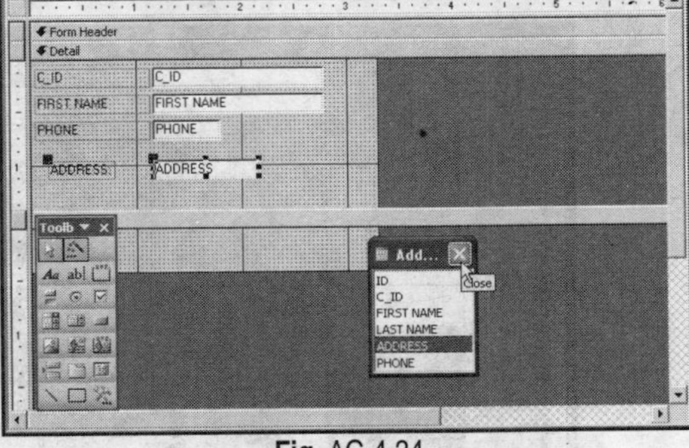

Fig. AC-4.34

Sometimes while positioning the Address field, you may release the left mouse-button before placing it properly at the desired place. Then the Address field does not get positioned at the desired place. It may get displayed at the corner. To correct the new field placement, you may undertake the following steps.

1. Place the mouse-pointer on the field name Address and press the left mouse-button. Immediately, a hand-like symbol appears at a particular point on the field name (Fig.AC-4.35).
2. Keeping the left mouse-button pressed, drag the hand-like symbol to the place where you want to set the Address field and then, release the left mouse-button.
3. Click anywhere else inside the form to remove the highlight from the field name.

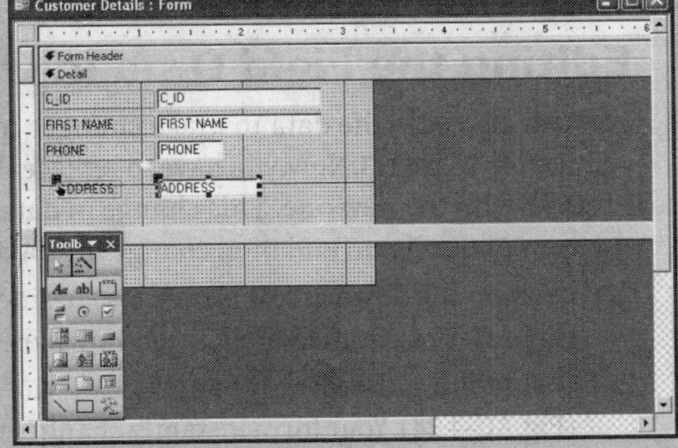

Fig. AC-4.35

Changing the Name of a Field

In the form displayed in Fig.AC-4.33, some field names are shown abbreviated. For example, the field name C_ID. To make the Form more user-friendly, it is better if you could write the full name of this field. So let us change the field name C_ID to **CUSTOMER ID**. To do so, you may follow the steps given below.

1. First of all, you have to highlight the first field name. To do so, *move* the mouse-pointer over the field name **C_ID** (Fig.AC-4.36) and *click* the

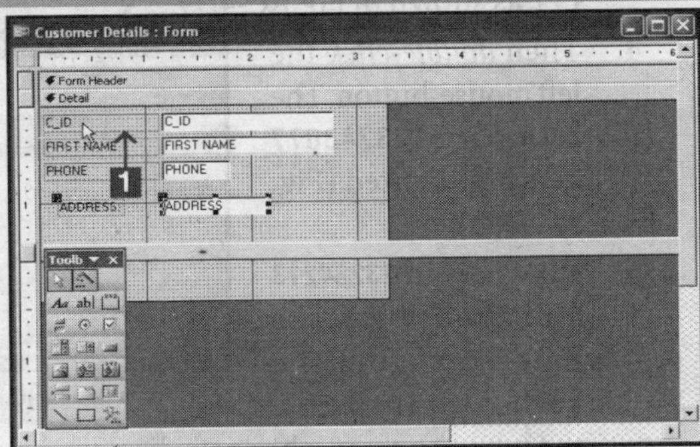

Fig. AC-4.36

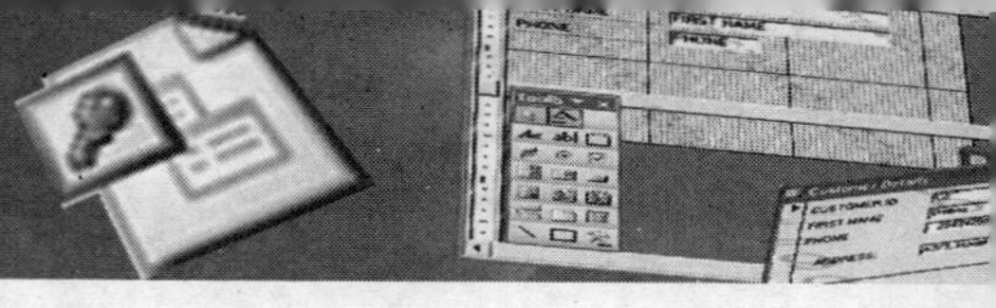

left mouse-button. Immediately, the first field name gets lighted up, and the mouse-pointer changes to **cursor** (I).

2. Now *click* again on the field name **C_ID**. The field name gets highlighted (Fig.AC-4.37).
3. *Type* the name **CUSTOMER ID** in capital letters (Fig.AC-4.38).
4. Next, *click* anywhere else on the screen. You will now clearly see the field name **CUSTOMER ID** (Fig.AC-4.38).

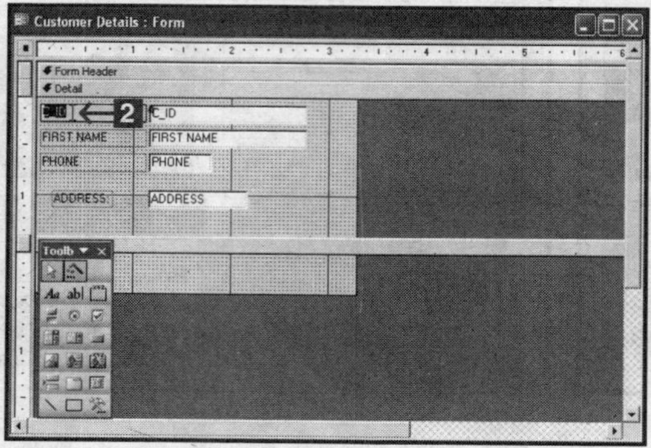

Fig. AC-4.37

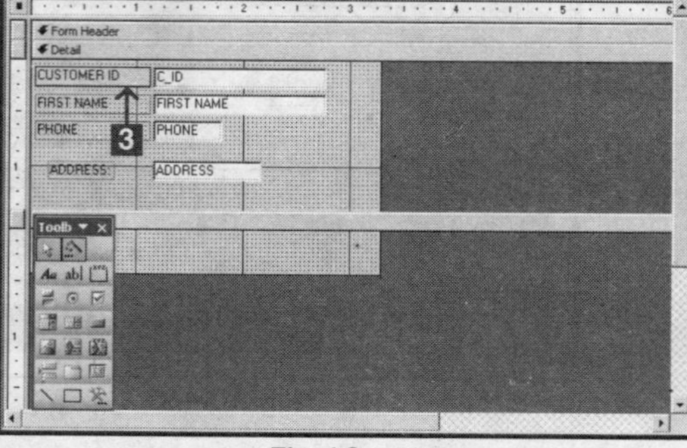

Fig. AC-4.38

Editing the Field Data in the Form

You can also edit, the data to make changes in a form. Suppose, the phone number of **Vikas** has been changed to **23284213**. Now, you have to replace the old phone number of **Vikas** given beside the field name **PHONE** with the new one. This change in data is possible only in the **Form View.** So let us first change the view of our Form and then change the data. To do so, you may undertake the following steps.

1. *Click* on the down arrow button (▼) beside the **View** button (Fig.AC-4.24). Immediately, a pull-down menu gets displayed.
2. Inside the pull-down menu, *click* on the **Form View** option (Fig.AC-4.24). Your form instantly changes to the **Form View** (Fig.AC-4.39). The form by default shows you the first record.
3. You must have noticed that the phone number of the first record is **23243077**. To change this number, *move* the mouse-pointer over it. Immediately, the mouse-pointer changes into (I), as shown in Fig.AC-4.39.

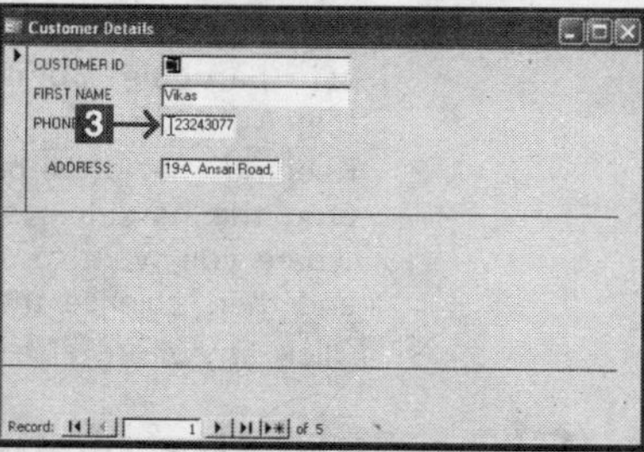

Fig. AC-4.39

4. Then *double-click* the left mouse-button. The number **23243077** gets highlighted (Fig. AC-4.40).
5. Now *type* in **23284213** and then *press* the **Enter** key from the keyboard. Instantly, the new phone number gets displayed at the highlighted point (Fig.AC-4.41).

Fig. AC-4.40

Fig. AC-4.41

Deleting a Record from the Form

A record you no longer need can be deleted from your form. Suppose, the customer **Deepa** has stopped purchasing goods from you and she is no longer your customer. In such a case, it is better to remove her name from the customers list. To delete the details of **Deepa**, i.e. the second record, you first have to display it and then proceed in the following way.

1. In our case, Fig.AC-4.41 displays the first record. So, to display **Deepa's** record, *move* the mouse-pointer over the **Next record** button (▶) and *click* on it once. Immediately, the information about **Deepa** gets displayed before you (Fig.AC-4.42).
2. Now *move* the mouse-pointer over the **Edit** option of the Menu bar and *click* over it. A pull-down menu appears (Fig. AC-4.43).
3. Inside the pull-down menu, *move* the mouse-point over the **Delete Record** option and *click* over it (Fig.AC-4.43).
4. *Move* the mouse-pointer on the **Yes** option of this warning box (Fig.AC-4.44) and *click* the left mouse-button. The record now gets deleted and the next record appears in the form (Fig.AC-4.45).

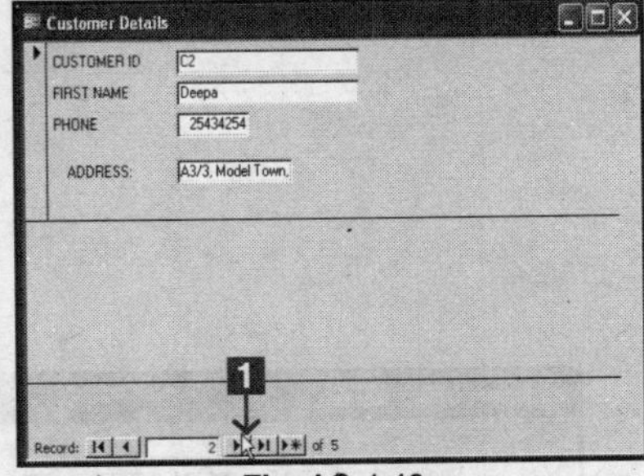

Fig. AC-4.42

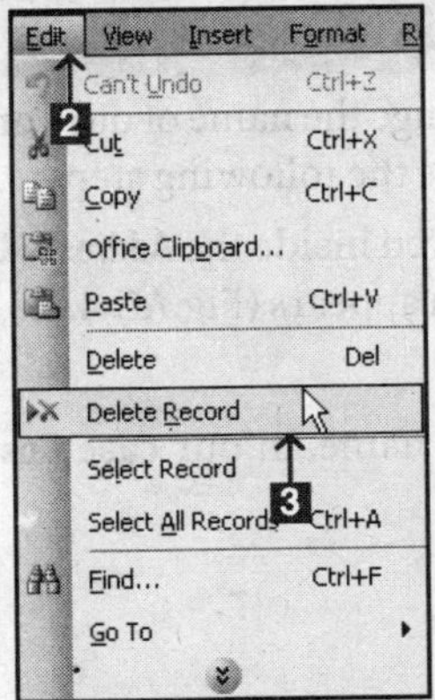

Fig. AC-4.43

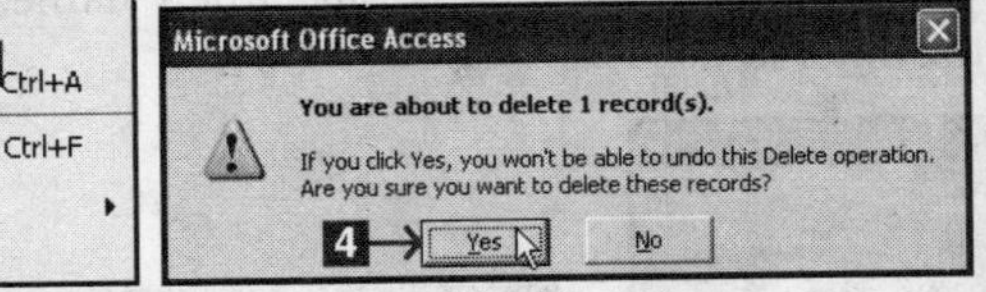

Fig. AC-4.44

Customer Details
CUSTOMER ID
FIRST NAME Mohan
PHONE 27899989
ADDRESS: A-172, Vikas Puri, N
Record: 2 of 4

Fig. AC-4.45

Closing the Form

So, you have learnt the method of creating forms. And now you know how to work in them. Let us now close our form **Customer Details**. To do so, you may undertake the following steps:

1. *Click* over the **File** Menu bar option. Immediately, a pull-down menu gets displayed (Fig.AC-4.46).
2. Inside the pull-down menu, *click* over the **Close** option (Fig.AC-4.46). Immediately, a message box (Fig.AC-4.47) gets displayed asking whether you want to save the changes made to the form.

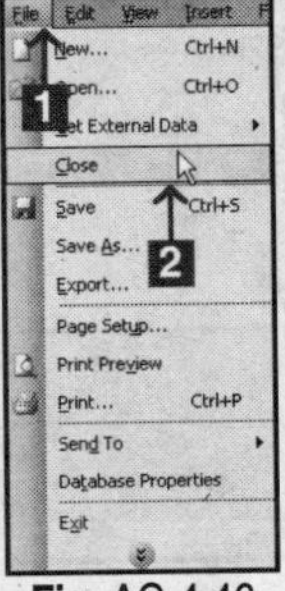

Fig. AC-4.46

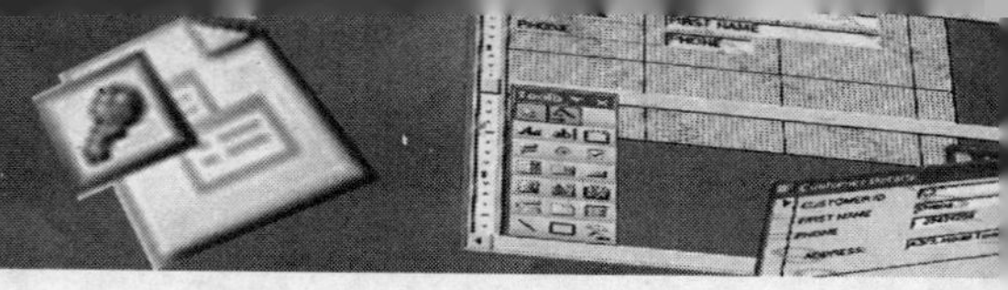

3. *Click* on the **Yes** option to save the changes (Fig.AC-4.47). Immediately, the Form disappears from the screen and the **Address : Database** box gets displayed (Fig.AC-4.48).

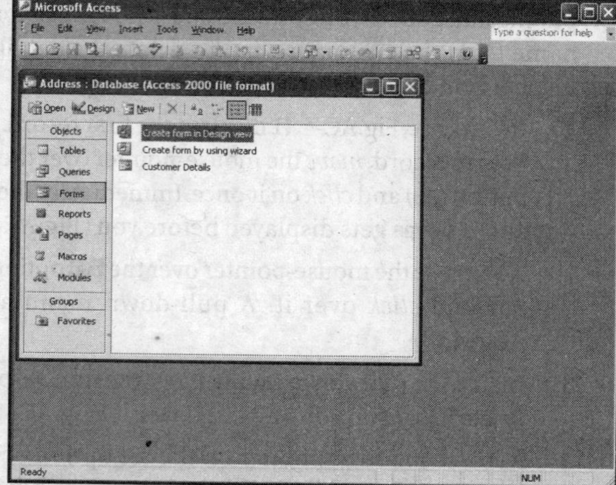

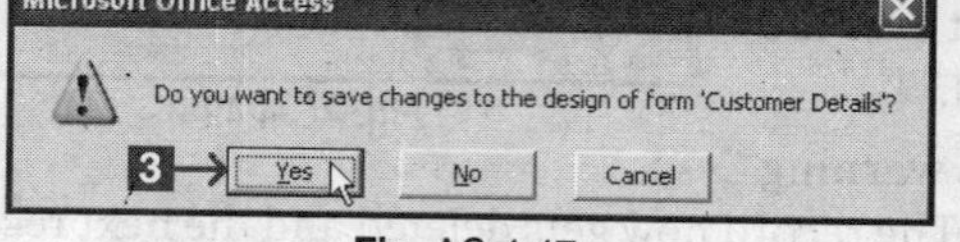

Fig. AC-4.47

Fig. AC-4.48

Renaming the Form and Quitting Microsoft Access

You can change the name of your Form to suit your needs. Let us now change the name of our Form from **CUSTOMER DETAILS** to **CUST DETAILS**. To do so, you may undertake the following steps:

1. *Move* the mouse-pointer over the name **Customer Details form** displayed inside the **Address : Database** box and *click* the right mouse-button. Immediately, a shortcut menu appears (Fig.AC-4.49).
2. Inside the shortcut menu, *click* on the **Rename** option (Fig.AC-4.49).
3. Instantly, **Customer Details** gets highlighted. Then start *type* a new name, in our case **Cust Details** (Fig.AC-4.50) and then *press* the Enter key.

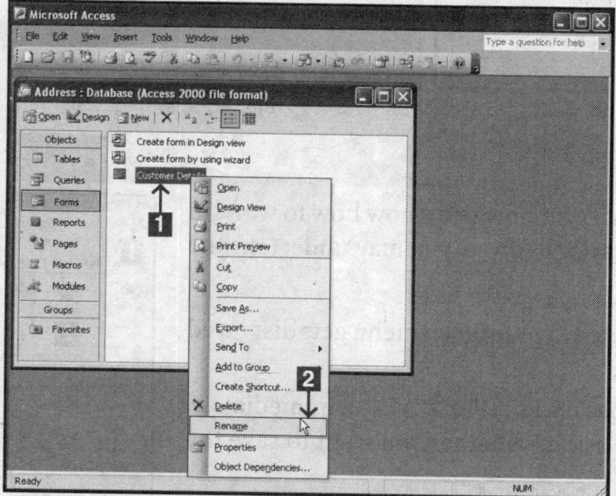

Fig. AC-4.49

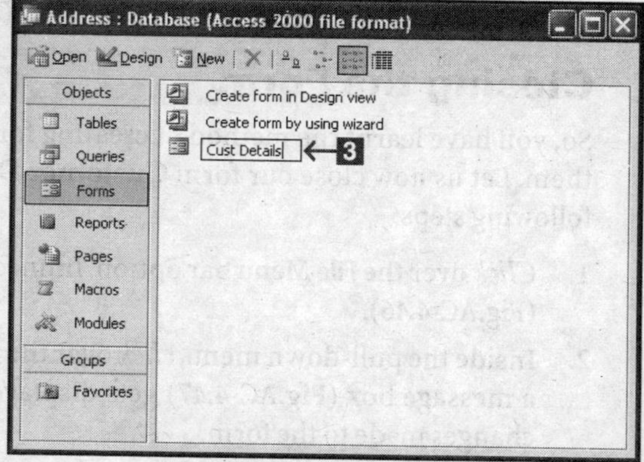

Fig. AC-4.50

4. Let us now close the **Address : Database** box. To do so, *click* on the **File** Menu bar option. Instantly, a pull-down menu gets displayed (Fig.AC-4.51).
5. Inside this pull-down menu, *click* on the **Close** option (Fig.AC-4.51). Immediately, the **Address : Database** box closes.
6. Now to quit Microsoft Access, *move* the mouse-pointer over the **Close** button (☒) present on the **Title bar**. Instantly, the Microsoft Access window closes.

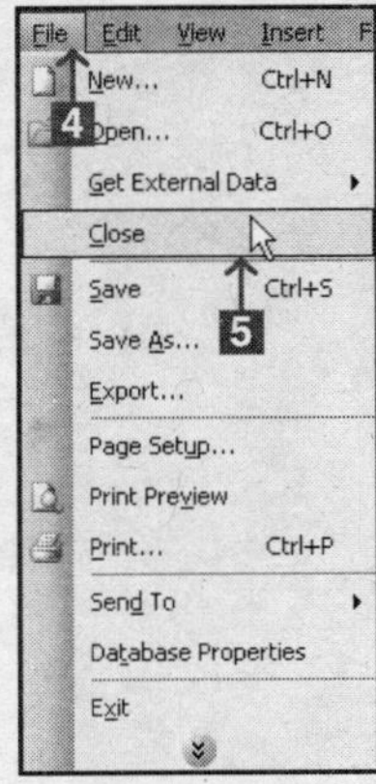

Fig. AC-4.51

Exercise

Fill in the Blanks

1. Access offers three views options. These are ________________, ____________ and ________________.
2. View button is present on the ________________.
3. To display the next record, click the ________________ button.
4. For adding a new field I the form you have to bring the _______ view on the screen.
5. There are __________ navigation buttons for moving through the records.

True/False

1. The navigation buttons are placed at the bottom of the Form View.
2. To move to the Last record directly, click the Next record button.
3. The data in a form can be edited in all the three views.
4. A record once entered in a form cannot be deleted.
5. The Previous record button is used to display the record previous to the Last record.

MICROSOFT ACCESS

Handling Queries 5

IN THIS CHAPTER

- Opening a Table in Microsoft Access
- Creating a Query on a Table
- Sorting Records
- Hiding a Field
- Unhiding a Field
- Setting Criterion
- Deleting Criterion
- Performing Calculations
- Saving a Query
- Closing the Query and Quitting Access

Queries are an essential part of any database. **Query** is a tool to extract the desired information. For retrieving the desired information from a database, queries specify a series of conditions. And, the information satisfying these conditions gets sorted out from the database. As explained in Chapter 2, database is a combination of Tables, Queries, Forms and Reports. So, queries are the medium to access selective information in tables or forms. When Microsoft Access executes a query on a table, it displays only those records which match the specified condition set out in the query.

In this chapter, you will use queries to extract information stored in one or more tables. Let us now try creating a query. Suppose you wish to know the codes (**C_ID**) and names of the customer (**FIRST NAME**), along with the name (**PRODUCT NAME**), cost (**PRICE**) and quantity (**QUANTITY**) of products purchased by them from the **Address** database. To find out such specific information, you have to create a **Query**. Before proceeding to create the desired query, let us first open Microsoft Access in the following way.

Opening a Table in Microsoft Access

1. *Switch* on your computer. Within a few seconds, Windows XP **Desktop** gets displayed.
2. *Move* the mouse-pointer over the **Start** button ( ) on the **Taskbar**, and *click* the left mouse-button. Immediately, a push-up menu appears on the screen.
3. Next, *move* the mouse-pointer and *place* it over the **All Programs** option. Immediately, a second menu appears on the screen.
4. Inside the second menu, *move* the mouse-pointer and *place* it over the **Microsoft Office** option. A third menu appears.
5. Inside the third menu, *move* the mouse-pointer over the **Microsoft Office Access 2003** option and *click* the left mouse-button.
6. Immediately, a **Microsoft Access** window appears on the right side of the window you can see the **Getting Started** Task pane containing various options (Fig.AC-5.1).
7. Inside the **Getting Started** Task pane, *move* the mouse-pointer over the **Open** option and *click* the left mouse-button (Fig.AC-5.1).
8. Instantly, the **Open** dialog box appears on the screen displaying the contents of **My Documents** folder, which is also the same folder where Address database was saved earlier (Fig.AC-5.2).
9. *Move* the mouse-pointer over the **Address** database and *click* the left mouse-button just once. The database name gets highlighted (Fig.AC-5.2).
10. Lastly, *move* the mouse-pointer over the **Open** button and *click* the left mouse-button (Fig.AC-5.2). Immediately, the Address:Database box appears (Fig.AC-5.3).

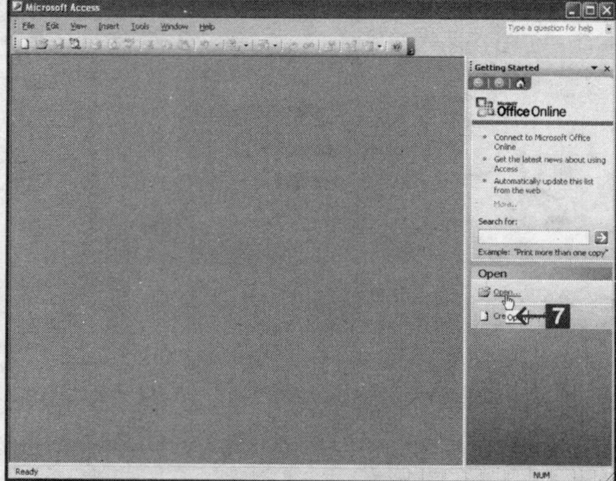

Fig. AC-5.1

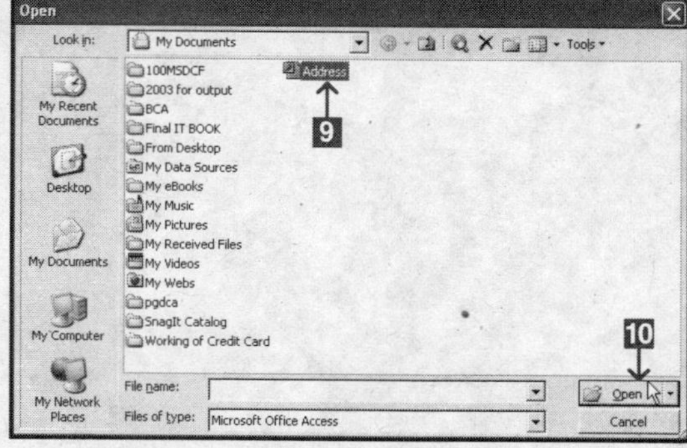

Fig. AC-5.2

Creating a Query on a Table

Let us now create a query in the Address database. As specified earlier, this query should give information about the codes **(C_ID)** and names of the customer **(FIRST NAME)**, along with the name **(PRODUCT NAME)**, cost **(PRICE)** and quantity of products **(QUANTITY)** purchased by them. For this, we will proceed along the following steps:

1. *Move* the mouse-pointer over the **Queries** tab (Fig.AC-5.3), and *click* the left mouse-button. Immediately, the **Queries** tab gets selected.
2. Then *click* on the **New** button of the **Address : Database** box (Fig.AC-5.4). Immediately, a **New Query** box opens up on the screen (Fig.AC-5.5).

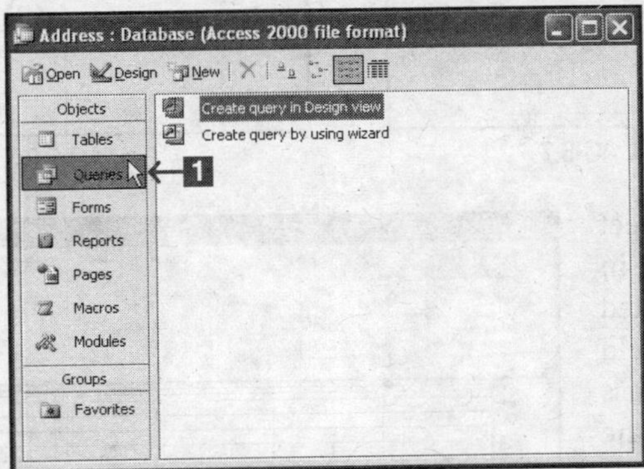

Fig. AC-5.3

Fig. AC-5.4

3. In the **New Query** box, the **Design View** is highlighted by default. If not, then *move* the mouse-pointer over this option, and *click* on it once to highlight it (Fig.AC-5.5).
4. Then *click* on the **OK** button, (Fig.AC-5.5). Immediately, a **Show Table** box appears on the screen (Fig.AC-5.6).
   You will notice that the **Show Table** box displays the names of the tables created by you in Chapter 2, i.e. **Address Details** table and **Order Details** table.

Fig. AC-5.5

5. In this box, you will have to select the tables whose fields you want to include in the Query. Since these fields are taken from the two tables of **Address : Database** i.e. **Address Details** and **Order Details,** both these tables have to be selected. The **Address Detail** table is highlighted by default (Fig.AC-5.6).
6. Now, *click* on the **Add** button (Fig.AC-5.6).
7. Now, *click* on the **Order Details** table to highlight it (Fig.AC-5.7).
8. Then *click* on the **Add** button. The **Order Details** table also gets selected (Fig.AC-5.7).

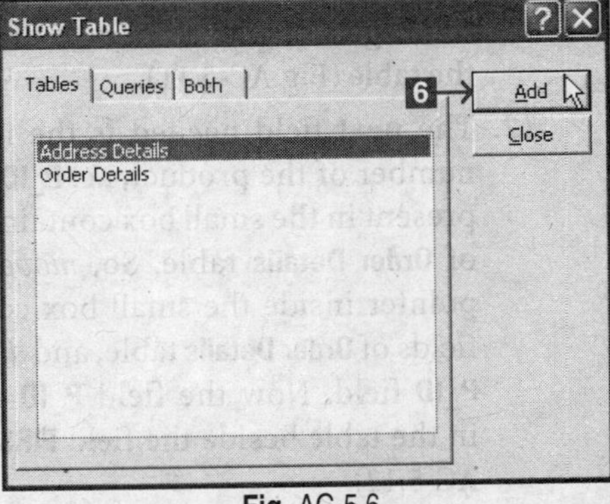

Fig. AC-5.6

9. After selecting the required tables, *click* on the **Close** button to close the **Show Table** box (Fig.AC-5.8). Now a **Query1 : Select Query** box gets displayed on the screen (Fig.AC-5.9).

Inside the **Query1 : Select Query** box, you will see two small boxes containing the fields of two tables– **Address Details** and **Order Details.** These small boxes are used for creating a query based on the fields of the two databases.

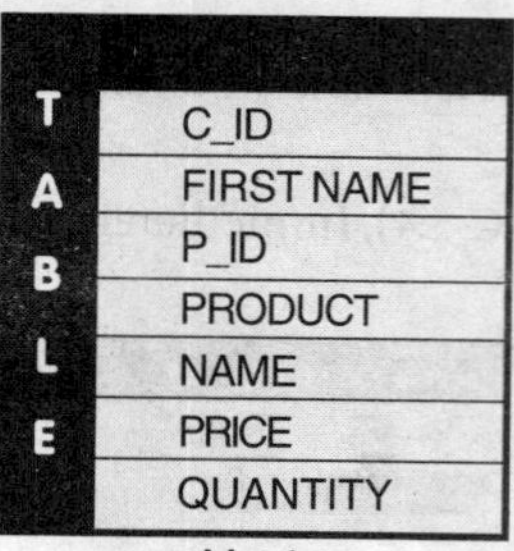

List 1

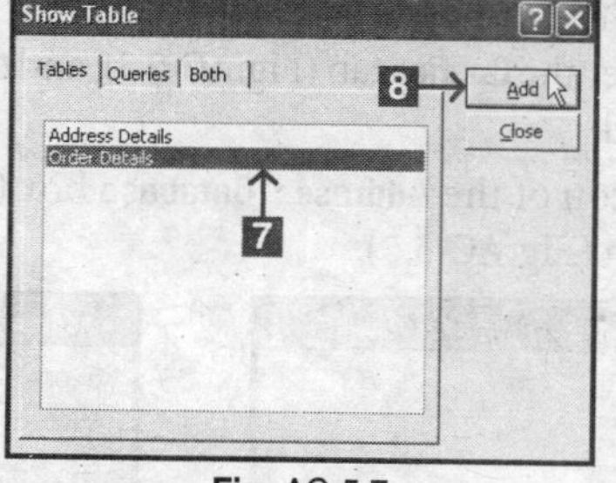

Fig. AC-5.7

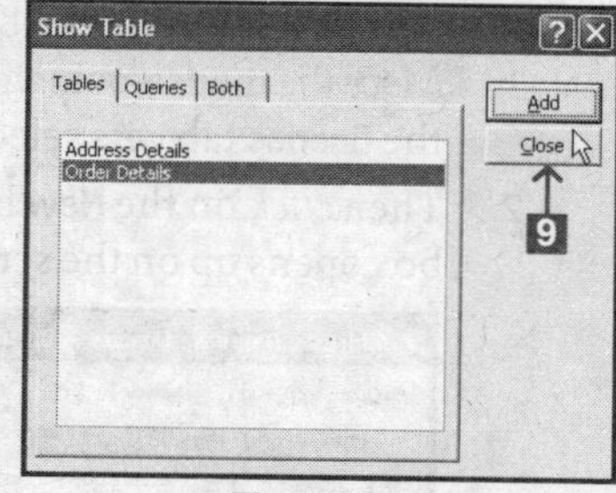

Fig. AC-5.8

10. Inside the two small boxes, you have to select only those fields which you wish to include in the **Query**. Therefore, the first field to be selected is the customer identification number field **(C_ID)**. This field is present in the **Address Details** table. So, *move* the mouse-pointer inside the small box containing the fields of **Address Details** table, and *double-click* on the **C_ID** field. You will notice that the field **C_ID** gets displayed in the table displayed at the bottom of **Query1 : Select Query** box (Fig AC-5.10).

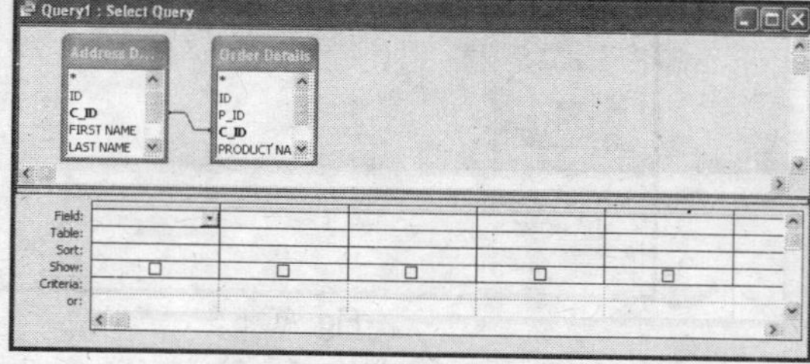

Fig. AC-5.9

11. The next field to be selected is the name of the customer, i.e. **FIRST NAME**. This field is also present in the small box containing the fields of **Address Details** table. So *move* the mouse-pointer on the field **FIRST NAME**, in the **Address Details** table (Fig.AC-5.11), and *double-click* the left mouse-button. Immediately, the field **FIRST NAME** gets displayed next to the **C_ID** field in the table (Fig.AC-5.11).

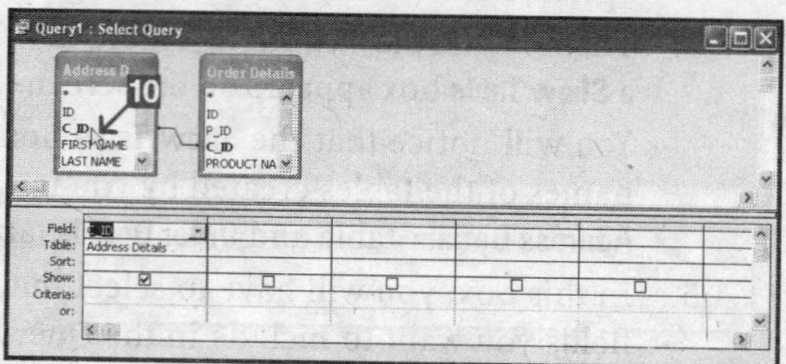

Fig. AC-5.10

12. The next field needed is the identification number of the product, i.e. **P_ID**. This field is present in the small box containing the fields of **Order Details** table. So, *move* the mouse-pointer inside the small box containing the fields of **Order Details** table, and *double-click* on **P_ID** field. Now the field **P_ID** also appears in the table beside the field **FIRST NAME** (Fig. AC-5.12).

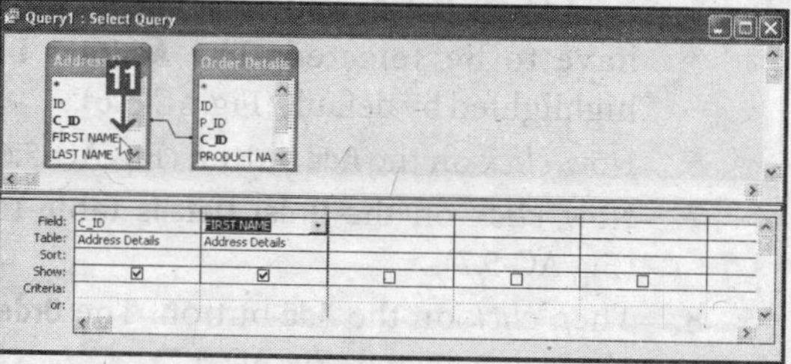

Fig. AC-5.11

13. Similarly, you can select each of the fields – **PRODUCT NAME, PRICE** and **QUANTITY** from the small box containing the fields of **Order Details** table (Fig.AC-5.10). *Double-click* on the field you want to select. Once all these fields get selected, your screen will look like Fig.AC-5.13.

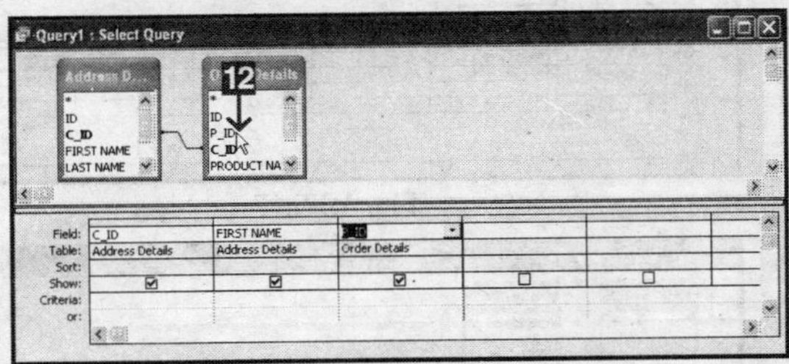

Fig. AC-5.12

Fig. AC-5.13

14. Let us perform a query on all the fields selected for your query. To do so, *move* the mouse-pointer over the **Run** button (!) present on the **Standard Toolbar** (Fig.AC-5.14) and *click* the left mouse-button.

Fig. AC-5.14

Immediately, the **Select Query** box displays all the details of customers who have purchased a product and the respective product details (Fig.AC-5.15).

Query1 : Select Query

C_ID	FIRST NAME	P_ID	PRODUCT NAM	PRICE	QUANTITY
C1	Vikas	P01	ERASER	8.00	50
C3	Mohan	P03	PEN	25.00	100
C4	Chandani	P04	PENCIL BOX	45.00	25

Record: 1 of 3

Fig. AC-5.15

So now you know how to create a query and how does it functions.

Sorting Records

After learning the procedure for creating a query, the next step for you is to arrange or sort the results of a query in a particular order so as to easily find specific information. There are two ways you can arrange or sort data. These are:

- **Sort Ascending** — It sorts the alphabets from A to Z and numbers from 1 to 9.
- **Sort Descending** — It sorts the alphabets from Z to A and numbers from 9 to 1.

Sorting Records according to a Field

Let us now arrange all the records of the result of our query in ascending order according to a field, say FIRST NAME. To do so, first you will need to display the query in Design View and then proceed.

1. *Move* the mouse-pointer over the down arrow button (▾) of the **View** button ( ) and *click* the left mouse-button on it. Instantly, a pull-down menu gets displayed (Fig.AC-5.16).

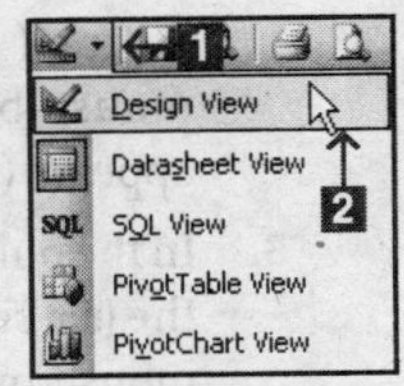

Fig. AC-5.16

2. Inside the pull-down menu, *click* on the **Design View** option. Immediately, the view of the Query changes to Design View (Fig.AC-5.17).

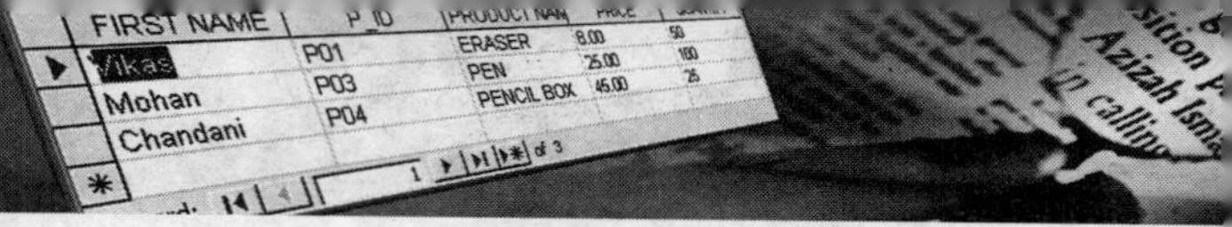

3. Now *click* the left mouse-button beside the **Sort** option (Fig.AC-5.18). Immediately, a down arrow button (▾) appears at that point.
4. *Click* on the down-arrow button (▾). Instantly, a pull-down menu appears (Fig. AC-5.19).

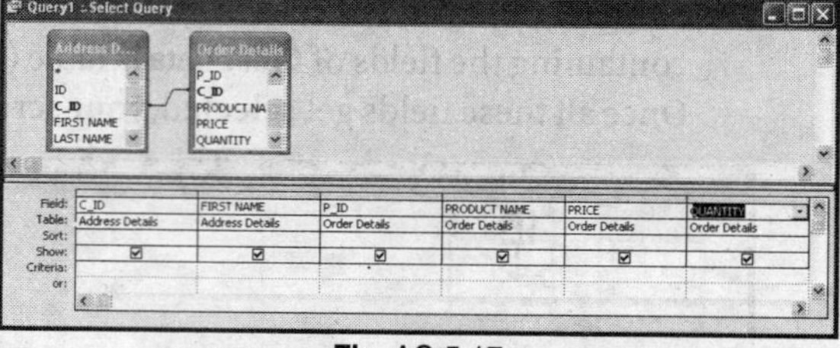

Fig. AC-5.17

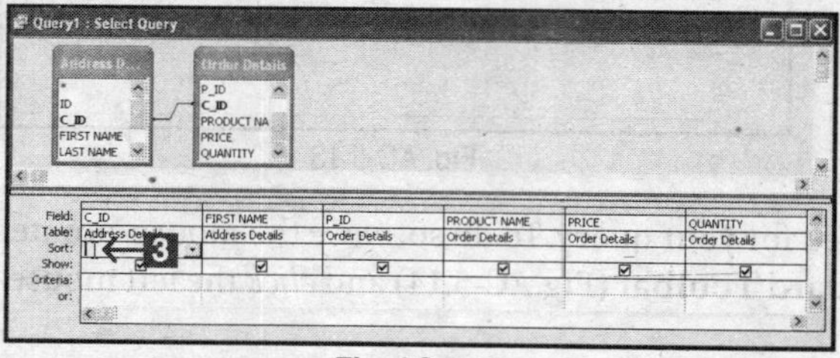

Fig. AC-5.18

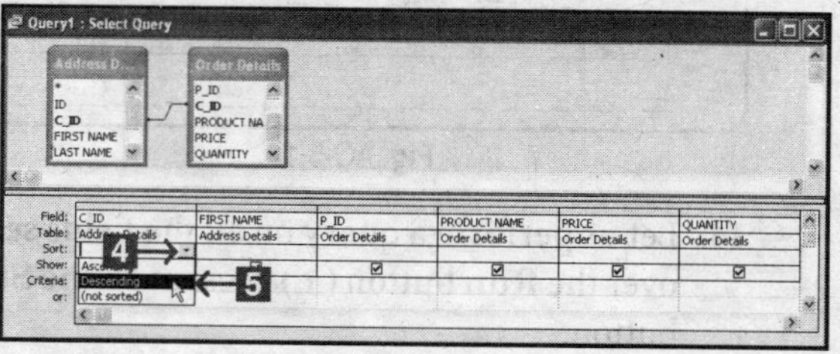

Fig. AC-5.19

5. Inside the pull-down menu, *click* on the **Ascending** option. **Ascending** option gets displayed in the column of the field **FIRST NAME** (Fig.AC-5.20).
6. Now *click* on the **Run** button (!) (Fig.AC-5.14). Immediately, the names under the field **FIRST NAME** appears in the ascending order (Fig.AC-5.21).

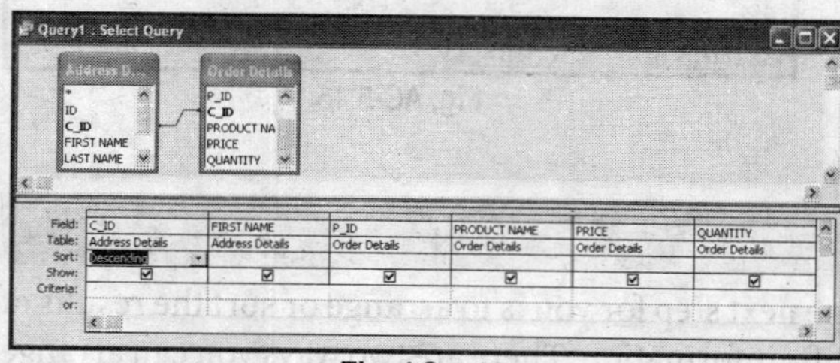

Fig. AC-5.20

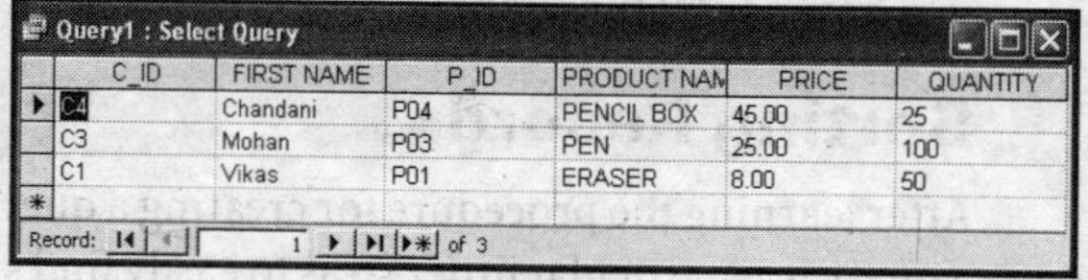

C_ID	FIRST NAME	P_ID	PRODUCT NAM	PRICE	QUANTITY
C4	Chandani	P04	PENCIL BOX	45.00	25
C3	Mohan	P03	PEN	25.00	100
C1	Vikas	P01	ERASER	8.00	50

Fig. AC-5.21

Removing Sort from a Field

You can also remove sorting from a field. Let us now remove sorting from the field **FIRST NAME**. To perform this operation also, you have to first move to Design View, and then proceed further. To do so, you may undertake the following steps:

1. Perform Steps 1 and 2 of the topic **Sorting Records according to a Field.**
2. Now, to remove the sorting of the field **FIRST NAME**, *move* the mouse-pointer on the down-arrow button (▾) beside the **Sort** option and *click* the left mouse-button. Immediately, a pull-down menu appears (Fig.AC-5.22).
3. In the pull-down menu, *move* the mouse-pointer over the **(not sorted)** option (Fig.AC-5.23) and *click* the left mouse-button.

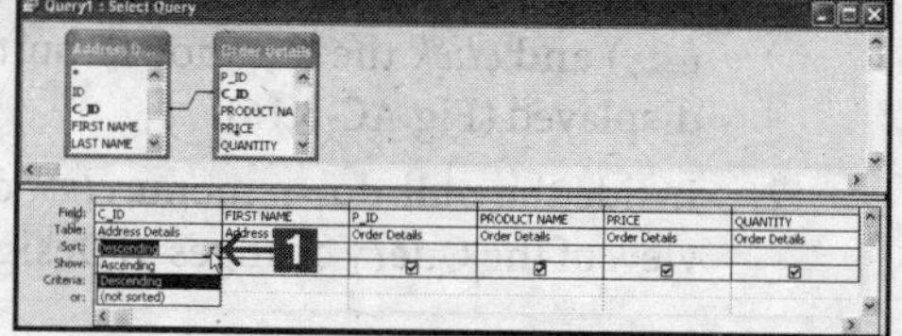

Fig. AC-5.22

4. Finally, *click* on the **Run** button (!) of the **Standard Toolbar** (Fig.AC-5.14). Now, all the records of the field **FIRST NAME** will once again appear in the previous order (Fig.AC-5.15).

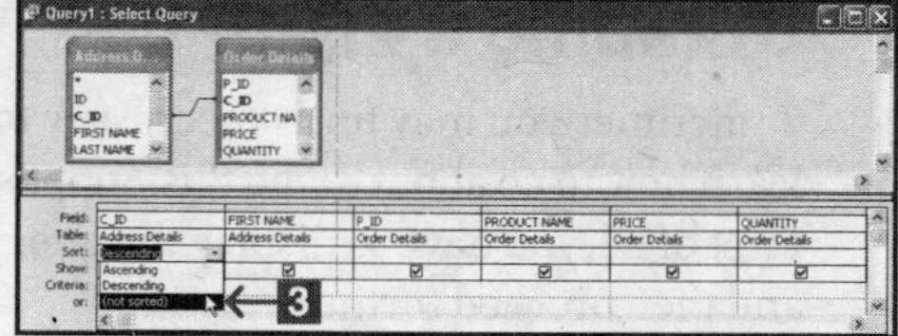

Fig. AC-5.23

Hiding a Field

Hiding a field is useful when you want to extract information from your database using a field name, but do not wish the field to be shown in the Query result. Let us hide a field, say the field **C_ ID**. This operation is possible only when the Query is displayed in Design View. Follow the steps given below to hide the field.

1. *Move* the mouse over the down-arrow button (▾) of the **View** button (▾) as shown in Fig.AC-5.16, and *click* the left mouse button. A pull-down menu gets displayed (Fig.AC-5.16).
2. Inside the pull-down menu, *click* on **Design View** option (Fig.AC-5.16). Immediately, the query gets changed to **Design View** (Fig.AC-5.17).
3. At the bottom of the **Query 1 : Select Query** box, you will notice a tick mark (✔) displayed under each field at the **Show** option (Fig.AC-5.24).
4. Since field **C_ID** is not to be displayed, *move* the mouse-pointer over the tick mark (✔) under the field **C_ID** and *click* the left mouse-button on the tick mark. The tick mark disappears instantly (Fig.AC-5.25).

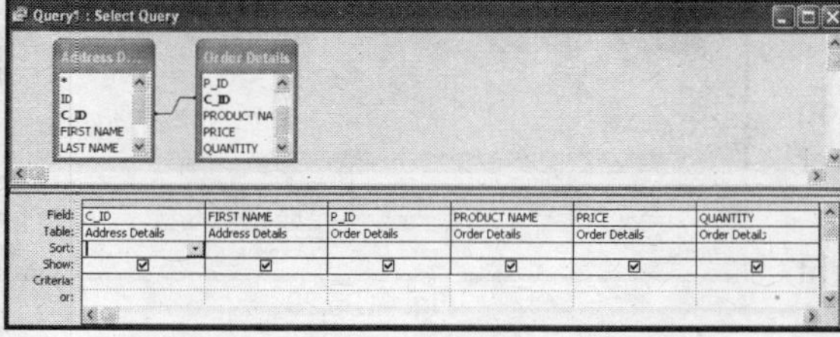

Fig. AC-5.24

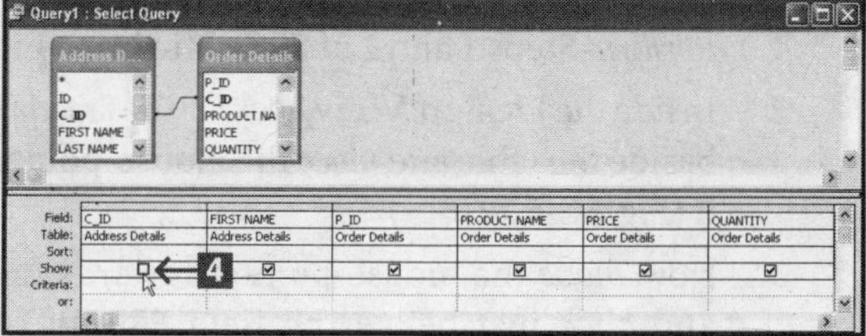

Fig. AC-5.25

> Sometimes you may not see the field C_ID inside the table. In that case, keep clicking on the Left arrow scroll button (◂) of the table, as shown in Fig.AC-5.20, until you see the field C_ID. Then move the mouse-pointer over the tick mark under the field C_ID, as shown in Fig.AC-5.21.

5. Now to execute the Query, *move* the mouse-pointer over the **Run** button (!) of the **Standard Toolbar** and *click* on it. Now, in the Query result (Fig.AC-5.26), you will not see the field **C_ID** which has been hidden.

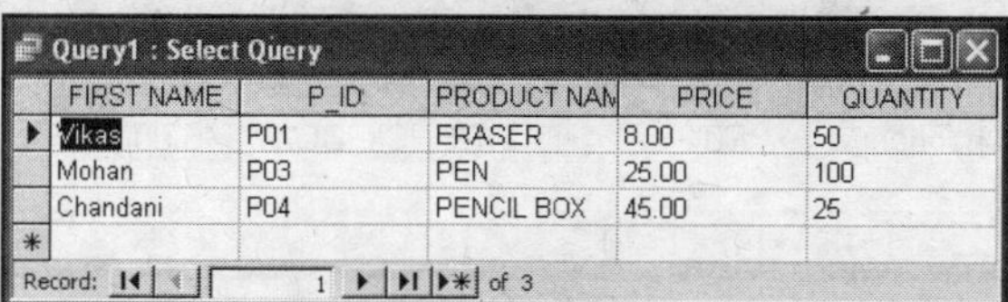

Query1 : Select Query

FIRST NAME	P_ID	PRODUCT NAM	PRICE	QUANTITY
Vikas	P01	ERASER	8.00	50
Mohan	P03	PEN	25.00	100
Chandani	P04	PENCIL BOX	45.00	25

Record: 1 of 3

Fig. AC-5.26

Unhiding a Field

Sometimes you may find it necessary to again display, i.e. unhide, the field you have hidden. Read on to learn how to go about doing this. Suppose, you wish to display the field C_ID, which you have just hidden. First of all, you have to display the query in **Design View**, and then proceed further.

1. *Perform* Steps 1 and 2 of the topic **Hiding a Field**.
2. Then *move* the mouse-pointer inside the blank square (☐) beside the **Show** option of the field **C_ID** and *click* inside it. A tick mark re-appears inside the box (Fig. AC-5.27).
3. Finally, *click* on the **Run** button (!) present on the **Standard Toolbar** (Fig.AC-5.14). Immediately, you will notice that the field **C_ID** reappears and your table now looks like Fig. AC-5.28.

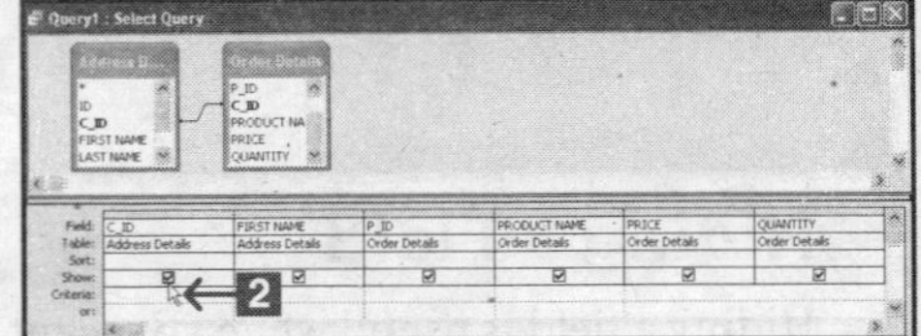

Fig. AC-5.27

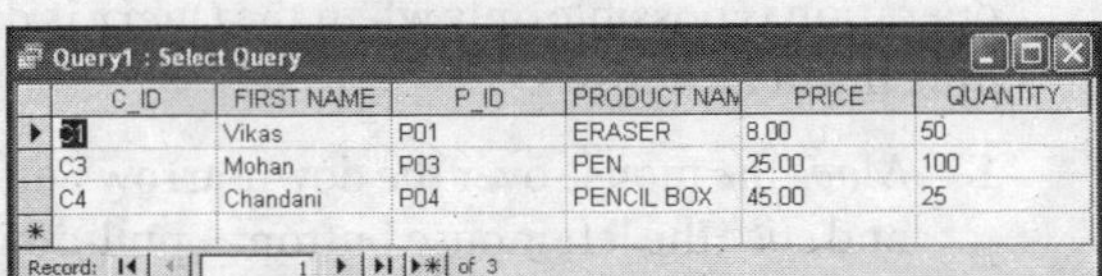

Query1 : Select Query

C_ID	FIRST NAME	P_ID	PRODUCT NAM	PRICE	QUANTITY
C1	Vikas	P01	ERASER	8.00	50
C3	Mohan	P03	PEN	25.00	100
C4	Chandani	P04	PENCIL BOX	45.00	25

Record: 1 of 3

Fig. AC-5.28

Setting Criterion

Criteria are conditions you set to display the specific records. Let us now set a criterion to display details of only those customers who have bought a product named **PENCIL BOX**.

For setting a criterion, first display the Query in Design View. To do so, you may undertake the following steps:

1. *Perform* Steps 1 and 2 of topic **Hiding a Field**.
2. Inside the **Design View**, *look for* the **Criteria** option beside the table and *place* the mouse-pointer over it (Fig.AC-5.29).
3. Now, *move* the mouse-pointer towards the right and *click* just below the field **PRODUCT NAME**. Immediately, a blinking cursor appears at that location (Fig.AC-5.29).
4. *Type* the Criteria as **=pencil box** (Fig.AC-5.30).
5. Finally, *click* on the **Run** button (!) of the **Standard Toolbar** (Fig.AC-5.14). The result of the query appears (Fig.AC-5.31).

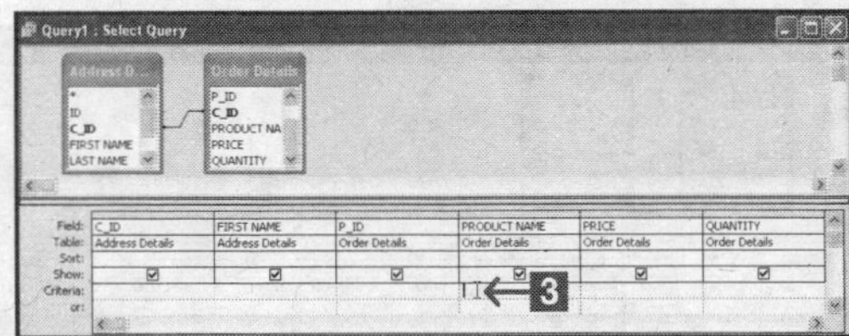

Fig. AC-5.29

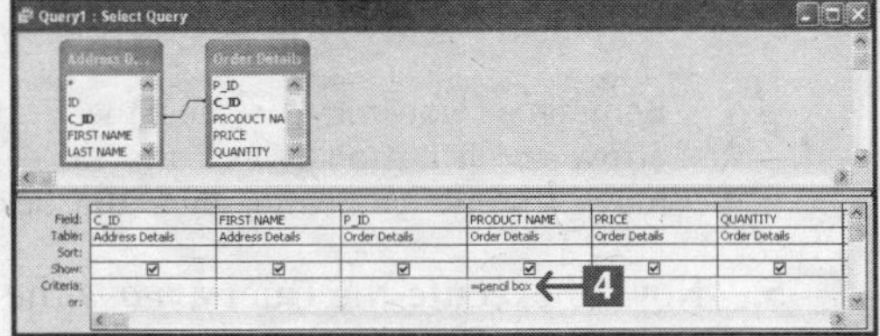

Fig. AC-5.30

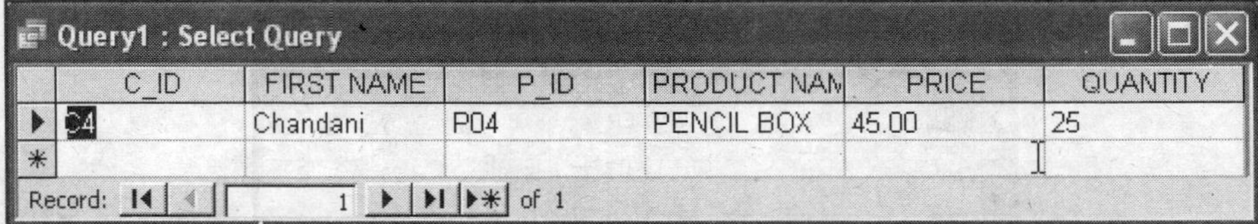

Query1 : Select Query

C_ID	FIRST NAME	P_ID	PRODUCT NAM	PRICE	QUANTITY
C4	Chandani	P04	PENCIL BOX	45.00	25

Record: 1 of 1

Fig. AC-5.31

6. All conditions in a query are automatically displayed within double quotes. Let us now see whether the condition =**pencil box** has also been displayed within double quotes ("").

   To do so, you have to bring the **Design View** on the screen. So perform Steps 1 and 2 of topic **Hiding a Field.**

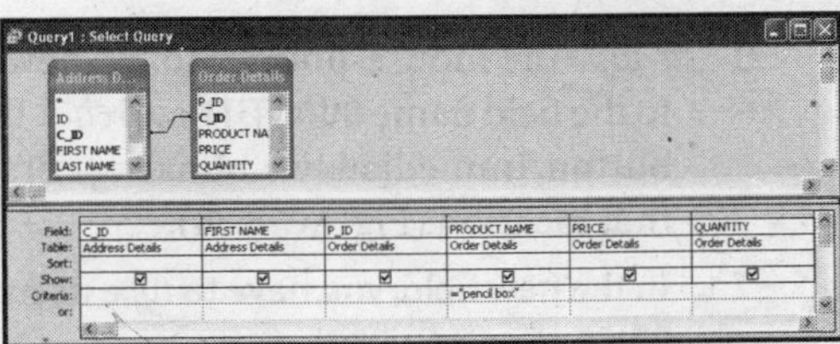

Fig. AC-5.32

You will now notice that Access adds quotations (" ") to the criterion, = **pencil box,** which you had typed (Fig.AC-5.32).

Deleting Criterion

When you wish to display all the records without imposing any conditions on them then you must remove all criteria from the records. For example, if you wish to display all the records (Fig.AC-5.12) then undertake the following steps:

1. Start with Fig.AC-5.32. *Move* the mouse-pointer to the left of the text written at **Criteria** option, in our case ="**pencil box**" and *click* the left mouse-button.
2. Then *press* the left mouse-button, and keeping it *pressed*, *drag* it such that the ="**pencil box**" criterion gets highlighted (Fig.AC-5.33).
3. Once the entire criterion text has been highlighted, *release* the mouse-button.
4. Then *press* the **Delete** key of your keyboard. Immediately, the criterion gets deleted.

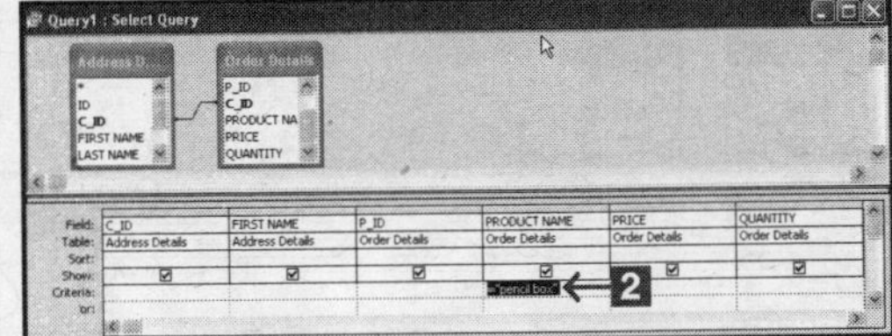

Fig. AC-5.33

5. Now *click* on **Run** button (!) of the **Standard Toolbar.** Immediately, Fig.AC-5.13 gets displayed.

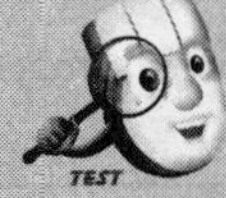

How to perform a Query to find the name of the product whose PRICE is 20.

- *Perform* step 1 of the topic '**Hiding a Field**'.
- *Move* the mouse-pointer over the **Criteria** option.
- *Click* on the Left arrow scroll button (◄) of the table to see field **PRICE.**
- *Move* the mouse-pointer towards right and *click* just under the field **PRICE.**
- Now *type* in the criteria as =20.
- Then *press* the **Run** button(!).

Performing Calculations

You can perform calculations for each record of your database, then review and analyze the result. Let us also calculate the total price to be paid by each customer depending upon the number of products he/she has purchased.

Before doing the actual calculations, first bring the Query's Design View on the screen and then proceed further. To do so, you may undertake the following steps.

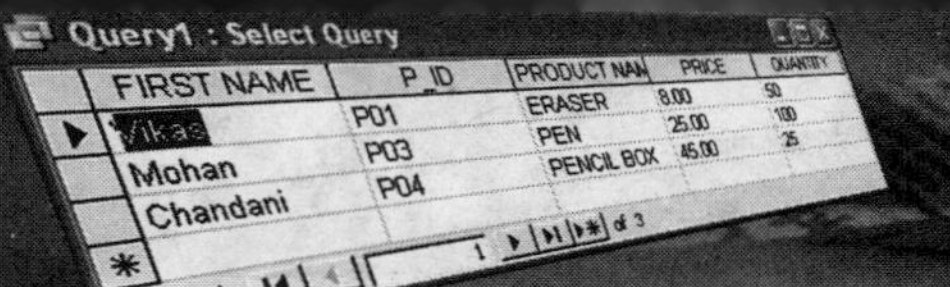

1. *Move* the mouse-pointer to the new column next to the field name **QUANTITY** and *click* the left mouse-button. Immediately, a blinking cursor appears at that location (Fig. AC-5.34).
2. In the new field, you have to *type* its name, say **TOTAL PRICE** (Fig. AC-5.35).
3. Just next to the line **TOTAL PRICE**, you have to type a command. So *type* : (colon).
4. Then *press* the **Space bar** key.
5. And *type* **[PRICE]*[QUANTITY]**. After typing this command, your screen looks like Fig. AC-5.36.
6. Finally, *click* on the **Run** button( ) present on the **Standard Toolbar**. You will notice that the new field gets added and the result, i.e. total price paid by each customer, appears on the screen (Fig. AC-5.37).

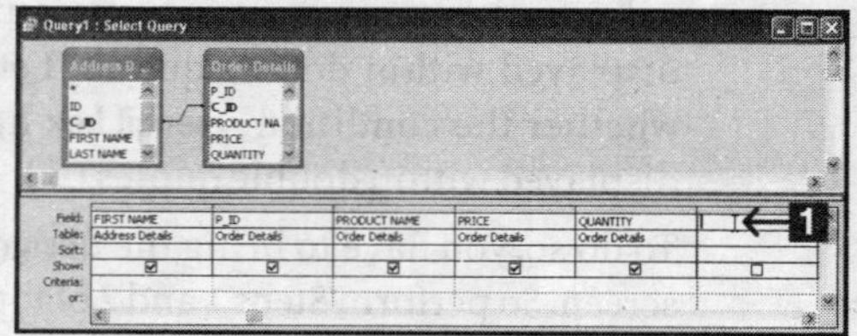

Fig. AC-5.34

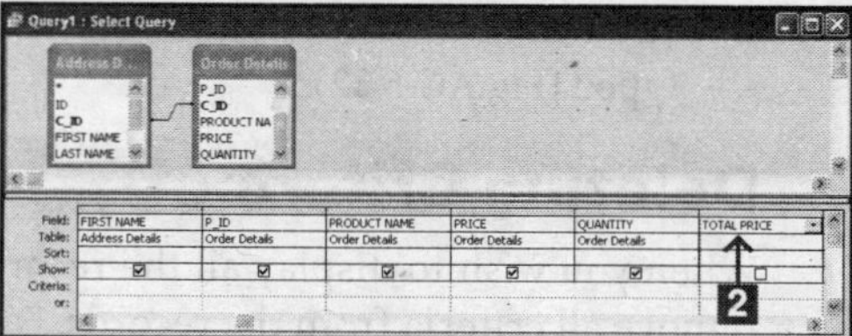

Fig. AC-5.35

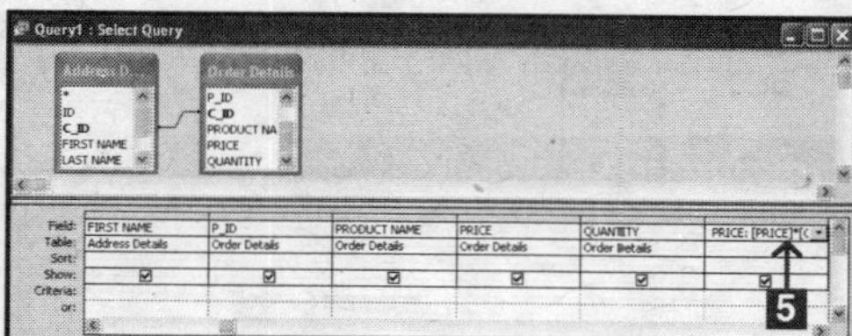

Fig. AC-5.36

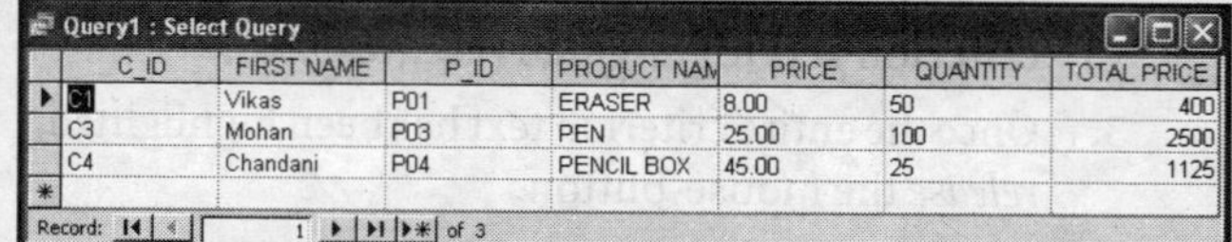

Fig. AC-5.37

Saving a Query

You can also save a Query for future use. To do so, you may undertake the following steps:

1. *Move* the mouse-pointer on the **Save** button ( ) of the **Standard Toolbar** (Fig. AC-5.38), and *click* the left mouse-button. Immediately, a **Save As** box appears on the screen (Fig. AC-5.39).

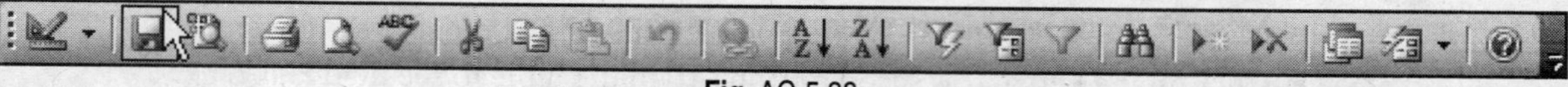

Fig. AC-5.38

2. Now *type* in a name, say **Product Query**, for this query (Fig. AC-5.40).
3. Next, *click* on the **OK** button (Fig. AC-5.40). Immediately, your query gets saved with the name **Product Query**.

Fig. AC-5.39

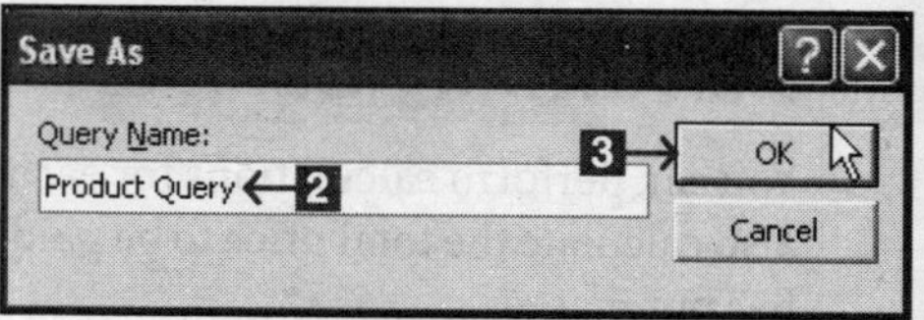

Fig. AC-5.40

Closing the Query and Quitting Access

Hope, now you would find it easy to create queries and work in them. Let us close our query before going for a break. To do so, you may undertake the following steps:

1. *Click* on the **File** Menu bar option. Immediately, a pull-down menu gets displayed (Fig.AC-5.41).
2. Inside the pull-down menu, *click* over the **Close** option (Fig.AC-5.41). Your query closes and you return to the **Address : Database** box. This box displays the query name inside it (Fig.AC-5.42).
3. Again, *click* on the **File** Menu bar option to close the **Address : Database** box (Fig.AC-5.43).
4. Then *click* on the **Close** option (Fig.AC-5.43). Now the **Address : Database** box also closes.
5. Finally, *move* the mouse-pointer to the extreme right corner of the **Title bar** and *click* on the **Close** button (☒). Microsoft Access window closes instantly. Now you can proceed to enjoy your well-earned break and return refreshed for going through a new topic.

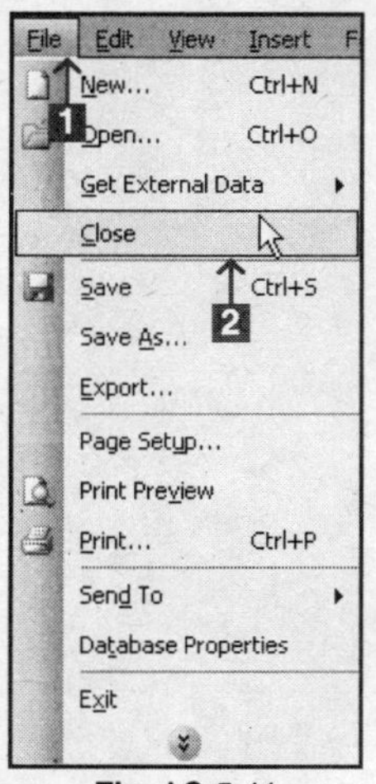

Fig. AC-5.41

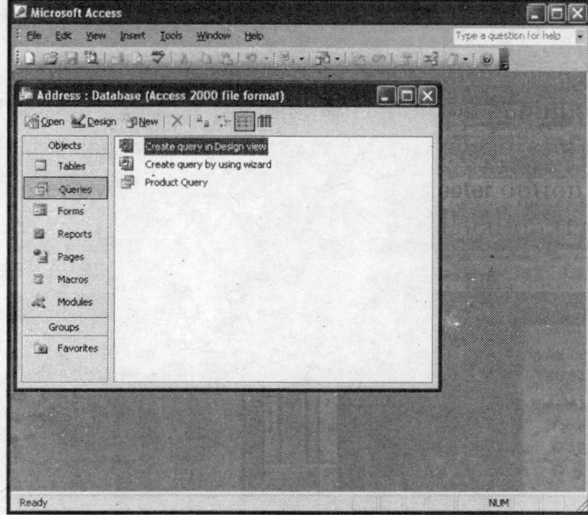

Fig. AC-5.42

Fig. AC-5.43

Exercise

Fill in the Blanks

1. ________ is a tool to extract the desired information.
2. Database is a combination of __________, __________, __________ and __________.
3. To remove sorting from a field you have to first move to the _________ view.
4. Queries specify a series of _____________ for retrieving the desired information from the database.

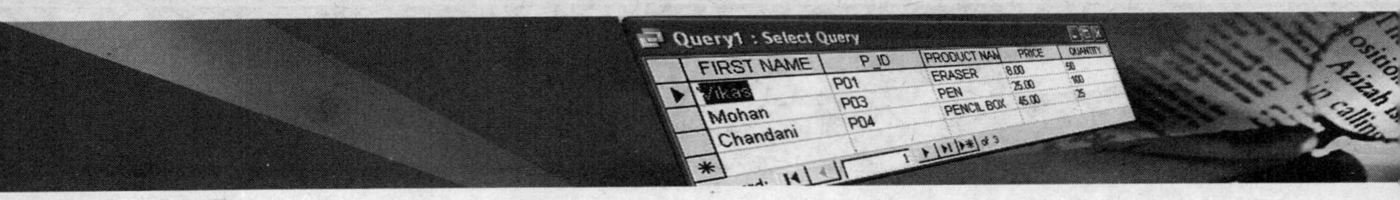

True/False

1. Queries are an essential part of any database.
2. Criteria are the conditions you set to display specific records.
3. A query cannot be saved for future use.
4. A criteria once set cannot be deleted.
5. There are four ways you can arrange or sort data.

MICROSOFT ACCESS

Generating Reports 6

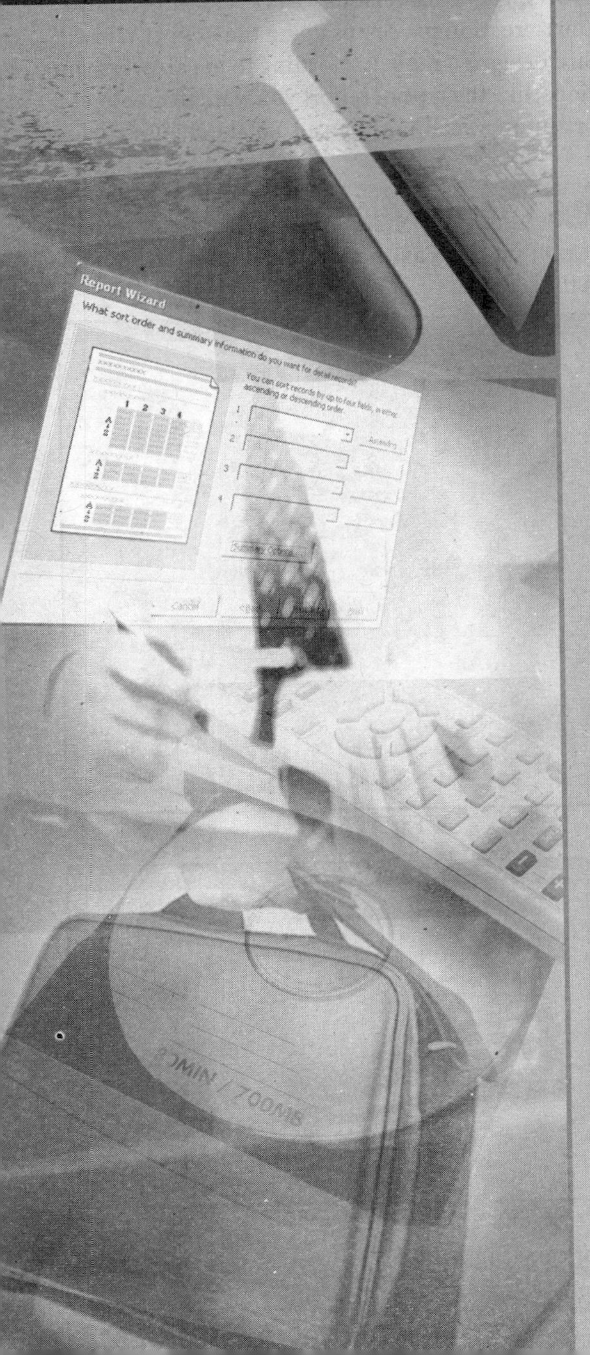

IN THIS CHAPTER

- Starting MS Access and Opening the Database
- Creating a Report with Report Wizards
- Printing a Report
- Closing the Report and Quitting Microsoft Access

Reports provide the most flexible way of viewing and printing information in your database. They enable you to display detailed information in almost any format. Like Queries, Reports also take information from other objects of your database, i.e. tables or queries, and then organize that information according to your instructions.

Report Wizard give you the basic layout for your reports. There are various ways of creating reports. However, in this Chapter, you will go through the report-creation processes using the Report Wizard. This is the easiest way to design a report. Report Wizard designs a report according to the answers you give to a series of questions. It asks you various questions, like the type of report you want to create, etc. After all its questions are answered, it creates the report automatically. You can also make changes in the report which you have created.

Starting MS Access and Opening the Database

1. *Move* the mouse-pointer over the **Start** button (start) on the **Taskbar**, and *click* the left mouse-button. Immediately, a push-up menu appears on the screen.
2. Next, *move* the mouse-pointer and *place* it over the **All Programs** option. Immediately, a second menu appears on the screen.
3. Inside the second menu, *move* the mouse-pointer and *place* it over the **Microsoft Office** option. A third menu appears.
4. Inside the third menu, *move* the mouse-pointer over the **Microsoft Office Access 2003** option and *click* the left mouse-button.
5. Immediately, a **Microsoft Access** window appears. On the right side of the window you can see the **Getting Started** Task pane containing various options (Fig.AC-6.1).

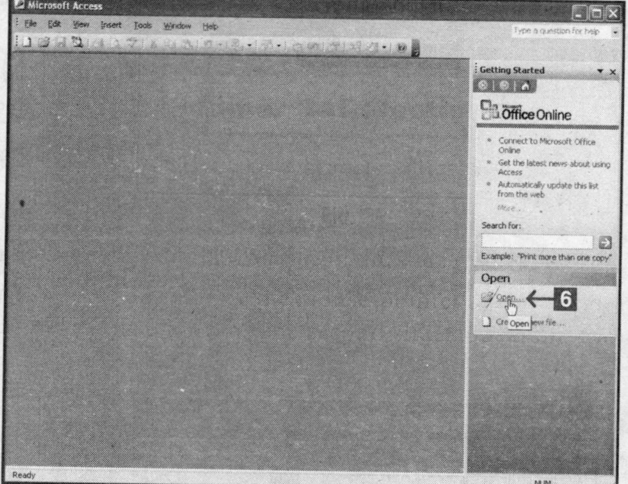

Fig. AC-6.1

6. Inside the **Getting Started** Task pane, *move* the mouse-pointer over the **Open** option and *click* the left mouse-button (Fig.AC-6.1).
7. Instantly, the **Open** dialog box appears on the screen displaying the contents of **My Documents** folder, which is also the same folder where Address database was saved earlier (Fig.AC-6.2).
8. *Move* the mouse-pointer over the **Address** database and *click* the left mouse-button just once. The database name gets highlighted (Fig.AC-6.2).
9. Lastly, *move* the mouse-pointer over the **Open** button and *click* the left mouse-button (Fig. AC-6.2). Immediately, the **Address : Database** box appears (Fig.AC-6.3).

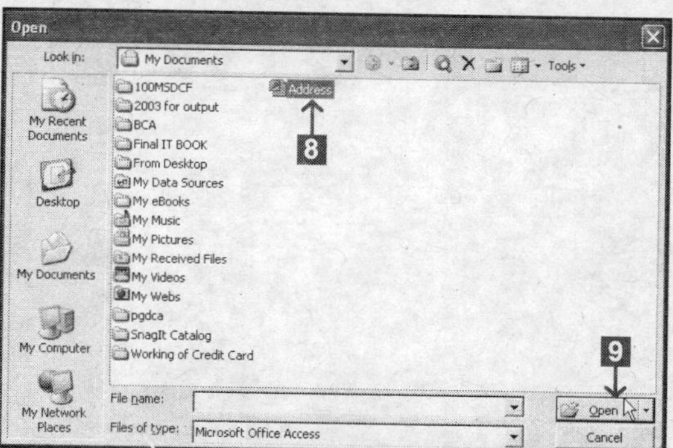

Fig. AC-6.2

Creating a Report with Report Wizard

For creating a report through the Report Wizard, you may follow the steps given below.

1. Inside the **Address : Database** box, *move* the mouse-pointer over the **Reports** tab (Fig.AC-6.3), and *click* the left mouse-button on it. Instantly, the tab gets selected.
2. Now, *click* on the **New** button of the **Address : Database** box (Fig.AC-6.3) to create a new report. A **New Report** box opens up on the screen (Fig.AC-6.4). The **New Report** box offers you six different ways to create a report which are described in the following table: Among all the options listed above, the Report Wizard is the easiest way to design a report.

TABLE

• **Design View**	Displays a completely blank Report Design window for you to start with.
• **Report Wizard**	Creates a tabular report depending upon the answers given by you to its questions.
• **AutoReport: Columnar**	Displays one or more records in a column.
• **AutoReport: Tabular**	Displays data in next rows and columns.
• **Chart Wizard**	Helps you create a business graph.
• **Label Wizard**	Helps you create a set of mailing labels.

3. Now, suppose you wish to create a report in **Report Wizard.** So *move* the mouse-pointer over the **Report Wizard** option (Fig.AC-6.4) and *click* on it to highlight it.

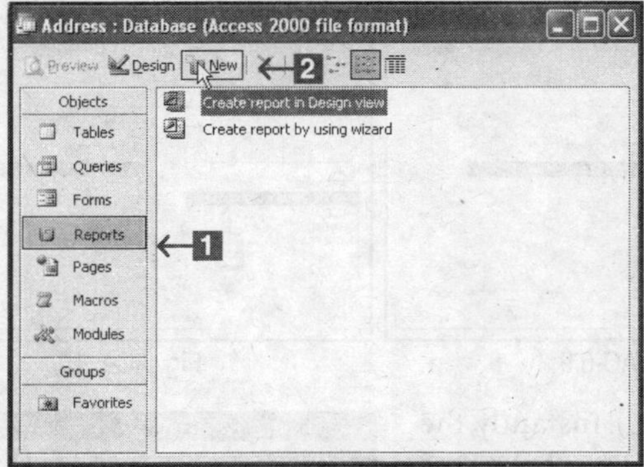

Fig. AC-6.3

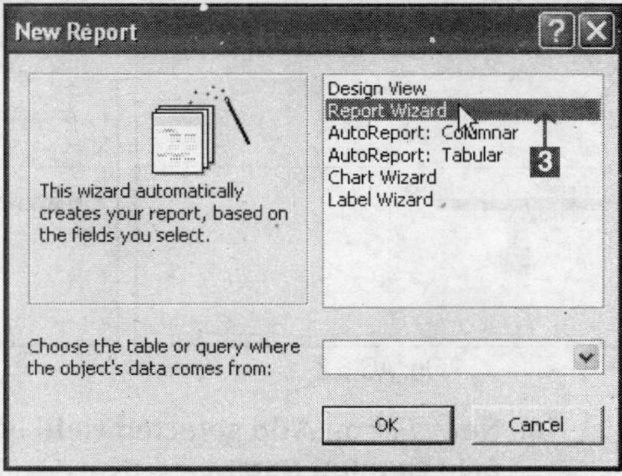

Fig. AC-6.4

4. Inside the **New Report** box, notice a small rectangular box (Fig.AC-6.5), which has the option **Choose the table or query where the object's data comes from**. A down arrow button ( ) is displayed beside this option. In this option, you have to display the table or query name from which the report will be created. Suppose you decide to create a report from the query called **Product Query** (designed in Chapter 5). So *move* the mouse-pointer over the down-arrow button ( ) and *click* on it (Fig.AC-6.5). A pull-down menu appears.
5. Inside the pull-down menu (Fig.AC-6.6), *move* the mouse-pointer over the query name **Product Query,** and *click* the left mouse-button. Instantly, this query name gets displayed in the rectangular box.
6. Finally *click* on the **OK** button. Immediately, a **Report Wizard** box opens up on the screen (Fig.AC-6.7). The **Product Query** has seven fields. Among them you have to choose the fields which you wish to display in your report. Suppose, you decide to create a report on details of products. Then the fields required are as shown in the Table 1.

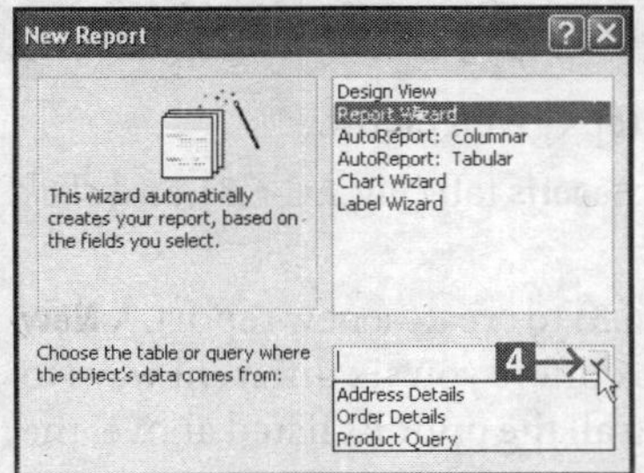

Fig. AC-6.5

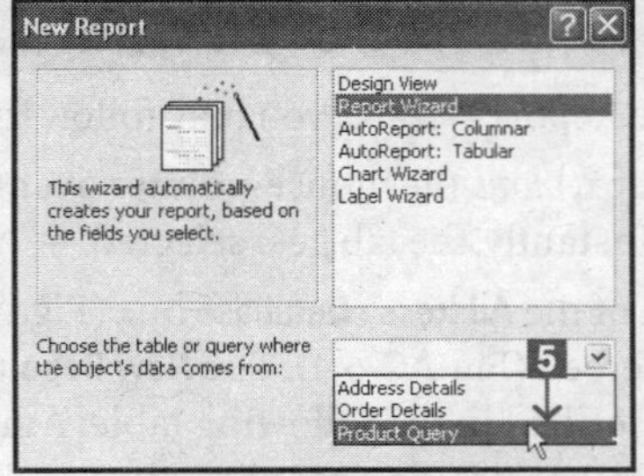

Fig. AC-6.6

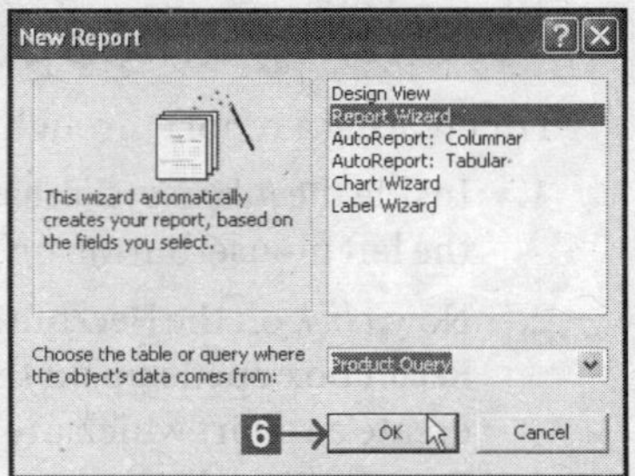

Fig. AC-6.7

P_ID
PRODUCT NAME
PRICE
QUANTITY
TOTAL PRICE

Table 1

7. Now, let us proceed to select the required fields one by one. For this, we first *move* the mouse-pointer over the field **P_ID** (Fig.AC-6.8) inside the box below the **Available Fields** option, and *click* on it to highlight it.
8. Next, *move* the mouse-pointer over the **Add selected field** button (>) (Fig. AC-6.9), and *click* on it. Immediately, the selected field moves inside the **Selected Fields** option box.
9. The next field to be added is the **PRODUCT NAME.** So *click* over this field name displayed inside the box below **Available Fields** option to highlight it (Fig.AC-6.10).

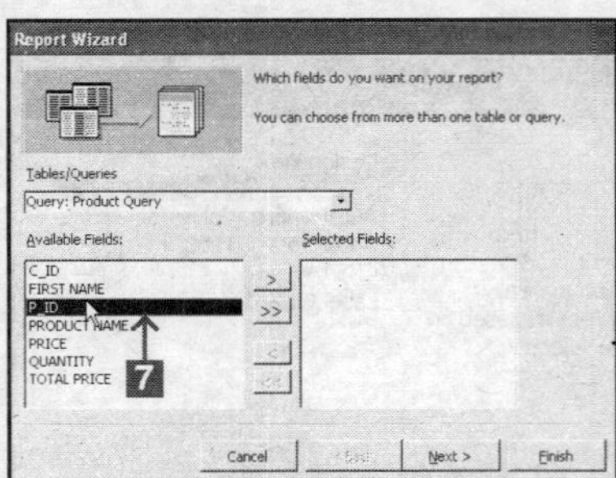

Fig. AC-6.8

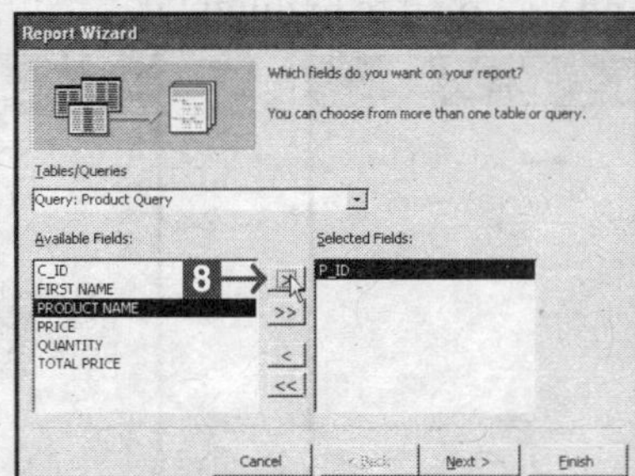

Fig. AC-6.9

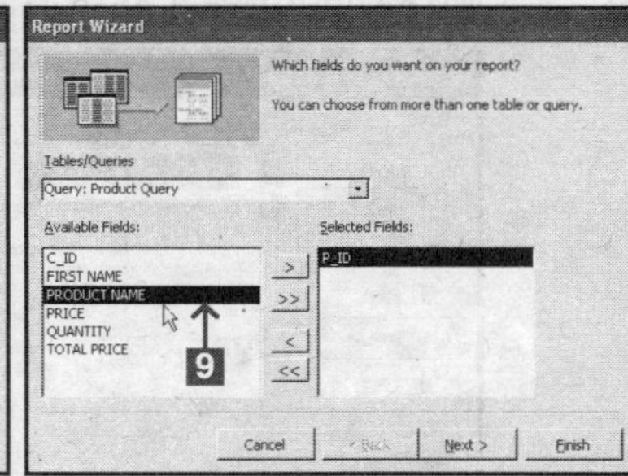

Fig. AC-6.10

10. Now *click* on **Add selected field** button (>). Instantly, the field **PRODUCT NAME** gets displayed inside the box below the **Selected Fields** option (Fig.AC-6.11).
11. Similarly, move the rest of the fields **PRICE, QUANTITY** and **TOTAL PRICE** from the box below the **Available Fields** option to the box below the **Selected Fields** option. Once you have moved all the required fields, the screen will look like Fig. AC-6.12.

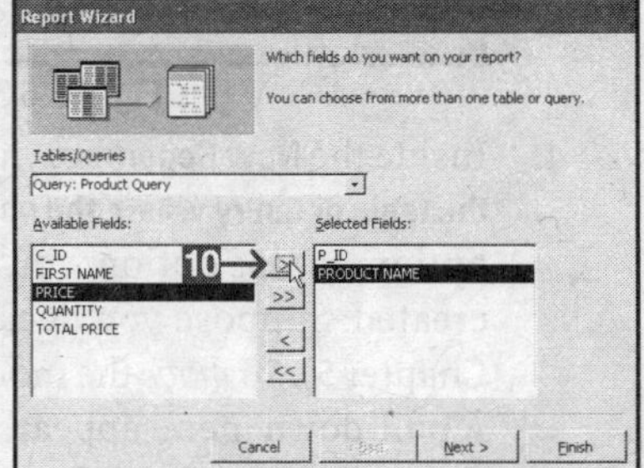

Fig. AC-6.11

12. Now *move* the mouse-pointer over the **Next** button of the **Report Wizard** box (Fig.AC-6.13) and *click* over it. Immediately, a second **Report Wizard** box gets displayed on the screen with some more questions (Fig.AC-6.14).

    The second **Report Wizard** box is used for grouping the information in your report according to a field.

    Grouping the information according to a field, say **P_ID**, means records in your report will be grouped on the basis of the product identification number. In other words, the report will show all records that match the first product identification number **P01**, then the records matching the second product identification number **P02**, and so on.

13. Suppose, you want to group the records in your report according to the **P_ID** field. For this, *move* the mouse-pointer over the field **P_ID** and *click* on it. **P_ID** gets instantly highlighted (Fig.AC-6.14).
14. Then *click* on the **Add selected field** button (>) (Fig.AC-6.14). This makes the field **P_ID** appear inside a box at the top of all the field names. This means, that records in the report have been grouped according to the **P_ID** field.

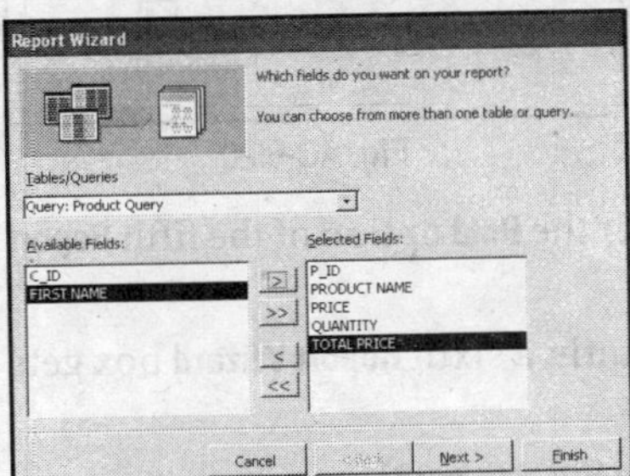

Fig. AC-6.12

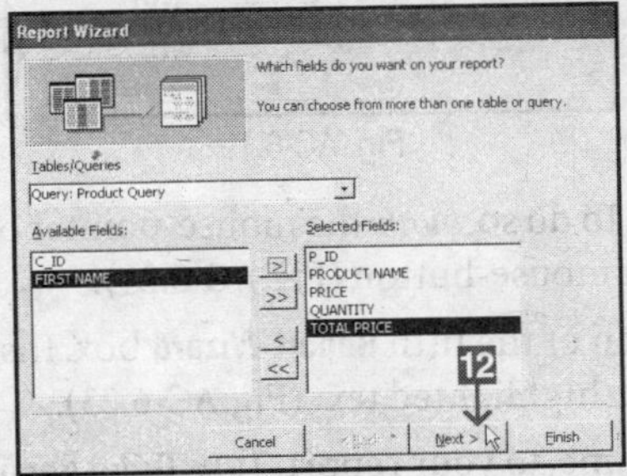

Fig. AC-6.13

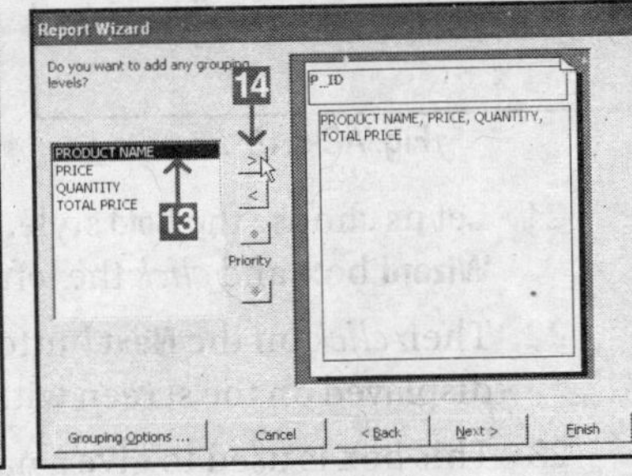

Fig. AC-6.14

15. Now *move* the mouse-pointer over the **Next** button (Fig.AC-6.15), and *click* the left mouse-button. Immediately, a third **Report Wizard** box opens up on the screen (Fig.AC-6.16).
16. The box shown in Fig.AC-6.16 is for sorting a field. Right now, you don't require this box. So, *click* on the **Summary Options** button (Fig.AC-6.16). Immediately, the **Summary Options** box opens up on the screen (Fig.AC-6.17). This box lists all the numeric fields of your report.
17. Suppose in your report, you would also like to calculate the grand total of the field **TOTAL PRICE.** In that case, *click* on the **Sum** option of the field **TOTAL PRICE.** Immediately, a tick mark (☑) appears inside the empty box beside the field **TOTAL PRICE** (Fig.AC-6.17).

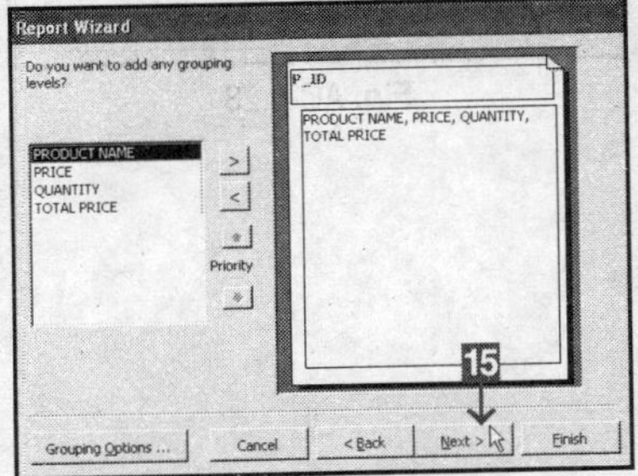

Fig. AC-6.15

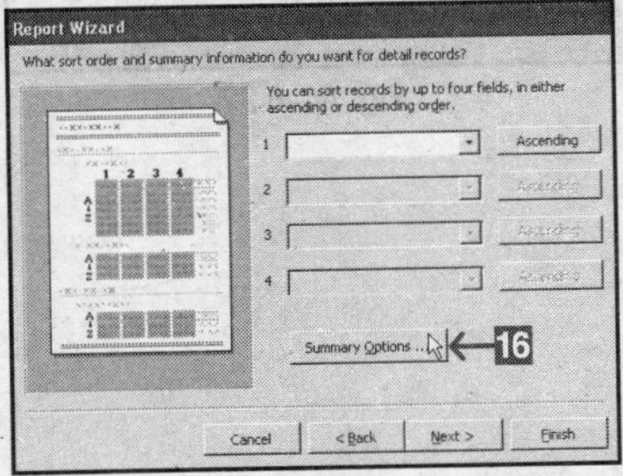

Fig. AC-6.16

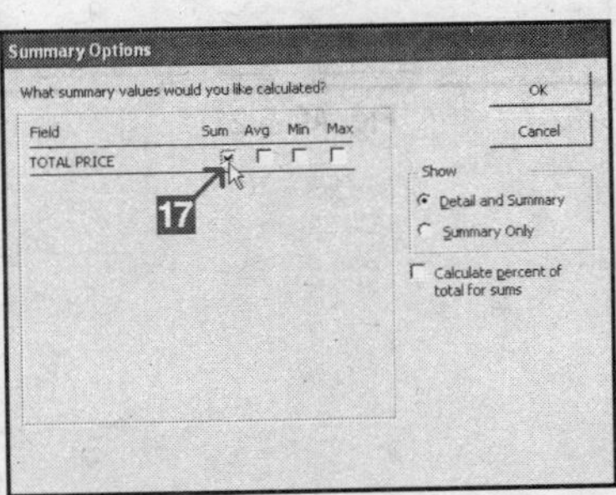

Fig. AC-6.17

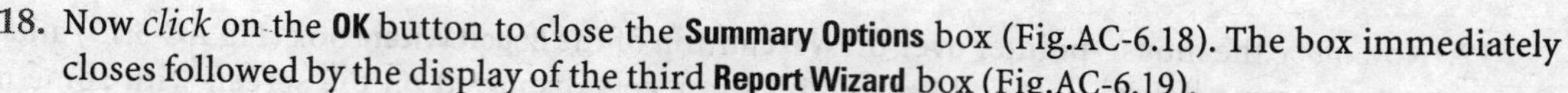

18. Now *click* on the **OK** button to close the **Summary Options** box (Fig.AC-6.18). The box immediately closes followed by the display of the third **Report Wizard** box (Fig.AC-6.19).
19. Inside the third **Report Wizard** box, *click* on the **Next** button (Fig. AC-6.19). Instantly a fourth **Report Wizard** box gets displayed (Fig.AC-6.20).
20. Again, *click* on the **Next** button of the fourth **Report Wizard** box. A fifth **Report Wizard** box comes up on the screen. This box allows you to choose a style for the text or data of your report such as applying fonts, borders and spacing to a report (Fig.AC-6.21).

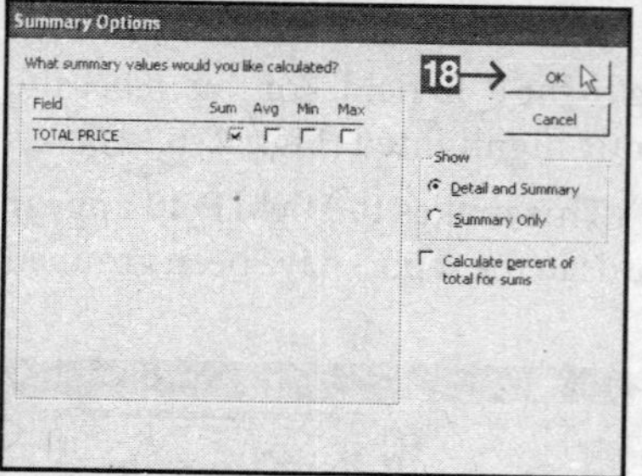

Fig. AC-6.18

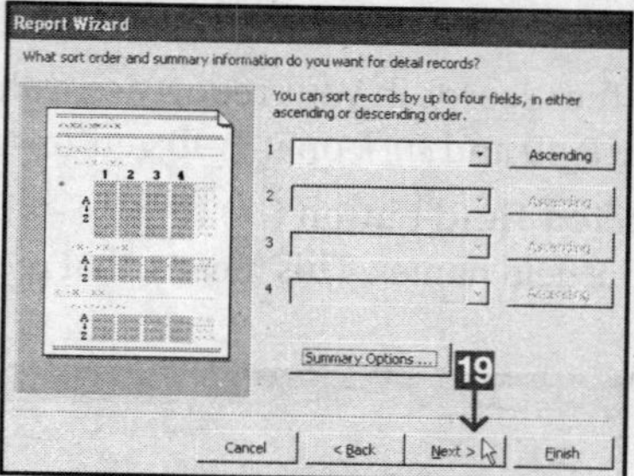

Fig. AC-6.19

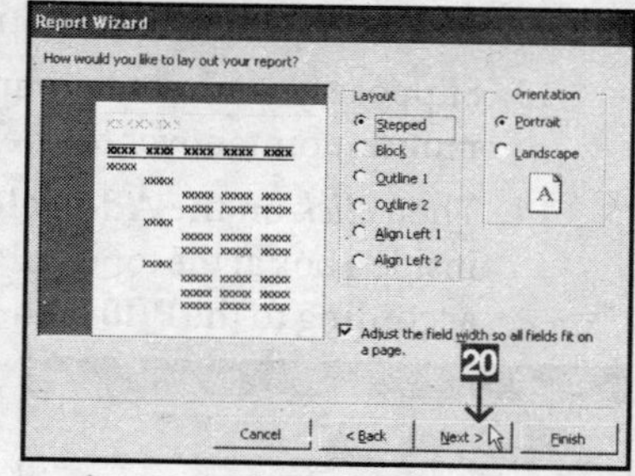

Fig. AC-6.20

21. Let us choose the **Bold** style. To do so, *move* the mouse-pointer over the **Bold** option of the fifth **Report Wizard** box, and *click* the left mouse-button (Fig.AC-6.21).
22. Then *click* on the **Next** button of the fifth **Report Wizard** box. Instantly, a sixth **Report Wizard** box gets displayed on the screen with highlighted text (Fig.AC-6.23).
23. This box is used to give a name, to your report. *Type* **Order Report** (Fig.AC-6.23).
24. Finally, *click* on the **Finish** button (Fig.AC-6.23). Immediately, the preview screen of the complete report named **Order Report** gets displayed on the screen (Fig.AC-6.24).

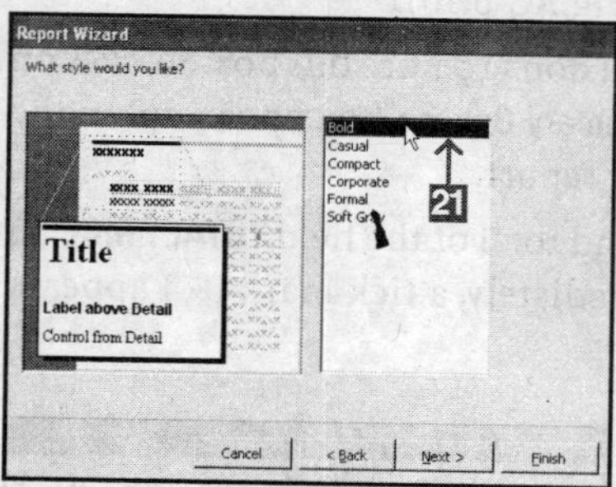

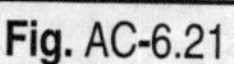

Fig. AC-6.21

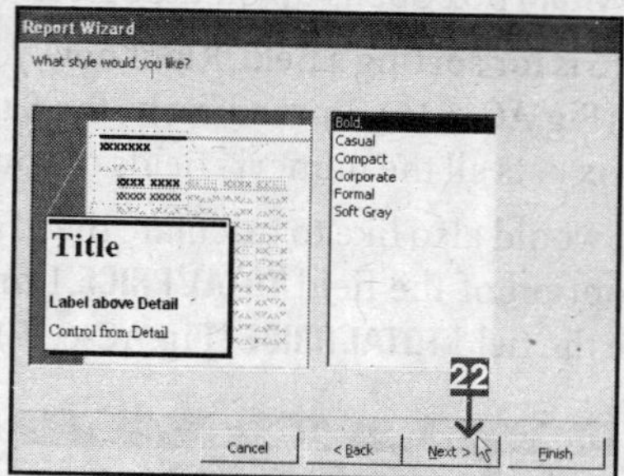

Fig. AC-6.22

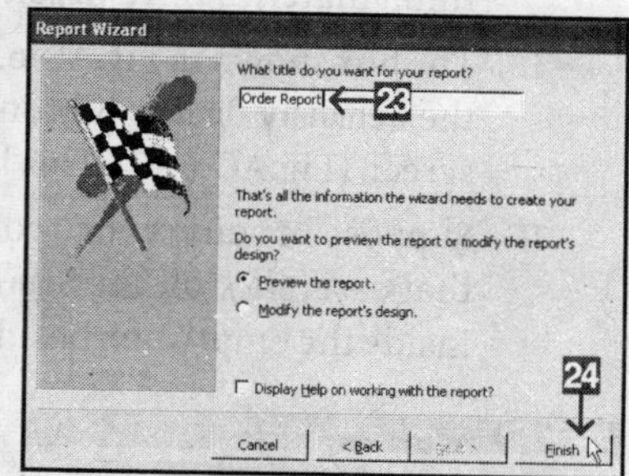

Fig. AC-6.23

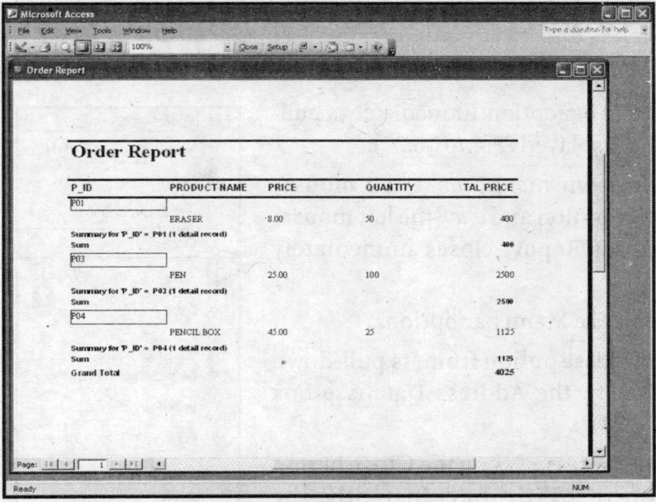

Fig. AC-6.24

Fig.AC-6.24 shows you only some records of your newly-created report. If you wish to see the entire report then undertake the following steps.

1. Move the mouse-pointer inside the Order Report. Immediately, the mouse-pointer changes into a magnifier symbol(🔍).
2. Then click the left mouse-button. Instantly, the screen gets minimized (Fig.AC-6.25), and the mouse-pointer changes to 🔍.
3. To read the report clearly, click again on the report. The report gets enlarged.

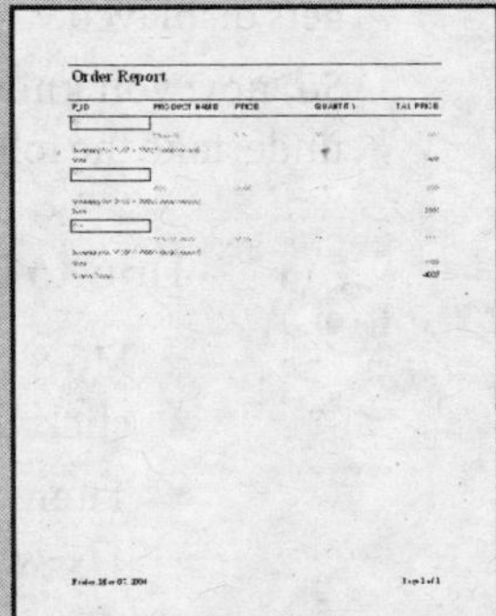

Fig. AC-6.25

Printing a Report

To print your report named **Order Report**, you may undertake the following steps:

1. Inside the preview screen itself, *move* the mouse-pointer over the **Print** button (🖨) present on the **Toolbar** (Fig.AC-6.26). Then *click* the left mouse-button. Immediately, the report gets printed.

Fig. AC-6.26

Closing the Report and Quitting Microsoft Access

Let us now close the report Order Report. To do so, undertake the following steps.

1. *Click* over **File** Menu bar option. Immediately, a pull-down menu gets displayed (Fig.AC-6.27).
2. Inside the pull-down menu, *move* the mouse-pointer over **Close** option and *click* the left mouse-button. The Order Report closes immediately (Fig.AC-6.27).
3. *Click* again on the **File** Menu bar option.
4. Then *click* on the **Close** option from its pull-down menu. Immediately, the Address Database box closes (Fig.AC-6.28).
5. To quit Microsoft Access, *click* on the **Close** button (☒) present on the **Title bar**. Instantly, the **Microsoft Access** window closes and the desktop gets displayed.

   So, now you know how to create a report. Let us undertake the following workout.

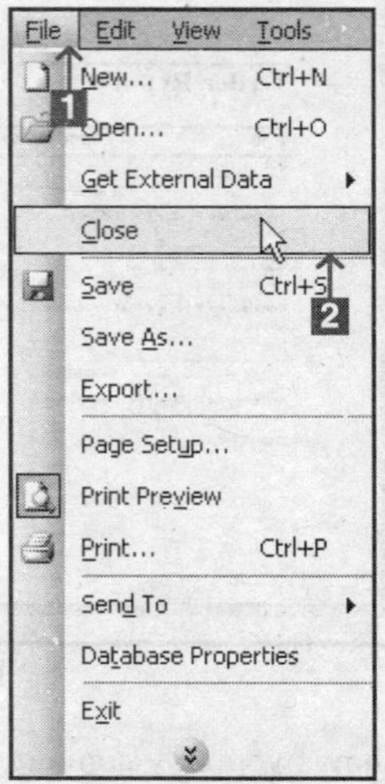

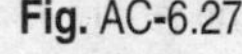
Fig. AC-6.27

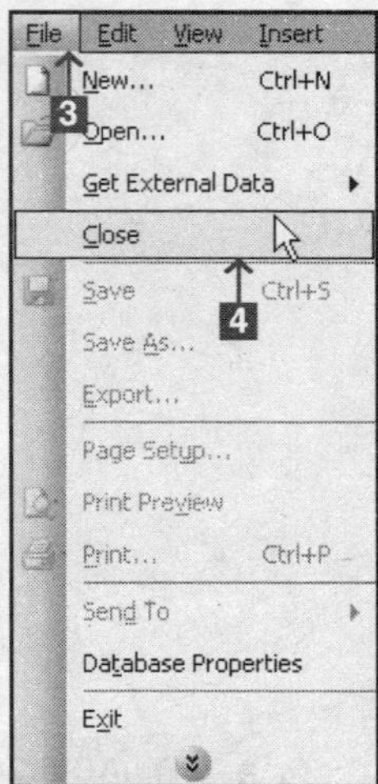

Fig. AC-6.28

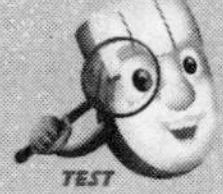

How to Display the contents of Address Details table in columns:

- Move the mouse-pointer over the Report tab of the Address : Database box and click the left mouse-button on it.
- Then move the mouse-pointer over New button and click on it. Immediately, a New Report box appears on the screen
- Now move the mouse-pointer over AutoReport: Columnar option inside the New Report box and click on it. You will notice that the option gets highlighted.
- Move the mouse-pointer over the down arrow button (⌄) beside the Choose the table or query where the object's data comes from option and click on it. Immediately a pull-down menu appears.
- Then select Address Details table from the pull-down menu.
- Finally, click on the OK button. Immediately, the report appears on the screen in columns (Fig.AC-6.20).
- Click on the File menu bar option. A pull-down menu appears.
- Then click on Save option. A Save As box appears on the screen.
- Now type the report name Add Report.
- Then click on the Save button of the Save As box.
- Finally, close the report by clicking on the File menu bar option and then on the Close option inside the pull-down menu.

Microsoft PowerPoint

IN THIS SECTION

- Working in Microsoft PowerPoint
- Adding Animation in Slides

MICROSOFT POWERPOINT

Working in Microsoft PowerPoint 1

IN THIS CHAPTER

- Starting PowerPoint
- Creating a Presentation using AutoContent Wizard
- Saving the Presentation
- Working with Text in Slides
- Formatting the Text
- Closing the Presentation
- Downloading a PowerPoint Design Template

If you want to make your point powerfully then PowerPoint is the right choice. Microsoft PowerPoint is a feature-rich program widely used for designing professional presentations like product profiles, research papers and dissertations. PowerPoint has a host of design templates that you can use to make your presentations. In PowerPoint presentations, you communicate your message to the target audience through slides. In the past, there used to be presentations consisting of physical slides requiring overhead projectors for display. However, they have been made obsolete by the electronic slides that run on computers. PowerPoint presentations consist of these electronic slides. Mostly these are dynamic slides that automatically change after a set time. PowerPoint offers tools and techniques for designing and running dynamic slide presentations. With these tools, you can easily design slides, insert text and graphics and then animate slides and their objects. PowerPoint presentations can be run on the network and the changes made by the presenter relayed to all connected computers. So, you may be eager to work in the PowerPoint. Let us quickly start the PowerPoint program.

Starting PowerPoint

Let us open the PowerPoint program through following steps.

1. *Move* the mouse-pointer over the **Start** button (start) on the **Taskbar** and *click* the left mouse-button. A push-up menu appears on the screen (Fig.PP-1.1).
2. Inside the push-up menu, *place* the mouse-pointer over the **All Programs** option. A second menu appears (Fig.PP-1.1).
3. Inside the second menu, *place* the mouse-pointer over the **Microsoft Office** option. A third menu appears (Fig.PP-1.1).
4. Inside the third menu, *move* the mouse-pointer over the **Microsoft Office PowerPoint 2003** option and *click* the left mouse-pointer (Fig.PP-1.1).
5. Instantly, the **Microsoft PowerPoint** window opens up on the screen (Fig.PP-2). Before working in the PowerPoint window, let us first know about its various components.

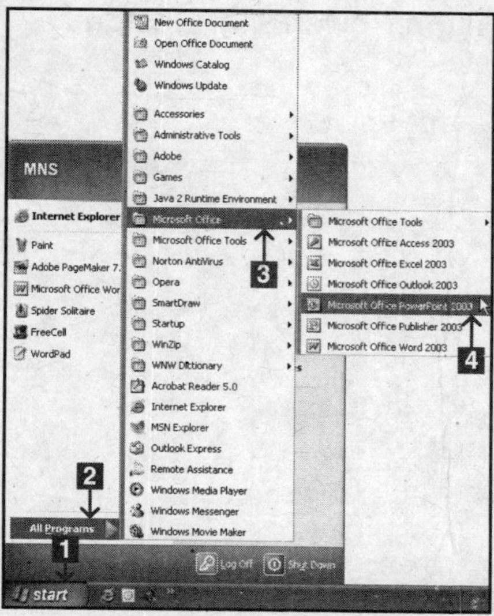

Fig. PP--1.1

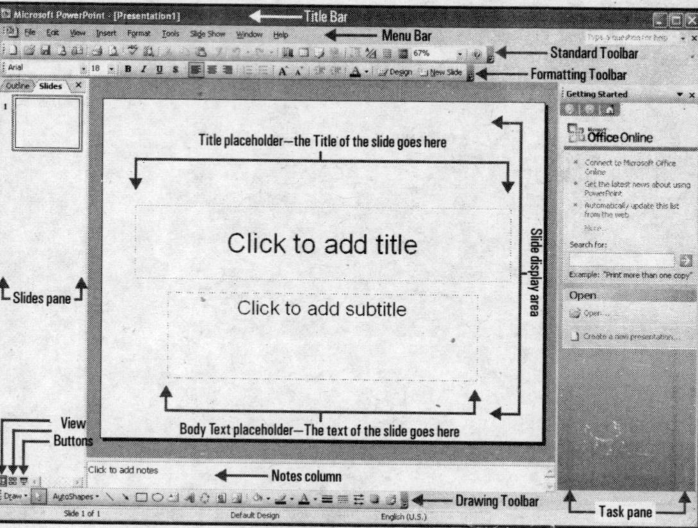

Fig. PP-1.2

PowerPoint Window Components

The PowerPoint window has many useful tools which help you in creating your presentations. A brief description of various components of the PowerPoint window (Fig.PP-1.2) is given below:

Title bar: It displays the name of the currently open presentation, apart from the **maximize, restore** and **close** buttons. In Fig.PP-1.2, the Title bar shows the default name, **Presentation1**.

Menu bar: It shows a list of commands used in PowerPoint to do various tasks.

Formatting Toolbar: It contains buttons for frequently performed formatting tasks such as **bold, italics,** etc.

Standard Toolbar: It contains buttons for commands like opening the presentation, saving the presentation, etc. Each button has an image that helps us identify its function.

Presentation display area: This area displays the newly created presentation. It is also used to add text to presentation slides.

Slide pane: It displays the miniature form of the current slide. The slide pane gets transformed into the outline pane when a presentation is displayed on the PowerPoint window.

Placeholder: It is a place represented by a dotted box on the slide where you can type the desired text. A slide may have many placeholders.

Notes column: It provides a quick way of entering notes that are displayed with the slides.

View buttons: With these buttons, you can quickly change the display of the presentation screen.

Drawing Toolbar: It provides buttons for inserting various objects in the presentation.

Outline pane: As explained earlier, the outline pane appears on the left of the PowerPoint window along with a finished presentation. It replaces the slide pane. The outline pane displays each slide with its text, number, etc. It is used to reorganize the presentation. You can modify, delete, or add to the slide text in the outline pane.

Task pane: The Task pane allows you to create a new presentation and open an existing presentation. The opening window of PowerPoint (Fig.PP-1.2) shows the **Getting Started** Task pane. However, to create a presentation, you need to access the **New Presentation** Task pane. To access this Task pane, click over the **Create a new presentation** option in the **Getting Started** Task pane.

If the Getting Started Task pane is not visible on the PowerPoint window, undertake the following steps to make it visible.

1. Move the mouse-pointer over the View menu bar option and click the left mouse-button. A pull-down menu appears (Fig.PP-1.3).
2. In the pull-down menu, click on the Task pane option. Instantly, the Task pane appears (Fig.PP-1.4).

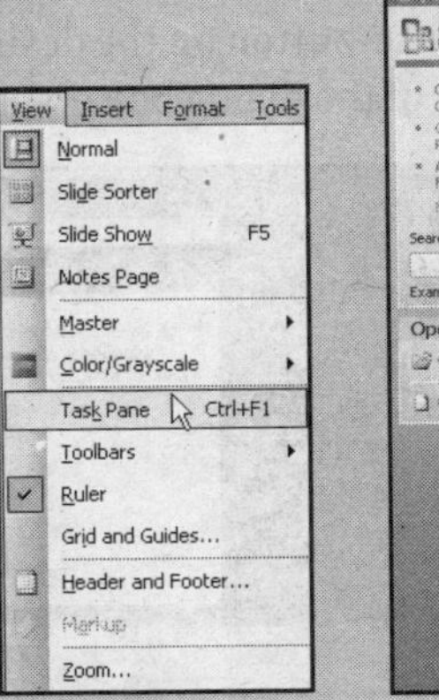

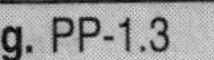

Fig. PP-1.3

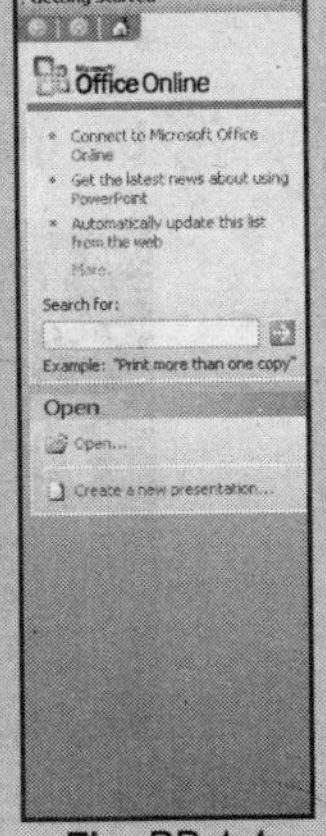

Fig. PP-1.4

Let us now create a PowerPoint presentation with the help of the New Presentation Task pane shown in (Fig.PP-1.6). In this pane under the New option, four ways are available for creating a new presentation. Of these ways, three are used commonly. These are:

- From AutoContent Wizard
- From Design Template
- Blank Presentation

We will create presentations using all the three methods mentioned above. First, we will use the **AutoContent Wizard** to create our presentation.

Creating a Presentation using AutoContent Wizard

The AutoContent Wizard asks you some questions during the process of presentation creation. And, based on your answers, it designs the presentation.

Let us now undertake the following steps to create a presentation through the AutoContent Wizard.

1. The **Microsoft PowerPoint** window (PP-1.2) is open your screen. In this window, *move* the mouse-pointer over the **Create a new Presentation** option in the **Getting Started** Task pane and *click* the left mouse-button (Fig.PP-1.5).
2. The **New Presentation** Task pane appears (Fig.PP-1.6). In this Task pane, *move* the mouse-pointer over the **From AutoContent wizard** option and *click* the left mouse-button
3. The first dialog box of the **AutoContent Wizard** appears (Fig. PP-1.7). *Click* on the **Next** button to begin the process of presentation creation (Fig.PP-1.7).
4. The second dialog box of the **AutoContent Wizard** appears (Fig.PP-1.8). In this box you need to select the type of presentation. Among the available types, the **General** category appears highlighted. On the right side of the dialog box, a list shows various presentations available in the **General** category. *Click* the left mouse-button on the desired presentation type, say **Certificate** (Fig.PP-1.8). Immediately, the **Title bar** of the dialog box displays the name of the selected presentation type.

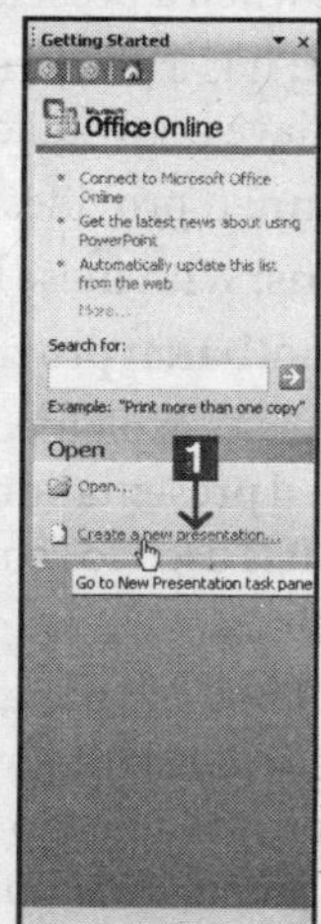

Fig. PP-1.5

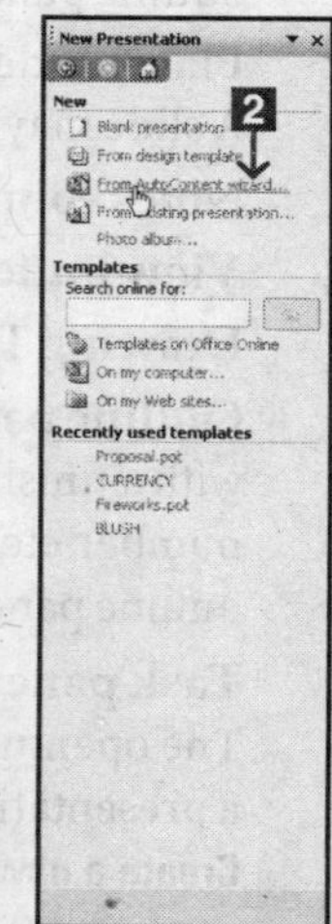

Fig. PP-1.6

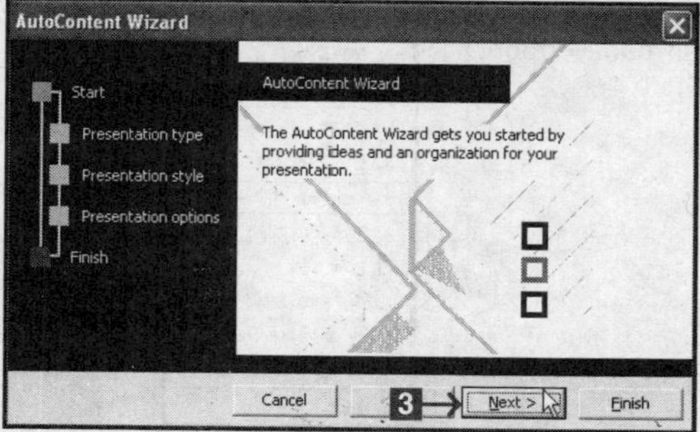

Fig. PP-1.7

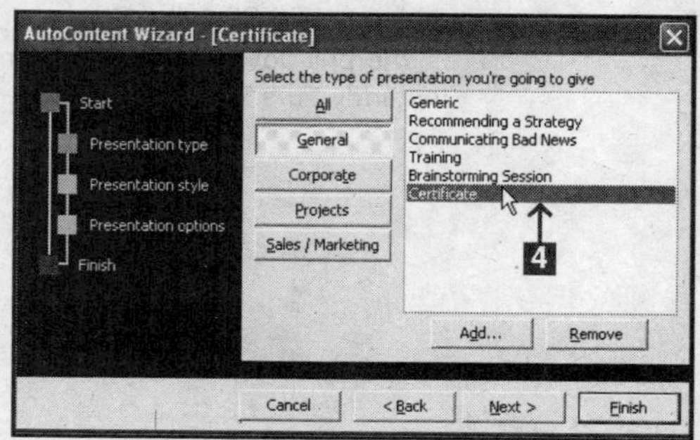

Fig. PP-1.8

5. After selecting the type of presentation, *move* the mouse-pointer over the **Next** button and *click* the left mouse-button (Fig. PP-1.9).
6. The third dialog box of the **AutoContent Wizard** appears (Fig.PP-1.10). In this dialog box, you need to specify the type of output you want to use for your presentation. By default, the **On-screen presentation** option appears selected. Let us use this default option as the type of output for our presentation. *Click* on the **Next** button (Fig. PP-1.10).

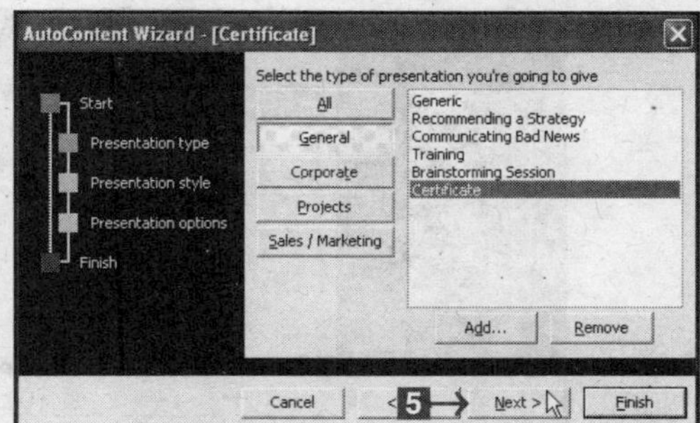

Fig. PP-1.9

7. The fourth dialog box of the **AutoContent Wizard** appears (Fig.PP-1.11). Using the options of this dialog box, you can assign a title for your presentation, slide number, footnote and date to the slides of your presentation.
8. Let us first assign a title to our presentation. To do so, *move* the mouse-pointer over the text box under the **Presentation title** option and *click* the left mouse-button. A blinking cursor appears in the box. *Type* **Certificate for Outstanding Contribution** as the title for our presentation (Fig.PP-1.11)
9. Next, *move* the mouse-pointer over the text box beside the **Footer** option and *click* the left mouse-button. Now, *type* **Dreamtech Press** as the footer for your presentation (Fig.PP-1.11). This text will appear at the bottom of each slide in your presentation.

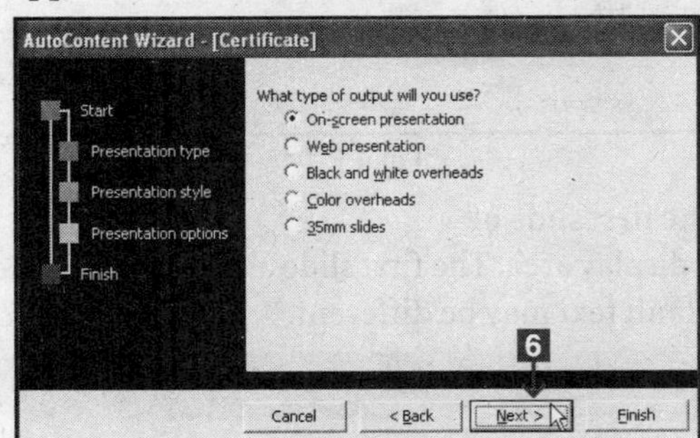

Fig. PP-1.10

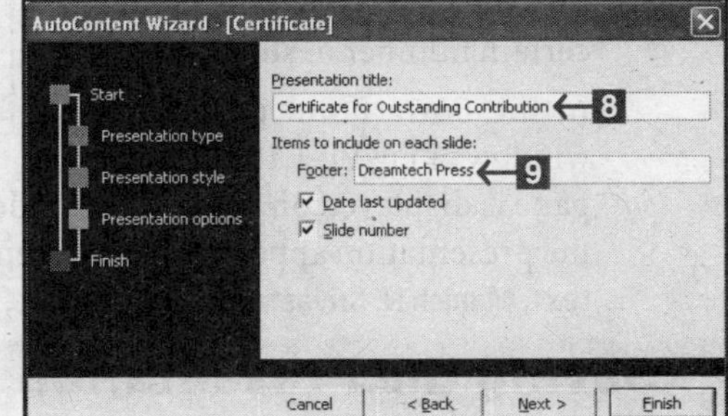

Fig. PP-1.11

10. If you don't want to display the date on which the slide was last updated then *move* the mouse-pointer over the square box beside the **Date last updated** option and *click* the left mouse-button. The check sign disappears from the square box and the option gets de-selected (Fig.PP-1.12).
11. After setting options for slides, *move* the mouse-pointer over the **Next** button and *click* the left mouse-button (Fig. PP-1.13).

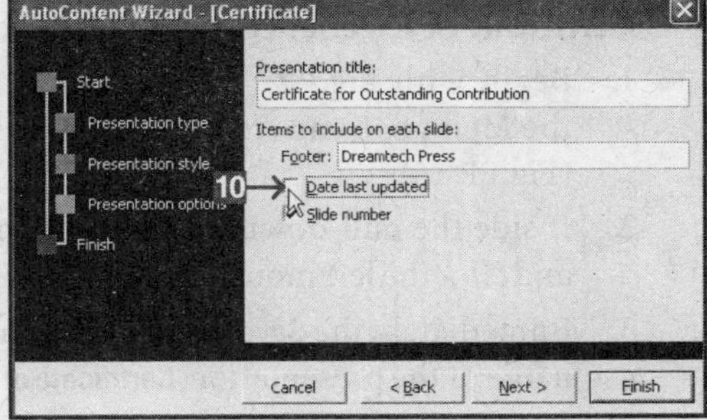

Fig. PP-1.12

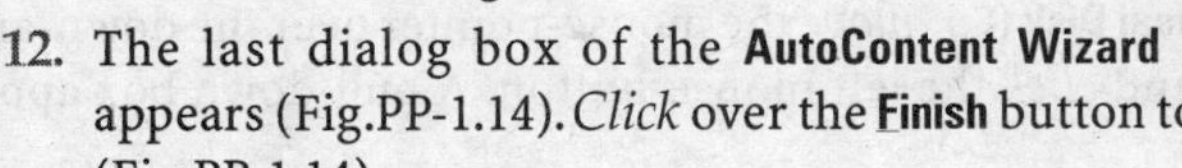

12. The last dialog box of the **AutoContent Wizard** appears (Fig.PP-1.14). *Click* over the **Finish** button to complete the process of presentation creation (Fig.PP-1.14).

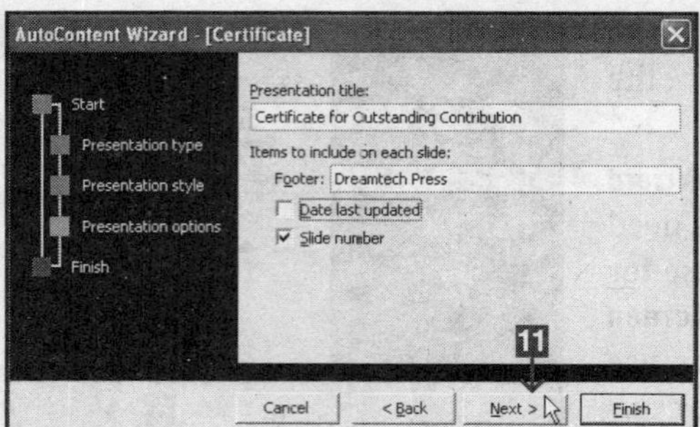

Fig. PP-1.13

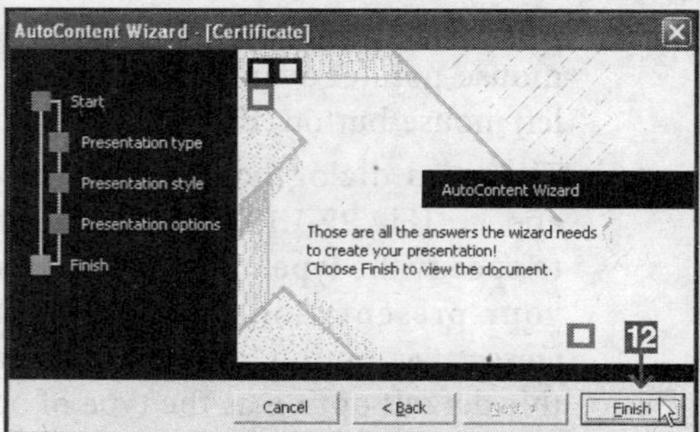

Fig. PP-1.14

13. The information supplied by you through AutoContent Wizard dialog boxes is used to create your presentation. In a few moments, this presentation appears on the screen (Fig.PP-1.15). This presentation by default has three slides. The number of slides depends on the type of presentation chosen by the user. Every presentation type by default has a certain number of slides.

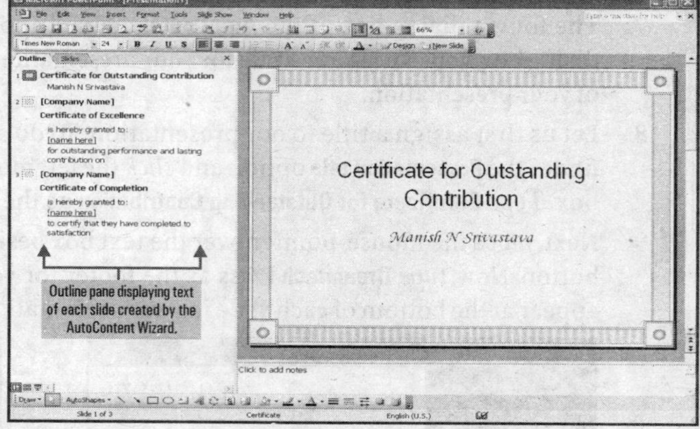

Fig. PP-1.15

In the PowerPoint presentation window of Fig.PP-1.15, the Outline pane is displayed on the left hand side and the first slide of the presentation appears in the presentation display area. The first slide also displays some default text, **Manish N. Srivastava**. In your case, the default text may be different.

Saving the Presentation

If you want to use the presentation you have just created in future then you must save it on the hard disk of your computer. Now, we will name our presentation file as **Certificate of Excellence** and save it in **Local Disk (C:)**. Let us proceed as follows:

1. Begin with Fig.PP-1.15. *Move* the mouse-pointer over the **File** option of the Menu bar and *click* the left mouse-button. A pull-down menu appears (Fig.PP-16).
2. Inside the pull-down menu, *move* the mouse-pointer over the **Save** option and *click* the left mouse-button (Fig.PP-1.16).
3. Immediately, the **Save As** dialog box appears (Fig.PP-17). In this box, *type* the name of the presentation, **Certificate of Excellence**, in the box beside the **File name** option (Fig.PP-1.17).
4. Now, to save the presentation in the **Local Disk (C:)**, *move* the mouse-pointer over the down-arrow button (▾) beside the **Save in** option and *click* the left mouse-button. A pull-down box appears (Fig. PP-1.18).

File Edit View Insert
New... Ctrl+N
Open... Ctrl+O
Close
Save Ctrl+S
Save As...
Save as Web Page...
Package for CD...

Fig. PP-1.16

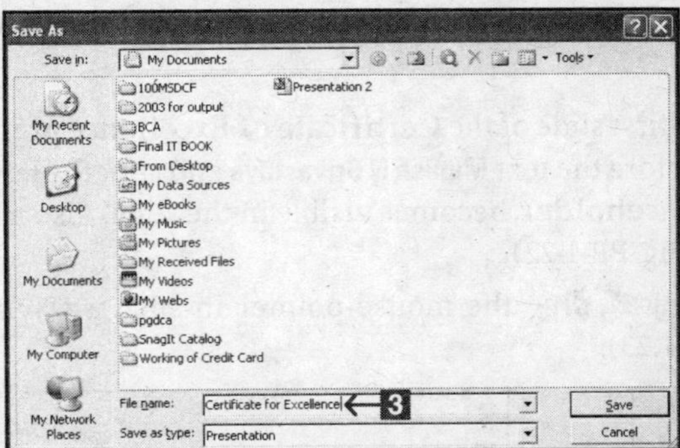

Fig. PP-1.17

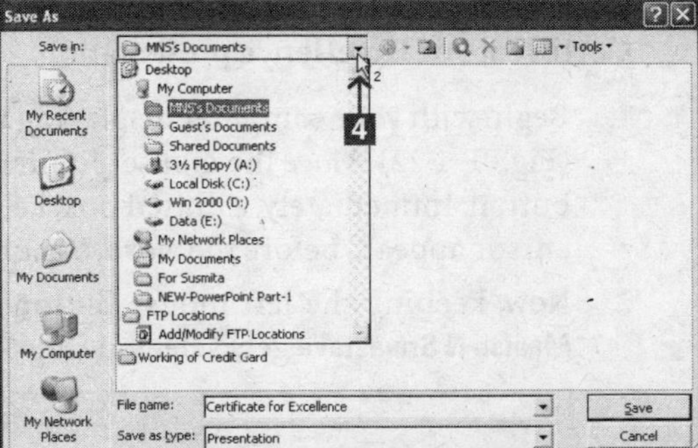

Fig. PP-1.18

5. Inside the pull-down box, *move* the mouse-pointer over the **Local Disk(C:)** and *click* the left mouse-button (Fig.PP-1.19). The **Local Disk (C:)** gets displayed inside the box beside the **Save in** option (Fig. PP-1.20).
6. Finally, *move* the mouse-pointer over **Save** button and *click* the left mouse-button (Fig. PP-1.20)

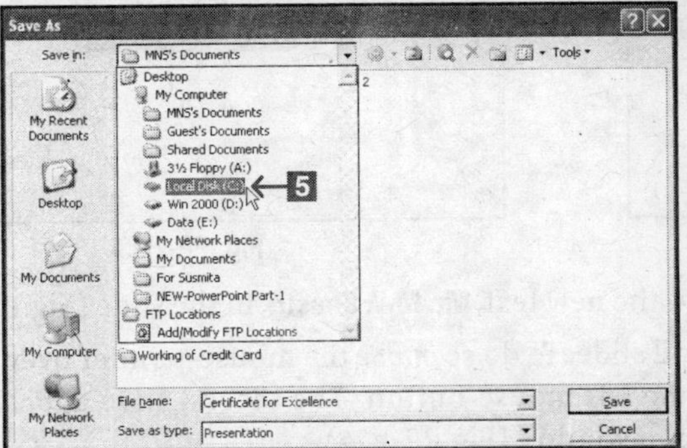

Fig. PP-1.19

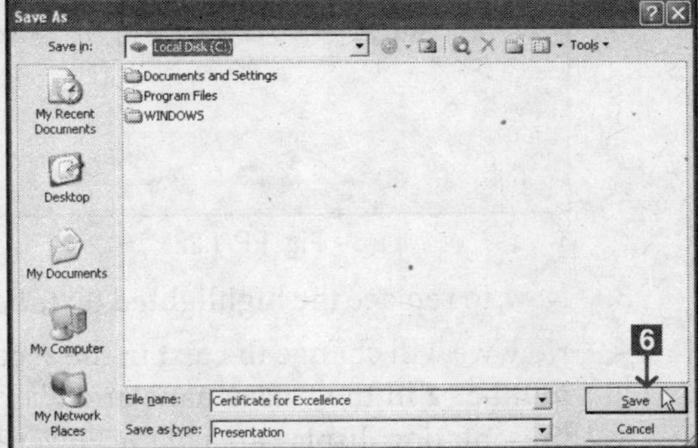

Fig. PP-1.20

7. Your presentation gets saved as **Certificate of Excellence** in the **Local Disk (C:)**. The **Title bar** of the PowerPoint window on your computer shows the name **Certificate of Excellence** (Fig.PP-1.21).

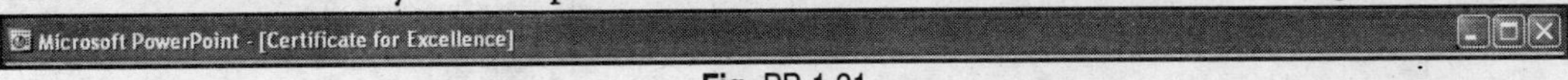

Fig. PP-1.21

Working with Text in Slides

Let us go back to Fig.PP-1.15. In the Outline pane of this figure, along with every slide some default text like (**Company name**), (**name here**), etc has been shown. When you click on a slide in the Outline pane, the slide with its default text gets displayed in the presentation display area. Some default images or logos may also be displayed in the slide. Remember, the default text in the slide varies for different types of presentation. You can replace the default text with the information of your choice in the slide. The placement of the default text is decided by the AutoContent wizard in such a way that if fully integrates with the remaining text of the slide. You can change or delete the entire text of a slide. You can add or change a slide's text in two ways—through the Outline Pane or in the slide.

In the first way, we select the slide (represented by a number) from the Outline pane and then make necessary changes to the text in the Outline pane itself. The second way is straight forward. You simply select the slide in the Outline pane and start making changes in the slide itself.

Now, we will use the second method, i.e. the slide method, to change text in various slides of the **Certificate of Excellence** presentation.

1. Begin with your computer displaying the first slide of the **Certificate of Excellence** presentation (Fig.PP-1.22). *Move* the mouse-pointer before the text **Manish N Srivastava** and *click* the left mouse-button. Immediately, a dotted box, i.e. **placeholder**, becomes visible in the slide. Also a blinking cursor appears before the word, **Manish** (Fig. PP-1.22).
2. Now, keeping the left mouse-button *pressed*, *drag* the mouse-pointer in such a way that text **Manish N Srivastava** gets selected (Fig. PP-1.23).

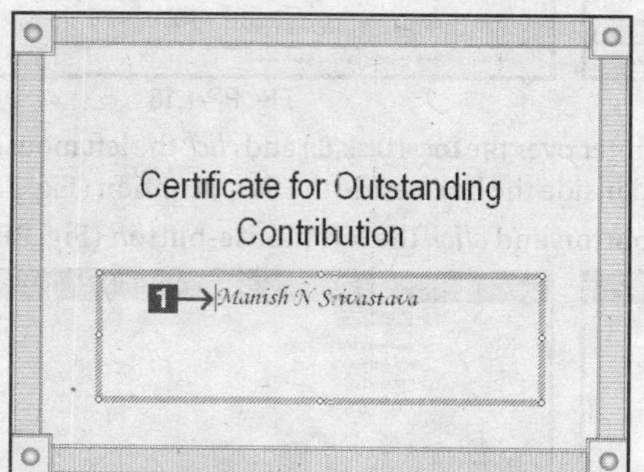

Fig. PP-1.22

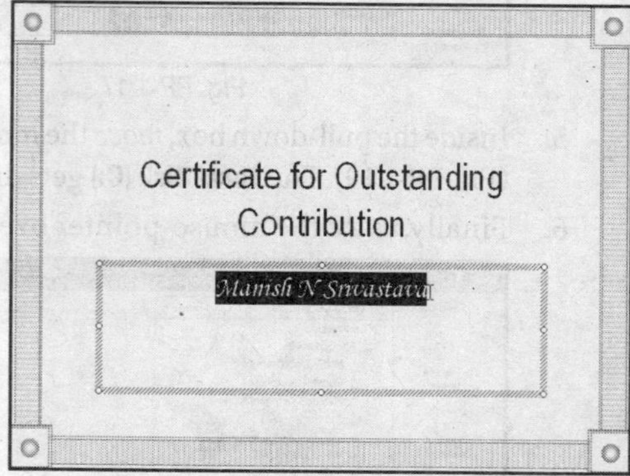

Fig. PP-1.23

3. Now, to replace the highlighted text, *type* the new text, **Mr. M.V. Shastri**, in the slide (Fig.PP-1.24).
4. Now, we will change the text in the second slide. To do so, *move* the mouse-pointer over the slide number **2** in the **Outline** pane and *click* the left mouse-button. The second slide appears in the presentation display area of the PowerPoint window (Fig.PP-1.25).

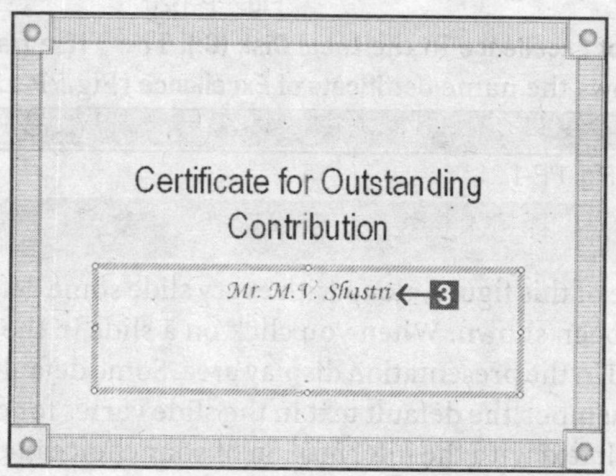

Fig. PP-1.24

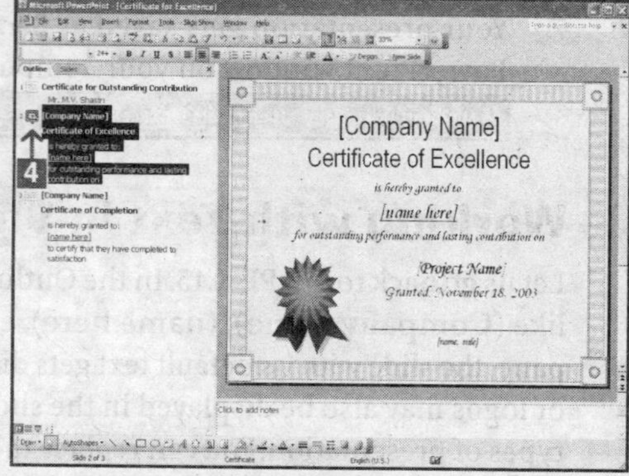

Fig. PP-1.25

5. In the second slide, we will change three default texts— [Company Name], [Name here] and [Project Name]. First, *move* the mouse-pointer over the text **[Company Name]** and *click* the left mouse-button. Then keeping the left mouse-button *pressed*, *drag* the mouse-pointer in such a way that the text **[Company Name]** gets highlighted (Fig.PP-1.26).

6. Now, to change the highlighted text, *type* **Dreamtech** (Fig.PP-1.27).

Fig. PP-1.26

Fig. PP-1.27

7. Next, following the procedure in Step 5 highlight the text **[Name here]** (Fig.PP-1.28).
8. Now, *type* **Mr. Chopra.** This text replaces the text **[Name here]** in the slide (Fig.PP-1.29).

Fig. PP-1.28

Fig. PP-1.29

9. Next, *highlight* the text **[Project Name]** (Fig.PP-1.30).
10. *Type* **The Science of Debugging.** This text replaces the text **[Project Name]** in the slide (Fig.PP-1.31).

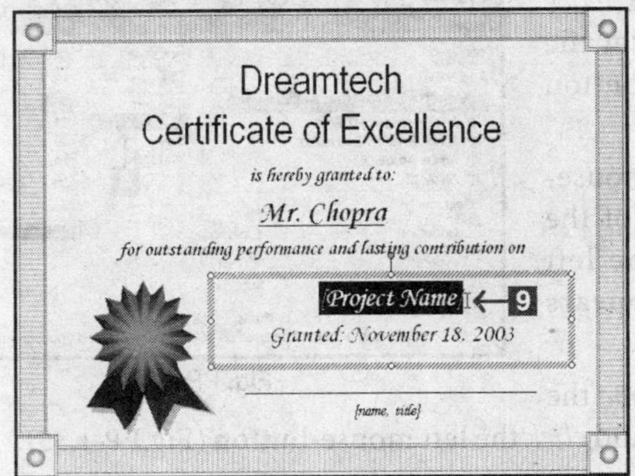

Fig. PP-1.30

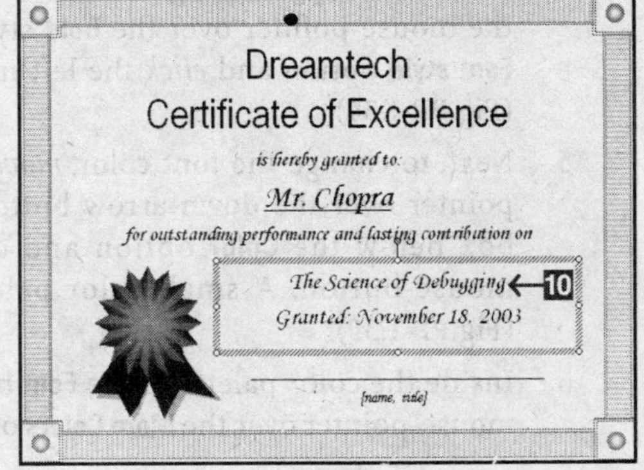

Fig. PP-1.31

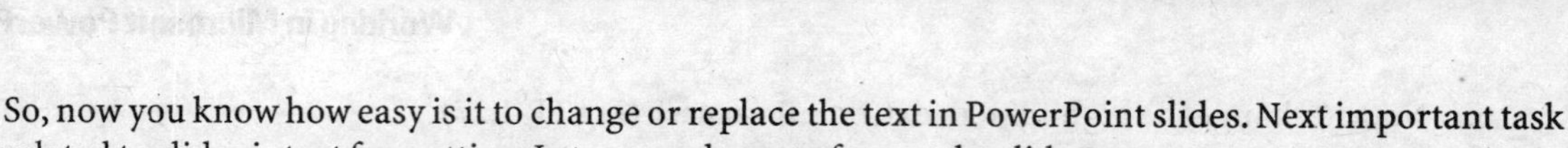

So, now you know how easy is it to change or replace the text in PowerPoint slides. Next important task related to slides is text formatting. Let us now learn to format the slide text.

Formatting the Text

You can make your presentation more attractive by applying various formatting features to text. Using text formatting features of PowerPoint, you can change the size of the text, underline the text, add color to text, etc. Now, we will use these features on the currently active second slide of **Certificate of Excellence** presentation. We will learn to change the text font, font color and background of the slide.

Changing Font and Font Color

1. Start with Fig.PP-1.31. *Move* the mouse-pointer to the left of the text **Dreamtech** and *click* the left mouse-button. Keeping the left mouse-button *pressed*, *drag* the mouse-pointer in such a way that the text **Dreamtech** gets selected (Fig.PP-1.32).
2. Now, we will change the font of the highlighted text. To do so, *move* the mouse-pointer over the **Format** option of the Menu bar and *click* the left mouse button. A pull-down menu appears (Fig.PP-1.33).
3. Inside the pull-down menu, *move* the mouse-pointer over the **Font** option and *click* the left mouse-button (Fig.PP-1.33).

Fig. PP-1.32

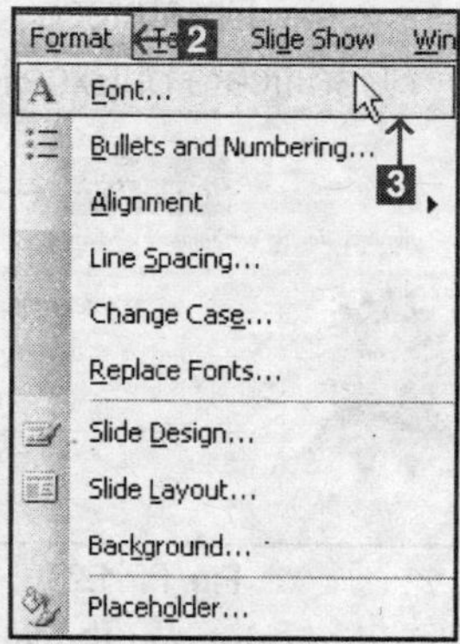

Fig. PP-1.33

4. The **Font** box appears (Fig.PP-1.34). In this box, *move* the mouse-pointer over the **Bold** style under the **Font style** option and *click* the left mouse-button (Fig.PP-1.34).
5. Next, to change the font color, *move* the mouse-pointer over the down-arrow button (▾) of the box below the **Color** option and *click* the left mouse-button. A small color palette appears (Fig.PP-1.35).
6. Inside the color palette of the **Font** box, *move* the mouse-pointer over the **More Colors** option and *click* the left mouse-button (Fig.PP-1.35).

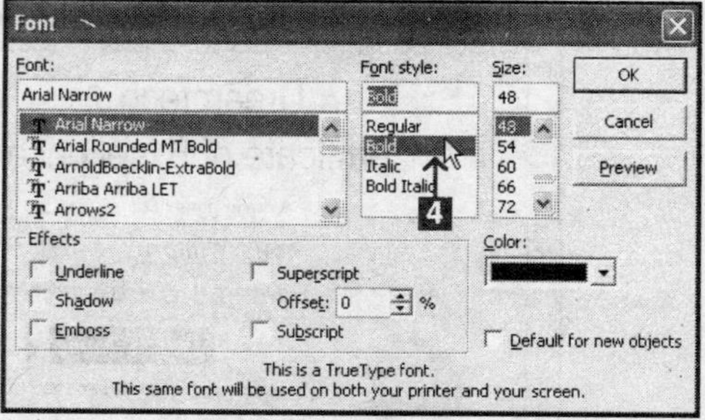

Fig. PP-1.34

7. The **Colors** box appears with two tabs – **Standard** and **Custom** (Fig.PP-1.39). By default, the **Standard** tab appears active with various colors shown under the **Colors**: option. We will use the **Standard** tab to select a color for our font. To do so, *move* the mouse-pointer over the desired color and *click* over it (Fig.PP-1.36). The **Colors** box has a box with two thick bars at its right side bottom. The top bar represents the newly selected color while the bottom bar shows the current color.

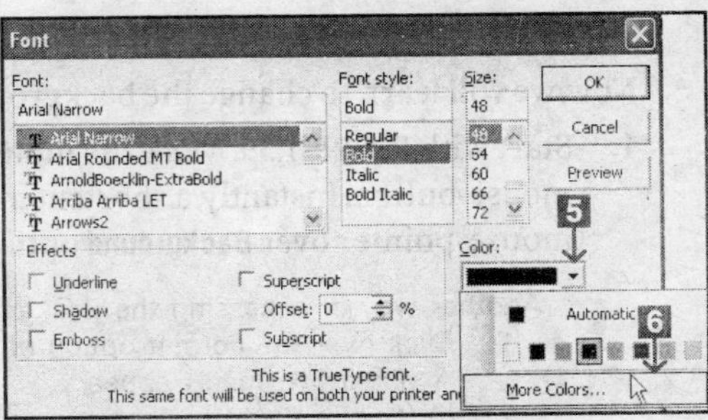

Fig. PP-1.35

8. Next, *move* the mouse-pointer over the **OK** button of the **Color** box and *click* the left mouse-button (Fig.PP-1.37).

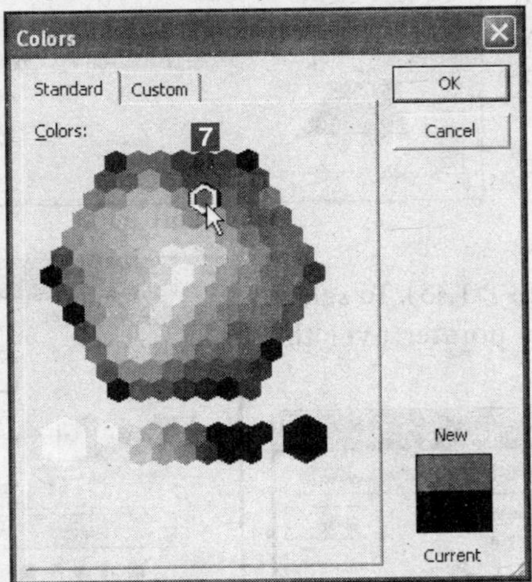

Fig. PP-1.36

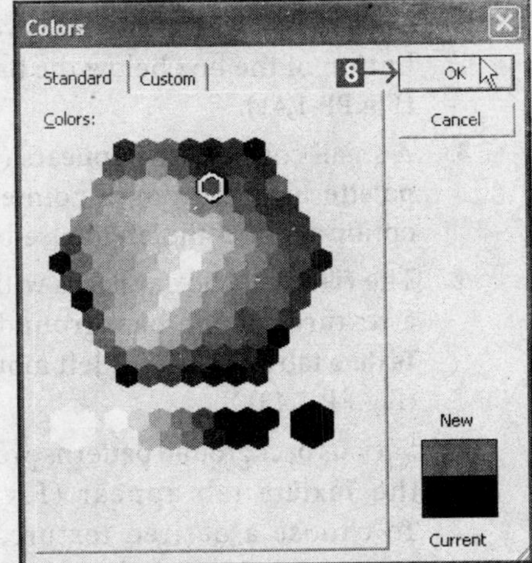

Fig. PP-1.37

9. The **Font** box re-appears (Fig.PP-1.38). Now, *move* the mouse-pointer over the **OK** button of the **Font** box and *click* the left mouse-button (Fig.PP-1.38).

10. The **Font** box disappears and the changes made to the selected text, i.e. **Dreamtech**, get reflected in the slide (Fig.PP-1.39).

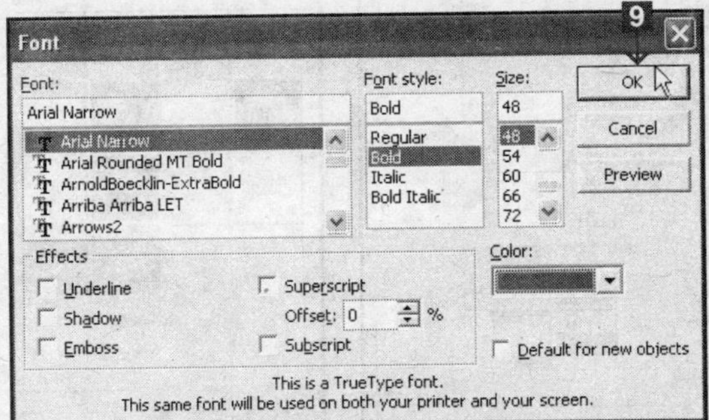

Fig. PP-1.38

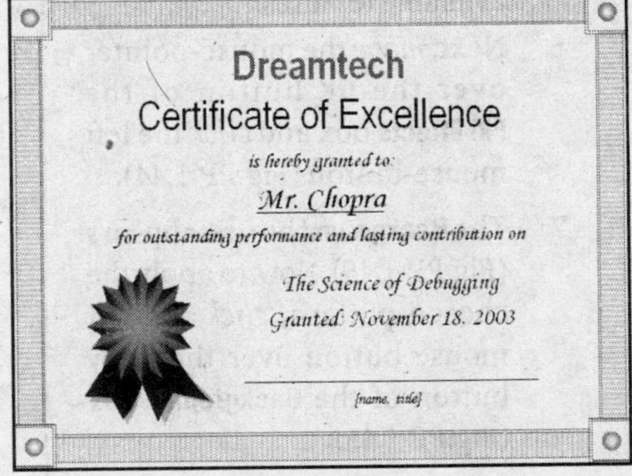

Fig. PP-1.39

Changing the Background

Now, we will learn to change the background of a PowerPoint slide.

1. Start with Fig.PP-1.39. *Move* the mouse-pointer over the empty area in the slide and *click* the right mouse-button. Instantly, a shortcut menu appears (Fig.PP-1.40). Inside the shortcut menu, *move* the mouse-pointer over **Background** option and *click* the left mouse-button (Fig.PP-1.40).

Another way of accessing the Background option is:
1. Click over the Format option of the Menu bar. A pull-down menu appears.
2. In the pull-down menu, click over the Background option.

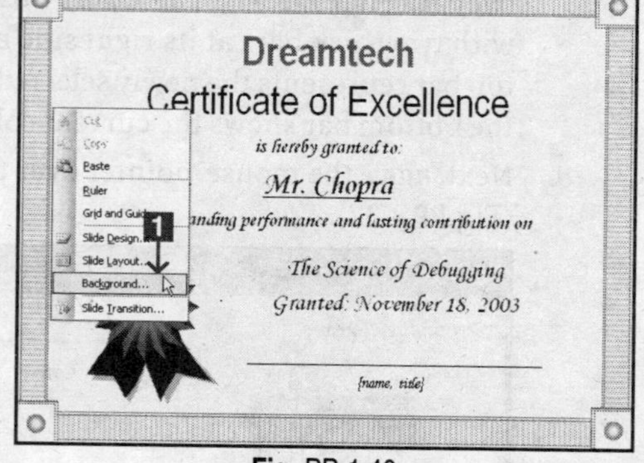

Fig. PP-1.40

2. The **Background** box appears (Fig.PP-1.41). This box has the **Background fill** option. To select a colour for the slide background, *click* over the down-arrow button of the box below the **Background fill** option (Fig.PP-1.41).
3. A small color palette appears (Fig.PP-1.42). In the palette, *move* the mouse-pointer over the **Fill Effects** option and *click* the left mouse-button (Fig.PP-1.42).
4. The **Fill Effects** box appears with several tabs (Fig.PP-1.43). To select a texture for the background, *move* the mouse-pointer over the **Texture** tab and *click* the left mouse-button (Fig.PP-1.43).

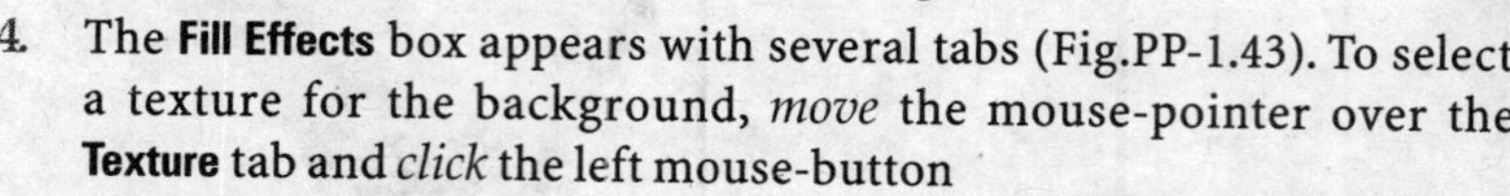

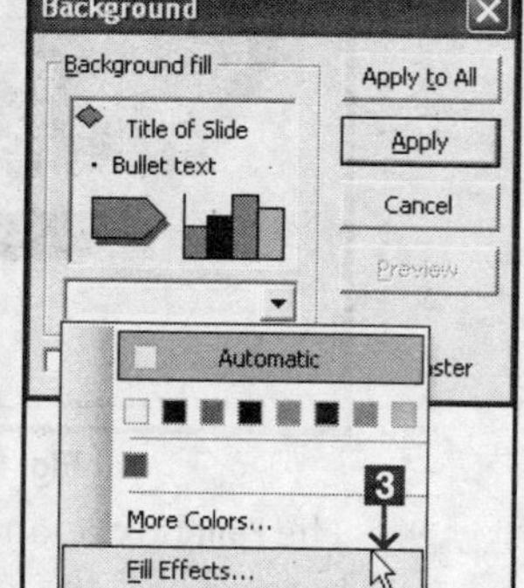

Fig. PP-1.41

Fig. PP-1.42

5. Various background patterns present under the **Texture** tab appear (Fig.PP-1.44). To choose a desired texture, *move* the mouse-pointer over it and *click* the left mouse-button. In Fig.PP-1.44, the **White marble** texture has been selected. The name of the selected texture appears in a bar below the box showing the available textures.
6. Next, *move* the mouse-pointer over the **OK** button of the **Fill Effects** box and *click* the left mouse-button (Fig.PP-1.44).
7. The **Background** box re-appears (Fig.PP-1.45). Now, to apply the chosen pattern, *click* the left mouse button over the **Apply** button of the **Background** box (Fig.PP-1.45).

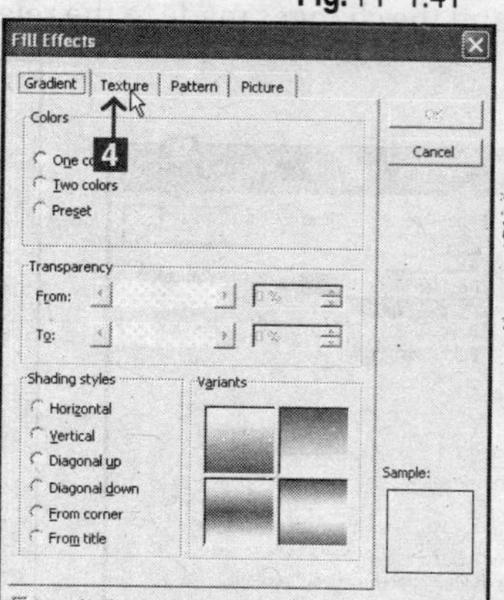

Fig. PP-1.43

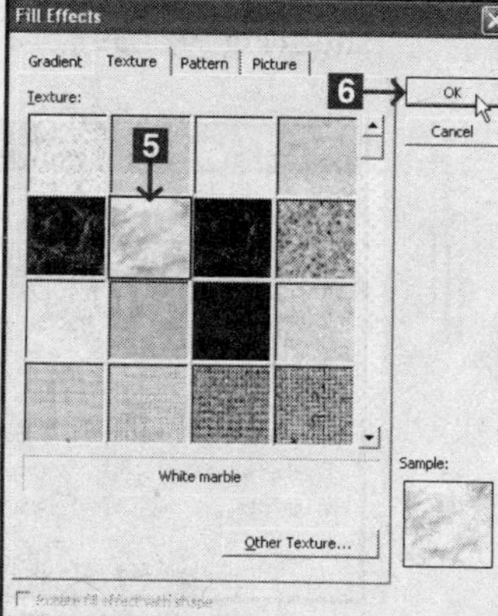

Fig. PP-1.44

8. The selected background pattern gets applied to the second slide (Fig.PP-1.46).

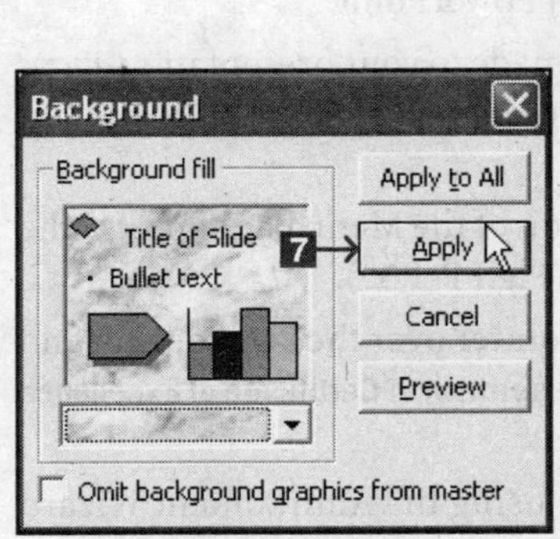

Fig. PP-1.45

Fig. PP-1.46

If you want to apply the selected background to all slides in a presentation then click over the Apply to All button of the Background box.

Deleting a Slide

You can delete any slide from your presentation. Suppose, of the three slides in the **Certificate of Excellence** presentation, you want to delete the **third slide.** Let us learn how to delete a desired slide.

1. Start with Fig.PP-1.46. In the **Outline** pane, *move* the mouse-pointer over slide number **3** and *click* the left mouse-button (Fig.PP-1.47).
2. Next, *move* the mouse-pointer over the **Edit** option of the Menu bar and *click* the left mouse-button. A pull-down menu appears (Fig.PP-1.48).
3. Inside the pull-down menu, *move* the mouse-pointer over the **Delete Slide** option and *click* the left mouse-button (Fig.PP-1.48).
4. The third slide gets deleted from the presentation. After this deletion, the **Outline** pane displays only two slides (Fig.PP-1.49).

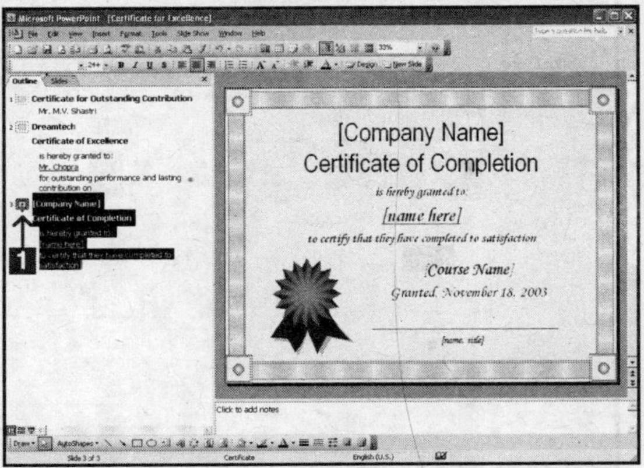

Fig. PP-1.47

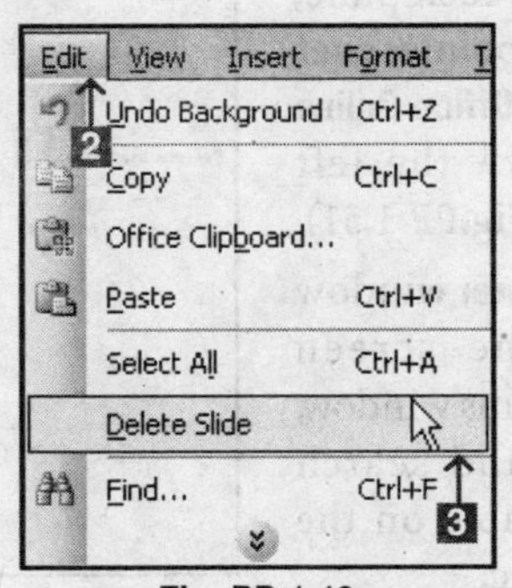

Fig. PP-1.48

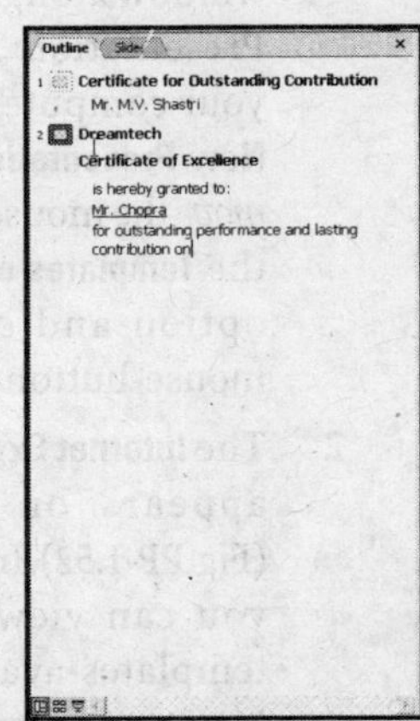

Fig. PP-1.49

Closing the Presentation

So, you have added a new dimension to your computer skills by learning the Microsoft PowerPoint program. In the next chapter, you will learn more about this program. Let us now close our presentation and quit the Microsoft PowerPoint.

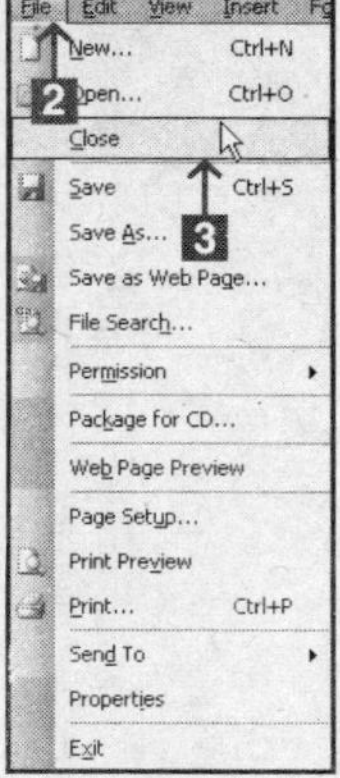

Fig. PP-1.50

1. Start with Fig.PP-1.49. First, to save the changes made to your presentation, *move* the mouse-pointer over the **Save** button ( ) present on the **Standard Toolbar** and *click* the left mouse-button.
2. Next, *move* the mouse-pointer over the **File** option of the Menu bar and *click* the left mouse-button. A pull-down menu appears (Fig.PP-1.50).
3. Inside the pull-down menu, move the mouse-pointer over the **Close** option and *click* the left mouse-button (Fig.PP-1.50). The presentation **Certificate of Excellence** closes down.

We have just closed the presentation that we made using the AutoContent Wizard option of the New Presentation Task pane. We will also create a presentation through a PowerPoint Design Template. You can use a default template of the PowerPoint program or download a new one from the Internet. We will first download a PowerPoint design template and then use it for making our presentation.

Downloading a PowerPoint Design Template

A PowerPoint template offers you readymade formatting and design styles for applying to your presentation. In other words, **Template** is a file that contains various formatting and design styles, including the type and size of bullets and fonts; placeholder sizes and positions; background design and fill color schemes. The Microsoft PowerPoint has its own collection of templates which you can use to create different presentations. If you don't want to use the default templates then you can download a PowerPoint template from the official website of the Microsoft and use it for creating presentations. Let us now learn to download a template from the official website of the Microsoft. Proceed as follows:

1. First, display the PowerPoint window along with the New Presentation Task pane on your computer. Then in the **New Presentation** Task pane, *move* the mouse-pointer over the **Templates on Office Online** option and *click* the left mouse-button (Fig.PP-1.51).
2. The **Internet Explorer** window appears on the screen (Fig.PP-1.52). In this window, you can view and search templates available on the Microsoft website.

Fig. PP-1.51

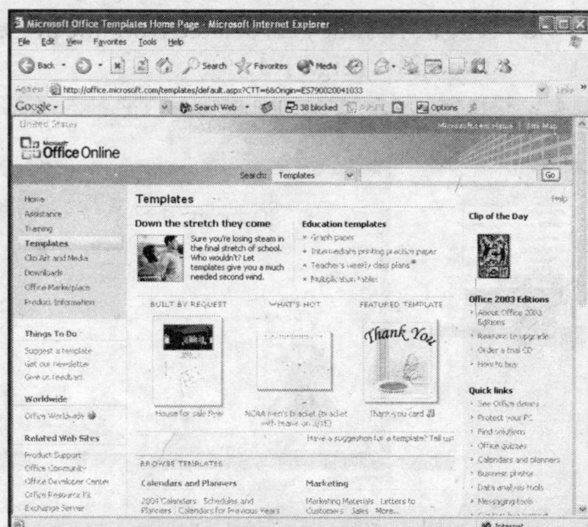

Fig. PP-1.52

3. In the Internet Explorer window, the **Search** option has two boxes. In our case, one box by default shows the text **Templates.** But the second box is empty. Now to search PowerPoint templates, *move* the mouse-pointer over the empty box beside the **Search** option and *click* the left mouse-button. Then *Type* **PowerPoint Design Templates**, and *click* over the **Go** button (Fig. PP-1.53).
4. In a few moments, names of various PowerPoint templates appear on the screen (Fig.PP-1.54). In this screen, **Page[1]** appears highlighted. It means we are on page number 1 of the website section that displays various PowerPoint templates.

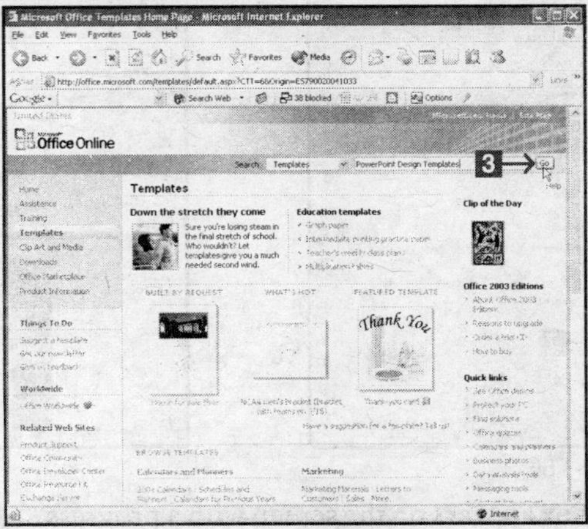

Fig. PP-1.53

5. Suppose, you want to download a template, **Bull's eye darts**, that appears on page 3 of the PowerPoint templates section. To download this template, *move* the mouse-pointer over **page number 3** of the website and *click* the left mouse-button (Fig. PP-1.54).
6. The templates present on page number **3** appear on the screen (Fig.PP-1.55). *Move* the mouse-pointer over the down-arrow scroll button (▾) of the PowerPoint window and *click* the left mouse-button. Keep *clicking* the left mouse-button until you reach the **Bull's eye darts** template (Fig. PP-1.55).

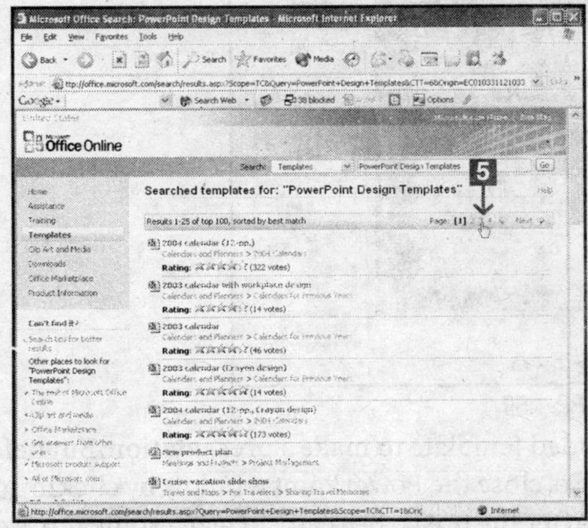

Fig. PP-1.54

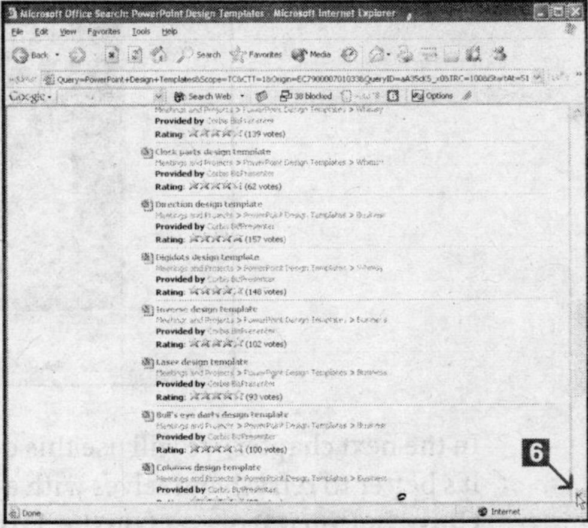

Fig. PP-1.55

7. Now, *move* the mouse-pointer over the **Bull's eye darts** template and *click* the left mouse-button (Fig. PP-1.56).

8. In few moments the preview of the selected template appears on the screen along with the button to download it (Fig.PP-1.57). After viewing the template's preview, *move* the mouse-pointer over the **Download Now** button and *click* the left mouse-button (Fig. PP-1.57).

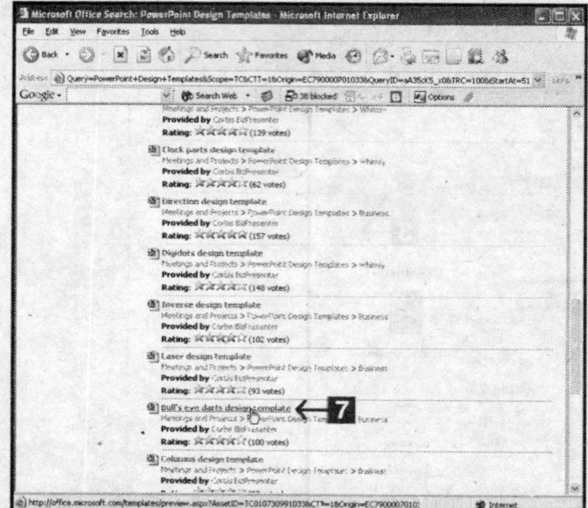

Fig. PP-1.56

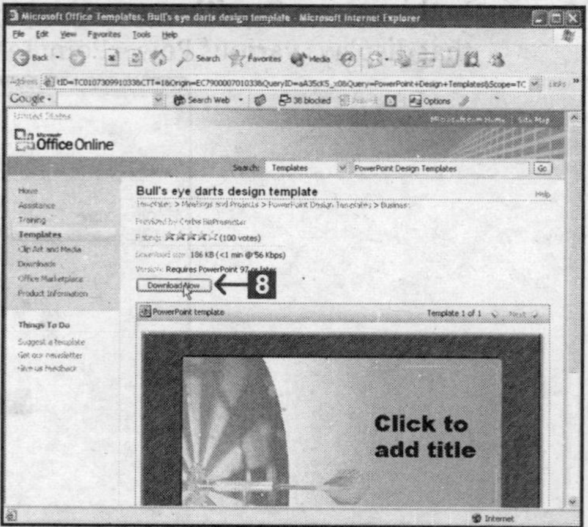

Fig. PP-1.57

9. A **Downloading Template** box appears on the screen with a progress bar (Fig.PP-1.58). Once the template is completely downloaded on your computer, the **Downloading Template** box disappears. Now, your computer displays the PowerPoint window with the first slide, also known as Title slide, of the newly-downloaded template (Fig.PP-1.59).

Fig. PP-1.58

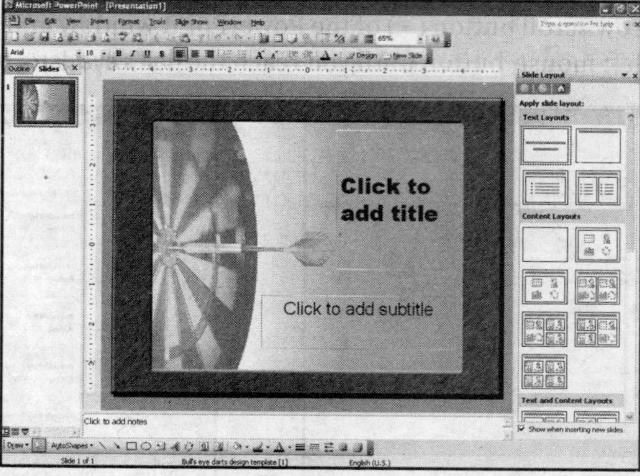

Fig. PP-1.59

In the next chapter, we will use this downloaded template to make a presentation. But before that it's better to refresh ourselves with a break. So, close the PowerPoint window by clicking over the **Close** button (☒) present on the **Title bar**. After the break, be ready to learn some more exciting features of the PowerPoint program.

Adding Animation in Slides 2

IN THIS CHAPTER

- Creating a Presentation using Design Template
- Adding Transition Effects to Slides
- Animating Individual Slide Elements with Custom Animation
- Previewing Animation Effects in the Slide
- Saving the Presentation and Quitting Microsoft PowerPoint
- Exercise
- Summary

In this chapter, we will create a presentation using a design template. In the last chapter we had introduced you to the design templates and also downloaded one such template, **Bull's eye darts.** You already know how to create a presentation through the AutoContent wizard, which is basically a readymade method to make a presentation of fixed number of slides. However, a design template offers you liberty to decide how many slides you want in a presentation. Besides setting the number of slides, you can add same or different animation effects to slides in the presentation.

We will work on two ways of adding animation effects to slides. The first way is **Transition Effect.** Using this option you can control how one slide leaves the screen and another one appears. The second way of adding animation effects is **Custom Animation** that lets you control the appearance of various slide elements. A slide element could be some text, image, chart etc. You can set same or different Custom Animation effects to slide elements.

Let's now open the Microsoft PowerPoint. In the previous chapter, you had learnt to open the Microsoft PowerPoint. Just to refresh your memory, the steps for opening the PowerPoint are listed hereunder:

1. *Move* the mouse-pointer over the **Start** button (start) on the **Taskbar** and *click* the left mouse-button. A push-up menu appears on the screen.
2. Inside the push-up menu, *place* the mouse-pointer over the **All Programs** option. A second menu appears.
3. Inside the second menu, *place* the mouse-pointer over the **Microsoft Office** option. A third menu appears.
4. Inside the third menu, *move* the mouse-pointer over the **Microsoft Office PowerPoint 2003** option and *click* the left mouse-pointer.
5. Instantly, the **Microsoft PowerPoint** window opens up on the screen.

Creating a Presentation using Design Template

Already, the PowerPoint window is open your screen. Let's now proceed to make a presentation based on the **Bull's eye darts** template.

1. *Move* the mouse-pointer over the **File** option of the Menu bar and *click* the left mouse-button. A pull-down menu appears (Fig.PP-2.1). Inside the pull-down menu, *move* the mouse-pointer over the **New** option and *click* the left mouse-button (Fig.PP-2.1).
2. The **New Presentation** Task pane appears on the right side of the **Microsoft PowerPoint** window (Fig.PP-2.2).

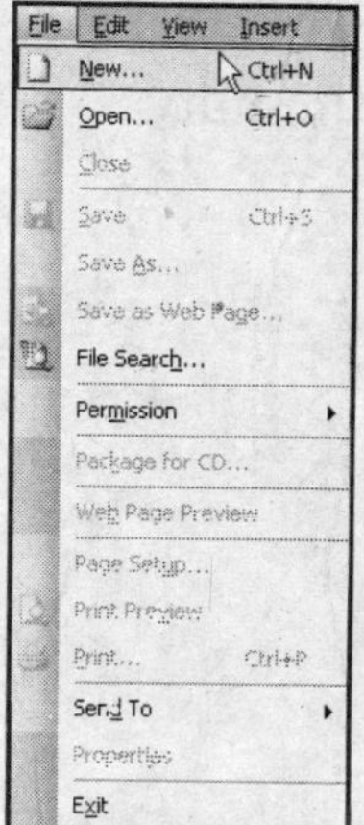

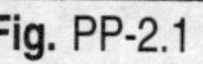
Fig. PP-2.1

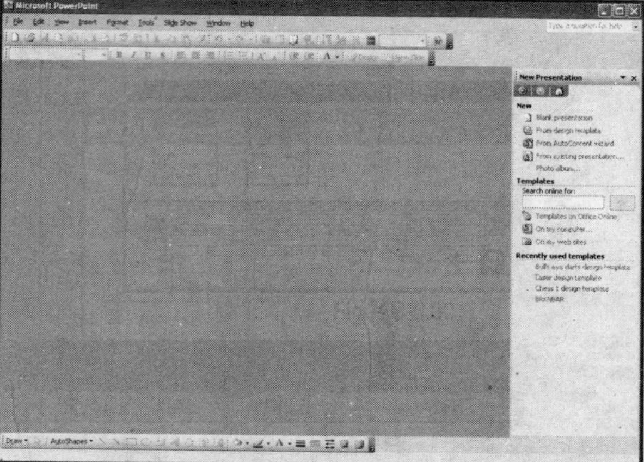

Fig. PP-2.2

3. In the **New Presentation** Task pane, *move* the mouse-pointer over the **From design template** option and *click* the left mouse-button (Fig.PP-2.3).
4. Instantly, the **Slide Design** Task pane replaces the **New Presentation** Task pane (Fig.PP-2.4). The **Slide Design** Task pane displays various design templates for creating a presentation. Let us choose a design template, say **Bull's eye darts**, for our presentation.
5. To access the **Bull's eye darts** template, *move* the mouse-pointer over the down scroll arrow button (⌄) of the **Slide Design** Task pane and *click* the left mouse-button (Fig.PP-2.5). More design templates appear in the **Slide Design** Task pane.
6. Now, *move* the mouse-pointer over the **Bull's eye darts** design template and *click* the left mouse-button (Fig.PP-2.6).

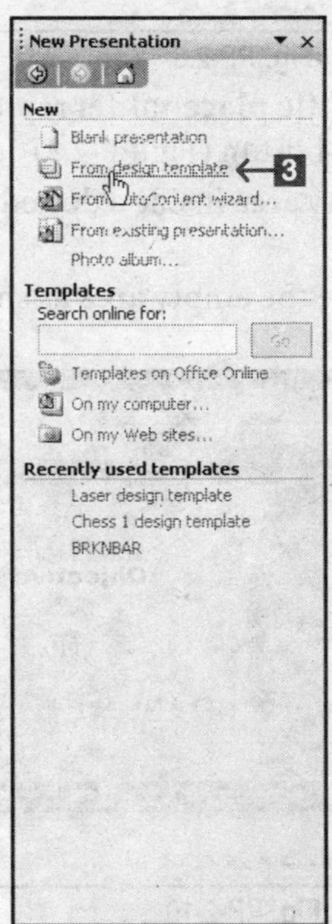

Fig. PP-2.3

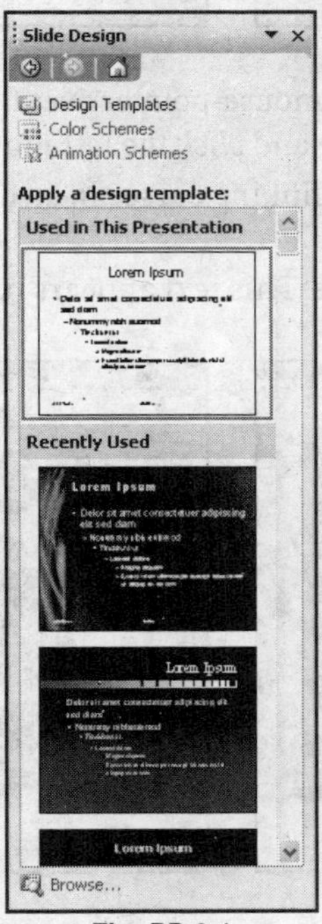

Fig. PP-2.4

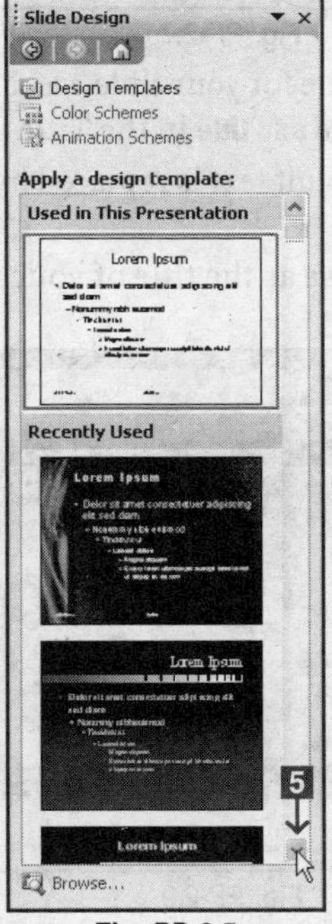

Fig. PP-2.5

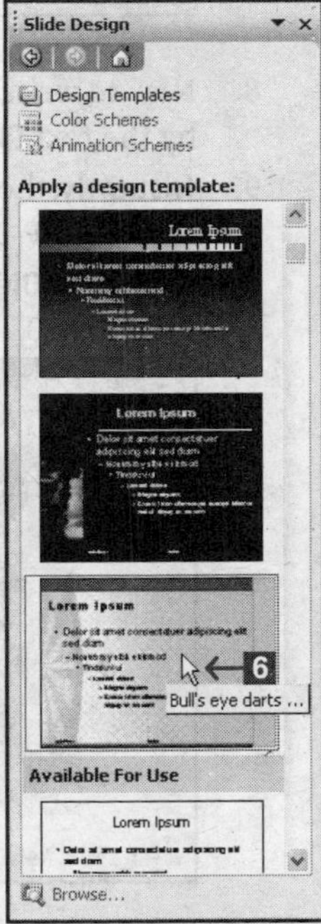

Fig. PP-2.6

7. In a few moments, the Microsoft PowerPoint generates the first slide of the **Bull's eye darts** template (Fig.PP-2.7). The first slide of a template is known as **Title slide.** All other slides which you would add after the Title slide using the template may be termed as secondary slides.

   The PowerPoint window of Fig.PP-7.7 also displays the **Slides** pane on its left. The **Slides** pane displays all slides of a presentation in miniature form. It displays serial numbers of slides and other relevant details. The **Slides** pane of Fig.PP-2.7 shows only one slide that is the Title slide of the **Bull's eye darts** template because so far we have not added any secondary slide.

   In every slide, there is place for writing the slide's title, subtitle or simple text. This place is actually a box with dotted borders, and is known as **placeholder.** The Title placeholder appears at the top of each slide followed by placeholders for the subtitle and text. These placeholders usually display some default text in bold or normal fonts.

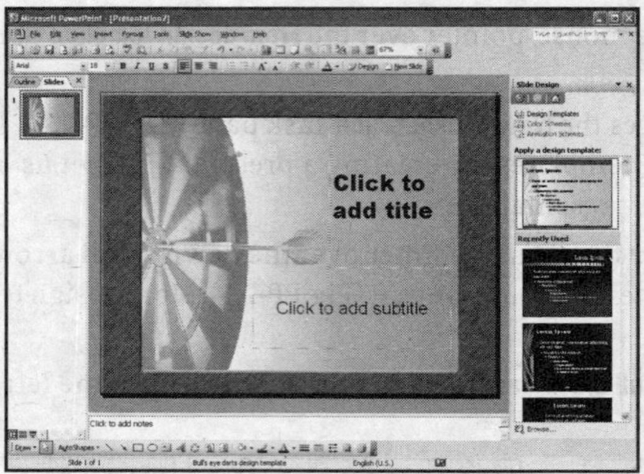

Fig. PP-2.7

Fig. PP-2.8

8. Now, to write a title for your slide, *move* the mouse-pointer over the **Title placeholder** represented by the text **Click to add title** in the Title slide and *click* the left mouse-button (Fig.PP-2.8)
9. Instantly, the default text is replaced by a blinking cursor in an empty area inside a dotted border box (Fig.PP-2.9).
10. Now, *type* **Objective** as the title of your slide. This text appears inside the empty area as shown in Fig.PP-2.10.

Fig. PP-2.9

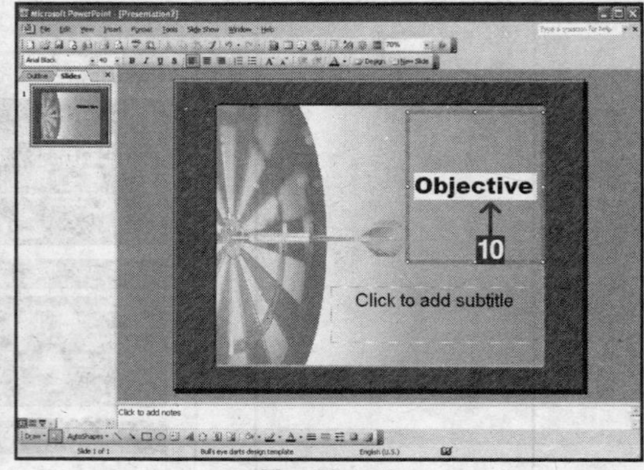

Fig. PP-2.10

11. To make the Title placeholder, i.e. the dotted border box, invisible, *click* anywhere in the slide. The text of the Title slide appears without placeholder (Fig.PP-2.11).
12. Next, *move* the mouse-pointer over the text **Click to add subtitle** that represents the placeholder for subtitle or text. We will use this placeholder to write names for our three secondary slides (Fig.PP-2.11).
13. Now, *click* on the default text **Click to add subtitle.** A blinking cursor replaces the default text. *Type* **Customer Satisfaction** as the name of your first secondary slide as shown in Fig.PP-2.12.

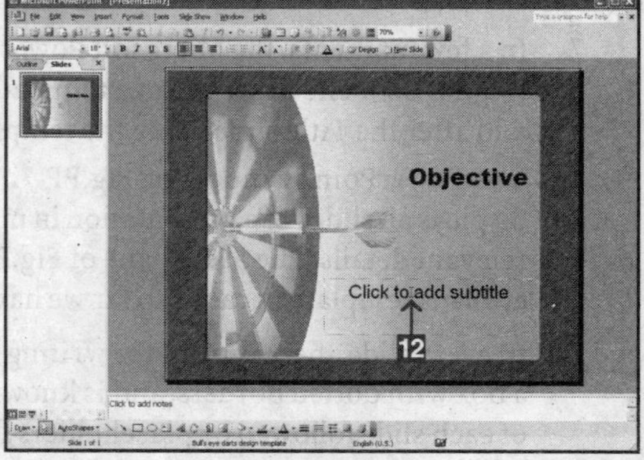

Fig. PP-2.11

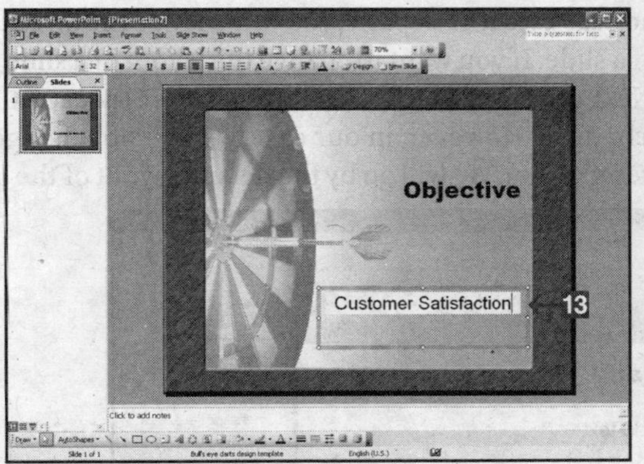

Fig. PP-2.12

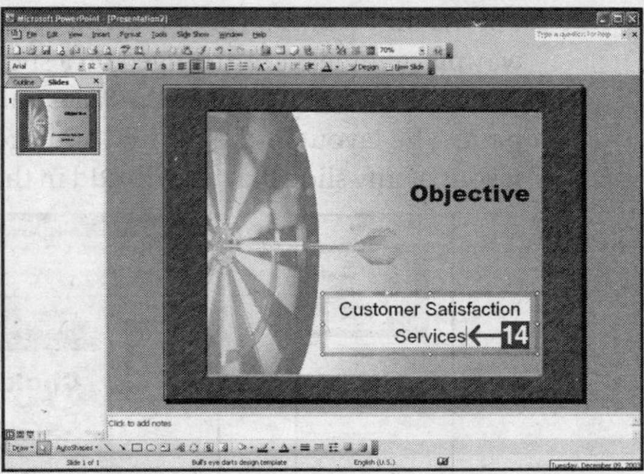

Fig. PP-2.13

14. Next, *press* the **Enter** key. A blank line gets inserted in the subtitle placeholder. Now, *type* **Services** as the name of your second secondary slide (Fig.PP-2.13).
15. Once again *press* the **Enter** key. Another blank line gets inserted in the subtitle placeholder. *Type* **Cost Analysis** as the name of your third secondary slide (Fig.PP-2.14).
16. After typing the names of the secondary slides, the first slide i.e. the Title slide of your presentation appears like Fig.PP-2.15.

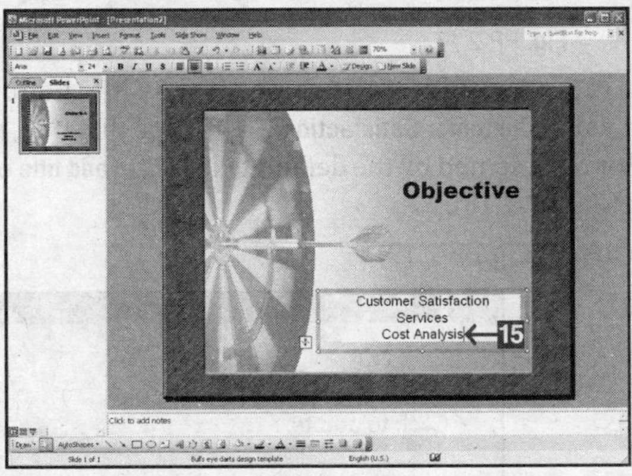

Fig. PP-2.14

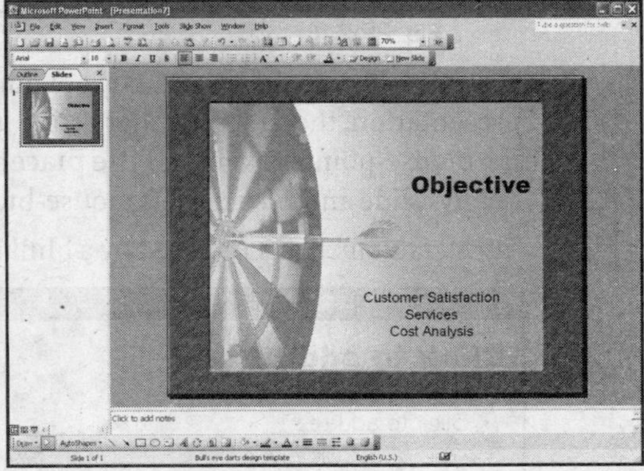

Fig. PP-2.15

Adding a New Slide

In the preceding topic, we have given names for our three secondary slides. Let us now add these slides one by one to our presentation.

1. Start with Fig. PP-2.15. *Move* the mouse-pointer over the empty area in the **Slides** pane and *click* the right mouse-button. A shortcut menu appears (Fig.PP-2.16). Inside the shortcut menu, *move* the mouse-pointer over the **New Slide** option and *click* the left mouse-button (Fig.PP-2.16).
2. A new slide gets inserted in your presentation as shown in Fig.PP-2.17. Now, the Slides pane displays two slides. Number **2** slide is the newly-inserted one. The new slide also has placeholders for the title and text. With the insertion of Slide 2, the **Slide Layout** Task pane also appears on the right of the

PowerPoint window (Fig.PP-2.17). Using the **Slide Layout** Task pane, you can change the layout (the way placeholders are arranged on a slide) of a slide. If you want to change the layout of a slide then first click over that slide in the **Slides** pane. Next, *click* over the desired layout in the **Slide Layout** Task pane. The layout of the desired slide gets changed. However, in our case, we will not change the layout of any slide that we will add in the presentation. We will go by the default layout of the slide.

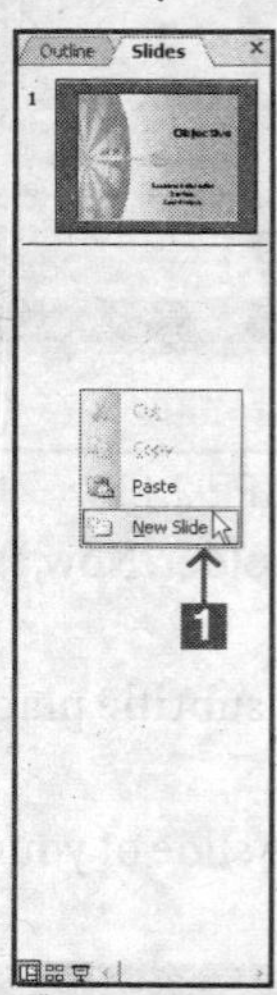

Fig. PP-2.16

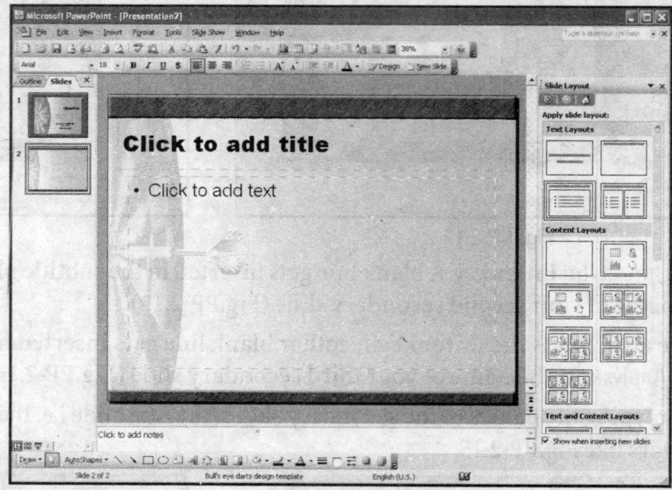

Fig. PP-2.17

3. Now, we will type the title and text of our first secondary slide. As you know, in the Title slide of our presentation, the first secondary slide is named as **Customer Satisfaction.** So, to type this title, *move* the mouse-pointer over the **Title placeholder** represented by the default text **Click to add title** of the second slide and *click* the left mouse-button (Fig.PP-2.18).
4. The default text gets replaced by a blinking cursor (Fig.PP-2.19).

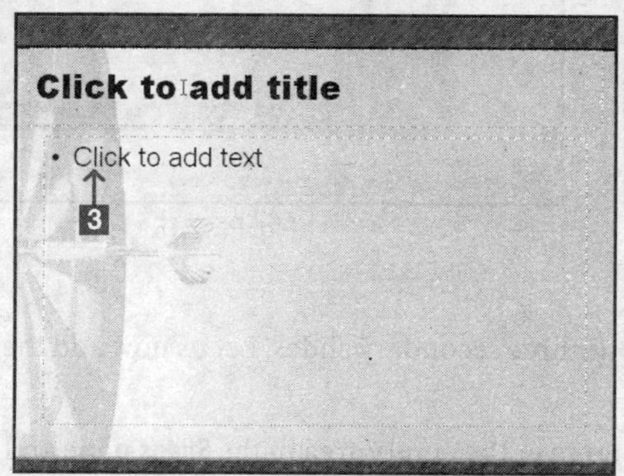

Fig. PP-2.18

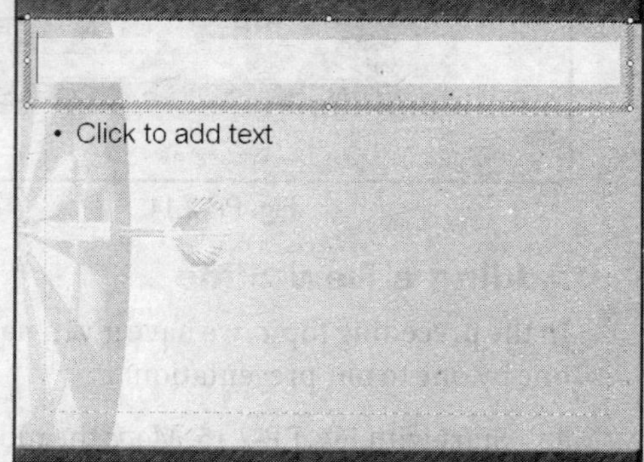

Fig. PP-2.19

5. *Type* **Customer Satisfaction.** This text appears inside the **Title placeholder** (Fig.PP-2.20).
6. Next, *move* the mouse-pointer over the **Body Text placeholder** represented by the default text **Click to add text** and *click* the left mouse-button (Fig.PP-2.21). The default text disappears but a bullet symbol remains with the blinking cursor.

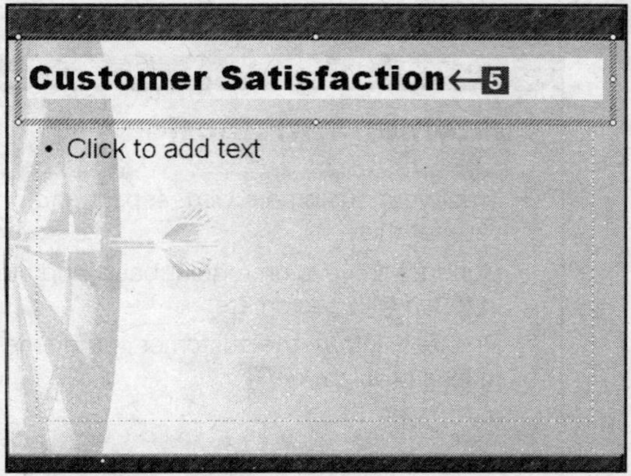

Fig. PP-2.20

Customer Satisfaction

• Click to add text

6

Fig. PP-2.21

7. Now, *type* **Treat your customers with respect and care for them.**, as shown in Fig.PP-2.22.
8. *Press* the **Enter** key. A blank line gets inserted inside the **Body Text placeholder** with a bullet symbol and the blinking cursor (Fig.PP-2.23).

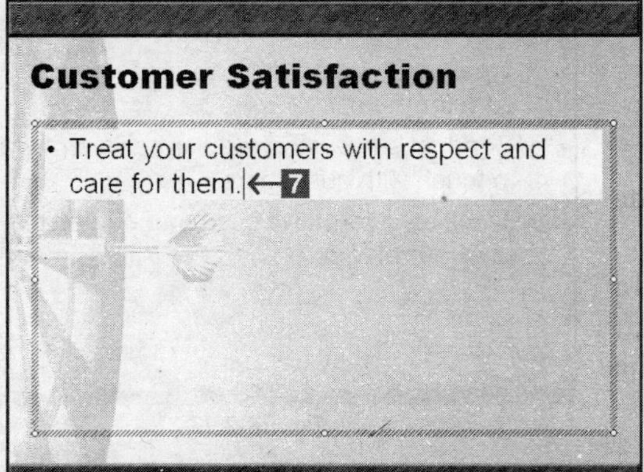

Fig. PP-2.22

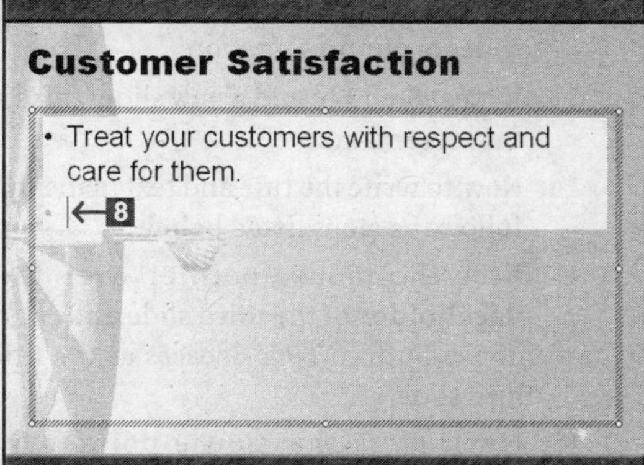

Fig. PP-2.23

9. Now, *type* **Conduct surveys on regular basis and stay in touch with customers.**, as shown in Fig.PP-2.24.
10. Once again *press* the **Enter** key. Another blank line gets inserted inside the **Body Text placeholder** with a bullet symbol and the blinking cursor (Fig.PP-2.25).

Customer Satisfaction

• Treat your customers with respect and care for them.
• Conduct surveys on regular basis and stay in touch with customers.

9

Fig. PP-2.24

11. *Type* **Precisely inform the customer of the time to fix a problem** as shown in Fig.PP-2.26.

Customer Satisfaction

- Treat your customers with respect and care for them.
- Conduct surveys on regular basis and stay in touch with customers.
- | ← 10

Fig. PP-2.25

Customer Satisfaction

- Treat your customers with respect and care for them.
- Conduct surveys on regular basis and stay in touch with customers.
- Precisely inform the customer of the time to fix a problem. ← 11

Fig. PP-2.26

12. Now, the second slide of our presentation looks like Fig.PP-2.27.

    Let us now proceed to create remaining two slides of our presentation.

13. Repeat Step 1 to add a new slide (third slide) in the presentation.

14. Now, to write the title and text in the third slide follow the steps listed below.

- *Place* the mouse-pointer over the **Title placeholder** of the third slide and *click* the left mouse-button. *Type* **Services** as the title of the third slide.
- Next, *place* the mouse-pointer over the **Body Text placeholder** of the third slide and click the left mouse-button. *Type* **Give him the correct information** and *press* the **Enter** key. A blank line gets inserted in the **Body Text placeholder**.
- Next, *type* the text **Send company literature to the customer on regular basis** and *press* the **Enter** key. Another blank line gets inserted in the **Body Text placeholder**.
- Lastly, *type* the text **Invite your customers for seminars and events.** Now, the third slide appears like Fig.PP-2.28.

Customer Satisfaction

- Treat your customers with respect and care for them.
- Conduct surveys on regular basis and stay in touch with customers.
- Precisely inform the customer of the time to fix a problem.

Fig. PP-2.27

Services

- Give him the correct information.
- Send company literature to the customer on regular basis.
- Invite your customers for seminars and events.

Fig. PP-2.28

15. Once again repeat Step 1 to add a new slide (fourth slide) in the presentation.
16. Now follow the steps listed below to add the title and text in the new slide.

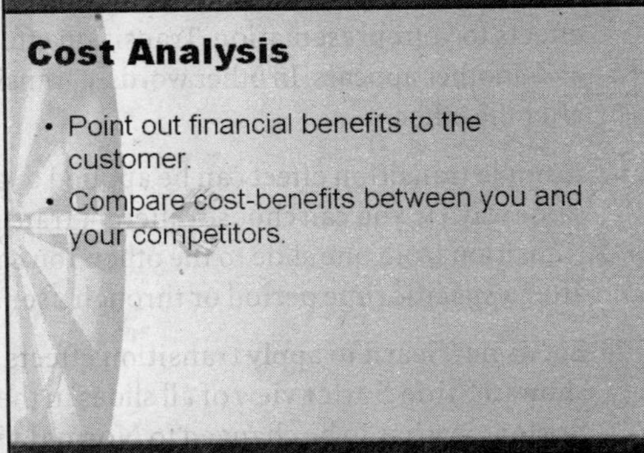

Fig. PP-2.29

- *Place* the mouse-pointer over the **Title placeholder** of the fourth slide and *click* the left mouse-button. *Type* **Cost Analysis** as the title of the slide.
- Now, *place* the mouse-pointer over the **Body Text placeholder** of the slide and *click* the left mouse-button. *Type* **Point out financial benefits to the customer** and *press* the **Enter** key. A blank line gets inserted in the **Body Text placeholder.**
- Finally, *type* the text **Compare cost-benefits between you and your competitors** . With this step we have created our fourth slide that appears like Fig.PP-2.29. Let us now view all the slides of our presentation together. To do so, proceed as follows.

17. *Move* the mouse-pointer over the **View** option of the Menu and *click* the left mouse-button. A pull-down menu appears (Fig.PP-2.30).
18. Inside the pull-down menu, *move* the mouse-pointer over the **Slide Sorter** option and *click* the left mouse-button (Fig.PP-2.30). Instantly, the miniature forms of all the four slides of our presentation appear in the PowerPoint window as shown in Fig. PP-2.31.

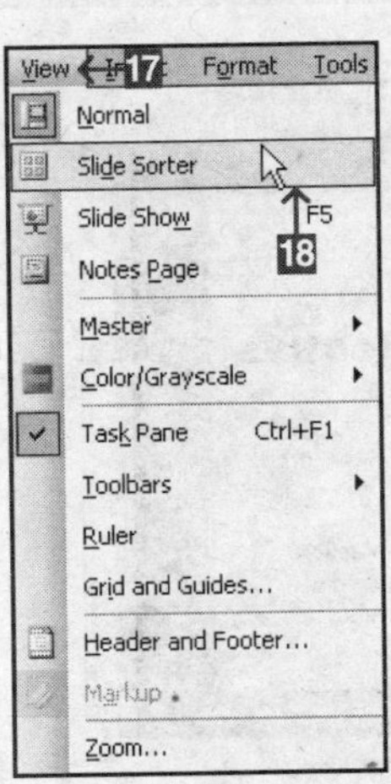

Fig. PP-2.30

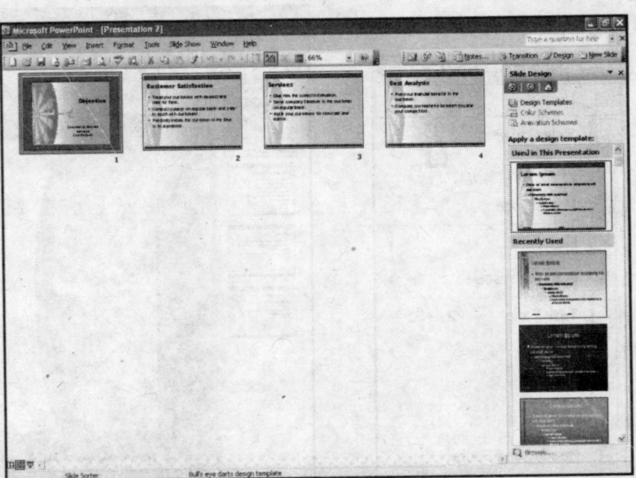

Fig. PP-2.31

The Slide Sorter view allows us to change the order of slides in a presentation. It displays the miniatures of all the slides of a presentation. You can then simply click and drag these miniatures from one location to another to change the order of occurrence of their slides in a slide show.

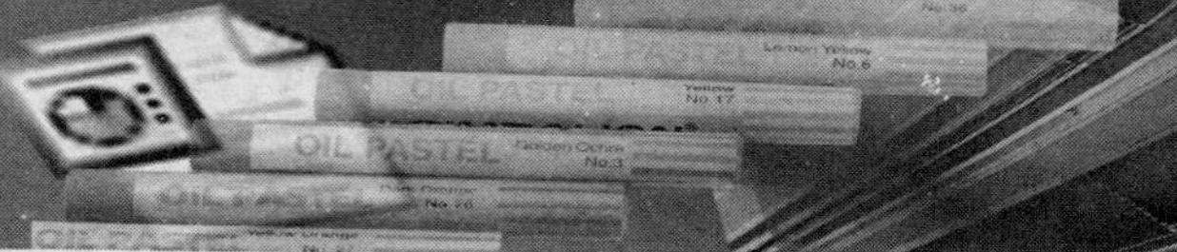

Adding Transition Effects to Slides

To enhance the visual appeal of your presentaiton, you may take advantage of PowerPoint's multimedia tools for animating slides and their individual elements. First step in this direction is to apply transition effects to your presentation. Transition effects are animations that occur as one slide leaves the screen and another appears. In other words, a transition effect fills the time gap between appearance of one slide after the other.

A single transition effect can be applied to the entire presentation so that each slide transitions in the same way. Or, you can choose different transition effects for different slides. You can control the speed of transition from one slide to the other. You can also decide whether the next slide appears automatically after a specific time period or through user's action like mouse click.

Let us now learn to apply transition effects to our presentation. We will begin with Fig.PP-2.31, which shows a **Slide Sorter** view of all slides in the presentation. Before applying transition effects, the **Slide Sorter** view has to be changed to **Normal** view. Let us proceed as follows:

1. Start with Fig.PP-2.31. *Move* the mouse-pointer over the **View** option of the Menu Bar and *click* the left mouse-button. A pull-down menu appears (Fig.PP-2.32).
2. In the pull-down menu, *move* the mouse-pointer over the **Normal** option and *click* the left mouse-button. The presentation view changes to normal as shown in Fig.PP-2.33.

Now, we will apply a transition effect to Slide 1, i.e. Title slide, of our presentation. To proceed ahead, undertake the following steps.

1. *Move* the mouse-pointer over Slide **1** (Title slide) in the Slides pane and *click* the left mouse-button.

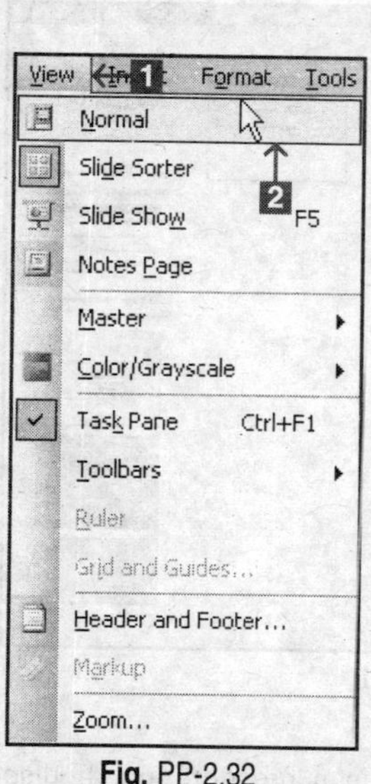

Fig. PP-2.32

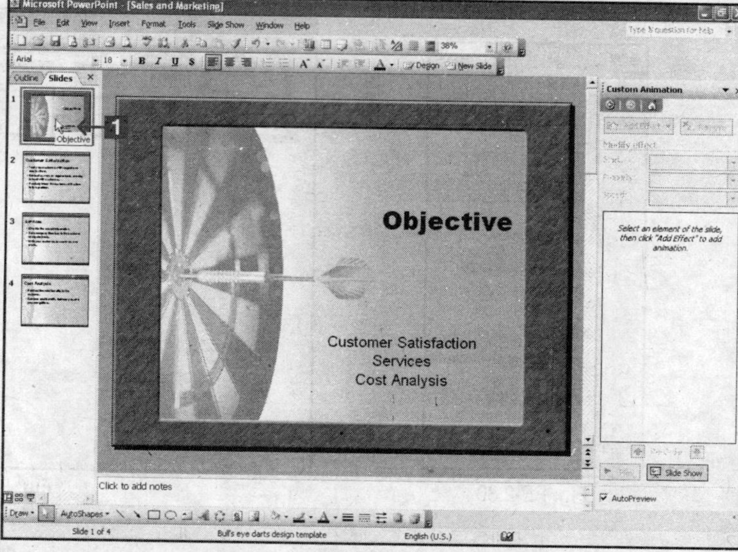

Fig. PP-2.33

2. Next, *move* the mouse-pointer over the **Slide Show** option of the Menu bar and *click* the left mouse-button. A pull-down menu appears (Fig.PP-2.34).

3. In the pull-down menu, *move* the mouse-pointer over the **Slide Transition** option and *click* the left mouse-button (Fig.PP-2.34).

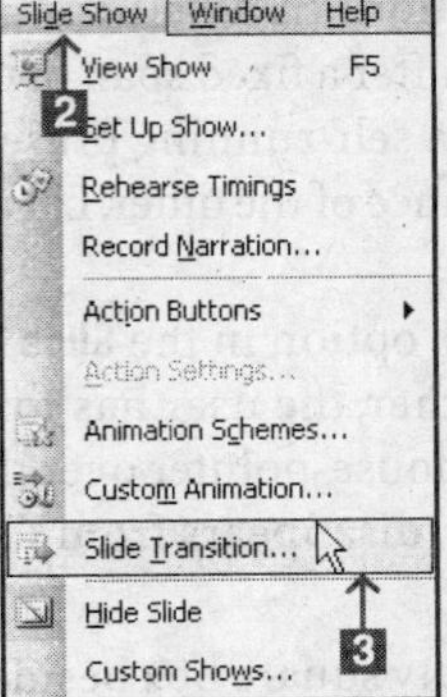

Fig. PP-2.34

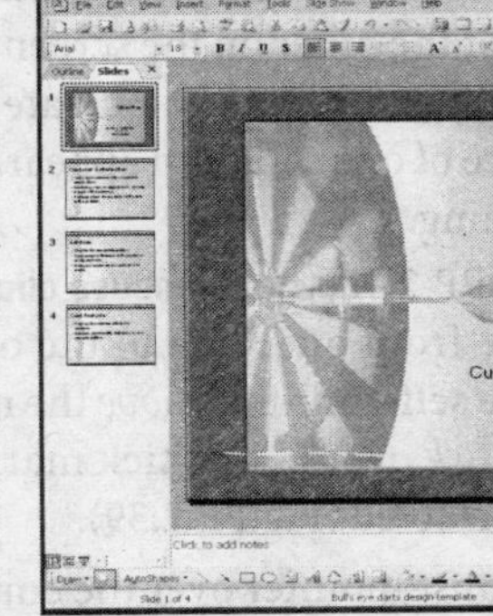

Fig. PP-2.35

4. Instantly, the **Slide Transition** Task pane appears at the right side of the window with names of various transition effects (Fig.PP-2.35).
5. In the **Slide Transition** Task pane, *move* the mouse-pointer over the name of a transition effect, say **Checkerboard Across**, and *click* the left mouse-button (Fig.PP-2.36).
6. Now, you have to set the transition speed. This you can do using the **Speed** option of the **Slide Transition** Task pane. Suppose, you want to change the transition speed from fast to medium. To do so, *move* the mouse-pointer over the down-arrow button (▾) beside the **Speed** option and *click* the left mouse-button. A small pull-down box appears with different speed levels for the selected transition (Fig.PP-2.37).
7. *Move* the mouse-pointer over the **Medium** speed level and *click* the left mouse-button (Fig.PP-2.38).

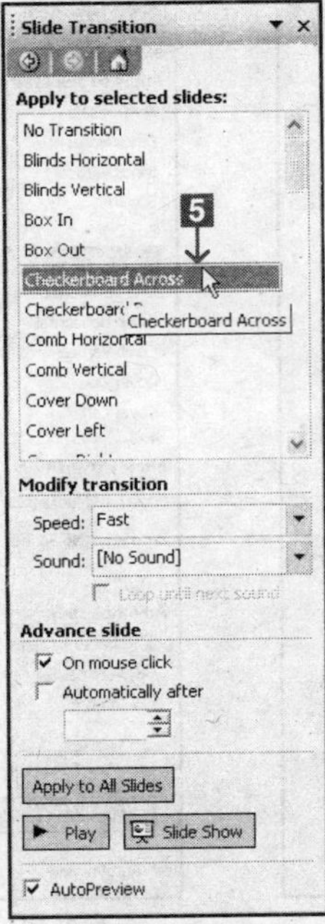

Fig. PP-2.36

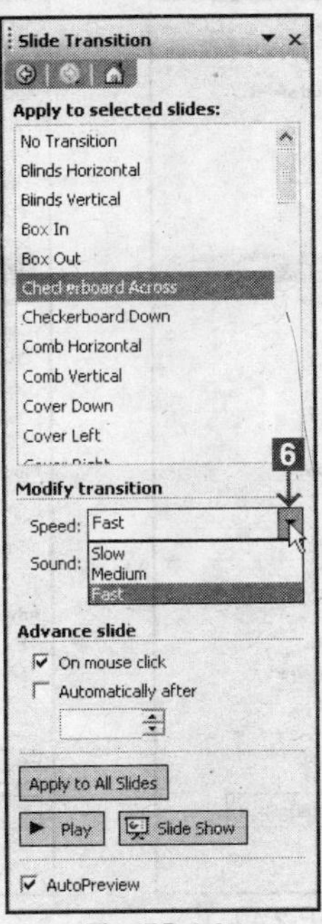

Fig. PP-2.37

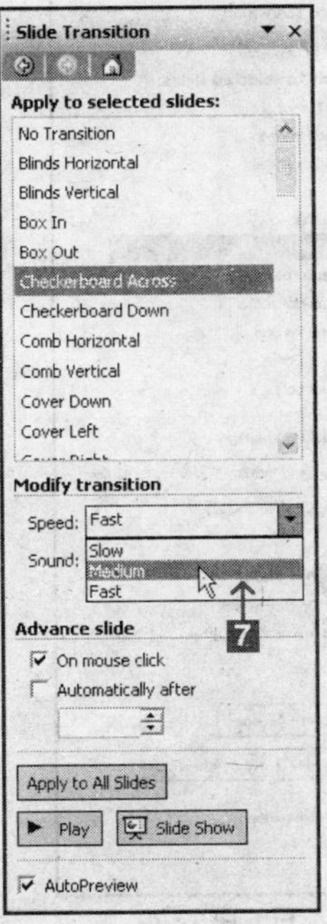

Fig. PP-2.38

So, you have learnt how to apply a transition effect to a slide and control the speed of transition. Let us now learn to create a self-running presentation. In a self-running presentation, slides appear automatically one after the other on the screen after a fixed span of time. The **Automatically After** option of the **Slide Transition** Task pane lets you create a self-running presentation and set the time interval between disappearance of one slide and appearance of the other. Let us now proceed ahead to make our presentation self-running.

8. As you see in Fig.PP-2.38, the **On mouse click** option in the **Slide Transition** pane is shown selected. It means, to move from one slide to the other, the user has to click the mouse. As we want our presentation to be self-running, *move* the mouse-pointer over the square box beside the **On mouse click** option and *click* over it. The tick mark disappears from the square box, indicating that the option has been disabled (Fig.PP-2.39).
9. Next, *move* the mouse-pointer over the empty square box beside the **Automatically after** option and *click* the left mouse-button. A tick mark appears inside the square box indicating the selection of the option (Fig.PP-2.40).
10. Now, you have to set time interval for transition from one slide to the other. To do so, *move* the mouse-pointer over the up-arrow scroll button (▲) present just below the **Automatically after** option and *click* the left mouse-button two times. The value inside the box becomes **00:02**, which means slides will appear after two seconds (Fig.PP-2.41).
11. If you want to apply the selected transition effect and timing to all slides then *click* over the **Apply to All Slides** button (Fig.PP-2.42). Otherwise, repeat Steps 1 to 9 to apply different transition effects to different slides in the presentation.

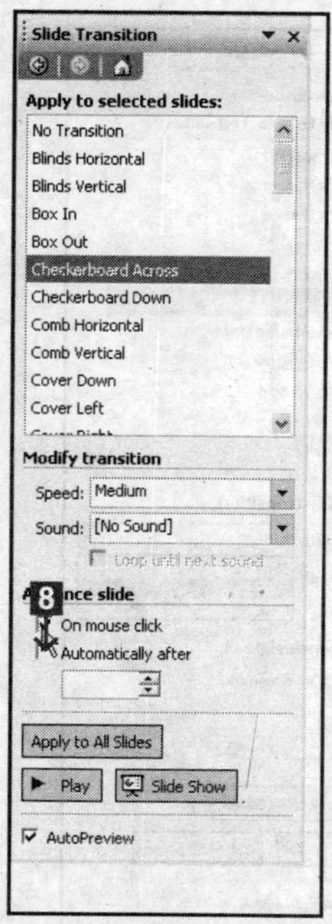

Fig. PP-2.39

Fig. PP-2.40

Fig. PP-2.41

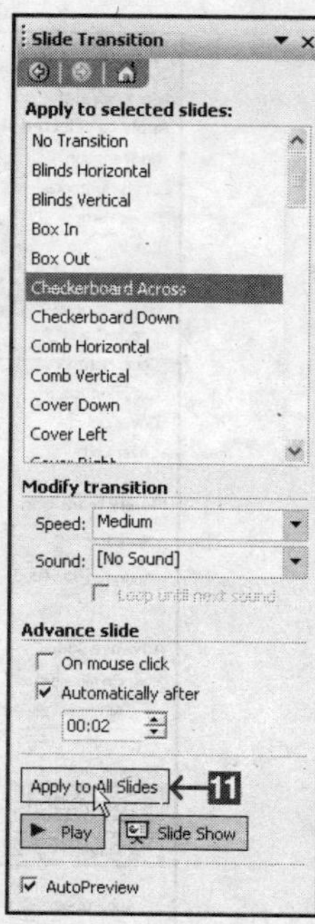

Fig. PP-2.42

A small star (☆) appears beside every slide to which a transition effect has been applied. This star is known as **Play Animation** star and its presence indicates that a transition or animation effect is present in the slide. You can click over the **Play Animation** star to preview the transition and other animation effects applied to an individual slide.

Animating Individual Slide Elements with Custom Animation

You can also apply animation effects to individual items in your slides, like text, graphics and chart objects. You can achieve this by using the **Custom Animation** feature of Microsoft PowerPoint. Custom Animation helps you decide how individual items of a slide would emerge on screen.

Now, we will learn to add Custom Animation to the title and body text of the Title slide of our presentation. But before proceeding ahead make sure that the presentation appears in the **Normal view** so that you could select individual elements of each slide easily.

NOTE

If the presentation is not appearing in the Normal view then click over the View option of the Menu bar. A pull-down menu appears. In the pull-down menu, click over the Normal option.

1. Start with Fig.PP-2.33. *Move* the mouse-pointer over the title text of the **Title Slide** and *click* the left mouse-button. Instantly, a placeholder appears around the text **Objective** (Fig.PP-2.43).
2. Now, *move* the mouse-pointer over the **Slide Show** option of the Menu bar and *click* the left mouse-button. A pull-down menu appears (Fig.PP-2.44).
3. In the pull-down menu, *move* the mouse-pointer over the **Custom Animation** option and *click* the left mouse-button (Fig.PP-2.44). Instantly, the **Custom Animation** Task pane appears on the right side of the window (Fig.PP-2.45).

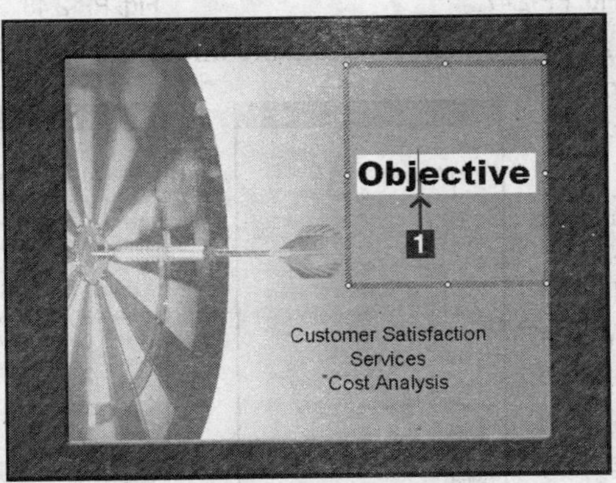

Fig. PP-2.43

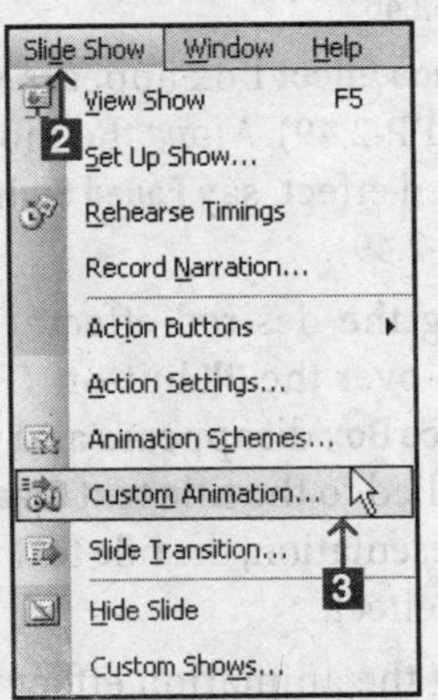

Fig. PP-2.44

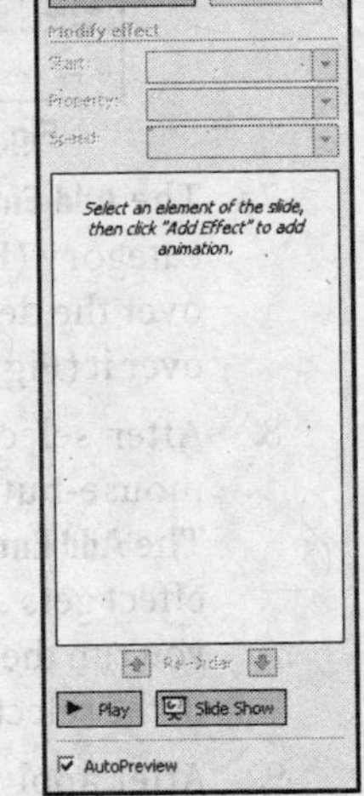

Fig. PP-2.45

4. In the **Custom Animation** Task pane, *move* the mouse-pointer over the **Add Effect** button and *click* the left mouse-button. Instantly, a list of four types of effect appears (Fig.PP-2.46). These effects are: **Entrance, Emphasis, Exit,** and **Motion Paths.** Let us understand function of these effects. Through the **Entrance** effect, you can decide how would an individual item of a slide emerge on the screen. The **Emphasis** effect enables you to emphasis individual items. If an individual item won't stay on the screen then using the **Exit** effect you can determine the way it should leave the slide. The last effect, **Motion Paths,** is used to make a slide item move from one point to the other on the screen.

5. Let us now learn to apply the **Entrance** effect. *Place* the mouse-pointer over the **Entrance** effect in the effects list (Fig.PP-2.47). Instantly, a sub-menu appears listing effects available in the Entrance effect category (Fig.PP-2.47).

6. In the sub-menu, *move* the mouse-pointer over the **More Effects** option and *click* the left mouse-button (Fig.PP-2.48).

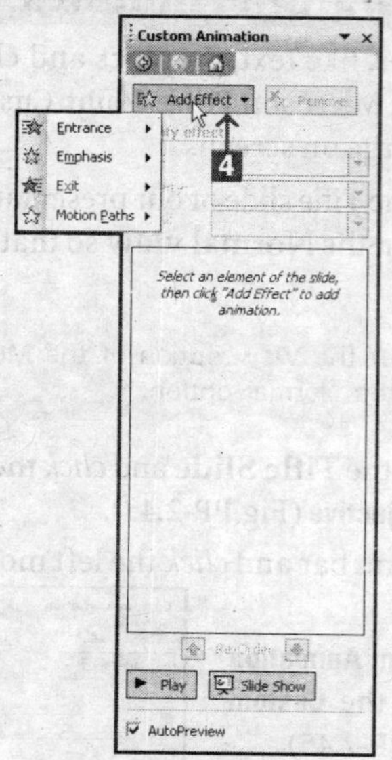

Fig. PP-2.46

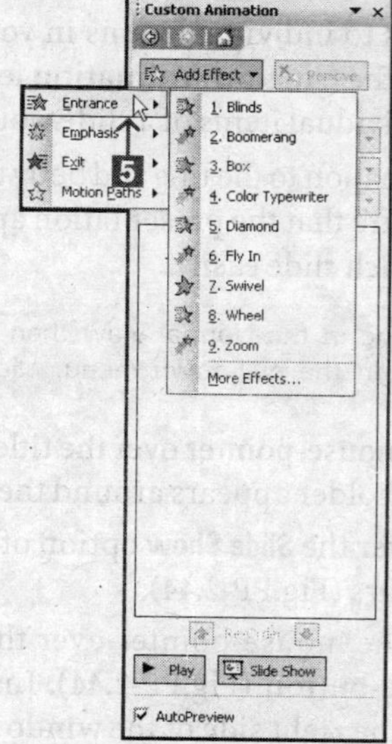

Fig. PP-2.47

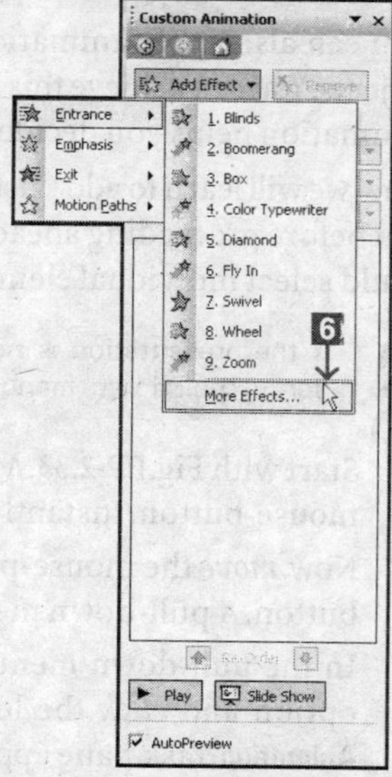

Fig. PP-2.48

7. The **Add Entrance Effect** box appears with names of all effects available under the **Entrance** effect category (Fig.PP-2.49). *Move* the mouse-pointer over the desired effect, say **Faded Swivel**, and *click* over it (Fig.PP-2.49).

8. After selecting the desired effect, *click* the left mouse-button over the **OK** button. (Fig.PP-2.50). The **Add Entrance Box** disappears and the selected effect gets applied to the title text **Objective**. When you run the presentation, the title text will animate in the selected effect.

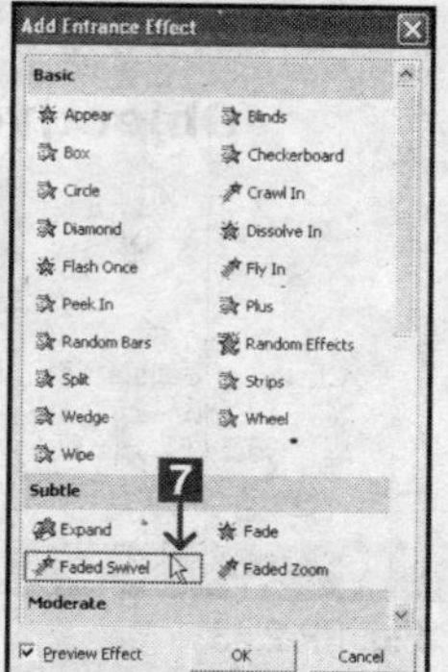

Fig. PP-2.49

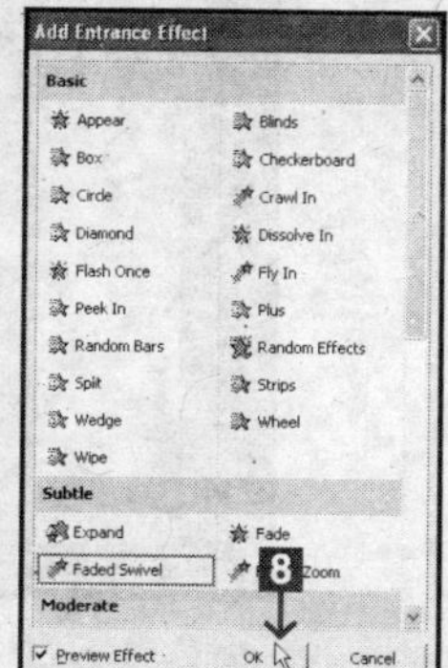

Fig. PP-2.50

9. After applying the animation effect to title text, you see that a number (in our case **1**) gets placed beside the title placeholder (Fig.PP-2.51). This number is known as **Animation tag.** The **Custom Animation** Task pane shows additional information about the animation tag (Fig.PP-2.52). As you add more animation effects to individual slide items, more tags appear beside them. Whenever you run the presentation, the effects added to a slide appear in the same order as they are shown in the **Custom Animation** Task pane. By default, effects are arranged in serial order.

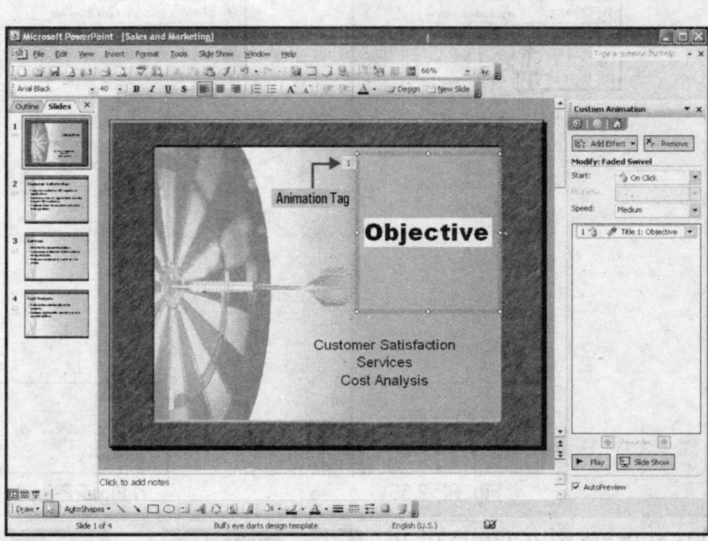

Fig. PP-2.51

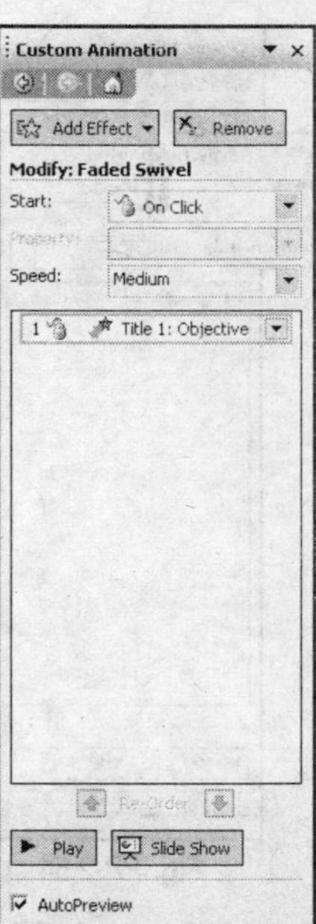

Fig. PP-2.52

10. Now we will apply another effect, say **Emphasis**, to the remaining text in the Title slide. To do so, *move* the mouse-pointer over the body text and *click* the left mouse-button. A placeholder surrounds the body text (Fig.PP-2.53).

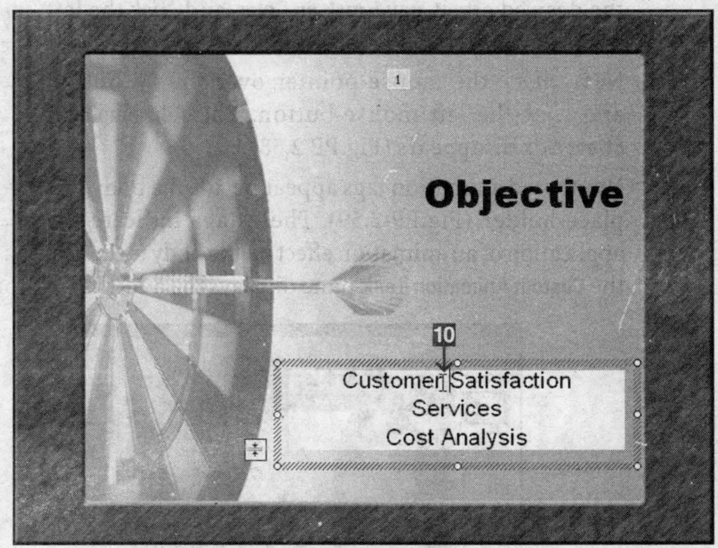

Fig. PP-2.53

11. In the **Custom Animation** Task pane, *move* the mouse-pointer over the **Add Effect** button and *click* the left mouse-button (Fig.PP-2.54). Instantly, a list of four types of effect appears.
12. In the list, *place* the mouse-pointer over the **Emphasis** effect. Instantly, a sub-menu appears listing effects available in the **Emphasis** effect category (Fig.PP-2.55).
13. In the sub-menu, *move* the mouse-pointer over the **More Effects** option and *click* the left mouse-button (Fig.PP-2.56).

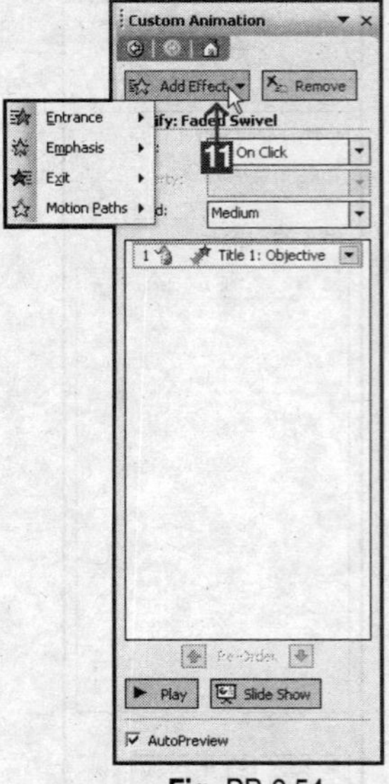

Fig. PP-2.54

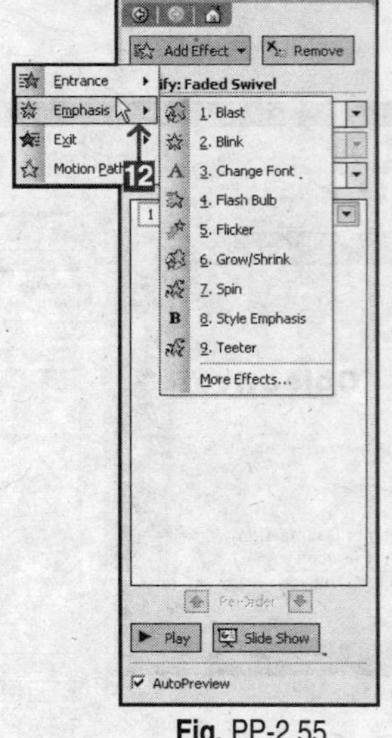

Fig. PP-2.55

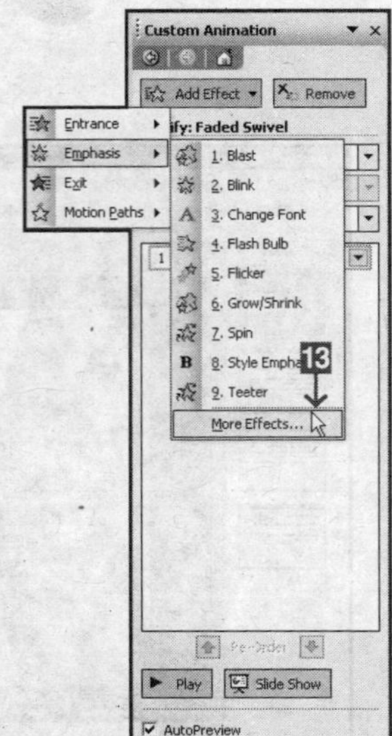

Fig. PP-2.56

14. The **Add Emphasis Effect** box appears with names of all animation effects present under the **Emphasis** effect category (Fig.PP-2.57). *Move* the mouse-pointer over the desired effect, say **Brush on Color,** and *click* the left mouse-button (Fig.PP-2.57).

15. Next, *move* the mouse-pointer over the **OK** button and *click* the left mouse-button. The **Add Emphasis Effect** box disappears (Fig.PP-2.58).

16. Numbered animation tags appear beside the body text place-holder (Fig.PP-2.59). These tags indicate the application of an animation effect on the body text. Also, the **Custom Animation** Task pane displays the additional information about these tags (Fig.PP-2.60).

Fig. PP-2.57

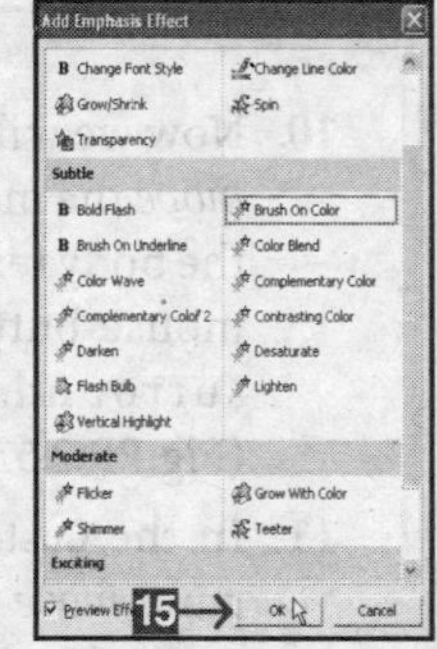

Fig. PP-2.58

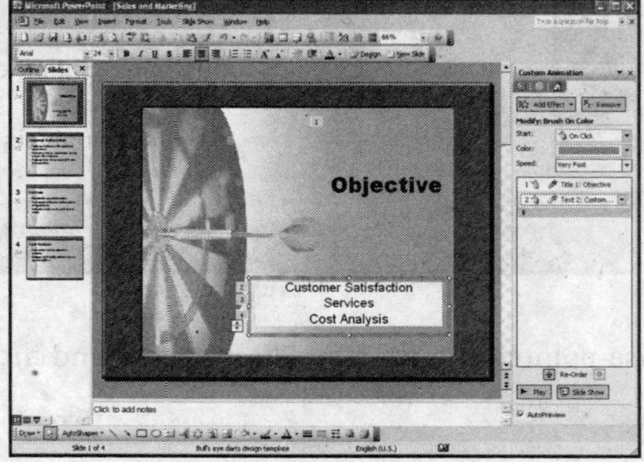

Fig. PP-2.59

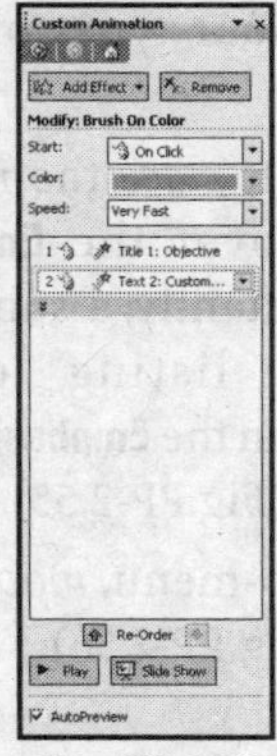

Fig. PP-2.60

Previewing Animation Effects in the Slide

By applying animation effects to the Title slide, you have learnt the procedure of applying Custom Animation to the individual elements in a slide. Now you must be keen to view the animation effects applied to the Title slide. To preview the animation effects, you need to click the **Play** button of the **Custom Animation** Task pane. But, first you have to click the desired slide in the **Slides** pane and then click over the Play button. After these steps, the effects (both Transition and Custom Animation) of the selected slide start appearing in the PowerPoint window. The preview actually helps you see how would the slide appear with the applied animation effects. If you are satisfied with the actual view, you can deliver the presentation to the target audience. After previewing the effects, if you find any scope for improvements in effects like changing their speed, timing of appearance on the screen, adding separate transition effect to the slide etc. then you can readily effect these improvements from the PowerPoint window. Let us now preview the slide effects by undertaking the following steps.

1. Start with Fig.PP-2.59. In the **Custom Animation** Task pane, *move* the mouse-pointer over the **Play** button and *click* the left mouse-button (Fig.PP-2.61).
2. The transition effect gets executed first and as a result the first slide of the presentation appears with the **Checkerboard Across** transition effect (Fig.PP-2.62).
3. Next, the title text of the first slide appears in the **Faded Swivel** effect (Fig.PP-2.63).
4. Lastly, the body text appears in the **Brush On Color** effect (Fig.PP-2.64).

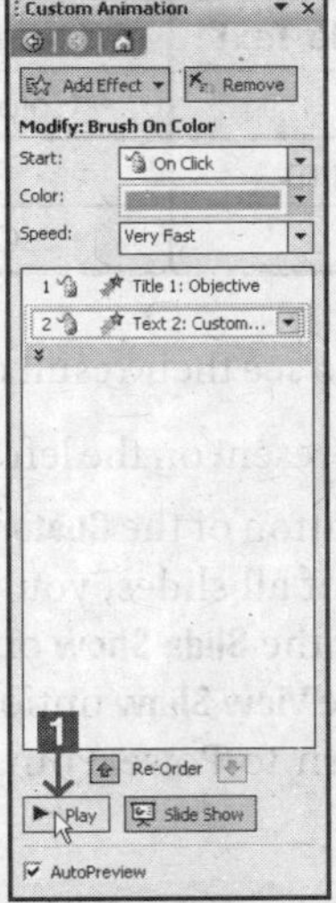

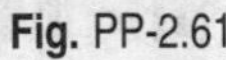

Fig. PP-2.61

Fig. PP-2.62

Fig. PP-2.63

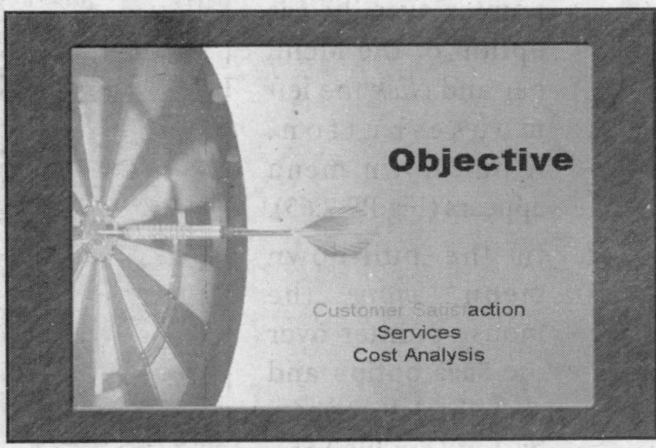

Fig. PP-2.64

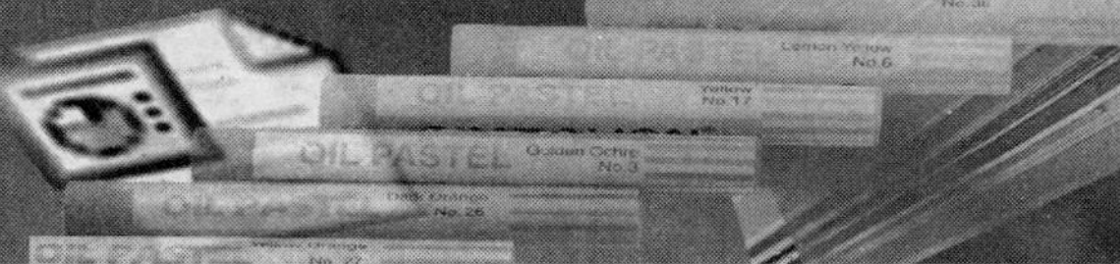

HOT TIP! To quickly preview the effects of any slide, click over the Play Animation star (☆) present beside each slide in the Slide pane.

So, you have previewed the Title slide with applied animation effects. Now, you may be eager to apply these effects on other slides of the presentation. To do so, repeat steps 1 to 15 of the topic, **Animating Individual Slide Elements with Custom Animation**. For your practice, we have listed below some animation effects of the Emphasis category and the slide numbers to whom these have to be applied. Apply these effects and see how do your slides animate.

TABLE

Slide Number	Effects for Title Text	Effects for Body Text
2	Wheel	Color Type Writer
3	Grow and Turn	Glide
4	Unfold	Compress

Once all necessary effects are added in the slides, to see their result on a slide,

(i) *Click* over the desired slide in the **Slides** pane present on the left side of the window.

(ii) Next, *move* the mouse-pointer over the **Play** button of the **Custom Animation** Task pane and *click* the left mouse-button. After previewing effects of all slides, you wish to show to your friends and colleagues on full-screen. To do so, *click* over the **Slide Show** option of the Menu bar. In the pull-down menu, *move* the mouse-pointer over the **View Show** option and *click* the left mouse-button. To stop the slide show in between and return to PowerPoint window, *press* the **Esc** key from keyboard.

Saving the Presentation and Quitting Microsoft PowerPoint

Now let us save our presentation with a name, **Sales and Marketing**, in **Local Disk (C:)**. proceed as follows:

1. *Move* the mouse-pointer over the **File** option of the Menu bar and *click* the left mouse-button. A pull-down menu appears (Fig.PP-2.65).
2. In the pull-down menu, *move* the mouse-pointer over the **Save** option and *click* the left mouse-button (Fig.PP-2.65).

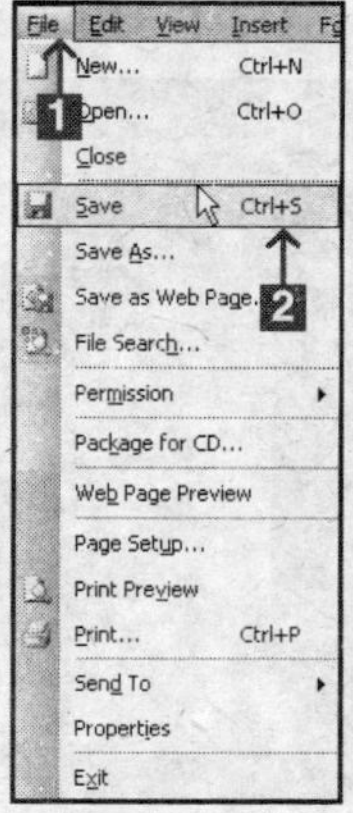

Fig. PP-2.65

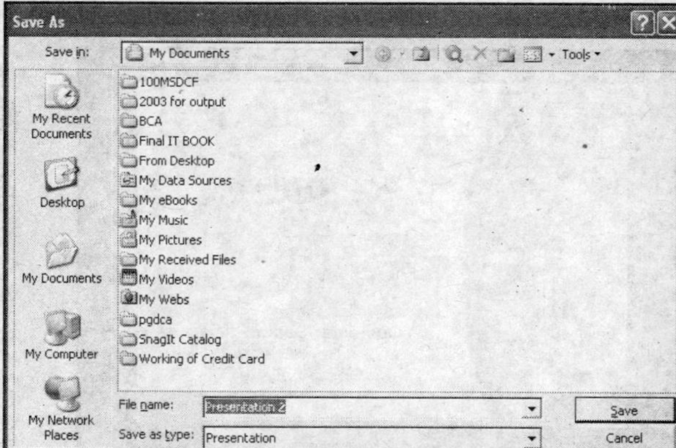

Fig. PP-2.66

The **Save As** box appears on the screen with some highlighted text inside the box beside the **File name** option (Fig.PP-2.66).

3. *Type* **Sales and Marketing.** This text overwrites the highlighted text beside the **File name** option (Fig.PP-2.67).
4. Now, to select the save location, *move* the mouse-pointer over the down-arrow button (▾) beside the **Save in** option and click the left mouse-button. Instantly, a pull-down box appears (Fig.PP-2.68).
5. In the pull-down box, *move* the mouse-pointer over the **Local Disk (C:)** and *click* the left mouse-button (Fig.PP-2.69).

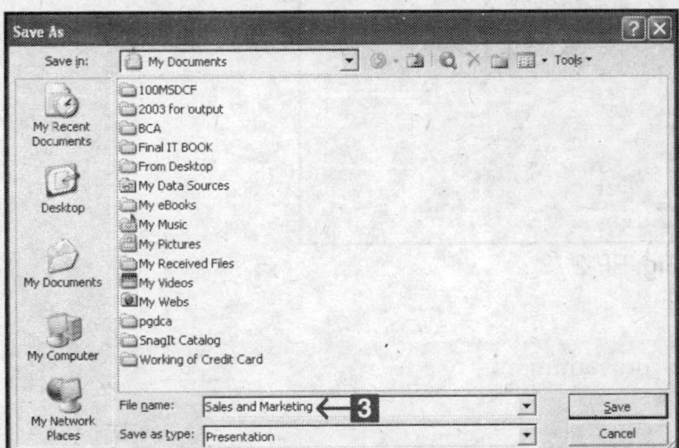

Fig. PP-2.67

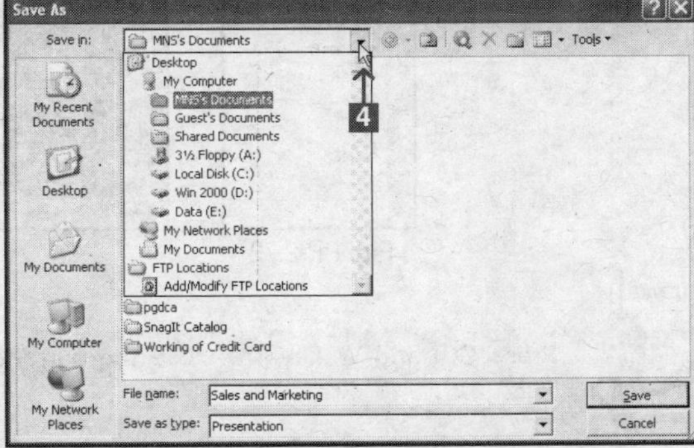

Fig. PP-2.68

6. The **Local Disk (C:)** appears beside the **Save in** option. *Move* the mouse-pointer over the **Save** button and *click* the left mouse-button (Fig.PP-2.70).

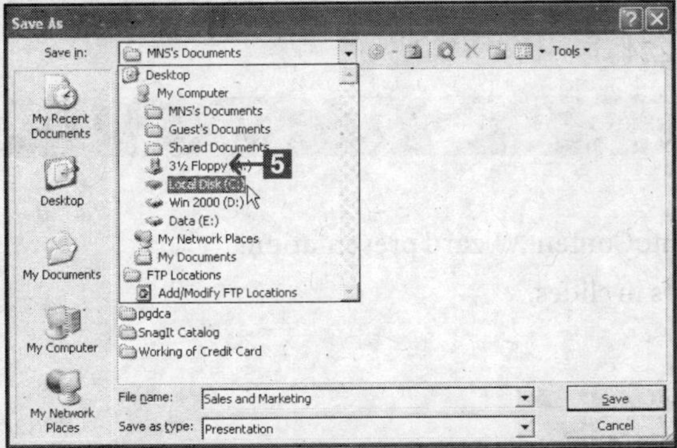

Fig. PP-2.69

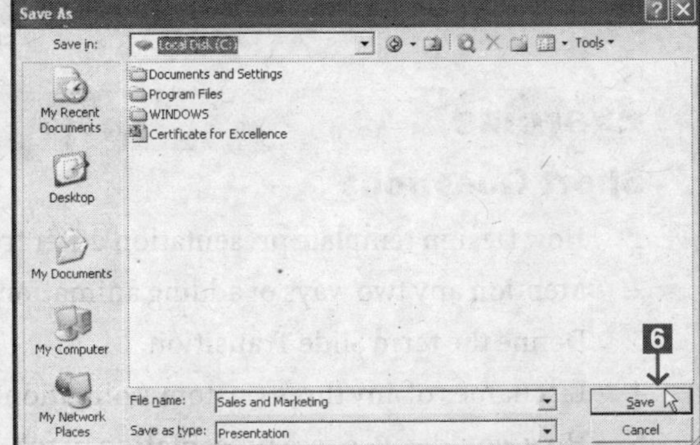

Fig. PP-2.70

7. Your presentation gets the name **Sales and Marketing** that appears on its Title bar (Fig.PP-2.71).

Fig. PP-2.71

8. Now, we will close the presentation. To do so, *move* the mouse-pointer over the **File** option of the Menu bar and *click* the left mouse-button. A pull-down menu appears (Fig.PP-2.72).

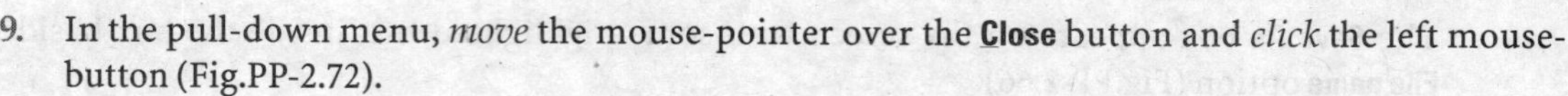

9. In the pull-down menu, *move* the mouse-pointer over the **Close** button and *click* the left mouse-button (Fig.PP-2.72).

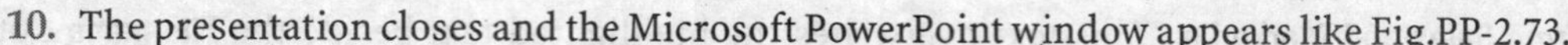

10. The presentation closes and the Microsoft PowerPoint window appears like Fig.PP-2.73.

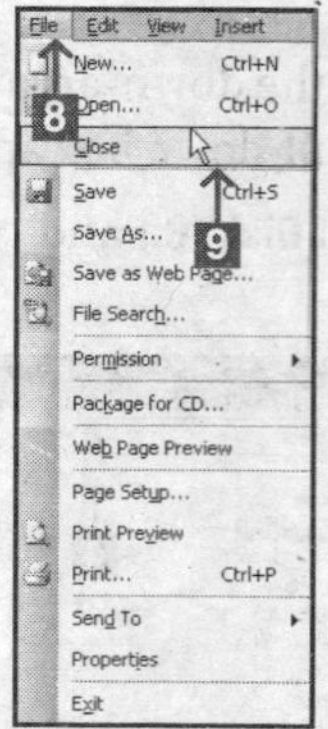

Fig. PP-2.72

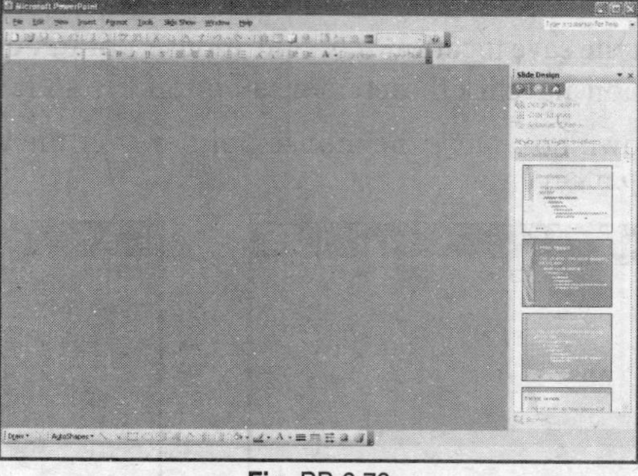

Fig. PP-2.73

HOT TIP!

Press Ctrl and W keys to close the currently open presentation.

11. Now, to quit the PowerPoint program, *move* the mouse-pointer over the **Close** button (☒) present on the **Title bar** and *click* the left mouse-button (Fig.PP-2.74). The PowerPoint program closes and you return to your Desktop.

11

Microsoft PowerPoint

Fig. PP-2.74

Exercise

Short Questions

1. How Design template presentation differ from AutoContent Wizard presentation?
2. Mention any two ways of adding animation effects in slides.
3. Define the term Slide Transition.
4. List names of any three Custom Animation effects.
5. How would you view a presentation in full-screen mode?

Summary

Microsoft PowerPoint is the presentation graphics program that helps you create lasting visual impact either in person or online. With multimedia support, you can animate slides and elements present in them. You can animate slides with the help of visual effects present under Slide Transition and Custom Animation. The user-friendly interface of Microsoft PowerPoint lets you view and create high-impact presentations more easily.

CHAPTER 9

Internet and Outlook Express

IN THIS CHAPTER

- What is Internet?
- Internet in India
- Scope of Internet
- Surfing the Net
- Creating Icon of ISP on Desktop
- Connecting to the Internet
- Sending and Receiving Emails using Outlook Express
- Replying an Email using Outlook Express
- Sending an Email using Outlook Express
- Closing Outlook Express Window
- Browsing the WWW
- Opening an Email Account
- Email with Attachment
- Sending an Email with Attachment File
- Viewing the Email with Attachment
- Internet Relay Chat & Instant Messenger
- Downloading from the Internet
- Online Shopping
- Steps for Online Shopping
- Wireless Internet
- Computer Virus and Antivirus Software
- How did I get Virus, anyway?
- General Virus Types
- Practice Safe Computing to Avoid Virus Attack
- Disconnecting from the Internet
- Other Internet Connection Services
- List of Popular Websites
- Conclusion

You often write letters to your friends living in distant places – may be in neighbouring cities or states or a far-off country like Australia or Canada. However, a doubt lingers in your mind whether your letter would reach your friend in time. Now you need not bother anymore about your friends getting your letters in time. For, the Internet is here to facilitate easy and instant communication between you and your friends. The Internet also saves you postal charges. The role of a postman being played by the Internet is just one of its myriad applications. It is, in fact, a storehouse of unlimited knowledge on any topic under the sun. Besides, this knowledge is also getting updated regularly. The Internet also plays a major role in bringing together various cultures, nations and peoples.

What is Internet?

Internet, also called the Net, is a global collection of computers connected to each other. This global network links thousands of computers at universities, research institutions, government agencies and business houses throughout the world. Using a small PC at your home and a telephone connection, you can reach anywhere in the world through the Internet. You can access information on thousands of topics ranging from designing toys to making atomic bombs. Each computer connected to the Internet can communicate with other computers. Messages or information sent or received on the Internet is in the form of files. Information travels over the Internet via a variety of languages known as protocols. In Internet, computers communicate with each other through the Transmission Control Protocol/Internet Protocol (TCP/IP).

Internet in India

In a vast country like India, the Internet is of great significance. With the Internet, distance is no barrier to instant communication. Whereas a letter might take 4-5 days to reach from one end of this country to another, an Internet message hardly takes seconds to reach from one end of the world to the other. For this to happen, only a computer connected to Internet at each end is needed. Communication in INDIA has advanced in leaps and bounds through the Internet. Apart from personal communication, Internet is now widely being used in business, distant education, defence, research etc.

Scope of Internet

The most interesting thing about the Internet is that no organisation owns or controls it. There is no government regulation and no one censors the information made available on the Internet. No matter wherever you are located, if your computer has an Internet connection, you can access any information related to any field, be it computers, sports, education, movies, etc., from any part of the world. You can even subscribe to mailing lists and engage in online shopping. Let us now have a look at a few things you can do on Internet.

Email – Your new postman

Electronic mail or Email is the most widely used feature of the Internet. It has now become a vital tool of communication for people. Email has not only bedazzled technocrats but also caught the fancy of all – be it a school kid, a housewife or a business tycoon. Many Internet users use it for emailing only. This service has enabled millions of Internet users all over the world to send and receive written messages in a few seconds. Email is basically a file that is sent from one computer to another through a network. In the 1970s Email was just about sending text messages but today you can send different types of files such as scanned/faxed images, computer graphics or sound and video files along with your email messages.

Advantages of Email

- It saves lot of paper and the chance of email getting misplaced is almost nil.
- Messages can be transmitted in a few seconds.
- Messages can be sent at any time of the day as per sender's convenience.
- Copies of a single email can be sent to multiple users.
- Both incoming and outgoing messages can be saved for future reference.

Chatting

The Chatting feature of the Internet lets you instantly communicate with people anywhere in the world by sending and receiving messages in real time. Using IRC you can also converse on the Net with more than one individual simultaneously. IRC is a chat protocol that uses the Internet to exchange text messages among users.

Chat room is the hub of Internet chatting. A chat room is actually a computer (chat server) that allows many persons to log on at the same time. When you enter a chat room, you see the names of the people who are already there, and a window in which a few lines of text are constantly moving upwards. These lines are the messages being sent by various members of the chat room to their chat partners. Once you join a room, you can read other person's messages and then send your messages to one or all the chatters. Every chatter has a login name, which he uses for his identification, and whatever is typed appears in the general conversation window. However, if you want to chat with only one chatter, you and that person can enter a private room to have a private conversation. Broadly, there are two categories of chatting, discussed here under.

(a) **Text-based Chat:** It is the oldest, the simplest and the most popular mode of chat on the Internet. This mode enables you to communicate, through messages, with one or more persons. During chatting when you type text in the message window, the text appears on the computer screen of every person participating in your conversation (that is, the individuals that are there in the message window). The text gets transferred quickly across Internet.

(b) **e-based or Multimedia Chat:** In this type of conversation, you make use of multimedia. e-based chat enables you to have voice conversations with your friends through live video over the Internet. Since sound and video signals get transferred slowly across the Internet, it is recommended that you use a high-speed modem for e-based chat.

Search Engine – Master Key to Information

Huge amount of information is available on the Internet. Finding the required information from the colossus Internet is quite a cumbersome task. But thanks to search engines, one can easily search the required information on the Net.

Search engine is a software that searches a particular piece of information according to the specified criteria. You can just log on to any search engine and get the required information without much effort and wastage of time. A search engine hunts for the specified criteria through its own database. It is better to use more than one search engine when trying to find something on the Net. This is because different search engines use different databases, so they produce different lists of web pages meeting the given criteria. Some popular search engines are Google, Yahoo, MSN, AltaVista, Look Smart, Netscape and Info space.

Educate yourself with e-Learning

Electronic Learning (e-Learning) is the mode of acquiring knowledge by means of the Internet, and computer based training programs. In this type of education, students study on their own at home or office and communicate with the faculty and other students via email, electronic forums, video-conferencing, chat rooms, bulletin boards, instant messaging and other forms of computer-based communication. In e-learning, you can learn about any subject anytime, anywhere with the help of a computer. E-learning can be divided into four broad categories described below.

Knowledge-based e-Learning: This type of e-Learning involves giving step-by-step instructions to perform a particular task. Usually, software manufacturers use this type of e-Learning to solve their clients' software-related problems. A client posts his query related to some software task to the manufacturer's website and gets the step-up-step guidance to undertake the task.

Online Support-based e-Learning: In Online Support-based e-Learning, the user puts up his query on forums, chat rooms, online bulletin boards, emails etc. and gets the answer to his query online. Online support offers the opportunity to get relatively quick answers to more specific questions.

Synchronous-based e-Learning: The Synchronous-based e-Learning operates in real-time environment where an instructor provides learning and training to students. In this type of e-learning, students and their instructor can set a time for direct interaction over the Internet. Direct real-time communication with the instructor and fellow students creates a virtual classroom in every student's living place. This type of training usually takes place via websites, audio or video-conferencing and Internet telephony.

Asynchronous-based e-learning: This type of e-Learning is most common as it involves self-learning by means of Internet, Intranet and CD-ROM. It may include access to instructors through online bulletin boards, online discussion groups, and emails.

e-Commerce – Way of doing business on the Net

Today, when one talks of the Internet, e-Commerce invariably comes into picture. The concept of e-Commerce is similar to commerce, which means transaction/exchange of goods and services for their worth. However, e-Commerce differs from commerce in that it involves selling and purchasing of commodities and services using a computer network, usually the Internet. The main elements of e-Commerce are listed below.

- **Product:** To conduct e-Commerce, you must have some product to sell.
- **Selling place:** In e-Commerce, the place of selling and ordering goods is a website.
- **Accessibility to people:** This element decides how people would access the website that is hosting e-Commerce.
- **How to place orders:** The website must have some on-line forms that people can use to place their orders.
- **How to accept money from customers:** In e-Commerce, credit card is the most convenient and commonly used means of accepting money from customers.
- **Delivery mechanism:** The website that is hosting e-Commerce must have the provision to deliver commodities to their customers. If the nature of the commodity is such that it can be delivered online, like some music, e-book, images etc., then delivery could be made online, otherwise the website must deliver the commodity manually at the customer's doorstep.

Using Internet for Entertainment

Apart from doing some serious work on the Internet, you can also entertain yourself by availing its entertainment services. Several websites offer free music and videos, which you can download and play on your computer. The concept of distributing such entertainment services originated from the popularity of the Kazaa.com website that offered free music to its subscribers. Following into the Kazaa.com footsteps, many websites such as PlanetM, Amazon and Yahoo started providing such facilities to their users. Some websites adopt music and video as the primary product for e-Commerce, where the users can place orders for CDs and DVDs online. If you are downloading music or video files from the Internet, you must have a download accelerator software such as FlashGet, which helps you download the files quickly. The download time also depends on the speed of the Internet connection and the type of network you are using.

Surfing the Net

You must have heard people talking about Surfing or Browsing the Net. Someone is surfing the Net means he or she is checking out sites on the Internet. As you know, the Internet contains a graphical, easy to use system that offers vast amount of information. This system is called the **World Wide Web (WWW)** or **Web.** It consists of a huge collection of pages containing information, images, sounds and video clips stored in computers around the world. Each page on WWW is called a **Webpage.** The site which stores webpages is called a **Website.** Various companies, universities, government agencies, etc. have their own websites which contain several webpages of information about the services provided by them. The first page of any website is called the **Home Page.** The Web lets you move around different webpages and websites and gather information with a click of your computer mouse. We will explain you how to open the desired sites and surf the Net later in the chapter.

Equipment Required for an Internet Connection

For using the Internet, you need the following equipment:

Computer

Any good IBM compatible, Macintosh or Windows based computer that has good memory (4 GB or more), at least 128MB RAM or more and P-III 533mHz processor.

Modem

Modem is a device that is used to transmit data over the network. Your computer sends data in **binary code** to your modem which converts the binary-coded data to an **analogue signal.** This data then travels along the telephone network. When the data reaches the destination computer, the modem connected to that computer converts the analogue signal back into binary-coded data which can be read by the computer. Thus the modem transmits data over the network.

There are two types of modem: **External modem** and **Internal modem.** The **External modem** has to be connected to your computer and your telephone line with cables and electric socket while the **Internal modem** is built inside your computer. The billing meter of your telephone starts moving the moment you get connected to the Internet. So a modem with good speed ensures low telephone bills. Modem with a speed of 28,800 bps is recommended, but you can also use the one having a speed of 14,000 bps.

Web Browser

The software used to navigate through the Net is known as **web browser.** The most popular browser types today are Netscape Navigator and Microsoft Internet Explorer. Make sure you have a web browser in your computer, otherwise you will not be able to surf the Net. The Microsoft Internet Explorer comes installed along with MS Office 2000/XP.

Telephone Line

It is essential to have a telephone connection to get connected to the Internet. All the data and information pass through telephone lines as analogue signals.

Internet Service Provider (ISP)

If you have a computer with a web browser, a modem and a telephone line connected to your computer, you now need an Internet connection. You can get an Internet connection from various Internet Service Providers (ISPs). You can choose your ISP from among 120 companies which have been granted ISP licences by the Government of India. Among the most popular ISPs are VSNL, MTNL and Mantra Online.

Creating Icon of ISP on Desktop

Let us now get connected to the Internet and understand how to use its various features. First, we will learn how to Email. For this, we will have to connect to the Internet. As you know, we need an ISP (Internet Service Provider) connection to enter the Internet. Therefore, first of all, we will create an ISP icon on our Desktop through the following steps:

1. *Switch on* your computer as well as your modem. Windows XP **Desktop** gets displayed on the screen.
2. *Move* the mouse-pointer over the **Start** button and *click* on it. A start-up menu appears on the screen (Fig.IN-1).
3. *Click* on the **All Programs** option in the start-up menu, a second menu gets displayed (Fig.IN-1).
4. *Move* the mouse-pointer over the **Accessories** option. A third menu appears (Fig.IN-1).
5. Now, *move* the mouse-pointer over the **Communication** option. A fourth menu gets displayed (Fig.IN-1).
6. In the fourth menu, *click* on the **Network Connections** option (Fig.IN-1). The **Network Connections** window box appears on the screen (Fig.IN-2).
7. Inside the **Network Connections** window, *locate* the **vsnl** icon. Now, we will make a shortcut of this icon on the **Desktop**. *Click* the right mouse-button on the **vsnl** icon. Instantly, a shortcut menu gets displayed on the screen (Fig.IN-3).

Fig. IN-1

Fig. IN-2

8. Inside the shortcut menu, *click* on **Create Shortcut** option (Fig.IN-3). Immediately, a **Shortcut** box gets displayed on the screen (Fig.IN-4), asking you whether you wish to place the shortcut on the Desktop.
9. Inside the **Shortcut** box, *click* on the **Yes** button. Instantly, a **Shortcut to vsnl** icon gets displayed on the Desktop (Fig.IN-5).

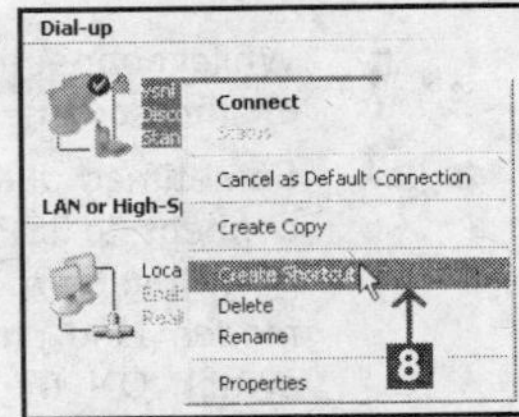

Fig. IN-3

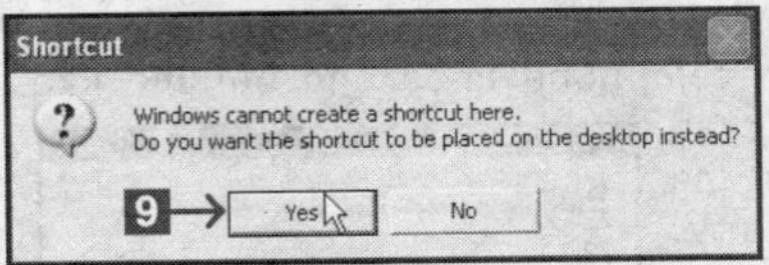

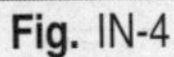

Fig. IN-4

Fig. IN-5

It is always better to make a shortcut of the vsnl icon on the Desktop, for it will make it convenient for you to quickly connect to the Internet.

Connecting to the Internet

Now, before we get connected to the Internet using the **Shortcut to vsnl** icon, it is better to close the **Network Connections** window. To close this window, undertake the following steps:

1. *Click* the left mouse-button on the **Close** button (☒) of the **Network Connections** window. Instantly, the window closes.
2. Now *move* the mouse-pointer over the **Shortcut to vsnl** icon displayed on the **Desktop** and *double-click* the left mouse-button. Instantly, a **Connect vsnl** box appears on the screen (Fig.IN-6).
3. In this box, *move* the mouse-pointer over the **Dial** button (Fig.IN-6) and *click* the left mouse-button on it. Another box called **Connecting vsnl** with a ringing sound appears on the screen (Fig.IN-7). The ringing sound indicates that your computer is getting ready to get connected to the Internet service provider, i.e. VSNL.

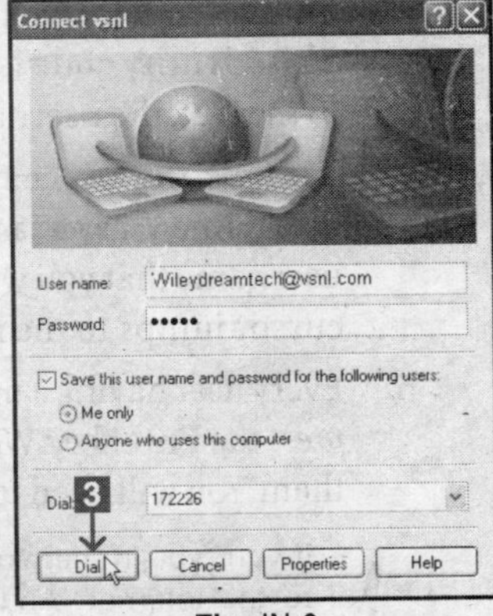

Fig. IN-6

4. Once you are connected, a box called **Post-Dial Terminal Screen** appears on your computer (Fig.IN-8).

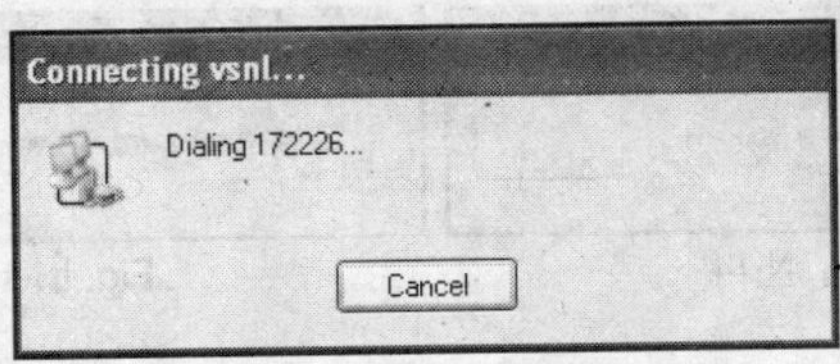

Fig. IN-7

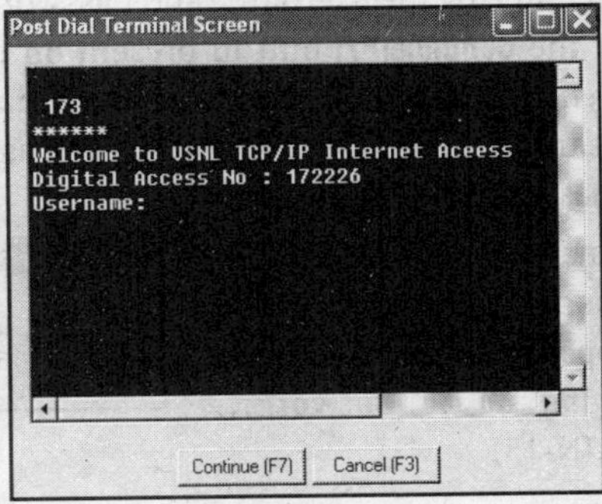

Fig. IN-8

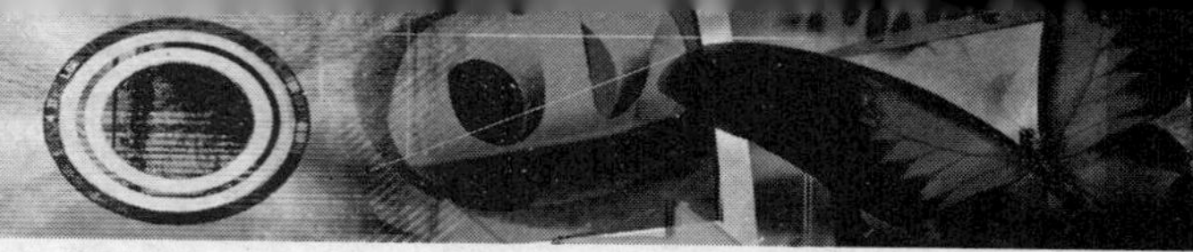

While connecting to an ISP, an error message (Fig.IN-9) may appear on the screen. Just click on the OK button and try connecting again.

Sometimes due to loose connections your modem may not be able to connect to ISP properly. So an error message gets displayed (Fig.IN-10). In such a case, first click on the OK button. Then switch OFF your modem and check all connections. After checking all the connections, switch ON the modem again.

Modems are connected through telephone lines and behave like telephones. Sometimes you hear an engaged tone on your phone when the number you are calling is busy. Similarly, if the ISP number you are dialling is busy, a message as shown in Fig.IN-11 appears on your computer screen. In that case, press Enter key to start re-dialling. Repeat this procedure until you get connected.

Disconnected from vsnl.
Dial-Up Networking was unable to complete the connection.
Error: 676
The line is busy
Try again later.
More Help
OK

Fig. IN-9

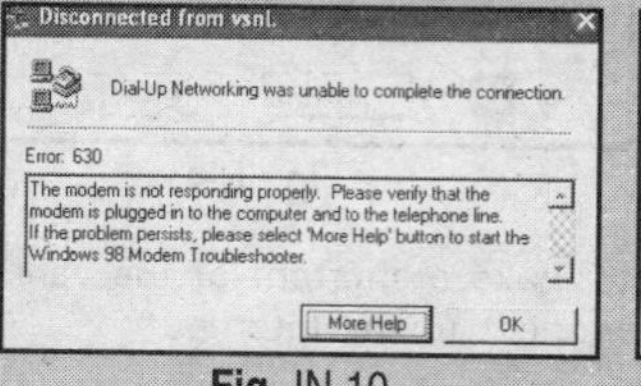

Fig. IN-10

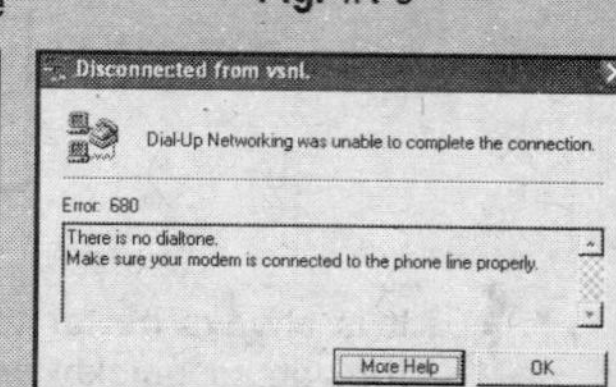

Fig. IN-11

5. Your screen now looks similar to Fig.IN-8. Every user is uniquely identified on the Net by using an identity code. This identity code is called the **username.** For connecting to the Net, the username has to be entered first.

   So, *type* the username. In Fig.IN-13, we have typed our username **Wileydreamtech@vsnl.com.** You should enter your username that you would like to have for your Net connection. Next, *press* the **Enter** key. Instantly, the cursor jumps to the next line, that is **Password** (Fig.IN-12).

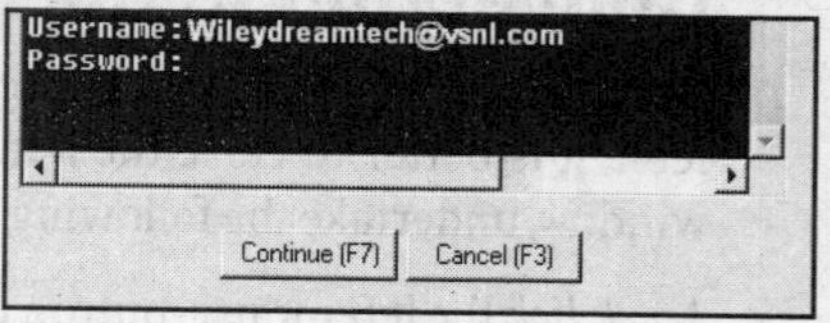

Fig. IN-12

6. Every user having a username is assigned a **password.** Now *type* in a password of your choice and then *press* the **Enter** key. Write down your username and password in your diary so that you should not forget them. You will need to enter the username and password whenever you intend to access the Internet.

If you type in the wrong password, you won't be able to get connected to the Internet. And, a message gets displayed on the screen saying Username/Password Incorrect, as shown in Fig.IN-13. Now try again. Type your username and password correctly and press the Enter key again.

Post Dial Terminal Screen
173
***
Welcome to VSNL TCP/IP Internet Aceess
Digital Access No : 172226
Username : Wileydreamtech@vsnl.com
Password:
Authentication failure
Username/Password Incorrect
Username:
Continue (F7)
Cancel (F3)

Fig. IN-13

7. After entering the username and password, *move* the mouse-pointer over the **Continue[F7]** button present on the **Post-Dial Terminal Screen** and *click* the left mouse-button. Immediately, a **Connecting to vsnl** box appears on your screen with the message **Status: Verifying user name and password...** (Fig.IN-14).

   After a few seconds, another message appears in the **Connecting to vsnl** box saying **Logging on to network...** (Fig.IN-15).

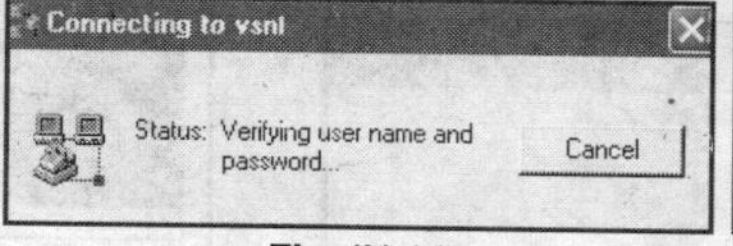

Fig. IN-14

Fig. IN-15

Within a few seconds, the **Connecting to vsnl** box appears displaying some information like time taken by your computer to log on to the Internet, speed of your modem, etc. (Fig.IN-16). *Click* on the **OK** button. The box disappears from the screen and turns into an icon on the left side of the clock present on the **Taskbar.**

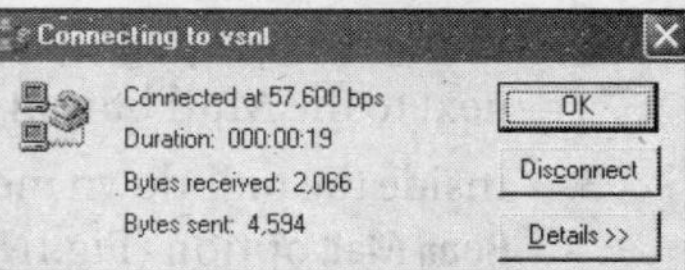

Fig. IN-16

8. Now you have to open a browser, **Internet Explorer** or **Netscape Navigator.** We will open the Internet Explorer which comes in-built with Windows XP.
   To do so, *double-click* on the **Internet Explorer** icon (Fig.IN-17), present on the **Desktop.** Immediately, the **Home page** of Internet Explorer gets displayed on your screen (Fig. IN-18).

Fig. IN-17

9. From this **Home page,** you can visit many other web pages linked to it. Actually, every Home page topic has a corresponding web page. You just have to click on the topic to open its page. For example, if you wish to display the current news on the screen, *click* on the **News** hyperlink, as shown in Fig. IN-18. Instantly, the **News** page gets displayed before you (Fig.IN-19).

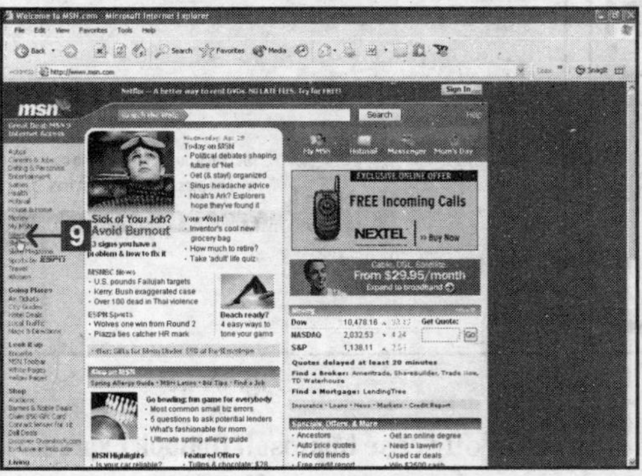

Fig. IN-18

Fig. IN-19

On getting disconnected from Internet, a message box appears on the screen, as shown in Fig.IN-20. If you wish to connect again, click on the Reconnect button

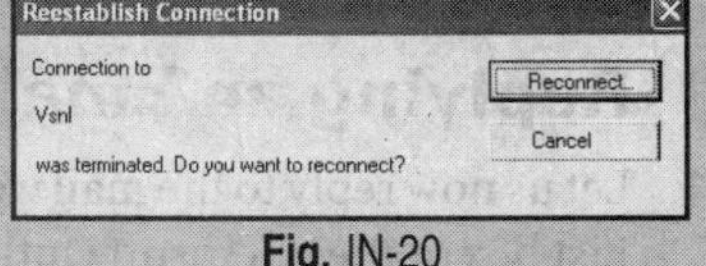

Fig. IN-20

Sending and Receiving Emails using Outlook Express

The Outlook Express is a message or Email handling software. This comes along with the Windows operating system. Outlook Express is used to exchange Email messages in the form of text or images. In the following section, we will learn how to work with Emails using Outlook Express.

Receiving an Email

To read an Email message which you have received undertake the following steps.

1. *Move* the mouse-pointer over the **Mail** button ( ) on the **Standard Toolbar** of the **Microsoft Internet Explorer** screen. Then *click* the left mouse button on it (Fig.IN-21).

2. Immediately, a pull-down menu appears next to the **Mail** button (Fig.IN-21).
3. Inside the pull-down menu, *click* on the **Read Mail** option (Fig.IN-21).

   Immediately, a Microsoft Outlook Express logo appears on the screen for a few seconds. Finally, the **Outlook Express** window opens up on your screen (Fig.IN-22).

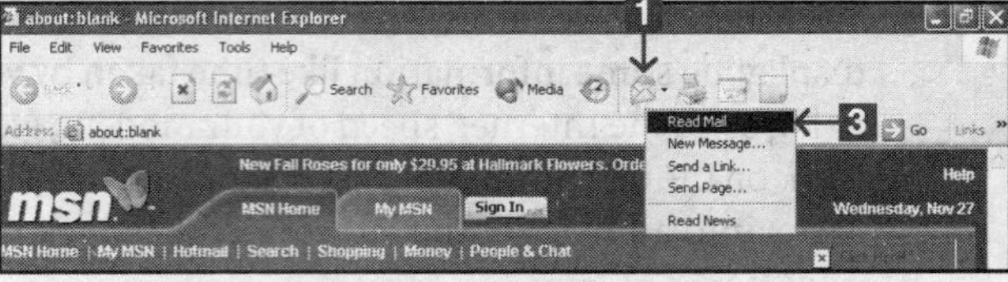

Fig. IN-21

4. Now, to view all the Emails you have received, *move* the mouse-pointer over the **Inbox** option inside the **Folders** box and *click* the left mouse-button (Fig.IN-22). Instantly, an **Inbox - Outlook Express** window appears giving details of all Email messages sent to your address (Fig.IN-23). In our case, we have received only one mail, i.e. from Microsoft Outlook Express.

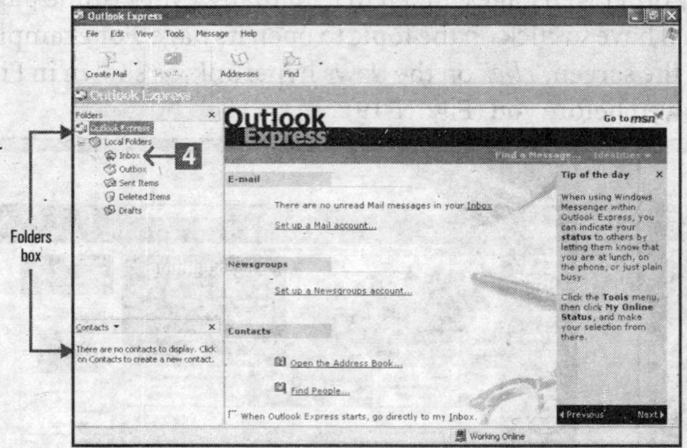

Fig. IN-22

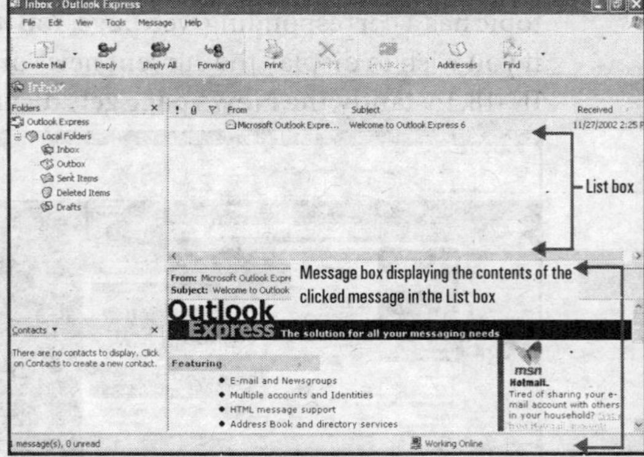

Fig. IN-23

5. If you wish to read the contents of a particular mail, in our case **Microsoft Outlook Express**, just *move* the mouse-pointer over it and *double-click* the left mouse-button. Immediately, a message box opens up on your screen displaying the contents of the message.

Replying an Email using Outlook Express

Let us now reply to the mail we have received from Microsoft Outlook Express, which is displayed in the List box of the Microsoft Outlook window. To do so, undertake the following steps:

1. Begin with Fig.IN-23. *Click* over the **Microsoft Outlook Express** email in the **List box**. The mail gets highlighted.

NOTE: If the mail is already highlighted then proceed from Step 2.

2. Now, *click* on the **Reply** button ( ) as shown in Fig.IN-24. A **Re: Welcome to Outlook Express 6** box appears on the screen (Fig.IN-25). This box has different boxes for typing the receiver's email address, subject of the email and message.

   In Fig.IN-25, you see the text, **Microsoft Outlook Express Team,** beside the **To** option. This text represents the address where the mail has to be sent. Here you may type your friend's email address. Beside the **Subject** option, topic of the mail to be sent is displayed.

3. We will go by the default text in **To** and **Subject** options. Also, we would not type any message in the text box. So, we will send a blank email. However, you may type any message if you want. Now, to send a blank email to Microsoft Outlook Express Team, *click* on the **Send** button (Send icon) (Fig.IN-26).

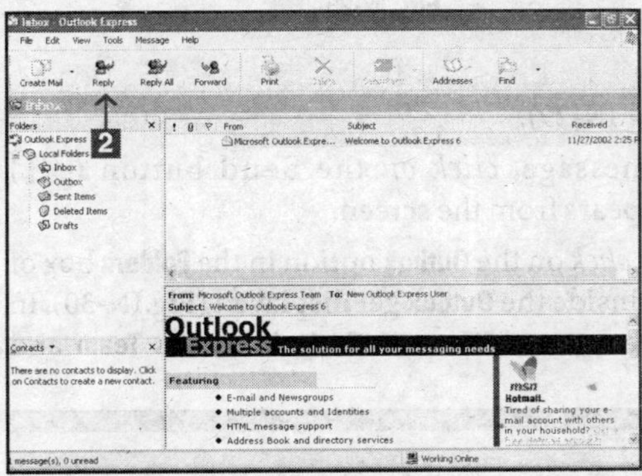

Fig. IN-24

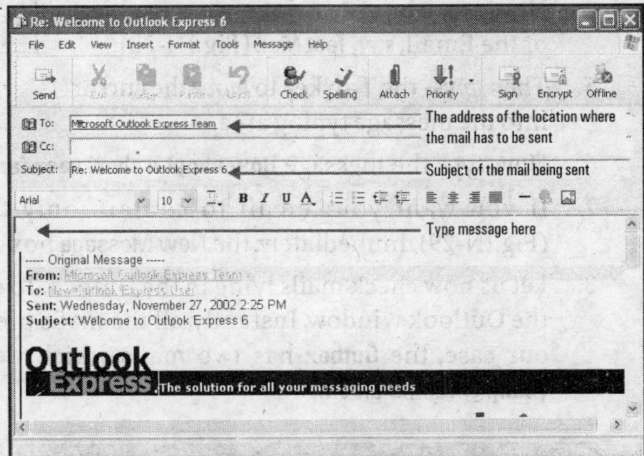

Fig. IN-25

Fig. IN-26

Immediately, the **Re: Welcome to Outlook Express 6** box disappears from the screen. This indicates that the mail has been sent.

All mails that are sent get collected inside the **Outbox** of the Outlook Express window. We will look inside the **Outbox** later. Let us now learn how to create a new mail in Outlook Express window and then send it.

When you click on the Send button (Send icon), your message gets stored in the Outbox (Outbox icon). This mail will be sent automatically from the Outbox when you start Outlook Express the next time.

Sending an Email using Outlook Express

To create a new email and send it, undertake the following steps:

1. *Start* with Fig.IN-24 displayed on your screen. *Click* on the **Create Mail** button (Create Mail icon) present on the **Standard Toolbar**. Immediately, a **New Message** box gets displayed on the screen (Fig.IN-27).

Fig. IN-27

2. Now, beside the **To** option, *type* the Email address, say, **yoanji@123india.com**, where you wish to send a message (Fig.IN-28). If you want the same mail to go to two persons then *type* another address in the box beside the **Cc**: option (in our case, **shwetasharma47@rediffmail.com**) (Fig.IN-28). Beside the **To**: and **Cc**: options, you may type your friends' email addresses.

3. Then *press* the **Tab** key two times to *move* the cursor in the box beside the **Subject** option.
4. Next, *type* a brief description of the subject of the Email, say, **Test Mail** (Fig.IN-28).

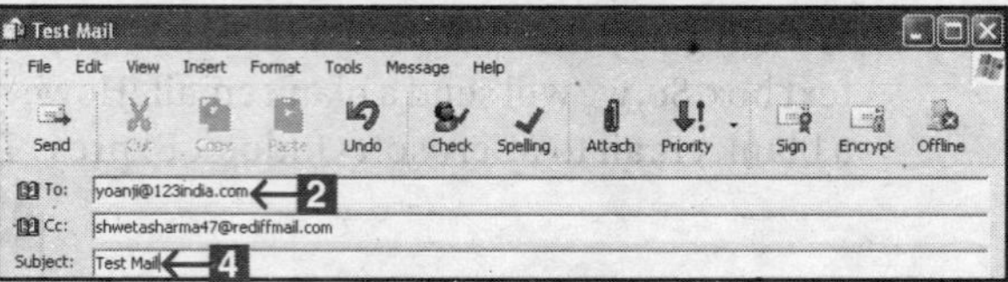

Fig. IN-28

5. Then, *press* the **Tab** key to *move* the cursor into the message typing area.
6. Now, *type* the message **How about a short vacation?** (Fig.IN-29).
7. If you want your email to contain only this message, *click on* the **Send** button (Send icon) (Fig.IN-29). Immediately, the **New Message** box disappears from the screen.
8. Let us now check mails lying in the Outbox. To do so, *click* on the **Outbox** option in the **Folders** box of the Outlook window. Instantly, all the mails present inside the **Outbox** get displayed (Fig.IN-30). In our case, the **Outbox** has two mails which we have sent to **Microsoft Outlook Express Team** and **yoanji@123india.com**.

Fig. IN-29

Fig. IN-30

If you want to deliver the mail instantly, click on the Send and Receive button (Send/Recv icon). On clicking this button, your message will instantly get delivered instead of getting stored in the Outbox. A message box (Fig.IN-31) gets displayed on the screen, indicating the same.

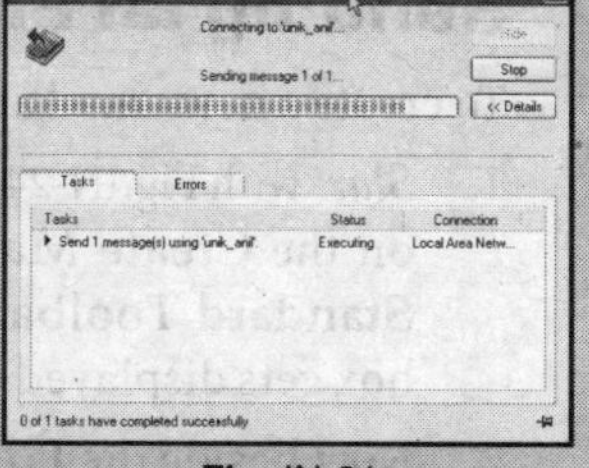

Fig. IN-31

Closing the Outlook Express Window

So, now you can easily send and read your mails in Outlook Express. Let us quit the Outlook Express window. To do so, undertake the following steps:

1. *Move* the mouse-pointer over the **Close** button (☒) of the Outlook Express window.
2. Then *click* the left mouse-button. Immediately, the Outlook Express window closes.

While closing Microsoft Outlook, if you have mails lying in the Outbox then a message box gets displayed asking you whether you wish to send the mails (Fig.IN-32).

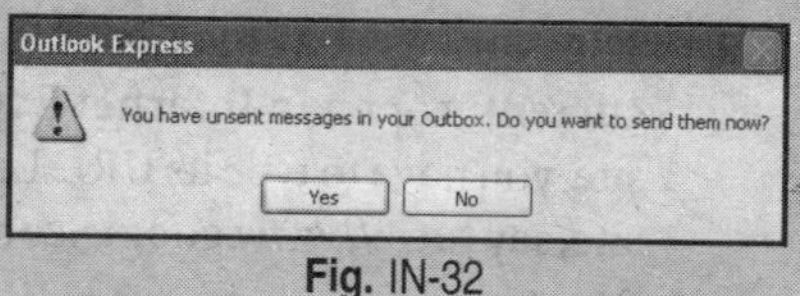

Fig. IN-32

Browsing the WWW

When you open the Internet Explorer browser, the home page of Microsoft Internet Explorer will open by default. If you have the Netscape browser, the home page of Netscape Incorporation opens on your screen by default.

Each web page on the web has a unique address. This address is called **URL (Uniform Resource Locator)**. The URLs of web pages start with **http: //** where http stands for **Hyper Text Transfer Protocol.** To view a particular website, you will have to write the address or URL of that website in the **Address bar** of the Internet Explorer window shown in Fig.IN-33.

Let us now learn to open different pages in a website. You already know that each web page contains text, images, sound and video clips. Images and text on some web pages may contain links to other web pages. Such a link is known as **Hyperlink.** Hyperlink is often indicated by underline or shown in a different colour from the main text. Some graphics are also used as hyperlinks (☝).

You may find the text links on a website's home page by moving the mouse-pointer to different locations, text or images. If the mouse cursor changes into a hand symbol (☝), it is an indication of a link to a different web page in that site. You may click on any hyperlink (☝), and a web page giving details of that particular topic opens up.

Let us now surf the web to find the sites of our interest. Before you begin web surfing, first get connected to the Internet as explained in the topic **Connecting to the Internet.** Then proceed as follows:

1. Begin with Fig.IN-19. This is the News page of the **Internet Explorer.** As you know, we had reached this page by clicking on the **News** topic on the home page of the **Internet Explorer** (Fig.IN-18). Now, to move to a previous page from the current one, in our case the home page of the Internet Explorer, just *click* on the **Back** button (◀) displayed on the **Standard Toolbar** of the **Internet Explorer** window. Immediately, the **Internet Explorer** home page gets displayed (Fig.IN-33).

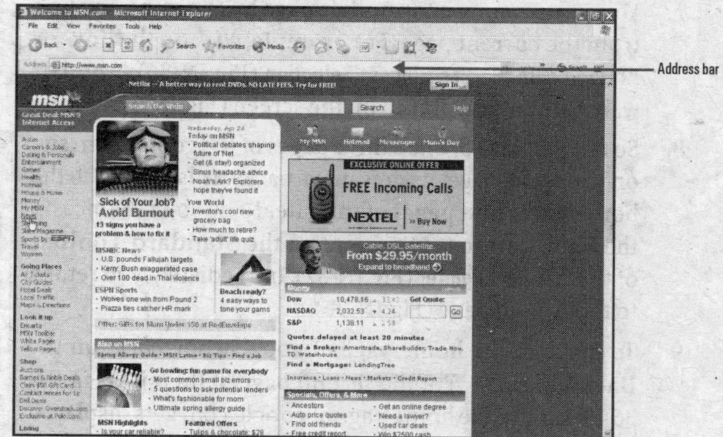

Fig. IN-33

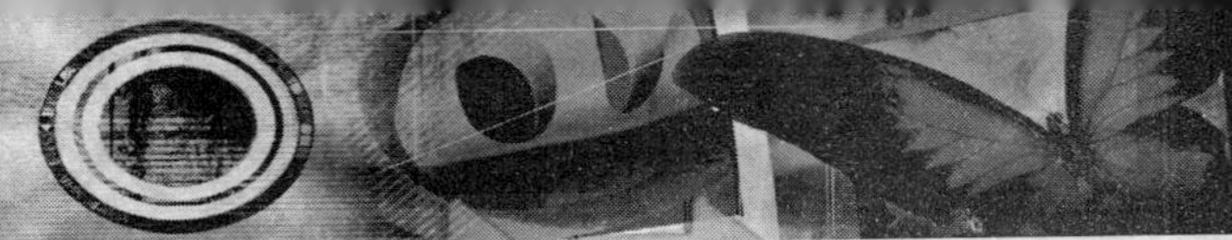

2. The **Address bar** of the home page displays the Uniform Resource Locator (URL) of the site that is currently open in Internet Explorer. To move to another site, you have to type its URL. Let us type the URL of another site, say http://www.google.com.

   To do so, *move* the mouse-pointer inside the **Address bar** and *click* the left mouse-button. The existing URL gets highlighted.

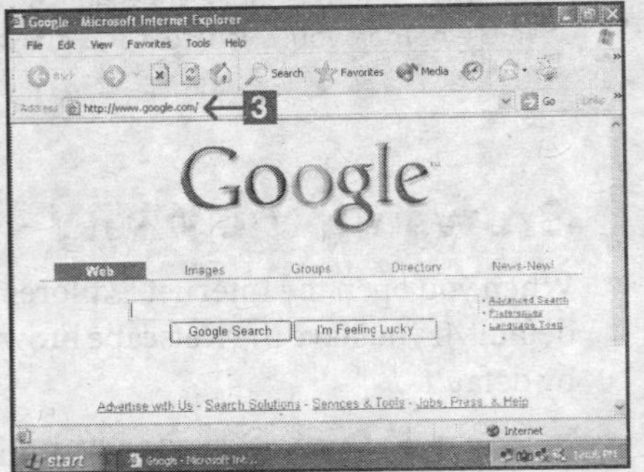

Fig. IN-34

3. Now, *type* the URL **http://www.google.com** and then *press* the **Enter** key. This URL gets highlighted and after a few seconds, the home page of google.com website appears on your screen (Fig.IN-34).
4. Now, *move* the mouse-pointer all over the screen. You will notice that at some places the mouse-pointer changes into a hand symbol (☝). The hand indicates the point from where you can go to another page. As you know, such a point is called hyperlink. To go to another page, *click* the left mouse-button on its hyperlink.

Fig. IN-35

5. Let us now move to the next page of the google.com site. Suppose, you wish to search for books available on the Internet. To do so, *click* the left mouse-button inside the box above the **Google Search** button. Instantly, a blinking cursor gets displayed in the box.
6. Now *type* **Books** (Fig.IN-35), and *click* over the **Google Search**. Immediately, a list of hyperlinks appears on the screen. Each hyperlink represents the name of a website offering books and briefly displays the information that can be obtained from that website (Fig.IN-36).

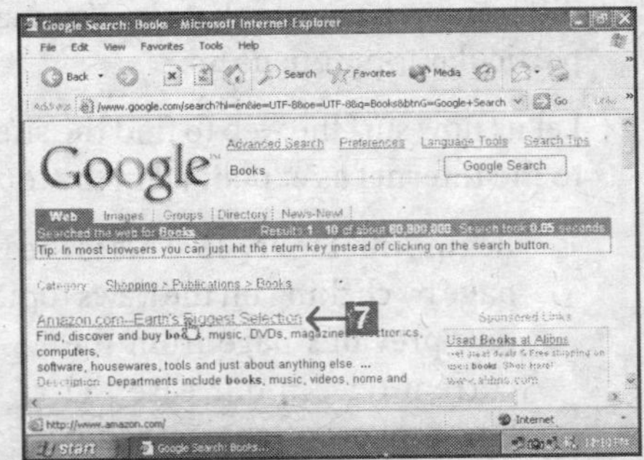

Fig. IN-36

7. You can now move to another page by choosing any link from the current page. For example, *click* on the link for **Amazon.com--Earth's Biggest Selection** (Fig.IN-36). Another web page gets displayed on the screen (Fig.IN-37).
8. So far, you have opened three pages of the google.com site on your screen. Let us now move backwards and reach the home page (first page) of this site. To do so, *click* once on the **Back** button (◀) present on the **Standard Toolbar** of the **Internet Explorer** (Fig.IN-37). Immediately, you return to the second page (Fig.IN-36).

Fig. IN-37

9. To move to the home page of google.com, *click* on the **Back** button (◀) of the second page of this site (Fig.IN-36). Instantly, the home page of google.com gets displayed on the screen (Fig.IN-34). If you no more want to continue searching the sites then to end browsing *click* on the **Stop** button (✖).

Opening an Email Account

Before you actually settle down to send an email, you need to create an email account. There are innumerable websites where you can create an email account. Some of the most popular sites in India where you can make an email account are:

- www.rediff.com
- www.indiatimes.com
- www.hotmail.com
- www.yahoomail.com
- www.mail.com
- www.indya.com.

Let us now create an account in www.rediff.com. Begin with the Internet Explorer window. *Type* address **www.rediff.com** in the **Address bar** and *press* the **Enter** key. Within a few seconds a page, as shown in Fig.IN-38, gets displayed on your screen.

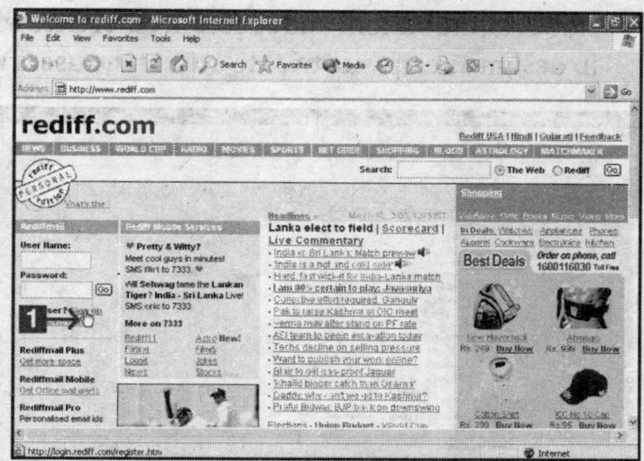

Fig. IN-38

In this page, two boxes are displayed: one for the **Login ID** and another for the **Password.** And just below these boxes, there are two options:

(a) Sign In **(b) New user? Sign up**

To create a new email account, undertake the following steps:

1. *Take* the mouse-pointer to the **New user? Sign up** option. Instantly, the cursor turns into the handshape. (Fig.IN-38). *Click* the left mouse button. A new page appears, with various email options (Fig.IN-39).
2. In the new page, take the mouse-pointer to the **Sign-Up Now** option under **Rediffmail Free** option and *click* the left mouse-button (Fig.IN-39). A new page that is the **Rediff Registration** appears (Fig.IN-40).
3. In the **Rediff Registration** page (Fig.IN-40), we have written the login ID as **mn_srivastava110478** and entered a password. But, you should enter both the login ID and the password of your choice. An ideal login ID should be the one which can be remembered easily. It should be 6 to 10 characters long. While writing a login ID, you should be careful not to use spaces and special characters like %, !, @, #, etc.
4. After finishing filling up the **Rediff Registration** page, *click* on the **Register Me** button that is located at the end of the page (Fig.IN-41). Instantly, a new page appears which confirms your registration (Fig.IN-42).

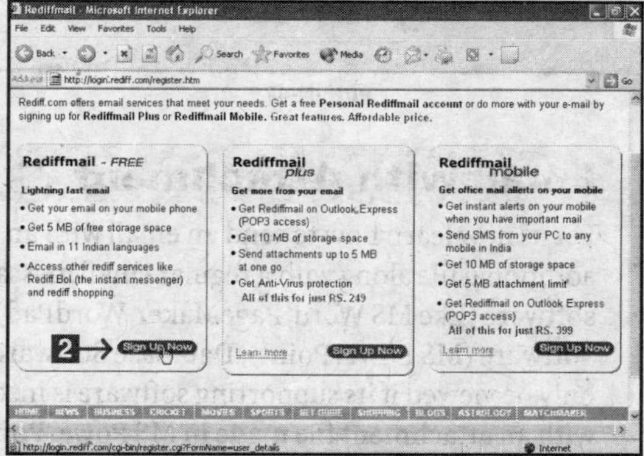

Fig. IN-39

Fig. IN-40

5. Now whenever you want to enter into your email account, *type* the address **www. rediffmail.com** in the **Address bar** of the **Internet Explorer** window and press the **Enter** key. Fig.IN-38 will appear. In this figure, *type* your ID and the Password that you had supplied while filling up the registration form. Then, *click* on the **Go** button to enter your email account.

Following the above method, you can open an email account in any other site. The process is same. However, the buttons and spaces in other sites will not be exactly the same. You will notice some differences in design as each site tries to attract the users with a unique design.

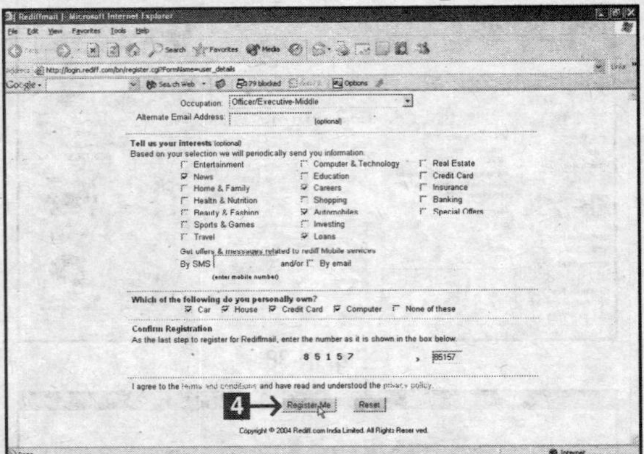

Fig. IN-41

Fig. IN-42

Email with Attachment

Let us now learn how to send an email with an attachment file. By attachment file, we mean attaching an additional file along with a regular email message. An attachment file could be a file of a word processing software (like MS Word, PageMaker, WordPad), Accounting Software (like Tally, MS Excel), Presentation Software (MS PowerPoint), Database Software (Access, FoxPro) or HTML page. An attachment file can only be viewed if its supporting software is installed on your computer. For example, you receive an email with an attachment file made in MS PowerPoint. In that case, MS PowerPoint must be installed on your computer, otherwise you won't be able to view the attachment file.

In this section, we will learn how an email message with an attachment file is exchanged between two users having email accounts on two different websites. In our example, a user having an email account on **hotmail.com** website sends an email message to the user having an email account on **indiatimes.com** website. The file attached to the email message is an MS Word document which is created in MS Word 2000/XP. The flow chart on the next page (Fig.IN-43) describes a broad outline of the procedure of sending and receiving an email with attachment file. Detailed explanation of the procedure follows the flow chart.

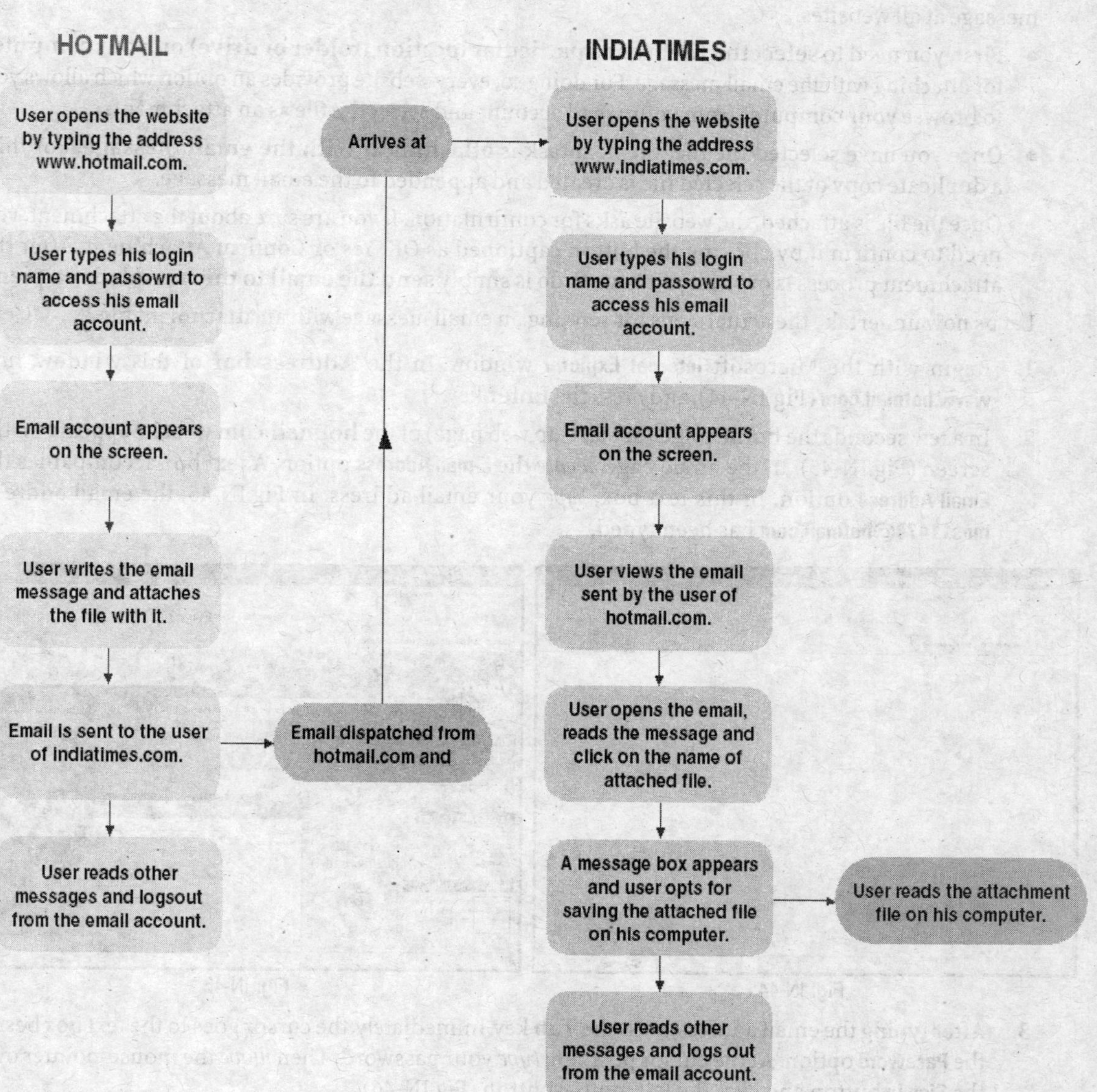
HOTMAIL
INDIATIMES
User opens the website by typing the address www.hotmail.com.
User types his login name and passowrd to access his email account.
Email account appears on the screen.
User writes the email message and attaches the file with it.
Email is sent to the user of indiatimes.com.
User reads other messages and logsout from the email account.
Email dispatched from hotmail.com and
Arrives at
User opens the website by typing the address www.indiatimes.com.
User types his login name and passowrd to access his email account.
Email account appears on the screen.
User views the email sent by the user of hotmail.com.
User opens the email, reads the message and click on the name of attached file.
A message box appears and user opts for saving the attached file on his computer.
User reads the attachment file on his computer.
User reads other messages and logs out from the email account.

Fig. IN-43

Sending an Email with Attachment File

Let us understand some basic steps that are commonly followed for attaching a file with an email message at all websites.

- First, you need to **select the file from a particular location (folder or drive) on your computer** for attaching with the email message. For doing so, every website provides an option which allows you to browse your computer from your email account and select the file as an attachment.
- Once you have selected the file, the next task is **attaching it with the email message.** For this, a duplicate copy of the selected file is created and appended to the email message.
- Once the file is attached, the website asks for confirmation. If you are sure about the attachment, you need to confirm it by clicking the button captioned as OK, Yes or Confirm Attachment. After the attachment process is over, all you have to do is simply **send the email to the intended recipient.**

Let us now undertake the actual steps for sending an email message with an attachment file.

1. Begin with the Microsoft **Internet Explorer** window. In the **Address bar** of this window, *type* **www.hotmail.com** (Fig.IN-44), and *press* the **Enter** key.
2. In a few seconds the **home page** (or start-up web page) of the **hotmail.com** website appears on the screen (Fig.IN-45). In the home page, *locate* the **E-mail Address** option. A text box accompanies the **Email Address** option. In this text box, *type* your email address. In Fig.IN-45, the email address, **mns11478@hotmail.com** has been typed.

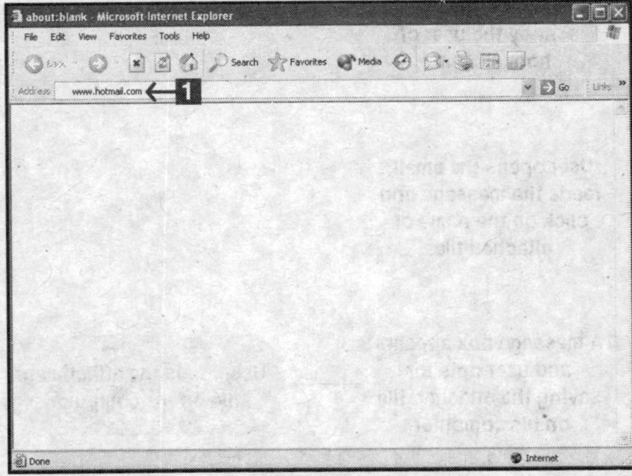

Fig. IN-44

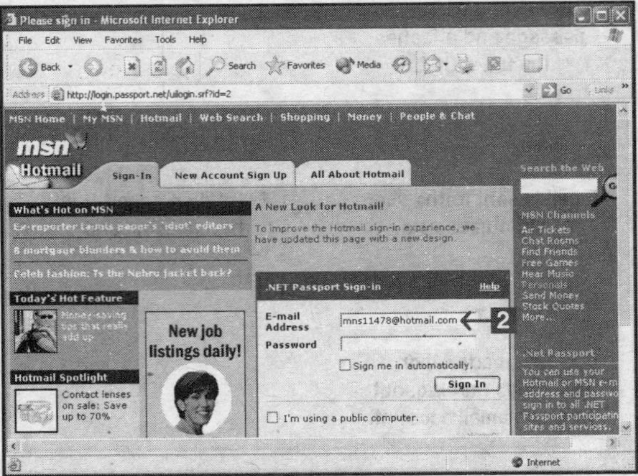

Fig. IN-45

3. After typing the email address, *press* the **Tab** key. Immediately, the cursor goes to the text box beside the **Password** option. At the cursor position, *type* your password. Then *move* the mouse-pointer over the **Sign In** button and *click* the left mouse-button (Fig.IN-46).
4. After a short while, the desired email account appears on the screen (Fig.In-47). Inside the email account window, locate the **Compose** tab and *click* over it (Fig.IN-47). The **Compose** window (Fig.IN-48) appears on the screen. Using this window, you can write emails and append attachments to them.

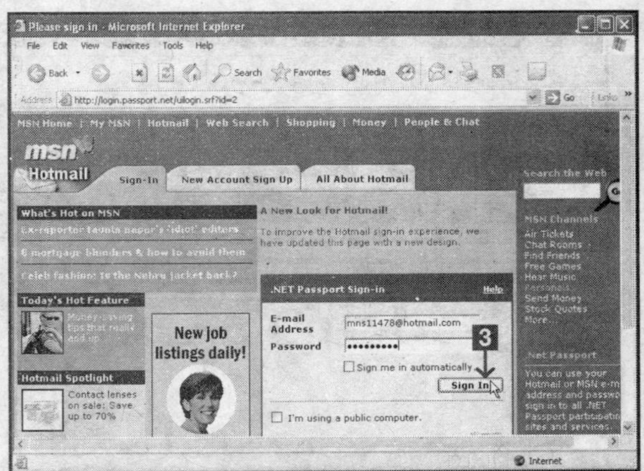

Fig. IN-46

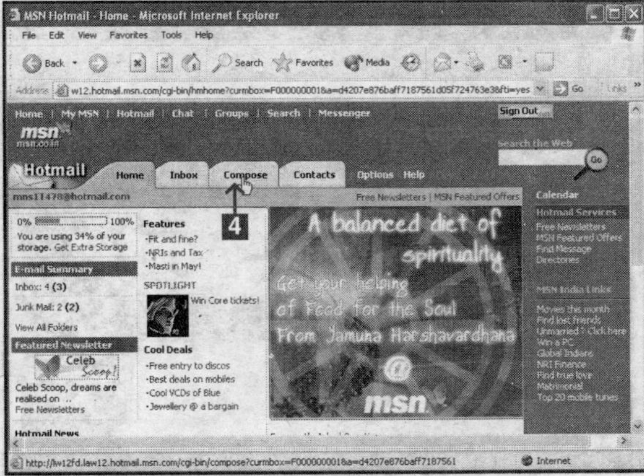

Fig. IN-47

5. Inside the **Compose** window, *move* the mouse-pointer over the text box beside the **To :** option and *click* the left mouse-button. Instantly a blinking cursor appears inside the box. Now, *type* the email address of the person whom you want to send the email. We have typed **anujgoswami@indiatimes.com** as the recipient of email (Fig.IN-48). You may type your friend's email address.
6. Now, *move* the mouse-pointer to the text box beside the **Subject:** option and *click* the left mouse-button. A blinking cursor appears in the box (Fig.IN-49).

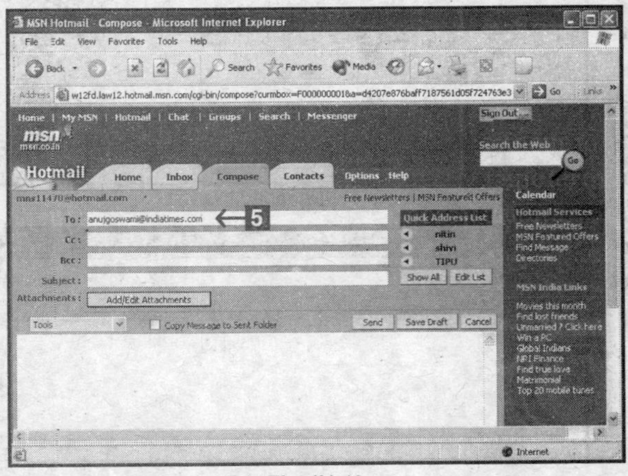

Fig. IN-48

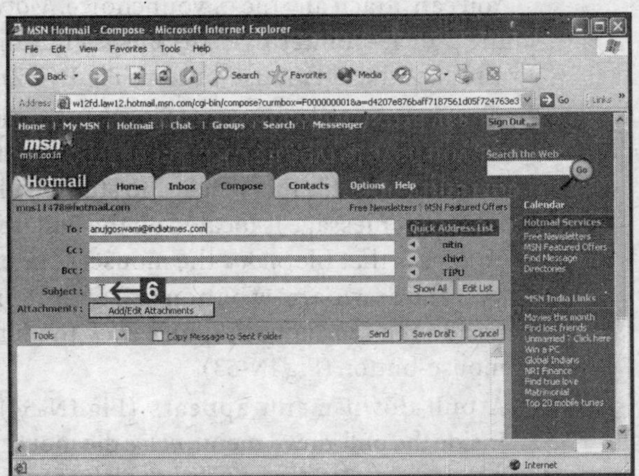

Fig. IN-49

7. In the text box of the **Subject:** option, *type* few words to describe the purpose or nature of email so that the recipient could easily guess the message written in the email. For example, *type* **Reply to your letter** (Fig.IN-50).
8. Now, *move* the mouse-pointer over **Add/Edit Attachment** button and *click* the left mouse-button (Fig.IN-51).

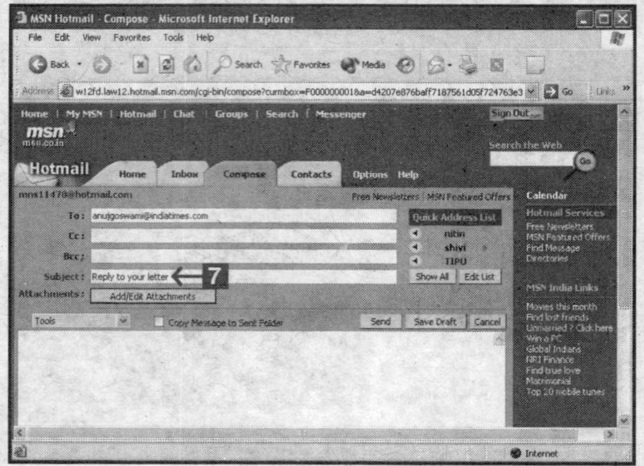

Fig. IN-50

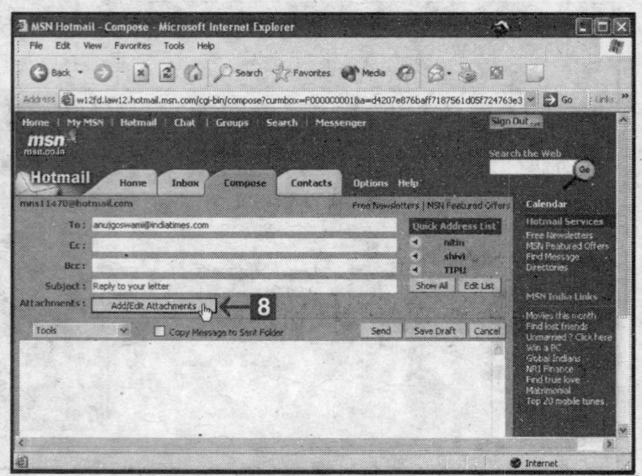

Fig. IN-51

9. In a few moments the **Attachment** window appears (Fig.IN-52). Through this window, you can select any file from your computer for attaching with the email message. Let us now understand the procedure of attaching a file with an email message. We will attach a file, **Letter.doc**, that is located in the **Desktop**. You can attach any file of your choice. *Move* the mouse-pointer over the **Browse** button and *click* the left mouse-button (Fig.IN-52).
10. The **Choose file** box appears (Fig.IN-53). This box displays a file present under the **gagan** folder. But the file that we need to attach with the email message is located on the **Desktop**. To access that file, *move* the mouse-pointer over the down-arrow button (▾) of the box beside the **Look in** option and *click* the left mouse-button (Fig.IN-53).
11. A pull-down menu appears (Fig.IN-54). Inside the pull-down menu, *move* the mouse-pointer over **Desktop** and *click* the left mouse-button (Fig.IN-54)
12. The **Desktop** folder appears beside the **Look in** option and files and folders present under the **Desktop** folder appear inside the big rectangular box (Fig.IN-55). Now *move* the mouse-pointer over the desired file, i.e. **Letter.doc** in the rectangular box and *click* the left mouse-button (Fig.IN-55). Instantly, the **Letter.doc** file gets highlighted and its name is displayed inside the box beside the **File name** option (Fig.IN-55)

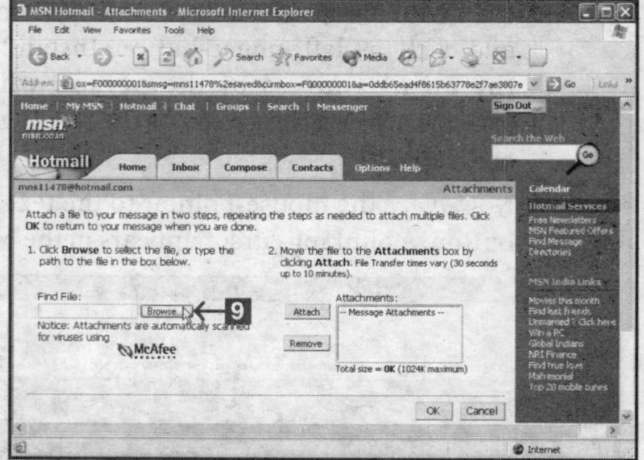

Fig. IN-52

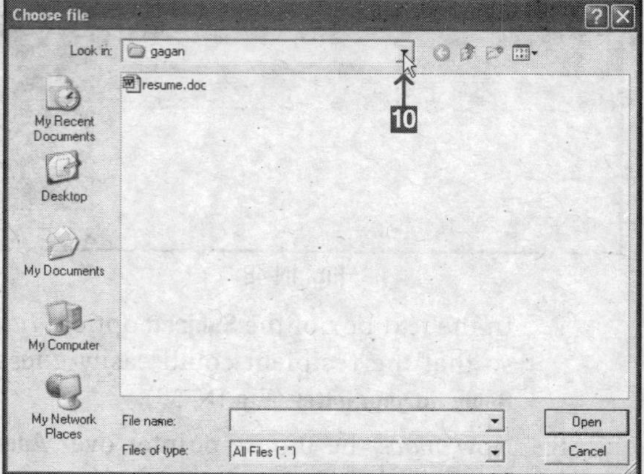

Fig. IN-53

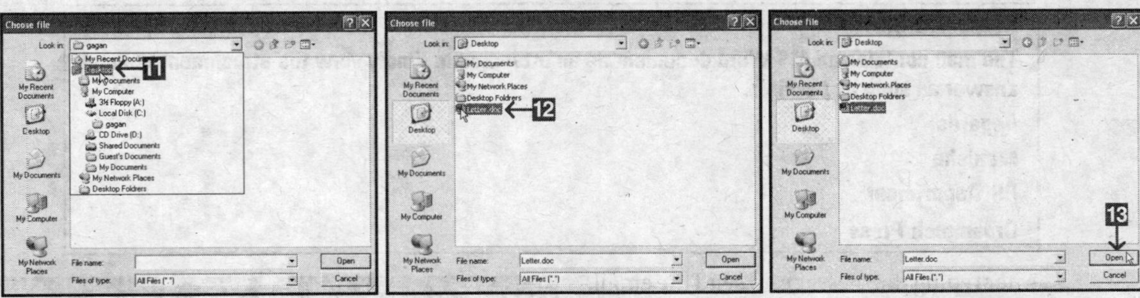

Fig. IN-54 Fig. IN-55 Fig. IN-56

13. After selecting the file, *click* over the **Open** button (Fig.IN-56).
14. Now, you return to the **Attachment** window (Fig.IN-57). *Move* the mouse-pointer over the **Attach** button and *click* the left mouse-button (Fig.IN-57).
15. In a few moments, the **Letter.doc** file gets attached with the email message and its name and size appear inside the small rectangular box beside the **Attach** button (Fig.IN-58). It confirms the successful attachment of the file with the email message.
16. Now *move* the mouse-pointer over the **OK** button and *click* the left mouse-button (Fig.IN-58).

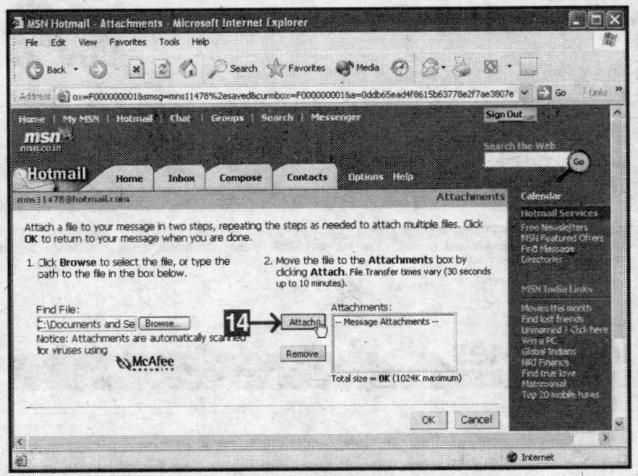

Fig. IN-57

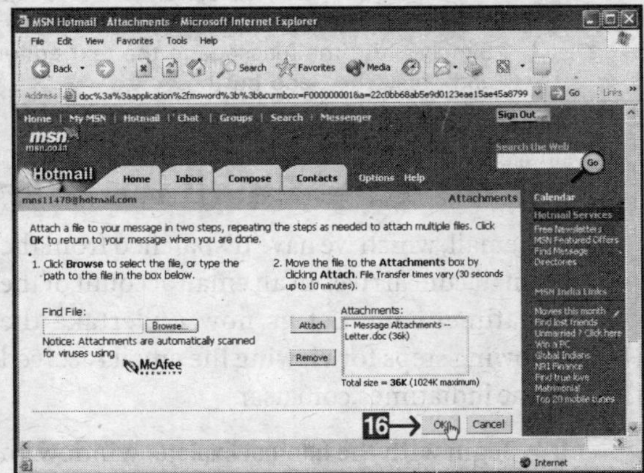

Fig. IN-58

17. The **Compose** window re-appears on the screen (Fig.IN-59). Inside the **Compose** window, the white region below the **Send** button is a small **text editor** that you can use for writing message. To write a message, *move* the mouse-pointer in the text editor and *click* the left mouse-button. At the position of the blinking cursor, *type* the following message.

Respected Sir,

The mail contains an MS Word document as an attachment. Kindly view the attachment file and answer as soon as possible.

Regards.

Manisha

PR Department

Dreamtech Press

After typing the message, to send the email, *move* the mouse-pointer over the **Send** button and *click* the left mouse-button (Fig.IN-59).

18. Now if you want to log out from your email account, *move* the mouse-pointer over the **Sign Out** button (Sign Out), present on the top right corner of the window, and *click* over it. Your email account windows gets closed.

If you do not want to attach a file to the email message then skip Steps 8 to 15. Simply write the message in the text editor and press the Send button.

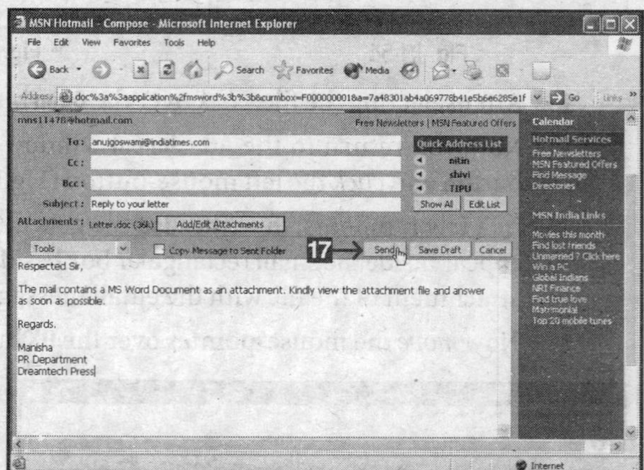

Fig. IN-59

Viewing the Email with Attachment

The email, which we have dispatched from the hotmail.com arrives in an email account of the indiatimes.com. Let us now undertake the following steps for viewing the email received by the indiatimes.com user.

1. Begin with the **Internet Explorer** window. In the Address bar of this window *type* address **www.indiatimes.com** and *press* the **Enter** key. The home page of **Indiatimes** website appears on the screen (Fig.IN-60)
2. Inside the home page, *move* the mouse-pointer over the **Email** icon and *click* the left mouse-button (Fig.IN-60).

Fig. IN-60

3. The email **login page** appears on the screen (Fig.IN-61). Inside the **login page**, you need to *type* the login name and password. We have typed the login name as **anujgoswami** inside the box below the **Indiatimes ID** option (Fig.IN-61). You may type the login name of your friend to whom you have sent email with an attachment file.

4. Now, *press* the **Tab** key. The cursor jumps to the box below the **Password** option. At the cursor position, *type* the password. Now, *move* the mouse-pointer over **Sign in** button and *click* the left mouse-button (Fig.IN-62).

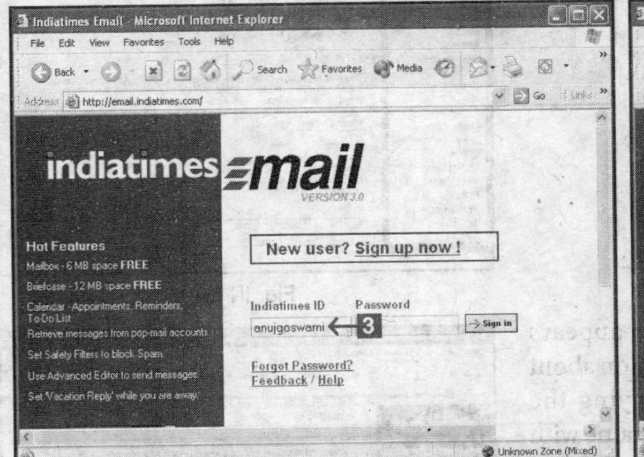

Fig. IN-61

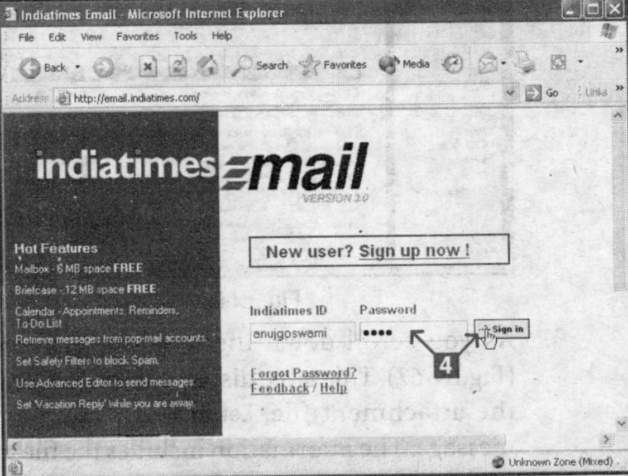

Fig. IN-62

5. In a few moments, the email account window of the Indiatimes.com user appears on the screen (Fig.IN-63). Inside this window, *move* the mouse-pointer over the **Inbox** option, present on the left hand side, and *click* the left mouse-button (Fig.IN-63).

6. A list of emails received by the user appears (Fig.IN-64). The list also has the email sent by the user of **hotmail.com** (mns11478@hotmail.com) to the user of **indiatimes.com** (anujgoswami@indiatimes.com) with subject as **Reply to your letter.**

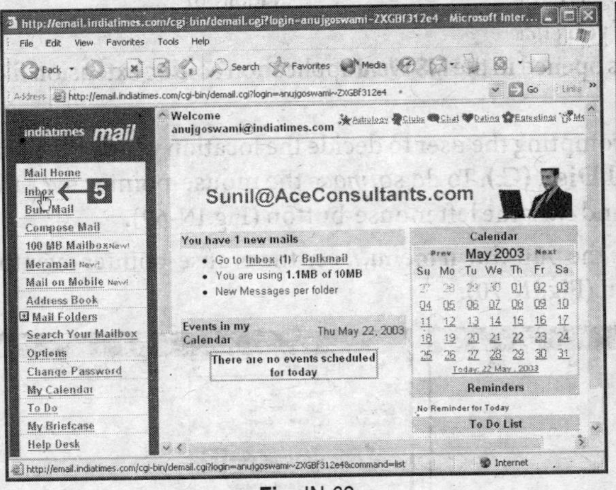

Fig. IN-63

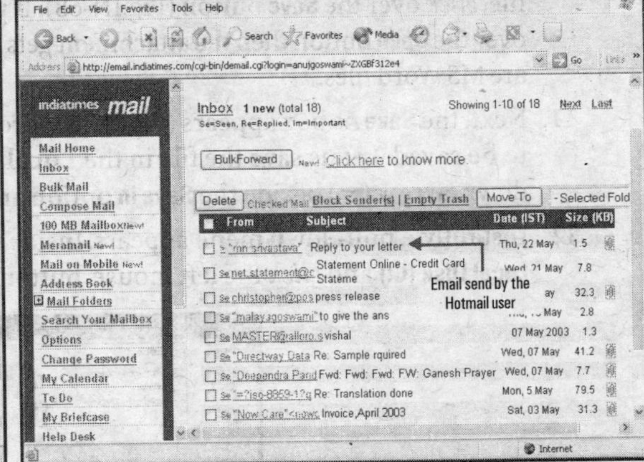

Fig. IN-64

7. To view email with subject **Reply to your letter** and its attachment file, *move* the mouse-pointer over the user name who sent the email i.e. **mn_srivastava** and *click* the left mouse-button (Fig.IN-65).

8. In a few moments, the message of the email appears on the screen (Fig.IN-66). After reading the message, *move* the mouse-pointer over the down-scroll arrow button and *click* the left mouse-button (Fig.IN-66).

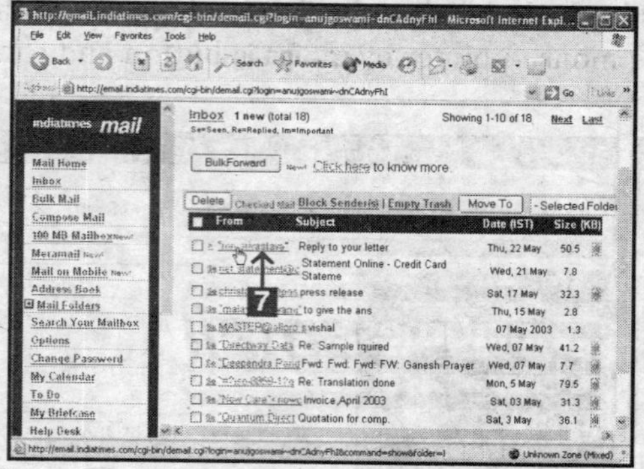

Fig. IN-65

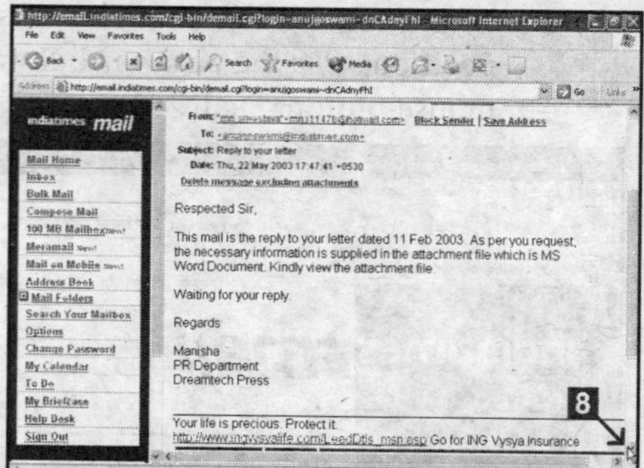

Fig. IN-66

9. As you scroll down the window, a table appears (Fig.IN-67). This table displays the information about the attachment file, **Letter.doc**, accompanying the message. The information includes the file name with its extension and size so that the user can identify the application for viewing the file. Inside the table, *move* the mouse-pointer over the file name **Letter.doc** and *click* the left mouse-button (Fig.IN-67).

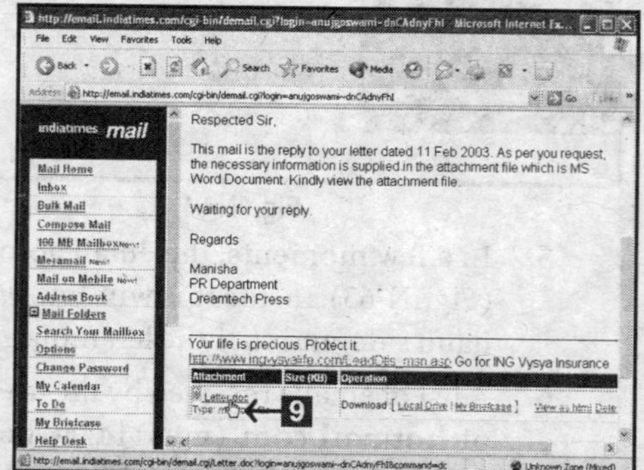

Fig. IN-67

10. Instantly, a **File Download** box appears on the screen (Fig.IN-68). It asks you whether you would like to view the attachment file or save it on your computer. Let us save the attachment file on the computer. To save the file, *click* over the **Save** button (Fig.IN-68). If you *click* over the **Open** button then the attachment gets opened in the **MS Word** application as **.doc** extension files are MS Word files.

11. Next, the **Save As** box appears (Fig.IN-69) prompting the user to decide the location where the file is to be saved. Let us save the file in the **Local Disk (C:)**. To do so, *move* the mouse-pointer over the down-arrow (▾) beside the **Save in** option and *click* the left mouse-button (Fig.IN-69).

12. Instantly, a pull-down menu appears. Inside the pull-down menu, *move* the mouse-pointer over the **Local Disk (C:)** and *click* the left mouse-button (Fig.IN-70).

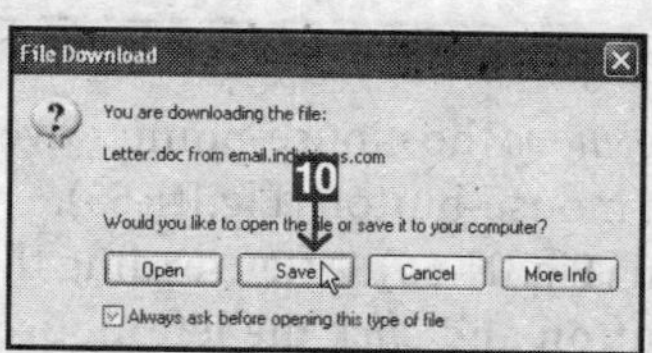

Fig. IN-68

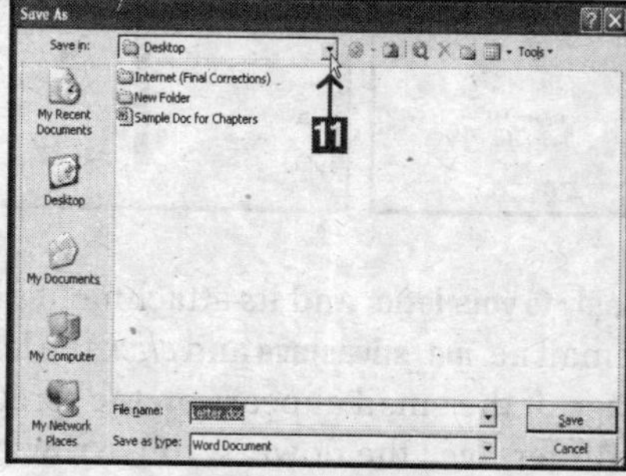

Fig. IN-69

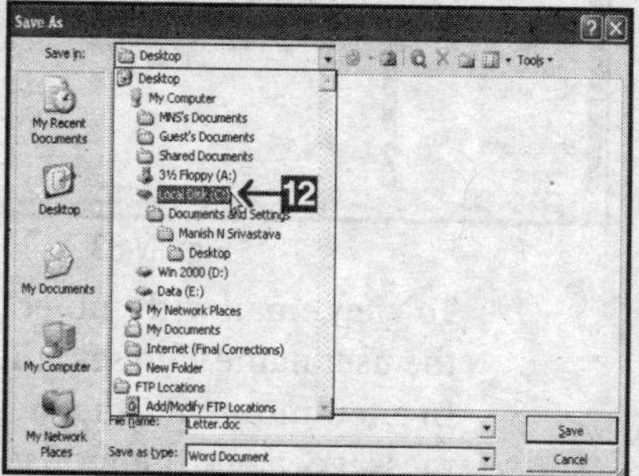

Fig. IN-70

13. The **Local Disk (C:)** appears beside the **Save in** option. Now, *move* the mouse-pointer over the **Save** button in the **Save As** box and *click* the left mouse-button (Fig.IN-71). The file gets saved on the computer.

14. After saving the file on the computer and performing other tasks like reading and sending email messages, locate the **Logout** option and *click* over it to close the email account.

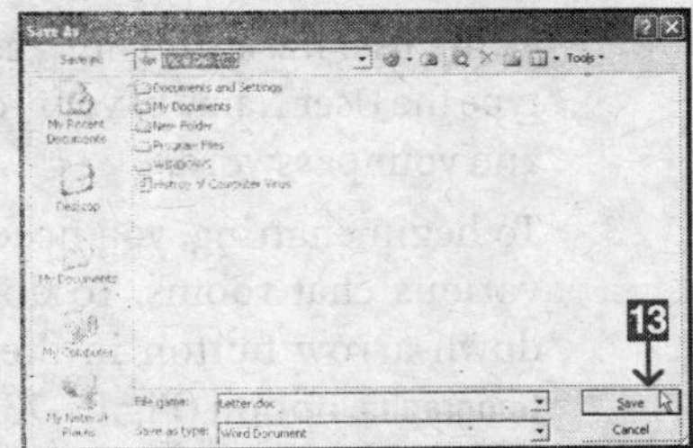

Fig. IN-71

Internet Relay Chat

Chatting is an interesting feature of the Internet. It is informative and thrilling and is an extension of the earlier popular penfriendship. The Internet Relay Chat (IRC) feature lets you instantly communicate with people around the world. Using IRC you can converse on the Net with one or more persons simultaneously by simply typing back and forth. This is a great way to meet people and exchange ideas. Unlike talking on the telephone, the IRC lets you chat with friends and colleagues in other cities, states or countries without your having to pay hefty long distance charges. In India, text-based chatting is popular with the young and the old alike.

Types of Chat

a) **Text-based Chat:** It is the oldest and most popular mode of chat on the Internet. This mode enables you to converse with one or more people simultaneously by typing text on your computer monitor. The text you type appears on the computer screen of every person participating in your conversation. The text gets transferred quickly across the Internet through the modem. So you do not need a high-speed modem for text-based chat.

b) **Multimedia Chat:** In this conversation, you make use of multimedia. It is also known as multimedia chat that is a new feature of the Internet. This feature enables you to communicate with other people through voice and live video over the Internet. Since sound and video signals get transferred slowly across Internet, it is recommended that you use a high speed modem for multimedia chat. However, multimedia chat is not functional in India as yet because of the narrow band-width.

How to Chat using rediff.com website

Let us see how to start the text-based chat. Here, we will learn the process of chatting in the rediff.com site through the following steps:

1. *Open* the **Internet Explorer** window and *type* the address **http://www.rediff.com** in its **Address bar.** Instantly, the home page of the site opens up on your desktop (Fig.IN-72).

2. In the rediff.com home page, *locate* the **Chat** option and *click* over it (Fig.IN-72). Another page of the website related to the **Chat** option opens on your screen (Fig.IN-73). In this page, we have typed **V.K.B.**

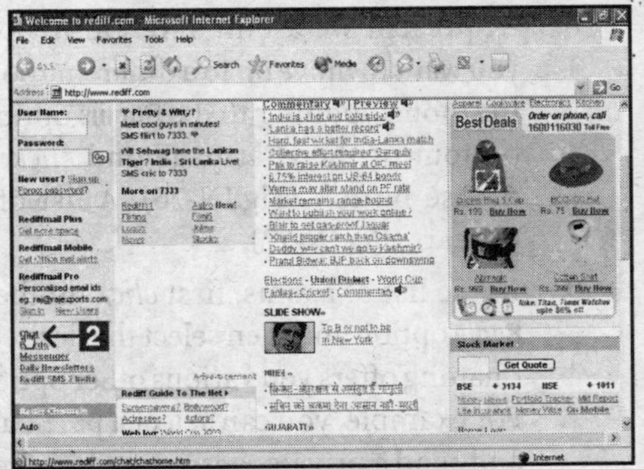

Fig. IN-72

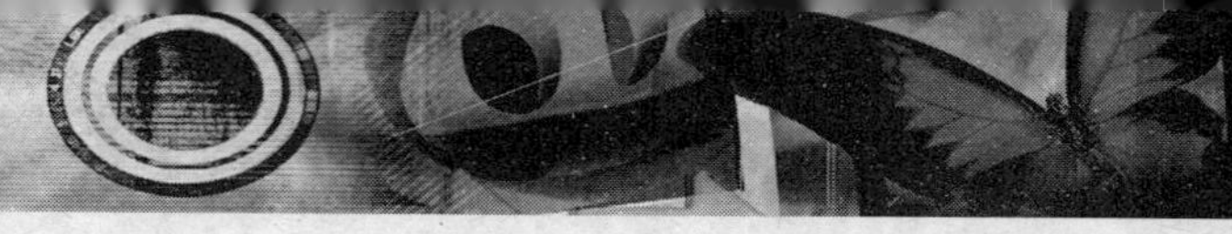

as the **User Name** and our Password. You may type the User Name of your rediffmail account and your password.

3. To begin chatting, you need to enter one of various chat rooms. To do so, *click* on the down-arrow button in the box beside the **Geographic** option (Fig.IN-73). A list of rooms appears (Fig.IN-74).
4. In the list of rooms, select a chat room say, **The Delhi Room** (Fig.IN-74).
5. Now, *click* over the **login** button (Fig.IN-75). Immediately a Chat page opens up on your screen (Fig.IN-76). In this page, the ID (in our case, **V.K.B.**) has been displayed in a box on the right hand side along with the IDs of all other users who are logged on for chatting in the site. The bigger box on the left displays chat messages of those currently chatting on the site. You may call it the message display box.
6. In the Chat page below the message display box a horizontal box is provided for you to type the chat message which you want to send. When sent, the message will be displayed in the message display box.
7. Now, *type* a chat message, say **HELLO EVERYBODY ! ANYONE FOR A CHAT ?** and *press* the Enter key. Instantly the message gets transferred to the message display box (Fig.IN-76). This means that your message has been sent to all those currently chatting on the site.
8. At present we are in **The Delhi Room**. If you want to move on to a different room, *move* the mouse-pointer to the **Rooms** option at the bottom of the chat page and *click* the left mouse button (Fig.IN-76). A list of rooms appears (Fig.IN-77).
9. In the list of rooms, first *click* on the **Change Room** option and then select the desired room. Chatting offers you various other options also. For example, you can select a particular user and send a private message to him/her. You can create your own room, change your profile, invite a friend etc.

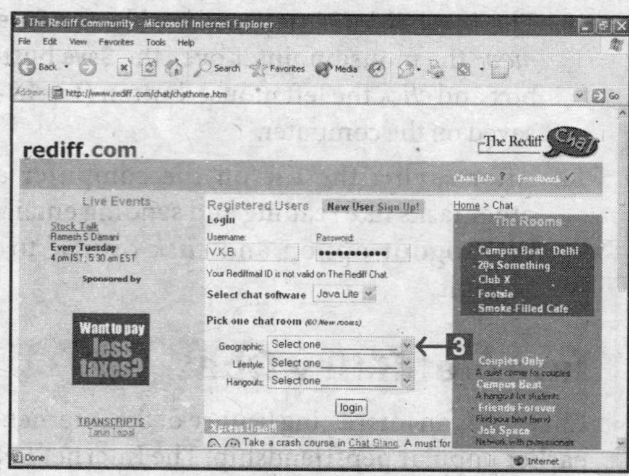

Fig. IN-73

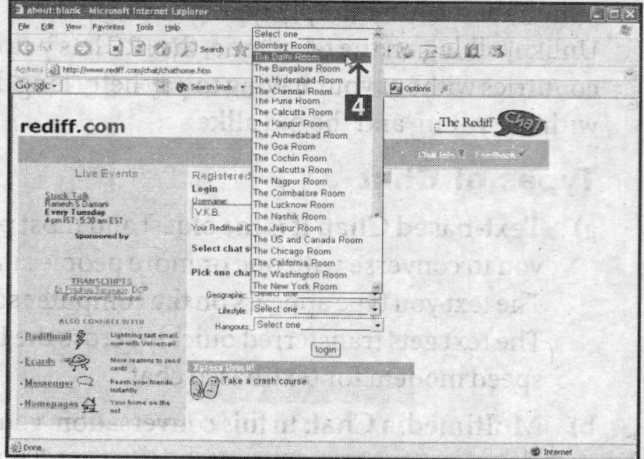

Fig. IN-74

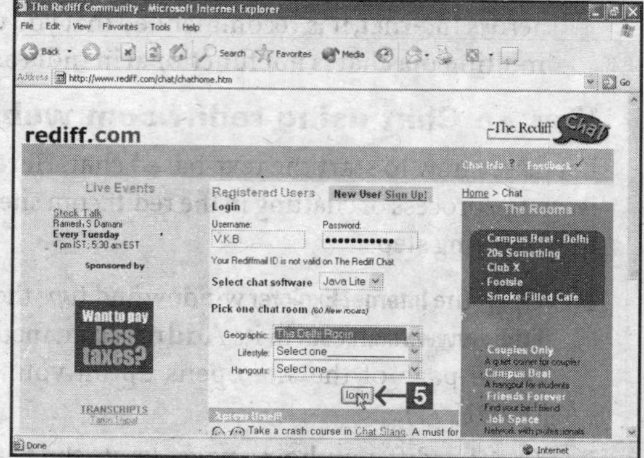

Fig. IN-75

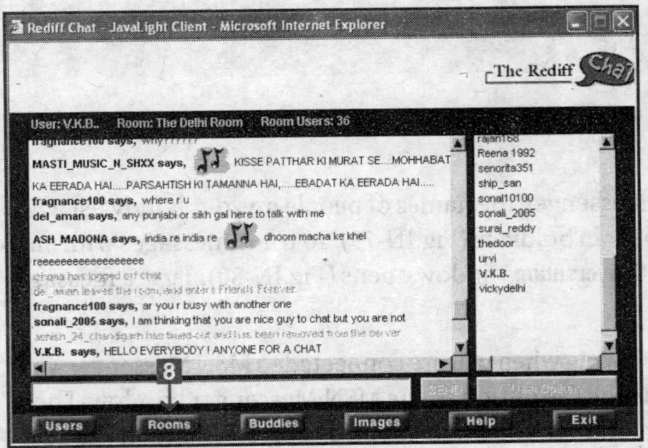

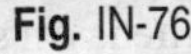

Fig. IN-76

Fig. IN-77

Instant Messenger

You already know about chatting and email. There is another way to communicate with your friends. it is known an instant messaging. It is something between chatting online and exchanging email messages. Instant messaging is popular with teenagers and others because it enables one to know which of one's friends are online. At the same time, it provides the facility to communicate with all your friends who are online. So, through instant messaging gives you can have an instant online party, or, in a business setting, an instant online meeting.

Instant messaging programs have a version of the "buddy list," a box that shows which of your friends are online. As soon as the name of someone you want to gossip with appears on the list, it's time for you to indulge in gossip. The three most popular instant messaging programs are: AOL Instant Messenger, MSN Messenger, and Yahoo! Messenger.

MSN Messenger

To exchange instant messages with your friends through MSN Messenger, you need two things: Windows XP and a .NET passport. You need a .NET passport to identify yourself to the Microsoft Network when you go online to instant-message. You can obtain the passport at this web address: http://register.passport.com. To obtain it, you provide information about yourself and select a password. Instant messaging with MSN Messenger is free.

Logging on to MSN Messenger

To start MSN Messenger, *double-click* the **MSN Messenger** icon in the lower-right corner of the window (near the clock). Once the MSN Messenger dialog box (Fig.IN-78) appears, proceed as follows:

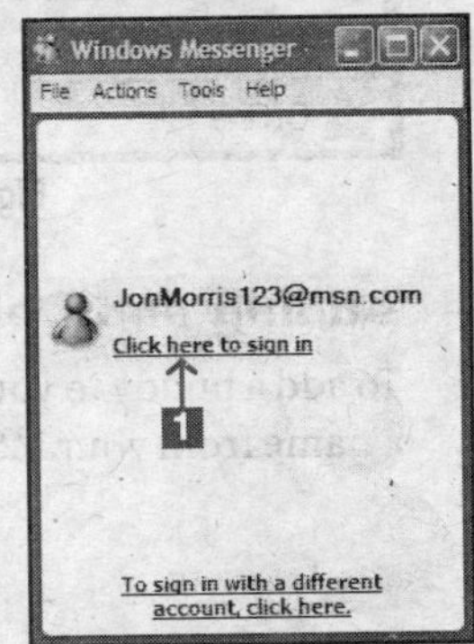

Fig. IN-78

1. *Click* over the **Click here to sign in** option, *type* your email address and password, and then *click* over the **OK** button. Another MSN Messenger window appears (Fig.IN-79).

If you want to login as some other user then do not follow Step 1. Instead, click over the "To sign in with a different account, click here" option.

Engaging in a chat session

After you have successfully logged on to the MSN Messenger, the names of people on your buddy list who are currently signed in at the MSN Messenger appear in boldface (Fig.IN-79). To trade messages with any of these people, *double-click* his or her name. The **Conversation** window opens (Fig.IN-80). *Type* a message and *click* the **Send** button (Fig.IN-80).

To defend your privacy and prevent others from knowing when you are connected to MSN Messenger, you can choose the **Offline** option. For this, first choose the **File** option in the MSN Messenger window. Then *click* over the **My Status** option in the pull-down menu. Another sub-menu appears. Finally, in the sub-menu, select the **Appear offline** option. After this selection, even if your name is on someone's buddy list, it won't appear there, and your erstwhile friend or some co-worker won't know that you are connected.

Fig. IN-79

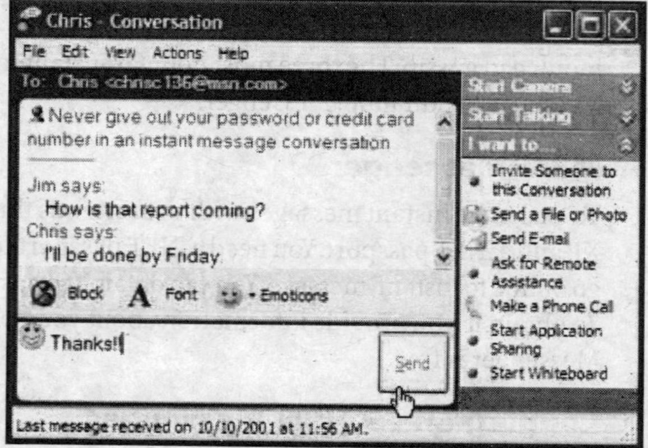

Fig. IN-80

Adding and Deleting Buddies

To add a buddy to your list, *click* the **Add** button, and, in the wizard dialog boxes that appear, either select a name from your MSN Messenger dialog box or enter an email address.

Downloading from the Internet

You can get any information and lot of software free of cost from the Internet. All you have to do is simply locate the website providing the required information or software. But you may ask how to save the information or software available on the Internet on your computer? The answer to this question is: Go for download. In the Internet context, term **download** implies transferring some information or data from the Internet to your PC. Various websites, like www.download.com, provide valuable information for free download. Let us now learn to download a card game from the www.download.com.

1. Begin with the Internet Explorer window. In the **Address bar** of this window, *type* **www.download.com** and *press* the **Enter** key (Fig.IN-81).
2. In a few moments, a web page like Fig.IN-82 appears on the screen. In this web page, *locate* the **Games** tab and *click* over it (Fig.IN-82).

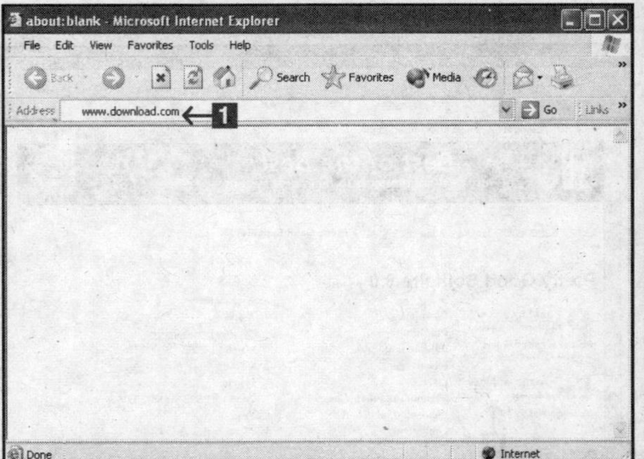

Fig. IN-81

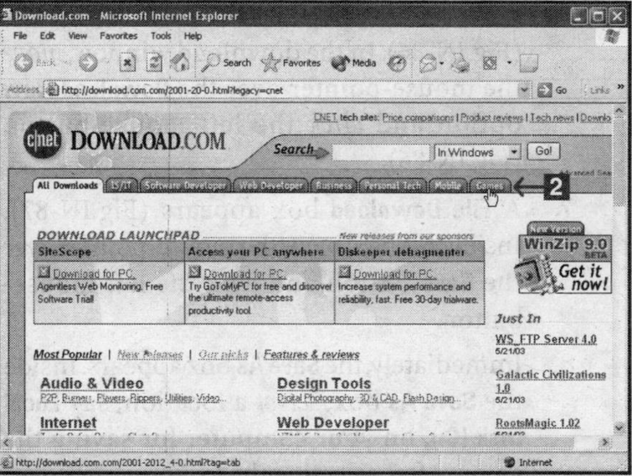

Fig. IN-82

3. Soon, you are presented with various options present under the **Games** tab. To access a card game, *move* the mouse-pointer over the down-scroll arrow button (⌄) and *click* the left mouse-button just once (Fig.IN-83).
4. As you scroll down the web page, you see the **Games Categories** option. Under this option, *move* the mouse-pointer over the **Cards** option and *click* the left mouse-button (Fig.IN-84).
5. A list of various card games appears on the screen (Fig.IN-85). Now to select a card game, say **Pretty Good Solitaire,** *move* the mouse-pointer over it and *click* the left mouse-button (Fig.IN-85).
6. Instantly, a window for downloading the selected game appears on the screen

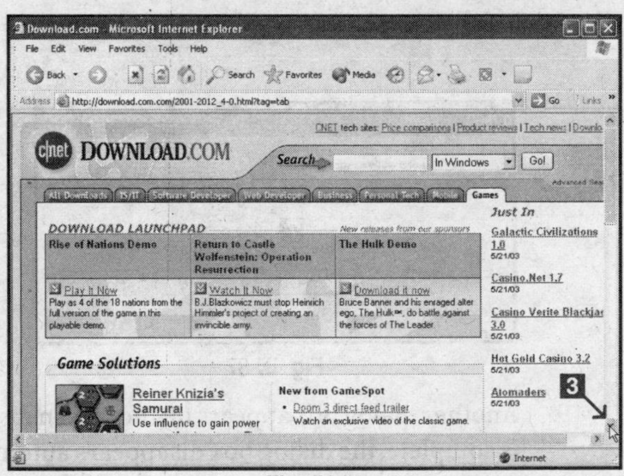

Fig. IN-83

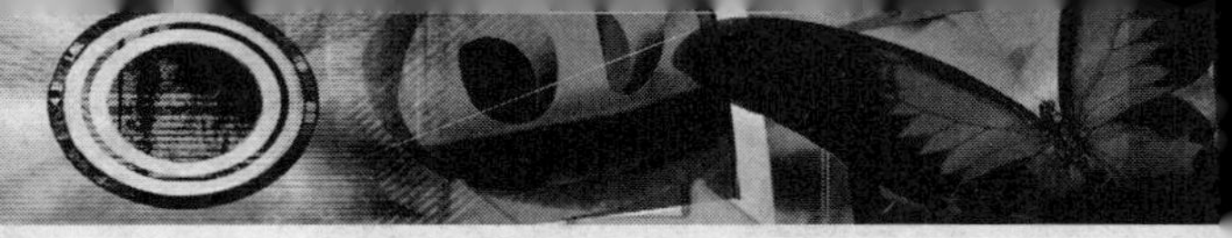

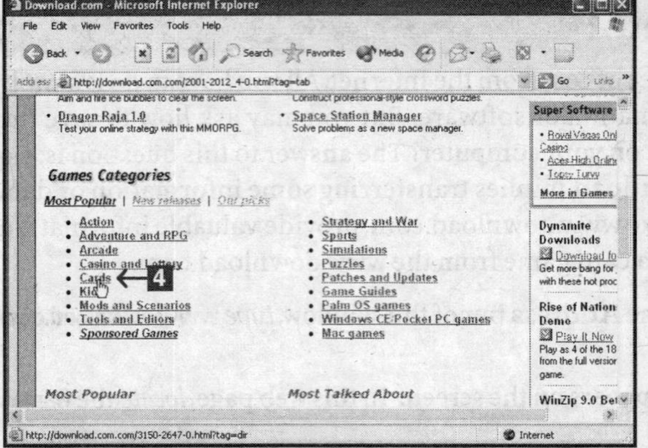

Fig. IN-84

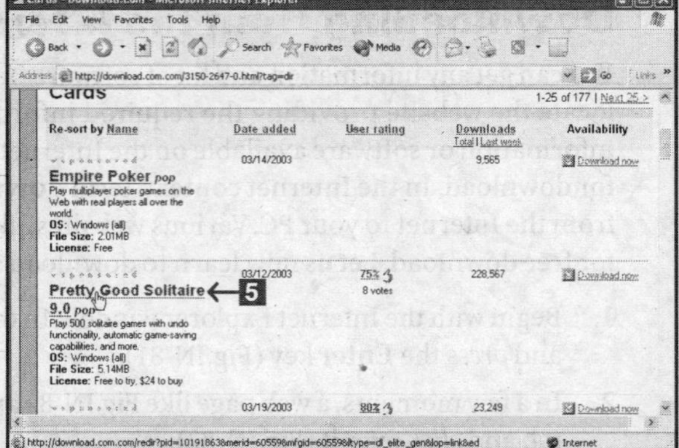

Fig. IN-85

(Fig.IN-86). In the download window, *move* the mouse-pointer over the **Download Now** option and *click* the left mouse-button (Fig.IN-86).

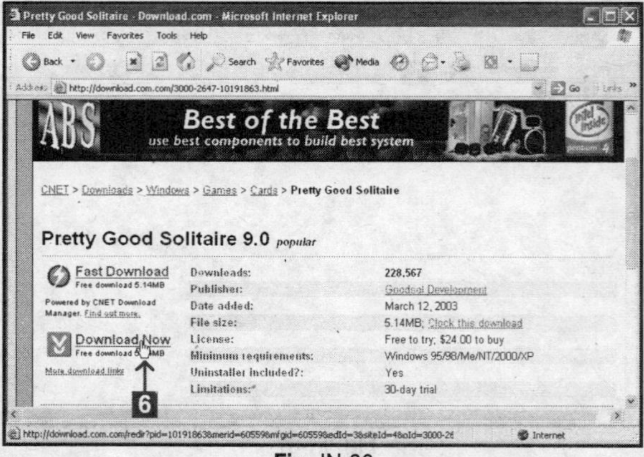

Fig. IN-86

7. A **File Download** box appears (Fig.IN-87). Inside this box, *move* the mouse-pointer over the **Save** button and *click* the left mouse-button.
8. Immediately, the **Save As** box appears. Inside the **Save As** box, *select* a location, say **Local Disk (C:)**, on your computer for saving the game. After selecting the location, *click* over the **Save** button (Fig.IN-88).

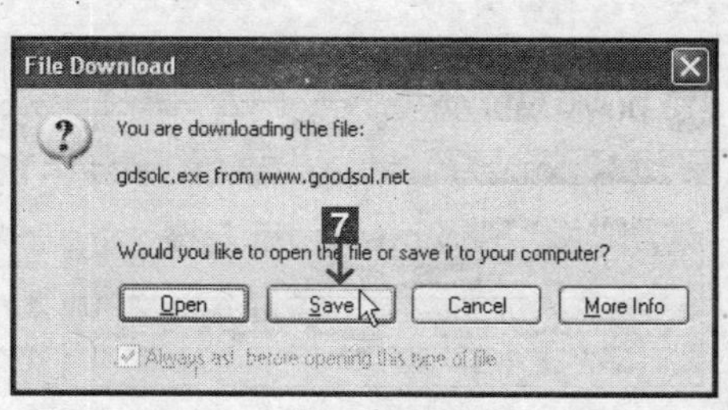

Fig. IN-87

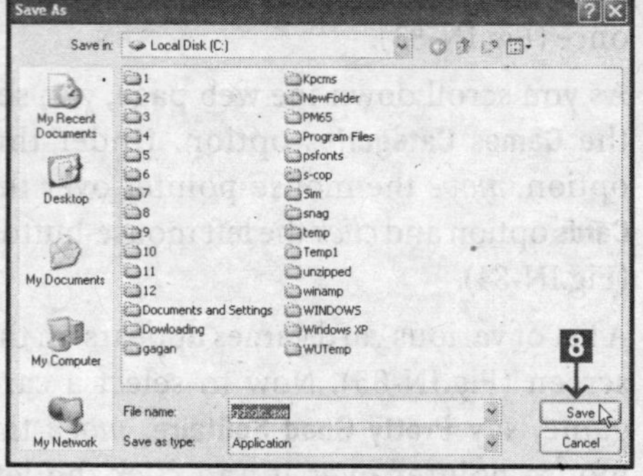

Fig. IN-88

9. Another dialog box appears on the screen displaying the progress of download. Once the download is complete, the dialog box disappears automatically.

10. Now to open the saved game, **Pretty Good Solitaire,** search it in the contents of the **Local Disk(C:).** Once you locate the game, *double-click* the left mouse-button over it and start playing.

Online Shopping

Online Shopping is another very useful feature of the Internet. It helps the user purchase and receive goods sitting at his home using an Internet-enabled computer. Online Shopping is blessing for elderly and all those busy professionals who can't make their way to shopping malls. If you are not busy or old, even then Online Shopping is a great help to you in the following ways:

- Online Shopping provides one-stop buying for all types of customer. All you need to own a product is to perform few mouse clicks to locate and select the product and pay for it.
- You don't have to frequent shopping malls in search of desired products.
- No headache of traffic jam and vehicle parking.
- No burden of carrying cash and shopping bags.
- Weather is no longer a barrier for shopping. Whether it's scorching summer, heavy rain or chilly winter, you can still do online shopping while relaxing at your home.

Almost all websites provide Online Shopping for their customers. To do online shopping, you must fulfil the following prerequisites:

Good Internet connection: You should have a good Internet connection which does not hang up frequently. A dial-up connection from a good ISP will also work.

Registered user of the host website: For security reasons, every website registers its customers. To prove that you are a registered user of the host website, you need to provide some credentials. The credentials include a login name or email address. The website uses these credentials to authenticate you and process your orders. Whenever you shop on the host website, you will be instructed to mention the name and password that you provided during registration. If you are not a registered user then you can become one by following the registration process of the host website.

Credit card: This is the most preferred mode of payment for Online Shopping. Most online purchases are paid by the credit card. For paying through credit card, you need to supply the credit card number, name of the card holder and its expiry date. Some domestic websites are also offering alternate modes of payment, like by demand draft or cash on receiving the goods. You receive the goods at the address, which you are instructed to provide during online shopping.

Steps for Online Shopping

Let us now learn how to shop online. We will demonstrate the process of Online Shopping at **Indiatimes.com** website. We assume that you are a registered user of this website and have an email account. Now, undertake the following steps for doing online shopping.

1. Begin with the Internet Explorer window. In the **Address bar** of this window, *type* **www.indiatimes.com.** In a few moments, the home page of indiatimes.com website appears on the screen (Fig.IN-89). In the home page, *click* over the **Shopping** option (Fig.IN-89).

2. Another page of indiatimes website appears, displaying a list of a shopping categories (Fig.IN-90). In this page, *click* over the **Audio/Video** option.

Fig. IN-89

Fig. IN-90

3. Another web page appears, displaying various items present under the **Audio/Video** shopping category (Fig.IN-91). In this page, *click* over the **Accessories** option (Fig. IN-91).

4. Another web page appears, displaying various **Audio/Video** accessories products along with their images, prices, and buttons to select them for purchasing (Fig.IN-92). Suppose you want to purchase a headphone (with mike). To locate it, *click* over the down-scroll arrow button (▾) (Fig. IN-92).

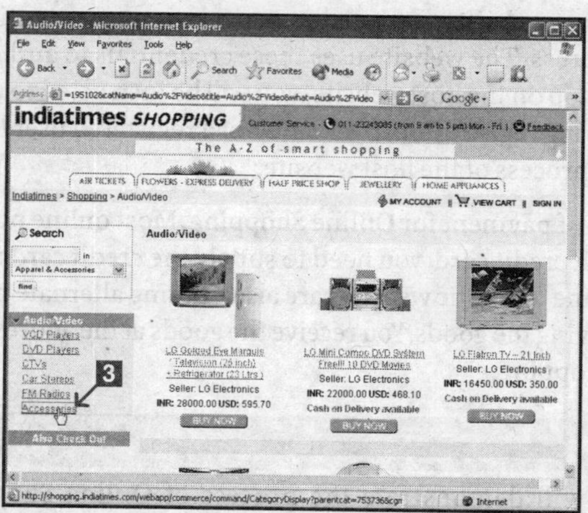

Fig. IN-91

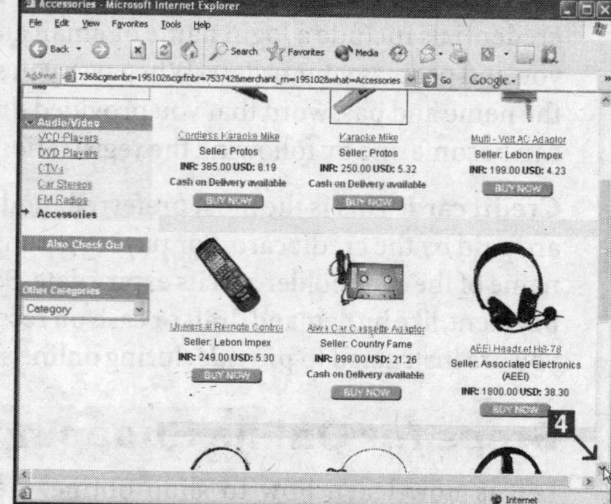

Fig. IN-92

5. When you find the desired headphone on the web page, stop clicking over the down-arrow scroll button. Now, move the mouse-pointer over the **BUY NOW** button beside the picture of headphone, and *click* the left mouse-button (Fig. IN-93).

6. In a few moments, the authentication screen appears (Fig.IN-94). In this screen, you need to provide your credentials to prove that you are a registered user of **indiatimes.com**. Usually, the user needs to provide his email address and the password of the email account as credentials. To complete the authentication process, *click* in the text box beside the **Indiatimes ID** option. In this box, we have typed the email address **mn_srivastava114** as our identification of being a registered user. You may provide your email address registered with **indiatimes.com**. Next, press the **Tab** key from the keyboard. The blinking cursor jumps to the text box beside the **Password** option. *Type* the password of your email account and *click* over the **Login** button (Fig. IN-94).

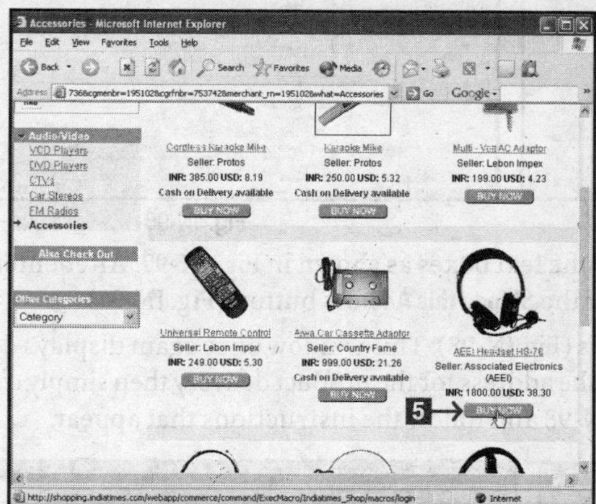

Fig. IN-93

Fig. IN-94

7. The **Shopping Cart** window appears (Fig.IN-95). This window displays the order information like name of the product, quantity, unit price and total amount. After viewing the order information, *click* over the **Proceed to Check Out** button (Fig. IN-95).

   If you want to purchase more than one microphone then *click* in the text box below the **Quantity** option and *type* **2.** Next, *click* over the **Update** button. Your order information is changed accordingly and is displayed before you. This process may take some time.

   If you change your mind and want to purchase some other accessory item instead of headphone then *click* over the **Remove** button. The selected product i.e. headphone disappears from the Shopping Cart window. Next, *click* over the **Buy More Items** button. You reach the window where you can view and select products for purchasing.

8. After your *click* on the **Proceed to check out** button, the **Billing Option** window appears (Fig.IN-96). In this window, you need to provide the address where the product is to be delivered. To do so, *click* over the down-arrow scroll button (▾). You find some options with empty text boxes. Mandatory options that can't be left blank are marked with some sign (usually * sign).

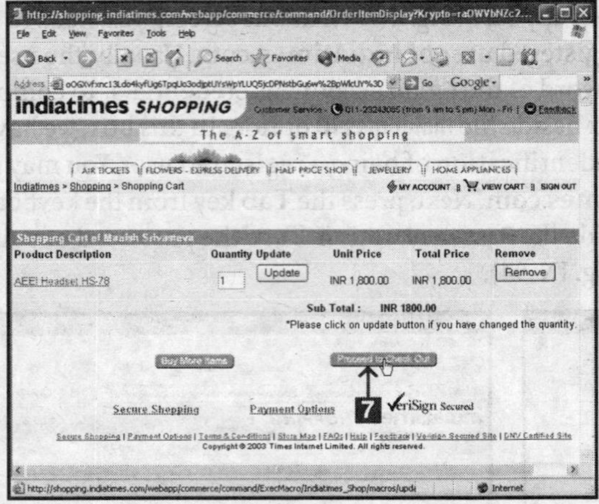

Fig. IN-95

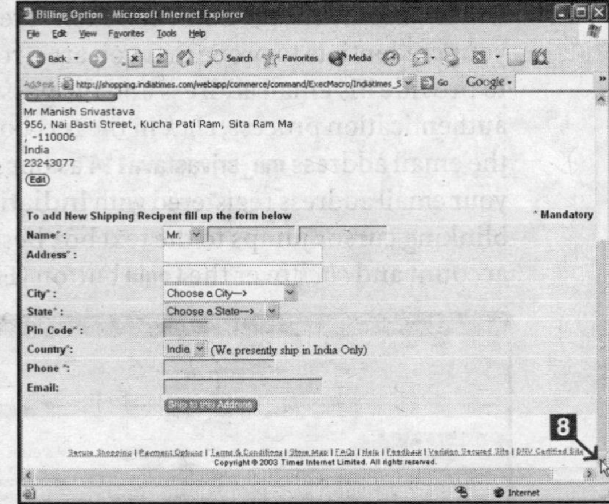

Fig. IN-96

9. *Type* the required address information in the text boxes as shown in Fig. IN-97. After entering the address for the product delivery, *click* over the **Ship to this Address** button (Fig. IN-97).
10. Another window of the **Billing Option** appears (Fig.IN-98). This window once again displays details of the product ordered. If you want to change the address for the product delivery then simply *click* over the **Change Shipping Address** button in Fig.IN-98 and follow the instructions that appear.

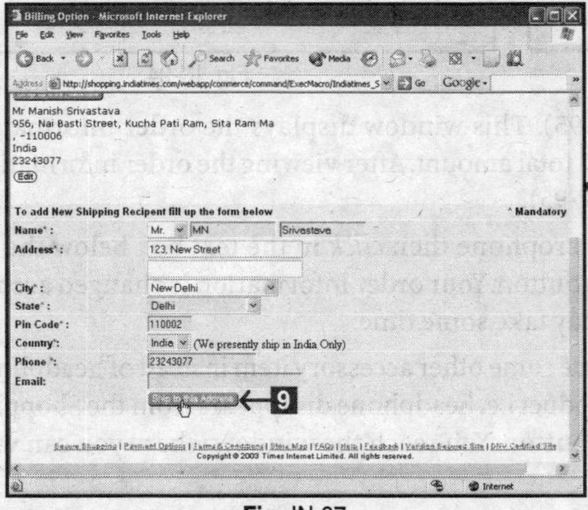

Fig. IN-97

Fig. IN-98

11. After viewing or changing the order details, *click* over the down-arrow scroll button (▾) to locate the mode of payment (Fig.IN-99). When you reach the mode of payment option, *stop clicking* the down-arrow scroll button (▾).
12. Among the displayed payment modes, select the one that suits you. Let us select the **Credit Card (Master/Visa)** option by *clicking* over the round button beside it (Fig.IN-99).
13. Next, *click* over the **Pay Now** button (Fig. IN-99). In a few moments, a payment window appears (Fig.IN-100).

14. In the payment window (Fig.IN-100), we need to enter appropriate information regarding our credit card in the relative text boxes. The information includes name of the credit card holder, credit card number and its expiry date (in month and year)
15. After entering the required information, *click* over the **Pay** button. In a few moments, your order gets processed. And, the product will reach your doorsteps within the duration specified by the website.

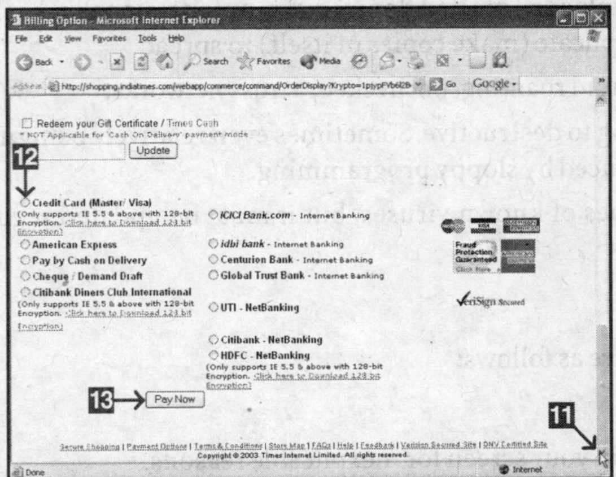

Fig. IN-99

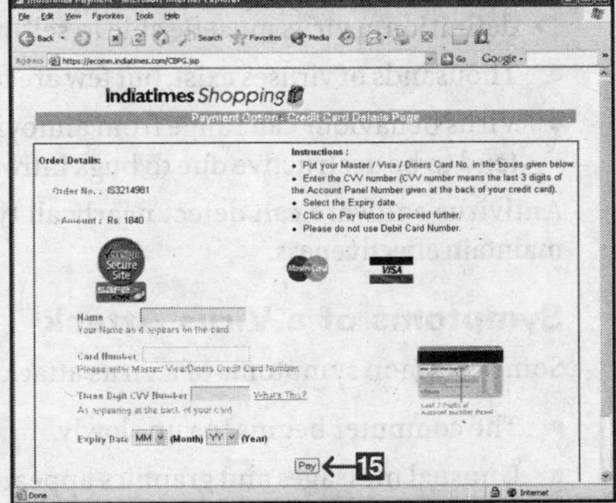

Fig. IN-100

Wireless Internet

People around the world use the Internet every day—to communicate with others, follow the stock market, keep up with the news, check weather, conduct business, shop, entertain and learn. Staying connected has become so important that it's hard to get away from your Internet-enabled computer. Get disconnected, and you may miss an important email message, a crucial update on your stock or some news you need to know. With your business or your personal life becoming more dependent on Internet communication, you may be searching for a device that allows you to access the Internet anytime and anywhere. To provide round-the-clock Internet access, the concept of wireless Internet came into existence. This technology is specially useful for handheld devices such as mobile phone, laptop computers, PDA etc. The most important factor in the birth of wireless Internet has been the phenomenal increase in the number of cell phones in the last few years. Now most mobile phones are web-enabled and they display the downloaded information in text based format instead of full graphical mode. Now with mobile phone in your hand, you can read news, stock market prices, download ring tones for the mobile phone.

Computer Virus

Computer virus is a self-replicating piece of computer code that can partially or fully attach itself to computer files or applications. Like any other program, it contains instructions that tell your computer what to do. But unlike an application, a virus usually tells your computer to do something you don't want it to do. Computer viruses are the common cold of modern technology. They can spread swiftly across open networks such as the Internet, causing crores of rupees worth of damage in a short span of time. If

you're lucky, a virus will execute only a benign "personality quirk," such as causing your computer to make seemingly random bleeps. But some viruses can be very destructive; they can format your hard drive, overwrite your hard drive boot sector, or delete files and render your machine inoperable. Five years ago, the chance you'd receive a virus over a 12-month period was about 1 in 1000; today, your chances have dropped to about 1 in 10.

- Viruses enter your system via email, downloads, infected floppy disks, or (occasionally) hacking. By definition, a virus must be able to self-replicate (make copies of itself) to spread.
- Thousands of viruses exist, but few are found roaming, unchecked, across networks.
- Virus behaviour can range from annoying to destructive. Sometimes even relatively benign viruses tend to be destructive due to bugs introduced by sloppy programming.

Antivirus software can detect nearly all types of known viruses, but it must be updated regularly to maintain effectiveness.

Symptoms of a Virus Attack

Some common symptoms of a virus attack are as follows:

- The computer begins to run slowly.
- Unusual messages and graphics appear on your screen for inexplicable reasons.
- Music, not associated with any of the current programs, begins to play.
- Some of the program and/or data files have either been corrupted or become difficult to locate.
- Unknown files or sub-directories have been created.
- The sizes/dates of executable files change automatically.
- The computer does not remember CMOS settings.
- The disk volume label has been changed mysteriously.
- The sizes of total and free memory are changed unexpectedly.
- The hardware devices begin to exhibit unusual behaviour.

Antivirus Software

Virus experts have recorded more than 40,000 viruses and their variant strains over the years, though only about 200 of those viruses are actively spreading in the wild. While most viruses are just annoying time-wasters, the ones that do deliver a destructive payload are a real threat.

Viruses have been around since the early 1960s, almost the same time when the early computers came into being. However, until the 1980s viruses were largely laboratory specimens, created by researchers and released in a controlled environment to examine their effect. When viruses first appeared in the wild in the 1980s, they spread slowly and passed via the "sneaker net": floppy disks traded by people and shared between computers. Later on, widely available Internet and email access hastened their spread.

Two years ago, the advent of viruses that spread rapidly via email (see "Melissa-like virus lurks" and "Love Letter's legacy," links below) significantly increased the odds that an average computer user would confront a virus. Email viruses today account for about 81 per cent of virus infections and can infect thousands of machines in a matter of minutes.

How did I get Virus, anyway?

You get a virus when you copy virus-infected application or files to your computer. The virus code inside the infected application or file gets activated when you run the application or open the file. How do you copy infected files is irrelevant: Viruses don't care if you get them as an email attachment, a download, or via a shared floppy disk. However, email attachments are the most prevalent — and easiest — mode of virus transmission. Once you open an infected file or application, the malicious code copies itself into a file on your system, where it waits to deliver its payload — whatever the programmer designed it to do to your system. Simply deleting the email after you open the attachment won't get rid of the virus, since it has already entered the machine. A virus writer can set the payload to trigger immediately, at a preset future time or date, or upon the execution of a specific command, such as when you save or open a file. The Michelangelo virus, for example, was programmed to release its payload on March 6 of any year — the artist's birthday.

General Virus Types

While there are thousands of virus variations, most fall into one of the following six general categories, each of which works its magic slightly differently:

- **Boot Sector Virus**: It replaces or implants itself in the boot sector—an area of the hard drive (or any other disk) accessed first when you turn on your computer. This kind of virus can prevent you from booting your hard disk.
- **File Virus:** It infects applications. The infected applications spread the virus by infecting associated documents and other applications whenever they're opened or run.
- **Macro Virus:** Written using a simplified macro programming language, these viruses affect Microsoft Office applications, such as Word and Excel. This virus type accounts for about 75 per cent of viruses found in the wild. A document infected with a macro virus generally modifies a pre-existing, commonly used command (such as Save) to trigger its payload upon execution of that command.
- **Multipartite Virus:** It infects both files and the boot sector—a double whammy that can reinfect your system dozens of times before it is caught.
- **Polymorphic Virus:** It changes code whenever it passes to another machine. In theory, these viruses should be more difficult for antivirus scanners to detect, but in practice they're usually not that well written.
- **Stealth Virus:** It hides its presence by making an infected file not appear infected. However, it doesn't usually stand up to antivirus software.

Worm and Trojan Horse

Worm, like a virus, is a program that harms the computer and destroys data stored in it. A computer worm is designed to copy itself from one computer to another over a network (e.g. by using emails). Worms are considered more harmful than viruses because they rely less (or not at all) on human behaviour to spread themselves from one computer to another. Computer worms spread much more rapidly than computer viruses. Worms use parts of an operating system that are automatic and are usually invisible to the user. It is common for worms to be noticed only when their uncontrolled replication consumes system resources, slowing or halting other tasks.

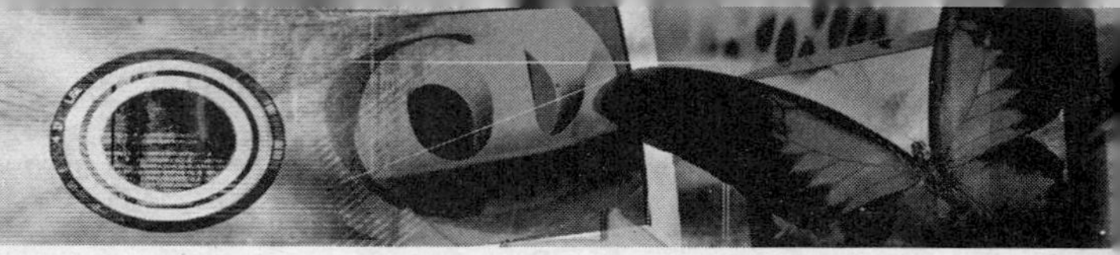

In computers, **Trojan horse** is a program in which malicious or harmful code is contained inside apparently harmless programming or data in such a way that it can get control and do its chosen form of damage, such as ruining the file allocation table on your hard disk. A Trojan horse may be widely redistributed as part of a computer virus. Unlike viruses, Trojan horses do not replicate themselves but they can just be as destructive.

Practice Safe Computing to Avoid Virus Attack

Follow the old saying—prevention is better than cure. To protect your computer from virus attacks during Internet surfing, follow the preventive steps listed below:

- The best protection against a virus attack is to avoid opening unexpected email attachments and downloads from unreliable sources. Resist the urge to double-click everything in your mailbox. If you get an unexpected file attachment, send an enquiry email to its sender. Ask him about the nature and function of the file attachment.
- For added safety, you need to install a reliable antivirus scanning software and download its updates regularly. Major antivirus software vendors, including Symantec, Network Associates, Computer Associates, and Trend Micro, provide regular updates. Some vendors also offer a service that will automatically retrieve updates on your computer from the company's website.
- Regular updates are essential. Researchers at Computer Economics estimate that 30 per cent of small businesses are vulnerable to viruses because either they don't keep their virus-scanning software updated or they don't install it correctly.

How anti- virus software works

Scanning software installed in your system looks for a virus in two ways—whether the virus is a known one or unknown. If it's a known virus (one that has already been detected in the wild and has an antidote written for it), the software will look for the virus's signature — a unique string of bytes that identifies the virus like a fingerprint — and will remove it from your system. Most scanning software will catch not only an initial virus but many of its variants as well, because the signature code usually remains intact.

In the case of new viruses for which no antidote has been created, the virus scanning software employs heuristics that look for unusual virus-like activity on your system. If the program sees any suspected activity, it quarantines the questionable program and broadcasts a warning to you about what the program may be trying to do (such as modify your Windows Registry). Quarantine means keeping the virus in some isolated place on your computer under strict vigilance so that it could not do further harm to your computer. If you and the software think the program may be a virus, you can send the quarantined file to the antivirus vendor, where researchers examine it, determine its signature, name and catalog it, and release its antidote. It's now a known virus. If the virus never appears again — which often happens when the virus is too poorly written to spread — then vendors categorize the virus as dormant. But viruses are like earthquakes: because their initial outbreak is usually followed by aftershocks. Variants (copycat viruses that emerge in droves after the initial outbreak) make up the bulk of known viruses.

You can easily purchase an anti-virus software from the market or download a free version of some anti-virus software from its company's website. But it is recommended that you purchase a genuine copy of anti-virus software as it comes with future support for your computer like updating the software against new virus threats and various additional features. Description of some popular anti-virus softwares follows.

- **Norton Anti-Virus:** This anti-virus software is most widely used and can easily be purchased from the market. Norton Anti-Virus has direct patch up with software firm Symantec, which specially deals in anti-virus operations. For more details about this anti-virus software visit **www.symantec.com.**
- **McAfee:** Software giant Microsoft uses this anti-virus software for its email website Hotmail. Whenever you open some email or download some file from Hotmail, the McAfee antivirus software automatically checks the files for viruses. For more details about this anti-virus software visit **www.mcafee.com.**
- **Smart Cop:** This is the first and most complete anti-virus software for the Internet era developed in India by **avsoft technologies.** This indigenous software can easily compete with any international anti-virus software. Smart Cop comes in different flavors for different types of operating systems. You can even deploy Smart Cop over the local network and easily monitor your computers. For more details about this anti-virus software visit **www.s-cop.com.**

Disconnecting from the Internet

Hope now you have a better understanding of important features of the Internet. This knowledge will help you use the Internet effectively and conveniently. Let us now take a break. To *move* out of the Internet, undertake the following steps.

1. *Move* the mouse-pointer over the **Stop** button (⊗) on the **Standard Toolbar** of the Internet Explorer screen and *click* the left mouse-button.
2. Then *click* over the minimized **Connecting to vsnl** button on the System Tray. Immediately, the **Connecting to vsnl** box appears on the screen.
3. Now *move* the mouse-pointer over the **Disconnect** button of the **Connecting to vsnl box** (Fig.IN-16, pg 164) and *click* the left mouse-button.
   The modem icon present on the right hand side of the **Taskbar** disappears from the screen. This indicates that you have successfully disconnected from the Internet.
4. Finally, *switch off* your modem.

Other Internet Connection Services

Integrated Service Digital Network (ISDN)

As the name of ISDN suggests, it allows digital communication. It allows communication over high speed, high quality digital channels. The digital technology is a lot faster and more accurate than the old analogue lines as it doesn't require the process of modulation and demodulation. ISDN relies on already existing copper cable systems, facilitating its smoother integration with the existing communication system. The media ISDN supports include Telex, fax, voice telephone, video telephone, audio, high definition TV and computer networking.

Digital Subscriber Line (DSL)

DSL is a very high-speed communication connection that uses the same wires as a regular telephone line. With the help of DSL connection, you can leave your Internet connection open and still use the phone line for voice calls. DSL connection has a high speed of 1.5 Mbps as compared to 56 Kbps supported by a regular modem. The company that offers DSL will usually provide the modem as part of line installation.

List of Popular Websites

Following is a list of the popular websites that are used by Internet surfers in India:

- www.rediff.com
- www.timesofindia.com
- www.hindustantimes.com
- www.filmfare.com
- www.google.com
- www.wileydreamtech.com
- www.yahoo.com
- www.computershope.com
- www.screensaver.com
- www.britannica.com
- www.msn.com
- www.aajtak.com
- www.hotmail.com
- www.khel .com
- www.dreamtechpress.com
- www.shareware.com
- www.sbpprojectfinder.com
- www.cnn.com

Conclusion

So, that's the end of your journey to the computer world. Hope you have enjoyed the trip with us. For you, it may be just a beginning. But, your newly acquired computer skills will go a long way in helping you improve your performance, no matter whatever the field you are connected with. In this venture, we have tried our best to acquaint you thoroughly with almost all aspects of computers. Hope you have also enriched your practical knowledge with the interactive CD and gained hands-on experience of the textual concepts.

In this increasingly competitive world, the skills that you have learnt from this book will stand you in good stead in all your pursuits. These will equip you with confidence and the extra edge that is essential for excelling in the academic as well as the job arena. Finally, we wish you a successful and prosperous future. Good Luck !

APPENDIX: About the CD

The CD-ROM provided with this book at no extra cost is especially designed to give you hands-on practice of what you have learnt through the book. It is a unique self-learning system. This comprehensive system ensures that all your requirements as a learner must be taken care of. Its objective is to enable you gain practical mastery of the MS-Office suite. The CD-ROM is a collection of softwares plus comprehensive examples and tutorials that provide a complete practical learning platform for the beginners. It also contains a powerful financial accounting software–BUSYLITE. Besides, it includes SmartCOP, an anti-virus software specially designed to easily detect and eradicate most of the computer viruses. It's a complete anti-virus solution for the Internet era.

Idea Behind the CD

- The CD has been designed keeping in mind the needs of all computer users and professionals.
- No prior knowledge of computers is required to use this CD.
- The examples and illustrations in this CD can be run in two modes viz. **Demo mode** and **Practice mode,** which equip the user with all the know-how needed to master the MS-Office suite.

Dual Language Feature

The CD also provides the feature to run the audio either in Hindi or in English as per your choice. The Overview (brief explanation about a simulation) as well as the instructions in audio can be run in either Hindi or English.

Minimum System Requirements

To run the CD-ROM, the following hardware and software are required:

- A PC with a Pentium or better processor
- 128 MB of RAM
- CD-ROM Drive
- Speakers
- Microsoft Windows XP/2000/98/Me
- 100MB of Hard Drive space
- Sound Card

Overview of CD Contents

The CD contains the following products/applications :

- Comdex Computer Course Self Training Software
- BUSYLITE (Accounting Software)
- SmartCOP (Anti-virus Software)

Just go through the following sections to get a better understanding of the CD contents.

Comdex Computer Course Self Training Software

The Comdex Computer Course Self Training Software consists of a unique three-stage learning system. Given below is a brief explanation of the various stages/modes:

1. **Explanation Mode :** This stage is all about what has been explained to you in the book. All topics, big or small, are described in detail, along with hundreds of screenshots in real colour and graphics. But your learning does not stop here. From here, the accompanying CD takes over. The CD shows you the actual working of various concepts and topics explained in the book.

2. **Audio Video Demo Mode :** Insert the accompanying software (CD) into your computer and *click* on the topic you wish to learn. The software automatically starts you teaching step by step through audio-video and graphic simulations. It shows the practical demo of what you have already read in the book.
3. **Self-Testing/Practice Mode :** The self-testing software evaluates your skills by instructing you to carry out the steps of a given topic. If you do it right, you go to the next step. And, if you do it wrong, the software helps you correct your mistake. Only when you have done it right, you can proceed further.

BUSYLITE

It is a very popular application for handling accounts. In the CD, the simple and easy-to-handle BUSYLITE software comes with a comprehensive introduction to the basic principles of accounting pertaining to the double-entry system of book-keeping. The CD tutorial explains how the concepts of accounting are implemented manually as well as using the BUSYLITE software. The processes are explained step by step through examples so that anyone new to accounting can easily learn the practical aspects of the subject.

SmartCOP

The CD contains the SmartCOP anti-virus software that is very resourceful and powerful. It is equipped to outsmart the most destructive of computer viruses. This comprehensive package detects as well as cleans up almost all the viruses from a system. It is equipped with a very fast and reliable scan engine. Its real-time scanning feature traps viruses before they enter a computer. It keeps a constant eye on Internet downloads and E-mail attachments.

Getting Started With the CD

Before starting the CD, close all the running applications. When you insert the CD in the CD-ROM Drive, the Comdex Computer Course Self Training Software starts automatically. You see the Splash screen (Fig.CD-1) followed by another screen (Fig.CD-2) that provides options for the audio language. Indicate your choice of the language as Hindi or English for the audio in Fig.CD-2. Audio instructions are available only for the **Audio/Video Demo mode**. Whatever audio language you choose, written instructions on the screen will be in English only.

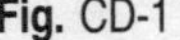

Fig. CD-1

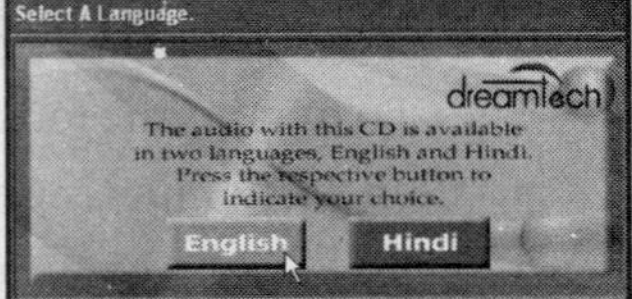

Fig. CD-2

To listen to the audio instructions, your system must be equipped with a Sound Card and speakers. If these are not available on your system then deselect the Sound option in the Control Bar before proceeding further. De-selection means there shouldn't be a tick mark in the check box beside the Sound option as shown in Fig.CD-3.

Fig. CD-3

Failing to deselect this option will display an error message as shown in (Fig. CD-4.

Fig. CD-4

After specifying the audio language, the next screen (Fig.CD-5) asks you whether you would like to be briefed on the features of the CD. If you select the **Yes** button, a screen showing CD features appears (Fig.CD-6). *Click* on the **Continue** button of this screen to proceed to the **Select a Topic** screen (Fig.CD-7). If you select the **No** button, you directly go to the **Select a Topic** Screen (Fig.CD-7).

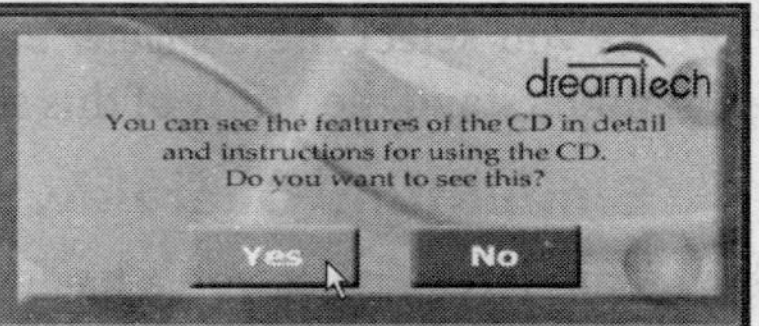

Fig. CD-5

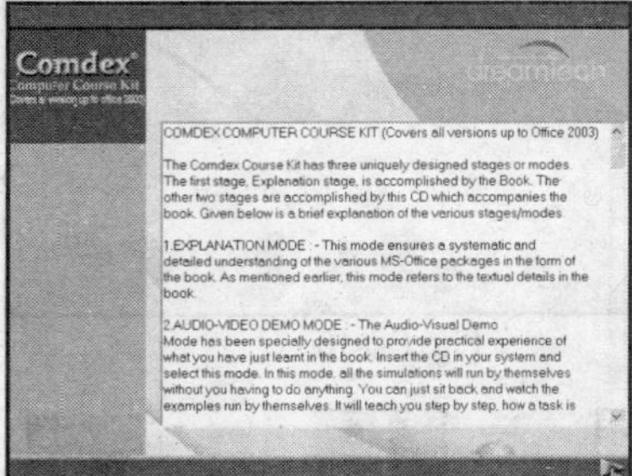

Fig. CD-6

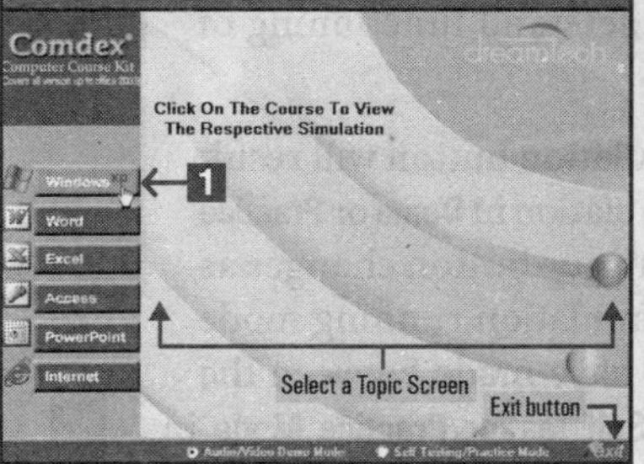

Fig. CD-7

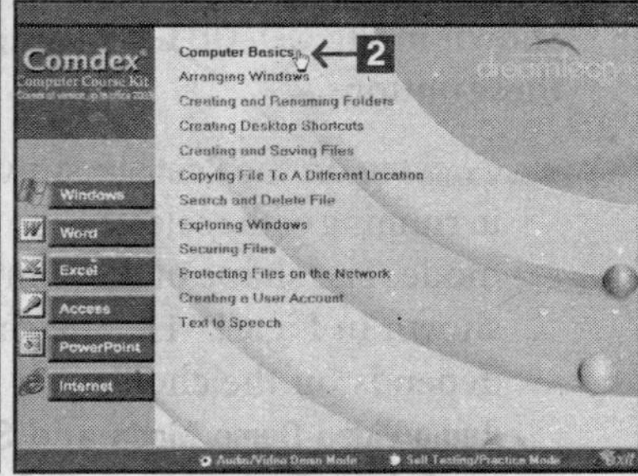

Fig. CD-8

Viewing Simulation of a Topic

All the self-training topics are listed in the left panel of the **Select a Topic** screen. When you click on a particular topic, a list of simulations available under that topic gets displayed in the right panel of the screen. Select any simulation to view it. By default, the selected simulation starts in the **Demo mode**. For selecting the **Practice mode**, go to the bottom of the screen and *click* on the radio button beside the **Self Testing/Practice Mode** as shown in Fig.CD-9.

Fig. CD-9

Demo-mode

In the **Demo mode**, the simulation runs by itself. You need not do anything. Just sit back and observe how does the simulation explain the selected topic.

In the Demo mode, if the audio is running, you cannot work with any other control of the Control Bar. If you want to Pause or Stop the simulation wait for the audio to stop and then click on the respective control.

Practice-mode

In the **Practice mode** simulation, you are guided to perform one step at a time. By following these simple guidelines, you can quickly learn to perform a particular function.

Let us now learn to view a desired simulation. We will view a simulation under the **Windows** topic. To do so, undertake the following steps.

1. *Click* on the **Windows** topic in the left panel of the **Select a Topic** Screen (Fig.CD-7). All the simulations under the **Windows** topic get displayed in the right panel (Fig.CD-8).
2. *Select* a simulation, say, **Computer Basics** by clicking on it (Fig.CD-8). Caption label of the selected simulation assumes a different colour (Fig.CD-8).

As you select the **Computer Basics** simulation, its **Simulation Overview** screen appears (CD-10). Let us understand the utility of this screen.

Simulation Overview Screen

This screen gives you a basic idea of what the selected simulation is going to accomplish. It has three buttons — **Continue** simulation, **Pause** audio and **Stop** audio, as shown in Fig.CD-10. Let us understand functioning of these buttons.

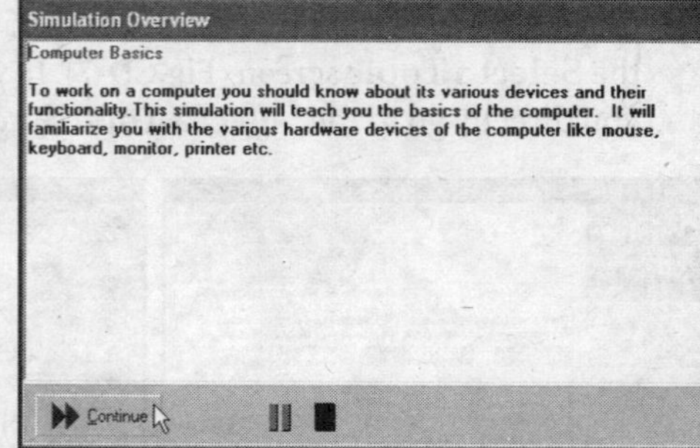

Fig. CD-10

Fig. CD-11

Fig. CD-12

Fig. CD-13

- *Clicking* on the **Continue** simulation button will result in running of the selected simulation in **Demo** or **Practice** mode. The shape of the Continue button changes as shown in Fig.CD-11. The simulation running mode depends on the choice you have made between the **Audio/Video Demo Mode** and **Self Testing/Practice Mode** in the **Select a Topic** screen as shown in Fig.CD-9.
- With the **Pause** audio button (Fig.CD-12), you can stop the simulation audio at any point and then restart the audio from that point. When you *click* on the **Pause** audio button, it changes to the **Continue** button (Fig.CD-11). To restart the audio from where it was paused, *click* on the **Continue** button.
- The **Stop** audio button (Fig.CD-13) helps you stop the simulation audio at any point and then restart it from the beginning. *Clicking* on the **Stop** audio button halts the simulation audio and the **Stop** button changes to the **Play** audio button. To start audio from the beginning of the simulation, *click* on the **Play** button.

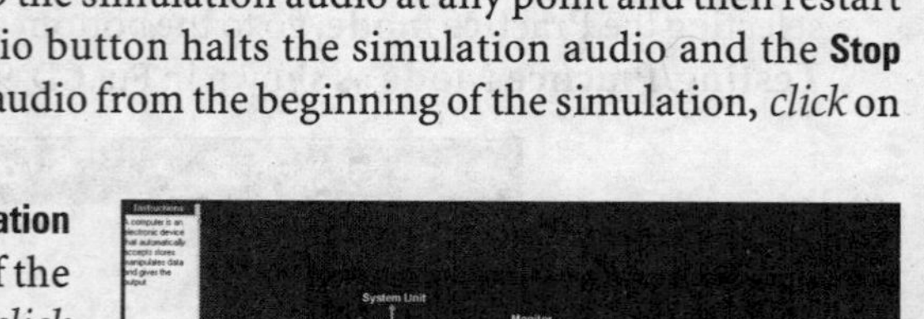

Let us now learn to move ahead from the **Simulation Overview** Screen. First, carefully read the overview of the **Computer Basics** simulation (Fig.CD-10), and then, *click* on the **Continue** button to run the simulation. A **Simulation Screen** appears (Fig.CD-14). Let us understand the utility of this screen.

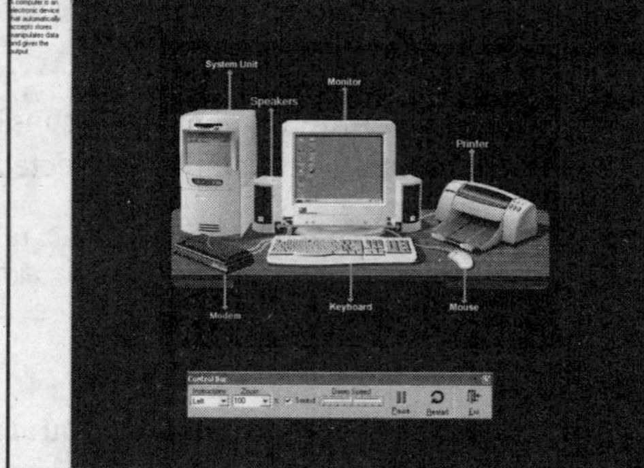

Fig. CD-14

Simulation Screen

It is the **Simulation Screen** where you see a selected simulation run in either **Demo** or **Practice** mode. Let us now understand functions of various controls and buttons of the Simulation Screen.

Controls and Buttons of Simulation Screen

The Simulation Screen has a **Control Bar** on which various buttons are present, as shown in Fig.CD-15. Functions of various Control Bar buttons are described below.

Fig. CD-15

Instructions Control

The first control, i.e. **Instructions**, on the Control Bar is a drop-down menu (Fig.CD-16), that can be used to select the location where you want the instructions bar to be placed on the Simulation Screen—on the Left, Bottom, Right or Top. By default, the **Left** option is selected (Fig.CD-16).

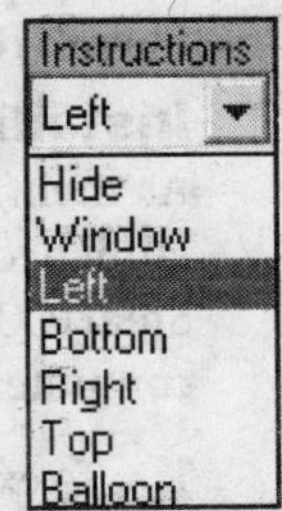

Fig. CD-16

You can also specify whether the instructions should appear in a **Window** or **Balloon**. For those who are completely new to computers, **Balloon** shape is the most suitable option. The **Balloon** is placed right on the screen and points out the location for the current action if the simulation is being run in the **Practice** mode. This gives you a clear idea of what is to be done in the current step. You may also hide the instructions bar by selecting the **Hide** option.

Zoom Control

This control also contains a drop-down menu which can be used to magnify or diminish the Simulation Screen. The degree of magnification is indicated in percentage as shown in Fig.CD-17. By default, **100**, which represents the normal size, is selected.

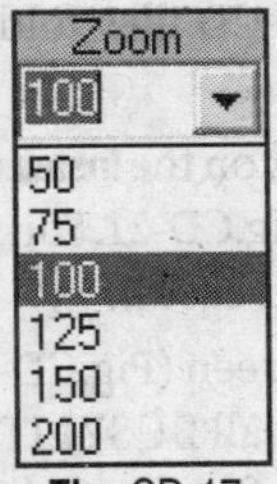

Fig. CD-17

Fig. CD-18

Sound Control

The **Sound** control (Fig.CD-18) applies only to the **Demo Mode.** With this control you can turn the audio on or off. By default, the Sound option is selected. Subsequent clicks will de-select and select the Sound option alternately.

Demo Speed Control

In **Demo mode**, you can also control the speed of the simulation with the help of the **Demo Speed** control (Fig.CD-19). The indicator on the timer bar can be dragged left or right with the mouse pointer to decrease or increase the simulation speed.

Restart Control

This button when clicked will restart the currently running simulation from the beginning. It is shown in Fig.CD-20.

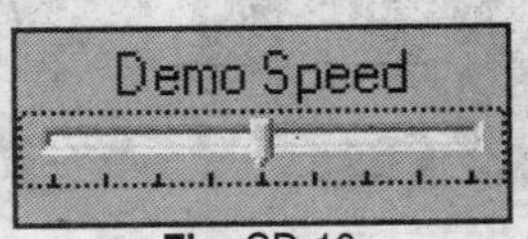

Fig. CD-19

Fig. CD-20

Pause and Stop buttons

You already know about the functioning of the other two Control Bar buttons—**Pause** and **Stop**, with respect to the Overview Screen, where these buttons are used to regulate the audio. But, in the Simulation Screen, these buttons are used to regulate the simulation. By clicking on the **Pause** button you can suspend the running of the simulation at any point. When clicked, the **Pause** button gets converted into the **Continue** button. To run the simulation from the point where it was stopped, click on the continue button.

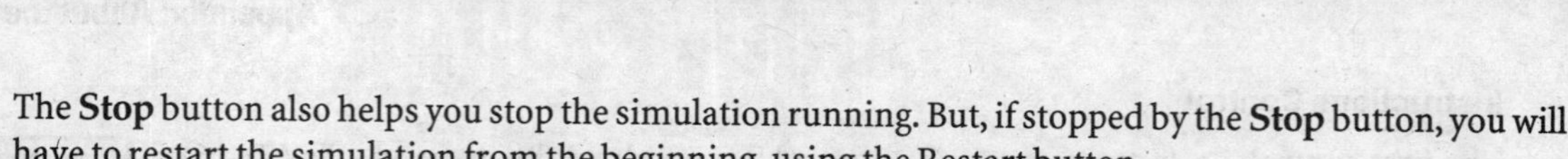

The **Stop** button also helps you stop the simulation running. But, if stopped by the **Stop** button, you will have to restart the simulation from the beginning, using the Restart button.

Installing BUSYLITE : Financial Accounting Package

As mentioned earlier, on inserting the CD, the Comdex Computer Course Self Training Software is launched by default. But the CD also contains the BUSYLITE Financial Accounting Package and the SmartCOP Anti-Virus Software. Let us learn to install these softwares. To install BUSYLITE on your computer's Hard Disk, undertake the following steps.

1. To exit from the default selection, that is, the Comdex Course Self Training software, *click* on the **exit** button of the **Select a topic** screen (Fig.CD-7).
2. *Open* the Windows Explorer and *click* on the CD-ROM Drive. All the files/folders of the root folder of the CD appear. By default, D drive is the CD-ROM drive. In your computer, the default CD-ROM drive may be represented by some other drive letter.
3. Among the CD files/folders, *double-click* on the **BUSYLITE** folder. All the files/folders of this folder appear.
4. *Double-click* on the **Install.exe** file. This will start the Installation Program of BUSYLITE and your monitor looks like Fig.CD-21. You are asked to specify the source drive. *Type* the drive letter of your CD-ROM drive, in our case **D**.
5. The next screen (Fig.CD-22) asks you to specify the target drive. *Type* in the drive letter on which you want to install BUSYLITE (default is C). After these steps, the BUSYLITE Installation Program will copy all the files to your target drive and then expand them.

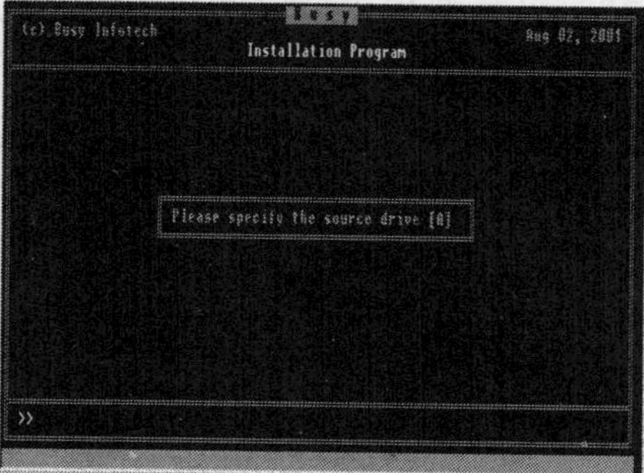

Fig. CD-21

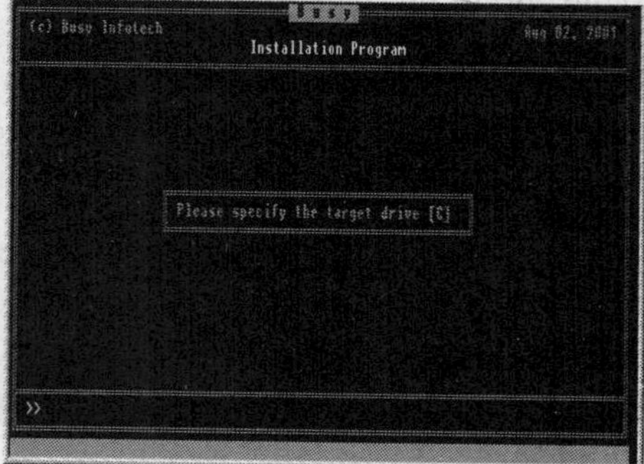

Fig. CD-22

Running BUSYLITE

After the installation of BUSYLITE in C:drive, undertake the following steps to run BUSYLITE:

1. *Launch* the MS DOS program. In the window of MS DOS program *type* C:\WINDOWS>**cd..** and *press* the **Enter** key.
2. Now *type* C:\>**cd Busy** and *press* the **Enter** key. The DOS prompt appears as C:\Busy>.
3. *Type* C:\Busy>**BUSYLITE** and *press* the **Enter** key. BUSYLITE gets loaded on your computer.

Installing SmartCOP Anti-Virus Software

The installation procedure of SmartCOP is very simple. Let us understand this procedure. To install SmartCOP on your computer's Hard Disk carry, undertake the following steps.

1. *Exit* from the default selection, that is the Comdex Computer Course Self Training Software, by *clicking* on the **exit** button of the **Select a topic** screen (Fig.CD-7).
2. *Open* the Windows Explorer and *click* on the CD-ROM Drive. All the files/folders of the root folder of the CD appear.
3. *Double-click* on the SmartCOP folder. All the files/folders of this folder appears.
4. Among the SmartCOP folder contents, *double-click* on the **Setup.exe** file. This starts the Installation Program of SmartCOP.
5. After the **InstallShield**, the next screen, known as the **Welcome** screen gets displayed
6. In the **Welcome** screen, when you *click* on the **Next** button, the **SmartCOP Setup** box gets displayed. If you select **Yes**, the **Smart Scan** module is loaded and it automatically starts scanning the C: drive. This is necessary to ensure that your system is free of viruses before SmartCOP is installed on it. You can select **No** to skip the initial scanning.
7. Once the scanning is complete, another box showing the license agreement is displayed. *Click* on the **Yes** button for accepting the license agreement. Then follow instructions of the installation wizard for installing the SmartCop on your computer.

Installing SmartCOP Anti-Virus Software

The installation procedure of SmartCOP is very simple. Let us understand this procedure. To install SmartCOP on your computer's Hard Disk easily, undertake the following steps:

1. Exit from the default selection, that is the Comdex Computer Course Self Training Software, by clicking on the **exit** button of the **Select a topic** screen (Fig. CD-7).
2. Open the Windows Explorer and click on the CD-ROM Drive. All the files/folders of the root folder of the CD appear.
3. Double-click on the SmartCOP folder. All the files/folders of this folder appears.
4. Among the SmartCOP folder contents, double-click on the **Setup.exe** file. This starts the Installation Program of SmartCOP.
5. After the InstallShield, the next screen, known as the **Welcome** screen gets displayed.
6. In the Welcome screen, when you click on the **Next** button, the **SmartCOP Scan** box gets displayed. If you select **Yes**, the **Smart Scan** module is loaded and it automatically starts scanning the C drive. This is necessary to ensure that your system is free of viruses before SmartCOP is installed on it. You can select **No** to skip the initial scanning.
7. Once the scanning is complete, another box showing the license agreement is displayed. Click on the **Yes** button for accepting the license agreement. Then follow instructions of the installation wizard for installing the SmartCop on your computer.

❖ ❖ ❖